ISBN 978-0-260-41346-8
PIBN 11126065

FDO 79
SEPT. 7, 1943

WAR FOOD ADMINISTRATION

[FDO 79]

PART 1401—DAIRY PRODUCTS

CONSERVATION AND DISTRIBUTION OF FLUID MILK AND CREAM

The fulfillment of requirements for the defense of the United States will result in a shortage in the supply of milk, cream, and milk byproducts for defense, for private account, and for export; and the following order is deemed necessary and appropriate in the public interest and to promote the national defense:

§ 1401.29 *Fluid milk and cream*—(a) *Definitions.* When used in this order, unless otherwise distinctly expressed or manifestly incompatible with the intent thereof:

(1) The term "person" means any individual, partnership, corporation, association, or any other business entity.

(2) The term "handler" means any person engaged in the handling or processing of milk, milk byproduct, or cream for sale or delivery in a milk sales area, irrespective of whether such sale or delivery is to other handlers, and irrespective of whether such person is also a milk producer; except that stores, restaurants, hotels, or similar establishments, in their capacity as such shall not be considered handlers; and no person shall be considered a handler in a milk sales area with respect to those operations which are carried on in a plant from which no milk, milk byproduct, or cream is delivered in such sales area.

(3) The term "milk" means cow's milk or any product of cow's milk which contains less than 5 percent butterfat and which is sold as milk or reconstituted milk.

(4) The term "milk byproduct" means (i) skim milk, buttermilk, flavored milk drink, or beverage containing more than 85 percent of skim milk; and (ii) cottage, pot, or bakers' cheese.

(5) The term "cream" means (i) the class of food defined in the regulations (5 F.R. 2442; 21 CFR, 1940 Supp., 18.500 *et seq.*) promulgated by the Secretary of Agriculture on June 28, 1940, and includes light cream, coffee cream, table cream, whipping cream, heavy cream, and any other cream whether sweet or sour by whatever name known; and (ii) milk and cream mixtures containing 5 percent or more of butterfat.

(6) The term "Director" means the Director of Food Distribution, War Food Administration.

(7) The term "market agent" means the market agent provided for in (c) (1) hereof.

(8) The term "advisory committee" means the advisory committee provided for in paragraph (c) (3) hereof.

(9) The term "base period" means any period designated by the Director for a milk sales area for the purpose of establishing quotas.

(10) The term "quota period" means any period designated by the Director for a milk sales area during which quotas established pursuant to this order shall be applicable.

(11) The term "quota" means the quantity, as established by the Director from time to time, of each of milk, milk byproducts, and cream, which a handler may deliver within a milk sales area during a quota period, in relation to the quantity of deliveries made by handlers during the base period.

(12) The term "milk sales area" means any geographical area designated by the Director for the purposes of this order.

(b) *Quotas and general restrictions.* (1) The Director shall designate or establish, from time to time, milk sales areas, base periods, quotas, and quota periods. The Director shall, in establishing milk sales areas, take into consideration, among other things, the density of population of each such area and the territory served by handlers making deliveries in that area. In establishing quotas, the Director (i) may establish separate quotas for handlers who are also producers, (ii) may establish separate quotas applicable to deliveries to various classes of purchasers, (iii) shall exclude, in the computation of quotas, deliveries to the agencies, persons, or groups specified in or pursuant to the provisions of paragraph (d) (1) hereof, (iv) may attach specific apportionments of quotas to wholesale and other buyers of milk, cream, or milk byproducts, which the buyer within his discretion may transfer from the quota of the handler, holding such apportionment, to the quota of another, and (v) may establish a quota for milk, one or more quotas for the several milk byproducts, and a quota for cream.

(2) No handler shall, during any quota period, deliver, within a milk sales area, a total quantity of milk, milk byproducts, or cream in excess of his respective quotas for such milk, milk byproducts, and cream during such period, except for deliveries exempt from such quotas.

(3) Each handler shall make an equitable distribution of milk, milk byproducts, and cream delivered by him, taking into consideration the schedules prepared in accordance with the provisions of paragraph (c) (2) (iii) and the persons and types of outlets supplied by such handler during the base period, and shall not favor purchasers who buy other products from him and shall not discriminate against purchasers who do not buy other products from him.

(4) All quotas hereunder shall be calculated quantitatively as specified by the Director: (i) for milk, in terms of pounds of milk, butterfat, or both; (ii) for cream, in terms of pounds of butterfat, cream, or both; and (iii) for milk byproducts, in terms of pounds of product, skim milk equivalent, or both: *Provided,* That the skim milk equivalent shall be computed in accordance with conversion factors announced by the Director.

(c) *Administration.* (1) The Director shall designate a market agent for each milk sales area or for a combination of several such areas and shall fix the amount of his salary. Insofar as he performs functions for the United States, the market agent will act under his appointment as collaborator without compensation from the United States. The market agent shall be subject to removal by the Director at any time, and all his acts shall be subject to the continuing right of the Director to disapprove at any time. Upon such disapproval, his acts shall be deemed null and void except insofar as any other person has acted in reliance thereon or in compliance therewith prior to such disapproval.

(2) The market agent is authorized and directed to:

(i) Obtain and assemble reports from handlers; assemble data with respect to the production, shipments, sales and delivery of milk, milk byproducts, and cream in the area, and with respect to the handlers under his jurisdiction; and furnish to the Director such available information as may be requested;

(ii) Receive petitions for relief from hardship; compile all necessary facts and data concerning such petitions; and transmit such petitions to the Director together with his recommendations;

(iii) With the advice of the advisory committee, prepare schedules establishing for various purchasers or classes of purchasers priorities to the purchase of milk, milk byproducts, and cream from handlers and transmit such schedules for approval to the Director, and such approved schedules shall be made available to handlers as schedules to be followed by them in the disposition of milk, milk byproducts, and cream;

(iv) Upon the request and with the advice of the advisory committee, devise plans which will permit handlers to share equitably in available supplies of milk and administer such plans upon approval by the Director;

(v) Keep books and records which will clearly reflect all of his acts and transactions, such books and records to be subject at any time to examination by the Director;

(vi) Collect the assessments as provided in this order from handlers required to pay such assessments;

(vii) Deliver to the Director promptly after his designation a bond in an amount and with surety thereon satisfactory to the Director, conditioned upon the faithful performance of the market agent's duties under this order;

(viii) Employ and fix the compensation of such persons as may be necessary to enable him to perform his duties hereunder;

(ix) Obtain a bond with reasonable surety thereon covering each employee of his office who handles funds under this order;

(x) Investigate and report to the Director any violation of this order;

(xi) Submit to the Director for approval a budget of expenses hereunder of the market agent;

(xii) Pay out of the funds collected by him as market agent the cost of his bond and of the bonds of his employees, his own compensation and that of his employees, and all other expenses necessarily incurred by him in the performance of his duties hereunder;

(xiii) Audit or inspect the books, records and other writings, premises, or inventories of milk, milk byproducts, and cream of any handler operating within the milk sales area subject to the jurisdiction of the market agent; and

(xiv) Perform such other duties as the Director may from time to time specify.

(3) The Director may designate for each milk sales area, or for a group of such areas, three or more persons to act as members of an advisory committee, and an alternate member for each of the members. Any such alternate shall act only in the event that the member for whom he is alternate is unable to act. The market agent shall be an additional member ex officio and shall act as chairman of the advisory committee. Each member of the committee shall be subject to removal by the Director at any time. The advisory committee shall meet at the call of the chairman. The advisory committee shall counsel with the market agent and shall recommend to the Director such amendments to this order and such changes in the administration thereof as it deems advisable.

(4) Each handler shall pay the market agent, within 20 days after the close of each calendar month, after the date of appointment of the market agent, an assessment upon the milk, milk byproducts, and cream, or any such portion thereof as may be specified by the Director, delivered by such handler during each such calendar month. This assessment shall be fixed, and may be modified from time to time, by the Director to meet the expenses which the Director finds will be necessarily incurred by the operations of this order in connection with an order issued pursuant hereto by the Director: *Provided, however*, That the assessment shall not exceed $0.03 per hundredweight of milk, cream, and skim milk equivalent of milk byproducts.

(d) *Quota exemptions.* (1) Notwithstanding the restrictions of paragraph (b) hereof, and without charge to his quota thereunder, any handler may deliver milk, milk byproducts, or cream to or for the following agencies or persons:

(i) The armed forces (Army, Navy, Marine Corps, and Coast Guard); any person feeding, pursuant to a written contract with any agency of the United States, personnel of the Army, Navy, Marine Corps, Coast Guard of the United States messed under the command of a commissioned or non-commissioned officer, to the extent necessary to feed such personnel;

(ii) Food Distribution Administration;

(iii) War Shipping Administration;

(iv) Veterans' Administration; and

(v) Any other agency or group named by the Director.

(e) *Audits and inspections.* The Director shall be entitled to make such audit or inspection of the books, records and other writings, premises, or inventories of milk, milk byproducts, or cream of any handler, and to make such investigations as may be necessary or appropriate, in his discretion, to the enforcement or administration of the provisions of this order.

(f) *Records and reports.* The Director shall be entitled to obtain such information from, and require such reports and the keeping of such records by, any person, as may be necessary or appropriate, in his discretion, to the enforcement or administration of the provisions of this order, subject to the approval of the Bureau of the Budget, pursuant to the Federal Reports Act of 1942.

(g) *Petition for relief from hardship.* Any person affected by this order who considers that compliance herewith would work an exceptional and unreasonable hardship on him may apply in writing for relief to the Director, setting forth in such petition all pertinent facts and the nature of the relief sought. The petition shall be submitted to the market agent of the milk sales area for which relief is sought. The Director may thereupon take such action as he deems appropriate, which action shall be final.

(h) *Violations.* The War Food Administrator may suspend, revoke, or reduce the quota of any person who violates any provision of this order, may prohibit by order such person from receiving, or using milk, cream, or any other material subject to priority or allocation control by the War Food Administrator, and may recommend that any such person be prohibited from receiving, making any deliveries of, or using materials subject to the priority or allocation control of other governmental agencies. In addition, any person who wilfully violates any provision of this order is guilty of a crime and may be prosecuted under any and all applicable laws. Further, civil action may be instituted to enforce any liability or duty created by, or to enjoin any violation of, any provision of this order.

(i) *Delegation of authority.* The administration of this order and the powers vested in the War Food Administrator, insofar as such powers relate to the administration of this order, are hereby delegated to the Director. The Director is authorized to redelegate to any employee of the United States Department of Agriculture any or all of the authority vested in him by this order.

(j) *Territorial scope.* The provisions of this order shall apply in the United States and the District of Columbia.

(k) *Communications.* All reports required to be filed hereunder and all communications concerning this order shall, unless instructions to the contrary are issued by the Director, be addressed to the Director of Food Distribution, War Food Administration, Washington 25, D. C., Ref. FD-79.

(l) *Effective date.* This order shall become effective at 12:01 a. m., e. w. t., September 10, 1943.

(E.O. 9280, 7 F.R. 10179; E.O. 9322, 8 F.R. 3807; E.O. 9334, 8 F.R. 5423)

Issued this 7th day of September 1943.

MARVIN JONES,
War Food Administrator.

Press Release Immediate:
Wednesday, September 8, 1943.

In an effort to maintain production of manufactured dairy products (principally evaporated milk, butter, cheese, and dry milk) at levels sufficient to supply essential civilian wartime needs, the War Food Administration today authorized its Director of Food Distribution to regulate expanding fluid milk sales through a system of dealer quotas.

Milk sales areas will be established and distributors will be assigned quotas which will represent the maximum sales or deliveries of fluid milk, cream, and fluid milk products they may make. This milk conservation and control program, established under Food Distribution Order 79 issued today, will go into effect first in the areas of heavy urban population where milk supply problems are most critical, and will be extended to other areas as administrative facilities permit.

Details of the program in each area will vary in accordance with local needs. WFA officials anticipate, however, that in most instances dealers' quotas will be set at approximately the quantity of fluid milk sold in recent months. Sales of cream and fluid milk by-products (skim milk, buttermilk, flavored milk drinks and cottage cheese) may be reduced somewhat below current or recent levels.

Dealers' quotas based on the current rate of deliveries would permit consumers to purchase more milk than they consumed in 1942, and considerably more than in pre-war years. Consumption of fluid milk and cream thus far in 1943 has been at a rate of more than 41 billion pounds annually compared with 37.7 billion pounds in 1942 and an average of 32.6 billion pounds in pre-war years (1936-40).

This increase in fluid milk sales, resulting largely from the sharp rise in consumer incomes, is continually decreasing the quantity of milk available for the manufacture of essential products such as butter, cheese, evaporated milk, ice cream, and milk powder. Already 20 percent above the 1941 level and 10 to 12 percent over 1942, consumption of fluid milk and cream has continued to rise at the rate of about 1 percent a month.

Total milk production has been mounting steadily in recent years—from 101 billion pounds in 1935 to 119 billion pounds in 1942—an all-time high. Production during the first 7 months of this year has been equal to production during the first 7 months of 1942. The encroachment of fluid milk markets on supplies normally used for manufacturing purposes has been so heavy, however, WFA officials stated, that practically the entire increase in whole milk deliveries since 1941 has been absorbed in fluid milk sales. This means that although war has greatly expanded the requirements for manufactured dairy products, both on the home and battle fronts, the supply of milk available for manufacturing uses at present is but little greater than it was during 1941, and promises to be lower, especially if fluid sales continue unchecked.

Primary purpose of the milk conservation and control program is to arrest this increasing diversion of supplies from manufacturing uses. WFA officials believe this can be accomplished by the stabilization of fluid milk consumption at approximately current levels, through a limitation of dealers' deliveries. Success of the program depends largely on trade and consumer cooperation, it was stated.

If this type of regulation does not succeed, the WFA said, consumer rationing of fluid milk and fluid milk products may be necessary in many areas. Rationing of such highly perishable products would be extremely complex at the consumer level, and would almost necessarily result in substantial reductions in fluid milk sales in many markets. Rationing will be necessary however, if this system of dealer quotas does not operate equitably and effectively to regulate the total volume sold in fluid channels.

Civilian consumption of every other major dairy product already is controlled. Butter, cheese, and evaporated milk are rationed. The quantity of milk solids which can be used in the manufacture of frozen dairy foods for civilians has been limited to 65 percent of that used last year. A limitation on heavy cream has been in effect since last November. Governmental agencies are taking 75 percent of the dry skim milk and an even larger proportion of the dry whole milk produced.

In addition to effectuating a more strategic division of the milk supply between fluid and manufacturing uses, the program also is expected to alleviate present unfavorable conditions in fluid milk marketing. Especially in markets where fluid milk supplies are short in relation to the continually rising demand, disruptive competition for milk supplies has arisen among some dealers. Stabilization of sales should eliminate the incentive for this type of competition.

Boundaries of the milk sales areas will be designated by the Director of Food Distribution, who also will appoint market agents to administer the orders for each area or group of areas. Expenses of administering the order in each area will be met by an assessment on the handlers for whom the quotas are established.

Authority for controlling sales of all fluid milk dealers, including producers who distribute milk or cream directly to consumers, is provided in today's action. Quotas for producer-distributors may be handled on a slightly different basis than quotas for other distributors, and will be closely aligned to the quantities of milk they produce.

Separate quotas also may be applied to deliveries to various classes of purchasers such as wholesale outlets, retail stores, restaurants, homes, etc. If supplies are not adequate to meet all demands, those considered most essential—such as for hospitals, pregnant and nursing mothers, and young children—will be met first. As a further protection to consumers, the order requires that each dealer make equitable distribution of his sales and prohibits discriminatory practices.

Sales of fluid milk and fluid milk products to the Armed Forces and to designated governmental agencies will be quota-exempt.

The over-all plan, WFA officials said, represents an opportunity for milk producers, milk dealers, health authorities, and the consuming public in each area to cooperate in the milk conservation program and assure equitable distribution of the available supply. It is believed that the plan can accomplish its basic purpose if the industry and the public cooperate to provide fair treatment to all consumers.

WAR FOOD ADMINISTRATION

[FDO 79, Amdt. 1]

PART 1401—DAIRY PRODUCTS

CONSERVATION AND DISTRIBUTION OF FLUID MILK AND CREAM

Food Distribution Order No. 79 (8 F.R 12426), issued by the War Food Administrator on September 7, 1943, is hereby amended as follows:

1. By deleting therefrom the provisions of § 1401.29 (a) (3) and inserting, in lieu thereof, the following:

(3) The term "milk" means cow's milk or any product of cow's milk which contains at least 3 percent but less than 6 percent butterfat, and which is sold as milk or reconstituted milk.

2. By inserting after § 1401.29 (a) (12) the following additional provision:

(13) The term "skim milk" means milk containing less than 3 percent butterfat as aforesaid the following additional provision

3. By inserting after § 1401.29 (a) (13), as aforesaid the following additional provision

(14) The term "delivery" means the act of delivering, transferring, or surrendering physical or constructive possession and control of milk, milk byproducts, or cream from one person to another person in a milk sales area.

4. By deleting therefrom the provisions in § 1401 29 (b) (1) (v) and inserting, in lieu thereof, the following:

(v) * * * may establish one or more quotas for milk, one or more quotas for the several milk byproducts, and one or more quotas for cream.

5. By deleting therefrom the provisions in § 1401.29 (b) (4) and inserting, in lieu thereof, the following:

(4) All quotas hereunder shall be calculated quantitatively as specified by the Director.

6. By deleting from § 1401.29 (c) (2) (iii) the words "with the advice of the advisory committee," wherever the same appear therein; and by capitalizing the word "prepare" which immediately follows the aforesaid words which are deleted.

7. By deleting the proviso in § 1401.29 (c) (4) and inserting, in lieu thereof, the following proviso:

Provided, however, That the assessment shall not exceed $0.03 per hundredweight of milk, milk equivalent of cream, and skim milk equivalent of milk byproducts.

This amendment to said Food Distribution Order No. 79 shall become effective 12:01 a. m., e. w. t., October 1, 1943.

(E.O. 9280, 7 F.R. 10179; E.O. 9322, 8 F.R. 3807; E.O. 9334, 8 F.R. 5423)

Issued this 28th day of September 1943.

MARVIN JONES,
War Food Administrator.

Press Release Immediate:
Wednesday, September 29, 1943.

Several changes in the milk conservation and control order (Food Distribution Order 79) designed to facilitate operation and administration of the order were made today by the War Food Administration.

Under the amended order, effective October 1, 1943, market agents in the milk sales areas to be established by the Director of Food Distribution may determine priorities for various classes of purchasers of milk, cream, and milk byproducts without the advice of any advisory committee which may be appointed. The original order provided that these distribution schedules were to be prepared with the advice of the advisory committee.

The amended order also differentiates milk and skim milk according to butterfat content, defining milk as containing between 3 and 6 percent butterfat, and skim milk as milk containing less than 3 percent butterfat. The original order did not define skim milk and defined milk as containing less than 5 percent butterfat.

The word "delivery" as used in the order is specifically defined, and the amendment also authorizes the Director of Food Distribution to establish more than one quota for milk and more than one quota for cream, at his discretion.

Other minor changes of a technical nature are provided in the amendment.

749985

FDO 79
AMDT. 1
SEPT. 28, 1943

WAR FOOD ADMINISTRATION

[FDO 79, Amdt. 1]

PART 1401—DAIRY PRODUCTS

CONSERVATION AND DISTRIBUTION OF FLUID MILK AND CREAM

Food Distribution Order No. 79 (8 F.R 12426), issued by the War Food Administrator on September 7, 1943, is hereby amended as follows:

1. By deleting therefrom the provisions of § 1401.29 (a) (3) and inserting, in lieu thereof, the following:

(3) The term "milk" means cow's milk or any product of cow's milk which contains at least 3 percent but less than 6 percent butterfat, and which is sold as milk or reconstituted milk.

2. By inserting after § 1401.29 (a) (12) the following additional provision:

(13) The term "skim milk" means milk containing less than 3 percent butterfat

3 By inserting after § 1401.29 (a) (13), as aforesaid the following additional provision

(14) The term "delivery" means the act of delivering, transferring, or surrendering physical or constructive possession and control of milk, milk byproducts, or cream from one person to another person in a milk sales area.

4. By deleting therefrom the provisions in § 1401 29 (b) (1) (v) and inserting, in lieu thereof, the following:

(v) * * * may establish one or more quotas for milk, one or more quotas for the several milk byproducts, and one or more quotas for cream.

5. By deleting therefrom the provisions in § 1401.29 (b) (4) and inserting, in lieu thereof, the following:

(4) All quotas hereunder shall be calculated quantitatively as specified by the Director.

6. By deleting from § 1401.29 (c) (2) (iii) the words "with the advice of the advisory committee," wherever the same appear therein; and by capitalizing the word "prepare" which immediately follows the aforesaid words which are deleted.

7. By deleting the proviso in § 1401.29 (c) (4) and inserting, in lieu thereof, the following proviso:

Provided, however, That the assessment shall not exceed $0.03 per hundredweight of milk, milk equivalent of cream, and skim milk equivalent of milk byproducts.

This amendment to said Food Distribution Order No. 79 shall become effective 12:01 a. m., e. w. t., October 1, 1943.

(E.O. 9280, 7 F.R. 10179; E.O. 9322, 8 F.R. 3807; E.O. 9334, 8 F.R. 5423)

Issued this 28th day of September 1943.

MARVIN JONES,
War Food Administrator.

Press Release Immediate:
Wednesday, September 29, 1943.

Several changes in the milk conservation and control order (Food Distribution Order 79) designed to facilitate operation and administration of the order were made today by the War Food Administration.

Under the amended order, effective October 1, 1943, market agents in the milk sales areas to be established by the Director of Food Distribution may determine priorities for various classes of purchasers of milk, cream, and milk byproducts without the advice of any advisory committee which may be appointed. The original order provided that these distribution schedules were to be prepared with the advice of the advisory committee.

The amended order also differentiates milk and skim milk according to butterfat content, defining milk as containing between 3 and 6 percent butterfat, and skim milk as milk containing less than 3 percent butterfat. The original order did not define skim milk and defined milk as containing less than 5 percent butterfat.

The word "delivery" as used in the order is specifically defined, and the amendment also authorizes the Director of Food Distribution to establish more than one quota for milk and more than one quota for cream, at his discretion.

Other minor changes of a technical nature are provided in the amendment.

WAR FOOD ADMINISTRATION
Food Distribution Administration
Washington 25, D. C.

CORRECTION NOTICE - FDO-79 Special Amendment 1.

In printing Food Distribution Order No.79 Special Amendment 1 the following error occurred:

In paragraph "Effective Date" "This amendment shall become effective at 12:01 a.m.c.w.t., December 1, 1943." Should read "This amendment shall become effective at 12:01 a.m. e.w.t., December 1, 1943"

FDO 79
SPECIAL AMDT. 1
NOV. 30, 1943

WAR FOOD ADMINISTRATION

[FDO 79-49 to 79-54, Amendment]

Part 1401—Dairy Products

FLUID MILK AND CREAM IN VARIOUS NEW YORK MILK SALES AREAS

Pursuant to Food Distribution Order No. 79 (8 F.R. 12426), dated September 7, 1943, as amended, and to effectuate the purposes thereof, the following orders issued by the Director of Food Distribution relative to the conservation and distribution of fluid milk and cream are amended in the respects hereinafter set forth:

FDO No. 79-49 (8 F.R. 14184) for Syracuse, New York, sales area, § 1401.92;

FDO No. 79-50 (8 F.R. 14186) for Utica-Rome, New York, sales area, § 1401.91;

FDO No. 79-51 (8 F.R. 14187) for Rochester, New York, sales area, § 1401.94;

FDO No. 79-52 (8 F.R. 14188) for Binghamton, New York, sales area, § 1401.93;

FDO No. 79-53 (8 F.R. 14190) for Albany-Schenectady-Troy, New York, sales area, § 1401.90; and

FDO No. 79-54 (8 F.R. 14191) for Niagara Frontier, New York, sales area, § 1401.89.

1. By deleting from each of the foregoing orders issued by the Director the provisions in (a) (8) of the respective order and inserting, in lieu thereof, the following:

(8) The term "wholesale purchasers" means any person who purchases milk, milk byproducts or cream, including sour cream, for purposes of resale, or use in other than personal, family, or household consumption, except (i) other handlers; (ii) purchasers engaged in the processing of milk, milk byproducts, or cream, who do not distribute milk, milk byproducts, or cream, including sour cream, in the sales area; (iii) industrial users; (iv) those purchasers specifically exempt from quota restrictions by FDO 79; (v) nursery, elementary, junior high, and high schools; and (vi) hospitals.

2. By inserting in each of the aforesaid orders issued by the Director an additional definition to be designated as (a) (13) in each of said orders:

(13) The term "industrial user" means a person, as determined by the market agent, who uses milk, cream (sweet or sour), skim milk beverage, and cottage, pot, or baker's cheese, in making other foods and who sells such foods primarily for resale to consumers off the premises where made.

Effective date. This amendment shall become effective at 12:01 a. m., c. w. t., December 1, 1943. With respect to violations, rights accrued, or liabilities incurred prior to the effective time of this amendment, the aforesaid orders issued by the Director shall be deemed to be in full force and effect for the purpose of sustaining any proper suit, action, or other proceeding with respect to any such violation, right, or liability.

(E.O. 9280, 8 F.R. 10179; E.O. 9322, 8 F.R. 3807; E.O. 9334, 8 F.R. 5423; E.O. 9392, 8 F.R. 14783; FDO 79, 8 F.R. 12426, 13283)

Issued this 30th day of November 1943.

C. W. Kitchen,
Acting Director of Food Distribution.

3? 3

FDO 79
GENERAL AMDT.
APR. 20, 1944

WAR FOOD ADMINISTRATION

[FDO 79-1 to 79-33, inc.; 79-35; 79-38 to 79-101, inc.; 79-103 to 79-114, inc.; 79-116 to 79-139, inc.; 79-141, 79-142, and 79-144, Amdt.]

PART 1401—DAIRY PRODUCTS

GENERAL AMENDMENT TO CERTAIN DIRECTOR'S ORDERS ALLOCATING MILK, MILK BYPRODUCTS, AND CREAM PURSUANT TO FOOD DISTRIBUTION ORDER NO. 79, AS AMENDED

In the determination of quotas for milk, milk byproducts, and cream for the quota periods of May and June 1944, respectively, wherever the term "75 percent" appears in each of the following orders, substitute, for said term, the term "100 percent":

The following orders issued by the Director of Food Distribution in accordance with the provisions of Food Distribution Order No. 79 (8 F.R. 12426) dated September 7, 1943, as amended, and said orders issued by the Director are designated as Nos. 79.1 to 79.33, inclusive; 79.35; 79.38 to 79.101, inclusive; 79.103 to 79.114, inclusive; 79.116 to 79.139, inclusive; 79.141, 79.142, and 79.144.

This order shall become effective at 12:01 a. m., e. w. t., May 1, 1944.

(E.O. 9280, 7 F.R. 10179; E.O. 9322, 8 F.R. 3807; E.O. 9334, 8 F.R. 5423; E.O. 9392, 8 F.R. 14783; FDO 79, 8 F.R. 12426, 13283)

Issued this 20th day of April 1944.

C. W. KITCHEN,
Acting Director of Distribution.

War Food Administration,
Summary 79-1 to 79-33, inclusive; FDO 79-35; 79-38; 79-101, 79-103 to 79-114, inclusive; 79-116 to 79-139, inclusive; 79-141, 79-142 and 79-144.

Quotas limiting sales of fluid cream and fluid milk byproducts will be adjusted during May and June to help assure the utilization of milk produced during these 2 months of peak output, the War Food Administration has announced.

Milk dealers in practically all the metropolitan areas which have been established as milk sales areas under Food Distribution Order 79 will be permitted to sell 100 percent as much cream and milk byproducts (chocolate drink, buttermilk, cottage cheese, etc.) as they sold in June 1943. At present, their sales are limited to 75 percent of the quantities of these products sold last June.

Sales quotas on fluid milk remain at 100 percent, but as quotas on cream and byproducts are transferable to fluid milk, in most cases dealers may distribute their increased allotment of milk in fluid milk, cream, or byproducts, according to local demand.

These adjustments in milk conservation quotas were made in anticipation of a heavier-than-usual production of milk during May and June. More milk normally is produced during these 2 months than during other months of the year, but this year an even greater than normal percentage of total annual milk output is expected to be concentrated during these 2 months.

WFA officials said that the production payments, which are being made to farmers to offset increases in dairy costs, are helping to encourage milk production. Present production reports show that the downward trend has been halted and that production this year may equal that of 1943, or be slightly higher.

With manpower and containers short and transportation facilities already overburdened, it would be difficult to market all the milk produced during the two peak production months in permitted uses without some revision of the quotas.

Complete removal of the quotas, even for a temporary period, is not considered justifiable, the WFA said, in view of the increasing war requirements for manufactured dairy products, nor is it considered necessary to relax completely in order to assure the use of all milk. If consumers cooperate and the trade makes full use of all available manufacturing facilities no milk need be wasted for lack of a market, they emphasized Should any dealer find that he is not able to market all his milk, even with the increased quotas granted for May and June, he may petition his market agent for further specific relief. Thirty-four market agents located in all sections of the country will be able to give prompt attention to these petitions and to make decisions based on a knowledge of local conditions.

Members of the fluid milk industry advisory committee who met in Washington recently reported that the fluid milk order has succeeded in diverting substantial quantities of milk to the manufacturing plants. Previous to the enactment of FDO 79, an increasing quantity of milk and cream was being bottled for fluid use, and a continually declining quantity was being offered for sale to creameries, condensaries, cheese plants and dried milk plants. By June 1943, fluid milk sales had reached an all time high. At the same time statistics showed that continuance of this trend would threaten the production of essential civilian and war supplies of manufactured dairy products.

The following figures illustrate why a milk conservation order was necessary: During the 2 years between 1941 and 1943, War requirements for dairy products, in terms of milk equivalent, increased from 5.4 billion pounds to 16.7 billion pounds. These increased requirements resulted primarily from the growth of our armed forces, and the increased numbers overseas, most of whom must depend on manufactured dairy products to obtain their milk nutrients. During the same period, U. S. civilian consumption of fluid milk and cream increased from 31.8 billion pounds to 38.1 billion pounds. Total milk production during that period, however, increased only 2.8 billion pounds—from 115.4 billion pounds to 118.2 billion pounds.

The difference between increased demand and increased supply was made up through restrictions on the use of milk and butterfat in the cream, fluid cream, through rationing butter, cheese, and evaporated milk and through an increase in whole milk deliveries from farms. Any further expansion in fluid milk consumption would have nullified many of those gains. The fact that total milk production had started trending downward and that war requirements were increasing made it all the more imperative to check fluid milk and cream sales in some way. The method finally decided upon—that of controlling sales through a system of dealer quotas—was an alternative to coupon rationing and was endorsed by the milk industry.

WAR FOOD ADMINISTRATION

[FDO 79-1]

PART 1401—DAIRY PRODUCTS

CONSERVATION AND DISTRIBUTION OF FLUID MILK AND CREAM IN THE BALTIMORE, MD., SALES AREA

Pursuant to the authority vested in me by Food Distribution Order No. 79 (8 F.R. 12426), issued on September 7, 1943, as amended, and to effectuate the purposes of such order, it is hereby ordered as follows:

§ 1401.34 *Quota restrictions*—(a) *Definitions.* When used in this order, unless otherwise distinctly expressed or manifestly incompatible with the intent hereof:

(1) Each term defined in Food Distribution Order No. 79, as amended, shall, when used herein, have the same meaning as is set forth for such term in Food Distribution Order No. 79, as amended.

(2) The term "order" means Food Distribution Order No. 79, issued on September 7, 1943, as amended.

(3) The term "sub-handler" means any handler, such as a peddler, vendor, sub-dealer, or secondary dealer, who purchases in a previously packaged and processed form milk, milk byproducts, or cream for delivery.

(b) *Milk sales area.* The following area is hereby designated as a "milk sales area" to be known as the Baltimore, Maryland, sales area, and is referred to hereinafter as the "sales area": The city of Baltimore; election district 5 in Carroll County; election districts 1, 2, 3, 9, 12, 13, 14, and 15 in Baltimore County; election districts 2, 3, and 5 in Anne Arundel County; and election districts 1 and 2 in Howard County. All of the sales area is in the State of Maryland.

(c) *Base period.* The calendar month of June 1943 is hereby designated as the base period for the sales area.

(d) *Quota period.* The remainder of the calendar month in which the provisions hereof become effective and each subsequent calendar month, respectively, is hereby designated as a quota period for the sales area.

(e) *Handler quotas.* Quotas for each handler in the sales area in each quota period shall be determined as follows:

(1) Divide the total deliveries of each of milk, milk byproducts, and cream (and of butterfat in milk or in cream where percentages of pounds of butterfat are specified in (e) (3) (i) or (e) (3) (ii) hereof) made in the sales area by such handler during the base period, after excluding the quota-exempt deliveries described in (h) hereof and adjusting such deliveries for the transfers set out in (i) hereof, by the number of days in the base period;

(2) Multiply the result of the foregoing calculation by the number of days in the quota period; and

(3) Multiply the aforesaid resulting amount by the following applicable percentage: (i) Milk: 100 percent of pounds of milk and ____ percent of pounds of butterfat; (ii) Cream: 75 percent of pounds of cream and 75 percent of pounds of butterfat; and (iii) Milk byproducts: 75 percent of pounds of milk byproducts other than cottage, pot, or baker's cheese and of the pounds of skim milk equivalent of cottage, pot, or baker's cheese. (For the purpose of this order, one pound of cottage, pot, or baker's cheese shall be considered as the equivalent of 7 pounds of skim milk.)

(f) *Quotas for handlers who are also producers.* Quotas for handlers who are also producers and who purchase no milk shall be 100 percent of the total production of such handlers in the base period.

(g) *Handler exemptions.* Quotas shall not apply to any handler who delivers in a quota period a daily average of less than 300 units of milk, cream, and milk byproducts. For the purpose of this order, a unit shall be the equivalent in volume of the following:

(1) Milk, one quart of milk;

(2) Cream, one-half pint of cream; and

(3) Milk byproduct, one quart of skim milk, buttermilk, flavored milk drink, or other beverage containing more than 85 percent of skim milk, or one-half pound of cottage, pot, or baker's cheese.

(h) *Quota exclusions and exemptions.* Deliveries of milk, milk byproducts, or cream (1) to other handlers, except for such deliveries to subhandlers, (2) to plants engaged in the handling or processing of milk, milk byproducts, or cream from which no milk, milk byproducts, or cream is delivered in the sales area, and (3) to the agencies or groups specified in (d) of the order, shall be excluded from the computation of deliveries in the base period and exempt from charges to quotas.

(i) *Transfers and apportionment of quotas.* The market agent is empowered to deduct an amount of base period deliveries to purchasers from the total of deliveries made by a handler or other person in the base period upon the application and a showing of unreasonable hardship by the handler making deliveries to such purchasers on the effective date of this order, and to add the amount of such deliveries to the total base period deliveries of the applicant handler. Denials of transfers or transfers granted by the market agent shall be reviewed by the Director upon application.

(j) *Petition for relief from hardship.* (1) Any person affected by the order or the provisions hereof who considers that compliance therewith would work an exceptional and unreasonable hardship on him, may file with the market agent a petition addressed to the Director. The petition shall contain the correct name, address and principal place of business of the petitioner, a full statement of the facts upon which the petition is based, and the hardship involved and the nature of the relief desired.

(2) Upon receiving such petition, the market agent shall immediately investigate the representations and facts stated therein.

(3) After investigation, the petition shall be certified to the Director, but prior to certification the market agent may (i) deny the petition; or (ii) grant temporary relief for a total period not to exceed 60 days.

(4) Denials or grants of relief by the market agent shall be reviewed by the Director and may be affirmed, modified, or reversed by the Director.

(k) *Reports.* Each handler shall transmit to the market agent on forms prescribed by the market agent the following reports:

(1) Within 20 days following the effective date of this order, reports which show the information required by the market agent to establish such handlers' quotas;

(2) Within 20 days following the close of each quota period, the information required by the market agent to establish volumes of deliveries of milk, cream, and milk byproducts during the preceding quota period; and

(3) Handlers exempt from quotas pursuant to (f) hereof shall, upon the request of the market agent, submit the information required by the market agent to establish volumes of deliveries of milk, cream, and milk byproducts.

(l) *Records.* Handlers shall keep and shall make available to the market agent such records of receipts, sales, deliveries, and production as the market agent shall require for the purpose of obtaining information which the Director may require for the establishment of quotas as prescribed in (b) of the order.

(m) *Bureau of the Budget approval.* The record-keeping and reporting requirements of this order have been approved by the Bureau of the Budget in accordance with the Federal Reports Act of 1942. Subsequent record-keeping or reporting requirements will be subject to the approval of the Bureau of the Budget pursuant to the Federal Reports Act of 1942.

(n) *Expense of administration.* Each handler shall pay to the market agent, within 20 days after the close of each calendar month an assessment of $0.01 per hundredweight of each of milk, cream, skim milk, buttermilk, flavored milk drinks, beverages containing more than 85 percent of skim milk, and skim milk equivalent of cottage, pot, or baker's cheese delivered during the preceding quota period and subject to quota regulations under the provisions hereof.

(o) *Distribution schedules.* The distribution schedules, if any, to be followed by the handlers in making deliveries shall be made effective in the terms of approval by the Director of such schedules.

(p) *Violations.* The market agent shall report all violations to the Director together with the information quired for the prosecution of such vi tions, except in a case where a han has made deliveries in a quota perio excess of a quota in an amount no exceed 5 percent of such quota, and the succeeding quota period makes liveries below that quota by at least same percent.

(q) This order shall take effect 12:01 a. m., e. w. t., October 4, 1943.

Issued this 30th day of September 1

ROY F. HENDRICKSON,
Director of Food Distributio

Press Release Immediate:
Thursday, September 30, 1943.

Federal control over fluid milk sales, through the establishment of quotas on deliveries of milk, cream, and milk byproducts, will go into effect in 13 eastern and midwestern metropolitan areas beginning October 4, the War Food Administration announced today.

These areas, and the market agents designated by the Food Distribution Administration to administer the milk conservation and control program in each, are:

Baltimore, Md., Washington, D. C., Roanoke, Va., Richmond, Va., Norfolk-Portsmouth-Newport News, Va.: George Irvine, 1731 I Street NW., Washington, D. C.

Cincinnati, Ohio, Toledo, Ohio, Dayton, Ohio, Canton, Ohio, Cleveland, Ohio: Fred W. Issler, 152 East Fourth Street, Cincinnati, Ohio.

Chicago, Illinois: A. W. Colebank, 135 South LaSalle St., Chicago, Ill.

Omaha-Neb.-Council Bluffs, Iowa: Wayne McPherson, Rm. 408, Post Office Bldg., Omaha, Nebraska.

St. Louis, Missouri: William C. Eckles, 4030 Chouteau Ave., St. Louis, Missouri.

Consumers in regulated areas will be able to purchase as much milk as they have been buying—within the limits of local supplies, officials said. The basic purpose of the program is to prevent a further increase in the consumption of fluid milk (rather than to reduce present consumption) so that enough milk will be available to produce the cheese, butter, and other manufactured dairy products required by the armed services and civilians. As milk conservation and control will be effected at the dealer level, consumer point rationing is not involved.

Milk dealers in the 13 initial milk sales areas will be allowed to sell as much fluid milk each month as they sold last June, (1943), the peak production month. To help assure that enough fluid milk will be available during the season of low production to enable dealers to sell as much as their quotas allow, cream sales will be limited to 75 percent of the quantity sold in June; and the sales quota for fluid milk by-products as a group (including cottage cheese, chocolate milk, and buttermilk) also is set at 75 percent of June sales.

Producer-distributors who purchase no milk (except those whose volume of sales is small enough to exempt them from the quota) will be allowed to sell an amount of fluid milk, cream, and fluid milk byproducts equal to 100 percent of their total milk production in June. "Quota-exempt" producer-distributors are defined separately for each area, but in general they are those whose deliveries are relatively small, and who produce the milk they sell from their own herds.

Milk distributors will be responsible for the fair distribution of supplies in their markets. Under Food Distribution Order 79, however, which authorizes the establishment of individual milk orders for each area, the various market agents may recommend distribution schedules to assure that, in the event of short supplies, the most essential needs will be met first.

Success of the milk conservation and control program depends largely on trade and consumer cooperation, WFA officials pointed out. It is believed that stabilization of milk consumption can be accomplished equitably through this system of dealer control without resorting to consumer rationing. Individual rationing of such a highly perishable product as milk would be very complex, difficult to administer, and would almost necessarily result in substantial reductions in fluid milk sales in many markets. Rationing at the consumer level undoubtedly will be necessary if control over dealers' sales does not effectively regulate fluid milk consumption, the officials said.

Under the individual orders established for each area, the milk control program may be modified to fit production and consumption conditions in each market. These orders will be administered by market agents appointed by the Director of Food Distribution.

Milk sales in all other cities of at least 100,000 population will be regulated as soon as administrative arrangements can be completed—with most areas of this size to be operating under the program by November 1. It is expected that the program will then be extended to smaller population areas until all markets of at least 50,000 population are included.

Distributor quotas for milk sales areas to be named later may be the same as those for the areas announced today, or they may vary if local conditions indicate that different bases are necessary.

Milk handlers (that is, all persons or firms engaged in the sale or transfer of milk, except such groups as retail stores, hotels, restaurants, etc.) will compute the quantity of milk and fluid milk byproducts which they may sell e month in terms of pounds of milk pounds of milk byproducts, and t cream sales in terms of pounds of cr and butterfat. In months which c tain more or less days than the period, handlers will determine amount of milk they may sell by m plying the average of daily deliveri June by 28, 29, or 31, whichever is plicable.

Dealers may exceed their mon quotas by up to 5 percent greater s providing they make up this exces reducing their deliveries proportiona the next month, without the ma agent being required to report such cess sales.

Deliveries to the armed forces, plants processing dairy products, an other handlers (except special classe handlers such as peddlers) are q exempt.

To facilitate administration, the n ket agent for each milk sales area act upon petitions for relief from h ship which may be submitted to him, his decision will be effective for a 60 period.

Dealers' quotas based on June d eries will permit consumers to purc more milk than they consumed in and considerably more than in pre- years. Consumption of fluid milk cream thus far in 1943 has been at a of more than 41 billion pounds ann compared with 37.7 billion pound 1942 and an average of 32.6 billion po in pre-war years (1936-40).

Total milk production has been mo ing steadily in recent years—from billion pounds in 1935 to 119 bi pounds in 1942—an all-time high. duction during the first 7 months of year equalled production during the months of 1942.

Increasing fluid milk sales, how resulting largely from the sharp ri consumer incomes, have reduced quantity of milk available for the m facture of essential products such as ter, cheese, evaporated milk, ice cr and milk powder. Previously u trolled, consumption of fluid milk cream has been rising at the ra about 1 percent a month, and alrea 20 percent above the 1941 level and 12 percent over 1942.

This has necessitated the stabiliz of fluid milk consumption in order to the requirements for manufactured products, both on the home and fronts, WFA officials explained.

FDO 79-1
AMDT. 1
OCTOBER 28, 1943

WAR FOOD ADMINISTRATION

[FDO 79-1, Amdt. 1]

PART 1401—DAIRY PRODUCTS

FLUID MILK AND CREAM IN BALTIMORE, MD., MILK SALES AREA

Pursuant to the authority vested in the Director by Food Distribution Order No. 79, dated September 7, 1943 (8 F.R. 12426), as amended, and to effectuate the purposes thereof, Director Food Distribution Order No. 79.1 § 1401.34, relative to the conservation of fluid milk in the Baltimore, Maryland, milk sales area (8 F.R. 13364), issued by the Director of Food Distribution on September 30, 1943, is amended as follows:

The milk sales area described in § 1401.34 (b) of the original order is modified in the following particulars: Add "election districts 4 and 8 in Baltimore County and the city of Annapolis in Anne Arundel County, Maryland."

Effective date. This amendment of FDO No. 79-1 shall become effective at 12:01 a. m., e. w. t., November 1, 1943.

(E.O. 9280, 8 F.R. 10179; E.O. 9322, 8 F.R. 3807; E.O. 9334, 8 F.R. 5423; FDO 79, 8 F.R. 12426, 13283)

Issued this 28th day of October 1943.

ROY F. HENDRICKSON,
Director of Food Distribution.

733 F
Cop 1

FDO 79-1
AMDT. 2
MAR. 29, 1944

WAR FOOD ADMINISTRATION

[FDO 79-1, Amdt. 2]

PART 1401—DAIRY PRODUCTS

FLUID MILK AND CREAM IN BALTIMORE, MD., SALES AREA

Pursuant to Food Distribution Order No. 79 (8 F.R. 12426), dated September 7, 1943, as amended, and to effectuate the purposes thereof, Food Distribution Order No. 79-1 (8 F.R. 13364), relative to the conservation and distribution of fluid milk in the Baltimore, Maryland, milk sales area, issued by the Director of Food Distribution on September 30, 1943, as amended, is hereby further amended as follows:

1. By deleting the numeral "20" wherever it appears in § 1401.34 (k) (2) and inserting, in lieu thereof, the numeral "10."

2. By deleting the numeral "$0.01" wherever it appears in § 1401.34 (n) and inserting, in lieu thereof, the numeral "$0.005."

The provisions of this amendment shall become effective at 12:01 a. m., e. w. t., April 1, 1944. With respect to violations of said Food Distribution Order No. 79-1, as amended, rights accrued, or liabilities incurred prior to the effective time of this amendment, said Food Distribution Order No. 79-1, as amended, shall be deemed to be in full force and effect for the purpose of sustaining any proper suit, action, or other proceeding with respect to any such violation, right, or liability.

(E.O. 9280, 7 F.R. 10179; E.O. 9322, 8 F.R. 3807; E.O. 9334, 8 F.R. 5423; E.O. 9392, 8 F.R. 14783; FDO 79, 8 F.R. 12426, 13283)

Issued this 29th day of March 1944.

LEE MARSHALL,
Director of Food Distribution.

77337 Cc. 1

FDO 79-2

SEPT. 30, 1943

WAR FOOD ADMINISTRATION

[FDO 79-2]

PART 1401—DAIRY PRODUCTS

CONSERVATION AND DISTRIBUTION OF FLUID MILK AND CREAM IN THE ST. LOUIS METROPOLITAN SALES AREA

Pursuant to the authority vested in me by Food Distribution Order No. 79 (8 F.R. 12426), issued on September 7, 1943, as amended, and to effectuate the purposes of such order, it is hereby ordered as follows:

§ 1401.45 *Quota restrictions*—(a) *Definitions.* When used in this order, unless otherwise distinctly expressed or manifestly incompatible with the intent hereof:

(1) Each term defined in Food Distribution Order No. 79, as amended, shall, when used herein, have the same meaning as is set forth for such term in Food Distribution Order No. 79, as amended.

(2) The term "order" means Food Distribution Order No. 79, issued on September 7, 1943, as amended.

(3) The term "sub-handler" means any handler, such as a peddler, vendor, sub-dealer, or secondary dealer, who purchases in a previously packaged and processed form milk, milk byproducts, or cream for delivery.

(b) *Milk sales area.* The following area is hereby designed as a "milk sales area" to be known as the St. Louis Metropolitan sales area, and is referred to hereinafter as the "sales area": All municipal corporations, military reservations and unincorporated territory within the geographical limits of the city of St. Louis and all townships except Meramec in St. Louis County, the township of St. Charles in St. Charles County, all in the State of Missouri; the townships of East St. Louis, Stites, Canteen, Centerville, Sugar Loaf, Stookey, St. Clair, Shiloh Valley, Mascoutah, Lebanon, O'Fallon, Caseyville, Millstadt, in St. Clair County, Columbia and Waterloo precincts in Monroe County, the townships of Helvetia, St. Jacob, Jarvis, Collinsville, Nameoki, Venice, Edwardsville, Chouteau, Wood River, Godfrey and Alton in Madison County, all in the State of Illinois.

(c) *Base period.* The calendar month of June 1943 is hereby designated as the base period for the sales area.

(d) *Quota period.* The remainder of the calendar month in which the provisions hereof become effective and each subsequent calendar month, respectively, is hereby designated as a quota period for the sales area.

(e) *Handler quotas.* Quotas for each handler in the sales area in each quota period shall be determined as follows:

(1) Divide the total deliveries of each of milk, milk byproducts, and cream (and of butterfat in milk or in cream where percentages of pounds of butterfat are specified in (e) (3) (i) or (e) (3) (ii) hereof) made in the sales area by such handler during the base period, after excluding the quota-exempt deliveries described in (h) hereof and adjusting such deliveries for the transfers set out in (i) hereof, by the number of days in the base period;

(2) Multiply the result of the foregoing calculation by the number of days in the quota period; and

(3) Multiply the aforesaid resulting amount by the following applicable percentage: (i) Milk: 100 percent of pounds of milk and ---- percent of pounds of butterfat; (ii) Cream: 75 percent of pounds of cream and 75 percent of pounds of butterfat; and (iii) Milk byproducts: 75 percent of pounds of milk byproducts other than cottage, pot, or baker's cheese and of the pounds of skim milk equivalent of cottage, pot, or baker's cheese. (For the purpose of this order, one pound of cottage, pot, or baker's cheese shall be considered as the equivalent of 7 pounds of skim milk.)

(f) *Quotas for handlers who are also producers.* Quotas for handlers who are also producers and who purchase no milk shall be 100 percent of the total production of such handlers in the base period.

(g) *Handler exemptions.* Quotas shall not apply to any handler who delivers in a quota period a daily average of less than 300 units of milk, cream, and milk byproducts. For the purpose of this order, a unit shall be the equivalent in volume of the following:

(1) Milk, one quart of milk;

(2) Cream, one-half pint of cream; and

(3) Milk byproducts, one quart of skim milk, buttermilk, flavored milk drink, or other beverage containing more than 85 percent of skim milk, or one-half pound of cottage, pot, or baker's cheese.

(h) *Quota exclusions and exemptions.* Deliveries of milk, milk byproducts, or cream (1) to other handlers, except for such deliveries to sub-handlers, (2) to plants engaged in the handling or processing of milk, milk byproducts, or cream from which no milk, milk byproducts, or cream is delivered in the sales area, and (3) to the agencies or groups specified in (d) of the order, shall be excluded from the computation of deliveries in the base period and exempt from charges to quotas.

(i) *Transfers and apportionment of quotas.* The market agent is empowered to deduct an amount of base period deliveries to purchasers from the total of deliveries made by a handler or other person in the base period upon the application and a showing of unreasonable hardship by the handler making deliveries to such purchasers on the effective date of this order, and to add the amount of such deliveries to the total base period deliveries of the applicant handler. Denials of transfers or transfers granted by the market agent shall be reviewed by the Director upon application.

(j) *Petition for relief from hardships.* (1) Any person affected by the order or the provisions hereof who considers that compliance therewith would work an exceptional and unreasonable hardship on him, may file with the market agent a petition addressed to the Director. The petition shall contain the correct name, address and principal place of business of the petitioner, a full statement of the facts upon which the petition is based, and the hardship involved and the nature of the relief desired.

(2) Upon receiving such petition, the market agent shall immediately investigate the representations and facts stated therein.

(3) After investigation, the petition shall be certified to the Director, but prior to certification the market agent may (i) deny the petition; or (ii) grant temporary relief for a total period not to exceed 60 days.

(4) Denials or grants of relief by the market agent shall be reviewed by the Director and may be affirmed, modified, or reversed by the Director.

(k) *Reports.* Each handler shall transmit to the market agent on forms prescribed by the market agent the following reports:

(1) Within 20 days following the effective date of this order, reports which show the information required by the market agent to establish such handlers' quotas;

(2) Within 20 days following the close of each quota period, the information required by the market agent to establish volumes of deliveries of milk, cream, and milk byproducts during the preceding quota period; and

(3) Handlers exempt from quotas pursuant to (f) hereof shall, upon the request of the market agent, submit the information required by the market agent to establish volumes of deliveries of milk, cream, and milk byproducts.

(l) *Records.* Handlers shall keep and shall make available to the market agent such records of receipts, sales, deliveries, and production as the market agent shall require for the purpose of obtaining information which the Director may require for the establishment of quotas as prescribed in (b) of the order.

(m) *Distribution schedules.* The distribution schedules, if any, to be followed by the handlers in making deliveries shall be made effective in the terms of approval by the Director of such schedules.

(n) *Expense of administration.* Each handler shall pay to the market agent, within 20 days after the close of each calendar month an assessment of $0.01 per hundredweight of each of milk, cream, skim milk, buttermilk, flavored milk drinks, beverages containing more than 85 percent of skim milk, and skim milk equivalent of cottage, pot, or baker's cheese delivered during the preceding quota period and subject to quota regulations under the provisions hereof.

(o) *Violations.* The market agent shall report all violations to the Director together with the information required for the prosecution of such violations, except in a case where a handler has made deliveries in a quota period in excess of a quota in an amount not to exceed 5 percent of such quota, and in the succeeding quota period makes deliveries below that quota by at least the same percent.

(p) *Bureau of the Budget approval.* The record-keeping and reporting requirements of this order have been ap proved by the Bureau of the Budge in accordance with the Federal Report Act of 1942. Subsequent record-keepin or reporting requirements will be subje to the approval of the Bureau of th Budget pursuant to the Federal Report Act of 1942.

(q) This order shall take effect a 12:01 a. m., e. w. t., October 4, 1943.

Issued this 30th day of Septembe 1943.

Roy F. Hendrickson,
Director of Food Distribution.

Press Release Immediate:
Thursday, September 30, 1943.

Federal control over fluid milk sales, through the establishment of quotas on deliveries of milk, cream, and milk byproducts, will go into effect in 13 eastern and midwestern metropolitan areas beginning October 4, the War Food Administration announced today.

These areas, and the market agents designated by the Food Distribution Administration to administer the milk conservation and control program in each, are:

Baltimore, Md., Washington, D. C., Roanoke, Va., Richmond, Va., Norfolk-Portsmouth-Newport News, Va.: George Irvine, 1731 I Street, NW., Washington, D. C.

Cincinnati, Ohio, Toledo, Ohio, Dayton, Ohio, Canton, Ohio, Cleveland, Ohio: Fred W. Issler, 152 East Fourth Street, Cincinnati, Ohio.

Chicago, Illinois: A. W. Colebank, 135 South LaSalle St., Chicago, Ill.

Omaha, Nebr.-Council Bluffs, Iowa: Wayne McPherren, Rm. 408, Post Office Bldg., Omaha, Nebraska.

St. Louis, Missouri: William C. Eckles, 4030 Chouteau Ave., St. Louis, Missouri.

Consumers in regulated areas will be able to purchase as much milk as they have been buying—within the limits of local supplies, officials said. The basic purpose of the program is to prevent a further increase in the consumption of fluid milk (rather than to reduce present consumption) so that enough milk will be available to produce the cheese, butter, and other manufactured dairly products required by the armed services and civilians. As milk conservation and control will be effected at the dealer level, consumer point rationing is not involved.

Milk dealers in the 13 initial milk sales areas will be allowed to sell as much fluid milk each month as they sold last June (1943), the peak production month. To help assure that enough fluid milk will be available during the season of low production to enable dealers to sell as much as their quotas allow, cream sales will be limited to 75 percent of the quantity sold in June, and the sales quota for fluid milk by-products as a group (including cottage cheese, chocolate milk, and buttermilk) also is set at 75 percent of June sales.

Producer-distributors who purchase no milk (except those whose volume of sales is small enough to exempt them from the quota) will be allowed to sell an amount of fluid milk, cream, and fluid milk byproducts equal to 100 percent of their total milk production in June. "Quota-exempt" producer-distributors are defined separately for each area, but in general they are those whose deliveries are relatively small, and who produce the milk they sell from their own herds.

Milk distributors will be responsible for the fair distribution of supplies in their markets. Under Food Distribution Order 79, however, which authorizes the establishment of individual milk orders for each area, the various market agents may recommend distribution schedules to assure that, in the event of short supplies, the most essential needs will be met first.

Success of the milk conservation and control program depends largely on trade and consumer cooperation, WFA officials pointed out. It is believed that stabilization of milk consumption can be accomplished equitably through this system of dealer control without resorting to consumer rationing. Individual rationing of such a highly perishable product as milk would be very complex, difficult to administer, and would almost necessarily result in substantial reductions in fluid milk sales in many markets. Rationing at the consumer level undoubtedly will be necessary if control over dealers' sales does not effectively regulate fluid milk consumption, the officials said.

Under the individual orders established for each area, the milk control program may be modified to fit production and consumption conditions in each market. These orders will be administered by market agents appointed by the Director of Food Distribution.

Milk sales in all other cities of at least 100,000 population will be regulated as soon as administrative arrangements can be completed—with most areas of this size to be operating under the program by November 1. It is expected that the program will then be extended to smaller population areas until all markets of at least 50,000 population are included.

Distributor quotas for milk sales areas to be named later may be the same as those for the areas announced today, or they may vary if local conditions indicate that different bases are necessary.

Milk handlers (that is, all persons or firms engaged in the sale or transfer of milk, except such groups as retail stores, hotels, restaurants, etc.) will compute the quantity of milk and fluid milk byproducts which they may sell each mont in terms of pounds of milk and pounc of milk byproducts, and their cream sale in terms of pounds of cream and butter fat. In months which contain more c less days than the base period, handle will determine the amount of milk the may sell by multiplying the average c daily deliveries in June by 28, 29, or 3 whichever is applicable.

Dealers may exceed their monthly quo tas by up to 5 percent greater sales pro viding they make up this excess b reducing their deliveries proportionate the next month, without the mark agent being required to report such ex cess sales.

Deliveries to the armed forces, t plants processing dairy products, and t other handlers (except special classes c handlers such as peddlers) are quot exempt.

To facilitate administration, the mar ket agent for each milk sales area ma act upon petitions for relief from hard ship which may be submitted to him, an his decision will be effective for a 60-da period.

Dealers' quotas based on June de liveries will permit consumers to pu chase more milk than they consume in 1942, and considerably more tha in pre-war years. Consumption of flu milk and cream thus far in 1943 h been at a rate of more than 41 billic pounds annually compared with 37 billion pounds in 1942 and an averag of 32.6 billion pounds in pre-war yea (1936-40).

Total milk production has been moun ing steadily in recent years—from 10 billion pounds in 1935 to 119 billic pounds in 1942—an all-time high. Pro duction during the first 7 months of th year equalled production during th same months of 1942.

Increasing fluid milk sales, howeve resulting largely from the sharp ri in consumer incomes, have reduced th quantity of milk available for the manu facture of essential products such a butter, cheese, evaporated milk, ic cream, and milk powder. Previously un controlled, consumption of fluid milk an cream has been rising at the rate c about 1 percent a month, and alreac is 20 percent above the 1941 level an 10 to 12 percent over 1942.

This has necessitated the stabilizatic of fluid milk consumption in order t meet the requirements for manufacture dairy products, both on the home an battle fronts, WFA officials explained.

FDO 79-2
AMDT. 1
OCTOBER 28, 1943

WAR FOOD ADMINISTRATION

[FDO 79-2. Amdt. 1]

Part 1401—Dairy Products

FLUID MILK AND CREAM IN ST. LOUIS, METROPOLITAN MILK SALES AREA

Pursuant to the authority vested in the Director by Food Distribution Order No. 79, dated September 7, 1943 (8 F.R. 12426), as amended, and to effectuate the purposes thereof, Director Food Distribution Order No. 79-2 § 1401.45, relative to the conservation of fluid milk in the St. Louis, Metropolitan milk sales area (8 F.R. 13365), issued by the Director of Food Distribution on September 30, 1943, is amended as follows:

The milk sales area described in § 1401.45 (b) of the original order is modified in the following particulars: Add the townships of Saline, Granite City and Ft. Russell in Madison County, Illinois; and substitute the township of "Centreville" for the township of "Centerville" in St. Clair County.

Effective date. This amendment of FDO No. 79-2 shall become effective at 12:01 a. m., e. w. t., November 1, 1943.

(E.O. 9280, 8 F.R. 10179; E.O. 9322, 8 F.R. 3807; E.O. 9334, 8 F.R. 5423; FDO 79, 8 F.R. 12426, 13283)

Issued this 28th day of October 1943.

Roy F. Hendrickson,
Director of Food Distribution.

33 F
.1

FDO 79-2
AMDT. 2
FEB. 19, 1944

WAR FOOD ADMINISTRATION

[FDO 79-2, Amdt. 2]

PART 1401—DAIRY PRODUCTS

FLUID MILK AND CREAM IN THE ST. LOUIS METROPOLITAN MILK SALES AREA

Pursuant to Food Distribution Order No. 79 (8 F.R. 12426), dated September 7, 1943, as amended, and to effectuate the purposes thereof, Food Distribution Order No. 79-2 (8 F.R. 13365), relative to the conservation and distribution of fluid milk in the St. Louis metropolitan milk sales area, issued by the Director of Food Distribution on September 30, 1943, as amended, is hereby further amended by deleting therefrom the provisions in § 1401.45 (h) and inserting, in lieu thereof, the following:

(h) *Quota exclusions and exemptions.* Deliveries of milk, milk byproducts, or cream (1) to other handlers, except for such deliveries to sub-handlers, (2) to plants engaged in the handling or processing of milk, milk byproducts, or cream from which no milk, milk byproducts or cream is delivered in the sales area, (3) to nursery, elementary, junior high, and high schools, and (4) to the agencies or groups specified in (d) of the order, shall be excluded from the computation of deliveries in the base period and exempt from charges to quotas.

The provisions of this amendment shall become effective at 12:01 a. m., e. w. t., March 1, 1944. With respect to violations of said Food Distribution Order No. 79-2, as amended, rights accrued, or liabilities incurred, prior to the effective time of this amendment, said Food Distribution Order No. 79-2, as amended, shall be deemed to be in full force and effect for the purpose of sustaining any proper suit, action, or other proceeding with respect to any such violation, right, or liability.

(E.O. 9280, 7 F.R. 10179; E.O. 9322, 8 F.R. 3807; E.O. 9334, 8 F.R. 5423; E.O. 9392, 8 F.R. 14783; FDO 79, 8 F.R. 12426, 13283)

Issued this 19th day of February 1944.

LEE MARSHALL,
Director of Food Distribution.

133 F
Jan 1

FDO 79-2

AMDT. 3
MAR. 29, 1944

WAR FOOD ADMINISTRATION

[FDO 79-2, Amdt. 3]

PART 1401—DAIRY PRODUCTS

FLUID MILK AND CREAM IN ST. LOUIS METROPOLITAN SALES AREA

Pursuant to Food Distribution Order No. 79 (8 F.R. 12426), dated September 7, 1943, as amended, and to effectuate the purposes thereof, Food Distribution Order No. 79-2 (8 F.R. 13365), relative to the conservation and distribution of fluid milk, milk byproducts, and cream in the St. Louis metropolitan milk sales area, issued by the Director of Food Distribution on September 30, 1943, as amended, is hereby further amended by deleting the numeral "20" wherever it appears in § 1401.45 (k) (2) thereof and inserting, in lieu thereof, the numeral "10."

The provisions of this amendment shall become effective at 12:01 a. m., e. w. t., April 1, 1944. With respect to violations of said Food Distribution Order No. 79-2, as amended, rights accrued, or liabilities incurred prior to the effective time of this amendment, said Food Distribution Order No. 79-2, as amended, shall be deemed to be in full force and effect for the purpose of sustaining any proper suit, action, or other proceeding with respect to any such violation, right, or liability.

(E.O. 9280, 7 F.R. 10179; E.O. 9322, 8 F.R. 3807; E.O. 9334, 8 F.R. 5423; E.O. 9392, 8 F.R. 14783; FDO 79, 8 F.R. 12426, 13283)

Issued this 29th day of March 1944.

LEE MARSHALL,
Director of Distribution.

FDO 79-3
SEPT. 30, 1943

WAR FOOD ADMINISTRATION

[FDO 79-3]

PART 1401—DAIRY PRODUCTS

CONSERVATION AND DISTRIBUTION OF FLUID MILK AND CREAM IN THE CLEVELAND, OHIO, SALES AREA

Pursuant to the authority vested in me by Food Distribution Order No. 79 (8 F.R. 12426), issued on September 7, 1943, as amended, and to effectuate the purposes of such order, it is hereby ordered as follows:

§ 1401.46 *Quota restrictions*—(a) *Definitions.* When used in this order, unless otherwise distinctly expressed or manifestly incompatible with the intent hereof.

(1) Each term defined in Food Distribution Order No. 79, as amended, shall, when used herein, have the same meaning as is set forth for such term in Food Distribution Order No. 79, as amended.

(2) The term "order" means Food Distribution Order No. 79, issued on September 7, 1943, as amended.

(3) The term "sub-handler" means any handler, such as a peddler, vendor, sub-dealer, or secondary dealer, who purchases in a previously packaged and processed form milk, milk byproducts, or cream for delivery.

(b) *Milk sales area.* The following area is hereby designated as a "milk sales area" to be known as the Cleveland, Ohio, sales area, and is referred to hereinafter as the "sales area":

The city of Cleveland, Cuyahoga County, the villages of Avon and Avon Lake, the townships of Ridgeville and Columbia, in Lorain County, the townships of Northfield Center and Twinsburg, in Summit County, the township of Aurora in Portage County, the townships of Bainbridge, Russell and Chester in Geauga County, the townships of Kirtland, Willoughby and Mentor in Lake County, all in the State of Ohio.

(c) *Base period.* The calendar month of June 1943 is hereby designated as the base period for the sales area.

(d) *Quota period.* The remainder of the calendar month in which the provisions hereof become effective and each subsequent calendar month, respectively, is hereby designated as a quota period for the sales area.

(e) *Handler quotas.* Quotas for each handler in the sales area in each quota period shall be determined as follows:

(1) Divide the total deliveries of each of milk, milk byproducts, and cream (and of butterfat in milk or in cream where percentages of pounds of butterfat are specified in (e) (3) (i) or (e) (3) (ii) hereof) made in the sales area by such handler during the base period, after excluding the quota-exempt deliveries described in (h) hereof and adjusting such deliveries for the transfers set out in (i) hereof, by the number of days in the base period;

(2) Multiply the result of the foregoing calculation by the number of days in the quota period; and

(3) Multiply the aforesaid resulting amount by the following applicable percentage: (i) Milk: 100 percent of pounds of milk and ---- percent of pounds of butterfat; (ii) Cream: 75 percent of pounds of cream and 75 percent of pounds of butterfat; and (iii) Milk byproducts: 75 percent of pounds of milk byproducts other than cottage, pot, or baker's cheese and of the pounds of skim milk equivalent of cottage, pot, or baker's cheese. (For the purpose of this order, one pound of cottage, pot, or baker's cheese shall be considered as the equivalent of 7 pounds of skim milk.)

(f) *Quotas for handlers who are also producers.* Quotas for handlers who are also producers and who purchase no milk shall be 100 percent of the total production of such handlers in the base period.

(g) *Handler exemptions.* Quotas shall not apply to any handler who delivers in a quota period a daily average of less than 150 units of milk, cream, and milk byproducts. For the purpose of this order, a unit shall be the equivalent in volume of the following:

(1) Milk, one quart of milk;

(2) Cream, one-half pint of cream; and

(3) Milk byproduct, one quart of skim milk, buttermilk, flavored milk drink, or other beverage containing more than 85 percent of skim milk, or one-half pound of cottage, pot, or baker's cheese.

(h) *Quota exclusions and exemptions.* Deliveries of milk, milk byproducts, or cream (1) to other handlers, except for such deliveries to sub-handlers, (2) to plants engaged in the handling or processing of milk, milk byproducts, or cream from which no milk, milk byproducts, or cream is delivered in the sales area, and (3) to the agencies or groups specified in (d) of the order, shall be excluded from the computation of deliveries in the base period and exempt from charges to quotas.

(i) *Transfers and apportionment of quotas.* The market agent is empowered to deduct an amount of base period deliveries to purchasers from the total of deliveries made by a handler or other person in the base period upon the application and a showing of unreasonable hardship by the handler making deliveries to such purchasers on the effective date of this order, and to add the amount of such deliveries to the total base period deliveries of the applicant handler. Denials of transfers or transfers granted by the market agent shall be reviewed by the Director upon application.

(j) *Petition for relief from hardships.* (1) Any person affected by the order or the provisions hereof who considers that compliance therewith would work an exceptional and unreasonable hardship on him, may file with the market agent a petition addressed to the Director. The petition shall contain the correct name, address and principal place of business of the petitioner, a full statement of the facts upon which the petition is based, and the hardship involved and the nature of the relief desired.

(2) Upon receiving such petition, the market agent shall immediately investigate the representations and facts stated therein.

(3) After investigation, the petition shall be certified to the Director, but prior to certification the market agent may (i) deny the petition; or (ii) grant temporary relief for a total period not to exceed 60 days.

(4) Denials or grants of relief by the market agent shall be reviewed by the Director and may be affirmed, modified, or reversed by the Director.

(k) *Reports.* Each handler shall transmit to the market agent on forms prescribed by the market agent the following reports:

(1) Within 20 days following the effective date of this order, reports which show the information required by the market agent to establish such handlers' quotas;

(2) Within 20 days following the close of each quota period, the information required by the market agent to establish volumes of deliveries of milk, cream, and milk byproducts during the preceding quota period; and

(3) Handlers exempt from quotas pursuant to (f) hereof shall, upon the request of the market agent, submit the information required by the market agent to establish volumes of deliveries of milk, cream, and milk byproducts.

(l) *Records.* Handlers shall keep and shall make available to the market agent such records of receipts, sales, deliveries, and production as the market agent shall require for the purpose of obtaining information which the Director may re-

quire for the establishment of quotas as prescribed in (b) of the order.

(m) *Distribution schedules.* The distribution schedules, if any, to be followed by the handlers in making deliveries shall be made effective in the terms of approval by the Director of such schedules.

(n) *Expense of administration.* Each handler shall pay to the market agent, within 20 days after the close of each calendar month an assessment of $.01 per hundredweight of each of milk, cream, skim milk, buttermilk, flavored milk drinks, beverages containing more than 85 percent of skim milk, and skim milk equivalent of cottage, pot, or baker's cheese delivered during the preceding quota period and subject to quota regulations under the provisions hereof.

(o) *Violations.* The market agent shall report all violations to the Director together with the information required for the prosecution of such violations, except in a case where a handler has made deliveries in a quota period in excess of a quota in an amount not to exceed 5 percent of such quota, and in the succeeding quota period makes deliveries below that quota by at least the same percent.

(p) *Bureau of the Budget approval.* The record-keeping and reporting requirements of this order have been approved by the Bureau of the Budget in accordance with the Federal Reports Act of 1942. Subsequent record-keeping or reporting requirements will be subject to the approval of the Bureau of the Budget pursuant to the Federal Reports Act of 1942.

(q) This order shall take effect at 12:01 a. m., e. w. t., October 4, 1943.

Issued this 30th day of September, 1943.

ROY F. HENDRICKSON,
Director of Distribution.

Press Release Immediate:
Thursday, September 30, 1943.

Federal control over fluid milk sales, through the establishment of quotas on deliveries of milk, cream, and milk by-products, will go into effect in 13 eastern and midwestern metropolitan areas beginning October 4, the War Food Administration announced today.

These areas, and the market agents designated by the Food Distribution Administration to administer the milk conservation and control program in each, are:

Baltimore, Md., Washington, D. C., Roanoke, Va., Richmond, Va., Norfolk-Portsmouth-Newport News, Va.: George Irvine, 1731 I Street NW., Washington, D. C.

Cincinnati, Ohio, Toledo, Ohio, Dayton, Ohio, Canton, Ohio, Cleveland, Ohio: Fred W. Issler, 152 East Fourth Street, Cincinnati, Ohio.

Chicago, Illinois: A. W. Colebank, 135 South LaSalle St, Chicago, Ill.

Omaha-Neb.-Council Bluffs, Iowa: Wayne McPherren, Rm 408, Post Office Bldg., Omaha, Nebraska.

St. Louis, Missouri: William C. Eckles, 4030 Chouteau Ave, St. Louis, Missouri.

Consumers in regulated areas will be able to purchase as much milk as they have been buying—within the limits of local supplies, officials said. The basic purpose of the program is to prevent a further increase in the consumption of fluid milk (rather than to reduce present consumption) so that enough milk will be available to produce the cheese, butter, and other manufactured dairy products required by the armed services and civilians. As milk conservation and control will be effected at the dealer level, consumer point rationing is not involved.

Milk dealers in the 13 initial milk sales areas will be allowed to sell as much fluid milk each month as they sold last June, (1943), the peak production month. To help assure that enough fluid milk will be available during the season of low production to enable dealers to sell as much as their quotas allow, cream sales will be limited to 75 percent of the quantity sold in June, and the sales quota for fluid milk by-products as a group (including cottage cheese, chocolate milk, and buttermilk) also is set at 75 percent of June sales.

Producer-distributors who purchase no milk (except those whose volume of sales is small enough to exempt them from the quota) will be allowed to sell an amount of fluid milk, cream, and fluid milk by-products equal to 100 percent of their total milk production in June. "Quota-exempt" producer-distributors are defined separately for each area, but in general they are those whose deliveries are relatively small, and who produce the milk they sell from their own herds.

Milk distributors will be responsible for the fair distribution of supplies in their markets. Under Food Distribution Order 79, however, which authorizes the establishment of individual milk orders for each area, the various market agents may recommend distribution schedules to assure that, in the event of short supplies, the most essential needs will be met first.

Success of the milk conservation and control program depends largely on trade and consumer cooperation, WFA officials pointed out. It is believed that stabilization of milk consumption can be accomplished equitably through this system of dealer control without resorting to consumer rationing. Individual rationing of such a highly perishable product as milk would be very complex, difficult to administer, and would almost necessarily result in substantial reductions in fluid milk sales in many markets. Rationing at the consumer level undoubtedly will be necessary if control over dealers' sales does not effectively regulate fluid milk consumption, the officials said.

Under the individual orders established for each area, the milk control program may be modified to fit production and consumption conditions in each market. These orders will be administered by market agents appointed by the Director of Food Distribution.

Milk sales in all other cities of at least 100,000 population will be regulated as soon as administrative arrangements can be completed—with most areas of this size to be operating under the program by November 1. It is expected that the program will then be extended to smaller population areas until all markets of at least 50,000 population are included.

Distributor quotas for milk sales areas to be named later may be the same as those for the areas announced today, or they may vary if local conditions indicate that different bases are necessary.

Milk handlers (that is, all persons or firms engaged in the sale or transfer of milk, except such groups as retail stores, hotels, restaurants, etc.) will compute the quantity of milk and fluid milk byproducts which they may sell each month in terms of pounds of milk and pounds of milk byproducts, and their cream sales in terms of pounds of cream and butterfat. In months which contain more or less days than the base period, handlers will determine the amount of milk they may sell by multiplying the average of daily deliveries in June by 28, 29, or 31, whichever is applicable.

Dealers may exceed their monthly quotas by up to 5 percent greater sales providing they make up this excess by reducing their deliveries proportionately the next month, without the market agent being required to report such excess sales.

Deliveries to the armed forces, to plants processing dairy products, and to other handlers (except special classes of handlers such as peddlers) are quota exempt.

To facilitate administration, the market agent for each milk sales area may act upon petitions for relief from hardship which may be submitted to him, and his decision will be effective for a 60-day period.

Dealers' quotas based on June deliveries will permit consumers to purchase more milk than they consumed in 1942, and considerably more than in pre-war years. Consumption of fluid milk and cream thus far in 1943 has been at a rate of more than 41 billion pounds annually compared with 37.7 billion pounds in 1942 and an average of 32.6 billion pounds in pre-war years (1936–40).

Total milk production has been mounting steadily in recent years—from 101 billion pounds in 1935 to 119 billion pounds in 1942—an all-time high. Production during the first 7 months of this year equalled production during the same months of 1942.

Increasing fluid milk sales, however, resulting largely from the sharp rise in consumer incomes, have reduced the quantity of milk available for the manufacture of essential products such as butter, cheese, evaporated milk, ice cream, and milk powder. Previously uncontrolled, consumption of fluid milk and cream has been rising at the rate of about 1 percent a month, and already is 20 percent above the 1941 level and 10 to 12 percent over 1942.

This has necessitated the stabilization of fluid milk consumption in order to meet the requirements for manufactured dairy products, both on the home and battle fronts, WFA officials explained.

.erve

1337

FDO 79-3
AMDT. 1
OCTOBER 28, 1943

WAR FOOD ADMINISTRATION

A [FDO 79-3, Amdt. 1]

PART 1401—DAIRY PRODUCTS

FLUID MILK AND CREAM IN CLEVELAND, OHIO, MILK SALES AREA

Pursuant to the authority vested in the Director by Food Distribution Order No. 79, dated September 7, 1943 (8 F.R. 12426), as amended, and to effectuate the purposes thereof, Director Food Distribution Order No. 79-3 § 1401.46, relative to the conservation of fluid milk in the Cleveland, Ohio, milk sales area (8 F.R. 13367) isued by the Director of Food Distribution on September 30, 1943, is amended as follows:

The milk sales area described in § 1401.46 (b) of the original order is modified in the following particulars: Add "the township of Macedonia and the villages of Northfield and Sagamore Hills in Summit County, Ohio."

Effective date. This amendment of FDO No. 79-3 shall become effective at 12:01 a. m., e. w. t., November 1, 1943.

(E.O. 9280, 8 F.R. 10179; E.O. 9322, 8 F.R. 3807; E.O. 9334, 8 F.R. 5423; FDO 79, 8 F.R. 12426, 13283)

Issued this 28th day of October 1943.

ROY F. HENDRICKSON,
Director of Food Distribution.

337
9.2

FDO 79-3
AMDT. 2
JAN. 27, 1944

WAR FOOD ADMINISTRATION

[FDO 79-3, Amdt. 2]

PART 1401—DAIRY PRODUCTS

FLUID MILK AND CREAM IN CLEVELAND, OHIO, SALES AREA

Pursuant to Food Distribution Order No. 79 (8 F.R. 12426), dated September 7, 1943, as amended, and to effectuate the purposes thereof, Food Distribution Order No. 79-3 (8 F.R. 13367), relative to the conservation and distribution of fluid milk in the Cleveland, Ohio, milk sales area, issued by the Director of Food Distribution on September 30, 1943, as amended, is hereby further amended as follows:

1. By deleting therefrom the provisions in § 1401.46 (f) and substituting therefor the following:

(f) *Quotas for handlers who are also producers.* Quotas for handlers who are also producers and who purchase no milk shall be computed in accordance with (e) hereof, except that the applicable percentages shall be 100 percent in lieu of the percentages specified in (e) (3).

2. By deleting therefrom the provisions of § 1401.46 (h) and substituting therefor the following:

(h) *Quota exclusions and exemptions.* Deliveries of milk, milk byproducts, or cream (1) to other handlers, except for such deliveries to subhandlers, (2) to plants engaged in the handling or processing of milk, milk byproducts, or cream from which no milk, milk byproducts, or cream is delivered in the sales area, (3) to nursery, elementary, junior high, and high schools, and (4) to the agencies or groups specified in (d) of the order, shall be excluded from the computation of deliveries in the base period and exempt from charges to quotas.

The provisions of this amendment shall become effective at 12:01 a. m. e. w. t., February 1, 1944. With respect to violations of said Food Distribution Order No. 79-3, as amended, rights accrued, or liabilities incurred prior to the effective time of this amendment, said Food Distribution Order No. 79-3, as amended, shall be deemed to be in full force and effect for the purpose of sustaining any proper suit, action, or other proceeding with respect to any such violation, right, or liability.

(E.O. 9280, 7 F.R. 10179; E.O. 9322, 8 F.R. 3807; E.O. 9334, 8 F.R. 5423; E.O. 9392, 8 F.R. 14783; FDO 79, 8 F.R. 12426, 13283)

Issued this 27th day of January 1944.

LEE MARSHALL,
Director of Food Distribution.

WAR FOOD ADMINISTRATION

[FDO 79-4]

PART 1401—DAIRY PRODUCTS

CONSERVATION AND DISTRIBUTION OF FLUID MILK AND CREAM IN THE WASHINGTON, D. C., SALES AREA

Pursuant to the authority vested in me by Food Distribution Order No. 79 (8 F.R. 12426), issued on September 7, 1943, as amended, and to effectuate the purposes of such order, it is hereby ordered as follows:

§ 1401.38 *Quota restrictions*—(a) *Definitions.* When used in this order, unless otherwise distinctly expressed or manifestly incompatible with the intent hereof;

(1) Each term defined in Food Distribution Order No. 79, as amended, shall, when used herein, have the same meaning as is set forth for such term in Food Distribution Order No. 79, as amended.

(2) The term "order" means Food Distribution Order No. 79, issued on September 7, 1943, as amended.

(3) The term "sub-handler" means any handler, such as a peddler, vendor, subdealer, or secondary dealer, who purchases in a previously packaged and processed form milk, milk byproducts, or cream for delivery.

(b) *Milk sales area.* The following area is hereby designated as a "milk sales area" to be known as the Washington, D. C. sales area, and is referred to hereinafter as the "sales area." The city of Washington, D. C., and the entire area encompassed by and including the election districts of Potomac, Rockville, Gaithersburg, Olney, and Colesville in Montgomery County, Maryland; Laurel, Bowie, Queen Anne, Marlboro, Mellwood, Surratts, and Oxon Hill in Prince Georges County, Maryland; Alexandria City, Virginia; the election districts of Occoquan in Prince William County, Virginia; and Mt. Vernon, Lee, Providence, and Dranesville in Fairfax County, Virginia.

(c) *Base period.* The calendar month of June 1943 is hereby designated as the base period for the sales area.

(d) *Quota period.* The remainder of the calendar month in which the provisions hereof become effective and each subsequent calendar month, respectively, is hereby designated as a quota period for the sales area.

(e) *Handler quotas.* Quotas for each handler in the sales area in each quota period shall be determined as follows:

(1) Divide the total deliveries of each of milk, milk byproducts, and cream (and of butterfat in milk or in cream where percentages of pounds of butterfat are specified in (e) (3) (i) or (e) (3) (ii) hereof) made in the sales area by such handler during the base period, after excluding the quota-exempt deliveries described in (h) hereof and adjusting such deliveries for the transfers set out in (i) hereof, by the number of days in the base period;

(2) Multiply the result of the foregoing calculation by the number of days in the quota period; and

(3) Multiply the aforesaid resulting amount by the following applicable percentages: (i) Milk: 100 percent of pounds of milk and ---- percent of pounds of butterfat; (ii) Cream: 75 percent of pounds of cream and 75 percent of pounds of butterfat; and (iii) Milk byproducts: 75 percent of pounds of milk byproducts other than cottage, pot, or baker's cheese and of the pounds of skim milk equivalent of cottage, pot, or baker's cheese. (For the purpose of this order, one pound of cottage, pot, or baker's cheese shall be considered as the equivalent of 7 pounds of skim milk.)

(f) *Quotas for handlers who are also producers.* Quotas for handlers who are also producers and who purchase no milk shall be 100 percent of the total production of such handlers in the base period.

(g) *Handler exemptions.* Quotas shall not apply to any handler who delivers in a quota period a daily average of less than 350 units of milk, cream, and milk byproducts. For the purpose of this order, a unit shall be the equivalent in volume of the following:

(1) Milk, one quart of milk;

(2) Cream, one-half pint of cream; and

(3) Milk byproduct, one quart of skim milk, buttermilk, flavored milk drink, or other beverage containing more than 85 percent of skim milk, or one-half pound of cottage, pot, or baker's cheese.

(h) *Quota exclusions and exemptions.* Deliveries of milk, milk byproducts, or cream (1) to other handlers, except for such deliveries to sub-handlers, (2) to plants engaged in the handling or processing of milk, milk byproducts, or cream from which no milk, milk byproducts, or cream is delivered in the sales area, and (3) to the agencies or groups specified in (d) of the order, shall be excluded from the computation of deliveries in the base period and exempt from charges to quotas.

(i) *Transfers and apportionment of quotas.* The market agent is empowered to deduct an amount of base period deliveries to purchasers from the total of deliveries made by a handler or other person in the base period upon the application and a showing of unreasonable hardship by the handler making deliveries to such purchasers on the effective date of this order, and to add the amount of such deliveries to the total base period deliveries of the applicant handler. Denials of transfers or transfers granted by the market agent shall be reviewed by the Director upon application.

(j) *Petition for relief from hardships.* (1) Any person affected by the order or the provisions hereof who considers that compliance therewith would work an exceptional and unreasonable hardship on him, may file with the market agent a petition addressed to the Director. The petition shall contain the correct name, address and principal place of business of the petitioner, a full statement of the facts upon which the petition is based, and the hardship involved and the nature of the relief desired.

(2) Upon receiving such petition, the market agent shall immediately investigate the representations and facts stated therein.

(3) After investigation, the petition shall be certified to the Director, but prior to certification the market agent may (i) deny the petition; or (ii) grant temporary relief for a total period not to exceed 60 days.

(4) Denials or grants of relief by the market agent shall be reviewed by the Director and may be affirmed, modified, or reversed by the Director.

(k) *Reports.* Each handler shall transmit to the market agent on forms prescribed by the market agent the following reports:

(1) Within 20 days following the effective date of this order, reports which show the information required by the market agent to establish such handlers' quotas;

(2) Within 20 days following the close of each quota period, the information required by the market agent to establish volumes of deliveries of milk, cream, and milk byproducts during the preceding quota period; and

(3) Handlers exempt from quotas pursuant to (f) hereof shall, upon the request of the market agent, submit the information required by the market agent to establish volumes of deliveries of milk, cream, and milk byproducts.

(l) *Records.* Handlers shall keep and shall make available to the market agent such records of receipts, sales, deliveries, and production as the market agent shall require for the purpose of obtaining information which the Director may require for the establishment of quotas as prescribed in (b) of the order.

(m) *Distribution schedules.* The distribution schedules, if any, to be followed by the handlers in making deliveries shall be made effective in the terms of approval by the Director of such schedules.

(n) *Expense of administration.* Each handler shall pay to the market agent, within 20 days after the close of each calendar month an assessment of $0.01 per hundredweight of each of milk, cream, skim milk, buttermilk, flavored milk drinks, beverages containing more than 85 percent of skim milk, and skim milk equivalent of cottage, pot, or baker's cheese delivered during the preceding quota period and subject to quota regulations under the provisions hereof.

(o) *Violations.* The market agent shall report all violations to the Director together with the information required for the prosecution of such violations, except in a case where a handler has made deliveries in a quota period in excess of a quota in an amount not to exceed 5 percent of such quota, and in the succeeding quota period makes deliveries below that quota by at least the same percent.

(p) *Bureau of the Budget approval.* The record-keeping and reporting requirements of this order have been approved by the Bureau of the Budget in accordance with the Federal Reports Act of 1942. Subsequent record-keeping or reporting requirements will be subject to the approval of the Bureau of the Budget pursuant to the Federal Reports Act of 1942.

(q) This order shall take effect at 12:01 a. m., e. w. t., October 4, 1943.

Issued this 30th day of September 1943.

ROY F. HENDRICKSON,
Director of Food Distribution.

Press Release Immediate:
Thursday, September 30, 1943.

Federal control over fluid milk sales, through the establishment of quotas on deliveries of milk, cream, and milk by-products, will go into effect in 13 eastern and midwestern metropolitan areas beginning October 4, the War Food Administration announced today.

These areas, and the market agents designated by the Food Distribution Administration to administer the milk conservation and control program in each, are:

Baltimore, Md., Washington, D. C., Roanoke, Va., Richmond, Va., Norfolk-Portsmouth-Newport News, Va.: George Irvine, 1731 I Street NW., Washington, D. C.

Cincinnati, Ohio, Toledo, Ohio, Dayton, Ohio, Canton, Ohio, Cleveland, Ohio: Fred W. Issler, 152 East Fourth Street, Cincinnati, Ohio.

Chicago, Illinois: A. W. Colebank, 135 South LaSalle St., Chicago, Ill.

Omaha, Neb.-Council Bluffs, Iowa: Wayne McPherron, Rm. 408, Post Office Bldg., Omaha, Nebraska.

St. Louis, Missouri: William C. Eckles, 4030 Chouteau Ave., St. Louis, Missouri.

Consumers in regulated areas will be able to purchase as much milk as they have been buying—within the limits of local supplies, officials said. The basic purpose of the program is to prevent a further increase in the consumption of fluid milk (rather than to reduce present consumption) so that enough milk will be available to produce the cheese, butter, and other manufactured dairy products required by the armed services and civilians. As milk conservation and control will be effected at the dealer level, consumer point rationing is not involved.

Milk dealers in the 13 initial milk sales areas will be allowed to sell as much fluid milk each month as they sold last June, (1943), the peak production month. To help assure that enough fluid milk will be available during the season of low production to enable dealers to sell as much as their quotas allow, cream sales will be limited to 75 percent of the quantity sold in June, and the sales quota for fluid milk byproducts as a group (including cottage cheese, chocolate milk, and buttermilk) also is set at 75 percent of June sales.

Producer-distributors who purchase no milk (except those whose volume of sales is small enough to exempt them from the quota) will be allowed to sell an amount of fluid milk, cream, and fluid milk byproducts equal to 100 percent of their total milk production in June. "Quota-exempt" producers-distributors are defined separately for each area, but in general they are those whose deliveries are relatively small, and who produce the milk they sell from their own herds.

Milk distributors will be responsible for the fair distribution of supplies in their markets. Under Food Distribution Order 79, however, which authorizes the establishment of individual milk orders for each area, the various market agents may recommend distribution schedules to assure that, in the event of short supplies, the most essential needs will be met first.

Success of the milk conservation and control program depends largely on trade and consumer cooperation, WFA officials pointed out. It is believed that stabilization of milk consumption can be accomplished equitably through this system of dealer control without resorting to consumer rationing. Individual rationing of such a highly perishable product as milk would be very complex, difficult to administer, and would almost necessarily result in substantial reductions in fluid milk sales in many markets. Rationing at the consumer level undoubtedly will be necessary if control over dealers' sales does not effectively regulate fluid milk consumption, the officials said.

Under the individual orders established for each area, the milk control program may be modified to fit production and consumption conditions in each market. These orders will be administered by market agents appointed by the Director of Food Distribution.

Milk sales in all other cities of at least 100,000 population will be regulated as soon as administrative arrangements can be completed—with most areas of this size to be operating under the program by November 1. It is expected that the program will then be extended to smaller population areas until all markets of at least 50,000 population are included.

Distributor quotas for milk sales areas to be named later may be the same as those for the areas announced today, or they may vary if local conditions indicate that different bases are necessary.

Milk handlers (that is, all persons or firms engaged in the sale or transfer of milk, except such groups as retail stores, hotels, restaurants, etc.) will compute the quantity of milk and fluid milk byproducts which they may sell each month in terms of pounds of milk and pounds of milk byproducts, and their cream sales in terms of pounds of cream and butterfat. In months which contain more or less days than the base period, handler will determine the amount of milk they may sell by multiplying the average of daily deliveries in June by 28, 29, or 31, whichever is applicable.

Dealers may exceed their monthly quotas by up to 5 percent greater sales providing they make up this excess by reducing their deliveries proportionately the next month, without the market agent being required to report such excess sales.

Deliveries to the armed forces, to plants processing dairy products, and to other handlers (except special classes of handlers such as peddlers) are quota exempt.

To facilitate administration, the market agent for each milk sales area may act upon petitions for relief from hardships which may be submitted to him, and his decision will be effective for a 60-day period.

Dealers' quotas based on June deliveries will permit consumers to purchase more milk than they consumed in 1942, and considerably more than in pre-war years. Consumption of fluid milk and cream thus far in 1943 has been at a rate of more than 41 billion pounds annually compared with 37.7 billion pounds in 1942 and an average of 32.6 billion pounds in pre-war years (1936-40).

Total milk production has been mounting steadily in recent years—from 101 billion pounds in 1935 to 119 billion pounds in 1942—an all-time high. Production during the first 7 months of this year equalled production during the same months of 1942.

Increasing fluid milk sales, however, resulting largely from the sharp rise in consumer incomes, have reduced the quantity of milk available for the manufacture of essential products such as butter, cheese, evaporated milk, ice cream, and milk powder. Previously uncontrolled, consumption of fluid milk and cream has been rising at the rate of about 1 percent a month, and already is 20 percent above the 1941 level and 10 to 12 percent over 1942.

This has necessitated the stabilization of fluid milk consumption in order to meet the requirements for manufactured dairy products, both on the home and battle fronts, WFA officials explained.

#1337
Am. 1

FDO 79-4
AMDT. 1
OCTOBER 28, 1943

WAR FOOD ADMINISTRATION

[FDO 79-4. Amdt. 1]

PART 1401—DAIRY PRODUCTS

FLUID MILK AND CREAM IN WASHINGTON, D. C., MILK SALES AREA

Pursuant to the authority vested in the Director by Food Distribution Order No. 79, dated September 7, 1943 (8 F.R. 12426), as amended, and to effectuate the purposes thereof, Director Food Distribution Order No. 79-4 § 1401.38, relative to the conservation of fluid milk in the Washington, D. C., milk sales area (8 F.R. 13368) issued by the Director of Food Distribution on September 30, 1943, is amended as follows:

The milk sales area described in § 1401.38 (b) of the original order is modified in the following particulars: Delete the election district of "Dranesville" in Fairfax County, Virginia.

Effective date. This amendment of FDO No. 79-4, shall become effective at 12:01 a. m., e. w. t., November 1, 1943.

(E.O. 9280, 8 F.R. 10179; E.O. 9322, 8 F.R. 3807; E.O. 9334, 8 F.R. 5423; FDO 79, 8 F.R. 12426, 13283)

Issued this 28th day of October 1943.

ROY F. HENDRICKSON,
Director of Food Distribution.

133F
Cop 1

FDO 79-4

AMDT. 2
MAR. 29, 1944

WAR FOOD ADMINISTRATION

[FDO 79-4, Amdt. 2]

PART 1401—DAIRY PRODUCTS

FLUID MILK AND CREAM IN THE WASHINGTON, D. C., SALES AREA

Pursuant to Food Distribution Order No. 79 (8 F.R. 1246), dated September 7, 1943, as amended, and to effectuate the purposes thereof, Food Distribution Order No. 79-4 (8 F.R. 13368), relative to the conservation and distribution of fluid milk in the Washington, D. C., milk sales area, issued by the Director of Food Distribution on September 30, 1943, as amended, is hereby further amended as follows:

1. By deleting the numeral "20" wherever it appears in § 1401.38 (k) (2) and inserting, in lieu thereof, the numeral "10."

2. By deleting the numeral "$0.01" wherever it appears in § 1401.38 (n) and inserting, in lieu thereof, the numeral "$0.005."

The provisions of this amendment shall become effective at 12:01 a. m., e. w. t., April 1, 1944. With respect to violations of said Food Distribution Order No. 79-4, as amended, rights accrued, or liabilities incurred prior to the effective time of this amendment, said Food Distribution Order No. 79-4, as amended, shall be deemed to be in full force and effect for the purpose of sustaining any proper suit, action, or other proceeding with respect to any such violation, right, or liability.

(E.O. 9280, 7 F.R. 10179; E.O. 9322, 8 F.R. 3607; E.O. 9334, 8 F.R. 5423; E.O. 9398, 8 F.R. 14783; FDO 79, 8 F.R. 12426, 13283)

Issued this 29th day of March 1944.

LEE MARSHALL,
Director of Food Distribution.

GPO—WFA 559—p 1

WAR FOOD ADMINISTRATION

[FDO 79-5]

PART 1401—DAIRY PRODUCTS

CONSERVATION AND DISTRIBUTION OF FLUID MILK AND CREAM IN THE NORFOLK-PORTSMOUTH-NEWPORT NEWS, VA., SALES AREA

Pursuant to the authority vested in me by Food Distribution Order No. 79 (8 F.R. 12426), issued on September 7, 1943, as amended, and to effectuate the purposes of such order, it is hereby ordered as follows:

§ 1401.37 *Quota restrictions*—(a) *Definitions.* When used in this order, unless otherwise distinctly expressed or manifestly incompatible with the intent hereof:

(1) Each term defined in Food Distribution Order No. 79, as amended, shall, when used herein, have the same meaning as is set forth for such term in Food Distribution Order No. 79, as amended.

(2) The term "order" means Food Distribution Order No. 79, issued on September 7, 1943, as amended.

(3) The term "sub-handler" means any handler, such as a peddler, vendor, sub-dealer, or secondary dealer, who purchases in a previously packaged and processed form milk, milk byproducts, or cream for delivery.

(b) *Milk sales area.* The following area is hereby designated as a "milk sales area" to be known as the Norfolk-Portsmouth-Newport News, Va., sales area, and is referred to hereinafter as the "sales area": The cities of Norfolk, Portsmouth, and Newport News, and the cities of Hampton and South Norfolk; the magisterial districts of Chesapeake and Wythe in Elizabeth City County; the districts of Deep Creek, Tanners Creek, Washington, and Western Branch in Norfolk County; the district of Kempsville in Princess Anne County; and the district of Newport in Warwick County, all in the State of Virginia.

(c) *Base period.* The calendar month of June 1943 is hereby designated as the base period for the sales area.

(d) *Quota period.* The remainder of the calendar month in which the provisions hereof become effective and each subsequent calendar month, respectively, is hereby designated as a quota period for the sales area.

(e) *Handler quotas.* Quotas for each handler in the sales area in each quota period shall be determined as follows:

(1) Divide the total deliveries of each of milk, milk byproducts, and cream (and of butterfat in milk or in cream where percentages of pounds of butterfat are specified in (e) (3) (i) or (e) (3) (ii) hereof) made in the sales area by such handler during the base period, after excluding the quota-exempt deliveries described in (h) hereof and adjusting such deliveries for the transfers set out in (i) hereof, by the number of days in the base period;

(2) Multiply the result of the foregoing calculation by the number of days in the quota period; and

(3) Multiply the aforesaid resulting amount by the following applicable percentage: (i) Milk: 100 percent of pounds of milk and ---- percent of pounds of butterfat; (ii) Cream: 75 percent of pounds of cream and 75 percent of pounds of butterfat; and (iii) Milk byproducts: 75 percent of pounds of milk byproducts other than cottage, pot, or baker's cheese and of the pounds of skim milk equivalent of cottage, pot, or baker's cheese. (For the purpose of this order, one pound of cottage, pot, or baker's cheese shall be considered as the equivalent of 7 pounds of skim milk.)

(f) *Quotas for handlers who are also producers.* Quotas for handlers who are also producers and who purchase no milk shall be 100 percent of the total production of such handlers in the base period.

(g) *Handler exemptions.* Quotas shall not apply to any handler who delivers in a quota period a daily average of less than 400 units of milk, cream, and milk byproducts. For the purpose of this order, a unit shall be the equivalent in volume of the following:

(1) Milk, one quart of milk;

(2) Cream, one-half pint of cream; and

(3) Milk byproduct, one quart of skim milk, buttermilk, flavored milk drink, or other beverage containing more than 85 percent of skim milk, or one-half pound of cottage, pot, or baker's cheese.

(h) *Quota exclusions and exemptions.* Deliveries of milk, milk byproducts, or cream (1) to other handlers, except for such deliveries to sub-handlers, (2) to plants engaged in the handling or processing of milk, milk byproducts, or cream from which no milk, milk byproducts, or cream is delivered in the sales area, and (3) to the agencies or groups specified in (d) of the order, shall be excluded from the computation of deliveries in the base period and exempt from charges to quotas.

(i) *Transfers and apportionment of quotas.* The market agent is empowered to deduct an amount of base period deliveries to purchasers from the total of deliveries made by a handler or other person in the base period upon the application and a showing of unreasonable hardship by the handler making deliveries to such purchasers on the effective date of this order, and to add the amount of such deliveries to the total base period deliveries of the applicant handler. Denials of transfers or transfers granted by the market agent shall be reviewed by the Director upon application.

(j) *Petition for relief from hardships.* (1) Any person affected by the order or the provisions hereof who considers that compliance therewith would work an exceptional and unreasonable hardship on him, may file with the market agent a petition addressed to the Director. The petition shall contain the correct name, address and principal place of business of the petitioner, a full statement of the facts upon which the petition is based, and the hardship involved and the nature of the relief desired.

(2) Upon receiving such petition, the market agent shall immediately investigate the representations and facts stated therein.

(3) After investigation, the petition shall be certified to the Director, but prior to certification the market agent may (i) deny the petition; or (ii) grant temporary relief for a total period not to exceed 60 days.

(4) Denials or grants of relief by the market agent shall be reviewed by the Director and may be affirmed, modified, or reversed by the Director.

(k) *Reports.* Each handler shall transmit to the market agent on forms prescribed by the market agent the following reports:

(1) Within 20 days following the effective date of this order, reports which show the information required by the market agent to establish such handlers' quotas;

(2) Within 20 days following the close of each quota period, the information required by the market agent to establish volumes of deliveries of milk, cream, and milk byproducts during the preceding quota period; and

(3) Handlers exempt from quotas pursuant to (f) hereof shall, upon the request of the market agent, submit the information required by the market agent to establish volumes of deliveries of milk, cream, and milk byproducts.

(l) *Records.* Handlers shall keep and shall make available to the market agent such records of receipts, sales, deliveries, and production as the market agent shall require for the purpose of obtaining information which the Director may require for the establishment of quotas as prescribed in (b) of the order.

(m) *Distribution schedules.* The distribution schedules, if any, to be followed by the handlers in making deliveries shall be made effective in the terms of approval by the Director of such schedules.

(n) *Expense of administration.* Each handler shall pay to the market agent, within 20 days after the close of each

iar month an assessment of $0.01
ıundredweight of each of milk,
, skim milk, buttermilk, flavored
irinks, beverages containing more
85 percent of skim milk, and skim
equivalent of cottage, pot, or bak-
heese delivered during the pre-
; quota period and subject to quota
tions under the provisions hereof.
Violations. The market agent
report all violations to the Director
ıer with the information required

for the prosecution of such violations, except in a case where a handler has made deliveries in a quota period in excess of a quota in an amount not to exceed 5 percent of such quota, and in the succeeding quota period makes deliveries below that quota by at least the same percent.

(p) *Bureau of the Budget approval.* The record-keeping and reporting requirements of this order have been approved by the Bureau of the Budget

in accordance
Act of 1942. S
or reporting
ject to the app
Budget pursua
Act of 1942.
(q) This ord
a. m., e. w. t.,

Issued this 3

Direct

Release Immediate:
day, September 30, 1943.

eral control over fluid milk sales,
gh the establishment of quotas on
ries of milk, cream, and milk by-
cts, will go into effect in 13 eastern
nidwestern metropolitan areas be-
ıg October 4, the War Food Ad-
ration announced today.
se areas, and the market agents
ıated by the Food Distribution Ad-
ration to administer the milk con-
ion and control program in each,

imore, Md., Washington, D. C.,
ke, Va., Richmond, Va., Norfolk-
nouth-Newport News, Va.: George
, 1731 I Street NW., Washington,

cinnati, Ohio, Toledo, Ohio, Day-
Ohio, Canton, Ohio, Cleveland,
Fred W. Issler, 152 East Fourth
, Cincinnati, Ohio.
cago, Illinois: A. W. Colebank, 135
LaSalle St.; Chicago, Ill.
aha-Neb.-Council Bluffs, Iowa:
e McPherren, Rm. 408, Post Office
Omaha, Nebraska.
Louis, Missouri: William C. Eckles,
Chouteau Ave., St. Louis, Missouri.
sumers in regulated areas will be
o purchase as much milk as they
been buying—within the limits of
supplies, officials said. The basic
se of the program is to prevent a
er increase in the consumption of
nilk (rather than to reduce present
mption) so that enough milk will
ilable to produce the cheese, but-
d other manufactured dairy prod-
equired by the armed services and
ns. As milk conservation and
ol will be effected at the dealer
consumer point rationing is not
ed.
: dealers in the 13 initial milk sales
will be allowed to sell as much fluid
each month as they sold last June,
, the peak production month. To
ssure that enough fluid milk will be
ble during the season of low pro-
n to enable dealers to sell as much
ir quotas allow, cream sales will be
d to 75 percent of the quantity sold
ne, and the sales quota for fluid
byproducts as a group (including
e cheese, chocolate milk, and but-
k) also is set at 75 percent of June

ducer-distributors who purchase no
except those whose volume of sales
ll enough to exempt them from the

quota) will be allowed to sell an amount of fluid milk, cream, and fluid milk byproducts equal to 100 percent of their total milk production in June. "Quota-exempt" producer-distributors are defined separately for each area, but in general they are those whose deliveries are relatively small, and who produce the milk they sell from their own herds.

Milk distributors will be responsible for the fair distribution of supplies in their markets. Under Food Distribution Order 79, however, which authorizes the establishment of individual milk orders for each area, the various market agents may recommend distribution schedules to assure that, in the event of short supplies, the most essential needs will be met first.

Success of the milk conservation and control program depends largely on trade and consumer cooperation, WFA officials pointed out. It is believed that stabilization of milk consumption can be accomplished equitably through this system of dealer control without resorting to consumer rationing. Individual rationing of such a highly perishable product as milk would be very complex, difficult to administer, and would almost necessarily result in substantial reductions in fluid milk sales in many markets. Rationing at the consumer level undoubtedly will be necessary if control over dealers' sales does not effectively regulate fluid milk consumption, the officials said.

Under the individual orders established for each area, the milk control program may be modified to fit production and consumption conditions in each market. These orders will be administered by market agents appointed by the Director of Food Distribution.

Milk sales in all other cities of at least 100,000 population will be regulated as soon as administrative arrangements can be completed—with most areas of this size to be operating under the program by November 1. It is expected that the program will then be extended to smaller population areas until all markets of at least 50,000 population are included.

Distributor quotas for milk sales areas to be named later may be the same as those for the areas announced today, or they may vary if local conditions indicate that different bases are necessary.

Milk handlers (that is, all persons or firms engaged in the sale or transfer of milk, except such groups as retail stores, hotels, restaurants, etc.) will compute the quantity of milk and fluid milk by-

products whicl
in terms of po
milk byproduc
in terms of po
fat. In mont
less days than
will determine
may sell by n
daily deliverie
whichever is a
Dealers ma
quotas by up
providing the
reducing their
the next mo
agent being r
cess sales.
Deliveries t
plants process
other handler
handlers such
exempt.
To facilitat
ket agent for
act upon peti
ship which n
and his decis
60-day period
Dealers' qu
eries will perr
more milk tha
and considera
years. Consu
cream thus f
rate of more t
nually compai
in 1942 and
pounds in pre
Total milk p
ing steadily i
billion pound
pounds in 194
duction durin
year equalled
same months
Increasing
resulting larg
consumer inc
quantity of mi
facture of esse
ter, cheese, ev
and milk po
trolled, consu
cream has be
about 1 perce
is 20 percent a
to 12 percent
This has n
tion of fluid r
to meet the r
tured dairy pr
and battle f
plained.

7337

FDO 79-5

AMDT. 1
OCTOBER 28, 1943

A

WAR FOOD ADMINISTRATION

[FDO 79-5, Amdt. 1]

PART 1401—DAIRY PRODUCTS

FLUID MILK AND CREAM IN NORFOLK-PORTSMOUTH-NEWPORT NEWS, VA., MILK SALES AREA

Pursuant to the authority vested in the Director by Food Distribution Order No. 79, dated September 7, 1943 (8 F.R. 12426), as amended, and to effectuate the purposes thereof, Director Food Distribution Order No. 79-5, § 1401.37, relative to the conservation of fluid milk in the Norfolk-Portsmouth-Newport News, Virginia, milk sales area (8 F.R. 13369), issued by the Director of Food Distribution on September 30, 1943, is amended as follows:

The milk sales area described in § 1401.37 (b) of the original order is modified in the following particulars: Delete all the area specified following the city of "South Norfolk" and substitute therefor "the counties of Princess Anne, Norfolk, Elizabeth City, York, Warwick and James City, all in the State of Virginia."

Effective date. This amendment of FDO No. 79-5 shall become effective at 12:01 a. m., e. w. t., November 1, 1943.

(E.O. 9280, 8 F.R. 10179; E.O. 9322, 8 F.R. 3807; E.O. 9334, 8 F.R. 5423; FDO 79, 8 F.R. 12426, 13283)

Issued this 28th day of October 1943.

ROY F. HENDRICKSON,
Director of Food Distribution.

FDO 79-5

AMDT. 2
MAR. 29, 1944

WAR FOOD ADMINISTRATION

[FDO 79-5, Amdt. 2]

PART 1401—DAIRY PRODUCTS

FLUID MILK AND CREAM IN NORFOLK-PORTSMOUTH-NEWPORT NEWS VA., SALES AREA

Pursuant to Food Distribution Order No. 79 (8 F.R. 12426), dated September 7, 1943, as amended, and to effectuate the purposes thereof Food Distribution Order No. 79-5 (8 F.R. 13369), relative to the conservation and distribution of fluid milk in the Norfolk-Portsmouth-Newport News, Virginia, milk sales area, issued by the Director of Food Distribution on September 30, 1943, as amended, is hereby further amended as follows:

1. By deleting the numeral "20" wherever it appears in § 1401.37 (k) (2) and inserting, in lieu thereof, the numeral "10."

2. By deleting the numeral "$0.01" wherever it appears in § 1401.37 (n) and inserting, in lieu thereof, the numeral "$0.005."

The provisions of this amendment shall become effective at 12:01 a. m., e. w. t., April 1, 1944. With respect to violations of said Food Distribution Order No. 79-5, as amended, rights accrued, or liabilities incurred prior to the effective time of this amendment, said Food Distribution Order No. 79-5, as amended, shall be deemed to be in full force and effect for the purpose of sustaining any proper suit, action, or other proceeding with respect to any such violation, right, or liability.

(E.O. 9280, 7 F.R. 10179; E.O. 9322, 8 F.R. 3807; E.O. 9334, 8 F.R. 5423; E.O. 9392, 8 F.R. 14783; FDO 79, 8 F.R. 12426, 13283)

Issued this 29th day of March 1944.

LEE MARSHALL,
Director of Food Distribution.

WAR FOOD ADMINISTRATION

[FDO 79-6]

PART 1401—DAIRY PRODUCTS

CONSERVATION AND DISTRIBUTION OF FLUID MILK AND CREAM IN THE RICHMOND, VA., SALES AREA

Pursuant to the authority vested in me by Food Distribution Order No. 79 (8 F. R. 12426), issued on September 7, 1943, as amended, and to effectuate the purposes of such order, it is hereby ordered as follows:

§ 1401.39 *Quota restrictions*—(a) *Definitions.* When used in this order, unless otherwise distinctly expressed or manifestly incompatible with the intent hereof:

(1) Each term defined in Food Distribution Order No. 79, as amended, shall, when used herein, have the same meaning as is set forth for such term in Food Distribution Order No. 79, as amended.

(2) The term "order" means Food Distribution Order No. 79, issued on September 7, 1943, as amended.

(3) The term "sub-handler" means any handler, such as a peddler, vendor, sub-dealer, or secondary dealer, who purchases in a previously packaged and processed form milk, milk byproducts, or cream for delivery.

(b) *Milk sales area.* The following area is hereby designated as a "milk sales area" to be known as the Richmond, Virginia, sales area, and is referred to hereinafter as the "sales area": The city of Richmond and the magisterial district of Manchester in Chesterfield County, Virginia; the magisterial districts of Brookland, Fairfield, Tuckahoe and Varina in Henrico County, Virginia.

(c) *Base period.* The calendar month of June 1943 is hereby designated as the base period for the sales area.

(d) *Quota period.* The remainder of the calendar month in which the provisions hereof become effective and each subsequent calendar month, respectively, is hereby designated as a quota period for the sales area.

(e) *Handler quotas.* Quotas for each handler in the sales area in each quota period shall be determined as follows:

(1) Divide the total deliveries of each of milk, milk byproducts, and cream (and of butterfat in milk or in cream where percentages of pounds of butterfat are specified in (e) (3) (i) or (e) (3) (ii) hereof) made in the sales area by such handler during the base period, after excluding the quota-exempt deliveries described in (h) hereof and adjusting such deliveries for the transfers set out in (i) hereof, by the number of days in the base period;

(2) Multiply the result of the foregoing calculation by the number of days in the quota period; and

(3) Multiply the aforesaid resulting amount by the following applicable percentage: (i) Milk: 100 percent of pounds of milk and ___ percent of pounds of butterfat; (ii) Cream: 75 percent of pounds of cream and 75 percent of pounds of butterfat; and (iii) Milk byproducts: 75 percent of pounds of milk byproducts other than cottage, pot, or baker's cheese and of the pounds of skim milk equivalent of cottage, pot, or baker's cheese. (For the purpose of this order, one pound of cottage, pot, or baker's cheese shall be considered as the equivalent of 7 pounds of skim milk.)

(f) *Quotas for handlers who are also producers.* Quotas for handlers who are also producers and who purchase no milk shall be 100 percent of the total production of such handlers in the base period.

(g) *Handler exemptions.* Quotas shall not apply to any handler who delivers in a quota period a daily average of less than 300 units of milk, cream, and milk byproducts. For the purpose of this order, a unit shall be the equivalent in volume of the following:

(1) Milk, one quart of milk;

(2) Cream, one-half pint of cream; and

(3) Milk byproduct, one quart of skim milk, buttermilk, flavored milk drink, or other beverage containing more than 85 percent of skim milk, or one-half pound of cottage, pot, or baker's cheese.

(h) *Quota exclusions and exemptions.* Deliveries of milk, milk byproducts, or cream (1) to other handlers, except for such deliveries to sub-handlers, (2) to plants engaged in the handling or processing of milk, milk byproducts, or cream from which no milk, milk byproducts, or cream is delivered in the sales area, and (3) to the agencies or groups specified in (d) of the order, shall be excluded from the computation of deliveries in the base period and exempt from charges to quotas.

(i) *Transfers and apportionment of quotas.* The market agent is empowered to deduct an amount of base period deliveries to purchasers from the total of deliveries made by a handler or other person in the base period upon the application and a showing of unreasonable hardship by the handler making deliveries to such purchasers on the effective date of this order, and to add the amount of such deliveries to the total base period deliveries of the applicant handler. Denials or transfers or transfers granted by the market agent shall be reviewed by the Director upon application.

(j) *Petition for relief from hardships.* (1) Any person affected by the order or the provisions hereof who considers that compliance therewith would work an exceptional and unreasonable hardship on him, may file with the market agent a petition addressed to the Director. The petition shall contain the correct name, address and principal place of business of the petitioner, a full statement of the facts upon which the petition is based, and the hardship involved and the nature of the relief desired.

(2) Upon receiving such petition, the market agent shall immediately investigate the representations and facts stated therein.

(3) After investigation, the petition shall be certified to the Director, but prior to certification the market agent may (i) deny the petition; or (ii) grant temporary relief for a total period not to exceed 60 days.

(4) Denials or grants of relief by the market agent shall be reviewed by the Director and may be affirmed, modified or reversed by the Director.

(k) *Reports.* Each handler shall transmit to the market agent on forms prescribed by the market agent the following reports:

(1) Within 20 days following the effective date of this order, reports which show the information required by the market agent to establish such handlers' quotas;

(2) Within 20 days following the close of each quota period, the information required by the market agent to establish volumes of deliveries of milk, cream, and milk byproducts during the preceding quota period; and

(3) Handlers exempt from quotas pursuant to (f) hereof shall, upon the request of the market agent, submit the information required by the market agent to establish volumes of deliveries of milk, cream, and milk byproducts.

(l) *Records.* Handlers shall keep and shall make available to the market agent such records of receipts, sales, deliveries, and production as the market agent shall require for the purpose of obtaining information which the Director may require for the establishment of quotas as prescribed in (b) of the order.

(m) *Distribution schedules.* The distribution schedules, if any, to be followed by the handlers in making deliveries shall be made effective in the terms of approval by the Director of such schedules.

(n) *Expense of administration.* Each handler shall pay to the market agent within 20 days after the close of each calendar month an assessment of $0.01 per hundredweight of each of milk, cream, skim milk, buttermilk, flavored milk drinks, beverages containing more than 85 percent of skim milk, and skim milk equivalent of cottage, pot, or baker's cheese delivered during the preceding quota period and subject to quota regulations under the provisions hereof.

(o) *Violations.* The market agent shall report all violations to the Director together with the information required for the prosecution of such violations, except in a case where a handler has made deliveries in a quota period in excess of a quota in an amount not to exceed 5 percent of such quota, and in the succeeding quota period makes deliveries below that quota by at least the same percent.

(p) *Bureau of the Budget approval.* The record-keeping and reporting requirements of this order have been approved by the Bureau of the Budget in accordance with the Federal Reports Act of 1942. Subsequent record-keeping or reporting requirements will be subject to the approval of the Bureau of the Budget pursuant to the Federal Reports Act of 1942.

(q) This order shall take effect at 12:01 a. m., e. w. t., October 4, 1943.

Issued this 30th day of September 1943.

ROY F. HENDRICKSON,
Director of Food Distribution.

Press Release Immediate:
Thursday, September 30, 1943.

Federal control over fluid milk sales, through the establishment of quotas on deliveries of milk, cream, and milk byproducts, will go into effect in 13 eastern and midwestern metropolitan areas beginning October 4, the War Food Administration announced today.

These areas, and the market agents designated by the Food Distribution Administration to administer the milk conservation and control program in each, are:

Baltimore, Md., Washington, D. C., Roanoke, Va., Richmond, Va., Norfolk-Portsmouth-Newport News, Va.: George Irvine, 1731 I Street NW., Washington, D. C.

Cincinnati, Ohio, Toledo, Ohio, Dayton, Ohio, Canton, Ohio, Cleveland, Ohio: Fred W. Issler, 152 East Fourth Street, Cincinnati, Ohio.

Chicago, Illinois: A. W. Colebank, 135 South LaSalle St., Chicago, Ill.

Omaha, Nebr.-Council Bluffs, Iowa: Wayne McPherren, Rm. 408, Post Office Bldg., Omaha, Nebraska.

St. Louis, Missouri: William C. Eckles, 4030 Chouteau Ave., St. Louis, Missouri.

Consumers in regulated areas will be able to purchase as much milk as they have been buying—within the limits of local supplies, officials said. The basic purpose of the program is to prevent a further increase in the consumption of fluid milk (rather than to reduce present consumption) so that enough milk will be available to produce the cheese, butter, and other manufactured dairy products required by the armed services and civilians. As milk conservation and control will be effected at the dealer level, consumer point rationing is not involved.

Milk dealers in the 13 initial milk sales areas will be allowed to sell as much fluid milk each month as they sold last June, (1943), the peak production month. To help assure that enough fluid milk will be available during the season of low production to enable dealers to sell as much as their quotas allow, cream sales will be limited to 75 percent of the quantity sold in June, and the sales quota for fluid milk by-products as a group (including cottage cheese, chocolate milk, and buttermilk) also is set at 75 percent of June sales.

Producer-distributors who purchase no milk (except those whose volume of sales is small enough to exempt them from the quota) will be allowed to sell an amount of fluid milk, cream, and fluid milk byproducts equal to 100 percent of their total milk production in June. "Quota-exempt" producer-distributors are defined separately for each area, but in general they are those whose deliveries are relatively small, and who produce the milk they sell from their own herds.

Milk distributors will be responsible for the fair distribution of supplies in their markets. Under Food Distribution Order 79, however, which authorizes the establishment of individual milk orders for each area, the various market agents may recommend distribution schedules to assure that, in the event of short supplies, the most essential needs will be met first.

Success of the milk conservation and control program depends largely on trade and consumer cooperation, WFA officials pointed out. It is believed that stabilization of milk consumption can be accomplished equitably through this system of dealer control without resorting to consumer rationing. Individual rationing of such a highly perishable product as milk would be very complex, difficult to administer, and would almost necessarily result in substantial reductions in fluid milk sales in many markets. Rationing at the consumer level undoubtedly will be necessary if control over dealers' sales does not effectively regulate fluid milk consumption, the officials said.

Under the individual orders established for each area, the milk control program may be modified to fit production and consumption conditions in each market. These orders will be administered by market agents appointed by the Director of Food Distribution.

Milk sales in all other cities of at least 100,000 population will be regulated as soon as administrative arrangements can be completed—with most areas of this size to be operating under the program by November 1. It is expected that the program will then be extended to smaller population areas until all markets of at least 50,000 population are included.

Distributor quotas for milk sales areas to be named later may be the same as those for the areas announced today, or they may vary if local conditions indicate that different bases are necessary.

Milk handlers (that is, all persons or firms engaged in the sale or transfer of milk, except such groups as retail stores, hotels, restaurants, etc.) will compute the quantity of milk and fluid milk byproducts which they may sell each month in terms of pounds of milk and pounds of milk byproducts, and their cream sales in terms of pounds of cream and butterfat. In months which contain more or less days than the base period handlers will determine the amount of milk they may sell by multiplying the average of daily deliveries in June by 28, 29, or 31, whichever is applicable.

Dealers may exceed their monthly quotas by up to 5 percent greater sales providing they make up their excess by reducing their deliveries proportionately the next month, without the market agent being required to report such excess sales.

Deliveries to the armed forces, to plants processing dairy products, and to other handlers (except special classes of handlers such as peddlers) are quota exempt.

To facilitate administration, the market agent for each milk sales area may act upon petitions for relief from hardship which may be submitted to him, and his decision will be effective for a 60-day period.

Dealers' quotas based on June deliveries will permit consumers to purchase more milk than they consumed in 1942, and considerably more than in pre-war years. Consumption of fluid milk and cream thus far in 1943 has been at a rate of more than 41 billion pounds annually compared with 37.7 billion pounds in 1942 and an average of 32.6 billion pounds in pre-war years (1936–40).

Total milk production has been mounting steadily in recent years—from 101 billion pounds in 1935 to 119 billion pounds in 1942—an all-time high. Production during the first 7 months of this year equalled production during the same months of 1942.

Increasing fluid milk sales, however, resulting largely from the sharp rise in consumer incomes, have reduced the quantity of milk available for the manufacture of essential products such as butter, cheese, evaporated milk, ice cream, and milk powder. Previously uncontrolled, consumption of fluid milk and cream has been rising at the rate of about 1 percent a month, and already is 20 percent above the 1941 level and 10 to 12 percent over 1942.

This has necessitated the stabilization of fluid milk consumption in order to meet the requirements for manufactured dairy products, both on the home and battle fronts, WFA officials explained.

serve
/
7337

FDO 79-6
AMDT. 1
NOV. 22, 1943

WAR FOOD ADMINISTRATION

[FDO 79-6, Amdt. 1]

PART 1401—DAIRY PRODUCTS

FLUID MILK AND CREAM IN RICHMOND, VA., SALES AREA

Pursuant to the authority vested in the Director by Food Distribution Order No. 79, dated September 7, 1943 (8 F.R. 12426), as amended, and to effectuate the purposes thereof, Director Food Distribution Order No. 79-6, § 1401.39, relative to the conservation of fluid milk in the Richmond, Virginia, milk sales area (8 F.R. 13370), issued by the Director of Food Distribution on September 30, 1943, is amended as follows:

The milk sales area described in § 1401.39 (b) of the original order is modified in the following particulars: Add the magisterial district of Ashland in Hanover County; the magisterial district of Dale in Chesterfield County; and the magisterial district of Dover in Goochland County.

Effective date. This amendment of FDO No. 79-6, shall become effective at 12:01 a. m., e. w. t., December 1, 1943.

(E.O. 9280, 8 F.R. 10179; E.O. 9322, 8 F.R. 3807; E.O. 9334, 8 F.R. 5423; FDO 79, 8 F.R. 12426, 13283)

Issued this 22d day of November 1943.

ROY F. HENDRICKSON,
Director of Food Distribution.

FDO 79-6

AMDT. 2
MAR. 29, 1944

WAR FOOD ADMINISTRATION

PART 1401—DAIRY PRODUCTS

[FDO 79-6, Amdt. 2]

FLUID MILK AND CREAM IN RICHMOND, VA., SALES AREA

Pursuant to Food Distribution Order No. 79 (8 F.R. 12426), dated September 7, 1943, as amended, and to effectuate the purposes thereof, Food Distribution Order No. 79-6 (8 F.R. 13370), relative to the conservation and distribution of fluid milk in the Richmond, Virginia, milk sales area, issued by the Director of Food Distribution on September 30, 1943, as amended, is hereby further amended, as follows:

1. By deleting the numeral "20" wherever it appears in § 1401.39 (k) (2) and inserting, in lieu thereof, the numeral "10."

2. By deleting the numeral "$0.01" wherever it appears in § 1401.39 (n) and inserting, in lieu thereof, the numeral "$0.005."

3. By deleting therefrom the provisions of § 1401.39 (h) and substituting therefor, the following:

(h) *Quota exclusions and exemptions.* Deliveries of milk, milk byproducts, or cream (1) to other handlers, except for such deliveries to sub-handlers, (2) to plants engaged in the handling or processing of milk, milk byproducts, or cream from which no milk, milk byproducts, or cream is delivered in the sales area, (3) to nursery, elementary, junior high, and high schools, and (4) to the agencies or groups specified in (d) of the order, shall be excluded from the computation of deliveries in the base period and exempt from charges to quota.

The provisions of this amendment shall become effective at 12:01 a. m., e. w. t., April 1, 1944. With respect to violations of said Food Distribution Order No. 79-6, as amended, rights accrued, or liabilities incurred prior to the effective time of this amendment, said Food Distribution Order No. 79-6, as amended, shall be deemed to be in full force and effect for the purpose of sustaining any proper suit, action, or other proceeding with respect to any such violation, right, or liability.

(E.O. 9280, 7 F.R. 10179; E.O. 9322, 8 F.R. 3807; E.O. 9334, 8 F.R. 5423; E.O. 9392, 8 F.R. 14783; FDO 79, 8 F.R. 12426, 13283)

Issued this 29th day of March 1944.

LEE MARSHALL,
Director of Food Distribution.

7337

FDO 79-7

SEPT. 30, 1943

WAR FOOD ADMINISTRATION

[FDO 79-7]

PART 1401—DAIRY PRODUCTS

CONSERVATION AND DISTRIBUTION OF FLUID MILK AND CREAM IN THE CHICAGO, ILL., METROPOLITAN MILK SALES AREA

Pursuant to the authority vested in me by Food Distribution Order No. 79 (8 F.R. 12426), issued on September 7, 1943, as amended, and to effectuate the purposes of such order, it is hereby ordered as follows:

§ 1401.40 *Quota restrictions* — (a) *Definitions.* When used in this order, unless otherwise distinctly expressed or manifestly incompatible with the intent hereof:

(1) Each term defined in Food Distribution Order No. 79, as amended, shall, when used herein, have the same meaning as is set forth for such term in Food Distribution Order No. 79, as amended.

(2) The term "order" means Food Distribution Order No. 79, issued on September 7, 1943, as amended.

(3) The term "sub-handler" means any handler, such as a peddler, vendor, sub-dealer, or secondary dealer, who purchases in a previously packaged and processed form milk, milk byproducts, or cream for delivery.

(b) *Milk sales area.* The following area is hereby designated as a "milk sales area" to be known as the Chicago, Illinois, metropolitan milk sales area, and is referred to hereinafter as the "sales area". The city of Chicago and the entire area included in:

The townships of Waukegan, Shields, Deerfield, and West Deerfield in Lake County, Illinois; the counties of Cook and DuPage in Illinois; the townships of Aurora, Batavia, Dundee, Elgin, Geneva, and St. Charles in Kane County, Illinois; the townships of Calumet, Hobart, and North in Lake County, Indiana.

(c) *Base period.* The calendar month of June 1943 is hereby designated as the base period for the sales area.

(d) *Quota period.* The remainder of the calendar month in which the provisions hereof become effective and each subsequent calendar month, respectively, is hereby designated as a quota period for the sales area.

(e) *Handler quotas.* Quotas for each handler in the sales area in each quota period shall be determined as follows:

(1) Divide the total deliveries of each of milk, milk byproducts, and cream (and of butterfat in milk or in cream where percentages of pounds of butterfat are specified in (e) (3) (i) or (e) (3) (ii) hereof) made in the sales area by such handler during the base period, after excluding the quota-exempt deliveries described in (h) hereof and adjusting such deliveries for the transfers set out in (i) hereof, by the number of days in the base period;

(2) Multiply the result of the foregoing calculation by the number of days in the quota period; and

(3) Multiply the aforesaid resulting amount by the following applicable percentage: (i) Milk: 100 percent of pounds of milk and ____ percent of pounds of butterfat; (ii) Cream: 75 percent of pounds of cream and 75 percent of pounds of butterfat; and (iii) Milk byproducts: 75 percent of pounds of milk byproducts other than cottage, pot, or baker's cheese and of the pounds of skim milk equivalent of cottage, pot, or baker's cheese. (For the purpose of this order, one pound of cottage, pot, or baker's cheese shall be considered as the equivalent of 7 pounds of skim milk.).

(f) *Quotas for handlers who are also producers.* Quotas for handlers who are also producers and who purchase no milk shall be 100 percent of the total production of such handlers in the base period.

(g) *Handler exemptions.* Quotas shall not apply to any handler who delivers in a quota period a daily average of less than 400 units of milk, cream, and milk byproducts. For the purpose of this order, a unit shall be the equivalent in volume of the following:

(1) Milk, one quart of milk;

(2) Cream, one-half pint of cream; and

(3) Milk byproduct, one quart of skim milk, buttermilk, flavored milk drink, or other beverage containing more than 85 percent of skim milk, or one-half pound of cottage, pot, or baker's cheese.

(h) *Quota exclusions and exemptions.* Deliveries of milk, milk byproducts, or cream (1) to other handlers, except for such deliveries to sub-handlers, (2) to plants engaged in the handling or processing of milk, milk byproducts, or cream from which no milk, milk byproducts, or cream is delivered in the sales area, and (3) to the agencies or groups specified in (d) of the order, shall be excluded from the computation of deliveries in the base period and exempt from charges to quotas.

(i) *Transfers and apportionment of quotas.* The market agent is empowered to deduct an amount of base period deliveries to purchasers from the total of deliveries made by a handler or other person in the base period upon the application and a showing of unreasonable hardship by the handler making deliveries to such purchasers on the effective date of this order, and to add the amount of such deliveries to the total base period deliveries of the applicant handler. Denials of transfers or transfers granted by the market agent shall be reviewed by the Director upon application.

(j) *Petition for relief from hardships.* (1) Any person affected by the order or the provisions hereof who considers that compliance therewith would work an exceptional and unreasonable hardship on him, may file with the market agent a petition addressed to the Director. The petition shall contain the correct name, address and principal place of business of the petitioner, a full statement of the facts upon which the petition is based, and the hardship involved and the nature of the relief desired.

(2) Upon receiving such petition, the market agent shall immediately investigate the representations and facts stated therein.

(3) After investigation, the petition shall be certified to the Director, but prior to certification the market agent may (i) deny the petition; or (ii) grant temporary relief for a total period not to exceed 60 days.

(4) Denials or grants of relief by the market agent shall be reviewed by the Director and may be affirmed, modified, or reversed by the Director.

(k) *Reports.* Each handler shall transmit to the market agent on forms prescribed by the market agent the following reports:

(1) Within 20 days following the effective date of this order, reports which show the information required by the market agent to establish such handlers' quotas;

(2) Within 20 days following the close of each quota period, the information required by the market agent to establish volumes of deliveries of milk, cream, and milk byproducts during the preceding quota period; and

(3) Handlers exempt from quotas pursuant to (f) hereof shall, upon the request of the market agent, submit the information required by the market agent to establish volumes of deliveries of milk, cream, and milk byproducts.

(l) *Records.* Handlers shall keep and shall make available to the market agent such records of receipts, sales, deliveries, and production as the market agent shall require for the purpose of obtaining information which the Director may re-

quire for the establishment of quotas as prescribed in (b) of the order.

(m) *Distribution schedules.* The distribution schedules, if any, to be followed by the handlers in making deliveries shall be made effective in the terms of approval by the Director of such schedules.

(n) *Expense of administration.* Each handler shall pay to the market agent, within 20 days after the close of each calendar month an assessment of $0.01 per hundredweight of each of milk, cream, skim milk, buttermilk, flavored milk drinks, beverages containing more than 85 percent of skim milk, and skim milk equivalent of cottage, pot, or baker's cheese delivered during the preceding quota period and subject to quota regulations under the provisions hereof.

(o) *Violations.* The market agent shall report all violations to the Director together with the information required for the prosecution of such violations, except in a case where a handler has made deliveries in a quota period in excess of a quota in an amount not to exceed 5 percent of such quota, and in the succeeding quota period makes deliveries below that quota by at least the same percent.

(p) *Bureau of the Budget approval.* The record-keeping and reporting requirements of this order have been approved by the Bureau of the Budget in accordance with the Federal Reports Act of 1942. Subsequent record-keeping or reporting requirements will be subject to the approval of the Bureau of the Budget pursuant to the Federal Reports Act of 1942.

(q) This order shall take effect at 12:01 a. m., e. w. t., October 4, 1943.

Issued this 30th day of September 1943.

ROY F. HENDRICKSON,
Director of Food Distribution.

Press Release Immediate:
Thursday, September 30, 1943.

Federal control over fluid milk sales, through the establishment of quotas on deliveries of milk, cream, and milk byproducts, will go into effect in 13 eastern and midwestern metropolitan areas beginning October 4, the War Food Administration announced today.

These areas, and the market agents designated by the Food Distribution Administration to administer the milk conservation and control program in each are:

Baltimore, Md., Washington, D. C., Roanoke, Va., Richmond, Va., Norfolk-Portsmouth-Newport News, Va.: George Irvine, 1731 I Street, NW., Washington, D. C.

Cincinnati, Ohio, Toledo, Ohio, Dayton, Ohio, Canton, Ohio, Cleveland, Ohio: Fred W. Issler, 152 East Fourth Street, Cincinnati, Ohio.

Chicago, Illinois: A. W. Colebank, 135 South LaSalle St., Chicago, Ill.

Omaha, Neb.-Council Bluffs, Iowa: Wayne McPherren, Rm. 408, Post Office Bldg., Omaha, Nebraska.

St. Louis, Missouri: William C. Eckles, 4030 Chouteau Ave., St. Louis, Missouri.

Consumers in regulated areas will be able to purchase as much milk as they have been buying—within the limits of local supplies, officials said. The basic purpose of the program is to prevent a further increase in the consumption of fluid milk (rather than to reduce present consumption) so that enough milk will be available to produce the cheese, butter, and other manufactured dairy products required by the armed services and civilians. As milk conservation and control will be affected at the dealer level, consumer point rationing is not involved.

Milk dealers in the 13 initial milk sales areas will be allowed to sell as much fluid milk each month as they sold last June, (1943), the peak production month. To help assure that enough fluid milk will be available during the season of low production to enable dealers to sell as much as their quotas allow, cream sales will be limited to 75 percent of the quantity sold in June, and the sales quota for fluid milk by-products as a group (including cottage cheese, chocolate milk, and buttermilk) also is set at 75 percent of June sales.

Producer-distributors who purchase no milk (except those whose volume of sales is small enough to exempt them from the quota) will be allowed to sell an amount of fluid milk, cream, and fluid milk byproducts equal to 100 percent of their total milk production in June. "Quota-exempt" producer-distributors are defined separately for each area, but in general they are those whose deliveries are relatively small, and who produce the milk they sell from their own herds.

Milk distributors will be responsible for the fair distribution of supplies in their markets. Under Food Distribution Order 79, however, which authorizes the establishment of individual milk orders for each area, the various market agents may recommend distribution schedules to assure that, in the event of short supplies, the most essential needs will be met first.

Success of the milk conservation and control program depends largely on trade and consumer cooperation, WFA officials pointed out. It is believed that stabilization of milk consumption can be accomplished equitably through this system of dealer control without resorting to consumer rationing. Individual rationing of such a highly perishable product as milk would be very complex, difficult to administer, and would almost necessarily result in substantial reductions in fluid milk sales in many markets. Rationing at the consumer level undoubtedly will be necessary if control over dealers' sales does not effectively regulate fluid milk consumption, the officials said.

Under the individual orders established for each area, the milk control program may be modified to fit production and consumption conditions in each market. These orders will be administered by market agents appointed by the Director of Food Distribution.

Milk sales in all other cities of at least 100,000 population will be regulated as soon as administrative arrangements can be completed—with most areas of this size to be operating under the program by November 1. It is expected that the program will then be extended to smaller population areas until all markets of at least 50,000 population are included.

Distributor quotas for milk sales areas to be named later may be the same as those for the areas announced today, or they may vary if local conditions indicate that different bases are necessary.

Milk handlers (that is, all persons or firms engaged in the sale or transfer of milk, except such groups as retail stores, hotels, restaurants, etc.) will compute the quantity of milk and fluid milk byproducts which they may sell each month in terms of pounds of milk and pounds of milk byproducts, and their cream sales in terms of pounds of cream and butterfat. In months which contain more or less days than the base period, handlers will determine the amount of milk they may sell by multiplying the average of daily deliveries in June by 28, 29, or 31, whichever is applicable.

Dealers may exceed their monthly quotas by up to 5 percent greater sales providing they make up this excess by reducing their deliveries proportionately the next month, without the market agent being required to report such excess sales.

Deliveries to the armed forces, to plants processing dairy products, and to other handlers (except special classes of handlers such as peddlers) are quota exempt.

To facilitate administration, the market agent for each milk sales area may act upon petitions for relief from hardship which may be submitted to him, and his decision will be effective for a 60-day period.

Dealers' quotas based on June deliveries will permit consumers to purchase more milk than they consumed in 1942, and considerably more than in pre-war years. Consumption of fluid milk and cream thus far in 1943 has been at a rate of more than 41 billion pounds annually compared with 37.7 billion pounds in 1942 and an average of 32.6 billion pounds in pre-war years (1936–40).

Total milk production has been mounting steadily in recent years—from 101 billion pounds in 1935 to 119 billion pounds in 1942—an all-time high. Production during the first 7 months of this year equalled production during the same months of 1942.

Increasing fluid milk sales, however, resulting largely from the sharp rise in consumer incomes, have reduced the quantity of milk available for the manufacture of essential products such as butter, cheese, evaporated milk, ice cream, and milk powder. Previously uncontrolled, consumption of fluid milk and cream has been rising at the rate of about 1 percent a month, and already is 20 percent above the 1941 level and 10 to 12 percent over 1942.

This has necessitated the stabilization of fluid milk consumption in order to meet the requirements for manufactured dairy products, both on the home and battle fronts, WFA officials explained.

FDO 79-7

AMDT. 1
NOV. 3, 1943

WAR FOOD ADMINISTRATION

[FDO 79-7, Amdt. 1]

A PART 1401—DAIRY PRODUCTS

FLUID MILK AND CREAM IN CHICAGO, ILL., METROPOLITAN MILK SALES AREA

Pursuant to the authority vested in the Director by Food Distribution Order No. 79, dated September 7, 1943 (8 F.R. 12426), as amended, and to effectuate the purposes thereof, Director Food Distribution Order No. 79-7, § 1401.40, relative to the conservation of fluid milk in the Chicago, Illinois, metropolitan milk sales area (8 F.R. 13371), issued by the Director of Food Distribution on September 30, 1943, is amended as follows:

The assessment specified in § 1401.40 (n) of the original order is reduced to $0.005 per cwt.

Effective date. This amendment of FDO No. 79-7, shall become effective at 12:01 a. m. e. w. t., November 5, 1943.

(E.O. 9280, 8 F.R. 10179; E.O. 9322, 8 F.R. 3807; E.O. 9334, 8 F.R. 5423; FDO 79, 8 F.R. 12426, 13283)

Issued this 3d day of November 1943.

ROY F. HENDRICKSON,
Director of Food Distribution.

WAR FOOD ADMINISTRATION

[FDO 79-7, Amdt. 2]

PART 1401—DAIRY PRODUCTS

FLUID MILK AND CREAM IN CHICAGO, ILL., METROPOLITAN SALES AREA

Pursuant to Food Distribution Order No. 79 (8 F.R. 12426), dated September 7, 1943, as amended, and to effectuate the purposes thereof, Food Distribution Order No. 79-7 (8 F.R. 13371), relative to the conservation and distribution of fluid milk in the Chicago, Illinois, metropolitan milk sales area, issued by the Director of Food Distribution on September 30, 1943, as amended, is hereby further amended by deleting therefrom the provisions in § 1401.40 (h) and inserting, in lieu thereof, the following:

(h) *Quota exclusions and exemptions.* Deliveries of milk, milk byproducts, or cream (1) to other handlers, except for such deliveries to sub-handlers, (2) to plants engaged in the handling or processing of milk, milk byproducts, or cream from which no milk, milk byproducts, or cream is delivered in the sales area, (3) to nursery, elementary, junior high, and high schools, and (4) to the agencies or groups specified in (d) of the order, shall be excluded from the computation of deliveries in the base period and exempt from charges to quotas.

The provisions of this amendment shall become effective at 12:01 a. m., e. w. t., March 1, 1944. With respect to violations of said Food Distribution Order No. 79-7, as amended, rights accrued, or liabilities incurred prior to the effective time of this amendment, said Food Distribution Order No. 79-7, as amended, shall be deemed to be in full force and effect for the purpose of sustaining any proper suit, action, or other proceeding with respect to any such violation, right, or liability.

(E.O. 9280, 7 F.R. 10179; E.O. 9322, 8 F.R. 3807; E.O. 9334, 8 F.R. 5423; E.O. 9392, 8 F.R. 14783; FDO 79, 8 F.R. 12426, 13283)

Issued this 19th day of February 1944.

LEE MARSHALL,
Director of Food Distribution.

FDO 79-7
AMDT. 3
MAR. 31, 1944

WAR FOOD ADMINISTRATION

[FDO 79-7, Amdt. 3]

PART 1401—DAIRY PRODUCTS

FLUID MILK AND CREAM IN CHICAGO, ILL., METROPOLITAN SALES AREA

Pursuant to Food Distribution Order No. 79 (8 F.R. 12426), dated September 7, 1943, as amended, and to effectuate the purposes thereof, Food Distribution Order No. 79-7 (8 F.R. 13371), relative to the conservation and distribution of fluid milk, milk byproducts, and cream in the Chicago, Illinois, metropolitan milk sales area, issued by the Director of Food Distribution on September 30, 1943, as amended, is further amended so as to read as follows:

§ 1401.40 *Quota restrictions*—(a) *Definitions.* When used in this order, unless otherwise distinctly expressed or manifestly incompatible with the intent hereof:

(1) Each term defined in Food Distribution Order No. 79, as amended, shall, when used herein, have the same meaning as is set forth for such term in Food Distribution Order No. 79, as amended.

(2) The term "FDO 79" means Food Distribution Order No. 79, issued on September 7, 1943, as amended.

(3) The term "sub-handler" means any handler, such as a peddler, vendor, sub-dealer, or secondary dealer, who purchases in a previously packaged and processed form milk, milk byproducts other than cottage, pot, or baker's cheese, or cream for delivery, and does not operate facilities for the processing and bottling of fluid milk.

(b) *Milk sales area.* The following area is hereby designated as a "milk sales area" to be known as the Chicago, Illinois, metropolitan milk area, and is referred to hereinafter as the "sales area":

The city of Chicago and the entire area included in:

The townships of Waukegan, Shields, Deerfield, and West Deerfield in Lake County, Illinois; the counties of Cook and DuPage in Illinois; the townships of Aurora, Batavia, Dundee, Elgin, Geneva, and St. Charles in Kane County, Illinois; the townships of Calumet, Hobart, and North in Lake County, Indiana.

(c) *Base period.* The calendar month of June 1943 is hereby designated as the base period for the sales area.

(d) *Quota period.* Each calendar month subsequent to the effective date of this order is hereby designated as a quota period for the sales area.

(e) *Handler quotas.* Quotas for each handler in the sales area in each quota period shall be determined as follows:

(1) Divide the total deliveries of each of milk, milk byproducts, cream and butterfat in cream made in the sales area by such handler during the base period, after excluding the base period deliveries of the character described in (h) hereof, and after adjusting such deliveries for transfers made pursuant to (j) and for relief as granted pursuant to (k), by the number of days in the base period;

(2) Multiply the result of the foregoing calculation by the number of days in the quota period; and

(3) Multiply the aforesaid resulting amount by the following applicable percentage: (i) Milk, 100 percent of pounds of milk; (ii) Cream, 75 percent of pounds of cream and 75 percent of pounds of butterfat; and (iii) Milk byproducts, 75 percent of pounds of milk byproducts other than cottage, pot, or baker's cheese and of the pounds of skim milk equivalent of cottage, pot, or baker's cheese. (For the purpose of this order, one pound of cottage, pot, or baker's cheese shall be considered as the equivalent of 7 pounds of skim milk.)

(f) *Quotas for handlers who are also producers.* Quotas for handlers who are also producers and who purchase no milk shall be 100 percent of the total production of such handlers in the base period.

(g) *Handler exemptions.* Quotas shall not apply to any handler who delivers in a quota period a daily average of less than 400 units of milk, cream, and milk byproducts: *Provided,* That not more than 200 units of such total consist of cream or of any one milk byproduct. For the purpose of this order, a unit shall be the equivalent in volume of the following:

(1) One quart of milk;

(2) One-half pint of cream; and

(3) One quart of fluid byproduct, or one-half pound of cottage, pot, or baker's cheese.

(h) *Quota exclusions and exemptions.* The following deliveries of milk, milk byproducts, or cream shall be excluded from the computation of deliveries in the base period and exempt from charges to quotas:

(1) To other handlers, except for such deliveries to sub-handlers.

(2) To plants engaged in the handling or processing of milk, milk byproducts, or cream from which no milk, milk byproducts, or cream is delivered in the sales area.

(3) To the agencies or groups specified in (d) of FDO 79.

(4) To industrial users in their capacity as such users and as determined by the market agent to be manufacturing products which require as an ingredient, milk, cream or milk byproducts, which are disposed of primarily for resale to consumers off the premises where made, and

(5) To schools determined by the market agent to be at high-school level or below.

(i) *Quota adjustments.* Within each quota period, a handler may at his discretion:

(1) Increase the pounds of cream in his cream quota to the extent that the substitution of the figure 100 for the figure 75 set out in (e) (3) (ii) will permit as follows:

(i) By reducing the average butterfat test of his cream deliveries below the average butterfat test of his cream quota, with the result that for each such reduction of 1 percent, the pounds of cream he may deliver may be increased by 4.5 percent of the pounds of cream in his cream quota computed pursuant to (e);

(ii) By transferring byproducts quota to cream quota, with the result that for each reduction of one pound in byproducts quota, the pounds of cream he may deliver may be increased at the following rates:

1 lb. of byproducts quota = .34 lbs. of 20% cream quota.
1 lb. of byproducts quota = .36 lbs. of 19% cream quota.
1 lb. of byproducts quota = .37 lbs. of 18% cream quota.
1 lb. of byproducts quota = .38 lbs. of 17% cream quota.
1 lb. of byproducts quota = .40 lbs. of 16% cream quota.
1 lb. of byproducts quota = .41 lbs. of 15% cream quota.
1 lb. of byproducts quota = .43 lbs. of 14% cream quota.
1 lb. of byproducts quota = .45 lbs. of 13% cream quota.
1 lb. of byproducts quota = .47 lbs. of 12% cream quota.

or, (iii) by reducing the butterfat content of cream deliveries and transferring byproducts quota to cream quota through the use of a combination of (i) and (ii).

(2) Increase the pounds of milk byproducts in milk byproducts quota by

transferring cream quota at the following rates:

1 lb. of 20% cream quota=2.91 lbs. of byproducts quota.
1 lb. of 19% cream quota=2.81 lbs. of byproducts quota.
1 lb. of 18% cream quota=2.72 lbs. of byproducts quota.
1 lb. of 17% cream quota=2.62 lbs. of byproducts quota.
1 lb. of 16% cream quota=2.52 lbs. of byproducts quota.
1 lb. of 15% cream quota=2.43 lbs. of byproducts quota.
1 lb. of 14% cream quota=2.33 lbs. of byproducts quota.
1 lb. of 13% cream quota=2.24 lbs. of byproducts quota.
1 lb. of 12% cream quota=2.14 lbs. of byproducts quota.

(3) Increase the pounds of milk in milk quota by:

(i) Transferring milk byproducts quota to milk quota at the rate of one pound of milk byproducts quota for each 0.75 pound of milk quota;

(ii) Transferring cream quota to milk quota at the following rates:

1 lb. of 20% cream quota=2.19 lbs. of milk quota.
1 lb. of 19% cream quota=2.12 lbs. of milk quota.
1 lb. of 18% cream quota=2.05 lbs. of milk quota.
1 lb. of 17% cream quota=1.97 lbs. of milk quota.
1 lb. of 16% cream quota=1.90 lbs. of milk quota.
1 lb. of 15% cream quota=1.83 lbs. of milk quota.
1 lb. of 14% cream quota=1.76 lbs. of milk quota.
1 lb. of 13% cream quota=1.69 lbs. of milk quota.
1 lb. of 12% cream quota=1.61 lbs. of milk quota.

(j) *Transfers of quotas between handlers.* The market agent is empowered to transfer quota between handlers as follows:

(1) Upon application and after written notice to the director and to each handler involved to:

(i) Reflect transfers of accounts occurring between the base period and October 4, 1943;

(ii) Permit deliveries to purchasers whose handlers have denied them service;

(iii) Permit a handler to serve an account which customarily rotates among handlers, inclusive of any account with a public agency or institution which is let on a bid basis: *Provided*, That the amounts of quota transferred to serve such accounts shall not exceed deliveries to such accounts in the base period or in the quota period next preceding the transfer, whichever is less; and

(2) Upon receipt of a request in writing from each handler involved to permit an exchange of quota between such handlers, except that a transfer of quota made up of deliveries to sub-handlers shall require proof of prior written notice of such request to each sub-handler affected and shall be subject for a period of seven days, from the date of filing of request and proof of notice, to a further transfer, to be made upon application by the sub-handler and the prospective supplying handler and notice to the other handlers affected.

(k) *Petition for relief from hardships.* (1) Any person affected by FDO 79 or the provisions hereof who considers that compliance therewith would work an exceptional and unreasonable hardship on him may file with the market agent a petition addressed to the Director. The petition shall contain the correct name, address and principal place of business of the petitioner, a full statement of the facts upon which the petition is based, and the hardship involved and the nature of the relief desired.

(2) Upon receiving such petition, the market agent shall immediately investigate the representations and facts stated therein.

(3) After investigation, the petition shall be certified to the Director, but prior to certification the market agent may (i) deny the petition; or (ii) grant temporary relief for a total period not to exceed 60 days.

(4) Denials or grants of relief by the market agent shall be reviewed by the Director and may be affirmed, modified, or reversed by the Director.

(l) *Reports.* Each handler shall transmit to the market agent on forms prescribed by the market agent the following reports:

(1) Within 20 days following the effective date of this order, reports which show the information required by the market agent to establish handler's quotas;

(2) Within 10 days following the close of each quota period, the information required by the market agent to establish volumes of deliveries of milk, cream, and milk byproducts during the preceding quota period; and

(3) Handlers exempt from quotas pursuant to (g) hereof shall, upon the request of the market agent, submit the information required by the market agent to establish volumes of deliveries of milk, cream, and milk byproducts.

(m) *Records.* Handlers shall keep and shall make available to the market agent such records of receipts, sales, deliveries, and production as the market agent shall require for the purpose of obtaining information which the Director may require for the establishment of quotas as prescribed in (b) of FDO 79.

(n) *Expense of administration.* Each handler shall pay to the market agent within 10 days after the close of each calendar month, an assessment of $0.005 per hundredweight of each of milk, cream, fluid milk byproducts, and skim milk equivalent of cottage, pot, or baker's cheese delivered during the preceding quota period and subject to quota regulations under the provisions hereof.

(o) *Violations.* The market agent shall report all violations to the Director together with the information required for the prosecution of such violations, except in a case where a handler has made deliveries in a quota period (other than a quota period during which offsetting deliveries below quota are to be made under this provision) in excess of a quota in an amount not to exceed 5 percent of such quota, and in the succeeding quota period makes deliveries below that quota by at least the same percent.

(p) *Bureau of the Budget approval.* The record-keeping and reporting requirements of this order have been approved by the Bureau of the Budget in accordance with the Federal Reports Act of 1942. Subsequent record-keeping or reporting requirements will be subject to the approval of the Bureau of the Budget pursuant to the Federal Reports Act of 1942.

(q) *Effective date.* This amendment shall become effective at 11:59 p. m., e. w. t., March 31, 1944. With respect to violations of said Food Distribution Order No. 79.7, as amended, rights accrued, or liabilities incurred prior to the effective time of this amendment, said Food Distribution Order No. 79–7, as amended, shall be deemed to be in full force and effect for the purpose of sustaining any proper suit, action, or other proceeding with respect to any such violation, right, or liability.

(E.O. 9280, 7 F.R. 10179; E.O. 9322, 8 F.R. 3807; E.O. 9334, 8 F.R. 3423; E.O. 9392, 8 F.R. 14783; FDO 79, 8 F.R. 12426, 13283)

Issued this 31st day of March 1944.

C. W. KITCHEN,
Acting Director of Food Distribution.

p. 3

WAR FOOD ADMINISTRATION

[FDO 79—8]

PART 1401—DAIRY PRODUCTS

CONSERVATION AND DISTRIBUTION OF FLUID MILK AND CREAM IN THE OMAHA-COUNCIL BLUFFS SALES AREA

Pursuant to the authority vested in me by Food Distribution Order No. 79 (8 F.R. 12426), issued on September 7, 1943, as amended, and to effectuate the purposes of such order, it is hereby ordered as follows:

§ 1401.35 *Quota restrictions*—(a) *Definitions.* When used in this order, unless otherwise distinctly expressed or manifestly incompatible with the intent hereof:

(1) Each term defined in Food Distribution Order No. 79, as amended, shall, when used herein, have the same meaning as is set forth for such term in Food Distribution Order No. 79, as amended.

(2) The term "order" means Food Distribution Order No. 79, issued on September 7, 1943, as amended.

(3) The term "sub-handler" means any handler, such as a peddler, vendor, sub-dealer, or secondary dealer, who purchases in a previously packaged and processed form milk, milk byproducts, or cream for delivery.

(b) *Milk sales area.* The following area is hereby designated as a "milk sales area" to be known as the Omaha-Council Bluffs sales area, and is referred to hereinafter as the "sales area"; the territory within the cities of Omaha, Nebraska, and Council Bluffs, Iowa; the territory within Kane, Lake, Garner, and Lewis Townships in Pottawattamie County, Iowa; the territory within East Omaha, Florence, Union, Benson, McHugh, Moorehead, McArdle, Loveland, Ralston, Ashland, and May Precincts in Douglas County, Nebraska; and the territory within Gilmore, Highland, and Bellevue Townships in Sarpy County, Nebraska.

(c) *Base period.* The calendar month of June 1943 is hereby designated as the base period for the sales area.

(d) *Quota period.* The remainder of the calendar month in which the provisions hereof become effective and each subsequent calendar month, respectively, is hereby designated as a quota period for the sales area.

(e) *Handler quotas.* Quotas for each handler in the sales area in each quota period shall be determined as follows:

(1) Divide the total deliveries of each milk, milk byproducts, and cream (and of butter fat in milk or in cream where percentages of pounds of butterfat are specified in (e) (3) (i) or (e) (3) (ii) hereof) made in the sales area by such handler during the base period, after excluding the quota-exempt deliveries described in (h) hereof and adjusting such deliveries for the transfers set out in (i) hereof, by the number of days in the base period;

(2) Multiply the result of the foregoing calculation by the number of days in the quota period; and

(3) Multiply the aforesaid resulting amount by the following applicable percentage: (i) Milk: 100 percent of pounds of milk and 100 percent of pounds of butterfat; (ii) Cream: 75 percent of pounds of cream and 75 percent of pounds of butterfat; and (iii) Milk byproducts: 75 percent of pounds of milk byproducts other than cottage, pot, or baker's cheese and of the pounds of skim milk equivalent of cottage, pot, or baker's cheese. (For the purpose of this order, one pound of cottage, pot, or baker's cheese shall be considered as the equivalent of 7 pounds of skim milk.)

(f) *Quotas for handlers who are also producers.* Quotas for handlers who are also producers and who purchase no milk shall be 100 percent of the total production of such handlers in the base period.

(g) *Handler exemptions.* Quotas shall not apply to any handler who delivers in a quota period a daily average of less than 125 units of milk, cream, and milk byproducts. For the purpose of this order, a unit shall be the equivalent in volume of the following:

(1) Milk, one quart of milk;

(2) Cream, one-half pint of cream; and

(3) Milk byproduct, one quart of skim milk, buttermilk, flavored milk drink, or other beverage containing more than 85 percent of skim milk, or one-half pound of cottage, pot, or baker's cheese.

(h) *Quota exclusions and exemptions.* Deliveries of milk, milk byproducts, or cream (1) to other handlers, except for such deliveries to sub-handlers, (2) to plants engaged in the handling or processing of milk, milk byproducts, or cream from which no milk, milk byproducts, or cream is delivered in the sales area, and (3) to the agencies or groups specified in (d) of the order, shall be excluded from the computation of deliveries in the base period and exempt from charges to quotas.

(i) *Transfers and apportionment of quotas.* The market agent is empowered to deduct an amount of base period deliveries to purchasers from the total of deliveries made by a handler or other person in the base period upon the application and a showing of unreasonable hardship by the handler making deliveries to such purchasers on the effective date of this order, and to add the amount of such deliveries to the total base period deliveries of the applicant handler. Denials of transfers or transfers granted by the market agent shall be reviewed by the Director upon application.

(j) *Petition for relief from hardships.* (1) Any person affected by the order or the provisions hereof who considers that compliance therewith would work an exceptional and unreasonable hardship on him, may file with the market agent a petition addressed to the Director. The petition shall contain the correct name, address and principal place of business of the petitioner, a full statement of the facts upon which the petition is based, and the hardship involved and the nature of the relief desired.

(2) Upon receiving such petition, the market agent shall immediately investigate the representations and facts stated therein.

(3) After investigation, the petition shall be certified to the Director, but prior to certification the market agent may (i) deny the petition; or (ii) grant temporary relief for a total period not to exceed 60 days.

(4) Denials or grants of relief by the market agent shall be reviewed by the Director and may be affirmed, modified, or reversed by the Director.

(k) *Reports.* Each handler shall transmit to the market agent on forms prescribed by the market agent the following reports:

(1) Within 20 days following the effective date of this order, reports which show the information required by the market agent to establish such handlers' quotas;

(2) Within 20 days following the close of each quota period, the information required by the market agent to establish volumes of deliveries of milk, cream, and milk byproducts during the preceding quota period; and

(3) Handlers exempt from quotas pursuant to (f) hereof shall, upon the request of the market agent, submit the information required by the market agent to establish volumes of deliveries of milk, cream, and milk byproducts.

(l) *Records.* Handlers shall keep and shall make available to the market agent such records of receipts, sales, deliveries, and production as the market agent shall require for the purpose of obtaining information which the Director may require for the establishment of quotas as prescribed in (b) of the order.

(m) *Distribution schedules.* The distribution schedules, if any, to be followed by the handlers in making deliveries shall be made effective in the terms of approval by the Director of such schedules.

(n) *Expense of administration.* Each handler shall pay to the market agent, within 20 days after the close of each calendar month an assessment of $0.01 per hundredweight of each of milk, cream, skim milk, buttermilk, flavored milk drinks, beverages containing more than 85 percent of skim milk, and skim milk equivalent of cottage, pot, or baker's cheese delivered during the preceding quota period and subject to quota regulations under the provisions hereof.

(o) *Violations.* The market agent shall report all violations to the Director together with the information required for the prosecution of such violations, except in a case where a handler has made deliveries in a quota period in excess of a quota in an amount not to exceed 5 percent of such quota, and in the succeeding quota period makes deliveries below that quota by at least the same percent.

(p) *Bureau of the Budget approval.* The record-keeping and reporting requirements of this order have been approved by the Bureau of the Budget in accordance with the Federal Reports Act of 1942. Subsequent record-keeping or reporting requirements will be subject to the approval of the Bureau of the Budget pursuant to the Federal Reports Act of 1942.

(q) This order shall take affect at 12:01 a. m., e. w. t., October 4, 1943.

Issued this 30th day of September 1943.

ROY F. HENDRICKSON,
Director of Food Distribution.

Press Release Immediate:
Thursday, September 30, 1943.

Federal control over fluid milk sales, through the establishment of quotas on deliveries of milk, cream, and milk byproducts, will go into effect in 13 eastern and midwestern metropolitan areas beginning October 4, the War Food Administration announced today.

These areas, and the market agents designated by the Food Distribution Administration to administer the milk conservation and control program in each, are:

Baltimore, Md., Washington, D. C., Roanoke, Va., Richmond, Va., Norfolk-Portsmouth-Newport News, Va.; George Irvine, 1731 I Street, N.Y., Washington, D. C.

Cincinnati, Ohio, Toledo, Ohio, Dayton, Ohio, Canton, Ohio, Cleveland, Ohio: Fred W. Issler, 152 East Fourth Street, Cincinnati, Ohio.

Chicago, Illinois: A. W. Colebank, 135 South LaSalle Street, Chicago, Ill.

Omaha Neb.-Council Bluffs, Iowa: Wayne McPherren, Rm. 408, Post Office Bldg., Omaha, Nebraska.

St. Louis, Missouri: William C. Eckles, 4030 Chouteau Ave., St. Louis, Missouri.

Consumers in regulated areas will be able to purchase as much milk as they have been buying—within the limits of local supplies, officials said. The basic purpose of the program is to prevent a further increase in the consumption of fluid milk (rather than to reduce present consumption) so that enough milk will be available to produce the cheese, butter, and other manufactured dairy products required by the armed services and civilians. As milk conservation and control will be effected at the dealer level, consumer point rationing is not involved

Milk dealers in the 13 initial milk sales areas will be allowed to sell as much fluid milk each month as they sold last June, (1943), the peak production month. To help assure that enough fluid milk will be available during the season of low production to enable dealers to sell as much as their quotas allow, cream sales will be limited to 75 percent of the quantity sold in June, and the sales quota for fluid milk byproducts as a group (including cottage cheese, chocolate milk, and buttermilk) also is set at 75 percent of June sales.

Producer-distributors who purchase no milk (except those whose volume of sales is small enough to exempt them from the quota) will be allowed to sell an amount of fluid milk, cream, and fluid milk byproducts equal to 100 percent of their total milk production in June. "Quota-exempt" producer-distributors are defined separately for each area, but in general they are those whose deliveries are relatively small, and who produce the milk they sell from their own herds.

Milk distributors will be responsible for the fair distribution of supplies in their markets. Under Food Distribution Order 79, however, which authorizes the establishment of individual milk orders for each area, the various market agents may recommend distribution schedules to assure that, in the event of short supplies, the most essential needs will be met first.

Success of the milk conservation and control program depends largely on trade and consumer cooperation, WFA officials pointed out. It is believed that stabilization of milk consumption can be accomplished equitably through this system of dealer control without resorting to consumer rationing. Individual rationing of such a highly perishable product as milk would be very complex, difficult to administer, and would almost necessarily result in substantial reductions in fluid milk sales in many markets. Rationing at the consumer level undoubtedly will be necessary if control over dealers' sales does not effectively regulate fluid milk consumption, the officials said.

Under the individual orders established for each area, the milk control program may be modified to fit production and consumption conditions in each market. These orders will be administered by market agents appointed by the Director of Food Distribution.

Milk sales in all other cities of at least 100,000 population will be regulated as soon as administrative arrangements can be completed—with most areas of this size to be operating under the program by November 1. It is expected that the program will then be extended to smaller population areas until all markets of at least 50,000 population are included.

Distributor quotas for milk sales areas to be named later may be the same as those for the areas announced today, or they may vary if local conditions indicate that different bases are necessary.

Milk handlers (that is, all persons or firms engaged in the sale or transfer of milk, except such groups as retail stores, hotels, restaurants, etc.) will compute the quantity of milk and fluid milk byproducts which they may sell each month in terms of pounds of milk and pounds of milk byproducts, and their cream sales in terms of pounds of cream and butterfat. In months which contain more or less days than the base period, handlers will determine the amount of milk they may sell by multiplying the average of daily deliveries in June by 28, 29, or 31, whichever is applicable.

Dealers may exceed their monthly quotas by up to 5 percent greater sales providing they make up this excess by reducing their deliveries proportionately the next month, without the market agent being required to report such excess sales.

Deliveries to the armed forces, to plants processing dairy products, and to other handlers (except special classes of handlers such as peddlers) are quota exempt.

To facilitate administration, the market agent for each milk sales area may act upon petitions for relief from hardship which may be submitted to him, and his decision will be effective for a 60-day period.

Dealers' quotas based on June deliveries will permit consumers to purchase more milk than they consumed in 1942, and considerably more than in pre-war years. Consumption of fluid milk and cream thus far in 1943 has been at a rate of more than 41 billion pounds annually compared with 37.7 billion pounds in 1942 and an average of 32.6 billion pounds in pre-war years (1936–40).

Total milk production has been mounting steadily in recent years—from 101 billion pounds in 1935 to 119 billion pounds in 1942—an all-time high. Production during the first 7 months of this year equalled production during the same months of 1942.

Increasing fluid milk sales, however, resulting largely from the sharp rise in consumer incomes, have reduced the quantity of milk available for the manufacture of essential products such as butter, cheese, evaporated milk, ice cream, and milk powder. Previously uncontrolled, consumption of fluid milk and cream has been rising at the rate of about 1 percent a month, and already is 20 percent above the 1941 level and 10 to 12 percent over 1942.

This has necessitated the stabilization of fluid milk consumption in order to meet the requirements for manufactured dairy products, both on the home and battle fronts, WFA officials explained.

FDO 79-8
AMDT. 1
FEB. 28, 1944

WAR FOOD ADMINISTRATION

[FDO 79-8, Amdt. 1]

PART 1401—DAIRY PRODUCTS

FLUID MILK AND CREAM IN THE OMAHA-COUNCIL BLUFFS SALES AREA

Pursuant to Food Distribution Order No. 79 (8 F.R. 12426), dated September 7, 1943, as amended, and to effectuate the purposes thereof, Food Distribution Order No. 79-8 (8 F.R. 13372), relative to the conservation and distribution of fluid milk in the Omaha-Council Bluffs milk sales area, issued by the Director of Food Distribution on September 30, 1943, is hereby amended by deleting therefrom the provisions in § 1401.35 (f) and inserting, in lieu thereof, the following:

(f) *Quotas for handlers who are also producers.* Quotas for handlers who are also producers and who purchase no milk shall be computed in accordance with (e) hereof, except that the applicable percentages shall be 100 percent in lieu of the percentages specified in (e) (3).

The provisions of this amendment shall become effective at 12:01 a. m., e. w. t., March 1, 1944. With respect to violations of said Food Distribution Order No. 79-8, rights accrued, or liabilities incurred prior to the effective time of this amendment, said Food Distribution Order No. 79-8, shall be deemed to be in full force and effect for the purpose of sustaining any proper suit, action, or other proceeding with respect to any such violation, right, or liability.

(E.O. 9280, 7 F.R. 10179; E.O. 9322, 8 F.R. 3807; E.O. 9334, 8 F.R. 5423; E.O. 9392, 8 F.R. 14785; FDO 79, 8 F.R. 12426, 13283.

Issued this 28th day of February 1944.

C. W. KITCHEN,
Acting Director of Food Distribution.

FDO 79-9

SEPT. 30, 1943

WAR FOOD ADMINISTRATION

[FDO 79-9]

PART 1401—DAIRY PRODUCTS

CONSERVATION AND DISTRIBUTION OF FLUID MILK AND CREAM IN THE CINCINNATI, OHIO, SALES AREA

Pursuant to the authority vested in me by Food Distribution Order No. 79 (8 F.R. 12426), issued on September 7, 1943, as amended, and to effectuate the purposes of such order, it is hereby ordered as follows:

§ 1401.44 *Quota restrictions*—(a) *Definitions.* When used in this order, unless otherwise distinctly expressed or manifestly incompatible with the intent hereof.

(1) Each term defined in Food Distribution Order No. 79, as amended, shall, when used herein, have the same meaning as is set forth for such term in Food Distribution Order No. 79, as amended.

(2) The term "order" means Food Distribution Order No. 79, issued on September 7, 1943, as amended.

(3) The term "sub-handler" means any handler, such as a peddler, vendor, sub-dealer, or secondary dealer, who purchases in a previously packaged and processed form milk, milk byproducts, or cream for delivery.

(b) *Milk sales area.* The following area is hereby designated as a "Milk sales area" to be known as the Cincinnati, Ohio sales area, and is referred to hereinafter as the "sales area": The city of Cincinnati and Hamilton County, in the State of Ohio; magisterial districts 4 and 7 in Kenton, that part of district 6 lying in Kenton County, and district 4 in Campbell County, all in the State of Kentucky.

(c) *Base period.* The calendar month of June 1943 is hereby designated as the base period for the sales area.

(d) *Quota period.* The remainder of the calendar month in which the provisions hereof become effective and each subsequent calendar month, respectively, is hereby designated as a quota period for the sales area.

(e) *Handler quotas.* Quotas for each handler in the sales area in each quota period shall be determined as follows:

(1) Divide the total deliveries of each of milk, milk byproducts, and cream (and of butterfat in milk or in cream where percentages of pounds of butterfat are specified in (e) (3) (i) or (e) (3) (ii) hereof) made in the sales area by such handler during the base period, after excluding the quota-exempt deliveries described in (h) hereof and adjusting such deliveries for the transfers set out in (i) hereof, by the number of days in the base period;

(2) Multiply the result of the foregoing calculation by the number of days in the quota period; and

(3) Multiply the aforesaid resulting amount by the following applicable percentages: (i) Milk: 100 percent of pounds of milk and ---- percent of pounds of butterfat; (ii) Cream: 75 percent of pounds of cream and 75 percent of pounds of butterfat; and (iii) Milk byproducts: 75 percent of pounds of milk byproducts other than cottage, pot, or baker's cheese and of the pounds of skim milk equivalent of cottage, pot, or baker's cheese. (For the purpose of this order, one pound of cottage, pot, or baker's cheese shall be considered as the equivalent of 7 pounds of skim milk.)

(f) *Quotas for handlers who are also producers.* Quotas for handlers who are also producers and who purchase no milk shall be 100 percent of the total production of such handlers in the base period.

(g) *Handler exemptions.* Quotas shall not apply to any handler who delivers in a quota period a daily average of less than 150 units of milk, cream, and milk byproducts. For the purpose of this order, a unit shall be the equivalent in volume of the following:

(1) Milk, one quart of milk;

(2) Cream, one-half pint of cream; and

(3) Milk byproduct, one quart of skim milk, buttermilk, flavored milk drink, or other beverage containing more than 85 percent of skim milk, or one-half pound of cottage, pot, or baker's cheese.

(h) *Quota exclusions and exemptions.* Deliveries of milk, milk byproducts, or cream (1) to other handlers, except for such deliveries to sub-handlers, (2) to plants engaged in the handling or processing of milk, milk byproducts, or cream from which no milk, milk byproducts, or cream is delivered in the sales area, and (3) to the agencies or groups specified in (d) of the order, shall be excluded from the computation of deliveries in the base period and exempt from charges to quotas.

(i) *Transfers and apportionment of quotas.* The market agent is empowered to deduct an amount of base period deliveries to purchasers from the total of deliveries made by a handler or other person in the base period upon the application and a showing of unreasonable hardship by the handler making deliveries to such purchasers on the effective date of this order, and to add the amount of such deliveries to the total base period deliveries of the applicant handler. Denials of transfers or transfers granted by the market agent shall be reviewed by the Director upon application.

(j) *Petition for relief from hardships.* (1) Any person affected by the order or the provisions hereof who considers that compliance therewith would work an exceptional and unreasonable hardship on him, may file with the market agent a petition addressed to the Director. The petition shall contain the correct name, address and principal place of business of the petitioner, a full statement of the facts upon which the petition is based, and the hardship involved and the nature of the relief desired.

(2) Upon receiving such petition, the market agent shall immediately investigate the representations and facts stated therein.

(3) After investigation, the petition shall be certified to the Director, but prior to certification the market agent may (i) deny the petition; or (ii) grant temporary relief for a total period not to exceed 60 days.

(4) Denials or grants of relief by the market agent shall be reviewed by the Director and may be affirmed, modified, or reversed by the Director.

(k) *Reports.* Each handler shall transmit to the market agent on forms prescribed by the market agent the following reports:

(1) Within 20 days following the effective date of this order, reports which show the information required by the market agent to establish such handlers' quotas;

(2) Within 20 days following the close of each quota period, the information required by the market agent to establish volumes of deliveries of milk, cream, and milk byproducts during the preceding quota period; and

(3) Handlers exempt from quotas pursuant to (f) hereof shall, upon the request of the market agent, submit the information required by the market agent to establish volumes of deliveries of milk, cream, and milk byproducts.

(l) *Records.* Handlers shall keep and shall make available to the market agent such record of receipts, sales, deliveries, and production as the market agent shall require for the purpose of obtaining information which the Director may require for the establishment of quotas as prescribed in (b) of the order.

(m) *Distribution schedules.* The distribution schedules, if any, to be followed by the handlers in making deliveries shall be made effective in the terms of approval by the Director of such schedules.

(n) *Expense of administration.* Each handler shall pay to the market agent, within 20 days after the close of each calendar month, an assessment of $.01 per hundredweight of each of milk, cream, skim milk, buttermilk, flavored milk drinks, beverages containing more than 85 percent of skim milk, and skim milk equivalent of cottage, pot, or baker's cheese delivered during the preceding quota period and subject to quota regulations under the provisions hereof.

(o) *Violations.* The market agent shall report all violations to the Director together with the information required for the prosecution of such violations, except in a case where a handler has made deliveries in a quota period in excess of a quota in an amount not to exceed 5 percent of such quota, and in the succeeding quota period makes deliveries below that quota by at least the same percent.

(p) *Bureau of the Budget approval.* The record-keeping and reporting requirements of this order have been approved by the Bureau of the Budget in accordance with the Federal Reports Act of 1942. Subsequent record-keeping or reporting requirements will be subject to the approval of the Bureau of the Budget pursuant to the Federal Reports Act of 1942.

(q) This order shall take effect at 12:01 a. m., e. w. t., October 4, 1943.

Issued this 30th day of September 1943.

ROY F. HENDRICKSON,
Director of Food Distribution.

Press Release Immediate:
Thursday, September 30, 1943.

Federal control over fluid milk sales, through the establishment of quotas on deliveries of milk, cream, and milk byproducts, will go into effect in 13 eastern and midwestern metropolitan areas beginning October 4, the War Food Administration announced today.

These areas, and the market agents designated by the Food Distribution Administration to administer the milk conservation and control program in each are:

Baltimore, Md., Washington, D. C., Roanoke, Va., Richmond, Va., Norfolk-Portsmouth-Newport News, Va.: George Irvine, 1731 I Street NW., Washington, D. C.

Cincinnati, Ohio, Toledo, Ohio, Dayton, Ohio, Canton, Ohio, Cleveland, Ohio: Fred W. Issler, 152 East Fourth Street, Cincinnati, Ohio.

Chicago, Illinois: A. W. Colebank, 135 South LaSalle St., Chicago, Ill.

Omaha-Neb.-Council Bluffs, Iowa: Wayne McPherren, Rm. 408, Post Office Bldg., Omaha, Nebraska.

St. Louis, Missouri: William C. Eckles, 4030 Chouteau Ave., St. Louis, Missouri.

Consumers in regulated areas will be able to purchase as much milk as they have been buying—within the limits of local supplies, officials said. The basic purpose of the program is to prevent a further increase in the consumption of fluid milk (rather than to reduce present consumption) so that enough milk will be available to produce the cheese, butter, and other manufactured dairy products required by the armed services and civilians. As milk conservation and control will be effected at the dealer level, consumer point rationing is not involved.

Milk dealers in the 13 initial milk sales areas will be allowed to sell as much fluid milk each month as they sold last June, (1943), the peak production month. To help assure that enough fluid milk will be available during the season of low production to enable dealers to sell as much as their quotas allow, cream sales will be limited to 75 percent of the quantity sold in June, and the sales quota for fluid milk by-products as a group (including cottage cheese, chocolate milk, and buttermilk) also is set at 75 percent of June sales.

Producer-distributors who purchase no milk (except those whose volume of sales is small enough to exempt them from the quota) will be allowed to sell an amount of fluid milk, cream, and fluid milk byproducts equal to 100 percent of their total milk production in June. "Quota-exempt" producer-distributors are defined separately for each area, but in general they are those whose deliveries are relatively small, and who produce the milk they sell from their own herds.

Milk distributors will be responsible for the fair distribution of supplies in their markets. Under Food Distribution Order 79, however, which authorizes the establishment of individual milk orders for each area, the various market agents may recommend distribution schedules to assure that, in the event of short supplies, the most essential needs will be met first.

Success of the milk conservation and control program depends largely on trade and consumer cooperation, WFA officials pointed out. It is believed that stabilization of milk consumption can be accomplished equitably through this system of dealer control without resorting to consumer rationing. Individual rationing of such a highly perishable product as milk would be very complex, difficult to administer, and would almost necessarily result in substantial reductions in fluid milk sales in many markets. Rationing at the consumer level undoubtedly will be necessary if control over dealers' sales does not effectively regulate fluid milk consumption, the officials said.

Under the individual orders established for each area, the milk control program may be modified to fit production and consumption conditions in each market. These orders will be administered by market agents appointed by the Director of Food Distribution.

Milk sales in all other cities of at least 100,000 population will be regulated as soon as administrative arrangements can be completed—with most areas of this size to be operating under the program by November 1. It is expected that the program will then be extended to smaller population areas until all markets of at least 50,000 population are included.

Distributor quotas for milk sales areas to be named later may be the same as those for the areas announced today, or they may vary if local conditions indicate that different bases are necessary.

Milk handlers (that is, all persons or firms engaged in the sale or transfer of milk, except such groups as retail stores, hotels, restaurants, etc.) will compute the quantity of milk and fluid milk byproducts which they may sell each month in terms of pounds of milk and pounds of milk byproducts, and their cream sales in terms of pounds of cream and butterfat. In months which contain more or less days than the base period, handlers will determine the amount of milk they may sell by multiplying the average of daily deliveries in June by 28, 29, or 31, whichever is applicable.

Dealers may exceed their monthly quotas by up to 5 percent greater sales providing they make up this excess by reducing their deliveries proportionately the next month, without the market agent being required to report such excess sales.

Deliveries to the armed forces, to plants processing dairy products, and to other handlers (except special classes of handlers such as peddlers) are quota exempt.

To facilitate administration, the market agent for each milk sales area may act upon petitions for relief from hardship which may be submitted to him, and his decision will be effective for a 60-day period.

Dealers' quotas based on June deliveries will permit consumers to purchase more milk than they consumed in 1942, and considerably more than in pre-war years. Consumption of fluid milk and cream thus far in 1943 has been at a rate of more than 41 billion pounds annually compared with 37.7 billion pounds in 1942 and an average of 32.6 billion pounds in pre-war years (1936–40).

Total milk production has been mounting steadily in recent years—from 101 billion pounds in 1935 to 119 billion pounds in 1942—an all-time high. Production during the first 7 months of this year equalled production during the same months of 1942.

Increasing fluid milk sales, however, resulting largely from the sharp rise in consumer incomes, have reduced the quantity of milk available for the manufacture of essential products such as butter, cheese, evaporated milk, ice cream, and milk powder. Previously uncontrolled, consumption of fluid milk and cream has been rising at the rate of about 1 percent a month, and already is 20 percent above the 1941 level and 10 to 12 percent over 1942.

This has necessitated the stabilization of fluid milk consumption in order to meet the requirements for manufactured dairy products, both on the home and battle fronts, WFA officials explained.

337

FDO 79-9
AMDT. 1
OCTOBER 28, 1943

WAR FOOD ADMINISTRATION

[FDO 79-9, Amdt. 1]

PART 1401—DAIRY PRODUCTS

CINCINNATI, OHIO, MILK SALES AREA

Pursuant to the authority vested in the Director by Food Distribution Order No. 79, dated September 7, 1943 (8 F.R. 12426), as amended, and to effectuate the purposes thereof, Director Food Distribution Order No. 79-9 § 1401.44, relative to the conservation of fluid milk in the Cincinnati, Ohio, milk sales area (8 F.R. 13373) issued by the Director of Food Distribution on September 30, 1943, is amended as follows:

The milk sales area described in § 1401.44 (b) of the original order is modified in the following particulars:

Délete all territory within the State of Kentucky and substitute therefor "the city of Newport, those parts of magisterial districts 1 and 3 outlying the city of Newport, and magisterial district 4 in Campbell County, the city of Covington, those parts of magisterial districts 3 and 6 outlying the city of Covington, and magisterial districts 4 and 7 in Kenton County, all in the State of Kentucky."

Effective date. This amendment of FDO No. 79-9, shall become effective at 12:01 a. m. e. w. t., November 1, 1943.

(E.O. 9280, 8 F.R. 10179; E.O. 9322, 8 F.R. 3807; E.O. 9334, 8 F.R. 5423; FDO 79, 8 F.R. 12426, 13283)

Issued this 28th day of October 1943.

ROY F. HENDRICKSON,
Director of Food Distribution.

35
4 p 1

FDO 79-9

AMDT. 2
JAN. 27, 1944

WAR FOOD ADMINISTRATION

[FDO 79-9, Amdt. 2]

PART 1401—DAIRY PRODUCTS

FLUID MILK AND CREAM IN CINCINNATI, OHIO, SALES AREA

Pursuant to Food Distribution Order No. 79 (8 F.R. 12426), dated September 7, 1943, as amended, and to effectuate the purposes thereof, Food Distribution Order No. 79-9 (8 F. R. 13373), relative to the conservation and distribution of fluid milk in the Cincinnati, Ohio, milk sales area, issued by the Director of Food Distribution on September 30, 1943, as amended, is hereby further amended as follows:

1. By deleting therefrom the provisions in § 1401.44 (f) and substituting therefor the following:

(f) *Quotas for handlers who are also producers.* Quotas for handlers who are also producers and who purchase no milk shall be computed in accordance with (e) hereof, except that the applicable percentages shall be 100 percent in lieu of the percentages specified in (e) (3).

2. By deleting therefrom the provisions of § 1401.44 (h) and substituting therefor the following:

(h) *Quota exclusions and exemptions.* Deliveries of milk, milk byproducts, or cream (1) to other handlers, except for such deliveries to sub-handlers, (2) to plants engaged in the handling or processing of milk, milk byproducts, or cream from which no milk, milk byproducts, or cream is delivered in the sales area, (3) to nursery, elementary, junior high, and high schools, and (4) to the agencies or groups specified in (d) of the order, shall be excluded from the computation of deliveries in the base period and exempt from charges to quotas.

The provisions of this amendment shall become effective at 12:01 a. m., e. w. t., February 1, 1944. With respect to violations of said Food Distribution Order No. 79-9, as amended, rights accrued, or liabilities incurred prior to the effective time of this amendment, said Food Distribution Order No. 79-9, as amended, shall be deemed to be in full force and effect for the purpose of sustaining any proper suit, action, or other proceeding with respect to any violation, right, or liability.

(E.O. 9280, 7 F.R. 10179; E.O. 9322, 8 F.R. 3807; E.O. 9334, 8 F.R. 5423; E.O. 9392, 8 F.R. 14783; FDO 79, 8 F.R. 12426, 13283)

Issued this 27th day of January 1944.

LEE MARSHALL,
Director of Food Distribution.

FDO 79-10

SEPT. 30, 1943

WAR FOOD ADMINISTRATION

[FDO 79-10]

PART 1401—DAIRY PRODUCTS

CONSERVATION AND DISTRIBUTION OF FLUID MILK AND CREAM IN THE CANTON, OHIO, SALES AREA

Pursuant to the authority vested in me by Food Distribution Order No. 79 (8 F.R. 12426), issued on September 7, 1943, as amended, and to effectuate the purposes of such order, it is hereby ordered as follows:

§ 1401.43 *Quota restrictions*—(a) *Definitions.* When used in this order, unless otherwise distinctly expressed or manifestly incompatible with the intent hereof:

(1) Each term defined in Food Distribution Order No. 79, as amended, shall, when used herein, have the same meaning as is set forth for such term in Food Distribution Order No. 79, as amended.

(2) The term "order" means Food Distribution Order No. 79, issued on September 7, 1943, as amended.

(3) The term "sub-handler" means any handler, such as a peddler, vendor, sub-dealer, or secondary dealer, who purchases in a previously packaged and processed form milk, milk byproducts, or cream for delivery.

(b) *Milk sales area.* The following area is hereby designated as a "milk sales area" to be known as the Canton, Ohio sales area, and is referred to hereinafter as the "sales area": The city of Canton and Stark County, in the State of Ohio.

(c) *Base period.* The calendar month of June 1943 is hereby designated as the base period for the sales area.

(d) *Quota period.* The remainder of the calendar month in which the provisions hereof become effective and each subsequent calendar month, respectively, is hereby designated as a quota period for the sales area.

(e) *Handler quotas.* Quotas for each handler in the sales area in each quota period shall be determined as follows:

(1) Divide the total deliveries of each of milk, milk byproducts, and cream (and of butterfat in milk or in cream where percentages of pounds of butterfat are specified in (e)(3)(i) or (e)(3)(ii) hereof) made in the sales area by such handler during the base period, after excluding the quota-exempt deliveries described in (h) hereof and adjusting such deliveries for the transfers set out in (i) hereof, by the number of days in the base period;

(2) Multiply the result of the foregoing calculation by the number of days in the quota period; and

(3) Multiply the aforesaid resulting amount by the following applicable percentage: (i) Milk: 100 percent of pounds of milk and ____ percent of pounds of butterfat; (ii) Cream: 75 percent of pounds of cream and 75 percent of pounds of butterfat; and (iii) Milk byproducts: 75 percent of pounds of milk byproducts other than cottage, pot, or baker's cheese and of the pounds of skim milk equivalent of cottage, pot, or baker's cheese. (For the purpose of this order, one pound of cottage, pot or baker's cheese shall be considered as the equivalent of 7 pounds of skim milk.)

(f) *Quotas for handlers who are also producers.* Quotas for handlers who are also producers and who purchase no milk shall be 100 percent of the total production of such handlers in the base period.

(g) *Handler exemptions.* Quotas shall not apply to any handler who delivers in a quota period a daily average of less than 150 units of milk, cream, and milk byproducts. For the purpose of this order, a unit shall be the equivalent in volume of the following:

(1) Milk, one quart of milk;

(2) Cream, one-half pint of cream; and

(3) Milk byproduct, one quart of skim milk, buttermilk, flavored milk drink, or other beverage containing more than 85 percent of skim milk, or one-half pound of cottage, pot, or baker's cheese.

(h) *Quota exclusions and exemptions.* Deliveries of milk, milk byproducts, or cream (1) to other handlers, except for such deliveries to sub-handlers, (2) to plants engaged in the handling or processing of milk, milk byproducts, or cream from which no milk, milk byproducts, or cream is delivered in the sales area, and (3) to the agencies or groups specified in (d) of the order, shall be excluded from the computation of deliveries in the base period and exempt from charges to quotas.

(i) *Transfers and apportionment of quotas.* The market agent is empowered to deduct an amount of base period deliveries to purchasers from the total of deliveries made by a handler or other person in the base period upon the application and a showing of unreasonable hardship by the handler making deliveries to such purchasers on the effective date of this order, and to add the amount of such deliveries to the total base period deliveries of the applicant handler. Denials of transfers or transfers granted by the market agent shall be reviewed by the Director upon application.

(j) *Petition for relief from hardships.* (1) Any person affected by the order or the provisions hereof who considers that compliance therewith would work an exceptional and unreasonable hardship on him, may file with the market agent a petition addressed to the Director. The petition shall contain the correct name, address and principal place of business of the petitioner, a full statement of the facts upon which the petition is based, and the hardship involved and the nature of the relief desired.

(2) Upon receiving such petition, the market agent shall immediately investigate the representations and facts stated therein.

(3) After investigation, the petition shall be certified to the Director, but prior to certification the market agent may (i) deny the petition; or (ii) grant temporary relief for a total period not to exceed 60 days.

(4) Denials or grants of relief by the market agent shall be reviewed by the Director and may be affirmed, modified, or reversed by the Director.

(k) *Reports.* Each handler shall transmit to the market agent on forms prescribed by the market agent the following reports:

(1) Within 20 days following the effective date of this order, reports which show the information required by the market agent to establish such handlers' quotas;

(2) Within 20 days following the close of each quota period, the information required by the market agent to establish volumes of deliveries of milk, cream, and milk byproducts during the preceding quota period; and

(3) Handlers exempt from quotas pursuant to (f) hereof shall, upon the request of the market agent, submit the information required by the market agent to establish volumes of deliveries of milk, cream, and milk byproducts.

(l) *Records.* Handlers shall keep and shall make available to the market agent such records of receipts, sales, deliveries, and production as the market agent shall require for the purpose of obtaining information which the Director may require for the establishment of quotas as prescribed in (b) of the order.

(m) *Distribution schedules.* The distribution schedules, if any, to be followed by the handlers in making deliveries shall be made effective in the terms of approval by the Director of such schedules.

(n) *Expense of administration.* Each handler shall pay to the market agent, within 20 days after the close of each calendar month an assessment of $.01 per hundredweight of each of milk, cream, skim milk, buttermilk, flavored milk drinks, beverages containing more than 85 percent of skim milk, and skim milk equivalent of cottage, pot, or baker's cheese delivered during the preceding quota period and subject to quota regulations under the provisions hereof.

(o) *Violations.* The market agent shall report all violations to the Director together with the information required for the prosecution of such violations, except in a case where a handler has made deliveries in a quota period in excess of a quota in an amount not to exceed 5 percent of such quota, and in the succeeding quota period makes deliveries below that quota by at least the same percent.

(p) *Bureau of the Budget approval.* The record-keeping and reporting requirements of this order have been approved by the Bureau of the Budget in accordance with the Federal Reports Act of **1942**. Subsequent record-keeping or reporting requirements will be subject to the approval of the Bureau of the Budget pursuant to the Federal Reports Act of **1942**.

(q) This order shall take effect at 12:01 a. m., e. w. t., October **4**, **1943**.

Issued this 30th day of September 1943.

ROY F. HENDRICKSON,
Director of Food Distribution.

Press Release Immediate:
Thursday, September 30, 1943.

Federal control over fluid milk sales, through the establishment of quotas on deliveries of milk, cream, and milk byproducts, will go into effect in 13 eastern and midwestern metropolitan areas beginning October 4, the War Food Administration announced today.

These areas, and the market agents designated by the Food Distribution Administration to administer the milk conservation and control program in each, are:

Baltimore, Md., Washington, D. C., Roanoke, Va., Richmond, Va., Norfolk-Portsmouth-Newport News, Va.: George Irvine, 1731 I Street NW., Washington, D. C.

Cincinnati, Ohio, Toledo, Ohio, Dayton, Ohio, Canton, Ohio, Cleveland, Ohio: Fred W. Issler, 152 East Fourth Street, Cincinnati, Ohio.

Chicago, Illinois: A. W. Colebank, 135 South LaSalle St., Chicago, Ill.

Omaha, Nebr.,-Council Bluffs, Iowa: Wayne McPherren, Rm. 408, Post Office Bldg., Omaha, Nebraska.

St. Louis, Missouri: William C. Eckles, 4030 Chouteau Ave., St. Louis, Missouri.

Consumers in regulated areas will be able to purchase as much milk as they have been buying—within the limits of local supplies, officials said. The basic purpose of the program is to prevent a further increase in the consumption of fluid milk (rather than to reduce present consumption) so that enough milk will be available to produce the cheese, butter, and other manufactured dairy products required by the armed services and civilians. As milk conservation and control will be effected at the dealer level, consumer point rationing is not involved.

Milk dealers in the 13 initial milk sales areas will be allowed to sell as much fluid milk each month as they sold last June, (1943), the peak production month. To help assure that enough fluid milk will be available during the season of low production to enable dealers to sell as much as their quotas allow, cream sales will be limited to 75 percent of the quantity sold in June, and the sales quota for fluid milk byproducts as a group (including cottage cheese, chocolate milk, and buttermilk) also is set at 75 percent of June sales.

Producer-distributors who purchase no milk (except those whose volume of sales is small enough to exempt them from the quota) will be allowed to sell an amount of fluid milk, cream, and fluid milk byproducts equal to 100 percent of their total milk production in June. "Quota-exempt" producer-distributors are defined separately for each area, but in general they are those whose deliveries are relatively small, and who produce the milk they sell from their own herds.

Milk distributors will be responsible for the fair distribution of supplies in their markets. Under Food Distribution Order 79, however, which authorizes the establishment of individual milk orders for each area, the various market agents may recommend distribution schedules to assure that, in the event of short supplies, the most essential needs will be met first.

Success of the milk conservation and control program depends largely on trade and consumer cooperation, WFA officials pointed out. It is believed that stabilization of milk consumption can be acomplished equitably through this system of dealer control without resorting to consumer rationing. Individual rationing of such a highly perishable product as milk would be very complex, difficult to administer, and would almost necessarily result in substantial reductions in fluid milk sales in many markets. Rationing at the consumer level undoubtedly will be necessary if control over dealers' sales does not effectively regulate fluid milk consumption, the officials said.

Under the individual orders established for each area, the milk control program may be modified to fit production and consumption conditions in each market. These orders will be administered by market agents appointed by the Director of Food Distribution.

Milk sales in all other cities of at least 100,000 population will be regulated as soon as administrative arrangements can be completed—with most areas of this size to be operating under the program by November 1. It is expected that the program will then be extended to smaller population areas until all markets of at least 50,000 population are included.

Distributor quotas for milk sales areas to be named later may be the same as those for the areas announced today, or they may vary if local conditions indicate that different bases are necessary.

Milk handlers (that is, all persons or firms engaged in the sale or transfer of milk, except such groups as retail stores, hotels, restaurants, etc.) will compute the quantity of milk and fluid milk byproducts which they may sell each month in terms of pounds of milk and pounds of milk byproducts, and their cream sales in terms of pounds of cream and butterfat. In months which contain more or less days than the base period, handlers will determine the amount of milk they may sell by multiplying the average of daily deliveries in June by **28**, **29**, or **31**, whichever is applicable.

Dealers may exceed their monthly quotas by up to 5 percent greater sales providing they make up this excess by reducing their deliveries proportionately the next month, without the market agent being required to report such excess sales.

Deliveries to the armed forces, to plants processing dairy products, and to other handlers (except special classes of handlers such as peddlers) are quota exempt.

To facilitate administration, the market agent for each milk sales area may act upon petitions for relief from hardship which may be submitted to him, and his decision will be effective for a 60-day period.

Dealers' quotas based on June deliveries will permit consumers to purchase more milk than they consumed in **1942**, and considerably more than in pre-war years. Consumption of fluid milk and cream thus far in **1943** has been at a rate of more than **41** billion pounds annually compared with **37.7** billion pounds in **1942** and an average of **32.6** billion pounds in pre-war years (**1936-40**).

Total milk production has been mounting steadily in recent years—from **101** billion pounds in **1935** to **119** billion pounds in **1942**—an all-time high. Production during the first **7** months of this year equalled production during the same months of **1942**.

Increasing fluid milk sales, however, resulting largely from the sharp rise in consumer incomes, have reduced the quantity of milk available for the manufacture of essential products such as butter, cheese, evaporated milk, ice cream, and milk powder. Previously uncontrolled, consumption of fluid milk and cream has been rising at the rate of about 1 percent a month, and already is **20** percent above the **1941** level and **10** to **12** percent over **1942**.

This has necessitated the stabilization of fluid milk consumption in order to meet the requirements for manufactured dairy products, both on the home and battle fronts, WFA officials explained.

FDO 79-10
AMDT. 1
NOV. 22, 1943

WAR FOOD ADMINISTRATION

[FDO 79-10, Amdt. 1]

Part 1401—Dairy Products

FLUID MILK AND CREAM IN CANTON, OHIO, SALES AREA

Pursuant to the authority vested in the Director by Food Distribution Order No. 79, dated September 7, 1943, (8 F.R. 12426), as amended, and to effectuate the purposes thereof, Director Food Distribution Order No. 79-10, § 1401.43, relative to the conservation of fluid milk in the Canton, Ohio, milk sales area (8 F.R. 13374), issued by the Director of Food Distribution on September 30, 1943, is amended as follows:

Reduce the quota exemption specified in § 1401.43 (g) of the original order to 50 units, so that the first line reads, "Quotas shall not apply to any handler who delivers in a quota period a daily average of less than 50 units of milk, cream, and milk byproducts".

Effective date. This amendment of DFDO No. 79-10, shall become effective at 12:01 a. m., e. w. t., December 1, 1943.

(E.O. 9280, 8 F.R. 10179; E.O. 9322, 8 F.R. 3807; E.O. 9334, 8 F.R. 5423; E.O. 9392, 8 F.R. 14783; FDO 79, 8 F.R. 12426, 13283)

Issued this 22d day of November 1943.

Roy F. Hendrickson,
Director of Food Distribution.

FDO 79-10
AMDT. 2
DEC. 28, 1943

WAR FOOD ADMINISTRATION

[FDO 79-10, Amdt. 2]

PART 1401—DAIRY PRODUCTS

FLUID MILK AND CREAM IN THE CANTON, OHIO MILK SALES AREA

Pursuant to Food Distribution Order No. 79 (8 F.R. 12426), dated September 7, 1943, as amended, and to effectuate the purposes thereof, Food Distribution Order No. 79-10 (8 F.R. 13374), relative to the conservation and distribution of fluid milk in the Canton, Ohio, milk sales area, issued by the Director of Food Distribution on September 30, 1943, as amended, is hereby further amended by adding to § 1401.43 (b) the following: "The townships of Knox and West in Columbiana County, and Smith township in Mahoning County, all in the State of Ohio."

The provisions of this amendment shall become effective at 12:01 a. m., e. w. t., January 1, 1944. With respect to violations of said Food Distribution Order No. 79-10, as amended, rights accrued, or liabilities incurred prior to the effective time of this amendment, said Food Distribution Order No. 79-10, as amended, shall be deemed to be in full force and effect for the purpose of sustaining any proper suit, action, or other proceeding with respect to any such violation, right or liability.

(E.O. 9280, 7 F.R. 10179; E.O. 9322, 8 F.R. 3807; E.O. 9334, 8 F.R. 5423; E.O. 9392, 8 F.R. 14783; FDO 79, 8 F.R. 12426, 13283)

Issued this 28th day of December 1943.

ROY F. HENDRICKSON,
Director of Food Distribution.

'3.3 4
Cop. 1

FDO 79-10
AMDT. 3
JAN. 27, 1944

WAR FOOD ADMINISTRATION

[FDO 79-10, Amdt. 3]

PART 1401—DAIRY PRODUCTS

FLUID MILK AND CREAM IN CANTON, OHIO, SALES AREA

Pursuant to Food Distribution Order No. 79 (8 F.R. 12426), dated September 7, 1943, as amended, and to effectuate the purposes thereof, Food Distribution Order No. 79-10 (8 F.R. 13374) relative to the conservation and distribution of fluid milk in the Canton, Ohio, milk sales area, issued by the Director of Food Distribution on September 30, 1943, as amended, is hereby further amended as follows:

1. By deleting therefrom the provisions in § 1401.43 (f) and substituting therefor the following:

(f) *Quotas for handlers who are also producers.* Quotas for handlers who are also producers and who purchase no milk shall be computed in accordance with (e) hereof, except that the applicable percentages shall be 100 percent in lieu of the percentages specified in (e) (3).

2. By deleting therefrom the provisions of § 1401.43 (h) and substituting therefor the following:

(h) *Quota exclusions and exemptions.* Deliveries of milk, milk byproducts, or cream (1) to other handlers, except for such deliveries to sub-handlers, (2) to plants engaged in the handling or processing of milk, milk byproducts, or cream from which no milk, milk byproducts, or cream is delivered in the sales area, (3) to nursery, elementary, junior high, and high schools, and (4) to the agencies or groups specified in (d) of the order, shall be excluded from the computation of deliveries in the base period and exempt from charges to quotas.

The provisions of this amendment shall become effective at 12:01 a. m., e. w. t., February 1, 1944. With respect to violations of said Food Distribution Order No. 79-10, as amended, rights accrued, or liabilities incurred prior to the effective time of this amendment, said Food Distribution Order No. 79-10, as amended, shall be deemed to be in full force and effect for the purpose of sustaining any proper suit, action, or other proceeding with respect to any such violation, right, or liability.

(E.O. 9280, 7 F.R. 10179; E.O. 9322, 8 F.R. 3807; E.O. 9334, 8 F.R. 5423; E.O. 9392, 8 F.R. 14783; FDO 79, 8 F.R. 12426, 13283)

Issued this 27th day of January 1944.

LEE MARSHALL,
Director of Food Distribution.

FDO 79-11

SEPTEMBER 30, 1943

WAR FOOD ADMINISTRATION

[FDO 79-11]

PART 1401—DAIRY PRODUCTS

CONSERVATION AND DISTRIBUTION OF FLUID MILK AND CREAM IN THE TOLEDO, OHIO, SALES AREA

Pursuant to the authority vested in me by Food Distribution Order No. 79 (8 F. R. 12426), issued on September 7, 1943, as amended, and to effectuate the purposes of such order, it is hereby ordered as follows:

§ 1401.42 *Quota restrictions*—(a) *Definitions.* When used in this order, unless otherwise distinctly expressed or manifestly incompatible with the intent hereof:

(1) Each term defined in Food Distribution Order No. 79, as amended, shall, when used herein, have the same meaning as is set forth for such term in Food Distribution Order No. 79, as amended.

(2) The term "order" means Food Distribution Order No. 79, issued on September 7, 1943, as amended.

(3) The term "sub-handler" means any handler, such as a peddler, vendor, sub-dealer, or secondary dealer, who purchases in a previously packaged and processed form milk, milk byproducts or cream for delivery.

(b) *Milk sales area.* The following area is hereby designated as a "milk sales area" to be known as the Toledo, Ohio sales area, and is referred to hereinafter as the "sales area": The city of Toledo; the villages of Ottawa Hills, Maumee, Sylvania, Harbor View, Rossford and Trilby in Lucas County, the townships of Monclova, Springfield, Adams, Sylvania, Washington, Jerusalem and Oregon in Lucas County, and the townships of Perrysburg, Ross and Lake in Wood County, all in the State of Ohio; the village of Lakeside and the townships of Whiteford, Bedford and Erie in Monroe County, all in the State of Michigan.

(c) *Base period.* The calendar month of June 1943 is hereby designated as the base period for the sales area.

(d) *Quota period.* The remainder of the calendar month in which the provisions hereof become effective and each subsequent calendar month, respectively, is hereby designated as a quota period for the sales area.

(e) *Handler quotas.* Quotas for each handler in the sales area in each quota period shall be determined as follows:

(1) Divide the total deliveries of each of milk, milk byproducts, and cream (and of butterfat in milk or in cream where percentages of pounds of butterfat are specified in (e) (3) (i) or (e) (3) (ii) hereof) made in the sales area by such handler during the base period, after excluding the quota-exempt deliveries described in (h) hereof and adjusting such deliveries for the transfers set out in (i) hereof, by the number of days in the base period;

(2) Multiply the result of the foregoing calculation by the number of days in the quota period; and

(3) Multiply the aforesaid resulting amount by the following applicable percentage: (i) Milk: 100 percent of pounds of milk and ---- percent of pounds of butterfat; (ii) Cream: 75 percent of pounds of cream and 75 percent of pounds of butterfat; and (iii) Milk byproducts: 75 percent of pounds of milk byproducts other than cottage, pot, or baker's cheese and of the pounds of skim milk equivalent of cottage, pot, or baker's cheese. (For the purpose of this order, one pound of cottage, pot, or baker's cheese shall be considered as the equivalent of 7 pounds of skim milk.)

(f) *Quotas for handlers who are also producers.* Quotas for handlers who are also producers and who purchase no milk shall be 100 percent of the total production of such handlers in the base period.

(g) *Handler exemptions.* Quotas shall not apply to any handler who delivers in a quota period a daily average of less than 150 units of milk, cream, and milk byproducts. For the purpose of this order, a unit shall be the equivalent in volume of the following:

(1) Milk, one quart of milk;

(2) Cream, one-half pint of cream; and

(3) Milk byproduct, one quart of skim milk, buttermilk, flavored milk drink, or other beverage containing more than 85 percent of skim milk, or one-half pound of cottage, pot, or baker's cheese.

(h) *Quota exclusions and exemptions.* Deliveries of milk, milk byproducts, or cream (1) to other handlers, except for such deliveries to sub-handlers, (2) to plants engaged in the handling or processing of milk, milk byproducts, or cream from which no milk, milk byproducts, or cream is delivered in the sales area, and (3) to the agencies or groups specified in (d) of the order, shall be excluded from the computation of deliveries in the base period and exempt from charges to quotas.

(i) *Transfers and apportionment of quotas.* The market agent is empowered to deduct an amount of base period deliveries to purchasers from the total of deliveries made by a handler or other person in the base period upon the application and a showing of unreasonable hardship by the handler making deliveries to such purchasers on the effective date of this order, and to add the amount of such deliveries to the total base period deliveries of the applicant handler. Denials of transfers or tranfers granted by the market agent shall be reviewed by the Director upon application.

(j) *Petition for relief from hardships.* (1) Any person affected by the order or the provisions hereof who considers that compliance therewith would work an exceptional and unreasonable hardship on him, may file with the market agent a petition addressed to the Director. The petition shall contain the correct name, address and principal place of business of the petitioner, a full statement of the facts upon which the petition is based, and the hardship involved and the nature of the relief desired.

(2) Upon receiving such petition, the market agent shall immediately investigate the representations and facts stated therein.

(3) After investigation, the petition shall be certified to the Director, but prior to certification the market agent may (i) deny the petition; or (ii) grant temporary relief for a total period not to exceed 60 days.

(4) Denials or grants of relief by the market agent shall be reviewed by the Director and may be affirmed, modified, or reversed by the Director.

(k) *Reports.* Each handler shall transmit to the market agent on forms prescribed by the market agent the following reports:

(1) Within 20 days following the effective date of this order, reports which show the information required by the market agent to establish such handlers' quotas;

(2) Within 20 days following the close of each quota period, the information required by the market agent to establish volumes of deliveries of milk, cream, and milk byproducts during the preceding quota period; and

(3) Handlers exempt from quotas pursuant to (f) hereof shall, upon the request of the market agent, submit the information required by the market agent to establish volumes of deliveries of milk, cream, and milk byproducts.

(l) *Records.* Handlers shall keep and shall make available to the market agent such records of receipts, sales, deliveries, and production as the market agent shall require for the purpose of obtaining information which the Director may require for the establishment of quotas as prescribed in (b) of the order.

(m) *Distribution schedules.* The distribution schedules, if any, to be followed by the handlers in making deliveries shall be made effective in the terms of approval by the Director of such schedules.

(n) *Expense of administration.* Each handler shall pay to the market agent, within 20 days after the close of each calendar month an assessment of $.01

per hundredweight of each of milk, cream, skim milk, buttermilk, flavored milk drinks, beverages containing more than 85 percent of skim milk, and skim milk equivalent of cottage, pot, or baker's cheese delivered during the preceding quota period and subject to quota regulations under the provisions hereof.

(o) *Violations.* The market agent shall report all violations to the Director together with the information required for the prosecution of such violations, except in a case where a handler has made deliveries in a quota period in excess of a quota in an amount not to exceed 5 percent of such quota, and in the succeeding quota period makes deliveries below that quota by at least the same percent.

(p) *Bureau of the Budget approval.* The record-keeping and reporting requirements of this order have been approved by the Bureau of the Budget in accordance with the Federal Reports Act of 1942. Subsequent record-keeping or reporting requirements will be subject to the approval of the Bureau of the Budget pursuant to the Federal Reports Act of 1942.

(q) This order shall take effect at 12:01 a. m., e. w. t., October 4, 1943.

Issued this 30th day of September 1943.

ROY F. HENDRICKSON,
Director of Food Distribution.

Press Release Immediate:
Thursday, September 30, 1943.

Federal control over fluid milk sales, through the establishment of quotas on deliveries of milk, cream, and milk byproducts, will go into effect in 13 eastern and midwestern metropolitan areas beginning October 4, the War Food Administration announced today.

These areas, and the market agents designated by the Food Distribution Administration to administer the milk conservation and control program in each, are:

Baltimore, Md., Washington, D. C. Roanoke, Va., Richmond, Va., Norfolk-Portsmouth-Newport News, Va.: George Irvine, 1731 I Street, NW., Washington, D. C.

Cincinnati, Ohio, Toledo, Ohio, Dayton, Ohio, Canton, Ohio, Cleveland, Ohio; Fred W. Issler, 152 East Fourth Street, Cincinnati, Ohio.

Chicago, Illinois: A. W. Colebank, 135 South LaSalle St., Chicago, Ill.

Omaha, Neb.-Council Bluffs, Iowa: Wayne McPherren, Rm. 408, Post Office Bldg., Omaha, Nebraska.

St. Louis, Missouri: William C. Eckles, 4030 Chouteau Ave., St. Louis, Missouri.

Consumers in regulated areas will be able to purchase as much milk as they have been buying—within the limits of local supplies, officials said. The basic purpose of the program is to prevent a further increase in the consumption of fluid milk (rather than to reduce present consumption) so that enough milk will be available to produce the cheese, butter, and other manufactured dairy products required by the armed services and civilians. As milk conservation and control will be effected at the dealer level, consumer point rationing is not involved.

Milk dealers in the 13 initial milk sales areas will be allowed to sell as much fluid milk each month as they sold last June, (1943), the peak production month. To help assure that enough fluid milk will be available during the season of low production to enable dealers to sell as much as their quotas allow, cream sales will be limited to 75 percent of the quantity sold in June, and the sales quota for fluid milk byproducts as a group (including cottage cheese, chocolate milk, and buttermilk) also is set at 75 percent of June sales.

Producer-distributors who purchase no milk (except those whose volume of sales is small enough to exempt them from the quota) will be allowed to sell an amount of fluid milk, cream, and fluid milk byproducts equal to 100 percent of their total milk production in June. "Quota-exempt" producer-distributors are defined separately for each area, but in general they are those whose deliveries are relatively small, and who produce the milk they sell from their own herds.

Milk distributors will be responsible for the fair distribution of supplies in their markets. Under Food Distribution Order 79, however, which authorizes the establishment of individual milk orders for each area, the various market agents may recommend distribution schedules to assure that, in the event of short supplies, the most essential needs will be met first.

Success of the milk conservation and control program depends largely on trade and consumer cooperation, WFA officials pointed out. It is believed that stabilization of milk consumption can be accomplished equitably through this system of dealer control without resorting to consumer rationing. Individual rationing of such a highly perishable product as milk would be very complex, difficult to administer, and would almost necessarily result in substantial reductions in fluid milk sales in many markets. Rationing at the consumer level undoubtedly will be necessary if control over dealers' sales does not effectively regulate fluid milk consumption, the officials said.

Under the individual orders established for each area, the milk control program may be modified to fit production and consumption conditions in each market. These orders will be administered by market agents appointed by the Director of Food Distribution.

Milk sales in all other cities of at least 100,000 population will be regulated as soon as administrative arrangements can be completed—with most areas of this size to be operating under the program by November 1. It is expected that the program will then be extended to smaller population areas until all markets of at least 50,000 population are included.

Distributor quotas for milk sales areas to be named later may be the same as those for the areas announced today, or they may vary if local conditions indicate that different bases are necessary.

Milk handlers (that is, all persons or firms engaged in the sale or transfer of milk, except such groups as retail stores, hotels, restaurants, etc.) will compute the quantity of milk and fluid milk byproducts which they may sell each month in terms of pounds of milk and pounds of milk byproducts, and their cream sales in terms of pounds of cream and butterfat. In months which contain more or less days than the base period, handlers will determine the amount of milk they may sell by multiplying the average of daily deliveries in June by 28, 29, or 31, whichever is applicable.

Dealers may exceed their monthly quotas by up to 5 percent greater sales providing they make up this excess by reducing their deliveries proportionately the next month, without the market agent being required to report such excess sales.

Deliveries to the armed forces, to plants processing dairy products, and to other handlers (except special classes of handlers such as peddlers) are quota exempt.

To facilitate administration, the market agent for each milk sales area may act upon petitions for relief from hardship which may be submitted to him, and his decision will be effective for a 60-day period.

Dealers' quotas based on June deliveries will permit consumers to purchase more milk than they consumed in 1942, and considerably more than in pre-war years. Consumption of fluid milk and cream thus far in 1943 has been at a rate of more than 41 billion pounds annually compared with 37.7 billion pounds in 1942 and an average of 32.6 billion pounds in pre-war years (1936–40).

Total milk production has been mounting steadily in recent years—from 101 billion pounds in 1935 to 119 billion pounds in 1942—an all-time high. Production during the first 7 months of this year equalled production during the same months of 1942.

Increasing fluid milk sales, however, resulting largely from the sharp rise in consumer incomes, have reduced the quantity of milk available for the manufacture of essential products such as butter, cheese, evaporated milk, ice cream, and milk powder. Previously uncontrolled, consumption of fluid milk and cream has been rising at the rate of about 1 percent a month, and already is 20 percent above the 1941 level and 10 to 12 percent over 1942.

This has necessitated the stabilization of fluid milk consumption in order to meet the requirements for manufactured dairy products, both on the home and battle fronts, WFA officials explained.

337

FDO 79-11
AMDT. 1
OCTOBER 28, 1943

WAR FOOD ADMINISTRATION

[FDO 79-11, Amdt. 1]

PART 1401—DAIRY PRODUCTS

TOLEDO, OHIO, MILK SALES AREA

Pursuant to the authority vested in the Director by Food Distribution Order No. 79, dated September 7, 1943 (8 F.R. 12426), as amended, and to effectuate the purposes thereof, Director Food Distribution Order No. 79-11, § 1401.42, relative to the conservation of fluid milk in the Toledo, Ohio, milk sales area (8 F.R. 13375), issued by the Director of Food Distribution on September 30, 1943, is amended as follows:

The milk sales area described in § 1401.42 (b) of the original order is modified in the following particulars:

Delete the description of the sales area and substitute in lieu thereof the following: "The city of Toledo and the townships of Monclova, Springfield, Adams, Sylvania, Washington, Jerusalem and Oregon in Lucas County, the townships of Perrysburg, Ross and Lake in Wood County, all in the State of Ohio; the townships of Whiteford, Bedford and Erie in Monroe County, all in the State of Michigan".

Effective date. This amendment of FDO No. 79-11 shall become effective at 12:01 a. m., e. w. t., November 1, 1943.

(E.O. 9280, 8 F.R. 10179; E.O. 9322, 8 F.R. 3807; E.O. 9334, 8 F.R. 5423; FDO 79, 8 F.R. 12426, 13283)

Issued this 28th day of October 1943.

ROY F. HENDRICKSON,
Director of Food Distribution.

FDO 79-11
AMDT. 2
JAN. 27, 1944

WAR FOOD ADMINISTRATION

[FDO 79-11, Amdt. 2]

PART 1401—DAIRY PRODUCTS

FLUID MILK AND CREAM IN TOLEDO, OHIO, SALES AREA

Pursuant to Food Distribution Order No. 79 (8 F. R. 12426), dated September 7, 1943, as amended, and to effectuate the purposes thereof, Food Distribution Order No. 7911 (13375), relative to the conservation and distribution of fluid milk in the Toledo, Ohio, milk sales area, issued by the Director of Food Distribution on September 30, 1943, as amended, is hereby further amended as follows:

1. By deleting therefrom the provisions in § 1401.42 (f) and substituting therefor the following:

(f) *Quotas for handlers who are also producers.* Quotas for handlers who are also producers and who purchase no milk shall be computed in accordance with (e) hereof, except that the applicable percentages shall be 100 percent in lieu of the percentages specified in (e) (3).

2. By deleting therefrom the provisions of § 1401.42 (h) and substituting therefor the following:

(h) *Quota exclusions and exemptions.* Deliveries of milk, milk byproducts, or cream (1) to other handlers, except for such deliveries to sub-handlers, (2) to plants, engaged in the handling or processing of milk, milk byproducts, or cream from which no milk, milk byproducts, or cream is delivered in the sales area, (3) to nursery, elementary, junior high, and high schools, and (4) to the agencies or groups specified in (d) of the order, shall be excluded from the computation of deliveries in the base period and exempt from charges to quotas.

The provisions of this amendment shall become effective at 12:01 a. m., e. w. t., February 1, 1944. With respect to violations of said Food Distribution Order No. 79-11, as amended, rights accrued, or liabilities incurred prior to the effective time of this amendment, said Director Food Distribution Order No. 79-11, as amended, shall be deemed to be in full force and effect for the purpose of sustaining any proper suit, action, or other proceeding with respect to any such violation, right, or liability.

(E.O. 9280, 7 F.R. 10179; E.O. 9322, 8 F.R. 3807; E.O. 9334, 8 F.R. 5423; E.O. 9392, 8 F.R. 14783; FDO 79, 8 F.R. 12426, 13283)

Issued this 27th day of January 1944.

LEE MARSHALL,
Director of Food Distribution.

WAR FOOD ADMINISTRATION

[FDO 79-12]

PART 1401—DAIRY PRODUCTS

CONSERVATION AND DISTRIBUTION OF FLUID MILK AND CREAM IN THE ROANOKE, VA., SALES AREA

Pursuant to the authority vested in me by Food Distribution Order No. 79 (8 F.R. 12426), issued on September 7, 1943, as amended, and to effectuate the purposes of such order, it is hereby ordered as follows:

§ 1401.36 *Quota restrictions*—(a) *Definitions.* When used in this order, unless otherwise distinctly expressed or manifestly incompatible with the intent hereof:

(1) Each term defined in Food Distribution Order No. 79, as amended, shall, when used herein, have the same meaning as is set forth for such term in Food Distribution Order No. 79, as amended.

(2) The term "order" means Food Distribution Order No. 79, issued on September 7, 1943, as amended.

(3) The term "sub-handler" means any handler, such as a peddler, vendor, sub-dealer, or secondary dealer, who purchases in a previously packaged and processed form milk, milk byproducts, or cream for delivery.

(b) *Milk sales area.* The following area is hereby designated as a "milk sales area" to be known as the Roanoke, Virginia, sales area, and is referred to hereinafter as the "sales area": The city of Roanoke and the magisterial districts of Big Lick, Cave Spring, and Salem, all in Roanoke County, Virginia.

(c) *Base period.* The calendar month of June 1943 is hereby designated as the base period for the sales area.

(d) *Quota period.* The remainder of the calendar month in which the provisions hereof become effective and each subsequent calendar month, respectively, is hereby designated as a quota period for the sales area.

(e) *Handler quotas.* Quotas for each handler in the sales area in each quota period shall be determined as follows:

(1) Divide the total deliveries of each of milk, milk byproducts, and cream (and of butterfat in milk or in cream where percentages of pounds of butterfat are specified in (e)(3)(i) or (e)(3)(ii) hereof) made in the sales area by such handler during the base period, after excluding the quota-exempt deliveries described in (h) hereof and adjusting such deliveries for the transfers set out in (i) hereof, by the number of days in the base period;

(2) Multiply the result of the foregoing calculation by the number of days in the quota period; and

(3) Multiply the aforesaid resulting amount by the following applicable percentage: (i) Milk: 100 percent of pounds of milk and ---- percent of pounds of butterfat; (ii) Cream: 75 percent of pounds of cream and 75 percent of pounds of butterfat; and (iii) Milk byproducts: 75 percent of pounds of milk byproducts other than cottage, pot, or baker's cheese and of the pounds of skim milk equivalent of cottage, pot, or baker's cheese. (For the purpose of this order, one pound of cottage, pot, or baker's cheese shall be considered as the equivalent of 7 pounds of skim milk.)

(f) *Quotas for handlers who are also producers.* Quotas for handlers who are also producers and who purchase no milk shall be 100 percent of the total production of such handlers in the base period.

(g) *Handler exemptions.* Quotas shall not apply to any handler who delivers in a quota period a daily average of less than 300 units of milk, cream, and milk byproducts. For the purpose of this order, a unit shall be the equivalent in volume of the following:

(1) Milk, one quart of milk;

(2) Cream, one-half pint of cream; and

(3) Milk byproduct, one quart of skim milk, buttermilk, flavored milk drink, or other beverage containing more than 85 percent of skim milk, or one-half pound of cottage, pot, or baker's cheese.

(h) *Quota exclusions and exemptions.* Deliveries of milk, milk byproducts, or cream (1) to other handlers, except for such deliveries to sub-handlers, (2) to plants engaged in the handling or processing of milk, milk byproducts, or cream from which no milk, milk byproducts, or cream is delivered in the sales area, and (3) to the agencies or groups specified in (d) of the order, shall be excluded from the computation of deliveries in the base period and exempt from charges to quotas.

(i) *Transfers and apportionment of quotas.* The market agent is empowered to deduct an amount of base period deliveries to purchasers from the total of deliveries made by a handler or other person in the base period upon the application and a showing of unreasonable hardship by the handler making deliveries to such purchasers on the effective date of this order, and to add the amount of such deliveries to the total base period deliveries of the applicant handler. Denials of transfers or transfers granted by the market agent shall be reviewed by the Director upon application.

(j) *Petition for relief from hardships.* (1) Any person affected by the order or the provisions hereof who considers that compliance therewith would work an exceptional and unreasonable hardship on him, may file with the market agent a petition addressed to the Director. The petition shall contain the correct name, address and principal place of business of the petitioner, a full statement of the facts upon which the petition is based, and the hardship involved and the nature of the relief desired.

(2) Upon receiving such petition, the market agent shall immediately investigate the representations and facts stated therein.

(3) After investigation, the petition shall be certified to the Director, but prior to certification the market agent may (i) deny the petition; or (ii) grant temporary relief for a total period not to exceed 60 days.

(4) Denials or grants of relief by the market agent shall be reviewed by the Director and may be affirmed, modified, or reversed by the Director.

(k) *Reports.* Each handler shall transmit to the market agent on forms prescribed by the market agent the following reports:

(1) Within 20 days following the effective date of this order, reports which show the information required by the market agent to establish such handlers' quotas;

(2) Within 20 days following the close of each quota period, the information required by the market agent to establish volumes of deliveries of milk, cream, and milk byproducts during the preceding quota period; and

(3) Handlers exempt from quotas pursuant to (f) hereof shall, upon the request of the market agent, submit the information required by the market agent to establish volumes of deliveries of milk, cream, and milk byproducts.

(l) *Records.* Handlers shall keep and shall make available to the market agent such records of receipts, sales, deliveries, and production as the market agent shall require for the purpose of obtaining information which the Director may require for the establishment of quotas as prescribed in (b) of the order.

(m) *Distribution schedules.* The distribution schedules, if any, to be followed by the handlers in making deliveries shall be made effective in the terms of approval by the Director of such schedules.

(n) *Expense of administration.* Each handler shall pay to the market agent, within 20 days after the close of each calendar month an assessment of $0.01 per hundredweight of each of milk, cream, skim milk, buttermilk, flavored milk drinks, beverages containing more than 85 percent of skim milk, and skim milk equivalent of cottage, pot, or baker's cheese delivered during the preceding quota period and subject to quota regulations under the provisions hereof.

(o) *Violations.* The market agent shall report all violations to the Director together with the information required for the prosecution of such violations, except in a case where a handler has made deliveries in a quota period in excess of a quota in an amount not to exceed 5 percent of such quota, and in the succeeding quota period makes deliveries below that quota by at least the same percent.

(p) *Bureau of the Budget approval.* The record-keeping and reporting requirements of this order have been approved by the Bureau of the Budget in accordance with the Federal Reports Act of 1942. Subsequent record-keeping or reporting requirements will be subject to the approval of the Bureau of the Budget pursuant to the Federal Reports Act of 1942.

(q) This order shall take effect at 12:01 a. m., e. w. t., October 4, 1943.

Issued this 30th day of September 1943.

ROY F. HENDRICKSON,
Director of Food Distribution.

Press Release Immediate:
Thursday, September 30, 1943

Federal control over fluid milk sales, through the establishment of quotas on deliveries of milk, cream, and milk byproducts, will go into effect in 13 eastern and midwestern metropolitan areas beginning October 4, the War Food Administration announced today.

These areas, and the market agents designated by the Food Distribution Administration to administer the milk conservation and control program in each, are:

Baltimore, Md., Washington, D. C., Roanoke, Va., Richmond, Va., Norfolk-Portsmouth-Newport News, Va.: George Irvine, 1731 I Street NW., Washington, D. C.

Cincinnati, Ohio, Toledo, Ohio, Dayton, Ohio, Canton, Ohio, Cleveland, Ohio: Fred W. Issler, 152 East Fourth Street. Cincinnati, Ohio.

Chicago, Illinois: A. W. Colebank, 135 South LaSalle St., Chicago, Ill.

Omaha, Neb.-Council Bluffs, Iowa: Wayne McPherren, Rm. 408, Post Office Bldg., Omaha, Nebraska.

St. Louis, Missouri: William C. Eckles, 4030 Chouteau Ave., St. Louis, Missouri.

Consumers in regulated areas will be able to purchase as much milk as they have been buying—within the limits of local supplies, officials said. The basic purpose of the program is to prevent a further increase in the consumption of fluid milk (rather than to reduce present consumption) so that enough milk will be available to produce the cheese, butter, and other manufactured dairy products required by the armed services and civilians. As milk conservation and control will be effected at the dealer level, consumer point rationing is not involved.

Milk dealers in the 13 initial milk sales areas will be allowed to sell as much fluid milk each month as they sold last June, (1943), the peak production month. To help assure that enough fluid milk will be available during the season of low production to enable dealers to sell as much as their quotas allow, cream sales will be limited to 75 percent of the quantity sold in June, and the sales quota for fluid milk by-products as a group (including cottage cheese, chocolate milk, and buttermilk) also is set at 75 percent of June sales.

Producer-distributors who purchase no milk (except those whose volume of sales is small enough to exempt them from the quota) will be allowed to sell an amount of fluid milk, cream, and fluid milk byproducts equal to 100 percent of their total milk production in June. "Quota-exempt" producer-distributors are defined separately for each area, but in general they are those whose deliveries are relatively small, and who produce the milk they sell from their own herds.

Milk distributors will be responsible for the fair distribution of supplies in their markets. Under Food Distribution Order 79, however, which authorizes the establishment of individual milk orders for each area, the various market agents may recommend distribution schedules to assure that, in the event of short supplies, the most essential needs will be met first.

Success of the milk conservation and control program depends largely on trade and consumer cooperation, WFA officials pointed out. It is believed that stabilization of milk consumption can be accomplished equitably through this system of dealer control without resorting to consumer rationing. Individual rationing of such a highly perishable product as milk would be very complex, difficult to administer, and would almost necessarily result in substantial reductions in fluid milk sales in many markets. Rationing at the consumer level undoubtedly will be necessary if control over dealers' sales does not effectively regulate fluid milk consumption, the officials said.

Under the individual orders established for each area, the milk control program may be modified to fit production and consumption conditions in each market. These orders will be administered by market agents appointed by the Director of Food Distribution.

Milk sales in all other cities of at least 100,000 population will be regulated as soon as administrative arrangements can be completed—with most areas of this size to be operating under the program by November 1. It is expected that the program will then be extended to smaller population areas until all markets of at least 50,000 population are included.

Distributor quotas for milk sales areas to be named later may be the same as those for the areas announced today, or they may vary if local conditions indicate that different bases are necessary.

Milk handlers (that is, all persons or firms engaged in the sale or transfer of milk, except such groups as retail stores, hotels, restaurants, etc.) will compute the quantity of milk and fluid milk byproducts which they may sell each month in terms of pounds of milk and pounds of milk byproducts, and their cream sales in terms of pounds of cream and butterfat. In months which contain more or less days than the base period, handlers will determine the amount of milk they may sell by multiplying the average of daily deliveries in June by 28, 29, or 31, whichever is applicable.

Dealers may exceed their monthly quotas by up to 5 percent greater sales providing they make up this excess by reducing their deliveries proportionately the next month, without the market agent being required to report such excess sales.

Deliveries to the armed forces, to plants processing dairy products, and to other handlers (except special classes of handlers such as peddlers) are quota exempt.

To facilitate administration, the market agent for each milk sales area may act upon petitions for relief from hardship which may be submitted to him, and his decision will be effective for a 60-day period.

Dealers' quotas based on June deliveries will permit consumers to purchase more milk than they consumed in 1942, and considerably more than in pre-war years. Consumption of fluid milk and cream thus far in 1943 has been at a rate of more than 41 billion pounds annually compared with 37.7 billion pounds in 1942 and an average of 32.6 billion pounds in pre-war years (1936–40).

Total milk production has been mounting steadily in recent years—from 101 billion pounds in 1935 to 119 billion pounds in 1942—an all-time high. Production during the first 7 months of this year equalled production during the same months of 1942.

Increasing fluid milk sales, however, resulting largely from the sharp rise in consumer incomes, have reduced the quantity of milk available for the manufacture of essential products such as butter, cheese, evaporated milk, ice cream, and milk powder. Previously uncontrolled, consumption of fluid milk and cream has been rising at the rate of about 1 percent a month, and already is 20 percent above the 1941 level and 10 to 12 percent over 1942.

This has necessitated the stabilization of fluid milk consumption in order to meet the requirements for manufactured dairy products, both on the home and battle fronts, WFA officials explained.

WAR FOOD ADMINISTRATION

[FDO 79-13]

PART 1401—DAIRY PRODUCTS

CONSERVATION AND DISTRIBUTION OF FLUID MILK AND CREAM IN THE DAYTON, OHIO, SALES AREA

Pursuant to the authority vested in me by Food Distribution Order No. 79 (8 F.R. 12426), issued on September 7, 1943, as amended, and to effectuate the purposes of such order, it is hereby ordered as follows:

§ 1401.41 *Quota restrictions*—(a) *Definitions.* When used in this order, unless otherwise distinctly expressed or manifestly incompatible with the intent hereof:

(1) Each term defined in Food Distribution Order No. 79, as amended, shall, when used herein, have the same meaning as is set forth for such term in Food Distribution Order No. 79, as amended.

(2) The term "order" means Food Distribution Order No. 79, issued on September 7, 1943, as amended.

(3) The term "sub-handler" means any handler, such as a peddler, vendor, sub-dealer, or secondary dealer, who purchases in a previously packaged and processed form milk, milk byproducts, or cream for delivery.

(b) *Milk sales area.* The following area is hereby designated as a "milk sales area" to be known as the Dayton, Ohio, sales area, and is referred to hereinafter as the "sales area": The city of Dayton, Montgomery County, and the townships of Bath, Beaver Creek, Sugar Creek in Greene County, all in the State of Ohio.

(c) *Base period.* The calendar month of June 1943 is hereby designated as the base period for the sales area.

(d) *Quota period.* The remainder of the calendar month in which the provisions hereof become effective and each subsequent calendar month, respectively, is hereby designated as a quota period for the sales area.

(e) *Handler quotas.* Quotas for each handler in the sales area in each quota period shall be determined as follows:

(1) Divide the total deliveries of each of milk, milk byproducts, and cream (and of butterfat in milk or in cream where percentages of pounds of butterfat are specified in (e) (3) (i) or (e) (3) (ii) hereof) made in the sales area by such handler during the base period, after excluding the quota-exempt deliveries described in (h) hereof and adjusting such deliveries for the transfers set out in (i) hereof, by the number of days in the base period;

(2) Multiply the result of the foregoing calculation by the number of days in the quota period; and

(3) Multiply the aforesaid resulting amount by the following applicable percentage: (i) Milk: 100 percent of pounds of milk and ---- percent of pounds of butterfat; (ii) Cream: 75 percent of pounds of cream and 75 percent of pounds of butterfat; and (iii) Milk byproducts: 75 percent of pounds of milk byproducts other than cottage, pot or baker's cheese and of the pounds of skim milk equivalent of cottage, pot, or baker's cheese. (For the purpose of this order, one pound of cottage, pot, or baker's cheese shall be considered as the equivalent of 7 pounds of skim milk.)

(f) *Quotas for handlers who are also producers.* Quotas for handlers who are also producers and who purchase no milk shall be 100 percent of the total production of such handlers in the base period.

(g) *Handler exemptions.* Quotas shall not apply to any handler who delivers in a quota period a daily average of less than 150 units of milk, cream, and milk byproducts. For the purpose of this order, a unit shall be the equivalent in volume of the following:

(1) Milk, one quart of milk;

(2) Cream, one-half pint of cream; and

(3) Milk byproduct, one quart of skim milk, buttermilk, flavored milk drink, or other beverage containing more than 85 percent of skim milk, or one-half pound of cottage, pot, or baker's cheese.

(h) *Quota exclusions and exemptions.* Deliveries of milk, milk byproducts, or cream (1) to other handlers, except for such deliveries to sub-handlers, (2) to plants engaged in the handling or processing of milk, milk byproducts, or cream from which no milk, milk byproducts, or cream is delivered in the sales area, and (3) to the agencies or groups specified in (d) of the order, shall be excluded from the computation of deliveries in the base period and exempt from charges to quotas.

(i) *Transfers and apportionment of quotas.* The market agent is empowered to deduct an amount of base period deliveries to purchasers from the total of deliveries made by a handler or other person in the base period upon the application and a showing of unreasonable hardship by the handler making deliveries to such purchasers on the effective date of this order, and to add the amount of such deliveries to the total base period deliveries of the applicant handler. Denials of transfers or transfers granted by the market agent shall be reviewed by the Director upon application.

(j) *Petition for relief from hardships.* (1) Any person affected by the order or the provisions hereof who considers that compliance therewith would work an exceptional and unreasonable hardship on him, may file with the market agent a petition addressed to the Director. The petition shall contain the correct name, address and principal place of business of the petitioner, a full statement of the facts upon which the petition is based, and the hardship involved and the nature of the relief desired.

(2) Upon receiving such petition, the market agent shall immediately investigate the representations and facts stated therein.

(3) After investigation, the petition shall be certified to the Director, but prior to certification the market agent may (i) deny the petition; or (ii) grant temporary relief for a total period not to exceed 60 days.

(4) Denials or grants of relief by the market agent shall be reviewed by the Director and may be affirmed, modified, or reversed by the Director.

(k) *Reports.* Each handler shall transmit to the market agent on forms prescribed by the market agent the following reports:

(1) Within 20 days following the effective date of this order, reports which show the information required by the market agent to establish such handlers' quotas;

(2) Within 20 days following the close of each quota period, the information required by the market agent to establish volumes of deliveries of milk, cream, and milk byproducts during the preceding quota period; and

(3) Handlers exempt from quotas pursuant to (f) hereof shall, upon the request of the market agent, submit the information required by the market agent to establish volumes of deliveries of milk, cream, and milk byproducts.

(l) *Records.* Handlers shall keep and shall make available to the market agent such records of receipts, sales, deliveries, and production as the market agent shall require for the purpose of obtaining information which the Director may require for the establishment of quotas as prescribed in (b) of the order.

(m) *Distribution schedules.* The distribution schedules, if any, to be followed by the handlers in making deliveries shall be made effective in the terms of approval by the Director of such schedules.

(n) *Expense of administration.* Each handler shall pay to the market agent, within 20 days after the close of each calendar month an assessment of $.01 per hundredweight of each of milk, cream, skim milk, buttermilk, flavored milk drinks, beverages containing more than 85 percent of skim milk, and skim milk equivalent of cottage, pot, or baker's cheese delivered during the preceding quota period and subject to quota regulations under the provisions hereof.

(o) *Violations.* The market agent shall report all violations to the Director together with the information required for the prosecution of such violations, except in a case where a handler has made deliveries in a quota period in excess of a quota in an amount not to exceed 5 percent of such quota, and in the succeeding quota period makes deliveries below that quota by at least the same percent.

(p) *Bureau of the Budget approval.* The record-keeping and reporting requirements of this order have been approved by the Bureau of the Budget in accordance with the Federal Reports Act of 1942. Subsequent record-keeping or reporting requirements will be subject to the approval of the Bureau of the Budget pursuant to the Federal Reports Act of 1942.

(q) This order shall take effect at 12:01 a. m., e. w. t., October 4, 1943.

Issued this 30th day of September 1943.

ROY F. HENDRICKSON,
Director of Food Distribution.

Press Release Immediate:
Thursday, September 30, 1943.

Federal control over fluid milk sales, through the establishment of quotas on deliveries of milk, cream and milk byproducts, will go into effect in 13 eastern and midwestern metropolitan areas beginning October 4, the War Food Administration announced today.

These areas, and the market agents designated by the Food Distribution Administration to administer the milk conservation and control program in each, are:

Baltimore, Md., Washington, D. C., Roanoke, Va., Richmond, Va., Norfolk-Portsmouth-Newport News, Va.: George Irvine, 1731 I Street NW., Washington, D. C.

Cincinnati, Ohio, Toledo, Ohio, Dayton, Ohio, Canton, Ohio, Cleveland, Ohio: Fred W. Issler, 152 East Fourth Street, Cincinnati, Ohio.

Chicago, Illinois: A. W. Colebank, 135 South LaSalle St., Chicago, Ill.

Omaha, Neb.-Council Bluffs, Iowa: Wayne McPherren, Rm. 408, Post Office Bldg., Omaha, Nebraska.

St. Louis, Missouri: William C. Eckles, 4030 Chouteau Ave., St. Louis, Missouri.

Consumers in regulated areas will be able to purchase as much milk as they have been buying—within the limits of local supplies, officials said. The basic purpose of the program is to prevent a further increase in the consumption of fluid milk (rather than to reduce present consumption) so that enough milk will be available to produce the cheese, butter, and other manufactured dairy products required by the armed services and civilians. As milk conservation and control will be effected at the dealer level, consumer point rationing is not involved.

Milk dealers in the 13 initial milk sales areas will be allowed to sell as much fluid milk each month as they sold last June (1943), the peak production month. To help assure that enough fluid milk will be available during the season of low production to enable dealers to sell as much as their quotas allow, cream sales will be limited to 75 percent of the quantity sold in June, and the sales quota for fluid milk byproducts as a group (including cottage cheese, chocolate milk, and buttermilk) also is set at 75 percent of June sales.

Producer-distributors who purchase no milk (except those whose volume of sales is small enough to exempt them from the quota) will be allowed to sell an amount of fluid milk, cream, and fluid milk byproducts equal to 100 percent of their total milk production in June. "Quota-exempt" producer-distributors are defined separately for each area, but in general they are those whose deliveries are relatively small, and who produce the milk they sell from their own herds.

Milk distributors will be responsible for the fair distribution of supplies in their markets. Under Food Distribution Order 79, however, which authorizes the establishment of individual milk orders for each area, the various market agents may recommend distribution schedules to assure that, in the event of short supplies, the most essential needs will be met first.

Success of the milk conservation and control program depends largely on trade and consumer cooperation, WFA officials pointed out. It is believed that stabilization of milk consumption can be accomplished equitably through this system of dealer control without resorting to consumer rationing. Individual rationing of such a highly perishable product as milk would be very complex difficult to administer, and would almost necessarily result in substantial reductions in fluid milk sales in many markets. Rationing at the consumer level undoubtedly will be necessary if control over dealers' sales does not effectively regulate fluid milk consumption, the officials said.

Under the individual orders established for each area, the milk control program may be modified to fit production and consumption conditions in each market. These orders will be administered by market agents appointed by the Director of Food Distribution.

Milk sales in all other cities of at least 100,000 population will be regulated as soon as administrative arrangements can be completed—with most areas of this size to be operating under the program by November 1. It is expected that the program will then be extended to smaller population areas until all markets of at least 50,000 population are included.

Distributor quotas for milk sales areas to be named later may be the same as those for the areas announced today, or they may vary if local conditions indicate that different bases are necessary.

Milk handlers, that is, all persons or firms engaged in the sale or transfer of milk, except such groups as retail stores, hotels, restaurants, etc.) will compute the quantity of milk and fluid milk byproducts which they may sell each month in terms of pounds of milk and pounds of milk byproducts, and their cream sales in terms of pounds of cream and butterfat. In months which contain more or less days than the base period, handlers will determine the amount of milk they may sell by multiplying the average of daily deliveries in June by 28, 29, or 31, whichever is applicable.

Dealers may exceed their monthly quotas by up to 5 percent greater sales providing they make up this excess by reducing their deliveries proportionately the next month, without the market agent being required to report such excess sales.

Deliveries to the armed forces, to plants processing dairy products, and to other handlers (except special classes of handlers such as peddlers) are quota exempt.

To facilitate administration, the market agent for each milk sales area may act upon petitions for relief from hardship which may be submitted to him, and his decision will be effective for a 60-day period.

Dealers' quotas based on June deliveries will permit consumers to purchase more milk than they consumed in 1942, and considerably more than in prewar years. Consumption of fluid milk and cream thus far in 1943 has been at a rate of more than 41 billion pounds annually compared with 37.7 billion pounds in 1942 and an average of 32.6 billion pounds in pre-war years (1936–40).

Total milk production has been mounting steadily in recent years—from 101 billion pounds in 1935 to 119 billion pounds in 1942—an all-time high. Production during the first 7 months of this year equalled production during the same months of 1942.

Increasing fluid milk sales, however, resulting largely from the sharp rise in consumer incomes, have reduced the quantity of milk available for the manufacture of essential products such as butter, cheese, evaporated milk, ice cream, and milk powder. Previously uncontrolled, consumption of fluid milk and cream has been rising at the rate of about 1 percent a month, and already is 20 percent above the 1941 level and 10 to 12 percent over 1942.

This has necessitated the stabilization of fluid milk consumption in order to meet the requirements for manufactured dairy products, both on the home and battle fronts, WFA officials explained.

10, 337

FDO 79-13

AMDT. 1
JAN. 27, 1944

WAR FOOD ADMINISTRATION

[FDO 79-13, Amdt. 1]

PART 1401—DAIRY PRODUCTS A

FLUID MILK AND CREAM IN DAYTON, OHIO, SALES AREA

Pursuant to Food Distribution Order No. 79 (8 F.R. 12426), dated September 7, 1943, as amended, and to effectuate the purposes thereof, Food Distribution Order No. 79-13 (8 F.R. 13377), relative to the conservation and distribution of fluid milk in the Dayton, Ohio, milk sales area, issued by the Director of Food Distribution on September 30, 1943, is amended as follows:

1. By deleting therefrom the provisions in § 1401.41 (f) and substituting therefor the following:

(f) *Quotas for handlers who are also producers.* Quotas for handlers who are also producers and who purchase no milk shall be computed in accordance with (e) hereof, except that the applicable percentages shall be 100 percent in lieu of the percentages specified in (e) (3).

2. By deleting therefrom the provisions of § 1401.41 (h) and substituting therefor the following:

(h) *Quota exclusions and exemptions.* Deliveries of milk, milk byproducts, or cream (1) to other handlers, except for such deliveries to sub-handlers, (2) to plants engaged in the handling or processing of milk, milk byproducts, or cream from which no milk, milk byproducts, or cream is delivered in the sales area, (3) to nursery, elementary, junior high, and high schools, and (4) to the agencies or groups specified in (d) of the order, shall be excluded from the computation of deliveries in the base period and exempt from charges to quotas.

The provisions of this amendment shall become effective at 12:01 a. m., e. w. t., February 1, 1944. With respect to violations of said Food Distribution Order No. 79-13, rights accrued, or liabilities incurred prior to the effective time of this amendment, said Food Distribution Order No. 79-13 shall be deemed to be in full force and effect for the purpose of sustaining any proper suit, action, or other proceeding with respect to any such violation, right, or liability.

(E.O. 9280, 7 F.R. 10179; E.O. 9322, 8 F.R. 3807; E.O. 9334, 8 F.R. 5423; E.O. 9392, 8 F.R. 14783; FDO 79, 8 F.R. 12426, 13283)

Issued this 27th day of January 1944.

LEE MARSHALL,
Director of Food Distribution.

7337

FDO 79-14
OCTOBER 1, 1943

WAR FOOD ADMINISTRATION

[FDO 79-14]

PART 1401—DAIRY PRODUCTS

CONSERVATION AND DISTRIBUTION OF FLUID MILK AND CREAM IN THE AKRON, OHIO, SALES AREA

Pursuant to the authority vested in me by Food Distribution Order No. 79 (8 F.R. 12426), issued on September 7, 1943, as amended, and to effectuate the purposes of such order, it is hereby ordered as follows:

§ 1401.49 *Quota restrictions*—(a) *Definitions.* When used in this order, unless otherwise distinctly expressed or manifestly incompatible with the intent hereof:

(1) Each term defined in Food Distribution Order No. 79, as amended, shall, when used herein, have the same meaning as is set forth for such term in Food Distribution Order No. 79, as amended.

(2) The term "order" means Food Distribution Order No. 79, issued on September 7, 1943, as amended.

(3) The term "sub-handler" means any handler, such as a peddler, vendor, sub-dealer, or secondary dealer, who purchases in a previously packaged and processed form milk, milk byproducts, or cream for delivery.

(b) *Milk sales area.* The following area is hereby designated as a "milk sales area" to be known as the Akron, Ohio, sales area, and is referred to hereinafter as the "sales area". The cities of Akron, Barberton, and Cuyahoga Falls, the townships of Copley, Coventry, Springfield, Norton, and Stow, and the Villages of Lakemore, Mogadore, Munroe Falls, Silver Lake, and Tallmadge in Summit County; the townships of Ravenna and Franklin, and that part of Suffield township comprising the part of the village of Mogadore which is in Portage County; and Wadsworth township in Medina County, all in the State of Ohio.

(c) *Base period.* The calendar month of June 1943 is hereby designated as the base period for the sales area.

(d) *Quota period.* The remainder of the calendar month in which the provisions hereof become effective and each subsequent calendar month, respectively, is hereby designated as a quota period for the sales area.

(e) *Handler quotas.* Quotas for each handler in the sales area in each quota period shall be determined as follows:

(1) Divide the total deliveries of each of milk, milk byproducts, and cream (and of butterfat in milk or in cream where percentages of pounds of butterfat are specified in (e) (3) (i) or (e) (3) (ii) hereof) made in the sales area by such handler during the base period, after excluding the quota-exempt deliveries described in (h) hereof and adjusting such deliveries for the transfers set out in (i) hereof, by the number of days in the base period;

(2) Multiply the result of the foregoing calculation by the number of days in the quota period; and

(3) Multiply the aforesaid resulting amount by the following applicable percentage: (i) Milk: 100 percent of pounds of milk and ______ percent of pounds of butterfat; (ii) Cream: 75 percent of pounds of cream and 75 percent of pounds of butterfat; and (iii) Milk byproducts: 75 percent of pounds of milk byproducts other than cottage, pot. or baker's cheese and of the pounds of skim milk equivalent of cottage, pot, or baker's cheese. (For the purpose of this order, one pound of cottage, pot, or baker's cheese shall be considered as the equivalent of 7 pounds of skim milk.)

(f) *Quotas for handlers who are also producers.* Quotas for handlers who are also producers and who purchase no milk shall be 100 percent of the total production of such handlers in the base period.

(g) *Handler exemptions.* Quotas shall not apply to any handler who delivers in a quota period a daily average of less than 150 units of milk, cream, and milk byproducts. For the purpose of this order, a unit shall be the equivalent in volume of the following:

(1) Milk, one quart of milk;

(2) Cream, one-half pint of cream; and

(3) Milk byproduct, one quart of skim milk, buttermilk, flavored milk drink, or other beverage containing more than 85 percent of skim milk, or one-half pound of cottage, pot, or baker's cheese.

(h) *Quota exclusions and exemptions.* Deliveries of milk, milk byproducts, or cream (1) to other handlers, except for such deliveries to sub-handlers, (2) to plants engaged in the handling or processing of milk, milk byproducts, or cream from which no milk, milk byproducts, or cream is delivered in the sales area, and (3) to the agencies or groups specified in (d) of the order, shall be excluded from the computation of deliveries in the base period and exempt from charges to quotas.

(i) *Transfers and apportionment of quotas.* The market agent is empowered to deduct an amount of base period deliveries to purchasers from the total of deliveries made by a handler or other person in the base period upon the application and a showing of unreasonable hardship by the handler making deliveries to such purchasers on the effective date of this order, and to add the amount of such deliveries to the total base period deliveries of the applicant handler. Denials of transfers or transfers granted by the market agent shall be reviewed by the Director upon application.

(j) *Petition for relief from hardships.* (1) Any person affected by the order or the provisions hereof who considers that compliance therewith would work an exceptional and unreasonable hardship on him, may file with the market agent a petition addressed to the Director. The petition shall contain the correct name, address and principal place of business of the petitioner, a full statement of the facts upon which the petition is based, and the hardship involved and the nature of the relief desired.

(2) Upon receiving such petition, the market agent shall immediately investigate the representations and facts stated therein.

(3) After investigation, the petition shall be certified to the Director, but prior to certification the market agent may (i) deny the petition; or (ii) grant temporary relief for a total period not to exceed 60 days.

(4) Denials or grants of relief by the market agent shall be reviewed by the Director and may be affirmed, modified, or reversed by the Director.

(k) *Reports.* Each handler shall transmit to the market agent on forms prescribed by the market agent the following reports:

(1) Within 20 days following the effective date of this order, reports which show the information required by the market agent to establish such handlers' quotas;

(2) Within 20 days following the close of each quota period, the information required by the market agent to establish volumes of deliveries of milk, cream, and milk byproducts during the preceding quota period; and

(3) Handlers exempt from quotas pursuant to (f) hereof shall, upon the request of the market agent, submit the information required by the market

agent to establish volumes of deliveries of milk, cream, and milk byproducts.

(l) *Records.* Handlers shall keep and shall make available to the market agent such records of receipts, sales, deliveries, and production as the market agent shall require for the purpose of obtaining information which the Director may require for the establishment of quotas as prescribed in (b) of the order.

(m) *Distribution schedules.* The distribution schedules, if any, to be followed by the handlers in making deliveries shall be made effective in the terms of approval by the Director of such schedules.

(n) *Expense of administration.* Each handler shall pay to the market agent, within 20 days after the close of each calendar month an assessment of $.01 per hundredweight of each of milk, cream, skim milk, buttermilk, flavored milk drinks, beverages containing more than 85 percent of skim milk, and skim milk equivalent of cottage, pot, or baker's cheese delivered during the preceding quota period and subject to quota regulations under the provisions hereof.

(o) *Violations.* The market agent shall report all violations to the Director together with the information required for the prosecution of such violations, except in a case where a handler has made deliveries in a quota period in excess of a quota in an amount not to exceed 5 percent of such quota, and in the succeeding quota period makes deliveries below that quota by at least the same percent.

(p) *Bureau of the Budget approval.* The record-keeping and reporting requirements of this order have been approved by the Bureau of the Budget in accordance with the Federal Reports Act of 1942. Subsequent record-keeping or reporting requirements will be subject to the approval of the Bureau of the Budget pursuant to the Federal Reports Act of 1942.

(q) This order shall take effect at 12:01 a. m., e. w. t., October 5, 1943.

Issued this 1st day of October 1943.

ROY F. HENDRICKSON,
Director of Food Distribution.

Press Release Immediate:
Saturday, October 2, 1943.

Eleven additional metropolitan areas will be brought under the Food Distribution Administration's fluid milk conservation and control program beginning October 5, the War Food Administration said today.

The new milk sales areas, and the market agents who will administer the program in each, are:

St. Joseph County, Ind.: M. E. Drake, 116 S. William St., South Bend, Ind.

Akron, Ohio; Huntington, W. Va.-Ashland, Ky.; Hamilton-Middletown, Ohio; Columbus, Ohio; Youngstown, Ohio: Fred Issler, 152 E. Fourth St., Cincinnati, Ohio.

Davenport, Ia.-Rock Island, Ill-Moline, Ill.: Howard E. Eisaman, 335 Federal Building, Rock Island, Ill.

Fort Wayne, Ind.: William J. Cline, 707 Citizens Trust Building, Fort Wayne, Ind.

Wichita, Kans., Greater Kansas City (Mo.-Kan.): M. M. Morehouse, 512 Porter Building, 406 W. 34th St., Kansas City, Mo.

Duluth, Minn.-Superior, Wis.: O. F. Kirkendall, 2002-4 W. Superior St., Duluth, Minn.

Dealers' monthly fluid milk sales in these areas may not exceed their June deliveries, and their sales of cream and of fluid milk byproducts (such as cottage cheese, chocolate milk and buttermilk) will be reduced to three-fourths of the quantities sold in June. Milk dealers include all persons or firms engaged in the sale or transfer of milk, but not retail stores, hotels, restaurants, etc.

Producer-distributors who purchase no milk (except those whose volume of sales is small enough to make them quota-exempt) will be allowed to sell an amount of fluid milk, cream and fluid milk byproducts equal to 100 percent of their total milk production in June. Quota-exempt producer distributors are defined separately for each area, but in general they are those whose deliveries are relatively small.

Consumers in these areas generally will be able to purchase as much milk under the milk conservation program as they have been buying—an amount considerably greater than that bought in pre-war years, and about 10 percent above last year's purchases. Sales quotas on cream and on fluid milk byproducts have been set below June deliveries to boost fluid milk supplies where milk production is low, and to conserve milk for manufacturing purposes in other areas.

Fluid milk sales are being stabilized in these and other metropolitan areas, FDA officials explained, to help assure sufficient milk for manufacturing the cheese, butter, evaporated milk and milk powder required by the armed services and civilians for good nutrition and properly balanced diets.

Largely due to expanded consumer demand, sales of fluid milk have been increasing steadily and are now about 20 percent higher than in pre-war years (1936–40) and 10 to 12 percent above those in 1942. With total milk production levelled off, and even declining somewhat, this expanding volume of milk sold for fluid uses has inevitably reduced the supply of "manufacturing milk;" and, consequently, the production of cheese, butter and other dairy foods.

The FDA's dealer-quota plan is an attempt to stabilize fluid milk consumption without resorting to individual consumer rationing. Point rationing of milk, a bulky and highly perishable commodity, would be very difficult to administer and would almost necessarily reduce fluid milk sales in many areas. If consumers and the trade cooperate with the present program to assure that sales are held within quotas and quantities available are distributed fairly, FDA officials believe consumer rationing will not be necessary.

Milk handlers in the sales areas named today, except Greater Kansas City and Wichita, Kansas, will compute the quantity of milk which they may sell each month in terms of pounds of milk, their cream sales in terms of pounds of cream and butterfat, and their milk products sales in terms of pounds of milk byproducts. In Great Kansas City and Wichita, milk handlers will determine their fluid milk quotas in terms of pounds of milk and butterfat.

Deliveries to the Armed Forces, to plants processing dairy products, and to other handlers (except special classes of handlers such as peddlers) are quota exempt.

To facilitate administration, the market agent for each milk sales area may act upon petitions for relief from hardship which may be submitted to him, and after investigation, he may grant temporary relief for a total period not to exceed 60 days.

Milk sales in 13 eastern and midwestern areas previously were brought under federal regulation. Sales quotas in these initial milk sales areas are the same as for those named today.

7793%
Cop.

WAR FOOD ADMINISTRATION

[FDO 79-14, Amdt. 1]

PART 1401—DAIRY PRODUCTS

FLUID MILK AND CREAM IN AKRON, OHIO, SALES AREA

Pursuant to Food Distribution Order No. 79 (8 F.R. 12426), dated September 7, 1943, as amended, and to effectuate the purposes thereof, Food Distribution Order No. 79-14 (8 F.R. 13424), relative to the conservation and distribution of fluid milk in the Akron, Ohio, milk sales area, issued by the Director of Food Distribution on October 1, 1943, is amended as follows:

1. By deleting therefrom the provisions in § 1401.49 (f) and substituting therefor the following:

(f) *Quotas for handlers who are also producers.* Quotas for handlers who are also producers and who purchase no milk shall be computed in accordance with (e) hereof, except that the applicable percentages shall be 100 percent in lieu of the percentages specified in (e) (3).

2. By deleting therefrom the provisions of § 1401.49 (h) and substituting therefor the following:

(h) *Quota exclusions and exemptions.* Deliveries of milk, milk byproducts, or cream (1) to other handlers, except for such deliveries to sub-handlers, (2) to plants engaged in the handling or processing of milk, milk byproducts, or cream from which no milk, milk byproducts, or cream is delivered in the sales area, (3) to nursery, elementary, junior high, and high schools, and (4) to the agencies or groups specified in (d) of the order, shall be excluded from the computation of deliveries in the base period and exempt from charges to quotas.

The provisions of this amendment shall become effective at 12:01 a. m. e. w. t., February 1, 1944. With respect to violations of said Food Distribution Order No. 79-14, rights accrued, or liabilities incurred prior to the effective time of this amendment, said Director Food Distribution Order No. 79-14 shall be deemed to be in full force and effect for the purpose of sustaining any proper suit, action, or other proceeding with respect to any such violation, right, or liability.

(E.O. 9280, 7 F.R. 10179; E.O. 9322, 8 F.R. 3807; E.O. 9334, 8 F.R. 5423; E.O. 9392, 8 F.R. 14783; FDO 79, 8 F.R. 12426, 13283)

Issued this 27th day of January 1944.

LEE MARSHALL,
Director of Food Distribution.

/ 7327

FDO 79-15
OCTOBER 1, 1943

WAR FOOD ADMINISTRATION

[FDO 79-15]

PART 1401—DAIRY PRODUCTS

CONSERVATION AND DISTRIBUTION OF FLUID MILK AND CREAM IN THE GREATER KANSAS CITY SALES AREA

Pursuant to the authority vested in me by Food Distribution Order No. 79 (8 F.R. 12426), issued on September 7, 1943, as amended, and to effectuate the purposes of such order, it is hereby ordered as follows:

§ 1401.57 *Quota restrictions*—(a) *Definitions.* When used in this order, unless otherwise distinctly expressed or manifestly incompatible with the intent hereof:

(1) Each term defined in Food Distribution Order No. 79, as amended, shall, when used herein, have the same meaning as is set forth for such term in Food Distribution Order No. 79, as amended.

(2) The term "order" means Food Distribution Order No. 79, issued on September 7, 1943, as amended.

(3) The term "sub-handler" means any handler, such as a peddler, vendor, sub-dealer, or secondary dealer, who purchases in a previously packaged and processed form milk, milk byproducts, or cream for delivery.

(b) *Milk sales area.* The following area is hereby designated as a "milk sales area" to be known as the Greater Kansas City sales area, and is referred to hereinafter as the "sales area"; all the territory within Jackson County, Missouri, that part of Clay County, Missouri, south of Highway 92, beginning at the Platte County and Clay County line, east to the west section line of section 26 in Washington Township, north to the north section line of said section 26, east to the Clay County and Ray County line; Lee, Waldron, May, and Pettis Townships in Platte County, Missouri; Wyandotte County, Kansas; Shawnee, Mission, Monticello and Lexington Townships in Johnson County, Kansas; and Delaware, Leavenworth, and that part of Kickapoo and High Prairie Townships east of the 95th principal meridian in Leavenworth County, Kansas.

(c) *Base period.* The calendar month of June 1943 is hereby designated as the base period for the sales area.

(d) *Quota period.* The remainder of the calendar month in which the provisions hereof become effective and each subsequent calendar month, respectively, is hereby designated as a quota period for the sales area.

(e) *Handler quotas.* Quotas for each handler in the sales area in each quota period shall be determined as follows:

(1) Divide the total deliveries of each of milk, milk byproducts, and cream (and of butterfat in milk or in cream where percentages of pounds of butterfat are specified in (e) (3) (i) or (e) (3) (ii) hereof) made in the sales area by such handler during the base period, after excluding the quota-exempt deliveries described in (h) hereof and adjusting such deliveries for the transfers set out in (i) hereof, by the number of days in the base period;

(2) Multiply the result of the foregoing calculation by the number of days in the quota period; and

(3) Multiply the aforesaid resulting amount by the following applicable percentages: (i) Milk: 100 percent of pounds of milk and 100 percent of pounds of butterfat; (ii) Cream: 75 percent of pounds of cream and 75 percent of pounds of butterfat; and (iii) Milk byproducts: 75 percent of pounds of milk byproducts other than cottage, pot, or baker's cheese and of the pounds of skim milk equivalent of cottage, pot, or baker's cheese. (For the purpose of this order, one pound of cottage, pot, or baker's cheese shall be considered as the equivalent of 7 pounds of skim milk.)

(f) *Quotas for handlers who are also producers.* Quotas for handlers who are also producers and who purchase no milk shall be 100 percent of the total production of such handlers in the base period.

(g) *Handler exemptions.* Quotas shall not apply to any handler who delivers in a quota period a daily average of less than 350 units of milk, cream, and milk byproducts. For the purpose of this order, a unit shall be the equivalent in volume of the following:

(1) Milk, one quart of milk;

(2) Cream, one-half pint of cream; and

(3) Milk byproduct, one quart of skim milk, buttermilk, flavored milk drink, or other beverage containing more than 85 percent of skim milk, or one-half pound of cottage, pot, or baker's cheese.

(h) *Quota exclusions and exemptions.* Deliveries of milk, milk byproducts, or cream (1) to other handlers, except for such deliveries to sub-handlers, (2) to plants engaged in the handling or processing of milk, milk byproducts, or cream from which no milk, milk byproducts, or cream is delivered in the sales area, and (3) to the agencies or groups specified in (d) of the order, shall be excluded from the computation of deliveries in the base period and exempt from charges to quotas.

(i) *Transfers and apportionment of quotas.* The market agent is empowered to deduct an amount of base period deliveries to purchasers from the total of deliveries made by a handler or other person in the base period upon the application and a showing of unreasonable hardship by the handler making deliveries to such purchasers on the effective date of this order, and to add the amount of such deliveries to the total base period deliveries of the applicant handler. Denials of transfers or transfers granted by the market agent shall be reviewed by the Director upon application.

(j) *Petition for relief from hardships.* (1) Any person affected by the order or the provisions hereof who considers that compliance therewith would work an exceptional and unreasonable hardship on him, may file with the market agent a petition addressed to the Director. The petition shall contain the correct name, address and principal place of business of the petitioner, a full statement of the facts upon which the petition is based, and the hardship involved and the nature of the relief desired.

(2) Upon receiving such petition, the market agent shall immediately investigate the representations and facts stated therein.

(3) After investigation, the petition shall be certified to the Director, but prior to certification the market agent may (i) deny the petition; or (ii) grant temporary relief for a total period not to exceed 60 days.

(4) Denials or grants of relief by the market agent shall be reviewed by the Director and may be affirmed, modified, or reversed by the Director.

(k) *Reports.* Each handler shall transmit to the market agent on forms prescribed by the market agent the following reports:

(1) Within 20 days following the effective date of this order, reports which show the information required by the market agent to establish such handlers' quotas;

(2) Within 20 days following the close of each quota period, the information required by the market agent to

establish volumes of deliveries of milk, cream, and milk byproducts during the preceding quota period; and

(3) Handlers exempt from quotas pursuant to (f) shall, upon the request of the market agent, submit the information required by the market agent to establish volumes of deliveries of milk, cream, and milk byproducts.

(l) *Records.* Handlers shall keep and shall make available to the market agent such records of receipts, sales, deliveries, and production as the market agent shall require for the purpose of obtaining information which the Director may require for the establishment of quotas as prescribed in (b) of the order.

(m) *Distribution schedules.* The distribution schedules, if any, to be followed by the handlers in making deliveries shall be made effective in the terms of approval by the Director of such schedules.

(n) *Expense of administration.* Each handler shall pay to the market agent, within 20 days after the close of each calendar month an assessment of $0.01 per hundredweight of each of milk, cream, skim milk, buttermilk, flavored milk drinks, beverages containing more than 85 percent of skim milk, and skim milk equivalent of cottage, pot, or baker's cheese delivered during the preceding quota period and subject to quota regulations under the provisions hereof.

(o) *Violations.* The market agent shall report all violations to the Director together with the information required for the prosecution of such violations, except in a case where a handler has made deliveries in a quota period in excess of a quota in an amount not to exceed 5 percent of such quota, an the succeeding quota period makes liveries below that quota by at least same percent.

(p) *Bureau of the Budget appr* The record-keeping and reporting quirements of this order have been proved by the Bureau of the Budg accordance with the Federal Reports of 1942. Subsequent record-keepin reporting requirements will be subje the approval of the Bureau of the Bu pursuant to the Federal Reports A 1942.

(q) This order shall take effec 12:01 a. m., e. w. t., October 5, 1943.

Issued this 1st day of October 194

ROY F. HENDRICKSON,
Director of Food Distributio

Press Release Immediate:
Saturday, October 2, 1943.

Eleven additional metropolitan areas will be brought under the Food Distribution Administration's fluid milk conservation and control program beginning October 5, the War Food Administration said today.

The new milk sales areas, and the market agents who will administer the program in each, are:

St. Joseph County, Ind.: M. E. Drake, 116 S. William St., South Bend, Ind.

Akron, Ohio; Huntington, W. Va.-Ashland, Ky.; Hamilton - Middletown, Ohio; Columbus, Ohio; Youngstown, Ohio: Fred Issler, 152 E. Fourth St., Cincinnati, Ohio.

Davenport, Ia.-Rock Island, Ill.-Moline, Ill.: Howard E. Eisaman, 335 Federal Building, Rock Island, Ill.

Fort Wayne, Ind.: William J. Kline, 707 Citizens Trust Building, Fort Wayne, Ind.

Wichita, Kans., Greater Kansas City (Mo.-Kan.): M. M. Morehouse, 512 Porter Building, 406 W. 34th St., Kansas City, Mo.

Duluth, Minn.-Superior, Wis.: O. F. Kirkendall, 2002-4 W. Superior St., Duluth, Minn.

Dealers' monthly fluid milk sales in these areas may not exceed their June deliveries, and their sales of cream and of fluid milk byproducts, (such as cottage cheese, chocolate milk and buttermilk) will be reduced to three-fourths of the quantities sold in June. Milk dealers include all persons or firms engaged in the sale or transfer of milk, but not retail stores, hotels, restaurants, etc.

Producer-distributors who purchase no milk (except those whose volume of sales is small enough to make them quota-exempt) will be allowed to sell an amount of fluid milk, cream and fluid milk byproducts equal to 100 percent of their total milk production in June. Quota-exempt producer distributors are defined separately for each area, but in general they are those whose deliveries are relatively small.

Consumers in these areas generally will be able to purchase as much milk under the milk conservation program as they have been buying—an amount considerably greater than that bought in pre-war years, and about 10 percent above last year's purchases. Sales quotas on cream and on fluid milk byproducts have been set below June deliveries to boost fluid milk supplies where milk production is low, and to conserve milk for manufacturing purposes in other areas.

Fluid milk sales are being stabilized in these and other metropolitan areas, FDA officials explained, to help assure sufficient milk for manufacturing the cheese, butter, evaporated milk and milk powder required by the armed services and civilians for good nutrition and properly balanced diets.

Largely due to expanded consumer demand, sales of fluid milk have been increasing steadily and are now about 20 percent higher than in pre-war years (1936–40) and 10 to 12 percent above those in 1942. With total milk production leveled off, and even declining somewhat, this expanding volume of milk sold for fluid uses has inevitably reduced the supply of "manufacturing milk," and, consequently, the production of cheese, butter and other dairy foods.

The FDA's dealer-quota plan is attempt to stabilize fluid milk consu tion without resorting to individual sumer rationing. Point rationing milk, a bulky and highly perishable c modity, would be very difficult to adn ister and would almost necessa reduce fluid milk sales in many ar If consumers and the trade coope with the present program to assure sales are held within quotas and qua ties available are distributed fairly, officials believe consumer rationing not be necessary.

Milk handlers in the sales areas na today, except Greater Kansas City Wichita, Kansas, will compute the qu tity of milk which they may sell e month in terms of pounds of milk, t cream sales in terms of pounds of cr and butterfat, and their milk prod sales in terms of pounds of milk bypr ucts. In Greater Kansas City and Wi ita, milk handlers will determine t fluid milk quotas in terms of pound milk and butterfat.

Deliveries to the Armed Forces, plants processing dairy products, an other handlers (except special classe handlers such as peddlers) are quota empt.

To facilitate administration, the m ket agent for each milk sales area act upon petitions for relief from ha ship which may be submitted to him, after investigation, he may grant tem rary relief for a total period not to ex 60 days.

Milk sales in 13 eastern and m western areas previously were brou under federal regulation. Sales qu in these initial milk sales areas are same as for those named today.

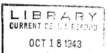

FDO 79-16
OCTOBER 1, 1943

WAR FOOD ADMINISTRATION

[FDO 79-16]

PART 1401—DAIRY PRODUCTS

CONSERVATION AND DISTRIBUTION OF FLUID MILK AND CREAM IN THE YOUNGSTOWN, OHIO, SALES AREA

Pursuant to the authority vested in me by Food Distribution Order No. 79 (8 F.R. 12426), issued on September 7, 1943, as amended, and to effectuate the purposes of such order, it is hereby ordered as follows:

§ 1401.55 *Quota restrictions*—(a) *Definitions.* When used in this order, unless otherwise distinctly expressed or manifestly incompatible with the intent hereof:

(1) Each term defined in Food Distribution Order No. 79, as amended, shall, when used herein, have the same meaning as is set forth for such term in Food Distribution Order No. 79, as amended.

(2) The term "order" means Food Distribution Order No. 79, issued on September 7, 1943, as amended.

(3) The term "sub-handler" means any handler, such as a peddler, vendor, sub-dealer, or secondary dealer, who purchases in a previously packaged and processed form milk, milk byproducts, or cream for delivery.

(b) *Milk sales area.* The following area is hereby designated as a "milk sales area" to be known as the Youngstown, Ohio sales area, and is referred to hereinafter as the "sales area": The city of Youngstown and the townships of Austintown, Boardman, Canfield, Coitsville, and Poland in Mahoning County, Ohio; the townships of Brookfield, Howland, Hubbard, Liberty, Vienna, Warren, and Weathersfield in Trumbull County, Ohio; the cities of Farrell and Sharon, the township of Hickory, and the boroughs of Sharpsville and Wheatland in Mercer County, Pa.

(c) *Base period.* The calendar month of June 1943 is hereby designated as the base period for the sales area.

(d) *Quota period.* The remainder of the calendar month in which the provisions hereof become effective and each subsequent calendar month, respectively, is hereby designated as a quota period for the sales area.

(e) *Handler quotas.* Quotas for each handler in the sales area in each quota period shall be determined as follows:

(1) Divide the total deliveries of each of milk, milk byproducts, and cream (and of butterfat in milk or in cream where percentages of pounds of butterfat are specified in (e) (3) (i) or (e) (3) (ii) hereof) made in the sales area by such handler during the base period, after excluding the quota-exempt deliveries described in (h) and adjusting such deliveries for the transfers set out in (i) hereof by the number of days in the base period;

(2) Multiply the result of the foregoing calculation by the number of days in the quota period; and

(3) Multiply the aforesaid resulting amount by the following applicable percentage: (i) Milk: 100 percent of pounds of milk and ______ percent of pounds of butterfat; (ii) Cream: 75 percent of pounds of cream and 75 percent of butterfat; and (iii) Milk byproducts: 75 percent of pounds of milk byproducts other than cottage, pot, or baker's cheese and of the pounds of skim milk equivalent of cottage, pot, or baker's cheese. (For the purpose of this order, one pound of cottage, pot, or baker's cheese shall be considered as the equivalent of 7 pounds of skim milk.)

(f) *Quotas for handlers who are also producers.* Quotas for handlers who are also producers and who purchase no milk shall be 100 percent of the total production of such handlers in the base period.

(g) *Handler exemptions.* Quotas shall not apply to any handler who delivers in a quota period a daily average of less than 150 units of milk, cream, and milk byproducts. For the purpose of this order, a unit shall be the equivalent in volume of the following:

(1) Milk, one quart of milk;

(2) Cream, one-half pint of cream; and

(3) Milk byproduct, one quart of skim milk, buttermilk, flavored milk drink, or other beverage containing more than 85 percent of skim milk, or one-half pound of cottage, pot, or baker's cheese.

(h) *Quota exclusions and exemptions.* Deliveries of milk, milk byproducts, or cream (1) to other handlers, except for such deliveries to sub-handlers, (2) to plants engaged in the handling or processing of milk, milk byproducts, or cream from which no milk, milk byproducts, or cream is delivered in the sales area, and (3) to the agencies or groups specified in (d) of the order, shall be excluded from the computation of deliveries in the base period and exempt from charges to quotas.

(i) *Transfers and apportionment of quotas.* The market agent is empowered to deduct an amount of base period deliveries to purchasers from the total of deliveries made by a handler or other person in the base period upon the application and a showing of unreasonable hardship by the handler making deliveries to such purchasers on the effective date of this order, and to add the amount of such deliveries to the total base period deliveries of the applicant handler. Denials of transfers or transfers granted by the market agent shall be reviewed by the Director upon application.

(j) *Petition for relief from hardships.* (1) Any person affected by the order or the provisions hereof who considers that compliance therewith would work an exceptional and unreasonable hardship on him, may file with the market agent a petition addressed to the Director. The petition shall contain the correct name, address and principal place of business of the petitioner, a full statement of the facts upon which the petition is based, and the hardship involved and the nature of the relief desired.

(2) Upon receiving such petition, the market agent shall immediately investigate the representations and facts stated therein.

(3) After investigation, the petition shall be certified to the Director, but prior to certification the market agent may (i) deny the petition; or (ii) grant temporary relief for a total period not to exceed 60 days.

(4) Denials or grants of relief by the market agent shall be reviewed by the Director and may be affirmed, modified, or reversed by the Director.

(k) *Reports.* Each handler shall transmit to the market agent on forms prescribed by the market agent the following reports:

(1) Within 20 days following the effective date of this order, reports which show the information required by the market agent to establish such handlers' quotas;

(2) Within 20 days following the close of each quota period, the information required by the market agent to establish volumes of deliveries of milk, cream, and milk byproducts during the preceding quota period; and

(3) Handlers exempt from quotas pursuant to (f) hereof shall, upon the request of the market agent, submit the information required by the market agent to establish volumes of deliveries of milk, cream, and milk byproducts.

(l) *Records.* Handlers shall keep and shall make available to the market agent such records of receipts, sales, deliveries, and production as the market agent shall require for the purpose of obtaining information which the Director may require for the establishment of quotas as prescribed in (b) of the order.

(m) *Distribution schedules.* The distribution schedules, if any, to be followed by the handlers in making deliveries shall be made effective in the terms of approval by the Director of such schedules.

(n) *Expense of administration.* Each handler shall pay to the market agent, within 20 days after the close of each calendar month an assessment of $0.01 per hundredweight of each of milk, cream, skim milk, buttermilk, flavored milk drinks, beverages containing more than 85 percent of skim milk, and skim milk equivalent of cottage, pot, or baker's cheese delivered during the preceding quota period and subject to quota regulations under the provisions hereof.

(o) *Violations.* The market agent shall report all violations to the Director together with the information required for the prosecution of such violations, except in a case where a handler has made deliveries in a quota period in excess of a quota in an amount not to exceed 5 percent of such quota, and in the succeeding quota period makes deliveries below that quota by at least the same percent.

(p) *Bureau of the Budget approval* The record-keeping and reporting requirements of this order have been approved by the Bureau of the Budget ir accordance with the Federal Reports Ac of 1942. Subsequent record-keeping o reporting requirements will be subject t the approval of the Bureau of the Budge pursuant to the Federal Reports Act o 1942.

(q) This order shall take affect a 12:01 a. m., e. w. t., October 5, 1943.

Issued this 1st day of October 1943.

Roy F. Hendrickson,
Director of Food Distribution.

Press Release Immediate:
Saturday, October 2, 1943.

Eleven additional metropolitan areas will be brought under the Food Distribution Administration's fluid milk conservation and control program beginning October 5, the War Food Administration said today.

The new milk sales areas, and the market agents who will administer the program in each, are:

St. Joseph County, Ind.: M. E. Drake, 116 S. William St., South Bend, Ind.

Akron, Ohio; Huntington, W. Va.-Ashland, Ky.; Hamilton-Middletown, Ohio; Columbus, Ohio; Youngstown, Ohio: Fred Issler, 152 E. Fourth St., Cincinnati, Ohio.

Davenport, Ia.-Rock Island, Ill.-Moline, Ill.: Howard E. Eisaman, 335 Federal Building, Rock Island, Ill.

Fort Wayne, Ind.: William J. Cline, 707 Citizens Trust Building, Fort Wayne, Ind.

Wichita, Kans., Greater Kansas City (Mo.-Kan.): M. M. Morehouse, 512 Porter Building, 406 W. 34th St., Kansas City, Mo.

Duluth, Minn.-Superior, Wis.: O. F. Kirkendall, 2002-4 W. Superior St., Duluth, Minn.

Dealers' monthly fluid milk sales in these areas may not exceed their June deliveries, and their sales of cream and of fluid milk byproducts, (such as cottage cheese, chocolate milk and buttermilk) will be reduced to three-fourths of the quantities sold in June. Milk dealers include all persons or firms engaged in the sale or transfer of milk, but not retail stores, hotels, restaurants, etc.

Producer-distributors who purchase no milk (except those whose volume of sales is small enough to make them quota-exempt) will be allowed to sell an amount of fluid milk, cream and fluid milk byproducts equal to 100 percent of their total milk production in June. Quota-exempt producer distributors are defined separately for each area, but in general they are those whose deliveries are relatively small.

Consumers in these areas generally will be able to purchase as much milk under the milk conservation program as they have been buying—an amount considerably greater than that bought in pre-war years, and about 10 percent above last year's purchases. Sales quotas on cream and on fluid milk byproducts have been set below June deliveries to boost fluid milk supplies where milk production is low, and to conserve milk for manufacturing purposes in other areas.

Fluid milk sales are being stabilized in these and other metropolitan areas. FDA officials explained, to help assure sufficient milk for manufacturing the cheese, butter, evaporated milk and milk powder required by the armed services and civilians for good nutrition and properly balanced diets.

Largely due to expanded consumer demand, sales of fluid milk have been increasing steadily and are now about 20 percent higher than in pre-war years (1936-40) and 10 to 12 percent above those in 1942. With total milk production levelled off, and even declining somewhat, this expanding volume of milk sold for fluid uses has inevitably reduced the supply of "manufacturing milk," and, consequently, the production of cheese, butter and other dairy foods.

The FDA's dealer-quota plan is an at tempt to stabilize fluid milk consumptio without resorting to individual con sumer rationing. Point rationing o milk, a bulky and highly perishable com modity, would be very difficult to admin ister and would almost necessarily re duce fluid milk sales in many areas. I consumers and the trade cooperate witl the present program to assure that sale are held within quotas and quantitie available are distributed fairly, FDA of ficials believe consumer rationing wi not be necessary.

Milk handlers in the sales areas name today, except Greater Kansas City an Wichita, Kansas, will compute the quan tity of milk which they may sell eac month in terms of pounds of milk, thei cream sales in terms of pounds of crea and butterfat, and their milk product sales in terms of pounds of milk by products. In Greater Kansas City an Wichita, milk handlers will determin their fluid milk quotas in terms of pound of milk and butterfat.

Deliveries to the Armed Forces, t plants processing dairy products, and t other handlers (except special classes o handlers such as peddlers) are quot exempt.

To facilitate administration, the mar ket agent for each milk sales area ma act upon petitions for relief from har ship which may be submitted to hi and after investigation, he may gra temporary relief for a total period n to exceed 60 days.

Milk sales in 13 eastern and midwe ern areas previously were brought unc federal regulation. Sales quotas these initial milk sales areas are t same as for those named today.

3 7

FDO 79-16

AMDT. 1
JAN. 27, 1944

WAR FOOD ADMINISTRATION

[FDO 79-16, Amdt. 1]

Part 1401—Dairy Products

FLUID MILK AND CREAM IN YOUNGSTOWN, OHIO, SALES AREA

Pursuant to Food Distribution Order No. 79 (8 F.R. 12426), dated September 7, 1943, as amended, and to effectuate the purposes thereof, Food Distribution Order No. 79-16 (8 F.R. 13427), relative to the conservation and distribution of fluid milk in the Youngstown, Ohio, milk sales area, issued by the Director of Food Distribution on October 1, 1943, is amended as follows:

1. By deleting therefrom the provisions in § 1401.55 (f) and substituting therefor the following:

(f) *Quotas for handlers who are also producers.* Quotas for handlers who are also producers and who purchase no milk shall be computed in accordance with (e) hereof, except that the applicable percentages shall be 100 percent in lieu of the percentages specified in (e) (3).

2. By deleting therefrom the provisions of § 1401.55 (h) and substituting therefor the following:

(h) *Quota exclusions and exemptions.* Deliveries of milk, milk byproducts, or cream (1) to other handlers, except for such deliveries to sub-handlers, (2) to plants engaged in the handling or processing of milk, milk byproducts, or cream from which no milk, milk byproducts, or cream is delivered in the sales area, (3) to nursery, elementary, junior high, and high schools, and (4) to the agencies or groups specified in (d) of the order, shall be excluded from the computation of deliveries in the base period and exempt from charges to quotas.

3. By deleting therefrom the numerals "150" wherever they appear in § 1401.55 (g) and inserting in lieu thereof, the numerals "50."

4. By adding to the description of the sales area in § 1401.55 (b) the following:

The townships of Beaver and Springfield in Mahoning County, and Newton, Braceville, Southington, Champion and Bazetta in Trumbull County, Ohio.

The provisions of this amendment shall become effective at 12:01 a. m., e. w. t., February 1, 1944. With respect to violations of said Food Distribution Order No. 79-16, rights accrued, or liabilities incurred prior to the effective time of this amendment, said Food Distribution Order No. 79-16 shall be deemed to be in full force and effect for the purpose of sustaining any proper suit, action, or other proceeding with respect to any such violation, right, or liability.

(E.O. 9280, 7 F.R. 10179; E.O. 9322, 8 F.R. 3807; E.O. 9334, 8 F.R. 5423; E.O. 9392, 8 F.R. 14783; FDO 79, 8 F.R. 12426, 13283)

Issued this 27th day of January 1944.

Lee Marshall,
Director of Food Distribution.

FDO 79-17

OCTOBER 1, 1943

WAR FOOD ADMINISTRATION

[FDO 79-17]

PART 1401—DAIRY PRODUCTS

CONSERVATION AND DISTRIBUTION OF FLUID MILK AND CREAM IN THE COLUMBUS, OHIO, SALES AREA

Pursuant to the authority vested in me by Food Distribution Order No. 79 (8 F.R. 12426), issued on September 7, 1943, as amended, and to effectuate the purposes of such order, it is hereby ordered as follows:

§ 1401.54 *Quota restrictions*—(a) *Definitions.* When used in this order, unless otherwise distinctly expressed or manifestly incompatible with the intent hereof:

(1) Each term defined in Food Distribution Order No. 79, as amended, shall, when used herein, have the same meaning as is set forth for such term in Food Distribution Order No. 79, as amended.

(2) The term "order" means Food Distribution Order No. 79, issued on September 7, 1943, as amended.

(3) The term "sub-handler" means any handler, such as a peddler, vendor, sub-dealer, or secondary dealer, who purchases in a previously packaged and processed form milk, milk byproducts, or cream for delivery.

(b) *Milk sales area.* The following area is hereby designated as a "milk sales area" to be known as the Columbus, Ohio sales area, and is referred to hereinafter as the "sales area": The city of Columbus (Montgomery Township) and the townships of Bexley, Blendon, Clinton, Franklin, Marion, Mifflin, Perry, Sharon, and Truro, all in Franklin County, Ohio.

(c) *Base period.* The calendar month of June 1943 is hereby designated as the base period for the sales area.

(d) *Quota period.* The remainder of the calendar month in which the provisions hereof become effective and each subsequent calendar month, respectively, is hereby designated as a quota period for the sales area.

(e) *Handler quotas.* Quotas for each handler in the sales area in each quota period shall be determined as follows:

(1) Divide the total deliveries of each of milk, milk byproducts, and cream (and of butterfat in milk or in cream where percentages of pounds of butterfat are specified in (e) (3) (i) or (e) (3) (ii) hereof) made in the sales area by such handler during the base period, after excluding the quota-exempt deliveries described in (h) hereof and adjusting such deliveries for the transfers set out in (i) hereof, by the number of days in the base period;

(2) Multiply the result of the foregoing calculation by the number of days in the quota period; and

(3) Multiply the aforesaid resulting amount by the following applicable percentage: (i) Milk: 100 percent of pounds of milk and ______ percent of pounds of butterfat; (ii) Cream: 75 percent of pounds of cream and 75 percent of pounds of butterfat; and (iii) Milk byproducts: 75 percent of pounds of milk byproducts other than cottage, pot, or baker's cheese and of the pounds of skim milk equivalent of cottage, pot, or baker's cheese. (For the purpose of this order, one pound of cottage, pot, or baker's cheese shall be considered as the equivalent of 7 pounds of skim milk.)

(f) *Quotas for handlers who are also producers.* Quotas for handlers who are also producers and who purchase no milk shall be 100 percent of the total production of such handlers in the base period.

(g) *Handler exemptions.* Quotas shall not apply to any handler who delivers in a quota period a daily average of less than 150 units of milk, cream, and milk byproducts. For the purpose of this order, a unit shall be the equivalent in volume of the following:

(1) Milk, one quart of milk;

(2) Cream, one-half pint of cream; and

(3) Milk byproduct, one quart of skim milk, buttermilk, flavored milk drink, or other beverage containing more than 85 percent of skim milk, or one-half pound of cottage, pot, or baker's cheese.

(h) *Quota exclusions and exemptions.* Deliveries of milk, milk byproducts, or cream (1) to other handlers, except for such deliveries to sub-handlers, (2) to plants engaged in the handling or processing of milk, milk byproducts, or cream from which no milk, milk byproducts, or cream is delivered in the sales area, and (3) to the agencies or groups specified in (d) of the order, shall be excluded from the computation of deliveries in the base period and exempt from charges to quotas.

(i) *Transfers and apportionment of quotas.* The market agent is empowered to deduct an amount of base period deliveries to purchasers from the total of deliveries made by a handler or other person in the base period upon the application and a showing of unreasonable hardship by the handler making deliveries to such purchasers on the effective date of this order, and to add the amount of such deliveries to the total base period deliveries of the applicant handler. Denials of transfers or transfers granted by the market agent shall be reviewed by the Director upon application.

(j) *Petition for relief from hardships.* (1) Any person affected by the order or the provisions hereof who considers that compliance therewith would work an exceptional and unreasonable hardship on him, may file with the market agent a petition addressed to the Director. (The petition shall contain the correct name, address and principal place of business of the petitioner, a full statement of the facts upon which the petition is based, and the hardship involved and the nature of the relief desired.

(2) Upon receiving such petition, the market agent shall immediately investigate the representations and facts stated therein.

(3) After investigation, the petition shall be certified to the Director, but prior to certification the market agent may (i) deny the petition; or (ii) grant temporary relief for a total period not to exceed 60 days.

(4) Denials or grants of relief by the market agent shall be reviewed by the Director and may be affirmed, modified, or reversed by the Director.

(k) *Reports.* Each handler shall transmit to the market agent on forms prescribed by the market agent the following reports:

(1) Within 20 days following the effective date of this order, reports which show the information required by the market agent to establish such handlers' quotas;

(2) Within 20 days following the close of each quota period, the information required by the market agent to establish volumes of deliveries of milk, cream, and milk byproducts during the preceding quota period; and

(3) Handlers exempt from quotas pursuant to (f) hereof shall, upon the request of the market agent, submit the information required by the market agent to establish volumes of deliveries of milk, cream, and milk byproducts.

(l) *Records.* Handlers shall keep and shall make available to the market agent such records of receipts, sales, deliveries, and production as the market agent shall require for the purpose of obtaining information which the Director may require for the establishment of quotas as prescribed in (b) of the order.

(m) *Distribution schedules.* The distribution schedules, if any, to be followed by the handlers in making deliveries shall be made effective in the terms of aproval by the Director of such schedules.

(n) *Expense of administration.* Each handler shall pay to the market agent, within 20 days after the close of each calendar month an assessment of $.01 per hundredweight of each of milk, cream, skim milk, buttermilk, flavored milk drinks, beverages containing more than 85 percent of skim milk, and skim milk equivalent of cottage, pot, or baker's cheese delivered during the preceding quota period and subject to quota regulations under the provisions hereof.

(o) *Violations.* The market agent shall report all violations to the Director together with the information required for the prosecution of such violations, except in a case where a handler has made deliveries in a quota period in excess of a quota in an amount not to exceed 5 percent of such quota, and in the succeeding quota period makes deliveries below that quota by at least the [illegible] percent.

(p) *Bureau of the Budget appr*[illegible] The record-keeping and reporting requirements of this order have been approved by the Bureau of the Budg[illegible] accordance with the Federal Report[illegible] of 1942. Subsequent record-keepin[illegible] reporting requirements will be subje[illegible] the approval of the Bureau of the Bu[illegible] pursuant to the Federal Reports A[illegible] 1942.

(q) This order shall take effec[illegible] 12:01 a. m., e. w. t., October 5, 1943.

Issued this 1st day of October 194[illegible]

ROY F. HENDRICKSON,
Director of Food Distributi[illegible]

Press Release Immediate:
Saturday, October 2, 1943.

Eleven additional metropolitan areas will be brought under the Food Distribution Administration's fluid milk conservation and control program beginning October 5, the War Food Administration said today.

The new milk sales areas, and the market agents who will administer the program in each are:

St. Joseph County, Ind.: M. E. Drake, 116 S. William St., South Bend, Ind.

Akron, Ohio; Huntington, W. Va.-Ashland, Ky.; Hamilton-Middletown, Ohio; Columbus, Ohio; Youngstown, Ohio: Fred Issler, 152 E. Fourth St., Cincinnati, Ohio.

Davenport, Ia.-Rock Island, Ill.-Moline, Ill.: Howard E. Eisaman, 335 Federal Building, Rock Island, Ill.

Fort Wayne, Ind.: William J. Cline, 707 Citizens Trust Building, Fort Wayne, Ind.

Wichita, Kans., Greater Kansas City (Mo.-Kan.): M. M. Morehouse, 512 Porter Building, 406 W. 34th St., Kansas City, Mo.

Duluth, Minn.-Superior, Wis.: O. F. Kirkendall, 2002-4 W. Superior St., Duluth, Minn.

Dealers' monthly fluid milk sales in these areas may not exceed their June deliveries, and their sales of cream and of fluid milk byproducts (such as cottage cheese, chocolate milk and buttermilk), will be reduced to three-fourths of the quantities sold in June. Milk dealers include all persons or firms engaged in the sale or transfer of milk, but not retail stores, hotels, restaurants, etc.

Producer-distributors who purchase no milk (except those whose volume of sales is small enough to make them quota-exempt) will be allowed to sell an amount of fluid milk, cream and fluid milk byproducts equal to 100 percent of their total milk production in June. Quota-exempt producer distributors are defined separately for each area, but in general they are those whose deliveries are relatively small.

Consumers in these areas generally will be able to purchase as much milk under the milk conservation program as they have been buying—an amount considerably greater than that bought in pre-war years, and about 10 percent above last year's purchases. Sales quotas on cream and on fluid milk byproducts have been set below June deliveries to boost fluid milk supplies where milk production is low, and to conserve milk for manufacturing purposes in other areas.

Fluid milk sales are being stabilized in these and other metropolitan areas, FDA officials explained, to help assure sufficient milk for manufacturing the cheese, butter, evaporated milk and milk powder required by the armed services and civilians for good nutrition and properly balanced diets.

Largely due to expanded consumer demand, sales of fluid milk have been increasing steadily and are now about 20 percent higher than in pre-war years (1936–40) and 10 to 12 percent above those in 1942. With total milk production levelled off, and even declining somewhat, this expanding volume of milk sold for fluid uses has inevitably reduced the supply of "manufacturing milk," and, consequently, the production of cheese, butter and other dairy foods.

The FDA's dealer-quota plan is a[illegible] tempt to stabilize fluid milk consum[illegible] without resorting to individual cons[illegible] rationing. Point rationing of mil[illegible] bulky and highly perishable commo[illegible] would be very difficult to administer would almost necessarily reduce milk sales in many areas. If consu[illegible] and the trade cooperate with the pr[illegible] program to assure that sales are within quotas and quantities avai[illegible] are distributed fairly, FDA officials lieve consumer rationing will no[illegible] necessary.

Milk handlers in the sales areas n[illegible] today, except Greater Kansas City Wichita, Kansas, will compute quantity of milk which they may each month in terms of pounds of [illegible] their cream sales in terms of poun[illegible] cream and butterfat, and their [illegible] products sales in terms of pound milk byproducts. In Greater Ka[illegible] City of Wichita, milk handlers wil[illegible] termine their fluid milk quotas in t[illegible] of pounds of milk and butterfat.

Deliveries to the Armed Force[illegible] plants processing dairy products, a[illegible] other handlers (except special class handlers such as peddlers) are [illegible] exempt.

To facilitate administration market agent for each milk sales may act upon petitions for relief [illegible] hardship which may be submitte[illegible] him, and after investigation, he grant temporary relief for a total p[illegible] not to exceed 60 days.

Milk sales in 13 eastern and [illegible] western areas previously were bro[illegible] under federal regulation. Sales q[illegible] in these initial milk sales areas ar[illegible] same as for those named today.

FDO 79-17
AMDT. 1
JAN. 27, 1944

WAR FOOD ADMINISTRATION

[FDO 79-17, Amdt. 1]

PART 1401—DAIRY PRODUCTS

FLUID MILK AND CREAM IN COLUMBUS, OHIO, SALES AREA

Pursuant to Food Distribution Order No. 79 (8 F.R. 12426), dated September 7, 1943, as amended, and to effectuate the purposes thereof, Food Distribution Order No. 79–17 (8 F.R. 13428), relative to the conservation and distribution of fluid milk in the Columbus, Ohio, milk sales area, issued by the Director of Food Distribution on October 1, 1943, is amended as follows:

1. By deleting therefrom the provisions in § 1401.54 (f) and substituting therefor the following:

(f) *Quotas for handlers who are also producers.* Quotas for handlers who are also producers and who purchase no milk shall be computed in accordance with (e) hereof, except that the applicable percentages shall be 100 percent in lieu of the percentages specified in (e) (3).

2. By deleting therefrom the provisions of § 1401.54 (h) and substituting therefor the following:

(h) *Quota exclusions and exemptions.* Deliveries of milk, milk byproducts, or cream (1) to other handlers, except for such deliveries to sub-handlers, (2) to plants engaged in the handling or processing of milk, milk byproducts, or cream from which no milk, milk byproducts, or cream is delivered in the sales area, (3) to nursery, elementary, junior high, and high schools, and (4) to the agencies or groups specified in (d) of the order, shall be excluded from the computation of deliveries in the base period and exempt from charges to quotas.

The provisions of this amendment shall become effective at 12:01 a. m., e. w. t., February 1, 1944. With respect to violations of said Food Distribution Order No. 79–17, rights accrued, or liabilities incurred prior to the effective time of this amendment, said Food Distribution Order No. 79–17 shall be deemed to be in full force and effect for the purpose of sustaining any proper suit, action, or other proceeding with respect to any such violation, right, or liability.

(E.O. 9280, 7 F. R. 10179; E.O. 9322, 8 F.R. 3807; E.O. 9334, 8 F.R. 5423; E.O. 9392, 8 F.R. 14783; FDO 79, 8 F.R. 12426, 13283)

Issued this 27th day of January 1944.

LEE MARSHALL,
Director of Food Distribution.

FDO 79-18

OCTOBER 1, 1943

WAR FOOD ADMINISTRATION

[FDO 79-18]

PART 1401—DAIRY PRODUCTS

CONSERVATION AND DISTRIBUTION OF FLUID MILK AND CREAM IN THE FT. WAYNE, IND., SALES AREA

Pursuant to the authority vested in me by Food Distribution Order No. 79 (8 F.R. 12426), issued on September 7, 1943, as amended, and to effectuate the purposes of such order, it is hereby ordered as follows:

§ 1401.53 *Quota restrictions*—(a) *Definitions*. When used in this order, unless otherwise distinctly expressed or manifestly incompatible with the intent hereof:

(1) Each term defined in Food Distribution Order No. 79, as amended, shall, when used herein, have the same meaning as is set forth for such term in Food Distribution Order No. 79, as amended.

(2) The term "order" means Food Distribution Order No. 79, issued on September 7, 1943, as amended.

(3) The term "sub-handler" means any handler, such as a peddler, vendor, sub-dealer, or secondary dealer, who purchases in a previously packaged and processed form milk, milk byproducts, or cream for delivery.

(b) *Milk sales area*. The following area is hereby designated as a "milk sales area" to be known as the Ft. Wayne, Ind. sales area, and is referred to hereinafter as the "sales area": The city of Ft. Wayne, Ind., and the townships of Adams, St. Joseph, Washington and Wayne in Allen County, Indiana.

(c) *Base period*. The calendar month of June 1943 is hereby designated as the base period for the sales area.

(d) *Quota period*. The remainder of the calendar month in which the provisions hereof become effective and each subsequent calendar month, respectively, is hereby designated as a quota period for the sales area.

(e) *Handler quotas*. Quotas for each handler in the sales area in each quota period shall be determined as follows:

(1) Divide the total deliveries of each of milk, milk byproducts, and cream (and of butterfat in milk or in cream where percentages of pounds of butterfat are specified in (e) (3) (i) or (e) (3) (ii) hereof) made in the sales area by such handler during the base period, after excluding the quota-exempt deliveries described in (h) and adjusting such deliveries for the transfers set out in (i) hereof, by the number of days in the base period;

(2) Multiply the result of the foregoing calculation by the number of days in the quota period; and

(3) Multiply the aforesaid resulting amount by the following applicable percentage: (i) Milk: 100 percent of pounds of milk and ______ percent of pounds of butterfat; (ii) Cream: 75 percent of pounds of cream and 75 percent of pounds of butterfat; and (iii) Milk byproducts: 75 percent of pounds of milk byproducts other than cottage, pot, or baker's cheese and of the pounds of skim milk equivalent of cottage, pot, or baker's cheese. (For the purpose of this order, one pound of cottage, pot, or baker's cheese shall be considered as the equivalent of 7 pounds of skim milk.)

(f) *Quotas for handlers who are also producers*. Quotas for handlers who are also producers and who purchase no milk shall be 100 percent of the total production of such handlers in the base period.

(g) *Handler exemptions*. Quotas shall not apply to any handler who delivers in a quota period a daily average of less than 100 units of milk, cream, and milk byproducts. For the purpose of this order, a unit shall be the equivalent in volume of the following:

(1) Milk, one quart of milk;

(2) Cream, one-half pint of cream; and

(3) Milk byproduct, one quart of skim milk, buttermilk, flavored milk drink, or other beverage containing more than 85 percent of skim milk, or one-half pound of cottage, pot, or baker's cheese.

(h) *Quota exclusions and exemptions*. Deliveries of milk, milk byproducts, or cream (1) to other handlers, except for such deliveries to sub-handlers, (2) to plants engaged in the handling or processing of milk, milk byproducts, or cream from which no milk, milk byproducts, or cream is delivered in the sales area, and (3) to the agencies or groups specified in (d) of the order, shall be excluded from the computation of deliveries in the base period and exempt from charges to quotas.

(i) *Transfers and apportionment of quotas*. The market agent is empowered to deduct an amount of base period deliveries to purchasers from the total of deliveries made by a handler or other person in the base period upon the application and a showing of unreasonable hardship by the handler making deliveries to such purchasers on the effective date of this order, and to add the amount of such deliveries to the total base period deliveries of the applicant handler. Denials of transfers or transfers granted by the market agent shall be reviewed by the Director upon application.

(j) *Petition for relief from hardships*. (1) Any person affected by the order or the provisions hereof who considers that compliance therewith would work an exceptional and unreasonable hardship on him, may file with the market agent a petition addressed to the Director. The petition shall contain the correct name, address and principal place of business of the petitioner, a full statement of the facts upon which the petition is based, and the hardship involved and the nature of the relief desired.

(2) Upon receiving such petition, the market agent shall immediately investigate the representations and facts stated therein.

(3) After investigation, the petition shall be certified to the Director, but prior to certification the market agent may (i) deny the petition; or (ii) grant temporary relief for a total period not to exceed 60 days.

(4) Denials or grants of relief by the market agent shall be reviewed by the Director and may be affirmed, modified, or reversed by the Director.

(k) *Reports*. Each handler shall transmit to the market agent on forms prescribed by the market agent the following reports:

(1) Within 20 days following the effective date of this order, reports which show the information required by the market agent to establish such handlers' quotas;

(2) Within 20 days following the close of each quota period, the information required by the market agent to establish volumes of deliveries of milk, cream, and milk byproducts during the preceding quota period; and

(3) Handlers exempt from quotas pursuant to (f) hereof shall, upon the request of the market agent, submit the information required by the market agent to establish volumes of deliveries of milk, cream, and milk byproducts.

(l) *Records*. Handlers shall keep and shall make available to the market agent such records of receipts, sales, deliveries, and production as the market agent shall require for the purpose of obtaining information which the Director may require for the establishment of quotas as prescribed in (b) of the order.

(m) *Distribution schedules.* The distribution schedules, if any, to be followed by the handlers in making deliveries shall be made effective in the terms of approval by the Director of such schedules.

(n) *Expense of administration.* Each handler shall pay to the market agent, within 20 days after the close of each calendar month an assessment of $0.01 per hundredweight of each of milk, cream, skim milk, buttermilk, flavored milk drinks, beverages containing more than 85 percent of skim milk, and skim milk equivalent of cottage, pot, or baker's cheese delivered during the preceding quota period and subject to quota regulations under the provisions hereof.

(o) *Violations.* The market agent shall report all violations to the Director together with the information required for the prosecution of such violations, except in a case where a handler has made deliveries in a quota period in excess of a quota in an amount not to exceed 5 percent of such quota, and in the succeeding quota period makes deliveries below that quota by at least the same percent.

(p) *Bureau of the Budget approval.* The record-keeping and reporting requirements of this order ha proved by the Bureau of th accordance with the Federal of 1942. Subsequent record reporting requirements will l the approval of the Bureau o pursuant to the Federal Re 1942.

(q) This order shall tal 12:01 a. m., e. w. t., October 5

Issued this 1st day of Octo

ROY F. HEND

Director of Food Di

Press Release, Immediate:
Saturday, October 2, 1943.

Eleven additional metropolitan areas will be brought under the Food Distribution Administration's fluid milk conservation and control program beginning October 5, the War Food Administration said today.

The new milk sales areas, and the market agents who will administer the program in each, are:

St. Joseph County, Ind.: M. E. Drake, 116 S. William St., South Bend, Ind.

Akron, Ohio; Huntington, W. Va.-Ashland, Ky.; Hamilton-Middletown, Ohio; Columbus, Ohio; Youngstown, Ohio: Fred Issler, 152 E. Fourth St., Cincinnati, Ohio.

Davenport, Ia.-Rock Island, Ill.,-Moline, Ill.; Howard E. Eisaman, 335 Federal Building, Rock Island, Ill.

Fort Wayne, Ind.: William J. Cline, 707 Citizens Trust Building, Fort Wayne, Ind.

Wichita, Kans., Greater Kansas City (Mo.-Kan.): M. M. Morehouse, 512 Porter Building, 406 W. 34th St., Kansas City, Mo.

Duluth, Minn.-Superior, Wis.: O. F. Kirkendall, 2002-4 W. Superior St., Duluth, Minn.

Dealer's monthly fluid milk sales in these areas may not exceed their June deliveries, and their sales of cream and of fluid milk byproducts (such as cottage cheese, chocolate milk and buttermilk) will be reduced to three-fourths of the quantities sold in June. Milk dealers include all persons or firms engaged in the sale or transfer of milk, but not retail stores, hotels, restaurants, etc.

Producer-distributors who purchase no milk (except those whose volume of sales is small enough to make them quota-exempt) will be allowed to sell an amount of fluid milk, cream and fluid milk byproducts equal to 100 percent of their total milk production in June. Quota-exempt producer distributors are defined separately for each area, but in general they are those whose deliveries are relatively small.

Consumers in these areas generally will be able to purchase as much milk under the milk conservation program as they have been buying—an amount considerably greater than that bought in pre-war years, and about 10 percent above last year's purchases. Sales quotas on cream and on fluid milk byproducts have been set below June deliveries to boost fluid milk supplies where milk production is low, and to conserve milk for manufacturing purposes in other areas.

Fluid milk sales are being stabilized in these and other metropolitan areas, FDA officials explained, to help assure sufficient milk for manufacturing the cheese, butter, evaporated milk and milk powder required by the armed services and civilians for good nutrition and properly balanced diets.

Largely due to expanded consumer demand, sales of fluid milk have been increasing steadily and are now about 20 percent higher than in pre-war years (1936-40) and 10 to 12 percent above those in 1942. With total milk production levelled off, and even declining somewhat, this expanding volume of milk sold for fluid uses has inevitably reduced the supply of "manufacturing milk," and, consequently, the production of cheese, butter and other dairy foods.

The FDA's dealer-quota attempt to stabilize fluid mi tion without resorting to inc sumer rationing. Point r milk, a bulky and highly per modity, would be very difficu ister and would almost neces fluid milk sales in many ar sumers and the trade cooper present program to assure t held within quotas and qua able are distributed fairly, believe consumer rationing necessary.

Milk handlers in the sales today, except Greater Kans Wichita, Kansas, will compu tity of milk which they m month in terms of pounds o cream sales in terms of pou and butterfat, and their m sales in terms of pounds of ucts. In Greater Kansas Ci ita, milk handlers will det fluid milk quotas in terms milk and butterfat.

Deliveries to the Arme plants processing dairy pro other handlers (except spec handlers such as peddlers exempt.

To facilitate administrati ket agent for each milk sa act upon petitions for relie ship which may be submitte after investigation, he may porary relief for a total p exceed 60 days.

Milk sales in 13 eastern a ern areas previously were b federal regulation. Sales q initial milk sales areas are for those named today.

FDO 79-18

AMDT. 1
FEB. 28, 1944

WAR FOOD ADMINISTRATION

[FDO 79-18, Amdt. 1]

PART 1401—DAIRY PRODUCTS

FLUID MILK AND CREAM IN THE FT. WAYNE, INDIANA, SALES AREA

Pursuant to Food Distribution Order No. 79 (8 F.R. 12426), dated September 7, 1943, as amended, and to effectuate the purposes thereof, Food Distribution Order No. 79-18 (8 F.R. 13429), relative to the conservation and distribution of fluid milk in the Ft. Wayne, Indiana, milk sales area, issued by the Director of Food Distribution on October 1, 1943, is hereby amended by deleting therefrom the provisions in § 1401.53 (h) and inserting, in lieu thereof, the following:

(h) *Quota exclusions and exemptions.* Deliveries of milk, milk byproducts, or cream (1) to other handlers, except for such deliveries to sub-handlers, (2) to plants engaged in the handling or processing of milk, milk byproducts, or cream from which no milk, milk byproducts, or cream is delivered in the sales area, (3) to nursery, elementary, junior high, and high schools, and (4) to the agencies or groups specified in (d) of the order, shall be excluded from the computation of deliveries in the base period and exempt from charges to quotas.

The provisions of this amendment shall become effective at 12:01 a. m., e. w. t., March 1, 1944. With respect to violations of said Food Distribution Order No. 79-18 rights accrued, or liabilities incurred prior to the effective time of this amendment, said Food Distribution Order No. 79-18, shall be deemed to be in full force and effect for the purpose of sustaining any proper suit, action, or other proceeding with respect to any such violation, right, or liability.

(E.O. 9280, 7 F.R. 10179; E.O. 9322, 8 F.R. 3807; E.O. 9334, 8 F.R. 5423; E.O. 9392, 8 F.R. 14783; FDO 79, 8 F.R. 12426, 13283)

Issued this 28th day of February 1944.

C. W. KITCHEN,
Acting Director of Food Distribution.

FDO 79-19

OCTOBER 1, 1943

WAR FOOD ADMINISTRATION

[FDO 79-19]

PART 1401—DAIRY PRODUCTS

CONSERVATION AND DISTRIBUTION OF FLUID MILK AND CREAM IN THE HUNTINGTON-ASHLAND METROPOLITAN SALES AREA

Pursuant to the authority vested in me by Food Distribution Order No. 79 (8 F.R. 12426), issued on September 7, 1943, as amended, and to effectuate the purposes of such order, it is hereby ordered as follows:

§ 1401.50 *Quota restrictions* — (a) *Definitions.* When used in this order, unless otherwise distinctly expressed or manifestly incompatible with the intent hereof:

(1) Each term defined in Food Distribution Order No. 79, as amended, shall, when used herein, have the same meaning as is set forth for such term in Food Distribution Order No. 79, as amended.

(2) The term "order" means Food Distribution Order No. 79, issued on September 7, 1943, as amended.

(3) The term "sub-handler" means any handler, such as a peddler, vendor, sub-dealer, or secondary dealer, who purchases in a previously packaged and processed form milk, milk byproducts, or cream for delivery.

(b) *Milk sales area.* The following area is hereby designated as a "milk sales area" to be known as the Huntington-Ashland Metropolitan sales area, and is referred to hereinafter as the "sales area": The cities of Huntington, W. Va., and Ashland, Ky.; the city of Ironton and the townships of Union, Fayette, Perry, and Upper in Lawrence County, Ohio; the magisterial district of Russell in Greenup County, and the districts of Catlettsburg, Lower Ashland, and Upper Ashland in Boyd County, Ky.; and the magisterial districts of Ceredo and Westmoreland in Wayne County, W. Va.; and the districts of Gideon, Guyandot, and Kyle in Cabell County, W. Va.

(c) *Base period.* The calendar month of June 1943 is hereby designated as the base period for the sales area.

(d) *Quota period.* The remainder of the calendar month in which the provisions hereof become effective and each subsequent calendar month, respectively, is hereby designated as a quota period for the sales area.

(e) *Handler quotas.* Quotas for each handler in the sales area in each quota period shall be determined as follows:

(1) Divide the total deliveries of each of milk, milk byproducts, and cream (and of butterfat in milk or in cream where percentages of pounds of butterfat are specified in (e) (3) (i) or (e) (3) (ii) hereof) made in the sales area by such handler during the base period, after excluding the quota-exempt deliveries described in (h) hereof and adjusting such deliveries for the transfers set out in (i) hereof, by the number of days in the base period;

(2) Multiply the result of the foregoing calculation by the number of days in the quota period; and

(3) Multiply the aforesaid resulting amount by the following applicable percentage: (i) Milk: 100 percent of pounds of milk and ______ percent of pounds of butterfat; (ii) Cream: 75 percent of pounds of cream and 75 percent of pounds of butterfat; and (iii) Milk byproducts: 75 percent of pounds of milk byproducts other than cottage, pot, or baker's cheese and of the pounds of skim milk equivalent of cottage, pot or baker's cheese. (For the purpose of this order, one pound of cottage, pot, or baker's cheese shall be considered as the equivalent of 7 pounds of skim milk.)

(f) *Quotas for handlers who are also producers.* Quotas for handlers who are also producers and who purchase no milk shall be 100 percent of the total production of such handlers in the base period.

(g) *Handler exemptions.* Quotas shall not apply to any handler who delivers in a quota period a daily average of less than 150 units of milk, cream, and milk byproducts. For the purpose of this order, a unit shall be the equivalent in volume of the following:

(1) Milk, one quart of milk;

(2) Cream, one-half pint of cream; and

(3) Milk byproduct, one quart of skim milk, buttermilk, flavored milk drink, or other beverage containing more than 85 percent of skim milk, or one-half pound of cottage, pot, or baker's cheese.

(h) *Quota exclusions and exemptions.* Deliveries of milk, milk byproducts, or cream (1) to other handlers, except for such deliveries to sub-handlers, (2) to plants engaged in the handling or processing of milk, milk byproducts, or cream from which no milk, milk byproducts, or cream is delivered in the sales area, and (3) to the agencies or groups specified in (d) of the order, shall be excluded from the computation of deliveries in the base period and exempt from charges to quotas.

(i) *Transfers and apportionment of quotas.* The market agent is empowered to ~~deduct an amount of base-period~~ deliveries to purchasers from the total of deliveries made by a handler or other person in the base period upon the application and a showing of unreasonable hardship by the handler making deliveries to such purchasers on the effective date of this order, and to add the amount of such deliveries to the total base period deliveries of the applicant handler. Denials of transfers or transfers granted by the market agent shall be reviewed by the Director upon application.

(j) *Petition for relief from hardships.* (1) Any person affected by the order or the provisions hereof who considers that compliance therewith would work an exceptional and unreasonable hardship on him, may file with the market agent a petition addressed to the Director. The petition shall contain the correct name, address and principal place of business of the petitioner, a full statement of the facts upon which the petition is based, and the hardship involved and the nature of the relief desired.

(2) Upon receiving such petition, the market agent shall immediately investigate the representations and facts stated therein.

(3) After investigation, the petition shall be certified to the Director, but prior to certification the market agent may (i) deny the petition; or (ii) grant temporary relief for a total period not to exceed 60 days.

(4) Denials or grants of relief by the market agent shall be reviewed by the Director and may be affirmed, modified, or reversed by the Director.

(k) *Reports.* Each handler shall transmit to the market agent on forms prescribed by the market agent the following reports:

(1) Within 20 days following the effective date of this order, reports which show the information required by the market agent to establish such handlers' quotas;

(2) Within 20 days following the close of each quota period, the information required by the market agent to establish volumes of deliveries of milk, cream, and milk byproducts during the preceding quota period; and

(3) Handlers exempt from quotas pursuant to (f) hereof shall, upon the request of the market agent, submit the information required by the market agent to establish volumes of deliveries of milk, cream, and milk byproducts.

(l) *Records.* Handlers shall keep and shall make available to the market agent such records of receipts, sales, deliveries, and production as the market agent shall require for the purpose of obtaining information which the Director may require for the establishment of quotas as prescribed in (b) of the order.

(m) *Distribution schedules.* The distribution schedules, if any, to be followed by the handlers in making deliveries shall be made effective in the terms of approval by the Director of such schedules.

(n) *Expense of administration.* Each handler shall pay to the market agent, within 20 days after the close of each calendar month an assessment of $0.01 per hundredweight of each of milk, cream, skim milk, buttermilk, flavored milk drinks, beverages containing more than 85 percent of skim milk, and skim milk equivalent of cottage, pot, or baker's cheese delivered during the preceding quota period and subject to quota regulations under the provisions hereof.

(o) *Violations.* The market agent shall report all violations to the Director together with the information required for the prosecution of such violations, except in a case where a handler has made deliveries in a quota period in excess of a quota in an amount not to exceed 5 percent of such quota, and in the succeeding quota period makes deliveries below that quota by at least the same percent.

(p) *Bureau of the Budget approval.* The record-keeping and reporting requirements of this order have been approved by the Bureau of the Budget in accordance with the Federal Reports Act of 1942. Subsequent record-keeping or reporting requirements will be subject to the approval of the Bureau of the Budget pursuant to the Federal Reports Act of 1942.

(q) This order shall take effect at 12:01 a. m., e. w. t., October 5, 1943.

Issued this 1st day of October 1943.

ROY F. HENDRICKSON,
Director of Food Distribution.

Press Release Immediate:
Saturday, October 2, 1943.

Eleven additional metropolitan areas will be brought under the Food Distribution Administration's fluid milk conservation and control program beginning October 5, the War Food Administration said today.

The new milk sales areas, and the market agents who will administer the program in each, are:

St. Joseph County, Ind.: M. E. Drake, 116 S. William St., South Bend, Ind.

Akron, Ohio; Huntington, W. Va.-Ashland, Ky.; Hamilton - Middletown, Ohio; Columbus, Ohio; Youngstown, Ohio: Fred Issler, 152 E. Fourth St., Cincinnati, Ohio.

Davenport, Ia.-Rock Island, Ill.-Moline, Ill.: Howard E. Eisaman, 335 Federal Building, Rock Island, Ill.

Fort Wayne, Ind.: William J. Cline, 707 Citizens Trust Building, Fort Wayne, Ind.

Wichita, Kan.; Greater Kansas City (Mo.-Kan.): M. M. Morehouse, 612 Porter Building, 406 W. 34th St., Kansas City, Mo.

Duluth, Minn.-Superior, Wis.: O. F. Kirkendall, 2002-4 W. Superior St., Duluth, Minn.

Dealers' monthly fluid milk sales in these areas may not exceed their June deliveries, and their sales of cream and of fluid milk byproducts (such as cottage cheese, chocolate milk and buttermilk) will be reduced to three-fourths of the quantities sold in June. Milk dealers include all persons or firms engaged in the sale or transfer of milk, but not retail stores, hotels, restaurants, etc.

Producer-distributors who purchase no milk (except those whose volume of sales is small enough to make them quota-exempt) will be allowed to sell an amount of fluid milk, cream and fluid milk byproducts equal to 100 percent of their total milk production in June. Quota-exempt producer-distributors are defined separately for each area, but in general they are those whose deliveries are relatively small.

Consumers in these areas generally will be able to purchase as much milk under the milk conservation program as they have been buying—an amount considerably greater than that bought in pre-war years, and about 10 percent above last year's purchases. Sales quotas on cream and on fluid milk byproducts have been set below June deliveries to boost fluid milk supplies where milk production is low, and to conserve milk for manufacturing purposes in other areas.

Fluid milk sales are being stabilized in these and other metropolitan areas, FDA officials explained, to help assure sufficient milk for manufacturing the cheese, butter, evaporated milk and milk powder required by the armed services and civilians for good nutrition and properly balanced diets.

Largely due to expanded consumer demand, sales of fluid milk have been increasing steadily and are now about 20 percent higher than in pre-war years (1936-40) and 10 to 12 percent above those in 1942. With total milk production levelled off, and even declining somewhat, this expanding volume of milk sold for fluid uses has inevitably reduced the supply of "manufacturing milk," and, consequently, the production of cheese, butter and other dairy foods.

The FDA's dealer-quota plan is an attempt to stabilize fluid milk consumption without resorting to individual consumer rationing. Point rationing of milk, a bulky and highly perishable commodity, would be very difficult to administer and would almost necessarily reduce fluid milk sales in many areas. If consumers and the trade cooperate with the present program to assure that sales are held within quotas and quantities available are distributed fairly, FDA officials believe consumer rationing will not be necessary.

Milk handlers in the sales areas named today, except Greater Kansas City and Wichita, Kansas, will compute the quantity of milk which they may sell each month in terms of pounds of milk, their cream sales in terms of pounds of cream and butterfat, and their milk products sales in terms of pounds of milk byproducts. In Greater Kansas City and Wichita, milk handlers will determine their fluid milk quotas in terms of pounds of milk and butterfat.

Deliveries to the armed forces, to plants processing dairy products, and to other handlers (except special classes of handlers such as peddlers) are quota exempt.

To facilitate administration, the market agent for each milk sales area may act upon petitions for relief from hardship which may be submitted to him, and after investigation, he may grant temporary relief for a total period not to exceed 60 days.

Milk sales in 13 eastern and midwestern areas previously were brought under federal regulation. Sales quotas in these initial milk sales areas are the same as for those named today.

337

FDO 79-19

AMDT. 1
JAN. 27, 1944

WAR FOOD ADMINISTRATION

[FDO 79-19, Amdt. 1]

PART 1401—DAIRY PRODUCTS

FLUID MILK AND CREAM IN HUNTINGTON-ASHLAND METROPOLITAN SALES AREA

Pursuant to Food Distribution Order No. 79 (8 F.R. 12426), dated September 7, 1943, as amended, and to effectuate the purposes thereof, Food Distribution Order No. 79-19 (8 F.R. 13430), relative to the conservation and distribution of fluid milk in the Huntington-Ashland metropolitan milk sales area, issued by the Director of Food Distribution on October 1, 1943, is amended as follows:

1. By deleting therefrom the provisions in § 1401.50 (f) and substituting therefor the following:

(f) *Quotas for handlers who are also producers.* Quotas for handlers who are also producers and who purchase no milk shall be computed in accordance with (e) hereof, except that the applicable percentages shall be 100 percent in lieu of the percentages specified in (e) (3).

2. By deleting therefrom the provisions of § 1401.50 (h) and substituting therefor the following:

(h) *Quota exclusions and exemptions.* Deliveries of milk, milk byproducts, or cream (1) to other handlers, except for such deliveries to sub-handlers, (2) to plants engaged in the handling or processing of milk, milk byproducts, or cream from which no milk, milk byproducts, or cream is delivered in the sales area, (3) to nursery, elementary, junior high, and high schools, and (4) to the agencies or groups specified in (d) of the order, shall be excluded from the computation of deliveries in the base period and exempt from charges to quotas.

The provisions of this amendment shall become effective at 12:01 a. m., e. w. t., February 1, 1944. With respect to violations of said Food Distribution Order No. 79-19, rights accrued, or liabilities incurred prior to the effective time of this amendment, said Food Distribution Order No. 79-19 shall be deemed to be in full force and effect for the purpose of sustaining any proper suit, action, or other proceeding with respect to any such violation, right, or liability.

(E.O. 9280, 7 F.R. 10179; E.O. 9322, 8 F.R. 3807; E.O. 9334, 8 F.R. 5423; E.O. 9392, 8 F.R. 14783; FDO 79, 8 F.R. 12426, 13283)

Issued this 27th day of January 1944.

LEE MARSHALL,
Director of Food Distribution.

CURRENT SERIAL RECORD

FDO 79-20

OCTOBER 1, 1943

WAR FOOD ADMINISTRATION

[FDO 79-20]

PART 1401—DAIRY PRODUCTS

CONSERVATION AND DISTRIBUTION OF FLUID MILK AND CREAM IN THE DAVENPORT-ROCK ISLAND-MOLINE SALES AREA

Pursuant to the authority vested in me by Food Distribution Order No. 79 (8 F.R. 12426), issued on September 7, 1943, as amended, and to effectuate the purposes of such order, it is hereby ordered as follows:

§ 1401.52 *Quota restrictions*—(a) *Definitions.* When used in this order, unless otherwise distinctly expressed or manifestly incompatible with the intent hereof:

(1) Each term defined in Food Distribution Order No. 79, as amended, shall, when used herein, have the same meaning as is set forth for such term in Food Distribution Order No. 79, as amended.

(2) The term "order" means Food Distribution Order No. 79, issued on September 7, 1943, as amended.

(3) The term "sub-handler" means any handler, such as a peddler, vendor, sub-dealer, or secondary dealer, who purchases in a previously packaged and processed form milk, milk byproducts, or cream for delivery.

(b) *Milk sales area.* The following area is hereby designated as a "milk sales area" to be known as the Davenport-Rock Island-Moline sales area, and is referred to hereinafter as the "sales area"; the territory lying within the corporate limits of the cities of Davenport and Bettendorf, both in Iowa; and Rock Island, Moline, East Moline, and Silvis, all in Illinois; together with the territory within the following townships: Davenport, Rockingham, and Pleasant Valley in Scott County, Iowa, and South Moline, Moline, Blackhawk, Coal Valley, Hampton, Port Byron, and South Rock Island in Rock Island County, Illinois.

(c) *Base period.* The calendar month of June 1943 is hereby designated as the base period for the sales area.

(d) *Quota period.* The remainder of the calendar month in which the provisions hereof become effective and each subsequent calendar month, respectively, is hereby designated as a quota period for the sales area.

(e) *Handler quotas.* Quotas for each handler in the sales area in each quota period shall be determined as follows:

(1) Divide the total deliveries of each of milk, milk byproducts, and cream (and of butterfat in milk or in cream where percentages of pounds of butterfat are specified in (e) (3) (i) or (e) (3) (ii) hereof) made in the sales area by such handler during the base period, after excluding the quota-exempt deliveries described in (h) and adjusting such deliveries for the transfers set out in (i) hereof, by the number of days in the base period;

(2) Multiply the result of the foregoing calculation by the number of days in the quota period; and

(3) Multiply the aforesaid resulting amount by the following applicable percentage: (i) Milk: 100 percent of pounds of milk and ______ percent of pounds of butterfat; (ii) Cream: 75 percent of pounds of cream and 75 percent of pounds of butterfat; and (iii) Milk byproducts: 75 percent of pounds of milk byproducts other than cottage, pot, or baker's cheese and of the pounds of skim milk equivalent of cottage, pot, or baker's cheese. (For the purpose of this order, one pound of cottage, pot, or baker's cheese shall be considered as the equivalent of 7 pounds of skim milk.)

(f) *Quotas for handlers who are also producers.* Quotas for handlers who are also producers and who purchase no milk shall be 100 percent of the total production of such handlers in the base period.

(g) *Handler exemptions.* Quotas shall not apply to any handler who delivers in a quota period a daily average of less than 200 units of milk, cream, and milk byproducts. For the purpose of this order, a unit shall be the equivalent in volume of the following:

(1) Milk, one quart of milk;

(2) Cream, one-half pint of cream; and

(3) Milk byproduct, one quart of skim milk, buttermilk, flavored milk drink, or other beverage containing more than 85 percent of skim milk, or one-half pound of cottage, pot, or baker's cheese.

(h) *Quota exclusions and exemptions.* Deliveries of milk, milk byproducts, or cream (1) to other handlers, except for such deliveries to sub-handlers, (2) to plants engaged in the handling or processing of milk, milk byproducts, or cream from which no milk, milk byproducts, or cream is delivered in the sales area, and (3) to the agencies or groups specified in (d) of the order, shall be excluded from the computation of deliveries in the base period and exempt from charges to quotas.

(i) *Transfers and apportionment of quotas.* The market agent is empowered to deduct an amount of base period deliveries to purchasers from the total of deliveries made by a handler or other person in the base period upon the application and a showing of unreasonable hardship by the handler making deliveries to such purchasers on the effective date of this order, and to add the amount of such deliveries to the total base period deliveries of the applicant handler. Denials of transfers or transfers granted by the market agent shall be reviewed by the Director upon application.

(j) *Petition for relief from hardships.* (1) Any person affected by the order or the provisions hereof who considers that compliance therewith would work an exceptional and unreasonable hardship on him, may file with the market agent a petition addressed to the Director. The petition shall contain the correct name, address and principal place of business of the petitioner, a full statement of the facts upon which the petition is based, and the hardship involved and the nature of the relief desired.

(2) Upon receiving such petition, the market agent shall immediately investigate the representations and facts stated therein.

(3) After investigation, the petition shall be certified to the Director, but prior to certification the market agent may (i) deny the petition; or (ii) grant temporary relief for a total period not to exceed 60 days.

(4) Denials or grants of relief by the market agent shall be reviewed by the Director and may be affirmed, modified, or reversed by the Director.

(k) *Reports.* Each handler shall transmit to the market agent on forms prescribed by the market agent the following reports:

(1) Within 20 days following the effective date of this order, reports which show the information required by the market agent to establish such handlers' quotas;

(2) Within 20 days following the close of each quota period, the information required by the market agent to establish volumes of deliveries of milk, cream, and milk byproducts during the preceding quota period; and

(3) Handlers exempt from quotas pursuant to (f) hereof shall, upon the request of the market agent, submit the information required by the market

agent to establish volumes of deliveries of milk, cream, and milk byproducts.

(l) *Records.* Handlers shall keep and shall make available to the market agent such records of receipts, sales, deliveries, and production as the market agent shall require for the purpose of obtaining information which the Director may require for the establishment of quotas as prescribed in (b) of the order.

(m) *Distribution schedules.* The distribution schedules, if any, to be followed by the handlers in making deliveries shall be made effective in the terms of approval by the Director of such schedules.

(n) *Expense of administration.* Each handler shall pay to the market agent, within 20 days after the close of each calendar month an assessment of $0.01 per hundredweight of each of milk, cream, skim milk, buttermilk, flavored milk drinks, beverages containing more than 85 percent of skim milk, and skim milk equivalent of cottage, pot, or baker's cheese delivered during the preceding quota period and subject to quota regulations under the provisions hereof.

(o) *Violations.* The market agent shall report all violations to the Director together with the information required for the prosecution of such violations, except in a case where a handler has made deliveries in a quota period in excess of a quota in an amount not to exceed 5 percent of such quota, and in the succeeding quota period makes deliveries below that quota by at least the same percent.

(p) *Bureau of the Budget approval.* The record-keeping and reporting requirements of this order have been approved by the Bureau of the Budget in accordance with the Federal Reports Act of 1942. Subsequent record-keeping or reporting requirements will be subject to the approval of the Bureau of the Budget pursuant to the Federal Reports Act of 1942.

(q) This order shall take effect at 12:01 a. m., e. w. t., October 5, 1943.

Issued this 1st day of October 1943.

ROY F. HENDRICKSON,
Director of Food Distribution.

Press Release Immediate:
Saturday, October 2, 1943.

Eleven additional metropolitan areas will be brought under the Food Distribution Administration's fluid milk conservation and control program beginning October 5, the War Food Administration said today.

The new milk sales areas, and the market agents who will administer the program in each, are:

St. Joseph County, Ind.: M. E. Drake, 116 S. William St., South Bend, Ind.

Akron, Ohio; Huntington, W. Va.-Ashland, Ky.; Hamilton-Middletown, Ohio; Columbus, Ohio; Youngstown, Ohio: Fred Issler, 152 E. Fourth St., Cincinnati, Ohio.

Davenport, Ia.-Rock Island, Ill.-Moline, Ill.; Howard E. Eisaman, 335 Federal Building, Rock Island, Ill.

Fort Wayne, Ind.: William J. Cline, 707 Citizens Trust Building, Fort Wayne, Ind.

Wichita, Kans.; Greater Kansas City (Mo.-Kan.): M. M. Morehouse, 512 Porter Building, 406 W. 34th St., Kansas City, Mo.

Duluth, Minn.-Superior, Wis.: O. F. Kirkendall, 2002-4 W. Superior St., Duluth, Minn.

Dealers' monthly fluid milk sales in these areas may not exceed their June deliveries, and their sales of cream and of fluid milk byproducts, (such as cottage cheese, chocolate milk and buttermilk) will be reduced to three-fourths of the quantities sold in June. Milk dealers include all persons or firms engaged in the sale or transfer of milk, but not retail stores, hotels, restaurants, etc.

Producer-distributors who purchase no milk (except those whose volume of sales is small enough to make them quota-exempt) will be allowed to sell an amount of fluid milk, cream and fluid milk byproducts equal to 100 percent of their total milk production in June. Quota-exempt producer distributors are defined separately for each area, but in general they are those whose deliveries are relatively small.

Consumers in these areas generally will be able to purchase as much milk under the milk conservation program as they have been buying—an amount considerably greater than that bought in pre-war years, and about 10 percent above last year's purchases. Sales quotas on cream and on fluid milk byproducts have been set below June deliveries to boost fluid milk supplies where milk production is low, and to conserve milk for manufacturing purposes in other areas.

Fluid milk sales are being stabilized in these and other metropolitan areas, FDA officials explained, to help assure sufficient milk for manufacturing the cheese, butter, evaporated milk and milk powder required by the armed services and civilians for good nutrition and properly balanced diets.

Largely due to expanded consumer demand, sales of fluid milk have been increasing steadily and are now about 20 percent higher than in pre-war years (1936–40) and 10 to 12 percent above those in 1942. With total milk production levelled off, and even declining somewhat, this expanding volume of milk sold for fluid uses has inevitably reduced the supply of 'manufacturing milk," and, consequently, the production of cheese, butter and other dairy foods.

The FDA's dealer-quota plan is an attempt to stabilize fluid milk consumption without resorting to individual consumer rationing. Point rationing of milk, a bulky and highly perishable commodity, would be very difficult to administer and would almost necessarily reduce fluid milk sales in many areas. If consumers and the trade cooperate with the present program to assure that sales are held within quotas and quantities available are distributed fairly, FDA officials believe consumer rationing will not be necessary.

Milk handlers in the sales areas named today, except Greater Kansas City and Wichita, Kansas, will compute the quantity of milk which they may sell each month in terms of pounds of milk, their cream sales in terms of pounds of cream and butterfat, and their milk products sales in terms of pounds of milk by-products. In Greater Kansas City and Wichita, milk handlers will determine their fluid milk quotas in terms of pounds of milk and butterfat.

Deliveries to the armed forces, to plants processing dairy products, and to other handlers (except special classes of handlers such as peddlers) are quota exempt.

To facilitate administration, the market agent for each milk sales area may act upon petitions for relief from hardship which may be submitted to him, and after investigation, he may grant temporary relief for a total period not to exceed 60 days.

Milk sales in 13 eastern and midwestern areas, previously were brought under federal regulation. Sales quotas in these initial milk sales areas are the same as for those named today.

WAR FOOD ADMINISTRATION

[FDO 79-20, Amdt. 1]

PART 1401—DAIRY PRODUCTS

FLUID MILK AND CREAM IN DAVENPORT-ROCK ISLAND-MOLINE, SALES AREA

Pursuant to Food Distribution Order No. 79 (8 F.R. 12426), dated September 7, 1943, as amended, and to effectuate the purposes thereof, Food Distribution Order No. 79-20 (8 F.R. 13431), relative to the conservation and distribution of fluid milk, milk byproducts, and cream in the Davenport-Rock Island-Moline milk sales area, issued by the Director of Food Distribution on October 1, 1943, is hereby amended by deleting therefrom the provisions in § 1401.52 (h) and inserting, in lieu thereof, the following:

(h) *Quota exclusions and exemptions.* Deliveries of milk, milk byproducts, or cream (1) to other handlers, except for such deliveries to sub-handlers, (2) to plants engaged in the handling or processing of milk, milk byproducts, or cream from which no milk, milk byproducts, or cream is delivered in the sales area, (3) to nursery, elementary, junior high, and high schools, and (4) to the agencies or groups specified in (d) of the order shall be excluded from the computation of deliveries in the base period and exempt from charges to quotas.

The provisions of this amendment shall become effective at 12:01 a. m., e. w. t., April 1, 1944. With respect to violations of said Food Distribution Order No. 79-20, rights accrued, or liabilities incurred prior to the effective time of this amendment, said Food Distribution Order No. 79-20, shall be deemed to be in full force and effect for the purpose of sustaining any proper suit, action, or other proceeding with respect to any such violation, right, or liability.

(E.O. 9280, 7 F.R. 10179; E.O. 9322, 8 F.R. 3807; E.O. 9334, 8 F.R. 5423; E.O. 9392, 8 F.R. 14783; FDO 79, 8 F.R. 12426, 13283)

Issued this 29th day of March 1944.

LEE MARSHALL,
Director of Distribution.

FDO 79-21

OCTOBER 1, 1943

WAR FOOD ADMINISTRATION

[FDO 79-21]

PART 1401—DAIRY PRODUCTS

CONSERVATION AND DISTRIBUTION OF FLUID MILK AND CREAM IN THE ST. JOSEPH COUNTY, IND., SALES AREA

Pursuant to the authority vested in me by Food Distribution Order No. 79 (8 F.R. 12426), issued on September 7, 1943, as amended, and to effectuate the purposes of such order, it is hereby ordered as follows:

§ 1401.48 *Quota restrictions*—(a) *Definitions.* When used in this order, unless otherwise distinctly expressed or manifestly incompatible with the intent hereof.

(1) Each term defined in Food Distribution Order No. 79, as amended, shall, when used herein, have the same meaning as is set forth for such term in Food Distribution Order No. 79, as amended.

(2) The term "order" means Food Distribution Order No. 79, issued on September 7, 1943, as amended.

(3) The term "sub-handler" means any handler, such as a peddler, vendor, sub-dealer, or secondary dealer, who purchases in a previously packaged and processed form milk, milk byproducts, or cream for delivery.

(b) *Milk sales area.* The following area is hereby designated as a "milk sales area" to be known as the St. Joseph County, Ind., sales area, and is referred to hereinafter as the "sales area": All municipal corporations and unincorporated territory within the geographical limits of St. Joseph County, Ind., excepting the townships of Olive, Liberty, and Lincoln.

(c) *Base period.* The calendar month of June 1943 is hereby designated as the base period for the sales area.

(d) *Quota period.* The remainder of the calendar month in which the provisions hereof become effective and each subsequent calendar month, respectively, is hereby designated as a quota period for the sales area.

(e) *Handler quotas.* Quotas for each handler in the sales area in each quota period shall be determined as follows:

(1) Divide the total deliveries of each of milk, milk byproducts, and cream (and of butterfat in milk or in cream where percentages of pounds of butterfat are specified in (e) (3) (i) or (e) (3) (ii) hereof) made in the sales area by such handler during the base period, after excluding the quota-exempt deliveries described in (h) and adjusting such deliveries for the transfers set out in (i) hereof, by the number of days in the base period;

(2) Multiply the result of the foregoing calculation by the number of days in the quota period; and

(3) Multiply the aforesaid resulting amount by the following applicable percentage: (i) Milk: 100 percent of pounds of milk and ---- percent of pounds of butterfat; (ii) Cream: 75 percent of pounds of cream and 75 percent of pounds of butterfat; and (iii) Milk byproducts: 75 percent of pounds of milk byproducts other than cottage, pot, or baker's cheese and of the pounds of skim milk equivalent of cottage, pot, or baker's cheese. (For the purpose of this order, one pound of cottage, pot, or baker's cheese shall be considered as the equivalent of 7 pounds of skim milk.)

(f) *Quotas for handlers who are also producers.* Quotas for handlers who are also producers and who purchase no milk shall be 100 percent of the total production of such handlers in the base period.

(g) *Handler exemptions.* Quotas shall not apply to any handler who delivers in a quota period a daily average of less than 100 units of milk, cream, and milk byproducts. For the purpose of this order, a unit shall be the equivalent in volume of the following:

(1) Milk, one quart of milk;

(2) Cream, one-half pint of cream; and

(3) Milk byproducts, one quart of skim milk, buttermilk, flavored milk drink, or other beverage containing more than 85 percent of skim milk, or one-half pound of cottage, pot, or baker's cheese.

(h) *Quota exclusions and exemptions.* Deliveries of milk, milk byproducts, or cream (1) to other handlers, except for such deliveries to sub-handlers, (2) to plants engaged in the handling or processing of milk, milk byproducts, or cream from which no milk, milk byproducts, or cream is delivered in the sales area, and (3) to the agencies or groups specified in (d) of the order, shall be excluded from the computation of deliveries in the base period and exempt from charges to quotas.

(i) *Transfers and apportionment of quotas.* The market agent is empowered to deduct an amount of base period deliveries to purchasers from the total of deliveries made by a handler or other person in the base period upon the application and a showing of unreasonable hardship by the handler making deliveries to such purchasers on the effective date of this order, and to add the amount of such deliveries to the total base period deliveries of the applicant handler. Denials of transfers or transfers granted by the market agent shall be reviewed by the Director upon application.

(j) *Petition for relief from hardships.* (1) Any person affected by the order or the provisions hereof who considers that compliance therewith would work an exceptional and unreasonable hardship on him, may file with the market agent a petition addressed to the Director. The petition shall contain the correct name, address, and principal place of business of the petitioner, a full statement of the facts upon which the petition is based, and the hardship involved and the nature of the relief desired.

(2) Upon receiving such petition, the market agent shall immediately investigate the representations and facts stated therein.

(3) After investigation, the petition shall be certified to the Director, but prior to certification the market agent may (i) deny the petition; or (ii) grant temporary relief for a total period not to exceed 60 days.

(4) Denials or grants of relief by the market agent shall be reviewed by the Director and may be affirmed, modified, or reversed by the Director.

(k) *Reports.* Each handler shall transmit to the market agent on forms prescribed by the market agent the following reports:

(1) Within 20 days following the effective date of this order, reports which show the information required by the market agent to establish such handlers' quotas;

(2) Within 20 days following the close of each quota period, the information required by the market agent to establish volumes of deliveries of milk, cream, and milk byproducts during the preceding quota period; and

(3) Handlers exempt from quotas pursuant to (f) hereof shall, upon the request of the market agent, submit the information required by the market agent to establish volumes of deliveries of milk, cream, and milk byproducts.

(l) *Records.* Handlers shall keep and shall make available to the market agent such records of receipts, sales, deliveries, and production as the market agent shall require for the purpose of obtaining information which the Director may re-

quire for the establishment of quotas as prescribed in (b) of the order.

(m) *Distribution schedules.* The distribution schedules, if any, to be followed by the handlers in making deliveries shall be made effective in the terms of approval by the Director of such schedules.

(n) *Expense of administration.* Each handler shall pay to the market agent within 20 days after the close of each calendar month an assessment of $0.01 per hundredweight of each of milk, cream, skim milk, buttermilk, flavored milk drinks, beverages containing more than 85 percent of skim milk, and skim milk equivalent of cottage, pot, or baker's cheese delivered during the preceding quota period and subject to quota regulations under the provisions hereof.

(o) *Violations.* The market agent shall report all violations to the Director together with the information required for the prosecution of such violations, except in a case where a handler has made deliveries in a quota period in excess of a quota in an amount not to exceed 5 percent of such quota, and in the succeeding quota period makes deliveries below that quota by at least the same percent.

(p) *Bureau of the Budget approval.* The record-keeping and reporting requirements of this order have been approved by the Bureau of the Budget in accordance with the Federal Reports Act of 1942. Subsequent record-keeping or reporting requirements will be subject to the approval of the Bureau of the Budget pursuant to the Federal Reports Act of 1942.

(q) This order shall take effect at 12:01 a. m., e. w. t., October 5, 1943.

Issued this 1st day of October 1943.

ROY F. HENDRICKSON,
Director of Food Distribution.

Press Release Immediate:
Saturday, October 2, 1943.

Eleven additional metropolitan areas will be brought under the Food Distribution Administration's fluid milk conservation and control program beginning October 5, the War Food Administration said today.

The new milk sales areas, and the market agents who will administer the program in each, are:

St. Joseph County, Ind.: M. E. Drake, 116 S. William St., South Bend, Ind.

Akron, Ohio; Huntington, W. Va.-Ashland, Ky.; Hamilton-Middletown, Ohio; Columbus, Ohio; Youngstown, Ohio: Fred Issler, 152 E. Fourth St., Cincinnati, Ohio.

Davenport, Ia.-Rock Island, Ill.-Moline, Ill.; Howard E. Eisaman, 335 Federal Building, Rock Island, Ill.

Fort Wayne, Ind.: William J. Cline, 707 Citizens Trust Building, Fort Wayne, Ind.

Wichita, Kans; Greater Kansas City, (Mo.-Kan.): M. M. Morehouse, 512 Porter Building, 406 W. 34th St., Kansas City, Mo.

Duluth, Minn.-Superior, Wis.: O. F. Kirkendall, 2002-4 W. Superior St., Duluth, Minn.

Dealers' monthly fluid milk sales in these areas may not exceed their June deliveries, and their sales of cream and of fluid milk byproducts, (such as cottage cheese, chocolate milk and buttermilk) will be reduced to three-fourths of the quantities sold in June. Milk dealers include all persons or firms engaged in the sale or transfer of milk, but not retail stores, hotels, restaurants, etc.

Producer-distributors who purchase no milk (except those whose volume of sales is small enough to make them quota-exempt) will be allowed to sell an amount of fluid milk, cream and fluid milk byproducts equal to 100 percent of their total milk production in June. Quota-exempt producer-distributors are defined separately for each area, but in general they are those whose deliveries are relatively small.

Consumers in these areas generally will be able to purchase as much milk under the milk conservation program as they have been buying—an amount considerably greater than that bought in pre-war years, and about 10 percent above last year's purchases. Sales quotas on cream and on fluid milk byproducts have been set below June deliveries to boost fluid milk supplies where milk production is low, and to conserve milk for manufacturing purposes in other areas.

Fluid milk sales are being stabilized in these and other metropolitan areas, FDA officials explained, to help assure sufficient milk for manufacturing the cheese, butter, evaporated milk and milk powder required by the armed services and civilians for good nutrition and properly balanced diets.

Largely due to expanded consumer demand, sales of fluid milk have been increasing steadily and are now about 20 percent higher than in pre-war years (1936-40) and 10 to 12 percent above those in 1942. With total milk production levelled off, and even declining somewhat, this expanding volume of milk sold for fluid uses has inevitably reduced the supply of "manufacturing milk," and, consequently, the production of cheese, butter and other dairy foods.

The FDA's dealer-quota plan is an attempt to stabilize fluid milk consumption without resorting to individual consumer rationing. Point rationing of milk, a bulky and highly perishable commodity, would be very difficult to administer and would almost necessarily reduce fluid milk sales in many areas. If consumers and the trade cooperate with the present program to assure that sales are held within quotas and quantities available are distributed fairly, FDA officials believe consumer rationing will not be necessary.

Milk handlers in the sales areas named today, except Greater Kansas City and Wichita, Kansas, will compute the quantity of milk which they may sell each month in terms of pounds of milk, their cream sales in terms of pounds of cream and butterfat, and their milk products sales in terms of pounds of milk byproducts. In Greater Kansas City and Wichita, milk handlers will determine their fluid milk quotas in terms of pounds of milk and butterfat.

Deliveries to the armed forces, to plants processing dairy products, and to other handlers (except special classes of handlers such as peddlers) are quota-exempt.

To facilitate administration, the market agent for each milk sales area may act upon petitions for relief from hardship which may be submitted to him, and after investigation, he may grant temporary relief for a total period not to exceed 60 days.

Milk sales in 13 eastern and midwestern areas previously were brought under federal regulation. Sales quotas in these initial milk sales areas are the same as for those named today.

FDO 79-22

OCT. 1, 1943

WAR FOOD ADMINISTRATION

(1) Divide the total deliveries of each of milk, milk byproducts, and cream (and of butterfat in milk or in cream where percentages of pounds of butterfat are specified in (e) (3) (i) or (e) (3) (ii) hereof) made in the sales area by such handler during the base period, after excluding the quota-exempt deliveries described in (h) hereof and adjusting such deliveries for the transfers set out in (i) hereof, by the number of days in the base period;

(2) Multiply the result of the foregoing calculation by the number of days in the quota period; and

(3) Multiply the aforesaid resulting amount by the following applicable percentage: (i) Milk: 100 percent of pounds of milk and ______ percent of pounds of butterfat; (ii) Cream: 75 percent of pounds of cream and 75 percent of pounds of butterfat; and (iii) Milk byproducts: 75 percent of pounds of milk byproducts other than cottage, pot, or baker's cheese and of the pounds of skim milk equivalent of cottage, pot, or baker's cheese. (For the purpose of this order, one pound of cottage, pot, or baker's cheese shall be considered as the equivalent of 7 pounds of skim milk.)

(f) *Quotas for handlers who are also producers.* Quotas for handlers who are also producers and who purchase no milk shall be 100 percent of the total production of such handlers in the base period.

(g) *Handler exemptions.* Quotas shall not apply to any handler who delivers in a quota period a daily average of less than 125 units of milk, cream, and milk byproducts. For the purpose of this order, a unit shall be the equivalent in volume of the following:

(1) Milk, one quart of milk;

(2) Cream, one-half pint of cream; and

(3) Milk byproducts, one quart of skim milk, buttermilk, flavored milk drink, or other beverage containing more than 85 percent of skim milk, or one-half pound of cottage, pot, or baker's cheese.

(h) *Quota exclusions and exemptions.* Deliveries of milk, milk byproducts, or cream (1) to other handlers, except for such deliveries to sub-handlers, (2) to plants engaged in the handling or processing of milk, milk byproducts, or cream from which no milk, milk byproducts, or cream is delivered in the sales area, and (3) to the agencies or groups specified in (d) of the order, shall be excluded from the competition of deliveries in the base period and exempt from charges to quotas.

(i) *Transfers and apportionment of quotas.* The market agent is empowered to deduct an amount of base period deliveries to purchasers from the total of deliveries made by a handler or other person in the base period upon the application and a showing of unreasonable hardship by the handler making deliveries to such purchasers on the effective date of this order, and to add the amount of such deliveries to the total base period deliveries of the applicant handler. Denials of transfers or transfers granted by the market agent shall be reviewed by the Director upon application.

(j) *Petition for relief from hardships.* (1) Any person affected by the order or the provisions hereof who considers that compliance therewith would work an exceptional and unreasonable hardship on him, may file with the market agent a petition addressed to the Director. The petition shall contain the correct name, address and principal place of business of the petitioner, a full statement of the facts upon which the petition is based, and the hardship involved and the nature of the relief desired.

(2) Upon receiving such petition, the market agent shall immediately investigate the representations and facts stated therein.

(3) After investigation, the petition shall be certified to the Director, but prior to certification the market agent may (i) deny the petition; or (ii) grant temporary relief for a total period not to exceed 60 days.

(4) Denials or grants of relief by the market agent shall be reviewed by the Director and may be affirmed, modified. or reversed by the Director.

(k) *Reports.* Each handler shall transmit to the market agent on forms prescribed by the market agent the following reports:

(1) Within 20 days following the effective date of this order, reports which show the information required by the market agent to establish such handlers' quotas;

(2) Within 20 days following the close of each quota period, the information required by the market agent to establish volumes of deliveries of milk, cream, and milk byproducts during the preceding quota period; and

(3) Handlers exempt from quotas pursuant to (f) hereof shall, upon the request of the market agent, submit the information required by the market agent to establish volumes of deliveries of milk, cream, and milk byproducts.

(l) *Records.* Handlers shall keep and shall make available to the market agent such records of receipts, sales, deliveries, and production as the market agent shall require for the purpose of obtaining information which the Director may require for the establishment of quotas as prescribed in (b) of the order.

(m) *Distribution schedules.* The distribution schedules, if any, to be followed by the handlers in making deliveries shall be made effective in the terms of approval by the Director of such schedules.

(n) *Expense of administration.* Each handler shall pay to the market agent, within 20 days after the close of each calendar month an assessment of $0.01 per hundredweight of each of milk, cream, skim milk, buttermilk, flavored milk drinks, beverages containing more than 85 percent of skim milk, and skim milk equivalent of cottage, pot, or baker's cheese delivered during the preceding quota period and subject to quota regulations under the provisions hereof.

(o) *Violations.* The market agent shall report all violations to the Director together with the information required for the prosecution of such violations, except in a case where a handler has made deliveries in a quota period in excess of a quota in an amount not to exceed 5 percent of such quota, and in the succeeding quota period makes deliveries below that quota by at least the same percent.

(p) *Bureau of the Budget approval.* The record-keeping and reporting requirements of this order have been approved by the Bureau of the Budget in accordance with the Federal Reports Act of 1942. Subsequent record-keeping or reporting requirements will be subject to the approval of the Bureau of the Budget pursuant to the Federal Reports Act of 1942.

(q) This order shall take effect at 12:01 a. m., e. w. t., October 5, 1943.

Issued this 1st day of October 1943.

ROY F. HENDRICKSON,
Director of Food Distribution.

Press Release, Immediate:
Saturday, October 2, 1943.

Eleven additional metropolitan areas will be brought under the Food Distribution Administration's fluid milk conservation and control program beginning October 5, the War Food Administration said today.

The new milk sales areas, and the market agents who will administer the program in each, are:

St. Joseph County, Ind.: M. E. Drake, 116 S. William St., South Bend, Ind.

Akron, Ohio, Huntington, W. Va.-Ashland, Ky., Hamilton-Middletown, Ohio, Columbus, Ohio, Youngstown, Ohio: Fred Issler, 152 E. Fourth St., Cincinnati, Ohio.

Davenport, Ia.-Rock Island, Ill.-Moline, Ill.: Howard E. Eisaman, 335 Federal Building, Rock Island, Ill.

Fort Wayne, Ind.: William J. Cline, 707 Citizens Trust Building, Fort Wayne, Ind.

Wichita, Kans., Greater Kansas City (Mo.-Kan.): M. M. Morehouse, 512 Porter Building, 406 W. 34th St., Kansas City, Mo.

Duluth, Minn.-Superior, Wis.: O. F. Kirkendall, 2002-4 W. Superior St., Duluth, Minn.

Dealers' monthly fluid milk sales in these areas may not exceed their June deliveries, and their sales of cream and of fluid milk byproducts (such as cottage cheese, chocolate milk and buttermilk) will be reduced to three-fourths of the quantities sold in June. Milk dealers include all persons or firms engaged in the sale or transfer of milk, but not retail stores, hotels, restaurants, etc.

Producer-distributors who purchase no milk (except those whose volume of sales is small enough to make them quota-exempt) will be allowed to sell an amount of fluid milk, cream and fluid milk byproducts equal to 100 percent of their total milk production in June. Quota-exempt producer distributors are defined separately for each area, but in general they are those whose deliveries are relatively small.

Consumers in these areas generally will be able to purchase as much milk under the milk conservation program as they have been buying—an amount considerably greater than that bought in pre-war years, and about 10 percent above last year's purchases. Sales quotas on cream and on fluid milk byproducts have been set below June deliveries to boost fluid milk supplies where milk production is low, and to conserve milk for manufacturing purposes in other areas.

Fluid milk sales are being stabilized in these and other metropolitan areas, FDA officials explained, to help assure sufficient milk for manufacturing the cheese, butter, evaporated milk and milk powder required by the armed services and civilians for good nutrition and properly balanced diets.

Largely due to expanded consumer demand, sales of fluid milk have been increasing steadily and are now about 20 percent higher than in pre-war years (1936-40) and 10 to 12 percent above those in 1942. With total milk production levelled off, and even declining somewhat, this expanding volume of milk sold for fluid uses has inevitably reduced the supply of "manufacturing milk," and, consequently, the production of cheese, butter and other dairy foods.

The FDA's dealer-quota plan is an attempt to stabilize fluid milk consumption without resorting to individual consumer rationing. Point rationing of milk, a bulky and highly perishable commodity, would be very difficult to administer and would almost necessarily reduce fluid milk sales in many areas. If consumers and the trade cooperate with the present program to assure that sales are held within quotas and quantities available are distributed fairly, FDA officials believe consumer rationing will not be necessary.

Milk handlers in the sales areas named today, except Greater Kansas City and Wichita, Kansas, will compute the quantity of milk which they may sell each month in terms of pounds of milk, their cream sales in terms of pounds of cream and butterfat, and their milk products sales in terms of pounds of milk byproducts. In Greater Kansas City and Wichita, milk handlers will determine their fluid milk quotas in terms of pounds of milk and butterfat.

Deliveries to the Armed Forces, to plants processing dairy products, and to other handlers (except special classes of handlers such as peddlers) are quota exempt.

To facilitate administration, the market agent for each milk sales area may act upon petitions for relief from hardship which may be submitted to him, and after investigation, he may grant temporary relief for a total period not to exceed 60 days.

Milk sales in 13 eastern and midwestern areas previously were brought under federal regulation. Sales quotas in these initial milk sales areas are the same as for those named today.

FDO 79-22
AMDT. 1
OCTOBER 28, 1943

WAR FOOD ADMINISTRATION

[FDO 79-22, Amdt. 1]

PART 1401—DAIRY PRODUCTS

DULUTH-SUPERIOR, WIS., MILK SALES AREA

Pursuant to the authority vested in the Director by Food Distribution Order No. 79, dated September 7, 1943 (8 F.R. 12426), as amended, and to effectuate the purposes thereof, Director Food Distribution Order No. 79-22, § 1401.58, relative to the conservation of fluid milk in the Duluth-Superior milk sales area (8 F.R. 13433), issued by the Director of Food Distribution on October 1, 1943, is amended as follows:

§ 1401.58 *Quota restrictions*—(a) *Milk sales area.* The milk sales area described in § 1401.58 (b) of the original order is modified in the following particulars:

Substitute "Thomson Township" for "Thompson Township" in Carlton County, Minnesota.

Effective date. This amendment of FDO No. 79-22, shall become effective at 12:01 a. m., e. w. t., November 1, 1943.

(E.O. 9280, 8 F.R. 10179; E.O. 9322, 8 F.R. 3807; E.O. 9334, 8 F.R. 5423; FDO 79, 8 F.R. 12426, 13283)

Issued this 28th day of October 1943.

ROY F. HENDRICKSON,
Director of Food Distribution.

WAR FOOD ADMINISTRATION

[FDO 79-23]

PART 1401—DAIRY PRODUCTS

CONSERVATION AND DISTRIBUTION OF FLUID MILK AND CREAM IN THE HAMILTON-MIDDLETOWN, OHIO, SALES AREA

Pursuant to the authority vested in me by Food Distribution Order No. 79 (8 F.R. 12426), issued on September 7, 1943, as amended, and to effectuate the purposes of such order, it is hereby ordered as follows:

§ 1401.51 *Quota restrictions*—(a) *Definitions.* When used in this order, unless otherwise distinctly expressed or manifestly incompatible with the intent hereof:

(1) Each term defined in Food Distribution Order No. 79, as amended, shall, when used herein, have the same meaning as is set forth for such term in Food Distribution Order No. 79, as amended.

(2) The term "order" means Food Distribution Order No. 79, issued on September 7, 1943, as amended.

(3) The term "sub-handler" means any handler, such as a peddler, vendor, sub-dealer, or secondary dealer, who purchases in a previously packaged and processed form milk, milk byproducts, or cream for delivery.

(b) *Milk sales area.* The following area is hereby designated as a "milk sales area" to be known as the Hamilton-Middletown, Ohio, sales area, and is referred to hereinafter as the "sales area". The cities of Hamilton and Middletown and the townships of Fairfield, Hanover, Lemon, Madison, St. Clair, that part of Ross township comprising part of Millville village, and that part of Wayne township comprising part of Seven Mile village, in Butler County; and the township of Franklin in Warren County, all in the State of Ohio.

(c) *Base period.* The calendar month of June 1943 is hereby designated as the base period for the sales area.

(d) *Quota period.* The remainder of the calendar month in which the provisions hereof become effective and each subsequent calendar month, respectively, is hereby designated as a quota period for the sales area.

(e) *Handler quotas.* Quotas for each handler in the sales area in each quota period shall be determined as follows:

(1) Divide the total deliveries of each of milk, milk byproducts, and cream (and of butterfat in milk or in cream where percentages of pounds of butterfat are specified in (e) (3) (i) or (e) (3) (ii) hereof) made in the sales area by such handler during the base period, after excluding the quota-exempt deliveries described in (h) hereof and adjusting such deliveries for the transfers set out in (i) hereof, by the number of days in the base period;

(2) Multiply the result of the foregoing calculation by the number of days in the quota period; and

(3) Multiply the aforesaid resulting amount by the following applicable percentage: (i) Milk: 100 percent of pounds of milk and ______ percent of pounds of butterfat; (ii) Cream: 75 percent of pounds of cream and 75 percent of pounds of butterfat; and (iii) Milk byproducts: 75 percent of pounds of milk byproducts other than cottage, pot, or baker's cheese and of the pounds of skim milk equivalent of cottage, pot, or baker's cheese. (For the purpose of this order, one pound of cottage, pot, or baker's cheese shall be considered as the equivalent of 7 pounds of skim milk.)

(f) *Quotas for handlers who are also producers.* Quotas for handlers who are also producers and who purchase no milk shall be 100 percent of the total production of such handlers in the base period.

(g) *Handler exemptions.* Quotas shall not apply to any handler who delivers in a quota period a daily average of less than 150 units of milk, cream, and milk byproducts. For the purpose of this order, a unit shall be the equivalent in volume of the following:

(1) Milk, one quart of milk;

(2) Cream, one-half pint of cream; and

(3) Milk byproduct, one quart of skim milk, buttermilk, flavored milk drink, or other beverage containing more than 85 percent of skim milk, or one-half pound of cottage, pot, or baker's cheese.

(h) *Quota exclusions and exemptions.* Deliveries of milk, milk byproducts, or cream (1) to other handlers, except for such deliveries to sub-handlers, (2) to plants engaged in the handling or processing of milk, milk byproducts, or cream from which no milk, milk byproducts, or cream is delivered in the sales area, and (3) to the agencies or groups specified in (d) of the order, shall be excluded from the computation of deliveries in the base period and exempt from charges to quotas.

(i) *Transfers and apportionment of quotas.* The market agent is empowered to deduct an amount of base period deliveries to purchasers from the total of deliveries made by a handler or other person in the base period upon the application and a showing of unreasonable hardship by the handler making deliveries to such purchasers on the effective date of this order, and to add the amount of such deliveries to the total base period deliveries of the applicant handler. Denials of transfers or transfers granted by the market agent shall be reviewed by the Director upon application.

(j) *Petition for relief from hardships.* (1) Any person affected by the order or the provisions hereof who considers that compliance therewith would work an exceptional and unreasonable hardship on him, may file with the market agent a petition addressed to the Director. The petition shall contain the correct name, address and principal place of business of the petitioner, a full statement of the facts upon which the petition is based, and the hardship involved and the nature of the relief desired.

(2) Upon receiving such petition, the market agent shall immediately investigate the representations and facts stated therein.

(3) After investigation, the petition shall be certified to the Director, but prior to certification the market agent may (i) deny the petition; or (ii) grant temporary relief for a total period not to exceed 60 days.

(4) Denials or grants of relief by the market agent shall be reviewed by the Director and may be affirmed, modified, or reversed by the Director.

(k) *Reports.* Each handler shall transmit to the market agent on forms prescribed by the market agent the following reports:

(1) Within 20 days following the effective date of this order, reports which show the information required by the market agent to establish such handlers' quotas;

(2) Within 20 days following the close of each quota period, the information required by the market agent to establish volumes of deliveries of milk, cream, and milk byproducts during the preceding quota period; and

(3) Handlers exempt from quotas pursuant to (f) hereof shall, upon the request of the market agent, submit the

information required by the market agent to establish volumes of deliveries of milk, cream, and milk byproducts.

(l) *Records.* Handlers shall keep and shall make available to the market agent such records of receipts, sales, deliveries, and production as the market agent shall require for the purpose of obtaining information which the Director may require for the establishment of quotas as prescribed in (b) of the order.

(m) *Distribution schedules.* The distribution schedules, if any, to be followed by the handlers in making deliveries shall be made effective in the terms of approval by the Director of such schedules.

(n) *Expense of administration.* Each handler shall pay to the market agent, within 20 days after the close of each calendar month an assessment of $.01 per hundredweight of each of milk, cream, skim milk, buttermilk, flavored milk drinks, beverages containing more than 85 percent of skim milk, and skim milk equivalent of cottage, pot, or baker's cheese delivered during the preceding quota period and subject to quota regulations under the provisions hereof.

(o) *Violations.* The market agent shall report all violations to the Director together with the information required for the prosecution of such violations, except in a case where a handler has made deliveries in a quota period in excess of a quota in an amount not to exceed 5 percent of such quota, and in the succeeding quota period makes deliveries below that quota by at least the same percent.

(p) *Bureau of the Budget approval.* The record-keeping and reporting requirements of this order have been approved by the Bureau of the Budget in accordance with the Federal Reports Act of 1942. Subsequent record-keeping or reporting requirements will be subject to the approval of the Bureau of the Budget pursuant to the Federal Reports Act of 1942.

(q) This order shall take effect at 12:01 a. m., e. w. t., October 5, 1943.

Issued this 1st day of October 1943.

ROY F. HENDRICKSON,
Director of Food Distribution.

Press Release, Immediate:
Saturday, October 2, 1943.

Eleven additional metropolitan areas will be brought under the Food Distribution Administration's fluid milk conservation and control program beginning October 5, the War Food Administration said today.

The new milk sales areas, and the market agents who will administer the program in each, are:

St. Joseph County, Ind.: M. E. Drake, 116 S. William St., South Bend, Ind.

Akron, Ohio; Huntington, W. Va.-Ashland, Ky.; Hamilton-Middletown, Ohio; Columbus, Ohio; Youngstown, Ohio: Fred Issler, 152 E. Fourth St., Cincinnati, Ohio.

Davenport, Ia.-Rock Island, Ill.-Moline, Ill.: Howard E. Eisaman, 335 Federal Building, Rock Island, Ill.

Fort Wayne, Ind.: William J. Cline, 707 Citizens Trust Building, Fort Wayne, Ind.

Wichita, Kans.: Greater Kansas City (Mo.-Kans.): M. M. Morehouse, 512 Porter Building, 406 W. 34th St., Kansas City, Mo.

Duluth, Minn.-Superior, Wis.: O. F. Kirkendall, 2002-4 W. Superior St., Duluth, Minn.

Dealers' monthly fluid milk sales in these areas may not exceed their June deliveries, and their sales of cream and of fluid milk byproducts (such as cottage cheese, chocolate milk and buttermilk) will be reduced to three-fourths of the quantities sold in June. Milk dealers include all persons or firms engaged in the sale or transfer of milk, but not retail stores, hotels, restaurants, etc.

Producer-distributors who purchase no milk (except those whose volume of sales is small enough to make them quota-exempt) will be allowed to sell an amount of fluid milk, cream and fluid milk byproducts equal to 100 percent of their total milk production in June. Quota-exempt producer distributors are defined separately for each area, but in general they are those whose deliveries are relatively small.

Consumers in these areas generally will be able to purchase as much milk under the milk conservation program as they have been buying—an amount considerably greater than that bought in pre-war years, and about 10 percent above last year's purchases. Sales quotas on cream and on fluid milk byproducts have been set below June deliveries to boost fluid milk supplies where milk production is low, and to conserve milk for manufacturing purposes in other areas.

Fluid milk sales are being stabilized in these and other metropolitan areas, FDA officials explained, to help assure sufficient milk for manufacturing the cheese, butter, evaporated milk and milk powder required by the armed services and civilians for good nutrition and properly balanced diets.

Largely due to expanded consumer demand, sales of fluid milk have been increasing steadily and are now about 20 percent higher than in pre-war years (1936–40) and 10 to 12 percent above those in 1942. With total milk production levelled off, and even declining somewhat, this expanding volume of milk sold for fluid uses has inevitably reduced the supply of "manufacturing milk," and, consequently, the production of cheese, butter and other dairy foods.

The FDA's dealer-quota plan is an attempt to stabilize fluid milk consumption without resorting to individual consumer rationing. Point rationing of milk, a bulky and highly perishable commodity, would be very difficult to administer and would almost necessarily reduce fluid milk sales in many areas. If consumers and the trade cooperate with the present program to assure that sales are held within quotas and quantities available are distributed fairly, FDA officials believe consumer rationing will not be necessary.

Milk handlers in the sales areas named today, except Greater Kansas City and Wichita, Kansas, will compute the quantity of milk which they may sell each month in terms of pounds of milk, their cream sales in terms of pounds of cream and butterfat, and their milk products sales in terms of pounds of milk byproducts. In Greater Kansas City and Wichita, milk handlers will determine their fluid milk quotas in terms of pounds of milk and butterfat.

Deliveries to the Armed Forces, to plants processing dairy products, and to other handlers (except special classes of handlers such as peddlers) are quota exempt.

To facilitate administration, the market agent for each milk sales area may act upon petitions for relief from hardship which may be submitted to him, and after investigation, he may grant temporary relief for a total period not to exceed 60 days.

Milk sales in 13 eastern and midwestern areas previously were brought under federal regulation. Sales quotas in these initial milk sales areas are the same as for those named today.

1/
357

FDO 79-23

AMDT. 1
JAN. 27, 1944

WAR FOOD ADMINISTRATION

[FDO 79-23, Amdt. 1]

PART 1401—DAIRY PRODUCTS

FLUID MILK AND CREAM IN HAMILTON-MIDDLETOWN, OHIO, SALES AREA

Pursuant to Food Distribution Order No. 79 (8 F.R. 12426), dated September 7, 1943, as amended, and to effectuate the purposes thereof, Food Distribution Order No. 79-23 (8 F.R. 13435), relative to the conservation and distribution of fluid milk in the Hamilton-Middletown, Ohio, milk sales area, issued by the Director of Food Distribution on October 1, 1943, is amended as follows:

1. By deleting therefrom the provisions in § 1401.51 (f) and substituting therefor the following:

(f) *Quotas for handlers who are also producers.* Quotas for handlers who are also producers and who purchase no milk shall be computed in accordance with (e) hereof, except that the applicable percentages shall be 100 percent in lieu of the percentages specified in (e) (3).

2. By deleting therefrom the provisions of § 1401.51 (h) and substituting therefor the following:

(h) *Quota exclusions and exemptions.* Deliveries of milk, milk byproducts, or cream (1) to other handlers, except for such deliveries to sub-handlers, (2) to plants engaged in the handling or processing of milk, milk byproducts, or cream from which no milk, milk byproducts, or cream is delivered in the sales area, (3) to nursery, elementary, junior high, and high schools, and (4) to the agencies or groups specified in (d) of the order, shall be excluded from the computation of deliveries in the base period and exempt from charges to quotas.

The provisions of this amendment shall become effective at 12:01 a. m., e. w. t., February 1, 1944. With respect to violations of said Food Distribution Order No. 79-23, rights accrued, or liabilities incurred prior to the effective time of this amendment, said Food Distribution Order No. 79-23 shall be deemed to be in full force and effect for the purpose of sustaining any proper suit, action, or other proceeding with respect to any such violation, right, or liability.

(E.O. 9280, 7 F.R. 10179; E.O. 9322, 8 F.R. 3807; EO. 9334, 8 F.R. 5423; E.O. 9392, 8 F.R. 14783; FDO 79, 8 F.R. 12426, 13283)

Issued this 27th day of January 1944.

LEE MARSHALL,
Director of Food Distribution.

FDO 79-24

OCT. 1, 1943

WAR FOOD ADMINISTRATION

[FDO 79-24]

PART 1401—DAIRY PRODUCTS

CONSERVATION AND DISTRIBUTION OF FLUID MILK AND CREAM IN THE WICHITA, KANSAS, SALES AREA

Pursuant to the authority vested in me by Food Distribution Order No. 79 (8 F.R. 12426), issued on September 7, 1943, as amended, and to effectuate the purposes of such order, it is hereby ordered as follows:

§ 1401.56 *Quota restrictions*—(a) *Definitions.* When used in this order, unless otherwise distinctly expressed or manifestly incompatible with the intent hereof:

(1) Each term defined in Food Distribution Order No. 79, as amended, shall, when used herein, have the same meaning as is set forth for such term in Food Distribution Order No. 79, as amended.

(2) The term "order" means Food Distribution Order No. 79, issued on September 7, 1943, as amended.

(3) The term "sub-handler" means any handler, such as a peddler, vendor, sub-dealer, or secondary dealer, who purchases in a previously packaged and processed form milk, milk byproducts, or cream for delivery.

(b) *Milk sales area.* The following area is hereby designated as a "milk sales area" to be known as the Wichita, Kansas, sales area, and is referred to hereinafter as the "sales area": All the territory within the corporate limits of the city of Wichita, Kansas, and the territory within Delano, Kechi, Riverside, Wichita, and Minneha Townships and the city of Eastborough, all in Sedgwick County, Kansas.

(c) *Base period.* The calendar month of June 1943 is hereby designated as the base period for the sales area.

(d) *Quota period.* The remainder of the calendar month in which the provisions hereof become effective and each subsequent calendar month, respectively, is hereby designated as a quota period for the sales area.

(e) *Handler quotas.* Quotas for each handler in the sales area in each quota period shall be determined as follows:

(1) Divide the total deliveries of each of milk, milk byproducts, and cream (and of butterfat in milk or in cream where percentages of pounds of butterfat are specified in (e) (3) (i) or (e) (3) (ii) hereof) made in the sales area by such handler during the base period, after excluding the quota-exempt deliveries described in (h) hereof and adjusting such deliveries for the transfers set out in (i) hereof, by the number of days in the base period;

(2) Multiply the result of the foregoing calculation by the number of days in the quota period; and

(3) Multiply the aforesaid resulting amount by the following applicable percentage: (i) Milk: 100 percent of pounds of milk and 100 percent of pounds of butterfat; (ii) Cream: 75 percent of pounds of cream and 75 percent of pounds of butterfat; and (iii) Milk byproducts: 75 percent of pounds of milk byproducts other than cottage, pot, or baker's cheese and of the pounds of skim milk equivalent of cottage, pot, or baker's cheese. (For the purpose of this order, one pound of cottage, pot, or baker's cheese shall be considered as the equivalent of 7 pounds of skim milk.)

(f) *Quotas for handlers who are also producers.* Quotas for handlers who are also producers and who purchase no milk shall be 100 percent of the total production of such handlers in the base period.

(g) *Handler exemptions.* Quotas shall not apply to any handler who delivers in a quota period a daily average of less than 350 units of milk, cream, and milk byproducts. For the purpose of this order, a unit shall be the equivalent in volume of the following:

(1) Milk, one quart of milk;

(2) Cream, one-half pint of cream; and

(3) Milk byproduct, one quart of skim milk, buttermilk, flavored milk drink, or other beverage containing more than 85 percent of skim milk, or one-half pound of cottage, pot, or baker's cheese.

(h) *Quota exclusions and exemptions.* Deliveries of milk, milk byproducts, or cream (1) to other handlers, except for such deliveries to sub-handlers, (2) to plants engaged in the handling or processing of milk, milk byproducts, or cream from which no milk, milk byproducts, or cream is delivered in the sales area, and (3) to the agencies or groups specified in (d) of the order, shall be excluded from the computation of deliveries in the base period and exempt from charges to quotas.

(i) *Transfers and apportionment of quotas.* The market agent is empowered to deduct an amount of base period deliveries to purchasers from the total of deliveries made by a handler or other person in the base period upon the application and a showing of unreasonable hardship by the handler making deliveries to such purchasers on the effective date of this order, and to add the amount of such deliveries to the total base period deliveries of the applicant handler. Denials of transfers or transfers granted by the market agent shall be reviewed by the Director upon application.

(j) *Petition for relief from hardships.* (1) Any person affected by the order or the provisions hereof who considers that compliance therewith would work an exceptional and unreasonable hardship on him, may file with the market agent a petition addressed to the Director. The petition shall contain the correct name, address and principal place of business of the petitioner, a full statement of the facts upon which the petition is based, and the hardship involved and the nature of the relief desired.

(2) Upon receiving such petition, the market agent shall immediately investigate the representations and facts stated therein.

(3) After investigation, the petition shall be certified to the Director, but prior to certification the market agent may (i) deny the petition; or (ii) grant temporary relief for a total period not to exceed 60 days.

(4) Denials or grants of relief by the market agent shall be reviewed by the Director and may be affirmed, modified, or reversed by the Director.

(k) *Reports.* Each handler shall transmit to the market agent on forms prescribed by the market agent the following reports:

(1) Within 20 days following the effective date of this order, reports which show the information required by the market agent to establish such handlers' quotas;

(2) Within 20 days following the close of each quota period, the information required by the market agent to establish volumes of deliveries of milk, cream, and milk byproducts during the preceding quota period; and

(3) Handlers exempt from quotas pursuant to (f) hereof shall, upon the request of the market agent, submit the information required by the market agent to establish volumes of deliveries of milk, cream, and milk byproducts.

(l) *Records.* Handlers shall keep and shall make available to the market agent such records of receipts, sales, deliveries, and production as the market agent shall require for the purpose of obtaining information which the Director may require for the establishment of quotas as prescribed in (b) of the order.

(m) *Distribution schedules.* The distribution schedules, if any, to be followed by the handlers in making deliveries shall be made effective in the terms of approval by the Director of such schedules.

(n) *Expense of administration.* Each handler shall pay to the market agent, within 20 days after the close of each calendar month an assessment of $0.01 per hundredweight of each of milk, cream, skim milk, buttermilk, flavored milk drinks, beverages containing more than 85 percent of skim milk, and skim milk equivalent of cottage, pot, or baker's cheese delivered during the preceding quota period and subject to quota regulations under the provisions hereof.

(o) *Violations.* The market agent shall report all violations to the Director together with the information required for the prosecution of such violations, except in a case where a handler has made deliveries in a quota period in excess of a quota in an amount not to exceed 5 percent of such quota, and in the succeeding quota period makes deliveries below that quota by at least the same percent.

(p) *Bureau of the Budget approval.* The record-keeping and reporting requirements of this order have been approved by the Bureau of the Budget in accordance with the Federal Reports Act of 1942. Subsequent record-keeping or reporting requirements will be subject to the approval of the Bureau of the Budget pursuant to the Federal Reports Act of 1942.

(q) This order shall take effect at 12:01 a. m., e. w. t., October 5, 1943.

Issued this 1st day of October 1943.

ROY F. HENDRICKSON,
Director of Food Distribution.

Press Release, Immediate:
Saturday, October 2, 1943.

Eleven additional metropolitan areas will be brought under the Food Distribution Administration's fluid milk conservation and control program beginning October 5, the War Food Administration said today.

The new milk sales areas, and the market agents who will administer the program in each, are:

St. Joseph County, Ind.: M. E. Drake, 116 S. William St., South Bend, Ind.

Akron, Ohio, Huntington, W. Va.-Ashland, Ky., Hamilton-Middletown, Ohio, Columbus, Ohio, Youngstown, Ohio: Fred Issler, 152 E. Fourth St., Cincinnati, Ohio.

Davenport, Ia.-Rock Island, Ill.-Moline, Ill.: Howard E. Eisaman, 335 Federal Building, Rock Island, Ill.

Fort Wayne, Ind.: William J. Cline, 707 Citizens Trust Building, Fort Wayne, Ind.

Wichita, Kans., Greater Kansas City (Mo.-Kan.): M. M. Morehouse, 512 Porter Building, 406 W. 34th St., Kansas City, Mo.

Duluth, Minn.-Superior, Wis.: O. F. Kirkendall, 2002-4 W. Superior St., Duluth, Minn.

Dealers' monthly fluid milk sales in these areas may not exceed their June deliveries, and their sales of cream and of fluid milk byproducts (such as cottage cheese, chocolate milk and buttermilk) will be reduced to three-fourths of the quantities sold in June. Milk dealers include all persons or firms engaged in the sale or transfer of milk, but not retail stores, hotels, restaurants, etc.

Producer-distributors who purchase no milk (except those whose volume of sales is small enough to make them quota-exempt) will be allowed to sell an amount of fluid milk, cream and fluid milk byproducts equal to 100 percent of their total milk production in June. Quota-exempt producer distributors are defined separately for each area, but in general they are those whose deliveries are relatively small.

Consumers in these areas generally will be able to purchase as much milk under the milk conservation program as they have been buying—an amount considerably greater than that bought in pre-war years, and about 10 percent above last year's purchases. Sales quotas on cream and on fluid milk byproducts have been set below June deliveries to boost fluid milk supplies where milk production is low, and to conserve milk for manufacturing purposes in other areas.

Fluid milk sales are being stabilized in these and other metropolitan areas, FDA officials explained, to help assure sufficient milk for manufacturing the cheese, butter, evaporated milk and milk powder required by the armed services and civilians for good nutrition and properly balanced diets.

Largely due to expanded consumer demand, sales of fluid milk have been increasing steadily and are now about 20 percent higher than in pre-war years (1935-40) and 10 to 12 percent above those in 1942. With total milk production levelled off, and even declining somewhat, this expanding volume of milk sold for fluid uses has inevitably reduced the supply of "manufacturing milk," and, consequently, the production of cheese, butter and other dairy foods.

The FDA's dealer-quota plan is an attempt to stabilize fluid milk consumption without resorting to individual consumer rationing. Point rationing of milk, a bulky and highly perishable commodity, would be very difficult to administer and would almost necessarily reduce fluid milk sales in many areas. If consumers and the trade cooperate with the present program to assure that sales are held within quotas and quantities available are distributed fairly, FDA officials believe consumer rationing will not be necessary.

Milk handlers in the sales areas named today, except Greater Kansas City and Wichita, Kansas, will compute the quantity of milk which they may sell each month in terms of pounds of milk, their cream sales in terms of pounds of cream and butterfat, and their milk products sales in terms of pounds of milk byproducts. In Greater Kansas City and Wichita, milk handlers will determine their fluid milk quotas in terms of pounds of milk and butterfat.

Deliveries to the Armed Forces, to plants processing dairy products, and to other handlers (except special classes of handlers such as peddlers) are quota exempt.

To facilitate administration, the market agent for each milk sales area may act upon petitions for relief from hardship which may be submitted to him, and after investigation, he may grant temporary relief for a total period not to exceed 60 days.

Milk sales in 13 eastern and midwestern areas previously were brought under federal regulation. Sales quotas in these initial milk sales areas are the same as for those named today.

FDO 79-25

OCTOBER 2, 1943

WAR FOOD ADMINISTRATION

[FDO 79-25]

PART 1401—DAIRY PRODUCTS

CONSERVATION AND DISTRIBUTION OF FLUID MILK AND CREAM IN HARRISBURG, PA., SALES AREA

Pursuant to the authority vested in me by Food Distribution Order No. 79 (8 F.R 12426), issued on September 7, 1943, as amended, and to effectuate the purposes of such order, it is hereby ordered as follows:

§ 1401.66 *Quota restrictions*—(a) *Definitions.* When used in this order, unless otherwise distinctly expressed or manifestly incompatible with the intent hereof:

(1) Each term defined in Food Distribution Order No. 79, as amended, shall, when used herein, have the same meaning as is set forth for such term in Food Distribution Order No. 79, as amended.

(2) The term "order" means Food Distribution Order No. 79, issued on September 7, 1943, as amended.

(3) The term "sub-handler" means any handler, such as a peddler, vendor, sub-dealer, or secondary dealer, who purchases in a previously packaged and processed form milk, milk byproducts or cream for delivery.

(b) *Milk sales area.* The following area is hereby designated as a "milk sales area" to be known as the Harrisburg, Pennsylvania, sales area, and is referred to hereinafter as the "sales area": The city of Harrisburg, the townships of Derry, Lower Swatara, Susquehanna, and Swatara, the boroughs of Highspire, Hummelstown, Middletown, Paxtang, Penbrook, Royalton, and Steelton, in Dauphin County, Pennsylvania; and

The townships of East Pennsboro, Hampden, and Lower Allen, the boroughs of Camp Hill, Lemoyne, Mechanicsburg, New Cumberland, Shiremanstown, West Fairview, and Wormleysburg, in Cumberland County, Pennsylvania.

(c) *Base period.* The calendar month of June 1943 is hereby designated as the base period for the sales area.

(d) *Quota period.* The remainder of the calendar month in which the provisions hereof become effective and each subsequent calendar month, respectively, is hereby designated as a quota period for the sales area.

(e) *Handler quotas.* Quotas for each handler in the sales area in each quota period shall be determined as follows:

(1) Divide the total deliveries of each of milk, milk byproducts, and cream (and of butterfat in milk or in cream where percentages of pounds of butterfat are specified in (e) (3) (i) or (e) (3) (ii) hereof) made in the sales area by such handler during the base period, after excluding the quota-exempt deliveries described in (h) hereof and adjusting such deliveries for the transfers set out in (i) hereof, by the number of days in the base period;

(2) Multiply the result of the foregoing calculation by the number of days in the quota period; and

(3) Multiply the aforesaid resulting amount by the following applicable percentage: (i) Milk: 100 percent of pounds of milk and ---- percent of pounds of butterfat; (ii) Cream: 75 percent of pounds of cream and 75 percent of pounds of butterfat; and (iii) Milk byproducts: 75 percent of pounds of milk byproducts other than cottage, pot, or bakers' cheese and of the pounds of skim milk equivalent of cottage, pot, or baker's cheese. (For the purpose of this order, one pound of cottage, pot, or baker's cheese shall be considered as the equivalent of 7 pounds of skim milk.)

(f) *Quotas for handlers who are also producers.* Quotas for handlers who are also producers and who purchase no milk shall be 100 percent of the total production of such handlers in the base period.

(g) *Handler exemptions.* Quotas shall not apply to any handler who delivers in a quota period a daily average of less than 400 units of milk, cream, and milk byproducts. For the purpose of this order, a unit shall be the equivalent in volume of the following: (1) Milk, one quart of milk; (2) cream, one-half pint of cream; and (3) milk byproducts, one quart of skim milk, buttermilk, flavored milk drink, or other beverage containing more than 85 percent of skim milk, or one-half pound of cottage, pot, or baker's cheese.

(h) *Quota exclusions and exemptions.* Deliveries of milk, milk byproducts, or cream (1) to other handlers, except for such deliveries to sub-handlers, (2) to plants engaged in the handling or processing of milk, milk byproducts, or cream from which no milk, milk byproducts, or cream is delivered in the sales area, and (3) to the agencies or groups specified in (d) of the order, shall be excluded from the computation of deliveries in the base period and exempt from charges to quotas.

(i) *Transfers and apportionment of quotas.* The market agent is empowered to deduct an amount of base period deliveries to purchasers from the total of deliveries made by a handler or other person in the base period upon the application and a showing of unreasonable hardship by the handler making deliveries to such purchasers on the effective date of this order, and to add the amount of such deliveries to the total base period deliveries of the applicant handler. Denials of transfers or transfers granted by the market agent shall be reviewed by the Director upon application.

(j) *Petition for relief from hardships.* (1) Any person affected by the order or the provisions hereof who considers that compliance therewith would work an exceptional and unreasonable hardship on him, may file with the market agent a petition addressed to the Director. The petition shall contain the correct name, address and principal place of business of the petitioner, a full statement of the facts upon which the petition is based, and the hardship involved and the nature of the relief desired.

(2) Upon receiving such petition, the market agent shall immediately investigate the representations and facts stated therein.

(3) After investigation, the petition shall be certified to the Director, but prior to certification the market agent may (i) deny the petition; or (ii) grant temporary relief for a total period not to exceed 60 days.

(4) Denials or grants of relief by the market agent shall be reviewed by the Director and may be affirmed, modified, or reversed by the Director.

(k) *Reports.* Each handler shall transmit to the market agent on forms prescribed by the market agent the following reports:

(1) Within 20 days following the effective date of this order, reports which show the information required by the market agent to establish such handlers' quotas;

(2) Within 20 days following the close of each quota period, the information required by the market agent to establish volumes of deliveries of milk, cream, and

milk byproducts during the preceding quota period; and

(3) Handlers exempt from quotas pursuant to (f) hereof shall, upon the request of the market agent, submit the information required by the market agent to establish volumes of deliveries of milk, cream, and milk byproducts.

(l) *Records.* Handlers shall keep and shall make available to the market agent such records of receipts, sales, deliveries, and production as the market agent shall require for the purpose of obtaining information which the Director may require for the establishment of quotas as prescribed in (b) of the order.

(m) *Distribution schedules.* The distribution schedules, if any, to be followed by the handlers in making deliveries shall be made effective in the terms of approval by the Director of such schedules.

(n) *Expense of administration.* Each handler shall pay to the market agent, within 20 days after the close of each calendar month an assessment of $0.005 per hundredweight of each of milk, cream, skim milk, buttermilk, flavored milk drinks, beverages containing more than 85 percent of skim milk, and skim milk equivalent of cottage, pot, or baker's cheese delivered during the preceding quota period and subject to quota regulations under the provisions hereof.

(o) *Violations.* The market agent shall report all violations to the Director together with the information required for the prosecution of such violations, except in a case where a handler has made deliveries in a quota period in excess of a quota in an amount not to exceed 5 percent of such quota, and in the succeeding quota period makes deliveries below that quota by at least the same percent.

(p) *Bureau of the Budget approval.* The record-keeping and reporting requirements of this order have been approved by the Bureau of the Budget in accordance with the Federal Reports Act of 1942. Subsequent record-keeping or reporting requirements will be subject to the approval of the Bureau of the Budget pursuant to the Federal Reports Act of 1942.

(q) This order shall take effect at 12:01 a. m., e. w. t., October 10, 1943.

Issued this 2d day of October 1943.

ROY F. HENDRICKSON,
Director of Food Distribution.

Press Release, Immediate:
Saturday, October 2, 1943.

The War Food Administration's fluid milk conservation and control program will be extended to cover eight new sales areas, effective October 10, 1943.

The newly designated sales areas are:

- Wilmington, Del.
- Lancaster, Pa.
- Reading, Pa.
- Scranton-Wilkes-Barre, Pa.
- Allentown-Bethlehem-Easton, Pa.
- Harrisburg, Pa.
- Trenton, N. J.
- Atlantic City, N. J.

William P. Sadler, 11 N. Juniper St., Philadelphia, Pennsylvania, will administer the program in each of these eight areas.

Dealers' monthly fluid milk sales in these areas may not exceed their June deliveries, and their sales of cream and of fluid milk byproducts (such as cottage cheese, chocolate milk and buttermilk) will be reduced to three-fourths of the quantities sold in June. Milk dealers include all persons or firms engaged in the sale or transfer of milk, but not retail stores, hotels, restaurants, etc.

Consumers in these areas, however, will be able to purchase as much milk under the milk conservation program as they have been buying within the limits of local supplies—in general an amount considerably greater than that bought in pre-war years, and about 10 percent above last year's purchases. Sales quotas on cream and fluid milk byproducts have been set below June deliveries to boost fluid milk supplies where milk production is low, and to conserve milk for manufacturing purposes.

Producer-distributors who purchase no milk will be allowed to sell an amount of fluid milk, cream and fluid milk byproducts equal to 100 percent of their total milk production in June. Quota-exempt producer distributors are defined separately for each area, but in general they are those whose deliveries are relatively small.

To help assure sufficient milk for manufacturing the cheese, butter, evaporated milk and milk powder required by the armed services and civilians for good nutrition and properly balanced diets, fluid milk sales are being stabilized in these and other metropolitan areas, FDA officials explained.

The FDA's dealer-quota plan is an attempt to stabilize fluid milk consumption without resorting to individual consumer rationing. Point rationing of milk, a bulky and highly perishable commodity, would be very difficult to administer and would almost necessarily reduce fluid milk sales in many areas. If consumers and the trade cooperate with the present program to assure that sales are held within quotas and quantities available are distributed fairly, FDA officials believe that consumer rationing will not be necessary.

Milk handlers in the sales areas named will compute the quantity of milk which they may sell each month in terms of pounds of milk, their cream sales in terms of pounds of cream and butterfat, and their milk byproducts sales in terms of pounds of milk byproducts.

Deliveries to the Armed Forces, to plants processing dairy products, and other handlers (except special classes of handlers such as peddlers) are quota exempt.

To facilitate administration, the market agent, Mr. Sadler, may act upon petitions for relief from hardships which may be submitted to him.

Milk sales in several other eastern and midwestern areas have been previously brought under federal regulation. Sales quotas are the same in all areas named to date.

WAR FOOD ADMINISTRATION

[FDO 79-26]

PART 1401—DAIRY PRODUCTS

CONSERVATION AND DISTRIBUTION OF FLUID MILK AND CREAM IN SCRANTON-WILKES-BARRE, PA., SALES AREA

Pursuant to the authority vested in me by Food Distribution Order No. 7 (8 F.R. 12426), issued on September 7, 1943, as amended, and to effectuate the purposes of such order, it is hereby ordered as follows:

§ 1401.64 *Quota restrictions*—(a) *Definitions.* When used in this order, unless otherwise distinctly expressed or manifestly incompatible with the intent hereof:

(1) Each term defined in Food Distribution Order No. 79, as amended, shall, when used herein, have the same meaning as is set forth for such term in Food Distribution Order No. 79, as amended.

(2) The term "order" means Food Distribution Order No. 79, issued on September 7, 1943, as amended.

(3) The term "sub-handler" means any handler, such as a peddler, vendor, sub-dealer, or secondary dealer, who purchases in a previously packaged and processed form milk, milk byproducts, or cream for delivery.

(b) *Milk sales area.* The following area is hereby designated as a "milk sales area" to be known as the Scranton-Wilkes-Barre, Pa., sales area, and is referred to hereinafter as the "sales area": The cities of Scranton in Lackawanna County and Wilkes-Barre in Luzerne County and the entire area included in:

The city of Carbondale, the townships of Abington, Carbondale, Fell, Glenburn, Lackawanna, La Plume, Ransom, Roaring Brook, and South Abington, the boroughs of Archbald, Blakely, Clarks Green, Clarks Summit, Dalton, Dickson City, Dunmore, Elmhurst, Jermyn, Mayfield, Moosic, Moscow, Old Forge, Olyphant, Taylor, Throop, Vandling, and Winton in Lackawanna County, Pa.;

The cities of Nanticoke and Pittston, the townships of Conyngham, Hanover, Jenkins, Kingston, Newport, Pittston, Plains, Plymouth, and Wilkes-Barre, the boroughs of Ashley, Avoca, Courtdale, Dupont, Duryea, Edwardsville, Exeter, Forty Fort, Hughestown, Kingston, Laflin, Larksville, Laurel Run, Luzerne, Nuangola, Plymouth, Pringle, Shickshinny, Sugar Notch, Swoyerville, Warrior Run, West Pittston, West Wyoming, Wyoming, and Yatesville in Luzerne County, Pa.;

The borough of Forest City in Susquehanna County, Pa.; and

The borough of Factoryville in Wyoming County, Pa.

(c) *Base period.* The calendar month of June 1943 is hereby designated as the base period for the sales area.

(d) *Quota period.* The remainder of the calendar month in which the provisions hereof become effective and each subsequent calendar month, respectively, is hereby designated as a quota period for the sales area.

(e) *Handler quotas.* Quotas for each handler in the sales area in each quota period shall be determined as follows:

(1) Divide the total deliveries of each of milk, milk byproducts, and cream (and of butterfat in milk or in cream where percentages of pounds of butterfat are specified in (e) (3) (i) or (e) (3) (ii) hereof) made in the sales area by such handler during the base period, after excluding the quota-exempt deliveries described in (h) hereof and adjusting such deliveries for the transfers set out in (i) hereof, by the number of days in the base period;

(2) Multiply the result of the foregoing calculation by the number of days in the quota period; and

(3) Multiply the aforesaid resulting amount by the following applicable percentage: (i) Milk: 100 percent of pounds of milk and ---- percent of pounds of butterfat; (ii) Cream: 75 percent of pounds of cream and 75 percent of pounds of butterfat; and (iii) Milk byproducts other than cottage, pot, or baker's cheese and of the pounds of skim milk equivalent of cottage, pot, or baker's cheese. (For the purpose of this order, one pound of cottage, pot, or baker's cheese shall be considered as the equivalent of 7 pounds of skim milk.)

(f) *Quotas for handlers who are also producers.* Quotas for handlers who are also producers and who purchase no milk shall be 100 percent of the total production of such handlers in the base period.

(g) *Handler exemptions.* Quotas shall not apply to any handler who delivers in a quota period a daily average of less than 400 units of milk, cream, and milk byproducts. For the purpose of this order, a unit shall be the equivalent in volume of the following: (1) Milk, one quart of milk; (2) cream, one-half pint of cream; and (3) milk byproduct, one quart of skim milk, buttermilk, flavored milk drink, or other beverage containing more than 85 percent of skim milk, or one-half pound of cottage, pot, or baker's cheese.

(h) *Quota exclusions and exemptions.* Deliveries of milk, milk byproducts, or cream (1) to other handlers, except for such deliveries to sub-handlers, (2) to plants engaged in the handling or processing of milk, milk byproducts, or cream from which no milk, milk byproducts, or cream is delivered in the sales area, and (3) to the agencies or groups specified in (d) of the order, shall be excluded from the computation of deliveries in the base period and exempt from charges to quotas.

(i) *Transfers and apportionment of quotas.* The market agent is empowered to deduct an amount of base period deliveries to purchasers from the total of deliveries made by a handler or other person in the base period upon the application and a showing of unreasonable hardship by the handler making deliveries to such purchasers on the effective date of this order, and to add the amount of such deliveries to the total base period deliveries of the applicant handler. Denials of transfers or transfers granted by the market agent shall be reviewed by the Director upon application.

(j) *Petition for relief from hardships.* (1) Any person affected by the order or the provisions hereof who considers that compliance therewith would work an exceptional and unreasonable hardship on him, may file with the market agent a petition addressed to the Director. The petition shall contain the correct name, address and principal place of business of the petitioner, a full statement of the facts upon which the petition is based, and the hardship involved and the nature of the relief desired.

(2) Upon receiving such petition, the market agent shall immediately investigate the representations and facts stated therein.

(3) After investigation, the petition shall be certified to the Director, but prior to certification the market agent may (i) deny the petition; or (ii) grant temporary relief for a total period not to exceed 60 days.

(4) Denials or grants of relief by the market agent shall be reviewed by the Director and may be affirmed, modified, or reversed by the Director.

(k) *Reports.* Each handler shall transmit to the market agent on forms prescribed by the market agent the following reports:

(1) Within 20 days following the effective date of this order, reports which show the information required by the market agent to establish such handlers' quotas;

(2) Within 20 days following the close of each quota period, the information required by the market agent to establish volumes of deliveries of milk, cream, and milk byproducts during the preceding quota period; and

(3) Handlers exempt from quotas pursuant to (f) hereof shall, upon the request of the market agent, submit the information required by the market agent to establish volumes of deliveries of milk, cream, and milk byproducts.

(l) *Records.* Handlers shall keep and shall make available to the market agent such records of receipts, sales, deliveries, and production as the market agent shall require for the purpose of obtaining information which the Director may require for the establishment of quotas as prescribed in (b) of the order.

(m) *Distribution schedules.* The distribution schedules, if any, to be followed by the handlers in making deliveries shall be made effective in the terms of approval by the Director of such schedules.

(n) *Expense of administration.* Each handler shall pay to the market agent, within 20 days after the close of each calendar month an assessment of $0.005 per hundredweight of each of milk, cream, skim milk, buttermilk, flavored milk drinks, beverages containing more than 85 percent of skim milk, and skim milk equivalent of cottage, pot, or baker's cheese delivered during the preceding quota period and subject to quota regulations under the provisions hereof.

(o) *Violations.* The market agent shall report all violations to the Director together with the information required for the prosecution of such violations, except in a case where a handler has made deliveries in a quota period in excess of a quota in an amount not to exceed 5 percent of such quota, and in the succeeding quota period makes deliveries below that quota by at least the same percent.

(p) *Bureau of the Budget approval.* The record-keeping and reporting requirements of this order have been approved by the Bureau of the Budget in accordance with the Federal Reports Act of 1942. Subsequent record-keeping or reporting requirements will be subject to the approval of the Bureau of the Budget pursuant to the Federal Reports Act of 1942.

(q) This order shall take effect at 12:01 a. m., e. w. t., October 10, 1943.

Issued this 2d day of October 1943.

ROY F. HENDRICKSON,
Director of Food Distribution.

Press Release, Immediate:
Saturday, October 2, 1943.

The War Food Administration's fluid milk conservation and control program will be extended to cover eight new sales areas, effective October 10, 1943.

The newly designated sales areas are:

- Wilmington, Del.
- Lancaster, Pa.
- Reading, Pa.
- Scranton-Wilkes-Barre, Pa.
- Allentown-Bethlehem-Easton, Pa.
- Harrisburg, Pa.
- Trenton, N. J.
- Atlantic City, N. J.

William P. Sadler, 11 N. Juniper St., Philadelphia, Pennsylvania, will administer the program in each of these eight areas.

Dealers' monthly fluid milk sales in these areas may not exceed their June deliveries, and their sales of cream and of fluid milk byproducts (such as cottage cheese, chocolate milk and buttermilk) will be reduced to three-fourths of the quantities sold in June. Milk dealers include all persons or firms engaged in the sale or transfer of milk, but not retail stores, hotels, restaurants, etc.

Consumers in these areas however, will be able to purchase as much milk under the milk conservation program as they have been buying within the limits of local supplies—in general an amount considerably greater than that bought in pre-war years, and about 10 percent above last year's purchases. Sales quotas on cream and fluid milk byproducts have been set below June deliveries to boost fluid milk supplies where milk production is low, and to conserve milk for manufacturing purposes.

Producer-distributors who purchase no milk will be allowed to sell an amount of fluid milk, cream and fluid milk byproducts equal to 100 percent of their total milk production in June. Quota-exempt producer-distributors are defined separately for each area, but in general they are those whose deliveries are relatively small.

To help assure sufficient milk for manufacturing the cheese, butter, evaporated milk and milk powder required by the armed services and civilians for good nutrition and properly balanced diets, fluid milk sales are being stabilized in these and other metropolitan areas, FDA officials explained.

The FDA's dealer-quota plan is an attempt to stabilize fluid milk consumption without resorting to individual consumer rationing. Point rationing of milk, a bulky and highly perishable commodity, would be very difficult to administer and would almost necessarily reduce fluid milk sales in many areas. If consumers and the trade cooperate with the present program to assure that sales are held within quotas and quantities available are distributed fairly, FDA officials believe that consumer rationing will not be necessary.

Milk handlers in the sales areas named will compute the quantity of milk which they may sell each month in terms of pounds of milk, their cream sales in terms of pounds of cream and butterfat, and their milk byproducts sales in terms of pounds of milk byproducts.

Deliveries to the Armed Forces, to plants processing dairy products, and other handlers (except special classes of handlers such as peddlers) are quota exempt.

To facilitate administration, the market agent, Mr. Sadler, may act upon petitions for relief from hardships which may be submitted to him.

Milk sales in several other eastern and midwestern areas have been previously brought under federal regulation. Sales quotas are the same in all areas named to date.

7233-
Cafi

FDO 79-27
OCT. 2, 1943

WAR FOOD ADMINISTRATION

[FDO 79-27]

PART 1401—DAIRY PRODUCTS

CONSERVATION AND DISTRIBUTION OF FLUID MILK AND CREAM IN ALLENTOWN-BETHLEHEM-EASTON, PA., SALES AREA

Pursuant to the authority vested in me by Food Distribution Order No. 79 (8 F.R. 12426), issued on September 7, 1943, as amended, and to effectuate the purposes of such order, it is hereby ordered as follows:

§ 1401.61 *Quota restrictions*—(a) *Definitions.* When used in this order, unless otherwise distinctly expressed or manifestly incompatible with the intent hereof.

(1) Each term defined in Food Distribution Order No. 79, as amended, shall, when used herein, have the same meaning as is set forth for such term in Food Distribution Order No. 79, as amended.

(2) The term "order" means Food Distribution Order No. 79, issued on September 7, 1943, as amended.

(3) The term "sub-handler" means any handler, such as a peddler, vendor, sub-dealer, or secondary dealer, who purchases in a previously packaged and processed form milk, milk byproducts, or cream for delivery.

(b) *Milk sales area.* The following area is hereby designated as a "milk sales area" to be known as the Allentown-Bethlehem-Easton, Pa., sales area, and is referred to hereinafter as the "sales area": The cities of Allentown and Bethlehem in Lehigh County, Pennsylvania, and the city of Easton and part of Bethlehem in Northampton County, Pennsylvania, and the entire area included in:

The borough of Riegelsville in Bucks County, Pennsylvania; The townships of Hanover, Lower Macungie, North Whitehall, Salisbury, South Whitehall, Upper Saucon, Washington, and Whitehall, the boroughs of Alburtis, Catasauqua, Coopersburg, Coplay, Emmaus, Fountain Hill, Macungie, Slatington, in Lehigh County, Pennsylvania;

The townships of Bethlehem, Forks, Hanover, Lower Nazareth, Lower Saucon, Palmer, Upper Nazareth, Williams, the boroughs of Freemansburg, Glendon, Hellertown, Nazareth, Northampton, North Catasauqua Stockertown, Tatamy, Walnutport, West Easton, and Wilson in Northampton County, Pennsylvania; and

The townships of Lopatcong and Pohatcong, the town of Phillipsburg, and the borough of Alpha in Warren County, New Jersey.

(c) *Base period.* The calendar month of June 1943 is hereby designated as the base period for the sales area.

(d) *Quota period.* The remainder of the calendar month in which the provisions hereof become effective and each subsequent calendar month, respectively, is hereby designated as a quota period for the sales area.

(e) *Handler quotas.* Quotas for each handler in the sales area in each quota period shall be determined as follows:

(1) Divide the total deliveries of each of milk, milk byproducts, and cream (and of butterfat in milk or in cream where percentages of pounds of butterfat are specified in (e) (3) (i) or (e) (3) (ii) hereof) made in the sales area by such handler during the base period, after excluding the quota-exempt deliveries described in (h) hereof and adjusting such deliveries for the transfers set out in (i) hereof, by the number of days in the base period;

(2) Multiply the result of the foregoing calculation by the number of days in the quota period; and

(3) Multiply the aforesaid resulting amount by the following applicable percentage: (i) Milk: 100 percent of pounds of milk and ______ percent of pounds of butterfat; (ii) Cream: 75 percent of pounds of cream and 75 percent of pounds of butterfat; and (iii) Milk byproducts: 75 percent of pounds of milk byproducts other than cottage, pot, or baker's cheese and of the pounds of skim milk equivalent of cottage, pot, or baker's cheese. (For the purpose of this order, one pound of cottage, pot, or baker's cheese shall be considered as the equivalent of 7 pounds of skim milk.)

(f) *Quotas for handlers who are also producers.* Quotas for handlers who are also producers and who purchase no milk shall be 100 percent of the total production of such handlers in the base period.

(g) *Handler exemptions.* Quotas shall not apply to any handler who delivers in a quota period a daily average of less than 400 units of milk, cream, and milk byproducts. For the purpose of this order, a unit shall be the equivalent in volume of the following: (1) Milk, one quart of milk; (2) cream, one-half point of cream; and (3) milk byproduct, one quart of skim milk, buttermilk, flavored milk drink, or other beverage containing more than 85 percent of skim milk, or one-half pound of cottage, pot, or baker's cheese.

(h) *Quota exclusions and exemptions.* Deliveries of milk, milk byproducts, or cream (1) to other handlers, except for such deliveries to sub-handlers, (2) to plants engaged in the handling or processing of milk, milk byproducts, or cream from which no milk, milk byproducts, or cream is delivered in the sales area, and (3) to the agencies or groups specified in (d) of the order, shall be excluded from the computation of deliveries in the base period and exempt from charges to quotas.

(i) *Transfers and apportionment of quotas.* The market agent is empowered to deduct an amount of base period deliveries to purchasers from the total of deliveries made by a handler or other person in the base period upon the application and a showing of unreasonable hardship by the handler making deliveries to such purchasers on the effective date of this order, and to add the amount of such deliveries to the total base period deliveries of the applicant handler. Denials of transfers or transfers granted by the market agent shall be reviewed by the Director upon application.

(j) *Petition for relief from hardships.* (1) Any person affected by the order or the provisions hereof who considers that compliance therewith would work an exceptional and unreasonable hardship on him, may file with the market agent a petition addressed to the Director. The petition shall contain the correct name, address and principal place of business of the petitioner, a full statement of the facts upon which the petition is based, and the hardship involved and the nature of the relief desired.

(2) Upon receiving such petition, the market agent shall immediately investigate the representations and facts stated therein.

(3) After investigation, the petition shall be certified to the Director, but prior to certification the market agent may (i) deny the petition; or (ii) grant temporary relief for a total period not to exceed 60 days.

(4) Denials or grants of relief by the market agent shall be reviewed by the Director and may be affirmed, modified, or reversed by the Director.

(k) *Reports.* Each handler shall transmit to the market agent on forms prescribed by the market agent the following reports:

(1) Within 20 days following the effective date of this order, reports which show the information required by the

and production as the market agent shall require for the purpose of obtaining information which the Director may require for the establishment of quotas as prescribed in (b) of the order.

(m) *Distribution schedules.* The distribution schedules, if any, to be followed by the handlers in making deliveries shall be made effective in the terms of approval by the Director of such schedules.

(n) *Expense of administration.* Each handler shall pay to the market agent, within 20 days after the close of each calendar month an assessment of $0.005 per hundredweight of each of milk, cream, skim milk, buttermilk, flavored milk drinks, beverages containing more than 85 percent of skim milk, and skim milk equivalent of cottage, pot, or baker's cheese delivered during the preceding quota period and subject to quota regulations under the provisions hereof.

(o) *Violations.* The market agent shall report all violations to the Director together with the information required for the prosecution of such violations, except in a case where a handler has made deliveries in a quota period in excess of a quota in an amount not to exceed 5 percent of such quota, and in the succeeding quota period makes deliveries below that quota by at least the same percent.

(p) *Bureau of the Budget approval.* The record keeping and reporting requirements of this order have been approved by the Bureau of the Budget in accordance with the Federal Reports Act of 1942. Subsequent record-keeping or reporting requirements will be subject to the approval of the Bureau of the Budget pursuant to the Federal Reports Act of 1942.

(q) This order shall take effect at 12:01 a. m., e. w. t., October 10, 1943.

Issued this 2d day of October 1943.

ROY F. HENDRICKSON,
Director of Food Distribution.

Press Release, Immediate:
Saturday, October 2, 1943.

The War Food Administration's fluid milk conservation and control program will be extended to cover eight new sales areas, effective October 10, 1943.

The newly designated sales areas are:

- Wilmington, Del.
- Lancaster, Pa.
- Reading, Pa.
- Scranton-Wilkes-Barre, Pa.
- Allentown-Bethlehem-Easton, Pa.
- Harrisburg, Pa.
- Trenton, N. J.
- Atlantic City, N. J.

William P. Sadler, 11 N. Juniper St., Philadelphia, Pennsylvania, will administer the program in each of these eight areas.

Dealers' monthly fluid milk sales in these areas may not exceed their June deliveries, and their sales of cream and of fluid milk byproducts (such as cottage cheese, chocolate milk and buttermilk) will be reduced to three-fourths of the quantities sold in June. Milk dealers include all persons or firms engaged in the sale or transfer of milk, but not retail stores, hotels, restaurants, etc.

Consumers in these areas, however, will be able to purchase as much milk under the milk conservation program as they have been buying within the limits of local supplies—in general an amount considerably greater than that bought in pre-war years, and about 10 percent above last year's purchases. Sales quotas on cream and fluid milk byproducts have been set below June deliveries to boost fluid milk supplies where milk production is low, and to conserve milk for manufacturing purposes.

Producer-distributors who purchase no milk will be allowed to sell an amount of fluid milk, cream and fluid milk byproducts equal to 100 percent of their total milk production in June. Quota-exempt producer distributors are defined separately for each area, but in general they are those whose deliveries are relatively small.

To help assure sufficient milk for manufacturing the cheese, butter, evaporated milk and milk powder required by the armed services and civilians for good nutrition and properly balanced diets, fluid milk sales are being stabilized in these and other metropolitan areas, FDA officials explained.

The FDA's dealer-quota plan is an attempt to stabilize fluid milk consumption without resorting to individual consumer rationing. Point rationing of milk, a bulky and highly perishable commodity, would be very difficult to administer and would almost necessarily reduce fluid milk sales in many areas. If consumers and the trade cooperate with the present program to assure that sales are held within quotas and quantities available are distributed fairly, FDA officials believe that consumer rationing will not be necessary.

Milk handlers in the sales areas named will compute the quantity of milk which they may sell each month in terms of pounds of milk, their cream sales in terms of pounds of cream and butterfat, and their milk byproducts sales in terms of pounds of milk byproducts.

Deliveries to the Armed Forces, to plants processing dairy products, and other handlers (except special classes of handlers such as peddlers) are quota exempt.

To facilitate administration, the market agent, Mr. Sadler, may act upon petitions for relief from hardships which may be submitted to him.

Milk sales in several other eastern and midwestern areas have been previously brought under federal regulation. Sales quotas are the same in all areas named to date.

Cop. 1

FDO 79-29
OCT. 2, 1943

WAR FOOD ADMINISTRATION

[FDO 79-29]

PART 1401—DAIRY PRODUCTS

CONSERVATION AND DISTRIBUTION OF FLUID MILK AND CREAM IN READING, PA., SALES AREA

Pursuant to the authority vested in me by Food Distribution Order No. 79 (8 F.R. 12426), issued on September 7, 1943, as amended, and to effectuate the purposes of such order, it is hereby ordered as follows:

§ 1401.59 *Quota restrictions*—(a) *Definitions.* When used in this order, unless otherwise distinctly expressed or manifestly incompatible with the intent hereof:

(1) Each term defined in Food Distribution Order No. 79, as amended, shall, when used herein, have the same meaning as is set forth for such term in Food Distribution Order No. 79, as amended.

(2) The term "order" means Food Distribution Order No. 79, issued on September 7, 1943, as amended.

(3) The term "sub-handler" means any handler, such as a peddler, vendor, sub-dealer, or secondary dealer, who purchases in a previously packaged and processed form milk, milk byproducts, or cream for delivery.

(b) *Milk sales area.* The following area is hereby designated as a "milk sales area" to be known as the Reading, Pennsylvania, sales area, and is referred to hereinafter as the "sales area": The city of Reading, the townships of Bern, Cumru, Exeter, Muhlenburg, Lower Alsace, Maidencreed, Ontelaunee, South Heidelberg, and Spring, the boroughs of Birdsboro, Kenhorst, Laureldale, Mohnton, Mount Penn, St. Lawrence, Skillington, Sinking Spring, Temple, Wernersville, West Lawn, West Leesport, West Reading, Wyomissing, and Wyomissing Hills, all in Berks County, Pa.

(c) *Base period.* The calendar month of June 1943 is hereby designated as the base period for the sales area.

(d) *Quota period.* The remainder of the calendar month in which the provisions hereof become effective and each subsequent calendar month, respectively, is hereby designated as a quota period for the sales area.

(e) *Handler quotas.* Quotas for each handler in the sales area in each quota period shall be determined as follows:

(1) Divide the total deliveries of each of milk, milk byproducts, and cream (and of butterfat in milk or in cream where percentages of pounds of butterfat are specified in (e) (3) (i) or (e) (3) (ii) hereof) made in the sales area by such handler during the base period, after excluding the quota-exempt deliveries described in (h) hereof and adjusting such deliveries for the transfers set out in (i) hereof, by the number of days in the base period;

(2) Multiply the result of the foregoing calculation by the number of days in the quota period; and

(3) Multiply the aforesaid resulting amount by the following applicable percentage: (i) [illegible]: 100 percent of pounds of milk an[illegible] percent of pounds of butterfat; [illegible] Cream: 75 percent of pounds of [illegible]am and 75 percent of pounds of butterfat; and (iii) Milk byproducts: 75 percent of pounds of milk byproducts other than cottage, pot, or bakers' cheese and of the pounds of skim milk equivalent of cottage, pot, or baker's cheese. (For the purpose of this order, one pound of cottage, pot, or baker's cheese shall be considered as the equivalent of 7 pounds of skim milk.)

(f) *Quotas for handlers who are also producers.* Quotas for handlers who are also producers and who purchase no milk shall be 100 percent of the total production of such handlers in the base period.

(g) *Handler exemptions.* Quotas shall not apply to any handler who delivers in a quota period a daily average of less than 400 units of milk, cream, and milk byproducts. For the purpose of this order, a unit shall be the equivalent in volume of the following: (1) milk, one quart of milk; (2) cream, one-half pint of cream; and (3) milk byproduct, one quart of skim milk, buttermilk, flavored milk drink, or other beverage containing more than 85 percent of skim milk, or one-half pound of cottage, pot, or bakers' cheese.

(h) *Quota exclusions and exemptions.* Deliveries of milk, milk byproducts, or cream (1) to other handlers, except for such deliveries to sub-handlers, (2) to plants engaged in the handling or processing of milk, milk byproducts, or cream from which no milk, milk byproducts, or cream is delivered in the sales area, and (3) to the agencies or groups specified in (d) of the order, shall be excluded from the computation of deliveries in the base period and exempt from charges to quotas.

(i) *Transfers and apportionment of quotas.* The market agent is empowered to deduct an amount of base period deliveries to purchasers from the total of deliveries made by a handler or other person in the base period upon the application and a showing of unreasonable hardship by the handler making deliveries to such purchasers on the effective date of this order, and to add the amount of such deliveries to the total base period deliveries of the applicant handler. Denials of transfers or transfers granted by the market agent shall be reviewed by the Director upon application.

(j) *Petition for relief from hardships.* (1) Any person affected by the order or the provisions hereof who considers that compliance therewith would work an exceptional and unreasonable hardship on him; may file with the market agent a petition addressed to the Director. The petition shall contain the correct name, address and principal place of business of the petitioner, a full statement of the facts upon which the petition is based, and the hardship involved and the nature of the relief desired.

(2) Upon receiving such petition, the market agent shall immediately investigate the representations and facts stated therein.

(3) After investigation, the petition shall be certified to the Director, but prior to certification the market agent may (i) deny the petition; or (ii) grant temporary relief for a total period not to exceed 60 days.

(4) Denials or grants of relief by the market agent shall be reviewed by the Director and may be affirmed, modified, or reversed by the Director.

(k) *Reports.* Each handler shall transmit to the market agent on forms prescribed by the market agent the following reports:

(1) Within 20 days following the effective date of this order, reports which show the information required by the market agent to establish such handlers' quotas;

(2) Within 20 days following the close of each quota period, the information required by the market agent to establish volumes of deliveries of milk, cream, and milk byproducts during the preceding quota period; and

(3) Handlers exempt from quotas pursuant to (f) hereof shall, upon the request of the market agent, submit the information required by the market agent

to establish volumes of deliveries of milk, cream, and milk byproducts.

(l) *Records.* Handlers shall keep and shall make available to the market agent such records of receipts, sales, deliveries, and production as the market agent shall require for the purpose of obtaining information which the Director may require for the establishment of quotas as prescribed in (b) of the order.

(m) *Distribution schedules.* The distribution schedules, if any, to be followed by the handlers in making deliveries shall be made effective in the terms of approval by the Director of such schedules.

(n) *Expense of administration.* Each handler shall pay to the market agent, within 20 days after the close of each calendar month an assessment of $0.005 per hundredweight of each of milk, cream, skim milk, buttermilk, flavored milk drinks, beverages containing more than 85 percent of skim milk, and skim milk equivalent of cottage, pot, or baker's cheese delivered during the preceding quota period and subject to quota regulations under the provisions hereof.

(o) *Violations.* The market agent shall report all violations to the Director together with the information required for the prosecution of such violations, except in a case where a handler has made deliveries in a quota period in excess of a quota in an amount not to exceed 5 percent of such quota, and in the succeeding quota period makes deliveries below quota by at least the same percent.

(p) *Bureau of the Budget appr* The record keeping and reporting quirements of this order have been proved by the Bureau of the Budge accordance with the Federal Rep Act of 1942. Subsequent record-kee or reporting requirements will be sub to the approval of the Bureau of Budget pursuant to the Federal Rep Act of 1942.

(q) This order shall take effec 12:01 a. m., e. w. t., October 10, 19

Issued this 2d day of October 19

ROY F. HENDRICKSON,
Director of Food Distributio

Press Release, Immediate:
Saturday, October 2, 1943.

The War Food Administration's fluid milk conservation and control program will be extended to cover eight new sales areas, effective October 10, 1943.

The newly designated sales areas are:

- Wilmington, Del.
- Lancaster, Pa.
- Reading, Pa.
- Scranton-Wilkes-Barre, Pa.
- Allentown-Bethlehem-Easton, Pa.
- Harrisburg, Pa.
- Trenton, N. J.
- Atlantic City, N. J.

William P. Sadler, 11 N. Juniper St., Philadelphia, Pennsylvania, will administer the program in each of these eight areas.

Dealers' monthly fluid milk sales in these areas may not exceed their June deliveries, and their sales of cream and of fluid milk byproducts (such as cottage cheese, chocolate milk and buttermilk) will be reduced to three-fourths of the quantities sold in June. Milk dealers include all persons or firms engaged in the sale or transfer of milk, but not retail stores, hotels, restaurants, etc.

Consumers in these areas however, will be able to purchase as much milk under the milk conservation program as they have been buying within the limits of local supplies—in general an amount considerably greater than that bought in pre-war years, and about 10 percent above last year's purchases. Sales quotas on cream and fluid milk byproducts have been set below June deliveries to boost fluid milk supplies where milk production is low, and to conserve milk for manufacturing purposes.

Producers-distributors who purchase no milk will be allowed to sell an amount of fluid milk, cream and fluid milk byproducts equal to 100 percent of their total milk production in June. Quota-exempt producer-distributors are defined separately for each area, but in general they are those whose deliveries are relatively small.

To help assure sufficient milk for manufacturing the cheese, butter, evaporated milk and milk powder required by the armed services and civilians for good nutrition and properly balanced diets, fluid milk sales are being stabilized in these and other metropolitan areas, FDA officials explained.

The FDA's dealer-quota plan is an attempt to stabilize fluid milk consumption without resorting to individual sumer rationing. Point rationin milk, a bulky and highly perishable c modity, would be very difficult to ad ister and would almost necessarily re fluid milk sales in many areas. If sumers and the trade cooperate with present program to assure that sale held within quotas and quantities a able are distributed fairly, FDA offi believe that consumer rationing will be necessary.

Milk handlers in the sales areas na will compute the quantity of milk w they may sell each month in term pounds of milk, their cream sale terms of pounds of cream and butte and their milk byproducts sales in te of pounds of milk byproducts.

Deliveries to the Armed Forces plants processing dairy products, other handlers (except special class handlers such as peddlers) are quot empt.

To facilitate administration, the ket agent, Mr. Sadler, may act upon tions for relief from hardships w may be submitted to him.

Milk sales in several other eastern midwestern areas have been previ brought under federal regulation. quotas are the same in all areas n to date.

WAR FOOD ADMINISTRATION

[FDO 79-30]

PART 1401—DAIRY PRODUCTS

CONSERVATION AND DISTRIBUTION OF FLUID MILK AND CREAM IN WILMINGTON, DEL., SALES AREA

Pursuant to the authority vested in me by Food Distribution Order No. 79 (8 F.R. 12426), issued on September 7, 1943, as amended, and to effectuate the purposes of such order, it is hereby ordered as follows:

§ 1401.65 *Quota restrictions*—(a) *Definitions.* When used in this order, unless otherwise distinctly expressed or manifestly incompatible with the intent hereof:

(1) Each term defined in Food Distribution Order No. 79, as amended, shall, when used herein, have the same meaning as is set forth for such term in Food Distribution Order No. 79, as amended.

(2) The term "order" means Food Distribution Order No. 79, issued on September 7, 1943, as amended.

(3) The term "sub-handler" means any handler, such as a peddler, vendor, sub-dealer, or secondary dealer, who purchases in a previously packaged and processed form milk, milk byproducts, or cream for delivery.

(b) *Milk sales area.* The following area is hereby designated as a "milk sales area" to be known as the Wilmington, Delaware sales area, and is referred to hereinafter as the "sales area": The city of Wilmington, the representative districts 1 to 10, inclusive, and that part of district 11 comprising part of the town of Newark, in New Castle, Delaware; the townships of Lower Penns Neck and Upper Penns Neck and the borough of Penns Grove in Salem County, New Jersey; and the township of New Garden and the borough of Avondale in Chester County, Pa., and the township of Bethel in Delaware County, Pa.

(c) *Base period.* The calendar month of June 1943 is hereby designated as the base period for the sales area.

(d) *Quota period.* The remainder of the calendar month in which the provisions hereof become effective and each subsequent calendar month, respectively, is hereby designated as a quota period for the sales area.

(e) *Handler quotas.* Quotas for each handler in the sales area in each quota period shall be determined as follows:

(1) Divide the total deliveries of each of milk, milk byproducts, and cream (and of butterfat in milk or in cream where percentages of pounds of butterfat are specified in (e) (3) (i) or (e) (3) (ii) hereof) made in the sales area by such handler during the base period, after excluding the quota-exempt deliveries described in (h) hereof and adjusting such deliveries for the transfers set out in (i) hereof, by the number of days in the base period;

(2) Multiply the result of the foregoing calculation by the number of days in the quota period; and

(3) Multiply the aforesaid resulting amount by the following applicable percentage: (i) Milk: 100 percent of pounds of milk and ____ percent of pounds of butterfat; (ii) Cream: 75 percent of pounds of cream and 75 percent of pounds of butterfat; and (iii) Milk byproducts: 75 percent of pounds of milk byproducts other than cottage, pot, or baker's cheese and of the pounds of skim milk equivalent of cottage, pot, or baker's cheese. (For the purpose of this order, one pound of cottage, pot, or baker's cheese shall be considered as the equivalent of 7 pounds of skim milk.)

(f) *Quotas for handlers who are also producers.* Quotas for handlers who are also producers and who purchase no milk shall be 100 percent of the total production of such handlers in the base period.

(g) *Handler exemptions.* Quotas shall not apply to any handler who delivers in a quota period a daily average of less than 400 units of milk, cream, and milk byproducts. For the purpose of this order, a unit shall be the equivalent in volume of the following: (1) milk, one quart of milk; (2) cream, one-half pint of cream; and (3) milk byproduct, one quart of skim milk, buttermilk, flavored milk drink, or other beverage containing more than 85 percent of skim milk, or one-half pound of cottage, pot, or bakers' cheese.

(h) *Quota exclusions and exemptions.* Deliveries of milk, milk byproducts, or cream (1) to other handlers, except for such deliveries to sub-handlers, (2) to plants engaged in the handling or processing of milk, milk byproducts, or cream from which no milk, milk byproducts, or cream is delivered in the sales area, and (3) to the agencies or groups specified in (d) of the order, shall be excluded from the computation of deliveries in the base period and exempt from charges to quotas.

(i) *Transfers and apportionment of quotas.* The market agent is empowered to deduct an amount of base period deliveries to purchasers from the total of deliveries made by a handler or other person in the base period upon the application and a showing of unreasonable hardship by the handler making deliveries to such purchasers on the effective date of this order, and to add the amount of such deliveries to the total base period deliveries of the applicant handler. Denials of transfers or transfers granted by the market agent shall be reviewed by the Director upon application.

(j) *Petition for relief from hardships.* (1) Any person affected by the order or the provisions hereof who considers that compliance therewith would work an exceptional and unreasonable hardship on him, may file with the market agent a petition addressed to the Director. The petition shall contain the correct name, address and principal place of business of the petitioner, a full statement of the facts upon which the petition is based, and the hardship involved and the nature of the relief desired.

(2) Upon receiving such petition, the market agent shall immediately investigate the representations and facts stated therein.

(3) After investigation, the petition shall be certified to the Director, but prior to certification the market agent may (i) deny the petition; or (ii) grant temporary relief for a total period not to exceed 60 days.

(4) Denials or grants of relief by the market agent shall be reviewed by the Director and may be affirmed, modified, or reversed by the Director.

(k) *Reports.* Each handler shall transmit to the market agent on forms prescribed by the market agent the following reports:

(1) Within 20 days following the effective date of this order, reports which show the information required by the market agent to establish such handlers' quotas;

(2) Within 20 days following the close of each quota period, the information required by the market agent to establish volumes of deliveries of milk, cream, and milk byproducts during the preceding quota period; and

(3) Handlers exempt from quotas pursuant to (f) hereof shall, upon the request of the market agent, submit the

information required by the market agent to establish volumes of deliveries of milk, cream, and milk byproducts.

(l) *Records.* Handlers shall keep and shall make available to the market agent such records of receipts, sales, deliveries, and production as the market agent shall require for the purpose of obtaining information which the Director may require for the establishment of quotas as prescribed in (b) of the order.

(m) *Distribution schedules.* The distribution schedules, if any, to be followed by the handlers in making deliveries shall be made effective in the terms of approval by the Director of such schedules.

(n) *Expense of administration.* Each handler shall pay to the market agent, within 20 days after the close of each calendar month an assessment of $0.005 per hundredweight of each of milk, cream, skim milk, buttermilk, flavored milk drinks, beverages containing more than 85 percent of skim milk, and skim milk equivalent of cottage, pot, or baker's cheese delivered during the preceding quota period and subject to quota regulations under the provisions hereof.

(o) *Violations.* The market agent shall report all violations to the Director together with the information required for the prosecution of such violations, except in a case where a handler has made deliveries in a quota period in excess of a quota in an amount not to exceed 5 percent of such quota, and in the succeeding quota period makes deliveries below that quota by at least th[e] same percent.

(p) *Bureau of the Budget approv[al].* The record-keeping and reporting r[e]quirements of this order have been a[p]proved by the Bureau of the Budget [in] accordance with the Federal Repor[ts] Act of 1942. Subsequent record-keepi[ng] or reporting requirements will be su[b]ject to the approval of the Bureau [of] the Budget pursuant to the Federal R[e]ports Act of 1942.

(q) This order shall take effect [at] 12:01 a. m., e. w. t., October 10, 1943.

Issued this 2d day of October 1943.

ROY F. HENDRICKSON,
Director of Food Distribution.

Press Release, Immediate:
Saturday, October 2, 1943.

The War Food Administration's fluid milk conservation and control program will be extended to cover eight new sales areas, effective October 10, 1943.

The newly designated sales areas are:

Wilmington, Del.
Lancaster, Pa.
Reading, Pa.
Scranton-Wilkes-Barre, Pa.
Allentown-Bethlehem-Easton, Pa.
Harrisburg, Pa.
Trenton, N. J.
Atlantic City, N. J.

William P. Sadler, 11 N. Juniper St., Philadelphia, Pennsylvania, will administer the program in each of these eight areas.

Dealers' monthly fluid milk sales in these areas may not exceed their June deliveries, and their sales of cream and of fluid milk byproducts (such as cottage cheese, chocolate milk and buttermilk) will be reduced to three-fourths of the quantities sold in June. Milk dealers include all persons or firms engaged in the sale or transfer of milk, but not retail stores, hotels, restaurants, etc.

Consumers in these areas, however, will be able to purchase as much milk under the milk conservation program as they have been buying within the limits of local supplies—in general an amount considerably greater than that bought in pre-war years, and about 10 percent above last year's purchases. Sales quotas on cream and fluid milk byproducts have been set below June deliveries to boost fluid milk supplies where milk production is low, and to conserve milk for manufacturing purposes.

Producer-distributors who purchase no milk will be allowed to sell an amount of fluid milk, cream and fluid milk byproducts equal to 100 percent of their total milk production in June. Quota-exempt producer distributors are defined separately for each area, but in general they are those whose deliveries are relatively small.

To help assure sufficient milk for manufacturing the cheese, butter, evaporated milk and milk powder required by the armed services and civilians for good nutrition and properly balanced diets, fluid milk sales are being stabilized in these and other metropolitan areas, FDA officials explained.

The FDA's dealer-quota plan is an attempt to stabilize fluid milk consumption without resorting to individual consumer rationing. Point rationing of milk, a bulky and highly perishab[le] commodity, would be very difficult [to] administer and would almost necessari[ly] reduce fluid milk sales in many are[as]. If consumers and the trade coopera[te] with the present program to assure th[at] sales are held within quotas and qua[n]tities available are distributed fair[ly], FDA officials believe that consum[er] rationing will not be necessary.

Milk handlers in the sales areas nam[ed] will compute the quantity of milk whi[ch] they may sell each month in terms [of] pounds of milk, their cream sales [in] terms of pounds of cream and butterf[at] and their milk byproducts sales in ter[ms] of pounds of milk byproducts.

Deliveries to the Armed Forces, [to] plants processing dairy products, a[nd] other handlers (except special classes [of] handlers such as peddlers) are quo[ta] exempt.

To facilitate administration, t[he] market agent, Mr. Sadler, may act up[on] petitions for relief from hardships whi[ch] may be submitted to him.

Milk sales in several other eastern a[nd] midwestern areas have been previous[ly] brought under federal regulation. Sa[les] quotas are the same in all areas nam[ed] to date.

FDO 79-31

OCT. 2, 1943

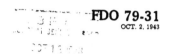

WAR FOOD ADMINISTRATION

[FDO 79-31]

PART 1401—DAIRY PRODUCTS

CONSERVATION AND DISTRIBUTION OF FLUID MILK AND CREAM IN TRENTON, N. J., SALES AREA

Pursuant to the authority vested in me by Food Distribution Order No. 79 (8 F.R. 12426), issued on September 7, 1943, as amended, and to effectuate the purposes of such order, it is hereby ordered as follows:

§ 1401.63 *Quota restrictions*—(a) *Definitions.* When used in this order, unless otherwise distinctly expressed or manifestly incompatible with the intent hereof:

(1) Each term defined in Food Distribution Order No. 79, as amended, shall, when used herein, have the same meaning as is set forth for such term in Food Distribution Order No. 79, as amended.

(2) The term "order" means Food Distribution Order No. 79, issued on September 7, 1943, as amended.

(3) The term "sub-handler" means any handler, such as a peddler, vendor, sub-dealer, or secondary dealer, who purchases in a previously packaged and processed form milk, milk byproducts, or cream for delivery.

(b) *Milk sales area.* The following area is hereby designated as a "milk sales area" to be known as the Trenton, N. J., sales area, and is referred to hereinafter as the "sales area": The city of Trenton, the townships of Ewing, Hamilton, Lawrence, and Princeton, and the borough of Princeton in Mercer County, N. J.; the township of Bordentown, the city of Bordentown, and the borough of Fieldboro in Burlington County, N. J.; the townships of Falls and Lower Makefield, the boroughs of Morrisville, Tullytown, and Yardley in Bucks County, Pa.

(c) *Base period.* The calendar month of June 1943 is hereby designated as the base period for the sale area.

(d) *Quota period.* The remainder of the calendar month in which the provisions hereof become effective and each subsequent calendar month, respectively, is hereby designated as a quota period for the sales area.

(e) *Handler quotas.* Quotas for each handler in the sales area in each quota period shall be determined as follows:

(1) Divide the total deliveries of each of milk, milk byproducts, and cream (and of butterfat in milk or in cream where percentages of pounds of butterfat are specified in (e) (3) (i) or (e) (3) (ii) hereof) made in the sales area by such handler during the base period, after excluding the quota-exempt deliveries described in (h) hereof and adjusting such deliveries for the transfers set out in (i) hereof, by the number of days in the base period;

(2) Multiply the result of the foregoing calculation by the number of days in the quota period; and

(3) Multiply the aforesaid resulting amount by the following applicable percentage: (i) Milk: 100 percent of pounds of milk and ---- percent of pounds of butterfat; (ii) Cream: 75 percent of pounds of cream and 75 percent of pounds of butterfat; and (iii) Milk byproducts: 75 percent of pounds of milk byproducts other than cottage, pot, or baker's cheese and of the pounds of skim milk equivalent of cottage, pot, or baker's cheese. (For the purpose of this order, one pound of cottage, pot, or baker's cheese shall be considered as the equivalent of 7 pounds of skim milk.)

(f) *Quotas for handlers who are also producers.* Quotas for handlers who are also producers and who purchase no milk shall be 100 percent of the total production of such handlers in the base period.

(g) *Handler exemptions.* Quotas shall not apply to any handler who delivers in a quota period a daily average of less than 400 units of milk, cream, and milk byproducts. For the purpose of this order, a unit shall be the equivalent in volume of the following: (1) milk, one quart of milk; (2) cream, one-half pint of cream; and (3) milk byproduct, one quart of skim milk, buttermilk, flavored milk drink, or other beverage containing more than 85 percent of skim milk, or one-half pound of cottage, pot, or baker's cheese.

(h) *Quota exclusions and exemptions.* Deliveries of milk, milk byproducts, or cream (1) to other handlers, except for such deliveries to sub-handlers, (2) to plants engaged in the handling or processing of milk, milk byproducts, or cream from which no milk, milk byproducts, or cream is delivered in the sales area, and (3) to the agencies or groups specified in (d) of the order, shall be excluded from the computation of deliveries in the base period and exempt from charges to quotas.

(i) *Transfers and apportionment of quotas.* The market agent is empowered to deduct an amount of base period deliveries to purchasers from the total of deliveries made by a handler or other person in the base period upon the application and a showing of unreasonable hardship by the handler making deliveries to such purchasers on the effective date of this order, and to add the amount of such deliveries to the total base period deliveries of the applicant handler. Denials of transfers or transfers granted by the market agent shall be reviewed by the Director upon application.

(j) *Petition for relief from hardships.* (1) Any person affected by the order or the provisions hereof who considers that compliance therewith would work an exceptional and unreasonable hardship on him, may file with the market agent a petition addressed to the Director. The petition shall contain the correct name, address and principal place of business of the petitioner, a full statement of the facts upon which the petition is based, and the hardship involved and the nature of the relief desired.

(2) Upon receiving such petition, the market agent shall immediately investigate the representations and facts stated therein.

(3) After investigation, the petition shall be certified to the Director, but prior to certification the market agent may (i) deny the petition; or (ii) grant temporary relief for a total period not to exceed 60 days.

(4) Denials or grants of relief by the market agent shall be reviewed by the Director and may be affirmed, modified, or reversed by the Director.

(k) *Reports.* Each handler shall transmit to the market agent on forms prescribed by the market agent the following reports:

(1) Within 20 days following the effective date of this order; reports which show the information required by the market agent to establish such handlers' quotas;

(2) Within 20 days following the close of each quota period, the information required by the market agent to establish

volumes of deliveries of milk, cream, and milk byproducts during the preceding quota period; and

(3) Handlers exempt from quotas pursuant to (f) hereof shall, upon the request of the market agent, submit the information required by the market agent to establish volumes of deliveries of milk, cream, and milk byproducts.

(l) *Records.* Handlers shall keep and shall make available to the market agent such records of receipts, sales, deliveries, and production as the market agent shall require for the purpose of obtaining information which the Director may require for the establishment of quotas as prescribed in (b) of the order.

(m) *Distribution schedules.* The distribution schedules, if any, to be followed by the handlers in making deliveries shall be made effective in the terms of approval by the Director of such schedules.

(n) *Expense of administration.* Each handler shall pay to the market agent, within 20 days after the close of each calendar month an assessment of $0.005 per hundredweight of each of milk, cream, skim milk, buttermilk, flavored milk drinks, beverages containing more than 85 percent of skim milk, and skim milk equivalent of cottage, pot, or baker's cheese delivered during the preceding quota period and subject to quota regulations under the provisions hereof.

(o) *Violations.* The market agent shall report all violations to the Director together with the information required for the prosecution of such violations, except in a case where a handler has made deliveries in a quota period in excess of a quota in an amount not to exceed 5 percent of such quota, and in the succeeding quota period makes deliveries below that quota by at least the same percent.

(p) *Bureau of Budget approval.* The record-keeping and reporting requirements of this order have been approved by the Bureau of the Budget in accordance with the Federal Reports Act of 1942. Subsequent record-keeping or reporting requirements will be subject to the approval of the Bureau of the Budget pursuant to the Federal Reports Act of 1942.

(q) This order shall take effect at 12:01 a. m., e. w. t., October 10, 1943.

Issued this 2d day of October 1943.

ROY F. HENDRICKSON,
Director of Food Distribution.

Press Release, Immediate:
Saturday, October 2' 1943.

The War Food Administration's fluid milk conservation and control program will be extended to cover eight new sales areas, effective October 10, 1943.

The newly designated sales areas are:

- Wilmington, Del.
- Lancaster, Pa.
- Reading, Pa.
- Scranton-Wilkes-Barre, Pa.
- Allentown-Bethlehem-Easton, Pa.
- Harrisburg, Pa.
- Trenton, N. J.
- Atlantic City, N. J.

William P. Sadler, 11 N. Juniper St., Philadelphia, Pennsylvania, will administer the program in each of these eight areas.

Dealers' monthly fluid milk sales in these areas may not exceed their June deliveries, and their sales of cream and of fluid milk byproducts (such as cottage cheese, chocolate milk and buttermilk) will be reduced to three-fourth of the quantities sold in June. Milk dealers include all persons or firms engaged in the sale or transfer of milk, but not retail stores, hotels, restaurants, etc.

Consumers in these areas, however, will be able to purchase as much milk under the milk conservation program as they have been buying within the limits of local supplies—in general an amount considerably greater than that bought in pre-war years, and about 10 percent above last year's purchases. Sales quotas on cream and fluid milk byproducts have been set below June deliveries to boost fluid milk supplies where milk production is low, and to conserve milk for manufacturing purposes.

Producer-distributors who purchase no milk will be allowed to sell an amount of fluid milk, cream and fluid milk byproducts equal to 100 percent of their total milk production in June. Quota-exempt producer distributors are defined separately for each area, but in general they are those whose deliveries are relatively small.

To help assure sufficient milk for manufacturing the cheese, butter, evaporated milk and milk powder required by the armed services and civilians for good nutrition and properly balanced diets, fluid milk sales are being stabilized in these and other metropolitan areas, FDA officials explained.

The FDA's dealer-quota plan is an attempt to stabilize fluid milk consumption without resorting to individual consumer rationing. Point rationing of milk, a bulky and highly perishable commodity, would be very difficult to administer and would almost necessarily reduce fluid milk sales in many areas. If consumers and the trade cooperate with the present program to assure that sales are held within quotas and quantities available are distributed fairly, FDA officials believe that consumer rationing will not be necessary.

Milk handlers in the sales areas named will compute the quantity of milk which they may sell each month in terms of pounds of milk, their cream sales in terms of pounds of cream and butterfat and their milk byproducts sales in terms of pounds of milk byproducts.

Deliveries to the Armed Forces, to plants processing dairy products, and other handlers (except special classes of handlers such as peddlers) are quota exempt.

To facilitate administration, the market agent, Mr. Sadler, may act upon petitions for relief from hardships which may be submitted to him.

Milk sales in several other eastern and midwestern areas have been previously brought under federal regulation. Sales quotas are the same in all areas named to date.

F 133 F

FDO 79-32
OCT. 2, 1943

WAR FOOD ADMINISTRATION

[FDO 79-32]

PART 1401—DAIRY PRODUCTS

CONSERVATION AND DISTRIBUTION OF FLUID MILK AND CREAM IN ATLANTIC CITY, N. J., SALES AREA

Pursuant to the authority vested in me by Food Distribution Order No. 79 (8 F.R. 12426), issued on September 7, 1943, as amended, and to effectuate the purposes of such order, it is hereby ordered as follows:

§ 1401.62 *Quota restrictions*—(a) *Definitions.* When used in this order, unless otherwise distinctly expressed or manifestly incompatible with the intent hereof:

(1) Each term defined in Food Distribution Order No. 79, as amended, shall, when used herein, have the same meaning as is set forth for such term in Food Distribution Order No. 79, as amended.

(2) The term "order" means Food Distribution Order No. 79, issued on September 7, 1943, as amended.

(3) The term "sub-handler" means any handler, such as a peddler, vendor, sub-dealer, or secondary dealer, who purchases in a previously packaged and processed form milk, milk byproducts, or cream for delivery.

(b) *Milk sales area.* The following area is hereby designated as a "milk sales area" to be known as the Atlantic City, New Jersey, sales area, and is referred to hereinafter as the "sales area": The city of Atlantic City, the cities of Absecon, Brigantine, Linwood, Margate, Northfield, Pleasantville, Somers Point, and Ventnor City, and the borough of Longport in Atlantic County, New Jersey; the city of Ocean City in Cape May County, New Jersey.

(c) *Base period.* The calendar month of June 1943 is hereby designated as the base period for the sales area.

(d) *Quota period.* The remainder of the calendar month in which the provisions hereof become effective and each subsequent calendar month, respectively, is hereby designated as a quota period for the sales area.

(e) *Handler quotas.* Quotas for each handler in the sales area in each quota period shall be determined as follows:

(1) Divide the total deliveries of each of milk, milk byproducts, and cream (and of butterfat in milk or in cream where percentages of pounds of butterfat are specified in (e) (3) (i) or (e) (3) (ii) hereof) made in the sales area by such handler during the base period, after excluding the quota-exempt deliveries described in (h) hereof and adjusting such deliveries for the transfers set out in (i) hereof, by the number of days in the base period;

(2) Multiply the result of the foregoing calculation by the number of days in the quota period; and

(3) Multiply the aforesaid resulting amount by the following applicable percentage: (i) Milk: 100 percent of pounds of milk and ---- percent of pounds of butterfat; (ii) Cream: 75 percent of pounds of cream and 75 percent of pounds of butterfat; and (iii) Milk byproducts: 75 percent of pounds of milk byproducts other than cottage, pot, or baker's cheese and of the pounds of skim milk equivalent of cottage, pot, or baker's cheese. (For the purpose of this order, one pound of cottage, pot, or baker's cheese shall be considered as the equivalent of 7 pounds of skim milk.)

(f) *Quotas for handlers who are also producers.* Quotas for handlers who are also producers and who purchase no milk shall be 100 percent of the total production of such handlers in the base period.

(g) *Handler exemptions.* Quotas shall not apply to any handler who delivers in a quota period a daily average of less than 400 units of milk, cream, and milk byproducts. For the purpose of this order, a unit shall be the equivalent in volume of the following: (1) Milk, one quart of milk; (2) cream, one-half pint of cream; and (3) milk byproduct, one quart of skim milk, buttermilk, flavored milk drink, or other beverage containing more than 85 percent of skim milk, or one-half pound of cottage, pot, or baker's cheese.

(h) *Quota exclusions and exemptions.* Deliveries of milk, milk byproducts, or cream (1) to other handlers, except for such deliveries to sub-handlers, (2) to plants engaged in the handling of processing of milk, milk byproducts, or cream from which no milk, milk byproducts, or cream is delivered in the sales area, and (3) to the agencies or groups specified in (d) of the order, shall be excluded from the computation of deliveries in the base period and exempt from charges to quotas.

(i) *Transfers and apportionment of quotas.* The market agent is empowered to deduct an amount of base period deliveries to purchasers from the total of deliveries made by a handler or other person in the base period upon the application and a showing of unreasonable hardship by the handler making deliveries to such purchasers on the effective date of this order, and to add the amount of such deliveries to the total base period deliveries of the applicant handler. Denials of transfers or transfers granted by the market agent shall be reviewed by the Director upon application.

(j) *Petition for relief from hardships.* (1) Any person affected by the order or the provisions hereof who considers that compliance therewith would work an exceptional and unreasonable hardship on him, may file with the market agent a petition addressed to the Director. The petition shall contain the correct name, address and principal place of business of the petitioner, a full statement of the facts upon which the petition is based, and the hardship involved and the nature of the relief desired.

(2) Upon receiving such petition, the market agent shall immediately investigate the representations and facts stated therein.

(3) After investigation, the petition shall be certified to the Director, but prior to certification the market agent may (i) deny the petition; or (ii) grant temporary relief for a total period not to exceed 60 days.

(4) Denials or grants of relief by the market agent shall be reviewed by the Director and may be affirmed, modified, or reversed by the Director.

(k) *Reports.* Each handler shall transmit to the market agent on forms prescribed by the market agent the following reports:

(1) Within 20 days following the effective date of this order, reports which show the information required by the market agent to establish such handlers' quotas;

(2) Within 20 days following the close of each quota period, the information required by the market agent to establish volumes of deliveries of milk, cream, and milk byproducts during the preceding quota period; and

(3) Handlers exempt from quotas pursuant to (f) hereof shall, upon the request of the market agent, submit the information required by the market agent to establish volumes of deliveries of milk, cream, and milk byproducts.

(l) *Records.* Handlers shall keep and shall make available to the market agent such records of receipts, sales, deliveries, and production as the market agent shall require for the purpose of obtaining information which the Director may require for the establishment of quotas as prescribed in (b) of the order.

(m) *Distribution schedules.* The distribution schedules, if any, to be followed by the handlers in making deliveries shall be made effective in the terms of approval by the Director of such schedules.

(n) *Expense of administration.* Each handler shall pay to the market agent, within 20 days after the close of each calendar month an assessment of $0.005 per hundredweight of each of milk, cream, skim milk, buttermilk, flavored milk drinks, beverages containing more than 85 percent of skim milk, and skim milk equivalent of cottage, pot, or baker's cheese delivered during the preceding quota period and subject to quota regulations under the provisions hereof.

(o) *Violations.* The market agent shall report all violations to the Director together with the information required for the prosecution of such violations, except in a case where a handler has made deliveries in a quota period in excess of a quota in an amount not to exceed 5 percent of such quota, and in the succeeding quota period makes deliveries below that quota by at least the same percent.

(p) *Bureau of the Budget approval.* The record-keeping and reporting requirements of this order have been approved by the Bureau of the Budget in accordance with the Federal Reports Act of 1942. Subsequent record-keeping or reporting requirements will be subject to the approval of the Bureau of the Budget pursuant to the Federal Reports Act of 1942.

(q) This order shall take effect at 12:01 a. m., e. w. t., October 10, 1943.

Issued this 2d day of October 1943.

ROY F. HENDRICKSON,
Director of Food Distribution.

Press Release, Immediate:
Saturday, October 2, 1943.

The War Food Administration's fluid milk conservation and control program will be extended to cover eight new sales areas, effective October 10, 1943.

The newly designated sales areas are:

- Wilmington, Del.
- Lancaster, Pa.
- Reading, Pa.
- Scranton-Wilkes-Barre, Pa.
- Allentown-Bethlehem-Easton, Pa.
- Harrisburg, Pa.
- Trenton, N. J.
- Atlantic City, N. J.

William P. Sadler, 11 N. Juniper St., Philadelphia, Pennsylvania, will administer the program in each of these eight areas.

Dealers' monthly fluid milk sales in these areas may not exceed their June deliveries, and their sales of cream and of fluid milk byproducts (such as cottage cheese, chocolate milk and buttermilk) will be reduced to three-fourths of the quantities sold in June. Milk dealers include all persons or firms engaged in the sale or transfer of milk, but not retail stores, hotels, restaurants, etc.

Consumers in these areas however, will be able to purchase as much milk under the milk conservation program as they have been buying within the limits of local supplies—in general an amount considerably greater than that bought in pre-war years, and about 10 percent above last year's purchases. Sales quotas on cream and fluid milk byproducts have been set below June deliveries to boost fluid milk supplies where milk production is low, and to conserve milk for manufacturing purposes.

Producer-distributors who purchase no milk will be allowed to sell an amount of fluid milk, cream and fluid milk byproducts equal to 100 percent of their total milk production in June. Quota-exempt producer distributors are defined separately for each area, but in general they are those whose deliveries are relatively small.

To help assure sufficient milk for manufacturing the cheese, butter, evaporated milk and milk powder required by the armed services and civilians for good nutrition and properly balanced diets, fluid milk sales are being stabilized in these and other metropolitan areas, FDA officials explained.

The FDA's dealer-quota plan is an attempt to stabilize fluid milk consumption without resorting to individual consumer rationing. Point rationing of milk, a bulky and highly perishable commodity, would be very difficult to administer and would almost necessarily reduce fluid milk sales in many areas. If consumers and the trade cooperate with the present program to assure that sales are held within quotas and quantities available are distributed fairly, FDA officials believe that consumer rationing will not be necessary.

Milk handlers in the sales areas named will compute the quantity of milk which they may sell each month in terms of pounds of milk, their cream sales in terms of pounds of cream and butterfat, and their milk byproducts sales in terms of pounds of milk byproducts.

Deliveries to the Armed Forces, to plants processing dairy products, and other handlers (except special classes of handlers such as peddlers) are quota exempt.

To facilitate administration, the market agent, Mr. Sadler, may act upon petitions for relief from hardships which may be submitted to him.

Milk sales in several other eastern and midwestern areas have been previously brought under federal regulation. Sales quotas are the same in all areas named to date.

cc/n1

FDO 79-33

OCT. 2, 1943

WAR FOOD ADMINISTRATION

[FDO 79-33]

PART 1401—DAIRY PRODUCTS

CONSERVATION AND DISTRIBUTION OF FLUID MILK AND CREAM IN PHILADELPHIA, PA., METROPOLITAN SALES AREA

Pursuant to the authority vested in me by Food Distribution Order No. 79 (8 F.R. 12426), issued on September 7, 1943, as amended, and to effectuate the purposes of such order, it is hereby ordered as follows:

§ 1401.67 *Quota restrictions*—(a) *Definitions.* When used in this order, unless otherwise distinctly expressed or manifestly incompatible with the intent hereof:

(1) Each term defined in Food Distribution Order No. 79, as amended, shall, when used herein, have the same meaning as is set forth for such term in Food Distribution Order No. 79, as amended.

(2) The term "order" means Food Distribution Order No. 79, issued on September 7, 1943, as amended.

(3) The term "sub-handler" means any handler, such as a peddler, vendor, sub-dealer, or secondary dealer, who purchases in a previously packaged and processed form milk, milk byproducts, or cream for delivery.

(b) *Milk sales area.* The following area is hereby designated as a "milk sales area" to be known as the Philadelphia, Pennsylvania, metropolitan sales area, and is referred to hereinafter as the "sales area": The city of Philadelphia, coincident with Philadelphia County, Pennsylvania;

The townships of Bensalem, Bristol, Lower Southampton, Middletown, Upper Southampton, and Warminster, and the boroughs of Bristol, Hulmeville, Ivyland, Langhorne, Langhorne Manor, and South Langhorne in Bucks County, Pennsylvania;

The townships of East Pikeland, Easttown, Schuylkill, Tredyffrin, and Willistown, and the boroughs of Malvern, Phoenixville, and Spring City in Chester County, Pennsylvania;

The city of Chester, the townships of Aston, Chester, Darby, Edgemont, Haverford, Lower Chichester, Marple, Middletown, Nether Providence, Newton, Radnor, Ridley, Springfield, Thornbury, Tinicum, Upper Chichester, Upper Darby, and Upper Providence, the boroughs of Aldan, Clifton Heights, Collingdale, Colwyn, Darby, East Lansdowne, Eddystone, Folcroft, Glenolden, Lansdowne, Marcus Hook, Media, Millbourne, Morton, Norwood, Parkside, Prospect Park, Ridley Park, Rose Valley, Rutledge, Sharon Hill, Swarthmore, Trainer, Upland, and Yeadon in Delaware County, Pennsylvania; The townships of Abington, Cheltenham, East Norriton, Hatfield, Horsham, Lower Gwynedd, Lower Merion, Lower Moreland, Lower Providence, Montgomery, Perkiomen, Plymouth, Springfield, Upper Dublin, Upper Gwynedd, Upper Merion, Upper Moreland, Upper Providence, West Norriton, Whitemarsh, and Whitpain, and the boroughs of Ambler, Bridgeport, Bryn Athyn, Collegeville, Conshohocken, Hatboro, Hatfield, Jenkintown, Lansdale, Narbeth, Norristown, North Wales, Rockledge, Royersford, Schwenksville, Trappe, and West Conshohocken in Montgomery County, Pennsylvania;

The cities of Beverly and Burlington, the townships of Burlington, Chester, Cinnaminson, Delanco, Delran, Edgewater Park, Florence, Morrestown, and Riverside, the boroughs of Palmyra and Riverton in Burlington County, New Jersey;

The cities of Camden and Gloucester, the townships of Berlin, Delaware, Gloucester, Haddon, Pennsauken, and Voorhees, the boroughs of Audubon, Barrington, Bellmawr, Berlin, Brooklawn, Clementon, Collingswood, Gibbsboro, Haddonfield, Haddon Heights, Hi-Nella, Laurel Springs, Lawnside, Lindenwold, Magnolia, Merchantville, Mount Ephraim, Oaklyn, Pine Hill, Pine Valley, Runnemede, Somerdale, Stratford, Tavistock, and Wood-Lynne in Camden County, New Jersey;

The city of Woodbury, the townships of Deptford, East Greenwich, Greenwich, Mantua, Washington, and West Deptford, the boroughs of Clayton, Glassboro, National Park, Paulsboro, Pittman, Wenonah, Westville, and Woodbury Heights, in Gloucester County, New Jersey.

(c) *Base period.* The calendar month of June 1943 is hereby designated as the base period for the sales area.

(d) *Quota period.* The remainder of the calendar month in which the provisions hereof become effective and each subsequent calendar month, respectively, is hereby designated as a quota period for the sales area.

(e) *Handler quotas.* Quotas for each handler in the sales area in each quota period shall be determined as follows:

(1) Divide the total deliveries of each of milk, milk byproducts, and cream (and of butterfat in milk or in cream where percentages of pounds of butterfat are specified in (e) (3) (i) or (e) (3) (ii) hereof) made in the sales area by such handler during the base period, after excluding the quota-exempt deliveries described in (h) hereof and adjusting such deliveries for the transfers set out in (i) hereof, by the number of days in the base period;

(2) Multiply the result of the foregoing calculation by the number of days in the quota period; and

(3) Multiply the aforesaid resulting amount by the following applicable percentage: (i) Milk: 100 percent of pounds of milk and ____ percent of pounds of butterfat; (ii) Cream: 75 percent of pounds of cream and 75 percent of pounds of butterfat; and (iii) Milk byproducts; 75 percent of pounds of milk byproducts other than cottage, pot, or baker's cheese and of the pounds of skim milk equivalent of cottage, pot, or baker's cheese. (For the purpose of this order, one pound of cottage, pot, or baker's cheese shall be considered as the equivalent of 7 pounds of skim milk.)

(f) *Quotas for handlers who are also producers.* Quotas for handlers who are also producers and who purchase no milk shall be 100 per cent of the total production of such handlers in the base period.

(g) *Handler exemptions.* Quotas shall not apply to any handler who delivers in a quota period a daily average of less than 400 units of milk, cream, and milk byproducts. For the purpose of this order, a unit shall be the equivalent in volume of the following: (1) Milk, one quart of milk; (2) cream, one-half pint of cream; and (3) milk byproduct, one quart of skim milk, buttermilk, flavored milk drink, or other beverage containing more than 85 percent of skim milk, or one-half pound of cottage, pot, or baker's cheese.

(h) *Quota exclusions and exemptions.* Deliveries of milk, milk byproducts, or cream (1) to other handlers, except for such deliveries to sub-handlers, (2) to plants engaged in the handling or processing of milk, milk byproducts, or cream from which no milk, milk byproducts, or cream is delivered in the sales area, and

(3) to the agencies or groups specified in (d) of the order, shall be excluded from the computation of deliveries in the base period and exempt from charges to quotas.

(i) *Transfers and apportionment of quotas.* The market agent is empowered to deduct an amount of base period deliveries to purchasers from the total of deliveries made by a handler or other person in the base period upon the application and a showing of unreasonable hardship by the handler making deliveries to such purchasers on the effective date of this order, and to add the amount of such deliveries to the total base period deliveries of the applicant handler. Denials of transfers or transfers granted by the market agent shall be reviewed by the Director upon application.

(j) *Petition for relief from hardships.* (1) Any person affected by the order or the provisions hereof who considers that compliance therewith would work an exceptional and unreasonable hardship on him, may file with the market agent a petition addressed to the Director. The petition shall contain the correct name, address, and principal place of business of the petitioner, a full statement of the facts upon which the petition is based, and the hardship involved and the nature of the relief desired.

(2) Upon receiving such petition, the market agent shall immediately investigate the representations and facts stated therein.

(3) After investigation, the petition shall be certified to the Director, but prior to certification the market agent may (i) deny the petition; or (ii) grant temporary relief for a total period not to exceed 60 days.

(4) Denials or grants of relief by the market agent shall be reviewed by the Director and may be affirmed, modified, or reversed by the Director.

(k) *Reports.* Each handler shall transmit to the market agent on forms prescribed by the market agent the following reports:

(1) Within 20 days following the effective date of this order, reports which show the information required by the market agent to establish such handlers' quotas;

(2) Within 20 days following the close of each quota period, the information required by the market agent to establish volumes of deliveries of milk, cream, and milk byproducts during the preceding quota period; and

(3) Handlers exempt from quotas pursuant to (f) hereof shall, upon the request of the market agent, submit the information required by the market agent to establish volumes of deliveries of milk, cream, and milk byproducts.

(l) *Records.* Handlers shall keep and shall make available to the market agent such records of receipts, sales deliveries, and production as the market agent shall require for the purpose of obtaining information which the Director may require for the establishment of quotas as prescribed in (b) of the order.

(m) *Distribution schedules.* The distribution schedules, if any, to be followed by the handlers in making deliveries shall be made effective in the terms of approval by the Director of such schedules.

(n) *Expense of administration.* Each handler shall pay to the market agent, within 20 days after the close of each calendar month an assessment of $0.005 per hundredweight of each of milk, cream, skim milk, buttermilk, flavored milk drinks, beverages containing more than 85 percent of skim milk, and skim milk equivalent of cottage, pot, or baker's cheese delivered during the preceding quota period and subject to quota regulations under the provisions hereof.

(o) *Violations.* The market agent shall report all violations to the Director together with the information required for the prosecution of such violations, except in a case where a handler has made deliveries in a quota period in excess of a quota in an amount not to exceed 5 percent of such quota, and in the succeeding quota period makes deliveries below that quota by at least the same percent.

(p) *Bureau of the Budget approval.* The record keeping and reporting requirements of this order have been approved by the Bureau of the Budget in accordance with the Federal Reports Act of 1942. Subsequent record-keeping or reporting requirements will be subject to the approval of the Bureau of the Budget pursuant to the Federal Reports Act of 1942.

(q) This order shall take effect at 12:01 a. m., e. w. t., October 10, 1943.

Issued this 2d day of October 1943.

ROY F. HENDRICKSON,
Director of Food Distribution.

Press Release, Immediate:
Saturday, October 2, 1943.

The War Food Administration's fluid milk conservation and control program will be extended to cover eight new sales areas, effective October 10, 1943.

The newly designated sales areas are:

Wilmington, Del.
Lancaster, Pa.
Reading, Pa.
Scranton-Wilkes-Barre, Pa.
Allentown-Bethlehem-Easton, Pa.
Harrisburg, Pa.
Trenton, N. J.
Atlantic City, N. J.

William P. Sadler, 11 N. Juniper St., Philadelphia, Pennsylvania, will administer the program in each of these eight areas.

Dealers' monthly fluid milk sales in these areas may not exceed their June deliveries, and their sales of cream and of fluid milk byproducts (such as cottage cheese, chocolate milk and buttermilk) will be reduced to three-fourths of the quantities sold in June. Milk dealers include all persons or firms engaged in the sale or transfer of milk, but not retail stores, hotels, restaurants, etc.

Consumers in these areas however, will be able to purchase as much milk under the milk conservation program as they have been buying within the limits of local supplies—in general an amount considerably greater than that bought in pre-war years, and about 10 percent above last year's purchases. Sales quotas on cream and fluid milk byproducts have been set below June deliveries to boost fluid milk supplies where milk production is low, and to conserve milk for manufacturing purposes.

Producer-distributors who purchase no milk will be allowed to sell an amount of fluid milk, cream and fluid milk byproducts equal to 100 percent of their total milk production in June. Quota-exempt producer distributors are defined separately for each area, but in general they are those whose deliveries are relatively small.

To help assure sufficient milk for manufacturing the cheese, butter, evaporated milk and milk powder required by the armed services and civilians for good nutrition and properly balanced diets, fluid milk sales are being stabilized in these and other metropolitan areas, FDA officials explained.

The FDA's dealer-quota plan is an attempt to stabilize fluid milk consumption without resorting to individual consumer rationing. Point rationing of milk, a bulky and highly perishable commodity, would be very difficult to administer and would almost necessarily reduce fluid milk sales in many areas. If consumers and the trade cooperate with the present program to assure that sales are held within quotas and quantities available are distributed fairly, FDA officials believe that consumer rationing will not be necessary.

Milk handlers in the sales areas named will compute the quantity of milk which they may sell each month in terms of pounds of milk, their cream sales in terms of pounds of cream and butterfat, and their milk byproducts sales in terms of pounds of milk byproducts.

Deliveries to the Armed Forces, to plants processing dairy products, and other handlers (except special classes of handlers such as peddlers) are quota exempt.

To facilitate administration, the market agent, Mr. Sadler, may act upon petitions for relief from hardships which may be submitted to him.

Milk sales in several other eastern and midwestern areas have been previously brought under federal regulation. Sales quotas are the same in all areas named to date.

Reserve
1
733.7

FDO 79-34
OCTOBER 8, 1943

WAR FOOD ADMINISTRATION

[FDO No. 79-34]

PART 1401—DAIRY PRODUCTS

CONSERVATION AND DISTRIBUTION OF FLUID MILK AND CREAM IN BRIDGEPORT-NEW HAVEN, CONN., SALES AREA

Pursuant to the authority vested in me by Food Distribution Order No. 79 (8 F.R. 12426), issued on September 7, 1943, as amended, and to effectuate the purposes of such order, it is hereby ordered as follows:

§ 1401.68 *Quota restrictions*—(a) *Definitions*. When used in this order, unless otherwise distinctly expressed or manifestly incompatible with the intent hereof:

(1) Each term defined in Food Distribution Order No. 79, as amended, shall, when used herein, have the same meaning as is set forth for such term in Food Distribution Order No. 79, as amended.

(2) The term FDO 79 means Food Distribution Order No. 79, issued on September 7, 1943, as amended.

(3) The term "sub-handler" means any handler, such as a peddler, vendor, sub-dealer, or secondary dealer, who purchases in a previously packaged and processed form milk, milk byproducts, or cream for delivery.

(b) *Milk sales area*. The following area is hereby designated as a "milk sales area" to be known as the Bridgeport-New Haven, Connecticut, sales area, and is referred to hereinafter as the "sales area": The territory included within the boundary lines of the following Connecticut cities and towns: Dairen, Norwalk, Westfort, Fairfield, Bridgeport, Stratford, Milford, Orange, West Haven, New Haven, East Haven, North Haven, Wallingford, Middlefield, Middletown, Meriden, Ansonia, Hamden, Derby, Trumbull, Easton, Weston, Wilton, New Canaan, Stamford and Greenwich.

(c) *Base period*. The calendar month of June 1943 is hereby designated as the base period for the sales area.

(d) *Quota period*. The remainder of the calendar month in which the provisions hereof become effective and each subsequent calendar month, respectively, is hereby designated as a quota period for the sales area.

(e) *Handler quotas*. Quotas for each handler in the sales area in each quota period shall be calculated in terms of pounds of each of the items for which percentages are specified in (3) below and shall be determined as follows:

(1) Divide the total deliveries of each such item made in the sales area by such handler during the base period, after excluding the quota-exempt deliveries described in (i) hereof, by the number of days in the base period;

(2) Multiply the result of the foregoing calculation by the number of days in the quota period;

(3) Multiply the aforesaid resulting amount by the following applicable percentage: (i) Milk: 100 percent; (ii) Butterfat in milk: -- percent; (iii) Cream: 75 percent; (iv) Butterfat in cream: 75 percent; (v) Milk byproducts other than cottage, pot or baker's cheese, 75 percent; and (vi) Cottage, pot, or baker's cheese: 75 percent of skim milk equivalent. (For the purpose of this order, one pound of cottage, pot, or baker's cheese shall be considered as the equivalent of 7 pounds of skim milk.)

(f) *Quota limitations*. No handler shall, during any quota period, make deliveries in the sales area in excess of his respective quotas, except as set out in (i) hereof: *Provided*, That a handler may, after application to and approval by the market agent, secure an increase in milk quotas through an equivalent reduction as determined by the market agent, in cream and milk byproducts quotas, and an increase in milk byproducts quota through an equivalent reduction as determined by the market agent, in cream quotas.

(g) *Quotas for handlers who are also producers*. Quotas for handlers who are also producers and who purchase no milk shall be 100 percent of the total production of such handlers in the base period.

(h) *Handler exemptions*. Quotas shall not apply to any handler who delivers in a quota period a daily average of less than 200 units of milk, cream, and milk byproducts. For the purpose of this order, a unit shall be the equivalent in volume of the following: (1) milk, one quart of milk; (2) cream, one-half pint of cream; and (3) milk byproduct, one quart of skim milk, buttermilk, flavored milk drink, or other beverage containing more than 85 percent of skim milk, or one-half pound of cottage, pot, or baker's cheese.

(i) *Quota exclusions and exemptions*. Deliveries of milk, milk byproducts, or cream (1) to other handlers, except for such deliveries to sub-handlers, (2) to plants engaged in the handling or processing of milk, milk byproducts, or cream from which no milk, milk byproducts, or cream is delivered in the sales area, (3) to nursery, elementary and junior high schools; and (4) to the agencies or groups specified in (d) of FDO 79, shall be excluded from the computation of deliveries in the base period and exempt from charges to quotas.

(j) *Transfers and apportionment of quotas*. The market agent is empowered to deduct an amount of base period deliveries to purchasers from the total of deliveries made by a handler or other person in the base period upon the application and a showing of unreasonable hardship by the handler making deliveries to such purchasers on the effective date of this order, and to add the amount of such deliveries to the total base period deliveries of the applicant handler. Denials of transfers or transfers granted by the market agent shall be reviewed by the Director upon application.

(k) *Petition for relief from hardships*. (1) Any person affected by FDO 79 or the provisions hereof who considers that compliance therewith would work an exceptional and unreasonable hardship on him, may file with the market agent a petition addressed to the Director. The petition shall contain the correct name, address and principal place of business of the petitioner, a full statement of the facts upon which the petition is based, and the hardship involved and the nature of the relief desired.

(2) Upon receiving such petition, the market agent shall immediately investigate the representations and facts stated therein.

(3) After investigation, the petition shall be certified to the Director, but prior to certification the market agent may (i) deny the petition, or (ii) grant temporary relief for a total period not to exceed 60 days.

(4) Denials or grants of relief by the market agent shall be reviewed by the Director and may be affirmed, modified, or reversed by the Director.

(l) *Reports*. Each handler shall transmit to the market agent on forms prescribed by the market agent the following reports:

(1) Within 20 days following the effective date of this order, reports which show the information required by the market agent to establish such handlers' quotas:

(2) Within 20 days following the close of each quota period, the information required by the market agent to establish volumes of deliveries of milk, cream,

and milk byproducts during the preceding quota period; and

(3) Handlers exempt from quotas pursuant to (h) hereof shall, upon the request of the market agent, submit the information required by the market agent to establish volumes of deliveries of milk, cream, and milk byproducts.

(m) *Records.* Handlers shall keep and shall make available to the market agent such records of receipts, sales, deliveries, and production as the market agent shall require for the purpose of obtaining information which the Director may require for the establishment of quotas as prescribed in (b) of FDO 79.

(n) *Distribution schedules.* The distribution schedules, if any, to be followed by the handlers in making deliveries shall be made effective in the terms of approval by the Director of such schedules.

(o) *Expense of administration.* Each handler shall pay to the market agent, within 20 days after the close of each calendar month an assessment of $.01 per hundredweight of each of milk, cream, skim milk, buttermilk, flavored milk drink, beverages containing more than 85 percent of skim milk, and skim milk equivalent of cottage, pot, or baker's cheese delivered during the preceding quota period and subject to quota regulations under the provisions hereof.

(p) *Violations.* The market agent shall report all violations to the Director together with the information required for the prosecution of such violations, except in a case where a handler has made deliveries in a quota period in excess of a quota in an amount not to exceed 5 percent of such quota, and in the succeeding quota period makes deliveries below that quota by at least the same percent.

(q) *Bureau of the Budget approval.* The record keeping and reporting requirements of this order have been approved by the Bureau of the Budget in accordance with the Federal Reports Act of 1942. Subsequent record keeping or reporting requirements will be subject to the approval of the Bureau of the Budget pursuant to the Federal Reports Act of 1942.

(r) This order shall take effect at 12:01 a. m., e. w. t., October 17, 1943.

Issued this 8th day of October 1943.

C. W. KITCHEN,
Acting Director of Food Distribution.

Press Release Immediate:
Saturday, October 9, 1943.

Effective October 17, the Food Distribution Administration's fluid milk conservation and control program will be extended to cover five more metropolitan areas, the War Food Administration said today.

The new milk sales areas, and the market agents who will administer the program in each, are:

Bridgeport-New Haven, Conn.; Hartford-New Britain, Conn.; Waterbury, Conn. — (Market Agent to be named later.)

New Orleans, La.—J. B. McCroskey, 1421 Carondelet Building, New Orleans, La.

Louisville, Ky.—L. S. Iverson, 455 S. 4th St., Louisville, Ky.

Dealers' milk sales in these areas will be limited to 100 percent of their June sales for fluid milk; 75 percent of June sales for cream, and 75 percent of June sales for milk byproducts as a group (including such products as cottage cheese, chocolate milk and buttermilk). However, a dealer may, upon approval of the market agent, increase his milk sales above the June level if he reduces his sales of cream and milk byproducts by an equivalent amount of milk. He also may increase his sales of milk pyproducts beyond the 75 percent quota by reducing his cream sales. Milk dealers include all persons or firms engaged in the sale or transfer of milk, but not retail stores, hotels, restaurants, etc.

Producer-distributors who purchase no milk (except those whose volume of sales is small enough to make them quota-exempt) will be allowed to sell an amount of fluid milk, cream, and fluid milk byproduct equal to 100 percent of their total milk production in June. Quota-exempt producer-distributors are defined separately for each area, but in general they are those whose deliveries are relatively small.

Deliveries of milk, milk byproducts and cream to plants manufacturing dairy products; to military agencies, and to other milk dealers (except special classes of dealers, such as peddlers) are quota-exempt. In the three Connecticut sales areas deliveries to nursery, elementary, and junior high schools also will be quota-exempt.

Consumers in these and other designated milk sales areas generally will be able to purchase as much milk under the milk conservation program as they have been buying—an amount considerably greater than that bought in pre-war years, and about 10 percent above last year's purchases. Sales quotas on cream and on fluid milk byproducts have been set below June deliveries to boost fluid milk supplies where milk production is low, and to conserve milk for manufacturing purposes.

Fluid milk sales are being stabilized in these and other metropolitan areas, FDA officials explained, to help assure sufficient milk for manufacturing the cheese, butter, evaporated milk and milk powder required by the armed services and civilians for good nutrition and properly balanced diets.

Largely due to expanded consumer demand, sales of fluid milk have been increasing steadily and are now about 20 percent higher than in pre-war years (1936-40) and 10 to 12 percent above those in 1942. With total milk production leveled off, and even declining somewhat, this expanding volume of milk sold for fluid uses has inevitably reduced the supply of "manufacturing milk," and, consequently, the production of cheese, butter and other dairy foods.

The FDA dealer-quota plan is an attempt to stabilize fluid milk consumption without resorting to individual consumer rationing. Point rationing of milk, a bulky and highly perishable commodity, would be very difficult to administer. If consumers and the trade cooperate with the present program to assure that sales are held within quotas and quantities available are distributed fairly, FDA officials believe consumer rationing will not be necessary.

Milk handlers in the 5 sales areas named today, will compute the quantity of milk which may sell each month in terms of pounds of milk, their cream sales in terms of pounds of cream and butterfat, and their milk byproducts sales in terms of pounds of milk byproducts or skim milk equivalent.

To facilitate administration, the market agent for each milk sales area may act upon petitions for relief from hardship which may be submitted to him, and after investigation, he may grant temporary relief for a total period not to exceed 60 days.

Milk sales in 33 eastern and midwestern areas previously were brought under federal regulation. Sales quotas in these initial milk sales areas are the same as for those named today.

77377
C/15

FDO 79-34
OCTOBER 8, 1943

WAR FOOD ADMINISTRATION

[FDO No. 79-34]

PART 1401—DAIRY PRODUCTS

CONSERVATION AND DISTRIBUTION OF FLUID MILK AND CREAM IN BRIDGEPORT-NEW HAVEN, CONN., SALES AREA

Pursuant to the authority vested in me by Food Distribution Order No. 79 (8 F.R. 12426), issued on September 7, 1943, as amended, and to effectuate the purposes of such order, it is hereby ordered as follows:

§ 1401.68 *Quota restrictions*—(a) *Definitions.* When used in this order, unless otherwise distinctly expressed or manifestly incompatible with the intent hereof:

(1) Each term defined in Food Distribution Order No. 79, as amended, shall, when used herein, have the same meaning as is set forth for such term in Food Distribution Order No. 79, as amended.

(2) The term FDO 79 means Food Distribution Order No. 79, issued on September 7, 1943, as amended.

(3) The term "sub-handler" means any handler, such as a peddler, vendor, sub-dealer, or secondary dealer, who purchases in a previously packaged and processed form milk, milk byproducts, or cream for delivery.

(b) *Milk sales area.* The following area is hereby designated as a "milk sales area" to be known as the Bridgeport-New Haven, Connecticut, sales area, and is referred to hereinafter as the "sales area": The territory included within the boundary lines of the following Connecticut cities and towns: Dairen, Norwalk, Westfort, Fairfield, Bridgeport, Stratford, Milford, Orange, West Haven, New Haven, East Haven, North Haven, Wallingford, Middlefield, Middletown, Meriden, Ansonia, Hamden, Derby, Trumbull, Easton, Weston, Wilton, New Canaan, Stamford and Greenwich.

(c) *Base period.* The calendar month of June 1943 is hereby designated as the base period for the sales area.

(d) *Quota period.* The remainder of the calendar month in which the provisions hereof become effective and each subsequent calendar month, respectively, is hereby designated as a quota period for the sales area.

(e) *Handler quotas.* Quotas for each handler in the sales area in each quota period shall be calculated in terms of pounds of each of the items for which percentages are specified in (3) below and shall be determined as follows:

(1) Divide the total deliveries of each such item made in the sales area by such handler during the base period, after excluding the quota-exempt deliveries described in (i) hereof, by the number of days in the base period;

(2) Multiply the result of the foregoing calculation by the number of days in the quota period;

(3) Multiply the aforesaid resulting amount by the following applicable percentage: (i) Milk: 100 percent; (ii) Butterfat in milk: -- percent; (iii) Cream: 75 percent; (iv) Butterfat in cream: 75 percent; (v) Milk byproducts other than cottage, pot or baker's cheese, 75 percent; and (vi) Cottage, pot, or baker's cheese: 75 percent of skim milk equivalent. (For the purpose of this order, one pound of cottage, pot, or baker's cheese shall be considered as the equivalent of 7 pounds of skim milk.)

(f) *Quota limitations.* No handler shall, during any quota period, make deliveries in the sales area in excess of his respective quotas, except as set out in (i) hereof: *Provided,* That a handler may, after application to and approval by the market agent, secure an increase in milk quotas through an equivalent reduction as determined by the market agent, in cream and milk byproducts quotas, and an increase in milk byproducts quota through an equivalent reduction as determined by the market agent, in cream quotas.

(g) *Quotas for handlers who are also producers.* Quotas for handlers who are also producers and who purchase no milk shall be 100 percent of the total production of such handlers in the base period.

(h) *Handler exemptions.* Quotas shall not apply to any handler who delivers in a quota period a daily average of less than 200 units of milk, cream, and milk byproducts. For the purpose of this order, a unit shall be the equivalent in volume of the following: (1) milk, one quart of milk; (2) cream, one-half pint of cream; and (3) milk byproduct, one quart of skim milk, buttermilk, flavored milk drink, or other beverage containing more than 85 percent of skim milk, or one-half pound of cottage, pot, or baker's cheese.

(i) *Quota exclusions and exemptions.* Deliveries of milk, milk byproducts, or cream (1) to other handlers, except for such deliveries to sub-handlers, (2) to plants engaged in the handling or processing of milk, milk byproducts, or cream from which no milk, milk byproducts, or cream is delivered in the sales area, (3) to nursery, elementary and junior high schools; and (4) to the agencies or groups specified in (d) of FDO 79, shall be excluded from the computation of deliveries in the base period and exempt from charges to quotas.

(j) *Transfers and apportionment of quotas.* The market agent is empowered to deduct an amount of base period deliveries to purchasers from the total of deliveries made by a handler or other person in the base period upon the application and a showing of unreasonable hardship by the handler making deliveries to such purchasers on the effective date of this order, and to add the amount of such deliveries to the total base period deliveries of the applicant handler. Denials of transfers or transfers granted by the market agent shall be reviewed by the Director upon application.

(k) *Petition for relief from hardships.* (1) Any person affected by FDO 79 or the provisions hereof who considers that compliance therewith would work an exceptional and unreasonable hardship on him, may file with the market agent a petition addressed to the Director. The petition shall contain the correct name, address and principal place of business of the petitioner, a full statement of the facts upon which the petition is based, and the hardship involved and the nature of the relief desired.

(2) Upon receiving such petition, the market agent shall immediately investigate the representations and facts stated therein.

(3) After investigation, the petition shall be certified to the Director, but prior to certification the market agent may (i) deny the petition, or (ii) grant temporary relief for a total period not to exceed 60 days.

(4) Denials or grants of relief by the market agent shall be reviewed by the Director and may be affirmed, modified, or reversed by the Director.

(l) *Reports.* Each handler shall transmit to the market agent on forms prescribed by the market agent the following reports:

(1) Within 20 days following the effective date of this order, reports which show the information required by the market agent to establish such handlers' quotas:

(2) Within 20 days following the close of each quota period, the information required by the market agent to establish volumes of deliveries of milk, cream,

and milk byproducts during the preceding quota period; and

(3) Handlers exempt from quotas pursuant to (h) hereof shall, upon the request of the market agent, submit the information required by the market agent to establish volumes of deliveries of milk, cream, and milk byproducts.

(m) *Records*. Handlers shall keep and shall make available to the market agent such records of receipts, sales, deliveries, and production as the market agent shall require for the purpose of obtaining information which the Director may require for the establishment of quotas as prescribed in (b) of FDO 79.

(n) *Distribution schedules*. The distribution schedules, if any, to be followed by the handlers in making deliveries shall be made effective in the terms of approval by the Director of such schedules.

(o) *Expense of administration*. Each handler shall pay to the market agent, within 20 days after the close of each calendar month an assessment of $.01 per hundredweight of each of milk, cream, skim milk, buttermilk, flavored milk drink, beverages containing more than 85 percent of skim milk, and skim milk equivalent of cottage, pot, or baker's cheese delivered during the preceding quota period and subject to quota regulations under the provisions hereof.

(p) *Violations*. The market agent shall report all violations to the Director together with the information required for the prosecution of such violations, except in a case where a handler has made deliveries in a quota period in excess of a quota in an amount not to exceed 5 percent of such quota, and in the succeeding quota period makes deliveries below that quota by at least the same percent.

(q) *Bureau of the Budget approval*. The record keeping and reporting requirements of this order have been approved by the Bureau of the Budget in accordance with the Federal Reports Act of 1942. Subsequent record keeping or reporting requirements will be subject to the approval of the Bureau of the Budget pursuant to the Federal Reports Act of 1942.

(r) This order shall take effect at 12:01 a. m., e. w. t., October 17, 1943.

Issued this 8th day of October 1943.

C. W. KITCHEN,
Acting Director of Food Distribution.

Press Release Immediate:
Saturday, October 9, 1943.

Effective October 17, the Food Distribution Administration's fluid milk conservation and control program will be extended to cover five more metropolitan areas, the War Food Administration said today.

The new milk sales areas, and the market agents who will administer the program in each, are:

Bridgeport-New Haven, Conn.; Hartford-New Britain, Conn.; Waterbury, Conn. — (Market Agent to be named later.)
New Orleans, La.—J. B. McCroskey, 1421 Carondelet Building, New Orleans, La.
Louisville, Ky.—L. S. Iverson, 455 S. 4th St.; Louisville, Ky.

Dealers' milk sales in these areas will be limited to 100 percent of their June sales for fluid milk; 75 percent of June sales for cream, and 75 percent of June sales for milk byproducts as a group (including such products as cottage cheese, chocolate milk and buttermilk). However, a dealer may, upon approval of the market agent, increase his milk sales above the June level if he reduces his sales of cream and milk byproducts by an equivalent amount of milk. He also may increase his sales of milk pyproducts beyond the 75 percent quota by reducing his cream sales. Milk dealers include all persons or firms engaged in the sale or transfer of milk, but not retail stores, hotels, restaurants, etc.

Producer-distributors who purchase no milk (except those whose volume of sales is small enough to make them quota-exempt) will be allowed to sell an amount of fluid milk, cream, and fluid milk byproduct equal to 100 percent of their total milk production in June. Quota-exempt producer-distributors are defined separately for each area, but in general they are those whose deliveries are relatively small.

Deliveries of milk, milk byproducts and cream to plants manufacturing dairy products; to military agencies, and to other milk dealers (except special classes of dealers, such as peddlers) are quota-exempt. In the three Connecticut sales areas deliveries to nursery, elementary, and junior high schools also will be quota-exempt.

Consumers in these and other designated milk sales areas generally will be able to purchase as much milk under the milk conservation program as they have been buying—an amount considerably greater than that bought in pre-war years, and about 10 percent above last year's purchases. Sales quotas on cream and on fluid milk byproducts have been set below June deliveries to boost fluid milk supplies where milk production is low, and to conserve milk for manufacturing purposes.

Fluid milk sales are being stabilized in these and other metropolitan areas, FDA officials explained, to help assure sufficient milk for manufacturing the cheese, butter, evaporated milk and milk powder required by the armed services and civilians for good nutrition and properly balanced diets.

Largely due to expanded consumer demand, sales of fluid milk have been increasing steadily and are now about 20 percent higher than in pre-war years (1936-40) and 10 to 12 percent above those in 1942. With total milk production leveled off, and even declining somewhat, this expanding volume of milk sold for fluid uses has inevitably reduced the supply of "manufacturing milk," and, consequently, the production of cheese, butter and other dairy foods.

The FDA dealer-quota plan is an attempt to stabilize fluid milk consumption without resorting to individual consumer rationing. Point rationing of milk, a bulky and highly perishable commodity, would be very difficult to administer. If consumers and the trade cooperate with the present program to assure that sales are held within quotas and quantities available are distributed fairly, FDA officials believe consumer rationing will not be necessary.

Milk handlers in the 5 sales areas named today, will compute the quantity of milk which may sell each month in terms of pounds of milk, their cream sales in terms of pounds of cream and butterfat, and their milk byproducts sales in terms of pounds of milk byproducts or skim milk equivalent.

To facilitate administration, the market agent for each milk sales area may act upon petitions for relief from hardship which may be submitted to him, and after investigation, he may grant temporary relief for a total period not to exceed 60 days.

Milk sales in 33 eastern and midwestern areas previously were brought under federal regulation. Sales quotas in these initial milk sales areas are the same as for those named today.

servs
/
17337

FDO 79-35
OCTOBER 8, 1943

WAR FOOD ADMINISTRATION

[FDO 79-35]

PART 1401—DAIRY PRODUCTS

CONSERVATION AND DISTRIBUTION OF FLUID MILK AND CREAM IN NEW ORLEANS, LA., SALES AREA

Pursuant to the authority vested in me by Food Distribution Order No. 79 (8 F.R. 12426), issued on September 7, 1943, as amended, and to effectuate the purposes of such order, it is hereby ordered as follows:

§ 1401.70 *Quota restrictions*—(a) *Definitions.* When used in this order, unless otherwise distinctly expressed or manifestly incompatible with the intent hereof:

(1) Each term defined in Food Distribution Order No. 79, as amended, shall, when used herein, have the same meaning as is set forth for such term in Food Distribution Order No. 79, as amended.

(2) The term FDO 79 means Food Distribution Order No. 79, issued on September 7, 1943, as amended.

(3) The term "sub-handler" means any handler, such as a peddler, vendor, sub-dealer, or secondary dealer, who purchases in a previously packaged and processed form milk, milk byproducts, or cream for delivery.

(b) *Milk sales area.* The following area is hereby designated as a "milk sales area" to be known as the New Orleans, Louisiana, sales area, and is referred to hereinafter as the "sales area": The cities, towns, and villages of New Orleans in Orleans Parish; Gretna, Westwego, Marrero, Harvey, Metairie, Harahan, and Belle Chasse in Jefferson Parish; Poydras, St. Bernard, Violet, Meraux, Chalmette, and Arabi in St. Bernard Parish; all in the State of Louisiana.

(c) *Base period.* The calendar month of June 1943 is hereby designated as the base period for the sales area.

(d) *Quota period.* The remainder of the calendar month in which the provisions hereof become effective and each subsequent calendar month, respectively, is hereby designated as a quota period for the sales area.

(e) *Handler quotas.* Quotas for each handler in the sales area in each quota period shall be calculated in terms of pounds of each of the items for which percentages are specified in (3) below and shall be determined as follows:

(1) Divide the total deliveries of each such item made in the sales area by such handler during the base period, after excluding the quota-exempt deliveries described in (i) hereof, by the number of days in the base period;

(2) Multiply the result of the foregoing calculation by the number of days in the quota period;

(3) Multiply the aforesaid resulting amount by the following applicable percentage: (i) Milk: 100 percent; (ii) Butterfat in milk: __ percent; (iii) Cream: 75 percent; (iv) Butterfat in cream: 75 percent; (v) Milk byproducts other than cottage, pot or baker's cheese: 75 percent; and (vi) Cottage, pot, or baker's cheese: 75 percent of skim milk equivalent. (For the purpose of this order, one pound of cottage, pot or baker's cheese shall be considered as the equivalent of 7 pounds of skim milk.)

(f) *Quota limitations.* No handler shall, during any quota period, make deliveries in the sales area in excess of his respective quotas, except as set out in (i) hereof: *Provided,* That a handler may; after application to and approval by the market agent, secure an increase in milk quotas through an equivalent reduction as determined by the market agent, in cream and milk byproducts quotas, and an increase in milk byproducts quota through an equivalent reduction as determined by the market agent, in cream quotas.

(g) *Quotas for handlers who are also producers.* Quotas for handlers who are also producers and who purchase no milk shall be 100 percent of the total production of such handlers in the base period.

(h) *Handler exemptions.* Quotas shall not apply to any handler who delivers in a quota period a daily average of less than 450 units of milk, cream, and milk byproducts. For the purpose of this order, a unit shall be the equivalent in volume of the following: (1) milk, one quart of milk; (2) cream, one-half pint of cream; and (3) milk byproduct, one quart of skim milk, buttermilk, flavored milk drink, or other beverage containing more than 85 percent of skim milk, or one-half pound of cottage, pot, or baker's cheese.

(i) *Quota exclusions and exemptions.* Deliveries of milk, milk byproducts, or cream (1) to other handlers, except for such deliveries to sub-handlers, (2) to plants engaged in the handling or processing of milk, milk byproducts, or cream from which no milk, milk byproducts, or cream is delivered in the sales area, and (3) to the agencies or groups specified in (d) of FDO 79, shall be excluded from the computation of deliveries in the base period and exempt from charges to quotas.

(j) *Transfers and apportionment of quotas.* The market agent is empowered to deduct an amount of base period deliveries to purchasers from the total of deliveries made by a handler or other person in the base period upon the application and a showing of unreasonable hardship by the handler making deliveries to such purchasers on the effective date of this order, and to add the amount of such deliveries to the total base period deliveries of the applicant handler. Denials of transfers or transfers granted by the market agent shall be reviewed by the Director upon application.

(k) *Petition for relief from hardships.* (1) Any person affected by FDO 79 or the provisions hereof who considers that compliance therewith would work an exceptional and unreasonable hardship on him, may file with the market agent a petition addressed to the Director. The petition shall contain the correct name, address and principal place of business of the petitioner, a full statement of the facts upon which the petition is based, and the hardship involved and the nature of the relief desired.

(2) Upon receiving such petition, the market agent shall immediately investigate the representations and facts stated therein.

(3) After investigation, the petition shall be certified to the Director, but prior to certification the market agent may (i) deny the petition, or (ii) grant temporary relief for a total period not to exceed 60 days.

(4) Denials or grants of relief by the market agent shall be reviewed by the Director and may be affirmed, modified, or reversed by the Director.

(l) *Reports.* Each handler shall transmit to the market agent on forms prescribed by the market agent the following reports:

(1) Within 20 days following the effective date of this order, reports which show the information required by the market agent to establish such handlers' quotas;

(2) Within 20 days following the close of each quota period, the information required by the market agent to establish volumes of deliveries of milk, cream, and milk byproducts during the preceding quota period; and

(3) Handlers exempt from quotas pursuant to (h) hereof shall, upon the request of the market agent, submit the information required by the market agent to establish volumes of deliveries of milk, cream, and milk byproducts.

(m) *Records.* Handlers shall keep and shall make available to the market agent such records of receipts, sales, deliveries, and production as the market agent shall require for the purpose of obtaining information which the Director may require for the establishment of quotas as prescribed in (b) of FDO 79.

(n) *Distribution schedules.* The distribution schedules, if any, to be followed by the handlers in making deliveries shall be made effective in the terms of approval by the Director of such schedules.

(o) *Expense of administration.* Each handler shall pay to the market agent, within 20 days after the close of each calendar month an assessment of $0.01 per hundredweight of each of milk cream, skim milk, buttermilk, flavored milk drinks, beverages containing more than 85 percent of skim milk, and skim milk equivalent of cottage, pot, or baker's cheese delivered during the preceding quota period and subject to quota regulations under the provisions hereof.

(p) *Violations.* The market agent shall report all violations to the Director together with the information required for the prosecution of such violations, except in a case where a handler has made deliveries in a quota period in excess of a quota in an amount not to exceed 5 percent of such quota, and in the succeeding quota period makes deliveries below that quota by at least the same percent.

(q) *Bureau of the Budget approval.* The record keeping and reporting requirements of this order have been approved by the Bureau of the Budget in accordance with the Federal Reports Act of 1942. Subsequent record keeping or reporting requirements will be subject to the approval of the Bureau of the Budget pursuant to the Federal Reports Act of 1942.

(r) This order shall take effect at 12:01 a. m., e. w. t., October 17, 1943.

Issued this 8th day of October 1943.

C. W. KITCHEN,
Acting Director of Food Distribution.

Press Release Immediate:
Saturday, October 9, 1943.

Effective October 17, the Food Distribution Administration's fluid milk conservation and control program will be extended to cover five more metropolitan areas, the War Food Administration said today.

The new milk sales areas, and the market agents who will administer the program in each, are:

Bridgeport-New Haven, Conn.; Hartford-New Britain, Conn.; Waterbury, Conn. — (Market Agent to be named later.)
New Orleans, La.—J. B. McCroskey, 1421 Carondelet Building, New Orleans, La.
Louisville, Ky.—L. S. Iverson, 455 S. 4th St., Louisville, Ky.

Dealers' milk sales in these areas will be limited to 100 percent of their June sales for fluid milk; 75 percent of June sales for cream, and 75 percent of June sales for milk byproducts as a group (including such products as cottage cheese, chocolate milk and buttermilk). However, a dealer may, upon approval of the market agent, increase his milk sales above the June level if he reduces his sales of cream and milk byproducts by an equivalent amount of milk. He also may increase his sales of milk byproducts beyond the 75 percent quota by reducing his cream sales. Milk dealers include all persons or firms engaged in the sale or transfer of milk, but not retail stores, hotels, restaurants, etc.

Producer-distributors who purchase no milk (except those whose volume of sales is small enough to make them quota-exempt) will be allowed to sell an amount of fluid milk, cream, and fluid milk byproducts equal to 100 percent of their total milk production in June. Quota-exempt producer-distributors are defined separately for each area, but in general they are those whose deliveries are relatively small.

Deliveries of milk, milk byproducts and cream to plants manufacturing dairy products; to military agencies, and to other milk dealers (except special classes of dealers, such as peddlers) are quota-exempt. In the three Connecticut sales areas deliveries to nursery, elementary, and junior high schools also will be quota-exempt.

Consumers in these and other designated milk sales areas generally will be able to purchase as much milk under the milk conservation program as they have been buying—an amount considerably greater than that bought in pre-war years, and about 10 percent above last year's purchases. Sales quotas on cream and on fluid milk byproducts have been set below June deliveries to boost fluid milk supplies where milk production is low, and to conserve milk for manufacturing purposes.

Fluid milk sales are being stabilized in these and other metropolitan areas, FDA officials explained, to help assure sufficient milk for manufacturing the cheese, butter, evaporated milk and milk powder required by the armed services and civilians for good nutrition and properly balanced diets.

Largely due to expanded consumer demand, sales of fluid milk have been increasing steadily and are now about 20 percent higher than in pre-war years (1936–40) and 10 to 12 percent above those in 1942. With total milk production levelled off, and even declining somewhat, this expanding volume of milk sold for fluid uses has inevitably reduced the supply of "manufacturing milk," and, consequently, the production of cheese, butter and other dairy foods.

The FDA dealer-quota plan is an attempt to stabilize fluid milk consumption without resorting to individual consumer rationing. Point rationing of milk, a bulky and highly perishable commodity, would be very difficult to administer. If consumers and the trade cooperate with the present program to assure that sales are held within quotas and quantities available are distributed fairly, FDA officials believe consumer rationing will not be necessary.

Milk handlers in the 5 sales areas named today, will compute the quantity of milk which may sell each month in terms of pounds of milk, their cream sales in terms of pounds of cream and butterfat, and their milk byproducts sales in terms of pounds of milk byproducts or skim milk equivalent.

To facilitate administration, the market agent for each milk sales area may act upon petitions for relief from hardship which may be submitted to him, and after investigation, he may grant temporary relief for a total period not to exceed 60 days.

Milk sales in 33 eastern and midwestern areas previously were brought under federal regulation. Sales quotas in these initial milk sales areas are the same as for those named today.

73 3
Cop. 1

WAR FOOD ADMINISTRATION

[FDO 79-36]

PART 1401—DAIRY PRODUCTS

CONSERVATION AND DISTRIBUTION OF FLUID MILK AND CREAM IN WATERBURY, CONN., SALES AREA

Pursuant to the authority vested in me by Food Distribution Order No. 79 (8 F.R. 12426), issued on September 7, 1943, as amended, and to effectuate the purposes of such order, it is hereby ordered as follows:

§ 1401.71 *Quota restrictions*—(a) *Definitions.* When used in this order, unless otherwise distinctly expressed or manifestly incompatible with the intent hereof:

(1) Each term defined in Food Distribution Order No. 79, as amended, shall, when used herein, have the same meaning as is set forth for such term in Food Distribution Order No. 79, as amended.

(2) The term FDO 79 means Food Distribution Order No. 79, issued on September 7, 1943, as amended.

(3) The term "sub-handler" means any handler, such as a peddler, vendor, sub-dealer, or secondary dealer, who purchases in a previously packaged and processed form milk, milk byproducts, or cream for delivery.

(b) *Milk sales area.* The following area is hereby designated as a "milk sales area" to be known as the Waterbury, Connecticut, sales area, and is referred to hereinafter as the "sales area":

The territory included within the boundary lines of the following Connecticut cities and towns: Waterbury and Naugatuck.

(c) *Base period.* The calendar month of June 1943 is hereby designated as the base period for the sales area.

(d) *Quota period.* The remainder of the calendar month in which the provisions hereof become effective and each subsequent calendar month, respectively, is hereby designated as a quota period for the sales area.

(e) *Handler quotas.* Quotas for each handler in the sales area in each quota period shall be calculated in terms of pounds of each of the items for which percentages are specified in (3) below and shall be determined as follows:

(1) Divide the total deliveries of each such item made in the sales area by such handler during the base period, after excluding the quota-exempt deliveries described in (i) hereof, by the number of days in the base period;

(2) Multiply the result of the foregoing calculation by the number of days in the quota period;

(3) Multiply the aforesaid resulting amount by the following applicable percentage: (i) Milk: 100 percent; (ii) Butterfat in milk: __ percent; (iii) Cream: 75 percent; (iv) Butterfat in cream: 75 percent; (v) Milk byproducts other than cottage, pot or baker's cheese: 75 percent; and (vi) Cottage, pot, or baker's cheese: 75 percent of skim milk equivalent. (For the purpose of this order, one pound of cottage, pot, or baker's cheese shall be considered as the equivalent of 7 pounds of skim milk.)

(f) *Quota limitations.* No handler shall, during any quota period, make deliveries in the sales area in excess of his respective quotas, except as set out in (i) hereof: *Provided,* That a handler may, after application to and approval by the market agent, secure an increase in milk quotas through an equivalent reduction as determined by the market agent, in cream and milk byproducts quotas, and an increase in milk byproducts quota through an equivalent reduction as determined by the market agent, in cream quotas.

(g) *Quotas for handlers who are also producers.* Quotas for handlers who are also producers and who purchase no milk shall be 100 percent of the total production of such handlers in the base period.

(h) *Handler exemptions.* Quotas shall not apply to any handler who delivers in a quota period a daily average of less than 200 units of milk, cream, and milk byproducts. For the purpose of this order, a unit shall be the equivalent in volume of the following: (1) milk, one quart of milk; (2) cream, one-half pint of cream; and (3) milk byproduct, one quart of skim milk, buttermilk, flavored milk drink, or other beverage containing more than 85 percent of skim milk, or one-half pound of cottage, pot, or bakers' cheese.

(i) *Quota exclusions and exemptions.* Deliveries of milk, milk byproducts, or cream (1) to other handlers, except for such deliveries to sub-handlers, (2) to plants engaged in the handling or processing of milk, milk byproducts, or cream from which no milk, milk byproducts, or cream is delivered in the sales area, (3) to nursery, elementary and junior high schools; and (4) to the agencies or groups specified in (d) of FDO 79, shall be excluded from the computation of deliveries in the base period and exempt from charges to quotas.

(j) *Transfers and apportionment of quotas.* The market agent is empowered to deduct an amount of base period deliveries to purchasers from the total of deliveries made by a handler or other person in the base period upon the application and a showing of unreasonable hardship by the handler making deliveries to such purchasers on the effective date of this order, and to add the amount of such deliveries to the total base period deliveries of the applicant handler. Denials of transfers or transfers granted by the market agent shall be reviewed by the Director upon application.

(k) *Petition for relief from hardships.* (1) Any person affected by FDO 79 or the provisions hereof who considers that compliance therewith would work exceptional and unreasonable hardship on him, may file with the market agent a petition addressed to the Director. The petition shall contain the correct name, address and principal place of business of the petitioner, a full statement of the facts upon which the petition is based, and the hardship involved and the nature of the relief desired.

(2) Upon receiving such petition, the market agent shall immediately investigate the representations and facts stated therein.

(3) After investigation, the petition shall be certified to the Director, but prior to certification the market agent may (i) deny the petition, or (ii) grant temporary relief for a total period not to exceed 60 days.

(4) Denials or grants of relief by the market agent shall be reviewed by the Director and may be affirmed, modified, or reversed by the Director.

(l) *Reports.* Each handler shall transmit to the market agent on forms prescribed by the market agent the following reports:

(1) Within 20 days following the effective date of this order, reports which show the information required by the market agent to establish such handlers' quotas;

(2) Within 20 days following the close of each quota period, the information required by the market agent to establish volumes of deliveries of milk, cream, and milk byproducts during the preceding quota period; and

(3) Handlers exempt from quotas pursuant to (h) hereof shall, upon the re-

quest of the market agent, submit the information required by the market agent to establish volumes of deliveries of milk, cream, and milk byproducts.

(m) *Records.* Handlers shall keep and shall make available to the market agent such records of receipts, sales, deliveries, and production as the market agent shall require for the purpose of obtaining information which the Director may require for the establishment of quotas as prescribed in (b) of FDO 79.

(n) *Distribution schedules.* The distribution schedules, if any, to be followed by the handlers in making deliveries shall be made effective in the terms of approval by the Director of such schedules.

(o) *Expense of administration.* Each handler shall pay to the market agent, within 20 days after the close of each calendar month an assessment of $0.01 per hundredweight of each of milk, cream, skim milk, buttermilk, flavored milk drinks, beverages containing more than 85 percent of skim milk, and skim milk equivalent of cottage, pot, or baker's cheese delivered during the preceding quota period and subject to quota regulations under the provisions hereof.

(p) *Violations.* The market agent shall report all violations to the Director together with the information required for the prosecution of such violations, except in a case where a handler has made deliveries in a quota period in excess of a quota in an amount not to exceed 5 percent of such quota, and in the succeeding quota period makes deliveries below that quota by at least the same percent.

(q) *Bureau of the Budget approval.* The record keeping and reporting requirements of this order have been approved by the Bureau of the Budget in accordance with the Federal Reports Act of 1942. Subsequent record keeping or reporting requirements will be subject to the approval of the Bureau of the Budget pursuant to the Federal Reports Act of 1942.

(r) This order shall take effect at 12:01 a. m., e. w. t., October 17, 1943.

Issued this 8th day of October 1943.

C. W. KITCHEN,
Acting Director of Food Distribution.

Press Release, Immediate:
Saturday, October 9, 1943.

Effective October 17, the Food Distribution Administration's fluid milk conservation and control program will be extended to cover five more metropolitan areas, the War Food Administration said today.

The new milk sales areas, and the market agents who will administer the program in each, are:

Bridgeport-New Haven, Conn.; Hartford-New Britain, Conn.; Waterbury, Conn.—(Market Agent to be named later.)

New Orleans, La.—J. B. McCroskey, 1421 Carondelet Building, New Orleans, La.

Louisville, Ky.—L. S. Iverson, 455 S. 4th St., Louisville, Ky.

Dealers' milk sales in these areas will be limited to 100 percent of their June sales for fluid milk; 75 percent of June sales for cream, and 75 percent of June sales for milk byproducts as a group (including such products as cottage cheese, chocolate milk and buttermilk). However, a dealer may, upon approval of the market agent, increase his milk sales above the June level if he reduces his sales of cream and milk byproducts by an equivalent amount of milk. He also may increase his sales of milk byproducts beyond the 75 percent quota by reducing his cream sales. Milk dealers include all persons or firms engaged in the sale or transfer of milk, but not retail stores, hotels, restaurants, etc.

Producer-distributors who purchase no milk (except those whose volume of sales is small enough to make them quota-exempt) will be allowed to sell an amount of fluid milk, cream, and fluid milk byproducts equal to 100 percent of their total milk production in June. Quota-exempt producer-distributors are defined separately for each area, but in general they are those whose deliveries are relatively small.

Deliveries of milk, milk byproducts and cream to plants manufacturing dairy products; to military agencies, and to other milk dealers (except special classes of dealers, such as peddlers) are quota-exempt. In the three Connecticut sales areas deliveries to nursery, elementary, and junior high schools also will be quota-exempt.

Consumers in these and other designated milk sales areas generally will be able to purchase as much milk under the milk conservation program as they have been buying—an amount considerably greater than that bought in pre-war years, and about 10 percent above last year's purchases. Sales quotas on cream and on fluid milk byproducts have been set below June deliveries to boost fluid milk supplies where milk production is low, and to conserve milk for manufacturing purposes.

Fluid milk sales are being stabilized in these and other metropolitan areas, FDA officials explained, to help assure sufficient milk for manufacturing the cheese, butter, evaporated milk and milk powder required by the armed services and civilians for good nutrition and properly balanced diets.

Largely due to expanded consumer demand, sales of fluid milk have been increasing steadily and are now about 20 percent higher than in pre-war years (1936-40) and 10 to 12 percent above those in 1942. With total milk production levelled off, and even declining somewhat, this expanding volume of milk sold for fluid uses has inevitably reduced the supply of "manufacturing milk," and, consequently, the production of cheese, butter and other dairy foods.

The FDA dealer-quota plan is an attempt to stabilize fluid milk consumption without resorting to individual consumer rationing. Point rationing of milk, a bulky and highly perishable commodity, would be very difficult to administer. If consumers and the trade cooperate with the present program to assure that sales are held within quotas and quantities available are distributed fairly, FDA officials believe consumer rationing will not be necessary.

Milk handlers in the 5 sales areas named today, will compute the quantity of milk which they may sell each month in terms of pounds of milk, their cream sales in terms of pounds of cream and butterfat, and their milk byproducts sales in terms of pounds of milk byproducts or skim milk equivalent.

To facilitate administration, the market agent for each milk sales area may act upon petitions for relief from hardship which may be submitted to him, and after investigation, he may grant temporary relief for a total period not to exceed 60 days.

Milk sales in 33 eastern and midwestern areas previously were brought under federal regulation. Sales quotas in these initial milk sales areas are the same as for those named today.

Co:.6

FDO 79-37

OCT. 8, 1943

WAR FOOD ADMINISTRATION

[FDO 79-37]

PART 1401—DAIRY PRODUCTS

CONSERVATION AND DISTRIBUTION OF FLUID MILK AND CREAM IN HARTFORD-NEW BRITAIN, CONN., SALES AREA

Pursuant to the authority vested in me by Food Distribution Order No. 79 (8 F.R. 12426), issued on September 7, 1943, as amended, and to effectuate the purposes of such order, it is hereby ordered as follows:

§ 1401.72 *Quota restrictions*—(a) *Definitions.* When used in this order, unless otherwise distinctly expressed or manifestly incompatible with the intent hereof:

(1) Each term defined in Food Distribution Order No. 79, as amended, shall, when used herein, have the same meaning as is set forth for such term in Food Distribution Order No. 79, as amended.

(2) The term FDO 79 means Food Distribution Order No. 79, issued on September 7, 1943, as amended.

(3) The term "sub-handler" means any handler, such as a peddler, vendor, sub-dealer, or secondary dealer, who purchases in a previously packaged and processed form milk, milk byproducts, or cream for delivery.

(b) *Milk sales area.* The following area is hereby designated as a "milk sales area" to be known as the Hartford-New Britain, Connecticut, sales area, and is referred to hereinafter as the "sales area": The territory included within the boundary lines of the following-Connecticut cities and towns: West Hartford, Hartford, East Hartford, Manchester, New Britain, Newington and Wethersfield.

(c) *Base period.* The calendar month of June 1943 is hereby designated as the base period for the sales area.

(d) *Quota period.* The remainder of the calendar month in which the provisions hereof become effective and each subsequent calendar month, respectively, is hereby designated as a quota period for the sales area.

(e) *Handler quotas.* Quotas for each handler in the sales area in each quota period shall be calculated in terms of pounds of each of the items for which percentages are specified in (3) below and shall be determined as follows:

(1) Divide the total deliveries of each such item made in the sales area by such handler during the base period, after excluding the quota-exempt deliveries described in (i) hereof, by the number of days in the base period;

(2) Multiply the result of the foregoing calculation by the number of days in the quota period;

(3) Multiply the aforesaid resulting amount by the following applicable percentage: (i) Milk: 100 percent; (ii) Butterfat in milk, -- percent; (iii) Cream: 75 percent; (iv) Butterfat in cream: 75 percent; (v) Milk byproducts other than cottage, pot or baker's cheese: 75 percent; and (vi) cottage, pot, or baker's cheese: 75 percent of skim milk equivalent. (For the purpose of this order, one pound of cottage, pot, or baker's cheese shall be considered as the equivalent of 7 pounds of skim milk.)

(f) *Quota limitations.* No handler shall, during any quota period, make deliveries in the sales area in excess of his respective quotas, except as set out in (i) hereof; *Provided,* That a handler may, after application to and approval by the market agent, secure an increase in milk quotas through an equivalent reduction as determined by the market agent, in cream and milk byproducts quotas, and an increase in milk byproducts quota through an equivalent reduction as determined by the market agent, in cream quotas.

(g) *Quotas for handlers who are also producers.* Quotas for handlers who are also producers and who purchase no milk shall be 100 percent of the total production of such handlers in the base period.

(h) *Handler exemptions.* Quotas shall not apply to any handler who delivers in a quota period a daily average of less than 200 units of milk, cream, and milk byproducts. For the purpose of this order, a unit shall be the equivalent in volume of the following: (1) milk, one quart of milk; (2) cream, one-half pint of cream; and (3) milk byproduct, one quart of skim milk, buttermilk, flavored milk drink, or other beverage containing more than 85 percent of skim milk, or one-half pound of cottage, pot, or baker's cheese.

(i) *Quota exclusions and exemptions.* Deliveries of milk, milk byproducts, or cream (1) to other handlers, except for such deliveries to sub-handlers, (2) to plants engaged in the handling or processing of milk, milk byproducts, or cream from which no milk, milk byproducts, or cream is delivered in the sales area, (3) to nursery, elementary and junior high schools; and (4) to the agencies or groups specified in (d) of FDO 79, shall be excluded from the computation of deliveries in the base period and exempt from charges to quotas.

(j) *Transfers and apportionment of quotas.* The market agent is empowered to deduct an amount of base period deliveries to purchasers from the total of deliveries made by a handler or other person in the base period upon the application and a showing of unreasonable hardship by the handler making deliveries to such purchasers on the effective date of this order, and to add the amount of such deliveries to the total base period deliveries of the applicant handler. Denials of transfers or transfers granted by the market agent shall be reviewed by the Director upon application.

(k) *Petition for relief from hardships.* (1) Any person affected by FDO 79 or the provisions hereof who considers that compliance therewith would work an exceptional and unreasonable hardship on him, may file with the market agent a petition addressed to the Director. The petition shall contain the correct name, address and principal place of business of the petitioner, a full statement of the facts upon which the petition is based, and the hardship involved and the nature of the relief desired.

(2) Upon receiving such petition, the market agent shall immediately investigate the representations and facts stated therein.

(3) After investigation, the petition shall be certified to the Director, but prior to certification the market agent may (i) deny the petition, or (ii) grant temporary relief for a total period not to exceed 60 days.

(4) Denials or grants of relief by the market agent shall be reviewed by the Director and may be affirmed, modified, or reversed by the Director.

(l) *Reports.* Each handler shall transmit to the market agent on forms prescribed by the market agent the following reports:

(1) Within 20 days following the effective date of this order, reports which show the information required by the market agent to establish such handlers' quotas;

(2) Within 20 days following the close of each quota period, the information required by the market agent to establish volumes of deliveries of milk, cream, and milk byproducts during the preceding quota period; and

(l) Handlers exempt from quotas pursuant to (h) hereof shall, upon the request of the market agent, submit the information required by the market agent to establish volumes of deliveries of milk, cream, and milk byproducts.

(m) *Records.* Handlers shall keep and shall make available to the market agent such records of receipts, sales, deliveries, and production as the market agent shall require for the purpose of obtaining information which the Director may require for the establishment of quotas as prescribed in (b) of FDO 79.

(n) *Distribution schedules.* The distribution schedules, if any, to be followed by the handlers in making deliveries shall be made effective in the terms of approval by the Director of such schedules.

(o) *Expense of administration.* Each handler shall pay to the market agent, within 20 days after the close of each calendar month an assessment of $.01 per hundredweight of each of milk, cream, skim milk, buttermilk, flavored milk drinks, beverages containing more than 85 percent of skim milk, and skim milk equivalent of cottage, pot, or baker's cheese delivered during the preceding quota period and subject to quota regulations under the provisions hereof.

(p) *Violations.* The market agent shall report all violations to the Director together with the information required for the prosecution of such violations, except in a case where a handler has made deliveries in a quota period in excess of a quota in an amount not to exceed 5 percent of such quota, and in the succeeding quota peri
liveries below that quota
the same percent.

(q) *Bureau of the Bud*
The record keeping and
quirements of this order h
proved by the Bureau of t
accordance with the Feder
of 1942. Subsequent reco
reporting requirements wil
the approval of the Bureau
pursuant to the Federal R
1942.

(r) This order shall t
12:01 a. m., e. w. t., Octobe

Issued this 8th day of O

C. W. K
Acting D
Food 1

Press Release Immediate:
Saturday, October 9, 1943.

Effective October 17, the Food Distribution Administration's fluid milk conservation and control program will be extended to cover five more metropolitan areas, the War Food Administration said today.

The new milk sales areas, and the market agents who will administer the program in each, are:

- Bridgeport-New Haven, Conn.; Hartford-New Britain, Conn.; Waterbury, Conn.—(Market Agent to be named later.)
- New Orleans, La.—J. B. McCroskey, 1421 Carondelet Building, New Orleans, La.
- Louisville, Ky.—L. S. Iverson, 455 S. 4th St., Louisville, Ky.

Dealers' milk sales in these areas will be limited to 100 percent of their June sales for fluid milk; 75 percent of June sales for cream; and 75 percent of June sales for milk byproducts as a group (including such products as cottage cheese, chocolate milk and buttermilk). However, a dealer may, upon approval of the market agent, increase his milk sales above the June level if he reduces his sales of cream and milk byproducts by an equivalent amount of milk. He also may increase his sales of milk byproducts beyond the 75 percent quota by reducing his cream sales. Milk dealers include all persons or firms engaged in the sale or transfer of milk, but not retail stores, hotels, restaurants, etc.

Producer-distributors who purchase no milk except those whose volume of sales is small enough to make them quota-exempt) will be allowed to sell an amount of fluid milk, cream, and fluid milk byproducts equal to 100 percent of their total milk production in June. Quota-exempt producer-distributors are defined separately for each area, but in general they are those whose deliveries are relatively small.

Deliveries of milk, milk byproducts and cream to plants manufacturing dairy products; to military agencies, and to other milk dealers (except special classes of dealers, such as peddlers) are quota-exempt. In the three Connecticut sales areas deliveries to nursery, elementary, and junior high schools also will be quota-exempt.

Consumers in these and other designated milk sales areas generally will be able to purchase as much milk under the milk conservation program as they have been buying—an amount considerably greater than that bought in pre-war years, and about 10 percent above last year's purchases. Sales quotas on cream and on fluid milk byproducts have been been set below June deliveries to boost fluid milk supplies where milk production is low, and to conserve milk for manufacturing purposes.

Fluid milk sales are being stabilized in these and other metropolitan areas, FDA officials explained, to help assure sufficient milk for manufacturing the cheese, butter, evaporated milk and milk powder required by the armed services and civilians for good nutrition and properly balanced diets.

Largely due to expanded consumer demand, sales of fluid milk have been increasing steadily and are now about 20 percent higher than in p
(1936–40) and 10 to 12 p
those in 1942. With total
tion levelled off, and e
somewhat, this expandin
milk sold for fluid uses h
reduced the supply of "n
milk," and, consequently, t
of cheese, butter and other

The FDA dealer-quota p
tempt to stabilize fluid milk
without resorting to indivi
rationing. Point rationin
bulky and highly perishab
would be very difficult to a
consumers and the trade c
the present program to ass
are held within quotas a
available are distributed
officials believe consumer
not be necessary.

Milk handlers in the
named today, will comput
of milk which may sell e
terms of pounds of milk,
sales in terms of pounds
butterfat, and their mil
sales in terms of pounds
products or skim milk equ

To facilitate administra
ket agent for each milk s
act upon petitions for reli
ship which may be submitt
after investigation, he may
rary relief for a total perio
60 days.

Milk sales in 33 eastern
ern areas previously were
federal regulation. Sales q
initial milk sales areas ar
for those named today.

FDO 79-38

OCTOBER 9, 1943

WAR FOOD ADMINISTRATION

[FDO 79-38]

PART 1401—DAIRY PRODUCTS

CONSERVATION AND DISTRIBUTION OF FLUID MILK AND CREAM IN LOUISVILLE, KY., METROPOLITAN SALES AREA

Pursuant to the authority vested in me by Food Distribution Order No. 79 (8 F.R. 12426), issued on September 7, 1943, as amended, and to effectuate the purposes of such order, it is hereby ordered as follows:

§ 1401.69 *Quota restrictions*—(a) *Definitions.* When used in this order, unless otherwise distinctly expressed or manifestly incompatible with the intent hereof:

(1) Each term defined in Food Distribution Order No. 79, as amended, shall, when used herein, have the same meaning as is set forth for such term in Food Distribution Order No. 79, as amended.

(2) The term FDO 79 means Food Distribution Order No. 79, issued on September 7, 1943, as amended.

(3) The term "sub-handler" means any handler, such as a peddler, vendor, sub-dealer, or secondary dealer, who purchases in a previously packaged and processed form milk, milk byproducts, or cream for delivery.

(b) *Milk sales area.* The following area is hereby designated as a "milk sales area" to be known as the Louisville, Kentucky, metropolitan sales area, and is referred to hereinafter as the "sales area": The city of Louisville, Fort Knox Military Reservation, and Jefferson County, Kentucky; and all municipal corporations and unincorporated territory within Clark and Floyd Counties, Indiana.

(c) *Base period.* The calendar month of June 1943 is hereby designated as the base period for the sales area.

(d) *Quota period.* The remainder of the calendar month in which the provisions hereof become effective and each subsequent calendar month, respectively, is hereby designated as a quota period for the sales area.

(e) *Handler quotas.* Quotas for each handler in the sales area in each quota period shall be calculated in terms of pounds of each of the items for which percentages are specified in (3) below and shall be determined as follows:

(1) Divide the total deliveries of each such item made in the sales area by such handler during the base period, after excluding the quota-exempt deliveries described in (i) hereof, by the number of days in the base period;

(2) Multiply the result of the foregoing calculation by the number of days in the quota period;

(3) Multiply the aforesaid resulting amount by the following applicable percentage: (i) Milk: 100 percent; (ii) Butterfat in milk: ____ percent; (iii) Cream: 75 percent; (iv) Butterfat in cream: 75 percent; (v) Milk byproducts other than cottage, pot or baker's cheese: 75 percent; and (vi) Cottage, pot, or baker's cheese: 75 percent of skim milk equivalent. (For the purpose of this order, one pound of cottage, pot, or baker's cheese shall be considered as the equivalent of 7 pounds of skim milk.)

(f) *Quota limitations.* No handler shall, during any quota period, make deliveries in the sales area in excess of his respective quotas, except as set out in (i) hereof: *Provided,* That a handler may, after application to and approval by the market agent, secure an increase in milk quotas through an equivalent reduction as determined by the market agent, in cream and milk byproducts quotas, and an increase in milk byproducts quota through an equivalent reduction as determined by the market agent, in cream quotas.

(g) *Quotas for handlers who are also producers.* Quotas for handlers who are also producers and who purchase no milk shall be 100 percent of the total production of such handlers in the base period.

(h) *Handler exemptions.* Quotas shall not apply to any handler who delivers in a quota period a daily average of less than 250 units of milk, cream, and milk byproducts. For the purpose of this order, a unit shall be the equivalent in volume of the following: (1) milk, one quart of milk; (2) cream, one-half pint of cream; and (3) milk byproduct, one quart of skim milk, buttermilk, flavored milk drink, or other beverage containing more than 85 percent of skim milk, or one-half pound of cottage, pot, or baker's cheese.

(i) *Quota exclusions and exemptions.* Deliveries of milk, milk byproducts, or cream (1) to other handlers, except for such deliveries to sub-handlers, (2) to plants engaged in the handling or processing of milk, milk byproducts, or cream from which no milk, milk byproducts, or cream is delivered in the sales area, and (3) to the agencies or groups specified in (d) of FDO 79, shall be excluded from the computation of deliveries in the base period and exempt from charges to quotas.

(j) *Transfers and apportionment of quotas.* The market agent is empowered to deduct an amount of base period deliveries to purchasers from the total of deliveries made by a handler or other person in the base period upon the application and a showing of unreasonable hardship by the handler making deliveries to such purchasers on the effective date of this order, and to add the amount of such deliveries to the total base period deliveries of the applicant handler. Denials of transfers or transfers granted by the market agent shall be reviewed by the Director upon application.

(k) *Petition for relief from hardships.* (1) Any person affected by FDO 79 or the provisions hereof who considers that compliance therewith would work an exceptional and unreasonable hardship on him, may file with the market agent a petition addressed to the Director. The petition shall contain the correct name, address and principal place of business of the petitioner, a full statement of the facts upon which the petition is based, and the hardship involved and the nature of the relief desired.

(2) Upon receiving such petition, the market agent shall immediately investigate the representations and facts stated therein.

(3) After investigation, the petition shall be certified to the Director, but prior to certification the market agent may (i) deny the petition, or (ii) grant temporary relief for a total period not to exceed 60 days.

(4) Denials or grants of relief by the market agent shall be reviewed by the Director and may be affirmed, modified, or reversed by the Director.

(l) *Reports.* Each handler shall transmit to the market agent on forms prescribed by the market agent the following reports:

(1) Within 20 days following the effective date of this order, reports which show the information required by the market agent to establish such handlers' quotas;

(2) Within 20 days following the close of each quota period, the information required by the market agent to establish volumes of deliveries of milk, cream, and milk byproducts during the preceding quota period; and

(3) Handlers exempt from quotas pursuant to (h) hereof, shall, upon the request of the market agent, submit the information required by the market

agent to establish volumes of deliveries of milk, cream, and milk byproducts.

(m) *Records.* Handlers shall keep and shall make available to the market agent such records of receipts, sales, deliveries, and production as the market agent shall require for the purpose of obtaining information which the Director may require for the establishment of quotas as prescribed in (b) of FDO 79.

(n) *Distribution schedules.* The distribution schedules, if any, to be followed by the handlers in making deliveries shall be made effective in the terms of approval by the Director of such schedules.

(o) *Expense of administration.* Each handler shall pay to the market agent, within 20 days after the close of each calendar month an assessment of $.01 per hundredweight of each of milk, cream, skim milk, buttermilk, flavored milk drinks, beverages containing more than 85 percent of skim milk, and skim milk the equivalent of cottage, pot, or baker's cheese delivered during the preceding quota period and subject to quota regulations under the provisions hereof.

(p) *Violations.* The market agent shall report all violations to the Director together with the information required for the prosecution of such violations, except in a case where a handler has made deliveries in a quota period in excess of a quota in an amount not to exceed 5 percent of such quota, and in th.. succeeding quota period makes deliveries below that quota by at least the same percent.

(q) *Bureau of the Budget approval.* The record keeping and reporting requirements of this order have been approved by the Bureau of the Budget in accordance with the Federal Reports Act of 1942. Subsequent record keeping or reporting requirements will be subject to the approval of the Bureau of the Budget pursuant to the Federal Reports Act of 1942.

(r) This order shall take effect at 12:01 a. m., e. w. t., October 17, 1943.

Issued this 8th day of October 1943.

C. W. KITCHEN,
Acting Director of Food Distribution.

Press Release, Immediate:
Saturday, October 9, 1943.

Effective October 17, the Food Distribution Administration's fluid milk conservation and control program will be extended to cover five more metropolitan areas, the War Food Administration said today.

The new milk sales areas, and the market agents who will administer the program in each, are:

- Bridgeport-New Haven, Conn.; Hartford-New Britain, Conn.; Waterbury, Conn.—(Market Agent to be named later.)
- New Orleans, La.—J. B. McCroskey, 1421 Carondelet Building, New Orleans, La.
- Louisville, Ky.—L. S. Iverson, 455 S. 4th St., Louisville, Ky.

Dealers' milk sales in these areas will be limited to 100 percent of their June sales for fluid milk; 75 percent of June sales for cream, and 75 percent of June sales for milk byproducts as a group (including such products as cottage cheese, chocolate milk and buttermilk). However, a dealer may, upon approval of the market agent, increase his milk sales above the June level if he reduces his sales of cream and milk byproducts by an equivalent amount of milk. He also may increase his sales of milk byproducts beyond the 75 percent quota by reducing his cream sales. Milk dealers include all persons or firms engaged in the sale or transfer of milk, but not retail stores, hotels, restaurants, etc.

Producer-distributors who purchase no milk (except those whose volume of sales is small enough to make them quota-exempt) will be allowed to sell an amount of fluid milk, cream, and fluid milk byproducts equal to 100 percent of their total milk production in June. Quota-exempt producer-distributors are defined separately for each area, but in general they are those whose deliveries are relatively small.

Deliveries of milk, milk byproducts and cream to plants manufacturing dairy products; to military agencies, and to other milk dealers (except special classes of dealers, such as peddlers) are quota-exempt. In the three Connecticut sales areas deliveries to nursery, elementary, and junior high schools also will be quota-exempt.

Consumers in these and other designated milk sales areas generally will be able to purchase as much milk under the milk conservation program as they have been buying—an amount considerably greater than that bought in pre-war years, and about 10 percent above last year's purchases. Sales quotas on cream and on fluid milk byproducts have been set below June deliveries to boost fluid milk supplies where milk production is low, and to conserve milk for manufacturing purposes.

Fluid milk sales are being stabilized in these and other metropolitan areas, FDA officials explained, to help assure sufficient milk for manufacturing the cheese, butter, evaporated milk and milk powder required by the armed services and civilians for good nutrition and properly balanced diets.

Largely due to expanded consumer demand, sales of fluid milk have been increasing steadily and are now about 20 percent higher than in pre-war years (1936–40) and 10 to 12 percent above those in 1942. With total milk production leveled off, and even declining somewhat, this expanding volume of milk sold for fluid uses has inevitably reduced the supply of "manufacturing milk," and, consequently, the production of cheese, butter and other dairy foods.

The FDA dealer-quota plan is an attempt to stabilize fluid milk consumption without resorting to individual consumer rationing. Point rationing of milk, a bulky and highly perishable commodity, would be very difficult to administer. If consumers and the trade cooperate with the present program to assure that sales are held within quotas and quantities available are distributed fairly, FDA officials believe consumer rationing will not be necessary.

Milk handlers in the 5 sales areas named today, will compute the quantity of milk which may sell each month in terms of pounds of milk, their cream sales in terms of pounds of cream and butterfat, and their milk byproducts sales in terms of pounds of milk byproducts or skim milk equivalent.

To facilitate administration, the market agent for each milk sales area may act upon petitions for relief from hardship which may be submitted to him, and after investigation, he may grant temporary relief for a total period not to exceed 60 days.

Milk sales in 33 eastern and midwestern areas previously were brought under federal regulation. Sales quotas in these initial milk sales areas are the same as for those named today.

3 3 F

FDO 79-38
AMDT. 1
FEB. 19, 1944

WAR FOOD ADMINISTRATION

[FDO 79-38, Amdt. 1]

PART 1401—DAIRY PRODUCTS

FLUID MILK AND CREAM IN LOUISVILLE, KY., METROPOLITAN SALES AREA

Pursuant to Food Distribution Order No. 79 (8 F.R. 12426), dated September 7, 1943, as amended, and to effectuate the purposes thereof, Food Distribution Order No. 79-38 (8 F.R. 13840), relative to the conservation and distribution of fluid milk in the Louisville, Kentucky, metropolitan milk sales area, issued by the Director of Food Distribution on October 8, 1943, is hereby amended by deleting therefrom the provisions in § 1409.69 (i) and inserting, in lieu thereof, the following:

(i) *Quota exclusions and exemptions.* Deliveries of milk, milk byproducts, or cream (1) to other handlers, except for such deliveries to sub-handlers, (2) to plants engaged in the handling or processing of milk, milk byproducts, or cream from which no milk, milk byproducts or cream is delivered in the sales area, (3) to nursery, elementary, junior high, and high schools, and (4) to the agencies or groups specified in (d) of FDO 79, shall be excluded from the computation of deliveries in the base period and exempt from charges to quotas.

The provisions of this amendment shall become effective at 12:01 a. m., e. w. t., March 1, 1944. With respect to violations of said Food Distribution Order No. 79-38, rights accrued, or liabilities incurred, prior to the effective time of this amendment, said Food Distribution Order No. 79-38 shall be deemed to be in full force and effect for the purpose of sustaining any proper suit, action, or other proceeding with respect to any such violation, right, or liability.

(E.O. 9280, 7 F.R. 10179; E.O. 9322, 8 F.R. 3807; E.O. 9334, 8 F.R. 5423; E.O. 9392, 8 F.R. 14783; FDO 79, 8 F.R. 12426, 13283)

Issued this 19th day of February 1944.

LEE MARSHALL,
Director of Food Distribution.

eserve
1
77327

FDO 79-39

OCTOBER 11, 1943

WAR FOOD ADMINISTRATION

[FDO 79-39]

PART 1401—DAIRY PRODUCTS

CONSERVATION AND DISTRIBUTION OF FLUID MILK AND CREAM IN SEATTLE, WASH., METROPOLITAN SALES AREA

Pursuant to the authority vested in me by Food Distribution Order No. 79 (8 F.R. 12426), issued on September 7, 1943, as amended, and to effectuate the purposes of such order, it is hereby ordered as follows:

§ 1401.77 *Quota restrictions*—(a) *Definitions.* When used in this order, unless otherwise distinctly expressed or manifestly incompatible with the intent hereof:

(1) Each term defined in Food Distribution Order No. 79, as amended, shall, when used herein, have the same meaning as is set forth for such term in Food Distribution Order No. 79, as amended.

(2) The term "FDO 79" means Food Distribution Order No. 79, issued on September 7, 1943, as amended.

(3) The term "sub-handler" means any handler, such as a peddler, vendor, sub-dealer, or secondary dealer, who purchases in a previously packaged and processed form milk, milk byproducts, or cream for delivery.

(b) *Milk sales area.* The following area is hereby designated as a "milk sales area" to be known as the Seattle, Washington, metropolitan sales area, and is referred to hereinafter as the "sales area":

The city of Seattle and the election precincts of Arbor Heights, Athena, Bellevue 1 and 2, Beverly, Beverly Heights, Bitter Lake, Blue Ridge, Boddy, Bossert, Bothell 1 and 2, Bow Lake, Broadview, Bryn Mawr 1 and 2, Buchanan, Burien, Cedar River, Chelsea, Crescent, Crown Hill, Des Moines, Duwamish, Earlington, Echo Lake, Enatie, Endolyne, Evanston, Foster, Foy, Fruitland, Greenwood, Haller Lake, Harrison, Houghton, Jackson, Jefferson, Johnson, Juanita, Kenmore, Kennydale, Kirkland 1 and 2, Lake City, Lake Forest, Lake View, Lakewood, Licton Springs, McGilvra, McKinley, Manhattan, Maple Leaf 1 and 2, Meadow Point, Medina, Mercer, Moorlands, Morningside, Mount View, North Burien, North Park, North Riverton, North Trunk, Oak Lake, Panola, Polk, Ravenna, Renton 1st Ward 1 and 2, Renton 2d Ward 1 and 2, Renton 3d Ward, Richmond, Riverton, Riverton Heights, Ronald, Roosevelt, Rose Hill 1 and 2, Sand Point, Seahurst, Sonora, Southern Heights, Sunnydale, Sunrise, Sylvan, Taylor, Tukwila, Urbana, Van Buren, Victory Heights, Wilburton, Wilson, Woodland, Wynona, Xenia, Yarbo, Zenith and Zirconia, in King County; the election precincts of Curie, Edmonds, and Richmond, in Snohomish County; all in the State of Washington.

(c) *Base period.* The calendar month of June 1943 is hereby designated as the base period for the sales area.

(d) *Quota period.* The remainder of the calendar month in which the provisions hereof become effective and each subsequent calendar month, respectively, is hereby designated as a quota period for the sales area.

(e) *Handler quotas.* Quotas for each handler in the sales area in each quota period shall be calculated in terms of pounds of each of the items for which percentages are specified in (3) below and shall be determined as follows:

(1) Divide the total deliveries of each such item made in the sales area by such handler during the base period, after excluding the quota-exempt deliveries described in (i) hereof, by the number of days in the base period;

(2) Multiply the result of the foregoing calculation by the number of days in the quota period;

(3) Multiply the aforesaid resulting amount by the following applicable percentage: (i) Milk: 100 percent; (ii) butterfat in milk: 100 percent; (iii) cream: 75 percent; (iv) butterfat in cream: 75 percent; (v) milk byproducts other than cottage, pot, or baker's cheese: 75 percent; and (vi) cottage, pot, or baker's cheese: 75 percent of skim milk equivalent. (For the purpose of this order, one pound of cottage, pot, or baker's cheese shall be considered as the equivalent of 7 pounds of skim milk.)

(f) *Quota limitations.* No handler shall, during any quota period, make deliveries in the sales area in excess of his respective quotas, except as set out in (i) hereof: *Provided*, That a handler may, after application to and approval by the market agent, secure an increase in milk quotas through an equivalent reduction as determined by the market agent, in cream and milk byproducts quotas, and an increase in milk byproducts quota through an equivalent reduction as determined by the market agent, in cream quotas.

(g) *Quotas for handlers who are also producers.* Quotas for handlers who are also producers and who purchase no milk shall be 100 percent of the total production of such handlers in the base period.

(h) *Handler exemptions.* Quotas shall not apply to any handler who delivers in a quota period a daily average of less than 300 units of milk, cream, and milk byproducts. For the purpose of this order, a unit shall be the equivalent in volume of the following: (1) Milk, one quart of milk; (2) cream, one-half pint of cream; and (3) milk byproducts, one quart of skim milk, buttermilk, flavored milk drink, or other beverage containing more than 85 percent of skim milk, or one-half pound of cottage, pot, or baker's cheese.

(i) *Quota exclusions and exemptions.* Deliveries of milk, milk byproducts, or cream (1) to other handlers, except for such deliveries to sub-handlers, (2) to plants engaged in the handling or processing of milk, milk byproducts, or cream from which no milk, milk byproducts, or cream is delivered in the sales area, and (3) to the agencies or groups specified in (d) of FDO 79, shall be excluded from the computation of deliveries in the base period and exempt from charges to quotas.

(j) *Transfers and apportionment of quotas.* The market agent is empowered to deduct an amount of base period deliveries to purchasers from the total of deliveries made by a handler or other person in the base period upon the application and a showing of unreasonable hardship by the handler making deliveries to such purchasers on the effective date of this order, and to add the amount of such deliveries to the total base period deliveries of the applicant handler. Denials of transfers or transfers granted by the market agent shall be reviewed by the Director upon application.

(k) *Petition for relief from hardships.* (1) Any person affected by FDO 79 or the provisions hereof who considers that compliance therewith would work an exceptional and unreasonable hardship on him, may file with the market agent a petition addressed to the Director. The petition shall contain the correct name, address and principal place of business of the petitioner, a full statement of the facts upon which the petition is based, and the hardship involved and the nature of the relief desired.

(2) Upon receiving such petition, the market agent shall immediately investigate the representations and facts stated therein.

(3) After investigation, the position shall be certified to the Director, but prior to certification the market agent may (i) deny the petition, or (ii) grant temporary relief for a total period not to exceed 60 days.

(4) Denials or grants of relief by the market agent shall be reviewed by the Director and may be affirmed, modified, or reversed by the Director.

(l) *Reports.* Each handler shall transmit to the market agent on forms prescribed by the market agent the following reports:

(1) Within 20 days following the effective date of this order, reports which show the information required by the market agent to establish such handlers' quotas;

(2) Within 20 days following the close of each quota period, the information required by the market agent to establish volumes of deliveries of milk, cream, and milk byproducts during the preceding quota period; and

(3) Handlers exempt from quotas pursuant to (h) hereof shall, upon the request of the market agent, submit the information required by the market agent to establish volumes of deliveries of milk, cream, and milk byproducts.

(m) *Records.* Handlers shall keep and shall make available to the market agent such records of receipts, sales, deliveries, and production as the market agent shall require for the purpose of obtaining information which the Director may require for the establishment of quotas as prescribed in (b) of FDO 79.

(n) *Distribution schedules.* The distribution schedules, if any, to be followed by the handlers in making deliveries shall be made effective in the terms of approval by the Director of such schedules.

(o) *Expense of administration.* Each handler shall pay to the market agent, within 20 days after the close of each calendar month an assessment of $0.01 per hundredweight of each of milk, cream, skim milk, buttermilk, flavored milk drinks, beverages containing more than 85 percent of skim milk, and skim milk equivalent of cottage, pot, or baker's cheese delivered during the preceding quota period and subject to quota regulations under the provisions hereof.

(p) *Violations.* The market agent shall report all violations to the Director together with the informa
for the prosecution of su
except in a case where a
made deliveries in a quota
cess of a quota in an a
exceed 5 percent of such
the succeeding quota peri
liveries below that quota b
same percent.

(q) *Bureau of the Bud*
The record keeping and
quirements of this order l
proved by the Bureau of
accordance with the Feder
of 1942. Subsequent reco
reporting requirements wil
the approval of the Bureau
pursuant to the Federal
of 1942.

(r) This order shall t
12:01 a. m., e. w. t. Octobe

Issued this 11th day of O

C. W.
Acti

Press Release, Immediate:
Monday, October 11, 1943.

Federal control over fluid milk sales will be extended to the Far West for the first time beginning October 17, 1943 when maximum deliveries quotas will be assigned to milk dealers in three Washington metropolitan areas, the War Food Administration said today. The milk conservation and control program also will go into effect in three New England areas on the same date.

The new milk sales areas, and the market agents who will administer the program for the Food Distribution Administration in each area, are:

Springfield-Holyoke, Mass.: Eastern New England Metropolitan (including cities in Bristol, Middlesex, Plymouth, Worcester, Essex, Norfolk and Suffolk counties in Massachusetts, and 22 cities in Rhode Island)—Mr. Samuel W. Tator, 80 Federal Street, Boston, Mass.

Fall River - New Bedford - Taunton, Mass.—Mr. John J. Hogan, 103 Pleasant Street, Fall River, Mass.

Seattle, Washington, Metropolitan; Spokane, Washington, Metropolitan; Tacoma, Washington, Metropolitan—Mr. J. H. Mapes, 635 Elliot Avenue, West, Seattle, Wash.

Dealers' fluid milk sales in these areas will be limited to the quantity sold in June. Cream sales and sales of milk byproducts (such as cottage cheese, chocolate milk and buttermilk) will be limited to 75 percent of the quantities sold in June. Upon approval of the market agent, however, a dealer may increase his fluid milk quota if he reduces his cream and milk byproducts sales in an amount approved by the market agent. He may increase sales of milk byproducts over the basic quota by reducing his cream sales. Milk dealers include all persons or firms engaged in the sale or transfer of milk, but not retail stores, hotels, restaurants, etc.

Producer-distributors who purchase no milk (except those whose volume of sales is small enough to make them quota-exempt) will be allowed to sell an amount of fluid milk, cream and fluid milk byproducts equal to 100 percent of their total milk production in June. Quota-exempt producer-distribtors are defined separately for each area, but in general they are those whose deliveries are relatively small.

Milk handlers in the 3 New England sales areas will compute the quantity of milk which they may sell each month in terms of pounds of milk, their cream sales in terms of pounds of cream and butterfat, and their milk byproducts sales in terms of pounds of milk byproducts or skim milk equivalent. In the 3 Washington state areas, milk handlers will determine their fluid milk quotas in terms of pounds of milk and butterfat.

Deliveries to the Armed Forces, to plants processing dairy products, and to other handlers (except special classes of handlers such as peddlers) are quota-exempt.

To facilitate administration, the market agent for each milk sales area may act upon petitions for relief from hardship which may be submitted to him, and after investigation, he may grant temporary relief for a total period not to exceed 60 days.

Milk sales in 38 eastern and midwestern areas previously were brought under federal regulation. Basic sales quotas in these initial milk sales areas are the same as for those named today.

The Eastern New England Metropolitan milk sales area includes the following cities:

In Bistol County, Massachusetts, the towns and cities of:

Attleboro	N. At
Easton	Seek
Mansfield	

In Middlesex County, M
the towns and cities of:

Arlington	Medi
Ashland	Melr
Bedford	Nati
Belmont	Newt
Billerica	N. R
Burlington	Read
Cambridge	Sher
Chelmsford	Som
Concord	Ston
Dracut	Sudb
Everett	Tewk
Framingham	Tyng
Holliston	Wak
Hopkinton	Walt
Hudson	Wat
Lexington	Way
Lincoln	West
Lowell	Wiln
Malden	Winc
Marlboro	Wob
Maynard	

In Plymouth County, M
the towns and cities of:

Abington	Norw
Bridgewater	Rock
Brockton	Scitu
E. Bridgewater	W. B
Hanover	Whit
Hanson	

In Worcester County, M
the towns and cities of:

Auburn	Leice
Berlin	Men
Blackstone	Milf
Boylston	Millb
Clinton	Millv
Grafton	North
Holden	North
Hopedale	Paxt

Shrewsbury	Uxbridge
Southboro	Westboro
Spencer	W. Boylston
Upton	Worcester

All of the towns and cities in the counties of Essex, Norfolk, and Suffolk, Massachusetts.

In Rhode Island the towns and cities of:

Barington	Newport
Bristol	No. Providence
Central Falls	No. Smithfield
Cranston	Pawtucket
Cumberland	Portsmouth
E. Greenwich	Providence
E. Providence	Smithfield
Jamestown	Warren
Johnston	Warwick
Lincoln	W. Warwick
Middletown	Woonsocket

The Fall River-New Bedford-Taunton area includes the following cities and towns:

In Massachusetts:

Achusnet	Fall River
Berkley	Freetown
Dartmouth	New Bedford
Dighton	Norton
Fairhaven	Raynham
Rehoboth	Taunton
Somerset	Westport
Swansea	

In Rhode Island:

Little Compton	Tiverton

The Springfield-Holyoke area includes:

Amherst	Northampton
Agawam	Palmer
Chicopee	South Hadley
Easthampton	Southhampton
East Longmeadow	Springfield
Granby	Ware
Hadley	Westfield
Hatfield	West Springfield
Holyoke	Wilbraham
Longmeadow	also Enfield, Conn.
Ludlow	

Consumers in these areas generally will be able to purchase as much milk under the milk conservation program as they have been buying—an amount considerably greater than that bought in pre-war years, and about 10 percent above last year's purchases. Sales quotas on cream and on fluid milk by-products have been set below June deliveries to boost fluid milk supplies where milk production is low, and to conserve milk for manufacturing purposes.

Fluid milk sales are being stabilized in these and other metropolitan areas, FDA officials explained, to help assure sufficient milk for manufacturing the cheese, butter, evaporated milk, and milk powder required by the Armed Services and civilians for good nutrition and properly balanced diets.

Largely due to expanded consumer demand, sales of fluid milk have been increasing steadily and are now about 20 percent higher than in pre-war years (1936–40) and 10 to 12 percent above those in 1942. With total milk production levelled off, and even declining somewhat, this expanding volume of milk sold for fluid uses has inevitably reduced the supply of "manufacturing milk," and consequently, the production of cheese, butter, and other dairy foods.

The FDA's dealer-quota plan is an attempt to stabilize fluid milk consumption without resorting to individual consumer rationing. Point rationing of milk, a bulky and highly perishable commodity, would be very difficult to administer. If consumers and the trade cooperate with the present program to assure that sales are held within quotas and quantities available are distributed fairly, FDA officials believe consumer rationing will not be necessary.

FDO 79-40

OCTOBER 11, 1943

WAR FOOD ADMINISTRATION

[FDO 79-40]

PART 1401—DAIRY PRODUCTS

CONSERVATION AND DISTRIBUTION OF FLUID MILK AND CREAM IN TACOMA, WASH., METROPOLITAN SALES AREA

Pursuant to the authority vested in me by Food Distribution Order No. 79 (8 F.R. 12426), issued on September 7, 1943, as amended, and to effectuate the purposes of such order, it is hereby ordered as follows:

§ 1401.76 *Quota restrictions*—(a) *Definitions.* When used in this order, unless otherwise distinctly expressed or manifestly incompatible with the intent hereof:

(1) Each term defined in Food Distribution Order No. 79, as amended, shall, when used herein, have the same meaning as is set forth for such term in Food Distribution Order No. 79, as amended.

(2) The term "FDO 79" means Food Distribution Order No. 79, issued on September 7, 1943, as amended.

(3) The term "sub-handler" means any handler, such as a peddler, vendor, sub-dealer, or secondary dealer, who purchases in a previously packaged and processed form milk, milk byproducts, or cream for delivery.

(b) *Milk sales area.* The following area is hereby designated as a "milk sales area" to be known as the Tacoma, Washington, metropolitan sales area, and is referred to hereinafter as the "sales area":

The city of Tacoma and the election precincts of American Lake, Brookdale, Custer, Dash Point, Day Island, Edgewood, Fir Crest, Gardenville, Grant, Harvard, Hunts Prairie, Hyada Park, Interlaaken, Lake City, Lake View, Midland, Milton, Narrows View, North Puyallup, Parkland 1 and 2, Puyallup, Puyallup Ward 1, precincts 1, 2, and 3, Puyallup Ward 2, precincts 1, 2, and 3, Puyallup Ward 3, precincts 1, 2, and 3, Riverside, Ruston, Steilacoom, Sumner 1, 2, and 3, University Place, and Woodrow, in Pierce County; the precincts of Aaron, Algona, Auburn 1 to 6, Harding, Jovita, Pacific, and Stuck, in King County; all in the State of Washington.

(c) *Base period.* The calendar month of June 1943 is hereby designated as the base period for the sales area.

(d) *Quota period.* The remainder of the calendar month in which the provisions hereof become effective and each subsequent calendar month, respectively, is hereby designated as a quota period for the sales area.

(e) *Handler quotas.* Quotas for each handler in the sales area in each quota period shall be calculated in terms of pounds of each of the items for which percentages are specified in (3) below and shall be determined as follows:

(1) Divide the total deliveries of each such item made in the sales area by such handler during the base period, after excluding the quota-exempt deliveries described in (i) hereof, by the number of days in the base period;

(2) Multiply the result of the foregoing calculation by the number of days in the quota period;

(3) Multiply the aforesaid resulting amount by the following applicable percentage: (i) Milk: 100 percent; (ii) butterfat in milk: 100 percent; (iii) cream: 75 percent; (iv) butterfat in cream: 75 percent; (v) milk byproducts other than cottage, pot, or baker's cheese: 75 percent; and (vi) cottage, pot, or baker's cheese: 75 percent of skim milk equivalent. (For the purpose of this order, one pound of cottage, pot, or baker's cheese shall be considered as the equivalent of 7 pounds of skim milk.)

(f) *Quota limitations.* No handler shall, during any quota period, make deliveries in the sales area in excess of his respective quotas, except as set out in (i) hereof: *Provided,* That a handler may, after application to and approval by the market agent, secure an increase in milk quotas through an equivalent reduction as determined by the market agent, in cream and milk byproducts quotas, and an increase in milk byproducts quota through an equivalent reduction as determined by the market agent, in cream quotas.

(g) *Quotas for handlers who are also producers.* Quotas for handlers who are also producers and who purchase no milk shall be 100 percent of the total production of such handlers in the base period.

(h) *Handler exemptions.* Quotas shall not apply to any handler who delivers in a quota period a daily average of less than 300 units of milk, cream, and milk byproducts. For the purpose of this order, a unit shall be the equivalent in volume of the following: (1) milk, one quart of milk; (2) cream, one-half pint of cream; and (3) milk byproduct, one quart of skim milk, buttermilk, flavored milk drink, or other beverage containing more than 85 percent of skim milk, or one-half pound of cottage, pot, or baker's cheese.

(i) *Quota exclusions and exemptions.* Deliveries of milk, milk byproducts, or cream (1) to other handlers, except for such deliveries to sub-handlers, (2) to plants engaged in the handling or processing of milk, milk byproducts or cream from which no milk, milk byproducts, or cream is delivered in the sales area, and (3) to the agencies or groups specified in (d) of FDO 79, shall be excluded from the computation of deliveries in the base period and exempt from charges to quotas.

(j) *Transfers and apportionment of quotas.* The market agent is empowered to deduct an amount of base period deliveries to purchasers from the total of deliveries made by a handler or other person in the base period upon the application and a showing of unreasonable hardship by the handler making deliveries to such purchasers on the effective date of this order, and to add the amount of such deliveries to the total base period deliveries of the applicant handler. Denials of transfers or transfers granted by the market agent shall be reviewed by the Director upon application.

(k) *Petition for relief from hardships.* (1) Any person affected by FDO 79 or the provisions hereof who considers that compliance therewith would work an exceptional and unreasonable hardship on him, may file with the market agent a petition addressed to the Director. The petition shall contain the correct name, address and principal place of business of the petitioner, a full statement of the facts upon which the petition is based, and the hardship involved and the nature of the relief desired.

(2) Upon receiving such petition, the market agent shall be reviewed by the Digate the representations and facts stated therein.

(3) After investigation, the petition shall be certified to the Director, but prior to certification the market agent may (i) deny the petition, or (ii) grant temporary relief for a total period not to exceed 60 days.

(4) Denials or grants of relief by the market agent shall be reviewed by the Director and may be affirmed, modified, or reversed by the Director.

(l) *Reports.* Each handler shall transmit to the market agent on forms prescribed by the market agent the following reports:

(1) Within 20 days following the effective date of this order, reports which show the information required by the market agent to establish such handlers' quotas;

(2) Within 20 days following the close of each quota period, the information re-

quired by the market agent to establish volumes of deliveries of milk, cream, and milk byproducts during the preceding quota period; and

(3) Handlers exempt from quotas pursuant to (h) hereof shall, upon the request of the market agent, submit the information required by the market agent to establish volumes of deliveries of milk, cream, and milk byproducts.

(m) *Records.* Handlers shall keep and shall make available to the market agent such records of receipts, sales, deliveries, and production as the market agent shall require for the purpose of obtaining information which the Director may require for the establishment of quotas as prescribed in (b) of FDO 79.

(n) *Distribution schedules.* The distribution schedules, if any, to be followed by the handlers in making deliveries shall be made effective in the terms of approval by the Director of such schedules.

(o) *Expense of administration.* Each handler shall pay to the market agent, within 20 days after the close of each calendar month an assessment of $0.01 per hundredweight of each of milk, cream, skim milk, buttermilk, flavored milk drinks, beverages containing more than 85 percent of skim milk, and skim milk equivalent of cottage, pot, or baker's cheese delivered during the preceding quota period and subject to quota regulations under the provisions hereof.

(p) *Violations.* The market agent shall report all violations to the Director together with the information required for the prosecution of such violations, except in a case where a handler has made deliveries in a quota period in excess of a quota in an amount not to exceed 5 per cent of such quota, and in the succeedin quota period makes deliveries below the quota by at least the same percent.

(q) *Bureau of the Budget approva* The record keeping and reporting re quirements of this order have been ap proved by the Bureau of the Budget i accordance with the Federal Reports Ac of 1942. Subsequent record keeping c reporting requirements will be subject t the approval of the Bureau of the Budge pursuant to the Federal Reports Act c 1942.

(r) This order shall take effect at 12:(a. m., e. w. t. October 17, 1943.

Issued this 11th day of October 194

C. W. KITCHEN,
Acting Director.

Press Release, Immediate:
Monday, October 11, 1943.

Federal Control over fluid milk sales will be extended to the Far West for the first time beginning October 17, 1943 when maximum deliveries quotas will be assigned to milk dealers in three Washington metropolitan areas, the War Food Administration said today. The milk conservation and control program also will go into effect in three New England areas on the same date.

The new milk sales areas, and the market agents who will administer the program for the Food Distribution Administration in each area, are:

Springfield-Holyoke, Mass.: Eastern New England Metropolitan (including cities in Bristol, Middlesex, Plymouth, Worcester, Essex, Norfolk, and Suffolk Counties in Massachusetts, and 22 cities in Rhode Island)—Mr. Samuel W. Tator, 80 Federal Street, Boston, Mass.

Fall River-New Bedford-Taunton, Mass.: Mr. John J. Hogan, 103 Pleasant Street, Fall River, Mass.

Seattle, Washington, Metropolitan; Spokane, Washington, Metropolitan; Tacoma, Washington, Metropolitan: Mr. J. H. Mapes, 635 Elliot Avenue, West, Seattle, Wash.

Dealers' fluid milk sales in these areas will be limited to the quantity sold in June. Cream sales and sales of milk byproducts (such as cottage cheese, chocolate milk and buttermilk) will be limited to 75 percent of the quantities sold in June. Upon approval of the market agent, however, a dealer may increase his fluid milk quota if he reduces his cream and milk byproducts sales in an amount approved by the market agent. He may increase sales of milk byproducts over the basic quota by reducing his cream sales. Milk dealers include all persons or firms engaged in the sale or transfer of milk, but not retail stores, hotels, restaurants, etc.

Producer-distributors who purchase no milk (except those whose volume of sales is small enough to make them quota-exempt) will be allowed to sell an amount of fluid milk, cream and fluid milk byproducts equal to 100 percent of their total milk production in June. Quota-exempt producer-distributors are defined separately for each area, but in general they are those whose deliveries are relatively small.

Milk handlers in the 3 New England sales areas will compute the quantity of milk which they may sell each month in terms of pounds of milk, their cream sales in terms of pounds of cream and butterfat, and their milk byproducts sales in terms of pounds of milk byproducts or skim milk equivalent. In the 3 Washington state areas, milk handlers will determine their fluid milk quotas in terms of pounds of milk and butterfat.

Deliveries to the Armed Forces, to plants processing dairy products, and to other handlers (except special classes of handlers such as peddlers) are quota-exempt.

To facilitate administration, the market agent for each milk sales area may act upon petitions for relief from hardship which may be submitted to him, and after investigation, he may grant temporary relief for a total period not to exceed 60 days.

Milk sales in 38 eastern and midwestern areas previously were brought under federal regulation. Basic sales quotas in these initial milk sales areas are the same as for those named today.

The Eastern New England Metropolitan milk sales area includes the following cities:

In Bristol County, Massachusetts, the towns and cities of:

Attleboro	N. Attleboro
Easton	Seekonk
Mansfield	

In Middlesex County, Massachusetts, the towns and cities of:

Arlington	Belmont
Ashland	Billerica
Bedford	Burlington
Cambridge	Newton
Chelmsford	N. Reading
Concord	Reading
Dracut	Sherborn
Everett	Somerville
Framingham	Stoneham
Holliston	Sudbury
Hopkinton	Tewksbury
Hudson	Tyngsboro
Lexington	Wakefield
Lincoln	Waltham
Lowell	Watertown
Malden	Wayland
Marlboro	Weston
Maynard	Wilmington
Medford	Winchester
Melrose	Woburn
Natick	

In Plymouth County, Massachusett the towns and cities of:

Abington	Norwell
Bridgewater	Rockland
Brockton	Scituate
E. Bridgewater	W. Bridgewater
Hanover	Whitman
Hanson	

In Worcester County, Massachusett the towns and cities of:

Auburn	Millville
Berlin	Northboro
Blackstone	Northbridge
Boylston	Paxton
Clinton	Shrewsbury
Grafton	Southboro
Holden	Spencer
Hopedale	Upton
Leicester	Uxbridge
Mendon	Westboro
Milford	W. Boylston
Millbury	Worcester

All of the towns and cities in tl counties of Essex, Norfolk, and Suffol Massachusetts.

In Rhode Island the towns and citi of:

Barrington	Cumberland
Bristol	E. Greenwich
Central Falls	E. Providence
Cranston	Jamestown

Johnston	Portsmouth
Lincoln	Providence
Middletown	Smithfield
Newport	Warren
No. Providence	Warwick
No. Smithfield	W. Warwick
Pawtucket	Woonsocket

The Fall River-New Bedford-Taunton area includes the following cities and towns:

In Massachusetts:

Acushnet	Norton
Berkley	Raynham
Dartmouth	Rehoboth
Dighton	Somerset
Fairhaven	Swansea
Fall River	Taunton
Freetown	Westport
New Bedford	

In Rhode Island:

Little Compton	Tiverton

The Springfield-Holyoke area includes:

Amherst	Chicopee
Agawam	Easthampton
East Longmeadow	South Hadley
Granby	Southampton
Hadley	Springfield
Hatfield	Ware
Holyoke	Westfield
Longmeadow	West Springfield
Ludlow	Wilbraham
Northampton	also Enfield, Conn.
Palmer	

Consumers in these areas generally will be able to purchase as much milk under the milk conservation program as they have been buying—an amount considerably greater than that bought in pre-war years, and about 10 percent above last year's purchases. Sales quotas on cream and on fluid milk byproducts have been set below June deliveries to boost fluid milk supplies where milk production is low, and to conserve milk for manufacturing purposes.

Fluid milk sales are being stabilized in these and other metropolitan areas, FDA officials explained, to help assure sufficient milk for manufacturing the cheese, butter, evaporated milk, and milk powder required by the Armed Services and civilians for good nutrition and properly balanced diets.

Largely due to expanded consumer demand, sales of fluid milk have been increasing steadily and are now about 20 percent higher than in pre-war years (1936–40) and 10 to 12 percent above those in 1942. With total milk production levelled off, and even declining somewhat, this expanding volume of milk sold for fluid uses has inevitably reduced the supply of "manufacturing milk," and consequently, the production of cheese, butter, and other dairy foods.

The FDA's dealer-quota plan is an attempt to stabilize fluid milk consumption without resorting to individual consumer rationing. Point rationing of milk, a bulky and highly perishable commodity, would be very difficult to administer. If consumers and the trade cooperate with the present program to assure that sales are held within quotas and quantities available are distributed fairly, FDA officials believe consumer rationing will not be necessary.

WAR FOOD ADMINISTRATION

[FDO 79-41]

PART 1401—DAIRY PRODUCTS

CONSERVATION AND DISTRIBUTION OF FLUID MILK AND CREAM IN SPOKANE, WASH., METROPOLITAN SALES AREA

Pursuant to the authority vested in me by Food Distribution Order No. 79 (8 F.R. 12426), issued on September 7, 1943, as amended, and to effectuate the purposes of such order, it is hereby ordered as follows:

§ 1401.75 *Quota restrictions*—(a) *Definitions.* When used in this order, unless otherwise distinctly expressed or manifestly incompatible with the intent hereof:

(1) Each term defined in Food Distribution Order No. 79, as amended, shall, when used herein, have the same meaning as is set forth for such term in Food Distribution Order No. 79, as amended.

(2) The term "FDO 79" means Food Distribution Order No. 79, issued on September 7, 1943, as amended.

(3) The term "sub-handler" means any handler, such as a peddler, vendor, sub-dealer, or secondary dealer, who purchases in a previously packaged and processed form milk, milk byproducts, or cream for delivery.

(b) *Milk sales area.* The following area is hereby designated as a "milk sales area" to be known as the Spokane, Washington, metropolitan sales area, and is referred to hereinafter as the "sales area":

The city of Spokane, the townships of East Spokane, Five Mile, Marshall, Mead, Moran, Opportunity, Pleasant Prairie, Stevens, and West Spokane, and the town of Millwood, all in Spokane County, Washington.

(c) *Base period.* The calendar month of June 1943 is hereby designated as the base period for the sales area.

(d) *Quota period.* The remainder of the calendar month in which the provisions hereof become effective and each subsequent calendar month, respectively, is hereby designated as a quota period for the sales area.

(e) *Handler quotas.* Quotas for each handler in the sales area in each quota period shall be calculated in terms of pounds of each of the items for which percentages are specified in (3) below and shall be determined as follows:

(1) Divide the total deliveries of each such item made in the sales area by such handler during the base period, after excluding the quota-exempt deliveries described in (i) hereof, by the number of days in the base period;

(2) Multiply the result of the foregoing calculation by the number of days in the quota period;

(3) Multiply the aforesaid resulting amount by the following applicable percentage: (i) Milk: 100 percent; (ii) butterfat in milk: 100 percent; (iii) cream: 75 percent; (iv) butterfat in cream: 75 percent; (v) milk byproducts other than cottage, pot, or baker's cheese: 75 percent; and (vi) cottage, pot, or baker's cheese: 75 percent of skim milk equivalent. (For the purpose of this order, one pound of cottage, pot, or baker's cheese shall be considered as the equivalent of 7 pounds of skim milk.)

(f) *Quota limitations.* No handler shall, during any quota period, make deliveries in the sales area in excess of his respective quotas, except as set out in (i) hereof: *Provided,* That a handler may, after application to and approval by the market agent, secure an increase in milk quotas through an equivalent reduction as determined by the market agent, in cream and milk byproducts quotas, and an increase in milk byproducts quota through an equivalent reduction as determined by the market agent, in cream quotas.

(g) *Quotas for handlers who are also producers.* Quotas for handlers who are also producers and who purchase no milk shall be 100 percent of the total production of such handlers in the base period.

(h) *Handler exemptions.* Quotas shall not apply to any handler who delivers in a quota period a daily average of less than 300 units of milk, cream, and milk byproducts. For the purpose of this order, a unit shall be the equivalent in volume of the following: (1) Milk, one quart of milk; (2) cream, one-half pint of cream; and (3) milk byproduct, one quart of skim milk, buttermilk, flavored milk drink, or other beverage containing more than 85 percent of skim milk, or one-half pound of cottage, pot or baker's cheese.

(i) *Quota exclusions and exemptions.* Deliveries of milk, milk byproducts, or cream (1) to other handlers, except for such deliveries to sub-handlers, (2) to plants engaged in the handling or processing of milk, milk byproducts, or cream from which no milk, milk byproducts or cream is delivered in the sales area, and (3) to the agencies or groups specfied in (d) of FDO 79, shall be excluded from the computation of deliveries in the base period and exempt from charges to quotas.

(j) *Transfers and apportionment of quotas.* The market agent is empowered to deduct an amount of base period deliveries to purchasers from the total of deliveries made by a handler or other person in the base period upon the application and a showing of unreasonable hardship by the handler making deliveries to such purchasers on the effective date of this order, and to add the amount of such deliveries to the total base period deliveries of the applicant handler. Denials of transfer or transfers granted by the market agent shall be reviewed by the Director upon application.

(k) *Petition for relief from hardships.* (1) Any person affected by FDO 79 or the provisions hereof who considers that compliance therewith would work an exceptional and unreasonable hardship on him, may file with the market agent a petition addressed to the Director. The petition shall contain the correct name, address and principal place of business of the petitioner, a full statement of the facts upon which the petition is based, and the hardship involved and the nature of the relief desired.

(2) Upon receiving such petition, the market agent shall immediately investigate the representations and facts stated therein.

(3) After investigation, the petition shall be certified to the Director, but prior to certification the market agent may (i) deny the petition, or (ii) grant temporary relief for a total period not to exceed 60 days.

(4) Denials or grants of relief by the market agent shall be reviewed by the Director and may be affirmed, modified, or reversed by the Director.

(l) *Reports.* Each handler shall transmit to the market agent on forms prescribed by the market agent the following reports:

(1) Within 20 days following the effective date of this order, reports which show the information required by the market agent to establish such handlers' quotas;

(2) Within 20 days following the close of each quota period, the information required by the market agent to establish volumes of deliveries of milk, cream, and milk byproducts during the preceding quota periods; and

(3) Handlers exempt from quotas pursuant to (h) hereof shall, upon the request of the market agent, submit the information required by the marke

agent to establish volumes of deliveries of milk, cream, and milk byproducts.

(m) *Records.* Handlers shall keep and shall make available to the market agent such records of receipts, sales, deliveries, and production as the market agent shall require for the purpose of obtaining information which the Director may require for the establishment of quotas as prescribed in (b) of FDO 79.

(n) *Distribution schedules.* The distribution schedule, if any, to be followed by the handlers in making deliveries shall be made effective in the terms of approval by the Director of such schedules.

(o) *Expense of administration.* Each handler shall pay to the market agent, within 20 days after the close of each calendar month an assessment of $0.01 per hundredweight of each of milk, cream, skim milk, buttermilk, flavored milk drinks, beverages containing more than 85 percent of skim milk, and skim milk equivalent of cottage, pot, or baker's cheese delivered during the preceding quota period and subject to quota regulations under the provisions hereof.

(p) *Violations.* The market agent shall report all violations to the Director together with the information required for the prosecution of such violations, except in a case where a handler has made deliveries in a quota period in excess of a quota in an amount not to exceed 5 percent of such quota, and in the succeeding quota period makes deliveries below that quota by at least the same percent.

(q) *Bureau of the Budget approval.* The record keeping and reporting requirements of this order have been approved by the Bureau of the Budget in accordance with the Federal Reports Act of 1942. Subsequent record keeping or reporting requirements will be subject to the approval of the Bureau of the Budget pursuant to the Federal Reports Act of 1942.

(r) This order shall take effect at 12:01 a. m., e. w. t. October 17, 1943.

Issued this 11th day of October 1943.

C. W. KITCHEN,
Acting Director.

Press Release, Immediate:
Monday, October 11, 1943

Federal Control over fluid milk sales will be extended to the Far West for the first time beginning October 17, 1943 when maximum deliveries quotas will be assigned to milk dealers in three Washington metropolitan areas, the War Food Administration said today. The milk conservation and control program also will go into effect in three New England areas on the same date.

The new milk sales areas, and the market agents who will administer the program for the Food Distribution Administration in each area, are:

Springfield-Holyoke, Mass.: Eastern New England Metropolitan (including cities in Bristol, Middlesex, Plymouth, Worcester, Essex, Norfolk and Suffolk counties in Massachusetts, and 22 cities in Rhode Island)—Mr. Samuel W. Tator, 80 Federal Street, Boston, Mass.

Fall River-New Bedford-Taunton, Mass.—Mr. John J. Hogan, 103 Pleasant Street, Fall River, Mass.

Seattle, Washington, Metropolitan; Spokane, Washington, Metropolitan; Tacoma, Washington, Metropolitan—Mr. J. H. Mapes, 635 Elliot Avenue, West, Seattle, Wash.

Dealers' fluid milk sales in these areas will be limited to the quantity sold in June. Cream sales and sales of milk byproducts (such as cottage cheese, chocolate milk and buttermilk) will be limited to 75 percent of the quantities sold in June. Upon approval of the market agent, however, a dealer may increase his fluid milk quota if he reduces his cream and milk byproducts sales in an amount approved by the market agent. He may increase sales of milk byproducts over the basic quota by reducing his cream sales. Milk dealers include all persons or firms engaged in the sale or transfer of milk, but not retail stores, hotels, restaurants, etc.

Producer-distributors who purchase no milk (except those whose volume of sales is small enough to make them quota-exempt) will be allowed to sell an amount of fluid milk, cream and fluid milk byproducts equal to 100 percent of their total milk production in June. Quota-exempt producer-distributors are defined separately for each area, but in general they are those whose deliveries are relatively small.

Milk handlers in the 3 New England sales areas will compute the quantity of milk which they may sell each month in terms of pounds of milk, their cream sales in terms of pounds of cream and butterfat, and their milk byproducts sales in terms of pounds of milk byproducts or skim milk equivalent. In the 3 Washington state areas, milk handlers will determine their fluid milk quotas in terms of pounds of milk and butterfat.

Deliveries to the Armed Forces, to plants processing dairy products, and to other handlers (except special classes of handlers such as peddlers) are quota-exempt.

To facilitate administration, the market agent for each milk sales area may act upon petitions for relief from hardship which may be submitted to him, and after investigation, he may grant temporary relief for a total period not to exceed 60 days.

Milk sales in 38 eastern and midwestern areas previously were brought under federal regulation. Basic sales quotas in these initial milk sales areas are the same as for those named today.

The Eastern New England Metropolitan milk sales area includes the following cities:

In Bristol County, Massachuetts, the towns and cities of:

Attleboro	N. Attleboro
Easton	Seekonk
Mansfield	

In Middlesex County, Massachusetts, the towns and cities of:

Arlington	Concord
Ashland	Dracut
Bedford	Everett
Belmont	Framingham
Billerica	Holliston
Burlington	Hopkinton
Cambridge	Hudson
Chelmsford	Lexington
Lincoln	Stoneham
Lowell	Sudbury
Malden	Tewksbury
Marlboro	Tyngsboro
Maynard	Wakefield
Medford	Waltham
Melrose	Watertown
Natick	Wayland
Newton	Weston
N. Reading	Wilmington
Reading	Winchester
Sherborn	Woburn
Somerville	

In Plymouth County, Massachusetts, the towns and cities of:

Abington	Norwell
Bridgewater	Rockland
Brockton	Scituate
E. Bridgewater	W. Bridgewater
Hanover	Whitman
Hanson	

In Worcester County, Massachusetts, the towns and cities of:

Auburn	Millville
Berlin	Northboro
Blackstone	Northbridge
Boylston	Paxton
Clinton	Shrewsbury
Grafton	Southboro
Holden	Spencer
Hopedale	Upton
Leicester	Uxbridge
Mendon	Westboro
Milford	W. Bolyston
Millbury	Worcester

All of the towns and cities in the counties of Essex, Norfolk, and Suffolk, Massachusetts.

In Rhode Island the towns and cities of:

Barrington	Newport
Briston	No. Providence
Central Falls	No. Smithfield
Cranston	Pawtucket
Cumberland	Portsmouth
E. Greenwich	Providence
E. Providence	Smithfield
Jamestown	Warren
Johnston	Warwick
Lincoln	W. Warwick
Middletown	Woonsocket

The Fall River-New Bedford-Taunton area includes the following cities and towns:

In Massachusetts:

Acushnet	Norton
Berkley	Raynham
Dartmouth	Rehoboth
Dighton	Somerset
Fairhaven	Swansea
Fall River	Taunton
Freetown	Westport
New Bedford	

In Rhode Island: Little Compton. Tiverton.

The Springfield-Holyoke area includes:

Amherst	Hatfield
Agawam	Holyoke
Chicopee	Longmeadow
Easthampton	Ludlow
East Longmeadow	Northampton
Granby	Palmer
Hadley	South Hadley
Southampton	West Springfield
Springfield	Wilbraham
Ware	also Enfield, Conn.
Westfield	

Consumers in these areas generally will be able to purchase as much milk under the milk conservation program as they have been buying—an amount considerably greater than that bought in pre-war years, and about 10 percent above last year's purchasers. Sales quotas on cream and on fluid milk by-products have been set below June deliveries to boost fluid milk supplies where milk production is low, and to conserve milk for manufacturing purposes.

Fluid milk sales are being stabilized in these and other metropolitan areas, FDA officials explained, to help assure sufficient milk for manufacturing the cheese, butter, evaporated milk, and milk powder required by the Armed Services and civilians for good nutrition and properly balanced diets.

Largely due to expanded consumer demand, sales of fluid milk have been increasing steadily and are now about 20 percent higher than in pre-war years (1936–40) and 10 to 12 percent above those in 1942. With total milk production levelled off, and even declining somewhat, this expanding volume of milk sold for fluid uses has inevitably reduced the supply of "manufacturing milk," and consequently, the production of cheese, butter, and other dairy foods.

The FDA's dealer-quota plan is an attempt to stabilize fluid milk consumption without resorting to individual consumer rationing. Point rationing of milk, a bulky and highly perishable commodity, would be very difficult to administer. If consumers and the trade cooperate with the present program to assure that sales are held within quotas and quantities available are distributed fairly, FDA officials believe consumer rationing will not be necessary.

FDO 79-42
OCTOBER 11, 1943

WAR FOOD ADMINISTRATION

[FDO 79-42]

PART 1401—DAIRY PRODUCTS

CONSERVATION AND DISTRIBUTION OF FLUID MILK AND CREAM IN FALL RIVER-NEW BEDFORD-TAUNTON, MASS., SALES AREA

Pursuant to the authority vested in me by Food Distribution Order No. 79 (8 F.R. 12426), issued on September 7, 1943, as amended, and to effectuate the purposes of such order, it is hereby ordered as follows:

§ 1401.73 *Quota restrictions*—(a) *Definitions.* When used in this order, unless otherwise distinctly expressed or manifestly incompatible with the intent hereof:

(1) Each term defined in Food Distribution Order No. 79, as amended, shall, when used herein, have the same meaning as is set forth for such term in Food Distribution Order No. 79, as amended.

(2) The term FDO 79 means Food Distribution Order No. 79, issued on September 7, 1943, as amended.

(3) The term "sub-handler" means any handler, such as a peddler, vendor, sub-dealer, or secondary dealer, who purchases in a previously packaged and processed form milk, milk byproducts, or cream for delivery.

(b) *Milk sales area.* The following area is hereby designated as a "milk sales area" to be known as the Fall River-New Bedford-Taunton, Massachusetts, sales area, and is referred to hereinafter as the "sales area":

The territory included within the boundaries of the following cities and towns in Massachusetts:

Acushnet, Berkley, Dartmouth, Dighton, Fairhaven, Fall River, Freetown, New Bedford, Norton, Raynham, Rehoboth, Somerset, Swansea, Taunton, and Westport

And the following cities and towns in Rhode Island:

Little Compton, and Tiverton.

(c) *Base period.* The calendar month of June 1943 is hereby designated as the base period for the sales area.

(d) *Quota period.* The remainder of the calendar month in which the provisions hereof become effective and each subsequent calendar month, respectively is hereby designated as a quota period for the sales area.

(e) *Handler quotas.* Quotas for each handler in the sales area in each quota period shall be calculated in terms of pounds of each of the items for which percentages are specfied in (3) below and shall be determined as follows:

(1) Divide the total deliveries of each such item made in the sales area by such handler during the base period, after excluding the quota-exempt deliveries described in (i) hereof, by the number of days in the base period;

(2) Multiply the result of the foregoing calculation by the number of days in the quota period:

(3) Multiply the aforesaid resulting amount by the following applicable percentage; (i) Milk: 100 percent; (ii) Butterfat in milk: ______ percent; (iii) Cream: 75 percent; (iv) Butterfat in cream: 75 percent; (v) Milk byproducts other than cottage, pot or baker's cheese: 75 percent; and (vi) Cottage, pot, or baker's cheese: 75 percent of skim milk equivalent. (For the purpose of this order, one pound of cottage, pot, or baker's cheese shall be considered as the equivalent of 7 pounds of skim milk.)

(f) *Quota limitations.* No handler shall, during any quota period, make deliveries in the sales area in excess of his respective quotas, except as set out in (i) hereof: *Provided,* That a handler may, after application to and approval by the market agent, secure an increase in milk quotas through an equivalent reduction as determined by the market agent, in cream and milk byproducts quotas and an increase in milk byproducts quota through an equivalent reduction as determined by the market agent, in cream quotas.

(g) *Quotas for handlers who are also producers.* Quotas for handlers who are also producers and who purchase no milk shall be 100 percent of the total production of such handlers in the base period.

(h) *Handler exemptions.* Quotas shall not apply to any handler who delivers in a quota period a daily average of less than 100 units of milk, cream and milk byproducts. For the purpose of this order, a unit shall be the equivalent in volume of the following: (1) milk, one quart of milk; (2) cream, one-half pint of cream; and (3) milk byproduct, one quart of skim milk, buttermilk, flavored milk drink or other beverage containing more than 85 percent of skim milk, or one-half pound of cottage, pot, or bakers' cheese.

(i) *Quota exclusions and exemptions.* Deliveries of milk, milk byproducts, or cream (1) to other handlers, except for such deliveries to sub-handlers, (2) to plants engaged in the handling or processing of milk, milk byproducts, or cream from which no milk, milk byproducts, or cream is delivered in the sales area, and (3) to the agencies or groups specified in (d) of FDO 79, shall be excluded from the computation of deliveries in the base period and exempt from charges to quotas.

(j) *Transfers and apportionment of quotas.* The market agent is empowered to deduct an amount of base period deliveries to purchasers from the total of deliveries made by a handler or other person in the base period upon the application and a showing of unreasonable hardship by the handler making deliveries to such purchasers on the effective date of this order, and to add the amount of such deliveries to the total base period deliveries of the applicant handler. Denials of transfers or transfers granted by the market agent shall be reviewed by the Director upon application.

(k) *Petition for relief from hardships.* (1) Any person affected by FDO 79 or the provisions hereof who considers that compliance therewith would work an exceptional and unreasonable hardship on him, may file with the market agent a petition addressed to the Director. The petition shall contain the correct name, address and principal place of business of the petitioner, a full statement of the facts upon which the petition is based, and the hardship involved and the nature of the relief desired.

(2) Upon receiving such petition, the market agent shall immediately investigate the representations and facts stated therein.

(3) After investigation, the petition shall be certified to the Director but prior to certification the market agent may (i) deny the petition, or (ii) grant temporary relief for a total period not to exceed 60 days.

(4) Denials or grants of relief by the market agent shall be reviewed by the Director and may be affirmed, modified, or reversed by the Director.

(l) *Reports.* Each handler shall transmit to the market agent on forms prescribed by the market agent the following reports:

(1) Within 20 days following the effective date of this order, reports which show the information required by the market agent to establish such handlers' quotas;

(2) Within 20 days following the close of each quota period, the information required by the market agent to establish volumes of deliveries of milk, cream, and milk byproducts during the preceding quota period; and

(3) Handlers exempt from quotas pursuant to (h) hereof shall, upon the request of the market agent, submit the information required by the market agent to establish volumes of deliveries of milk, cream, and milk byproducts.

(m) *Records.* Handlers shall keep and shall make available to the market agent such records of receipts, sales, deliveries, and production as the market agent shall require for the purpose of obtaining information which the Director may require for the establishment of quotas as prescribed in (b) of FDO 79.

(n) *Distribution schedules.* The distribution schedules, if any, to be followed by the handlers in making deliveries shall be made effective in the terms of approval by the Director of such schedules.

(o) *Expense of administration.* Each handler shall pay to the market agent, within 20 days after the close of each calendar month an assessment of $0.015 per hundredweight of each of milk, cream, skim milk, buttermilk, flavored milk drinks, beverages containing more than 85 percent of skim milk, and skim milk equivalent of cottage, pot, or baker's cheese delivered during the preceding quota period and subject to quota regulations under the provisions hereof.

(p) *Violations.* The market agent shall report all violations to the Director together with the information required for the prosecution of such violations, except in a case where a handler has made deliveries in a quota period in excess of a quota in an amount not to exceed 5 percent of such quota, and in the succeeding quota period makes deliveries below that quota by at least the same percent.

(q) *Bureau o*
The record kee
quirements of th
proved by the
in accordance w
Act of 1942. S
ing or reportin
subject to the
of the Budget p
Reports Act of 1

(r) This order
a. m., e. w. t., O

Issued this 11t

Press Release, immediate:
Monday, October 11, 1943.

Federal control over fluid milk sales will be extended to the Far West for the first time beginning October 17, 1943 when maximum deliveries quotas will be assigned to milk dealers in three Washington metropolitan areas, the War Food Administration said today. The milk conservation and control program also will go into effect in three New England areas on the same date.

The new milk sales areas, and the market agents who will administer the program for the Food Distribution Administration in each area, are:

Springfield-Holyoke, Mass.: Eastern New England Metropolitan (including cities in Bristol, Middlesex, Plymouth, Worcester, Essex, Norfolk, and Suffolk counties in Massachusetts, and 22 cities in Rhode Island)—Mr. Samuel W. Tator, 80 Federal St., Boston, Mass.

Fall River - New Bedford - Taunton, Mass.—Mr. John J. Hogan, 103 Pleasant St., Fall River, Mass.

Seattle, Wash., Metropolitan; Spokane, Wash., Metropolitan; Tacoma, Wash., Metropolitan—Mr. J. H. Mapes, 635 Elliot Ave., West, Seattle, Wash.

Dealers' fluid milk sales in these areas will be limited to the quantity sold in June. Cream sales and sales of milk byproducts (such as cottage cheese, chocolate milk and buttermilk) will be limited to 75 percent of the quantities sold in June. Upon approval of the market agent, however, a dealer may increase his fluid milk quota if he reduces his cream and milk byproducts sales in an amount approved by the market agent. He may increase sales of milk byproducts over the basic quota by reducing his cream sales. Milk dealers include all persons or firms engaged in the sale or transfer of milk, but not retail stores, hotels, restaurants, etc.

Producer-distributors who purchase no milk (except those whose volume of sales is small enough to make them quota-exempt) will be allowed to sell an amount of fluid milk, cream and fluid milk byproducts equal to 100 percent of their total milk production in June. Quota-exempt producer-distributors are defined separately for each area, but in general they are those whose deliveries are relatively small.

Milk handlers in the 3 New England sales areas will compute the quantity of milk which they may sell each month in terms of pounds of milk, their cream sales in terms of pounds of cream and butterfat, and their milk byproducts sales in terms of pounds of milk byproducts or skim milk equivalent. In the 3 Washington state areas, milk handlers will determine their fluid milk quotas in terms of pounds of milk and butterfat.

Deliveries to the Armed Forces, to plants processing dairy products, and to other handlers (except special classes of handlers such as peddlers) are quota-exempt.

To facilitate administration, the market agent for each milk sales area may act upon petitions for relief from hardship which may be submitted to him, and after investigation, he may grant temporary relief for a total period not to exceed 60 days.

Milk sales in 38 eastern and midwestern areas previously were brought under federal regulation. Basic sales quotas in these initial milk sales areas are the same as for those named today.

The Eastern New England Metropolitan milk sales area includes the following cities:

In Bristol County, Massachusetts, the towns and cities of:

Attleboro	N. Attleboro
Easton	Seekonk
Mansfield	

In Middlesex County, Massachusetts, the towns and cities of:

Arlington	Concord
Ashland	Dracut
Bedford	Everett
Belmont	Framingham
Billerica	Holliston
Burlington	Hopkinton
Cambridge	Hudson
Chelmsford	Lexington

Lincoln
Lowell
Malden
Marlboro
Maynard
Medford
Melrose
Natick
Newton
N. Reading
Reading
Sherborn
Somerville

In Plymouth
the towns and c

Abington
Bridgewater
Brockton
E. Bridgewater
Hanover
Hanson

In Worcester
the towns and c

Auburn
Berlin
Blackstone
Boylston
Clinton
Grafton
Holden
Hopedale
Leicester
Mendon
Milford
Millbury

All of the town
ties of Essex,
Massachusetts.

In Rhode Is
cities of:

Barrington
Bristol
Central Falls
Cranston
Cumberland
E. Greenwich
E. Providence
Jamestown
Johnston
Lincoln
Middletown

The Fall River-New Bedford-Taunton area includes the following cities and towns:

In Massachusetts:

Acushnet	Norton
Berkley	Raynham
Dartmouth	Rehoboth
Dighton	Somerset
Fairhaven	Swansea
Fall River	Taunton
Freetown	Westport
New Bedford	

In Rhode Island:

Little Compton	Tiverton

The Springfield-Holyoke area includes:

Amherst	Holyoke
Agawam	Longmeadow
Chicopee	Ludlow
Easthampton	Northhampton
East Longmeadow	Palmer
Granby	South Hadley
Hadley	Southhampton
Hatfield	Springfield
Ware	Wilbraham
Westfield	also Enfield, Conn.
West Springfield	

Note to editors: Background material follows:

Consumers in these areas generally will be able to purchase as much milk under the milk conservation program as they have been buying—an amount considerably greater than that bought in pre-war years, and about 10 percent above last year's purchases. Sales quotas on cream and on fluid milk byproducts have been set below June deliveries to boost fluid milk supplies where milk production is low, and to conserve milk for manufacturing purposes.

Fluid milk sales are being stabilized in these and other metropolitan areas, FDA officials explained, to help assure sufficient milk for manufacturing the cheese, butter, exaporated milk, and milk powder required by the Armed Services and civilians for good nutrition and properly balanced diets.

Largely due to expanded consumer demand, sales of fluid milk have been increasing steadily and are now about 20 percent higher than in pre-war years (1936–40) and 10 to 12 percent above those in 1942. With total milk production levelled off, and even declining somewhat, this expanding volume of milk sold for fluid uses has inevitably reduced the supply of "manufacturing milk," and consequently, the production of cheese, butter, and other dairy foods.

The FDA's dealer-quota plan is an attempt to stabilize fluid milk consumption without resorting to individual consumer rationing. Point rationing of milk, a bulky and highly perishable commodity, would be very difficult to administer. If consumers and the trade cooperate with the present program to assure that sales are held within quotas and quantities available are distributed fairly, FDA officials believe consumer rationing will not be necessary.

331-
·121

FDO 79-42

AMDT. 1
MAR. 1, 1944

WAR FOOD ADMINISTRATION

[FDO 79-42, Amdt. 1]

PART 1401—DAIRY PRODUCTS

FLUID MILK AND CREAM IN FALL RIVER-NEW BEDFORD-TAUNTON, MASS., SALES AREA

Pursuant to Food Distribution Order No. 79 (8 F.R. 12426), dated September 7, 1943, as amended, and to effectuate the purposes thereof, Food Distribution Order No. 79-42 (8 F.R. 13966), relative to the conservation and distribution of fluid milk in the Fall River-New Bedford-Taunton, Massachusetts, milk sales area, issued by the Director of Food Distribution on October 11, 1943, is hereby amended as follows:

1. By deleting therefrom the provisions in § 1401.73 (g) and inserting, in lieu thereof, the following:

(g) *Quotas for handlers who are also producers.* Quotas for handlers who are also producers and who purchase no milk shall be computed in accordance with (e) hereof, except that the applicable percentages shall be 100 percent in lieu of the percentages specified in (e) (3).

2. By deleting therefrom the numeral "100" in § 1401.73 (h) wherever it appears, and inserting, in lieu thereof, the numeral "300."

The provisions of this amendment shall become effective at 12:01 a. m., e. w. t., March 1, 1944. With respect to violations of said Food Distribution Order No. 79-42, rights accrued, or liabilities incurred prior to the effective time of this amendment, said Food Distribution Order No. 79-42 shall be deemed to be in full force and effect for the purpose of sustaining any proper suit, action, or other proceeding with respect to any such violation, right, or liability.

(E.O. 9280, 7 F.R. 10179; E.O. 9322, 8 F.R. 3807; E.O. 9334, 8 F.R. 5423; E.O. 9392, 8 F.R. 14783; FDO 79, 8 F.R. 12426, 13283)

Issued this 1st day of March 1944.

C. W. KITCHEN,
Acting Director of Food Distribution.

"DAIRY PRODUCTS"

In section 1401.74, paragraph (b), Northbridge was omitted from the list of cities and towns in Worcester County, Mass.

77337
Cop. 2

FDO-79-43

OCTOBER 11, 1943

WAR FOOD ADMINISTRATION

[FDO 79-43]

PART 1401—DAIRY PRODUCTS

CONSERVATION AND DISTRIBUTION OF FLUID MILK AND CREAM IN EASTERN NEW ENGLAND METROPOLITAN SALES AREA

Pursuant to the authority vested in me by Food Distribution Order No. 79 (8 F.R. 12426), issued on September 7, 1943, as amended, and to effectuate the purposes of such order, it is hereby ordered as follows:

§ 1401.74 *Quota restrictions*—(a) *Definitions*. When used in this order, unless otherwise distinctly expressed or manifestly incompatible with the intent hereof:

(1) Each term defined in Food Distribution Order No. 79, as amended, shall, when used herein, have the same meaning as is set forth for such term in Food Distribution Order No. 79, as amended.

(2) The term FDO 79 means Food Distribution Order No. 79, issued on September 7, 1943, as amended.

(3) The term "sub-handler" means any handler, such as a peddler, vendor, sub-dealer, or secondary dealer, who purchases in a previously packaged and processed form milk, milk byproducts, or cream for delivery.

(b) *Milk sales area*. The following area is hereby designated as a "milk sales area" to be known as the Eastern New England, Metropolitan sales area, and is referred to hereinafter as the "sales area":

In Bristol County, Massachusetts, the towns and cities of:

Attleboro, Easton, Mansfield, N. Attleboro, Seekonk.

In Middlesex County, Massachusetts, the towns and cities of:

Arlington, Ashland, Bedford, Belmont, Billerica, Burlington, Cambridge, Chelmsford, Concord, Dracut, Everett, Framingham, Holliston, Hopkinton, Hudson, Lexington, Lincoln, Lowell, Malden, Marlboro, Maynard, Medford, Melrose, Natick, Newton, N. Reading, Reading, Sherborn, Somerville, Stoneham, Sudbury, Tewksbury, Tyngsboro, Wakefield, Waltham, Watertown, Wayland, Weston, Wilmington, Winchester, and Woburn.

In Plymouth County, Massachusetts, the towns and cities of:

Abington, Bridgewater, Brockton, E. Bridgewater, Hanover, Hanson, Norwell, Rockland, Scituate, W. Bridgewater, and Whitman.

In Worcester County, Massachusetts, the towns and cities of:

Auburn, Berlin, Blackstone, Boylston, Clinton, Grafton, Holden, Hopedale, Leicester, Mendon, Milford, Millbury, Millville, Northboro, Paxton, Shrewsbury, Southboro, Spencer, Upton, Uxbridge, Westboro, W. Boylston, and Worcester.

In Rhode Island the towns and cities of:

Barrington, Bristol, Central Falls, Cranston, Cumberland, E. Greenwich, E. Providence, Jamestown, Johnston, Lincoln, Middletown, Newport, No. Providence, No. Smithfield, Pawtucket, Portsmouth, Providence, Smithfield, Warren, Warwick, W. Warwick, and Woonsocket.

All of the towns and cities in the counties of Essex, Norfolk, and Suffolk, Massachusetts.

(c) *Base period*. The calendar month of June 1943 is hereby designated as the base period for the sales area.

(d) *Quota period*. The remainder of the calendar month in which the provisions hereof become effective and each subsequent calendar month, respectively, is hereby designated as a quota period for the sales area.

(e) *Handler quotas*. Quotas for each handler in the sales area in each quota period shall be calculated in terms of pounds of each of the items for which percentages are specified in (3) below and shall be determined as follows:

(1) Divide the total deliveries of each such item made in the sales area by such handler during the base period, after excluding the quota-exempt deliveries described in (i) hereof, by the number of days in the base period;

(2) Multiply the result of the foregoing calculation by the number of days in the quota period;

(3) Multiply the aforesaid resulting amount by the following applicable percentage: (i) Milk: 100 percent; (ii) Butterfat in milk: ______ percent; (iii) Cream: 75 percent; (iv) Butterfat in cream: 75 percent; (v) Milk byproducts other than cottage, pot or baker's cheese: 75 percent; and (vi) Cottage, pot, or baker's cheese: 75 percent of skim milk equivalent. (For the purpose of this order, one pound of cottage, pot, or baker's cheese shall be considered as the equivalent of 7 pounds of skim milk.)

(f) *Quota limitations*. No handler shall, during any quota period, make deliveries in the sales area in excess of his respective quotas, except as set out in (i) hereof: *Provided*, That a handler may, after application to and approval by the market agent, secure an increase in milk quotas through an equivalent reduction as determined by the market agent, in cream and milk byproducts quotas, and an increase in milk byproducts quota through an equivalent reduction as determined by the market agent, in cream quotas.

(g) *Quotas for handlers who are also producers*. Quotas for handlers who are also producers and who purchase no milk shall be 100 percent of the total production of such handlers in the base period.

(h) *Handler exemptions*. Quotas shall not apply to any handler who delivers in a quota period a daily average of less than 300 units of milk, cream, and milk byproducts. For the purpose of this order, a unit shall be the equivalent in volume of the following: (1) milk, one quart of milk; (2) cream, one-half pint of cream; and (3) milk byproduct, one quart of skim milk, buttermilk, flavored milk drink, or other beverage containing more than 85 percent of skim milk, or one-half pound of cottage, pot, or baker's cheese.

(i) *Quota exclusions and exemptions*. Deliveries of milk, milk byproducts, or cream (1) to other handlers, except for such deliveries to sub-handlers, (2) to plants engaged in the handling or processing of milk, milk byproducts, or cream from which no milk, milk byproducts, or cream is delivered in the sales area, and (3) to the agencies or groups specified in (d) of FDO 79, shall be excluded from the computation of deliveries in the base period and exempt from charges to quotas.

(j) *Transfers and apportionment of quotas*. The market agent is empowered to deduct an amount of base period deliveries to purchasers from the total of deliveries made by a handler or other person in the base period upon the application and a showing of unreasonable hardship by the handler making deliveries to such purchasers on the effective date of this order, and to add the amount of such deliveries to the total base period deliveries of the applicant handler. Denials of transfers or transfers granted by the market agent shall be reviewed by the Director upon application.

(k) *Petition for relief from hardships*. (1) Any person affected by FDO 79 or the provisions hereof who considers that compliance therewith would work an exceptional and unreasonable hardship on him, may file with the market agent a petition addressed to the Director. The petition shall contain the correct name, address and principal place of business of the petitioner, a full statement of the facts upon which the petition is based, and the hardship involved and the nature of the relief desired.

(2) Upon receiving such petition, the market agent shall immediately investigate the representations and facts stated therein.

(3) After investigation, the petition shall be certified to the Director, but prior to certification the market agent may (i) deny the petition, or (ii) grant temporary relief for a total period not to exceed 60 days.

(4) Denials or grants of relief by the market agent shall be reviewed by the Director and may be affirmed, modified, or reversed by the Director.

(l) *Reports.* Each handler shall transmit to the market agent on forms prescribed by the market agent the following reports:

(1) Within 20 days following the effective date of this order, reports which show the information required by the market agent to establish such handlers' quotas;

(2) Within 20 days following the close of each quota period, the information required by the market agent to establish volumes of deliveries of milk, cream, and milk byproducts during the preceding quota period; and

(3) Handlers exempt from quotas pursuant to (h) hereof shall, upon the request of the market agent, submit the information required by the market agent to establish volumes of deliveries of milk, cream, and milk byproducts.

(m) *Records.* Handlers shall keep and shall make available to the market agent such records of receipts, sales, deliveries, and production as the market agent shall require for the purpose of obtaining information which the Director may require for the establishment of quotas as prescribed in (b) of FDO 79.

(n) *Distribution schedules.* The distribution schedules, if any, to be followed by the handlers in making deliveries shall be made effective in the terms of approval by the Director of such schedules.

(o) *Expense of administration.* Each handler shall pay to the market agent, within 20 days after the close of each calendar month an assessment of $0.01 per hundredweight of each of milk, cream, skim milk, buttermilk, flavored milk drinks, beverages containing more than 85 percent of skim milk, and skim milk equivalent of cottage, pot, or baker's cheese delivered during the preceding quota period and subject to quota regulations under the provisions hereof.

(p) *Violations.* The market agent shall report all violations to the Director together with the information required for the prosecution of such violations, except in a case where a handler has made deliveries in a quota period in excess of a quota in an amount not to exceed 5 percent of such quota, and in the succeeding quota period makes deliveries below that quota by at least the same percent.

(q) *Bureau of the Budget approval.* The record keeping and reporting requirements of this order have been approved by the Bureau of the Budget in accordance with the Federal Reports Act of 1942. Subsequent record keeping or reporting requirements will be subject to the approval of the Bureau of the Budget pursuant to the Federal Reports Act of 1942.

(r) This order shall take effect at 12:01 a. m., e. w. t., October 17, 1943.

Issued this 11th day of October 1943.

C. W. KITCHEN,
Acting Director of Food Distribution.

Press Release, Immediate:
Monday, October 11, 1943.

Federal control over fluid milk sales will be extended to the Far West for the first time beginning October 17, 1943 when maximum deliveries quotas will be assigned to milk dealers in three Washington metropolitan areas, the War Food Administration said today. The milk conservation and control program also will go into effect in three New England areas on the same date.

The new milk sales areas, and the market agents who will administer the program for the Food Distribution Administration in each area, are:

Springfield-Holyoke, Mass.: Eastern New England Metropolitan (including cities in Bristol, Middlesex, Plymouth, Worcester, Essex, Norfolk and Suffolk counties in Massachusetts, and 22 cities in Rhode Island)—Mr. Samuel W. Tator, 80 Federal St., Boston, Mass.

Fall River - New Bedford - Taunton, Mass.—Mr. John J. Hogan, 103 Pleasant St., Fall River, Mass.

Seattle, Wash., Metropolitan; Spokane, Wash., Metropolitan; Tacoma, Wash., Metropolitan—Mr. J. H. Mapes, 635 Elliot Ave., West, Seattle, Wash.

Dealers' fluid milk sales in these areas will be limited to the quantity sold in June. Cream sales and sales of milk byproducts (such as cottage cheese, chocolate milk and buttermilk) will be limited to 75 percent of the quantities sold in June. Upon approval of the market agent, however, a dealer may increase his fluid milk quota if he reduces his cream and milk byproducts sales in an amount approved by the market agent. He may increase sales of milk byproducts over the basic quota by reducing his cream sales. Milk dealers include all persons or firms engaged in the sale or transfer of milk, but not retail stores, hotels, restaurants, etc.

Producer-distributors who purchase no milk (except those whose volume of sales is small enough to make them quota-exempt) will be allowed to sell an amount of fluid milk, cream and fluid milk byproducts equal to 100 percent of their total milk production in June. Quota-exempt producer-distributors are defined separately for each area, but in general they are those whose deliveries are relatively small.

Milk handlers in the 3 New England sales areas will compute the quantity of milk which they may sell each month in terms of pounds of milk, their cream sales in terms of pounds of cream and butterfat, and their milk byproducts sales in terms of pounds of milk byproducts or skim milk equivalent. In the 3 Washington state areas, milk handlers will determine their fluid milk quotas in terms of pounds of milk and butterfat.

Deliveries to the Armed Forces, to plants processing dairy products, and to other handlers (except special classes of handlers such as peddlers) are quota-exempt.

To facilitate administration, the market agent for each milk sales area may act upon petitions for relief from hardship which may be submitted to him, and after investigation, he may grant temporary relief for a total period not to exceed 60 days.

Milk sales in 38 eastern and midwestern areas previously were brought under federal regulation. Basic sales quotas in these initial milk sales areas are the same as for those named today.

The Eastern New England Metropolitan milk sales area includes the following cities:

In Bristol County, Massachusetts, the towns and cities of:

Attleboro	N. Attleboro
Easton	Seekonk
Mansfield	

In Middlesex County, Massachusetts, the towns and cities of:

Arlington	Medford
Ashland	Melrose
Bedford	Natick
Belmont	Newton
Billerica	N. Reading
Burlington	Reading
Cambridge	Sherborn
Chelmsford	Somerville
Concord	Stoneham
Dracut	Sudbury
Everett	Tewksbury
Framingham	Tyngsboro
Holliston	Wakefield
Hopkinton	Waltham
Hudson	Watertown
Lexington	Wayland
Lincoln	Weston
Lowell	Wilmington
Malden	Winchester
Marlboro	Woburn
Maynard	

In Plymouth County, Massachusetts, the towns and cities of:

Abington	Norwell
Bridgewater	Rockland
Brockton	Scituate
E. Bridgewater	W. Bridgewater
Hanover	Whitman
Hanson	

In Worcester County, Massachusetts, the towns and cities of:

Auburn	Millville
Berlin	Northboro
Blackstone	Northbridge
Boylston	Paxton
Clinton	Shrewsbury
Grafton	Southboro
Holden	Spencer
Hopedale	Upton
Leicester	Uxbridge
Mendon	Westboro
Milford	W. Boylston
Millbury	Worcester

All of the towns and cities in the counties of Essex, Norfolk, and Suffolk, Massachusetts.

In Rhode Island the towns and cities of:

Barrington	Newport
Bristol	No. Providence
Central Falls	No. Smithfield
Cranston	Pawtucket
Cumberland	Portsmouth
E. Greenwich	Providence
E. Providence	Smithfield
Jamestown	Warren
Johnston	Warwick
Lincoln	W. Warwick
Middletown	Woonsocket

The Fall River-New Bedford-Taunton area includes the following cities and towns:

In Massachusetts:

Acushnet	Dartmouth
Berkley	Dighton
Fairhaven	Rehoboth
Fall River	Somerset
Freetown	Swansea
New Bedford	Taunton
Norton	Westport
Raynham	

In Rhode Island:

Little Compton	Tiverton

The Springfield-Holyoke area includes:

Amherst	Northampton
Agawam	Palmer
Chicopee	South Hadley
Easthampton	Southamption
East Longmeadow	Springfield
Granby	Ware
Hadley	Westfield
Hatfield	West Springfield
Holyoke	Wilbraham
Longmeadow	also Enfield, Conn.
Ludlow	

Note to editors: Background material follows:

Consumers in these areas generally will be able to purchase as much milk under the milk conservation program as they have been buying—an amount considerably greater than that bought in pre-war years, and about 10 percent above last year's purchases. Sales quotas on cream and on fluid milk by-products have been set below June deliveries to boost fluid milk supplies where milk production is low, and to conserve milk for manufacturing purposes.

Fluid milk sales are being stabilized in these and other metropolitan areas, FDA officials explained, to help assure sufficient milk for manufacturing the cheese, butter, evaporated milk, and milk powder required by the Armed Services and civilians for good nutrition and properly balanced diets.

Largely due to expanded consumer demand, sales of fluid milk have been increasing steadily and are now about 20 percent higher than in pre-war years (1936–40) and 10 to 12 percent above those in 1942. With total milk production levelled off, and even declining somewhat, this expanding volume of milk sold for fluid uses has inevitably reduced the supply of "manufacturing milk," and consequently, the production of cheese, butter, and other dairy foods.

The FDA's dealer-quota plan is an attempt to stabilize fluid milk consumption without resorting to individual consumer rationing. Point rationing of milk, a bulky and highly perishable commodity, would be very difficult to administer. If consumers and the trade cooperate with the present program to assure that sales are held within quotas and quantities available are distributed fairly, FDA officials believe consumer rationing will not be necessary.

WAR FOOD ADMINISTRATION

[FDO 79-43, Amdt. 1]

Part 1401—Dairy Products

EASTERN NEW ENGLAND, METROPOLITAN MILK SALES AREA

Pursuant to the authority vested in the Director by Food Distribution Order No. 79, dated September 7, 1943 (8 F.R. 12426), as amended, and to effectuate the purposes thereof, Director Food Distribution Order No. 79-43, § 1401.74, relative to the conservation of fluid milk in the Eastern New England, Metropolitan, milk sales area (8 F.R. 13967), issued by the Director of Food Distribution on October 11, 1943, is amended as follows: The milk sales area described in § 1401.74 (b) of the original order is modified in the following particulars:

In the list of towns and cities in Plymouth County, Massachusetts, insert after the word "Hanson", the words "Hingham", and "Hull".

Effective date. This amendment of FDO No. 79-43, shall become effective at 12:01 a. m. e. w. t., November 1, 1943.

(E.O. 9280, 8 F.R. 10179; E.O. 9322, 8 F.R. 3807; E.O. 9334, 8 F.R. 5423; FDO 79, 8 F.R. 12426, 13283)

Issued this 28th day of October 1943.

Roy F. Hendrickson,
Director of Food Distribution.

1
7337
Copy 1

FDO 79-43
AMDT. 2
NOV. 30, 1943

WAR FOOD ADMINISTRATION

[FDO 79-43, Amdt. 2]

PART 1401—DAIRY PRODUCTS

DIRECTOR'S ORDER FOR THE EASTERN NEW ENGLAND METROPOLITAN MILK SALES AREA

Pursuant to the authority vested in the Director by Food Distribution Order No. 79, dated September 7, 1943 (8 F.R. 12426), as amended, and to effectuate the purposes thereof, Food Distribution Order No. 79-43, § 1401.74, relative to the conservation of fluid milk in the Eastern New England Metropolitan milk sales area (8 F.R. 13967) issued by the Director of Food Distribution on October 11, 1943, is amended as follows:

The quotas for handlers who are also producers, described in § 1401.74 (g) of the original order, is modified in the following particulars: Strike out (g) and insert in lieu thereof the following:

(g) *Quotas for handlers who are also producers.*—Quotas for handlers who are also producers and who purchase no milk shall be computed in accordance with (e) hereof, except that the applicable percentages shall be 100 percent in lieu of the percentages specified in (e) (3).

(b) *Effective date.*—This amendment of FDO No. 79-43 shall become effective at 12:01 a. m., e. w. t., December 1, 1943.

(E.O. 9280, 7 F.R., 10179; E.O. 9322, 8 F.R. 5807; E.O. 9354, 8 F.R. 5423; E.O. 9392, 8 F.R. 1478; FDO 79, 8 F.R. 12426, 13283)

Issued this 30th day of November 1943.

C. W. KITCHEN,
Acting Director of Food Distribution.

3F

FDO 79-43

AMDT. 3
FEB. 28, 1944

WAR FOOD ADMINISTRATION

[FDO 79-43 Amdt. 3]

PART 1401—DAIRY PRODUCTS

FLUID MILK AND CREAM IN THE EASTERN NEW ENGLAND METROPOLITAN SALES AREA

Pursuant to Food Distribution Order No. 79 (8 F.R. 12426), dated September 7, 1943, as amended, and to effectuate the purposes thereof, Food Distribution Order No. 79-43 (8 F.R. 13967), relative to the conservation and distribution of fluid milk in the Eastern New England metropolitan milk sales area, issued by the Director of Food Distribution on October 11, 1943, as amended, is hereby further amended by deleting therefrom the provisions in § 1401.74 (a) (3) and inserting, in lieu thereof, the following:

(3) The term "sub-handler" means any handler, who (i) receives in a previously packaged and processed form milk, milk byproducts, or cream for delivery, and (ii) does not operate facilities for the processing and bottling of fluid milk.

The provisions of this amendment shall become effective at 12:01 a. m., e. w. t., March 1, 1944. With respect to violations of said Food Distribution Order No. 79-43, as amended, rights accrued, or liabilities incurred prior to the effective time of this amendment, said Food Distribution Order No. 79-43, as amended, shall be deemed to be in full force and effect for the purpose of sustaining any proper suit, action, or other proceeding with respect to any such violation, right, or liability.

(E.O. 9280, 7 F.R. 10179; E.O. 9322, 8 F.R. 3807; E.O. 9334, 8 F.R. 5423; E.O. 9392, 8 F.R. 14783; FDO 79, 8 F.R. 12426, 13283)

Issued this 28th day of February 1944.

C. W. KITCHEN,
Acting Director of Food Distribution.

33F

erve

FDO 79-43

AMDT. 4
MAR. 1, 1944

WAR FOOD ADMINISTRATION

[FDO 79-43, Amdt. 4]

PART 1401—DAIRY PRODUCTS

FLUID MILK AND CREAM IN EASTERN NEW ENGLAND METROPOLITAN SALES AREA

Pursuant to Food Distribution Order No. 79 (8 F.R. 12426), dated September 7, 1943, as amended, and to effectuate the purposes thereof, Food Distribution Order No. 79-43 (8 F.R. 13967), relative to the conservation and distribution of fluid milk in the Eastern New England metropolitan milk sales area, issued by the Director of Food Distribution on October 11, 1943, as amended, is hereby further amended by deleting from the description of the sales area in § 1401.74 (b) the following:

The towns of Attleboro, North Attleboro and Seekonk in Bristol County, Massachusetts; the towns of Blackstone and Millville in Worcester County, Massachusetts; all the towns and cities listed as being in the State of Rhode Island; and Norfolk County, Massachusetts, and inserting in lieu of Norfolk County, Massachusetts, the following towns and cities located within said Norfolk County:

Avon, Braintree, Brookline, Canton, Cohasset, Dedham, Dover, Foxborough, Holbrook, Medfield, Medway, Millis, Milton, Needham, Norfolk, Norwood, Quincy, Randolph, Sharon, Stoughton, Walpole, Wellesley, Westwood, and Weymouth.

The complete description of the sales area is as follows:

In Bristol County, Massachusetts, the towns and cities of Easton and Mansfield.

In Middlesex County, Massachusetts, the towns and cities of:

Arlington, Ashland, Bedford, Belmont, Billerica, Burlington, Cambridge, Chelmsford, Concord, Dracut, Everett, Framingham, Holliston, Hopkinton, Hudson, Lexington, Lincoln, Lowell, Malden, Marlboro, Maynard, Medford, Melrose, Natick, Newton, N. Reading, Reading, Sherborn, Somerville, Stoneham, Sudbury, Tewksbury, Tyngsboro, Wakefield, Waltham, Watertown, Wayland, Weston, Wilmington, and Winchester.

In Plymouth County, Massachusetts, the towns and cities of:

Abington, Bridgewater, Brockton, E. Bridgewater, Hanover, Hanson, Hingham, Hull, Norwell, Rockland, Scituate, W. Bridgewater, and Whitman.

In Worcester County, Massachusetts, the towns and cities of:

Auburn, Berlin, Boylston, Clinton, Grafton, Holden, Hopedale, Leicester, Mendon, Milford, Millbury, Northboro, Northbridge, Paxton, Shrewsbury, Southboro, Spencer, Upton, Uxbridge, Westboro, W. Boylston, and Worcester.

In Norfolk County, Massachusetts, the towns and cities of:

Avon, Braintree, Brookline, Canton, Cohasset, Dedham, Dover, Foxborough, Holbrook, Medfield, Medway, Millis, Milton, Needham, Norfolk, Norwood, Quincy, Randolph, Sharon, Stoughton, Walpole, Wellesley, Westwood, and Weymouth.

All the towns and cities in the counties of Essex and Suffolk, Massachusetts.

The provisions of this amendment shall become effective at 12:01 a. m., e. w. t., March 1, 1944. With respect to violations of said Food Distribution Order No. 79-43, as amended, rights accrued, or liabilities incurred prior to the effective time of this amendment, said Food Distribution Order No. 79-43, as amended, shall be deemed to be in full force and effect for the purpose of sustaining any proper suit, action, or other proceeding with respect to any such violation, right, or liability.

(E.O. 9280, 7 F.R. 10179; E.O. 9322, 8 F.R. 3807; E.O. 9334, 8 F.R. 5423; E.O. 9392, 8 F.R. 14783; FDO 79, 8 F.R. 12426, 13283)

Issued this 1st day of March 1944.

C. W. KITCHEN,
Acting Director of Food Distribution.

FDO 79-43
AMDT. 5
MAR. 29, 1944

WAR FOOD ADMINISTRATION

[FDO 79-43, Amdt. 5]

PART 1401—DAIRY PRODUCTS

FLUID MILK CREAM IN EASTERN NEW ENGLAND METROPOLITAN SALES AREA

Pursuant to Food Distribution Order No. 79 (8 F.R. 12426), dated September 7, 1943, as amended, and to effectuate the purposes thereof, Food Distribution Order No. 79-43 (8 F.R. 13967), relative to the conservation and distribution of fluid milk in the Eastern New England metropolitan milk sales area, issued by the Director of Food Distribution on October 11, 1943, as amended, is hereby further amended by deleting therefrom the provisions in § 1401.74 (i) and inserting in lieu thereof, the following:

(i) *Quota exclusions and exemptions.* Deliveries of milk, milk byproducts, or cream (1) to other handlers, except for such deliveries to sub-handlers, (2) to plants engaged in the handling or processing of milk, milk byproducts, or cream from which no milk, milk byproducts, or cream is delivered in the sales area, (3) to nursery, elementary, junior high, and high schools, and (4) to the agencies or groups specified in (d) of FDO 79, shall be excluded from the computation of deliveries in the base period and exempt from charges to quotas.

The provisions of this amendment shall become effective at 12:01 a. m. e. w. t., April 1, 1944. With respect to violations of said Food Distribution Order No. 79-43, as amended, rights accrued, or liabilities incurred prior to the effective time of this amendment, said Food Distribution Order No. 79-43, as amended, shall be deemed to be in full force and effect for the purpose of sustaining any proper suit, action, or other proceeding with respect to any such violation, right, or liability.

(E.O. 9280, 7 F.R. 10179; E.O. 9322, 8 F.R. 3807; E.O. 9334, 8 F.R. 5423; E.O. 9392, 8 F.R. 14783; FDO 79, 8 F.R. 12426, 13283)

Issued this 29th day of March 1944.

LEE MARSHALL,
Director of Food Distribution.

FDO 79-43
AMDT. 6
APR. 5, 1944

WAR FOOD ADMINISTRATION

[FDO 79-43, Amdt. 6]

PART 1401—DAIRY PRODUCTS

FLUID MILK AND CREAM IN EASTERN NEW ENGLAND METROPOLITAN SALES AREA

Pursuant to Food Distribution Order No. 79 (8 F.R. 12426), dated September 7, 1943, as amended, and to effectuate the purposes thereof, Food Distribution Order No. 79-43 (8 F.R. 13967), relative to the conservation and distribution of fluid milk, milk byproducts, and cream in the Eastern New England metropolitan milk sales area, issued by the Director of Food Distribution on October 11, 1943, as amended, is hereby further amended by deleting from the description of the sales area in § 1401.74 (b) the following:

The cities and towns of Hopkinton, Hudson and Marlboro in Middlesex County, Massachusetts, and all the cities and towns listed as being in Worcester County, Massachusetts,

making the complete description of the sales area read as follows:

In Bristol County, Massachusetts, the towns of Easton and Mansfield.

In Middlesex County, Massachusetts, the towns and cities of:

Arlington, Ashland, Bedford, Belmont, Billerica, Burlington, Cambridge, Chelmsford, Concord, Dracut, Everett, Framingham, Holliston, Lexington, Lincoln, Lowell, Malden, Maynard, Medford, Melrose, Natick, Newton, N. Reading, Reading, Sherborn, Somerville, Stoneham, Sudbury, Tewksbury, Tyngsboro, Wakefield, Waltham, Watertown, Wayland, Weston, Wilmington, Winchester, and Woburn.

In Plymouth County, Massachusetts, the towns and cities of:

Abington, Bridgewater, Brockton, E. Bridgewater, Hanover, Hanson, Hingham, Hull, Norwell, Rockland, Scituate, W. Bridgewater, and Whitman.

In Norfolk County, Massachusetts, the towns and cities of:

Avon, Braintree, Brookline, Canton, Cohasset, Dedham, Dover, Foxborough, Holbrook, Medfield, Medway, Millis, Milton, Needham, Norfolk, Norwood, Quincy, Randolph, Sharon, Stoughton, Walpole, Wellesley, Westwood, and Weymouth.

All the towns and cities in the counties of Essex and Suffolk, Massachusetts.

The provisions of this amendment shall become effective at 12:01 a. m., e. w. t., May 1, 1944. With respect to violations of said Food Distribution Order No. 79-43, as amended, rights accrued, or liabilities incurred prior to the effective time of this amendment, said Food Distribution Order No. 79-43, as amended, shall be deemed to be in full force and effect for the purpose of sustaining any proper suit, action, or other proceeding with respect to any such violation, right, or liability.

(E.O. 9280, 7 F.R. 10179; E.O. 9322, 8 F.R. 3807; E.O. 9334, 8 F.R. 5423; E.O. 9392, 8 F.R. 14783; FDO 79, 8 F.R. 12426, 13283)

Issued this 5th day of April 1944.

LEE MARSHALL,
Director of Distribution.

47321

FDO 79-44

OCTOBER 11, 1943

WAR FOOD ADMINISTRATION

[FDO 79-44]

PART 1401—DAIRY PRODUCTS

CONSERVATION AND DISTRIBUTION OF FLUID MILK AND CREAM IN SPRINGFIELD-HOLYOKE, MASS., SALES AREA

Pursuant to the authority vested in me by Food Distribution Order No. 79 (8 F.R. 12426), issued on September 7, 1943, as amended, and to effectuate the purposes of such order, it is hereby ordered as follows:

§ 1401.78 *Quota restrictions*—(a) *Definitions.* When used in this order, unless otherwise distinctly expressed or manifestly incompatible with the intent hereof:

(1) Each term defined in Food Distribution Order No. 79, as amended, shall, when used herein, have the same meaning as is set forth for such term in Food Distribution Order No. 79, as amended.

(2) The term FDO 79 means Food Distribution Order No. 79, issued on September 7, 1943, as amended.

(3) The term "sub-handler" means any handler, such as peddler, vendor, sub-dealer, or secondary dealer, who purchases in a previously packaged and processed form milk, milk byproducts, or cream for delivery.

(b) *Milk sales area.* The following area is hereby designated as a "milk sales area" to be known as the Springfield-Holyoke, Massachusetts, sales area, and is referred to hereinafter as the "sales area":

The territory included within the boundaries of the following cities and towns in Massachusetts:

Amherst, Agawam, Chicopee, Easthampton, East Longmeadow, Granby, Hadley, Hatfield, Holyoke, Longmeadow, Ludlow, Northampton, Palmer, South Hadley, Southampton, Springfield, Ware, Westfield, West Springfield, and Wilbraham, and in Enfield, Connecticut.

(c) *Base period.* The calendar month of June 1943 is hereby designated as the base period for the sales area.

(d) *Quota period.* The remainder of the calendar month in which the provisions hereof become effective and each subsequent calendar month, respectively, is hereby designated as a quota period for the sales area.

(e) *Handler quotas.* Quotas for each handler in the sales area in each quota period shall be calculated in terms of pounds of each of the items for which percentages are specified in (3) below and shall be determined as follows:

(1) Divide the total deliveries of each item made in the sales area by such handler during the base period, after excluding the quota-exempt deliveries described in (i) hereof, by the number of days in the base period;

(2) Multiply the result of the foregoing calculation by the number of days in the quota period;

(3) Multiply the aforesaid resulting amount by the following applicable percentage: (i) Milk: 100 percent; (ii) Butterfat in milk: ------ percent; (iii) Cream: 75 percent; (iv) Butterfat in cream: 75 percent; (v) Milk by products other than cottage, pot or baker's cheese: 75 percent; and (vi) Cottage, pot or baker's cheese: 75 percent of skim milk equivalent. (For the purpose of this order, one pound of cottage, pot or baker's cheese shall be considered as the equivalent of 7 pounds of skim milk.)

(f) *Quota limitations.* No handler shall, during any quota period, make deliveries in the sales area in excess of his respective quotas, except as set out in (i) hereof: *Provided,* That a handler may, after application to and approval by the market agent, secure an increase in milk quotas through an equivalent reduction as determined by the market agent, in cream and milk byproducts quotas, and an increase in milk byproducts quota through an equivalent reduction as determined by the market agent in cream quotas.

(g) *Quotas for handlers who are also producers.* Quotas for handlers who are also producers and who purchase no milk shall be 100 percent of the total production of such handlers in the base period.

(h) *Handler exemptions.* Quotas shall not apply to any handler who delivers in a quota period a daily average of less than 200 units of milk, cream, and milk byproducts. For the purpose of this order, a unit shall be the equivalent in volume of the following: (1) milk, one quart of milk; (2) cream, one-half pint of cream; and (3) milk byproduct, one quart of skim milk, buttermilk, flavored milk drink, or other beverage containing more than 85 percent of skim milk, or one-half pound of cottage, pot, or baker's cheese.

(i) *Quota exclusions and exemptions.* Deliveries of milk, milk byproducts, or cream (1) to other handlers, except for such deliveries to sub-handlers, (2) to plants engaged in the handling or processing of milk, milk byproducts, or cream from which no milk, milk byproducts, or cream is delivered in the sales area, and (3) to the agencies or groups specified in (d) of FDO 79, shall be excluded from the computation of deliveries in the base period and exempt from charges to quotas.

(j) *Transfers and apportionment of quotas.* The market agent is empowered to deduct an amount of base period deliveries to purchasers from the total of deliveries made by a handler or other person in the base period upon the application and a showing of unreasonable hardship by the handler making deliveries to such purchasers on the effective date of this order, and to add the amount of such deliveries to the total base period deliveries of the applicant handler. Denials of transfers or transfers granted by the market agent shall be reviewed by the Director upon application.

(k) *Petition for relief from hardships.* (1) Any person affected by FDO 79 or the provisions hereof who considers that compliance therewith would work an exceptional and unreasonable hardship on him, may file with the market agent a petition addressed to the Director. The petition shall contain the correct name, address and principal place of business of the petitioner, a full statement of the facts upon which the petition is based, and the hardship involved and the nature of the relief desired.

(2) Upon receiving such petition, the market agent shall immediately investigate the representations and facts stated therein.

(3) After investigation, the petition shall be certified to the Director, but prior to certification the market agent may (i) deny the petition, or (ii) grant temporary relief for a total period of not to exceed 60 days.

(4) Denials or grants of relief by the market agent shall be reviewed by the Director and may be affirmed, modified, or reversed by the Director.

(l) *Reports.* Each handler shall transmit to the market agent on forms prescribed by the market agent the following reports:

(1) Within 20 days following the effective date of this order, reports which show the information required by the market agent to establish such handlers' quotas;

(2) Within 20 days following the close of each quota period, the information required by the market agent to establish volumes of deliveries of milk, cream, and milk byproducts during the preceding quota period; and

(3) Handlers exempt from quotas pursuant to (h) hereof shall, upon the re-

quest of the market agent, submit the information required by the market agent to establish volumes of deliveries of milk, cream, and milk byproducts.

(m) *Records.* Handlers shall keep and shall make available to the market agent such records of receipts, sales, deliveries, and production as the market agent shall require for the purpose of obtaining information which the Director may require for the establishment of quotas as prescribed in (b) of FDO 79.

(n) *Distribution schedules.* The distribution schedules, is any, to be followed by the handlers in making deliveries shall be made effective in the terms of approval by the Director of such schedules.

(o) *Expense of administration.* Each handler shall pay to the market agent, within 20 days after the close of each calendar month an assessment of $0.015 per hundredweight of each of milk, cream, skim milk, buttermilk, flavored milk drinks, beverages containing more than 85 percent of skim milk, and skim milk equivalent of cottage, pot, or baker's cheese delivered during the preceding quota period and subject to quota regulations under the provisions hereof.

(p) *Violations.* The market agent shall report all violations to the Director together with the information required for the prosecution of such violations, except in a case where a handler has made deliveries in a quota period in excess of a quota in an amount not to exceed 5 percent of such quota, and in the succeeding quota period makes deliveries below that quota by at least the same percent.

(q) *Bureau of the Budget approval.* The record keeping and reporting requirements of this order have been approved by the Bureau of the Budget in accordance with the Federal Reports Act of 1942. Subsequent record keeping or reporting requirements will be subject to the approval of the Bureau of the Budget pursuant to the Federal Reports Act of 1942.

(r) This order shall take effect at 12:01 a. m., e. w. t., October 17, 1943.

Issued this 11th day of October 1943.

C. W. KITCHEN,
Acting Director of Food Distribution.

Press Release, Immediate:
Monday, October 11, 1943.

Federal Control over fluid milk sales will be extended to the Far West for the first time beginning October 17, 1943 when maximum deliveries quotas will be assigned to milk dealers in three Washington metropolitan areas, the War Food Administration said today. The milk conservation and control program also will go into effect in three New England areas on the same date.

The new milk sales areas, and the market agents who will administer the program for the Food Distribution Administration in each area, are:

Springfield-Holyoke, Mass: Eastern New England Metropolitan (including cities in Bristol, Middlesex, Plymouth, Worcester, Essex, Norfolk and Suffolk counties in Massachusetts, and 22 cities in Rhode Island)—Mr. Samuel W. Tator, 80 Federal St., Boston, Mass.

Fall River - New Bedford - Taunton, Mass.—Mr. John J. Hogan, 103 Pleasant St., Fall River, Mass.

Seattle, Wash., Metropolitan; Spokane, Wash., Metropolitan; Tacoma, Wash., Metropolitan—Mr. J. H. Mapes, 635 Elliot Ave., West, Seattle, Wash.

Dealers' fluid milk sales in these areas will be limited to the quantity sold in June. Cream sales and sales of milk byproducts (such as cottage cheese, chocolate milk and buttermilk) will be limited to 75 percent of the quantities sold in June. Upon approval of the market agent, however, a dealer may increase his fluid milk quota if he reduces his cream and milk byproducts sales in an amount approved by the market agent. He may increase sales of milk byproducts over the basic quota by reducing his cream sales. Milk dealers include all persons or firms engaged in the sale or transfer of milk, but not retail stores, hotels, restaurants, etc.

Producer-distributors who purchase no milk (except those whose volume of sales is small enough to make them quota-exempt) will be allowed to sell an amount of fluid milk, cream and fluid milk byproducts equal to 100 percent of their total milk production in June. Quota-exempt producer-distributors are defined separately for each area, but in general they are those whose deliveries are relatively small.

Milk handlers in the 3 New England sales areas will compute the quantity of milk which they may sell each month in terms of pounds of milk, their cream sales in terms of pounds of cream and butterfat, and their milk byproducts sales in terms of pounds of milk byproducts or skim milk equivalent. In the 3 Washington state areas, milk handlers will determine their fluid milk quotas in terms of pounds of milk and butterfat.

Deliveries to the Armed Forces, to plants processing dairy products, and to other handlers (except special classes of handlers such as peddlers) are quota-exempt.

To facilitate administration, the market agent for each milk sales area may act upon petitions for relief from hardship which may be submitted to him, and after investigation, he may grant temporary relief for a total period not to exceed 60 days.

Milk sales in 38 eastern and midwestern areas previously were brought under federal regulation. Basic sales quotas in these initial milk sales areas are the same as for those named today.

The Eastern New England Metropolitan milk sales area includes the following cities:

In Bristol County, Massachusetts, the towns and cities of:

Attleboro	N. Attleboro
Easton	Seekonk
Mansfield	

In Middlesex County, Massachusetts, the towns and cities of:

Arlington	Concord
Ashland	Dracut
Bedford	Everett
Belmont	Framingham
Billerica	Holliston
Burlington	Hopkinton
Cambridge	Hudson
Chelmsford	Lexington
Lincoln	Stoneham
Lowell	Sudbury
Malden	Tewksbury
Marlboro	Tyngsboro
Maynard	Wakefield
Medford	Waltham
Melrose	Watertown
Natick	Wayland
Newton	Weston
N. Reading	Wilmington
Reading	Winchester
Sherborn	Woburn
Somerville	

In Plymouth County, Massachusetts, the towns and cities of:

Abington	Norwell
Bridgewater	Rockland
Brockton	Scituate
E. Bridgewater	W. Bridgewater
Hanover	Whitman
Hanson	

In Worcester County, Massachusetts, the towns and cities of:

Auburn	Millville
Berlin	Northboro
Blackstone	Northbridge
Boylston	Paxton
Clinton	Shrewsbury
Grafton	Southboro
Holden	Spencer
Hopedale	Upton
Leicester	Uxbridge
Mendon	Westboro
Milford	W. Boylston
Millbury	Worcester

All of the towns and cities in the counties of Essex, Norfolk, and Suffolk, Massachusetts.

In Rhode Island the towns and cities of:

Barrington	Newport
Bristol	No. Providence
Central Falls	No. Smithfield
Cranston	Pawtucket
Cumberland	Portsmouth
E. Greenwich	Providence
E. Providence	Smithfield
Jamestown	Warren
Johnston	Warwick
Lincoln	W. Warwick
Middletown	Woonsocket

The Fall River-New Bedford-Taunton area includes the following cities and towns:

In Massachusetts:

Acushnet	Norton
Berkley	Raynham
Dartmouth	Rehoboth
Dighton	Somerset
Fairhaven	Swansea
Fall River	Taunton
Freetown	Westport
New Bedford	

In Rhode Island:

Little Compton	Tiverton

The Springfield-Holyoke area includes:

Amherst	Hatfield
Agawam	Holyoke
Chicopee	Longmeadow
Easthampton	Ludlow
East Longmeadow	Northampton
Granby	Palmer
Hadley	South Hadley
Southampton	West Springfield
Springfield	Wilbraham
Ware	also Enfield, Conn.
Westfield	

Note to editors: Background material follows:

Consumers in these areas generally will be able to purchase as much milk under the milk conservation program as they have been buying—an amount considerably greater than that bought in pre-war years, and about 10 percent above last year's purchases. Sales quotas on cream and on fluid milk byproducts have been set below June deliveries to boost fluid milk supplies where milk production is low, and to conserve milk for manufacturing purposes.

Fluid milk sales are being stabilized in these and other metropolitan areas, FDA officials explained, to help assure sufficient milk for manufacturing the cheese, butter, evaporated milk, and milk powder required by the Armed Services and civilians for good nutrition and properly balanced diets.

Largely due to expanded consumer demand, sales of fluid milk have been increasing steadily and are now about 20 percent higher than in pre-war years (1936-40) and 10 to 12 percent above those in 1942. With total milk production levelled off, and even declining somewhat, this expanding volume of milk sold for fluid uses has inevitably reduced the supply of "manufacturing milk," and consequently, the production of cheese, butter, and other dairy foods.

The FDA's dealer-quota plan is an attempt to stabilize fluid milk consumption without resorting to individual consumer rationing. Point rationing of milk, a bulky and highly perishable commodity, would be very difficult to administer. If consumers and the trade cooperate with the present program to assure that sales are held within quotas and quantities available are distributed fairly, FDA officials believe consumer rationing will not be necessary.

WAR FOOD ADMINISTRATION

[FDO 79-44, Amdt. 1]

PART 1401—DAIRY PRODUCTS

DIRECTOR'S ORDER FOR THE SPRINGFIELD-HOLYOKE, MASS., MILK SALES AREA

Pursuant to the authority vested in the Director by Food Distribution Order No. 79, dated September 7, 1943 (8 F.R. 12426), as amended, and to effectuate the purposes thereof, Food Distribution Order No. 79-44, § 1401.78, relative to the conservation of fluid milk in the Springfield-Holyoke, Mass., milk sales area (8 F.R. 13968), issued by the Director of Food Distribution on October 11, 1943, is amended as follows:

The milk sales area described in § 1401.78 (b) of the original order is modified in the following particulars: Delete the words "and in Enfield, Connecticut."

Effective date. This amendment of FDO No. 79-44 shall become effective at 12:01 a. m., e. w. t., December 1, 1943.

(E.O. 9280, 7 F.R. 10179; E.O. 9322, 8 F.R. 3807; E.O. 9334, 8 F.R. 5423; E.O. 9392, 8 F.R. 14783; FDO 79, 8 F.R. 12426, 13283)

Issued this 29th day of November 1943.

ROY F. HENDRICKSON,
Director of Food Distribution.

serve

/

7337

FDO 79-44
AMDT. 2
NOV. 30, 1943

WAR FOOD ADMINISTRATION

[FDO 79-44, Amdt. 2]

PART 1401—DAIRY PRODUCTS

DIRECTOR'S ORDER FOR SPRINGFIELD-HOLYOKE, MASS., MILK SALES AREA

Pursuant to the authority vested in the Director by Food Distribution Order No. 79, dated September 7, 1943 (8 F.R. 12426), as amended, and to effectuate the purposes thereof, Food Distribution Order No. 79-44, § 1401.78, relative to the conservation of fluid milk in the Springfield-Holyoke, Massachusetts, milk sales area (8 F.R. 13968) issued by the Director of Food Distribution on October 11, 1943, is amended as follows:

Quotas for handlers who are also producers described in § 1401.78 (g) of the original order is modified in the following particulars: Strike out (g) and insert in lieu thereof the following:

(g) *Quotas for handlers who are also producers.*—Quotas for handlers who are also producers and who purchase no milk shall be computed in accordance with (e) hereof, except that the applicable percentages shall be 100 percent in lieu of the percentages specified in (e) (3).

(b) *Effective date.*—This amendment of FDO No. 79.44, shall become effective at 12:01 a. m., e. w. t., December 1, 1943.

(E.O. 9280, 7 F.R. 10179; E.O. 9322, 8 F.R. 3807; E.O. 9334, 8 F.R. 5423; E.O. 9392, 8 F.R. 14783; FDO 79, 8 F.R. 12426, 13283)

Issued this 30th day of November 1943.

C. W. KITCHEN,
Acting Director of Food Distribution.

FDO 79-44

AMDT. 3
FEB. 28, 1944

WAR FOOD ADMINISTRATION

[FDO 79-44, Amdt. 3]

PART 1401—DAIRY PRODUCTS

FLUID MILK AND CREAM IN SPRINGFIELD-HOLYOKE, MASS., SALES AREA

Pursuant to Food Distribution Order No. 79 (8 F.R. 12426), dated September 7, 1943, as amended, and to effectuate the purposes thereof, Food Distribution Order No. 79-44 (8 F.R. 13968), relative to the conservation and distribution of fluid milk in the Springfield-Holyoke, Massachusetts, milk sales area, issued by the Director of Food Distribution on October 11, 1943, as amended, is hereby further amended by deleting therefrom the provisions in § 1401.78 (a) (3) and inserting, in lieu thereof, the following:

(3) The term "sub-handler" means any handler, who (i) receives in a previously packaged and processed form milk, milk byproducts, or cream for delivery, and (ii) does not operate facilities for the processing and bottling of fluid milk.

The provisions of this amendment shall become effective at 12:01 a. m., e. w. t., March 1, 1944. With respect to violations of said Food Distribution Order No. 79-44, as amended, rights accrued, or liabilities incurred prior to the effective time of this amendment, said Food Distribution Order No. 79-44, as amended, shall be deemed to be in full force and effect for the purpose of sustaining any proper suit, action, or other proceeding with respect to any such violation, right, or liability.

(E.O. 9280, 7 F.R. 10179; E.O. 9322, 8 F.R. 3807; E.O. 9334, 8 F.R. 5423; E.O. 9392, 8 F.R. 14793; FDO 79, 8 F.R. 12426, 13283)

Issued this 28th day of February 1944.

C. W. KITCHEN,
Acting Director of Food Distribution.

FDO 79-44

AMDT. 4
MAR. 29, 1944

WAR FOOD ADMINISTRATION

[FDO 79-44, Amdt. 4]

PART 1401—DAIRY PRODUCTS

FLUID MILK AND CREAM IN SPRINGFIELD-HOLYOKE, MASS., SALES AREA

Pursuant to Food Distribution Order No. 79 (8 F.R. 12426), dated September 7, 1943, as amended, and to effectuate the purposes thereof, Food Distribution Order No. 79-44 (8 F.R. 13968), relative to the conservation and distribution of fluid milk in the Springfield-Holyoke, Massachusetts, milk sales area, issued by the Director of Food Distribution on October 11, 1943, as amended, is hereby further amended by deleting therefrom the provisions in § 1401.78 (i) and inserting, in lieu thereof, the following:

(i) *Quota exclusions and exemptions.* Deliveries of milk, milk byproducts, or cream (1) to other handlers, except for such deliveries to sub-handlers, (2) to plants engaged in the handling or processing of milk, milk byproducts, or cream from which no milk, milk byproducts, or cream is delivered in the sales area, (3) to nursery, elementary, junior high, and high schools, and (4) to the agencies or groups specified in (d) of FDO 79, shall be excluded from the computation of deliveries in the base period and exempt from charges to quotas.

The provisions of this amendment shall become effective at 12:01 a. m., e. w. t., April 1, 1944. With respect to violations of said Food Distribution Order No. 79-44, as amended, rights accrued, or liabilities incurred prior to the effective time of this amendment, said Food Distribution Order No. 79-44, as amended, shall be deemed to be in full force and effect for the purpose of sustaining any proper suit, action, or other proceeding with respect to any such violation, right, or liability.

(E.O. 9280, 7 F.R. 10179; E.O. 9322, 8 F.R. 3807; E.O. 9334, 8 F.R. 5423; E.O. 9392, 8 F.R. 14783; FDO 79, 8 F.R. 12426, 13283)

Issued this 29th day of March 1944.

LEE MARSHALL,
Director of Food Distribution.

WAR FOOD ADMINISTRATION

[FDO No. 79-45]

PART 1401—DAIRY PRODUCTS

FLUID MILK AND CREAM IN MINNEAPOLIS-ST. PAUL, MINN., SALES AREA

Pursuant to the authority vested in me by Food Distribution Order No. 79 (8 F.R. 12426), issued on September 7 1943, as amended, and to effectuate the purposes of such order, it is hereby ordered as follows:

§ 1401.114 *Quota restrictions*—(a) *Definitions.* When used in this order, unless otherwise distinctly expressed or manifestly incompatible with the intent hereof:

(1) Each term defined in Food Distribution Order No. 79, as amended, shall, when used herein, have the same meaning as is set forth for such term in Food Distribution Order No. 79, as amended.

(2) The term "FDO 79" means Food Distribution Order No. 79, issued on September 7, 1943, as amended.

(3) The term "sub-handler" means any handler, such as a peddler, vendor, subdealer, or secondary dealer, who purchases in a previously packaged and processed form milk, milk byproducts, or cream for delivery.

(b) *Milk sales area.* The following area is hereby designated as a "milk sales area" to be known as the Minneapolis-St. Paul, Minnesota, sales area, and is referred to hereinafter as the "sales area":

The cities of Minneapolis and St. Paul and the entire area, encompassed by and including:

On the north, the city of Anoka and the townships of Anoka and Fridley in Anoka County; the townships of Mounds View and White Bear in Ramsey County; the townships of Lincoln and Grant in Washington County;

On the west, the townships of Brooklyn and New Hope, the villages of Osseo and Golden Valley, the townships of Minnetonka, Orono, and Excelsior, the city of Wayzata, and the villages of Mound and Island Park, all in Hennepin County;

On the south, the township of Minnetonka and the villages of Edina and Richfield in Hennepin County; the township of Mendota, the cities of West St. Paul and South St. Paul, and the village of Inver Grove in Dakota County; and

On the east, the villages of St. Paul Park and Newport in Washington County; the township of New Canada and the village of North St. Paul in Ramsey County; the townships of Lincoln, Grant, Baytown and Stillwater, the village of Bayport, and the city of Stillwater in Washington County, all of the above being in the State of Minnesota.

(c) *Base period.* The calendar month of June 1943 is hereby designated as the base period for the sales area.

(d) *Quota period.* The remainder of the calendar month in which the provisions hereof become effective and each subsequent calendar month, respectively, is hereby designated as a quota period for the sales area.

(e) *Handler quotas.* Quotas for each handler in the sales area in each quota period shall be calculated in terms of pounds of each of the items for which percentages are specified in (3) below and shall be determined as follows:

(1) Divide the total deliveries of each such item made in the sales area by such handler during the base period, after excluding the quota-exempt deliveries described in (i) hereof, by the number of days in the base period;

(2) Multiply the result of the foregoing calculation by the number of days in the quota period;

(3) Multiply the aforesaid resulting amount by the following applicable percentage: (i) milk: 100 percent; (ii) butterfat in milk ______ percent; (iii) cream: 75 percent; (iv) butterfat in cream: 75 percent; (v) milk byproducts other than cottage, pot, or baker's cheese: 75 percent; and (vi) cottage, pot, or baker's cheese: 75 percent of skim milk equivalent. (For the purpose of this order, one pound of cottage, pot, or baker's cheese shall be considered as the equivalent of 7 pounds of skim milk.)

(f) *Quota limitations.* No handler shall, during any quota period, make deliveries in the sales area in excess of his respective quotas, except as set out in (i) hereof: *Provided*, That a handler may, after application to and approval by the market agent, secure an increase in milk quotas through an equivalent reduction as determined by the market agent, in cream and milk byproducts quotas, and an increase in milk byproducts quota through an equivalent reduction as determined by the market agent, in cream quotas.

(g) *Quotas for handlers who are also producers.* Quotas for handlers who are also producers and who purchase no milk shall be 100 percent of the total production of such handlers in the base period.

(h) *Handler exemptions.* Quotas shall not apply to any handler who delivers in a quota period a daily average of less than 200 units of milk, cream, and milk byproducts. For the purpose of this order, a unit shall be the equivalent in the volume of the following: (1) Milk, one quart of milk; (2) cream, one-half pint of cream; and (3) milk byproduct, one quart of skim milk, buttermilk, flavored milk drink, or other beverage containing more than 85 percent of skim milk, or one-half pound of cottage, pot, or baker's cheese.

(i) *Quota exclusions and exemptions.* Deliveries of milk, milk byproducts, or cream (1) to other handlers, except for such deliveries to sub-handlers, (2) to plants engaged in the handlings or processing of milk, milk byproducts, or cream from which no milk, milk byproducts, or cream is delivered in the sales area, and (3) to the agencies or groups specified in (d) of FDO 79, shall be excluded from the computation of deliveries in the base period and exempt from charges to quotas.

(j) *Transfers and apportionment of quotas.* The market agent is empowered to deduct an amount of base period deliveries to purchasers from the total of deliveries made by a handler or other person in the base period upon the application and a showing of unreasonable hardship by the handler making deliveries to such purchasers on the effective date of this order, and to add the amount of such deliveries to the total base period deliveries of the applicant handler. Denials of transfers or transfers granted by the market agent shall be reviewed by the Director upon application.

(k) *Petition for relief from hardships.* Any person affected by FDO 79 or the provisions hereof who considers that compliance therewith would work an exceptional and unreasonable hardship on him, may file with the market agent a petition addressed to the Director. The petition shall contain the correct name, address and principal place of business of the petitioner, a full statement of the facts upon which the petition is based, and the hardship involved and the nature of the relief desired.

(2) Upon receiving such petition, the market agent shall immediately investigate the representations and facts stated therein.

(3) After investigation, the petition shall be certified to the Director, but prior to certification the market agent may (i) deny the petition, or (ii) grant temporary relief for a total period not to exceed 60 days.

(4) Denials or grants of relief by the market agent shall be reviewed by the Director and may be affirmed, modified, or reversed by the Director.

(l) *Reports.* Each handler shall transmit to the market agent on forms prescribed by the market agent the following reports:

(1) Within 20 days following the effective date of this order, reports which show the information required by the market agent to establish such handlers' quotas;

(2) Within 20 days following the close of each quota period, the information required by the market agent to establish volumes of deliveries of milk, cream, and milk byproducts during the preceding quota period; and

(3) Handlers exempt from quotas pursuant to (h) hereof shall, upon the request of the market agent, submit the information required by the market agent to establish volumes of deliveries of milk, cream, and milk byproducts.

(m) *Records.* Handlers shall keep and shall make available to the market agent such records of receipts, sales, deliveries, and production as the market agent shall require for the purpose of obtaining information which the Director may require for the establishment of quotas as prescribed in (b) of FDO 79.

(n) *Distribution schedules.* The distribution schedules, if any, to be followed by the handlers in making deliveries shall be made effective in the terms of approval by the Director of such schedules.

(o) *Expense of administration.* Each handler shall pay to the market agent, within 20 days after the close of each calendar month an assessment of $0.01 per hundredweight of each of milk, cream, skim milk, buttermilk, flavored milk drinks, beverages containing more than 85 percent of skim milk, and skim milk equivalent of cottage, pot, or baker's cheese delivered during the preceding quota period and subject to quota regulations under the provisions hereof.

(p) *Violations.* The market agent shall report all violations to the Director together with the information required for the prosecution of such violat except in a case where a handler made deliveries in a quota period i cess of a quota in an amount not t ceed 5 percent of such quota, and i succeeding quota period makes deliv below that quota by at least the percent.

(q) *Bureau of the Budget appr* The record keeping and reporting quirements of this order have been proved by the Bureau of the Budg accordance with the Federal Report of 1942. Subsequent record keepin reporting requirements will be su to the approval of the Bureau of Budget pursuant to the Federal Re Act of 1942.

(r) This order shall take effec 12:01 a. m., e. w. t., October 22, 194

Issued this 19th day of October 19

C. W. KITCHEN
Acting Director of Food Distributi

Press Release, Immediate:
Wednesday, October 20, 1943.

Milk sales in 19 metropolitan areas in Illinois, Michigan, Colorado, Utah, Arizona, Oregon, Pennsylvania, Minnesota, Oklahoma and West Virginia will be regulated under the Food Distribution Administration's fluid milk conservation and control program, beginning November 1, 1943.

The new milk sales areas and the market agents who will administer the program in each are:

Johnstown, Pa., Erie, Pa., Altoona, Pa., Pittsburgh, Pa., Metropolitan, Charleston, W. Va., Wheeling, W. Va.: George A. Taylor, Century Building, Pittsburgh, Pa.

Peoria, Ill., Rockford, Ill.: A. W. Colebank, 135 S. LaSalle St., Chicago, Ill.

Phoenix, Ariz., Denver, Colo., Metropolitan, Salt Lake City, Utah, Metropolitan: Ben King, 503 Security Life Building, 810 14th St., Denver, Colo. (temp. address).

Portland, Oregon, Metropolitan: J. H. Mapes, 635 Elliot Avenue, West, Seattle, Washington.

Detroit, Michigan, Metropolitan, Saginaw-Bay City, Mich., Metropolitan, Lansing, Mich., Metropolitan, Flint, Mich., Metropolitan: (To be announced later.)

Oklahoma City, Oklahoma, Tulsa, Oklahoma: M. M. Morehouse, 512 Porter Bldg., 406 W. 34th St., Kansas City, Mo.

Minneapolis-St. Paul, Minnesota: D. F. Spencer, 404 Post Office Bldg., Minneapolis, Minn.

Under the program, milk dealers will be permitted to sell as much fluid milk as they sold in June and three-fourths as much cream and milk byproducts (such as cottage cheese, chocolate milk, and buttermilk) as they sold in June. Milk dealers include all persons or firms engaged in the sale or transfer of milk, but not such distributors as subhandlers ("peddlers"), retail stores, hotels, or restaurants.

Producer-distributors who purchase no milk will be permitted to sell as much milk as they produced in June.

Dealers will be allowed to exceed these base quotas by not more than 5 percent during any month, providing they decrease their deliveries the next month by the same amount, without being reported in violation.

A dealer also may increase his milk sales by reducing his cream and milk byproducts sales, and increase his sales of milk byproducts by reducing his cream sales, providing such an ad ment is approved by the market for the area.

Deliveries of milk, cream, and mil products to other dealers, to the A Forces, and to plants processing who do not distribute milk, cream, milk byproducts in the sales area quota-exempt.

Consumers in the milk sales named today and in others already ignated generally will be able to chase as much milk under the milk servation program as they have buying in recent months—within limits of local supplies. In some a production is not expected to be l enough to permit dealers to sell as n milk as their quotas allow.

Fluid milk sales are being stabil Food Distribution Administration cials said, to help assure sufficient for manufacturing, the cheese, bu evaporated milk, and milk powder quired by the Armed Services and vilians for food nutrition and pro balanced diets. Sales quotas on cr and on fluid milk byproducts have set below June deliveries to boost milk supplies where production is and to conserve milk for manufactu purposes.

FDO 79-45

AMDT. 1
FEB. 19, 1944

WAR FOOD ADMINISTRATION

§ 1401.114 (i) and inserting, in lieu thereof, the following:

(i) *Quota exclusions and exemptions.* Deliveries of milk, milk byproducts, or cream (1) to other handlers, except for such deliveries to subhandlers, (2) to plants engaged in the handling or processing of milk, milk byproducts, or cream from which no milk, milk byproducts, or cream is delivered in the sales area, (3) to nursery, elementary, junior high, and high schools, and (4) to the agencies or groups specified in (d) of FDO 79, shall be excluded from the computation of deliveries in the base period and exempt from charges to quotas.

The provisions of this amendment shall become effective at 12:01 a. m., e. w. t., March 1, 1944. With respect to violations of said Food Distribution Order No. 79-45, rights accrued, or liabilities incurred prior to the effective time of this amendment, said Food Distribution Order No. 79-45, shall be deemed to be in full force and effect for the purpose of sustaining any proper suit, action, or other proceeding with respect to any such violation, right, or liability.

(E.O. 9280, 7 F.R. 10179; E.O. 9322, 8 F.R. 3807; E.O. 9334, 8 F.R. 5423; E.O. 9392, 8 F.R. 14783; FDO 79, 8 F.R. 12426, 13283)

Issued this 19th day of February 1944.

LEE MARSHALL,
Director of Food Distribution.

FDO 79-46
OCTOBER 14, 1943

WAR FOOD ADMINISTRATION

[FDO 79-46]

PART 1401—DAIRY PRODUCTS

FLUID MILK AND CREAM IN GRAND RAPIDS, MICH., METROPOLITAN SALES AREA

Pursuant to the authority vested in me by Food Distribution Order No. 79 (8 F.R. 12426), issued on September 7, 1943, as amended, and to effectuate the purposes of such order, it is hereby ordered as follows:

§ 1401.80 *Quota restrictions*—(a) *Definitions*. When used in this order, unless otherwise distinctly expressed or manifestly incompatible with the intent hereof:

(1) Each term defined in Food Distribution Order No. 79, as amended, shall, when used herein, have the same meaning as is set forth for such term in Food Distribution Order No. 79, as amended.

(2) The term FDO 79 means Food Distribution Order No. 79, issued on September 7, 1943, as amended.

(3) The term "sub-handler" means any handler, such as a peddler, vendor, sub-dealer, or secondary dealer, who purchases in a previously packaged and processed form milk, milk byproducts, or cream for delivery.

(b) *Milk sales area*. The following area is hereby designated as a "milk sales area" to be known as the Grand Rapids, Michigan, metropolitan sales area, and is referred to hereinafter as the "sales area":

The cities of Grand Rapids, East Grand Rapids, and Grandville, and the townships of Grand Rapids, Walker, Wyoming, and Paris, all in Kent County, Michigan.

(c) *Base period*. The calendar month of June 1943 is hereby designated as the base period for the sales area.

(d) *Quota period*. The remainder of the calendar month in which the provisions hereof become effective and each subsequent calendar month, respectively, is hereby designated as a quota period for the sales area.

(e) *Handler quotas*. Quotas for each handler in the sales area in each quota period shall be calculated in terms of pounds of each of the items for which percentages are specified in (3) below and shall be determined as follows:

(1) Divide the total deliveries of each such item made in the sales area by such handler during the base period, after excluding the quota-exempt deliveries described in (i) hereof, by the number of days in the base period;

(2) Multiply the result of the foregoing calculation by the number of days in the quota period;

(3) Multiply the aforesaid resulting amount by the following applicable percentage: (i) milk: 100 percent; (ii) butterfat in milk: ____ percent; (iii) cream: 75 percent; (iv) butterfat in cream: 75 percent; (v) milk byproducts other than cottage, pot, or baker's cheese: 75 percent; and (vi) cottage, pot, or baker's cheese: 75 percent of skim milk equivalent. (For the purpose of this order, one pound of cottage, pot, or baker's cheese shall be considered as the equivalent of 7 pounds of skim milk.)

(f) *Quota limitations*. No handler shall, during any quota period, make deliveries in the sales area in excess of his respective quotas, except as set out in (i) hereof: *Provided*, That a handler may, after application to and approval by the market agent, secure an increase in milk quotas through an equivalent reduction as determined by the market agent, in cream and milk byproducts quotas, and an increase in milk byproducts quota through an equivalent reduction as determined by the market agent, in cream quotas.

(g) *Quotas for handlers who are also producers*. Quotas for handlers who are also producers and who purchase no milk shall be 100 percent of the total production of such handlers in the base period.

(h) *Handler exemptions*. Quotas shall not apply to any handler who delivers in a quota period a daily average of less than 300 units of milk, cream, and milk byproducts. For the purpose of this order, a unit shall be the equivalent in volume of the following: (1) milk, one quart of milk; (2) cream, one-half pint of cream; and (3) milk byproduct, one quart of skim milk, buttermilk, flavored milk drink, or other beverage containing more than 85 percent of skim milk, or one-half of cottage, pot, or baker's cheese.

(i) *Quota exclusions and exemptions*. Deliveries of milk, milk byproducts, or cream (1) to other handlers, except for such deliveries to sub-handlers, (2) to plants engaged in the handling or processing of milk, milk byproducts, or cream from which no milk, milk byproducts, or cream is delivered in the sales area, and (3) to the agencies or groups specified in (d) of FDO 79, shall be excluded from the computation of deliveries in the base period and exempt from charges to quotas.

(j) *Transfers and apportionment of quotas*. The market agent is empowered to deduct an amount of base period deliveries to purchasers from the total of deliveries made by a handler or other person in the base period upon the application and a showing of unreasonable hardship by the handler making deliveries to such purchasers on the effective date of this order, and to add the amount of such deliveries to the total base period deliveries of the applicant handler. Denials of transfers or transfers granted by the market agent shall be reviewed by the Director upon application.

(k) *Petition for relief from hardships*. (1) Any person affected by FDO 79 or the provisions hereof who considers that compliance therewith would work an exceptional and unreasonable hardship on him, may file with the market agent a petition addressed to the Director. The petition shall contain the correct name, address and principal place of business of the petitioner, a full statement of the facts upon which the petition is based, and the hardship involved and the nature of the relief desired.

(2) Upon receiving such petition, the market agent shall immediately investigate the representations and facts stated therein.

(3) After investigation, the petition shall be certified to the Director, but prior to certification the market agent may (i) deny the petition, or (ii) grant temporary relief for a total period not to exceed 60 days.

(4) Denials or grants of relief by the market agent shall be reviewed by the Director and may be affirmed, modified, or reversed by the Director.

(l) *Reports*. Each handler shall transmit to the market agent on forms prescribed by the market agent the following reports:

(1) Within 20 days following the effective date of this order, reports which show the information required by the market agent to establish such handlers' quotas;

(2) Within 20 days following the close of each quota period, the information required by the market agent to establish volumes of deliveries of milk, cream, and milk byproducts during the preceding quota period; and

(3) Handlers exempt from quotas pursuant to (h) hereof shall, upon the request of the market agent, submit the information required by the market agent to establish volumes of deliveries of milk, cream, and milk byproducts.

(m) *Records.* Handlers shall keep and shall make available to the market agent such records of receipts, sales, deliveries, and production as the market agent shall require for the purpose of obtaining information which the Director may require for the establishment of quotas as prescribed in (b) of FDO 79.

(n) *Distribution schedules.* The distribution schedules, if any, to be followed by the handlers in making deliveries shall be made effective in the terms of approval by the Director of such schedules.

(o) *Expense of administration.* Each handler shall pay to the market agent, within 20 days after the close of each calendar month an assessment of $0.01 per hundredweight of each of milk, cream, skim milk, buttermilk, flavored milk drinks, beverages containing more than 85 percent of skim milk, and skim milk equivalent of cottage, pot, or baker's cheese delivered during the preceding quota period and subject to quota regulations under the provisions hereof.

(p) *Violations.* The market agent shall report all violations to the Director together with the information required for the prosecution of such violations, except in a case where a handler has made deliveries in a quota period in excess of a quota in an amount not to exceed 5 percent of such quota, and in the succeeding quota period makes deliveries below that quota by at least the same percent.

(q) *Bureau of the Budget approval.* The record keeping and reporting requirements of this order have been approved by the Bureau of the Budget in accordance with the Federal Reports Act of 1942. Subsequent record keeping or reporting requirements will be subject to the approval of the Bureau of the Budget pursuant to the Federal Reports Act of 1942.

(r) This order shall take effect at 12:01 a. m., e. w. t., November 1, 1943.

Issued this 14th day of October 1943.

ROY F. HENDRICKSON,
Director of Food Distribution.

Press Release, Immediate:
Friday, October 15, 1943.

The War Food Administration announced today that three new metropolitan sales areas will be placed under the Food Distribution Administration's fluid milk conservation and control program, effective November 1, 1943.

The new market areas and market agents with addresses are:

Grand Rapids, Mich., M. E. Drake, 116 S. Williams St., South Bend 24, Ind.

Indianapolis, Ind., W. A. Wilson, 446 Illinois Bldg., Indianapolis, Ind.

Des Moines, Iowa, Wayne McPherren, 418 Post Office Bldg., Omaha, Nebr.

Under the provisions of this program, dealers' monthly fluid milk sales may not exceed their June deliveries and their sales of cream and of fluid milk byproducts (such as cottage cheese, chocolate milk and buttermilk), will be reduced to three-fourths of the quantities sold in June. Milk dealers include all persons or firms engaged in the sale or transfer of milk, but not such as retail stores, hotels and restaurants.

Consumers, within the limits of local supplies, will be able to purchase as much milk under this program as they have been buying, which is considerably more than they purchased in pre-war years.

Sales quotas on cream and fluid milk byproducts have been set below June deliveries to boost fluid milk supplies where milk production is low and to conserve milk for manufacturing purposes.

Deliveries to the Armed Forces, to plants processing dairy products, and other handlers (except special classes of handlers such as peddlers), are exempt from quotas.

7337
Cop. 2

FDO 79-46
AMDT. 1
OCTOBER 28, 1943

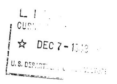

WAR FOOD ADMINISTRATION

[FDO 79-46, Amdt. 1]

PART 1401—DAIRY PRODUCTS

GRAND RAPIDS, MICH., METROPOLITAN MILK SALES AREA

Pursuant to the authority vested in the Director by Food Distribution Order No. 79, dated September 7, 1943 (8 F.R. 12426), as amended, and to effectuate the purposes thereof, Director Food Distribution Order No. 79-46, § 1401.80, relative to the conservation of fluid milk in the Grand Rapids, Michigan, Metropolitan milk sales area (8 F.R. 14067), issued by the Director of Food Distribution on October 14, 1943, is amended as follows:

The milk sales area described in § 1401.80 (b) of the original order is modified in the following particulars:

Add the townships of "Alpine" and "Plainfield" in Kent County, Michigan.

Effective date. This amendment of FDO No. 79-46 shall become effective at 12:01 a. m. e. w. t., November 1, 1943.

(E.O. 9280, 8 F.R. 10179; E.O. 9322, 8 F.R. 3807; E.O. 9334, 8 F.R. 5423; FDO 79, 8 F.R. 12426, 13283)

Issued this 28th day of October 1943.

ROY F. HENDRICKSON,
Director of Food Distribution.

WAR FOOD ADMINISTRATION

[FDO 79-47]

PART 1401—DAIRY PRODUCTS

FLUID MILK AND CREAM IN INDIANAPOLIS, IND., METROPOLITAN SALES AREA

Pursuant to the authority vested in me by Food Distribution Order No. 79 (8 F.R. 12426), issued on September 7, 1943, as amended, and to effectuate the purposes of such order, it is hereby ordered as follows:

§ 1401.79 *Quota restrictions*—(a) *Definitions.* When used in this order, unless otherwise distinctly expressed or manifestly incompatible with the intent hereof:

(1) Each term defined in Food Distribution Order No. 79, as amended, shall, when used herein, have the same meaning as is set forth for such term in Food Distribution Order No. 79, as amended.

(2) The term "FDO 79" means Food Distribution Order No. 79, issued on September 7, 1943, as amended.

(3) The term "sub-handler" means any handler, such as a peddler, vendor, sub-dealer, or secondary dealer, who purchases in a previously packaged and processed form milk, milk byproducts, or cream for delivery.

(b) *Milk sales area.* The following area is hereby designated as a "milk sales area" to be known as the Indianapolis, Indiana, metropolitan sales area, and is referred to hereinafter as the "sales area":

The city of Indianapolis and the townships of Center, Warren, Lawrence, Washington, Wayne, Decatur, Perry and that part of Franklin township comprising part of the city of Beech Grove, all in Marion County, Indiana.

(c) *Base period.* The calendar month of June 1943 is hereby designated as the base period for the sales area.

(d) *Quota period.* The remainder of the calendar month in which the provisions hereof become effective and each subsequent calendar month, respectively, is hereby designated as a quota period for the sales area.

(e) *Handler quotas.* Quotas for each handler in the sales area in each quota period shall be calculated in terms of pounds of each of the items for which percentages are specified in (3) below and shall be determined as follows:

(1) Divide the total deliveries of each such item made in the sales area by such handler during the base period, after excluding the quota-exempt deliveries described in (i) hereof, by the number of days in the base period;

(2) Multiply the result of the foregoing calculation by the number of days in the quota period;

(3) Multiply the aforesaid resulting amount by the following applicable percentage: (i) Milk: 100 percent; (ii) Butterfat in milk: ___ percent; (iii) Cream: 75 percent; (iv) Butterfat in cream: 75 percent; (v) Milk byproducts other than cottage, pot, or baker's cheese: 75 percent; and (vi) Cottage, pot, or baker's cheese: 75 percent of skim milk equivalent. (For the purpose of this order, one pound of cottage, pot, or baker's cheese shall be considered as the equivalent of 7 pounds of skim milk.)

(f) *Quota limitations.* No handler shall, during any quota period, make deliveries in the sales area in excess of his respective quotas, except as set out in (i) hereof: *Provided,* That a handler may, after application to and approval by the market agent, secure an increase in milk quotas through an equivalent reduction as determined by the market agent, in cream and milk byproducts quotas, and an increase in milk byproducts quota through an equivalent reduction as determined by the market agent, in cream quotas.

(g) *Quotas for handlers who are also producers.* Quotas for handlers who are also producers and who purchase no milk shall be 100 percent of the total production of such handlers in the base period.

(h) *Handler exemptions.* Quotas shall not apply to any handler who delivers in a quota period a daily average of less than 300 units of milk, cream, and milk byproducts. For the purpose of this order, a unit shall be the equivalent in volume of the following: (1) milk, one quart of milk; (2) cream, one-half pint of cream; and (3) milk byproduct, one quart of skim milk, buttermilk, flavored milk drink, or other beverage containing more than 85 percent of skim milk, or one-half pound of cottage, pot, or baker's cheese.

(i) *Quota exclusions and exemptions.* Deliveries of milk, milk byproducts, or cream (1) to other handlers, except for such deliveries to sub-handlers, (2) to plants engaged in the handling or processing of milk, milk byproducts, or cream from which no milk, milk byproducts, or cream is delivered in the sales area, and (3) to the agencies or groups specified in (d) of FDO 79, shall be excluded from the computation of deliveries in the base period and exempt from charges to quotas.

(j) *Transfers and apportionment of quotas.* The market agent is empowered to deduct an amount of base period deliveries to purchasers from the total of deliveries made by a handler or other person in the base period upon the application and a showing of unreasonable hardship by the handler making deliveries to such purchasers on the effective date of this order, and to add the amount of such deliveries to the total base period deliveries of the applicant handler. Denials of transfers or transfers granted by the market agent shall be reviewed by the Director upon application.

(k) *Petition for relief from hardships.* (1) Any person affected by FDO 79 or the provisions hereof who considers that compliance therewith would work an exceptional and unreasonable hardship on him, may file with the market agent a petition addressed to the Director. The petition shall contain the correct name, address and principal place of business of the petitioner, a full statement of the facts upon which the petition is based, and the hardship involved and the nature of the relief desired.

(2) Upon receiving such petition, the market agent shall immediately investigate the representations and facts stated therein.

(3) After investigation, the petition shall be certified to the Director, but prior to certification the market agent may (i) deny the petition, or (ii) grant temporary relief for a total period not to exceed 60 days.

(4) Denials or grants of relief by the market agent shall be reviewed by the Director and may be affirmed, modified, or reversed by the Director.

(l) *Reports.* Each handler shall transmit to the market agent on forms prescribed by the market agent the following reports:

(1) Within 20 days following the effective date of this order, reports which show the information required by the market agent to establish such handlers' quotas;

(2) Within 20 days following the close of each quota period, the information required by the market agent to establish volumes of deliveries of milk, cream, and milk byproducts during the preceding quota period; and

(3) Handlers exempt from quotas pursuant to (h) hereof shall, upon the re-

quest of the market agent, submit the information required by the market agent to establish volumes of deliveries of milk, cream, and milk byproducts.

(m) *Records.* Handlers shall keep and shall make available to the market agent such records of receipts, sales, deliveries, and production as the market agent shall require for the purpose of obtaining information which the Director may require for the establishment of quotas as prescribed in (b) of FDO 79.

(n) *Distribution schedules.* The distribution schedules, if any, to be followed by the handlers in making deliveries shall be made effective in the terms of approval by the Director of such schedules.

(o) *Expense of administration.* Each handler shall pay to the market agent, within 20 days after the close of each calendar month an assessment of $0.01 per hundredweight of each of milk, cream, skim milk, buttermilk, flavored milk drinks, beverages containing more than 85 percent of skim milk, and skim milk equivalent of cottage, pot, or baker's cheese delivered during the preceding quota period and subject to quota regulations under the provisions hereof.

(p) *Violations.* The market agent shall report all violations to the Director together with the information required for the prosecution of such violations, except in a case where a handler has made deliveries in a quota period in excess of a quota in an amount not to exceed 5 percent of such quota, and in the succeeding quota period makes deliveries below that quota by at least the same percent.

(q) *Bureau of the Budget approval.* The record keeping and reporting requirements of this order have been approved by the Bureau of the Budget in accordance with Federal Reports Act of 1942. Subsequent record keeping or reporting requirements will be subject to the approval of the Bureau of the Budget pursuant to the Federal Reports Act of 1942.

(r) This order shall take effect at 12:01 a. m., e. w. t., November 1, 1943.

Issued this 14th day of October 1943.

ROY F. HENDRICKSON,
Director of Food Distribution.

Press Release, Immediate:
Friday, October 15, 1943.

The War Food Administration announced today that three new metropolitan sales areas will be placed under the Food Distribution Administration's fluid milk conservation and control program, effective November 1, 1943.

The new market areas and market agents with addresses are:

Grand Rapids, Mich., M. E. Drake, 116 S. Williams St., South Bend 24, Ind.

Indianapolis, Ind., W. A. Wilson, 446 Illinois Bldg., Indianapolis, Ind.

Des Moines, Iowa, Wayne McPherren, 418 Post Office Bldg., Omaha, Nebr.

Under the provisions of this program, dealers' monthly fluid milk sales may not exceed their June deliveries and their sales of cream and of fluid milk byproducts (such as cottage cheese, chocolate milk and buttermilk), will be reduced to three-fourths of the quantities sold in June. Milk dealers include all persons or firms engaged in the sale or transfer of milk, but not such as retail stores, hotels and restaurants.

Consumers, within the limits of local supplies, will be able to purchase as much milk under this program as they have been buying, which is considerably more than they purchased in pre-war years.

Sales quotas on cream and fluid milk byproducts have been set below June deliveries to boost fluid milk supplies where milk production is low and to conserve milk for manufacturing purposes.

Deliveries to the Armed Forces, to plants processing dairy products, and other handlers (except special classes of handlers such as peddlers), are exempt from quotas.

FDO 79-47

AMDT. 1
FEB. 28, 1944

WAR FOOD ADMINISTRATION

[FDO 79-47, Amdt. 1]

PART 1401—DAIRY PRODUCTS

FLUID MILK AND CREAM IN INDIANAPOLIS, IND., METROPOLITAN SALES AREA

Pursuant to Food Distribution Order No. 79 (8 F.R. 12426), dated September 7, 1943, as amended, and to effectuate the purposes thereof, Food Distribution Order No. 79-47 (8 F.R. 14069), relative to the conservation and distribution of fluid milk in the Indianapolis, Indiana, milk sales area, issued by the Director of Food Distribution on October 14, 1943, is hereby amended by deleting therefrom the provisions of § 1401.79 (i) and inserting, in lieu thereof, the following:

(i) *Quota exclusions and exemptions.* Deliveries of milk, milk byproducts, or cream (1) to other handlers, except for such deliveries to sub-handlers, (2) to plants engaged in the handling or processing of milk, milk byproducts, or cream from which no milk, milk byproducts, or cream is delivered in the sales area, (3) to nursery, elementary, junior high, and high schools, and (4) to the agencies or groups specified in (d) of FDO 79, shall be excluded from the computation of deliveries in the base period and exempt from charges to quotas.

The provisions of this amendment shall become effective at 12:01 a. m., e. w. t., March 1, 1944. With respect to violations of said Food Distribution Order No. 79-47, rights accrued, or liabilities incurred prior to the effective time of this amendment, said Food Distribution Order No. 79-47 shall be deemed to be in full force and effect for the purpose of sustaining any proper suit, action, or other proceeding with respect to any such violation, right or liability.

(E.O. 9280, 7 F.R. 10179; E.O. 9322, 8 F.R. 3807; E.O. 9334, 8 F.R. 5423; E.O. 9392, 8 F.R. 14783; FDO 79, 8 F.R. 12426, 13283)

Issued this 28th day of February 1944.

C. W. KITCHEN,
Acting Director of Food Distribution.

7387
Cl-?

FDO 79-48

OCTOBER 14, 1943

WAR FOOD ADMINISTRATION

[FDO 79-48]

PART 1401—DAIRY PRODUCTS

FLUID MILK AND CREAM IN DES MOINES, IOWA, METROPOLITAN SALES AREA

Pursuant to the authority vested in me by Food Distribution Order No. 79 (8 F.R. 12426), issued on September 7, 1943, as amended, and to effectuate the purposes of such order, it is hereby ordered as follows:

§ 1401.81 *Quota restrictions*—(a) *Definitions.* When used in this order, unless otherwise distinctly expressed or manifestly incompatible with the intent hereof:

(1) Each term defined in Food Distribution Order No. 79, as amended, shall, when used herein, have the same meaning as is set forth for such term in Food Distribution Order No. 79, as amended.

(2) The term "FDO 79" means Food Distribution Order No. 79, issued on September 7, 1943, as amended.

(3) The term "sub-handler" means any handler, such as a peddler, vendor, sub-dealer, or secondary dealer, who purchases in a previously packaged and processed form milk, milk byproducts, or cream for delivery.

(b) *Milk sales area.* The following area is hereby designated as a "milk sales area" to be known as the Des Moines, Iowa, metropolitan sales area, and is referred to hereinafter as the "sales area";

The city of Des Moines and the townships of Allen, Bloomfield, Delaware, Des Moines, Four Mile, Lee, Saylor, Valley, Walnut, Webster and that part of Jefferson township in Grimes town, all in Polk County, Iowa.

(c) *Base period.* The calendar month of June 1943 is hereby designated as the base period for the sales area.

(d) *Quota period.* The remainder of the calendar month in which the provisions hereof become effective and each subsequent calendar month, respectively, is hereby designated as a quota period for the sales area.

(e) *Handler quotas.* Quotas for each handler in the sales area in each quota period shall be calculated in terms of pounds of each of the items for which percentages are specified in (3) below and shall be determined as follows:

(1) Divide the total deliveries of each such item made in the sales area by such handler during the base period, after excluding the quota-exempt deliveries described in (i) hereof, by the number of days in the base period;

(2) Multiply the result of the foregoing calculation by the number of days in the quota period;

(3) Multiply the aforesaid resulting amount by the following applicable percentage: (i) Milk: 100 percent; (ii) Butterfat in milk: ________ percent; (iii) cream: 75 percent; (iv) butterfat in cream: 75 percent; (v) milk byproducts other than cottage, pot or baker's cheese: 75 percent; and (vi) cottage, pot, or baker's cheese: 75 percent of skim milk equivalent. (For the purpose of this order, one pound of cottage, pot, or baker's cheese shall be considered as the equivalent of 7 pounds of skim milk.)

(f) *Quota limitations.* No handler shall, during any quota period, make deliveries in the sales area in excess of his respective quotas, except as set out in (i) hereof: *Provided*, That a handler may, after application to and approval by the market agent, secure an increase in milk quotas through an equivalent reduction as determined by the market agent, in cream and milk byproducts quotas, and an increase in milk byproducts quota through an equivalent reduction as determined by the market agent, in cream quotas.

(g) *Quotas for handlers who are also producers.* Quotas for handlers who are also producers and who purchase no milk shall be 100 percent of the total production of such handlers in the base period.

(h) *Handler exemptions.* Quotas shall not apply to any handler who delivers in a quota period a daily average of less than 200 units of milk, cream, and milk byproducts. For the purpose of this order, a unit shall be the equivalent in volume of the following: (1) milk, one quart of milk; (2) cream, one-half pint of cream; and (3) milk byproduct, one quart of skim milk, buttermilk, flavored milk drink, or other beverage containing more than 85 percent of skim milk; or one-half pound of cottage, pot, or baker's cheese.

(i) *Quota exclusions and exemptions.* Deliveries of milk, milk byproducts, or cream (1) to other handlers, except for such deliveries to sub-handlers, (2) to plants engaged in the handling or processing of milk, milk byproducts, or cream from which no milk, milk byproducts, or cream is delivered in the sales area, and (3) to the agencies or groups specified in (d) of FDO 79, shall be excluded from the computation of deliveries in the base period and exempt from charges to quotas.

(j) *Transfers and apportionment of quotas.* The market agent is empowered to deduct an amount of base period deliveries to purchasers from the total of deliveries made by a handler or other person in the base period upon the application and a showing of unreasonable hardship by the handler making deliveries to such purchasers on the effective date of this order, and to add the amount of such deliveries to the total base period deliveries of the applicant handler. Denials of transfers or transfers granted by the market agent shall be reviewed by the Director upon application.

(k) *Petition for relief from hardships.* (1) Any person affected by FDO 79 or the provisions hereof who considers that compliance therewith would work an exceptional and unreasonable hardship on him, may file with the market agent a petition addressed to the Director. The petition shall contain the correct name, address and principal place of business of the petitioner, a full statement of the facts upon which the petition is based, and the hardship involved and the nature of the relief desired.

(2) Upon receiving such petition, the market agent shall immediately investigate the representations and facts stated therein.

(3) After investigation, the petition shall be certified to the Director, but prior to certification the market agent may (i) deny the petition, or (ii) grant temporary relief for a total period not to exceed 60 days.

(4) Denials or grants of relief by the market agent shall be reviewed by the Director and may be affirmed, modified, or reversed by the Director.

(l) *Reports.* Each handler shall transmit to the market agent on forms prescribed by the market agent the following reports:

(1) Within 20 days following the effective date of this order, reports which show the information required by the market agent to establish such handlers' quotas;

(2) Within 20 days following the close of each quota period, the information required by the market agent to establish volumes of deliveries of milk, cream, and milk byproducts during the preceding quota period; and

(3) Handlers exempt from quotas pursuant to (h) hereof shall, upon the request of the market agent, submit the information required by the market agent to establish volumes of deliveries of milk, cream, and milk byproducts.

(m) *Records.* Handlers shall keep and shall make available to the market agent such records of receipts, sales, deliveries, and production as the market agent shall require for the purpose of obtaining information which the Director may require for the establishment of quotas as prescribed in (b) of FDO 79.

(n) *Distribution schedules.* The distribution schedules, if any, to be followed by the handlers in making deliveries shall be made effective in the terms of approval by the Director of such schedules.

(o) *Expense of administration.* Each handler shall pay to the market agent, within 20 days after the close of each calendar month an assessment of $0.01 per hundredweight of each of milk, cream, skim milk, buttermilk, flavored milk drinks, beverages containing more than 85 percent of skim milk, and skim milk equivalent of cottage, pot, or baker's cheese delivered during the preceding quota period and subject to quota regulations under the provisions hereof.

(p) *Violations.* The market agent shall report all violations to the Director together with the information required for the prosecution of such violations, except in a case where a handler has made deliveries in a quota period in excess of a quota in an amount not to exceed 5 percent of such quota, and in the succeeding quota period makes deliveries below that quota by at least the same percent.

(q) *Bureau of the Budget approval.* The record keeping and reporting requirements of this order have been approved by the Bureau of the Budget in accordance with the Federal Reports Act of 1942. Subsequent record keeping or reporting requirements will be subject to the approval of the Bureau of the Budget pursuant to the Federal Reports Act of 1942.

(r) This order shall take effect at 12:01 a. m., c. w. t., November 1, 1943.

Issued this 14th day of October 1943.

ROY F. HENDRICKSON,
Director of Food Distribution.

Press Release, Immediate:
Friday, October 15, 1943.

The War Food Administration announced today that three new metropolitan sales areas will be placed under the Food Distribution Administration's fluid milk conservation and control program, effective November 1, 1943.

The new market areas and market agents with addresses are:

Grand Rapids, Mich., M. E. Drake, 116 S. Williams St., South Bend 24, Ind.

Indianapolis, Ind., W. A. Wilson, 446 Illinois Bldg., Indianapolis, Ind.

Des Moines, Iowa, Wayne McPherren, 418 Post Office Bldg., Omaha, Nebr.

Under the provisions of this program, dealers' monthly fluid milk sales may not exceed their June deliveries and their sales of cream and of fluid milk byproducts (such as cottage cheese, chocolate milk and buttermilk), will be reduced to three-fourths of the quantities sold in June. Milk dealers include all persons or firms engaged in the sale or transfer of milk, but not such as retail stores, hotels and restaurants.

Consumers, within the limits of local supplies, will be able to purchase as much milk under this program as they have been buying, which is considerably more than they purchased in pre-war years.

Sales quotas on cream and fluid milk byproducts have been set below June deliveries to boost fluid milk supplies where milk production is low and to conserve milk for manufacturing purposes.

Deliveries to the Armed Forces, to plants processing dairy products, and other handlers, (except special classes of handlers such as peddlers), are exempt from quotas.

FDO 79-48
AMDT. 1
NOV. 3, 1943

WAR FOOD ADMINISTRATION

[FDO 79-48, Amdt. 1]

PART 1401—DAIRY PRODUCTS

FLUID MILK AND CREAM IN DES MOINES, IOWA, METROPOLITAN MILK SALES AREA

Pursuant to the authority vested in the Director by Food Distribution Order No. 79, dated September 7, 1943 (8 F.R. 12426), as amended, and to effectuate the purposes thereof, Director Food Distribution Order No. 79-48, § 1401.81, relative to the conservation of fluid milk in the Des Moines, Iowa, metropolitan milk sales area (8 F.R. 14070), issued by the Director of Food Distribution on October 14, 1943, is amended as follows:

The milk sales area described in § 1401.81 (b) of the original order is modified in the following particulars: Add Crocker township in Polk County, Iowa.

Effective date. This amendment of FDO No. 79-48, shall become effective at 12:01 a. m., e. w. t., November 5, 1943.

(E.O. 9280, 8 F.R. 10179; E.O. 9322, 8 F.R. 3807; E.O. 9334, 8 F.R. 5423; FDO 79, 8 F.R. 12426, 13283)

Issued this 3d day of November 1943.

ROY F. HENDRICKSON,
Director of Food Distribution.

77337
Cop. 1

FDO 79-49

OCTOBER 15, 1943

WAR FOOD ADMINISTRATION

[FDO 79-49]

PART 1401—DAIRY PRODUCTS

FLUID MILK AND CREAM IN SYRACUSE, N. Y., SALES AREA

Pursuant to authority vested in me by Food Distribution Order No. 79 (8 F.R. 12426), issued September 7, 1943, as amended, and to effectuate the purposes of such order, it is hereby ordered, as follows:

§ 1401.92 *Quota restrictions*—(a) *Definitions.* When used in this order, unless otherwise distinctly expressed or manifestly incompatible with the intent hereof:

(1) Each term defined in Food Distribution Order No. 79, as amended, shall, when used herein, have the same meaning as is set forth for such term in Food Distribution Order No. 79, as amended.

(2) The term "FDO 79" means Food Distribution Order No. 79, issued on September 7, 1943, as amended.

(3) The term "skim milk beverage" means skim milk, buttermilk, chocolate drink, or any other beverage containing more than 85 percent skim milk and less than 3 percent butterfat.

(4) The term "regulated" when used in conjunction with the terms "milk", "cream", "skim milk beverage", "cottage, pot, or baker's cheese", or "product" means milk, cream, skim milk beverage, cottage, pot, or bakers cheese, or product, delivered to retail purchasers, to stores, to public eating places, to other wholesale purchasers, and to sub-handlers for whom no bases and quotas have been established.

(5) The term "retail purchaser" means any person who purchases milk, milk byproducts, or cream at retail for personal, family, or household consumption.

(6) The term "store" means a merchandising establishment of fixed situs, the operator of which purchases milk and other food products for resale primarily for consumption off the premises.

(7) The term "public eating place" means any place in which food, prepared and ready for sale or consumption either on or off the premises where sold, is served, sold, or offered for sale; and such term includes, but is not necessarily limited to, any hotel, club, restaurant, cafe, cafeteria, caterer, inn, railroad diner, lunch room, sandwich stand, or drug store which serves, sells, or offers food for sale, as aforesaid. Any institution of voluntary or involuntary confinement, such as a hospital, sanitarium (or sanitorium), asylum, penal institution, or school, is not a "public eating place."

(8) The term "wholesale purchaser" means any person who purchases milk, milk byproducts, or cream, for purposes of resale, or use in other than personal, family or household consumption, except (i) other handlers, (ii) purchasers engaged in the processing of milk, milk byproducts, or cream who do not distribute milk, milk byproducts, or cream, in the sales area, (iii) those purchasers specifically exempt from quota restrictions by FDO 79, and (iv) nursery, elementary, junior high and high schools.

9. The term "producer-handler" means a handler who delivers milk produced only by his own herd and in a total quantity of less than 200 quarts per day.

(10) The term "sub-handler" means a handler, such as a peddler, or sub-dealer, who purchases milk in the same package in which it is delivered to purchasers: *Provided,* That a handler who handles more than 1,000 quarts of milk per day, or more than 500 quarts of cream per day, shall not be deemed a subhandler.

(11) The term "product" means milk, cream, skim milk beverage, or cottage, pot or baker's cheese.

(12) The term "b. f." used in conjunction with the title of the conversion table in (o) hereof means butter fat.

(b) *Milk sales area.* The following area is hereby designated as a milk sales area to be known as the Syracuse, New York, sales area, and is referred to hereinafter as the "sales area": The territory included within the boundaries of the following cities and towns:

The city of Syracuse and the towns of Camillus, Onondaga, DeWitt, Manlius, Salina, and Geddes in Onondaga County, New York.

(c) *Bases and base period.* The handler's daily average delivery of each regulated product in the base period adjusted for transfers in accordance with (h) hereof shall be his base. The base for milk and skim milk beverages shall be computed in terms of quarts, for cream, in terms of milk equivalent in accordance with the conversion table set forth in (o) hereof, and for cottage, pot, or baker's cheese in terms of pounds of product. The calendar month of June 1943, is hereby designated as the base period for the sales area.

(d) *Quota periods.* The remainder of the calendar month in which this order becomes effective and each subsequent calendar month is hereby designated as a quota period for the sales area.

(e) *Handler quotas.* No handler shall deliver during any quota period a quantity of any regulated product in excess of his base for that product, multiplied by the number of days in the quota period and by the following applicable percentages: (1) milk: 100 percent; (2) milk equivalent of cream: 75 percent; (3) skim milk beverages: 75 percent; (4) cottage, pot or baker's cheese: 75 percent: *Provided,* That a handler may, upon application to and approval by the market agent, secure an increase in milk quota through an equivalent reduction in cream and [illegible] byproduct quotas.

(f) *Producer-handler quotas.* Each producer-handler's quota shall be 100 percent of milk produced.

(g) *Sub-handler quotas.* No bases or quotas shall be established for deliveries by sub-handlers except as provided in (h) hereof.

(h) *Transfer and apportionment of bases and quotas.* The market agent is empowered to transfer bases upon application by a handler making the deliveries from which such bases were derived on the effective date of this order and upon a showing of unreasonable hardship by the applicant. Upon application by a sub-handler, the market agent is empowered to transfer from a handler to such sub-handler that part of the handler's base and quota derived from delivery in the base period by such handler to such sub-handler.

Denials or grants of transfers by the market agent shall be reviewed by the Director upon application.

(i) The distribution schedules, if any, to be followed by the handlers in making deliveries shall be made effective in the terms of approval by the Director of such schedules.

(j) *Petition for relief from hardship.* Any person considering that compliance with FDO 79, or any instrument issued thereunder, would work an exceptional and unreasonable hardship on him, may file with the market agent a petition addressed to the Director. The petition shall contain the correct name address and principal place of business of the petitioner, a full statement of the facts upon which the petition is based, and the hardship involved and the nature of the relief desired.

Upon receiving such petition, the market agent shall immediately investigate the representations and facts stated therein.

(j-1) *Relief.* After investigation, the market agent shall certify the petition to the Director, but prior to certification the market agent may: (1) deny the petition; or (2) grant temporary relief for a total period not to exceed 60 days.

Denials or grants of relief by the market agent shall be reviewed by the Director, and may be affirmed, modified or reversed by him.

(k) *Reports.* Each handler shall transmit to the market agent on forms prescribed by the market agent the following reports:

(1) Within 20 days following the effective date of this order, reports which show the information required by the market agent to establish such handlers' bases;

(2) Within 20 days following the close of each quota period, the information required by the market agent to establish volumes of deliveries of milk, cream, and milk byproducts during the preceding quota period; and

(3) Handlers whose deliveries are exempt from quotas shall, upon request of the market agent, submit the information required by the market agent to establish volumes of deliveries of milk, cream, and milk byproducts.

(l) *Records.* Handlers shall keep and shall make available to the market agent such records of receipts, sales, deliveries, and production as the market agent shall request for the purpose of obtaining information which the Director may require for the establishment of quotas as prescribed in (b) of FDO 79 and which is necessary to verify compliance with the provisions of this order.

(m) *Expense of administration.* Each handler except producer-handlers and sub-handlers having no bases and quotas shall pay to the market agent at the time of filing the reports required under (k) (2), an assessment of 2 cents per 100 quarts of regulated milk or milk equivalent of cream delivered during the quota period. Whenever verification by the market agent of information supplied by a handler discloses errors in assessment payment to the market agent, he shall bill the handler for any unpaid amount, and the handler shall, within 5 days, make payment to the market agent of the amount so billed. Whenever verification discloses that the handler made an overpayment, the market agent shall, within 5 days, return such overpayment to such handler.

(n) *Liquidation.* Upon the termination or suspension hereof, the market agent shall, if so directed by the Director, liquidate the business of the market agent's office and dispose of all funds and property then in his possession or under his control, together with claims receivable, unpaid and owing at the time of such temination or suspension. Any funds over and above the amounts necessary to meet outstanding obligations and the expenses necessarily incurred by the market agent in liquidating the business of the market agent's office shall be distributed by the market agent in accordance with instructions issued by the Director.

(o) *Conversion table.*

[Quarts of 3.5 percent b. f. milk equivalent of a qu
of cream at various butterfat tests]

Cream (percent b. f.)	Milk equivalent (quarts)	Cream (percent b. f.)	Milk equ alent (quarts
6	1.71	31	8.
7	2.00	32	8.
8	2.28	33	9.
9	2.56	34	9.
10	2.85	35	9.
11	3.13	36	10.
12	3.41	37	10.
13	3.69	38	10.
14	3.98	39	10.
15	4.26	40	11.
16	4.54	41	11.
17	4.82	42	11.
18	5.10	43	11.
19	5.38	44	12.
20	5.65	45	12
21	5.93	46	12
22	6.21	47	13.
23	6.49	48	13.
24	6.76	49	13.
25	7.04	50	13.
26	7.31	51	14.
27	7.58	52	14.
28	7.85	53	14.
29	8.13	54	14
30	8.40	55	15.

(p) *Bureau of the Budget approv* The record-keeping and reporting r quirements of this order have been a proved by the Bureau of the Budget accordance with the Federal Reports A of 1942. Subsequent record-keeping reporting requirements will be subject the approval of the Bureau of the Budg pursuant to the Federal Reports Act 1942.

(q) *Violations.* The market agent sha report all violations to the Director t gether with the information required f the prosecution of such violations, e cept in a case where a handler has ma deliveries in a quota period in excess a quota in an amount not to exceed percent of such quota, and in the su ceeding quota period makes deliveri below that quota by at least the sa percent.

(r) *Effective date.* This order shall b come effective at 12:01 a. m., e. w. t., N vember 1, 1943.

Issued this 15th day of October 1943.

C. W. KITCHEN,
Acting Director of Food Distribution.

Press Release, Immediate:
Saturday, October 16, 1943.

The War Food Administration announced today that milk sales in six New York areas will be regulated, beginning November 1, under the Food Distribution Administration's fluid milk conservation and control program.

The new milk sales areas, for which C. J. Blanford, 205 E. 42nd St., New York City, will be market agent, are: Niagara Frontier, Utica-Rome, Rochester, Syracuse, Binghamton, Albany-Schenectady-Troy.

Under the program, milk dealers will be permitted to sell as much fluid milk as they sold in June and three-fourths as much cream and milk byproducts (such as cottage cheese, chocolate milk, and buttermilk) as they sold in June. Milk dealers include all persons or firms engaged in the sale or transfer of milk, but not such distributors as subhandlers ("peddlers") who deliver less than 1,000 quarts of milk or 500 quarts of cream a day, retail stores, hotels, or restaurants.

To permit flexible adjustment to local production and consumption conditions, dealers will be allowed to exceed these base quotas by not more than 5 percent during any month, providing they decrease their deliveries the next month by the same amount.

A dealer may increase his milk sales also by reducing his cream and milk byproducts sales, providing such an adjustment is approved by the market agent for the area.

Producer-distributors, defined for these 6 areas as those who purchase no milk and sell less than 200 quarts a day, may sell as much milk as their herds produce.

Deliveries of milk, cream, and milk byproducts to nursery, elementary, junior high and high schools; to plants processing milk who do not distribute milk, cream, or other milk products in the sal area; to the Armed Forces, and to oth milk handlers are quota-exempt.

Consumers in the milk sales are named today and in others already de ignated generally will be able to purcha as much milk under the milk conserv tion program as they have been buyi in recent months—within the limits local supplies.

Fluid milk sales are being stabilize Food Distribution Administration offici said, to help assure sufficient milk f manufacturing the cheese, butter, eva orated milk, and milk powder requir by the Armed Services and civilians f good nutrition and properly balanc diets. Sales quotas on cream and fluid milk byproducts have been set b low June deliveries to boost fluid m supplies where production is low, and conserve milk for manufacturing p poses.

1337
Cop.1

FDO 79-49

AMDT. 1
NOV. 22, 1943

WAR FOOD ADMINISTRATION

[FDO 79-49, Amdt. 1]

PART 1401—DAIRY PRODUCTS

FLUID MILK AND CREAM, SYRACUSE, N. Y., SALES AREA

Pursuant to the authority vested in the Director by Food Distribution Order No. 79, dated September 7, 1943 (8 F.R. 12426), as amended, and to effectuate the purposes thereof, Director Food Distribution Order No. 79-49, § 1401.92, relative to the conservation of fluid milk in the Syracuse, New York, milk sales area (8 F.R. 14183), issued by the Director of Food Distribution on October 15, 1943, is amended as follows:

The milk sales area described in § 1401.92 (b) of the original order is modified in the following particulars: Add the towns of Cicero, Clay, and Marcellus, in Onandaga County, New York.

Effective date. This amendment of FDO No. 79-49 shall become effective at 12:01 a. m., e. w. t., December 1, 1943.

(E.O. 9280, 8 F.R. 10179; E.O. 9322, 8 F.R. 3807; E.O. 9334, 8 F.R. 5423; E.O. 9392, 8 F.R. 14783; F.D.O. 79, 8 F.R. 12426, 13283)

Issued this 22d day of November 1943.

ROY F. HENDRICKSON,
Director of Food Distribution.

FDO 79-50

OCTOBER 15, 1943

WAR FOOD ADMINISTRATION

[FDO 79-50]

PART 1401—DAIRY PRODUCTS

FLUID MILK AND CREAM IN UTICA-ROME, N. Y. SALES AREA

Pursuant to authority vested in me by Food Distribution Order No. 79 (8 F.R. 12426), issued September 7, 1943, as amended, and to effectuate the purposes of such order, it is hereby ordered as follows:

§ 1401.91 *Quota restrictions*—(a) *Definitions.* When used in this order, unless otherwise distinctly expressed or manifestly incompatible with the intent hereof:

(1) Each term defined in Food Distribution Order No. 79, as amended, shall, when used herein, have the same meaning as is set forth for such term in Food Distribution Order No. 79, as amended.

(2) The term "FDO 79" means Food Distribution Order No. 79, issued on September 7, 1943, as amended.

(3) The term "skim milk beverage" means skim milk, buttermilk, chocolate drink, or any other beverage containing more than 85 percent skim milk and less than 3 percent butterfat.

(4) The term "regulated" when used in conjunction with the terms "milk", "cream", "skim milk beverage", "cottage, pot, or baker's cheese", or "product" means milk, cream, skim milk beverage, cottage, pot, or baker's cheese, or product, delivered to retail purchasers, to stores, to public eating places, to other wholesale purchasers, and to sub-handlers for whom no bases and quotas have been established.

(5) The term "retail purchaser" means any person who purchases milk, milk byproducts, or cream at retail for personal, family, or household consumption.

(6) The term "store" means a merchandising establishment of fixed situs, the operator of which purchases milk and other food products for resale primarily for consumption off the premises.

(7) The term "public eating place" means any place in which food, prepared and ready for sale or consumption either on or off the premises where sold, is served, sold, or offered for sale; and such term includes, but is not necessarily limited to, any hotel, club, restaurant, cafe, cafeteria, caterer, inn, railroad diner, lunch room, sandwich stand, or drug store which serves, sells, or offers food for sale, as aforesaid. Any institution of voluntary or involuntary confinement, such as a hospital, sanitarium, (or sanitorium), asylum, penal institution, or school, is not a "public eating place".

(8) The term "wholesale purchaser" means any person who purchases milk, milk byproducts, or cream, for purposes of resale, or use in other than personal, family or household consumption, except (i) other handlers, (ii) purchasers engaged in the processing of milk, milk byproducts, or cream who do not distribute milk, milk byproducts, or cream, in the sales area, (iii) those purchasers specifically exempt from quota restrictions by FDO 79, and (iv) nursery, elementary, junior high and high schools.

(9) The term "producer-handler" means a handler who delivers milk produced only by his own herd and in a total quantity of less than 200 quarts per day.

(10) The term "sub-handler" means a handler, such as a peddler, or sub-dealer, who purchases milk in the same package in which it is delivered to purchaser; *Provided*, That a handler who handles more than 1,000 quarts of milk per day, or more than 500 quarts of cream per day, shall not be deemed a sub-handler.

(11) The term "product" means milk, cream, skim milk beverage, or cottage, pot or baker's cheese.

(12) The term "b. f." used in conjunction with the title of the conversion table in (o) hereof means butter fat.

(b) *Milk sales area.* The following area is hereby designated as a milk sales area to be known as the Utica-Rome, New York, sales area, and is referred to hereinafter as the "sales area": The territory included within the boundaries of the following cities and towns:

The cities of Rome and Utica, and the towns of Deerfield, Kirkland, Marcy, New Hartford, and Whitestown in Oneida County, New York; and the towns of Frankfort, German Flatts, Herkimer, and Schuyler in Herkimer County, New York.

(c) *Bases and base period.* The handler's daily average delivery of each regulated product in the base period adjusted for transfers in accordance with (h) hereof shall be his base. The base for milk and skim milk beverages shall be computed in terms of quarts, for cream, in terms of milk equivalent in accordance with the conversion table set forth in (o) hereof, and for cottage, pot, or baker's cheese in terms of pounds of product. The calendar month of June 1943, is hereby designated as the base period for the sales area.

(d) *Quota periods.* The remainder of the calendar month in which this order becomes effective and each subsequent calendar month is hereby designated as a quota period for the sales area.

(e) *Handler quotas.* No handler shall deliver during any quota period a quantity of any regulated product in excess of his base for that product, multiplied by the number of days in the quota period and by the following applicable percentages: (1) milk: 100 percent; (2) milk equivalent of cream: 75 percent; (3) skim milk beverages: 75 percent; (4) cottage, pot or baker's cheese: 75 percent; *Provided*, That a handler may, upon application to and approval by the market agent, secure an increase in milk quota through an equivalent reduction in cream and milk byproduct quotas.

(f) *Producer-handler quotas.* Each producer-handler's quota shall be 100 percent of milk produced.

(g) *Sub-handler quotas.* No bases or quotas shall be established for deliveries by sub-handlers except as provided in (h) hereof.

(h) *Transfer and apportionment of bases and quotas.* The market agent is empowered to transfer bases upon application by a handler making the deliveries from which such bases were derived on the effective date of this order and upon a showing of unreasonable hardship by the applicant. Upon application by a sub-handler, the market agent is empowered to transfer from a handler to such sub-handler that part of the handler's base and quota derived from delivery in the base period by such handler to such sub-handler.

Denials or grants of transfers by the market agent shall be reviewed by the Director upon application.

(i) The distribution schedules, if any, to be followed by the handlers in making deliveries shall be made effective in the terms of approval by the Director of such schedules.

(j) *Petition for relief from hardship.* Any person considering that compliance with FDO 79, or any instrument issued thereunder, would work an exceptional and unreasonable hardship on him, may file with the market agent a petition addressed to the Director. The petition shall contain the correct name, address and principal place of business of the petitioner, a full statement of the facts upon which the petition is based, and the hardship involved and the nature of the relief desired.

Upon receiving such petition, the market agent shall immediately investigate the representations and facts stated therein.

(j-1) *Relief.* After investigation, the market agent shall certify the petition to the Director, but prior to certification the market agent may: (1) deny the petition; or (2) grant temporary relief for a total period not to exceed 60 days.

Denials or grants of relief by the market agent shall be reviewed by the Director, and may be affirmed, modified or reversed by him.

(k) *Reports.* Each handler shall transmit to the market agent on forms prescribed by the market agent the following reports:

(1) Within 20 days following the effective date of this order, reports which show the information required by the market agent to establish such handlers' bases;

(2) Within 20 days following the close of each quota period, the information required by the market agent to establish volumes of deliveries of milk, cream, and milk byproducts during the preceding quota period; and

(3) Handlers whose deliveries are exempt from quotas shall, upon request of the market agent, submit the information required by the market agent to establish volumes of deliveries of milk, cream, and milk byproducts.

(l) *Records.* Handlers shall keep and shall make available to the market agent such records of receipts, sales, deliveries, and production as the market agent shall request for the purpose of obtaining information which the Director may require for the establishment of quotas as prescribed in (b) of FDO 79 and which is necessary to verify compliance with the provisions of this order.

(m) *Expense of administration.* Each handler except producer-handlers and sub-handlers having no bases and quotas shall pay to the market agent at the time of filing the reports required under (k) (2), an assessment of 2 cents per 100 quarts of regulated milk or milk equivalent of cream delivered during the quota period. Whenever verification by the market agent of information supplied by a handler discloses errors in assessment payment to the market agent, he shall bill the handler for any unpaid amount, and the handler shall, within 5 days, make payment to the market agent of the amount so billed. Whenever verification discloses that the handler made an overpayment, the market agent shall, within 5 days, return such overpayment to such handler.

(n) *Liquidation.* Upon the termination or suspension hereof, the market agent shall, if so directed by the Director, liquidate the business of the market agent's office and dispose of all funds and property then in his possession or under his control, together with claims receivable, unpaid and owing at the time of such termination or suspension. Any funds over and above the amounts necessary to meet outstanding obligations and the expenses necessarily incurred by the market agent in liquidating the business of the market agent's office shall be distributed by the market agent in accordance with instructions issued by the Director.

(o) *Conversion table.*

[Quarts of 3.5 percent b. f. milk equivalent of a quart of cream at various butterfat tests]

Cream (percent b. f.)	Milk equivalent (quarts)	Cream (percent b. f.)	Milk equivalent (quarts)
6	1.71	31	8.67
7	2.00	32	8.95
8	2.28	33	9.22
9	2.56	34	9.50
10	2.85	35	9.77
11	3.13	36	10.04
12	3.41	37	10.31
13	3.69	38	10.58
14	3.98	39	10.85
15	4.26	40	11.12
16	4.54	41	11.39
17	4.82	42	11.66
18	5.10	43	11.93
19	5.38	44	12.20
20	5.65	45	12.47
21	5.93	46	12.74
22	6.21	47	13.00
23	6.49	48	13.27
24	6.76	49	13.54
25	7.04	50	13.80
26	7.31	51	14.07
27	7.58	52	14.34
28	7.85	53	14.60
29	8.13	54	14.86
30	8.40	55	15.13

(p) *Bureau of the Budget approval.* The record-keeping and reporting requirements of this order have been approved by the Bureau of the Budget in accordance with the Federal Reports Act of 1942. Subsequent record-keeping or reporting requirements will be subject to the approval of the Bureau of the Budget pursuant to the Federal Reports Act of 1942.

(q) *Violations.* The market agent shall report all violations to the Director together with the information required for the prosecution of such violations except in a case where a handler has made deliveries in a quota period in excess of a quota in an amount not to exceed 5 percent of such quota, and in the succeeding quota period makes deliveries below that quota by at least the same percent.

(r) *Effective date.* This order shall become effective at 12:01 a. m., e. w. t., November 1, 1943.

Issued this 15th day of October 1943.

C. W. KITCHEN,
Acting Director of Food Distribution.

Press Release, Immediate:
Saturday, October 16, 1943.

The War Food Administration announced today that milk sales in six New York areas will be regulated, beginning November 1, under the Food Distribution Administration's fluid milk conservation and control program.

The new milk sales areas, for which C. J. Blanford, 205 E. 42nd St., New York City, will be market agent, are: Niagara Frontier, Utica-Rome, Rochester, Syracuse, Binghamton, Albany-Schenectady-Troy.

Under the program, milk dealers will be permitted to sell as much fluid milk as they sold in June and three-fourths as much cream and milk byproducts (such as cottage cheese, chocolate milk, and buttermilk) as they sold in June. Milk dealers include all persons or firms engaged in the sale or transfer of milk, but not such distributors as subhandlers ("peddlers") who deliver less than 1,000 quarts of milk or 500 quarts of cream a day, retail stores, hotels, or restaurants.

To permit flexible adjustment to local production and consumption conditions, dealers will be allowed to exceed these base quotas by not more than 5 percent during any month, providing they decrease their deliveries the next month by the same amount.

A dealer may increase his milk sales also by reducing his cream and milk byproducts sales, providing such an adjustment is approved by the market agent for the area.

Producer-distributors, defined for these 6 areas as those who purchase no milk and sell less than 200 quarts a day, may sell as much milk as their herds produce.

Deliveries of milk, cream, and milk byproducts to nursery, elementary, junior high and high schools; to plants processing milk who do not distribute milk, cream, or other milk products in the sales area; to the Armed Forces, and to other milk handlers are quota-exempt.

Consumers in the milk sales areas named today and in others already designated generally will be able to purchase as much milk under the milk conservation program as they have been buying in recent months—within the limits of local supplies.

Fluid milk sales are being stabilized, Food Distribution Administration officials said, to help assure sufficient milk for manufacturing the cheese, butter, evaporated milk, and milk powder required by the Armed Services and civilians for good nutrition and properly balanced diets. Sales quotas on cream and on fluid milk byproducts have been set below June deliveries to boost fluid milk supplies where production is low, and to conserve milk for manufacturing purposes.

Reserve

/ 733

FDO 79-51

OCTOBER 15, 1943

WAR FOOD ADMINISTRATION

[FDO 79-51]

PART 1401—DAIRY PRODUCTS

FLUID MILK AND CREAM IN ROCHESTER, N. Y., SALES AREA

Pursuant to authority vested in me by Food Distribution Order No. 79 (8 F.R. 12426), issued September 7, 1943, as amended, and to effectuate the purposes of such order, it is hereby ordered as follows:

§ 1401.94 *Quota restrictions*—(a) *Definitions.* When used in this order, unless otherwise distinctly expressed or manifestly incompatible with the intent hereof:

(1) Each term defined in Food Distribution Order No. 79, as amended, shall, when used herein, have the same meaning as is set forth for such term in Food Distribution Order No. 79, as amended.

(2) The term "FDO 79" means Food Distribution Order No. 79, issued on September 7, 1943, as amended.

(3) The term "skim milk beverage" means skim milk, buttermilk, chocolate drink, or any other beverage containing more than 85 percent skim milk and less than 3 percent butterfat.

(4) The term "regulated" when used in conjunction with the terms "milk", "cream", "skim milk beverage", "cottage pot, or baker's cheese", or "product" means milk, cream, skim milk beverage, cottage, pot, or baker's cheese, or product, delivered to retail purchasers, to stores, to public eating places, to other wholesale purchasers, and to sub-handlers for whom no bases and quotas have been established.

(5) The term "retail purchaser" means any person who purchases milk, milk byproducts, or cream at retail for personal, family, or household consumption.

(6) The term "store" means a merchandising establishment of fixed situs, the operator of which purchases milk and other food products for resale primarily for consumption off the premises.

(7) The term "public eating place" means any place in which food, prepared and ready for sale or consumption either on or off the premises where sold, is served, sold, or offered for sale; and such term includes, but is not necessarily limited to, any hotel, club, restaurant, cafe, cafeteria, caterer, inn, railroad diner, lunch room, sandwich stand, or drug store which serves, sells, or offers food for sale, as aforesaid. Any institution of voluntary or involuntary confinement, such as a hospital, sanitarium, (or sanitorium), asylum, penal institution, or school, is not a "public eating place".

(8) The term "wholesale purchaser" means any person who purchases milk, milk byproducts, or cream, for purposes of resale, or use in other than personal, family or household consumption, except (i) other handlers, (ii) purchasers engaged in the processing of milk, milk byproducts, or cream who do not distribute milk, milk byproducts, or cream, in the sales area, (iii) those purchasers specifically exempt from quota restrictions by FDO 79, and (iv) nursery, elementary, junior high and high schools.

(9) The term "producer-handler" means a handler who delivers milk produced only by his own herd and in a total quantity of less than 200 quarts per day.

(10) The term "sub-handler" means a handler, such as a peddler, or sub-dealer, who purchases milk in the same package in which it is delivered to purchasers: *Provided,* That a handler who handles more than 1,000 quarts of milk per day, or more than 500 quarts of cream per day, shall not be deemed a sub-handler.

(11) The term "product" means milk, cream, skim milk beverage, or cottage, pot or baker's cheese.

(12) The term "b. f." used in conjunction with the title of the conversion table in (o) hereof means butter fat.

(b) *Milk sales area.* The following area is hereby designated as a milk sales area to be known as the Rochester, New York, sales area, and is referred to hereinafter as the 'sales area": The territory included within the boundaries of the following New York cities and towns:

The city of Rochester, and the towns of Pittsford, Perinton, Irondequoit, Penfield, Webster, Greece, Gates, Chili, Brighton, Henrietta, Riga, Ogden, and Parma in Monroe County, New York.

(c) *Bases and base period.* The handler's daily average delivery of each regulated product in the base period adjusted for transfers in accordance with (h) hereof shall be his base. The base for milk and skim milk beverages shall be computed in terms of quarts, for cream, in terms of milk equivalent in accordance with the conversion table set forth in (o) hereof, and for cottage, pot, or baker's cheese in terms of pounds of product. The calendar month of June 1943, is hereby designated as the base period for the sales area.

(d) *Quota periods.* The remainder of the calendar month in which this order becomes effective and each subsequent calendar month is hereby designated as a quota period for the sales area.

(e) *Handler quotas.* No handler shall deliver during any quota period a quantity of any regulated product in excess of his base for that product, multiplied by the number of days in the quota period and by the following applicable percentages: (1) milk: 100 percent; (2) milk equivalent of cream: 75 percent; (3) skim milk beverages: 75 percent; (4) cottage, pot or baker's cheese: 75 percent; *Provided,* That a handler may, upon application to and approval by the market agent, secure an increase in milk quota through an equivalent reduction in cream and milk byproduct quotas.

(f) *Producer-handler quotas.* Each producer-handler's quota shall be 100 percent of milk produced.

(g) *Sub-handler quotas.* No bases or quotas shall be established for deliveries by sub-handlers except as provided in (h) hereof.

(h) *Transfer and apportionment of bases and quotas.* The market agent is empowered to transfer bases upon application by a handler making the deliveries from which such bases were derived on the effective date of this order and upon a showing of unreasonable hardship by the applicant. Upon application by a sub-handler, the market agent is empowered to transfer from a handler to such sub-handler that part of the handler's base and quota derived from delivery in the base period by such handler to such sub-handler.

Denials or grants of transfers by the market agent shall be reviewed by the Director upon application.

(i) The distribution schedules, if any, to be followed by the handlers in making deliveries shall be made effective in the terms of approval by the Director of such schedules.

(j) *Petition for relief from hardship.* Any person considering that compliance with FDO 79, or any instrument issued thereunder, would work an exceptional and unreasonable hardship on him, may file with the market agent a petition addressed to the Director. The petition shall contain the correct name, address and principal place of business of the petitioner, a full statement of the facts upon which the petition is based, and the hardship involved and the nature of the relief desired.

Upon receiving such petition, the market agent shall immediately investigate the representations and facts stated therein.

(j-1) *Relief.* After investigation, the market agent shall certify the petition to the Director, but prior to certification the market agent may: (1) deny the petition; or (2) grant temporary relief for a total period not to exceed 60 days.

Denials or grants of relief by the market agent shall be reviewed by the Director, and may be affirmed, modified or reversed by him.

(k) *Reports.* Each handler shall transmit to the market agent on forms prescribed by the market agent the following reports:

(1) Within 20 days following the effective date of this order, reports which show the information required by the market agent to establish such handlers' bases;

(2) Within 20 days following the close of each quota period, the information required by the market agent to establish volumes of deliveries of milk, cream, and milk byproducts during the preceding quota period; and

(3) Handlers whose deliveries are exempt from quotas shall, upon request of the market agent, submit the information required by the market agent to establish volumes of deliveries of milk, cream, and milk byproducts.

(l) *Records.* Handlers shall keep and shall make available to the market agent such records of receipts, sales, deliveries, and production as the market agent shall request for the purpose of obtaining information which the Director may require for the establishment of quotas as prescribed in (b) of FDO 79 and which is necessary to verify compliance with the provisions of this order.

(m) *Expense of administration.* Each handler except producer-handlers and sub-handlers having no bases and quotas shall pay to the market agent at the time of filing the reports required under (k) (2), an assessment of 2 cents per 100 quarts of regulated milk or milk equivalent of cream delivered during the quota period. Whenever verification by the market agent of information supplied by a handler discloses errors in assessment payment to the market agent, he shall bill the handler for any unpaid amount, and the handler shall, within 5 days, make payment to the market agent of the amount so billed. Whenever verification discloses that the handler made an overpayment, the market agent shall, within 5 days, return such overpayment to such handler.

(n) *Liquidation.* Upon the termination or suspension hereof, the market agent shall, if so directed by the Director, liquidate the business of the market agent's office and dispose of all funds and property then in his possession or under his control, together with claims receivable, unpaid and owing at the time of such termination or suspension. Any funds over and above the amounts necessary to meet outstanding obligations and the expenses necessarily incurred by the market agent in liquidating the business of the market agent's office shall be distributed by the market agent in accordance with instructions issued by the Director.

(o) *Conversion table.*

[Quarts of 3.5 percent b. f. milk equivalent of a quart of cream at various butterfat tests]

Cream (percent b. f.)	Milk equivalent (quarts)	Cream (percent b. f.)	Milk equivalent (quarts)
6	1.71	31	8.67
7	2.00	32	8.95
8	2.28	33	9.22
9	2.56	34	9.50
10	2.85	35	9.77
11	3.13	36	10.04
12	3.41	37	10.31
13	3.69	38	10.58
14	3.98	39	10.85
15	4.26	40	11.12
16	4.54	41	11.39
17	4.82	42	11.66
18	5.10	43	11.93
19	5.38	44	12.20
20	5.65	45	12.47
21	5.93	46	12.74
22	6.21	47	13.00
23	6.49	48	13.27
24	6.76	49	13.54
25	7.04	50	13.80
26	7.31	51	14.07
27	7.58	52	14.34
28	7.85	53	14.60
29	8.13	54	14.86
30	8.40	55	15.13

(p) *Bureau of the Budget approval.* The record-keeping and reporting requirements of this order have been approved by the Bureau of the Budget in accordance with the Federal Reports Act of 1942. Subsequent record-keeping or reporting requirements will be subject to the approval of the Bureau of the Budget pursuant to the Federal Reports Act of 1942.

(q) *Violations.* The market agent shall report all violations to the Director together with the information required for the prosecution of such violations, except in a case where a handler has made deliveries in a quota period in excess of a quota in an amount not to exceed 5 percent of such quota, and in the succeeding quota period makes deliveries below that quota by at least the same percent.

(r) *Effective date.* This order shall become effective at 12:01 a. m., e. w. t., November 1, 1943.

Issued this 15th day of October 1943.

C. W. KITCHEN,
Acting Director of Food Distribution.

Press Release, Immediate:
Saturday, October 16, 1943.

The War Food Administration announced today that milk sales in six New York areas will be regulated, beginning November 1, under the Food Distribution Administration's fluid milk conservation and control program.

The new milk sales areas, for which C. J. Blanford, 205 E. 42nd St., New York City, will be market agent, are: Niagara Frontier, Utica-Rome, Rochester, Syracuse, Binghamton, Albany-Schenectady-Troy.

Under the program, milk dealers will be permitted to sell as much fluid milk as they sold in June and three-fourths as much cream and milk byproducts (such as cottage cheese, chocolate milk, and buttermilk) as they sold in June. Milk dealers include all persons or firms engaged in the sale or transfer of milk, but not such distributors as subhandlers ("peddlers") who deliver less than 1,000 quarts of milk or 500 quarts of cream a day, retail stores, hotels, or restaurants.

To permit flexible adjustment to local production and consumption conditions, dealers will be allowed to exceed these base quotas by not more than 5 percent during any month, providing they decrease their deliveries the next month by the same amount.

A dealer may increase his milk sales also by reducing his cream and milk byproducts sales, providing such an adjustment is approved by the market agent for the area.

Producer-distributors, defined for these 6 areas as those who purchase no milk and sell less than 200 quarts a day, may sell as much milk as their herds produce.

Deliveries of milk, cream, and milk byproducts to nursery, elementary, junior high and high schools; to plants processing milk who do not distribute milk, cream, or other milk products in the sales area; to the Armed Forces, and to other milk handlers are quota-exempt.

Consumers in the milk sales areas named today and in others already designated generally will be able to purchase as much milk under the milk conservation program as they have been buying in recent months—within the limits of local supplies.

Fluid milk sales are being stabilized, Food Distribution Administration officials said, to help assure sufficient milk for manufacturing the cheese, butter, evaporated milk, and milk powder required by the Armed Services and civilians for good nutrition and properly balanced diets. Sales quotas on cream and on fluid milk byproducts have been set below June deliveries to boost fluid milk supplies where production is low, and to conserve milk for manufacturing purposes.

47337

FDO 79-52

OCTOBER 15, 1943

WAR FOOD ADMINISTRATION

[FDO 79-52]

PART 1401—DAIRY PRODUCTS

FLUID MILK AND CREAM IN BINGHAMTON, N. Y., SALES AREA

Pursuant to authority vested in me by Food Distribution Order No. 79 (8 F.R. 12426), issued September 7, 1943, as amended, and to effectuate the purposes of such order, it is hereby ordered as follows:

§ 1401.93 *Quota restrictions*—(a) *Definitions.* When used in this order, unless otherwise distinctly expressed or manifestly incompatable with the intent hereof:

(1) Each term defined in Food Distribution Order No. 79, as amended, shall, when used herein, have the same meaning as is set forth for such term in Food Distribution Order No. 79, as amended.

(2) The term "FDO 79" means Food Distribution Order No. 79, issued on September 7, 1943, as amended.

(3) The term "skim milk beverage" means skim milk, buttermilk, chocolate drink, or any other beverage containing more than 85 percent skim milk and less than 3 percent butterfat.

(4) The term "regulated" when used in conjunction with the terms "milk", "cream", "skim milk beverage", "cottage, pot, or baker's cheese", or "product", means milk, cream, skim milk beverage, cottage, pot, or baker's cheese, or product, delivered to retail purchasers, to stores, to public eating places, to other wholesale purchasers, and to sub-handlers for whom no bases and quotas have been established.

(5) The term "retail purchaser" means any person who purchases milk, milk byproducts, or cream at retail for personal, family, or household consumption.

(6) The term "store" means a merchandising establishment of fixed situs, the operator of which purchases milk and other food products for resale primarily for consumption off the premises.

(7) The term "public eating place" means any place in which food, prepared and ready for sale or consumption either on or off the premises where sold, is served, sold, or offered for sale; and such term includes, but is not necessarily limited to, any hotel, club, restaurant, cafe, cafeteria, caterer, inn, railroad diner, lunch room, sandwich stand, or drug store which serves, sells, or offers food for sale, as aforesaid. Any institution of voluntary or involuntary confinement, such as a hospital, sanitarium, (or sanitorium), asylum, penal institution, or school, is not a "public eating place".

(8) The term "wholesale purchaser" means any person who purchases milk, milk byproducts, or cream, for purposes of resale, or use in other than personal, family or household consumption, except (i) other handlers, (ii) purchasers engaged in the processing of milk, milk byproducts, or cream who do not distribute milk, milk byproducts, or cream, in the sales area, (iii) those purchasers specifically exempt from quota restrictions by FDO 79, and (iv) nursery, elementary, junior high and high schools.

(9) The term "producer-handler" means a handler who delivers milk produced only by his own herd and in a total quantity of less than 200 quarts per day.

(10) The term "sub-handler" means a handler, such as a peddler, or sub-dealer, who purchases milk in the same package in which it is delivered to purchasers: *Provided,* That a handler who handles more than 1,000 quarts of milk per day, or more than 500 quarts of cream per day, shall not be deemed a subhandler.

(11) The term "product" means milk, cream, skim milk beverage, or cottage, pot or baker's cheese.

(12) The term "b. f." used in conjunction with the title of the conversion table in (o) hereof means butter fat.

(b) *Milk sales area.* The following area is hereby designated as a milk sales area to be known as the Binghamton, New York, sales area, and is referred to hereinafter as the "sales area": The territory included within the boundaries of the following cities and towns:

The city of Binghamton and the towns of Binghamton, Conklin, Dickinson, Kirkwood, Union, and Vestal in Broome County, New York.

(c) *Bases and base period.* The handler's daily average delivery of each regulated product in the base period adjusted for transfers in accordance with (h) hereof shall be his base. The base for milk and skim milk beverages shall be computed in terms of quarts, for cream, in terms of milk equivalent in accordance with the conversion table set forth in (o) hereof, and for cottage, pot, or baker's cheese in terms of pounds of product. The calendar month of June 1943, is hereby designated as the base period for the sales area.

(d) *Quota periods.* The remainder of the calendar month in which this order becomes effective and each subsequent calendar month is hereby designated as a quota period for the sales area.

(e) *Handler quotas.* No handler shall deliver during any quota period a quantity of any regulated product in excess of his base for that product, multiplied by the number of days in the quota period and by the following applicable percentages: (1) milk, 100 percent; (2) milk equivalent of cream 75 percent; (3) skim milk beverages, 75 percent; (4) cottage, pot or baker's cheese, 75 percent: *Provided,* That a handler may, upon application to and approval by the market agent, secure an increase in milk quota through an equivalent reduction in cream and milk byproduct quotas.

(f) *Producer-handler quotas.* Each producer-handler's quota shall be 100 percent of milk produced.

(g) *Sub-handler quotas.* No bases or quotas shall be established for deliveries by sub-handlers except as provided in (h) hereof.

(h) *Transfer and apportionment of bases and quotas.* The market agent is empowered to transfer bases upon application by a handler making the deliveries from which such bases were derived on the effective date of this order and upon a showing of unreasonable hardship by the applicant. Upon application by a sub-handler, the market agent is empowered to transfer from a handler to such sub-handler that part of the handler's base and quota derived from delivery in the base period by such handler to such sub-handler.

Denials or grants of transfers by the market agent shall be reviewed by the Director upon application.

(i) The distribution schedules, if any, to be followed by the handlers in making deliveries shall be made effective in the terms of approval by the Director of such schedules.

(j) *Petition for relief from hardship.* Any person considering that compliance with FDO 79, or any instrument issued thereunder, would work an exceptional and unreasonable hardship on him, may file with the market agent a petition addressed to the Director. The petition shall contain the correct name, address and principal place of business of the petitioner, a full statement of the facts upon which the petition is based, and the hardship involved and the nature of the relief desired.

Upon receiving such petition, the market agent shall immediately investigate the representations and facts stated therein.

(j-1) *Relief.* After investigation, the market agent shall certify the petition to the Director, but prior to certification the market agent may: (1) deny the petition; or (2) grant temporary relief for a total period not to exceed 60 days.

Denials or grants of relief by the market agent shall be reviewed by the Director, and may be affirmed, modified or reversed by him.

(k) *Reports.* Each handler shall transmit to the market agent on forms prescribed by the market agent the following reports:

(1) Within 20 days following the effective date of this order, reports which show the information required by the market agent to establish such handlers' bases;

(2) Within 20 days following the close of each quota period, the information required by the market agent to establish volumes of deliveries of milk, cream, and milk byproducts during the preceding quota period; and

(3) Handlers whose deliveries are exempt from quotas shall, upon request of the market agent, submit the information required by the market agent to establish volumes of deliveries of milk, cream, and milk byproducts.

(l) *Records.* Handlers shall keep and shall make available to the market agent such records of receipts, sales, deliveries, and production as the market agent shall request for the purpose of obtaining information which the Director may require for the establishment of quotas as prescribed in (b) of FDO 79 and which is necessary to verify compliance with the provisions of this order.

(m) *Expense of administration.* Each handler except producer-handlers and sub-handlers having no bases and quotas shall pay to the market agent at the time of filing the reports required under (k) (2), an assessment of 2 cents per 100 quarts of regulated milk or milk equivalent of cream delivered during the quota period. Whenever verification by the market agent of information supplied by a handler discloses errors in assessment payment to the market agent, he shall bill the handler for any unpaid amount, and the handler shall, within 5 days, make payment to the market agent of the amount so billed. Whenever verification discloses that the handler made an overpayment, the market agent shall, within 5 days, return such overpayment to such handler.

(n) *Liquidation.* Upon the termination or suspension hereof, the market agent shall, if so directed by the Director, liquidate the business of the market agent's office and dispose of all funds and property then in his possession or under his control, together with claims receivable, unpaid and owing at the time of such termination or suspension. Any funds over and above the amounts necessary to meet outstanding obligations and the expenses necessarily incurred by the market agent in liquidating the business of the market agent's office shall be distributed by the market agent in accordance with instructions issued by the Director.

(o) *Conversion table.*

Quarts of 3.5 percent b. f. milk equivalent of a quart of cream at various butterfat tests]

Cream (percent b. f.)	Milk equivalent (quarts)	Cream (percent b. f.)	Milk equivalent (quarts)
6	1.71	31	8.67
7	2.00	32	8.95
8	2.28	33	9.22
9	2.56	34	9.50
10	2.85	35	9.77
11	3.13	36	10.04
12	3.41	37	10.31
13	3.69	38	10.59
14	3.98	39	10.85
15	4.26	40	11.12
16	4.54	41	11.39
17	4.82	42	11.66
18	5.10	43	11.93
19	5.38	44	12.20
20	5.65	45	12.47
21	5.93	46	12.74
22	6.21	47	13.00
23	6.49	48	13.27
24	6.76	49	13.54
25	7.04	50	13.81
26	7.31	51	14.07
27	7.58	52	14.34
28	7.85	53	14.60
29	8.13	54	14.86
30	8.40	55	15.13

(p) *Bureau of the Budget approval.* The record-keeping and reporting requirements of this order have been approved by the Bureau of the Budget in accordance with the Federal Reports Act of 1942. Subsequent record-keeping or reporting requirements will be subject to the approval of the Bureau of the Budget pursuant to the Federal Reports Act of 1942.

(q) *Violations.* The market agent shall report all violations to the Director together with the information required for the prosecution of such violations, except in a case where a handler has made deliveries in a quota period in excess of a quota in an amount not to exceed 5 percent of such quota, and in the succeeding quota period makes deliveries below that quota by at least the same percent.

(r) *Effective date.* This order shall become effective at 12:01 a. m., e. w. t., November 1, 1943.

Issued this 15th day of October 1943.

C. W. Kitchen,
Acting Director of Food Distribution.

Press Release, Immediate:
Saturday, October 16, 1943

The War Food Administration announced today that milk sales in six New York areas will be regulated, beginning November 1, under the Food Distribution Administration's fluid milk conservation and control program.

The new milk sales areas, for which C. J. Blanford, 205 E. 42nd St., New York City, will be market agent, are: Niagara Frontier, Utica-Rome, Rochester, Syracuse, Binghamton, Albany-Schenectady-Troy.

Under the program, milk dealers will be permitted to sell as much fluid milk as they sold in June and three-fourths as much cream and milk byproducts (such as cottage cheese, chocolate milk, and buttermilk) as they sold in June. Milk dealers include all persons or firms engaged in the sale or transfer of milk, but not such distributors as subhandlers ("peddlers") who deliver less than 1,000 quarts of milk or 500 quarts of cream a day, retail stores, hotels, or restaurants.

To permit flexible adjustment to local production and consumption conditions, dealers will be allowed to exceed these base quotas by not more than 5 percent during any month, providing they decrease their deliveries the next month by the same amount.

A dealer may increase his milk sales also by reducing his cream and milk byproducts sales, providing such an adjustment is approved by the market agent for the area.

Producer-distributors, defined for these 6 areas as those who purchase no milk and sell less than 200 quarts a day, may sell as much milk as their herds produce.

Deliveries of milk, cream, and milk byproducts to nursery, elementary, junior high and high schools; to plants processing milk who do not distribute milk, cream, or other milk products in the sales area; to the Armed Forces, and to other milk handlers are quota-exempt.

Consumers in the milk sales areas named today and in others already designated generally will be able to purchase as much milk under the milk conservation program as they have been buying in recent months—within the limits of local supplies.

Fluid milk sales are being stabilized, Food Distribution Administration officials said, to help assure sufficient milk for manufacturing the cheese, butter, evaporated milk, and milk powder required by the Armed Services and civilians for good nutrition and properly balanced diets. Sales quotas on cream and on fluid milk byproducts have been set below June deliveries to boost fluid milk supplies where production is low, and to conserve milk for manufacturing purposes.

FDO 79-52
AMDT. 1
NOV. 22, 1943

WAR FOOD ADMINISTRATION

[FDO 79-52, Amdt. 1]

Part 1401—Dairy Products

FLUID MILK AND CREAM IN BINGHAMTON, N. Y., SALES AREA

Pursuant to the authority vested in the Director by Food Distribution Order No. 79, dated September 7, 1943 (8 F.R. 12426), as amended, and to effectuate the purposes thereof, Director Food Distribution Order No. 79-52, § 1401.93, relative to the conservation of fluid milk in the Binghamton, New York, milk sales area (8 F.R. 14188), issued by the Director of Food Distribution on October 15, 1943, is amended as follows:

The milk sales area described in § 1401.93 (b) of the original order is modified in the following particulars: In line 2 of the description of the milk sales area, insert the word "Chenango" after the word "Binghamton" and insert the word "Fenton" after the word "Dickinson," making the description of the sales area read as follows:

The city of Binghamton, and the towns of Binghamton, Chenango, Conklin, Dickinson, Fenton, Kirkwood, Union, and Vestal in Broome County, New York.

Effective date. This amendment of FDO No. 79-52 shall become effective at 12:01 a. m., e. w. t., December 1, 1943.

(E.O. 9280, 8 F.R. 10179; E.O. 9322, 8 F.R. 3807; E.O. 9334, 8 F.R. 5423; E.O. 9392, 8 F.R. 14783, FDO 79, 8 F.R. 12426, 13283)

Issued this 22d day of November 1943.

Roy F. Hendrickson,
Director of Food Distribution.

GPO—WFA 310—p. 1

ierva
serve
/
735

FDO 79-53

OCTOBER 15, 1943

WAR FOOD ADMINISTRATION

[FDO 79-53] A

PART 1401—DAIRY PRODUCTS

FLUID MILK AND CREAM IN ALB'NY-SCHENECTADY-TROY, N. Y., SALES AREA

Pursuant to authority vested in me by Food Distribution Order No. 79 (8 F.R. 12426), issued September 7, 1943, as amended, and to effectuate the purposes of such order, it is hereby ordered as follows:

§ 1401.90 *Quota restrictions*—(a) *Definitions.* When used in this order, unless otherwise distinctly expressed or manifestly incompatible with the intent hereof:

(1) Each term defined in Food Distribution Order No. 79, as amended, shall, when used herein, have the same meaning as set forth for such term in Food Distribution Order No. 79, as amended.

(2) The term "FDO 79" means Food Distribution Order No. 79, issued on September 7, 1943, as amended.

(3) The term "skim milk beverage" means skim milk, buttermilk, chocolate drink, or any other beverage containing more than 85 percent skim milk and less than 3 percent butterfat.

(4) The term "regulated" when used in conjunction with the terms "milk", "cream", "skim milk beverage", "cottage, pot, or baker's cheese", or "product" means milk, cream, skim milk beverage, cottage, pot, or baker's cheese, or product, delivered to retail purchasers, to stores, to public eating places, to other wholesale purchasers, and to sub-handlers for whom no bases and quotas have been established.

(5) The term "retail purchaser" means any person who purchases milk, milk byproducts, or cream at retail for personal, family, or household consumption.

(6) The term "store" means a merchandising establishment of fixed situs, the operator of which purchases milk and other food products for resale primarily for consumption off the premises.

(7) The term "public eating place" means any place in which food, prepared and ready for sale or consumption either on or off the premises where sold, is served, sold, or offered for sale; and such term includes, but is not necessarily limited to, any hotel, club, restaurant, cafe, cafeteria, caterer, inn, railroad diner, lunch room, sandwich stand, or drug store which serves, sells, or offers food for sale, as aforesaid. Any institution of voluntary or involuntary confinement such as a hospital, sanitarium (or sanitorium), asylum, penal institution, or school is not a "public eating place".

(8) The term "wholesale purchaser" means any person who purchases milk, milk byproducts, or cream, for purposes of resale, or use in other than personal, family or household consumption, except (i) other handlers, (ii) purchasers engaged in the processing of milk, milk byproducts, or cream who do not distribute milk, milk byproducts, or cream in the sales area, (iii) those purchasers specifically exempt from quota restrictions by FDO 79, and (iv) nursery, elementary, junior high and high schools.

(9) The term "producer-handler" means a handler who delivers milk produced only by his own herd and in a total quantity of less than 200 quarts per day.

(10) The term "sub-handler" means a handler, such as a peddler, or sub-dealer, who purchases milk in the same package in which it is delivered to purchasers: *Provided*, That a handler who handles more than 1,000 quarts of milk per day, or more than 500 quarts of cream per day, shall not be deemed a sub-handler.

(11) The term "product" means milk, cream, skim milk beverage, or cottage, pot or baker's cheese.

(12) The term "b. f." used in conjunction with the title of the conversion table in (o) hereof means butter fat.

(b) *Milk sales area.* The following area is hereby designated as a milk sales area to be known as the Albany-Schenectady-Troy, New York, sales area, and is referred to hereinafter as the "sales area": The territory included within the boundaries of the following cities and towns:

The cities of Albany, Cohoes, and Watervliet, and the towns of Bethlehem, Colonie, Green Island and Guilderland in Albany County, New York; the city of Schenectady and the towns of Glenville, Niskayuna, and Rotterdam in Schenectady County, New York; and the cities of Troy and Rensselaer, and the towns of Brunswick, East Greenbush, North Greenbush, Schaghticoke, and that part of Pittstown comprising part of the village of Valley Falls in Rensselaer County, New York; and the town of Waterford in Saratoga County, New York.

(c) *Bases and base period.* The handler's daily average delivery of each regulated product in the base period adjusted for transfers in accordance with (h) hereof shall be his base. The base for milk and skim milk beverages shall be computed in terms of quarts, for cream, in terms of milk equivalent in accordance with the conversion table set forth in (o) hereof, and for cottage, pot, or baker's cheese in terms of pounds of product. The calendar month of June 1943, is hereby designated as the base period for the sales area.

(d) *Quota periods.* The remainder of the calendar month in which this order becomes effective and each subsequent calendar month is hereby designated as a quota period for the sales area.

(e) *Handler quotas.* No handler shall deliver during any quota period a quantity of any regulated product in excess of his base for that product, multiplied by the number of days in the quota period and by the following applicable percentages: (1) milk, 100 percent; (2) milk equivalent of cream, 75 percent; (3) skim milk beverages, 75 percent; (4) cottage, pot or baker's cheese, 75 percent;

Provided, That a handler may, upon application to and approval by the market agent, secure an increase in milk quota through an equivalent reduction in cream and milk byproduct quotas.

(f) *Producer-handler quotas.* Each producer-handler's quota shall be 100 percent of milk produced.

(g) *Sub-handler quotas.* No bases or quotas shall be established for deliveries by sub-handlers except as provided in (h) hereof.

(h) *Transfer and apportionment of bases and quotas.* The market agent is empowered to transfer bases upon application by a handler making the deliveries from which such bases were derived on the effective date of this order and upon a showing of unreasonable hardship by the applicant. Upon application by a sub-handler, the market agent is empowered to transfer from a handler to such sub-handler that part of the handler's base and quota derived from delivery in the base period by such handler to such sub-handler.

Denials or grants of transfers by the market agent shall be reviewed by the Director upon application:

(i) The distribution schedules, if any, to be followed by the handlers in making deliveries shall be made effective in the terms of approval by the Director of such schedules.

(j) *Petition for relief from hardship.* Any person considering that compliance with FDO 79, or any instrument issued thereunder, would work an exceptional and unreasonable hardship on him, may file with the market agent a petition addressed to the Director. The petition shall contain the correct name, address and principal place of business of the petitioner, a full statement of the facts upon which the petition is based, and the hardship involved and the nature of the relief desired.

Upon receiving such petition, the market agent shall immediately investigate the representations and facts stated therein.

(j-1) *Relief.* After investigation, the market agent shall certify the petition to the Director, but prior to certification the market agent may: (1) deny the petition; or (2) grant temporary relief for a total period not to exceed 60 days.

Denials or grants of relief by the market agent shall be reviewed by the Director, and may be affirmed, modified or reversed by him.

(k) *Reports.* Each handler shall transmit to the market agent on forms prescribed by the market agent the following reports:

(1) Within 20 days following the effective date of this order, reports which show the information required by the market agent to establish such handlers' bases;

(2) Within 20 days following the close of each quota period, the information required by the market agent to establish volumes of deliveries of milk, cream, and milk byproducts during the preceding quota period; and

(3) Handlers whose deliveries are exempt from quotas shall, upon request of the market agent, submit the information required by the market agent to establish volumes of deliveries of milk, cream, and milk byproducts.

(l) *Records.* Handlers shall keep and shall make available to the market agent such records of receipts, sales, deliveries, and production as the market agent shall request for the purpose of obtaining information which the Director may require for the establishment of quotas as prescribed in (b) of FDO 79 and which is necessary to verify compliance with the provisions of this order.

(m) *Expense of administration.* Each handler except producer-handlers and sub-handlers having no bases and quotas shall pay to the market agent at the time of filing the reports required under (k) (2), an assessment of 2 cents per 100 quarts of regulated milk or milk equivalent of cream delivered during the quota period. Whenever verification by the market agent of information supplied by a handler discloses errors in assessment payment to the market agent, he shall bill the handler for any unpaid amount, and the handler shall, within 5 days, make payment to the market agent of the amount so billed. Whenever verification discloses that the handler made an overpayment, the market agent shall, within 5 days, return such overpayment to such handler.

(n) *Liquidation.* Upon the termination or suspension hereof, the market agent shall, if so directed by the Director, liquidate the business of the market agent's office and dispose of all funds and property then in his possession or under his control, together with claims receivable, unpaid and owing at the time of such termination or suspension. Any funds over and above the amounts necessary to meet outstanding obligations and the expenses necessarily incurred by the market agent in liquidating the business of the market agent's office shall be distributed by the market agent in accordance with instructions issued by the Director.

(o) *Conversion table.*

Quarts of 3.5 percent b. f. milk equiv
of cream at various butterfat

Cream (percent b. f.)	Milk equivalent (quarts)	Cream (p cent b. f
6	1.71	31
7	2.00	32
8	2.28	33
9	2.56	34
10	2.85	35
11	3.13	36
12	3.41	37
13	3.69	38
14	3.98	39
15	4.26	40
16	4.54	41
17	4.82	42
18	5.10	43
19	5.38	44
20	5.65	45
21	5.93	46
22	6.21	47
23	6.49	48
24	6.76	49
25	7.04	50
26	7.31	51
27	7.58	52
28	7.85	53
29	8.13	54
30	8.40	55

(p) *Bureau of the Budg*
The record-keeping and re
quirements of this order ha
proved by the Bureau of th
accordance with the Federal
of 1942. Subsequent record
reporting requirements will
to the approval of the Bu
Budget pursuant to the Fed
Act of 1942.

(q) *Violations.* The ma
shall report all violations to
together with the informati
for the prosecution of such
except in a case where a
made deliveries in a quota p
cess of a quota in an amour
ceed 5 percent of such quota
succeeding quota period mak
below that quota by at lea
percent.

(r) *Effective date.* This
become effective at 12:01 a.
November 1, 1943.

Issued this 15th day of Oct

C. W. K

Acting Director of Food Di

Press Release, Immediate:
Saturday, October 16, 1943.

The War Food Administration announced today that milk sales in six New York areas will be regulated, beginning November 1, under the Food Distribution Administration's fluid milk conservation and control program.

The new milk sales areas, for which C. J. Blanford, 205 E. 42nd St., New York City, will be market agent, are: Niagara Frontier, Utica-Rome, Rochester, Syracuse, Binghamton, Albany-Schenectady-Troy.

Under the program, milk dealers will be permitted to sell as much fluid milk as they sold in June and three-fourths as much cream and milk byproducts (such as cottage cheese, chocolate milk, and buttermilk) as they sold in June. Milk dealers include all persons or firms engaged in the sale or transfer of milk, but not such distributors as subhandlers ("peddlers") who deliver less than 1,000 quarts of milk or 500 quarts of cream a day, retail stores, hotels, or restaurants.

To permit flexible adjustment to local production and consumption conditions, dealers will be allowed to exceed these base quotas by not more than 5 percent during any month, providing they decrease their deliveries the next month by the same amount.

A dealer may increase his milk sales also by reducing his cream and milk byproducts sales, providing such an adjustment is approved by the market agent for the area.

Producer-distributors, defined for these 6 areas as those who purchase no milk and sell less than 200 quarts a day, may sell as much milk as their herds produce.

Deliveries of milk, cream, and milk byproducts to nursery, elementary, junior high and high schools; to plants processing milk who do not distribute milk, cream, or other milk product
area; to the Armed Forces, a
milk handlers are quota-exe

Consumers in the milk
named today and in others al
nated generally will be able
as much milk under the mi
tion program as they have be
recent months—within the li
supplies.

Fluid milk sales are bein
Food Distribution Adminis
cials said, to help assure su
for manufacturing the che
evaporated milk, and milk
quired by the Armed Servic
ians for good nutrition and p
anced diets. Sales quotas or
on fluid milk byproducts ha
below June deliveries to boo
supplies where production is
conserve milk for manufac
poses.

FDO 79-53
AMDT. 1
NOV. 22, 1943

WAR FOOD ADMINISTRATION

PART 1401—DAIRY PRODUCTS

[FDO 79-53, Amdt. 1]

FLUID MILK AND CREAM IN ALBANY-SCHENECTADY-TROY, N. Y., SALES AREA

Pursuant to the authority vested in the Director by Food Distribution Order No. 79, dated September 7, 1943 (8 F.R. 12426), as amended, and to effectuate the purposes thereof, Food Distribution Order No. 79-53, § 1401.90, relative to the conservation of fluid milk in the Albany-Schenectady-Troy, N. Y., milk sales area (8 F.R. 14190), issued by the Director of Food Distribution on October 15, 1943, is amended as follows:

The milk sales area described in § 1401.90 (b) of the original order is modified in the following particulars: By deleting the words "town of Waterford", wherever the same appears therein, and by inserting in lieu thereof the words "towns of Halfmoon and Waterford".

Effective date. This amendment of FDO No. 79-53, shall become effective at 12:01 a. m, e. w. t., December 1, 1943.

(E.O. 9280, 8 F.R. 10179; E.O. 9322, 8 F.R. 3807; E.O. 9334, 8 F.R. 5423; E.O. 9392, 8 F.R. 14783; FDO 79, 8 F.R. 12426, 13283)

Issued this 22d day of November 1943.

ROY F. HENDRICKSON,
Director of Food Distribution.

WAR FOOD ADMINISTRATION
Office of Distribution
Washington 25, D. C.

CORRECTION NOTICE - FDO 79.53 Amendment 2.

In printing Food Distribution Order No. 79.53 Amendment 2 the following errors occurred:

Section 1401.90 (b) second paragraph the town "Rotterdom" should read "Rotterdam". The town of "Hamilton" erroneously appeared. This should read "Halfmoon".

WAR FOOD ADMINISTRATION

[FDO 79-53, Amdt. 2]

PART 1401—DAIRY PRODUCTS

FLUID MILK AND CREAM IN ALBANY-SCHENECTADY-TROY, N. Y., SALES AREA

Pursuant to Food Distribution Order No. 79 (8 F.R. 12426), dated September 7, 1943, as amended, and to effectuate the purposes thereof, Food Distribution Order No. 79-53 (8 F.R. 14190), relative to the conservation and distribution of fluid milk in the Albany-Schenectady-Troy, New York, milk sales area, issued by the Director of Food Distribution on October 15, 1943, as amended, is hereby further amended by deleting therefrom the description of the sales area in § 1401.90 (b) and inserting in lieu thereof the following:

The cities of Albany, Cohoes, and Watervliet, and the towns of Bethlehem, Colonie, Green Island and Guilderland in Albany County, New York; the city of Schenectady and the towns of Glenville, Niskayuna, and Rotterdom in Schenectady County, New York; and the cities of Troy and Rensselaer, and the towns of Brunswick, East Greenbush and North Greenbush in Rensselaer County, New York; and the towns of Hamilton and Waterford in Saratoga County, New York.

The provisions of this amendment shall become effective at 12:01 a. m., e. w. t., March 1, 1944. With respect to violations of said Food Distribution Order No. 79-53, as amended, rights accrued, or liabilities incurred prior to the effective time of this amendment, said Food Distribution Order No. 79-53, as amended, shall be deemed to be in full force and effect for the purpose of sustaining any proper suit, action, or other proceeding with respect to any such violation, right, or liability.

(E.O. 9280, 7 F.R. 10179; E.O. 9322, 8 F.R. 3807; E.O. 9334, 8 F.R. 5423; E.O. 9392, 8 F.R. 14783; FDO 79, 12426, 13283)

Issued this 11th day of February 1944.

C. W. KITCHEN,
Acting Director of Food Distribution.

Reserve
1
77337

FDO 79-54
OCTOBER 15, 1943

WAR FOOD ADMINISTRATION

[FDO 79-54]

PART 1401—DAIRY PRODUCTS

FLUID MILK AND CREAM IN NIAGARA FRONTIER, N. Y., SALES AREA

Pursuant to authority vested in me by Food Distribution Order No. 79 (8 F.R 12426), issued September 7, 1943, as amended, and to effectuate the purposes of such order, it is hereby ordered as follows:

§ 1401.89 *Quota restrictions*—(a) *Definitions.* When used in this order, unless otherwise distinctly expressed or manifestly incompatible with the intent hereof:

(1) Each term defined in Food Distribution Order No. 79, as amended, shall, when used herein, have the same meaning as is set forth for such term in Food Distribution Order No. 79, as amended.

(2) The term "FDO 79" means Food Distribution Order No. 79, issued on September 7, 1943, as amended.

(3) The term "skim milk beverage" means skim milk, buttermilk, chocolate drink, or any other beverage containing more than 85 percent skim milk and less than 3 percent butterfat.

(4) The term "regulated" when used in conjunction with the terms "milk", "cream", "skim milk beverage", "cottage, pot, or baker's cheese", or "product" means milk, cream, skim milk beverage, cottage, pot, or baker's cheese, or product, delivered to retail purchasers, to stores, to public eating places, to other wholesale purchasers, and to sub-handlers for whom no bases and quotas have been established.

(5) The term "retail purchaser" means any person who purchases milk, milk byproducts, or cream at retail for personal, family, or household consumption.

(6) The term "store" means a merchandising establishment of fixed situs, the operator of which purchases milk and other food products for resale primarily for consumption off the premises.

(7) The term "public eating place" means any place in which food, prepared and ready for sale or consumption either on or off the premises where sold, is served, sold, or offered for sale; and such term includes, but is not necessarily limited to, any hotel, club, restaurant, cafe, cafeteria, caterer, inn, railroad diner, lunch room, sandwich stand, or drug store which serves, sells, or offers food for sale, as aforesaid. Any institution of voluntary or involuntary confinement, such as a hospital, sanitarium (or sanitorium), asylum, penal institution or school, is not a "public eating place".

(8) The term "wholesale purchaser" means any person who purchases milk, milk byproducts, or cream, for purposes of resale, or use in other than personal, family or household consumption, except (i) other handlers, (ii) purchasers engaged in the processing of milk, milk byproducts, or cream who do not distribute milk, milk byproducts, or cream, in the sales area, (iii) those purchasers specifically exempt from quota restrictions by FDO 79, and (iv) nursery, elementary, junior high and high schools.

(9) The term "producer-handler" means a handler who delivers milk produced only by his own herd and in a total quantity of less than 200 quarts per day.

(10) The term "sub-handler" means a handler, such as a peddler, or subdealer, who purchases milk in the same package in which it is delivered to purchasers: *Provided*, That a handler who handles more than 1,000 quarts of milk per day, or more than 500 quarts of cream per day, shall not be deemed a sub-handler.

(11) The term "product" means milk, cream, skim milk beverage, or cottage, pot, or baker's cheese.

(12) The term "b. f." used in conjunction with the title of the conversion table in (o) hereof means butter fat.

(b) *Milk sales area.* The following area is hereby designated as a milk sales area to be known as the Niagara Frontier, New York, sales area, and is referred to hereinafter as the "sales area": The territory included within the boundaries of the following New York cities and towns:

The cities of Buffalo, Tonawanda and Lackawanna, and the towns of Clarence, Newstead, Evans, Hamburg, Aurora, West Seneca, Cheektowaga, Lancaster, Amherst, Tonawanda, Grand Island, and Orchard Park in Erie County, New York, and the cities of Niagara Falls, Lockport, and North Tonawanda, and the towns of Porter, Lewiston, Niagara, Wheatfield, Wilson, Newfane, Cambria, Pendleton, and Lockport in Niagara County, New York.

(c) *Bases and base period.* The handler's daily average delivery of each regulated product in the base period adjusted for transfers in accordance with (h) hereof shall be his base. The base for milk and skim milk beverages shall be computed in terms of quarts, for cream, in terms of milk equivalent in accordance with the conversion table set forth in (o) hereof, and for cottage, pot, or baker's cheese in terms of pounds of product. The calendar month of June 1943, is hereby designated as the base period for the sales area.

(d) *Quota periods.* The remainder of the calendar month in which this order becomes effective and each subsequent calendar month is hereby designated as a quota period for the sales area.

(e) *Handler quotas.* No handler shall deliver during any quota period a quantity of any regulated product in excess of his base for that product, multiplied by the number of days in the quota period and by the following applicable percentages: (1) milk, 100 percent; (2) milk equivalent of cream, 75 percent; (3) skim milk beverages, 75 percent; (4) cottage, pot or baker's cheese, 75 percent; *Provided*, That a handler may, upon application to and approval by the market agent, secure an increase in milk quota through an equivalent reduction in cream and milk byproduct quotas.

(f) *Producer-handler quotas.* Each producer-handler's quota shall be 100 percent of milk produced.

(g) *Sub-handler quotas.* No bases or quotas shall be established for deliveries by sub-handlers except as provided in (h) hereof.

(h) *Transfer and apportionment of bases and quotas.* The market agent is empowered to transfer bases upon application by a handler making the deliveries from which such bases were derived on the effective date of this order and upon a showing of unreasonable hardship by the applicant. Upon application by a sub-handler, the market agent is empowered to transfer from a handler to such sub-handler that part of the handler's base and quota derived from delivery in the base period by such handler to such sub-handler.

Denials or grants of transfers by the market agent shall be reviewed by the Director upon application.

(i) The distribution schedules, if any, to be followed by the handlers in making deliveries shall be made effective in the terms of approval by the Director of such schedules.

(j) *Petition for relief from hardship.* Any person considering that compliance with FDO 79, or any instrument issued thereunder, would work an exceptional and unreasonable hardship on him, may file with the market agent a petition addressed to the Director. The petition shall contain the correct name, address and principal place of business of the petitioner, a full statement of the facts upon which the petition is based, and the hardship involved and the nature of the relief desired.

Upon receiving such petition, the market agent shall immediately investigate the representations and facts stated therein.

(j-1) *Relief.* After investigation, the market agent shall certify the petition to the Director, but prior to certification the market agent may:

(1) Deny the petition; or

(2) Grant temporary relief for a total period not to exceed 60 days.

Denials or grants of relief by the market agent shall be reviewed by the Director, and may be affirmed, modified or reversed by him.

(k) *Reports.* Each handler shall transmit to the market agent on forms prescribed by the market agent the following reports:

(1) Within 20 days following the effective date of this order, reports which show the information required by the market agent to establish such handlers' bases;

(2) Within 20 days following the close of each quota period, the information required by the market agent to establish volumes of deliveries of milk, cream, and milk byproducts during the preceding quota period; and

(3) Handlers whose deliveries are exempt from quotas shall, upon request of the market agent, submit the information required by the market agent to establish volumes of deliveries of milk, cream, and milk byproducts.

(l) *Records.* Handlers shall keep and shall make available to the market agent such records of receipts, sales, deliveries, and production as the market agent shall request for the purpose of obtaining information which the Director may require for the establishment of quotas as prescribed in (b) of FDO 79 and which is necessary to verify compliance with the provisions of this order.

(m) *Expense of administration.* Each handler except producer-handlers and sub-handlers having no bases and quotas shall pay to the market agent at the time of filing the reports required under (k) (2), an assessment of 2 cents per 100 quarts of regulated milk or milk equivalent of cream delivered during the quota period. Whenever verification by the market agent of information supplied by a handler discloses errors in assessment payment to the market agent, he shall bill the handler for any unpaid amount, and the handler shall, within 5 days, make payment to the market agent of the amount so billed. Whenever verification discloses that the handler made an overpayment, the market agent shall, within 5 days, return such overpayment to such handler.

(n) *Liquidation.* Upon the termination or suspension hereof, the market agent shall, if so directed by the Director, liquidate the business of the market agent's office and dispose of all funds and property then in his possession or under his control, together with claims receivable, unpaid and owing at the time of such termination or suspension. Any funds over and above the amounts necessary to meet outstanding obligations and the expense necessarily incurred by the market agent in liquidating the business of the market agent's office shall be distributed by the market agent in accordance with instructions issued by the Director.

(o) *Con*

Quarts of 3.5 of c
Cream (percent b. f.)
6
7
8
9
10
11
12
13
14
15
16
17
18
19
20
21
22
23
24
25
26
27
28
29
30

(p) *Bur*
The recor
quirements
proved by
accordance
of 1942. S
reporting r
the approv
pursuant t
1942.

(q) *Viol*
shall repor
together w
for the pros
cept in a c
deliveries i
a quota in
percent of
ceeding quo
low that qu
cent.

(r) *Effec*
become eff
November

Issued th

Acting D

Press Release, Immediate:
Saturday, October 16, 1943.

The War Food Administration announced today that milk sales in six New York areas will be regulated, beginning November 1, under the Food Distribution Administration's fluid milk conservation and control program.

The new milk sales areas, for which C. J. Blanford, 205 E. 42nd St., New York City, will be market agent, are: Niagara Frontier, Utica-Rome, Rochester, Syracuse, Binghamton, Albany-Schenectady-Troy.

Under the program, milk dealers will be permitted to sell as much fluid milk as they sold in June and three-fourths as much cream and milk byproducts (such as cottage cheese, chocolate milk, and buttermilk) as they sold in June. Milk dealers include all persons or firms engaged in the sale or transfer of milk, but not such distributors as subhandlers ("peddlers") who deliver less than 1,000 quarts of milk or 500 quarts of cream a day, retail stores, hotels, or restaurants.

To permit flexible adjustment to local production and consumption conditions, dealers will be allowed to exceed these base quotas by not more than 5 percent during any month, providing they decrease their deliveries the next month by the same amount.

A dealer may increase his milk sales also by reducing his cream and milk byproducts sales, providing such an adjustment is approved by the market agent for the area.

Producer-distributors, defined for these 6 areas as those who purchase no milk and sell less than 200 quarts a day, may sell as much milk as their herds produce.

Deliveries of milk, cream, and milk byproducts to nursery, elementary, junior high and high schools; to plants processing milk who do not distribute milk, cream, or
sales area;
other milk

Consume
named too
designated
chase as m
servation p
buying in
limits of lo

Fluid mi
Food Dist
cials said,
for manuf
evaporated
quired by t
ians for g
balanced d
and on flui
set below
milk suppl
and to con
purposes.

WAR FOOD ADMINISTRATION

[FDO No. 79-55]

PART 1401—DAIRY PRODUCTS

FLUID MILK AND CREAM IN SALT LAKE CITY, UTAH, METROPOLITAN SALES AREA

Pursuant to the authority vested in me by Food Distribution Order No. 79 (8 F.R. 12426), issued on September 7, 1943, as amended, and to effectuate the purposes of such order, it is hereby ordered as follows:

§ 1401.105 *Quota restrictions*—(a) *Definitions.* When used in this order, unless otherwise distinctly expressed or manifestly incompatible with the intent hereof:

(1) Each term defined in Food Distribution Order No. 79, as amended, shall, when used herein, have the same meaning as is set forth for such term in Food Distribution Order No. 79, as amended.

(2 The term "FDO 79" means Food Distribution Order No. 79, issued on September 7, 1943, as amended.

(3) The term "sub-handler" means any handler, such as a peddler, vendor, sub-dealer, or secondary dealer, who purchases in a previously packaged and processed form milk, milk byproducts, or cream for delivery.

(b) *Milk sales area.* The following area is hereby designated as a "milk sales area" to be known as the Salt Lake City, Utah, metropolitan sales area, and is referred to hereinafter as the "sales area":

Salt Lake City and the election precincts 1, 2, 3, 4, 5, 6, 11, that part of precinct 7 comprising voting districts 166, 167, and 171, all in Salt Lake County; the precincts Bountiful, South Bountiful, and West Bountiful in Davis County, Utah.

(c) *Base period.* The calendar month of June 1943 is hereby designated as the base period for the sales area.

(d) *Quota period.* The remainder of the calendar month in which the provisions hereof become effective and each subsequent calendar month, respectively, is hereby designated as a quota period for the sales area.

(e) *Handler quotas.* Quotas for each handler in the sales area in each quota period shall be calculated in terms of pounds of each of the items for which percentages are specified in (3) below and shall be determined as follows:

(1) Divide the total deliveries of each such item made in the sales area by such handler during the base period, after excluding the quota-exempt deliveries described in (i) hereof, by the number of days in the base period;

(2) Multiply the result of the foregoing calculation by the number of days in the quota period;

(3) Multiply the aforesaid resulting amount by the following applicable percentage: (i) milk: 100 percent; (ii) butterfat in milk: 100 percent; (iii) cream: 75 percent; (iv) butterfat in cream: 75 percent; (v) milk byproducts other than cottage, pot, or baker's cheese: 75 percent; and (vi) cottage, pot, or baker's cheese: 75 percent of skim milk equivalent. (For the purpose of this order, one pound of cottage, pot, or baker's cheese shall be considered as the equivalent of 7 pounds of skim milk.)

(f) *Quota limitations.* No handler shall, during any quota period, make deliveries in the sales area in excess of his respective quotas, except as set out in (i) hereof: *Provided*, That a handler may, after application to and approval by the market agent, secure an increase in milk quotas through an equivalent reduction as determined by the market agent, in cream and milk byproducts quotas, and an increase in milk byproducts quota through an equivalent reduction as determined by the market agent, in cream quotas.

(g) *Quotas for handlers who are also producers.* Quotas for handlers who are also producers and who purchase no milk shall be 100 percent of the total production of such handlers in the base period.

(h) *Handler exemptions.* Quotas shall not apply to any handler who delivers in a quota period a daily average of less than 200 units of milk, cream, and milk byproducts. For the purpose of this order, a unit shall be the equivalent in volume of the following: (1) milk, one quart of milk; (2) cream, one-half pint of cream; and (3) milk byproduct, one quart of skim milk, buttermilk, flavored milk drink, or other beverage containing more than 85 percent of skim milk, or one-half pound of cottage, pot, or baker's cheese.

(i) *Quota exclusions and exemptions.* Deliveries of milk, milk byproducts, or cream (1) to other handlers, except for such deliveries to sub-handlers, (2) to plants engaged in the handling or processing of milk, milk byproducts, or cream from which no milk, milk byproducts or cream is delivered in the sales area, and (3) to the agencies or groups specified in (d) of FDO 79, shall be excluded from the computation of deliveries in the base period and exempt from charges to quotas.

(j) *Transfers and apportionment of quotas.* The market agent is empowered to deduct an amount of base period deliveries to purchasers from the total of deliveries made by a handler or other person in the base period upon the application and a showing of unreasonable hardship by the handler making deliveries to such purchasers on the effective date of this order, and to add the amount of such deliveries to the total base period deliveries of the applicant handler. Denials of transfers or transfers granted by the market agent shall be reviewed by the Director upon application.

(k) *Petition for relief from hardships.* (1) Any person affected by FDO 79 or the provisions hereof who considers that compliance therewith would work an exceptional and unreasonable hardship on him, may file with the market agent a petition addressed to the Director. The petition shall contain the correct name, address and principal place of business of the petitioner, a full statement of the facts upon which the petition is based, and the hardship involved and the nature of the relief desired.

(2) Upon receiving such petition, the market agent shall immediately investigate the representations and facts stated therein.

(3) After investigation, the petition shall be certified to the Director, but prior to certification the market agent may (i) deny the petition, or (ii) grant temporary relief for a total period of not to exceed 60 days.

(4) Denials or grants of relief by the market agent shall be reviewed by the Director and may be affirmed, modified, or reversed by the Director.

(l) *Reports.* Each handler shall transmit to the market agent on forms prescribed by the market agent the following reports:

(1) Within 20 days following the effective date of this order, reports which show the information required by the market agent to establish such handlers' quotas;

(2) Within 20 days following the close of each quota period, the information required by the market agent to establish volumes of deliveries of milk, cream, and milk byproducts during the preceding quota period; and

(3) Handlers exempt from quotas pursuant to (h) hereof shall, upon the re-

quest of the market agent, submit the information required by the market agent to establish volumes of deliveries of milk, cream, and milk byproducts.

(m) *Records.* Handlers shall keep and shall make available to the market agent such records of receipts, sales, deliveries, and production as the market agent shall require for the purpose of obtaining information which the Director may require for the establishment of quotas as prescribed in (b) of FDO 79.

(n) *Distribution schedules.* The distribution schedules, if any, to be followed by the handlers in making deliveries shall be made effective in the terms of approval by the Director of such schedules.

(o) *Expense of administration.* Each handler shall pay to the market agent, within 20 days after the close of each calendar month an assessment of $0.015 per hundredweight of each of milk, cream, skim milk, buttermilk, flavored milk drinks, beverages containing more than 85 percent of skim milk, and skim milk equivalent of cottage, pot, or baker's cheese delivered during the preceding quota period and subject to quota regulations under the provisions hereof.

(p) *Violations.* The market agent shall report all violations to the Director together with the information required for the prosecution of such violations, except in a case where a handler has made deliveries in a quota period in excess of a quota in an amount not to exceed 5 percent of such quota, and in the succeeding quota period makes deliveries below that quota by at least the sa percent.

(q) *Bureau of the Budget approv* The record keeping and reporting quirements of this order have been proved by the Bureau of the Budget accordance with the Federal Reports of 1942. Subsequent record keeping reporting requirements will be subj to the approval of the Bureau of Budget pursuant to the Federal Repo Act of 1942.

(r) This order shall take effect 12:01 a. m., e.w.t., November 1, 1943.

Issued this 19th day of October 194

C. W. KITCHEN,
Acting Director of Food Distribution

Press Release, Immediate:
Wednesday, October 20, 1943.

Milk sales in 19 metropolitan areas in Illinois, Michigan, Colorado, Utah, Arizona, Oregon, Pennsylvania, Minnesota, Oklahoma and West Virginia will be regulated under the Food Distribution Administration's fluid milk conservation and control program, beginning November 1, 1943.

The new milk sales areas and the market agents who will administer the program in each are:

Johnstown, Pa., Erie, Pa., Altoona, Pa., Pittsburgh, Pa., Metropolitan, Charleston, W. Va., Wheeling, W. Va.: George A. Taylor, Century Building, Pittsburgh, Pa.

Peoria, Ill., Rockford, Ill.: A. W. Colebank, 135 S. LaSalle St., Chicago, Ill.

Phoenix, Ariz., Denver, Col., Metropolitan, Salt Lake City, Utah, Metropolitan: Ben King, 503 Security Life Building, 810 14th St., Denver, Colo. (temp. address).

Portland, Oregon, Metropolitan: J. H. Mapes, 635 Elliot Avenue, West Seattle, Washington.

Detroit, Michigan, Metropolitan, Saginaw-Bay City, Mich., Metropolitan, Lansing, Mich., Metropolitan, Flint, Mich., Metropolitan: (To be announced later).

Oklahoma City, Oklahoma, Tulsa, Oklahoma: M. M. Morehouse, 512 Porter Bldg., 406 W. 34th St., Kansas City, Mo.

Minneapolis-St. Paul, Minnesota: D. F. Spencer, 404 Post Office Bldg., Minneapolis, Minn.

Under the program, milk dealers will be permitted to sell as much fluid milk as they sold in June and three-fourths as much cream and milk byproducts (such as cottage cheese, chocolate milk, and buttermilk) as they sold in June. Milk dealers include all persons or firms engaged in the sale or transfer of milk, but not such distributors as subhandlers ("peddlers"), retail stores, hotels, or restaurants.

Producer-distributors who purchase no milk will be permitted to sell as much milk as they produced in June.

Dealers will be allowed to exceed these base quotas by not more than 5 percent during any month, providing they decrease their deliveries the next month by the same amount, without being reported in violation.

A dealer also may increase his milk sales by reducing his cream and milk byproducts sales, and increase his sales of milk byproducts by reducing his cream sales, providing such an adjustment approved by the market agent for area.

Deliveries of milk, cream, and m byproducts to other dealers, to the Arm Forces, and to plants processing m who do not distribute milk, cream, a milk byproducts in the sales area quota-exempt.

Consumers in the milk sales ar named today and in others alrea designated generally will be able to pu chase as much milk under the milk co servation program as they have be buying in recent months—within t limits of local supplies. In some are production is not expected to be lar enough to permit dealers to sell as mu milk as their quotas allow.

Fluid milk sales are being stabiliz Food Distribution Administration of cials said, to help assure sufficient mi for manufacturing the cheese, butt evaporated milk, and milk powder r quired by the Armed Services and civ ians for food nutrition and properly ba anced diets. Sales quotas on cream a on fluid milk byproducts have been s below June deliveries to boost fluid mi supplies where production is low, and conserve milk for manufacturing pu poses.

7

FDO 79-56

OCTOBER 19, 1943

WAR FOOD ADMINISTRATION

[FDO 79-56]

PART 1401—DAIRY PRODUCTS

FLUID MILK AND CREAM, ALTOONA, PA., SALES AREA

Pursuant to the authority vested in me by Food Distribution Order No. 79 (8 F.R. 12426), issued on September 7, 1943, as amended, and to effectuate the purposes of such order, it is hereby ordered, as follows:

§ 1401.109 *Quota restrictions*—(a) *Definitions.* When used in this order, unless otherwise distinctly expressed or manifestly incompatible with the intent hereof:

(1) Each term defined in Food Distribution Order No. 79, as amended, shall when used herein, have the same meaning as is set forth for such term in Food Distribution Order No. 79, as amended.

(2) The term "FDO 79" means Food Distribution Order No. 79, issued on September 7, 1943, as amended.

(3) The term "sub-handler" means any handler, such as a peddler, vendor, sub-dealer, or secondary dealer, who purchases in a previously packaged and processed form milk, milk byproducts, or cream for delivery.

(b) *Milk sales area.* The following area is hereby designated as a "milk sales area" to be known as the Altoona, Pennsylvania, sales area, and is referred to hereinafter as the "sales area":

The city of Altoona, the townships of Allegheny, Blair, and Logan, the boroughs of Duncansville, Hollidaysburg, and Newry in Blair County; the townships of Cresson and Gallitzin, the boroughs of Ashville, Cresson, Gallitzin, Sankertown, and Tunnelhill in Cambria County; all in the State of Pennsylvania.

(c) *Base period.* The calendar month of June 1943 is hereby designated as the base period for the sales area.

(d) *Quota period.* The remainder of the calendar month in which the provisions hereof become effective and each subsequent calendar month, respectively, is hereby designated as a quota period for the sales area.

(e) *Handler quotas.* Quotas for each handler in the sales area in each quota period shall be calculated in terms of pounds of each of the items for which percentages are specified in (3) below and shall be determined as follows:

(1) Divide the total deliveries of each such item made in the sales area by such handler during the base period, after excluding the quota-exempt deliveries described in (i) hereof, by the number of days in the base period;

(2) Multiply the result of the foregoing calculation by the number of days in the quota period;

(3) Multiply the aforesaid resulting amount by the following applicable percentage: (i) milk, 100 percent; (ii) butterfat in milk, ______ percent; (iii) cream, 75 percent; (iv) butterfat in cream, 75 percent; (v) milk byproducts other than cottage, pot, or baker's cheese, 75 percent; and (vi) cottage, pot, or baker's cheese, 75 percent of skim milk equivalent. (For the purpose of this order, one pound of cottage, pot, or baker's cheese shall be considered as the equivalent of 7 pounds of skim milk.)

(f) *Quota limitations.* No handler shall, during any quota period, make deliveries in the sales area in excess of his respective quotas, except as set out in (i) hereof: *Provided*, That a handler may, after application to and approval by the market agent, secure an increase in milk quotas through an equivalent reduction as determined by the market agent, in cream and milk byproducts quotas, and an increase in milk byproducts quota through an equivalent reduction as determined by the market agent, in cream quotas.

(g) *Quotas for handlers who are also producers.* Quotas for handlers who are also producers and who purchase no milk shall be 100 percent of the total production of such handlers in the base period.

(h) *Handler exemptions.* Quotas shall not apply to any handler who delivers in a quota period a daily average of less than 350 units of milk, cream, and milk byproducts. For the purpose of this order, a unit shall be the equivalent in volume of the following: (1) milk, one quart of milk; (2) cream, one-half pint of cream; and (3) milk byproducts, one quart of skim milk, buttermilk, flavored milk drink, or other beverage containing more than 85 percent of skim milk, or one half pound of cottage, pot, or baker's cheese.

(i) *Quota exclusions and exemptions.* Deliveries of milk, milk byproducts, or cream (1) to other handlers, except for such deliveries to sub-handlers, (2) to plants engaged in the handling or processing of milk, milk byproducts, or cream from which no milk, milk byproducts, or cream is delivered in the sales area, and (3) to the agencies or groups specified in (d) of FDO 79, shall be excluded from the computation of deliveries in the base period and exempt from charges to quotas.

(j) *Transfers and apportionment of quotas.* The market agent is empowered to deduct an amount of base period deliveries to purchasers from the total of deliveries made by a handler or other person in the base period upon the application and a showing of unreasonable hardship by the handler making deliveries to such purchasers on the effective date of this order, and to add the amount of such deliveries to the total base period deliveries of the applicant handler. Denials of transfers or transfers granted by the market agent shall be reviewed by the Director upon application.

(k) *Petition for relief from hardships.* (1) Any person affected by FDO 79 or the provisions hereof who considers that compliance therewith would work an exceptional and unreasonable hardship on him, may file with the market agent a petition addressed to the Director. The petition shall contain the correct name, address and principal place of business of the petitioner, a full statement of the facts upon which the petition is based, and the hardship involved and the nature of the relief desired.

(2) Upon receiving such petition, the market agent shall immediately investigate the representations and facts stated therein.

(3) After investigation, the petition shall be certified to the Director, but prior to certification the market agent may (i) deny the petition, or (ii) grant temporary relief for a total period not to exceed 60 days.

(4) Denials or grants of relief by the market agent shall be reviewed by the Director and may be affirmed, modified, or reversed by the Director.

(l) *Reports.* Each handler shall transmit to the market agent on forms prescribed by the market agent the following reports:

(1) Within 20 days following the effective date of this order, reports which show the information required by the market agent to establish such handlers' quotas;

(2) Within 20 days following the close of each quota period, the information required by the market agent to establish volumes of deliveries of milk, cream, and milk byproducts during the preceding quota period; and

(3) Handlers exempt from quotas pursuant to (h) hereof shall, upon the request of the market agent, submit the information required by the market

agent to establish volumes of deliveries of milk, cream, and milk byproducts.

(m) *Records.* Handlers shall keep and shall make available to the market agent such records of receipts, sales, deliveries, and production as the market agent shall require for the purpose of obtaining information which the Director may require for the establishment of quotas as prescribed in (b) of FDO 79.

(n) *Distribution schedules.* The distribution schedules, if any, to be followed by the handlers in making deliveries shall be made effective in the terms of approval by the Director of such schedules.

(o) *Expense of administration.* Each handler shall pay to the market agent, within 20 days after the close of each calendar month an assessment of $0 01 per hundredweight of each of milk, cream, skim milk, buttermilk, flavored milk drinks, beverages containing more than 85 percent of skim milk, and skim milk equivalent of cottage, pot, or baker's cheese delivered during the preceding quota period and subject to quota regulations under the provisions hereof.

(p) *Violations.* The market agent shall report all violations to the Director together with the information required for the prosecution of such violations, except in a case where a handler has made deliveries in a quota period in excess of a quota in an amount not to exceed 5 percent of such quota, and in the succeeding quota period makes deliveries below that quota by at percent.

(q) *Bureau of the B* The record keeping an quirements of this orde proved by the Bureau o accordance with the F Act of 1942. Subsequent or reporting requirement to the approval of the Budget pursuant to the Act of 1942.

(r) This order shall 12:01 a. m., e. w. t., Noven

Issued this 19th day (

C. V
Acting Director of Foo

Press Release, Immediate:
Wednesday, October 20, 1943.

Milk sales in 19 metropolitan areas in Illinois, Michigan, Colorado, Utah, Arizona, Oregon, Pennsylvania, Minnesota, Oklahoma and West Virginia will be regulated under the Food Distribution Administration's fluid milk conservation and control program, beginning November 1, 1943.

The new milk sales areas and the market agents who will administer the program in each are:

Johnstown, Pa., Erie, Pa., Altoona, Pa., Pittsburgh, Pa., Metropolitan, Charleston, W. Va., Wheeling, W. Va.: George A. Taylor, Century Building, Pittsburgh, Pa.

Peoria, Ill., Rockford, Ill.: A. W. Colebank, 135 S. LaSalle St., Chicago, Ill.

Phoenix, Ariz., Denver, Colo., Metropolitan, Salt Lake City, Utah, Metropolitan: Ben King, 503 Security Life Building, 810 14th St., Denver, Colo. (temp. address).

Portland, Oregon, Metropolitan: J. H. Mapes, 635 Elliot Avenue, West Seattle, Washington.

Detroit, Michigan, Metropolitan, Saginaw-Bay City, Mich., Metropolitan, Lansing, Mich., Metropolitan, Flint, Mich., Metropolitan: (To be announced later).

Oklahoma City, Oklahoma, Tulsa, Oklahoma: M. M. Morehouse, 512 Porter Bldg., 406 W. 34th St., Kansas City, Mo.

Minneapolis-St. Paul, Minnesota: D. F. Spencer, 404 Post Office Bldg., Minneapolis, Minn.

Under the program, milk dealers will be permitted to sell as much fluid milk as they sold in June and three-fourths as much cream and milk byproducts (such as cottage cheese, chocolate milk, and buttermilk) as they sold in June. Milk dealers include all persons or firms engaged in the sale or transfer of milk, but not such distributors as subhandlers ("peddlers"), retail stores, hotels, or restaurants.

Producer-distributors who purchase no milk will be permitted to sell as much milk as they produced in June.

Dealers will be allowed to exceed these base quotas by not more than 5 percent during any month, providing they decrease their deliveries the next month by the same amount, without being reported in violation.

A dealer also may increase his milk sales by reducing his cream and milk byproducts sales, and increase his sales of milk byproducts by reducing his cream sales, providing such a approved by the marke area.

Deliveries of milk, c byproducts to other Armed Forces, and to p milk who do not distrib and milk byproducts in are quota-exempt.

Consumers in the m named today and in oth ignated generally will chase as much milk und servation program as buying in recent mon limits of local supplies. production is not expe enough to permit dealer milk as their quotas allo

Fluid milk sales are Food Distribution Adm cials said, to help assur for manufacturing the evaporated milk, and n quired by the Armed Se ians for food nutrition a anced diets. Sales quota on fluid milk byproduct below June deliveries to supplies where product to conserve milk for purposes.

Reserve
1
77337

FDO 79-57

OCTOBER 19, 1943

WAR FOOD ADMINISTRATION

[FDO 79-57]

PART 1401—DAIRY PRODUCTS

FLUID MILK AND CREAM IN PHOENIX, ARIZ., SALES AREA

Pursuant to the authority vested in me by Food Distribution Order No. 79 (8 F.R. 12426), issued on September 7, 1943, as amended, and to effectuate the purposes of such order, it is hereby ordered as follows:

§ 1401.104 *Quota restrictions*—(a) *Definitions.* When used in this order, unless otherwise distinctly expressed or manifestly incompatible with the intent hereof;

(1) Each term defined in Food Distribution Order No. 79, as amended, shall, when used herein, have the same meaning as is set forth for such term in Food Distribution Order No. 79, as amended.

(2) The term "FDO 79" means Food Distribution Order No. 79, issued on September 7, 1943, as amended.

(3) The term "sub-handler" means any handler, such as a peddler, vendor, sub-dealer, or secondary dealer, who purchases in a previously packaged and processed form milk, milk byproducts, or cream for delivery.

(b) *Milk sales area.* The following area is hereby designated as a "milk sales area" to be known as the Phoenix, Arizona, sales area, and is referred to hereinafter as the "sales area":

The city of Phoenix and the supervisorial districts described as follows:

That part of district 1 bounded by West 8th Street, Bartlet Road, Base Line Road, South Central Avenue, Laveen Road, and city limits;

That part of district 2 bounded by Lateral 19, Arizona Canal, Indian School Road, Chicago Avenue, Thomas Road, 40th Street, U. S. Highway 60, and city limits;

That part of district 3 bounded by Salt River, Lateral 17, Buckeye Road, Lateral 15, Van Buren Street, Lateral 16, and city limits, all in Maricopa County, Arizona.

(c) *Base period.* The calendar month of June 1943 is hereby designated as the base period for the sales area.

(d) *Quota period.* The remainder of the calendar month in which the provisions hereof become effective and each subsequent calendar month, respectively, is hereby designated as a quota period for the sales area.

(e) *Handler quotas.* Quotas for each handler in the sales area in each quota period shall be calculated in terms of pounds of each of the items for which percentages are specified in (3) below and shall be determined as follows:

(1) Divide the total deliveries of each such item made in the sales area by such handler during the base period, after excluding the quota-exempt deliveries described in (i) hereof, by the number of days in the base period;

(2) Multiply the result of the foregoing calculation by the number of days in the quota period;

(3) Multiply the aforesaid resulting amount by the following applicable percentage: (i) milk, 100 percent; (ii) butterfat in milk, 100 percent; (iii) cream, 75 percent; (iv) butterfat in cream, 75 percent; (v) milk byproducts other than cottage, pot, or baker's cheese, 75 percent; and (vi) cottage, pot, or baker's cheese, 75 percent of skim milk equivalent. (For the purpose of this order, one pound of cottage, pot, or baker's cheese shall be considered as the equivalent of 7 pounds of skim milk.)

(f) *Quota limitations.* No handler shall, during any quota period, make deliveries in the sales area in excess of his respective quotas, except as set out in (i) hereof: *Provided,* That a handler may, after application to and approval by the market agent, secure an increase in milk quotas through an equivalent reduction as determined by the market agent, in cream and milk byproducts quotas, and an increase in milk byproducts quota through an equivalent reduction as determined by the market agent, in cream quotas.

(g) *Quotas for handlers who are also producers.* Quotas for handlers who are also producers and who purchase no milk shall be 100 percent of the total production of such handlers in the base period.

(h) *Handler exemptions.* Quotas shall not apply to any handler who delivers in a quota period a daily average of less than 200 units of milk, cream, and milk byproducts. For the purpose of this order, a unit shall be the equivalent in volume of the following: (1) milk, one quart of milk; (2) cream, one-half pint of cream; and (3) milk byproduct, one quart of skim milk, buttermilk, flavored milk drink, or other beverage containing more than 85 percent of skim milk, or one-half pound of cottage, pot, or baker's cheese.

(i) *Quota exclusions and exemptions.* Deliveries of milk, milk byproducts, or cream (1) to other handlers, except for such deliveries to sub-handlers, (2) to plants engaged in the handling or processing of milk, milk byproducts, or cream from which no milk, milk byproducts, or cream is delivered in the sales area, and (3) to the agencies or groups specified in (d) of FDO 79, shall be excluded from the computation of deliveries in the base period and exempt from charges to quotas.

(j) *Transfers and apportionment of quotas.* The market agent is empowered to deduct an amount of base period deliveries to purchasers from the total of deliveries made by a handler or other person in the base period upon the application and a showing of unreasonable hardship by the handler making deliveries to such purchasers on the effective date of this order, and to add the amount of such deliveries to the total base period deliveries of the applicant handler. Denials of transfers or tranfers granted by the market agent shall be reviewed by the Director upon application.

(k) *Petition for relief from hardships.* (1) Any person affected by FDO 79 or the provisions hereof who considers that compliance therewith would work an exceptional and unreasonable hardship on him, may file with the market agent a petition addressed to the Director. The petition shall contain the correct name, address and principal place of business of the petitioner, a full statement of the facts upon which the petition is based, and the hardship involved and the nature of the relief desired.

(2) Upon receiving such petition, the market agent shall immediately investigate the representations and facts stated therein.

(3) After investigation, the petition shall be certified to the Director; but prior to certification the market agent may (i) deny the petition, or (ii) grant temporary relief for a total period not to exceed 60 days.

(4) Denials or grants of relief by the market agent shall be reviewed by the Director and may be affirmed, modified, or reversed by the Director.

(l) *Reports.* Each handler shall transmit to the market agent on forms prescribed by the market agent the following reports:

(1) Within 20 days following the effective date of this order, reports which show the information required by the market agent to establish such handlers' quotas;

(2) Within 20 days following the close of each quota period, the information required by the market agent to establish volumes of deliveries of milk, cream, and milk byproducts during the preceding quota period; and

(3) Handlers exempt from quotas pursuant to (h) hereof shall, upon the request of the market agent, submit the

information required by the market agent to establish volumes of deliveries of milk, cream, and milk byproducts.

(m) *Records.* Handlers shall keep and shall make available to the market agent such records of receipts, sales, deliveries, and production as the market agent shall require for the purpose of obtaining information which the Director may require for the establishment of quotas as prescribed in (b) of FDO 79.

(n) *Distribution schedules.* The distribution schedules, if any, to be followed by the handlers in making deliveries shall be made effective in the terms of approval by the Director of such schedules.

(o) *Expense of administration.* Each handler shall pay to the market agent, within 20 days after the close of each calendar month an assessment of $0.015 per hundredweight of each of milk, cream, skim milk, buttermilk, flavored milk drinks, beverages containing more than 85 percent of skim milk, and skim milk equivalent of cottage, pot, or baker's cheese delivered during the preceding quota period and subject to quota regulations under the provisions hereof.

(p) *Violations.* The market agent shall report all violations to the Director together with the information required for the prosecution of such violations, except in a case where a handler has made deliveries in a quota period in excess of a quota in an amount not to exceed 5 percent of such quota, and in the succeeding quota period makes deliveries below that quota by at least the same percent.

(q) *Bureau of the Budget approval.* The record keeping and reporting requirements of this order have been approved by the Bureau of the Budget in accordance with the Federal Reports Act of 1942. Subsequent record keeping or reporting requirements will be subject to the approval of the Bureau of the Budget pursuant to the Federal Reports Act of 1942.

(r) This order shall take effect at 12:01 a. m., e. w. t., November 1, 1943.

Issued this 19th day of October 1943.

C. W. KITCHEN,
Acting Director of Food Distribution.

Press Release, Immediate:
Wednesday, October 20, 1943.

Milk sales in 19 metropolitan areas in Illinois, Michigan, Colorado, Utah, Arizona, Oregon, Pennsylvania, Minnesota, Oklahoma and West Virginia will be regulated under the Food Distribution Administration's fluid milk conservation and control program, beginning November 1, 1943.

The new milk sales areas and the market agents who will administer the program in each are:

Johnstown, Pa., Erie, Pa., Altoona, Pa., Pittsburgh, Pa., Metropolitan, Charleston, W. Va., Wheeling, W. Va.: George A. Taylor, Century Building, Pittsburgh, Pa.

Peoria, Ill., Rockford, Ill.: A. W. Colebank, 135 S. LaSalle St., Chicago, Ill.

Phoenix, Ariz., Denver, Colo., Metropolitan, Salt Lake City, Utah, Metropolitan: Ben King, 503 Security Life Building, 810 14th St., Denver, Colo. (temp. address).

Portland, Oregon, Metropolitan: J. H. Mapes, 635 Elliot Avenue, West, Seattle, Washington.

Detroit, Michigan, Metropolitan, Saginaw-Bay City, Mich., Metropolitan, Lansing, Mich., Metropolitan, Flint, Mich., Metropolitan: (To be announced later).

Oklahoma City, Oklahoma, Tulsa, Oklahoma: M. M. Morehouse, 512 Porter Bldg., 406 W. 34th St., Kansas City, Mo.

Minneapolis-St. Paul, Minnesota: D. F. Spencer, 404 Post Office Bldg., Minneapolis, Minn.

Under the program, milk dealers will be permitted to sell as much fluid milk as they sold in June and three-fourths as much cream and milk byproducts (such as cottage cheese, chocolate milk, and buttermilk) as they sold in June. Milk dealers include all persons or firms engaged in the sale or transfer of milk, but not such distributors as subhandlers ("peddlers"), retail stores, hotels, or restaurants.

Producer-distributors who purchase no milk will be permitted to sell as much milk as they produced in June.

Dealers will be allowed to exceed these base quotas by not more than 5 percent during any month, providing they decrease their deliveries the next month by the same amount, without being reported in violation.

A dealer also may increase his milk sales by reducing his cream and milk byproducts sales, and increase his sales of milk byproducts by reducing his cream sales, providing such an adjustment is approved by the market agent for the area.

Deliveries of milk, cream, and milk byproducts to other dealers, to the Armed Forces, and to plants processing milk who do not distribute milk, cream, and milk byproducts in the sales area are quota-exempt.

Consumers in the milk sales areas named today and in others already designated generally will be able to purchase as much milk under the milk conservation program as they have been buying in recent months—within the limits of local supplies. In some areas, production is not expected to be large enough to permit dealers to sell as much milk as their quotas allow.

Fluid milk sales are being stabilized, Food Distribution Administration officials said, to help assure sufficient milk for manufacturing the cheese, butter, evaporated milk, and milk powder required by the Armed Services and civilians for food nutrition and properly balanced diets. Sales quotas on cream and on fluid milk byproducts have been set below June deliveries to boost fluid milk supplies where production is low, and to conserve milk for manufacturing purposes.

FDO 79-58

OCTOBER 19, 1943

WAR FOOD ADMINISTRATION

[FDO 79-58]

PART 1401—DAIRY PRODUCTS

FLUID MILK AND CREAM IN DENVER, COLO., METROPOLITAN SALES AREA

Pursuant to the authority vested in me by Food Distribution Order No. 79 (8 F.R. 12426), issued on September 7, 1943, as amended, and to effectuate the purposes of such order, it is hereby ordered as follows:

§ 1401.103 *Quota restrictions*—(a) *Definitions.* When used in this order, unless otherwise distinctly expressed or manifestly incompatible with the intent hereof:

(1) Each term defined in Food Distribution Order No. 79, as amended, shall, when used herein, have the same meaning as is set forth for such term in Food Distribution Order No. 79, as amended.

(2) The term "FDO 79" means Food Distribution Order No. 79, issued on September 7, 1943, as amended.

(3) The term "sub-handler" means any handler, such as a peddler, vendor, sub-dealer, or secondary dealer, who purchases in a previously packaged and processed form milk, milk byproducts, or cream for delivery.

(b) *Milk sales area.* The following area is hereby designated as a "milk sales area" to be known as the Denver Colorado, metropolitan sales area, and is referred to hereinafter as the "sales area":

The city of Denver (coincident with Denver County); the election precincts of Adams City, Aurora, Baker, College, East Aurora, Retreat Park, Rose Hill, Sable, and Utah Junction in Adams County; the precincts numbered 1 to 28, 30 to 37, 40, and 41 in Arapahoe County; the precincts of Bancroft, Berkeley, Columbia Heights, Daniels, Divinner, Edgewater 1 and 2, Golden 1, 2, 3, and 4, Golf Club, Griffith, Maple Grove, Mount Air, Northeast Arvada, North Lakewood, Northwest Arvada, Pleasant View, Pioneer, Southeast Arvada, South Lakewood, Southwest Arvada, Vasquez, and Wheat Ridge in Jefferson County, all in the State of Colorado.

(c) *Base period.* The calendar month of June 1943 is hereby designated as the base period for the sales area.

(d) *Quota period.* The remainder of the calendar month in which the provisions hereof become effective and each subsequent calendar month, respectively, is hereby designated as a quota period for the sales area.

(e) *Handler quotas.* Quotas for each handler in the sales area in each quota period shall be calculated in terms of pounds of each of the items for which percentages are specified in (3) below and shall be determined as follows:

(1) Divide the total deliveries of each such item made in the sales area by such handler during the base period, after excluding the quota-exempt deliveries described in (i) hereof, by the number of days in the base period;

(2) Multiply the result of the foregoing calculation by the number of days in the quota period;

(3) Multiply the aforesaid resulting amount by the following applicable percentage: (i) Milk: 100 percent; (ii) butterfat in milk: 100 percent; (iii) cream: 75 percent: (iv) butterfat in cream: 75 percent; (v) milk byproducts other than cottage, pot, or baker's cheese: 75 percent; and (vi) cottage, pot, or baker's cheese: 75 percent of skim milk equivalent. (For the purpose of this order, one pound of cottage, pot, or baker's cheese shall be considered as the equivalent of 7 pounds of skim milk.)

(f) *Quota limitations.* No handler shall, during any quota period make deliveries in the sales area in excess of his respective quotas except as set out in (i) hereof: *Provided,* That a handler may, after application to and approval by the market agent, secure an increase in milk quotas through an equivalent reduction as determined by the market agent, in cream and milk byproducts quotas, and an increase in milk byproducts quota through an equivalent reduction as determined by the market agent, in cream quotas.

(g) *Quotas for handlers who are also producers.* Quotas for handlers who are also producers and who purchase no milk shall be 100 percent of the total production of such handlers in the base period.

(h) *Handler exemptions.* Quotas shall not apply to any handler who delivers in a quota period a daily average of less than 200 units of milk, cream, and milk byproducts. For the purpose of this order, a unit shall be the equivalent in volume of the following: (1) milk, one quart of milk; (2) cream, one-half pint of cream; and (3) milk byproduct, one quart of skim milk, buttermilk, flavored milk drink, or other beverage containing more than 85 percent of skim milk, or one-half pound of cottage, pot, or baker's cheese.

(i) *Quota exclusions and exemptions.* Deliveries of milk, milk byproducts, or cream (1) to other handlers, except for such deliveries to sub-handlers, (2) to plants engaged in the handling or processing of milk, milk byproducts, or cream from which no milk, milk byproducts, or cream is delivered in the sales area, and (3) to the agencies or groups specified in (d) of FDO 79, shall be excluded from the computation of deliveries in the base period and exempt from charges to quotas.

(j) *Transfers and apportionment of quotas.* The market agent is empowered to deduct an amount of base period deliveries to purchasers from the total of deliveries made by a handler or other person in the base period upon the application and a showing of unreasonable hardship by the handler making deliveries to such purchasers on the effective date of this order, and to add the amount of such deliveries to the total base period deliveries of the applicant handler. Denials of transfers or transfers granted by the market agent shall be reviewed by the Director upon application.

(k) *Petition for relief from hardships.* (1) Any person affected by FDO 79 or the provisions hereof who considers that compliance therewith would work an exceptional and unreasonable hardship on him may file with the market agent a petition addressed to the Director. The petition shall contain the correct name, address and principal place of business of the petitioner, a full statement of the facts upon which the petition is based, and the hardship involved and the nature of the relief desired.

(2) Upon receiving such petition, the market agent shall immediately investigate the representations and facts stated therein.

(3) After investigation, the petition shall be certified to the Director, but prior to certification the market agent may (i) deny the petition, or (ii) grant temporary relief for a total period not to exceed 60 days.

(4) Denials or grants of relief by the market agent shall be reviewed by the Director and may be affirmed, modified, or reversed by the Director.

(l) *Reports.* Each handler shall transmit to the market agent on forms prescribed by the market agent the following reports:

(1) Within 20 days following the effective date of this order, reports which show the information required by the market agent to establish such handlers' quotas;

(2) Within 20 days following the close of each quota period, the information required by the market agent to establish

volumes of deliveries of milk, cream, and milk byproducts during the preceding quota period; and

(3) Handlers exempt from quotas pursuant to (h) hereof shall, upon the request of the market agent, submit the information required by the market agent to establish volumes of deliveries of milk, cream, and milk byproducts.

(m) *Records.* Handlers shall keep and shall make available to the market agent such records of receipts, sales, deliveries, and production as the market agent shall require for the purpose of obtaining information which the Director may require for the establishment of quotas as prescribed in (b) of FDO 79.

(n) *Distribution schedules.* The distribution schedules, if any, to be followed by the handlers in making deliveries shall be made effective in the terms of approval by the Director of such schedules.

(o) *Expense of administration.* Each handler shall pay to the market agent, within 20 days after the close of each calendar month an assessment of $0 015 per hundredweight of each of milk, cream, skim milk, buttermilk, flavored milk drinks, beverages containing more than 85 percent of skim milk, and skim milk equivalent of cottage, pot, or baker's cheese delivered during the preceding quota period and subject to quota regulations under the provisions hereof.

(p) *Violations.* The market agent shall report all violations to the Director together with the information required for the prosecution of such violations, except in a case where a handler has made deliveries in a quota period in excess of a quota in an amount n exceed 5 percent of such quota, a the succeeding quota period make liveries below that quota by at leas same percent.

(q) *Bureau of the Budget app* The record keeping and reportin quirements of this order have bee proved by the Bureau of the Budg accordance with the Federal Report of 1942. Subsequent record keepi reporting requirements will be subj the approval of the Bureau of the B pursuant to the Federal Reports A 1942.

(r) This order shall take effe 12:01 a. m., e. w. t., November 1, 19

Issued this 19th day of October 19

C. W. KITCHEN
Acting Director of Food Distributi

Press Release, Immediate:
Wednesday, October 20, 1943.

Milk sales in 19 metropolitan areas in Illinois, Michigan, Colorado, Utah, Arizona, Oregon, Pennsylvania, Minnesota, Oklahoma and West Virginia will be regulated under the Food Distribution Administration's fluid milk conservation and control program, beginning November 1, 1943.

The new milk sales areas and the market agents who will administer the program in each are:

Johnstown, Pa., Erie, Pa., Altoona, Pa., Pittsburgh, Pa., Metropolitan, Charleston, W. Va., Wheeling, W. Va.: George A. Taylor, Century Building, Pittsburgh, Pa.

Peoria, Ill, Rockford, Ill.: A. W. Colebank, 135 S. LaSalle St., Chicago, Ill.

Phoenix, Ariz., Denver, Colo., Metropolitan, Salt Lake City, Utah, Metropolitan: Ben King, 503 Security Life Building, 810 14th St., Denver, Colo. (temp. address).

Portland, Oregon, Metropolitan: J. H. Mapes, 635 Elliot Avenue, West, Seattle, Washington.

Detroit, Michigan, Metropolitan, Saginaw-Bay City, Mich., Metropolitan, Lansing, Mich., Metropolitan, Flint. Mich., Metropolitan: (To be announced later).

Oklahoma City, Oklahoma, Tulsa, Oklahoma: M. M. Morehouse, 512 Porter Bldg., 406 W. 34th St., Kansas City, Mo.

Minneapolis-St. Paul, Minnesota: D. F. Spencer, 404 Post Office Bldg., Minneapolis, Minn.

Under the program, milk dealers will be permitted to sell as much fluid milk as they sold in June and three-fourths as much cream and milk byproducts (such as cottage cheese, chocolate milk, and buttermilk) as they sold in June. Milk dealers include all persons or firms engaged in the sale or transfer of milk, but not such distributors as subhandlers ("peddlers"), retail stores, hotels, or restaurants.

Producer-distributors who purchase no milk will be permitted to sell as much milk as they produced in June.

Dealers will be allowed to exceed these base quotas by not more than 5 percent during any month, providing they decrease their deliveries the next month by the same amount, without being reported in violation.

A dealer also may increase his milk sales by reducing his cream and milk byproducts sales, and increase his sales of milk byproducts by reducing his cream sales, providing such an adjustme approved by the market agent fo area.

Deliveries of milk, cream, and byproducts to other dealers, to Armed Forces, and to plants proce milk who do not distribute milk, c and milk byproducts in the sales are quota-exempt.

Consumers in the milk sales named today and in others already ignated generally will be able to chase as much milk under the milk servation program as they have buying in recent months—withi limits of local supplies. In some production is not expected to be enough to permit dealers to sell as milk as their quotas allow.

Fluid milk sales are being stabi Food Distribution Administration cials said, to help assure sufficient for manufacturing the cheese, b evaporated milk, and milk powde quired by the Armed Services and ians for food nutrition and properl anced diets. Sales quotas on crean on fluid milk byproducts have bee below June deliveries to boost fluid supplies where production is low, a conserve milk for manufacturing poses.

FDO 79-59

OCTOBER 19, 1943

WAR FOOD ADMINISTRATION

[FDO 79-59]

PART 1401—DAIRY PRODUCTS

FLUID MILK AND CREAM IN CHARLESTON, W. VA., SALES AREA

Pursuant to the authority vested in me by Food Distribution Order No. 79 (8 F.R. 12426), issued on September 7, 1943, as amended, and to effectuate the purposes of such order, it is hereby ordered as follows:

§ 1401.111 *Quota restrictions*—(a) *Definitions.* When used in this order, unless otherwise distinctly expressed or manifestly incompatible with the intent hereof:

(1) Each term defined in Food Distribution Order No. 79, as amended, shall, when used herein, have the same meaning as is set forth for such term in Food Distribution Order No. 79, as amended.

(2) The term "FDO 79" means Food Distribution Order No. 79, issued on September 7, 1943, as amended.

(3) The term "sub-handler" means any handler, such as a peddler, vendor, sub-dealer, or secondary dealer, who purchases in a previously packaged and processed form milk, milk byproducts, or cream for delivery.

(b) *Milk sales area.* The following area is hereby designated as a "milk sales area" to be known as the Charleston, West Virginia, sales area, and is referred to hereinafter as the "sales area":

The city of Charleston and the magisterial districts of Charleston, Jefferson, Loudon, Malden, and Union in Kanawha County, West Virginia; that part of the district of Pocatalico comprising part of the town of Nitro, all in Putnam County, West Virginia.

(c) *Base period.* The calendar month of June 1943 is hereby designated as the base period for the sales area.

(d) *Quota period.* The remainder of the calendar month in which the provisions hereof become effective and each subsequent calendar month, respectively, is hereby designated as a quota period for the sales area.

(e) *Handler quotas.* Quotas for each handler in the sales area in each quota period shall be calculated in terms of pounds of each of the items for which percentages are specified in (3) below and shall be determined as follows:

(1) Divide the total deliveries of each such item made in the sales area by such handler during the base period, after excluding the quota-exempt deliveries described in (i) hereof, by the number of days in the base period;

(2) Multiply the result of the foregoing calculation by the number of days in the quota period;

(3) Multiply the aforesaid resulting amount by the following applicable percentage: (i) Milk: 100 percent; (ii) butterfat in milk: ------ percent; (iii) cream: 75 percent; (iv) butterfat in cream: 75 percent; (v) milk byproducts other than cottage, pot, or baker's cheese: 75 percent; and (vi) cottage, pot, or baker's cheese: 75 percent of skim milk equivalent. (For the purpose of this order, one pound of cottage, pot, or baker's cheese shall be considered as the equivalent of 7 pounds of skim milk.)

(f) *Quota limitations.* No handler shall, during any quota period, make deliveries in the sales area in excess of his respective quotas, except as set out in (i) hereof: *Provided*, That a handler may, after application to and approval by the market agent, secure an increase in milk quotas through an equivalent reduction as determined by the market agent, in cream and milk byproducts quotas, and an increase in milk byproducts quota through an equivalent reduction as determined by the market agent, in cream quotas.

(g) *Quotas for handlers who are also producers.* Quotas for handlers who are also producers and who purchase no milk shall be 100 percent of the total production of such handlers in the base period.

(h) *Handler exemptions.* Quotas shall not apply to any handler who delivers in a quota period a daily average of less than 350 units of milk, cream, and milk byproducts. For the purpose of this order, a unit shall be the equivalent in volume of the following: (1) milk, one quart of milk; (2) cream, one-half pint of cream; and (3) milk byproduct, one quart of skim milk, buttermilk, flavored milk drink, or other beverage containing more than 85 percent of skim milk, or one-half pound of cottage, pot, or baker's cheese.

(i) *Quota exclusions and exemptions.* Deliveries of milk, milk byproducts, or cream (1) to other handlers, except for such deliveries to sub-handlers, (2) to plants engaged in the handling or processing of milk, milk byproducts, or cream from which no milk, milk byproducts, or cream is delivered in the sales area, and (3) to the agencies or groups specified in (d) of FDO 79, shall be excluded from the computation of deliveries in the base period and exempt from charges to quotas.

(j) *Transfers and apportionment of quotas.* The market agent is empowered to deduct an amount of base period deliveries to purchasers from the total of deliveries made by a handler or other person in the base period upon the application and a showing of unreasonable hardship by the handler making deliveries to such purchasers on the effective date of this order, and to add the amount of such deliveries to the total base period deliveries of the applicant handler. Denials of transfers or transfers granted by the market agent shall be reviewed by the Director upon application.

(k) *Petition for relief from hardships.* (1) Any person affected by FDO 79 or the provisions hereof who considers that compliance therewith would work an exceptional and unreasonable hardship on him, may file with the market agent a petition addressed to the Director. The petition shall contain the correct name, address and principal place of business of the petitioner, a full statement of the facts upon which the petition is based, and the hardship involved and the nature of the relief desired.

(2) Upon receiving such petition, the market agent shall immediately investigate the representations and facts stated therein.

(3) After investigation, the petition shall be certified to the Director, but prior to certification the market agent may (i) deny the petition, or (ii) grant temporary relief for a total period not to exceed 60 days.

(4) Denials or grants of relief by the market agent shall be reviewed by the Director and may be affirmed, modified, or reversed by the Director.

(l) *Reports.* Each handler shall transmit to the market agent on forms prescribed by the market agent the following reports:

(1) Within 20 days following the effective date of this order, reports which show the information required by the market agent to establish such handlers' quotas;

(2) Within 20 days following the close of each quota period the information required by the market agent to establish volumes of deliveries of milk, cream, and milk byproducts during the preceding quota period; and

(3) Handlers exempt from quotas pursuant to (h) hereof shall, upon the request of the market agent, submit the information required by the market agent to establish volumes of deliveries of milk, cream, and milk byproducts.

(m) *Records.* Handlers shall keep and shall make available to the market agent such records of receipts, sales, deliveries, and production as the market agent shall require for the purpose of obtaining information which the Director may require for the establishment of quotas as prescribed in (b) of FDO 79.

(n) *Distribution schedules.* The distribution schedules, if any, to be followed by the handlers in making deliveries shall be made effective in the terms of approval by the Director of such schedules.

(o) *Expense of administration.* Each handler shall pay to the market agent, within 20 days after the close of each calendar month an assessment of $0.01 per hundredweight of each of milk, cream, skim milk, buttermilk, flavored milk drinks, beverages containing more than 85 percent of skim milk, and skim milk equivalent of cottage, pot, or baker's cheese delivered during the preceding quota period and subject to quota regulations under the provisions hereof.

(p) *Violations.* The market agent shall report all violations to the Director together with the information required for the prosecution of such violations, except in a case where a handler has made deliveries in a quota period in excess of a quota in an amount not to exceed 5 percent of such quota, and in the succeeding quota period makes deliveries below that quota by at least the same percent.

(q) *Bureau of the Budget approval.* The record keeping and reporting requirements of this order have been approved by the Bureau of the Budget in accordance with the Federal Reports Act of 1942. Subsequent record keeping or reporting requirements will be subject to the approval of the Bureau of the Budget pursuant to the Federal Reports Act of 1942.

(r) This order shall take effect at 12:01 a. m., e. w. t., November 1, 1943.

Issued this 19th day of October 1943.

C. W. KITCHEN,
Acting Director of Food Distribution.

Press Release, Immediate:
Wednesday, October 20, 1943.

Milk sales in 19 metropolitan areas in Illinois, Michigan, Colorado, Utah, Arizona, Oregon, Pennsylvania, Minnesota, Oklahoma and West Virginia will be regulated under the Food Distribution Administration's fluid milk conservation and control program, beginning November 1, 1943.

The new milk sales areas and the market agents who will administer the program in each are:

Johnstown, Pa., Erie, Pa., Altoona, Pa., Pittsburgh, Pa., Metropolitan, Charleston, W. Va., Wheeling, W. Va.: George A. Taylor, Century Building, Pittsburgh, Pa.

Peoria, Ill., Rockford, Ill.: A. W. Colebank, 135 S. LaSalle St., Chicago, Ill.

Phoenix, Ariz., Denver, Colo., Metropolitan, Salt Lake City, Utah, Metropolitan: Ben King, 503 Security Life Building, 810 14th St., Denver, Colo. (temp. address).

Portland, Oregon, Metropolitan: J. H. Mapes, 635 Elliot Avenue, West, Seattle, Washington.

Detroit, Michigan, Metropolitan, Saginaw-Bay City, Mich., Metropolitan, Lansing, Mich., Metropolitan, Flint, Mich., Metropolitan: (To be announced later).

Oklahoma City, Oklahoma, Tulsa, Oklahoma: M. M. Morehouse, 512 Porter Bldg., 406 W. 34th St., Kansas City, Mo.

Minneapolis-St. Paul, Minnesota: D. F. Spencer, 404 Post Office Bldg., Minneapolis, Minn.

Under the program, milk dealers will be permitted to sell as much fluid milk as they sold in June and three-fourths as much cream and milk byproducts (such as cottage cheese, chocolate milk, and buttermilk) as they sold in June. Milk dealers include all persons or firms engaged in the sale or transfer of milk, but not such distributors as subhandlers ("peddlers"), retail stores, hotels, or restaurants.

Producer-distributors who purchase no milk will be permitted to sell as much milk as they produced in June.

Dealers will be allowed to exceed these base quotas by not more than 5 percent during any month, providing they decrease their deliveries the next month by the same amount, without being reported in violation.

A dealer also may increase his milk sales by reducing his cream and milk byproducts sales, and increase his sales of milk byproducts by reducing his cream sales, providing such an adjustment is approved by the market agent for the area.

Deliveries of milk, cream, and milk byproducts to other dealers, to the Armed Forces, and to plants processing milk who do not distribute milk, cream, and milk byproducts in the sales area are quota-exempt.

Consumers in the milk sales areas named today and in others already designated generally will be able to purchase as much milk under the milk conservation program as they have been buying in recent months—within the limits of local supplies. In some areas, production is not expected to be large enough to permit dealers to sell as much milk as their quotas allow.

Fluid milk sales are being stabilized, Food Distribution Administration officials said, to help assure sufficient milk for manufacturing the cheese, butter, evaporated milk, and milk powder required by the Armed Services and civilians for food nutrition and properly balanced diets. Sales quotas on cream and on fluid milk byproducts have been set below June deliveries to boost fluid milk supplies where production is low, and to conserve milk for manufacturing purposes.

77354
Ag. 2

FDO 79-60

OCTOBER 19, 1943

WAR FOOD ADMINISTRATION

[FDO 79-60]

PART 1401—DAIRY PRODUCTS

FLUID MILK AND CREAM IN PEORIA, ILL., SALES AREA

Pursuant to the authority vested in me by Food Distribution Order No. 79 (8 F.R. 12426), issued on September 7, 1943, as amended, and to effectuate the purposes of such order, it is hereby ordered as follows:

§ 1401.98 *Quota restrictions*—(a) *Definitions.* When used in this order, unless otherwise distinctly expressed or manifestly incompatible with the intent hereof:

(1) Each term defined in Food Distribution Order No. 79, as amended, shall, when used herein, have the same meaning as is set forth for such term in Food Distribution Order No. 79, as amended.

(2) The term "FDO 79" means Food Distribution Order No. 79, issued on September 7, 1943, as amended.

(3) The term "sub-handler" means any handler, such as a peddler, vendor, sub-dealer, or secondary dealer, who purchases in a previously packaged and processed form milk, milk byproducts, or cream for delivery.

(b) *Milk sales area.* The following area is hereby designated as a "milk sales area" to be known as the Peoria, Illinois sales area, and is referred to hereinafter as the "sales area":

The city of Peoria and the townships of Limestone, Peoria, and Richwoods, in Peoria County; the townships of Fondulac, Pekin, and that part of Groveland Township comprising parts of the village of Crevecoeur and the city of East Peoria, in Tazewell County, all in the State of Illinois.

(c) *Base period.* The calendar month of June 1943 is hereby designated as the base period for the sales area.

(d) *Quota period.* The remainder of the calendar month in which the provisions hereof become effective and each subsequent calendar month, respectively, is hereby designated as a quota period for the sales area.

(e) *Handler quotas.* Quotas for each handler in the sales area in each quota period shall be calculated in terms of pounds of each of the items for which percentages are specified in (3) below and shall be determined as follows:

(1) Divide the total deliveries of each such item made in the sales area by such handler during the base period, after excluding the quota-exempt deliveries described in (i) hereof, by the number of days in the base period;

(2) Multiply the result of the foregoing calculation by the number of days in the quota period;

(3) Multiply the aforesaid resulting amount by the following applicable percentage: (i) milk: 100 percent; (ii) butterfat in milk: ______ percent; (iii) cream: 75 percent; (iv) butterfat in cream: 75 percent; (v) milk byproducts other than cottage, pot, or baker's cheese: 75 percent; and (vi) cottage, pot, or baker's cheese: 75 percent of skim milk equivalent. (For the purpose of this order, one pound of cottage, pot, or baker's cheese shall be considered as the equivalent of 7 pounds of skim milk.)

(f) *Quota limitations.* No handler shall, during any quota period, make deliveries in the sales area in excess of his respective quotas, except as set out in (i) hereof: *Provided,* That a handler may, after application to and approval by the market agent, secure an increase in milk quotas through an equivalent reduction as determined by the market agent, in cream and milk byproducts quotas, and an increase in milk byproducts quota through an equivalent reduction as determined by the market agent, in cream quotas.

(g) *Quotas for handlers who are also producers.* Quotas for handlers who are also producers and who purchase no milk shall be 100 percent of the total production of such handlers in the base period.

(h) *Handler exemptions.* Quotas shall not apply to any handler who delivers in a quota period a daily average of less than 300 units of milk, cream, and milk byproducts. For the purpose of this order, a unit shall be the equivalent in volume of the following: (1) Milk, one quart of milk; (2) cream, one-half pint of cream; and (3) milk byproduct, one quart of skim milk, buttermilk, flavored milk drink, or other beverage containing more than 85 percent of skim milk, or one-half pound of cottage, pot, or baker's cheese.

(i) *Quota exclusions and exemptions.* Deliveries of milk, milk byproducts, or cream (1) to other handlers, except for such deliveries to sub-handlers, (2) to plants engaged in the handling or processing of milk, milk byproducts, or cream from which no milk, milk byproducts, or cream is delivered in the sales area, and (3) to the agencies or groups specified in (d) of FDO 79, shall be excluded from the computation of deliveries in the base period and exempt from charges to quotas.

(j) *Transfers and apportionment of quotas.* The market agent is empowered to deduct an amount of base period deliveries to purchasers from the total of deliveries made by a handler or other person in the base period upon the application and a showing of unreasonable hardship by the handler making deliveries to such purchasers on the effective date of this order, and to add the amount of such deliveries to the total base period deliveries of the applicant handler. Denials of transfers or transfers granted by the market agent shall be reviewed by the Director upon application.

(k) *Petition for relief from hardships.* (1) Any person affected by FDO 79 or the provisions hereof who considers that compliance therewith would work an exceptional and unreasonable hardship on him, may file with the market agent a petition addressed to the Director. The petition shall contain the correct name, address and principal place of business of the petitioner, a full statement of the facts upon which the petition is based, and the hardship involved and the nature of the relief desired.

(2) Upon receiving such petition, the market agent shall immediately investigate the representations and facts stated therein.

(3) After investigation, the petition shall be certified to the Director, but prior to certification the market agent may (i) deny the petition, or (ii) grant temporary relief for a total period not to exceed 60 days.

(4) Denials or grants of relief by the market agent shall be reviewed by the Director and may be affirmed, modified, or reversed by the Director.

(l) *Reports.* Each handler shall transmit to the market agent on forms prescribed by the market agent the following reports:

(1) Within 20 days following the effective date of this order, reports which show the information required by the market agent to establish such handlers' quotas;

(2) Within 20 days following the close of each quota period, the information required by the market agent to establish volumes of deliveries of milk, cream, and milk byproducts during the preceding quota period; and

(3) Handlers exempt from quotas pursuant to (h) hereof shall, upon the request of the market agent, submit the

information required by the market agent to establish volumes of deliveries of milk, cream, and milk byproducts.

(m) *Records.* Handlers shall keep and shall make available to the market agent such records of receipts, sales, deliveries, and production as the market agent shall require for the purpose of obtaining information which the Director may require for the establishment of quotas as prescribed in (b) of FDO 79.

(n) *Distribution schedules.* The distribution schedules, if any, to be followed by the handlers in making deliveries shall be made effective in the terms of approval by the Director of such schedules.

(o) *Expense of administration.* Each handler shall pay to the market agent, within 20 days after the close of each calendar month an assessment of $.01 per hundredweight of each of milk, cream, skim milk, buttermilk, flavored milk drinks, beverages containing more than 85 percent of skim milk, and skim milk equivalent of cottage, pot or baker's cheese delivered during the preceding quota period and subject to quota regulations under the provisions hereof.

(p) *Violations.* The market agent shall report all violations to the Director together with the information required for the prosecution of such violations, except in a case where a handler has made deliveries in a quota period in excess of a quota in an amount not to exceed 5 percent of such quota, and in the succeeding quota period makes deliveries below that quota by at least the same percent.

(q) *Bureau of the Budget approval.* The record keeping and reporting requirements of this order have been approved by the Bureau of the Budget in accordance with the Federal Reports Act of 1942. Subsequent record keeping or reporting requirements will be subject to the approval of the Bureau of the Budget pursuant to the Federal Reports Act of 1942.

(r) This order shall take effect at 12:01 a. m., e. w. t., November 1, 1943.

Issued this 19th day of October 1943.

C. W. KITCHEN,
Acting Director of Food Distribution.

Press Release, Immediate:
Wednesday, October 20, 1943.

Milk sales in 19 metropolitan areas in Illinois, Michigan, Colorado, Utah, Arizona, Oregon, Pennsylvania, Minnesota, Oklahoma and West Virginia will be regulated under the Food Distribution Administration's fluid milk conservation and control program, beginning November 1, 1943.

The new milk sales areas and the market agents who will administer the program in each are:

Johnston, Pa., Erie, Pa., Altoona, Pa., Pittsburgh, Pa., Metropolitan, Charleston, W. Va., Wheeling, W. Va.: George A. Taylor, Century Building, Pittsburgh, Pa.

Peoria, Ill., Rockford, Ill.: A. W. Colebank, 135 S. LaSalle St., Chicago, Ill.

Phoenix, Ariz., Denver, Colo., Metropolitan, Salt Lake City, Utah, Metropolitan: Ben King, 503 Security Life Building, 810 14th St., Denver, Colo. (temp. address).

Portland, Oregon, Metropolitan: J. H. Mapes, 635 Elliot Avenue, West, Seattle, Washington.

Detroit, Michigan, Metropolitan, Saginaw-Bay City, Mich., Metropolitan, Lansing, Mich., Metropolitan, Flint, Mich., Metropolitan: (To be announced later).

Oklahoma City, Oklahoma, Tulsa, Oklahoma: M M. Morehouse, 512 Porter Bldg., 406 W. 34th St., Kansas City, Mo.

Minneapolis-St. Paul, Minnesota: D. F. Spencer, 404 Post Office Bldg., Minneapolis, Minn.

Under the program, milk dealers will be permitted to sell as much fluid milk as they sold in June and three-fourths as much cream and milk byproducts (such as cottage cheese, chocolate milk, and buttermilk) as they sold in June. Milk dealers include all persons or firms engaged in the sale or transfer of milk, but not such distributors as subhandlers ("peddlers"), retail stores, hotels, or restaurants.

Producer-distributors who purchase no milk will be permitted to sell as much milk as they produced in June.

Dealers will be allowed to exceed these base quotas by not more than 5 percent during any month, providing they decrease their deliveries the next month by the same amount, without being reported in violation.

A dealer also may increase his milk sales by reducing his cream and milk byproducts sales, and increase his sales of milk byproducts by reducing his cream sales, providing such an adjustment is approved by the market agent for the area.

Deliveries of milk, cream, and milk byproducts to other dealers, to the Armed Forces, and to plants processing milk who do not distribute milk, cream, and milk byproducts in the sales area are quota-exempt.

Consumers in the milk sales areas named today and in others already designated generally will be able to purchase as much milk under the milk conservation program as they have been buying in recent months—within the limits of local supplies. In some areas, production is not expected to be large enough to permit dealers to sell as much milk as their quotas allow.

Fluid milk sales are being stabilized, Food Distribution Administration officials said, to help assure sufficient milk for manufacturing the cheese, butter, evaporated milk, and milk powder required by the Armed Services and civilians for food nutrition and properly balanced diets. Sales quotas on cream and on fluid milk byproducts have been set below June deliveries to boost fluid milk supplies where production is low, and to conserve milk for manufacturing purposes.

WAR FOOD ADMINISTRATION

[FDO 79-61]

PART 1401—DAIRY PRODUCTS

FLUID MILK AND CREAM IN WHEELING, W. VA., MILK SALES AREA

Pursuant to the authority vested in me by Food Distribution Order No. 79 (8 F.R. 12426), issued on September 7 1943, as amended, and to effectuate the purposes of such order, it is hereby ordered as follows:

§ 1401.101 *Quota restrictions*—(a) *Definitions.* When used in this order, unless otherwise distinctly expressed or manifestly incompatible with the intent hereof:

(1) Each term defined in Food Distribution Order No. 79, as amended, shall, when used herein, have the same meaning as is set forth for such term in Food Distribution Order No. 79, as amended.

(2) The term "FDO 79" means Food Distribution Order No. 79, issued on September 7, 1943, as amended.

(3) The term "sub-handler" means any handler, such as a peddler, vendor, sub-dealer, or secondary dealer, who purchases in a previously packaged and processed form milk, milk byproducts, or cream for delivery.

(b) *Milk sales area.* The following area is hereby designated as a "milk sales area" to be known as the Wheeling, West Virginia, sales area, and is referred to hereinafter as the "sales area":

The city of Wheeling and the magisterial districts of Center, Clay, Liberty, Madison, Richland, Ritchie, Triadelphia, Union, Washington, and Webster in Ohio County, West Virginia; the magisterial districts of Buffalo and Wellsburg in Brooke County, West Virginia; the magisterial districts of Clay, Union, and Washington in Marshall County, West Virginia; the townships of Colerain, Mead, Pease, and Pultney in Belmont County, Ohio; and the townships of Mount Pleasant, Smithfield, and Warren in Jefferson County, Ohio.

(c) *Base period.* The calendar month of June 1943 is hereby designated as the base period for the sales area.

(d) *Quota period.* The remainder of the calendar month in which the provisions hereof become effective and each subsequent calendar month, respectively, is hereby designated as a quota period for the sales area.

(e) *Handler quotas.* Quotas for each handler in the sales area in each quota period shall be calculated in terms of pounds of each of the items for which percentages are specified in (3) below and shall be determined as follows:

(1) Divide the total deliveries of each such item made in the sales area by such handler during the base period, after excluding the quota-exempt deliveries described in (i) hereof, by the number of days in the base period;

(2) Multiply the result of the foregoing calculation by the number of days in the quota period;

(3) Multiply the aforesaid resulting amount by the following applicable percentage: (i) milk: 100 percent; (ii) butterfat in milk: ___ percent; (iii) cream: 75 percent; (iv) butterfat in cream: 75 percent; (v) milk byproducts other than cottage, pot, or baker's cheese: 75 percent; and (vi) cottage, pot, or baker's cheese: 75 percent of skim milk equivalent. (For the purpose of this order, one pound of cottage, pot, or baker's cheese shall be considered as the equivalent of 7 pounds of skim milk.)

(f) *Quota limitations.* No handler shall, during any quota period, make deliveries in the sales area in excess of his respective quotas, except as set out in (i) hereof: *Provided*, That a handler may, after application to and approval by the market agent, secure an increase in milk quotas through an equivalent reduction as determined by the market agent, in cream and milk byproducts quotas, and an increase in milk byproducts quota through an equivalent reduction as determined by the market agent, in cream quotas.

(g) *Quotas for handlers who are also producers.* Quotas for handlers who are also producers and who purchase no milk shall be 100 percent of the total production of such handlers in the base period

(h) *Handler exemptions.* Quotas shall not apply to any handler who delivers in a quota period a daily average of less than 350 units of milk, cream, and milk byproducts. For the purpose of this order, a unit shall be the equivalent in volume of the following: (1) milk, one quart of milk; (2) cream, one-half pint of cream; and (3) milk byproduct, one quart of skim milk, buttermilk, flavored milk drink, or other beverage containing more than 85 percent of skim milk, or one-half pound of cottage, pot, or baker's cheese.

(i) *Quota exclusions and exemptions.* Deliveries of milk, milk byproducts, or cream (1) to other handlers, except for such deliveries to sub-handlers, (2) to plants engaged in the handling or processing of milk, milk byproducts, or cream from which no milk, milk byproducts, or cream is delivered in the sales area, and (3) to the agencies or groups specified in (d) of FDO 79, shall be excluded from the computation of deliveries in the base period and exempt from charges to quotas.

(j) *Transfers and apportionment of quotas.* The market agent is empowered to deduct an amount of base period deliveries to purchasers from the total of deliveries made by a handler or other person in the base period upon the application and a showing of unreasonable hardship by the handler making deliveries to such purchasers on the effective date of this order, and to add the amount of such deliveries to the total base period deliveries of the applicant handler. Denials of transfers or transfers granted by the market agent shall be reviewed by the Director upon application.

(k) *Petition for relief from hardships.* (1) Any person affected by FDO 79 or the provisions hereof who considers that compliance therewith would work an exceptional and unreasonable hardship on him, may file with the market agent a petition addressed to the Director. The petition shall contain the correct name, address and principal place of business of the petitioner, a full statement of the facts upon which the petition is based, and the hardship involved and the nature of the relief desired.

(2) Upon receiving such petition, the market agent shall immediately investigate the representations and facts stated therein.

(3) After investigation, the petition shall be certified to the Director, but prior to certification the market agent may (i) deny the petition, or (ii) grant temporary relief for a total period not to exceed 60 days.

(4) Denials or grants of relief by the market agent shall be reviewed by the Director and may be affirmed, modified, or reversed by the Director.

(l) *Reports.* Each handler shall transmit to the market agent on forms prescribed by the market agent the following reports:

(1) Within 20 days following the effective date of this order, reports which show the information required by the market agent to establish such handlers' quotas;

(2) Within 20 days following the close of each quota period, the information

required by the market agent to establish volumes of deliveries of milk, cream, and milk byproducts during the preceding quota period; and

(3) Handlers exempt from quotas pursuant to (h) hereof shall, upon the request of the market agent, submit the information required by the market agent to establish volumes of deliveries of milk, cream, and milk byproducts.

(m) *Records.* Handlers shall keep and shall make available to the market agent such records of receipts, sales, deliveries, and production as the market agent shall require for the purpose of obtaining information which the Director may require for the establishment of quotas as prescribed in (b) of FDO 79.

(n) *Distribution schedules.* The distribution schedules, if any, to be followed by the handlers in making deliveries shall be made effective in the terms of approval by the Director of such schedules.

(o) *Expense of administration.* Each handler shall pay to the market agent, within 20 days after the close of each calendar month an assessment of $.01 per hundredweight of each of milk, cream, skim milk, buttermilk, flavored milk drinks, beverages containing more than 85 percent of skim milk, and skim milk equivalent of cottage, pot, or baker's cheese delivered during the preceding quota period and subject to quota regulations under the provisions hereof.

(p) *Violations.* The market agent shall report all violations to the Director together with the information required for the prosecution of such violations, except in a case where a handler has made deliveries in a quota period in excess of a quota in an amc exceed 5 percent of such qu the succeeding quota period liveries below that quota by same percent.

(q) *Bureau of the Budge* The record keeping and re quirements of this order ha proved by the Bureau of th accordance with the Federal of 1942. Subsequent reco or reporting requirements v ject to the approval of the Bu Budget pursuant to the Fede Act of 1942.

(r) This order shall tak 12:01 a. m., e. w. t., Novembe

Issued this 19th day of Oct

C. W. K
Acting Director of Food Dis

Press Release, Immediate:
Wednesday, October 20, 1943.

Milk sales in 19 metropolitan areas in Illinois, Michigan, Colorado, Utah, Arizona, Oregon, Pennsylvania, Minnesota, Oklahoma and West Virginia will be regulated under the Food Distribution Administration's fluid milk conservation and control program, beginning November 1, 1943.

The new milk sales areas and the market agents who will administer the program in each are:

Johnstown, Pa., Erie, Pa., Altoona, Pa., Pittsburgh, Pa., Metropolitan, Charleston, W. Va., Wheeling, W. Va.: George A. Taylor, Century Building, Pittsburgh, Pa.

Peoria, Ill., Rockford, Ill.: A. W. Colebank, 135 S. LaSalle St., Chicago, Ill.

Phoenix, Ariz., Denver, Colo., Metropolitan, Salt Lake City, Utah, Metropolitan: Ben King, 503 Security Life Building, 810 14th St., Denver, Colo. (temp. address).

Portland, Oregon, Metropolitan: J. H. Mapes, 635 Elliot Avenue, West, Seattle, Washington.

Detroit, Michigan, Metropolitan, Saginaw-Bay City, Mich., Metropolitan, Lansing, Mich., Metropolitan, Flint, Mich., Metropolitan: (To be announced later).

Oklahoma City, Oklahoma, Tulsa, Oklahoma: M. M. Morehouse, 512 Porter Bldg., 406 W. 34th St., Kansas City, Mo.

Minneapolis-St. Paul, Minnesota: D. F. Spencer, 404 Post Office Bldg., Minneapolis, Minn.

Under the program, milk dealers will be permitted to sell as much fluid milk as they sold in June and three-fourths as much cream and milk byproducts (such as cottage cheese, chocolate milk, and buttermilk) as they sold in June. Milk dealers include all persons or firms engaged in the sale or transfer of milk, but not such distributors as subhandlers ("peddlers"), retail stores, hotels, or restaurants.

Producer-distributors who purchase no milk will be permitted to sell as much milk as they produced in June.

Dealers will be allowed to exceed these base quotas by not more than 5 percent during any month, providing they decrease their deliveries the next month by the same amount, without being reported in violation.

A dealer also may increase his milk sales by reducing his cream and milk byproducts sales, and increase his sales of milk byproducts by reducing his cream sales, providing such an ad approved by the market ag area.

Deliveries of milk, cream, a products to other dealers, to Forces, and to plants proc who do not distribute milk, milk byproducts in the sal quota-exempt.

Consumers in the milk named today and in others a ignated generally will be a chase as much milk under th servation program as they buying in recent months— limits of local supplies. In production is not expected enough to permit dealers to s milk as their quotas allow.

Fluid milk sales are being Food Distribution Administ cials said, to help assure sui for manufacturing the che evaporated milk, and milk quired by the Armed Service ians for food nutrition and p anced diets. Sales quotas or on fluid milk byproducts ha below June deliveries to boo supplies where production to conserve milk for manufac poses.

WAR FOOD ADMINISTRATION

[FDO 79-61, Amdt. 1]

PART 1401—DAIRY PRODUCTS

FLUID MILK AND CREAM IN THE WHEELING, W. VA., MILK SALES AREA

Pursuant to Food Distribution Order No. 79 (8 F. R. 12426), dated September 7, 1943, as amended, and to effectuate the purposes thereof, Food Distribution Order No. 79-61 (8 F. R. 14263) relative to the conservation and distribution of fluid milk in the Wheeling, West Virginia milk sales area, issued by the Director of Food Distribution on October 19, 1943, is amended by deleting therefrom the numerals "350" wherever they appear in § 1401.101 (h) and inserting, in lieu thereof, the numerals "100."

The provisions of this amendment shall become effective at 12:01 a. m., e. w. t., January 1, 1944. With respect to violations of said Food Distribution Order No. 79-61, rights accrued, or liabilities incurred prior to the effective time of this amendment, said Food Distribution Order No. 79-61 shall be deemed to be in full force and effect for the purpose of sustaining any proper suit, action, or other proceeding with respect to any such violation, right, or liability.

(E.O. 9280, 7 F.R. 10179; E.O. 9322, 8 F.R. 3807; E.O. 9334, 8 F.R. 5423; E.O. 9392, 8 F.R. 14783; FDO 79, 8 F.R. 12426, 13283)

Issued this 28th day of December 1943.

ROY F. HENDRICKSON,
Director of Food Distribution.

FDO 79-62

OCTOBER 19, 1943

WAR FOOD ADMINISTRATION

[FDO 79-62]

PART 1401—DAIRY PRODUCTS

FLUID MILK AND CREAM IN PORTLAND, OREG., METROPOLITAN SALES AREA

Pursuant to the authority vested in me by Food Distribution Order No. 79 (8 F.R. 12426), issued on September 7, 1943, as amended, and to effectuate the purposes of such order, it is hereby ordered as follows:

§ 1401.107 *Quota restrictions*—(a) *Definitions.* When used in this order, unless otherwise distinctly expressed or manifestly incompatible with the intent hereof:

(1) Each term defined in Food Distribution Order No. 79, as amended, shall, when used herein, have the same meaning as is set forth for such term in Food Distribution Order No. 79, as amended.

(2) The term "FDO 79" means Food Distribution Order No. 79, issued on September 7, 1943, as amended.

(3) The term "sub-handler" means any handler, such as a peddler, vendor, sub-dealer, or secondary dealer, who purchases in a previously packaged and processed form milk, milk byproducts, or cream for delivery.

(b) *Milk sales area.* The following area is hereby designated as a "milk sales area" to be known as the Portland, Oregon, metropolitan sales area, and is referred to hereinafter as the "sales area":

The city of Portland (consisting of the election precincts 1 to 392), the precincts of Swift, Faloma, Englewood, Rigler, Community Acres, Rosaria, Lochknowe, Roseway, Rose Park, Columbia, Parkrose, Ascot Acres, Russellville, Kelly, Plympton, Skagway, North Kelly Butte, South Kelly Butte, Mount Scott, Sycamore, Eastwood, Rockwood, East Gresham, West Gresham, South Gresham, Holbrook, Skyline, Bonny Slope, Sylvan, Mount Zion, Hillsdale, Capitol Hill, Ryan, Multnomah, Primrose, Maplewood, West Portland, Kilpatrick-Collins, Riverdale, Errol Heights, Darlington, Brentwood, and Kendall in Multnomah County, Oregon; the precincts of Ardenwald 1 and 2, Bryant, Clackamas, Concord, Forest Hills, Garthwick, Gladstone 1 and 2, Harmony, Hazelia, Island, Jennings Lodge, Lake Grove, Meldrum, Milwaukie 1 and 2, Oak Grove 1 and 2, Oregon City 1 to 8, Oswego 1 and 2, Park Place, Rosemont, Silver Springs, West Linn 1 to 4, White City Park, and Wichita in Clackamas County, Oregon; the precincts numbered 6, 7, 8, 9, 41, 42, and 43 in Washington County, Oregon; and the city of Vancouver and an area extending 3 miles to the east, north, and west of the city limits of Vancouver in Clark County, Washington.

(c) *Base period.* The calendar month of June 1943 is hereby designated as the base period for the sales area.

(d) *Quota period.* The remainder of the calendar month in which the provisions hereof become effective and each subsequent calendar month, respectively, is hereby designated as a quota period for the sales area.

(e) *Handler quotas.* Quotas for each handler in the sales area in each quota period shall be calculated in terms of pounds of each of the items for which percentages are specified in (3) below and shall be determined as follows:

(1) Divide the total deliveries of each such item made in the sales area by such handler during the base period, after excluding the quota-exempt deliveries described in (i) hereof, by the number of days in the base period;

(2) Multiply the result of the foregoing calculation by the number of days in the quota period;

(3) Multiply the aforesaid resulting amount by the following applicable percentage: (i) milk: 100 percent; (ii) butterfat in milk: 100 percent; (iii) cream: 75 percent; (iv) butterfat in cream: 75 percent; (v) milk byproducts other than cottage, pot, or baker's cheese: 75 percent; and (vi) cottage, pot, or baker's cheese: 75 percent of skim milk equivalent. (For the purpose of this order, one pound of cottage, pot, or baker's cheese shall be considered as the equivalent of 7 pounds of skim milk.)

(f) *Quota limitations.* No handler shall, during any quota period, make deliveries in the sales area in excess of his respective quotas, except as set out in (i) hereof: *Provided*, That a handler may, after application to and approval by the market agent, secure an increase in milk quotas through an equivalent reduction as determined by the market agent, in cream and milk byproducts quotas, and an increase in milk byproducts quota through an equivalent reduction as determined by the market agent, in cream quotas.

(g) *Quotas for handlers who are also producers.* Quotas for handlers who are also producers and who purchase no milk shall be 100 percent of the total production of such handlers in the base period.

(h) *Handler exceptions.* Quotas shall not apply to any handler who delivers in a quota period a daily average of less than 300 units of milk, cream, and milk byproducts. For the purpose of this order, a unit shall be the equivalent in volume of the following: (1) milk, one quart of milk; (2) cream, one-half pint of cream; and (3) milk byproduct, one quart of skim milk, buttermilk, flavored milk drink, or other beverage containing more than 85 percent of skim milk, or one-half pound of cottage, pot, or baker's cheese.

(i) *Quota exclusions and exemptions.* Deliveries of milk, milk byproducts, or cream (1) to other handlers, except for such deliveries to sub-handlers, (2) to plants engaged in the handling or processing of milk, milk byproducts, or cream from which no milk, milk byproducts, or cream is delivered in the sales area, and (3) to the agencies or groups specified in (d) of FDO 79, shall be excluded from the computation of deliveries in the base period and exempt from charges to quotas.

(j) *Transfers and apportionment of quotas.* The market agent is empowered to deduct an amount of base period deliveries to purchaser from the total of deliveries made by a handler or other person in the base period upon the application and a showing of unreasonable hardship by the handler making deliveries to such purchasers on the effective date of this order, and to add the amount of such deliveries to the total base period deliveries of the applicant handler. Denials of transfers or transfers granted by the market agent shall be reviewed by the Director upon application.

(k) *Petition for relief from hardships.* (1) Any person affected by FDO 79 or the provisions hereof who considers that compliance therewith would work an exceptional and unreasonable hardship on him, may file with the market agent a petition addressed to the Director. The petition shall contain the correct name, address and principal place of business of the petitioner, a full statement of the facts upon which the petition is based, and the hardship involved and the nature of the relief desired.

(2) Upon receiving such petition, the market agent shall immediately investigate the representations and facts stated therein.

(3) After investigation, the petition shall be certified to the Director, but prior to certification the market agent may (i) deny the petition, or (ii) grant temporary relief for a total period not to exceed 60 days.

(4) Denials or grants of relief by the market agent shall be reviewed by the

Director and may be affirmed, modified, or reversed by the Director.

(l) *Reports.* Each handler shall transmit to the market agent on forms prescribed by the market agent the following reports:

(1) Within 20 days following the effective date of this order, reports which show the information required by the market agent to establish such handlers' quotas;

(2) Within 20 days following the close of each quota period, the information required by the market agent to establish volumes of deliveries of milk, cream, and milk byproducts during the preceding quota period; and

(3) Handlers exempt from quotas pursuant to (h) hereof shall, upon the request of the market agent, submit the information required by the market agent to establish volumes of deliveries of milk, cream, and milk byproducts.

(m) *Records.* Handlers shall keep and shall make available to the market agent such records of receipts, sales, deliveries, and production as the market agent shall require for the purpose of obtaining information which the Director may require for the establishment of quotas as prescribed in (b) of FDO 79.

(n) *Distribution schedules.* The distribution schedules, if any, to be followed by the handlers in making deliveries shall be made effective in the terms of approval by the Director of such schedules.

(o) *Expense of administration.* Each handler shall pay to the market agent, within 20 days after the close of each calendar month an assessment of $.01 per hundredweight of each milk, cream skim milk, buttermilk, flavored milk drinks, beverages containing more than 85 percent of skim milk, and skim milk equivalent of cottage, pot, or baker's cheese delivered during the preceding quota period and subject to quota regulations under the provisions hereof.

(p) *Violations.* The market agent shall report all violations to the Director together with the info
for the prosecution o
except in a case whe
made deliveries in a q
cess of a quota in an e
eeed 5 percent of such
succeeding quota perio
below that quota by
percent.

(q) *Bureau of the*
The record keeping a
quirements of this ord
proved by the Bureau
accordance with the Fe
of 1942. Subsequent
reporting requirements
the approval of the Bu
pursuant to the Feder
1942.

(r) This order sha
12:01 a. m. e. w. t., Nc

Issued this 19th day

C

Acting Director of Fo

Press Release, Immediate:
Wednesday, October 20, 1943.

Milk sales in 19 metropolitan areas in Illinois, Michigan, Colorado, Utah, Arizona, Oregon, Pennsylvania, Minnesota, Oklahoma and West Virginia will be regulated under the Food Distribution Administration's fluid milk conservation and control program, beginning November 1, 1943.

The new milk sales areas and the market agents who will administer the program in each are:

Johnstown, Pa., Erie, Pa., Altoona, Pa., Pittsburgh, Pa., Metropolitan, Charleston, W. Va., Wheeling, W. Va.: George A. Taylor, Century Building, Pittsburgh, Pa.

Peoria, Ill., Rockford, Ill.: A. W. Colebank, 135 S. LaSalle St., Chicago, Ill.

Phoenix, Ariz., Denver, Colo., Metropolitan, Salt Lake City, Utah, Metropolitan: Ben King, 503 Security Life Building, 810 14th St., Denver, Colo. (temp. address).

Portland, Oregon, Metropolitan: J. H. Mapes, 635 Elliot Avenue, West, Seattle, Wash.

Detroit, Michigan, Metropolitan, Saginaw-Bay City, Mich., Metropolitan, Lansing, Mich., Metropolitan, Flint, Mich., Metropolitan: (To be announced later).

Oklahoma City, Oklahoma, Tulsa, Oklahoma: M. M. Morehouse, 512 Porter Bldg., 406 W. 34th St., Kansas City, Mo.

Minneapolis-St. Paul, Minnesota: D. F. Spencer, 404 Post Office Bldg., Minneapolis, Minn.

Under the program, milk dealers will be permitted to sell as much fluid milk as they sold in June and three-fourths as much cream and milk byproducts (such as cottage cheese, chocolate milk, and buttermilk) as they sold in June. Milk dealers include all persons or firms engaged in the sale or transfer of milk, but not such distributors as subhandlers ("peddlers"), retail stores, hotels, or restaurants.

Producer-distributors who purchase no milk will be permitted to sell as much milk as they produced in June.

Dealers will be allowed to exceed these base quotas by not more than 5 percent during any month, providing they decrease their deliveries the next month by the same amount, without being reported in violation.

A dealer also may increase his milk sales by reducing his cream and milk byproducts sales, and increase his sales of milk byproducts by reducing his cream sales, providing such
approved by the marl
area.

Deliveries of milk,
byproducts to other dee
Forces, and to plants
who do not distribute
milk byproducts in t
quota-exempt.

Consumers in the
named today and in o
ignated generally will
chase as much milk ur
servation program as
buying in recent mc
limits of local supplie
production is not exp
enough to permit deal
milk as their quotas al

Fluid milk sales are
Food Distribution Ad
cials said, to help ass
for manufacturing th
evaporated milk, and
quired by the Armed
ians for food nutrition
anced diets. Sales qu
on fluid milk byprodu
below June deliveries
supplies where produc
conserve milk for ma
poses.

eserve

FDO 79-62

AMDT. 1
MAR. 30, 1944

WAR FOOD ADMINISTRATION

[FDO 79-62, Amdt. 1]

PART 1401—DAIRY PRODUCTS

FLUID MILK AND CREAM IN PORTLAND, OREG., METROPOLITAN SALES AREA

Pursuant to Food Distribution Order No. 79 (8 F.R. 12426), dated September 7, 1943, as amended, and to effectuate the purposes thereof, Food Distribution Order No. 79-62 (8 F.R. 14264), relative to the conservation and distribution of fluid milk and cream in the Portland, Oregon, metropolitan milk sales area, issued by the Director of Food Distribution on October 19, 1943, is amended by deleting therefrom the description of the sales area in § 1401.107 (b) thereof and inserting, in lieu thereof, the following:

The city of Portland and the precincts within the counties of Multnomah, Washington, and Clackamas, all in Oregon, as shown on the map on page 899 and listed in Table No. 4, pp. 887 to 894 of the Sixteenth Census of the United States: 1940 (Population, Volume 1); and the city of Vancouver and an area extending 3 miles to the east, north, and west of the city limits of Vancouver in Clark County, Washington.

The provisions of this amendment shall become effective at 12:01 a. m., e. w. t., April 1, 1944. With respect to violations of said Food Distribution Order No. 79-62, rights accrued, or liabilities incurred, prior to the effective time of this amendment, said Food Distribution Order No. 79-62, shall be deemed to be in full force and effect for the purpose of sustaining any proper suit, action, or other proceeding with respect to any such violation, right, or liability.

(E.O. 9280, 7 F.R. 10179; E.O. 9322, 8 F.R. 3807; E.O. 9334, 8 F.R. 5423; E.O. 9393, 8 F.R. 14783; FDO 79, 8 F.R. 12426, 13283)

Issued this 30th day of March 1944.

LEE MARSHALL,
Director of Distribution.

FDO 79-63
OCTOBER 19, 1943

WAR FOOD ADMINISTRATION

[FDO 79-63]

PART 1401—DAIRY PRODUCTS

FLUID MILK AND CREAM IN LANSING, MICH., METROPOLITAN SALES AREA

Pursuant to the authority vested in me by Food Distribution Order No. 79 (8 F.R. 12426), issued on September 7, 1943, as amended, and to effectuate the purposes of such order, it is hereby ordered as follows:

§ 1401.88 *Quota restrictions*—(a) *Definitions.* When used in this order, unless otherwise distinctly expressed or manifestly incompatible with the intent hereof:

(1) Each term defined in Food Distribution Order No. 79, as amended, shall, when used herein, have the same meaning as is set forth for such term in Food Distribution Order No. 79, as amended.

(2) The term "FDO 79" means Food Distribution Order No. 79, issued on September 7, 1943, as amended.

(3) The term "sub-handler" means any handler, such as a peddler, vendor, sub-dealer, or secondary dealer, who purchases in a previously packaged and processed form milk, milk byproducts, or cream for delivery.

(b) *Milk sales area.* The following area is hereby designated as a "milk sales area" to be known as the Lansing, Michigan, metropolitan sales area, and is referred to hereinafter as the "sales area":

The cities of Lansing and East Lansing, and the townships of Delhi, Lansing, and Meridian, all in Ingham County, Michigan.

(c) *Base period.* The calendar month of June 1943 is hereby designated as the base period for the sales area.

(d) *Quota period.* The remainder of the calendar month in which the provisions hereof become effective and each subsequent calendar month, respectively, is hereby designated as a quota period for the sales area.

(e) *Handler quotas.* Quotas for each handler in the sales area in each quota period shall be calculated in terms of pounds of each of the items for which percentages are specified in (3) below and shall be determined as follows:

(1) Divide the total deliveries of each such item made in the sales area by such handler during the base period, after excluding the quota-exempt deliveries described in (i) hereof, by the number of days in the base period;

(2) Multiply the result of the foregoing calculation by the number of days in the quota period;

(3) Multiply the aforesaid resulting amount by the following applicable percentage: (i) milk: 100 percent; (ii) butterfat in milk: ______ percent; (iii) cream: 75 percent; (iv) butterfat in cream: 75 percent; (v) milk byproducts other than cottage, pot, or baker's cheese: 75 percent: and (vi) cottage, pot, or baker's cheese, 75 percent of skim milk equivalent. (For the purpose of this order, one pound of cottage, pot, or baker's cheese shall be considered as the equivalent of 7 pounds of skim milk.)

(f) *Quota limitations.* No handler shall, during any quota period, make deliveries in the sales area in excess of his respective quotas, except as set out in (i) hereof: *Provided*, That a handler may, after application to and approval by the market agent, secure an increase in milk quotas through an equivalent reduction as determined by the market agent, in cream and milk byproducts quotas, and an increase in milk byproducts quota through an equivalent reduction as determined by the market agent in cream quotas.

(g) *Quotas for handlers who are also producers.* Quotas for handlers who are also producers and who purchase no milk shall be 100 percent of the total production of such handlers in the base period.

(h) *Handler exemptions.* Quotas shall not apply to any handler who delivers in a quota period a daily average of less than 300 units of milk, cream, and milk byproducts. For the purpose of this order, a unit shall be the equivalent in volume of the following: (1) milk, one quart of milk; (2) cream, one-half pint of cream; and (3) milk byproduct, one quart of skim milk, buttermilk, flavored milk drink, or other beverage containing more than 85 percent of skim milk, or one-half pound of cottage, pot, or baker's cheese.

(i) *Quota exclusions and exemptions.* Deliveries of milk, milk byproducts, or cream (1) to other handlers, except for such deliveries to sub-handlers, (2) to plants engaged in the handling or processing of milk, milk byproducts, or cream from which no milk, milk byproducts, or cream is delivered in the sales area, and (3) to the agencies or groups specified in (d) of FDO 79, shall be excluded from the computation of deliveries in the base period and exempt from charges to quotas.

(j) *Transfers and apportionment of quotas.* The market agent is empowered to deduct an amount of base period deliveries to purchasers from the total of deliveries made by a handler or other person in the base period upon the application and a showing of unreasonable hardship by the handler making deliveries to such purchasers on the effective date of this order, and to add the amount of such deliveries to the total base period deliveries of the applicant handler. Denials of transfers or transfers granted by the market agent shall be reviewed by the Director upon application.

(k) *Petition for relief from hardships.* (1) Any person affected by FDO 79 or the provisions hereof who considers that compliance therewith would work an exceptional and unreasonable hardship on him, may file with the market agent a petition addressed to the Director. The petition shall contain the correct name, address and principal place of business of the petitioner, a full statement of the facts upon which the petition is based, and the hardship involved and the nature of the relief desired.

(2) Upon receiving such petition, the market agent shall immediately investigate the representations and facts stated therein.

(3) After investigation, the petition shall be certified to the Director, but prior to certification the market agent may (i) deny the petition, or (ii) grant temporary relief for a total period not to exceed 60 days.

(4) Denials or grants of relief by the market agent shall be reviewed by the Director and may be affirmed, modified, or reversed by the Director.

(l) *Reports.* Each handler shall transmit to the market agent on forms prescribed by the market agent the following reports:

(1) Within 20 days following the effective date of this order, reports which show the information required by the market agent to establish such handlers' quotas;

(2) Within 20 days following the close of each quota period, the information required by the market agent to establish volumes of deliveries of milk, cream, and milk byproducts during the preceding quota period; and

(3) Handlers exempt from quotas pursuant to (h) hereof shall, upon the request of the market agent, submit the information required by the market

agent to establish volumes of deliveries of milk, cream, and milk byproducts.

(m) *Records.* Handlers shall keep and shall make available to the market agent such records of receipts, sales, deliveries, and production as the market agent shall require for the purpose of obtaining information which the Director may require for the establishment of quotas as prescribed in (b) of FDO 79.

(n) *Distribution schedules.* The distribution schedules, if any, to be followed by the handlers in making deliveries shall be made effective in the terms of approval by the Director of such schedules.

(o) *Expense of administration.* Each handler shall pay to the market agent, within 20 days after the close of each calendar month an assessment of $0.01 per hundredweight of each of milk, cream, skim milk, buttermilk, flavored milk drinks, beverages containing more than 85 percent of skim milk, and skim milk equivalent of cottage, pot, or baker's cheese delivered during the preceding quota period and subject to quota regulations under the provisions hereof.

(p) *Violations.* The market agent shall report all violations to the Director together with the information required for the prosecution of such violations, except in a case where a handler has made deliveries in a quota period in excess of a quota in an amount not to exceed 5 percent of such quota, and in the succeeding quota period makes deliveries below that quota by at least the same percent.

(q) *Bureau of the Budget approval.* The record keeping and reporting requirements of this order have been approved by the Bureau of the Budget in accordance with the Federal Reports Act of 1942. Subsequent record keeping or reporting requirements will be subject to the approval of the Bureau of the Budget pursuant to the Federal Reports Act of 1942.

(r) This order shall take effect at 12:01 a. m., e. w. t., November 1, 1943.

Issued this 19th day of October 1943.

C. W. KITCHEN,
Acting Director of Food Distribution.

Press Release Immediate:
Wednesday, October 20, 1943.

Milk sales in 19 metropolitan areas in Illinois, Michigan, Colorado, Utah, Arizona, Oregon, Pennsylvania, Minnesota, Oklahoma and West Virginia will be regulated under the Food Distribution Administration's fluid milk conservation and control program, beginning November 1, 1943.

The new milk sales areas and the market agents who will administer the program in each are:

Johnstown, Pa., Erie, Pa., Altoona, Pa., Pittsburgh, Pa., Metropolitan, Charleston, W. Va., Wheeling, W. Va.; George A. Taylor, Century Building, Pittsburgh, Pa.

Peoria, Ill., Rockford, Ill.; A. W. Colebank, 135 S. LaSalle St., Chicago, Ill.

Phoenix, Ariz., Denver, Colo., Metropolitan, Salt Lake City, Utah, Metropolitan; Ben King, 503 Security Life Building, 810 14th St., Denver, Colo. (temp. address).

Portland, Oregon, Metropolitan; J. H. Mapes, 635 Elliot Avenue, West, Seattle, Washington.

Detroit, Michigan, Metropolitan, Saginaw-Bay City, Mich., Metropolitan, Lansing, Mich., Metropolitan, Flint, Mich., Metropolitan; (To be announced later).

Oklahoma City, Oklahoma, Tulsa, Oklahoma; M. M. Morehouse, 512 Porter Bldg., 406 W. 34th St., Kansas City, Mo.

Minneapolis-St. Paul, Minnesota; D. F. Spencer, 404 Post Office Bldg., Minneapolis, Minn.

Under the program, milk dealers will be permitted to sell as much fluid milk as they sold in June and three-fourths as much cream and milk byproducts (such as cottage cheese, chocolate milk, and buttermilk) as they sold in June. Milk dealers include all persons or firms engaged in the sale or transfer of milk, but not such distributors as subhandlers ("peddlers"), retail stores, hotels, or restaurants.

Producer-distributors who purchase no milk will be permitted to sell as much milk as they produced in June.

Dealers will be allowed to exceed these base quotas by not more than 5 percent during any month, providing they decrease their deliveries the next month by the same amount, without being reported in violation.

A dealer also may increase his milk sales by reducing his cream and milk byproducts sales, and increase his sales of milk byproducts by reducing his cream sales, providing such an adjustment is approved by the market agent for the area.

Deliveries of milk, cream, and milk byproducts to other dealers, to the Armed Forces, and to plants processing milk who do not distribute milk, cream, and milk byproducts in the sales area are quota-exempt.

Consumers in the milk sales areas named today and in others already designated generally will be able to purchase as much milk under the milk conservation program as they have been buying in recent months—within the limits of local supplies. In some areas, production is not expected to be large enough to permit dealers to sell as much milk as their quotas allow.

Fluid milk sales are being stabilized, Food Distribution Administration officials said, to help assure sufficient milk for manufacturing the cheese, butter, evaporated milk, and milk powder required by the Armed Services and civilians for food nutrition and properly balanced diets. Sales quotas on cream and on fluid milk byproducts have been set below June deliveries to boost fluid milk supplies where production is low, and to conserve milk for manufacturing purposes.

. /.

FDO 79-64

OCTOBER 19, 1943

WAR FOOD ADMINISTRATION

[FDO 79-64]

PART 1401—DAIRY PRODUCTS

FLUID MILK AND CREAM IN DETROIT, MICH., METROPOLITAN SALES AREA

Pursuant to the authority vested in me by Food Distribution Order No. 79 (8 F.R. 12426), issued on September 7, 1943, as amended, and to effectuate the purposes of such order, it is hereby ordered as follows:

§ 1401.96 *Quota restrictions*—(a) *Definitions.* When used in this order, unless otherwise distinctly expressed or manifestly incompatible with the intent hereof:

(1) Each term defined in Food Distribution Order No. 79, as amended, shall, when used herein, have the same meaning as is set forth for such term in Food Distribution Order No. 79, as amended.

(2) The term "FDO 79" means Food Distribution Order No. 79, issued on September 7, 1943, as amended.

(3) The term "sub-handler" means any handler, such as a peddler, vendor, sub-dealer, or secondary dealer, who purchases in a previously packaged and processed form milk, milk byproducts, or cream for delivery.

(b) *Milk sales area.* The following area is hereby designated as a "milk sales area" to be known as the Detroit, Michigan, metropolitan sales area, and is referred to hereinafter as the "sales area":

The cities of Detroit, Dearborn, Garden City, Grosse Pointe, Hamtramck, Highland Park, Lincoln Park, Melvindale, Plymouth, River Rouge, and Wyandotte, the townships of Dearborn, Ecorse, Gratiot, Grosse Isle, Grosse Pointe, Livonia, Monguagon, Nankin, Northville, Plymouth, Redford, and Taylor in Wayne County; the cities of Center Line, East Detroit, Mount Clemens, and Utica, the townships of Clinton, Erin, Harrison, Lake, Sterling, and Warren, in Macomb County; the cities of Berkley, Birmingham, Bloomfield Hills, Farmington, Ferndale, Huntington Woods, Pleasant Ridge, Pontiac, and Royal Oak, the townships of Avon, Royal Oak, Bloomfield, Farmington, that part of Novi Township comprising part of Northville Village, Pontiac, Southfield, Troy, Waterford, and West Bloomfield in Oakland County, the entire area being in the State of Michigan.

(c) *Base period.* The calendar month of June 1943 is hereby designated as the base period for the sales area.

(d) *Quota period.* The remainder of the calendar month in which the provisions hereof become effective and each subsequent calendar month, respectively, is hereby designated as a quota period for the sales area.

(e) *Handler quotas.* Quotas for each handler in the sales area in each quota period shall be calculated in terms of pounds of each of the items for which percentages are specified in (3) below and shall be determined as follows:

(1) Divide the total deliveries of each such item made in the sales area by such handler during the base period, after excluding the quota-exempt deliveries described in (i) hereof, by the number of days in the base period;

(2) Multiply the result of the foregoing calculation by the number of days in the quota period;

(3) Multiply the aforesaid resulting amount by the following applicable percentage: (i) milk: 100 percent; (ii) butterfat in milk: ------ percent; (iii) cream: 75 percent; (iv) butterfat in cream: 75 percent; (v) milk byproducts other than cottage, pot, or baker's cheese, 75 percent; and (vi) cottage, pot, or baker's cheese, 75 percent of skim milk equivalent. (For the purpose of this order, one pound of cottage, pot, or baker's cheese shall be considered as the equivalent of 7 pounds of skim milk.)

(f) *Quota limitations.* No handler shall, during any quota period, make deliveries in the sales area in excess of his respective quotas, except as set out in (i) hereof; *Provided*, That a handler may, after application to and approval by the market agent, secure an increase in milk quotas through an equivalent reduction as determined by the market agent, in cream and milk byproducts quotas, and an increase in milk byproducts quota through an equivalent reduction as determined by the market agent, in cream quotas.

(g) *Quotas for handlers who are also producers.* Quotas for handlers who are also producers and who purchase no milk shall be 100 percent of the total production of such handlers in the base period.

(h) *Handler exemptions.* Quotas shall not apply to any handler who delivers in a quota period a daily average of less than 300 units of milk, cream, and milk byproducts. For the purpose of this order, a unit shall be the equivalent in volume of the following: (1) milk, one quart of milk; (2) cream, one-half pint of cream; and (3) milk byproduct, one quart of skim milk, buttermilk, flavored milk during, or other beverage containing more than 85 percent of skim milk, or one-half pound of cottage, pot, or baker's cheese.

(i) *Quota exclusions and exemptions.* Deliveries of milk, milk byproducts, or cream (1) to other handlers, except for such deliveries to sub-handlers, (2) to plants engaged in the handling or processing of milk, milk byproducts, or cream from which no milk, milk byproducts, or cream is delivered in the sales area, and (3) to the agencies or groups specified in (d) of FDO 79, shall be excluded from the computation of deliveries in the base period and exempt from charges to quotas.

(j) *Transfers and apportionment of quotas.* The market agent is empowered to deduct an amount of base period deliveries to purchasers from the total of deliveries made by a handler or other person in the base period upon the application and a showing of unreasonable hardship by the handler making deliveries to such purchasers on the effective date of this order, and to add the amount of such deliveries to the total base period deliveries of the applicant handler. Denials of transfers or transfers granted by the market agent shall be reviewed by the Director upon application.

(k) *Petition for relief from hardships* (1) Any person affected by FDO 79 or the provisions hereof who considers that compliance therewith would work an exceptional and unreasonable hardship on him, may file with the market agent a petition addressed to the Director. The petition shall contain the correct name, address and principal place of business of the petitioner, a full statement of the facts upon which the petition is based, and the hardship involved and the nature of the relief desired.

(2) Upon receiving such petition, the market agent shall immediately investigate the representations and facts stated therein.

(3) After investigation, the petition shall be certified to the Director, but prior to certification the market agent may (i) deny the petition, or (ii) grant temporary relief for a total period not to exceed 60 days.

(4) Denials or grants of relief by the market agent shall be reviewed by the Director and may be affirmed, modified, or reversed by the Director.

(l) *Reports.* Each handler shall transmit to the market agent on forms prescribed by the market agent the following reports:

(1) Within 20 days following the effective date of this order, reports which show the information required by the market agent to establish such handlers' quotas;

(2) Within 20 days following the close of each quota period, the information

required by the market agent to establish volumes of deliveries of milk, cream, and milk byproducts during the preceding quota period; and

(3) Handlers exempt from quotas pursuant to (h) hereof shall, upon the request of the market agent, submit the information required by the market agent to establish volumes of deliveries of milk, cream, and milk byproducts.

(m) *Records.* Handlers shall keep and shall make available to the market agent such records of receipts, sales, deliveries, and production as the market agent shall require for the purpose of obtaining information which the Director may require for the establishment of quotas as prescribed in (b) of FDO 79.

(n) *Distribution schedules.* The distribution schedules, if any, to be followed by the handlers in making deliveries shall be made effective in the terms of approval by the Director of such schedules.

(o) *Expense of administration.* Each handler shall pay to the market agent, within 20 days after the close of each calendar month an assessment of $0.01 per hundredweight of each of milk, cream, skim milk, buttermilk, flavored milk drinks, beverages containing more than 85 percent of skim milk, and skim milk equivalent of cottage, pot, or baker's cheese delivered during the preceding quota period and subject to quota regulations under the provisions hereof.

(p) *Violations.* The market agent shall report all violations to the Director together with the information required for the prosecution of such violations, except in a case where a handler has made deliveries in a quota period in excess of a quota in an amount not to exceed 5 percent of such quota, and in the succeeding quota period makes deliveries below that quota by at least the same percent.

(q) *Bureau of the Budget approval.* The record keeping and reporting requirements of this order have been approved by the Bureau of the Budget in accordance with the Federal Reports Act of 1942. Subsequent record keeping or reporting requirements will be subject to the approval of the Bureau of the Budget pursuant to the Federal Reports Act of 1942.

(r) This order shall take effect at 12:01 a. m., e. w. t., November 1, 1943.

Issued this 19th day of October 1943.

C. W. KITCHEN,
Acting Director of Food Distribution.

Press Release Immediate:
Wednesday, October 20, 1943.

Milk sales in 19 metropolitan areas in Illinois, Michigan, Colorado, Utah, Arizona, Oregon, Pennsylvania, Minnesota, Oklahoma and West Virginia will be regulated under the Food Distribution Administration's fluid milk conservation and control program, beginning November 1, 1943.

The new milk sales areas and the market agents who will administer the program in each are:

Johnstown, Pa., Erie, Pa., Altoona, Pa., Pittsburgh, Pa., Metropolitan, Charleston, W. Va., Wheeling, W. Va.; George A. Taylor, Century Building, Pittsburgh, Pa.

Peoria, Ill., Rockford, Ill.: A. W. Colebank, 135 S. La Salle St., Chicago, Ill.

Phoenix, Ariz., Denver, Colo., Metropolitan, Salt Lake City, Utah, Metropolitan; Ben King, 503 Security Life Building, 810 14th St., Denver, Colo. (temp. address).

Portland, Oregon, Metropolitan; C. H. Mapes, 625 Elliot Avenue, West Seattle, Washington.

Detroit, Mich., Metropolitan, Saginaw-Bay City, Mich., Metropolitan, Lansing, Mich., Metropolitan, Flint, Mich., Metropolitan (to be announced later).

Oklahoma City, Oklahoma, Tulsa, Oklahoma; M. M. Morehouse, 512 Porter Bldg., 406 W. 34th St., Kansas City, Mo.

Minneapolis-St. Paul, Minnesota; D. F. Spencer, 404 Post Office Bldg., Minneapolis, Minn.

Under the program, milk dealers will be permitted to sell as much fluid milk as they sold in June and three-fourths as much cream and milk byproducts (such as cottage cheese, chocolate milk, and buttermilk) as they sold in June. Milk dealers include all persons or firms engaged in the sale or transfer of milk, but not such distributors as subhandlers ("peddlers"), retail stores, hotels, or restaurants.

Producer-distributors who purchase no milk will be permitted to sell as much milk as they produced in June.

Dealers will be allowed to exceed these base quotas by not more than 5 percent during any month, providing they decrease their deliveries the next month by the same amount, without being reported in violation.

A dealer also may increase his milk sales by reducing his cream and milk byproducts sales, and increase his sales of milk byproducts by reducing his cream sales, providing such an adjustment is approved by the market agent for the area.

Deliveries of milk, cream, and milk byproducts to other dealers, to the Armed Forces, and to plants processing milk who do not distribute milk, cream, and milk byproducts in the sales area are quota-exempt.

Consumers in the milk sales areas named today and in others already designated generally will be able to purchase as much milk under the milk conservation program as they have been buying in recent months—within the limits of local supplies. In some areas, production is not expected to be large enough to permit dealers to sell as much milk as their quotas allow.

Fluid milk sales are being stabilized, Food Distribution Administration officials said, to help assure sufficient milk for manufacturing the cheese, butter, evaporated milk, and milk powder required by the Armed Services and civilians for food nutrition and properly balanced diets. Sales quotas on cream and on fluid milk byproducts have been set below June deliveries to boost fluid milk supplies where production is low, and to conserve milk for manufacturing purposes.

FDO 79-65

OCTOBER 19, 1943

WAR FOOD ADMINISTRATION

[FDO 79-65]

PART 1401—DAIRY PRODUCTS

FLUID MILK AND CREAM IN SAGINAW-BAY CITY, MICH., METROPOLITAN SALES AREA

Pursuant to the authority vested in me by Food Distribution Order No. 79 (8 F.R. 12426), issued on September 7, 1943, as amended, and to effectuate the purposes of such order, it is hereby ordered as follows:

§ 1401.100 *Quota restrictions*—(a) *Definitions.* When used in this order, unless otherwise distinctly expressed or manifestly incompatible with the intent hereof:

(1) Each term defined in Food Distribution Order No. 79, as amended, shall, when used herein, have the same meaning as is set forth for such term in Food Distribution Order No. 79, as amended.

(2) The term "FDO 79" means Food Distribution Order No. 79, issued on September 7, 1943, as amended.

(3) The term "sub-handler" means any handler, such as a peddler, vendor, sub-dealer, or secondary dealer, who purchases in a previously packaged and processed form milk, milk byproducts or cream for delivery.

(b) *Milk sales area.* The following area is hereby designated as a "milk sales area" to be known as the Saginaw-Bay City, metropolitan sales area, and is referred to hereinafter as the "sales area":

The cities of Saginaw in Saginaw County, and Bay City and Essexville in Bay County; the townships of Bangor, Hampton, and Portsmouth in Bay County; and the townships of Buena Vista, Carrollton, Saginaw, and Zilwaukee in Saginaw County, all in the State of Michigan.

(c) *Base period.* The calendar month of June 1943 is hereby designated as the base period for the sales area.

(d) *Quota period.* The remainder of the calendar month in which the provisions hereof become effective and each subsequent calendar month, respectively, is hereby designated as a quota period for the sales area.

(e) *Handler quotas.* Quotas for each handler in the sales area in each quota period shall be calculated in terms of pounds of each of the items for which percentages are specified in (3) below and shall be determined as follows:

(1) Divide the total deliveries of each such item made in the sales area by such handler during the base period, after excluding the quota-exempt deliveries described in (i) hereof, by the number of days in the base period;

(2) Multiply the result of the foregoing calculation by the number of days in the quota period;

(3) Multiply the aforesaid resulting amount by the following applicable percentage: (i) milk: 100 percent; (ii) butterfat in milk: ------ percent; (iii) cream: 75 percent; (iv) butterfat in cream: 75 percent; (v) milk byproducts other than cottage, pot, or baker's cheese: 75 percent; and (vi) cottage, pot, or baker's cheese: 75 percent of skim milk equivalent. (For the purpose of this order, one pound of cottage, pot, or baker's cheese shall be considered as the equivalent of 7 pounds of skim milk.)

(f) *Quota limitations.* No handler shall, during any quota period, make deliveries in the sales area in excess of his respective quotas, except as set out in (i) hereof: *Provided*, That a handler may, after application to and approval by the market agent, secure an increase in milk quotas through an equivalent reduction as determined by the market agent, in cream and milk byproducts quotas, and an increase in milk byproducts quota through an equivalent reduction as determined by the market agent, in cream quotas.

(g) *Quotas for handlers who are also producers.* Quotas for handlers who are also producers and who purchase no milk shall be 100 percent of the total production of such handlers in the base period.

(h) *Handler exemptions.* Quotas shall not apply to any handler who delivers in a quota period a daily average of less than 300 units of milk, cream, and milk byproducts. For the purpose of this order, a unit shall be the equivalent in volume of the following: (1) milk, one quart of milk; (2) cream, one-half pint of cream; and (3) milk byproduct, one quart of skim milk, buttermilk, flavored milk drink, or other beverage containing more than 85 percent of skim milk, or one-half pound of cottage, pot, or baker's cheese.

(i) *Quota exclusions and exemptions.* Deliveries of milk, milk byproducts, or cream (1) to other handlers, except for such deliveries to sub-handlers, (2) to plants engaged in the handling or processing of milk, milk byproducts, or cream from which no milk, milk byproducts, or cream is delivered in the sales area, and (3) to the agencies or groups specified in (d) of FDO 79, shall be excluded from the computation of deliveries in the base period and exempt from charges to quotas.

(j) *Transfers and apportionment of quotas.* The market agent is empowered to deduct an amount of base period deliveries to purchasers from the total of deliveries made by a handler or other person in the base period upon the application and a showing of unreasonable hardship by the handler making deliveries to such purchasers on the effective date of this order, and to add the amount of such deliveries to the total base period deliveries of the applicant handler. Denials of transfers or transfers granted by the market agent shall be reviewed by the Director upon application.

(k) *Petition for relief from hardships.* (1) Any person affected by FDO 79 or the provisions hereof who considers that compliance therewith would work an exceptional and unreasonable hardship on him, may file with the market agent a petition addressed to the Director. The petition shall contain the correct name, address and principal place of business of the petitioner, a full statement of the facts upon which the petition is based, and the hardship involved and the nature of the relief desired.

(2) Upon receiving such petition, the market agent shall immediately investigate the representations and facts stated therein.

(3) After investigation, the petition shall be certified to the Director, but prior to certification the market agent may (i) deny the petition, or (ii) grant temporary relief for a total period not to exceed 60 days.

(4) Denials or grants of relief by the market agent shall be reviewed by the Director and may be affirmed, modified or reversed by the Director.

(l) *Reports.* Each handler shall transmit to the market agent on forms prescribed by the market agent the following reports:

(1) Within 20 days following the effective date of this order, reports which show the information required by the market agent to establish such handlers' quotas;

(2) Within 20 days following the close of each quota period, the information required by the market agent to establish volumes of deliveries of milk, cream, and milk byproducts during the preceding quota period; and

(3) Handlers exempt from quotas pursuant to (h) hereof shall, upon the request of the market agent, submit the information required by the market agent to establish volumes of deliveries of milk, cream, and milk byproducts.

(m) *Records.* Handlers shall keep and shall make available to the market agent such records of receipts, sales, deliveries, and production as the market agent shall require for the purpose of obtaining information which the Director may require for the establishment of quotas as prescribed in (b) of FDO 79.

(n) *Distribution schedules.* The distribution schedules, if any, to be followed by the handlers in making deliveries shall be made effective in the terms of approval by the Director of such schedules.

(o) *Expense of administration.* Each handler shall pay to the market agent, within 20 days after the close of each calendar month an assessment of $0.01 per hundredweight of each of milk, cream, skim milk, buttermilk, flavored milk drinks, beverages containing more than 85 percent of skim milk, and skim milk equivalent of cottage, pot, or baker's cheese delivered during the preceding quota period and subject to quota regulations under the provisions hereof.

(p) *Violations.* The market agent shall report all violations to the Director together with the information required for the prosecution of such violations, except in a case where a handler has made deliveries in a quota period in excess of a quota in an amount not to exceed 5 percent of such quota, and in the succeeding quota period makes deliveries below that quota by at least the same percent.

(q) *Bureau of the Budget approval.* The record keeping and reporting requirements of this order have been approved by the Bureau of the Budget in accordance with the Federal Reports Act of 1942. Subsequent record keeping or reporting requirements will be subject to the approval of the Bureau of the Budget pursuant to the Federal Reports Act of 1942.

(r) This order shall take effect at 12.01 a. m., e. w. t., November 1, 1943.

Issued this 19th day of October 1943.

C. W. KITCHEN,
Acting Director of Food Distribution.

Press Release Immediate:
Wednesday, October 20, 1943.

Milk sales in 19 metropolitan areas in Illinois, Michigan, Colorado, Utah, Arizona, Oregon, Pennsylvania, Minnesota, Oklahoma and West Virginia will be regulated under the Food Distribution Administration's fluid milk conservation and control program, beginning November 1, 1943.

The new milk sales areas and the market agents who will administer the program in each are:

Johnstown, Pa., Erie, Pa., Altoona, Pa., Pittsburgh, Pa., Metropolitan, Charleston, W. Va., Wheeling, W. Va.; George A. Taylor, Century Building, Pittsburgh, Pa.

Peoria, Ill., Rockford, Ill.; A. W. Colebank, 135 S. La Salle St., Chicago, Ill.

Phoenix, Ariz., Denver, Colo., Metropolitan, Salt Lake City, Utah, Metropolitan; Ben King, 503 Security Life Building, 810 14th St., Denver, Colo. (temp. address).

Portland, Oregon, Metropolitan; J. H Mapes, 635 Elliot Avenue, West, Seattle, Wash.

Detroit, Mich., Metropolitan, Saginaw-Bay City, Mich., Metropolitan, Lansing, Mich., Metropolitan, Flint, Mich., Metropolitan (to be announced later).

Oklahoma City, Okla., Tulsa, Okla.; M. M. Morehouse, 512 Porter Bldg., 406 W. 34th St., Kansas City, Mo.

Minneapolis-St. Paul, Minn.; D. F. Spencer, 404 Post Office Bldg., Minneapolis, Minn.

Under the program, milk dealers will be permitted to sell as much fluid milk as they sold in June and three-fourths as much cream and milk byproducts (such as cottage cheese, chocolate milk, and buttermilk) as they sold in June. Milk dealers include all persons or firms engaged in the sale or transfer of milk, but not such distributors as subhandlers ("peddlers"), retail stores, hotels, or restaurants.

Producer-distributors who purchase no milk will be permitted to sell as much milk as they produced in June.

Dealers will be allowed to exceed these base quotas by not more than 5 percent during any month, providing they decrease their deliveries the next month by the same amount, without being reported in violation.

A dealer also may increase his milk sales by reducing his cream and milk byproducts sales, and increase his sales of milk byproducts by reducing his cream sales, providing such an adjustment is approved by the market agent for the area.

Deliveries of milk, cream, and milk byproducts to other dealers, to the Armed Forces, and to plants processing milk who do not distribute milk, cream, and milk byproducts in the sales area are quota-exempt.

Consumers in the milk sales areas named today and in others already designated generally will be able to purchase as much milk under the milk conservation program as they have been buying in recent months—within the limits of local supplies. In some areas, production is not expected to be large enough to permit dealers to sell as much milk as their quotas allow.

Fluid milk sales are being stabilized, Food Distribution Administration officials said, to help assure sufficient milk for manufacturing the cheese, butter, evaporated milk, and milk powder required by the Armed Services and civilians for food nutrition and properly balanced diets. Sales quotas on cream and on fluid milk byproducts have been set below June deliveries to boost fluid milk supplies where production is low, and to conserve milk for manufacturing purposes.

WAR FOOD ADMINISTRATION

[FDO 79-66]

PART 1401—DAIRY PRODUCTS

FLUID MILK AND CREAM IN ROCKFORD, ILL., SALES AREA

Pursuant to the authority vested in me by Food Distribution Order No. 79 (8 F.R. 12426), issued on September 7, 1943, as amended, and to effectuate the purposes of such order, it is hereby ordered as follows:

§ 1401.97 *Quota restrictions* — (a) *Definitions.* When used in this order, unless otherwise distinctly expressed or manifestly incompatible with the intent hereof:

(1) Each term defined in Food Distribution Order No. 79, as amended, shall, when used herein, have the same meaning as is set forth for such term in Food Distribution Order No. 79, as amended.

(2) The term "FDO 79" means Food Distribution Order No. 79, issued on September 7, 1943, as amended.

(3) The term "sub-handler" means any handler, such as a peddler, vendor, sub-dealer, or secondary dealer, who purchases in a previously packaged and processed form milk, milk byproducts, or cream for delivery.

(b) *Milk sales area.* The following area is hereby designated as a "milk sales area" to be known as the Rockford, Illinois, sales area, and is referred to hereinafter as the "sales area":

The city of Rockford and the townships of Rockford and Cherry Valley, in Winnebago County, Illinois.

(c) *Base period.* The calendar month of June 1943 is hereby designated as the base period for the sales area.

(d) *Quota period.* The remainder of the calendar month in which the provisions hereof become effective and each subsequent calendar month, respectively, is hereby designated as a quota period for the sales area.

(e) *Handler quotas.* Quotas for each handler in the sales area in each quota period shall be calculated in terms of pounds of each of the items for which percentages are specified in (3) below and shall be determined as follows:

(1) Divide the total deliveries of each such item made in the sales area by such handler during the base period, after excluding the quota-exempt deliveries described in (i) hereof, by the number of days in the base period;

(2) Multiply the result of the foregoing calculation by the number of days in the quota period;

(3) Multiply the aforesaid resulting amount by the following applicable percentage: (i) milk: 100 percent; (ii) butterfat in milk: ______ percent; (iii) cream: 75 percent; (iv) butterfat in cream: 75 percent; (v) milk byproducts other than cottage, pot, or baker's cheese: 75 percent; and (vi) cottage, pot, or baker's cheese: 75 percent of skim milk equivalent. (For the purpose of this order, one pound of cottage, pot, or baker's cheese shall be considered as the equivalent of 7 pounds of skim milk.)

(f) *Quota limitations.* No handler shall, during any quota period, make deliveries in the sales area in excess of his respective quotas, except as set out in (i) hereof: *Provided,* That a handler may, after application to and approval by the market agent, secure an increase in milk quotas through an equivalent reduction as determined by the market agent, in cream and milk byproducts quotas, and an increase in milk byproducts quota through an equivalent reduction as determined by the market agent, in cream quotas.

(g) *Quotas for handlers who are also producers.* Quotas for handlers who are also producers and who purchase no milk shall be 100 percent of the total production of such handlers in the base period.

(h) *Handler exemptions.* Quotas shall not apply to any handler who delivers in a quota period a daily average of less than 300 units of milk, cream, and milk byproducts. For the purpose of this order, a unit shall be the equivalent in volume of the following: (1) milk, one quart of milk; (2) cream, one-half pint of cream; and (3) milk byproduct, one quart of skim milk, buttermilk, flavored milk drink, or other beverage containing more than 85 percent of skim milk, or one-half pound of cottage, pot, or baker's cheese.

(i) *Quota exclusions and exemptions.* Deliveries of milk, milk byproducts, or cream (1) to other handlers, except for such deliveries to sub-handlers, (2) to plants engaged in the handling or processing of milk, milk byproducts, or cream from which no milk, milk byproducts, or cream is delivered in the sales area, and (3) to the agencies or groups specified in (d) of FDO 79, shall be excluded from the computation of deliveries in the base period and exempt from charges to quotas.

(j) *Transfers and apportionment of quotas.* The market agent is empowered to deduct an amount of base period deliveries to purchasers from the total of deliveries made by a handler or other person in the base period upon the application and a showing of unreasonable hardship by the handler making deliveries to such purchasers on the effective date of this order, and to add the amount of such deliveries to the total base period deliveries of the applicant handler. Denials of transfers or transfers granted by the market agent shall be reviewed by the Director upon application.

(k) *Petition for relief from hardships.* (1) Any person affected by FDO 79 or the provisions hereof who considers that compliance therewith would work an exceptional and unreasonable hardship on him, may file with the market agent a petition addressed to the Director. The petition shall contain the correct name, address and principal place of business of the petitioner, a full statement of the facts upon which the petition is based, and the hardship involved and the nature of the relief desired.

(2) Upon receiving such petition the market agent shall immediately investigate the representations and facts stated therein.

(3) After investigation, the petition shall be certified to the Director, but prior to certification the market agent may (i) deny the petition, or (ii) grant temporary relief for a total period not to exceed 60 days.

(4) Denials or grants of relief by the market agent shall be reviewed by the Director and may be affirmed, modified, or reversed by the Director.

(l) *Reports.* Each handler shall transmit to the market agent on forms prescribed by the market agent the following reports:

(1) Within 20 days following the effective date of this order, reports which show the information required by the market agent to establish such handlers' quotas;

(2) Within 20 days following the close of each quota period, the information required by the market agent to establish volumes of deliveries of milk, cream, and milk byproducts during the preceding quota period; and

(3) Handlers exempt from quotas pursuant to (h) hereof shall, upon the request of the market agent, submit the information required by the market agent to establish volumes of deliveries of milk, cream, and milk byproducts.

(m) *Records.* Handlers shall keep and shall make available to the market agent such records of receipts, sales, deliveries, and production as the market agent shall require for the purpose of obtaining information which the Director may require for the establishment of quotas as prescribed in (b) of FDO 79.

(n) *Distribution schedules.* The distribution schedules, if any, to be followed by the handlers in making deliveries shall be made effective in the terms of approval by the Director of such schedules.

(o) *Expense of administration.* Each handler shall pay to the market agent, within 20 days after the close of each calendar month an assessment of $0.01 per hundredweight of each of milk, cream, skim milk, buttermilk, flavored milk drinks, beverages containing more than 85 percent of skim milk, and skim milk equivalent of cottage, pot, or baker's cheese delivered during the preceding quota period and subject to quota regulations under the provisions hereof.

(p) *Violations.* The market agent shall report all violations to the Director together with the information required for the prosecution of such violations, except in a case where a handler has made deliveries in a quota period in excess of a quota in an amount not to exceed 5 percent of such quota, and in the succeeding quota period makes deliveries below that quota by at least the same percent.

(q) *Bureau of the Budget approval.* The record keeping and reporting requirements of this order have been approved by the Bureau of the Budget in accordance with the Federal Reports Act of 1942. Subsequent record keeping or reporting requirements will be subject to the approval of the Bureau of the Budget pursuant to the Federal Reports Act of 1942.

(r) This order shall take effect at 12:01 a. m., e. w. t., November 1, 1943.

Issued this 19th day of October 1943.

C. W. KITCHEN,
Acting Director of Food Distribution.

Press Release Immediate:
Wednesday, October 20, 1943.

Milk sales in 19 metropolitan areas in Illinois, Michigan, Colorado, Utah, Arizona, Oregon, Pennsylvania, Minnesota, Oklahoma and West Virginia will be regulated under the Food Distribution Administration's fluid milk conservation and control program, beginning November 1, 1943.

The new milk sales areas and the market agents who will administer the program in each are:

Johnstown, Pa.; Erie, Pa.; Altoona, Pa.; Pittsburgh, Pa., Metropolitan; Charleston, W. Va.; Wheeling, W. Va.: George A. Taylor, Century Building, Pittsburgh, Pa.

Peoria, Ill.; Rockford, Ill.: A. W. Colebank, 135 S. LaSalle St., Chicago, Ill.

Phoenix, Ariz.; Denver, Colo., Metropolitan; Salt Lake City, Utah, Metropolitan: Ben King, 503 Security Life Building, 810 14th St., Denver, Colo. (temp. address).

Portland, Oregon, Metropolitan: J. H. Mapes, 635 Elliot Avenue, West, Seattle, Washington.

Detroit, Michigan, Metropolitan; Saginaw-Bay City, Mich., Metropolitan; Lansing, Mich., Metropolitan; Flint, Mich., Metropolitan: (To be announced later).

Oklahoma City, Oklahoma; Tulsa, Oklahoma: M. M. Morehouse, 512 Porter Bldg., 406 W. 34th St., Kansas City, Mo

Minneapolis-St. Paul, Minnesota: D. F. Spencer, 404 Post Office Bldg., Minneapolis, Minn.

Under the program, milk dealers will be permitted to sell as much fluid milk as they sold in June and three-fourths as much cream and milk byproducts (such as cottage cheese, chocolate milk, and buttermilk) as they sold in June. Milk dealers include all persons or firms engaged in the sale or transfer of milk, but not such distributors as subhandlers ("peddlers"), retail stores, hotels, or restaurants.

Producer-distributors who purchase no milk will be permitted to sell as much milk as they produced in June.

Dealers will be allowed to exceed these base quotas by not more than 5 percent during any month, providing they decrease their deliveries the next month by the same amount, without being reported in violation.

A dealer also may increase his milk sales by reducing his cream and milk byproducts sales, and increase his sales of milk byproducts by reducing his cream sales, providing such an adjustment is approved by the market agent for the area.

Deliveries of milk, cream, and milk byproducts to other dealers, to the Armed Forces, and to plants processing milk who do not distribute milk, cream, and milk byproducts in the sales area are quota-exempt.

Consumers in the milk sales areas named today and in others already designated generally will be able to purchase as much milk under the milk conservation program as they have been buying in recent months—within the limits of local supplies. In some areas, production is not expected to be large enough to permit dealers to sell as much milk as their quotas allow.

Fluid milk sales are being stabilized, Food Distribution Administration officials said, to help assure sufficient milk for manufacturing the cheese, butter, evaporated milk, and milk powder required by the Armed Services and civilians for food nutrition and properly balanced diets. Sales quotas on cream and on fluid milk byproducts have been set below June deliveries to boost fluid milk supplies where production is low, and to conserve milk for manufacturing purposes.

'V8

FDO 79-66

AMDT. 1
JAN. 27, 1944

WAR FOOD ADMINISTRATION

[FDO 79-66, Amdt. 1] A

PART 1401—DAIRY PRODUCTS

FLUID MILK AND CREAM IN ROCKFORD, ILL., SALES AREA

Pursuant to Food Distribution Order No. 79 (8 F.R. 12426), dated September 7, 1943, as amended, and to effectuate the purposes thereof, Food Distribution Order No. 79-66 (8 F.R. 14268), relative to the conservation and distribution of fluid milk in the Rockford, Illinois, milk sales area, issued by the Director of Food Distribution on October 19, 1943, is hereby amended as follows:

Delete the numerals "300" wherever they appear in § 1401.97 (h) and insert in lieu thereof, the numerals "100".

The provisions of this amendment shall become effective at 12:01 a. m., e. w. t., February 1, 1944. With respect to violations of said Food Distribution Order No. 79-66, rights accrued, or liabilities incurred prior to the effective time of this amendment, said Food Distribution Order No. 79-66 shall be deemed to be in full force and effect for the purpose of sustaining any proper suit, action, or other proceeding with respect to any such violation, right, or liability.

(E.O. 9280, 7 F.R. 10179; E.O. 9322, 8 F.R. 3807; E.O. 9334, 8 F.R. 5423; E.O. 9392, 8 F.R. 14783; FDO 79, 8 F.R. 12426, 13283)

Issued this 27th day of January 1944.

LEE MARSHALL,
Director of Food Distribution.

FDO 79-67

OCTOBER 19, 1943

WAR FOOD ADMINISTRATION

[FDO 79-67]

PART 1401—DAIRY PRODUCTS

FLUID MILK AND CREAM IN FLINT, MICH., METROPOLITAN SALES AREA

Pursuant to the authority vested in me by Food Distribution Order No. 79 (8 F.R. 12426), issued on September 7, 1943, as amended, and to effectuate the purposes of such order, it is hereby ordered as follows:

§ 1401.95 *Quota restrictions*—(a) *Definitions.* When used in this order, unless otherwise distinctly expressed or manifestly incompatible with the intent hereof:

(1) Each term defined in Food Distribution Order No. 79, as amended, shall, when used herein, have the same meaning as is set forth for such term in Food Distribution Order No. 79, as amended.

(2) The term "FDO 79" means Food Distribution Order No. 79, issued on September 7, 1943, as amended.

(3) The term "sub-handler" means any handler, such as a peddler, vendor, sub-dealer, or secondary dealer, who purchases in a previously packaged and processed form milk, milk byproducts, or cream for delivery.

(b) *Milk sales area.* The following area is hereby designated as a "milk sales area" to be known as the Flint, Michigan, metropolitan sales area, and is referred to hereinafter as the "sales area":

The cities of Flint and Mount Morris and the townships of Burton, Flint, Genesee, and Mount Morris, all in Genesee County, Michigan.

(c) *Base period.* The calendar month of June 1943 is hereby designated as the base period for the sales area.

(d) *Quota period.* The remainder of the calendar month in which the provisions hereof become effective and each subsequent calendar month, respectively, is hereby designated as a quota period for the sales area.

(e) *Handler quotas.* Quotas for each handler in the sales area in each quota period shall be calculated in terms of pounds of each of the items for which percentages are specified in (3) below and shall be determined as follows:

(1) Divide the total deliveries of each such item made in the sales area by such handler during the base period, after excluding the quota-exempt deliveries described in (i) hereof, by the number of days in the base period;

(2) Multiply the result of the foregoing calculation by the number of days in the quota period;

(3) Multiply the aforesaid resulting amount by the following applicable percentage: (i) milk: 100 percent; (ii) butterfat in milk: ------ percent; (iii) cream: 75 percent; (iv) butterfat in cream: 75 percent; (v) milk byproducts other than cottage, pot, or baker's cheese: 75 percent; and (vi) cottage, pot, or baker's cheese: 75 percent of skim milk equivalent. (For the purpose of this order, one pound of cottage, pot, or baker's cheese shall be considered as the equivalent of 7 pounds of skim milk.)

(f) *Quota limitations.* No handler shall, during any quota period, make deliveries in the sales area in excess of his respective quotas, except as set out in (i) hereof: *Provided,* That a handler may, after application to and approval by the market agent, secure an increase in milk quotas through an equivalent reduction as determined by the market agent, in cream and milk byproducts quotas, and an increase in milk byproducts quota through an equivalent reduction as determined by the market agent, in cream quotas.

(g) *Quotas for handlers who are also producers.* Quotas for handlers who are also producers and who purchase no milk shall be 100 percent of the total production of such handlers in the base period.

(h) *Handler exemptions.* Quotas shall not apply to any handler who delivers in a quota period a daily average of less than 300 units of milk, cream, and milk byproducts. For the purpose of this order, a unit shall be the equivalent in volume of the following: (1) milk, one quart of milk; (2) cream, one-half pint of cream; and (3) milk byproduct, one quart of skim milk, buttermilk, flavored milk drink, or other beverage containing more than 85 percent of skim milk, or one-half pound of cottage, pot, or baker's cheese.

(i) *Quota exclusions and exemptions.* Deliveries of milk, milk byproducts, or cream (1) to other handlers, except for such deliveries to sub-handlers, (2) to plants engaged in the handling or processing of milk, milk byproducts, or cream from which no milk, milk byproducts, or cream is delivered in the sales area, and (3) to the agencies or groups specified in (d) of FDO 79, shall be excluded from the computation of deliveries in the base period and exempt from charges to quotas.

(j) *Transfers and apportionment of quotas.* The market agent is empowered to deduct an amount of base period deliveries to purchasers from the total of deliveries made by a handler or other person in the base period upon the application and a showing of unreasonable hardship by the handler making deliveries to such purchasers on the effective date of this order, and to add the amount of such deliveries to the total base period deliveries of the applicant handler. Denials of transfers or transfers granted by the market agent shall be reviewed by the Director upon application.

(k) *Petition for relief from hardships.* (1) Any person affected by FDO 79 or the provisions hereof who considers that compliance therewith would work an exceptional and unreasonable hardship on him, may file with the market agent a petition addressed to the Director. The petition shall contain the correct name, address and principal place of business of the petitioner, a full statement of the facts upon which the petition is based, and the hardship involved and the nature of the relief desired.

(2) Upon receiving such petition, the market agent shall immediately investigate the representations and facts stated therein.

(3) After investigation, the petition shall be certified to the Director, but prior to certification the market agent may (i) deny the petition, or (ii) grant temporary relief for a total period not to exceed 60 days.

(4) Denials or grants of relief by the market agent shall be reviewed by the Director and may be affirmed, modified, or reversed by the Director.

(l) *Reports.* Each handler shall transmit to the market agent on forms prescribed by the market agent the following reports:

(1) Within 20 days following the effective date of this order, reports which show the information required by the market agent to establish such handlers' quotas;

(2) Within 20 days following the close of each quota period, the information required by the market agent to establish volumes of deliveries of milk, cream, and milk byproducts during the preceding quota period; and

(3) Handlers exempt from quotas pursuant to (h) hereof shall, upon the request of the market agent, submit the information required by the market agent to establish volumes of deliveries of milk, cream, and milk byproducts.

(m) *Records.* Handlers shall keep and shall make available to the market agent such records of receipts, sales, deliveries, and production as the market agent shall require for the purpose of obtaining information which the Director may require for the establishment of quotas as prescribed in (b) of FDO 79.

(n) *Distribution schedules.* The distribution schedules, if any, to be followed by the handlers in making deliveries shall be made effective in the terms of approval by the Director of such schedules.

(o) *Expense of administration.* Each handler shall pay to the market agent, within 20 days after the close of each calendar month an assessment of $0.01 per hundredweight of each milk, cream, skim milk, buttermilk, flavored milk drinks, beverages containing more than 85 percent of skim milk, and skim milk equivalent of cottage, pot, or baker's cheese delivered during the preceding quota period and subject to quota regulations under the provisions hereof.

(p) *Violations.* The market agent shall report all violations to the Director together with the information required for the prosecution of such violations, except in a case where a handler has made deliveries in a quota period in excess of a quota in an amount not to exceed 5 percent of such quota, and in the succeeding quota period makes deliveries below that quota by at least the same percent.

(q) *Bureau of the Budget approval.* The record keeping and reporting requirements of this order have been approved by the Bureau of the Budget in accordance with the Federal Reports Act of 1942. Subsequent record keeping or reporting requirements will be subject to the approval of the Bureau of the Budget pursuant to the Federal Reports Act of 1942.

(r) This order shall take effect at 12:01 a. m., e. w. t., November 1, 1943.

Issued this 19th day of October 1943.

C. W. KITCHEN,
Acting Director of Food Distribution.

Press Release, Immediate:
Wednesday, October 20, 1943.

Milk sales in 19 metropolitan areas in Illinois, Michigan, Colorado, Utah, Arizona, Oregon, Pennsylvania, Minnesota, Oklahoma and West Virginia will be regulated under the Food Distribution Administration's fluid milk conservation and control program, beginning November 1, 1943.

The new milk sales areas and the market agents who will administer the program in each are:

Johnstown, Pa., Erie, Pa., Altoona, Pa., Pittsburgh, Pa., Metropolitan, Charleston, W. Va., Wheeling, W. Va.; George A. Taylor, Century Building, Pittsburgh, Pa.

Peoria, Ill., Rockford, Ill.; A. W. Colebank, 135 S. La Salle St., Chicago, Ill.

Phoenix, Ariz., Denver, Colo., Metropolitan, Salt Lake City, Utah, Metropolitan; Ben King, 503 Security Life Building, 810 14th St., Denver, Colo. (temp. address).

Portland, Oregon, Metropolitan; J. H. Mapes, 635 Elliot Avenue, West, Seattle, Washington.

Detroit, Mich., Metropolitan, Saginaw-Bay City, Mich., Metropolitan, Lansing, Mich., Metropolitan, Flint, Mich., Metropolitan (to be announced later).

Oklahoma City, Okla., Tulsa, Okla.; M. M. Morehouse, 512 Porter Bldg., 406 W. 34th St., Kansas City, Mo.

Minneapolis-St. Paul, Minn.; D. F. Spencer, 404 Post Office Bldg., Minneapolis, Minn.

Under the program, milk dealers will be permitted to sell as much fluid milk as they sold in June and three-fourths as much cream and milk byproducts (such as cottage cheese, chocolate milk, and buttermilk) as they sold in June. Milk dealers include all persons or firms engaged in the sale or transfer of milk, but not such distributors as subhandlers ("peddlers"), retail stores, hotels, or restaurants.

Producer-distributors who purchase no milk will be permitted to sell as much milk as they produced in June.

Dealers will be allowed to exceed these base quotas by not more than 5 percent during any month, providing they decrease their deliveries the next month by the same amount, without being reported in violation.

A dealer also may increase his milk sales by reducing his cream and milk byproducts sales, and increase his sales of milk byproducts by reducing his cream sales, providing such an adjustment is approved by the market agent for the area.

Deliveries of milk, cream, and milk byproducts to other dealers, to the Armed Forces, and to plants processing milk who do not distribute milk, cream, and milk byproducts in the sales area are quota-exempt.

Consumers in the milk sales areas named today and in others already designated generally will be able to purchase as much milk under the milk conservation program as they have been buying in recent months—within the limits of local supplies. In some areas, production is not expected to be large enough to permit dealers to sell as much milk as their quotas allow.

Fluid milk sales are being stabilized, Food Distribution Administration officials said, to help assure sufficient milk for manufacturing the cheese, butter, evaporated milk, and milk powder required by the Armed Services and civilians for food nutrition and properly balanced diets. Sales quotas on cream and on fluid milk byproducts have been set below June deliveries to boost fluid milk supplies where production is low, and to conserve milk for manufacturing purposes.

FDO 79-67

AMDT. 1
MAR. 29, 1944

WAR FOOD ADMINISTRATION

[FDO 79-67, Amdt. 1]

PART 1401—DAIRY PRODUCTS

FLUID MILK AND CREAM IN FLINT, MICH., METROPOLITAN SALES AREA

Pursuant to Food Distribution Order No. 79 (8 F.R. 12426), dated September 7, 1943, as amended, and to effectuate the purposes thereof, Food Distribution Order No. 79-67 (8 F. R. 14269), relative to the conservation and distribution of fluid milk in the Flint, Michigan, metropolitan milk sales area, issued by the Director of Food Distribution on October 19, 1943, is amended by deleting the description of the sales area in § 1401.95 (b) and inserting in lieu thereof, the following:

(b) The cities of Flint, Grand Blanc and Mount Morris, and the townships of Burton, Flint, Genesee, Grand Blanc and Mount Morris, all in Genesee County Michigan.

The provisions of this amendment shall become effective at 12:01 a. m., e. w. t., April 1, 1944. With respect to violations of said Food Distribution Order No. 79-67, rights accrued, or liabilities incurred prior to the effective time of this amendment, said Food Distribution Order No. 79-67 shall be deemed to be in full force and effect for the purpose of sustaining any proper suit, action, or other proceeding with respect to any such violation, right, or liability.

(E.O. 9280, 7 F.R. 10179; E.O. 9322, 8 F.R. 3807; E.O. 9334, 8 F.R. 5423; E.O. 9392, 8 F.R. 14783; FDO 79, 8 F.R. 12426, 13283)

Issued this 29th day of March 1944.

LEE MARSHALL,
Director of Food Distribution.

WAR FOOD ADMINISTRATION

[FDO 79-68]

PART 1401—DAIRY PRODUCTS

FLUID MILK AND CREAM IN PITTSBURGH, PA., METROPOLITAN SALES AREA

Pursuant to the authority vested in me by Food Distribution Order No. 79 (8 F.R. 12426), issued on September 7, 1943, as amended, and to effectuate the purposes of such order, it is hereby ordered as follows:

§ 1401.102 *Quota restrictions*—(a) *Definitions*. When used in this order, unless otherwise distinctly expressed or manifestly incompatible with the intent hereof:

(1) Each term defined in Food Distribution Order No. 79, as amended, shall, when used herein, have the same meaning as is set forth for such term in Food Distribution Order No. 79, as amended.

(2) The term "FDO 79" means Food Distribution Order No. 79, issued on September 7, 1943, as amended.

(3) The term "sub-handler" means any handler, such as a peddler, vendor, sub-dealer, or secondary dealer, who purchases in a previously packaged and processed form milk, milk byproducts, or cream for delivery.

(b) *Milk sales area*. The following area is hereby designated as a "milk sales area" to be known as the Pittsburgh, Pennsylvania, metropolitan sales area, and is referred to hereinafter as the "sales area":

The cities of Pittsburgh, Clairton, Duquesne, and McKeesport; the townships of Aleppo; Baldwin, Bethel, Braddock, Collier, Crescent, East Deer, Elizabeth, Forward, Frazer, Hampton, Harmar, Harrison, Indiana, Jefferson, Kennedy, Kilbuck, Leet, Lincoln, McCandless, Mifflin, Mount Lebanon, Neville, North Versailles, O'Hara, Ohio, Patton, Penn, Plum, Reserve, Robinson, Ross, Scott, Sewickley Heights, Shaler, Snowden, South Fayette, South Versailles, Springdale, Stowe, Upper St. Clair, Versailles, West Deer, and Wilkins; the boroughs of Aspinwall, Avalon, Bellvue, Ben Avon, Ben Avon Heights, Blawnox, Brackenridge, Braddock, Brentwood, Bridgeville, Carnegie, Castle Shannon, Chalfant, Cheswick, Churchill, Corapolis, Crafton, Dormont, Dravosburg, East McKeesport, East Pittsburgh, Edgewood, Edgeworth, Elizabeth, Emsworth, Etna, Forest Hills, Fox Chapel, Glassport, Glenfield, Greentree, Haysville, Heidelberg, Homestead, Ingram, Leetsdale, Liberty, McDonald (that part in Allegheny County), McKees Rocks, Millvale, Mount Oliver, Munhall, North Braddock, Oakdale, Oakmont, Osborne, Pitcairn, Port Vue, Rankin, Rosslyn Farms, Sewickley, Sewickley Heights, Sharpsburg, Springdale, Swissvale, Tarentum, Thornburg, Trafford (that part in Allegheny County), Turtle Creek, Verona, Versailles, Wall, West Elizabeth, West Homestead, West View, Whitaker, Wilkinsburg, and Wilmerding, in Allegheny County; the township of Harmony and the boroughs of Aliquippa, Ambridge, Baden and South Heights, in Beaver County; the city of Uniontown, the townships of Brownsville, Georges, German, Jefferson, Luzerne, Menallen, Nicholson, North Union, Perry, Redstone, South Union, Springhill, Upper Tyrone, and Washington, and the boroughs of Bellevernon, Brownsville, Everson, Fairchance, Fayette City, Masontown, Point Marion, and Smithfield, in Fayette County; the townships of Cumberland and Monongahela and the boroughs of Carmichaels, Greensboro, and Rices Landing, in Greene County; the cities of Monongahela and Washington, the townships of Canton, Carroll, Cecil, Chartiers, East Bethlehem, East Pike Run, Fallowfield, North Franklin, South Strabane, Union, and West Pike Run, and the boroughs of Allenport, Beallsville, Bentleyville, California, Canonsburg, Centerville, Charleroi, Coal Center, Donora, Dunlevy, East Washington, Elco, Ellsworth, Finleyville, Houston, Long Branch, McDonald (that part in Washington County), New Eagle, North Charleroi, Roscoe, Speers, Stockdale, Twilight, and West Brownsville, in Washington County; the cities of Greensburg, Jeannette, Monessen, and New Kensington, the townships of East Huntingdon, Hempfield, Lower Burrell, Mount Pleasant, North Huntingdon, Penn, Rostraver, Sewickley, South Huntingdon, and Unity, and the boroughs of Adamsburg, Arnold, Arona, Hunker, Irwin, Latrobe, Madison, Manor, Mount Pleasant, North Bellevernon, North Irwin, Penn, Scottdale, Smithton, South Greensburg, Southwest Greensburg, Suterville, Trafford (that part in Westmoreland County), West Newton, Youngstown and Youngwood, in Westmoreland County; all in the State of Pennsylvania.

(c) *Base period*. The calendar month of June 1943 is hereby designated as the base period for the sales area.

(d) *Quota period*. The remainder of the calendar month in which the provisions hereof become effective and each subsequent calendar month, respectively, is hereby designated as a quota period for the sales area.

(e) *Handler quotas*. Quotas for each handler in the sales area in each quota period shall be calculated in terms of pounds of each of the items for which percentages are specified in (3) below and shall be determined as follows:

(1) Divide the total deliveries of each such item made in the sales area by such handler during the base period, after excluding the quota-exempt deliveries described in (i) hereof, by the number of days in the base period;

(2) Multiply the result of the foregoing calculation by the number of days in the quota period;

(3) Multiply the aforesaid resulting amount by the following applicable percentage: (i) milk: 100 percent; (ii) butterfat in milk: -------- percent; (iii) cream: 75 percent; (iv) butterfat in cream: 75 percent~~; (v) milk~~ byproducts other than cottage, pot, or baker's cheese: 75 percent; and (vi) cottage, pot, or baker's cheese: 75 percent of skim milk equivalent. (For the purpose of this order, one pound of cottage, pot, or baker's cheese shall be considered as the equivalent of 7 pounds of skim milk.)

(f) *Quota limitations*. No handler shall, during any quota period, make deliveries in the sales area in excess of his respective quotas, except as set out in (i) hereof: *Provided*, That a handler may, after application to and approval by the market agent, secure an increase in milk quotas through an equivalent reduction as determined by the market agent, in cream and milk byproducts quotas, and an increase in milk byproducts quota through an equivalent reduction as determined by the market agent, in cream quotas.

(g) *Quotas for handlers who are also producers*. Quotas for handlers who are also producers and who purchase no milk shall be 100 percent of the total productions of such handlers in the base period.

(h) *Handler exemptions*. Quotas shall not apply to any handler who delivers in a quota period a daily average of less than 350 units of milk, cream, and milk byproducts. For the purpose of this order, a unit shall be the equivalent in volume of the following: (1) milk, one quart of milk; (2) cream, one-half pint of cream; and (3) milk byproduct, one quart of skim milk, buttermilk, flavored milk drink, or other beverage containing more than 85 percent of skim milk, or one-half pound of cottage, pot, or baker's cheese.

(i) *Quota exclusions and exemptions*. Deliveries of milk, milk byproducts, or cream (1) to other handlers, except for such deliveries to sub-handlers, (2) to plants engaged in the handling or processing of milk, milk byproducts, or cream from which no milk, milk byproducts, or cream is delivered in the sales area, and (3) to the agencies or groups specified in (d) of FDO 79, shall be excluded from the computation of deliveries in the base period and exempt from charges to quotas.

(j) *Transfers and apportionment of quotas*. The market agent is empowered to deduct an amount of base period deliveries to purchasers from the total of deliveries made by a handler or other person in the base period upon the application and a showing of unreasonable hardship by the handler making deliveries to such purchasers on the effective date of this order, and to add the amount of such deliveries to the total base period deliveries of the applicant handler. Denials of transfers or transfers granted by the market agent shall be reviewed by the Director upon application.

(k) *Petition for relief from hardships.* (1) Any person affected by FDO 79 or the provisions hereof who considers that compliance therewith would work an exceptional and unreasonable hardship on him, may file with the market agent a petition addressed to the Director. The petition shall contain the correct name, address and principal place of business of the petitioner, a full statement of the facts upon which the petition is based, and the hardship involved and the nature of the relief desired.

(2) Upon receiving such petition, the market agent shall immediately investigate the representations and facts stated therein.

(3) After investigation, the petition shall be certified to the Director, but prior to certification the market agent may (i) deny the petition, or (ii) grant temporary relief for a total period not to exceed 60 days.

(4) Denials or grants of relief by the market agent shall be reviewed by the Director and may be affirmed, modified, or reversed by the Director.

(l) *Reports.* Each handler shall transmit to the market agent on forms prescribed by the market agent the following reports:

(1) Within 20 days following the effective date of this order, reports which show the information required by the market agent to establish such handlers' quotas;

(2) Within 20 days following the close of each quota period, the information required by the market agent to establish volumes of deliveries of milk, cream, and milk byproducts during the preceding quota period; and

(3) Handlers exempt from quotas pursuant to (h) hereof shall, upon the request of the market agent, submit the information required by the market agent to establish volumes of deliveries of milk, cream, and milk byproducts.

(m) *Records.* Handlers shall keep and shall make available to the market agent such records of receipts, sales, deliveries, and production as the market agent shall require for the purpose of obtaining information which the Director may require for the establishment of quotas as prescribed in (b) of FDO 79.

(n) *Distribution schedules.* The distribution schedules, if any, to be followed by the handlers in making deliveries shall be made effective in the terms of approval by the Director of such schedules.

(o) *Expense of administration.* Each handler shall pay to the market agent, within 20 days after the close of each calendar month an assessment of $0.01 per hundredweight of each of milk, cream, skim milk, buttermilk, flavored milk drinks, beverages containing more than 85 percent of skim milk, and skim milk equivalent of cottage, pot, or baker's cheese delivered during the preceding quota period and subject to quota regulations under the provisions hereof.

(p) *Violations.* The market agent shall report all violations to the Director together with the information required for the prosecution of such violations, except in a case where a handler has made deliveries in a quota period in excess of a quota in an amount not to exceed 5 percent of such quota, and in the succeeding quota period makes deliveries below that quota by at least the same percent.

(q) *Bureau of the Budget approval.* The record keeping and reporting requirements of this order have been approved by the Bureau of the Budget in accordance with the Federal Reports Act of 1942. Subsequent record keeping or reporting requirements will be subject to the approval of the Bureau of the Budget pursuant to the Federal Reports Act of 1942.

(r) This order shall take effect at 12:01 a. m., e. w. t., November 1, 1943.

Issued this 19th day of October 1943.

C. W. KITCHEN,
Acting Director of Food Distribution

Press Release Immediate:
Wednesday, October 20, 1943.

Milk sales in 19 metropolitan areas in Illinois, Michigan, Colorado, Utah, Arizona, Oregon, Pennsylvania, Minnesota, Oklahoma and West Virginia will be regulated under the Food Distribution Administration's fluid milk conservation and control program, beginning November 1, 1943.

The new milk sales areas and the marget agents who will administer the program in each are:

Johnstown, Pa., Erie, Pa., Altoona, Pa., Pittsburgh, Pa., Metropolitan, Charleston, W. Va., Wheeling, W. Va.; George A. Taylor, Century Building, Pittsburgh, Pa.

Peoria, Ill., Rockford, Ill.; A. W. Colebank, 135 S. La Salle Street, Chicago, Ill.

Phoenix, Ariz., Denver, Colo.; Metropolitan, Salt Lake City, Utah, Metropolitan; Ben King, 503 Security Life Building, 810 14th St., Denver, Colo. (temp. address).

Portland, Oregon, Metropolitan; J. H. Mapes, 635 Elliot Avenue, West, Seattle, Washington.

Detroit, Michigan, Metropolitan, Saginaw-Bay City, Mich., Metropolitan, Lansing, Mich., Metropolitan, Flint, Mich., Metropolitan. (To be announced later).

Oklahoma City, Oklahoma, Tulsa, Oklahoma; M. M. Morehouse, 512 Porter Bldg., 406 W. 34th St., Kansas City, Mo.

Minneapolis-St. Paul, Minnesota; D. F. Spencer, 404 Post Office Bldg., Minneapolis, Minn.

Under the program, milk dealers will be permitted to sell as much fluid milk as they sold in June and three-fourths as much cream and milk byproducts (such as cottage cheese, chocolate milk, and buttermilk) as they sold in June. Milk dealers include all persons or firms engaged in the sale or transfer of milk, but not such distributors as subhandlers ("peddlers"), retail stores, hotels, or restaurants.

Producer-distributors who purchase no milk will be permitted to sell as much milk as they produced in June.

Dealers will be allowed to exceed these base quotas by not more than 5 percent during any month, providing they decrease their deliveries the next month by the same amount, without being reported in violation.

A dealer also may increase his milk sales by reducing his cream and milk byproducts sales, and increase his sales of milk byproducts by reducing his cream sales, providing such an adjustment is approved by the market agent for the area.

Deliveries of milk, cream, and milk byproducts to other dealers, to the Armed Forces, and to plants processing milk who do not distribute milk, cream, and milk byproducts in the sales area are quota-exempt.

Consumers in the milk sales areas named today and in others already designated generally will be able to purchase as much milk under the milk conservation program as they have been buying in recent months—within the limits of local supplies. In some areas, production is not expected to be large enough to permit dealers to sell as much milk as their quotas allow.

Fluid milk sales are being stabilized, Food Distribution Administration officials said, to help assure sufficient milk for manufacturing the cheese, butter, evaporated milk, and milk powder required by the Armed Services and civilians for food nutrition and properly balanced diets. Sales quotas on cream and on fluid milk byproducts have been set below June deliveries to boost fluid milk supplies where production is low, and to conserve milk for manufacturing purposes.

WAR FOOD ADMINISTRATION

[FDO 79-69]

PART 1401—DAIRY PRODUCTS

FLUID MILK AND CREAM IN JOHNSTOWN, PA., SALES AREA

Pursuant to the authority vested in me by Food Distribution Order No. 79 (8 F.R. 12426), issued on September 7, 1943, as amended, and to effectuate the purposes of such order, it is hereby ordered as follows:

§ 1401.110 *Quota restrictions*—(a) *Definitions.* When used in this order, unless otherwise distinctly expressed or manifestly incompatible with the intent hereof:

(1) Each term defined in Food Distribution Order No. 79, as amended, shall, when used herein, have the same meaning as is set forth for such term in Food Distribution Order No. 79, as amended.

(2) The term "FDO 79" means Food Distribution Order No. 79, issued on September 7, 1943, as amended.

(3) The term "sub-handler" means any handler, such as a peddler, vendor, sub-dealer, or secondary dealer, who purchases in a previously packaged and processed form milk, milk byproducts, or cream for delivery.

(b) *Milk sales area.* The following area is hereby designated as a "milk sales area" to be known as the Johnstown, Pennsylvania, sales area, and is referred to hereinafter as the "sales area":

The city of Johnstown, the townships of Conemaugh, Croyle, East Taylor, Lower Yoder, Middle Taylor, Portage, Richland, Stony Creek, Somerhill, Upper Yoder, and West Taylor, the boroughs of Brownstown, Daisytown, Dale, East Conemaugh, Ferndale, Franklin, Geistown, Lorain, Portage, Scalp Level, South Fork, Southmont, Summerhill, Westmont, and Wilmore in Cambria County; the township of Conemaugh and the boroughs of Benson, Paint, and Windber in Somerset County, all in the State of Pennsylvania.

(c) *Base period.* The calendar month of June 1943 is hereby designated as the base period for the sales area.

(d) *Quota period.* The remainder of the calendar month in which the provisions hereof become effective and each subsequent calendar month, respectively, is hereby designated as a quota period for the sales area.

(e) *Handler quotas.* Quotas for each handler in the sales area in each quota period shall be calculated in terms of pounds of each of the items for which percentages are specified in (3) below and shall be determined as follows:

(1) Divide the total deliveries of each such item made in the sales area by such handler during the base period, after excluding the quota-exempt deliveries described in (i) hereof, by the number of days in the base period;

(2) Multiply the result of the foregoing calculation by the number of days in the quota period;

(3) Multiply the aforesaid resulting amount by the following applicable percentage: (i) milk: 100 percent; (ii) butterfat in milk: ______ percent; (iii) cream: 75 percent; (iv) butterfat in cream: 75 percent; (v) milk byproducts other than cottage, pot, or baker's cheese: 75 percent; and (vi) cottage, pot, or baker's cheese: 75 percent of skim milk equivalent. (For the purpose of this order, one pound of cottage, pot, or baker's cheese shall be considered as the equivalent of 7 pounds of skim milk.)

(f) *Quota limitations.* No handler shall, during any quota period, make deliveries in the sales area in excess of his respective quotas, except as set out in (i) hereof: *Provided,* That a handler may, after application to and approval by the market agent, secure an increase in milk quotas through an equivalent reduction as determined by the market agent, in cream and milk byproducts quotas, and an increase in milk byproducts quota through an equivalent reduction as determined by the market agent, in cream quotas.

(g) *Quotas for handlers who are also producers.* Quotas for handlers who are also producers and who purchase no milk shall be 100 percent of the total production of such handlers in the base period.

(h) *Handler exemptions.* Quotas shall not apply to any handler who delivers in a quota period a daily average of less than 350 units of milk, cream, and milk byproducts. For the purpose of this order, a unit shall be the equivalent in volume of the following: (1) milk, one quart of milk; (2) cream, one-half pint of cream; and (3) milk byproduct, one quart of skim milk, buttermilk, flavored milk drink, or other beverage containing more than 85 percent of skim milk, or one-half pound of cottage, pot, or baker's cheese.

(i) *Quota exclusions and exemptions.* Deliveries of milk, milk byproducts, or cream (1) to other handlers, except for such deliveries to sub-handlers, (2) to plants engaged in the handling or processing of milk, milk byproducts, or cream from which no milk, milk byproducts, or cream is delivered in the sales area, and (3) to the agencies or groups specified in (d) of FDO 79, shall be excluded from the computation of deliveries in the base period and exempt from charges to quotas.

(j) *Transfers and apportionment of quotas.* The market agent is empowered to deduct an amount of base period deliveries to purchasers from the total of deliveries made by a handler or other person in the base period upon the application and a showing of unreasonable hardship by the handler making deliveries to such purchasers on the effective date of this order, and to add the amount of such deliveries to the total base period deliveries of the applicant handler. Denials of transfers or transfers granted by the market agent shall be reviewed by the Director upon application.

(k) *Petition for relief from hardships.* (1) Any person affected by FDO 79 or the provisions hereof who considers that compliance therewith would work an exceptional and unreasonable hardship on him, may file with the market agent a petition addressed to the Director. The petition shall contain the correct name, address and principal place of business of the petitioner, a full statement of the facts upon which the petition is based, and the hardship involved and the nature of the relief desired.

(2) Upon receiving such petition, the market agent shall immediately investigate the representations and facts stated therein.

(3) After investigation, the petition shall be certified to the Director, but prior to certification the market agent may (i) deny the petition, or (ii) grant temporary relief for a total period not to exceed 60 days.

(4) Denials or grants of relief by the market agent shall be reviewed by the Director and may be affirmed, modified, or reversed by the Director.

(l) *Reports.* Each handler shall transmit to the market agent on forms prescribed by the market agent the following reports:

(1) Within 20 days following the effective date of this order, reports which show the information required by the market agent to establish such handlers' quotas;

(2) Within 20 days following the close of each quota period, the information required by the market agent to establish volumes of deliveries of milk, cream, and milk byproducts during the preceding quota period; and

(3) Handlers exempt from quotas pursuant to (h) hereof shall, upon the request of the market agent, submit the

information required by the market agent to establish volumes of deliveries of milk, cream, and milk byproducts.

(m) *Records.* Handlers shall keep and shall make available to the market agent such records of receipts, sales, deliveries, and production as the market agent shall require for the purpose of obtaining information which the Director may require for the establishment of quotas as prescribed in (b) of FDO 79.

(n) *Distribution schedules.* The distribution schedules, if any, to be followed by the handlers in making deliveries shall be made effective in the terms of approval by the Director of such schedules

(o) *Expense of administration.* Each handler shall pay to the market agent, within 20 days after the close of each calendar month an assessment of $0.01 per hundredweight of each of milk, cream, skim milk, buttermilk, flavored milk drinks, beverages containing more than 85 percent of skim milk, and skim milk equivalent of cottage, pot or baker's cheese delivered during the preceding quota period and subject to quota regulations under the provisions hereof.

(p) *Violations.* The market agent shall report all violations to the Director together with the information required for the prosecution of such violations, except in a case where a handler has made deliveries in a quota period in excess of a quota in an amount not to exceed 5 percent of such quota, and in the succeeding quota period makes deliveries below that quota by at least the same percent.

(q) *Bureau of the Budget approval.* The record keeping and reporting requirements of this order have been approved by the Bureau of the Budget in accordance with the Federal Reports Act of 1942. Subsequent record keeping or reporting requirements will be subject to the approval of the Bureau of the Budget pursuant to the Federal Reports Act of 1942.

(r) This order shall take effect at 12:01 a. m., e. w. t., November 1, 1943.

Issued this 19th day of October 1943.

C. W. KITCHEN,
Acting Director of Food Distribution.

Press Release Immediate:
Wednesday, October 20, 1943.

Milk sales in 19 metropolitan areas in Illinois, Michigan, Colorado, Utah, Arizona, Oregon, Pennsylvania, Minnesota, Oklahoma and West Virginia will be regulated under the Food Distribution Administration's fluid milk conservation and control program, beginning November 1, 1943.

The new milk sales areas and the market agents who will administer the program in each are:

Johnstown, Pa., Erie, Pa., Altoona, Pa., Pittsburgh, Pa., Metropolitan, Charleston, W. Va., Wheeling, W. Va.; George A. Taylor, Century Building, Pittsburgh, Pa.

Peoria, Ill., Rockford, Ill.; A. W. Colebank, 135 S. La Salle St., Chicago, Ill.

Phoenix, Ariz., Denver, Colo., Metropolitan, Salt Lake City, Utah, Metropolitan; Ben King, 503 Security Life Building, 810 14th St., Denver, Colo. (temp. address).

Portland, Oregon, Metropolitan; J. H. Mapes, 635 Elliot Avenue, West, Seattle, Washington.

Detroit, Michigan, Metropolitan, Saginaw-Bay City, Mich., Metropolitan, Lansing, Mich., Metropolitan, Flint, Mich., Metropolitan (to be announced later).

Oklahoma City, Oklahoma, Tulsa, Oklahoma; M. M. Morehouse, 512 Porter Bldg., 406 W. 34th St., Kansas City, Mo.

Minneapolis-St. Paul, Minnesota; D. F. Spencer, 404 Post Office Bldg., Minneapolis, Minn.

Under the program, milk dealers will be permitted to sell as much fluid milk as they sold in June and three-fourths as much cream and milk byproducts (such as cottage cheese, chocolate milk, and buttermilk) as they sold in June. Milk dealers include all persons or firms engaged in the sale or transfer of milk, but not such distributors as subhandlers ("peddlers"), retail stores, hotels, or restaurants.

Producer-distributors who purchase no milk will be permitted to sell as much milk as they produced in June.

Dealers will be allowed to exceed these base quotas by not more than 5 percent during any month, providing they decrease their deliveries the next month by the same amount, without being reported in violation.

A dealer also may increase his milk sales by reducing his cream and milk byproducts sales, and increase his sales of milk byproducts by reducing his cream sales, providing such an adjustment is approved by the market agent for the area.

Deliveries of milk, cream, and milk byproducts to other dealers, to the Armed Forces, and to plants processing milk who do not distribute milk, cream, and milk byproducts in the sales area are quota-exempt.

Consumers in the milk sales areas named today and in others already designated generally will be able to purchase as much milk under the milk conservation program as they have been buying in recent months—within the limits of local supplies. In some areas, production is not expected to be large enough to permit dealers to sell as much milk as their quotas allow.

Fluid milk sales are being stabilized, Food Distribution Administration officials said, to help assure sufficient milk for manufacturing the cheese, butter, evaporated milk, and milk powder required by the Armed Services and civilians for food nutrition and properly balanced diets. Sales quotas on cream and on fluid milk byproducts have been set below June deliveries to boost fluid milk supplies where production is low, and to conserve milk for manufacturing purposes.

FDO 79-70

OCTOBER 19, 1943

WAR FOOD ADMINISTRATION

[FDO 79-70]

PART 1401—DAIRY PRODUCTS

FLUID MILK AND CREAM IN ERIE, PA., SALES AREA

Pursuant to the authority vested in me by Food Distribution Order No. 79 (8 F.R. 12426), issued on September 7, 1943, as amended, and to effectuate the purposes of such order, it is hereby ordered as follows:

§ 1401.108 *Quota restrictions*—(a) *Definitions.* When used in this order, unless otherwise distinctly expressed or manifestly incompatible with the intent hereof:

(1) Each term defined in Food Distribution Order No. 79, as amended, shall, when used herein, have the same meaning as is set forth for such term in Food Distribution Order No. 79, as amended.

(2) The term "FDO 79" means Food Distribution Order No. 79, issued on September 7, 1943, as amended.

(3) The term "sub-handler" means any handler, such as a peddler, vendor, sub-dealer, or secondary dealer, who purchases in a previously packaged and processed form milk, milk byproducts, or cream for delivery.

(b) *Milk sales area.* The following area is hereby designated as a "milk sales area" to be known as the Erie, Pennsylvania, sales area, and is referred to hereinafter as the "sales area":

The city of Erie, the townships of Harborcreek, Lawrence Park, and Millcreek, and the borough of Wesleyville all in Erie County, Pennsylvania.

(c) *Base period.* The calendar month of June 1943 is hereby designated as the base period for the sales area.

(d) *Quota period.* The remainder of the calendar month in which the provisions hereof become effective and each subsequent calendar month, respectively, is hereby designated as a quota period for the sales area.

(e) *Handler quotas.* Quotas for each handler in the sales area in each quota period shall be calculated in terms of pounds of each of the items for which percentages are specified in (3) below and shall be determined as follows:

(1) Divide the total deliveries of each such item made in the sales area by such handler during the base period, after excluding the quota-exempt deliveries described in (i) hereof, by the number of days in the base period;

(2) Multiply the result of the foregoing calculation by the number of days in the quota period;

(3) Multiply the aforesaid resulting amount by the following applicable percentage: (i) milk: 100 percent; (ii) butterfat in milk: ______ percent; (iii) cream: 75 percent; (iv) butterfat in cream: 75 percent; (v) milk byproducts other than cottage, pot, or baker's cheese: 75 percent; and (vi) cottage, pot, or baker's cheese: 75 percent of skim milk equivalent. (For the purpose of this order, one pound of cottage, pot, or baker's cheese shall be considered as the equivalent of 7 pounds of skim milk.)

(f) *Quota limitations.* No handler shall, during any quota period, make deliveries in the sales area in excess of his respective quotas, except as set out in (i) hereof: *Provided*, That a handler may, after application to and approval by the market agent, secure an increase in milk quotas through an equivalent reduction as determined by the market agent, in cream and milk byproducts quotas, and an increase in milk byproducts quota through an equivalent reduction as determined by the market agent, in cream quotas.

(g) *Quotas for handlers who are also producers.* Quotas for handlers who are also producers and who purchase no milk shall be 100 percent of the total production of such handlers in the base period.

(h) *Handler exemptions.* Quotas shall not apply to any handler who delivers in a quota period a daily average of less than 350 units of milk, cream, and milk byproducts. For the purpose of this order, a unit shall be the equivalent in volume of the following: (1) milk, one quart of milk; (2) cream, one-half pint of cream; and (3) milk byproduct, one quart of skim milk, buttermilk, flavored milk drink, or other beverage containing more than 85 percent of skim milk, or one-half pound of cottage, pot, or baker's cheese.

(i) *Quota exclusions and exemptions.* Deliveries of milk, milk byproducts, or cream (1) to other handlers, except for such deliveries to sub-handlers, (2) to plants engaged in the handling or processing of milk, milk byproducts, or cream from which no milk, milk byproducts or cream is delivered in the sales area, and (3) to the agencies or groups specified in (d) of FDO 79, shall be excluded from the computation of deliveries in the base period and exempt from charges to quotas.

(j) *Transfers and apportionment of quotas.* The market agent is empowered to deduct an amount of base period deliveries to purchasers from the total of deliveries made by a handler or other person in the base period upon the application and a showing of unreasonable hardship by the handler making deliveries to such purchasers on the effective date of this order, and to add the amount of such deliveries to the total base period deliveries of the applicant handler. Denials of transfers or transfers granted by the market agent shall be reviewed by the Director upon application.

(k) *Petition for relief from hardships.* (1) any person affected by FDO 79 or the provisions hereof who considers that compliance therewith would work an exceptional and unreasonable hardship on him, may file with the market agent a petition addressed to the Director. The petition shall contain the correct name, address and principal place of business of the petitioner, a full statement of the facts upon which the petition is based, and the hardship involved and the nature of the relief desired.

(2) Upon receiving such petition, the market agent shall immediately investigate the representations and facts stated therein.

(3) After investigation, the petition shall be certified to the Director, but prior to certification the market agent may (i) deny the petition, or (ii) grant temporary relief for a total period not to exceed 60 days.

(4) Denials or grants of relief by the market agent shall be reviewed by the Director and may be affirmed, modified, or reversed by the Director.

(l) *Reports.* Each handler shall transmit to the market agent on forms prescribed by the market agent the following reports:

(1) Within 20 days following the effective date of this order, reports which show the information required by the market agent to establish such handlers' quotas;

(2) Within 20 days following the close of each quota period, the information required by the market agent to establish volumes of deliveries of milk, cream, and milk byproducts during the preceding quota period; and

(3) Handlers exempt from quotas pursuant to (h) hereof shall, upon the request of the market agent, submit the information required by the market agent to establish volumes of deliveries of milk, cream, and milk byproducts.

(m) *Records.* Handlers shall keep and shall make available to the market agent such records of receipts, sales, deliveries, and production as the market agent shall require for the purpose of obtaining information which the Director may require for the establishment of quotas as prescribed in (b) of FDO 79.

(n) *Distribution schedules.* The distribution schedules, if any, to be followed by the handlers in making deliveries shall be made effective in the terms of approval by the Director of such schedules.

(o) *Expense of administration.* Each handler shall pay to the market agent, within 20 days after the close of each calendar month an assessment of $0 01 per hundredweight of each of milk, cream, skim milk, buttermilk, flavored milk drinks, beverages containing more than 85 percent of skim milk, and skim milk equivalent of cottage, pot, or baker's cheese delivered during the preceding quota period and subject to quota regulations under the provisions hereof.

(p) *Violations.* The market agent shall report all violations to the Director together with the information required for the prosecution of such violations, except in a case where a handler has made deliveries in a quota period in excess of a quota in an amount not to exceed 5 percent of such quota, and in the succeeding quota period makes deliveries below that quota by at least the same percent.

(q) *Bureau of the Budget approval.* The record keeping and reporting requirements of this order have been approved by the Bureau of the Budget in accordance with the Federal Reports Act of 1942. Subsequent record keeping or reporting requirements will be subject to the approval of the Bureau of the Budget pursuant to the Federal Reports Act of 1942.

(r) This order shall take effect at 12:01 a. m., e. w. t., November 1, 1943.

Issued this 19th day of October 1943.

C. W. KITCHEN,
Acting Director of Food Distribution.

Press Release Immediate:
Wednesday, October 20, 1943.

Milk sales in 19 metropolitan areas in Illinois, Michigan, Colorado, Utah, Arizona, Oregon, Pennsylvania, Minnesota, Oklahoma and West Virginia will be regulated under the Food Distribution Administration's fluid milk conservation and control program, beginning November 1, 1943.

The new milk sales areas and the market agents who will administer the program in each are:

Johnstown, Pa., Erie, Pa., Altoona, Pa., Pittsburgh, Pa., Metropolitan, Charleston, W. Va., Wheeling, W. Va.; George A. Taylor, Century Building, Pittsburgh, Pa.

Peoria, Ill., Rockford, Ill.; A. W. Colebank, 135 S. La Salle St., Chicago, Ill.

Phoenix, Ariz., Denver, Colo.; Metropolitan, Salt Lake City, Utah, Metropolitan; Ben King, 503 Security Life Building, 810 14th St., Denver, Colo. (temp. address).

Portland, Oregon, Metropolitan; J. H. Mapes, 635 Elliot Avenue, West, Seattle, Washington.

Detroit, Michigan, Metropolitan; Saginaw-Bay City, Mich., Metropolitan, Lansing, Mich., Metropolitan, Flint, Mich., Metropolitan; (To be announced later).

Oklahoma City, Oklahoma, Tulsa, Oklahoma; M. M. Morehouse, 512 Porter Bldg., 406 W. 34th St., Kansas City, Mo.

Minneapolis-St. Paul, Minnesota; D. F. Spencer, 404 Post Office Bldg., Minneapolis, Minn.

Under the program, milk dealers will be permitted to sell as much fluid milk as they sold in June and three-fourths as much cream and milk byproducts (such as cottage cheese, chocolate milk, and buttermilk) as they sold in June. Milk dealers include all persons or firms engaged in the sale or transfer of milk, but not such distributors as subhandlers ("peddlers"), retail stores, hotels, or restaurants.

Producer-distributors who purchase no milk will be permitted to sell as much milk as they produced in June.

Dealers will be allowed to exceed these base quotas by not more than 5 percent during any month, providing they decrease their deliveries the next month by the same amount, without being reported in violation.

A dealer also may increase his milk sales by reducing his cream and milk byproducts sales, and increase his sales of milk byproducts by reducing his cream sales, providing such an adjustment is approved by the market agent for the area.

Deliveries of milk, cream, and milk byproducts to other dealers, to the Armed Forces, and to plants processing milk who do not distribute milk, cream, and milk byproducts in the sales area are quota-exempt.

Consumers in the milk sales areas named today and in others already designated generally will be able to purchase as much milk under the milk conservation program as they have been buying in recent months—within the limits of local supplies. In some areas, production is not expected to be large enough to permit dealers to sell as much milk as their quotas allow.

Fluid milk sales are being stabilized, Food Distribution Administration officials said, to help assure sufficient milk for manufacturing the cheese, butter, evaporated milk, and milk powder required by the Armed Services and civilians for food nutrition and properly balanced diets. Sales quotas on cream and on fluid milk byproducts have been set below June deliveries to boost fluid milk supplies where production is low, and to conserve milk for manufacturing purposes.

FDO 79-70
AMDT. 1
DEC. 28, 1943

WAR FOOD ADMINISTRATION

[FDO 79-70, Amdt. 1]

PART 1401—DAIRY PRODUCTS

FLUID MILK AND CREAM IN THE ERIE, PA., MILK SALES AREA

Pursuant to Food Distribution Order No. 79 (8 F.R. 12426), dated September 7, 1943, as amended, and to effectuate the purposes thereof, Food Distribution Order No. 79-70 (8 F.R. 14273) relative to the conservation and distribution of fluid milk in the Erie, Pennsylvania, milk sales area, issued by the Director of Food Distribution on October 19, 1943, is amended by deleting therefrom the numerals "350" wherever they appear in § 1401.108 (h) and inserting in lieu thereof, the numerals "200."

The provisions of this amendment shall become effective at 12:01 a. m., e. w. t., January 1, 1944. With respect to violations of said Food Distribution Order No. 79-70, rights accrued, or liabilities incurred prior to the effective time of this amendment, said Food Distribution Order No. 79-70 shall be deemed to be in full force and effect for the purpose of sustaining any proper suit, action, or other proceeding with respect to any such violation, right, or liability.

(E.O. 9280, 7 F.R. 10179; E.O. 9322, 8 F.R. 3807; E.O. 9334, 8 F.R. 5423; E.O. 9392, 8 F.R. 14783; FDO 79, 8 F.R. 12426, 13283)

Issued this 28th day of December 1943.

ROY F. HENDRICKSON,
Director of Food Distribution.

eserve

7357

FDO 79-71

OCTOBER 19, 1943

WAR FOOD ADMINISTRATION

[FDO 79-71]

PART 1401—DAIRY PRODUCTS

FLUID MILK AND CREAM IN OKLAHOMA CITY, OKLA., METROPOLITAN SALES AREA

Pursuant to the authority vested in me by Food Distribution Order No. 79 (8 F.R. 12426), issued on September 7 1943, as amended, and to effectuate the purposes of such order, it is hereby ordered as follows:

§ 1401 112 *Quota restrictions*—(a) *Definitions.* When used in this order, unless otherwise distinctly expressed or manifestly incompatible with the intent hereof:

(1) Each term defined in Food Distribution Order No. 79, as amended, shall, when used herein, have the same meaning as is set forth for such term in Food Distribution Order No. 79, as amended.

(2) The term "FDO 79" means Food Distribution Order No. 79, issued on September 7, 1943, as amended.

(3) The term "sub-handler" means any handler, such as a peddler, vendor, sub-dealer, or secondary dealer, who purchases in a previously packaged and processed form milk, milk byproducts, or cream for delivery.

(b) *Milk sales area.* The following area is hereby designated as a "milk sales area" to be known as the Oklahoma City, Oklahoma, metropolitan sales area, and is referred to hereinafter as the "sales area":

The cities of Oklahoma City, Bethany, and Britton; the townships of Britton, Council Grove, Greeley, Mustang, and Oklahoma; and the town of Nichols Hill, all in Oklahoma County, Oklahoma.

(c) *Base period.* The calendar month of June 1943 is hereby designated as the base period for the sales area.

(d) *Quota period.* The remainder of the calendar month in which the provisions hereof become effective and each subsequent calendar month, respectively, is hereby designated as a quota period for the sales area.

(e) *Handler quotas.* Quotas for each handler in the sales area in each quota period shall be calculated in terms of pounds of each of the items for which percentages are specified in (3) below and shall be determined as follows:

(1) Divide the total deliveries of each such item made in the sales area by such handler during the base period, after excluding the quota-exempt deliveries described in (i) hereof, by the number of days in the base period;

(2) Multiply the result of the foregoing calculation by the number of days in the quota period;

(3) Multiply the aforesaid resulting amount by the following applicable percentage: (i) milk: 100 percent; (ii) butterfat in milk: 100 percent; (iii) cream: 75 percent; (iv) butterfat in cream: 75 percent; (v) milk byproducts other than cottage, pot, or baker's cheese: 75 percent; and (vi) cottage, pot, or baker's cheese: 75 percent of skim milk equivalent. (For the purpose of this order, one pound of cottage, pot, or baker's cheese shall be considered as the equivalent of 7 pounds of skim milk.)

(f) *Quota limitations.* No handler shall, during any quota period, make deliveries in the sales area in excess of his respective quotas, except as set out in (i) hereof: *Provided,* That a handler may, after application to and approval by the market agent, secure an increase in milk quotas through an equivalent reduction as determined by the market agent, in cream and milk byproducts quotas, and an increase in milk byproducts quota through an equivalent reduction as determined by the market agent, in cream quotas.

(g) *Quotas for handlers who are also producers.* Quotas for handlers who are also producers and who purchase no milk shall be 100 percent of the total production of such handlers in the base period

(h) *Handler exemptions.* Quotas shall not apply to any handler who delivers in a quota period a daily average of less than 150 units of milk, cream, and milk byproducts. For the purpose of this order, a unit shall be the equivalent in the volume of the following: (1) milk, one quart of milk; (2) cream, one-half pint of cream; and (3) milk byproduct, one quart of skim milk, buttermilk, flavored milk drink, or other beverage containing more than 85 percent of skim milk, or one-half pound of cottage, pot, or baker's cheese.

(i) *Quota exclusions and exemptions* Deliveries of milk, milk byproducts, or cream (1) to other handlers, except for such deliveries to sub-handlers, (2) to plants engaged in the handling or processing of milk, milk byproducts, or cream from which no milk, milk byproducts, or cream is delivered in the sales area, and (3) to the agencies or groups specified in (d) of FDO 79, shall be excluded from the computation of deliveries in the base period and exempt from charges to quotas.

(j) *Transfers and apportionment of quotas.* The market agent is empowered to deduct an amount of base period deliveries to purchasers from the total of deliveries made by a handler or other person in the base period upon the application and a showing of unreasonable hardship by the handler making deliveries to such purchasers on the effective date of this order, and to add the amount of such deliveries to the total base period deliveries of the applicant handler. Denials of transfers or transfers granted by the market agent shall be reviewed by the Director upon application.

(k) *Petition for relief from hardships.* (1) Any person affected by FDO 79 or the provisions hereof who considers that compliance therewith would work an exceptional and unreasonable hardship on him, may file with the market agent a petition addressed to the Director. The petition shall contain the correct name, address and principal place of business of the petitioner, a full statement of the facts upon which the petition is based, and the hardship involved and the nature of the relief desired.

(2) Upon receiving such petition, the market agent shall immediately investigate the representations and facts stated therein.

(3) After investigation, the petition shall be certified to the Director, but prior to certification the market agent may (i) deny the petition, or (ii) grant temporary relief for a total period not to exceed 60 days.

(4) Denials or grants of relief by the market agent shall be reviewed by the Director and may be affirmed, modified, or reversed by the Director.

(l) *Reports.* Each handler shall transmit to the market agent on forms prescribed by the market agent the following reports:

(1) Within 20 days following the effective date of this order, reports which show the information required by the market agent to establish such handlers' quotas;

(2) Within 20 days following the close of each quota period, the information required by the market agent to establish volumes of deliveries of milk, cream, and milk byproducts during the preceding quota period; and

(3) Handlers exempt from quotas pursuant to (h) hereof shall, upon the request of the market agent, submit the information required by the market agent to establish volumes of deliveries of milk, cream, and milk byproducts.

(m) *Records.* Handlers shall keep and shall make available to the market agent such records of receipts, sales, deliveries, and production as the market agent shall require for the purpose of obtaining information which the Director may require for the establishment of quotas as prescribed in (b) of FDO 79.

(n) *Distribution schedules.* The distribution schedules, if any, to be followed by the handlers in making deliveries shall be made effective in the terms of approval by the Director of such schedules.

(o) *Expense of administration.* Each handler shall pay to the market agent, within 20 days after the close of each calendar month an assessment of $0.01 per hundredweight of each of mil cream, skim milk, buttermilk, flavore milk drinks, beverages containing mo than 85 percent of skim milk, and ski milk equivalent of cottage, pot, (baker's cheese delivered during the pr ceding quota period and subject to quot regulations under the provisions hereo

(p) *Violations.* The market ager shall report all violations to the Directo together with the information require for the prosecution of such violation except in a case where a handler ha made deliveries in a quota period in ex cess of a quota in an amount not to ex ceed 5 percent of such quota, and in th succeeding quota period makes deliverie

---

Press Release, Immediate:
Wednesday, October 20, 1943.

Milk sales in 19 metropolitan areas in Illinois, Michigan, Colorado, Utah, Arizona, Oregon, Pennsylvania, Minnesota, Oklahoma and West Virginia will be regulated under the Food Distribution Administration's fluid milk conservation and control program, beginning November 1, 1943.

The new milk sales areas and the market agents who will administer the program in each are:

Johnstown, Pa., Erie, Pa., Altoona, Pa., Pittsburgh, Pa., Metropolitan, Charleston, W. Va., Wheeling, W. Va.: George A. Taylor, Century Building, Pittsburgh, Pa.

Peoria, Ill., Rockford, Ill.: A. W. Colebank, 135 S. La Salle St., Chicago, Ill.

Phoenix, Ariz., Denver, Colo., Metropolitan, Salt Lake City, Utah, Metropolitan: Ben King, 503 Security Life Building, 810 14th St., Denver, Colo. (temp. address).

Portland, Oregon, Metropolitan: J. H. Mapes, 635 Elliot Avenue, West, Seattle, Wash.

Detroit, Mich., Metropolitan, Saginaw-Bay City, Mich., Metropolitan, Lansing, Mich., Metropolitan, Flint, Mich., Metropolitan: (To be announced later).

Oklahoma City, Okla., Tulsa, Okla. M. M. Morehouse, 512 Porter Bldg., 40 W. 34th St., Kansas City, Mo.

Minneapolis-St. Paul, Minn.: D. F Spencer, 404 Post Office Bldg., Minneapolis, Minn.

Under the program, milk dealers wil be permitted to sell as much fluid milk a they sold in June and three-fourths a much cream and milk byproducts (suc as cottage cheese, chocolate milk, an buttermilk) as they sold in June. Mil dealers include all persons or firms engaged in the sale or transfer of milk, bu not such distributors as subhandle ("peddlers"), retail stores, hotels, o restaurants.

Producer-distributors who purchas no milk will be permitted to sell as muc milk as they produced in June.

Dealers will be allowed to exceed thes base quotas by not more than 5 percen during any month, providing they decrease their deliveries the next month b the same amount, without being reporte in violation.

A dealer also may increase his mil sales by reducing his cream and mil byproducts sales, and increase his sale of milk byproducts by reducing his crean sales, providing such an adjustment i

FDO 79-71

AMDT. 1

NOV. 3, 1943

WAR FOOD ADMINISTRATION

[FDO 79-71, Amdt. 1]

PART 1401—DAIRY PRODUCTS

FLUID MILK AND CREAM IN OKLAHOMA CITY, OKLA., METROPOLITAN MILK SALES AREA

Pursuant to the authority vested in the Director by Food Distribution Order No. 79, dated September 7, 1943 (8 F.R. 12426), as amended, and to effectuate the purposes thereof, Director Food Distribution Order No. 79-71, § 1401.112, relative to the conservation of fluid milk in the Oklahoma City, Oklahoma, metropolitan milk sales area (8 F.R. 14274), issued by the Director of Food Distribution on October 21, 1943, is amended as follows:

The milk sales area described in § 1401.112 (b) of the original order is modified in the following particulars: In line 2 of the description of the milk sales area, insert the word "Boone" after the townships of, and before the word "Britton." In line 3, insert the word "Crutcho" after the word "Council Grove," and before the word "Greeley," making the description of the sales area read as follows:

The cities of Oklahoma City, Bethany, Britton; the townships of Boone, Britton, Council Grove, Crutcho, Greeley, Mustang, and Oklahoma; and the town of Nichols Hill, all in Oklahoma County, Oklahoma.

Effective date. This amendment of FDO No. 79-71, shall become effective at 12:01 a. m., e. w. t., November 5, 1943.

(E.O. 9280, 8 F.R. 10179; E.O. 9322, 8 F.R. 3807; E.O. 9334, 8 F.R. 5423; FDO 79, 8 F.R. 12426, 13283)

Issued this 3d day of November 1943.

ROY F. HENDRICKSON,
Director of Food Distribution.

FDO 79-72

OCTOBER 19, 1943

WAR FOOD ADMINISTRATION

[FDO 79-72]

PART 1401—DAIRY PRODUCTS

FLUID MILK AND CREAM IN TULSA, OKLA., METROPOLITAN SALES AREA

Pursuant to the authority vested in me by Food Distribution Order No. 79 (8 F.R. 12426), issued on September 7, 1943, as amended, and to effectuate the purposes of such order, it is hereby ordered as follows:

§ 1401.113 *Quota restrictions*—(a) *Definitions.* When used in this order, unless otherwise distinctly expressed or manifestly incompatible with the intent hereof:

(1) Each term defined in Food Distribution Order No. 79, as amended, shall, when used herein, have the same meaning as is set forth for such term in Food Distribution Order No. 79, as amended.

(2) The term "FDO 79" means Food Distribution Order No. 79, issued on September 7, 1943, as amended.

(3) The term "sub-handler" means any handler, such as a peddler, vendor, sub-dealer, or secondary dealer, who purchases in a previously packaged and processed form milk, milk byproducts, or cre[illegible] for delivery.

(b) *Milk sales area.* The following area is hereby designated as a "milk sales area", to be known as the Tulsa, Oklahoma, metropolitan sales area, and is referred to hereinafter as the "sales area":

The cities of Tulsa and Sand Springs: the townships of Dawson, Lynn Lane, Red Fork, and Wekiwa, and the towns of Dawson and Garden City in Tulsa County, Oklahoma; the city of Sapulpa and the township of Sapulpa in Creek County, Oklahoma; and that part of Black Dog Township in township 20 N, ranges 10, 11, and 12 E, in Osage County, Oklahoma.

(c) *Base period.* The calendar month of June 1943 is hereby designated as the base period for the sales area.

(d) *Quota period.* The remainder of the calendar month in which the provisions hereof become effective and each subsequent calendar month, respectively, is hereby designated as a quota period for the sales area.

(e) *Handler quotas.* Quotas for each handler in the sales area in each quota period shall be calculated in terms of pounds of each of the items for which percentages are specified in (3) below and shall be determined as follows:

(1) Divide the total deliveries of each such item made in the sales area by such handler during the base period, after excluding the quota-exempt deliveries described in (i) hereof, by the number of days in the base period;

(2) Multiply the result of the foregoing calculation by the number of days in the quota period;

(3) Multiply the aforesaid resulting amount by the following applicable percentage: (i) milk: 100 percent; (ii) butterfat in milk: 100 percent; (iii) cream: 75 percent; (iv) butterfat in cream: 75 percent; (v) milk byproducts other than cottage, pot, or baker's cheese: 75 percent; and (vi) cottage, pot or baker's cheese: 75 percent of skim milk equivalent. (For the purpose of this order, one pound of cottage, pot, or baker's cheese shall be considered as the equivalent of 7 pounds of skim milk.)

(f) *Quota limitations.* No handler shall, during any quota period, make deliveries in the sales area in excess of his respective quotas, except as set out in (i) hereof: *Provided*, That a handler may, after application to and approval by the market agent, secure an increase in milk quotas through an equivalent reduction as determined by the market agent, in cream and milk byproducts quotas, and an increase in milk byproducts quota through an equivalent reduction as determined by the market agent, in cream quotas.

(g) *Quotas for handlers who are also producers.* Quotas for handlers who are also producers and who purchase no milk shall be 100 percent of the total production of such handlers in the base period.

(h) *Handler exemptions.* Quotas shall not apply to any handler who delivers in a quota period a daily average of less than 150 units of milk, cream, and milk byproducts. For the purpose of this order, a unit shall be the equivalent in the volume of the following: (1) milk, one quart of milk; (2) cream, one-half pint of cream; and (3) milk byproduct, one quart of skim milk, buttermilk, flavored milk drink, or other beverage containing more than 85 percent of skim milk, or one-half pound of cottage, pot, or baker's cheese.

(i) *Quota exclusions and exemptions.* Deliveries of milk, milk byproducts, or cream (1) to other handlers, except for such deliveries to sub-handlers, (2) to plants engaged in the handling or processing of milk, milk byproducts, or cream from which no milk, milk byproducts, or cream is delivered in the sales area, and (3) to the agencies or groups specified in (d) of FDO 79, shall be excluded from the computation of deliveries in the base period and exempt from charges to quotas.

(j) *Transfers and apportionment of quotas.* The market agent is empowered to deduct an amount of base period deliveries to purchasers from the total of deliveries made by a handler or other person in the base period upon the application and a showing of unreasonable hardship by the handler making deliveries to such purchasers on the effective date of this order, and to add the amount of such deliveries to the total base period deliveries of the applicant handler. Denials of transfers or transfers granted by the market agent shall be reviewed by the Director upon application.

(k) *Petition for relief from hardships.* (1) Any person affected by FDO 79 or the provisions hereof who considers that compliance therewith would work an exceptional and unreasonable hardship on him, may file with the market agent a petition addressed to the Director. The petition shall contain the correct name, address and principal place of business of the petitioner, a full statement of the facts upon which the petition is based, and the hardship involved and the nature of the relief desired.

(2) Upon receiving such petition, the market agent shall immediately investigate the representations and facts stated therein.

(3) After investigation, the petition shall be certified to the Director, but prior to certification the market agent may (i) deny the petition, or (ii) grant temporary relief for a total period not to exceed 60 days.

(4) Denials or grants of relief by the market agent shall be reviewed by the Director and may be affirmed, modified, or reversed by the Director.

(l) *Reports.* Each handler shall transmit to the market agent on forms prescribed by the market agent the following reports:

(1) Within 20 days following the effective date of this order, reports which show the information required by the market agent to establish such handlers' quotas;

(2) Within 20 days following the close of each quota period, the information required by the market agent to establish volumes of deliveries of milk, cream, and milk byproducts during the preceding quota period; and

(3) Handlers exempt from quotas pursuant to (h) hereof shall, upon the re-

quest of the market agent, submit the information required by the market agent to establish volumes of deliveries of milk, cream, and milk byproducts.

(m) *Records.* Handlers shall keep and shall make available to the market agent such records of receipts, sales, deliveries, and production as the market agent shall require for the purpose of obtaining information which the Director may require for the establishment of quotas as prescribed in (b) of FDO 79.

(n) *Distribution schedules.* The distribution schedules, if any, to be followed by the handlers in making deliveries shall be made effective in the terms of approval by the Director of such schedules.

(o) *Expense of administration.* Each handler shall pay to the market agent, within 20 days after the close of each calendar month an assessment of $0.01 per hundredweight of each of milk, cream, skim milk, buttermilk, flavored milk drinks, beverages containing more than 85 percent of skim milk, and skim milk equivalent of cottage, pot, or baker's cheese delivered during the preceding quota period and subject to quota regulations under the provisions hereof.

(p) *Violations.* The market agent shall report all violations to the Director together with the information required for the prosecution of such violations, except in a case where a handler has made deliveries in a quota period in excess of a quota in an amount not to ex-

ceed 5
succee
eries t
same p
(q)
The r
quirem
proved
in acc
Act of
or rep
ject tc
the Bu
ports
(r)
12:01
Issu
Actin

Press Release, Immediate:
Wednesday, October 20, 1943.

Milk sales in 19 metropolitan areas in Illinois, Michigan, Colorado, Utah, Arizona, Oregon, Pennsylvania, Minnesota, Oklahoma and West Virginia will be regulated under the Food Distribution Administration's fluid milk conservation and control program, beginning November 1, 1943.

The new milk sales areas and the market agents who will administer the program in each are:

Johnstown, Pa.; Erie, Pa.; Altoona, Pa.; Pittsburgh, Pa., Metropolitan; Charleston, W. Va.; Wheeling, W. Va.: George A. Taylor, Century Building, Pittsburgh, Pa.

Peoria, Ill.; Rockford, Ill.: A. W. Colebank, 135 S. La Salle St., Chicago, Ill.

Phoenix, Ariz.; Denver, Colo., Metropolitan; Salt Lake City, Utah, Metropolitan: Ben King, 503 Security Life Building, 810 14th St., Denver, Colo. (temp. address).

Portland, Oreg., Metropolitan: J. H. Mapes, 635 Elliot Avenue, West, Seattle, Washington.

Detroit, Michigan, Metropolitan; Saginaw-Bay City, Mich., Metropolitan; Lansing, Mich., Metropolitan; Flint, Mich., Metropolitan: (To be announced later).

Oklahoma City, Oklahoma; Tulsa, Oklahoma: M. M. Morehouse, 512 Porter Bldg., 406 W. 34th St., Kansas City, Mo.

Minneapolis-St. Paul, Minnesota: D. F. Spencer, 404 Post Office Bldg., Minneapolis, Minn.

Under the program, milk dealers will be permitted to sell as much fluid milk as they sold in June and three-fourths as much cream and milk byproducts (such as cottage cheese, chocolate milk, and buttermilk) as they sold in June. Milk dealers include all persons or firms engaged in the sale or transfer of milk, but not such distributors as subhandlers ("peddlers"), retail stores, hotels, or restaurants.

Producer-distributors who purchase no milk will be permitted to sell as much milk as they produced in June.

Dealers will be allowed to exceed these base quotas by not more than 5 percent during any month, providing they decrease their deliveries the next month by the same amount, without being reported in violation.

A dealer also may increase his milk sales by reducing his cream and milk byproducts sales, and increase his sales of milk byproducts by reducing his cream

sales,
approv
area.
Deli
produc
Forces
who d
milk i
quota-
Con
named
nated
as mu
tion p
in rec
local s
tion is
to pern
their c
Flui
Food
cials s
for ma
evapo
quired
vilians
balanc
and o
set be
milk s
and to
purpo

77387

FDO 79-73

OCTOBER 22, 1943

WAR FOOD ADMINISTRATION

[FDO 79-73]

PART 1401—DAIRY PRODUCTS

FLUID MILK AND CREAM IN SAN DIEGO, CALIF., SALES AREA

Pursuant to the authority vested in me by Food Distribution Order No. 79 (8 F.R. 12426), issued on September 7, 1943, as amended, and to effectuate the purposes of such order, it is hereby ordered as follows:

§ 1401.85 *Quota restrictions*—(a) *Definitions*. When used in this order, unless otherwise distinctly expressed or manifestly incompatible with the intent hereof:

(1) Each term defined in Food Distribution Order No. 79, as amended, shall, when used herein, have the same meaning as is set forth for such term in Food Distribution Order No. 79 as amended.

(2) The term "FDO 79" means Food Distribution Order No. 79, issued on September 7, 1943, as amended.

(3) The term "sub-handler" means any handler, such as a peddler, vendor, sub-dealer, or secondary dealer, who purchases in a previously packaged and processed form milk, milk byproducts, or cream for delivery.

(b) *Milk sales area*. The following area is hereby designated as a "milk sales area" to be known as the San Diego, California, sales area, and is referred to hereinafter as the "sales area":

The entire area included in the marketing area now designated by the Director of Agriculture of the State of California pursuant to the provisions of Chapter 10, Division 4, of the Agricultural Code of the State of California as the San Diego County Marketing Area.

(c) *Base period*. The calender month of June 1943 is hereby designated as the base period for the sales area.

(d) *Quota period*. The remainder of the calendar month in which the provisions hereof become effective and each subsequent calendar month, respectively, is hereby designated as a quota period for the sales area.

(e) *Handler quotas*. Quotas for each handler in the sales area in each quota period shall be calculated in terms of pounds of each of the items for which percentages are specified in (3) below and shall be determined as follows:

(1) Divide the total deliveries of each such item made in the sales area by such handler during the base period, after excluding the quota-exempt deliveries described in (i) hereof, by the number of days in the base period;

(2) Multiply the result of the foregoing calculation by the number of days in the quota period;

(3) Multiply the aforesaid resulting amount by the following applicable percentage: (i) Milk: 100 percent; (ii) butterfat in milk: 100 percent; (iii) cream: 75 percent; (iv) butterfat in cream: 75 percent; (v) milk byproducts other than cottage, pot, or baker's cheese: 75 percent; and (vi) cottage, pot, or baker's cheese: 75 percent of skim milk equivalent. (For the purpose of this order, one pound of cottage, pot, or baker's cheese shall be considered as the equivalent of 7 pounds of skim milk.)

(f) *Quota limitations*. No handler shall, during any quota period, make deliveries in the sales area in excess of his respective quotas, except as set out in (i) hereof: *Provided*, That a handler may, after application to and approval by the market agent, secure an increase in milk quotas through an equivalent reduction as determined by the market agent, in cream and milk byproducts quotas, and an increase in milk byproducts quota through an equivalent reduction as determined by the market agent, in cream quotas.

(g) *Quotas for handlers who are also producers*. Quotas for handlers who are also producers and who purchase no milk shall be 100 percent of the total production of such handlers in the base period.

(h) *Handler exemptions*. Quotas shall not apply to any handler who delivers in a quota period a daily average of less than 300 units of milk, cream, and milk byproducts. For the purpose of this order, a unit shall be the equivalent in volume of the following: (1) Milk, one quart of milk; (2) cream, one-half pint of cream; and (3) milk byproduct, one quart of skim milk, buttermilk, flavored milk drink, or other beverage containing more than 85 percent of skim milk, or one-half pound of cottage, pot, or baker's cheese.

(i) *Quota exclusions and exemptions*. Deliveries of milk, milk byproducts, or cream (1) to other handlers, except for such deliveries to sub-handlers, (2) to plants engaged in the handling or processing of milk, milk byproducts, or cream from which no milk, milk byproducts, or cream is delivered in the sales area, and (3) to the agencies or groups specified in (d) of FDO 79, shall be excluded from the computation of deliveries in the base period and exempt from charges to quotas.

(j) *Transfers and apportionment of quotas*. The market agent is empowered to deduct an amount of base period deliveries to purchasers from the total of deliveries made by a handler or other person in the base period upon the application and a showing of unreasonable hardship by the handler making deliveries to such purchasers on the effective date of this order, and to add the amount of such deliveries to the total base period deliveries of the applicant handler. Denials of transfers or transfers granted by the market agent shall be reviewed by the Director upon application.

(k) *Petition for relief from hardships*. (1) Any person affected by FDO 79 or the provisions hereof who considers that compliance therewith would work an exceptional and unreasonable hardship on him, may file with the market agent a petition addressed to the Director. The petition shall contain the correct name, address and principal place of business of the petitioner, a full statement of the facts upon which the petition is based, and the hardship involved and the nature of the relief desired.

(2) Upon receiving such petition, the market agent shall immediately investigate the representations and facts stated therein.

(3) After investigation, the petition shall be certified to the Director, but prior to certification the market agent may (i) deny the petition, or (ii) grant temporary relief for a total period not to exceed 60 days.

(4) Denials or grants of relief by the market agent shall be reviewed by the Director and may be affirmed, modified, or reversed by the Director.

(l) *Reports*. Each handler shall transmit to the market agent on forms prescribed by the market agent the following reports:

(1) Within 20 days following the effective date of this order, reports which show the information required by the market agent to establish such handlers' quotas;

(2) Within 20 days following the close of each quota period, the information required by the market agent to establish volumes of deliveries of milk, cream, and milk byproducts during the preceding quota period; and

(3) Handlers exempt from quotas pursuant to (h) hereof shall, upon the request of the market agent, submit the information required by the market agent to establish volumes of deliveries of milk, cream, and milk byproducts.

(m). *Records.* Handlers shall keep and shall make available to the market agent such records of receipts, sales, deliveries, and production as the market agent shall require for the purpose of obtaining information which the Director may require for the establishment of quotas as prescribed in (b) of FDO 79.

(n) *Distribution schedules.* The distribution schedules, if any, to be followed by the handlers in making deliveries shall be made effective in the terms of approval by the Director of such schedules.

(o) *Expense of administration.* Each handler shall pay to the market agent, within 20 days after the close of each calendar month an assessment of $0.01 per hundredweight of each of milk, cream, skim milk, buttermilk, flavored milk drinks, beverages containing more than 85 percent of skim milk, and skim milk equivalent of cottage, pot, or baker's cheese delivered during the preceding quota period and subject to quota regulations under the provisions hereof.

(p) *Violations.* The market agent shall report all violations to the Director together with the information required for the prosecution of such violations, except in a case where a handler has made deliveries in a quota period in excess of a quota in an amount not to exceed 5 percent of such quota, and in the succeeding quota period makes deliveries below that quota by at least the same percent.

(q) *Bureau of the Budget approval.* The record keeping and reporting requirements of this order have been approved by the Bureau of the Budget in accordance with the Federal Reports Act of 1942. Subsequent record keeping or reporting requirements will be subject to the approval of the Bureau of the Budget pursuant to the Federal Reports Act of 1942.

(r) This order shall take effect at 12:01 a. m., e. w. t., November 1, 1943.

Issued this 22d day of October 1943.

C. W. Kitchen,
Acting Director of Food Distribution.

Press Release, Immediate:
Friday, October 22, 1943.

Milk sales in 5 metropolitan areas in California will be regulated under the Food Distribution Administration's fluid milk conservation and control program, beginning November 1.

The new milk sales areas, and the market agents who will administer the program in each, are:

San Diego and Los Angeles (metropolitan), Martin Blank, 351 C. of C. Bldg., Los Angeles, Calif.

San Jose; San Francisco Bay Region, and Sacramento, E. L. Vehlow, Mull Bldg., Sacramento, Calif.

Under the program, milk dealers will be permitted to sell as much fluid milk as they sold in June and three-fourths as much cream and milk byproducts (such as cottage cheese, chocolate milk, and buttermilk) as they sold in June. Milk dealers include all persons or firms engaged in the sale or transfer of milk, but not such distributors as subhandlers ("peddlers"), retail stores, hotels, or restaurants.

Producer-distributors who purchase no milk will be permitted to sell as much milk as they produced in June.

Dealers will be allowed to exceed these base quotas by not more than 5 percent during any month, providing they decrease their deliveries the next month by the same amount, without being reported in violation.

A dealer may also increase his milk sales by reducing his cream and milk byproducts sales, and increase his sales of milk byproducts by reducing his cream sales, providing such an adjustment is approved by the market agent for the area.

Deliveries of milk, cream, and milk byproducts to other dealers; to the armed forces, and to plants processing milk who do not distribute milk, cream or milk byproducts in the sales area are quota exempt.

Consumers in the milk sales areas named today and in others already designated generally will be able to purchase as much milk under the milk conservation program as they have been buying in recent months—within the limits of local supplies.

Fluid milk sales are being stabilized FDA officials said, to help assure sufficient milk for manufacturing the cheese, butter, evaporated milk, and milk powder required by the Armed Services and civilians for good nutrition and properly balanced diets. Sales quotas on cream and on milk byproducts have been set below June deliveries to boost fluid milk supplies where production is low, and to conserve milk for manufacturing purposes.

FDO 79-73
AMDT. 1
DEC. 23, 1943

WAR FOOD ADMINISTRATION

[FDO 79-73, Amdt. 1]

PART 1401—DAIRY PRODUCTS

FLUID MILK AND CREAM IN THE SAN DIEGO, CALIF., SALES AREA

Pursuant to Food Distribution Order No. 79 (8 F.R. 12426), dated September 7, 1943, as amended, and to effectuate the purposes thereof, Food Distribution Order No. 79-73 (8 F.R. 14367), relative to the conservation and distribution of fluid milk in the San Diego, California, milk sales area, issued by the Director of Food Distribution on October 22, 1943, is amended by deleting therefrom the numerals "0·01" wherever they appear in § 1401.85 (o) and inserting, in lieu thereof, the numerals "0·005."

The provisions of this amendment shall become effective at 12:01 a. m., e. w. t., January 1, 1944. With respect to violations of said Food Distribution Order No. 79-73, rights accrued, or liabilities incurred prior to the effective time of this amendment, said Food Distribution Order No. 79-73 shall be deemed to be in full force and effect for the purpose of sustaining any proper suit, action, or other proceeding with respect to any such violation, right, or liability.

(E.O. 9280, 7 F.R. 10179; E.O. 9322, 8 F.R. 3807; E.O. 9334, 8 F.R. 5423; E.O. 9392, 8 F.R. 14783; FDO 79, 8 F.R. 12426, 13283)

Issued this 23d day of December 1943.

ROY F. HENDRICKSON,
Director of Food Distribution.

7337

FDO 79-73
AMDT. 2
FEB. 19, 1944

WAR FOOD ADMINISTRATION

[FDO 79-73, Amdt. 2] A

PART 1401—DAIRY PRODUCTS

FLUID MILK AND CREAM IN SAN DIEGO, CALIF., SALES AREA

Pursuant to Food Distribution Order No. 79 (8 F.R. 12426), dated September 7, 1943, as amended, said to effectuate the purposes thereof, Food Distribution Order No. 79-73 (8 F.R. 14367), relative to the conservation and distribution of fluid milk in the San Diego, California, milk sales area, issued by the Director of Food Distribution on October 22, 1943, as amended, is hereby further amended by deleting therefrom the provisions in § 1401.85 (i) and inserting, in lieu thereof, the following:

(i) *Quota exclusions and exemptions.* Deliveries of milk, milk byproducts, or cream (1) to other handlers, except for such deliveries to sub-handlers, (2) to plants engaged in the handling or processing of milk, milk byproducts, or cream from which no milk, milk byproducts, or cream is delivered in the sales area, (3) to nursery, elementary, junior high, and high schools, and (4) to the agencies or groups specified in (d) of FDO 79, shall be excluded from the computation of deliveries in the base period and exempt from charges to quotas.

The provisions of this amendment shall become effective at 12:01 a. m., e. w. t., March 1, 1944. With respect to violations of said Food Distribution Order No. 79-73, as amended, rights accrued, or liabilities incurred, prior to the effective time of this amendment, said Food Distribution Order No. 79-73, as amended, shall be deemed to be in full force and effect for the purpose of sustaining any proper suit, action, or other proceeding with respect to any such violation, right, or liability.

(E.O. 9280, 7 F.R. 10179; E.O. 9322, 8 F.R. 3807; E.O. 9334, 8 F.R. 5423; E.O. 9392, 8 F.R. 14783; FDO 79, 8 F.R. 12426, 13283)

Issued this 19th day of February 1944.

LEE MARSHALL,
Director of Food Distribution.

-733F
serve

FDO 79-73

AMDT. 3
FEB. 28, 1944

WAR FOOD ADMINISTRATION

[FDO 79-73, Amdt. 3]

PART 1401—DAIRY PRODUCTS

FLUID MILK AND CREAM IN SAN DIEGO, CALIF., SALES AREA

Pursuant to Food Distribution Order No. 79 (8 F.R. 12426), dated September 7, 1943, as amended, and to effectuate the purposes thereof, Food Distribution Order No. 79-73 (8 F.R. 14367), relative to the conservation and distribution of fluid milk in the San Diego, California, milk sales area, issued by the Director of Food Distribution on October 22, 1943, as amended, is hereby further amended by deleting therefrom the description of the sales area in § 1401.85 (b) and inserting in lieu thereof, the following:

Beginning at the intersection of the shore line of the Pacific Ocean with the northern boundary in the city of Oceanside and running thence north easterly at right angles to said shore line, a distance of two (2) miles; thence south easterly parallel to and two (2) miles distant at right angles from the shore line of said Pacific Ocean to an intersection with the northern boundary of township 14 S. Range 3 W., S. B. B. M. (Del Mar); thence east along township lines to the northeast corner of township 14 S. Range 1 W. (Foster); thence south along township lines to an intersection with the boundary line between the United States and Mexico; thence westerly along said boundary to an intersection with the shore line of the Pacific Ocean; thence in a general northern direction following said shore line to the place of beginning. The following communities are included in the above area; Oceanside, Carlsbad, South Coast Park, Encinitas, Cardiff, Solana Beach, Del Mar, Lakeside, the city of San Diego and communities embraced therein, the city of La Mesa, the city of El Cajon, the city of National City, the city of Chula Vista, Imperial Beach, Palm City, Otay and San Ysidro, and the city of Coronado.

The provisions of this amendment shall become effective at 12:01 a. m., e. w. t., March 1, 1944. With respect to violations of said Food Distribution Order No. 79-73, as amended, rights accrued, or liabilities incurred prior to the effective time of this amendment, said Food Distribution Order No. 79-73, as amended, shall be deemed to be in full force and effect for the purpose of sustaining any proper suit, action, or other proceeding with respect to any such violation, right, or liability.

(E.O. 9280, 7 F.R. 10179; E.O. 9322, 8 F.R. 3807; E.O. 9334, 8 F.R. 5423; E.O. 9392, 8 F.R. 14783; FDO 79, 8 F.R. 12426, 13283)

Issued this 28th day of February 1944.

C. W. KITCHEN,
Acting Director of Food Distribution.

FDO 79-74

OCTOBER 22, 1943

WAR FOOD ADMINISTRATION

[FDO 79-74]

PART 1401—DAIRY PRODUCTS

FLUID MILK AND CREAM IN SAN JOSE, CALIF., SALES AREA

Pursuant to the authority vested in me by Food Distribution Order No. 79 (8 F.R. 12426), issued on September 7, 1943, as amended, and to effectuate the purposes of such order, it is hereby ordered as follows:

§ 1401.84 *Quota restrictions*—(a) *Definitions.* When used in this order, unless otherwise distinctly expressed or manifestly incompatible with the intent hereof:

(1) Each term defined in Food Distribution Order No. 79, as amended, shall, when used herein, have the same meaning as is set forth for such term in Food Distribution Order No. 79, as amended.

(2) The term "FDO 79" means Food Distribution Order No. 79, issued on September 7, 1943, as amended.

(3) The term "sub-handler" means any handler, such as a peddler, vendor, sub-dealer, or secondary dealer, who purchases in a previously packaged and processed form milk, milk byproducts, or cream for delivery.

(b) *Milk sales area.* The following area is hereby designated as a "milk sales area" to be known as the San Jose, California, sales area, and is referred to hereinafter as the "sales area";

The entire area included in the marketing area now designated by the Director of Agriculture of the State of California pursuant to the provisions of Chapter 10, Division 4, of the Agricultural Code of the State of California as the Santa Clara County Marketing Area.

(c) *Base period.* The calendar month of June 1943 is hereby designated as the base period for the sales area.

(d) *Quota period.* The remainder of the calendar month in which the provisions hereof become effective and each subsequent calendar month, respectively, is hereby designated as a quota period for the sales area.

(e) *Handler quotas.* Quotas for each handler in the sales area in each quota period shall be calculated in terms of pounds of each of the items for which percentages are specified in (3) below and shall be determined as follows:

(1) Divide the total deliveries of each such item made in the sales area by such handler during the base period, after excluding the quota-exempt deliveries described in (i) hereof, by the number of days in the base period;

(2) Multiply the result of the foregoing calculation by the number of days in the quota period;

(3) Multiply the aforesaid resulting amount by the following applicable percentage: (i) Milk: 100 percent; (ii) butterfat in milk: 100 percent; (iii) cream: 75 percent; (iv) butterfat in cream: 75 percent; (v) milk byproducts other than cottage, pot, or baker's cheese: 75 percent; and (vi) cottage, pot, or baker's cheese: 75 percent of skim milk equivalent. (For the purpose of this order, 1 pound of cottage, pot, or baker's cheese shall be considered as the equivalent of 7 pounds of skim milk.)

(f) *Quota limitations.* No handler shall, during any quota period, make deliveries in the sales area in excess of his respective quotas, except as set out in (i) hereof: *Provided*, That a handler may, after application to and approval by the market agent, secure an increase in milk quotas through an equivalent reduction as determined by the market agent, in cream and milk byproducts quotas, and an increase in milk byproducts quota through an equivalent reduction as determined by the market agent in cream quotas.

(g) *Quotas for handlers who are also producers.* Quotas for handlers who are also producers and who purchase no milk shall be 100 percent of the total production of such handlers in the base period.

(h) *Handler exemptions.* Quotas shall not apply to any handler who delivers in a quota period a daily average of less than 300 units of milk, cream, and milk byproducts. For the purpose of this order, a unit shall be the equivalent in volume of the following: (1) Milk, one quart of milk; (2) cream, one-half pint of cream; and (3) milk byproduct, one quart of skim milk, buttermilk, flavored milk drink, or other beverage containing more than 85 percent of skim milk, or one-half pound of cottage, pot, or baker's cheese.

(i) *Quota exclusions and exemptions.* Deliveries of milk, milk byproducts, or cream (1) to other handlers, except for such deliveries to sub-handlers, (2) to plants engaged in the handling or processing of milk, milk byproducts or cream from which no milk, milk byproducts, or cream is delivered in the sales area, and (3) to the agencies or groups specified in (d) of FDO 79, shall be excluded from the computation of deliveries in the base period and exempt from charges to quotas.

(j) *Transfers and apportionment of quotas.* The market agent is empowered to deduct an amount of base period deliveries to purchasers from the total of deliveries made by a handler or other person in the base period upon the application and a showing of unreasonable hardship by the handler making deliveries to such purchasers on the effective date of this order, and to add the amount of such deliveries to the total base period deliveries of the applicant handler. Denials of transfers or transfers granted by the market agent shall be reviewed by the Director upon application.

(k) *Petition for relief from hardships.* (1) Any person affected by FDO 79 or the provisions hereof who considers that compliance therewith would work an exceptional and unreasonable hardship on him, may file with the market agent a petition addressed to the Director. The petition shall contain the correct name, address and principal place of business of the petitioner, a full statement of the facts upon which the petition is based, and the hardship involved and the nature of the relief desired.

(2) Upon receiving such petition, the market agent shall immediately investigate the representations and facts stated therein.

(3) After investigation, the petition shall be certified to the Director, but prior to certification the market agent may (i) deny the petition, or (ii) grant temporary relief for a total period not to exceed 60 days.

(4) Denials or grants of relief by the market agent shall be reviewed by the Director and may be affirmed, modified, or reversed by the Director.

(l) *Reports.* Each handler shall transmit to the market agent on forms prescribed by the market agent the following reports:

(1) Within 20 days following the effective date of this order, reports which show the information required by the market agent to establish such handlers' quotas;

(2) Within 20 days following the close of each quota period, the information required by the market agent to establish volumes of deliveries of milk, cream, and milk byproducts during the preceding quota period; and

(3) Handlers exempt from quotas pursuant to (h) hereof shall, upon the request of the market agent, submit the information required by the market agent to establish volumes of deliveries of milk, cream, and milk byproducts.

(m) *Records.* Handlers shall keep and shall make available to the market agent such records of receipts, sales, deliveries, and production as the market agent shall require for the purpose of obtaining information which the Director may require for the establishment of quotas as prescribed in (b) of FDO 79.

(n) *Distribution schedules.* The distribution schedules, if any, to be followed by the handlers in making deliveries shall be made effective in the terms of approval by the Director of such schedules.

(o) *Expense of administration.* Each handler shall pay to the market agent, within 20 days after the close of each calendar month an assesment of $0 01 per hundredweight of each of milk, cream, skim milk, buttermilk, flavored milk drinks, beverages containing more than 85 percent of skim milk, and skim milk equivalent of cottage, pot, or baker's cheese delivered during the preceding quota period and subject to quota regulations under the provisions hereof.

(p) *Violations.* The market agent shall report all violations to the Director together with the information required for the prosecution of such violations, except in a case where a handler has made deliveries in a quota period in excess of a quota in an amount not to exceed 5 percent of such quota, and in the succeeding quota period makes deliveries below that quota by at least the same percent.

(q) *Bureau of the Budget a* The record keeping and repor quirements of this order have t proved by the Bureau of the B accordance with the Federal Rep of 1942. Subsequent record ke reporting requirements will be to the approval of the Bureau Budget pursuant to the Federal Act of 1942.

(r) This order shall take (12.01 a. m., e. w. t. November 1,

Issued this 22d day of Octobe

C. W. Kitc
Acting Director of Food Distri

Press Release, Immediate:
Friday, October 22, 1943.

Milk sales in 5 metropolitan areas in California will be regulated under the Food Distribution Administration's fluid milk conservation and control program, beginning November 1.

The new milk sales areas, and the market agents who will administer the program in each, are:

San Diego and Los Angeles (metropolitan), Martin Blank, 351 C. of C. Bldg., Los Angeles, Calif.

San Jose; San Francisco Bay Region, and Sacramento, E. L. Vehlow, Mull Bldg., Sacramento, Calif.

Under the program, milk dealers will be permitted to sell as much fluid milk as they sold in June and three-fourths as much cream and milk byproducts (such as cottage cheese, chocolate milk, and buttermilk) as they sold in June. Milk dealers include all persons or firms engaged in the sale or transfer of milk, but not such distributors as subhandlers ("peddlers"), retail stores, hotels, or restaurants.

Producer-distributors who purchase no milk will be permitted to sell as much milk as they produced in June.

Dealers will be allowed to exceed these base quotas by not more than 5 percent during any month, providing they decrease their deliveries the next month by the same amount, without being reported in violation.

A dealer may also increase his milk sales by reducing his cream and milk byproducts sales, and increase his sales of milk byproducts by reducing his cream sales, providing such an adjustment is approved by the market agent for the area.

Deliveries of milk, cream, and milk byproducts to other dealers; to the armed forces, and to plants processing milk who do not distribute milk, cream byproducts in the sales area a exempt.

Consumers in the milk sal named today and in others alrea nated generally will be able to as much milk under the milk c tion program as they have been recent months—within the limit supplies.

Fluid milk sales are being FDA officials said, to help assu cient milk for manufacturing th butter, evaporated milk, and m der required by the Armed Serv civilians for good nutrition and balanced diets. Sales quotas o and on milk byproducts have below June deliveries to boost fl supplies where production is to conserve milk for manufactu poses.

serve
/
7337

FDO 79-75
OCTOBER 22, 1943

WAR FOOD ADMINISTRATION

[FDO 79-75] A

PART 1401—DAIRY PRODUCTS

FLUID MILK AND CREAM IN LOS ANGELES, CALIF., METROPOLITAN SALES AREA

Pursuant to the authority vested in me by Food Distribution Order No. 79 (8 F.R. 12426), issued on September 7, 1943, as amended, and to effectuate the purposes of such order, it is hereby ordered as follows:

§ 1401.87 *Quota restrictions*—(a) *Definitions.* When used in this order, unless otherwise distinctly expressed or manifestly incompatible with the intent hereof:

(1) Each term defined in Food Distribution Order No. 79, as amended, shall when used herein, have the same meaning as is set forth for such term in Food Distribution Order No. 79, as amended.

(2) The term "FDO 79" means Food Distribution Order No. 79, issued on September 7, 1943, as amended.

(3) The term "sub-handler" means any handler, such as a peddler, vendor, sub-dealer, or secondary dealer, who purchases in a prevously packaged and processed form milk, milk byproducts, or cream for delivery.

(b) *Milk sales area.* The following area is hereby designated as a "milk sales area" to be known as the Los Angeles, California, metropolitan sales area, and is referred to hereinafter as the "sales area":

The entire area included in the marketing areas now designated by the Director of Agriculture of the State of California pursuant to the provisions of Chapter 10, Division 4, of the Agricultural Code of the State of California, as the Los Angeles County Marketing Area, the Orange County Marketing Area, and the San Bernardino-Riverside Marketing Area.

(c) *Base period.* The calendar month of June 1943 is hereby designated as the base period for the sales area.

(d) *Quota period.* The remainder of the calendar month in which the provisions hereof become effective and each subsequent calendar month, respectively, is hereby designated as a quota period for the sales area.

(e) *Handler quotas.* Quotas for each handler in the sales area in each quota period shall be calculated in terms of pounds of each of the items for which percentages are specified in (3) below and shall be determined as follows:

(1) Divide the total deliveries of each such item made in the sales area by such handler during the base period, after excluding the quota-exempt deliveries described in (i) hereof, by the number of days in the base period;

(2) Multiply the result of the foregoing calculation by the number of days in the quota period;

(3) Multiply the aforesaid resulting amount by the following applicable percentage: (i) Milk: 100 percent; (ii) butterfat in milk: 100 percent; (iii) cream: 75 percent; (iv) butterfat in cream: 75 percent; (v) milk byproducts other than cottage, pot, or baker's cheese: 75 percent; and (vi) cottage, pot, or baker's cheese, 75 percent of skim milk equivalent. (For the purpose of this order, one pound of cottage, pot, or baker's cheese shall be considered as the equivalent of 7 pounds of skim milk.)

(f) *Quota limitations.* No handler shall, during any quota period, make deliveries in the sales area in excess of his respective quotas, except as set out in (i) hereof: *Provided,* That a handler may, after application to and approval by the market agent, secure an increase in milk quotas through an equivalent reduction as determined by the market agent, in cream and milk byproducts quotas, and an increase in milk byproducts quota through an equivalent reduction as determined by the market agent, in cream quotas.

(g) *Quotas for handlers who are also producers.* Quotas for handlers who are also producers and who purchase no milk shall be 100 percent of the total deliveries of such handlers in the base period.

(h) *Handler exemptions.* Quotas shall not apply to any handler who delivers in a quota period a daily average of less than 300 units of milk, cream, and milk byproducts. For the purpose of this order, a unit shall be the equivalent in volume of the following: (1) Milk, one quart of milk; (2) cream, one-half pint of cream; and (3) milk byproduct, one quart of skim milk, buttermilk, flavored milk drink, or other beverage containing more than 85 percent of skim milk, or one-half pound of cottage, pot, or baker's cheese.

(i) *Quota exclusions and exemptions.* Deliveries of milk, milk byproducts, or cream (1) to other handlers, except for such deliveries to sub-handlers, (2) to plants engaged in the handling or processing of milk, milk byproducts, or cream from which no milk, milk byproducts, or cream is delivered in the sales area, and (3) to the agencies or groups specified in (d) of FDO 79, shall be excluded from the computation of deliveries in the base period and exempt from charges to quotas.

(j) *Transfers and apportionment of quotas.* The market agent is empowered to deduct an amount of base period deliveries to purchasers from the total of deliveries made by a handler or other person in the base period upon the application and a showing of unreasonable hardship by the handler making deliveries to such purchasers on the effective date of this order, and to add the amount of such deliveries to the total base period deliveries of the applicant handler. Denials of transfers or transfers granted by the market agent shall be reviewed by the Director upon application.

(k) *Petition for relief from hardships.* (1) Any person affected by FDO 79 or the provisions hereof who considers that compliance therewith would work an exceptional and unreasonable hardship on him, may file with the market agent a petition addressed to the Director. The petition shall contain the correct name, address and principal place of business of the petitioner, a full statement of the facts upon which the petition is based, and the hardship involved and the nature of the relief desired.

(2) Upon receiving such petition, the market agent shall immediately investigate the representations and facts stated therein.

(3) After investigation, the petition shall be certified to the Director, but prior to certification the market agent may (i) deny the petition, or (ii) grant temporary relief for a total period not to exceed 60 days.

(4) Denials or grants of relief by the market agent shall be reviewed by the Director and may be affirmed, modified, or reversed by the Director.

(l) *Reports.* Each handler shall transmit to the market agent on forms prescribed by the market agent the following reports:

(1) Within 20 days following the effective date of this order, reports which show the information required by the market agent to establish such handlers' quotas;

(2) Within 20 days following the close of each quota period, the information required by the market agent to establish volumes of deliveries of milk, cream, and milk byproducts during the preceding quota period; and

(3) Handlers exempt from quotas pursuant to (h) hereof shall, upon the request of the market agent, submit the information required by the market agent to establish volumes of deliveries of milk, cream, and milk byproducts.

(m) *Records.* Handlers shall keep and shall make available to the market agent such records of receipts, sales, deliveries, and production as the market agent shall require for the purpose of obtaining information which the Director may require for the establishment of quotas as prescribed in (b) of FDO 79.

(n) *Distribution schedules.* The distribution schedules, if any, to be followed by the handlers in making deliveries shall be made effective in the terms of approval by the Director of such schedules.

(o) *Expense of administration.* Each handler shall pay to the market agent, within 20 days after the close of each calendar month an assessment of $0.01 per hundredweight of each of milk, cream, skim milk, buttermilk, flavored milk drinks, beverages containing more than 85 percent of skim milk, and skim milk equivalent of cottage, pot, or baker's cheese delivered during the preceding quota period and subject to quota regulations under the provisions hereof

(p) *Violations.* The market agent shall report all violations to the Director together with the information required for the prosecution of such violations, except in a case where a handler has made deliveries in a quota period in excess of a quota in an amount not to exceed 5 percent of such quota, and in the succeeding quota period makes deliveries below that quota by at least the same percent.

(q) *Bureau of the Budget approval.* The record keeping and reporting requirements of this order have been approved by the Bureau of the Budget in accordance with the Federal Reports Act of 1942. Subsequent record keeping or reporting requirements will be subject to the approval of the Bureau of the Budget pursuant to the Federal Reports Act of 1942.

(r) This order shall take effect at 12:01 a. m., e. w. t. November 1, 1943.

Issued this 22d day of October 1943.

C. W. KITCHEN,
Acting Director of Food Distribution.

Press Release, Immediate:
Friday, October 22, 1943.

Milk sales in 5 metropolitan areas in California will be regulated under the Food Distribution Administration's fluid milk conservation and control program, beginning November 1.

The new milk sales areas, and the market agents who will administer the program in each, are:

San Diego and Los Angeles (metropolitan), Martin Blank, 351 C. of C. Bldg., Los Angeles, Calif.

San Jose; San Francisco Bay Region, and Sacramento, E. L. Vehlow, Mull Bldg., Sacramento, Calif.

Under the program, milk dealers will be permitted to sell as much fluid milk as they sold in June and three-fourths as much cream and milk byproducts (such as cottage cheese, chocolate milk, and buttermilk) as they sold in June. Milk dealers include all persons or firms engaged in the sale or transfer of milk, but not such distributors as subhandlers ("peddlers"), retail stores, hotels, or restaurants.

Producer-distributors who purchase no milk will be permitted to sell as much milk as they produced in June.

Dealers will be allowed to exceed these base quotas by not more than 5 percent during any month, providing they decrease their deliveries the next month by the same amount, without being reported in violation.

A dealer may also increase his milk sales by reducing his cream and milk byproducts sales, and increase his sales of milk byproducts by reducing his cream sales, providing such an adjustment is approved by the market agent for the area.

Deliveries of milk, cream, and milk byproducts to other dealers; to the armed forces, and to plants processing milk who do not distribute milk, cream or milk byproducts in the sales area are quota exempt.

Consumers in the milk sales areas named today and in others already designated generally will be able to purchase as much milk under the milk conservation program as they have been buying in recent months—within the limits of local supplies.

Fluid milk sales are being stabilized FDA officials said, to help assure sufficient milk for manufacturing the cheese, butter, evaporated milk, and milk powder required by the Armed Services and civilians for good nutrition and properly balanced diets. Sales quotas on cream and on milk byproducts have been set below June deliveries to boost fluid milk supplies where production is low, and to conserve milk for manufacturing purposes.

WAR FOOD ADMINISTRATION

[FDO 79-75, Amdt. 1]

PART 1401—DAIRY PRODUCTS

FLUID MILK AND CREAM IN THE LOS ANGELES, CALIF., METROPOLITAN SALES AREA

Pursuant to Food Distribution Order No. 79 (8 F.R. 12426), dated September 7, 1943, as amended, and to effectuate the purposes thereof, Food Distribution Order No. 79-75 (8 F.R. 14370), relative to the conservation and distribution of fluid milk in the Los Angeles, California, metropolitan milk sales area, issued by the Director of Food Distribution on October 22, 1943, is amended by deleting therefrom the numerals "0.01" wherever they appear in § 1401.87 (o) and inserting, in lieu thereof, the numerals "0.005."

The provisions of this amendment shall become effective at 12:01 a. m., e. w. t., January 1, 1944. With respect to violations of said Food Distribution Order No. 79-75, rights accrued, or liabilities incurred prior to the effective time of this amendment, said Food Distribution Order No. 79-75 shall be deemed to be in full force and effect for the purpose of sustaining any proper suit, action, or other proceeding with respect to any such violation, right, or liability.

(E.O. 9280, 7 F.R. 10179; E.O. 9322, 8 F.R. 3807; E.O. 9334, 8 F.R. 5423; E.O. 9392, 8 F.R. 14783; FDO 79, 8 F.R. 12426, 13283)

Issued this 23d day of December 1943.

ROY F. HENDRICKSON,
Director of Food Distribution.

98A.F.21-
1
77337

FDO 79-75
AMDT. 2
FEB. 19, 1944

WAR FOOD ADMINISTRATION

[FDO 79-75, Amdt. 2] A

PART 1401—DAIRY PRODUCTS

FLUID MILK AND CREAM IN LOS ANGELES, CALIF. SALES AREA

Pursuant to Food Distribution Order No. 79 (8 F.R. 12426), dated September 7, 1943, as amended, and to effectuate the purposes thereof, Food Distribution Order No. 79-75 (8 F.R. 14370), relative to the conservation and distribution of fluid milk in the Los Angeles, California, milk sales area, issued by the Director of Food Distribution on October 22, 1943, as amended, is hereby further amended by deleting therefrom the provisions in § 1401.87 (i) and inserting, in lieu thereof, the following:

(i) *Quota exclusions and exemptions.* Deliveries of milk, milk byproducts, or cream (1) to other handlers, except for such deliveries to sub-handlers, (2) to plants engaged in the handling of processing of milk, milk byproducts, or cream from which no milk, milk byproducts, or cream is delivered in the sales area, (3) to nursery, elementary, junior high, and high schools, and (4) to the agencies or groups specified in (d) of FDO 79, shall be excluded from the computation of deliveries in the base period and exempt from charges to quotas.

The provisions of this amendment shall become effective at 12:01 a. m., e. w. t., March 1, 1944. With respect to violations of said Food Distribution Order No. 79-75, as amended, rights accrued, or liabilities incurred prior to the effective time of this amendment, said Food Distribution Order No. 79-75, as amended, shall be deemed to be in full force and effect for the purpose of sustaining any proper suit, action, or other proceeding with respect to any such violation, right, or liability.

(E.O. 9280, 7 F.R. 10179; E.O. 9322, 8 F.R. 3807; E.O. 9334, 8 F.R. 5423; E.O. 9392, 8 F.R. 14783; FDO 79, 8 F.R. 12426, 13283)

Issued this 19th day of February 1944.

LEE MARSHALL,
Director of Food Distribution.

33+

FDO 79-75

AMDT. 3
MAR. 31, 1944

WAR FOOD ADMINISTRATION

[FDO 79-75, Amdt. 3]

PART 1401—DAIRY PRODUCTS

FLUID MILK AND CREAM IN LOS ANGELES, CALIF., METROPOLITAN SALES AREA

Pursuant to Food Distribution Order No. 79 (8 F.R. 12426), dated September 7, 1943, as amended, and to effectuate the purposes thereof, Food Distribution Order No. 79-75 (8 F.R. 14370), relative to the conservation and distribution of fluid milk, milk byproducts, and cream in the Los Angeles, California, metropolitan milk sales area, issued by the Director of Food Distribution on October 22, 1943, as amended, is hereby further amended by deleting therefrom the description of the sales area in § 1401.87 (b) and inserting, in lieu thereof, the following:

The entire area within Los Angeles County, excluding the communities of Little Rock, Palmdale, Denis, Lancaster, Roosevelt, Oban and Hi Vista; the entire area within Orange County; that portion of San Bernardino County south of the township line between Townships Three and Four, north of the San Bernardino base meridian and west of 117 west longitude; and that portion of Riverside County north of the township line between Townships Four and Five, south of the San Bernardino base meridian and west of 117 West longitude, all within the State of California.

The provisions of this amendment shall become effective at 12:01 a. m., e. w. t., April 1, 1944. With respect to violations of said Food Distribution Order No. 79-75, as amended, rights accrued, or liabilities incurred prior to the effective time of this amendment, said Food Distribution Order No. 79-75, as amended, shall be deemed to be in full force and effect for the purpose of sustaining any proper suit, action, or other proceeding with respect to any such violation, right, or liability.

(E.O. 9280, 7 F.R. 10179; E.O. 9322, 8 F.R. 3807; E.O. 9334, 8 F.R. 5423; E.O. 9392, 8 F.R. 14783; FDO 79, 8 F.R. 12426, 13283)

Issued this 31st day of March 1944.

C. W. KITCHEN,
Acting Director of Distribution.

rve

F.D.J.-

WAR FOOD ADMINISTRATION

[FDO 79-76]

Part 1401—Dairy Products

FLUID MILK AND CREAM IN SAN FRANCISCO BAY REGION SALES AREA

Pursuant to the authority vested in me by Food Distribution Order No. 79 (8 F.R. 12426), issued on September 7, 1943, as amended, and to effectuate the purposes of such order, it is hereby ordered as follows:

§ 1401.83 *Quota restrictions*—(a) *Definitions.* When used in this order, unless otherwise distinctly expressed or manifestly incompatible with the intent hereof:

(1) Each term defined in Food Distribution Order No. 79, as amended, shall, when used herein, have the same meaning as is set forth for such term in Food Distribution Order No. 79, as amended.

(2) The term "FDO 79" means Food Distribution Order No. 79, issued on September 7, 1943, as amended.

(3) The term "sub-handler" means any handler, such as a peddler, vendor, sub-dealer, or secondary dealer, who purchases in a previously packaged and processed form milk, milk byproducts, or cream for delivery.

(b) *Milk sales area.* The following area is hereby designated as a "milk sales area" to be known as the San Francisco Bay region sales area, and is referred to hereinafter as the "sales area":

The entire area included in the marketing areas now designated by the Director of Agriculture of the State of California pursuant to the provisions of Chapter 10, Division 4, of the Agricultural Code of the State of California, as the San Francisco County Marketing Area, the San Mateo County Marketing Area, the Marin County Marketing Area, and the Alameda-Contra Costa Marketing Area.

(c) *Base period.* The calendar month of June 1943 is hereby designated as the base period for the sales area.

(d) *Quota period.* The remainder of the calendar month in which the provisions hereof become effective and each subsequent calendar month, respectively, is hereby designated as a quota period for the sales area.

(e) *Handler quotas.* Quotas for each handler in the sales area in each quota period shall be calculated in terms of pounds of each of the items for which percentages are specified in (3) below and shall be determined as follows:

(1) Divide the total deliveries of each such item made in the sales area by such handler during the base period, after excluding the quota-exempt deliveries described in (i) hereof, by the number of days in the base period;

(2) Multiply the result of the foregoing calculation by the number of days in the quota period;

(3) Multiply the aforesaid resulting amount by the following applicable percentage: (i) Milk: 100 percent; (ii) butterfat in milk: 100 percent; (iii) cream: 75 percent; (iv) butterfat in cream: 75 percent; (v) milk byproducts other than cottage, pot, or baker's cheese: 75 percent; and (vi) cottage, pot, or baker's cheese: 75 percent of skim milk equivalent. (For the purpose of this order, one pound of cottage, pot, or baker's cheese shall be considered as the equivalent of 7 pounds of skim milk.)

(f) *Quota limitations.* No handler shall, during any quota period, make deliveries in the sales area in excess of his respective quotas, except as set out in (i) hereof: *Provided,* That a handler may, after application to and approval by the market agent, secure an increase in milk quotas through an equivalent reduction as determined by the market agent, in cream and milk byproducts quotas, and an increase in milk byproducts quota through an equivalent reduction as determined by the market agent, in cream quotas.

(g) *Quotas for handlers who are also producers.* Quotas for handlers who are also producers and who purchase no milk shall be 100 percent of the total production of such handlers in the base period.

(h) *Handler exemptions.* Quotas shall not apply to any handler who delivers in a quota period a daily average of less than 300 units of milk, cream, and milk byproducts. For the purpose of this order, a unit shall be the equivalent in volume of the following: (1) Milk, one quart of milk; (2) cream, one-half pint of cream; and (3) milk byproduct, one quart of skim milk, buttermilk, flavored milk drink, or other beverage containing more than 85 percent of skim milk, or one-half pound of cottage, pot, or baker's cheese.

(i) *Quota exclusions and exemptions.* Deliveries of milk, milk byproducts, or cream (1) to other handlers, except for such deliveries to sub-handlers, (2) to plants engaged in the handling or processing of milk, milk byproducts, or cream from which no milk, milk byproducts, or cream is delivered in the sales area, and (3) to the agencies or groups specified in (d) of FDO 79, shall be excluded from the computation of deliveries in the base period and exempt from charges to quotas.

(j) *Transfers and apportionment of quotas.* The market agent is empowered to deduct an amount of base period deliveries to purchasers from the total of deliveries made by a handler or other person in the base period upon the application and a showing of unreasonable hardship by the handler making deliveries to such purchasers on the effective date of this order, and to add the amount of such deliveries to the total base period deliveries of the applicant handler. Denials of transfers or transfers granted by the market agent shall be reviewed by the Director upon application.

(k) *Petition for relief from hardships.* (1) Any person affected by FDO 79 or the provisions hereof who considers that compliance therewith would work an exceptional and unreasonable hardship on him, may file with the market agent a petition addressed to the Director. The petition shall contain the correct name, address and principal place of business of the petitioner, a full statement of the facts upon which the petition is based, and the hardship involved and the nature of the relief desired.

(2) Upon receiving such petition, the market agent shall immediately investigate the representations and facts stated therein.

(3) After investigation, the petition shall be certified to the Director, but prior to certification the market agent may (i) deny the petition, or (ii) grant temporary relief for a total period not to exceed 60 days.

(4) Denials or grants of relief by the market agent shall be reviewed by the Director and may be affirmed, modified, or reversed by the Director.

(l) *Reports.* Each handler shall transmit to the market agent on forms prescribed by the market agent the following reports:

(1) Within 20 days following the effective date of this order, reports which show the information required by the market agent to establish such handlers' quotas;

(2) Within 20 days following the close of each quota period, the information required by the market agent to establish volumes of deliveries of milk, cream, and milk byproducts during the preceding quota period; and

(3) Handlers exempt from quotas pursuant to (h) hereof shall, upon the request of the market agent, submit the information required by the market

agent to establish volumes of deliveries of milk, cream, and milk byproducts.

(m) *Records.* Handlers shall keep and shall make available to the market agent such records of receipts, sales, deliveries, and production as the market agent shall require for the purpose of obtaining information which the Director may require for the establishment of quotas as prescribed in (b) of FDO 79.

(n) *Distribution schedules.* The distribution schedules, if any, to be followed by the handlers in making deliveries shall be made effective in the terms of approval by the Director of such schedules.

(o) *Expense of administration.* Each handler shall pay to the market agent, within 20 days after the close of each calendar month an assessment of $0.01 per hundredweight of each of milk, cream, skim milk, buttermilk, flavored milk drinks, beverages containing more than 85 percent of skim milk, and skim milk equivalent of cottage, pot, or baker's cheese delivered during the preceding quota period and subject to quota regulations under the provisions hereof.

(p) *Violations.* The market agent shall report all violations to the Director together with the information required for the prosecution of such violations, except in a case where a handler has made deliveries in a quota period in excess of a quota in an amount not to exceed 5 percent of such quota, and in the succeeding quota period makes deliveries below that quota by at least the same percent.

(q) *Bureau of the Budget approval.* The record keeping and reporting requirements of this order have been approved by the Bureau of the Budget in accordance with the Federal Reports Act of 1942. Subsequent record keeping or reporting requirements will be subject to the approval of the Bureau of the Budget pursuant to the Federal Reports Act of 1942.

(r) This order shall take effect at 12:01 a. m., e. w. t., November 1, 1943.

Issued this 22d day of October 1943.

C. W. KITCHEN,
Acting Director of Food Distribution.

Press Release, Immediate:
Friday, October 22, 1943.

Milk sales in 5 metropolitan areas in California will be regulated under the Food Distribution Administration's fluid milk conservation and control program, beginning November 1.

The new milk sales areas, and the market agents who will administer the program in each, are:

San Diego and Los Angeles (metropolitan), Martin Blank, 351 C. of C. Bldg., Los Angeles, Calif.

San Jose; San Francisco Bay Region, and Sacramento, E. L. Vehlow, Mull Bldg., Sacramento, Calif.

Under the program, milk dealers will be permitted to sell as much fluid milk as they sold in June and three-fourths as much cream and milk byproducts (such as cottage cheese, chocolate milk, and buttermilk) as they sold in June. Milk dealers include all persons or firms engaged in the sale or transfer of milk, but not such distributors as subhandlers ("peddlers"), retail stores, hotels, or restaurants.

Producer-distributors who purchase no milk will be permitted to sell as much milk as they produced in June.

Dealers will be allowed to exceed these base quotas by not more than 5 percent during any month, providing they decrease their deliveries the next month by the same amount, without being reported in violation.

A dealer may also increase his milk sales by reducing his cream and milk byproducts sales, and increase his sales of milk byproducts by reducing his cream sales, providing such an adjustment is approved by the market agent for the area.

Deliveries of milk, cream, and milk byproducts to other dealers; to the armed forces, and to plants processing milk who do not distribute milk, cream or milk byproducts in the sales area are quota exempt.

Consumers in the milk sales areas named today and in others already designated generally will be able to purchase as much milk under the milk conservation program as they have been buying in recent months—within the limits of local supplies.

Fluid milk sales are being stabilized FDA officials said, to help assure sufficient milk for manufacturing the cheese, butter, evaporated milk, and milk powder required by the Armed Services and civilians for good nutrition and properly balanced diets. Sales quotas on cream and on milk byproducts have been set below June deliveries to boost fluid milk supplies where production is low, and to conserve milk for manufacturing purposes.

WAR FOOD ADMINISTRATION

[FDO 79-76, Amdt. 1]

PART 1401—DAIRY PRODUCTS

SAN FRANCISCO BAY REGION MILK SALES AREA

Pursuant to the authority vested in the Director by Food Distribution Order No. 79, dated September 7, 1943 (8 F.R. 12426), as amended, and to effectuate the purposes thereof, Food Distribution Order No. 79-76, § 1401.83 (b), relative to the conservation of fluid milk in the San Francisco Bay region milk sales area (8 F.R. 14371), issued by the Acting Director of Food Distribution on October 22, 1943, is amended as follows:

The milk sales area described in § 1401.83 (b) of the original order is modified in the following particulars; add:

That portion of Solano County starting at a point, being the intersection of the Napa-Solano County line, and the east bank of San Pablo Bay; thence easterly along said Napa-Solano County line to State Highway U. S. No. 40; thence southerly along State Highway U. S. No. 40 to County Road No. 233; thence easterly along said County Road No. 233 to County Road No. 91; thence southerly along County Road No. 91 to County Road No. 133; thence southeasterly along County Road No. 133 to the northwest corner of Benicia Arsenal; thence southerly along the boundary of Benicia Arsenal to the north boundary of Carquinez Straits; thence westerly along the north boundary of Carquinez Straits to San Pablo Bay; thence along the north and east boundary of San Pablo Bay to the point of beginning.

Effective date. This amendment of FDO 79-76, shall become effective at 12:01 a. m., e. w. t., January 1, 1944.

(E.O. 9280, 7 F.R. 10179; E.O. 9322, 8 F.R. 3807; E.O. 9334, 8 F.R. 5423; E.O. 9392, 8 F.R. 14783; FDO 79, 8 F.R. 12426, 13283)

Issued this 28th day of December 1943.

ROY F. HENDRICKSON,
Director of Food Distribution.

serve
/
7793

FDO 79-77

OCTOBER 22, 1943

WAR FOOD ADMINISTRATION

[FDO 79-77]

PART 1401—DAIRY PRODUCTS

FLUID MILK AND CREAM IN SACRAMENTO, CALIF., SALES AREA

Pursuant to the authority vested in me by Food Distribution Order No. 79 (8 F.R. 12426), issued on September 7, 1943, as amended, and to effectuate the purposes of such order, it is hereby ordered as follows:

§ 1401.86 *Quota restrictions*—(a) *Definitions.* When used in this order, unless otherwise distinctly expressed or manifestly incompatible with the intent hereof:

(1) Each term defined in Food Distribution Order No. 79, as amended, shall, when used herein, have the same meaning as is set forth for such term in Food Distribution Order No. 79, as amended.

(2) The term "FDO 79" means Food Distribution Order No. 79, issued on September 7, 1943, as amended.

(3) The term "sub-handler" means any handler, such as a peddler, vendor, sub-dealer, or secondary dealer, who purchases in a previously packaged and processed form milk, milk byproducts, or cream for delivery.

(b) *Milk sales area.* The following area is hereby designated as a "milk sales area" to be known as the Sacramento, California, sales area, and is referred to hereinafter as the "sales area":

The entire area included in the marketing area now designated by the Director of Agriculture of the State of California pursuant to the provisions of Chapter 10, Division 4, of the Agricultural Code of the State of California as the Sacramento Marketing Area.

(c) *Base period.* The calendar month of June 1943 is hereby designated as the base period for the sales area.

(d) *Quota period.* The remainder of the calendar month in which the provisions hereof become effective and each subsequent calendar month, respectively, is hereby designated as a quota period for the sales area.

(e) *Handler quotas.* Quotas for each handler in the sales area in each quota period shall be calculated in terms of pounds of each of the items for which percentages are specified in (3) below and shall be determined as follows:

(1) Divide the total deliveries of each such item made in the sales area by such handler during the base period, after excluding the quota-exempt deliveries described in (i) hereof, by the number of days in the base period;

(2) Multiply the result of the foregoing calculation by the number of days in the quota period;

(3) Multiply the aforesaid resulting amount by the following applicable percentage: (i) Milk: 100 percent; (ii) butterfat in milk: 100 percent; (iii) cream: 75 percent; (iv) butterfat in cream: 75 percent; (v) milk byproducts other than cottage, pot, or baker's cheese: 75 percent; and (vi) cottage, pot, or baker's cheese: 75 percent of skim milk equivalent. (For the purpose of this order, one pound of cottage, pot, or baker's cheese shall be considered as the equivalent of 7 pounds of skim milk.)

(f) *Quota limitations.* No handler shall, during any quota period, make deliveries in the sales area in excess of his respective quotas, except as set out in (i) hereof: *Provided,* That a handler may, after application to and approval by the market agent, secure an increase in milk quotas through an equivalent reduction as determined by the market agent, in cream and milk byproducts quotas, and an increase in milk byproducts quota through an equivalent reduction as determined by the market agent, in cream quotas.

(g) *Quotas for handlers who are also producers.* Quotas for handlers who are also producers and who purchase no milk shall be 100 percent of the total production of such handlers in the base period.

(h) *Handler exemptions.* Quotas shall not apply to any handler who delivers in a quota period a daily average of less than 300 units of milk, cream, and milk byproducts. For the purpose of this order, a unit shall be the equivalent in volume of the following: (1) Milk, one quart of milk; (2) cream, one-half pint of cream; and (3) milk byproduct, one quart of skim milk, buttermilk, flavored milk drink, or other beverage containing more than 85 percent of skim milk, or one-half pound of cottage, pot, or baker's cheese.

(i) *Quota exclusions and exemptions.* Deliveries of milk, milk byproducts, or cream (1) to other handlers, except for such deliveries to sub-handlers, (2) to plants engaged in the handling or processing of milk, milk byproducts, or cream from which no milk, milk byproducts, or cream is delivered in the sales area, and (3) to the agencies or groups specified in (d) of FDO 79, shall be excluded from the computation of deliveries in the base period and exempt from charges to quotas.

(j) *Transfers and apportionment of quotas.* The market agent is empowered to deduct an amount of base period deliveries to purchasers from the total of deliveries made by a handler or other person in the base period upon the application and a showing of unreasonable hardship by the handler making deliveries to such purchasers on the effective date of this order, and to add the amount of such deliveries to the total base period deliveries of the applicant handler. Denials of transfers or transfers granted by the market agent shall be reviewed by the Director upon application.

(k) *Petition for relief from hardships.* (1) Any person affected by FDO 79 or the provisions hereof who considers that compliance therewith would work an exceptional and unreasonable hardship on him may file with the market agent a petition addressed to the Director. The petition shall contain the correct name, address and principal place of business of the petitioner, a full statement of the facts upon which the petition is based, and the hardship involved and the nature of the relief desired.

(2) Upon receiving such petition, the market agent shall immediately investigate the representations and facts stated therein.

(3) After investigation, the petition shall be certified to the Director, but prior to certification the market agent may (i) deny the petition, or (ii) grant temporary relief for a total period not to exceed 60 days.

(4) Denials or grants of relief by the market agent shall be reviewed by the Director and may be affirmed, modified, or reversed by the Director.

(l) *Reports.* Each handler shall transmit to the market agent on forms prescribed by the market agent the following reports:

(1) Within 20 days following the effective date of this order, reports which show the information required by the market agent to establish such handlers' quotas;

(2) Within 20 days following the close of each quota period, the information required by the market agent to establish volumes of deliveries of milk, cream, and milk byproducts during the preceding quota period; and

(3) Handlers exempt from quotas pursuant to (h) hereof shall, upon the re-

quest of the market agent, submit the information required by the market agent to establish volumes of deliveries of milk, cream, and milk byproducts.

(m) *Records.* Handlers shall keep and shall make available to the market agent such records of receipts, sales, deliveries, and production as the market agent shall require for the purpose of obtaining information which the Director may require for the establishment of quotas as prescribed in (b) of FDO 79.

(n) *Distribution schedules.* The distribution schedules, if any, to be followed by the handlers in making deliveries shall be made effective in the terms of approval by the Director of such schedule.

(o) *Expense of administration.* Each handler shall pay to the market agent, within 20 days after the close of each calendar month, an assessment of $0.01 per hundredweight of each of milk, cream, skim milk, buttermilk, flavored milk drinks, beverages containing more than 85 percent of skim milk, and skim milk equivalent of cottage, pot, or baker's cheese delivered during the preceding quota period and subject to quota regulations under the provisions hereof.

(p) *Violations.* The market agent shall report all violations to the Director together with the information required for the prosecution of such violations, except in a case where a handler has made deliveries in a quota period in excess of a quota in an amount not to exceed 5 percent of such quota, and in the succeeding quota period makes deliveries below that quota by at least the same percent.

(q) *Bureau of the Budget approval.* The record keeping and reporting requirements of this order have been approved by the Bureau of the Budget in accordance with the Federal Reports Act of 1942. Subsequent record keeping or reporting requirements will be subject to the approval of the Bureau of the Budget pursuant to the Federal Reports Act of 1942.

(r) This order shall take effect at 12:01 a. m., e. w. t., November 1, 1943.

Issued this 22d day of October 1943.

C. W. KITCHEN,
Acting Director of Food Distribution.

Press Release, Immediate:
Friday, October 22, 1943.

Milk sales in 5 metropolitan areas in California will be regulated under the Food Distribution Administration's fluid milk conservation and control program, beginning November 1.

The new milk sales areas, and the market agents who will administer the program in each, are:

San Diego and Los Angeles (metropolitan), Martin Blank, 351 C. of C. Bldg., Los Angeles, Calif.

San Jose; San Francisco Bay Region, and Sacramento, E. L. Vehlow, Mull Bldg., Sacramento, Calif.

Under the program, milk dealers will be permitted to sell as much fluid milk as they sold in June and three-fourths as much cream and milk byproducts (such as cottage cheese, chocolate milk, and buttermilk) as they sold in June. Milk dealers include all persons or firms engaged in the sale or transfer of milk, but not such distributors as subhandlers ("peddlers"), retail stores, hotels, or restaurants.

Producer-distributors who purchase no milk will be permitted to sell as much milk as they produced in June.

Dealers will be allowed to exceed these base quotas by not more than 5 percent during any month, providing they decrease their deliveries the next month by the same amount, without being reported in violation.

A dealer may also increase his milk sales by reducing his cream and milk byproducts sales, and increase his sales of milk byproducts by reducing his cream sales, providing such an adjustment is approved by the market agent for the area.

Deliveries of milk, cream, and milk byproducts to other dealers; to the armed forces, and to plants processing milk who do not distribute milk, cream or milk byproducts in the sales area are quota exempt.

Consumers in the milk sales areas named today and in others already designated generally will be able to purchase as much milk under the milk conservation program as they have been buying in recent months—within the limits of local supplies.

Fluid milk sales are being stabilized FDA officials said, to help assure sufficient milk for manufacturing the cheese, butter, evaporated milk, and milk powder required by the Armed Services and civilians for good nutrition and properly balanced diets. Sales quotas on cream and on milk byproducts have been set below June deliveries to boost fluid milk supplies where production is low, and to conserve milk for manufacturing purposes.

rve
/
7 3 3 2

FDO 79-78

OCTOBER 26, 1943

WAR FOOD ADMINISTRATION

[FDO 79-78]

PART 1401—DAIRY PRODUCTS

FLUID MILK AND CREAM IN EVANSVILLE, IND., SALES AREA

Pursuant to the authority vested in me by Food Distribution Order No. 79 (8 F.R. 12426), issued on September 7, 1943, as amended, and to effectuate the purposes of such order, it is hereby ordered as follows:

§ 1401.117 *Quota restrictions*—(a) *Definitions.* When used in this order, unless otherwise distinctly expressed or manifestly incompatible with the intent hereof:

(1) Each term defined in Food Distribution Order No. 79, as amended, shall, when used herein, have the same meaning as is set forth for such term in Food Distribution Order No. 79, as amended.

(2) The term "FDO 79" means Food Distribution Order No. 79, issued on September 7, 1943, as amended.

(3) The term "sub-handler" means any handler, such as a peddler, vendor, sub-dealer, or secondary dealer, who purchases in a previously packaged and processed form milk, milk byproducts, or cream for delivery.

(b) *Milk sales area.* The following area is hereby designated as a "milk sales area" to be known as the Evansville, Indiana, sales area, and is referred to hereinafter as the "sales area":

The city of Evansville and the townships of Center, German, Knight, Perry, and Pigeon, in Vanderburgh County, Indiana; the magisterial districts of Upper Henderson and Lower Henderson, in Henderson County, Kentucky.

(c) *Base period.* The calendar month of June 1943 is hereby designated as the base period for the sales area.

(d) *Quota period.* The remainder of the calendar month in which the provisions hereof become effective and each subsequent calendar month, respectively, is hereby designated as a quota period for the sales area.

(e) *Handler quotas.* Quotas for each handler in the sales area in each quota period shall be calculated in terms of pounds of each of the items for which percentages are specified in (3) below and shall be determined as follows:

(1) Divide the total deliveries of each such item made in the sales area by such handler during the base period, after excluding the quota-exempt deliveries described in (i) hereof, by the number of days in the base period;

(2) Multiply the result of the foregoing calculation by the number of days in the quota period;

(3) Multiply the aforesaid resulting amount by the following applicable percentage: (i) Milk: 100 percent; (ii) butterfat in milk: ------ percent; (iii) cream: 75 percent; (iv) butterfat in cream: 75 percent; (v) milk byproducts other than cottage, pot, or baker's cheese: 75 percent; and (vi) cottage, pot, or baker's cheese: 75 percent of skim milk equivalent. (For the purpose of this order one pound of cottage, pot, or baker's cheese shall be considered as the equivalent of 7 pounds of skim milk.)

(f) *Quota limitations.* No handler shall, during any quota period, make deliveries in the sales area in excess of his respective quotas, except as set out in (i) hereof: *Provided,* That a handler may, after application to and approval by the market agent, secure an increase in milk quotas through an equivalent reduction as determined by the market agent, in cream and milk byproducts quotas, and an increase in milk byproducts quota through an equivalent reduction as determined by the market agent, in cream quotas.

(g) *Quotas for handlers who are also producers.* Quotas for handlers who are also producers and who purchase no milk shall be 100 percent of the total production of such handlers in the base period.

(h) *Handler exemptions.* Quotas shall not apply to any handler who delivers in a quota period a daily average of less than 300 units of milk, cream, and milk byproducts. For the purpose of this order, a unit shall be the equivalent in volume of the following: (1) Milk, one quart of milk; (2) cream, one-half pint of cream; and (3) milk byproduct, one quart of skim milk, buttermilk, flavored milk drink, or other beverage containing more than 85 percent of skim milk, or one-half pound of cottage, pot, or baker's cheese.

(i) *Quota exclusions and exemptions.* Deliveries of milk, milk byproducts, or cream (1) to other handlers, except for such deliveries to sub-handlers, (2) to plants engaged in the handling or processing of milk, milk byproducts, or cream from which no milk, milk byproducts, or cream is delivered in the sales area, and (3) to the agencies or groups specified in (d) of FDO 79, shall be excluded from the computation of deliveries in the base period and exempt from charges to quotas.

(j) *Transfers and apportionment of quotas.* The market agent is empowered to deduct an amount of base period deliveries to purchasers from the total of deliveries made by a handler or other person in the base period upon the application and a showing of unreasonable hardship by the handler making deliveries to such purchasers on the effective date of this order, and to add the amount of such deliveries to the total base period deliveries of the applicant handler. Denials of transfers or transfers granted by the market agent shall be reviewed by the Director upon application.

(k) *Petition for relief from hardships.* (1) Any person affected by FDO 79 or the provisions hereof who considers that compliance therewith would work an exceptional and unreasonable hardship on him, may file with the market agent a petition addressed to the Director. The petition shall contain the correct name, address and principal place of business of the petitioner, a full statement of the facts upon which the petition is based, and the hardship involved and the nature of the relief desired.

(2) Upon receiving such petition, the market agent shall immediately investigate the representations and facts stated therein.

(3) After investigation, the petition shall be certified to the Director, but prior to certification the market agent may (i) deny the petition, or (ii) grant temporary relief for a total period not to exceed 60 days.

(4) Denials or grants of relief by the market agent shall be reviewed by the Director and may be affirmed, modified, or reversed by the Director.

(l) *Reports.* Each handler shall transmit to the market agent on forms prescribed by the market agent the following reports:

(1) Within 20 days following the effective date of this order, reports which show the information required by the market agent to establish such handlers' quotas;

(2) Within 20 days following the close of each quota period, the information required by the market agent to establish volumes of deliveries of milk, cream, and milk byproducts during the preceding quota period; and

(3) Handlers exempt from quotas pursuant to (h) hereof shall, upon the request of the market agent, submit the information required by the market agent to establish volumes of deliveries of milk, cream, and milk byproducts.

(m) *Records.* Handlers shall keep and shall make available to the market agent such records of receipts, sales, deliveries, and production as the market agent shall require for the purpose of obtaining information which the Director may require for the establishment of quotas as prescribed in (b) of FDO 79.

(n) *Distribution schedules.* The distribution schedules, if any, to be followed by the handlers in making deliveries shall be made effective in the terms of approval by the Director of such schedules.

(o) *Expense of administration.* Each handler shall pay to the market agent, within 20 days after the close of each calendar month an assessment of $0.01 per hundredweight of each of milk, cream, skim milk, buttermilk, flavored milk drinks, beverages containing more than 85 percent of skim milk, and skim milk equivalent of cottage, pot, or baker's cheese delivered during the preceding quota period and subject to quota regulations under the provisions hereof.

(p) *Violations.* The market agent shall report all violations to the Director together with the information required for the prosecution of such violations, except in a case where a handler has made deliveries in a quota period in excess of a quota in an amount not to exceed 5 percent of such quota, and in the succeeding quota period makes deliveries below that quota by at least the same percent.

(q) *Bureau of the Budget approval.* The record keeping and reporting requirements of this order have been approved by the Bureau of the Budget in accordance with the Federal Reports Act of 1942. Subsequent record keeping or reporting requirements will be subject to the approval of the Bureau of the Budget pursuant to the Federal Reports Act of 1942.

(r) This order shall take effect at 12:01 a. m., e. w. t., November 1, 1943.

Issued this 26th day of October 1943.

C. W. Kitchen,
Acting Director of Food Distribution.

Press Release, Immediate:
Tuesday, October 26, 1943.

Milk sales in Evansville, Indiana, and 2 metropolitan areas in Wisconsin will be regulated under the Food Distribution Administration's fluid milk conservation and control program, beginning November 1.

The new milk sales areas, the applicable Food Distribution Orders (in parentheses) and the market agent who will administer the program in each, are: Milwaukee, Metropolitan (FDO-79.80) and Racine-Kenosha (FDO-79.79), H. H. Erdmann, 135 S. LaSalle St., Chicago, Ill.; Evansville, Indiana (FDO-79.78), L. S. Iverson, 455 S. 4th Street, Louisville, Kentucky.

Under the program, milk dealers will be permitted to sell as much fluid milk as they sold in June and three-fourths as much cream and milk byproducts (such as cottage cheese, chocolate milk, and buttermilk) as they sold in June. Milk dealers include all persons or firms engaged in the sale or transfer of milk, but not such distributors as subhandlers ("peddlers"), retail stores, hotels, or restaurants.

Producer-distributors who purchase no milk will be permitted to sell as much milk as they produced in June.

A dealer may also increase his milk sales by reducing his cream and milk byproducts sales, and increase his sales of milk byproducts by reducing his cream sales, providing such an adjustment is approved in advance by the market agent for the area.

Deliveries of milk, cream, and milk byproducts to other dealers; to the Armed Forces, and to plants processing milk who do not distribute milk, cream or milk byproducts in the sales area are quota exempt.

Consumers in the milk sales areas named today and in others already designated generally will be able to purchase as much milk under the milk conservation program as they have been buying in recent months—within the limits of local supplies.

Fluid milk sales are being stabilized, Food Distribution Administration officials said, to help assure sufficient milk for manufacturing the cheese, butter, evaporated milk, and milk powder required by the Armed Services and civilians for good nutrition and properly balanced diets. Sales quotas on cream and on milk byproducts have been set below June deliveries to boost fluid milk supplies where production is low, and to conserve milk for manufacturing purposes.

FDO 79-78

AMDT. 1
NOV. 22, 1943

WAR FOOD ADMINISTRATION

[FDO 79-78, Amdt. 1]

PART 1401—DAIRY PRODUCTS

FLUID MILK AND CREAM IN EVANSVILLE, IND., SALES AREA

Pursuant to the authority vested in the Director by Food Distribution Order No. 79, dated September 7, 1943 (8 F.R. 12426), as amended, and to effectuate the purposes thereof, Director Food Distribution Order No. 79-78, § 1401.117, relative to the conservation of fluid milk in the Evansville, Indiana, milk sales area (8 F.R. 14599), issued by the Director of Food Distribution on October 26, 1943, is amended as follows:

The milk sales area described in § 1401.117 (b) of the original order is modified in the following particulars: Delete the phrase, "the magisterial districts of Upper Henderson and Lower Henderson in Henderson County, Kentucky," making the description of the sales area read as follows:

The city of Evansville and the townships of Center, German, Knight, Perry, and Pigeon in Vanderburgh County, Indiana.

Effective date. This amendment of FDO No. 79-78 shall become effective at 12:01 a. m., e. w. t., December 1, 1943.

(E.O. 9280, 8 F.R. 10179; E.O. 9322, 8 F.R. 3807; E.O. 9334, 8 F.R. 5423; E.O. 9392, 8 F.R. 14783; FDO 79, 8 F.R. 12426, 13283)

Issued this 22d day of November 1943.

ROY F. HENDRICKSON,
Director of Food Distribution.

FDO 79-78
AMDT. 2
MAR. 1, 1944

WAR FOOD ADMINISTRATION

[FDO 79-78, Amdt. 2]

PART 1401—DAIRY PRODUCTS

FLUID MILK AND CREAM IN EVANSVILLE, IND., SALES AREA

Pursuant to Food Distribution Order No. 79 (8 F.R. 12426), dated September 7, 1943, as amended, and to effectuate the purposes thereof, Food Distribution Order No. 79-78 (8 F.R. 14599), relative to the conservation and distribution of fluid milk in the Evansville, Indiana, milk sales area, issued by the Director of Food Distribution on October 26, 1943, as amended, is hereby further amended by deleting therefrom the provisions in § 1401.117 (i) and inserting, in lieu thereof, the following:

(i) *Quota exclusions and exemptions.* Deliveries of milk, milk byproducts, or cream (1) to other handlers, except for such deliveries to sub-handlers, (2) to plants engaged in the handling or processing of milk, milk byproducts, or cream from which no milk, milk byproducts or cream is delivered in the sales area, (3) to nursery, elementary, junior high, and high schools, and (4) to the agencies or groups specified in (d) of FDO 79, shall be excluded from the computation of deliveries in the base period and exempt from charges to quotas.

The provisions of this amendment shall become effective at 12:01 a. m., e.w.t., March 1, 1944. With respect to violations of said Food Distribution Order No. 79-78, as amended, rights accrued, or liabilities incurred prior to the effective time of this amendment, said Food Distribution Order No. 79-78, as amended, shall be deemed to be in full force and effect for the purpose of sustaining any proper suit, action, or other proceeding with respect to any such violation, right, or liability.

(E.O. 9280, 7 F.R. 10179; E.O. 9322, 8 F.R. 3807; E.O. 9334, 8 F.R. 5423; E.O. 9392, 8 F.R. 14783; FDO 79, 8 F.R. 12426, 13283)

Issued this 1st day of March 1944.

C. W. KITCHEN,
Acting Director of Food Distribution.

FDO 79-79

OCTOBER 26, 1943

WAR FOOD ADMINISTRATION

[FDO 79-79]

PART 1401—DAIRY PRODUCTS

FLUID MILK AND CREAM IN RACINE-KENOSHA, WIS., SALES AREA

Pursuant to the authority vested in me by Food Distribution Order No. 79 (8 F.R. 12426), issued on September 7, 1943, as amended, and to effectuate the purposes of such order, it is hereby ordered as follows:

§ 1401.106 *Quota restrictions*—(a) *Definitions.* When used in this order, unless otherwise distinctly expressed or manifestly incompatible with the intent hereof:

(1) Each term defined in Food Distribution Order No. 79, as amended, shall, when used herein, have the same meaning as is set forth for such term in Food Distribution Order No. 79, as amended.

(2) The term "FDO 79" means Food Distribution Order No. 79, issued on September 7, 1943, as amended.

(3) The term "sub-handler" means any handler, such as a peddler, vendor, sub-dealer, or secondary dealer, who purchases in a previously packaged and processed form milk, milk byproducts, or cream for delivery.

(b) *Milk sales area.* The following area is hereby designated as a "milk sales area" to be known as the Racine-Kenosha, Wisconsin, sales area, and is referred to hereinafter as the "sales area":

The city of Racine in Racine County; the city of Kenosha and the towns of Pleasant Prairie and Somers in Kenosha County; the towns of Caledonia and Mount Pleasant and the village of Sturtevant in Racine County, all in the State of Wisconsin.

(c) *Base period.* The calendar month of June 1943 is hereby designated as the base period for the sales area.

(d) *Quota period.* The remainder of the calendar month in which the provisions hereof become effective and each subsequent calendar month, respectively, is hereby designated as a quota period for the sales area.

(e) *Handler quotas.* Quotas for each handler in the sales area in each quota period shall be calculated in terms of pounds of each of the items for which percentages are specified in (3) below and shall be determined as follows:

(1) Divide the total deliveries of each such item made in the sales area by such handler during the base period, after excluding the quota-exempt deliveries described in (i) hereof, by the number of days in the base period;

(2) Multiply the result of the foregoing calculation by the number of days in the quota period;

(3) Multiply the aforesaid resulting amount by the following applicable percentage: (i) Milk: 100 percent; (ii) butterfat in milk: ------ percent; (iii) cream: 75 percent; (iv) butterfat in cream: 75 percent; (v) milk byproducts other than cottage, pot, or baker's cheese: 75 percent; and (vi) cottage, pot, or baker's cheese: 75 percent of skim milk equivalent. (For the purpose of this order, one pound of cottage, pot, or baker's cheese shall be considered as the equivalent of 7 pounds of skim milk.)

(f) *Quota limitations.* No handler shall, during any quota period, make deliveries in the sales area in excess of his respective quotas, except as set out in (i) hereof: *Provided,* That a handler may, after application to and approval by the market agent, secure an increase in milk quotas through an equivalent reduction as determined by the market agent, in cream and milk byproducts quotas, and an increase in milk byproducts quota through an equivalent reduction as determined by the market agent, in cream quotas.

(g) *Quotas for handlers who are also producers.* Quotas for handlers who are also producers and who purchase no milk shall be 100 percent of the total production of such handlers in the base period.

(h) *Handler exemptions.* Quotas shall not apply to any handler who delivers in a quota period a daily average of less than 150 units of milk, cream, and milk byproducts. For the purpose of this order, a unit shall be the equivalent in volume of the following: (1) Milk, one quart of milk; (2) cream, one-half pint of cream; and (3) milk byproduct, one quart of skim milk, buttermilk, flavored milk drink, or other beverage containing more than 85 percent of skim milk, or one-half pound of cottage, pot, or baker's cheese.

(i) *Quota exclusions and exemptions.* Deliveries of milk, milk byproducts, or cream (1) to other handlers, except for such deliveries to sub-handlers, (2) to plants engaged in the handling or processing of milk, milk byproducts, or cream from which no milk, milk byproducts, or cream is delivered in the sales area, and (3) to the agencies or groups specified in (d) of FDO 79, shall be excluded from the computation of deliveries in the base period and exempt from charges to quotas.

(j) *Transfers and apportionment of quotas.* The market agent is empowered to deduct an amount of base period deliveries to purchasers from the total of deliveries made by a handler or other person in the base period upon the application and a showing of unreasonable hardship by the handler making deliveries to such purchasers on the effective date of this order, and to add the amount of such deliveries to the total base period deliveries of the applicant handler. Denials of transfers or transfers granted by the market agent shall be reviewed by the Director upon application.

(k) *Petition for relief from hardships.* (1) Any person affected by FDO 79 or the provisions hereof who considers that compliance therewith would work an exceptional and unreasonable hardship on him, may file with the market agent a petition addressed to the Director. The petition shall contain the correct name, address and principal place of business of the petitioner, a full statement of the facts upon which the petition is based, and the hardship involved and the nature of the relief desired.

(2) Upon receiving such petition, the market agent shall immediately investigate the representations and facts stated therein.

(3) After investigation, the petition shall be certified to the Director, but prior to certification the market agent may (i) deny the petition, or (ii) grant temporary relief for a total period not to exceed 60 days.

(4) Denials or grants of relief by the market agent shall be reviewed by the Director and may be affirmed, modified, or reversed by the Director.

(l) *Reports.* Each handler shall transmit to the market agent on forms prescribed by the market agent the following reports:

(1) Within 20 days following the effective date of this order, reports which show the information required by the market agent to establish such handlers' quotas;

(2) Within 20 days following the close of each quota period, the information required by the market agent to establish volumes of deliveries of milk, cream, and milk byproducts during the preceding quota period; and

(3) Handlers exempt from quotas pursuant to (h) hereof shall, upon the request of the market agent, submit the information required by the market agent to establish volumes of deliveries of milk, cream, and milk byproducts.

(m) *Records.* Handlers shall keep and shall make available to the market agent such records of receipts, sales, deliveries, and production as the market agent shall require for the purpose of obtaining information which the Director may require for the establishment of quotas as prescribed in (b) of FDO 79.

(n) *Distribution schedules.* The distribution schedules, if any, to be followed by the handlers in making deliveries shall be made effective in the terms of approval by the Director of such schedules.

(o) *Expense of administration.* Each handler shall pay to the market agent, within 20 days after the close of each calendar month an assessment of $.01 per hundredweight of each of milk, cream, skim milk, buttermilk, flavored milk drinks, beverages containing more than 85 percent of skim milk, and skim milk equivalent of cottage, pot, or baker's cheese delivered during the preceding quota period and subject to quota regulations under the provisions hereof.

(p) *Violations.* The market agent shall report all violations to the Director together with the information required for the prosecution of such violations, except in a case where a handler has made deliveries in a quota period in excess of a quota in an amount not to exceed 5 percent of such quota, and in the succeeding quota period makes deliveries below that quota by at least the same percent.

(q) *Bureau of the Budget approval.* The record keeping and reporting requirements of this order have been approved by the Bureau of the Budget in accordance with the Federal Reports Act of 1942. Subsequent record keeping or reporting requirements will be subject to the approval of the Bureau of the Budget pursuant to the Federal Reports Act of 1942.

(r) This order shall take effect at 12:01 a. m., e. w. t., November 1, 1943.

Issued this 26th day of October 1943.

C. W. KITCHEN,
Acting Director of Food Distribution.

Press Release, Immediate:
Tuesday, October 26, 1943.

Milk sales in Evansville, Indiana, and 2 metropolitan areas in Wisconsin will be regulated under the Food Distribution Administration's fluid milk conservation and control program, beginning November 1.

The new milk sales areas, the applicable Food Distribution Orders (in parentheses) and the market agent who will administer the program in each, are: Milwaukee, Metropolitan (FDO-79.80) and Racine-Kenosha (FDO-79.79), H. H. Erdmann, 135 S. LaSalle St., Chicago, Ill.; Evansville, Indiana (FDO-79.78), L. S. Iverson, 455 S. 4th Street, Louisville, Kentucky.

Under the program, milk dealers will be permitted to sell as much fluid milk as they sold in June and three-fourths as much cream and milk byproducts (such as cottage cheese, chocolate milk, and buttermilk) as they sold in June. Milk dealers include all persons or firms engaged in the sale or transfer of milk, but not such distributors as subhandlers ("peddlers"), retail stores, hotels, or restaurants.

Producer-distributors who purchase no milk will be permitted to sell as much milk as they produced in June.

A dealer may also increase his milk sales by reducing his cream and milk byproducts sales, and increase his sales of milk byproducts by reducing his cream sales, providing such an adjustment is approved in advance by the market agent for the area.

Deliveries of milk, cream, and milk byproducts to other dealers; to the Armed Forces, and to plants processing milk who do not distribute milk, cream or milk byproducts in the sales area are quota exempt.

Consumers in the milk sales areas named today and in others already designated generally will be able to purchase as much milk under the milk conservation program as they have been buying in recent months—within the limits of local supplies.

Fluid milk sales are being stabilized, Food Distribution Administration officials said, to help assure sufficient milk for manufacturing the cheese, butter, evaporated milk, and milk powder required by the Armed Services and civilians for good nutrition and properly balanced diets. Sales quotas on cream and on milk byproducts have been set below June deliveries to boost fluid milk supplies where production is low, and to conserve milk for manufacturing purposes.

FDO 79-80

OCTOBER 26, 1943

WAR FOOD ADMINISTRATION

(1) Divide the total deliveries of each such item made in the sales area by such handler during the base period, after excluding the quota-exempt deliveries described in (i) hereof, by the number of days in the base period;

(2) Multiply the result of the foregoing calculation by the number of days in the quota period;

(3) Multiply the aforesaid resulting amount by the following applicable percentage: (i) Milk: 100 percent; (ii) butterfat in milk: ______ percent; (iii) cream: 75 percent; (iv) butterfat in cream: 75 percent; (v) milk byproducts other than cottage, pot, or baker's cheese: 75 percent; and (vi) cottage, pot, or baker's cheese: 75 percent of skim milk equivalent. (For the purpose of this order, one pound of cottage, pot, or baker's cheese shall be considered as the equivalent of 7 pounds of skim milk.)

(f) *Quota limitations.* No handler shall, during any quota period, make deliveries in the sales area in excess of his respective quotas, except as set out in (i) hereof: *Provided*, That a handler may, after application to and approval by the market agent, secure an increase in milk quotas through an equivalent reduction as determined by the market agent, in cream and milk byproducts quotas, and an increase in milk byproducts quota through an equivalent reduction as determined by the market agent, in cream quotas.

(g) *Quotas for handlers who are also producers.* Quotas for handlers who are also producers and who purchase no milk shall be 100 percent of the total production of such handlers in the base period.

(h) *Handler exemptions.* Quotas shall not apply to any handler who delivers in a quota period a daily average of less than 250 units of milk, cream, and milk byproducts. For the purpose of this order, a unit shall be the equivalent in volume of the following: (1) Milk, one quart of milk; (2) cream, one-half pint of cream; and (3) milk byproduct, one quart of skim milk, buttermilk, flavored milk drink, or other beverage containing more than 85 percent of skim milk, or one-half pound of cottage, pot, or bakers' cheese.

(i) *Quota exclusions and exemptions.* Deliveries of milk, milk byproducts, or cream (1) to other handlers, except for such deliveries to sub-handlers, (2) to plants engaged in the handling or processing of milk, milk byproducts, or cream from which no milk, milk byproducts, or cream is delivered in the sales area, and (3) to the agencies or groups specified in (d) of FDO 79, shall be excluded from the computation of deliveries in the base period and exempt from charges to quotas.

(j) *Transfers and apportionment of quotas.* The market agent is empowered to deduct an amount of base period deliveries to purchasers from the total of deliveries made by a handler or other person in the base period upon the application and a showing of unreasonable hardship by the handler making deliveries to such purchasers on the effective date of this order, and to add the amount of such deliveries to the total base period deliveries of the applicant handler. Denials of transfers or transfers granted by the market agent shall be reviewed by the Director upon application.

(k) *Petition for relief from hardships.* (1) Any person affected by FDO 79 or the provisions hereof who considers that compliance therewith would work an exceptional and unreasonable hardship on him, may file with the market agent a petition addressed to the Director. The petition shall contain the correct name, address and principal place of business of the petitioner, a full statement of the facts upon which the petition is based, and the hardship involved and the nature of the relief desired.

(2) Upon receiving such petition, the market agent shall immediately investigate the representations and facts stated therein.

(3) After investigation, the petition shall be certified to the Director, but prior to certification the market agent may (i) deny the petition, or (ii) grant temporary relief for a total period not to exceed 60 days.

(4) Denials or grants of relief by the market agent shall be reviewed by the Director and may be affirmed, modified, or reversed by the Director.

(l) *Reports.* Each handler shall transmit to the market agent on forms prescribed by the market agent the following reports:

(1) Within 20 days following the effective date of this order, reports which show the information required by the market agent to establish such handlers' quotas;

(2) Within 20 days following the close of each quota period, the information required by the market agent to establish volumes of deliveries of milk, cream, and milk byproducts during the preceding quota period; and

(3) Handlers exempt from quotas pursuant to (h) hereof shall, upon the request of the market agent, submit the in-

information required by the market agent to establish volumes of deliveries of milk, cream, and milk byproducts.

(m) *Records.* Handlers shall keep and shall make available to the market agent such records of receipts, sales, deliveries, and production as the market agent shall require for the purpose of obtaining information which the Director may require for the establishment of quotas as prescribed in (b) of FDO 79.

(n) *Distribution schedules.* The distribution schedules, if any, to be followed by the handlers in making deliveries shall be made effective in the terms of approval by the Director of such schedules.

(o) *Expense of administration.* Each handler shall pay to the market agent, within 20 days after the close of each calendar month an assessment of $.01 per hundredweight of each of milk, cream, skim milk, buttermilk, flavored milk drinks, beverages containing more than 85 percent of skim milk, and skim milk equivalent of cottage, pot, or baker's cheese delivered during the preceding quota period and subject to quota regulations under the provisions hereof.

(p) *Violations.* The market agent shall report all violations to the Director together with the information required for the prosecution of such violations, except in a case where a handler has made deliveries in a quota period in excess of a quota in an amount not to exceed 5 percent of such quota, and in the succeeding quota period makes deliveries below that quota by at least the same percent.

(q) *Bureau of the Budget approval.* The record keeping and reporting requirements of this order have been approved by the Bureau of the Budget in accordance with the Federal Reports Act of 1942. Subsequent record keeping or reporting requirements will be subject to the approval of the Bureau of the Budget pursuant to the Federal Reports Act of 1942.

(r) This order shall take effect at 12:01 a. m., e. w. t., November 1, 1943.

Issued this 26th day of October 1943.

C. W. KITCHEN,
Acting Director of Food Distribution.

Press Release, Immediate:
Tuesday, October 26, 1943.

Milk sales in Evansville, Indiana, and 2 metropolitan areas in Wisconsin will be regulated under the Food Distribution Administration's fluid milk conservation and control program, beginning November 1.

The new milk sales areas, the applicable Food Distribution Orders (in parentheses) and the market agent who will administer the program in each, are: Milwaukee, Metropolitan (FDO-79.80) and Racine-Kenosha (FDO-79.79), H. H. Erdmann, 135 S. LaSalle St., Chicago, Ill.; Evansville, Indiana (FDO-79.78), L. S. Iverson, 455 S. 4th Street, Louisville, Kentucky.

Under the program, milk dealers will be permitted to sell as much fluid milk as they sold in June and three-fourths as much cream and milk byproducts (such as cottage cheese, chocolate milk, and buttermilk) as they sold in June. Milk dealers include all persons or firms engaged in the sale or transfer of milk, but not such distributors as subhandlers ("peddlers"), retail stores, hotels, or restaurants.

Producer-distributors who purchase no milk will be permitted to sell as much milk as they produced in June.

A dealer may also increase his milk sales by reducing his cream and milk byproducts sales, and increase his sales of milk byproducts by reducing his cream sales, providing such an adjustment is approved in advance by the market agent for the area.

Deliveries of milk, cream, and milk byproducts to other dealers; to the Armed Forces, and to plants processing milk who do not distribute milk, cream or milk byproducts in the sales area are quota exempt.

Consumers in the milk sales areas named today and in others already designated generally will be able to purchase as much milk under the milk conservation program as they have been buying in recent months—within the limits of local supplies.

Fluid milk sales are being stabilized, Food Distribution Administration officials said, to help assure sufficient milk for manufacturing the cheese, butter, evaporated milk, and milk powder required by the Armed Services and civilians for good nutrition and properly balanced diets. Sales quotas on cream and on milk byproducts have been set below June deliveries to boost fluid milk supplies where production is low, and to conserve milk for manufacturing purposes.

FDO 79-80
AMDT. 1
NOV. 22, 1943

WAR FOOD ADMINISTRATION

[FDO 79-80, Amdt. 1]

PART 1401—DAIRY PRODUCTS

FLUID MILK AND CREAM IN MILWAUKEE, WIS., METROPOLITAN SALES AREA

Pursuant to the authority vested in the Director by Food Distribution Order No. 79, dated September 7, 1943 (8 F.R. 12426), as amended, and to effectuate the purposes thereof, Director Food Distribution Order No. 79-80, § 1401.99, relative to the conservation of fluid milk in the Milwaukee, Wisconsin, metropolitan milk sales area (8 F.R. 14601), issued by the Director of Food Distribution on October 26, 1943, is amended as follows:

The milk sales area described in § 1401.99 (b) of the original order is modified in the following particulars: Delete the description of the milk sales area and substitute in lieu thereof the following:

The city of Milwaukee; the counties of Milwaukee, Ozaukee, and Waukesha; the city of West Bend, the towns and villages of Barton, Farmington, Germantown, Jackson, Kewaskum, Polk, Richfield, Slinger, Trenton, and West Bend in Washington County; and the town of Raymond in Racine County, all in the State of Wisconsin.

Reduce the quota exemption specified in § 1401.99 (h) of the original order from 250 to 100 units, making the first sentence read as follows: "Quotas shall not apply to any handler who delivers in a quota period a daily average of less than 100 units of milk, cream, and milk byproducts."

Effective date. This amendment of FDO 79-80 shall become effective at 12:01 a. m., e. w. t., December 1, 1943.

(E.O. 9280, 8 F.R. 10179; E.O. 9322, 8 F.R. 3807; E.O. 9334, 8 F.R. 5423; E.O. 9392, 8 F.R. 14783; FDO 79, 8 F.R. 12426, 13283)

Issued this 22d day of November 1943.

ROY F. HENDRICKSON,
Director of Food Distribution.

FDO 79-81
OCTOBER 21, 1943

WAR FOOD ADMINISTRATION

[FDO 79-81]

PART 1401—DAIRY PRODUCTS

FLUID MILK AND CREAM IN NEW YORK-NEW JERSEY METROPOLITAN MILK SALES AREA

Pursuant to authority vested in me by Food Distribution Order No. 79 (8 F.R. 12426), issued September 7, 1943, as amended, and to effectuate the purposes of such order, it is hereby ordered as follows:

§ 1401.47 *Quota restrictions*—(a) *Definitions.* When used in this order, unless otherwise distinctly expressed or manifestly incompatible with the intent hereof:

(1) Each term defined in Food Distribution Order No. 79, as amended, shall, when used herein, have the same meaning as is set forth for such term in Food Distribution Order No. 79, as amended;

(2) The term "Food Distribution Order No. 79" means Food Distribution Order No. 79, issued on September 7, 1943, as amended;

(3) The term "skim milk beverage" means skim milk, buttermilk, chocolate drink, or any other beverage containing more than 85 percent skim milk and less than 3 percent butterfat;

(4) The term "sour cream" means cream which has been fermented by means of a lactic acid or other harmless milk culture, and which is commonly sold under the name of sour cream.

(5) The term "regulated", when used in conjunction with the term "milk," "cream other than sour cream," "sour cream," "skim milk beverage," "cottage, pot, or baker's cheese," or "product," means milk, cream other than sour cream, sour cream, skim milk beverage, cottage, pot, or baker's cheese, or product, delivered to retail purchasers, to stores, to public eating places, to other wholesale purchasers, and to subhandlers for which latter no bases and quotas have been established;

(6) The term "retail purchaser" means any person who purchases milk, milk byproducts, or cream, including sour cream, at retail for personal, family, or household consumption;

(7) The term "store" means a merchandising establishment of fixed situs, the operator of which purchases milk and other food products for resale primarily for consumption off the premises;

(8) The term "public eating place" means any place in which food, prepared and ready for sale or consumption either on or off the premises where sold, is served, sold, or offered for sale; and such term includes, but is not necessarily limited to, any hotel, club, restaurant, cafe, cafeteria, caterer, inn, railroad diner, lunch room, sandwich stand, or drug store which serves, sells, or offers food for sale, as aforesaid. Any institution of voluntary or involuntary confinement, such as a hospital, sanitarium (or sanatorium), asylum, penal institution, or school, is not a "public eating place";

(9) The term "wholesale purchaser" means any person who purchases milk, milk byproducts, or cream, including sour cream, for purposes of resale, or use in other than personal, family, or household consumption, except (i) other handlers, (ii) purchasers engaged in the processing of milk, milk byproducts, or cream who do not distribute milk, milk byproducts, or cream, including sour cream, in the sales area, (iii) those purchasers specifically exempt from quota restrictions by Food Distribution Order No. 79 (iv) nursery, elementary, junior high and high school, and (v) hospitals.

(10) The term "producer-handler" means a handler who delivers milk produced only by his own herd and in a total quantity of less than 600 quarts per day;

(11) The term "subhandler" means a handler, such as a peddler or subdealer, who purchases milk in the same package in which it is delivered to purchasers: *Provided*, That a handler who handles more than 1,000 quarts of milk per day, or more than 500 quarts of cream per day, shall not be deemed a subhandler;

(12) The term "product" means milk, cream other than sour cream, sour cream, skim milk beverage, or cottage, pot, or baker's cheese;

(13) The term "b. f." used in connection with the title of the conversion table in (o) hereof means butter fat.

(b) *Milk sales area.* The following area is hereby designated as a milk sales area to be known as the New York-New Jersey Metropolitan Milk Sales Area and referred to hereinafter as the "sales area":

In the State of New York: City of New York; Nassau County; Rockland County; Suffolk County (except Fisher's Island); and Westchester County. In the State of New Jersey: Bergen County; Essex County; Hudson County; Union County; Middlesex County (except Cranbury township, Plainsboro township, and South Brunswick); Monmouth County (except Allentown borough, Atlantic township, Englishtown borough, Farmingdale borough, Freehold borough, Freehold township, Holmdel township, Howell township, Jersey Homesteads borough, Manalapan township, Marlboro township, Millstone township, Shrewbury township, Upper Freehold township, and Wall township); Morris County (except Chester borough, Chester township, Dover town, Jefferson township, Mendham borough, Mendham township, Mine hill township, Mount Arlington borough, Mount Olive township, Netcong borough, Randolph township, Rockaway township, Roxbury township, Washington township, and Wharton borough); and Passaic County (except Ringwood borough, and West Milford township.) The following minor civil divisions of Somerset County: Bound Brook borough, Green Brook township, North Plainfield borough, South Bound Brook borough, and Watchung borough, all in the State of New Jersey.

(c) *Bases and base period.* The handler's daily average delivery of each regulated product in the base period adjusted for transfers in accordance with (h) hereof shall be his base. The base for milk and skim milk beverages shall be computed in terms of quarts, for cream (including sour cream) in terms of milk equivalent in accordance with the conversion table set forth in (o) hereof, and for cottage, pot, or baker's cheese in terms of pounds of product. The calendar month of June 1943 is hereby designated as the base period for the sales area.

(d) *Quota periods.* The remainder of the calendar month in which this order becomes effective and each subsequent calendar month is hereby designated as a quota period for the sales area.

(e) *Handler quotas.* No handler shall deliver during any quota period a quantity of any regulated product in excess of his base for that product, multiplied by the number of days in the quota period and by the following applicable percentages: (1) Milk, 100 percent; (2) milk equivalent of cream other than sour cream, 75 percent; (3) milk equivalent of sour cream, 75 percent; (4) skim milk beverages, 75 percent; (5) cottage, pot or baker's cheese: 75 percent: *Provided*, That a handler may, upon application to and approval by the market agent, secure an increase in milk quota through an equivalent reduction in cream and milk byproduct quotas.

(f) *Producer-handler quotas.* Each producer-handler's quota shall be 100 percent of milk produced.

(g) *Subhandler quotas.* No bases or quotas shall be established for deliveries by subhandlers except as provided in (h) hereof.

(h) *Transfer and apportionment of bases and quotas.* The market agent is empowered to transfer bases upon application by a handler making the deliveries from which such bases were derived on the effective date of this order and upon a showing of unreasonable hardship by the applicant. Upon application by a subhandler, the market agent is empowered to transfer from a handler to such subhandler that part of the handler's base and quota derived from delivery in the base period by such handler to such subhandler.

Denials or grants of transfers by the market agent shall be reviewed by the Director upon application.

(i) The distribution schedules, if any, to be followed by the handlers in making deliveries shall be made effective in the terms of approval by the Director of such schedules.

(j) *Petition for relief from hardship.* Any person considering that compliance with Food Distribution Order No. 79, or any instrument issued thereunder, would work an exceptional and unreasonable hardship on him, may file with the market agent a petition addressed to the Director. The petition shall contain the correct name, address and principal place of business of the petitioner, a full statement of the facts upon which the petition is based, and the hardship involved and the nature of the relief desired.

Upon receiving such petition, the market agent shall immediately investigate the representations and facts stated therein.

(j-1) *Relief.* After investigation, the market agent shall certify the petition to the Director, but prior to certification the market agent may:

(1) Deny the petition; or

(2) Grant temporary relief for a total period not to exceed 60 days.

Denials or grant of relief by the market agent shall be reviewed by the Director, and may be affirmed, modified or reversed by him.

(k) *Reports.* Each handler shall transmit to the market agent on forms prescribed by the market agent the following reports:

(1) Within 20 days following the effective date of this order, reports which show the information required by the market agent to establish such handlers' bases;

(2) Within 20 days following the close of each quota period, the information required by the market agent to establish volumes of deliveries of milk, cream, and milk byproducts during the preceding quota period; and

(3) Handlers whose deliveries are exempt from quotas shall, upon request of the market agent, submit the information required by the market agent to establish volumes of deliveries of milk, cream, and milk byproducts.

(l) *Records.* Handlers shall keep and shall make available to the market agent such records of receipts, sales, deliveries, and production as the market agent shall request for the purpose of obtaining information which the Director may require for the establishment of quotas as prescribed in (b) of Food Distribution Order No. 79 and which is necessary to verify compliance with the provisions of this order.

(m) *Expense of administration.* Each handler except producer-handlers and subhandlers having no bases and quotas shall pay to the market agent at the time of filing the reports required under (k) (2), an assessment of 2 cents per 100 quarts of regulated milk, or milk equivalent of cream delivered during the quota period. Whenever verification by the market agent of information supplied by a handler discloses errors in assessment payment to the market agent, he shall bill the handler for any unpaid amount, and the handler shall, within 5 days, make payment to the market agent of the amount so billed. Whenever verification discloses that the handler made an overpayment, the market agent shall, within 5 days, return such overpayment to such handler.

(n) *Liquidation.* Upon the termination or suspension hereof, the market agent shall, if so directed by the Director, liquidate the business of the market agent's office and dispose of all funds and property then in his possession or under his control, together with claims receivable, unpaid and owing at the time of such termination or suspension. Any funds over and above the amounts necessary to meet outstanding obligations and the expenses necessarily incurred by the market agent in liquidating the business of the market agent's office shall be distributed by the market agent in accordance with instructions issued by the Director.

(c) *Conversion table.*

QUARTS OF 3.5 PERCENT B. F. MILK EQUIVALENT OF A QUART OF CREAM AT VARIOUS BUTTERFAT TESTS

Cream (percent b. f.):	*Milk equivalent (quarts)*
6	1.71
7	2.00
8	2.28
9	2.56
10	2.85
11	3.13
12	3.41
13	3.69
14	3.98
15	4.26
16	4.54
17	4.82
18	5.10
19	5.38
20	5.65
21	5.93
22	6.21
23	6.49
24	6.76
25	7.04
26	7.31
27	7.58
28	7.85
29	8.13
30	8.40
31	8.67
32	8.95
33	9.22
34	9.50
35	9.77
36	10.04
37	10.31
38	10.58
39	10.85
40	11.12
41	11.39
42	11.66
43	11.93
44	12.20
45	12.47
46	12.74
47	13.00
48	13.27
49	13.54
50	13.80
51	14.07
52	14.34
53	14.60
54	14.86
55	15.13

(p) *Bureau of the Budget approval.* The record-keeping and reporting requirements of this order have been approved by the Bureau of the Budget in accordance with the Federal Reports Act of 1942. Subsequent record-keeping or reporting requirements will be subject to the approval of the Bureau of the Budget pursuant to the Federal Reports Act of 1942.

(q) *Violations.* The market agent shall report all violations to the Director together with the information required for the prosecution of such violations, except in a case where a handler has made deliveries in a quota period in excess of a quota in an amount not to exceed 5 percent of such quota, and in the succeeding quota period makes deliveries below that quota by at least the same percent.

(r) *Effective date.* This order shall become effective at 12:01 a. m., e. w. t., November 1, 1943.

Issued this 21st day of October 1943.

ROY F. HENDRICKSON,
Director of Food Distribution.

Press Release, Immediate:
Friday, October 22, 1943

Milk dealers in Metropolitan New York City and northern New Jersey will be assigned quotas (by the WFA) representing the maximum quantities of milk, cream and milk byproducts which they may sell each month beginning November 1.

Under the quotas, dealers will be permitted to sell as much fluid milk as they sold in June and three-fourths as much cream, sour cream, skim milk beverages (including skim milk, chocolate milk and buttermilk), and cottage, pot and bakers' cheese as they sold in June. Milk dealers include all persons or firms engaged in the sale or transfer of milk, but not such distributors as subhandlers ("peddlers") who deliver less than 1,000 quarts of milk or 500 quarts of cream a day, retail stores, hotels, or restaurants.

Dealers will be allowed to exceed these base quotas by not more than 5 percent during any month, without being reported in violation, providing they decrease their deliveries the next month by the same amount.

A dealer may increase his milk sales also by reducing his cream and milk byproduct sales, providing such an adjustment is approved by the market agent for the area. Dr. C. J. Blanford, 205 E. 42nd St., New York City, will administer the Food Distribution Administration's fluid milk conservation and control program in the New York-New Jersey Metropolitan milk sales area.

Producer-distributors, defined for this area as those who purchase no milk and sell less than 600 quarts a day, may sell as much milk as their herds produce.

Deliveries of milk, cream, and milk byproducts to nursery, elementary, junior high, high schools; to hospitals; to plants processing milk who do not distribute milk, cream, or other milk products in the sales area; to the Armed Forces, and to other milk handlers are quota-exempt.

To facilitate administration, the market agent may act upon petitions for relief from hardship. If investigation warrants such action, he may grant temporary relief for a total period not to exceed 60 days.

Quotas assigned to dealers' deliveries in previously named milk sales areas are the same as for the New York-New Jersey area except that in the latter area, sour cream is classed separately from cream; and skim milk beverages, and cottage, pot and baker's cheese are recognized as two distinct classes of milk byproducts.

serve

/

7337

FDO 79-81

AMDT. 1
NOV. 30, 1943

WAR FOOD ADMINISTRATION

A

[FDO 79-81, Amdt. 1]

PART 1401—DAIRY PRODUCTS

FLUID MILK AND CREAM IN NEW YORK-NEW JERSEY METROPOLITAN MILK SALES AREA

Pursuant to the authority vested in the Director by Food Distribution Order No. 79, dated September 7, 1943, (8 F.R. 12426), as amended, and to effectuate the purposes thereof, Food Distribution Order No. 79-81, § 1401.47 relative to the conservation of fluid milk in the New York-New Jersey metropolitan milk sales area (8 F.R. 14373), issued by the Director of Food Distribution on October 21, 1943, is amended as follows:

1. By deleting the provisions in (a) (9) of said order and inserting, in lieu thereof, the following:

(9) The term "wholesale purchasers" means any person who purchases milk, milk byproducts or cream, including sour cream, for purposes of resale, or use in other than personal, family, or household consumption, except (i) other handlers; (ii) purchasers engaged in the processing of milk, milk byproducts, or cream, who do not distribute milk, milk byproducts, or cream, including sour cream, in the sales area; (iii) industrial users; (iv) those purchasers specifically exempt from quota restrictions by FDO 79; (v) nursery, elementary, junior high, and high schools; and (vi) hospitals.

2. By inserting in said order an additional definition to be designated as (a) (14):

(14) The term "industrial user" means a person, as determined by the market agent, who uses milk, cream (sweet or sour), skim milk beverage, and cottage, pot, or bakers' cheese, in making other foods and who sells such foods primarily for resale to consumers off the premises where made.

Effective date. This amendment shall become effective at 12:01 a. m., e. w. t., December 1, 1943. With respect to violations, rights accrued, or liabilities incurred prior to the effective time of this amendment, the aforesaid orders issued by the Director shall be deemed to be in full force and effect for the purpose of sustaining any proper suit, action, or other proceeding with respect to any such violation, right, or liability.

(E.O. 9280, 8 F.R. 10179; E.O. 9322, 8 F.R. 3807; E.O. 9334, 8 F.R. 5423; E.O. 9392, 8 F.R. 14783; FDO 79, 8 F.R. 12426, 13283.)

Issued this 30th day of November, 1943.

C. W. KITCHEN,
Acting Director of Food Distribution.

FDO 79-82
OCTOBER 28, 1943

WAR FOOD ADMINISTRATION

[FDO 79-82]

PART 1401—DAIRY PRODUCTS

DELEGATION OF AUTHORITY WITH RESPECT TO FLUID MILK AND CREAM

Pursuant to the authority vested in the Director by Food Distribution Order No. 79, issued by the War Food Administrator on September 7, 1943, as amended (8 F. R. 13283), and in order to effectuate the purposes thereof, it is hereby ordered as follows:

§ 1401.115 *Delegation of authority*—(a) *Definitions.* When used herein, unless otherwise distinctly expressed or manifestly incompatible with the intent hereof:

(1) The term "FDO 79" means Food Distribution Order No. 79, issued by the War Food Administrator on September 7, 1943, as amended.

(2) Each term defined in FDO 79 shall, when used herein, have the same meaning as set forth in said FDO 79.

(b) *Authority delegated.* The authority vested in the Director with respect to petitions for relief from hardship, submitted pursuant to FDO 79 or any Director's order issued thereunder, is hereby delegated to the Chief of the Dairy and Poultry Branch, Food Distribution Administration.

(c) *Retention of authority by Director.* Nothing contained herein shall be construed to abrogate any power or authority vested in the Director by FDO 79.

(d) *Effective date.* The provisions hereof shall become effective at 12:01 a. m., e. w. t., October 28, 1943.

(E.O. 9280, 7 F.R. 10179; E.O. 9322, 8 F.R. 3807; E.O. 9334, 8 F.R. 5423; FDO 79, 8 F.R. 12426, 13283)

Issued this 28th day of October 1943.

ROY F. HENDRICKSON,
Director of Food Distribution.

erve

FDO 79-83

OCTOBER 28, 1943

WAR FOOD ADMINISTRATION

[FDO 79-83]

PART 1401—DAIRY PRODUCTS

FLUID MILK AND CREAM IN PORTLAND, MAINE, SALES AREA

Pursuant to the authority vested in me by Food Distribution Order No. 79 (8 F.R. 12426), issued on September 7, 1943, as amended, and to effectuate the purposes of such order, it is hereby ordered as follows:

§ 1401.116 *Quota restrictions*—(a) *Definitions.* When used in this order, unless otherwise distinctly expressed or manifestly incompatible with the intent hereof:

(1) Each term defined in Food Distribution Order No. 79, as amended, shall, when used herein, have the same meaning as is set forth for such term in Food Distribution Order No. 79, as amended.

(2) The term "FDO 79" means Food Distribution Order No. 79, issued on September 7, 1943, as amended.

(3) The term "sub-handler" means any handler, such as a peddler, vendor, sub-dealer, or secondary dealer, who purchases in a previously packaged and processed form milk, milk byproducts, or cream for delivery.

(b) *Milk sales area.* The following area is hereby designated as a "milk sales area" to be known as the Portland, Maine, sales area, and is referred to hereinfter as the "sales area":

The cities of Portland, South Portland and Westbrook, and the towns of Cape Elizabeth and Falmouth, all in Cumberland County, Maine.

(c) *Base period.* The calendar month of June 1943 is hereby designated as the base period for the sales area.

(d) *Quota period.* The remainder of the calendar month in which the provisions hereof become effective and each subsequent calendar month, respectively, is hereby designated as a quota period for the sales area.

(e) *Handler quotas.* Quotas for each handler in the sales area in each quota period shall be calculated in terms of pounds of each of the items for which percentages are specified in (3) below and shall be determined as follows:

(1) Divide the total deliveries of each such item made in the sales area by such handler during the base period, after excluding the quota-exempt deliveries described in (i) hereof, by the number of days in the base period;

(2) Multiply the result of the foregoing calculation by the number of days in the quota period;

(3) Multiply the aforesaid resulting amount by the following applicable percentage: (i) Milk: 100 percent, (ii) butterfat in milk: ------ percent; (iii) cream: 75 percent; (iv) butterfat in cream: 75 percent; (v) milk byproducts other than cottage, pot, or baker's cheese: 75 percent; and (vi) cottage, pot, or baker's cheese: 75 percent of skim milk equivalent. (For the purpose of this order, one pound of cottage, pot, or baker's cheese shall be considered as the equivalent of 7 pounds of skim milk.)

(f) *Quota limitations.* No handler shall, during any quota period, make deliveries in the sales area in excess of his respective quotas, except as set out in (i) hereof: *Provided,* That a handler may, after application to and approval by the market agent, secure an increase in milk quotas through an equivalent reduction as determined by the market agent, in cream and milk byproducts quotas, and an increase in milk byproducts quota through an equivalent reduetion as determined by the market agent, in cream quotas.

(g) *Quotas for handlers who are also producers.* Quotas for handlers who are also producers and who purchase no milk shall be 100 percent of the total production of such handlers in the base period.

(h) *Handler exemptions.* Quotas shall not apply to any handler who delivers in a quota period a daily average of less than 200 units of milk, cream, and milk byproducts. For the purpose of this order, a unit shall be the equivalent in the volume of the following: (1) Milk, one quart of milk; (2) cream, one-half pint of cream; and (3) milk byproduct, one quart of skim milk, buttermilk, flavored milk drink, or other beverage containing more than 85 percent of skim milk, or one-half pound of cottage, pot, or baker's cheese.

(i) *Quota exclu 'ons and exemptions.* Deliveries of milk, milk byproducts, or cream (1) to other handlers, except for such deliveries to sub-handlers, (2) to plants engaged in the handling or processing of milk, milk byproducts, or cream from which no milk, milk byproducts, or cream is delivered in the sales area, and (3) to the agencies or groups specified in (d) of FDO 79, shall be excluded from the computation of deliveries in the base period and exempt from charges to quotas.

(j) *Transfers and apportionment of quotas.* The market agent is empowered to deduct an amount of base period deliveries to purchasers from the total of deliveries made by a handler or other person in the base period upon the application and a showing of unreasonable hardship by the handler making deliveries to such purchasers on the effective date of this order, and to add the amount of such deliveries to the total base period deliveries of the applicant handler. Denials of transfers or transfers granted by the market agent shall be reviewed by the Director upon application.

(k) *Petition for relief from hardships.* (1) Any person affected by FDO 79 or the provisions hereof who considers that compliance therewith would work an exceptional and unreasonable hardship on him, may file with the market agent a petition addressed to the Director. The petition shall contain the correct name, address and principal place of business of the petitioner, a full statement of the facts upon which the petition is based, and the hardship involved and the nature of the relief desired.

(2) Upon receiving such petition, the market agent shall immediately investigate the representations and facts stated therein.

(3) After investigation, the petition shall be certified to the Director, but prior to certification the market agent may (i) deny the petition, or (ii) grant temporary relief for a total period not to exceed 60 days.

(4) Denials or grants of relief by the market agent shall be reviewed by the Director and may be affirmed, modified, or reversed by the Director.

(l) *Reports.* Each handler shall transmit to the market agent on forms prescribed by the market agent the following reports:

(1) Within 20 days following the effective date of this order, reports which show the information required by the market agent to establish such handlers' quotas:

(2) Within 20 days following the close of each quota period, the information required by the market agent to establish volumes of deliveries of milk, cream, and milk byproducts during the preceding quota period; and

(3) Handlers exempt from quotas pursuant to (h) hereof shall, upon the request of the market agent, submit the information required by the market agent to establish volumes of deliveries of milk, cream, and milk byproducts.

(m) *Records.* Handlers shall keep and shall make available to the market agent such records of receipts, sales, deliveries, and production as the market agent shall require for the purpose of obtaining information which the Director may require for the establishment of quotas as prescribed in (b) of FDO 79.

(n) *Distribution schedules.* The distribution schedules, if any, to be followed by the handlers in making deliveries shall be made effective in the terms of approval by the Director of such schedules.

(o) *Expense of administration.* Each handler shall pay to the market agent, within 20 days after the close of each calendar month an assessment of $.015 per hundredweight of each of milk, cream, skim milk, buttermilk, flavored milk drinks, beverages containing more than 85 percent of skim milk, and skim milk equivalent of cottage, pot, or baker's cheese delivered during the preceding quota period and subject to quota regulations under the provisions hereof.

(p) *Violations.* The market agent shall report all violations to the Director together with the information required for the prosecution of such violations, except in a case where a handler has made deliveries in a quota period in excess of a quota in an amount not to exceed 5 percent of such quota, and in the succeeding quota period makes deliveries below that quota by at least the same percent.

(q) *Bureau of the Budget approval.* The record keeping and reporting requirements of this order have been approved by the Bureau of the Budget in accordance with the Federal Reports Act of 1942. Subsequent record keeping or reporting requirements will be subject to the approval of the Bureau of the Budget pursuant to the Federal Reports Act of 1942.

(r) This order shall take effect at 12:01 a. m., e. w. t., November 1, 1943.

Issued this 28th day of October 1943.

C. W. KITCHEN,
Acting Director of Food Distribution.

Press Release Immediate:
Friday, October 29, 1943

Milk sales in 5 areas in California, Iowa, Maine, Michigan, and Ohio will be regulated under the Food Distribution Administration's fluid milk conservation and control program.

The new milk sales areas, the applicable Food Distribution Order (in parentheses), and the market agents who will administer the program in each are:

Stockton, Calif., (FDO 79.84) Ernest L. Vehlow, Mull Building, Sacramento, Calif.

Sioux City, Iowa, Metropolitan (FDO 79.85) Wayne McPherren, Post Office Building, Omaha, Nebr.

Portland, Maine (FDO 79.83) Samuel Tator, 80 Federal Street, Boston, Mass.

Kalamazoo, Mich. (FDO 79.87) M. E. Drake, 116 S. William Street, South Bend, Ind.

Springfield Ohio (FDO 79.86) Fred W. Issler, 152 E. 4th Street, Cincinnati, Ohio.

The program will take effect November 1 in Portland, Maine and November 7 in the other areas.

Under the program milk dealers will be permitted to sell as much fluid milk as they sold in June and three-fourths as much cream and milk byproducts (such as cottage cheese, chocolate milk, and buttermilk) as they sold in June. Milk dealers include all persons or firms engaged in the sale or transfer of milk, but not such distributors as subhandlers ("peddlers"), retail stores, hotels, or restaurants.

WAR FOOD ADMINISTRATION
Food Distribution Administration
Washington 25, D. C.

/

CORRECTION NOTICE - FDO-79.83 Amendment 1.
Dairy Products

In printing Food Distribution Order No. 79.83 Amendment 1 the following error occurred:

In paragraph (b) Effective date-"FDO No. 79.116." Should read "FDO No. 79.83."

7337
2d ...

FDO 79-83

AMDT. 1
NOV. 30, 1943

WAR FOOD ADMINISTRATION

[FDO 79-83, Amdt. 1]

PART 1401—DAIRY PRODUCTS

DIRECTOR'S ORDER FOR THE PORTLAND, ME., MILK SALES AREA

Pursuant to the authority vested in the Director by Food Distribution Order No. 79, dated September 7, 1943 (8 F.R. 12426), as amended, and to effectuate the purposes thereof, Food Distribution Order No. 79-83, § 1401.116, relative to the conservation of fluid milk in the Portland, Maine, milk sales area (8 F.R. 14654), issued by the Director of Food Distribution on October 28, 1943, is amended as follows:

The quotas for handlers who are also producers, described in § 1401.116 (g) of the original order, is modified in the following particulars: Strike out (g) and insert in lieu thereof the following:

(g) *Quotas for handlers who are also producers.*—Quotas for handlers who are also producers and who purchase no milk shall be computed in accordance with (e) hereof, except that the applicable percentages shall be 100 percent in lieu of the percentages specified in (e) (3).

(b) *Effective date.*—This amendment of FDO No. 79.116 shall become effective at 12:01 a. m., e. w. t., December 1, 1943.

(E.O. 9280, 7 F.R. 10179; E.O. 9322, 8 F.R. 3807; E.O. 9334, 8 F.R. 5423; E.O. 9392, 8 F.R. 14783; FDO 79, 8 F.R. 12426, 13283)

Issued this 30th day of November 1943.

C. W. KITCHEN,
Acting Director of Food Distribution.

3 ✓
.1

FDO 79-83

AMDT. 2
JAN. 27, 1944

WAR FOOD ADMINISTRATION

[FDO 79-83, Amdt. 2]

PART 1401—DAIRY PRODUCTS

FLUID MILK AND CREAM IN PORTLAND, MAINE, SALES AREA

Pursuant to Food Distribution Order No. 79 (8 F.R. 12426), dated September 7, 1943, as amended, and to effectuate the purposes thereof, Food Distribution Order No. 79-83 (8 F.R. 14654), relative to the conservation and distribution of fluid milk in the Portland, Maine, milk sales area, issued by the Director of Food Distribution on October 28, 1943, as amended, is hereby further amended by deleting therefrom the description of the sales area in § 1401.116 (b) and inserting, in lieu thereof, the following:

The cities of Portland, South Portland, and Westbrook and the towns of Cape Elizabeth, Cumberland, Falmouth, and Scarborough in Cumberland County, and the town of Old Orchard Beach in York County, all in the State of Maine.

The provisions of this amendment shall become effective at 12:01 a. m., e. w. t., February 1, 1944. With respect to violations of said Food Distribution Order No. 79-83, as amended, rights accrued, or liabilities incurred prior to the effective time of this amendment, said Food Distribution Order No. 79-83, as amended, shall be deemed to be in full force and effect for the purpose of sustaining any proper suit, action, or other proceeding with respect to any such violation, right, or liability.

(E.O. 9280, 7 F.R. 10179; E.O. 9322, 8 F.R. 3807; E.O. 9334, 8 F.R. 5423; E.O. 9392, 8 F.R. 14783; FDO 79, 8 F.R. 12426, 13283)

Issued this 27th day of January 1944.

LEE MARSHALL,
Director of Food Distribution.

serve

FDO 79-83
AMDT. 3
FEB. 28, 1944

WAR FOOD ADMINISTRATION

[FDO 79-83, Amdt. 3]

PART 1401—DAIRY PRODUCTS

FLUID MILK AND CREAM IN PORTLAND, MAINE, SALES AREA

Pursuant to Food Distribution Order No. 79 (8 F.R. 12426), dated September 7, 1943, as amended, and to effectuate the purposes thereof, Food Distribution Order No. 79-83 (8 F.R. 14654), relative to the conservation and distribution of fluid milk in the Portland, Maine, milk sales area, issued by the Director of Food Distribution on October 28, 1943, as amended, is hereby further amended by deleting therefrom the provisions in § 1401.116 (a) (3) and inserting, in lieu thereof, the following:

(3) The term "sub-handler" means any handler, who (i) receives in a previously packaged and processed form milk, milk byproducts, or cream for delivery, and (ii) does not operate facilities for the processing and bottling of fluid milk.

The provisions of this amendment shall become effective at 12:01 a. m., e. w. t., March 1, 1944. With respect to violations of said Food Distribution Order No. 79-83, as amended, rights accrued, or liabilities incurred prior to the effective time of this amendment, said Food Distribution Order No. 79-83, as amended, shall be deemed to be in full force and effect for the purpose of sustaining any proper suit, action, or other proceeding with respect to any such violation, right, or liability.

(E.O. 9280, 7 F.R. 10179; E.O. 9322, 8 F.R. 3807; E.O. 9334, 8 F.R. 5423; E.O. 9392, 8 F.R. 14783; FDO 79, 8 F.R. 12426, 13283)

Issued this 28th day of February 1944.

C. W. KITCHEN,
Acting Director of Food Distribution.

FDO 79-83
AMDT. 4
MAR. 29, 1944

WAR FOOD ADMINISTRATION

[FDO 79-83, Amdt. 4]

PART 1401—DAIRY PRODUCTS

FLUID MILK AND CREAM IN PORTLAND, MAINE, SALES AREA

Pursuant to Food Distribution Order No. 79 (8 F.R. 12426), dated September 7, 1943, as amended, and to effectuate the purposes thereof, Food Distribution Order No. 79-83 (8 F.R. 14654), relative to the conservation and distribution of fluid milk in the Portland, Maine, milk sales area, issued by the Director of Food Distribution on October 28, 1943, as amended, is hereby further amended by deleting therefrom the provisions in § 1401.116 (i) and inserting, in lieu thereof, the following:

(i) *Quota exclusions and exemptions.* Deliveries of milk, milk byproducts, or cream (1) to other handlers, except for such deliveries to sub-handlers, (2) to plants engaged in the handling or processing of milk, milk byproducts, or cream from which no milk, milk byproducts, or cream is delivered in the sales area, (3) to nursery, elementary, junior high, and high schools, and (4) to the agencies or groups specified in (d) of FDO 79, shall be excluded from the computation of deliveries in the base period and exempt from charges to quotas.

The provisions of this amendment shall become effective at 12:01 a. m., e. w. t., April 1, 1944. With respect to violations of said Food Distribution Order No. 79-83, as amended, rights accrued, or liabilities incurred prior to the effective time of this amendment, said Food Distribution Order No. 79-83, as amended, shall be deemed to be in full force and effect for the purpose of sustaining any proper suit, action, or other proceeding with respect to any such violation, right, or liability.

(E.O. 9280, 7 F.R. 10179; E.O. 9322, 8 F.R. 3807; E.O. 9334, 8 F.R. 5423; E.O. 9392, 8 F.R. 14783; FDO 79, 8 F.R. 12426, 13283)

Issued this 29th day of March 1944.

LEE MARSHALL,
Director of Food Distribution.

WAR FOOD ADMINISTRATION

[FDO 79-84]

PART 1401—DAIRY PRODUCTS

FLUID MILK AND CREAM IN STOCKTON, CALIF., SALES AREA

Pursuant to the authority vested in me by Food Distribution Order No. 79 (8 F.R. 12426), issued on September 7, 1943, as amended, and to effectuate the purposes of such order, it is hereby ordered as follows:

§ 1401.118 *Quota restricting*—(a) *Definitions.* When used in this order, unless otherwise distinctly expressed or manifestly incompatible with the intent hereof:

(1) Each term defined in Food Distribution Order No. 79, as amended, shall, when used herein, have the same meaning as is set forth for such term in Food Distribution Order No. 79, as amended.

(2) The term "FDO 79" means Food Distribution Order No. 79, issued on September 7, 1943, as amended.

(3) The term "sub-handler" means any handler, such as a peddler, vendor, sub-dealer, or secondary dealer, who purchases in a previously packaged and processed form milk, milk byproducts, or cream for delivery.

(b) *Milk sales area.* The following area is hereby designated as a "milk sales area" to be known as the Stockton, California, sales area, and is referred to hereinafter as the 'sales area":

The entire area included in the marketing area now designated by the Director of Agriculture of the State of California pursuant to the provisions of Chapter 10, Division 4, of the Agricultural Code of the State of California, as the San Joaquin County Marketing Area.

(c) *Base period.* The calendar month of June 1943 is hereby designated as the base period for the sales area.

(d) *Quota period.* The remainder of the calendar month in which the provisions hereof become effective and each subsequent calendar month, respectively, is hereby designated as a quota period for the sales area.

(e) *Handler quotas.* Quotas for each handler in the sales area in each quota period shall be calculated in terms of pounds of each of the items for which percentages are specified in (3) below and shall be determined as follows:

(1) Divide the total deliveries of each such item made in the sales area by such handler during the base period, after excluding the quota-exempt deliveries described in (i) hereof, by the number of days in the base period;

(2) Multiply the result of the foregoing calculation by the number of days in the quota period;

(3) Multiply the aforesaid resulting amount by the following applicable percentage: (i) Milk: 100 percent; (ii) butterfat in milk: 100 percent; (iii) cream: 75 percent; (iv) butterfat in cream: 75 percent; (v) milk byproducts other than cottage, pot, or baker's cheese: 75 percent; and (vi) cottage, pot, or baker's cheese: 75 percent of skim milk equivalent. (For the purpose of this order, one pound of cottage, pot, or baker's cheese shall be considered as the equivalent of 7 pounds of skim milk.)

(f) *Quota limitations.* No handler shall, during any quota period, make deliveries in the sales area in excess of his respective quotas, except as set out in (i) hereof: *Provided,* That a handler may, after application to and approval by the market agent, secure an increase in milk quotas through an equivalent reduction as determined by the market agent, in cream and milk byproducts quotas, and an increase in milk byproducts quota through an equivalent reduction as determined by the market agent, in cream quotas.

(g) *Quotas for handlers who are also producers.* Quotas for handlers who are also producers and who purchase no milk shall be 100 percent of the total production of such handlers in the base period.

(h) *Handler exemptions.* Quotas shall not apply to any handler who delivers in a quota period a daily average of less than 300 units of milk, cream, and milk byproducts. For the purpose of this order, a unit shall be the equivalent in volume of the following: (1) Milk, one quart of milk; (2) cream, one-half pint of cream; and (3) milk byproduct, one quart of skim milk, buttermilk, flavored milk drink, or other beverage containing more than 85 percent of skim milk, or one-half pound of cottage, pot, or baker's cheese.

(i) *Quota exclusions and exemptions.* Deliveries of milk, milk byproducts, or cream (1) to other handlers, except for such deliveries to sub-handlers, (2) to plants engaged in the handling or processing of milk, milk byproducts, or cream from which no milk, milk byproducts, or cream is delivered in the sales area, and (3) to the agencies or groups specified in (d) of FDO 79, shall be excluded from the computation of deliveries in the base period and exempt from charges to quotas.

(j) *Transfers and apportionment of quotas.* The market agent is empowered to deduct an amount of base period deliveries to purchasers from the total of deliveries made by a handler or other person in the base period upon the application and a showing of unreasonable hardship by the handler making deliveries to such purchasers on the effective date of this order, and to add the amount of such deliveries to the total base period deliveries of the applicant handler. Denials of transfers or transfers granted by the market agent shall be reviewed by the Director upon application.

(k) *Petition for relief from hardships.* (1) Any person affected by FDO 79 or the provisions hereof who considers that compliance therewith would work an exceptional and unreasonable hardship on him, may file with the market agent a petition addressed to the Director. The petition shall contain the correct name, address and principal place of business of the petitioner, a full statement of the facts upon which the petition is based, and the hardship involved and the nature of the relief desired.

(2) Upon receiving such petition, the market agent shall immediately investigate the representations and facts stated therein.

(3) After investigation, the petition shall be certified to the Director, but prior to certification the market agent may (i) deny the petition, or (ii) grant temporary relief for a total period not to exceed 60 days.

(4) Denials or grants of relief by the market agent shall be reviewed by the Director and may be affirmed, modified, or reversed by the Director.

(l) *Reports.* Each handler shall transmit to the market agent on forms prescribed by the market agent the following reports:

(1) Within 20 days following the effective date of this order, reports which show the information required by the market agent to establish such handlers' quotas;

(2) Within 20 days following the close of each quota period, the information required by the market agent to establish volumes of deliveries of milk, cream, and milk byproducts during the preceding quota period; and

(3) Handlers exempt from quotas pursuant to (h) hereof shall, upon the request of the market agent, submit the information required by the market agent to establish volumes of deliveries of milk, cream, and milk byproducts.

(m) *Records.* Handlers shall keep and shall make available to the market agent such records of receipts, sales, deliveries, and production as the market agent shall require for the purpose of obtaining information which the Director may require for the establishment of quotas as prescribed in (b) of FDO 79.

(n) *Distribution schedules.* The distribution schedules, if any, to be followed by the handlers in making deliveries shall be made effective in the terms of approval by the Director of such schedules.

(o) *Expense of administration.* Each handler shall pay to the market agent, within 20 days after the close of each calendar month an assessment of $.01 per hundredweight of each of milk, cream, skim milk, buttermilk, flavored milk drinks, beverages containing more than 85 percent of skim milk, and skim milk equivalent of cottage, pot, or baker's cheese delivered during the preceding quota period and subject to quota regulations under the provisions hereof.

(p) *Violations.* The market agent shall report all violations to the Director together with the information required for the prosecution of such violations, except in a case where a handler has made deliveries in a quota period in excess of a quota in an amount not to exceed 5 percent of such quota, and in the succeeding quota period makes deliveries below that quota by at least the same percent.

(q) *Bureau of the Budget approval.* The record keeping and reporting requirements of this order have been approved by the Bureau of the Budget in accordance with the Federal Reports Act of 1942. Subsequent record keeping or reporting requirements will be subject to the approval of the Bureau of the Budget pursuant to the Federal Reports Act of 1942.

(r) This order shall take effect at 12:01 a. m., e. w. t., November 7, 1943.

Issued this 28th day of October 1943.

C. W. KITCHEN,
Acting Director of Food Distribution.

Press Release Immediate:
Friday, October 29, 1943

Milk sales in 5 areas in California, Iowa, Maine, Michigan, and Ohio will be regulated under the Food Distribution Administration's fluid milk conservation and control program.

The new milk sales areas, the applicable Food Distribution Order (in parentheses), and the market agents who will administer the program in each are:

Stockton, Calif., (FDO 79.84) Ernest L. Vehlow, Mull Building, Sacramento, Calif.

Sioux City, Iowa, Metropolitan (FDO 79.85) Wayne McPherren, Post Office Building, Omaha, Nebr.

Portland, Maine (FDO 79.83) Samuel Tator, 80 Federal Street, Boston, Mass.

Kalamazoo, Mich. (FDO 79.87) M. E. Drake, 116 S. William Street, South Bend, Ind.

Springfield Ohio (FDO 79.86) Fred W. Issler, 152 E. 4th Street, Cincinnati, Ohio.

The program will take effect November 1 in Portland, Maine and November 7 in the other areas.

Under the program milk dealers will be permitted to sell as much fluid milk as they sold in June and three-fourths as much cream and milk byproducts (such as cottage cheese, chocolate milk, and buttermilk) as they sold in June. Milk dealers include all persons or firms engaged in the sale or transfer of milk, but not such distributors as subhandlers ("peddlers"), retail stores, hotels, or restaurants.

47337
Cal. 1

FDO 79-85

OCTOBER 28, 1943

WAR FOOD ADMINISTRATION

[FDO 79-85]

PART 1401—DAIRY PRODUCTS

FLUID MILK AND CREAM IN SIOUX CITY, IOWA, METROPOLITAN SALES AREA

Pursuant to the authority vested in me by Food Distribution Order No. 79 (8 F.R. 12426), issued on September 7, 1943, as amended, and to effectuate the purposes of such order, it is hereby ordered as follows:

§ 1401.119 *Quota restrictions*—(a) *Definitions.* When used in this order, unless otherwise distinctly expressed or manifestly incompatible with the intent hereof:

(1) Each term defined in Food Distribution Order No. 79, as amended, shall, when used herein, have the same meaning as is set forth for such term in Food Distribution Order No. 79, as amended.

(2) The term "FDO 79" means Food Distribution Order No. 79, issued on September 7, 1943, as amended.

(3) The term "sub-handler" means any handler, such as a peddler, vendor, sub-dealer, or secondary dealer, who purchases in a previously packaged and processed form milk, milk byproducts, or cream for delivery.

(b) *Milk sales area.* The following area is hereby designated as a "milk sales area" to be known as the Sioux City Iowa, metropolitan sales area, and is referred to hereinafter as the "sales area":

The territory within the corporate limits of Sioux City, Iowa; South Sioux City, Nebraska; Stephens, South Dakota; and the territory within the following townships or precincts: Woodbury and Concord in Woodbury County, Iowa; Hancock, Perry, and Hungerford in Plymouth County, Iowa; Big Sioux and Jefferson in Union County, South Dakota; and Dakota and Covington in Dakota County, Nebraska.

(c) *Base period.* The calendar month of June 1943 is hereby designated as the base period for the sales area.

(d) *Quota.* The remainder of the calendar month in which the provisions hereof become effective and each subsequent calendar month, respectively, is hereby designated as a quota period for the sales area.

(e) *Handler quotas.* Quotas for each handler in the sales area in each quota period shall be calculated in terms of pounds of each of the items for which percentages are specified in (3) below and shall be determined as follows:

(1) Divide the total deliveries of each such item made in the sales area by such handler during the base period, after excluding the quota-exempt deliveries described in (i) hereof, by the number of days in the base period;

(2) Multiply the result of the foregoing calculation by the number of days in the quota period;

(3) Multiply the aforesaid resulting amount by the following applicable percentage: (i) Milk: 100 percent; (ii) butterfat in milk: xxx percent; (iii) cream: 75 percent; (iv) butterfat in cream: 75 percent; (v) milk byproducts other than cottage, pot, or baker's cheese: 75 percent; and (vi) cottage, pot, or baker's cheese: 75 percent of skim milk equivalent. (For the purpose of this order, one pound of cottage, pot, or baker's cheese shall be considered as the equivalent of 7 pounds of skim milk.)

(f) *Quota limitations.* No handler shall, during any quota period, make deliveries in the sales area in excess of his respective quotas, except as set out in (i) hereof: *Provided,* That a handler may, after application to and approval by the market agent, secure an increase in milk quotas through an equivalent reduction as determined by the market agent, in cream and milk byproducts quotas, and an increase in milk byproducts quota through an equivalent reduction as determined by the market agent, in cream quotas.

(g) *Quotas for handlers who are also producers.* Quotas for handlers who are also producers and who purchase no milk shall be 100 percent of the total production of such handlers in the base period.

(h) *Handler exemptions.* Quotas shall not apply to any handler who delivers in a quota period a daily average of less than 125 units of milk, cream, and milk byproducts. For the purpose of this order, a unit shall be the equivalent in volume of the following: (1) Milk, one quart of milk; (2) cream, one-half pint of cream; and (3) milk byproduct, one quart of skim milk, buttermilk, flavored milk drink, or other beverage containing more than 85 percent of skim milk, or one-half pound of cottage, pot, or baker's cheese.

(i) *Quota exclusions and exemptions.* Deliveries of milk, milk byproducts, or cream (1) to other handlers, except for such deliveries to sub-handlers, (2) to plants engaged in the handling or processing of milk, milk byproducts, or cream from which no milk, milk byproducts, or cream is delivered in the sales area, and (3) to the agencies or groups specified in (d) of FDO 79, shall be excluded from the computation of deliveries in the base period and exempt from charges to quotas.

(j) *Transfers and apportionment of quotas.* The market agent is empowered to deduct an amount of base period deliveries to purchasers from the total of deliveries made by a handler or other person in the base peirod upon the application and a showing of unreasonable hardship by the handler making deliveries to such purchasers on the effective date of this order, and to add the amount of such deliveries to the total base period deliveries of the applicant handler. Denials of transfers or transfers granted by the market agent shall be reviewed by the Director upon application.

(k) *Petition for relief from hardships.* (1) Any person affected by FDO 79 or the provisions hereof who considers that compliance therewith would work an exceptional and unreasonable hardship on him, may file with the market agent a petition addressed to the Director. The petition shall contain the correct name, address and principal place of business of the petitioner, a full statement of the facts upon which the petition is based, and the hardship involved and the nature of the relief desired.

(2) Upon receiving such petition, the market agent shall immediately investigate the representations and facts stated therein.

(3) After investigation, the petition shall be certified to the Director, but prior to certification the market agent may (i) deny the petition, or (ii) grant temporary relief for a total period not to exceed 60 days.

(4) Denials or grants of relief by the market agent shall be reviewed by the Director and may be affirmed, modified, or reversed by the Director.

(l) *Reports.* Each handler shall transmit to the market agent on forms prescribed by the market agent the following reports:

(1) Within 20 days following the effective date of this order, reports which show the information required by the market agent to establish such handlers' quotas;

(2) Within 20 days following the close of each quota period, the information re-

quired by the market agent to establish volumes of deliveries of milk, cream, and milk byproducts during the preceding quota period; and

(3) Handlers exempt from quotas pursuant to (h) hereof shall, upon the request of the market agent, submit the information required by the market agent to establish volumes of deliveries of milk, cream, and milk byproducts.

(m) *Records.* Handlers shall keep and shall make available to the market agent such records of receipts, sales, deliveries, and production as the market agent shall require for the purpose of obtaining information which the Director may require for the establishment of quotas as prescribed in (b) of FDO 79.

(n) *Distribution schedules.* The distribution schedules, if any, to be followed by the handlers in making deliveries shall be made effective in the terms of approval by the Director of such schedules.

(o) *Expense of administration.* Each handler shall pay to the market agent, within 20 days after the close of each calendar month an assessment of $0.01 per hundredweight of each of milk, cream, skim milk, buttermilk, flavored milk drinks, beverages containing more than 85 percent of skim milk, and skim milk equivalent of cottage, pot, or baker's cheese delivered during the preceding quota period and subject to quota regulations under the provisions hereof.

(p) *Violations.* The market agent shall report all violations to the Director together with the information required for the prosecution of such violations, except in a case where a handler has made deliveries in a quota period in excess of a quota in an amount not to exceed 5 percent o
the succeeding qu
liveries below thai
same percent.

(q) *Bureau of*
The record keepi
quirements of thi
proved by the Bu
accordance with t
of 1942. Subsequ
reporting require
to the approval of
get pursuant to tl
of 1942.

(r) This order
12:01 a. m., e. w. t

Issued this 28th

Acting Director

Press Release Immediate:
Friday, October 29, 1943

Milk sales in 5 areas in California, Iowa, Maine, Michigan, and Ohio will be regulated under the Food Distribution Administration's fluid milk conservation and control program.

The new milk sales areas, the applicable Food Distribution Order (in parentheses), and the market agents who will administer the program in each are:

Stockton, Calif., (FDO 79.84) Ernest L. Vehlow, Mull Building, Sacramento, Calif.

Sioux City, Iowa, Metropolitan (FDO 79.85) Wayne McPherren, Post Office Building, Omaha, Nebr.

Portland, Maine (FDO 79.83) Samuel Tator, 80 Federal Street, Boston, Mass.

Kalamazoo, Mich. (FDO 79.87) M. E. Drake, 116 S. William Street, South Bend, Ind.

Springfield Ohio (FDO 79.86) Fred W. Issler, 152 E. 4th Street, Cincinnati, Ohio.

The program wi
1 in Portland, Ma
the other areas.

Under the prog
be permitted to s
as they sold in Ju
much cream and
as cottage chees
buttermilk) as th
dealers include a
gaged in the sale
not such distrib
("peddlers"), ret
restaurants.

WAR FOOD ADMINISTRATION
Food Distribution Administration
Washington 25, D. C.

CORRECTION NOTICE - FDO 79.86 Dairy Products

In printing Food Distribution Order No. 79.86 the following error occurred:

In section 1401.121 (e) (3) Item (vi) should read: "Cottage, pot or baker's cheese: 75 percent of skim milk equivalent".

1
7735
Ap. 1

FDO 79-86

OCTOBER 28, 1943

DEC 7 - 1943

WAR FOOD ADMINISTRATION

[FDO 79-86]

PART 1401—DAIRY PRODUCTS

FLUID MILK AND CREAM, SPRINGFIELD, OHIO SALES AREA

Pursuant to the authority vested in me by Food Distribution Order No. 79 (8 F.R. 12426), issued on September 7, 1943, as amended, and to effectuate the purposes of such order, it is hereby ordered as follows:

§ 1401.121 *Quota restrictions*—(a) *Definitions.* When used in this order, unless otherwise distinctly expressed or manifestly incompatible with the intent hereof:

(1) Each term defined in Food Distribution Order No. 79, as amended, shall, when used herein, have the same meaning as is set forth for such term in Food Distribution Order No. 79, as amended.

(2) The term "FDO 79" means Food Distribution Order No. 79, issued on September 7, 1943, as amended.

(3) The term "sub-handler" means any handler, such as a peddler, vendor, sub-dealer, or secondary dealer, who purchases in a previously packaged and processed form milk, milk byproducts, or cream for delivery.

(b) *Milk sales area.* The following area is hereby designated as a "milk sales area" to be known as the Springfield, Ohio, sales area, and is referred to hereinafter as the "sales area":

The city of Springfield and Clark County, in the State of Ohio.

(c) *Base period.* The calendar month of June 1943 is hereby designated as the base period for the sales area.

(d) *Quota period.* The remainder of the calendar month in which the provisions hereof become effective and each subsequent calendar month, respectively, is hereby designated as a quota period for the sales area.

(e) *Handler quotas.* Quotas for each handler in the sales area in each quota period shall be calculated in terms of pounds of each of the items for which percentages are specified in (3) below and shall be determined as follows:

(1) Divide the total deliveries of each such item made in the sales area by such handler during the base period, after excluding the quota-exempt deliveries described in (i) hereof, by the number of days in the base period;

(2) Multiply the result of the foregoing calculation by the number of days in the quota period;

(3) Multiply the aforesaid resulting amount by the following applicable percentage: (i) Milk: 100 percent; (ii) butterfat in milk: ______ percent; (iii) cream: 75 percent; (iv) butterfat in cream: 75 percent; (v) milk byproducts other than cottage, pot, or baker's cheese: 75 percent; and (vi) cottage, pot, or baker's cheese: _____ percent of skim milk equivalent. (For the purpose of this order one pound of cottage, pot, or baker's cheese shall be considered as the equivalent of 7 pounds of skim milk.)

(f) *Quota limitations.* No handler shall, during any quota period, make deliveries in the sales area in excess of his respective quotas, except as set out in (i) hereof: *Provided,* That a handler may, after application to and approval by the market agent, secure an increase in milk quotas through an equivalent reduction as determined by the market agent, in cream and milk byproducts quotas, and an increase in milk byproducts quota through an equivalent reduction as determined by the market agent, in cream quotas.

(g) *Quotas for handlers who are also producers.* Quotas for handlers who are also producers and who purchase no milk shall be 100 percent of the total production of such handlers in the base period.

(h) *Handler exemptions.* Quotas shall not apply to any handler who delivers in a quota period a daily average of less than 150 units of milk, cream, and milk byproducts. For the purpose of this order, a unit shall be the equivalent in volume of the following: (1) Milk, one quart of milk; (2) cream, one-half pint of cream; and (3) milk byproduct, one quart of skim milk, buttermilk, flavored milk drink, or other beverage containing more than 85 percent of skim milk, or one-half pound of cottage, pot or baker's cheese.

(i) *Quota exclusions and exemptions.* Deliveries of milk, milk byproducts, or cream (1) to other handlers, except for such deliveries to sub-handlers, (2) to plants engaged in the handling or processing of milk, milk byproducts, or cream from which no milk, milk byproducts, or cream is delivered in the sales area, and (3) to the agencies or groups specified in (d) of FDO 79, shall be excluded from the computation of deliveries in the base period and exempt from charges to quotas.

(j) *Transfers and apportionment of quotas.* The market agent is empowered to deduct an amount of base period deliveries to purchasers from the total of deliveries made by a handler or other person in the base period upon the application and a showing of unreasonable hardship by the handler making deliveries to such purchasers on the effective date of this order, and to add the amount of such deliveries to the total base period deliveries of the applicant handler. Denials of transfers or transfers granted by the market agent shall be reviewed by the Director upon application.

(k) *Petition for relief from hardships.* (1) Any person affected by FDO 79 or the provisions hereof who considers that compliance therewith would work an exceptional and unreasonable hardship on him, may file with the market agent a petition addressed to the Director. The petition shall contain the correct name, address and principal place of business of the petitioner, a full statement of the facts upon which the petition is based, and the hardship involved and the nature of the relief desired.

(2) Upon receiving such petition, the market agent shall immediately investigate the representations and facts stated therein.

(3) After investigation, the petition shall be certified to the Director, but prior to certification the market agent may (i) deny the petition, or (ii) grant temporary relief for a total period not to exceed 60 days.

(4) Denials or grants of relief by the market agent shall be reviewed by the Director and may be affirmed, modified, or reversed by the Director.

(l) *Reports.* Each handler shall transmit to the market agent on forms prescribed by the market agent the following reports:

(1) Within 20 days following the effective date of this order, reports which show the information required by the market agent to establish such handlers' quotas;

(2) Within 20 days following the close of each quota period, the information required by the market agent to establish volumes of deliveries of milk, cream, and milk byproducts during the preceding quota period; and

(3) Handlers exempt from quotas pursuant to (h) hereof shall, upon the request of the market agent, submit the information required by the market

agent to establish volumes of deliveries of milk, cream, and milk byproducts.

(m) *Records*. Handlers shall keep and shall make available to the market agent such records of receipts, sales, deliveries, and production as the market agent shall require for the purpose of obtaining information which the Director may require for the establishment of quotas as prescribed in (b) of FDO 79.

(n) *Distribution schedules*. The distribution schedules, if any, to be followed by the handlers in making deliveries shall be made effective in the terms of approval by the Director of such schedules.

(o) *Expense of administration*. Each handler shall pay to the market agent, within 20 days after the close of each calendar month an assessment of $.01 per hundredweight of each of milk, cream, skim milk, buttermilk, flavored milk drinks, beverages containing more than 85 percent of skim milk, and skim milk equivalent of cottage, pot, or baker's cheese delivered during the preceding quota period and subject to quota regulations under the provisions hereof.

(p) *Violations*. The market agent shall report all violations to the Director together with the information required for the prosecution of such violations, except in a case where a handler has made deliveries in a quota period in excess of a quota in an amount not to exceed 5 percent of such quota, and in the succeeding quota period makes deliveries below same perce

(q) *Bure*
The record
quirements
proved by
accordance
of 1942. S
reporting r
the approva
pursuant t
1942.

(r) This
12:01 a. m.,

Issued th

Acting Dir

Press Release Immediate:
Friday, October 29, 1943

Milk sales in 5 areas in California, Iowa, Maine, Michigan, and Ohio will be regulated under the Food Distribution Administration's fluid milk conservation and control program.

The new milk sales areas, the applicable Food Distribution Order (in parentheses), and the market agents who will administer the program in each are:

Stockton, Calif., (FDO 79.84) Ernest L. Vehlow, Mull Building, Sacramento, Calif.

Sioux City, Iowa, Metropolitan (FDO 79.85) Wayne McPherren, Post Office Building, Omaha, Nebr.

Portland, Maine (FDO 79.83) Samuel Tator, 80 Federal Street, Boston, Mass.

Kalamazoo, Mich. (FDO 79.87) M. E. Drake, 116 S. William Street, South Bend, Ind.

Springfield Ohio (FDO 79.86) Fred W. Issler, 152 E. 4th Street, Cincinnati, Ohio.

The prog
1 in Portla
the other

Under th
be permitt
as they sold
much crea
as cottage
buttermilk
dealers inc
gaged in th
not such
("peddlers"
restaurants

WAR FOOD ADMINISTRATION

[FDO 79-86, Amdt. 1]

PART 1401—DAIRY PRODUCTS

FLUID MILK AND CREAM IN SPRINGFIELD, OHIO, SALES AREA

Pursuant to Food Distribution Order No. 79 (8 F.R. 12426), dated September 7, 1943, as amended, and to effectuate the purposes thereof, Food Distribution Order No. 79-86 (8 F.R. 14724), relative to the conservation and distribution of fluid milk in the Springfield, Ohio, milk sales area, issued by the Director of Food Distribution on October 28, 1943, is amended as follows:

1. By deleting therefrom the provisions in § 1401.121 (g) and substituting therefor the following:

(g) *Quotas for handlers who are also producers.* Quotas for handlers who are also producers and who purchase no milk shall be computed in accordance with (e) hereof, except that the applicable percentages shall be 100 percent in lieu of the percentages specified in (e) (3).

2. By deleting therefrom the provisions of § 1401.121 (i) and substituting therefor, the following:

(i) *Quota exclusions and exemptions.* Deliveries of milk, milk byproducts, or cream (1) to other handlers, except for such deliveries to sub-handlers, (2) to plants engaged in the handling or processing of milk, milk byproducts, or cream from which no milk, milk byproducts, or cream is delivered in the sales area, (3) to nursery, elementary, junior high, and high schools, and (4) to the agencies or groups specified in (d) of FDO 79, shall be excluded from the computation of deliveries in the base period and exempt from charges to quotas.

The provisions of this amendment shall become effective at 12:01 a. m., e. w. t., February 1, 1944. With respect to violations of said Food Distribution Order No. 79-86, rights accrued, or liabilities incurred prior to the effective time of this amendment, said Food Distribution Order No. 79-86, shall be deemed to be in full force and effect for the purpose of sustaining any proper suit, action, or other proceeding with respect to any such violation, right, or liability.

(E.O. 9280, 7 F.R. 10179; E.O. 9322, 8 F.R. 3807; E.O. 9334, 8 F.R. 5423; E.O. 9392, 8 F.R. 14783; FDO 79, 8 F.R. 12426, 13283)

Issued this 27th day of January 1944.

LEE MARSHALL,
Director of Food Distribution.

WAR FOOD ADMINISTRATION

[FDO 79-87]

PART 1401—DAIRY PRODUCTS

FLUID MILK AND CREAM, KALAMAZOO, MICH., SALES AREA

Pursuant to the authority vested in me by Food Distribution Order No. 79 (8 F.R. 12426), issued on September 7, 1943, as amended, and to effectuate the purposes of such order, it is hereby ordered as follows:

§ 1401.120 *Quota restrictions*—(a) *Definitions.* When used in this order, unless otherwise distinctly expressed or manifestly incompatible with the intent hereof:

(1) Each term defined in Food Distribution Order No. 79, as amended, shall, when used herein, have the same meaning as is set forth for such term in Food Distribution Order No. 79, as amended.

(2) The term "FDO 79" means Food Distribution Order No. 79, issued on September 7, 1943, as amended.

(3) The term "sub-handler" means any handler, such as a peddler, vendor, sub-dealer, or secondary dealer, who purchases in a previously packaged and processed form milk, milk byproducts, or cream for delivery.

(b) *Milk sales area.* The following area is hereby designated as a "milk sales area" to be known as the Kalamazoo, Michigan, sales area, and is referred to hereinafter as the "sales area":

The city of Kalamazoo, the townships of Comstock and Kalamazoo, and the cities of Galesburg and Parchment, all in Kalamazoo County, Michigan.

(c) *Base period.* The calendar month of June 1943 is hereby designated as the base period for the sales area.

(d) *Quota period.* The remainder of the calendar month in which the provisions hereof become effective and each subsequent calendar month, respectively, is hereby designated as a quota period for the sales area.

(e) *Handler quotas.* Quotas for each handler in the sales area in each quota period shall be calculated in terms of pounds of each of the items for which percentages are specified in (3) below and shall be determined as follows:

(1) Divide the total deliveries of each such item made in the sales area by such handler during the base period, after excluding the quota-exempt deliveries described in (i) hereof, by the number of days in the base period;

(2) Multiply the result of the foregoing calculation by the number of days in the quota period;

(3) Multiply the aforesaid resulting amount by the following applicable percentage: (i) Milk: 100 percent; (ii) butterfat in milk: ______ percent; (iii) cream: 75 percent; (iv) butterfat in cream: 75 percent; (v) milk byproducts other than cottage, pot, or baker's cheese: 75 percent; and (vi) cottage, pot, or baker's cheese: 75 percent of skim milk equivalent. (For the purpose of this order, one pound of cottage, pot, or baker's cheese shall be considered as the equivalent of 7 pounds of skim milk.)

(f) *Quota limitations.* No handler shall, during any quota period, make deliveries in the sales area in excess of his respective quotas, except as set out in (i) hereof: *Provided,* That a handler may, after application to and approval by the market agent, secure an increase in milk quotas through an equivalent reduction as determined by the market agent, in cream and milk byproducts quotas, and an increase in milk byproducts quota through an equivalent reduction as determined by the market agent, in cream quotas.

(g) *Quotas for handlers who are also producers.* Quotas for handlers who are also producers and who purchase no milk shall be 100 percent of the total production of such handlers in the base period.

(h) *Handler exemptions.* Quotas shall not apply to any handler who delivers in a quota period a daily average of less than 100 units of milk, cream, and milk byproducts. For the purpose of this order, a unit shall be the equivalent in volume of the following: (1) Milk, one quart of milk; (2) cream, one-half pint of cream; and (3) milk byproduct, one quart of skim milk, buttermilk, flavored milk drink, or other beverage containing more than 85 percent of skim milk, or one-half pound of cottage, pot, or baker's cheese.

(i) *Quota exclusions and exemptions.* Deliveries of milk, milk byproducts, or cream (1) to other handlers, except for such deliveries to sub-handlers, (2) to plants engaged in the handling or processing of milk, milk byproducts, or cream from which no milk, milk byproducts, or cream is delivered in the sales area, and (3) to the agencies or groups specified in (d) of FDO 79, shall be excluded from the computation of deliveries in the base period and exempt from charges to quotas.

(j) *Transfers and apportionment of quotas.* The market agent is empowered to deduct an amount of base period deliveries to purchasers from the total of deliveries made by a handler or other person in the base period upon the application and a showing of unreasonable hardship by the handler making deliveries to such purchasers on the effective date of this order, and to add the amount of such deliveries to the total base period deliveries of the applicant handler. Denials of transfers or transfers granted by the market agent shall be reviewed by the Director upon application.

(k) *Petition for relief from hardships.* (1) Any person affected by FDO 79 or the provisions hereof who considers that compliance therewith would work an exceptional and unreasonable hardship on him, may file with the market agent a petition addressed to the Director. The petition shall contain the correct name, address and principal place of business of the petitioner, a full statement of the facts upon which the petition is based, and the hardship involved and the nature of the relief desired.

(2) Upon receiving such petition, the market agent shall immediately investigate the representations and facts stated therein.

(3) After investigation, the petition shall be certified to the Director, but prior to certification the market agent may (i) deny the petition, or (ii) grant temporary relief for a total period not to exceed 60 days.

(4) Denials or grants of relief by the market agent shall be reviewed by the Director and may be affirmed, modified, or reversed by the Director.

(l) *Reports.* Each handler shall transmit to the market agent on forms prescribed by the market agent the following reports:

(1) Within 20 days following the effective date of this order, reports which show the information required by the market agent to establish such handlers' quotas;

(2) Within 20 days following the close of each quota period, the information required by the market agent to establish volumes of deliveries of milk, cream, and milk byproducts during the preceding quota period; and

(3) Handlers exempt from quotas pursuant to (h) hereof shall, upon the request of the market agent, submit the

information required by the market agent to establish volumes of deliveries of milk, cream, and milk byproducts.

(m) *Records.* Handlers shall keep and shall make available to the market agent such records of receipts, sales, deliveries, and production as the market agent shall require for the purpose of obtaining information which the Director may require for the establishment of quotas as prescribed in (b) of FDO 79.

(n) *Distribution schedules.* The distribution schedules, if any, to be followed by the handlers in making deliveries shall be made effective in the terms of approval by the Director of such schedules.

(o) *Expense of administration.* Each handler shall pay to the market agent, within 20 days after the close of each calendar month an assessment of $.01 per hundredweight of each of milk, cream, skim milk, buttermilk, flavored milk drinks, beverages containing more than 85 percent of skim milk, and skim milk equivalent of cottage, pot, or baker's cheese delivered during the preceding quota period and subject to quota regulations under the provisions hereof.

(p) *Violations.* The market agent shall report all violations to the Director together with the information required for the prosecution of such violations, except in a case where a handler has made deliveries in a quota period in excess of a quota in an amount not to exceed 5 percent of such quota, and in the succeeding quota period makes deliveries below that quota by at least the same percent.

(q) *Bureau of the Budget approval.* The record keeping and reporting requirements of this order have been approved by the Bureau of the Budget in accordance with the Federal Reports Act of 1942. Subsequent record keeping or reporting requirements will be subject to the approval of the Bureau of the Budget pursuant to the Federal Reports Act of 1942.

(r) This order shall take effect at 12:01 a. m., e. w. t., November 7, 1943.

Issued this 28th day of October 1943.

C. W. KITCHEN,
Acting Director of Food Distribution.

Press Release Immediate:
Friday, October 29, 1943.

Milk sales in 5 areas in California, Iowa, Maine, Michigan, and Ohio will be regulated under the Food Distribution Administration's fluid milk conservation and control program.

The new milk sales areas, the applicable Food Distribution Order (in parentheses), and the market agents who will administer the program in each are:

Stockton, Calif., (FDO 79.84) Ernest L. Vehlow, Mull Building, Sacramento, Calif.

Sioux City, Iowa, Metropolitan (FDO 79 85) Wayne McPherren, Post Office Building, Omaha, Nebr.

Portland, Maine (FDO 79.83) Samuel Tator, 80 Federal Street, Boston, Mass.

Kalamazoo, Mich. (FDO 79.87) M. E. Drake, 116 S. William Street, South Bend, Ind.

Springfield Ohio (FDO 79.86) Fred W. Issler, 152 E. 4th Street, Cincinnati, Ohio.

The program will take effect November 1 in Portland, Maine and November 7 in the other areas.

Under the program milk dealers will be permitted to sell as much fluid milk as they sold in June and three-fourths as much cream and milk byproducts (such as cottage cheese, chocolate milk, and buttermilk) as they sold in June. Milk dealers include all persons or firms engaged in the sale or transfer of milk, but not such distributors as subhandlers ("peddlers"), retail stores, hotels, or restaurants.

FDO 79-87
AMDT. 1
NOV. 24, 1943

WAR FOOD ADMINISTRATION

[FDO 79-87, Amdt. 1]

PART 1401—DAIRY PRODUCTS

FLUID MILK AND CREAM IN KALAMAZOO, MICH., SALES AREA

Pursuant to the authority vested in the Director by Food Distribution Order No. 79, dated September 7, 1943 (8 F.R. 12426), as amended, and to effectuate the purposes thereof, Director Food Distribution Order No. 79–87, § 1401,120, relative to the conservation of fluid milk in the Kalamazoo, Michigan, milk sales area (8 F.R. 14725), issued by the Director of Food Distribution on October 28, 1943, is amended as follows:

The milk sales area described in § 1401.120 (b) of the original order is modified in the following particulars: Add the following: "Sections 25 to 36 inclusive in Cooper Township, sections 1 to 18 inclusive in Portage Township, and sections 23 to 26 inclusive and sections 35 to 36 in Oshtemo Township, all in Kalamazoo County, Michigan."

Effective date. This amendment of DFDO No. 79–87, shall become effective at 12:01 a. m., e. w. t., December 1, 1943.

(E.O. 9280, 8 F.R. 10179; E.O. 9322, 8 F.R. 3807; E.O. 9334, 8 F.R. 5423; E.O. 9392, 8 F.R. 14783; FDO 79, 8 F.R. 12426, 13283)

Issued this 24th day of November 1943.

ROY F. HENDRICKSON,
Director of Food Distribution.

FDO 79-88

NOV. 6, 1943

WAR FOOD ADMINISTRATION

[FDO 79-88]

PART 1401—DAIRY PRODUCTS

FLUID MILK AND CREAM IN TERRE HAUTE, IND., SALES AREA

Pursuant to the authority vested in me by Food Distribution Order No. 79 (8 F.R. 12426), issued on September 7, 1943, as amended, and to effectuate the purposes of such order, it is hereby ordered as follows:

§ 1401.123 *Quota restrictions*—(a) *Definitions.* When used in this order, unless otherwise distinctly expressed or manifestly incompatible with the intent hereof:

(1) Each term defined in Food Distribution Order No. 79, as amended, shall, when used herein, have the same meaning as is set forth for such term in Food Distribution Order No. 79, as amended.

(2) The term "FDO 79" means Food Distribution Order No. 79, issued on September 7, 1943, as amended.

(3) The term "sub-handler" means any handler, such as a peddler, vendor, sub-dealer, or secondary dealer, who purchases in a previously packaged and processed form milk, milk byproducts, or cream for delivery.

(b) *Milk sales area.* The following area is hereby designated as a "milk sales area" to be known as the Terre Haute, Indiana, sales area, and is referred to hereinafter as the "sales area":

The city of Terre Haute, and the townships of Harrison, Honey Creek, and Sugar Creek, all in Vigo County, Indiana.

(c) *Base period.* The calendar month of June 1943 is hereby designated as the base period for the sales area.

(d) *Quota period.* The remainder of the calendar month in which the provisions hereof become effective and each subsequent calendar month, respectively, is hereby designated as a quota period for the sales area.

(e) *Handler quotas.* Quotas for each handler in the sales area in each quota period shall be calculated in terms of pounds of each of the items for which percentages are specified in (3) below and shall be determined as follows:

(1) Divide the total deliveries of each such item made in the sales area by such handler during the base period, after excluding the quota-exempt deliveries described in (i) hereof, by the number of days in the base period;

(2) Multiply the result of the foregoing calculation by the number of days in the quota period;

(3) Multiply the aforesaid resulting amount by the following applicable percentage: (i) Milk: 100 percent; (ii) butterfat in milk: ____ percent; (iii) cream: 75 percent; (iv) butterfat in cream: 75 percent; (v) milk byproducts other than cottage, pot, or baker's cheese: 75 percent; and (vi) cottage, pot, or baker's cheese: 75 percent of skim milk equivalent. (For the purpose of this order, one pound of cottage, pot, or baker's cheese shall be considered as the equivalent of 7 pounds of skim milk.)

(f) *Quota limitations.* No handler shall, during any quota period, make deliveries in the sales area in excess of his respective quotas, except as set out in (i) hereof: *Provided,* That a handler may, after application to and approval by the market agent, secure an increase in milk quotas through an equivalent reduction as determined by the market agent, in cream and milk byproducts quotas, and an increase in milk byproducts quota through an equivalent reduction as determined by the market agent, in cream quotas.

(g) *Quotas for handlers who are also producers.* Quotas for handlers who are also producers and who purchase no milk shall be 100 percent of the total production of such handlers in the base period.

(h) *Handler exemptions.* Quotas shall not apply to any handler who delivers in a quota period a daily average of less than 200 units of milk; cream, and milk byproducts. For the purpose of this order, a unit shall be the equivalent in volume of the following: (1) Milk, one quart of milk; (2) cream, one-half pint of cream; and (3) milk byproduct, one quart of skim milk, buttermilk, flavored milk drink, or other beverage containing more than 85 percent of skim milk, or one-half pound of cottage, pot, or baker's cheese.

(i) *Quota exclusions and exemptions.* Deliveries of milk, milk byproducts, or cream (1) to other handlers, except for such deliveries to sub-handlers, (2) to plants engaged in the handling or processing of milk, milk byproducts, or cream from which no milk, milk byproducts, or cream is delivered in the sales area, and (3) to the agencies or groups specified in (d) of FDO 79, shall be excluded from the computation of deliveries in the base period and exempt from charges to quotas.

(j) *Transfers and apportionment of quotas.* The market agent is empowered to deduct an amount of base period deliveries to purchasers from the total of deliveries made by a handler or other person in the base period upon the application and a showing of unreasonable hardship by the handler making deliveries to such purchasers on the effective date of this order, and to add the amount of such deliveries to the total base period deliveries of the applicant handler. Denials of transfers or transfers granted by the market agent shall be reviewed by the Director upon application.

(k) *Petition for relief from hardships.* (1) Any person affected by FDO 79 or the provisions hereof who considers that compliance therewith would work an exceptional and unreasonable hardship on him, may file with the market agent a petition addressed to the Director. The petition shall contain the correct name, address and principal place of business of the petitioner, a full statement of the facts upon which the petition is based, and the hardship involved and the nature of the relief desired.

(2) Upon receiving such petition, the market agent shall immediately investigate the representations and facts stated therein.

(3) After investigation, the petition shall be certified to the Director, but prior to certification the market agent may (i) deny the petition, or (ii) grant temporary relief for a total period not to exceed 60 days.

(4) Denials or grants of relief by the market agent shall be reviewed by the Director and may be affirmed, modified, or reversed by the Director.

(l) *Reports.* Each handler shall transmit to the market agent on forms prescribed by the market agent the following reports:

(1) Within 20 days following the effective date of this order, reports which show the information required by the market agent to establish such handlers' quotas;

(2) Within 20 days following the close of each quota period, the information required by the market agent to establish volumes of deliveries of milk, cream, and milk byproducts during the preceding quota period; and

(3) Handlers exempt from quotas pursuant to (h) hereof shall, upon the re-

quest of the market agent, submit the information required by the market agent to establish volumes of deliveries of milk, cream, and milk byproducts.

(m) *Records.* Handlers shall keep and shall make available to the market agent such records of receipts, sales, deliveries, and production as the market agent shall require for the purpose of obtaining information which the Director may require for the establishment of quotas as prescribed in (b) of FDO 79.

(n) *Distribution schedules.* The distribution schedules, if any, to be followed by the handlers in making deliveries shall be made effective in the terms of approval by the Director of such schedules.

(o) *Expense of administration.* Each handler shall pay to the market agent, within 20 days after the close of each calendar month an assessment of $0.01 per hundredweight of each of milk, cream, skim milk, buttermilk, flavored milk drinks, beverages containing more than 85 percent of skim milk, and skim milk equivalent of cottage, pot, or baker's cheese delivered during the preceding quota period and subject to quota regulations under the provisions hereof.

(p) *Violations.* The market agent shall report all violations to the Director together with the information required for the prosecution of such violations, except in a case where a handler has made deliveries in a quota period in excess of a quota in an amount not to exceed 5 percent of such quota, and in the succeeding quota period makes deliveries below that quota by at least the same percent.

(q) *Bureau of the Budget approval.* The record keeping and reporting requirements of this order have been approved by the Bureau of the Budget in accordance with the Federal Reports Act of 1942. Subsequent record keeping or reporting requirements will be subject to the approval of the Bureau of the Budget pursuant to the Federal Reports Act of 1942.

(r) This order shall take effect at 12:01 a. m., e. w. t., December 1, 1943.

Issued this 6th day of November 1943.

C. W. Kitchen,
Acting Director of Food Distribution.

Release—Immediate:
Washington, D. C., November 8, 1943.

Ten New Milk Sales Areas Named

Milk sales in 10 metropolitan areas in Iowa, Nebraska, New Hampshire, Missouri, Kansas, Colorado, Indiana, and California will be regulated under the Food Distribution Administration's fluid milk conservation and control program beginning December 1, 1943, the War Food Administration said today.

The new milk sales areas and the market agents who will administer the program in each, are:

Springfield, Mo., (FDO 79); St. Joseph, Mo., (FDO 79); Topeka, Kans., (FDO 79); M. M. Morehouse, 512 Porter Bldg., 406 W. 34th St., Kansas City, Mo.

Manchester, N. H., (FDO 79), Samuel Tator, 80 Federal Street, Boston, Mass.

Pueblo, Colo., (FDO 79), Ben King, 503 Security Life Bldg., 810 14th St., Denver, Colo.

Terre Haute, Ind., (FDO 79), W. A. Wilson, 446 Illinois Building, Indianapolis, Ind.

Fresno, Calif., (FDO 79), E. L. Vehlow, Mull Building, Sacramento, Calif.

Lincoln, Nebr., (FDO) 79), Wayne McPherren, 408 Post Office Building, Omaha, Nebr.

Cedar Rapids, Iowa, (FDO 79); Waterloo, Iowa, (FDO 79).

Under the program, milk dealers will be permitted to sell as much fluid milk as they sold in June and three-fourths as much cream and milk byproducts (such as cottage cheese, chocolate milk, and buttermilk) as they sold in June. Milk dealers include all persons or firms engaged in the sale or transfer of milk, but not such distributors as subhandlers ("peddlers"), retail stores, hotels, or restaurants.

Producer-distributors who purchase no milk will be permitted to sell as much milk as they produced in June.

A dealer may increase his milk sales by reducing his cream and milk byproducts sales, and increase his sales of milk byproducts by reducing his cream sales, providing such an adjustment is approved in advance by the market agent for the area.

Deliveries of milk, cream, and milk byproducts to other dealers: to the Armed Forces, and to plants processing milk who do not distribute milk, cream or milk byproducts in the sales area are quota exempt.

Consumers in the milk sales areas named today and in others already designated generally will be able to purchase as much milk under the milk conservation program as they have been buying in recent months—within the limits of local supplies.

Fluid milk sales are being stabilized, Food Distribution Administration officials said, to help assure sufficient milk for manufacturing the cheese, butter, evaporated milk, and milk powder required by the Armed Services and civilians for good nutrition and properly balanced diets. Sales quotas on cream and on milk byproducts have been set below June deliveries to boost fluid milk supplies where production is low, and to conserve milk for manufacturing purposes.

FDO 79-88

AMDT. 1
DEC. 28, 1943

WAR FOOD ADMINISTRATION

[FDO 79-88, Amdt. 1]

PART 1401—DAIRY PRODUCTS

FLUID MILK AND CREAM IN THE TERRE HAUTE, IND., MILK SALES AREA

Pursuant to Food Distribution Order No. 79 (8 F. R. 12426), dated September 7, 1943, as amended, and to effectuate the purposes thereof, Food Distribution Order No. 79-88 (8 F. R. 15471), relative to the conservation and distribution of fluid milk in the Terre Haute, Indiana, milk sales area, issued by the Director of Food Distribution on November 6, 1943, is amended by deleting therefrom the description of the sales area in § 1401.123 (b) and inserting, in lieu thereof, the following:

The city of Terre Haute, and all of the remaining territory within the corporate limits of Vigo County, Indiana.

The provisions of this amendment shall become effective at 12:01 a. m., e. w. t., January 1, 1944. With respect to violations of said Food Distribution Order No. 79-88, rights accrued, or liabilities incurred prior to the effective time of this amendment, said Food Distribution Order No. 79-88, shall be deemed to be in full force and effect for the purpose of sustaining any proper suit, action, or other proceeding with respect to any such violation, right, or liability.

(E.O. 9280, 7 F.R. 10179; E.O. 9322, 8 F.R. 3807; E.O. 9334, 8 F.R. 5423; E.O. 9392, 8 F.R. 14783; FDO 79, 8 F.R. 12426, 13283)

Issued this 28th day of December 1943.

ROY F. HENDRICKSON,
Director of Food Distribution.

WAR FOOD ADMINISTRATION
Food Distribution Administration
Washington 25, D. C.

CORRECTION NOTICE: FDO-79.89 "Dairy Products"

In printing Food Distribution Order 79.89 the following error occurred:

In section 1401.125 (k) the word "harishops" should read "hardships" so that (k) will read, "Petition for relief from hardships".

FDO 79-89

NOV. 6, 1943

WAR FOOD ADMINISTRATION

PART 1401—DAIRY PRODUCTS

[FDO 79-89]

FLUID MILK AND CREAM IN CEDAR RAPIDS, IOWA, SALES AREA

Pursuant to the authority vested in me by Food Distribution Order No. 79 (8 F.R. 12426), issued on September 7, 1943, as amended, and to effectuate the purposes of such order it is hereby ordered as follows:

§ 1401.125 *Quota restrictions*—(a) *Definitions.* When used in this order, unless otherwise distinctly expressed or manifestly incompatible with the intent hereof:

(1) Each term defined in Food Distribution Order No. 79, as amended, shall, when used herein, have the same meaning as is set forth for such term in Food Distribution Order No. 79, as amended.

(2) The term "FDO 79" means Food Distribution Order No. 79, issued on September 7, 1943, as amended.

(3) The term "sub-handler" means any handler, such as a peddler, vendor, sub-dealer, or secondary dealer, who purchases in a previously packaged and processed form milk, milk byproducts, or cream for delivery.

(b) *Milk sales area.* The following area is hereby designated as a "milk sales area" to be known as the Cedar Rapids, Iowa, sales area, and is referred to hereinafter as the "sales area":

The city of Cedar Rapids and the townships of Bertram, Clinton, College, Marion, and Monroe in Linn County, Iowa.

(c) *Base period.* The calendar month of June 1943 is hereby designated as the base period for the sales area.

(d) *Quota period.* The remainder of the calendar month in which the provisions hereof become effective and each subsequent calendar month, respectively, is hereby designated as a quota period for the sales area.

(e) *Handler quotas.* Quotas for each handler in the sales area in each quota period shall be calculated in terms of pounds of each of the items for which percentages are specified in (3) below and shall be determined as follows:

(1) Divide the total deliveries of each such item made in the sales area by such handler during the base period, after excluding the quota-exempt deliveries described in (i) hereof, by the number of days in the base period;

(2) Multiply the result of the foregoing calculation by the number of days in the quota period;

(3) Multiply the aforesaid resulting amount by the following applicable percentage: (i) Milk: 100 percent; (ii) butterfat in milk: — per cent; (iii) cream: 75 percent; (iv) butterfat in cream: 75 percent; (v) milk byproducts other than cottage, pot or baker's cheese: 75 percent; and (vi) cottage, pot, or baker's cheese: 75 percent of skim milk equivalent. (For the purpose of this order, one pound of cottage, pot, or baker's cheese shall be considered as the equivalent of 7 pounds of skim milk.)

(f) *Quota limitations.* No handler shall, during any quota period, make deliveries in the sales area in excess of his respective quotas, except as set out in (i) hereof: *Provided,* That a handler may, after application to and approval by the market agent, secure an increase in milk quotas through an equivalent reduction as determined by the market agent, in cream and milk byproducts quotas, and an increase in milk byproducts quota through an equivalent reduction as determined by the market agent, in cream quotas.

(g) *Quotas for handlers who are also producers.* Quotas for handlers who are also producers and who purchase no milk shall be 100 percent of the total production of such handlers in the base period.

(h) *Handler exemptions.* Quotas shall not apply to any handler who delivers in a quota period a daily average of less than 200 units of milk, cream, and milk byproducts. For the purpose of this order, a unit shall be the equivalent in volume of the following: (1) Milk, one quart of milk; (2) cream, one-half pint of cream; and (3) milk byproduct, one quart of skim milk, buttermilk, flavored milk drink, or other beverage containing more than 85 percent of skim milk, or one-half pound of cottage, pot, or baker's cheese.

(i) *Quota exclusions and exemptions.* Deliveries of milk, milk byproducts, or cream (1) to other handlers, except for such deliveries to sub-handlers, (2) to plants engaged in the handling or processing of milk, milk byproducts, or cream from which no milk, milk byproducts, or cream is delivered in the sales area, and (3) to the agencies or groups specified in (d) of FDO 79, shall be excluded from the computation of deliveries in the base period and exempt from charges to quotas.

(j) *Transfers and apportionment of quotas.* The market agent is empowered to deduct an amount of base period deliveries to purchasers from the total of deliveries made by a handler or other person in the base period upon the application and a showing of unreasonable hardship by the handler making deliveries to such purchasers on the effective date of this order, and to add the amount of such deliveries to the total base period deliveries of the applicant handler. Denials of transfers or transfers granted by the market agent shall be reviewed by the Director upon application.

(k) *Petition for relief from hardshops* (1) Any person affected by FDO 79 or the provisions hereof who considers that compliance therewith would work an exceptional and unreasonable hardship on him, may file with the market agent a petition addressed to the Director. The petition shall contain the correct name, address and principal place of business of the petitioner, a full statement of the facts upon which the petition is based, and the hardship involved and the nature of the relief desired.

(2) Upon receiving such petition, the market agent shall immediately investigate the representations and facts stated therein.

(3) After investigation, the petition shall be certified to the Director, but prior to certification the market agent may (i) deny the petition, or (ii) grant temporary relief for a total period not to exceed 60 days.

(4) Denials or grants of relief by the market agent shall be reviewed by the Director and may be affirmed, modified, or reversed by the Director.

(l) *Reports.* Each handler shall transmit to the market agent on forms prescribed by the market agent the following reports:

(1) Within 20 days following the effective date of this order, reports which show the information required by the market agent to establish such handlers' quotas;

(2) Within 20 days following the close of each quota period, the information required by the market agent to establish volumes of deliveries of milk, cream, and milk byproducts during the preceding quota period; and

(3) Handlers exempt from quotas pursuant to (h) hereof shall, upon the request of the marget agent, submit the information required by the market agent to establish volumes of deliveries of milk, cream, and milk byproducts.

(m) *Records.* Handlers shall keep and shall make available to the market agent such records of receipts, sales, deliveries, and production as the market agent shall require for the purpose of obtaining information which the Director may require for the establishment of quotas as prescribed in (b) of FDO 79.

(n) *Distribution schedules.* The distribution schedules, if any, to be followed by the handlers in making deliveries shall be made effective in the terms of approval by the Director of such schedules.

(o) *Expense of administration.* Each handler shall pay to the market agent, within 20 days after the close of each calendar month an assessment of $0.01 per hundredweight of each of milk, cream, skim milk, buttermilk, flavored milk drinks, beverages containing more than 85 percent of skim milk, and skim milk equivalent of cottage, pot, or baker's cheese delivered during the preceding quota period and subject to quota regulations under the provisions hereof.

(p) *Violations.* The market agent shall report all violations to the Director, together with the information required for the prosecution of such violations, except in a case where a handler has made deliveries in a quota period in excess of a quota in an amount not to exceed 5 percent of such quota, and in the succeeding quota period makes deliveries below that quota by at least the same percent.

(q) *Bureau of the Budget approval.* The record keeping and reporting requirements of this order have been approved by the Bureau of the Budget in accordance with the Federal Reports Act of 1942. Subsequent record keeping or reporting requirements will be subject to the approval of the Bureau of the Budget pursuant to the Federal Reports Act of 1942.

(r) This order shall take effect at 12:01 a. m., e. w. t., December 1, 1943.

Issued this 6th day of November 1943.

C. W. KITCHEN,
Acting Director of Food Distribution.

Release—Immediate:
Washington, D. C., November 8, 1943.

TEN NEW MILK SALES AREAS NAMED

Milk sales in 10 metropolitan areas in Iowa, Nebraska, New Hampshire, Missouri, Kansas, Colorado, Indiana, and California will be regulated under the Food Distribution Administration's fluid milk conservation and control program beginning December 1, 1943, the War Food Administration said today.

The new milk sales areas and the market agents who will administer the program in each, are:

Springfield, Mo., (FDO 79); St. Joseph, Mo., (FDO 79); Topeka, Kans., (FDO 79); M. M. Morehouse, 512 Porter Bldg., 406 W. 34th St., Kansas City, Mo.

Manchester, N. H., (FDO 79), Samuel Tator, 80 Federal Street, Boston, Mass.

Pueblo, Colo., (FDO 79), Ben King, 503 Security Life Bldg., 810 14th St., Denver, Colo.

Terre Haute, Ind., (FDO 79), W. A. Wilson, 446 Illinois Building, Indianapolis, Ind.

Fresno, Calif., (FDO 79), E. L. Vehlow, Mull Building, Sacramento, Calif.

Lincoln, Nebr., (FDO) 79), Wayne McPherren, 408 Post Office Building, Omaha, Nebr.

Cedar Rapids, Iowa, (FDO 79); Waterloo, Iowa, (FDO 79).

Under the program, milk dealers will be permitted to sell as much fluid milk as they sold in June and three-fourths as much cream and milk byproducts (such as cottage cheese, chocolate milk, and buttermilk) as they sold in June. Milk dealers include all persons or firms engaged in the sale or transfer of milk, but not such distributors as subhandlers ("peddlers"), retail stores, hotels, or restaurants.

Producer-distributors who purchase no milk will be permitted to sell as much milk as they produced in June.

A dealer may increase his milk sales by reducing his cream and milk byproducts sales, and increase his sales of milk byproducts by reducing his cream sales, providing such an adjustment is approved in advance by the market agent for the area.

Deliveries of milk, cream, and milk byproducts to other dealers: to the Armed Forces, and to plants processing milk who do not distribute milk, cream or milk byproducts in the sales area are quota exempt.

Consumers in the milk sales areas named today and in others already designated generally will be able to purchase as much milk under the milk conservation program as they have been buying in recent months—within the limits of local supplies.

Fluid milk sales are being stabilized, Food Distribution Administration officials said, to help assure sufficient milk for manufacturing the cheese, butter, evaporated milk, and milk powder required by the Armed Services and civilians for good nutrition and properly balanced diets. Sales quotas on cream and on milk byproducts have been set below June deliveries to boost fluid milk supplies where production is low, and to conserve milk for manufacturing purposes.

WAR FOOD ADMINISTRATION

[FDO 79-89, Amdt. 1]

PART 1401—DAIRY PRODUCTS

FLUID MILK IN CEDAR RAPIDS, IOWA, SALES AREA

Pursuant to the authority vested in the Director by Food Distribution Order No. 79, dated September 7, 1943 (8 F.R. 12426), as amended, and to effectuate the purposes thereof, Food Distribution Order No. 79-89, § 1401.125, relative to the conservation of fluid milk in the Cedar Rapids, Iowa, milk sales area (8 F.R. 15473), issued by the Acting Director of Food Distribution on November 6, 1943, is amended as follows:

The expense of administration specified in § 1401.125 (o) of the original order is increased from $0.01 to $0.02.

Effective date. This amendment of FDO 79-89, shall become effective at 12:01 a. m., e. w. t., February 1, 1944.

(E.O. 9280, 7 F.R. 10179; E.O. 9322, 8 F.R. 3807; E.O. 9334, 8 F.R. 5423; E.O. 9392, 8 F.R. 14783; FDO 79, 8 F.R. 12426, 13283).

Issued this 4th day of January, 1944.

ROY F. HENDRICKSON,
Director of Food Distribution.

FDO 79-89
AMDT. 2
MAR. 29, 1944

WAR FOOD ADMINISTRATION

[FDO 79-89, Amdt. 2]

PART 1401—DAIRY PRODUCTS

FLUID MILK AND CREAM IN CEDAR RAPIDS, IOWA, SALES AREA

Pursuant to Food Distribution Order No. 79 (8 F.R. 12426), dated September 7, 1943, as amended, and to effectuate the purposes thereof, Food Distribution Order No. 79-89 (8 F.R. 15473), relative to the conservation and distribution of fluid milk, milk byproducts, and cream in the Cedar Rapids, Iowa, milk sales area, issued by the Director of Food Distribution on November 6, 1943, as amended, is hereby further amended by deleting therefrom the provisions in § 1401.125 (i) and inserting, in lieu thereof, the following:

(i) *Quota exclusions and exemptions.* Deliveries of milk, milk byproducts, or cream (1) to other handlers, except for such deliveries to sub-handlers, (2) to plants engaged in the handling or processing of milk, milk byproducts, or cream from which no milk, milk byproducts, or cream is delivered in the sales area, (3) to nursery, elementary, junior high, and high schools, and (4) to the agencies or groups specified in (d) of FDO 79 shall be excluded from the computation of deliveries in the base period and exempt from charges to quotas.

The provisions of this amendment shall become effective at 12:01 a. m., e. w. t., April 1, 1944. With respect to violations of said Food Distribution Order No. 79-89, as amended, rights accrued, or liabilities incurred prior to the effective time of this amendment, said Food Distribution Order No. 79-89, as amended, shall be deemed to be in full force and effect for the purpose of sustaining any proper suit, action, or other proceeding with respect to any such violation, right, or liability.

(E.O. 9280, 7 F.R. 10179; E.O. 9322, 8 F.R. 3807; E.O. 9334, 8 F.R. 5423; E.O. 9392, 8 F.R. 14783; FDO 79, 8 F.R. 12426, 13283)

Issued this 29th day of March 1944.

LEE MARSHALL,
Director of Distribution.

FDO 79-90

NOV. 6, 1943

WAR FOOD ADMINISTRATION

PART 1401—DAIRY PRODUCTS

[FDO 79-90]

FLUID MILK AND CREAM IN WATERLOO, IOWA, SALES AREA

Pursuant to the authority vested in me by Food Distribution Order No. 79 (8 F.R. 12426), issued on September 7, 1943, as amended, and to effectuate the purposes of such order, it is hereby ordered as follows:

§ 1401.126 *Quota restrictions*—(a) *Definitions.* When used in this order, unless otherwise distinctly expressed or manifestly incompatible with the intent hereof:

(1) Each term defined in Food Distribution Order No. 79, as amended, shall, when used herein, have the same meaning as is set forth for such term in Food Distribution Order No. 79, as amended.

(2) The term "FDO 79" means Food Distribution Order No. 79, issued on September 7, 1943, as amended.

(3) The term "sub-handler" means any handler, such as a peddler, vendor, sub-dealer, or secondary dealer, who purchases in a previously packaged and processed form milk, milk byproducts, or cream for delivery.

(b) *Milk sales area.* The following area is hereby designated as a "milk sales area" to be known as the Waterloo, Iowa, sales area, and is referred to hereinafter as the "sales area":

The city of Waterloo and the townships of Cedar Falls, East Waterloo, and Waterloo, all in Black Hawk County, Iowa.

(c) *Base period.* The calendar month of June 1943 is hereby designated as the base period for the sales area.

(d) *Quota period.* The remainder of the calendar month in which the provisions hereof become effective and each subsequent calendar month, respectively, is hereby designated as a quota period for the sales area.

(e) *Handler quotas.* Quotas for each handler in the sales area in each quota period shall be calculated in terms of pounds of each of the items for which percentages are specified in (3) below and shall be determined as follows:

(1) Divide the total deliveries of each such item made in the sales area by such handler during the base period, after excluding the quota-exempt deliveries described in (i) hereof, by the number of days in the base period;

(2) Multiply the result of the foregoing calculation by the number of days in the quota period;

(3) Multiply the aforesaid resulting amount by the following applicable percentage: (i) Milk: 100 percent; (ii) butterfat in milk: ---- percent; (iii) cream: 75 percent; (iv) butterfat in cream: 75 percent; (v) milk byproducts other than cottage, pot, or baker's cheese: 75 percent; and (vi) cottage, pot, or baker's cheese: 75 percent of skim milk equivalent. (For the purpose of this order, one pound of cottage, pot, or baker's cheese shall be considered as the equivalent of 7 pounds of skim milk.)

(f) *Quota limitations.* No handler shall, during any quota period, make deliveries in the sales area in excess of his respective quotas, except as set out in (i) hereof: *Provided,* That a handler may, after application to and approval by the market agent, secure an increase in milk quotas through an equivalent reduction as determined by the market agent, in cream and milk byproducts quotas, and an increase in milk byproducts quota through an equivalent reduction as determined by the market agent, in cream quotas.

(g) *Quotas for handlers who are also producers.* Quotas for handlers who are also producers and who purchase no milk shall be 100 percent of the total production of such handlers in the base period.

(h) *Handler exemptions.* Quotas shall not apply to any handler who delivers in a quota period a daily average of less than 200 units of milk, cream, and milk byproducts. For the purpose of this order, a unit shall be the equivalent in volume of the following: (1) Milk, one quart of milk; (2) cream, one-half pint of cream; and (3) milk byproduct, one quart of skim milk, buttermilk, flavored milk drink, or other beverage containing more than 85 percent of skim milk, or one-half pound of cottage, pot, or baker's cheese.

(i) *Quota exclusions and exemptions.* Deliveries of milk, milk byproducts, or cream (1) to other handlers, except for such deliveries to sub-handlers, (2) to plants engaged in the handling or processing of milk, milk byproducts, or cream from which no milk, milk byproducts, or cream is delivered in the sales area, and (3) to the agencies or groups specified in (d) of FDO 79, shall be excluded from the computation of deliveries in the base period and exempt from charges to quotas.

(j) *Transfers and apportionment of quotas.* The market agent is empowered to deduct an amount of base period deliveries to purchasers from the total of deliveries made by a handler or other person in the base period upon the application and a showing of unreasonable hardship by the handler making deliveries to such purchasers on the effective date of this order, and to add the amount of such deliveries to the total base period deliveries of the applicant handler. Denials of transfers or transfers granted by the market agent shall be reviewed by the Director upon application.

(k) *Petition for relief from hardships.* (1) Any person affected by FDO 79 or the provisions hereof who considers that compliance therewith would work an exceptional and unreasonable hardship on him, may file with the market agent a petition addressed to the Director. The petition shall contain the correct name, address and principal place of business of the petitioner, a full statement of the facts upon which the petition is based, and the hardship involved and the nature of the relief desired.

(2) Upon receiving such petition, the market agent shall immediately investigate the representations and facts stated therein.

(3) After investigation, the petition shall be certified to the Director, but prior to certification the market agent may (i) deny the petition, or (ii) grant temporary relief for a total period not to exceed 60 days.

(4) Denials or grants of relief by the market agent shall be reviewed by the Director and may be affirmed, modified, or reversed by the Director.

(l) *Reports.* Each handler shall transmit to the market agent on forms prescribed by the market agent the following reports:

(1) Within 20 days following the effective date of this order, reports which show the information required by the market agent to establish such handlers' quotas;

(2) Within 20 days following the close of each quota period, the information required by the market agent to establish volumes of deliveries of milk, cream, and milk byproducts during the preceding quota period; and

(3) Handlers exempt from quotas pursuant to (h) hereof shall, upon the re-

quest of the market agent, submit the information required by the market agent to establish volumes of deliveries of milk, cream, and milk byproducts.

(m) *Records.* Handlers shall keep and shall make available to the market agent such records of receipts, sales, deliveries, and production as the market agent shall require for the purpose of obtaining information which the Director may require for the establishment of quotas as prescribed in (b) of FDO 79.

(n) *Distribution schedules.* The distribution schedules, if any, to be followed by the handlers in making deliveries shall be made effective in the terms of approval by the Director of such schedules.

(o) *Expense of administration.* Each handler shall pay to the market agent, within 20 days after the close of each calendar month an assessment of $0.01 per hundredweight of each of milk, cream, skim milk, buttermilk, flavored milk drinks, beverages containing more than 85 percent of skim milk, and skim milk equivalent of cottage, pot, or baker's cheese delivered during the preceding quota period and subject to quota regulations under the provisions hereof.

(p) *Violations.* The market agent shall report all violations to the Director together with the information required for the prosecution of such violations, except in a case where a handler has made deliveries in a quota period in excess of a quota in an amount not to exceed 5 percent of such quota, and in the succeeding quota period ma liveries below that quota by at l same percent.

(q) *Bureau of the Budget a* The record keeping and report quirements of this order have b proved by the Bureau of the Bu accordance with the Federal Rep of 1942. Subsequent record kee reporting requirements will be su the approval of the Bureau of the pursuant to the Federal Reports 1942.

(r) This order shall take effect a. m., e. w. t., December 1, 1943.

Issued this 6th day of Novemb

C. W. KITCH

Acting Director of Food Distrib

Release—Immediate:
Washington, D. C., November 8, 1943.

TEN NEW MILK SALES AREAS NAMED

Milk sales in 10 metropolitan areas in Iowa, Nebraska, New Hampshire, Missouri, Kansas, Colorado, Indiana, and California will be regulated under the Food Distribution Administration's fluid milk conservation and control program beginning December 1, 1943, the War Food Administration said today.

The new milk sales areas and the market agents who will administer the program in each, are:

Springfield, Mo., (FDO 79); St. Joseph, Mo., (FDO 79); Topeka, Kans., (FDO 79); M. M. Morehouse, 512 Porter Bldg., 406 W. 34th St., Kansas City, Mo.

Manchester, N. H., (FDO 79), Samuel Tator, 80 Federal Street, Boston, Mass.

Pueblo, Colo., (FDO 79), Ben King, 503 Security Life Bldg., 810 14th St., Denver, Colo.

Terre Haute, Ind., (FDO 79), W. A. Wilson, 446 Illinois Building, Indianapolis, Ind.

Fresno, Calif., (FDO 79), E. L. Vehlow, Mull Building, Sacramento, Calif.

Lincoln, Nebr., (FDO 79), Wayne McPherren, 408 Post Office Building, Omaha, Nebr.

Cedar Rapids, Iowa, (FDO 79); Waterloo, Iowa, (FDO 79).

Under the program, milk dealers will be permitted to sell as much fluid milk as they sold in June and three-fourths as much cream and milk byproducts (such as cottage cheese, chocolate milk, and buttermilk) as they sold in June. Milk dealers include all persons or firms engaged in the sale or transfer of milk, but not such distributors as subhandlers ("peddlers"), retail stores, hotels, or restaurants.

Producer-distributors who purchase no milk will be permitted to sell as much milk as they produced in June.

A dealer may increase his milk sales by reducing his cream and milk byproducts sales, and increase his sales of milk byproducts by reducing his cream sales, providing such an adjustment is approved in advance by the market agent for the area.

Deliveries of milk, cream, a byproducts to other dealers: Armed Forces, and to plants pr milk who do not distribute milk or milk byproducts in the sales quota exempt.

Consumers in the milk sale named today and in others designated generally will be able chase as much milk under the n servation program as they ha buying in recent months—wit limits of local supplies.

Fluid milk sales are being st Food Distribution Administrat cials said, to help assure suffici for manufacturing the cheese, evaporated milk, and milk pov quired by the Armed Services a ians for good nutrition and balanced diets. Sales quotas o and on milk byproducts have below June deliveries to boost fl supplies where production is l to conserve milk for manuf purposes.

FDO 79-90
AMDT. 1
JAN. 4, 1944

WAR FOOD ADMINISTRATION

[FDO 79-90, Amdt. 1]

PART 1401—DAIRY PRODUCTS

FLUID MILK IN WATERLOO, IOWA, SALES AREA

Pursuant to the authority vested in the Director by Food Distribution Order No. 79, dated September 7, 1943 (8 F.R. 12426), as amended, and to effectuate the purposes thereof, Food Distribution Order No. 79-90, § 1401.126, relative to the conservation of fluid milk in the Waterloo, Iowa, milk sales area (8 F.R. 15474), issued by the Acting Director of Food Distribution on November 6, 1943, is amended as follows:

The expense of administration specified in § 1401.126 (o) of the original order is increased from $0.01 to $0.02.

Effective date. This amendment of FDO 79-90, shall become effective at 12:01 a. m., e. w. t., February 1, 1944.

(E.O. 9280, 7 F.R. 10179; E.O. 9322, 8 F.R. 3807; E.O. 9334, 8 F.R. 5423; E.O. 9392, 8 F.R. 14783; FDO 79, 8 F.R. 12426, 13285)

Issued this 4th day of January 1944.

ROY F. HENDRICKSON,
Director of Food Distribution.

FDO 79-90
AMDT. 2
MAR. 29, 1944

WAR FOOD ADMINISTRATION

[FDO 79-90, Amdt. 2]

PART 1401—DAIRY PRODUCTS

FLUID MILK AND CREAM IN WATERLOO, IOWA, SALES AREA

Pursuant to Food Distribution Order No. 79 (8 F.R. 12426), dated September 7, 1943, as amended, and to effectuate the purposes thereof, Food Distribution Order No. 79-90 (8 F.R. 15474), relative to the conservation and distribution of fluid milk, milk byproducts, and cream in the Waterloo, Iowa, milk sales area, issued by the Director of Food Distribution on November 6, 1943, as amended, is hereby further amended by deleting therefrom the provisions in § 1401.126 (i) and inserting, in lieu thereof, the following:

(i) *Quota exclusions and exemptions.* Deliveries of milk, milk byproducts, or cream (1) to other handlers, except for such deliveries to subhandlers, (2) to plants engaged in the handling or processing of milk, milk byproducts, or cream from which no milk, milk byproducts, or cream is delivered in the sales area, (3) to nursery, elementary, junior high, and high schools, and (4) to the agencies or groups specified in (d) of FDO 79 shall be excluded from the computation of deliveries in the base period and exempt from charges to quotas.

The provisions of this amendment shall become effective at 12:01 a. m., e. w. t., April 1, 1944. With respect to violations of said Food Distribution Order No. 79-90, as amended, rights accrued, or liabilities incurred prior to the effective time of this amendment, said Food Distribution Order No. 79-90, as amended, shall be deemed to be in full force and effect for the purpose of sustaining any proper suit, action, or other proceeding with respect to any such violation, right, or liability.

(E.O. 9280, 7 F.R. 10179; E.O. 9322, 8 F.R. 3807; E.O. 9334, 8 F.R. 5423; E.O. 9392, 8 F.R. 14783; FDO 79, 8 F.R. 12426, 13283)

Issued this 29th day of March 1944.

LEE MARSHALL,
Director of Distribution.

733 7
2

FDO 79-91

NOV. 6, 1943

WAR FOOD ADMINISTRATION

[FDO 79-91]

PART 1401—DAIRY PRODUCTS

FLUID MILK AND CREAM IN PUEBLO, COLO., SALES AREA

Pursuant to the authority vested in me by Food Distribution Order No. 79 (8 F.R. 12426), issued on September 7, 1943, as amended, and to effectuate the purposes of such order, it is hereby ordered as follows:

§ 1401.130 *Quota restrictions*—(a) *Definitions.* When used in this order, unless otherwise distinctly expressed or manifestly incompatible with the intent hereof:

(1) Each term defined in Food Distribution Order No. 79, as amended, shall, when used herein, have the same meaning as is set forth for such term in Food Distribution Order No. 79, as amended.

(2) The term "FDO 79" means Food Distribution Order No. 79, issued on September 7, 1943, as amended.

(3) The term "sub-handler" means any handler, such as a peddler, vendor, sub-dealer, or secondary dealer, who purchases in a previously packaged and processed form milk, milk byproducts, or cream for delivery.

(b) *Milk sales area.* The following area is hereby designated as a "milk sales area" to be known as the Pueblo, Colorado, sales area, and is referred to hereinafter as the "sales area":

The city of Pueblo, those parts of the election precincts numbered 2 through 7, 10, 12, 16, 18, 19, 21, 23, and 37 which extend beyond the city limits of Pueblo, the election precincts numbered 112, 113, 115, 117, 124, and 125, that part of election precinct 1 which lies outside Pueblo and is surrounded by Pueblo city limits, and that part of election precinct 9 outside Pueblo comprising the Colorado State Hospital for the Insane, all in Pueblo County, Colorado.

(c) *Base period.* The calendar month of June 1943 is hereby designated as the base period for the sales area.

(d) *Quota period.* The remainder of the calendar month in which the provisions hereof become effective and each subsequent calendar month, respectively, is hereby designated as a quota period for the sales area.

(e) *Handler quotas.* Quotas for each handler in the sales area in each quota period shall be calculated in terms of pounds of each of the items for which percentages are specified in (3) below and shall be determined as follows:

(1) Divide the total deliveries of each such item made in the sales area by such handler during the base period, after excluding the quota-exempt deliveries described in (i) hereof, by the number of days in the base period;

(2) Multiply the result of the foregoing calculation by the number of days in the quota period;

(3) Multiply the aforesaid resulting amount by the following applicable percentage: (i) Milk: 100 percent; (ii) butterfat in milk: 100 percent; (iii) cream: 75 percent; (iv) Butterfat in cream: 75 percent; (v) Milk byproducts other than cottage, pot, or baker's cheese: 75 percent; and (vi) cottage, pot, or baker's cheese: 75 percent of skim milk equivalent. (For the purpose of this order, one pound of cottage, pot, or baker's cheese shall be considered as the equivalent of 7 pounds of skim milk.)

(f) *Quota limitations.* No handler shall, during any quota period, make deliveries in the sales area in excess of his respective quotas, except as set out in (i) hereof: *Provided,* That a handler may, after application to and approval by the market agent, secure an increase in milk quotas through an equivalent reduction as determined by the market agent, in cream and milk byproducts quotas, and an increase in milk byproducts quota through an equivalent reduction as determined by the market agent, in cream quotas.

(g) *Quotas for handlers who are also producers.* Quotas for handlers who are also producers and who purchase no milk shall be 100 percent of the total production of such handlers in the base period.

(h) *Handler exemptions.* Quotas shall not apply to any handler who delivers in a quota period a daily average of less than 200 units of milk, cream, and milk byproducts. For the purpose of this order, a unit shall be the equivalent in the volume of the following: (1) Milk, one quart of milk; (2) cream, one-half pint of cream; and (3) milk byproducts, one quart of skim milk, buttermilk, flavored milk drink, or other beverage containing more than 85 percent of skim milk, or one-half pound of cottage, pot, or baker's cheese.

(i) *Quota exclusions and exemptions.* Deliveries of milk, milk byproducts, or cream (1) to other handlers, except for such deliveries to sub-handlers, (2) to plants engaged in the handling or processing of milk, milk byproducts, or cream from which no milk, milk byproducts, or cream is delivered in the sales area, and (3) to the agencies or groups specified in (d) of FDO 79, shall be excluded from the computation of deliveries in the base period and exempt from charges to quotas.

(j) *Transfers and apportionment of quotas.* The market agent is empowered to deduct an amount of base period deliveries to purchasers from the total of deliveries made by a handler or other person in the base period upon the application and a showing of unreasonable hardship by the handler making deliveries to such purchasers on the effective date of this order, and to add the amount of such deliveries to the total base period deliveries of the applicant handler. Denials of transfers or transfers granted by the market agent shall be reviewed by the Director upon application.

(k) *Petition for relief from hardships.* (1) Any person affected by FDO 79 or the provisions hereof who considers that compliance therewith would work an exceptional and unreasonable hardship on him, may file with the market agent a petition addressed to the Director. The petition shall contain the correct name, address and principal place of business of the petitioner, a full statement of the facts upon which the petition is based, and the hardship involved and the nature of the relief desired.

(2) Upon receiving such petition, the market agent shall immediately investigate the representations and facts stated therein.

(3) After investigation, the petition shall be certified to the Director, but prior to certification the market agent may (i) deny the petition, or (ii) grant temporary relief for a total period not to exceed 60 days.

(4) Denials or grants of relief by the market agent shall be reviewed by the Director and may be affirmed, modified, or reversed by the Director.

(l) *Reports.* Each handler shall transmit to the market agent on forms prescribed by the market agent the following reports:

(1) Within 20 days following the effective date of this order, reports which show the information required by the

market agent to establish such handlers' quotas;

(2) Within 20 days following the close of each quota period, the information required by the market agent to establish volumes of deliveries of milk, cream, and milk byproducts during the preceding quota period; and

(3) Handlers exempt from quotas pursuant to (h) hereof shall, upon the request of the market agent, submit the information required by the market agent to establish volumes of deliveries of milk, cream, and milk byproducts.

(m) *Records.* Handlers shall keep and shall make available to the market agent such records of receipts, sales, deliveries, and production as the market agent shall require for the purpose of obtaining information which the Director may require for the establishment of quotas as prescribed in (b) of FDO 79.

(n) *Distribution schedules.* The distribution schedules, if any, to be followed by the handlers in making deliveries shall be made effective in the terms of approval by the Director of such schedules.

(o) *Expense of administration.* Each handler shall pay to the market agent, within 20 days after the close of each calendar month an assessment of $0.015 per hundredweight of each of milk, cream, skim milk, buttermilk, flavored milk drinks, beverages containing more than 85 percent of skim milk, and skim milk equivalent of cottage, pot, or baker's cheese delivered during the preceding quota period and subject to quota regulations under the provisions hereof.

(p) *Violations.* The market agent shall report all violations to the Director together with the information required for the prosecution of such violations, except in a case where a handler has made deliveries in a quota perioc excess of a quota in an amount no exceed 5 percent of such quota, anc the succeeding quota period makes liveries below that quota by at least same percent.

(q) *Bureau of the Budget appro* The record keeping and reporting quirements of this order have been proved by the Bureau of the Budge accordance with the Federal Reports of 1942. Subsequent record keeping reporting requirements will be sub to the approval of the Bureau of Budget pursuant to the Federal Rep Act of 1942.

(r) This order shall take effect 12:01 a. m., e. w. t., December 1, 194

Issued this 6th day of November 1

C. W. KITCHEN,
Acting Director of Food Distributio

Release—Immediate:
Washington, D. C., November 8, 1943.

TEN NEW MILK SALES AREAS NAMED

Milk sales in 10 metropolitan areas in Iowa, Nebraska, New Hampshire, Missouri, Kansas, Colorado, Indiana, and California will be regulated under the Food Distribution Administration's fluid milk conservation and control program beginning December 1, 1943, the War Food Administration said today.

The new milk sales areas and the market agents who will administer the program in each, are:

Springfield, Mo., (FDO 79); St. Joseph, Mo., (FDO 79); Topeka, Kans., (FDO 79); M. M. Morehouse, 512 Porter Bldg., 406 W. 34th St., Kansas City, Mo.

Manchester, N. H., (FDO 79), Samuel Tator, 80 Federal Street, Boston, Mass.

Pueblo, Colo., (FDO 79), Ben King, 503 Security Life Bldg., 810 14th St., Denver, Colo.

Terre Haute, Ind., (FDO 79), W. A. Wilson, 446 Illinois Building, Indianapolis, Ind.

Fresno, Calif., (FDO 79), E. L. Vehlow, Mull Building, Sacramento, Calif.

Lincoln, Nebr., (FDO) 79), Wayne McPherren, 408 Post Office Building, Omaha, Nebr.

Cedar Rapids, Iowa, (FDO 79); Waterloo, Iowa, (FDO 79).

Under the program, milk dealers will be permitted to sell as much fluid milk as they sold in June and three-fourths as much cream and milk byproducts (such as cottage cheese, chocolate milk, and buttermilk) as they sold in June. Milk dealers include all persons or firms engaged in the sale or transfer of milk, but not such distributors as subhandlers ("peddlers"), retail stores, hotels, or restaurants.

Producer-distributors who purchase no milk will be permitted to sell as much milk as they produced in June.

A dealer may increase his milk sales by reducing his cream and milk byproducts sales, and increase his sales of milk byproducts by reducing his cream sales, providing such an adjustment is approved in advance by the market agent for the area.

Deliveries of milk, cream, and 1 byproducts to other dealers: to Armed Forces, and to plants proces milk who do not distribute milk, cr or milk byproducts in the sales area quota exempt.

Consumers in the milk sales a named today and in others alre designated generally will be able to 1 chase as much milk under the milk c servation program as they have 1 buying in recent months—within limits of local supplies.

Fluid milk sales are being stabili Food Distribution Administration cials said, to help assure sufficient 1 for manufacturing the cheese, bu evaporated milk, and milk powder quired by the Armed Services and c ians for good nutrition and prop balanced diets. Sales quotas on cr and on milk byproducts have been below June deliveries to boost fluid 1 supplies where production is low, to conserve milk for manufactu purposes.

FDO 79-92
NOV. 6, 1943

WAR FOOD ADMINISTRATION

[FDO 79-92] A

PART 1401—DAIRY PRODUCTS

FLUID MILK AND CREAM IN SPRINGFIELD, MO., SALES AREA

Pursuant to the authority vested in me by Food Distribution Order No. 79 (8 F.R. 12426), issued on September 7, 1943, as amended, and to effectuate the purposes of such order, it is hereby ordered as follows:

§ 1401.129 *Quota restrictions*—(a) *Definitions.* When used in this order, unless otherwise distinctly expressed or manifestly incompatible with the intent hereof:

(1) Each term defined in Food Distribution Order No. 79, as amended, shall, when used herein, have the same meaning as is set forth for such term in Food Distribution Order No. 79, as amended.

(2) The term "FDO 79" means Food Distribution Order No. 79, issued on September 7, 1943, as amended.

(3) The term "sub-handler" means any handler, such as a peddler, vendor, sub-dealer, or secondary dealer, who purchases in a previously packaged and processed form milk, milk byproducts, or cream for delivery.

(b) *Milk sales area.* The following area is hereby designated as a "milk sales area" to be known as the Springfield, Missouri, sales area, and is referred to hereinafter as the "sales area":

The city of Springfield and the townships of Campbell and North Campbell, all in Greene County, Missouri.

(c) *Base period.* The calendar month of June 1943 is hereby designated as the base period for the sales area.

(d) *Quota period.* The remainder of the calendar month in which the provisions hereof become effective and each subsequent calendar month, respectively, is hereby designated as a quota period for the sales area.

(e) *Handler quotas.* Quotas for each handler in the sales area in each quota period shall be calculated in terms of pounds of each of the items for which percentages are specified in (3) below and shall be determined as follows:

(1) Divide the total deliveries of each such item made in the sales area by such handler during the base period, after excluding the quota-exempt deliveries described in (i) hereof, by the number of days in the base period;

(2) Multiply the result of the foregoing calculation by the number of days in the quota period;

(3) Multiply the aforesaid resulting amount by the following applicable percentage: (i) Milk: 100 percent; (ii) butterfat in milk: 100 percent; (iii) cream: 75 percent; (iv) butterfat in cream: 75 percent; (v) milk byproducts other than cottage, pot, or baker's cheese: 75 percent; and (vi) cottage, pot, or baker's cheese: 75 percent of skim milk equivalent. (For the purpose of this order, one pound of cottage, pot, or baker's cheese shall be considered as the equivalent of 7 pounds of skim milk.)

(f) *Quota limitations.* No handler shall, during any quota period, make deliveries in the sales area in excess of his respective quotas, except as set out in (i) hereof: *Provided,* That a handler may, after application to and approval by the market agent, secure an increase in milk quotas through an equivalent reduction as determined by the market agent, in cream and milk byproducts quotas, and an increase in milk byproducts quota through an equivalent reduction as determined by the market agent, in cream quotas.

(g) *Quotas for handlers who are also producers.* Quotas for handlers who are also producers and who purchase no milk shall be 100 percent of the total production of such handlers in the base period.

(h) *Handler exemptions.* Quotas shall not apply to any handler who delivers in a quota period a daily average of less than 350 units of milk, cream, and milk byproducts. For the purpose of this order, a unit shall be the equivalent in the volume of the following: (1) Milk, one quart of milk; (2) cream, one-half pint of cream; and (3) milk byproduct, one quart of skim milk, buttermilk, flavored milk drink, or other beverage containing more than 85 percent of skim milk, or one-half pound of cottage, pot, or baker's cheese.

(i) *Quota exclusions and exemptions.* Deliveries of milk, milk byproducts, or cream (1) to other handlers, except for such deliveries to sub-handlers, (2) to plants engaged in the handling or processing of milk, milk byproducts, or cream from which no milk, milk byproducts, or cream is delivered in the sales area, and (3) to the agencies or groups specified in (d) of FDO 79, shall be excluded from the computation of deliveries in the base period and exempt from charges to quotas.

(j) *Transfers and apportionment of quotas.* The market agent is empowered to deduct an amount of base period deliveries to purchasers from the total of deliveries made by a handler or other person in the base period upon the application and a showing of unreasonable hardship by the handler making deliveries to such purchasers on the effective date of this order, and to add the amount of such deliveries to the total base period deliveries of the applicant handler. Denials of transfers or transfers granted by the market agent shall be reviewed by the Director upon application.

(k) *Petition for relief from hardships.* (1) Any person affected by FDO 79 or the provisions hereof who considers that compliance therewith would work an exceptional and unreasonable hardship on him, may file with the market agent a petition addressed to the Director. The petition shall contain the correct name, address and principal place of business of the petitioner, a full statement of the facts upon which the petition is based, and the hardship involved and the nature of the relief desired.

(2) Upon receiving such petition, the market agent shall immediately investigate the representations and facts stated therein.

(3) After investigation, the petition shall be certified to the Director, but prior to certification the market agent may (i) deny the petition, or (ii) grant temporary relief for a total period not to exceed 60 days.

(4) Denials or grants of relief by the market agent shall be reviewed by the Director and may be affirmed, modified, or reversed by the Director.

(l) *Reports.* Each handler shall transmit to the market agent on forms prescribed by the market agent the following reports:

(1) Within 20 days following the effective date of this order, reports which show the information required by the market agent to establish such handlers' quotas;

(2) Within 20 days following the close of each quota period, the information required by the market agent to establish volumes of deliveries of milk, cream, and milk byproducts during the preceding quota period; and

(3) Handlers exempt from quotas pursuant to (h) hereof shall, upon the request of the market agent, submit the information required by the market agent to establish volumes of deliveries of milk, cream, and milk byproducts.

(m) *Records.* Handlers shall keep and shall make available to the market agent such records of receipts, sales, deliveries, and production as the market agent shall require for the purpose of obtaining information which the Director may require for the establishment of quotas as prescribed in (b) of FDO 79.

(n) *Distribution schedules.* The distribution schedules, if any, to be followed by the handlers in making deliveries shall be made effective in the terms of approval by the Director of such schedules.

(o) *Expense of administration.* Each handler shall pay to the market agent, within 20 days after the close of each calendar month an assessment of $.01 per hundredweight of each of milk, cream, skim milk, buttermilk, flavored milk drinks, beverages containing more than 85 percent of skim milk, and skim milk equivalent of cottage, pot, or baker's cheese delivered during the preceding quota period and subject to quota regulations under the provisions hereof.

(p) *Violations.* The market agent shall report all violations to the Director together with the information required for the prosecution of such violations, except in a case where a handler has made deliveries in a quota period in excess of a quota in an amount not to exceed 5 percent of such quota, and in the succeeding quota period makes deliverie below that quota by at least the sam percent.

(q) *Bureau of the Budget approval* The record keeping and reporting re quirements of this order have been ap proved by the Bureau of the Budget i accordance with the Federal Reports Ac of 1942. Subsequent record keeping o reporting requirements will be subjec to the approval of the Bureau of th Budget pursuant to the Federal Report Act of 1942.

(r) This order shall take effect a 12:01 a. m., e. w. t., December 1, 1943.

Issued this 6th day of November 1943

C. W. Kitchen,
Acting Director of Food Distribution.

Release—Immediate:
Washington, D. C., November 8, 1943.

TEN NEW MILK SALES AREAS NAMED

Milk sales in 10 metropolitan areas in Iowa, Nebraska, New Hampshire, Missouri, Kansas, Colorado, Indiana, and California will be regulated under the Food Distribution Administration's fluid milk conservation and control program beginning December 1, 1943, the War Food Administration said today.

The new milk sales areas and the market agents who will administer the program in each, are:

Springfield, Mo., (FDO 79); St. Joseph, Mo., (FDO 79); Topeka, Kans., (FDO 79); M. M. Morehouse, 512 Porter Bldg., 406 W. 34th St., Kansas City, Mo.

Manchester, N. H., (FDO 79), Samuel Tator, 80 Federal Street, Boston, Mass.

Pueblo, Colo., (FDO 79), Ben King, 503 Security Life Bldg., 810 14th St., Denver, Colo.

Terre Haute, Ind., (FDO 79), W. A. Wilson, 446 Illinois Building, Indianapolis, Ind.

Fresno, Calif., (FDO 79), E. L. Vehlow, Mull Building, Sacramento, Calif.

Lincoln, Nebr., (FDO) 79), Wayne McPherren, 408 Fost Office Building, Omaha, Nebr.

Cedar Rapids, Iowa, (FDO 79); Waterloo, Iowa, (FDO 79).

Under the program, milk dealers will be permitted to sell as much fluid milk as they sold in June and three-fourths as much cream and milk byproducts (such as cottage cheese, chocolate milk, and buttermilk) as they sold in June. Milk dealers include all persons or firms engaged in the sale or transfer of milk, but not such distributors as subhandlers ("peddlers"), retail stores, hotels, or restaurants.

Producer-distributors who purchase no milk will be permitted to sell as much milk as they produced in June.

A dealer may increase his milk sales by reducing his cream and milk byproducts sales, and increase his sales of milk byproducts by reducing his cream sales, providing such an adjustment is approved in advance by the market agent for the area.

Deliveries of milk, cream, and mill byproducts to other dealers: to th Armed Forces, and to plants processin milk who do not distribute milk, crean or milk byproducts in the sales area ar quota exempt.

Consumers in the milk sales area named today and in others alread designated generally will be able to pur chase as much milk under the milk con servation program as they have bee buying in recent months—within th limits of local supplies.

Fluid milk sales are being stabilized Food Distribution Administration offi cials said, to help assure sufficient mil for manufacturing the cheese, butte evaporated milk, and milk powder re quired by the Armed Services and civil ians for good nutrition and properl balanced diets. Sales quotas on crear and on milk byproducts have been se below June deliveries to boost fluid mil supplies where production is low, an to conserve milk for manufacturin purposes.

3F
/

FDO 79-92
AMDT. 1
DEC. 31, 19

WAR FOOD ADMINISTRATION

[FDO 79-92, Amdt. 1]

PART 1401—DAIRY PRODUCTS

FLUID MILK AND CREAM IN SPRINGFIELD, MO., SALES AREA

Pursuant to the authority vested in the Director by Food Distribution Order No. 79, dated September 7, 1943 (8 F.R. 12426) as amended, and to effectuate the purposes thereof, Food Distribution Order No. 79-92 (8 F.R. 15476), relative to the conservation and distribution of fluid milk in the Springfield, Missouri, milk sales area, issued by the Director of Food Distribution on November 6, 1943, is amended as follows:

Delete the numerals "350" wherever they appear in § 1401.129 (h) and insert, in lieu thereof, the numerals "150".

Effective date. This amendment of FDO 79-92, shall become effective at 12:01 a. m., e. w. t., January 1, 1944.

(E.O. 9280, 7 F.R. 10179; E.O. 9322, 8 F.R. 3807; E.O. 9334, 8 F.R. 5423; E.O. 9392, 8 F.R. 14783; FDO 79, 8 F.R. 12426, 13283)

Issued this 31st day of December 1943.

ROY F. HENDRICKSON,
Director of Food Distribution.

WAR FOOD ADMINISTRATION
Food Distribution Administration
Washington 25, D. C.

CORRECTION NOTICE: FDO-79.93 "Dairy Products"

In printing Food Distribution Order 79.93 the following error occurred:

In section 1401.127 (L) (1) the word "puotas" should read "quotas" so the sentence will read, "Within 20 days following the effective date of this order, reports which show the information required by the market agent to establish such handlers' quotas;".

337

FDO 79-93

NOV. 6, 1943

WAR FOOD ADMINISTRATION

PART 1401—DAIRY PRODUCTS

FLUID MILK AND CREAM IN TOPEKA, KANS., SALES AREA

Pursuant to the authority vested in me by Food Distribution Order No. 79 (8 F.R. 12426), issued on September 7, 1943, as amended, and to effectuate the purposes of such order, it is hereby ordered as follows:

§ 1401.127 *Quota restrictions*—(a) *Definitions.* When used in this order, unless otherwise distinctly expressed or manifestly incompatible with the intent hereof:

(1) Each term defined in Food Distribution Order No. 79, as amended, shall, when used herein, have the same meaning as is set forth for such term in Food Distribution Order No. 79, as amended.

(2) The term "FDO 79" means Food Distribution Order No. 79, issued on September 7, 1943, as amended.

(3) The term "sub-handler" means any handler, such as a peddler, vendor, sub-dealer, or secondary dealer, who purchases in a previously packaged and processed form milk, milk byproducts, or cream for delivery.

(b) *Milk sales area.* The following area is hereby designated as a "milk sales area" to be known as the Topeka, Kansas, sales area, and is referred to hereinafter as the "sales area":

The city of Topeka and the township of Topeka in Shawnee County, Kansas.

(c) *Base period.* The calendar month of June 1943 is hereby designated as the base period for the sales area.

(d) *Quota period.* The remainder of the calendar month in which the provisions hereof become effective and each subsequent calendar month, respectively, is hereby designated as a quota period of the sales area.

(e) *Handler quotas.* Quotas for each handler in the sales area in each quota period shall be calculated in terms of pounds of each of the items for which percentages are specified in (3) below and shall be determined as follows:

(1) Divide the total deliveries of each such item made in the sales area by such handler during the base period, after excluding the quota-exempt deliveries described in (i) hereof, by the number of days in the base period;

(2) Multiply the result of the foregoing calculation by the number of days in the quota period;

(3) Multiply the aforesaid resulting amount by the following applicable percentage: (i) Milk: 100 percent; (ii) butterfat in milk: 100 percent; (iii) cream: 75 percent; (iv) butterfat in cream: 75 percent; (v) milk byproducts other than cottage, pot, or baker's cheese: 75 percent; and (vi) cottage, pot, or baker's cheese: 75 percent of skim milk equivalent. (For the purpose of this order, one pound of cottage, pot, or baker's cheese shall be considered as the equivalent of 7 pounds of skim milk.)

(f) *Quota limitations.* No handler shall, during any quota period, make deliveries in the sales area in excess of his respective quotas, except as set out in (i) hereof: *Provided,* That a handler may, after application to and approval by the market agent, secure an increase in milk quotas through an equivalent reduction as determined by the market agent, in cream and milk byproducts quotas, and an increase in milk byproducts quota through an equivalent reduction as determined by the market agent, in cream quotas.

(g) *Quotas for handlers who are also producers.* Quotas for handlers who are also producers and who purchase no milk shall be 100 percent of the total production of such handlers in the base period.

(h) *Handler exemptions.* Quotas shall not apply to any handler who delivers in a quota period a daily average of less than 350 units of milk, cream, and milk byproducts. For the purpose of this order, a unit shall be the equivalent in the volume of the following: (1) Milk, one quart of milk; (2) cream, one-half pint of cream; and (3) milk byproduct, one quart of skim milk, buttermilk, flavored milk drink, or other beverage containing more than 85 percent of skim milk, or one-half pound of cottage, pot, or baker's cheese.

(i) *Quota exclusions and exemptions.* Deliveries of milk, milk byproducts, or cream (1) to other handlers, except for such deliveries to sub-handlers, (2) to plants engaged in the handling or processing of milk, milk byproducts, or cream from which no milk, milk byproducts, or cream is delivered in the sales area, and (3) to the agencies or groups specified in (d) of FDO 79, shall be excluded from the computation of deliveries in the base period and exempt from charges to quotas.

(j) *Transfers and apportionment of quotas.* The market agent is empowered to deduct an amount of base period deliveries to purchasers from the total of deliveries made by a handler or other person in the base period upon the application and a showing of unreasonable hardship by the handler making deliveries to such purchasers on the effective date of this order, and to add the amount of such deliveries to the total base period deliveries of the applicant handler. Denials of transfers or transfers granted by the market agent shall be reviewed by the Director upon application.

(k) *Petition for relief from hardships.* (1) Any person affected by FDO 79 or the provisions hereof who considers that compliance therewith would work an exceptional and unreasonable hardship on him, may file with the market agent a petition addressed to the Director. The petition shall contain the correct name, address and principal place of business of the petitioner, a full statement of the facts upon which the petition is based, and the hardship involved and the nature of the relief desired.

(2) Upon receiving such petition, the market agent shall immediately investigate the representations and facts stated therein.

(3) After investigation, the petition shall be certified to the Director, but prior to certification the market agent may (i) deny the petition, or (ii) grant temporary relief for a total period not to exceed 60 days.

(4) Denials or grants of relief by the market agent shall be reviewed by the Director and may be affirmed, modified, or reversed by the Director.

(l) *Reports.* Each handler shall transmit to the market agent on forms prescribed by the market agent the following reports:

(1) Within 20 days following the effective date of this order, reports which show the information required by the market agent to establish such handlers' quotas;

(2) Within 20 days following the close of each quota period, the information required by the market agent to establish volumes of deliveries of milk, cream, and milk byproducts during the preceding quota period; and

(3) Handlers exempt from quotas pursuant to (h) hereof shall, upon the request of the market agent, submit the information required by the market

agent to establish volumes of deliveries of milk, cream, and milk byproducts.

(m) *Records.* Handlers shall keep and shall make available to the market agent such records of receipts, sales, deliveries, and production as the market agent shall require for the purpose of obtaining information which the Director may require for the establishment of quotas as prescribed in (b) of FDO 79.

(n) *Distribution schedules.* The distribution schedules, if any, to be followed by the handlers in making deliveries shall be made effective in the terms of approval by the Director of such schedules.

(o) *Expense of administration.* Each handler shall pay to the market agent, within 20 days after the close of each calendar month an assessment of $.01 per hundredweight of each of milk, cream, skim milk, buttermilk, flavored milk drinks, beverages containing more than 85 percent of skim milk, and skim milk equivalent of cottage, pot, or baker's cheese delivered during the preceding quota period and subject to quota regulations under the provisions hereof.

(p) *Violations.* The market agent shall report all violations to the Director together with the information required for the prosecution of such violations, except in a case where a handler has made deliveries in a quota period in excess of a quota in an amount not to exceed 5 percent of such quota, and in the succeeding quota period makes deliveries belo[w] that quota by at least the same percen[tage].

(q) *Bureau of the Budget approv[al].* The record keeping and reporting re[quirements] of this order have been ap[proved] by the Bureau of the Budget i[n] accordance with the Federal Reports A[ct] of 1942. Subsequent record keeping [or] reporting requirements will be subject [to] the approval of the Bureau of the Budg[et] pursuant to the Federal Reports Act [of] 1942.

(r) This order shall take effect [at] 12:01 a. m., e. w. t., December 1, 1943.

Issued this 6th day of November 194[3].

C. W. Kitchen,
Acting Director of Food Distribution.

Release—Immediate:
Washington, D. C., November 8, 1943.

TEN NEW MILK SALES AREAS NAMED

Milk sales in 10 metropolitan areas in Iowa, Nebraska, New Hampshire, Missouri, Kansas, Colorado, Indiana, and California will be regulated under the Food Distribution Administration's fluid milk conservation and control program beginning December 1, 1943, the War Food Administration said today.

The new milk sales areas and the market agents who will administer the program in each, are:

Springfield, Mo., (FDO 79); St. Joseph, Mo., (FDO 79); Topeka, Kans., (FDO 79); M. M. Morehouse, 512 Porter Bldg., 406 W. 34th St., Kansas City, Mo.

Manchester, N. H., (FDO 79), Samuel Tator, 80 Federal Street, Boston, Mass.

Pueblo, Colo., (FDO 79), Ben King, 503 Security Life Bldg., 810 14th St., Denver, Colo.

Terre Haute, Ind., (FDO 79), W. A. Wilson, 446 Illinois Building, Indianapolis, Ind.

Fresno, Calif., (FDO 79), E. L. Vehlow, Mull Building, Sacramento, Calif.

Lincoln, Nebr., (FDO) 79), Wayne McPherren, 408 Post Office Building, Omaha, Nebr.

Cedar Rapids, Iowa, (FDO 79); Waterloo, Iowa, (FDO 79).

Under the program, milk dealers will be permitted to sell as much fluid milk as they sold in June and three-fourths as much cream and milk byproducts (such as cottage cheese, chocolate milk, and buttermilk) as they sold in June. Milk dealers include all persons or firms engaged in the sale or transfer of milk, but not such distributors as subhandlers ("peddlers"), retail stores, hotels, or restaurants.

Producer-distributors who purchase no milk will be permitted to sell as much milk as they produced in June.

A dealer may increase his milk sales by reducing his cream and milk byproducts sales, and increase his sales of milk byproducts by reducing his cream sales, providing such an adjustment is approved in advance by the market agent for the area.

Deliveries of milk, cream, and mi[lk] byproducts to other dealers: to t[he] Armed Forces, and to plants processi[ng] milk who do not distribute milk, crea[m] or milk byproducts in the sales area a[re] quota exempt.

Consumers in the milk sales are[as] named today and in others alrea[dy] designated generally will be able to pu[r]chase as much milk under the milk co[n]servation program as they have be[en] buying in recent months—within t[he] limits of local supplies.

Fluid milk sales are being stabilize[d,] Food Distribution Administration of[fi]cials said, to help assure sufficient mi[lk] for manufacturing the cheese, butte[r,] evaporated milk, and milk powder r[e]quired by the Armed Services and civi[l]ians for good nutrition and proper[ly] balanced diets. Sales quotas on crea[m] and on milk byproducts have been s[et] below June deliveries to boost fluid mi[lk] supplies where production is low, an[d] to conserve milk for manufacturi[ng] purposes.

FDO 79-93
AMDT. 1
DEC. 28, 1943

WAR FOOD ADMINISTRATION

[FDO 79-93, Amdt. 1]

PART 1401—DAIRY PRODUCTS

FLUID MILK AND CREAM IN THE TOPEKA, KANS., MILK SALES AREA

Pursuant to Food Distribution Order No. 79 (8 F. R. 12426), dated September 7, 1943, as amended, and to effectuate the purposes thereof. Food Distribution Order No. 79-93 (8 F. R. 15477), relative to the conservation and distribution of fluid milk in the Topeka, Kansas, milk sales area, issued by the Director of Food Distribution on November 6, 1943, is amended by deleting the description of the sales area in § 1401.127 (b) and inserting in lieu thereof, the following:

The territory within the corporate limits of the city of Topeka and the territory within the following boundary lines of Shawnee County, in the State of Kansas: Beginning at the southwest (SW) corner, section 35, township 12 S, range 15 E in Shawnee County, Kansas; thence north two miles; thence west one mile; thence north one mile; thence west one mile; thence north one mile; thence west two miles to the southwest corner section 7, township 12 S, range 15 E; thence north three and one-fourth (3¼) miles more or less, to the south bank of the Kansas River; thence easterly along said south bank three miles, more or less, to the west line of section 27, township 11 S, range 15 E; thence three and one-half (3½) miles, more or less, to the northwest corner, section 10, township 11 S, range 15 E; thence east two miles; thence north one mile to the northwest corner, section 1, township 11 S, range 15 E; thence east four miles to the Meriden road; thence south along said road one mile; thence east two miles to the east line of Shawnee County; thence south and easterly along said county line to the point of intersection with the west line of the east one-half of section 36, township 11 S, range 16 E; thence south two and one-half (2½) miles more or less, to the south quarter corner of section 12, township 12 S, range 16 E; thence west two and one-half (2½) miles to northeast corner, section 16, township 12 S, range 16 E; thence south one mile, thence west one mile; thence south three miles to the southeast corner, section 32, township 12 S, range 16 E; thence west four miles to the point of beginning.

The provisions of this amendment shall become effective at 12:01 a. m., e. w. t., January 1, 1944. With respect to violations of said Food Distribution Order No. 79-93, rights accrued, or liabilities incurred prior to the effective time of this amendment, said Food Distribution Order No. 79-93, shall be deemed to be in full force and effect for the purpose of sustaining any proper suit, action, or other proceeding with respect to any such violation, right, or liability.

(E.O. 9280, 7 F.R. 10179; E.O. 9322, 8 F.R. 3807; E.O. 9334, 8 F.R. 5423; E.O. 9392, 8 F.R. 14783; FDO 79, 8 F.R. 12426, 13283)

Issued this 28th day of December 1943.

ROY F. HENDRICKSON,
Director of Food Distribution.

WAR FOOD ADMINISTRATION
Food Distribution Administration
Washington 25, D. C.

CORRECTION NOTICE: FDO-79.94 "Dairy Products"

In printing Food Distribution Order 79.94 the following error occurred in punctuation:

In Section 1401.82 (f) a colon(:) instead of a semicolon(;) should be used after the word "hereof" so the sentence will be punctuated as follows: "No handler shall, during any quota period, make deliveries in the sales area in excess of his respective quotas, except as set out in (i) hereof:".

7733 ~

FDO 79-94

NOV. 6, 1943

WAR FOOD ADMINISTRATION

[FDO 79-94]

PART 1401—DAIRY PRODUCTS

FLUID MILK AND CREAM IN FRESNO, CALIF., SALES AREA

Pursuant to the authority vested in me by Food Distribution Order No. 79 (8 F.R. 12426), issued on September 7, 1943, as amended, and to effectuate the purposes of such order, it is hereby ordered as follows:

§ 1401.82 *Quota restrictions*—(a) *Definitions.* When used in this order, unless otherwise distinctly expressed or manifestly incompatible with the intent hereof:

(1) Each term defined in Food Distribution Order No. 79, as amended, shall, when used herein, have the same meaning as is set forth for such term in Food Distribution Order No. 79, as amended.

(2) The term "FDO 79" means Food Distribution Order No. 79, issued on September 7, 1943, as amended.

(3) The term "sub-handler" means any handler, such as a peddler, vendor, sub-dealer, or secondary dealer, who purchases in a previously packaged and processed form milk, milk byproducts, or cream for delivery.

(b) *Milk sales area.* The following area is hereby designated as a "milk sales area" to be known as the Fresno, California, sales area, and is referred to hereinafter as the "sales area":

The entire area included in the marketing area now designated by the Director of Agriculture of the State of California pursuant to the provisions of Chapter 10, Division 4, of the Agricultural Code of the State of California as the Fresno Marketing Area.

(c) *Base period.* The calendar month of June 1943 is hereby designated as the base period for the sales area.

(d) *Quota period.* The remainder of the calendar month in which the provisions hereof become effective and each subsequent calendar month, respectively, is hereby designated as a quota period for the sales area.

(e) *Handler quotas.* Quotas for each handler in the sales area in each quota period shall be calculated in terms of pounds of each of the items for which percentages are specified in (3) below and shall be determined as follows:

(1) Divide the total deliveries of each such item made in the sales area by such handler during the base period, after excluding the quota-exempt deliveries described in (i) hereof, by the number of days in the base period;

(2) Multiply the result of the foregoing calculation by the number of days in the quota period;

(3) Multiply the aforesaid resulting amount by the following applicable percentage: (i) Milk: 100 percent; (ii) butterfat in milk: 100 percent; (iii) cream: 75 percent; (iv) butterfat in cream: 75 percent; (v) milk byproducts other than cottage, pot, or baker's cheese: 75 percent; and (vi) cottage, pot, or baker's cheese: 75 percent of skim milk equivalent. (For the purpose of this order, one pound of cottage, pot, or baker's cheese shall be considered as the equivalent of 7 pounds of skim milk.)

(f) *Quota limitations.* No handler shall, during any quota period, make deliveries in the sales area in excess of his respective quotas, except as set out in (i) hereof; *Provided*, That a handler may, after application to and approval by the market agent, secure an increase in milk quotas through an equivalent reduction as determined by the market agent, in cream and milk byproducts quotas, and an increase in milk byproducts quota through an equivalent reduction as determined by the market agent, in cream quotas.

(g) *Quotas for handlers who are also producers.* Quotas for handlers who are also producers and who purchase no milk shall be 100 percent of the total production of such handlers in the base period.

(h) *Handler exemptions.* Quotas shall not apply to any handler who delivers in a quota period a daily average of less than 300 units of milk, cream, and milk byproducts. For the purpose of this order, a unit shall be the equivalent in volume of the following: (1) Milk, one quart of milk; (2) cream, one-half pint of cream; and (3) milk byproducts, one quart of skim milk, buttermilk, flavored milk drink, or other beverage containing more than 85 percent of skim milk, or one-half pound of cottage, pot, or baker's cheese.

(i) *Quota exclusions and exemptions.* Deliveries of milk, milk byproducts, or cream (1) to other handlers, except for such deliveries to sub-handlers, (2) to plants engaged in the handling or processing of milk, milk byproducts or cream from which no milk, milk byproducts, or cream is delivered in the sales area, and (3) to the agencies or groups specified in (d) of FDO 79, shall be excluded from the computation of deliveries in the base period and exempt from charges to quotas.

(j) *Transfers and apportionment of quotas.* The market agent is empowered to deduct an amount of base period deliveries to purchasers from the total of deliveries made by a handler or other person in the base period upon the application and a showing of unreasonable hardship by the handler making deliveries to such purchasers on the effective date of this order, and to add the amount of such deliveries to the total base period deliveries of the applicant handler. Denials of transfers or transfers granted by the market agent shall be reviewed by the Director upon application.

(k) *Petition for relief from hardships.* (1) Any person affected by FDO 79 or the provisions hereof who considers that compliance therewith would work an exceptional and unreasonable hardship on him, may file with the market agent a petition addressed to the Director. The petition shall contain the correct name, address and principal place of business of the petitioner, a full statement of the facts upon which the petition is based, and the hardship involved and the nature of the relief desired.

(2) Upon receiving such petition, the market agent shall immediately investigate the representations and facts stated therein.

(3) After investigation, the petition shall be certified to the Director, but prior to certification the market agent may (i) deny the petition, or (ii) grant temporary relief for a total period not to exceed 60 days.

(4) Denials or grants of relief by the market agent shall be reviewed by the Director and may be affirmed, modified, or reversed by the Director.

(l) *Reports.* Each handler shall transmit to the market agent on forms prescribed by the market agent the following reports:

(1) Within 20 days following the effective date of this order, reports which show the information required by the market agent to establish such handlers' quotas;

(2) Within 20 days following the close of each quota period, the information required by the market agent to establish volumes of deliveries of milk, cream, and

milk byproducts during the preceding quota period; and

(3) Handlers exempt from quotas pursuant to (h) hereof shall, upon the request of the market agent, submit the information required by the market agent to establish volumes of deliveries of milk, cream, and milk byproducts.

(m) *Records.* Handlers shall keep and shall make available to the market agent such records of receipts, sales, deliveries, and production as the market agent shall require for the purpose of obtaining information which the Director may require for the establishment of quotas as prescribed in (b) of FDO 79.

(n) *Distribution schedules.* The distribution schedules, if any, to be followed by the handlers in making deliveries shall be made effective in the terms of approval by the Director of such schedules.

(o) *Expense of administration.* Each handler shall pay to the market agent, within 20 days after the close of each calendar month an assessment of $0.01 per hundredweight of each of milk, cream, skim milk, buttermilk, flavored milk drinks, beverages containing more than 85 percent of skim milk, and skim milk equivalent of cottage, pot, or baker's cheese delivered during the preceding quota period and subject to quota regulations under the provisions hereof.

(p) *Violations.* The market agent shall report all violations to the Director together with the information required for the prosecution of such violations, except in a case where a handler has made deliveries in a quota period in excess of a quota in an amount not to exceed 5 percent of such quota, and in

the s
liveri
same

(q)
The
quire
provi
accou
of 19
repor
the a
pursu
1942.

(r)
a. m

Iss

Acti

Release—Immediate:
Washington, D. C., November 8, 1943.

TEN NEW MILK SALES AREAS NAMED

Milk sales in 10 metropolitan areas in Iowa, Nebraska, New Hampshire, Missouri, Kansas, Colorado, Indiana, and California will be regulated under the Food Distribution Administration's fluid milk conservation and control program beginning December 1, 1943, the War Food Administration said today.

The new milk sales areas and the market agents who will administer the program in each, are:

Springfield, Mo., (FDO 79); St. Joseph, Mo., (FDO 79); Topeka, Kans., (FDO 79); M. M. Morehouse, 512 Porter Bldg., 406 W. 34th St., Kansas City, Mo.

Manchester, N. H., (FDO 79), Samuel Tator, 80 Federal Street, Boston, Mass.

Pueblo, Colo., (FDO 79), Ben King, 503 Security Life Bldg., 810 14th St., Denver, Colo.

Terre Haute, Ind., (FDO 79), W. A. Wilson, 446 Illinois Building, Indianapolis, Ind.

Fresno, Calif., (FDO 79), E. L. Vehlow, Mull Building, Sacramento, Calif.

Lincoln, Nebr., (FDO) 79), Wayne McPherren, 408 Post Office Building, Omaha, Nebr.

Cedar Rapids, Iowa, (FDO 79); Waterloo, Iowa, (FDO 79).

Under the program, milk dealers will be permitted to sell as much fluid milk as they sold in June and three-fourths as much cream and milk byproducts (such as cottage cheese, chocolate milk, and buttermilk) as they sold in June. Milk dealers include all persons or firms engaged in the sale or transfer of milk, but not such distributors as subhandlers ("peddlers"), retail stores, hotels, or restaurants.

Producer-distributors who purchase no milk will be permitted to sell as much milk as they produced in June.

A dealer may increase his milk sales by reducing his cream and milk byproducts sales, and increase his sales of milk byproducts by reducing his cream sales, providing such an adjustment is approved in advance by the market agent for the area.

De
bypr
Arm
milk
or m
quot

Co
nam
desig
chas
servi
buyi
limit

Fl
Food
cials
for
evap
quir
ians
bala
and
belov
supp
to c
purp

77337
Op. 1

FDO 79-95
NOV. 6, 1943

WAR FOOD ADMINISTRATION

[FDO 79-95]

PART 1401—DAIRY PRODUCTS

FLUID MILK AND CREAM IN LINCOLN, NEBR., SALES AREA

Pursuant to the authority vested in me by Food Distribution Order No. 79 (8 F.R. 12426), issued on September 7, 1943, as amended, and to effectuate the purposes of such order, it is hereby ordered as follows:

§ 1401.124 *Quota restrictions*—(a) *Definitions.* When used in this order, unless otherwise distinctly expressed or manifestly incompatible with the intent hereof:

(1) Each term defined in Food Distribution Order No. 79, as amended, shall, when used herein, have the same meaning as is set forth for such term in Food Distribution Order No. 79, as amended.

(2) The term "FDO 79" means Food Distribution Order No. 79, issued on September 7, 1943, as amended.

(3) The term "sub-handler" means any handler, such as a peddler, vendor, sub-dealer, or secondary dealer, who purchases in a previously packaged and processed form milk, milk byproducts, or cream for delivery.

(b) *Milk sales area.* The following area is hereby designated as a "milk sales area" to be known as the Lincoln, Nebraska, sales area, and is referred to hereinafter as the "sales area":

The city of Lincoln and the precincts of Garfield, Lancaster, West Lincoln, and Yankee Hill, all in Lancaster County, Nebraska.

(c) *Base period.* The calendar month of June 1943 is hereby designated as the base period for the sales area.

(d) *Quota period.* The remainder of the calendar month in which the provisions hereof become effective and each subsequent calendar month, respectively, is hereby designated as a quota period for the sales area.

(e) *Handler quotas.* Quotas for each handler in the sales area in each quota period shall be calculated in terms of pounds of each of the items for which percentages are specified in (3) below and shall be determined as follows:

(1) Divide the total deliveries of each such item made in the sales area by such handler during the base period, after excluding the quota-exempt deliveries described in (i) hereof, by the number of days in the base period;

(2) Multiply the result of the foregoing calculation by the number of days in the quota period;

(3) Multiply the aforesaid resulting amount by the following applicable percentage: (i) Milk: 100 percent; (ii) butterfat in milk: 100 percent; (iii) cream: 75 percent; (iv) butterfat in cream: 75 percent; (v) milk byproducts other than cottage, pot, or baker's cheese: 75 percent; and (vi) cottage, pot, or baker's cheese: 75 percent of skim milk equivalent. (For the purpose of this order, one pound of cottage, pot, or baker's cheese shall be considered as the equivalent of 7 pounds of skim milk.)

(f) *Quota limitations.* No handler shall, during any quota period, make deliveries in the sales area in excess of his respective quotas, except as set out in (i) hereof: *Provided*, That a handler may, after application to and approval by the market agent, secure an increase in milk quotas through an equivalent reduction as determined by the market agent, in cream and milk byproducts quotas, and an increase in milk byproducts quota through an equivalent reduction as determined by the market agent, in cream quotas.

(g) *Quotas for handlers who are also producers.* Quotas for handlers who are also producers and who purchase no milk shall be 100 percent of the total production of such handlers in the base period.

(h) *Handler exemptions.* Quotas shall not apply to any handler who delivers in a quota period a daily average of less than 125 units of milk, cream, and milk byproducts. For the purpose of this order, a unit shall be the equivalent in volume of the following: (1) Milk, one quart of milk; (2) cream, one-half pint of cream; and (3) milk byproduct, one quart of skim milk, buttermilk, flavored milk drink, or other beverage containing more than 85 percent of skim milk, or one-half pound of cottage, pot, or baker's cheese.

(i) *Quota exclusions and exemptions.* Deliveries of milk, milk byproducts, or cream (1) to other handlers, except for such deliveries to sub-handlers, (2) to plants engaged in the handling or processing of milk, milk byproducts, or cream from which no milk, milk byproducts, or cream is delivered in the sales area, and (3) to the agencies or groups specified in (d) of FDO 79, shall be excluded from the computation of deliveries in the base period and exempt from charges to quotas.

(j) *Transfers and apportionment of quotas.* The market agent is empowered to deduct an amount of base period deliveries to purchasers from the total of deliveries made by a handler or other person in the base period upon the application and a showing of unreasonable hardship by the handler making deliveries to such purchasers on the effective date of this order, and to add the amount of such deliveries to the total base period deliveries of the applicant handler. Denials of transfers or transfers granted by the market agent shall be reviewed by the Director upon application.

(k) *Petition for relief from hardships.* (1) Any person affected by FDO 79 or the provisions hereof who considers that compliance therewith would work an exceptional and unreasonable hardship on him, may file with the market agent a petition addressed to the Director. The petition shall contain the correct name, address, and principal place of business of the petitioner, a full statement of the facts upon which the petition is based, and the hardship involved and the nature of the relief desired.

(2) Upon receiving such petition, the market agent shall immediately investigate the representations and facts stated therein.

(3) After investigation, the petition shall be certified to the Director, but prior to certification the market agent may (i) deny the petition, or (ii) grant temporary relief for a total period not to exceed 60 days.

(4) Denials or grants of relief by the market agent shall be reviewed by the Director and may be affirmed, modified, or reversed by the Director.

(l) *Reports.* Each handler shall transmit to the market agent on forms prescribed by the market agent the following reports:

(1) Within 20 days following the effective date of this order, reports which show the information required by the market agent to establish such handlers' quotas;

(2) Within 20 days following the close of each quota period, the information required by the market agent to establish volumes of deliveries of milk, cream, and milk byproducts during the preceding quota period; and

(3) Handlers exempt from quotas pursuant to (h) hereof shall, upon the request of the market agent, submit the information required by the market

agent to establish volumes of deliveries of milk, cream, and milk byproducts.

(m) *Records.* Handlers shall keep and shall make available to the market agent such records of receipts, sales, deliveries, and production as the market agent shall require for the purpose of obtaining information which the Director may require for the establishment of quotas as prescribed in (b) of FDO 79.

(n) *Distribution schedules.* The distribution schedules, if any, to be followed by the handlers in making deliveries shall be made effective in the terms of approval by the Director of such schedules.

(o) *Expense of administration.* Each handler shall pay to the market agent, within 20 days after the close of each calendar month an assessment of $0.01 per hundredweight of each of milk, cream, skim milk, buttermilk, flavored milk drinks, beverages containing more than 85 percent of skim milk, and skim milk equivalent of cottage, pot, or baker's cheese delivered during the preceding quota period and subject to quota regulations under the provisions hereof.

(p) *Violations.* The market agent shall report all violations to the Director together with the information required for the prosecution of such violations, except in a case where a handler has made deliveries in a quota period in excess of a quota in an amount not to exceed 5 percent of such quota, and in the succeeding quota period makes deliveries below that quota by at least the same percent.

(q) *Bureau of the Budget approval.* The record keeping and reporting requirements of this order have been approved by the Bureau of the Budget in accordance with the Federal Reports Act of 1942. Subsequent record keeping or reporting requirements will be subject to the approval of the Bureau of the Budget pursuant to the Federal Reports Act of 1942.

(r) This order shall take effect at 12:01 a. m., e. w. t., December 1, 1943.

Issued this 6th day of November 1943.

C. W. KITCHEN,
Acting Director of Food Distribution.

Release—Immediate:
Washington, D. C., November 8, 1943.

TEN NEW MILK SALES AREAS NAMED

Milk sales in 10 metropolitan areas in Iowa, Nebraska, New Hampshire, Missouri, Kansas, Colorado, Indiana, and California will be regulated under the Food Distribution Administration's fluid milk conservation and control program beginning December 1, 1943, the War Food Administration said today.

The new milk sales areas and the market agents who will administer the program in each, are:

Springfield, Mo., (FDO 79); St. Joseph, Mo., (FDO 79); Topeka, Kans., (FDO 79); M. M. Morehouse, 512 Porter Bldg., 406 W. 34th St., Kansas City, Mo.

Manchester, N. H., (FDO 79), Samuel Tator, 80 Federal Street, Boston, Mass.

Pueblo, Colo., (FDO 79), Ben King, 503 Security Life Bldg., 810 14th St., Denver, Colo.

Terre Haute, Ind., (FDO 79), W. A. Wilson, 446 Illinois Building, Indianapolis, Ind.

Fresno, Calif., (FDO 79), E. L. Vehlow, Mull Building, Sacramento, Calif.

Lincoln, Nebr., (FDO) 79), Wayne McPherren, 408 Post Office Building, Omaha, Nebr.

Cedar Rapids, Iowa, (FDO 79); Waterloo, Iowa, (FDO 79).

Under the program, milk dealers will be permitted to sell as much fluid milk as they sold in June and three-fourths as much cream and milk byproducts (such as cottage cheese, chocolate milk, and buttermilk) as they sold in June. Milk dealers include all persons or firms engaged in the sale or transfer of milk, but not such distributors as subhandlers ("peddlers"), retail stores, hotels, or restaurants.

Producer-distributors who purchase no milk will be permitted to sell as much milk as they produced in June.

A dealer may increase his milk sales by reducing his cream and milk byproducts sales, and increase his sales of milk byproducts by reducing his cream sales, providing such an adjustment is approved in advance by the market agent for the area.

Deliveries of milk, cream, and milk byproducts to other dealers: to the Armed Forces, and to plants processing milk who do not distribute milk, cream or milk byproducts in the sales area are quota exempt.

Consumers in the milk sales areas named today and in others already designated generally will be able to purchase as much milk under the milk conservation program as they have been buying in recent months—within the limits of local supplies.

Fluid milk sales are being stabilized, Food Distribution Administration officials said, to help assure sufficient milk for manufacturing the cheese, butter, evaporated milk, and milk powder required by the Armed Services and civilians for good nutrition and properly balanced diets. Sales quotas on cream and on milk byproducts have been set below June deliveries to boost fluid milk supplies where production is low, and to conserve milk for manufacturing purposes.

FDO 79-96

NOV. 6, 1943

WAR FOOD ADMINISTRATION

[FDO 79-96]

PART 1401—DAIRY PRODUCTS

FLUID MILK AND CREAM IN ST. JOSEPH, MO., SALES AREA

Pursuant to the authority vested in me by Food Distribution Order No. 79 (8 F.R. 12426), issued on September 7, 1943, as amended, and to effectuate the purposes of such order, it is hereby ordered as follows:

§ 1401.128 *Quota restrictions*—(a) *Definitions*. When used in this order, unless otherwise distinctly expressed or manifestly incompatible with the intent hereof;

(1) Each term defined in Food Distribution Order No. 79, as amended, shall, when used herein, have the same meaning as is set forth for such term in Food Distribution Order No. 79, as amended.

(2) The term "FDO 79" means Food Distribution Order No. 79, issued on September 7, 1943, as amended.

(3) The term "sub-handler" means any handler, such as a peddler, vendor, sub-dealer, or secondary dealer, who purchases in a previously packaged and processed form milk, milk byproducts, or cream for delivery.

(b) *Milk sales area*. The following area is hereby designated as a "milk sales area" to be known as the St. Joseph, Missouri, sales area, and is referred to hereinafter as the "sales area":

The city of St. Joseph and the township of Washington in Buchanan County, Missouri, and the township of Washington in Doniphan County, Kansas.

(c) *Base period*. The calendar month of June 1943 is hereby designated as the base period for the sales area.

(d) *Quota period*. The remainder of the calendar month in which the provisions hereof become effective and each subsequent calendar month, respectively, is hereby designated as a quota period for the sales area.

(e) *Handler quotas*. Quotas for each handler in the sales area in each quota period shall be calculated in terms of pounds of each of the items for which percentages are specified in (3) below and shall be determined as follows:

(1) Divide the total deliveries of each such item made in the sales area by such handler during the base period, after excluding the quota-exempt deliveries described in (i) hereof, by the number of days in the base period;

(2) Multiply the result of the foregoing calculation by the number of days in the quota period;

(3) Multiply the aforesaid resulting amount by the following applicable percentage: (i) Milk: 100 percent; (ii) butterfat in milk: 100 percent; (iii) cream: 75 percent; (iv) butterfat in cream: 75 percent; (v) milk byproducts other than cottage, pot, or baker's cheese: 75 percent; and (vi) cottage, pot, or baker's cheese: 75 percent of skim milk equivalent. (For the purpose of this order, one pound of cottage, pot, or baker's cheese shall be considered as the equivalent of 7 pounds of skim milk.)

(f) *Quota limitations*. No handler shall, during any quota period, make deliveries in the sales area in excess of his respective quotas, except as set out in (i) hereof: *Provided*, That a handler may, after application to and approval by the market agent, secure an increase in milk quotas through an equivalent reduction as determined by the market agent, in cream and milk byproducts quotas, and an increase in milk byproducts quota through an equivalent reduction as determined by the market agent, in cream quotas.

(g) *Quotas for handlers who are also producers*. Quotas for handlers who are also producers and who purchase no milk shall be 100 percent of the total production of such handlers in the base period.

(h) *Handler exemptions*. Quotas shall not apply to any handler who delivers in a quota period a daily average of less than 350 units of milk, cream, and milk byproducts. For the purpose of this order, a unit shall be the equivalent in the volume of the following: (1) Milk, one quart of milk; (2) cream, one-half pint of cream; and (3) milk byproduct, one quart of skim milk, buttermilk, flavored milk drink, or other beverage containing more than 85 percent of skim milk, or one-half pound of cottage, pot, or baker's cheese.

(i) *Quota exclusions and exemptions*. Deliveries of milk, milk byproducts, or cream (1) to other handlers, except for such deliveries to sub-handlers, (2) to plants engaged in the handling or processing of milk, milk byproducts, or cream from which no milk, milk byproducts, or cream is delivered in the sales area, and (3) to the agencies or groups specified in (d) of FDO 79, shall be excluded from the computation of deliveries in the base period and exempt from charges to quotas.

(j) *Transfers and apportionment of quotas*. The market agent is empowered to deduct an amount of base period deliveries to purchasers from the total of deliveries made by a handler or other person in the base period upon the application and a showing of unreasonable hardship by the handler making deliveries to such purchasers on the effective date of this order, and to add the amount of such deliveries to the total base period deliveries of the applicant handler. Denials of transfers or transfers granted by the market agent shall be reviewed by the Director upon application.

(k) *Petition for relief from hardships*. (1) Any person affected by FDO 79 or the provisions hereof who considers that compliance therewith would work an exceptional and unreasonable hardship on him, may file with the market agent a petition addressed to the Director. The petition shall contain the correct name, address and principal place of business of the petitioner, a full statement of the facts upon which the petition is based, and the hardship involved and the nature of the relief desired.

(2) Upon receiving such petition, the market agent shall immediately investigate the representations and facts stated therein.

(3) After investigation, the petition shall be certified to the Director, but prior to certification the market agent may (i) deny the petition, or (ii) grant temporary relief for a total period not to exceed 60 days.

(4) Denials or grants of relief by the market agent shall be reviewed by the Director and may be affirmed, modified, or reversed by the Director.

(l) *Reports*. Each handler shall transmit to the market agent on forms prescribed by the market agent the following reports:

(1) Within 20 days following the effective date of this order, reports which show the information required by the market agent to establish such handlers' quotas;

(2) Within 20 days following the close of each quota period, the information required by the market agent to establish volumes of deliveries of milk, cream, and milk byproducts during the preceding quota period; and

(3) Handlers exempt from quotas pursuant to (h) hereof shall, upon the request of the market agent, submit the information required by the market agent to establish volumes of deliveries of milk, cream, and milk byproducts.

(m) *Records.* Handlers shall keep and shall make available to the market agent such records of receipts, sales, deliveries, and production as the market agent shall require for the purpose of obtaining information which the Director may require for the establishment of quotas as prescribed in (b) of FDO 79.

(n) *Distribution schedules.* The distribution schedules, if any, to be followed by the handlers in making deliveries shall be made effective in the terms of approval by the Director of such schedules.

(o) *Expense of administration.* Each handler shall pay to the market agent, within 20 days after the close of each calendar month an assessment of $.01 per hundredweight of each of milk, cream, skim milk, buttermilk, flavored milk drinks, beverages containing more than 85 percent of skim milk, and skim milk equivalent of cottage, pot, or baker's cheese delivered during the preceding quota period and subject to quota regulations under the provisions hereof.

(p) *Violations.* The market agent shall report all violations to the Director together with the information required for the prosecution of such violations, except in a case where a handler has made deliveries in a quota period in excess of a quota in an amount not to exceed 5 percent of such quota, and in the succeeding quota period makes deliveries below that quota by at least the same percent.

(q) *Bureau of the Budget approval.* The record keeping and reporting requirements of this order have been approved by the Bureau of the Budget in accordance with the Federal Reports Act of 1942. Subsequent record keeping or reporting requirements will be subject to the approval of the Bureau of the Budget pursuant to the Federal Reports Act of 1942.

(r) This order shall take effect at 12:01 a. m., e. w. t., December 1, 1943.

Issued this 6th day of November 1943.

C. W. KITCHEN,
Acting Director of Food Distribution.

Release—Immediate:
Washington, D. C., November 8, 1943.

TEN NEW MILK SALES AREAS NAMED

Milk sales in 10 metropolitan areas in Iowa, Nebraska, New Hampshire, Missouri, Kansas, Colorado, Indiana, and California will be regulated under the Food Distribution Administration's fluid milk conservation and control program beginning December 1, 1943, the War Food Administration said today.

The new milk sales areas and the market agents who will administer the program in each, are:

Springfield, Mo., (FDO 79); St. Joseph, Mo., (FDO 79); Topeka, Kans., (FDO 79); M. M. Morehouse, 512 Porter Bldg., 406 W. 34th St., Kansas City, Mo.

Manchester, N. H., (FDO 79), Samuel Tator, 80 Federal Street, Boston, Mass.

Pueblo, Colo., (FDO 79), Ben King, 503 Security Life Bldg., 810 14th St., Denver, Colo.

Terre Haute, Ind., (FDO 79), W. A. Wilson, 446 Illinois Building, Indianapolis, Ind.

Fresno, Calif., (FDO 79), E. L. Vehlow, Mull Building, Sacramento, Calif.

Lincoln, Nebr., (FDO) 79), Wayne McPherren, 408 Post Office Building, Omaha, Nebr.

Cedar Rapids, Iowa, (FDO 79); Waterloo, Iowa, (FDO 79).

Under the program, milk dealers will be permitted to sell as much fluid milk as they sold in June and three-fourths as much cream and milk byproducts (such as cottage cheese, chocolate milk, and buttermilk) as they sold in June. Milk dealers include all persons or firms engaged in the sale or transfer of milk, but not such distributors as subhandlers ("peddlers"), retail stores, hotels, or restaurants.

Producer-distributors who purchase no milk will be permitted to sell as much milk as they produced in June.

A dealer may increase his milk sales by reducing his cream and milk byproducts sales, and increase his sales of milk byproducts by reducing his cream sales, providing such an adjustment is approved in advance by the market agent for the area.

Deliveries of milk, cream, and milk byproducts to other dealers: to the Armed Forces, and to plants processing milk who do not distribute milk, cream or milk byproducts in the sales area are quota exempt.

Consumers in the milk sales areas named today and in others already designated generally will be able to purchase as much milk under the milk conservation program as they have been buying in recent months—within the limits of local supplies.

Fluid milk sales are being stabilized, Food Distribution Administration officials said, to help assure sufficient milk for manufacturing the cheese, butter, evaporated milk, and milk powder required by the Armed Services and civilians for good nutrition and properly balanced diets. Sales quotas on cream and on milk byproducts have been set below June deliveries to boost fluid milk supplies where production is low, and to conserve milk for manufacturing purposes.

FDO 79-96
AMDT. 1
DEC. 28, 1943

WAR FOOD ADMINISTRATION

[FDO 79-96, Amdt. 1]

PART 1401—DAIRY PRODUCTS

FLUID MILK AND CREAM IN THE ST. JOSEPH, MO., MILK SALES AREA

Pursuant to Food Distribution Order No. 79 (8 F. R. 12426), dated September 7, 1943, as amended, and to effectuate the purposes thereof, Food Distribution Order No. 79-96 (8 F.R. 15480), relative to the conservation and distribution of fluid milk in the St. Joseph, Missouri, milk sales area, issued by the Director of Food Distribution on November 6, 1943, is amended as follows:

First: By deleting therefrom the description of the sales area in § 1401.128 (b) and inserting, in lieu thereof, the following:

The city of St. Joseph, the township of Washington, the north half of Wayne township and the north half of Center township, in Buchanan County, the south half of Jefferson township in Andrew County, all in the state of Missouri.

Second: Delete therefrom the numerals "350" wherever they appear in § 1401.128 (h) and insert in lieu thereof, the numerals "200".

The provisions of this amendment shall become effective at 12:01 a. m., e. w. t., January 1, 1944. With respect to violations of said Food Distribution Order No. 79-96, rights accrued, or liabilities incurred prior to the effective date of this amendment, said Food Distribution Order No. 79-96, shall be deemed to be in full force and effect for the purpose of sustaining any proper suit, action, or other proceeding with respect to any such violation, right, or liability.

(E.O. 9280, 7 F.R. 10179; E.O. 9322, 8 F.R. 3807; E.O. 9334, 8 F.R. 5423; E.O. 9392, 8 F.R. 14783; FDO 79, 8 F.R. 12426, 13283)

Issued this 28th day of December 1943.

ROY F. HENDRICKSON,
Director of Food Distribution.

WAR FOOD ADMINISTRATION
Food Distribution Administration
Washington 25, D. C.

CORRECTION NOTICE: FDO-79.97 "Dairy Products"

In printing Food Distribution Order 79.97 the following error occurred:

In section 1401.122 (H) Item (1) the word "cream" should read "milk" so that Item (1) reads, "Milk, one quart of milk;".

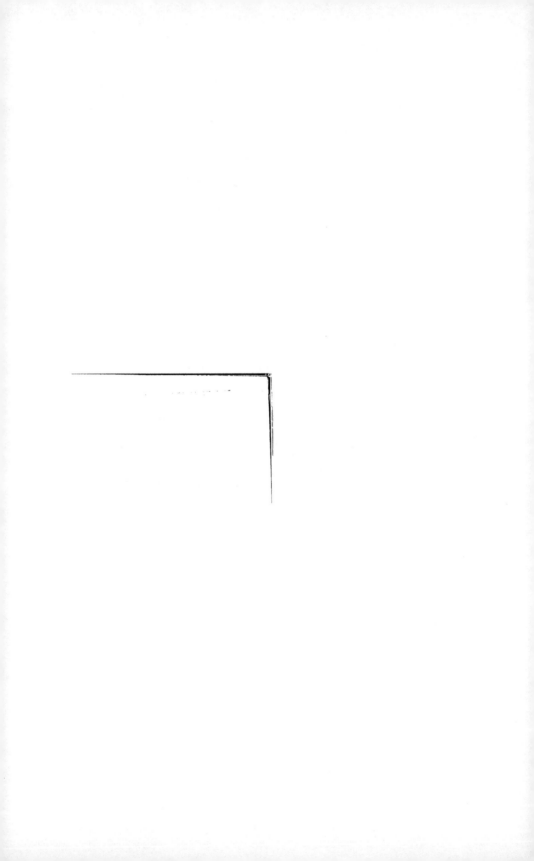

32 F
1/1

FDO 79-97

NOV. 6, 1943

WAR FOOD ADMINISTRATION

[FDO 79-97]

PART 1401—DAIRY PRODUCTS

FLUID MILK AND CREAM IN MANCHESTER, N. H., SALES AREA

Pursuant to the authority vested in me by Food Distribution Order No. 79 (8 F.R. 12426), issued on September 7, 1943, as amended, and to effectuate the purposes of such order, it is hereby ordered as follows:

§ 1401.122 *Quota restrictions*—(a) *Definitions*. When used in this order, unless otherwise distinctly expressed or manifestly incompatible with the intent hereof:

(1) Each term defined in Food Distribution Order No. 79, as amended, shall, when used herein, have the same meaning as is set forth for such term in Food Distribution Order No. 79, as amended.

(2) The term "FDO 79" means Food Distribution Order No. 79, issued on September 7, 1943, as amended.

(3) The term "sub-handler" means any handler, such as a peddler, vendor, sub-dealer, or secondary dealer, who purchases in a previously packaged and processed form milk, milk byproducts, or cream for delivery.

(b) *Milk sales area*. The following area is hereby designated as a "milk sales area" to be known as the Manchester, New Hampshire, sales area, and is referred to hereinafter as the "sales area":

The city of Manchester and the town of Goffstown, both in Hillsboro County, New Hampshire.

(c) *Base period*. The calendar month of June 1943 is hereby designated as the base period for the sales area.

(d) *Quota period*. The remainder of the calendar month in which the provisions hereof become effective and each subsequent calendar month, respectively, is hereby designated as a quota period for the sales area.

(e) *Handler quotas*. Quotas for each handler in the sales area in each quota period shall be calculated in terms of pounds of each of the items for which percentages are specified in (3) below and shall be determined as follows:

(1) Divide the total deliveries of each such item made in the sales area by such handler during the base period, after excluding the quota-exempt deliveries described in (i) hereof, by the number of days in the base period;

(2) Multiply the result of the foregoing calculation by the number of days in the quota period;

(3) Multiply the aforesaid resulting amount by the following applicable percentage: (i) Milk: 100 percent; (ii) butterfat in milk: ___ percent; (iii) cream: 75 percent; (iv) butterfat in cream: 75 percent; (v) milk byproducts other than cottage, pot, or baker's cheese, 75 percent; and (vi) cottage, pot, or baker's cheese, 75 percent of skim milk equivalent. (For the purpose of this order, one pound of cottage, pot, or baker's cheese shall be considered as the equivalent of 7 pounds of skim milk.)

(f) *Quota limitations*. No handler shall, during any quota period, make deliveries in the sales area in excess of his respective quotas, except as set out in (i) hereof: *Provided*, That a handler may, after application to and approval by the market agent, secure an increase in milk quotas through an equivalent reduction as determined by the market agent, in cream and milk byproducts quotas, and an increase in milk byproducts quota through an equivalent reduction as determined by the market agent, in cream quotas.

(g) *Quotas for handlers who are also producers*. Quotas for handlers who are also producers and who purchase no milk shall be 100 percent of the total production of such handlers in the base period.

(h) *Handler exemptions*. Quotas shall not apply to any handler who delivers in a quota period a daily average of less than 200 units of milk, cream, and milk byproducts. For the purpose of this order, a unit shall be the equivalent in volume of the following: (1) Milk, one quart of cream; (2) cream, one-half pint of cream; and (3) milk byproduct, one quart of skim milk, buttermilk, flavored milk drink, or other beverage containing more than 85 percent of skim milk, or one-half pound of cottage, pot, or baker's cheese.

(i) *Quota exclusions and exemptions*. Deliveries of milk, milk byproducts, or cream (1) to other handlers, except for such deliveries to sub-handlers, (2) to plants engaged in the handling or processing of milk, milk byproducts, or cream from which no milk, milk byproducts, or cream is delivered in the sales area, and (3) to the agencies or groups specified in (d) of FDO 79, shall be excluded from the computation of deliveries in the base period and exempt from charges to quotas.

(j) *Transfers and apportionment of quotas*. The market agent is empowered to deduct an amount of base period deliveries to purchasers from the total of deliveries made by a handler or other person in the base period upon the application and a showing of unreasonable hardship by the handler making deliveries to such purchasers on the effective date of this order, and to add the amount of such deliveries to the total base period deliveries of the applicant handler. Denials of transfers or transfers granted by the market agent shall be reviewed by the Director upon application.

(k) *Petition for relief from hardships*. (1) Any person affected by FDO 79 or the provisions hereof who considers that compliance therewith would work an exceptional and unreasonable hardship on him, may file with the market agent a petition addressed to the Director. The petition shall contain the correct name, address and principal place of business of the petitioner, a full statement of the facts upon which the petition is based, and the hardship involved and the nature of the relief desired.

(2) Upon receiving such petition, the market agent shall immediately investigate the representations and facts stated therein.

(3) After investigation, the petition shall be certified to the Director, but prior to certification the market agent may (i) deny the petition, or (ii) grant temporary relief for a total period not to exceed 60 days.

(4) Denials or grants of relief by the market agent shall be reviewed by the Director and may be affirmed, modified, or reversed by the Director.

(l) *Reports*. Each handler shall transmit to the market agent on forms prescribed by the market agent the following reports:

(1) Within 20 days following the effective date of this order, reports which show the information required by the market agent to establish such handlers' quotas;

(2) Within 20 days following the close of each quota period, the information required by the market agent to establish volumes of deliveries of milk, cream, and milk byproducts during the preceding quota period; and

(3) Handlers exempt from quotas pursuant to (h) hereof shall, upon the request of the market agent, submit the information required by the market

agent to establish volumes of deliveries of milk, cream, and milk byproducts.

(m) *Records.* Handlers shall keep and shall make available to the market agent such records of receipts, sales, deliveries, and production as the market agent shall require for the purpose of obtaining information which the Director may require for the establishment of quotas as prescribed in (b) of FDO 79.

(n) *Distribution schedules.* The distribution schedules, if any, to be followed by the handlers in making deliveries shall be made effective in the terms of approval by the Director of such schedules.

(o) *Expense of administration.* Each handler shall pay to the market agent, within 20 days after the close of each calendar month an assessment of $0.015 per hundredweight of each of milk, cream, skim milk, buttermilk, flavored milk drinks, beverages containing more than 85 percent of skim milk, and skim milk equivalent of cottage, pot, or baker's cheese delivered during the preceding quota period and subject to quota regulations under the provisions hereof.

(p) *Violations.* The market agent shall report all violations to the Director together with the information required for the prosecution of such violations, except in a case where a handler has made deliveries in a quota period in excess of a quota in an amount not to exceed 5 percent of such quota, and in the succeeding quota period makes delive[r]
quota by at least the same

(q) *Bureau of the Bu*[…]
The record keeping and
quirements of this order [...]
proved by the Bureau of
accordance with the Feder[…]
of 1942. Subsequent reco[…]
reporting requirements w[…]
to the approval of the I[…]
Budget pursuant to the F[…]
Act of 1942.

(r) This order shall t[…]
12:01 a. m., e. w. t., Dec[…]

Issued this 6th day of N[…]

C. W[…]

Acting Director of Food […]

7337
Cop 1

FDO 79-97
AMDT. 1
NOV. 29, 1943

WAR FOOD ADMINISTRATION

[FDO 79-97, Amdt. 1]

PART 1401—DAIRY PRODUCTS

DIRECTOR'S ORDER FOR THE MANCHESTER, N. H., MILK SALES AREA

Pursuant to the authority vested in the Director by Food Distribution Order No. 79, dated September 7, 1943 (8 F.R. 12426), as amended, and to effectuate the purposes thereof, Food Distribution Order No. 79-97, § 1401.122, relative to the conservation of fluid milk in the Manchester, New Hampshire, milk sales area (8 F.R. 15481), issued by the Director of Food Distribution on November 6, 1943, is amended as follows:

The milk sales area described in § 1401.122 (b) of the original order is modified in the following particulars: Add: "The town of Hooksett in the County of Merrimack, New Hampshire."

Effective date. This amendment of FDO No. 79-97, shall become effective at 12:01 a. m., e. w. t., December 1, 1943.

(E.O. 9280, 7 F.R. 10179; E.O. 9322, 8 F.R. 3807; E.O. 9334, 8 F.R. 5423; E.O. 9392, 8 F.R. 14783; FDO 79, 8 F.R. 12426, 13283)

Issued this 29th day of November 1943.

ROY F. HENDRICKSON,
Director of Food Distribution.

FDO 79-97
AMDT. 2
NOV. 30, 1943

WAR FOOD ADMINISTRATION

[FDO 79-97, Amdt. 2]

PART 1401—DAIRY PRODUCTS

DIRECTOR'S ORDER FOR MANCHESTER, N. H., MILK SALES AREA

Pursuant to the authority vested in the Director by Food Distribution Order No. 79, dated September 7, 1943, (8 F.R. 12426), as amended, and to effectuate the purposes thereof, Food Distribution Order No. 79-97, § 1401.122, relative to the conservation of fluid milk in the Manchester, New Hampshire, milk sales area (8 F.R. 15481) issued by the Director of Food Distribution on November 6, 1943, is amended as follows:

Quotas for handlers who are also producers described in § 1401.122 (g) of the original order is modified in the following particulars: Strike out (g) and insert in lieu thereof the following:

(g) *Quotas for handlers who are also producers.*—Quotas for handlers who are also producers and who purchase no milk shall be computed in accordance with (e) hereof, except that the applicable percentages shall be 100 percent in lieu of the percentages specified in (e) (3).

(b) *Effective date.*—This amendment of FDO No. 79-97, shall become effective at 12:01 a. m., e. w. t., December 1, 1943.

(E.O. 9280, 7 F.R. 10179; E.O. 9322, 8 F.R. 3807; E.O. 9334, 8 F.R. 5423; E.O. 9392, 8 F.R. 14783; FDO 79, 8 F.R. 12426, 13283)

Issued this 30th day of November 1943.

C. W. KITCHEN,
Acting Director of Food Distribution.

FDO 79-97

AMDT. 3
FEB. 28, 1944

WAR FOOD ADMINISTRATION

[FDO 79-97, Amdt. 3]

PART 1401—DAIRY PRODUCTS

FLUID MILK AND CREAM IN THE MANCHESTER, NEW HAMPSHIRE, SALES AREA

Pursuant to Food Distribution Order No. 79 (8 F.R. 12426), dated September 7, 1943, as amended, and to effectuate the purposes thereof, Food Distribution Order No. 79-97 (8 F.R. 15481), relative to the conservation and distribution of fluid milk in the Manchester, New Hampshire, milk sales area, issued by the Director of Food Distribution on November 6, 1943, as amended, is hereby further amended by deleting therefrom the provisions in § 1401.122 (a) (3) and inserting, in lieu thereof, the following:

(3) The term "sub-handler" means any handler, who (i) receives in a previously packaged and processed form milk, milk byproducts, or cream for delivery, and (ii) does not operate facilities for the processing and bottling of fluid milk.

The provisions of this amendment shall become effective at 12:01 a. m., e. w. t., March 1, 1944. With respect to violations of said Food Distribution Order No. 79-97, as amended, rights accrued, or liabilities incurred prior to the effective time of this amendment, said Food Distribution Order No. 79-97, as amended, shall be deemed to be in full force and effect for the purpose of sustaining any proper suit, action, or other proceeding with respect to any such violation, right, or liability.

(E.O. 9280, 7 F.R. 10179; E.O. 9322, 8 F.R. 3807; E.O. 9334, 8 F.R. 5423; E.O. 9392, 8 F.R. 14783; FDO 79, 8 F.R. 12426, 13283)

Issued this 28th day of February 1944.

C. W. KITCHEN,
Acting Director of Food Distribution.

733F
Cop

FDO 79-97
AMDT. 4
MAR. 29, 1944

WAR FOOD ADMINISTRATION

[FDO 79-97, Amdt. 4]

PART 1401—DAIRY PRODUCTS

FLUID MILK AND CREAM IN MANCHESTER, N. H., SALES AREA

Pursuant to Food Distribution Order No. 79 (8 F. R. 12426), dated September 7, 1943, as amended, and to effectuate the purposes thereof, Food Distribution Order No. 79-97 (8 F.R. 15481), relative to the conservation and distribution of fluid milk in the Manchester, New Hampshire, milk sales area, issued by the Director of Food Distribution on November 6, 1943, as amended, is hereby further amended by deleting therefrom the provisions in § 1401.122 (i) and inserting, in lieu thereof, the following:

(i) *Quota exclusions and exemptions.* Deliveries of milk, milk byproducts, or cream (1) to other handlers, except for such deliveries to sub-handlers, (2) to plants engaged in the handling or processing of milk, milk byproducts, or cream from which no milk, milk byproducts, or cream is delivered in the sales area, (3) to nursery, elementary, junior high, and high schools, and (4) to the agencies or groups specified in (d) of FDO 79, shall be excluded from the computation of deliveries in the base period and exempt from charges to quotas.

The provisions of this amendment shall become effective at 12:01 a. m., e. w. t., April 1, 1944. With respect to violations of said Food Distribution Order No. 79-97, as amended, rights accrued, or liabilities incurred prior to the effective time of this amendment, said Food Distribution Order No. 79-97, as amended, shall be deemed to be in full force and effect for the purpose of sustaining any proper suit, action, or other proceeding with respect to any such violation, right, or liability.

(E.O. 9280, 7 F.R. 10179; E.O. 9332, 8 F.R. 3807; E.O. 9334, 8 F.R. 5423; E.O. 9392, 8 F.R. 14783; FDO 79, 8 F.R. 12426, 13286)

Issued this 29th day of March 1944.

LEE MARSHALL,
Director of Food Distribution.

WAR FOOD ADMINISTRATION
Food Distribution Administration
Washington 25, D. C.

CORRECTION NOTICE - FDO-79-98

FLUID MILK AND CREAM, DECATUR, ILL., SALES AREA

In printing FDO-79-98 the following error occurred:

In section 1401.132 (0) the word "handler" was omitted. The sentence should read: "Each handler shall pay to the market agent, within 20 days after the close of each calendar month ...".

FDO 79-98

NOV. 16, 1943

WAR FOOD ADMINISTRATION

[FDO 79-98]

PART 1401—DAIRY PRODUCTS

FLUID MILK AND CREAM, DECATUR, ILL., SALES AREA

Pursuant to the authority vested in me by Food Distribution Order No. 79 (8 F.R. 12426), issued on September 7, 1943, as amended, and to effectuate the purposes of such order, it is hereby ordered as follows:

§ 1401.132 *Quota restrictions.*—(a) *Definitions.* When used in this order, unless otherwise distinctly expressed or manifestly incompatible with the intent hereof.

(1) Each term defined in Food Distribution Order No. 79, as amended, shall, when used herein, have the same meaning as is set forth for such term in Food Distribution Order No. 79, as amended.

(2) The term "FDO 79" means Food Distribution Order No. 79, issued on September 7, 1943, as amended.

(3) The term "sub-handler" means any handler, such as a peddler, vendor, sub-dealer, or secondary dealer, who purchases in a previously packaged and processed form milk, milk byproducts, or cream for delivery.

(b) *Milk sales area.* The following area is hereby designated as a "milk sales area" to be known as the Decatur, Illinois, sales area, and is referred to hereinafter as the "sales area".

The city of Decatur and the township of Decatur, in Macon County, Illinois.

(c) *Base period.* The calendar month of June 1943 is hereby designated as the base period for the sales area.

(d) *Quota period.* The remainder of the calendar month in which the provisions hereof become effective and each subsequent calendar month, respectively, is hereby designated as a quota period for the sales area.

(e) *Handler quotas.* Quotas for each handler in the sales area in each quota period shall be calculated in terms of pounds of each of the items for which percentages are specified in (3) below and shall be determined as follows:

(1) Divide the total deliveries of each such item made in the sales area by such handler during the base period, after excluding the quota-exempt deliveries described in (i) hereof, by the number of days in the base period;

(2) Multiply the result of the foregoing calculation by the number of days in the quota period;

(3) Multiply the aforesaid resulting amount by the following applicable percentages: (i) Milk, 100 percent; (ii) butterfat in milk, ______ percent; (iii) cream, 75 percent; (iv) butterfat, in cream, 75 percent; (v) milk byproducts other than cottage, pot, or baker's cheese, 75 percent; and (vi) cottage, pot, or baker's cheese, 75 percent of skim milk equivalent. (For the purpose of this order, one pound of cottage, pot, or baker's cheese shall be considered as the equivalent of 7 pounds of skim milk.)

(f) *Quota limitations.* No handler shall, during any quota period, make deliveries in the sales area in excess of his respective quotas, except as set out in (i) hereof: *Provided,* That a handler may, after application to and approval by the market agent, secure an increase in milk quotas through an equivalent reduction as determined by the market agent, in cream and milk byproducts quotas, and an increase in milk byproducts quota through an equivalent reduction as determined by the market agent, in cream quotas.

(g) *Quotas for handlers who are also producers.* Quotas for handlers who are also producers and who purchase no milk shall be 100 percent of the total production of such handlers in the base period.

(h) *Handler exemptions.* Quotas shall not apply to any handler who delivers in a quota period a daily average of less than 300 units of milk, cream, and milk byproducts. For the purpose of this order, a unit shall be the equivalent in volume of the following: (1) Milk, one quart of milk; (2) cream, one-half pint of cream; and (3) milk byproduct, one quart of skim milk, buttermilk, flavored milk drink, or other beverage containing more than 85 percent of skim milk, or one-half pound of cottage, pot, or baker's cheese.

(i) *Quota exclusions and exemptions.* Deliveries of milk, milk byproducts, or cream (1) to other handlers, except for such deliveries to sub-handlers, (2) to plants engaged in the handling or processing of milk, milk byproducts, or cream from which no milk, milk byproducts, or cream is delivered in the sales area, and (3) to the agencies or groups specified in (d) of FDO 79, shall be excluded from the computation of deliveries in the base period and exempt from charges to quotas.

(j) *Transfers and apportionment of quotas.* The market agent is empowered to deduct an amount of base period deliveries to purchasers from the total of deliveries made by a handler or other person in the base period upon the application and a showing of unreasonable hardship by the handler making deliveries to such purchasers on the effective date of this order, and to add the amount of such deliveries to the total base period deliveries of the applicant handler. Denials of transfers or transfers granted by the market agent shall be reviewed by the Director upon application.

(k) *Petition for relief from hardships.* (1) Any person affected by FDO 79 or the provisions hereof who considers that compliance therewith would work an exceptional and unreasonable hardship on him, may file with the market agent a petition addressed to the Director. The petition shall contain the correct name, address and principal place of business of the petitioner, a full statement of the facts upon which the petition is based, and the hardship involved and the nature of the relief desired.

(2) Upon receiving such petition, the market agent shall immediately investigate the representations and facts stated therein.

(3) After investigation, the petition shall be certified to the Director, but prior to certification the market agent may (i) deny the petition, or (ii) grant temporary relief for a total period not to exceed 60 days.

(4) Denials or grants of relief by the market agent shall be reviewed by the Director and may be affirmed, modified, or reversed by the Director.

(l) *Reports.* Each handler shall transmit to the market agent on forms prescribed by the market agent the following reports:

(1) Within 20 days following the effective date of this order, reports which show the information required by the market agent to establish such handlers' quotas;

(2) Within 20 days following the close of each quota period, the information required by the market agent to establish volumes of deliveries of milk, cream, and milk byproducts during the preceding quota period; and

(3) Handlers exempt from quotas pursuant to (h) hereof shall, upon the request of the market agent, submit the information required by the market

agent to establish volumes of deliveries of milk, cream, and milk byproducts.

(m) *Records.* Handlers shall keep and shall make available to the market agent such records of receipts, sales, deliveries, and production as the market agent shall require for the purpose of obtaining information which the Director may require for the establishment of quotas as prescribed in (b) of FDO 79.

(n) *Distribution schedules.* The distribution schedules, if any, to be followed by the handlers in making deliveries shall be made effective in the terms of approval by the Director of such schedules.

(o) *Expense of administration.* Each shall pay to the market agent, within 20 days after the close of each calendar month an assessment of $0.01 per hundredweight of each of milk, cream, skim milk, buttermilk, flavored milk drinks, beverages containing more than 85 percent of skim milk, and skim milk equivalent of cottage, pot, or baker's cheese delivered during the preceding quota period and subject to quota regulations under the provisions hereof.

(p) *Violations.* The market agent shall report all violations to the Director together with the information required for the prosecution of such violations, except in a case where a handler has made deliveries in a quota period in excess of a quota in an amount not to exceed 5 percent of such quota, and in the succeeding quota period makes deliveries below that same percent.

(q) *Bureau of* The record keep quirements of th proved by the B accordance with of 1942. Subseq reporting require the approval of tl pursuant to the 1942.

(r) This order a. m., e. w. t., D

Issued this 16tl

Release—Immediate.

WASHINGTON, D. C., 11-17, 1943.

FOUR NEW MILK SALES AREAS NAMED

Milk sales in 4 metropolitan areas in Wisconsin, Pennsylvania and Illinois will be regulated under the Food Distribution Administration's fluid milk conservation and control program, beginning December 1, the War Food Administration said today.

The new milk sales areas, and the market agents who will administer the program in each, are:

Madison, Wis., H. H. Erdmann, 135 S. La-Salle St., Chicago, Ill.
York, Pa., Wm. Sadler, 11 N. Juniper St., Philadelphia, Pa.
Springfield, Ill.
Decatur, Ill.

Under the program, milk dealers will be permitted to sell as much fluid milk as they sold in June and three-fourths as much cream and milk byproducts (such as cottage cheese, chocolate milk, and buttermilk) as they sold in June. Milk dealers include all persons or firms engaged in the sale or transfer of milk, but not such distributors as subhandlers ("peddlers"), retail stores, hotels, or restaurants.

Producer-distributors who purchase no milk will be permitted to sell as much milk as they produced in June.

A dealer may increase his milk sales by reducing his cream and milk byproducts sales, and increase his sales of milk byproducts by reducing his cream sales, providing such an adjustment is approved in advance by the market agent for the area.

Deliveries of milk, cream, and milk byproducts to other dealers; to the Armed Forces, and to plants processing milk who do not distribute milk, cream or milk byproduc quota exempt.

Consumers in named today and nated generally as much milk ur tion program as in recent month local supplies.

Fluid milk sal Food Distributio cials said, to hel for manufacturi evaporated milk quired by the Ar ians for good nut anced diets. Sal on milk byprodu June deliveries t plies where pro conserve milk f poses.

FDO 79-98

AMDT. 1
MAR. 29, 1944

WAR FOOD ADMINISTRATION

[FDO 79-98, Amdt. 1]

PART 1401—DAIRY PRODUCTS

FLUID MILK AND CREAM IN DECATUR, ILL., SALES AREA

Pursuant to Food Distribution Order No. 79 (8 F.R. 12426), dated September 7, 1943, as amended, and to effectuate the purposes thereof, Food Distribution Order No. 79–98 (8 F.R. 15767), relative to the conservation and distribution of fluid milk, milk byproducts, and cream in the Decatur, Illinois, milk sales area, issued by the Director of Food Distribution on November 16, 1943, is hereby amended by deleting the numeral "20" wherever it appears in § 1401.132 (1) (2) thereof and inserting, in lieu thereof, the numeral "10."

The provisions of this amendment shall become effective at 12:01 a. m., e. w. t., April 1, 1944. With respect to violations of said Food Distribution Order No. 79–98, rights accrued, or liabilities incurred prior to the effective time of this amendment, said Food Distribution Order No. 79–98, shall be deemed to be in full force and effect for the purpose of sustaining any proper suit, action or other proceeding with respect to any such violations, right, or liability.

(E.O. 9280, 7 F.R. 10179; E.O. 9322, 8 F.R. 3807; E.O. 9334, 8 F.R. 5423; E.O. 9392, 8 F.R. 14783; FDO 79, 8 F.R. 12426, 13283)

Issued this 29th day of March 1944.

LEE MARSHALL,
Director of Distribution.

FDO 79-99

NOV. 16, 1943

WAR FOOD ADMINISTRATION

[FDO 79-99]

PART 1401—DAIRY PRODUCTS

FLUID MILK AND CREAM, SPRINGFIELD, ILL., SALES AREA

Pursuant to the authority vested in me by Food Distribution Order No. 79 (8 F.R. 12426), issued on September 7, 1943, as amended, and to effectuate the purposes of such order, it is hereby ordered as follows:

§ 1401.133 *Quota restrictions*—(a) *Definitions.* When used in this order, unless otherwise distinctly expressed or manifestly incompatible with the intent hereof:

(1) Each term defined in Food Distribution Order No. 79, as amended, shall, when used herein, have the same meaning as is set forth for such term in Food Distribution Order No. 79, as amended.

(2) The term "FDO 79" means Food Distribution Order No. 79, issued on September 7, 1943, as amended.

(3) The term "sub-handler" means any handler, such as a peddler, vendor, sub-dealer, or secondary dealer, who purchases in a previously packaged and processed form milk, milk byproducts, or cream for delivery.

(b) *Milk sales area.* The following area is hereby designated as a "milk sales area" to be known as the Springfield, Illinois, sales area, and is referred to hereinafter as the "sales area":

The city of Springfield and the townships of Springfield, Capital, and Woodside, all in Sangamon County, Illinois.

(c) *Base period.* The calendar month of June 1943 is hereby designated as the base period for the sales area.

(d) *Quota period.* The remainder of the calendar month in which the provisions hereof become effective and each subsequent calendar month, respectively, is hereby designated as a quota period for the sales area.

(e) *Handler quotas.* Quotas for each handler in the sales area in each quota period shall be calculated in terms of pounds of each of the items for which percentages are specified in (3) below and shall be determined as follows:

(1) Divide the total deliveries of each such item made in the sales area by such handler during the base period, after excluding the quota-exempt deliveries described in (i) hereof, by the number of days in the base period;

(2) Multiply the result of the foregoing calculation by the number of days in the quota period;

(3) Multiply the aforesaid resulting amount by the following applicable percentage: (i) Milk, 100 percent; (ii) butterfat in milk, ------ percent; (iii) cream, 75 percent; (iv) butterfat in cream, 75 percent; (v) milk byproducts other than cottage, pot, or baker's cheese, 75 percent; and (vi) cottage, pot, or baker's cheese, 75 percent of skim milk equivalent. (For the purpose of this order, one pound of cottage, pot, or baker's cheese shall be considered as the equivalent of 7 pounds of skim milk.)

(f) *Quota limitations.* No handler shall, during any quota period, make deliveries in the sales area in excess of his respective quotas, except as set out in (i) hereof: *Provided*, That a handler may, after application to and approval by the market agent, secure an increase in milk quotas through an equivalent reduction as determined by the market agent, in cream and milk byproducts quotas, and an increase in milk byproducts quota through an equivalent reduction as determined by the market agent, in cream quotas.

(g) *Quotas for handlers who are also producers.* Quotas for handlers who are also producers and who purchase no milk shall be 100 percent of the total production of such handlers in the base period.

(h) *Handler exemptions.* Quotas shall not apply to any handler who delivers in a quota period a daily average of less than 250 units of milk, cream, and milk byproducts. For the purpose of this order, a unit shall be the equivalent in the volume of the following: (1) Milk, one quart of milk; (2) cream, one-half pint of cream; and (3) milk byproduct, one quart of skim milk, buttermilk, flavored milk drink, or other beverage containing more than 85 percent of skim milk, or one-half pound of cottage, pot, or baker's cheese.

(i) *Quota exclusions and exemptions.* Deliveries of milk, milk byproducts, or cream (1) to other handlers, except for such deliveries to sub-handlers, (2) to plants engaged in the handling or processing of milk, milk byproducts, or cream from which no milk, milk byproducts, or cream is delivered in the sales area, and (3) to the agencies or groups specified in (d) of FDO 79, shall be excluded from the computation of deliveries in the base period and exempt from charges to quotas.

(j) *Transfers and apportionment of quotas.* The market agent is empowered to deduct an amount of base period deliveries to purchasers from the total of deliveries made by a handler or other person in the base period upon the application and a showing of unreasonable hardship by the handler making deliveries to such purchasers on the effective date of this order, and to add the amount of such deliveries to the total base period deliveries of the applicant handler. Denials of transfers or transfers granted by the market agent shall be reviewed by the Director upon application.

(k) *Petition for relief from hardships.* (1) Any person affected by FDO 79 or the provisions hereof who considers that compliance therewith would work an exceptional and unreasonable hardship on him, may file with the market agent a petition addressed to the Director. The petition shall contain the correct name, address and principal place of business of the petitioner, a full statement of the facts upon which the petition is based, and the hardship involved and the nature of the relief desired.

(2) Upon receiving such petition, the market agent shall immediately investigate the representations and facts stated therein.

(3) After investigation, the petition shall be certified to the Director, but prior to certification the market agent may (i) deny the petition, or (ii) grant temporary relief for a total period not to exceed 60 days.

(4) Denials or grants of relief by the market agent shall be reviewed by the Director and may be affirmed, modified, or reversed by the Director.

(l) *Reports.* Each handler shall transmit to the market agent on forms prescribed by the market agent the following reports:

(1) Within 20 days following the effective date of this order reports which show the information required by the market agent to establish such handlers' quotas;

(2) Within 20 days following the close of each quota period, the information required by the market agent to establish volumes of deliveries of milk, cream, and milk byproducts during the preceding quota period; and

(3) Handlers exempt from quotas pursuant to (h) hereof shall, upon the request of the market agent, submit the information required by the market agent to establish volumes of deliveries of milk, cream, and milk byproducts.

(m) *Records.* Handlers shall keep and shall make available to the market agent such records of receipts, sales, deliveries, and production as the market agent shall require for the purpose of obtaining information which the Director may require for the establishment of quotas as prescribed in (b) of FDO 79.

(n) *Distribution schedules.* The distribution schedules, if any, to be followed by the handlers in making deliveries shall be made effective in the terms of approval by the Director of such schedules.

(o) *Expense of administration.* Each handler shall pay to the market agent, within 20 days after the close of each calendar month an assessment of $0.01 per hundredweight of each of milk, cream, skim milk, buttermilk, flavored milk drinks, beverages containing more than 85 percent of skim milk, and skim milk equivalent of cottage, pot, or baker's cheese delivered during the preceding quota period and subject to quota regulations under the provisions hereof.

(p) *Violations.* The market agent shall report all violations to the Director together with the information required for the prosecution of such violations, except in a case where a handler has made deliveries in a quota period in excess of a quota in an amount not to exceed 5 percent of such quota, and in the succeeding quota period makes deliveries below that quota by at least the same percent.

(q) *Bureau of the Budget approval.* The record keeping and reporting requirements of this order have been approved by the Bureau of the Budget in accordance with the Federal Reports Act of 1942. Subsequent record keeping or reporting requirements will be subject to the approval of the Bureau of the Budget pursuant to the Federal Reports Act of 1942.

(r) This order shall take effect at 12:01 a. m., e. w. t., December 1, 1943.

Issued this 16th day of November 1943.

S. R. SMITH,
Acting Director of Food Distribution.

Release—Immediate.

WASHINGTON, D. C., 11-17, 1943.

FOUR NEW MILK SALES AREAS NAMED

Milk sales in 4 metropolitan areas in Wisconsin, Pennsylvania and Illinois will be regulated under the Food Distribution Administration's fluid milk conservation and control program, beginning December 1, the War Food Administration said today.

The new milk sales areas, and the market agents who will administer the program in each, are:

Madison, Wis., H. H. Erdmann, 135 S. La-Salle St., Chicago, Ill.
York, Pa., Wm. Sadler, 11 N. Juniper St., Philadelphia, Pa.
Springfield, Ill.
Decatur, Ill.

Under the program, milk dealers will be permitted to sell as much fluid milk as they sold in June and three-fourths as much cream and milk byproducts (such as cottage cheese, chocolate milk, and buttermilk) as they sold in June. Milk dealers include all persons or firms engaged in the sale or transfer of milk, but not such distributors as subhandlers ("peddlers"), retail stores, hotels, or restaurants.

Producer-distributors who purchase no milk will be permitted to sell as much milk as they produced in June.

A dealer may increase his milk sales by reducing his cream and milk byproducts sales, and increase his sales of milk byproducts by reducing his cream sales; providing such an adjustment is approved in advance by the market agent for the area.

Deliveries of milk, cream, and milk byproducts to other dealers: to the Armed Forces, and to plants processing milk who do not distribute milk, cream or milk byproducts in the sales area are quota exempt.

Consumers in the milk sales areas named today and in others already designated generally will be able to purchase as much milk under the milk conservation program as they have been buying in recent months—within the limits of local supplies.

Fluid milk sales are being stabilized, Food Distribution Administration officials said, to help assure sufficient milk for manufacturing the cheese, butter, evaporated milk, and milk powder required by the Armed Services and civilians for good nutrition and properly balanced diets. Sales quotas on cream and on milk byproducts have been set below June deliveries to boost fluid milk supplies where production is low, and to conserve milk for manufacturing purposes.

FDO 79-99

AMDT. 1
MAR. 29, 1944

~~WAR FOOD~~ ADMINISTRATION

[FDO 79-99. Amdt. 1]

PART 1401—DAIRY PRODUCTS

FLUID MILK AND CREAM IN SPRINGFIELD, ILL., SALES AREA

Pursuant to Food Distribution Order No. 79 (8 F.R. 12426), dated September 7, 1943, as amended, and to effectuate the purposes thereof, Food Distribution Order No. 79-99 (8 F.R. 15769), relative to the conservation and distribution of fluid milk, milk byproducts, and cream, in the Springfield, Illinois, milk sales area, issued by the Director of Food Distribution on November 16, 1943, is hereby amended by deleting the numeral "20" wherever it appears in § 1401.133 (1) (2) thereof and inserting, in lieu thereof, the numeral "10."

The provisions of this amendment shall become effective at 12:01 a. m., e. w. t., April 1, 1944. With respect to violations of said Food Distribution Order No. 79-99, rights accrued, or liabilities incurred, prior to the effective time of this amendment, said Food Distribution Order No. 79-99 shall be deemed to be in full force and effect for the purpose of sustaining any proper suit, action, or other proceeding with respect to any such violation, right, or liability.

(E.O. 9280, 7 F.R. 10179; E.O. 9322, 8 F.R. 3807; E.O. 9334, 8 F.R. 5423; E.O. 9392, 8 F.R. 14783; FDO 79, 8 F.R. 12426, 13283)

Issued this 29th day of March 1944.

LEE MARSHALL,
Director of Distribution.

WAR FOOD ADMINISTRATION
Food Distribution Administration
Washington 25, D. C.

CORRECTION NOTICE - FDO-79-100

FLUID MILK AND CREAM, MADISON, WIS., SALES AREA

In printing FDO-79-100 the following error occurred:

In section 1401.134 (i) (2) the word "mlik" should read "milk" so that the sentence reads: "to plants engaged in the handling or processing of milk, milk by-products, or cream from which no milk, milk by-products, or cream is delivered in the sales area."

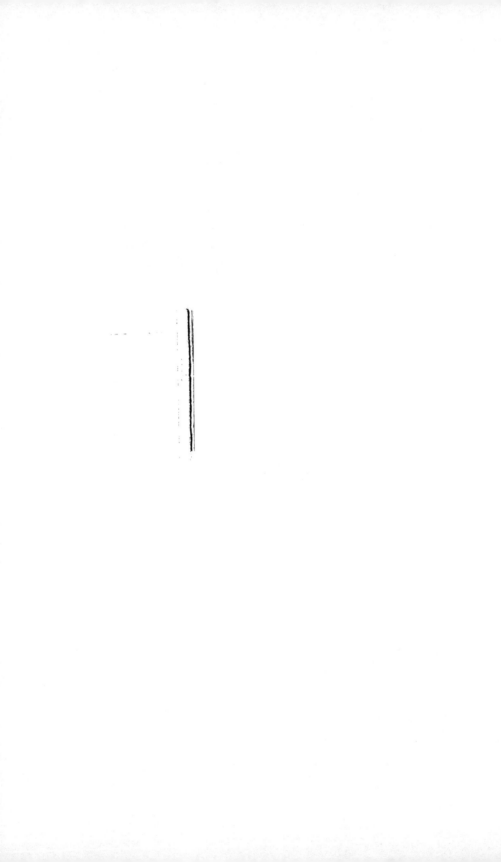

FDO 79-100
NOV. 16, 1943

WAR FOOD ADMINISTRATION

[FDO 79-100] A

Part 1401—Dairy Products

FLUID MILK AND CREAM, MADISON, WIS., SALES AREA

Pursuant to the authority vested in me by Food Distribution Order No. 79 (8 F.R. 12426), issued on September 7, 1943, as amended, and to effectuate the purposes of such order, it is hereby ordered as follows:

§ 1401.134 *Quota restrictions*—(a) *Definitions.* When used in this order, unless otherwise distinctly expressed or manifestly incompatible with the intent hereof:

(1) Each term defined in Food Distribution Order No. 79, as amended, shall, when used herein, have the same meaning as is set forth for such term in Food Distribution Order No. 79, as amended.

(2) The term "FDO 79" means Food Distribution Order No. 79, issued on September 7, 1943, as amended.

(3) The term "sub-handler" means any handler, such as a peddler, vendor, sub-dealer, or secondary dealer, who purchases in a previously packaged and processed form milk, milk byproducts, or cream for delivery.

(b) *Milk sales area.* The following area is hereby designated as a "milk sales area" to be known as the Madison, Wisconsin, sales area, and is referred to hereinafter as the "sales area":

The city of Madison, the towns of Blooming Grove and Madison, and the villages of Monona, Maple Bluff, and Shorewood Hills, all in Dane County, Wisconsin.

(c) *Base period.* The calendar month of June 1943 is hereby designated as the base period for the sales area.

(d) *Quota period.* The remainder of the calendar month in which the provisions hereof become effective and each subsequent calendar month, respectively, is hereby designated as a quota period for the sales area.

(e) *Handler quotas.* Quotas for each handler in the sales area in each quota period shall be calculated in terms of pounds of each of the items for which percentages are specified in (3) below and shall be determined as follows:

(1) Divide the total deliveries of each such item made in the sales area by such handler during the base period, after excluding the quota-exempt deliveries described in (i) hereof, by the number of days in the base period;

(2) Multiply the result of the foregoing calculation by the number of days in the quota period;

(3) Multiply the aforesaid resulting amount by the following applicable percentage: (i) Milk, 100 percent; (ii) butterfat in milk, ------ percent; (iii) cream, 75 percent; (iv) butterfat in cream, 75 percent; (v) milk byproducts other than cottage, pot or baker's cheese, 75 percent; and (vi) Cottage, pot or baker's cheese, 75 percent of skim milk equivalent. (For the purpose of this order, one pound of cottage, pot, or baker's cheese shall be considered as the equivalent of 7 pounds of skim milk.)

(f) *Quota limitations.* No handler shall, during any quota period, make deliveries in the sales area in excess of his respective quotas, except as set out in (j) hereof: *Provided,* That a handler may, after application to and approval by the market agent, secure an increase in milk quotas through an equivalent reduction as determined by the market agent, in cream and milk byproducts quotas, and an increase in milk byproducts quota through an equvalent reduction as determined by the market agent, in cream quotas.

(g) *Quotas for handlers who are also producers.* Quotas for handlers who are also producers and who purchase no milk shall be 100 percent of the total production of such handlers in the base period.

(h) *Handler exemptions.* Quotas shall not apply to any handler who delivers in a quota period a daily average of less than 150 units of milk, cream, and milk byproducts. For the purpose of this order, a unit shall be the equivalent in volume of the following: (1) Milk, one quart of milk; (2) cream, one-half pint of cream; and (3) milk byproduct, one quart of skim milk, buttermilk, flavored milk drink, or other beverage containing more than 85 percent of skim milk, or one-half pound of cottage, pot, or baker's cheese.

(i) *Quota exclusions and exemptions.* Deliveries of milk, milk byproducts, or cream (1) to other handlers, except for such deliveries to sub-handlers, (2) to plants engaged in the handling or processing of milk, milk byproducts, or cream from which no milk, milk byproducts, or cream is delivered in the sales area, and (3) to the agencies or groups specified in (d) of FDO 79, shall be excluded from the computations of deliveries in the base period and exempt from charges to quotas.

(j) *Transfers and apportionment of quotas.* The market agent is empowered to deduct an amount of base period deliveries to purchasers from the total of deliveries made by a handler or other person in the base period upon the application and a showing of unreasonable hardship by the handler making deliveries to such purchasers on the effective date of this order, and to add the amount of such deliveries to the total base period deliveries of the applicant handler. Denials of transfers or transfers granted by the market agent shall be reviewed by the Director upon application.

(k) *Petition for relief from hardships.* (1) Any person affected by FDO 79 or the provisions hereof who considers that compliance therewith would work an exceptional and unreasonable hardship on him, may file with the market agent a petition addressed to the Director. The petition shall contain the correct name, address and principal place of business of the petitioner, a full statement of the facts upon which the petition is based, and the hardship involved and the nature of the relief desired.

(2) Upon receiving such petition, the market agent shall immediately investigate the representations and facts stated therein.

(3) After investigation, the petition shall be certified to the Director, but prior to certification the market agent may (i) deny the petition, or (ii) grant temporary relief for a total period not to exceed 60 days.

(4) Denials or grants of relief by the market agent shall be reviewed by the Director and may be affirmed, modified, or reversed by the Director.

(l) *Reports.* Each handler shall transmit to the market agent on forms prescribed by the market agent the following reports:

(1) Within 20 days following the effective date of this order, reports which show the information required by the market agent to establish such handlers' quotas;

(2) Within 20 days following the close of each quota period, the information required by the market agent to establish volumes of deliveries of milk, cream, and milk byproducts during the preceding quota period; and

(3) Handlers exempt from quotas pursuant to (h) hereof shall, upon the request of the market agent, submit the information required by the market agent to establish volumes of deliveries of milk, cream, and milk byproducts.

(m) *Records.* Handlers shall keep and shall make available to the market agent such records of receipts, sales, deliveries, and production as the market agent shall require for the purpose of obtaining information which the Director may require for the establishment of quotas as prescribed in (b) of FDO 79.

(n) *Distribution schedules.* The distribution schedules, if any, to be followed by the handlers in making deliveries shall be made effective in the terms of approval by the Director of such schedules.

(o) *Expense of administration.* Each handler shall pay to the market agent, within 20 days after the close of each calendar month an assessment of $0.01 per hundredweight of each of milk, cream, skim milk, buttermilk, flavored milk drinks, beverages containing more than 85 percent of skim milk, and skim milk equivalent of cottage, pot, or baker's cheese delivered during the preceding quota period and subject to quota regulations under the provisions hereof.

(p) *Violations.* The market agent shall report all violations to the Director together with the information required for the prosecution of such violations, except in a case where a handler has made deliveries in a quota period in excess of a quota in an amount not to exceed 5 percent of such quota, and in the succeeding quota period makes deliveries below that quota by at least the same percent.

(q) *Bureau of the Bu* The record keeping and quirements of this order proved by the Bureau of accordance with the Feder of 1942. Subsequent reco reporting requirements v to the approval of the Budget pursuant to the F Act of 1942.

(r) This order shall 12:01 a. m., e. w. t., Dece

Issued this 16th day of

S. I
Acting
Food

Release—Immediate.

WASHINGTON, D. C., 11-17, 1943.

FOUR NEW MILK SALES AREAS NAMED

Milk sales in 4 metropolitan areas in Wisconsin, Pennsylvania and Illinois will be regulated under the Food Distribution Administration's fluid milk conservation and control program, beginning December 1, the War Food Administration said today.

The new milk sales areas, and the market agents who will administer the program in each, are:

Madison, Wis., H. H. Erdmann, 135 S. LaSalle St., Chicago, Ill.
York, Pa., Wm. Sadler, 11 N. Juniper St., Philadelphia, Pa.
Springfield, Ill.
Decatur, Ill.

Under the program, milk dealers will be permitted to sell as much fluid milk as they sold in June and three-fourths as much cream and milk byproducts (such as cottage cheese, chocolate milk, and buttermilk), as they sold in June. Milk dealers include all persons or firms engaged in the sale or transfer of milk, but not such distributors as subhandlers ("peddlers"), retail stores, hotels, or restaurants.

Producer-distributors who purchase no milk will be permitted to sell as much milk as they produced in June.

A dealer may increase his milk sales by reducing his cream and milk byproducts sales, and increase his sales of milk byproducts by reducing his cream sales, providing such an adjustment is approved in advance by the market agent for the area.

Deliveries of milk, cream, and milk byproducts to other dealers: to the Armed Forces, and to plants processing milk who do not distribute milk, cream or milk byproducts in the quota exempt.

Consumers in the mill named today and in others nated generally will be abl as much milk under the m tion program as they have in recent months—within local supplies.

Fluid milk sales are bei Food Distribution Admini cials said, to help assure s for manufacturing the c evaporated milk, and mil quired by the Armed Servi ians for good nutrition and anced diets. Sales quotas on milk byproducts have be June deliveries to boost flu plies where production is conserve milk for manufa poses.

FDO 79-100
AMDT. 1
DEC. 2, 1943

WAR FOOD ADMINISTRATION

A [FDO 79-100, Amdt. 1].

PART 1401—DAIRY PRODUCTS

DIRECTOR'S ORDER FOR THE MADISON, WISC., MILK SALES AREA

Pursuant to Food Distribution Order No. 79 (8 F.R. 12426), dated September 7, 1943, as amended, and to effectuate the purposes thereof, Food Distribution Order No. 79-100 (8 F.R. 15770), issued by the Director of Food Distribution on November 16, 1943, is amended by deleting therefrom the provisions in § 1401.134 (b) and inserting, in lieu thereof, the following:

(b) *Milk sales area.* The following area is hereby indicated as a "milk sales area" to be known as the Madison, Wisconsin, sales area, and is referred to hereafter as the "sales area":

The city of Madison; the villages of Shorewood Hills, Middleton, Pleasant Branch, and Maple Bluff; the town of Madison; sections 28 to 33, inclusive, in the town of Blooming Grove and that part of the town of Blooming Grove north of the line 300 feet south of U. S. highways 12 and 18 and west of the east line of sections 21, 16, 9, and 4; sections 31, 32, and 33 in the town of Burke; the south half of sections 21, 25, and 26, the east half of section 32 and all of the sections 27, 28, 33, 34, 35, and 36 in the town of Westport; sections 1, 11, 12, 13, 14, 24, 25, and 36 in the town of Middleton; sections 1 to 12, inclusive, in the town of Fitchburg; and sections 4 to 9, inclusive, in the town of Dunn. All of the foregoing sales area is in Dane County, Wisconsin.

The provisions of this amendment shall become effective at 12:01 a. m., e. w. t., December 2, 1943. With respect to violations, rights accrued, or liabilities incurred prior to the effective time of this amendment, the aforesaid order FDO No. 79-100, issued by the Director, shall be deemed to be in full force and effect, for the purpose of sustaining any proper suit, action, or other proceeding with respect to any such violation, right, or liability.

(E.O. 9280, 7 F.R. 10179; E.O. 9322, 8 F.R. 3807; E.O. 9334, 8 F.R. 5423; E.O. 9392, 8 F.R. 14783; FDO 79, 8 F.R. 12426, 13283)

Issued this 2d day of December 1943.

ROY F. HENDRICKSON,
Director of Food Distribution.

WAR FOOD ADMINISTRATION

[FDO 79–101]

PART 1410—DAIRY PRODUCTS

FLUID MILK AND CREAM, YORK, PA., SALES AREA

Pursuant to the authority vested in me by Food Distribution Order No. 79 (8 F.R. 12426), issued on September 7, 1943, as amended, and to effectuate the purposes of such order, it is hereby ordered as follows:

§ 1401.131 *Quota restrictions*—(a) *Definitions.* When used in this order, unless otherwise distinctly expressed or manifestly incompatible with the intent hereof:

(1) Each term defined in Food Distribution Order No. 79, as amended, shall, when used herein, have the same meaning as is set forth for such term in Food Distribution Order No. 79, as amended.

(2) The term "FDO 79" means Food Distribution Order No. 79, issued on September 7, 1943, as amended.

(3) The term "sub-handler" means any handler, such as a peddler, vendor, sub-dealer, or secondary dealer, who purchases in a previously packaged and processed form milk, milk byproducts, or cream for delivery.

(b) *Milk sales area.* The following area is hereby designated as a "milk sales area" to be known as the York, Pennsylvania, sales area, and is referred to hereinafter as the "sales area":

The city of York, the townships of Manchester, Springetsbury, Spring Garden, West Manchester, and York, and the boroughs of Dallastown, North York, Red Lion, West York, and Yoe, all in York County, Pennsylvania.

(c) *Base period.* The calendar month of June 1943 is hereby designated as the base period for the sales area.

(d) *Quota period.* The remainder of the calendar month in which the provisions hereof become effective and each subsequent calendar month, respectively, is hereby designated as a quota period for the sales area.

(e) *Handler quotas.* Quotas for each handler in the sales area in each quota period shall be calculated in terms of pounds of each of the items for which percentages are specified in (3) below and shall be determined as follows:

(1) Divide the total deliveries of each such item made in the sales area by such handler during the base period, after excluding the quota-exempt deliveries described in (i) hereof, by the number of days in the base period;

(2) Multiply the result of the foregoing calculation by the number of days in the quota period;

(3) Multiply the aforesaid resulting amount by the following applicable percentage: (i) Milk, 100 percent; (ii) butterfat in milk, ------ percent; (iii) cream, 75 percent; (iv) butterfat in cream, 75 percent; (v) milk byproducts other than cottage, pot, or baker's cheese, 75 percent; and (vi) cottage, pot, or baker's cheese, 75 percent of skim milk equivalent. (For the purpose of this order, one pound of cottage, pot, or baker's cheese shall be considered as the equivalent of 7 pounds of skim milk.)

(f) *Quota limitations.* No handler shall, during any quota period, make deliveries in the sales area in excess of his respective quotas, except as set out in (i) hereof: *Provided*, That a handler may, after application to and approval by the market agent, secure an increase in milk quotas through an equivalent reduction as determined by the market agent, in cream and milk byproducts quotas, and an increase in milk byproducts quota through an equivalent reduction as determined by the market agent, in cream quotas.

(g) *Quotas for handlers who are also producers.* Quotas for handlers who are also producers and who purchase no milk shall be 100 percent of the total production of such handlers in the base period.

(h) *Handler exemptions.* Quotas shall not apply to any handler who delivers in a quota period a daily average of less than 350 units of milk, cream, and milk byproducts. For the purpose of this order, a unit shall be the equivalent in the volume of the following: (1) Milk, one quart of milk; (2) cream, one-half pint of cream; and (3) milk byproduct, one quart of skim milk, buttermilk, flavored milk drink, or other beverage containing more than 85 percent of skim milk, or one-half pound of cottage, pot, or baker's cheese.

(i) *Quota exclusions and exemptions.* Deliveries of milk, milk byproducts, or cream (1) to other handlers, except for such deliveries to sub-handlers, (2) to plants engaged in the handling or processing of milk, milk byproducts, or cream from which no milk, milk byproducts, or cream is delivered in the sales area, and (3) to the agencies or groups specified in (d) of FDO 79, shall be excluded from the computation of deliveries in the base period and exempt from charges to quotas.

(j) *Transfers and apportionment of quotas.* The market agent is empowered to deduct an amount of base period deliveries to purchasers from the total of deliveries made by a handler or other person in the base period upon the application and a showing of unreasonable hardship by the handler making deliveries to such purchasers on the effective date of this order, and to add the amount of such deliveries to the total base period deliveries of the applicant handler. Denials of transfers or transfers granted by the market agent shall be reviewed by the Director upon application.

(k) *Petition for relief from hardships.* (1) Any person affected by FDO 79 or the provisions hereof who considers that compliance therewith would work an exceptional and unreasonable hardship on him, may file with the market agent a petition addressed to the Director. The petition shall contain the correct name, address and principal place of business of the petitioner, a full statement of the facts upon which the petition is based, and the hardship involved and the nature of the relief desired.

(2) Upon receiving such petition, the market agent shall immediately investigate the representations and facts stated therein.

(3) After investigation, the petition shall be certified to the Director, but prior to certification the market agent may (i) deny the petition, or (ii) grant temporary relief for a total period not to exceed 60 days.

(4) Denials or grants of relief by the market agent shall be reviewed by the Director and may be affirmed, modified, or reversed by the Director.

(l) *Reports.* Each handler shall transmit to the market agent on forms prescribed by the market agent the following reports:

(1) Within 20 days following the effective date of this order, reports which show the information required by the market agent to establish such handler's quotas;

(2) Within 20 days following the close of each quota period, the information required by the market agent to establish volumes of deliveries of milk, cream, and milk byproducts during the preceding quota period; and

(3) Handlers exempt from quotas pursuant to (h) hereof shall, upon the request of the market agent, submit the information required by the market

agent to establish volumes of deliveries of milk, cream, and milk byproducts.

(m) *Records*. Handlers shall keep and shall make available to the market agent such records of receipts, sales, deliveries, and production as the market agent shall require for the purpose of obtaining information which the Director may require for the establishment of quotas as prescribed in (b) of FDO 79.

(n) *Distribution schedules*. The distribution schedules, if any, to be followed by the handlers in making deliveries shall be made effective in the terms of approval by the Director of such schedules.

(o) *Expense of administration*. Each handler shall pay to the market agent, within 20 days after the close of each calendar month an assessment of $0.01 per hundredweight of each of milk, cream, skim milk, buttermilk, flavored milk drinks, beverages, containing more than 85 percent of skim milk, and skim milk equivalent of cottage, pot, or baker's cheese delivered during the preceding quota period and subject to quota regulations under the provisions hereof.

(p) *Violations*. The market agent shall report all violations to the Director together with the information required for the prosecution of such violations, except in a case where a handler has made deliveries in a quota period in excess of a quota in an amount not to exceed 5 percent of such quota, and in the succeeding quota period makes deliveries below that same percent.

(q) *Bureau of t* The record keepin quirements of this proved by the Bur accordance with Act of 1942. Subse or reporting requi ject to the approv the Budget pursua ports Act of 1942.

(r) This order 12:01 a. m., e. w. t.

Issued this 16th c

Acting Director o

Release—Immediate.

WASHINGTON, D. C., 11-17, 1943.

FOUR NEW MILK SALES AREAS NAMED

Milk sales in 4 metropolitan areas in Wisconsin, Pennsylvania and Illinois will be regulated under the Food Distribution Administration's fluid milk conservation and control program, beginning December 1, the War Food Administration said today.

The new milk sales areas, and the market agents who will administer the program in each, are:

Madison, Wis., H. H. Erdmann, 135 S. La-Salle St., Chicago, Ill.
York, Pa., Wm. Sadler, 11 N. Juniper St., Philadelphia, Pa.
Springfield, Ill.
Decatur, Ill.

Under the program, milk dealers will be permitted to sell as much fluid milk as they sold in June and three-fourths as much cream and milk byproducts (such as cottage cheese, chocolate milk, and buttermilk) as they sold in June. Milk dealers include all persons or firms engaged in the sale or transfer of milk, but not such distributors as subhandlers ("peddlers"), retail stores, hotels, or restaurants.

Producer-distributors who purchase no milk will be permitted to sell as much milk as they produced in June.

A dealer may increase his milk sales by reducing his cream and milk byproducts sales, and increase his sales of milk byproducts by reducing his cream sales, providing such an adjustment is approved in advance by the market agent for the area.

Deliveries of milk, cream, and milk byproducts to other dealers: to the Armed Forces, and to plants processing milk who do not distribute milk, cream or milk byproduct quota exempt.

Consumers in named today and i nated generally wi as much milk und tion program as t in recent months- local supplies.

Fluid milk sales Food Distribution cials said, to help for manufacturin evaporated milk, quired by the Arm ians for good nutri anced diets. Sale on milk byproduct June deliveries to plies where produ conserve milk for poses.

FDO 79-101
AMDT. 1
NOV. 29, 1943

WAR FOOD ADMINISTRATION

[FDO 79-101, Amdt. 1]

PART 1401—DAIRY PRODUCTS

DIRECTOR'S ORDER FOR THE YORK, PA., MILK SALES AREA

Pursuant to the authority vested in the Director by Food Distribution Order No. 79, dated September 7, 1943 (8 F.R. 12426), as amended, and to effectuate the purposes thereof, Food Distribution Order No. 79–101, § 1401.131, relative to the conservation of fluid milk in the York, Pennsylvania, milk sales area (8 F.R. 15771), issued by the Director of Food Distribution on November 16, 1943, is amended as follows:

The expense of administration specified in § 1401.131 (o) of the original order is reduced from $0.01 to $0.005.

Effective date. This amendment of FDO 79–101, shall become effective at 12:01 a. m., e. w. t., December 1, 1943.

(E.O. 9280, 7 F.R. 10179; E.O. 9322, 8 F.R. 3807; E.O. 9334, 8 F.R. 5423; E.O. 9392, 8 F.R. 14783; FDO 79, 8 F.R. 12426, 13283)

Issued this 29th day of November 1943.

ROY F. HENDRICKSON,
Director of Food Distribution.

F 7 3 F 1

FDO 79-102

NOV. 30, 1943

WAR FOOD ADMINISTRATION

[FDO 79-102]

PART 1401—DAIRY PRODUCTS

DELEGATION OF AUTHORITY TO MARKET AGENTS IN THE ADMINISTRATION OF FOOD DISTRIBUTION ORDERS FOR THE CONSERVATION AND DISTRIBUTION OF FLUID MILK AND CREAM

Pursuant to the authority vested in the Director by Food Distribution Order No. 79 (8 F.R. 12426) issued by the War Food Administrator on September 7, 1943, as amended, and in order to effectuate the purposes thereof, it is hereby ordered as follows:

§ 1401.135 *Fluid milk and cream*—(a) *Definitions.* When used in this order, unless otherwise distinctly expressed or manifestly incompatible with the intent hereof, each term defined in Food Distribution Order No. 79, as amended, shall, when used herein, have the same meaning as is set forth for such term in Food Distribution Order No. 79, as amended.

(b) *Delegation of authority.*—The market agent under any of the Director's orders, No. 79-1 through No. 79-101 (except No. 79-82), issued pursuant to ood Distribution Order No. 79, as mended, is hereby authorized:

(1) To exempt deliveries of milk, ream, and milk byproducts to industrial sers, in their capacity as such users, rom charges to quotas and exclude such eliveries from the computation of deliveries in the base period, and the term industrial user" shall be construed to ean a person, as determined by the market agent, manufacturing products which require, as an ingredient, milk, cream, or milk byproducts, and which are disposed of primarily for resale to consumers off the premises where made.

(2) To permit an exchange of quotas between handlers upon receipt of a request in writing from each handler affected.

(3) To increase or decrease the quotas of any handler, upon application from a handler and written notice to the Director and to each handler affected, (i) to permit deliveries to purchasers not being serviced, or (ii) permit a handler to serve a contractual account which customarily rotates among several handlers inclusive of any contract let by a public agency or institution on a bid basis: *Provided,* That the amount of quota transferred to serve such account shall not exceed deliveries to such account in the base period or in the quota period next preceding the transfer, whichever is less.

(4) To permit a handler to make the following compensating adjustments in quotas, to be made concurrently within each quota period: (i) In an area wherein a quota of butter fat in milk is not specified, milk quota may be increased 2.15 pounds for each one pound reduction in cream quota of a 20 percent butter fat content, and with each decline of one percent in the butter fat content of cream quota, the allowable increase in milk quota per pound of cream quota reduction shall be reduced .07 pound, and milk quota may be increased .75 pound with each one pound reduction in milk byproducts quota; (ii) in an area wherein a quota of butter fat in milk is specified, milk quota may be increased one pound for each one pound reduction in the cream or milk byproducts quota, and the quota of butter fat in milk may be increased one pound for each one pound reduction in the quota of butter fat in cream; (iii) cream quota may be increased one pound for each one pound reduction in milk byproducts quota: *Provided,* That the resulting cream quota shall not exceed 100 percent of deliveries of cream in the base period; and (iv) milk byproducts quota may be increased one pound for each one pound reduction in cream quota.

(c) *Review by the Director.*—A ruling by a market agent under the authority delegated herein may be reviewed by the Director upon petition by a handler affected by a change in quota, if filed within 15 days after issuance of written notice to the handler, or upon the initiative of the Director, and may be affirmed, modified or reversed by the Director. Compliance with the provisions set forth in FDO 79, § 1401.29 (b) (3), by the handlers affected by change in quota, shall be a consideration affecting such review.

(d) *Effective date.*—This order shall become effective at 12:01 a. m., e. w. t., December 1, 1943.

Issued this 30th day of November 1943.

C. W. KITCHEN,
Acting Director of Food Distribution.

ar Food Administration
ummary to FDO 79-102

Market agents in the 100 milk sales eas established to date will be given ore specific authority to adjust the fluid conservation program to actual arket conditions under the terms of ood Distribution Order No. 79-102 hich becomes effective December 1.

The major action taken today under is order authorizes market agents to ermit dealers to increase their delivers of milk, cream or milk by-products by reducing their quotas of cream or by-products at specified rates of exchange. The fluid milk quotas, however, cannot be reduced to provide additional cream or by-products.

Other changes in the conservation order include:

(1) Permitting transfer of quotas among handlers almost automatically in cases where there is full agreement between the receiving and relinquishing handler.

(2) Authorizing the transfer of quotas between handlers where necessary, notwithstanding the lack of agreement, to allow delivery to producers not being serviced by the handler whose quota was supposed to cover such deliveries and to allow for the shifting of accounts which have customarily passed from one handler to another. These transfers are conditioned from application from the handler and discretion on the part of the market agent.

(3) Making quota exempt the deliveries of milk, cream or milk by-products to an "industrial user", as defined in the order.

7337

FDO 79-102
AMDT. 1
JAN. 6, 1944

WAR FOOD ADMINISTRATION

[FDO 79-102, Amdt. 1] A.

PART 1401—DAIRY PRODUCTS

DELEGATION OF AUTHORITY TO MARKET AGENTS IN THE ADMINISTRATION OF FOOD DISTRIBUTION ORDERS FOR THE CONSERVATION AND DISTRIBUTION OF FLUID MILK AND CREAM

Pursuant to Food Distribution Order No. 79 (8 F.R. 12426), dated September 7, 1943, as amended, and to effectuate the purposes thereof, Food Distribution Order No. 79-102 (8 F.R. 16313), issued by the Director of Food Distribution on November 30, 1943, is amended as follows:

1. By adding as (5), in § 1401.135 (b) the following provision:

(5) To permit a determination of a handler's quotas as follows:

(i) Divide by 30 the total pounds of milk solids delivered by the handler in the base period within the sales area in the form of milk, and in the form of cream and milk byproducts, after excluding quota exempt deliveries;

(ii) Multiply the above results by the number of days in the quota period; and

(iii) Multiply the aforesaid resulting amounts by 100 percent in the case of milk solids delivered in the form of milk, and 75 percent in the case of milk solids delivered in the form of cream and milk byproducts: *Provided*, That the fluid volume of cream delivered subject to quota in any quota period shall not exceed 100 percent of cream deliveries of this character in the base period, irrespective of the milk solids content of such deliveries. (For the purpose of this order, the milk solids content of milk, and cream and milk byproducts shall be computed as follows: Each hundredweight of milk, and cream and milk byproducts other than cottage, pot, or baker's cheese, shall be considered the equivalent of 9.375 pounds of milk solids plus the number of pounds of solids calculated by multiplying the pounds of butterfat content in such milk, and cream and milk byproducts by .906; and each hundredweight of cottage, pot, or baker's cheese shall be considered the equivalent of 62.5 pounds of milk solids plus one pound of solids for each one percent of butterfat content of such cheese.)

2. By adding as (6) in § 1401.135 (b) the following provision:

(6) To permit each handler whose deliveries are governed by the quota determination described in (b) (5) hereof to increase his quota for milk in any quota period by one pound of milk solids for each one pound of milk solids he reduces his quota for cream and milk byproducts.

The provisions of this amendment shall become effective at 12:01 a. m., e. w. t., January 1, 1944. With respect to violations of said Food Distribution Order No. 79-102, rights accrued or liabilities incurred prior to the effective time of this amendment, said Food Distribution Order No. 79-102 shall be deemed to be in full force and effect for the purpose of sustaining any proper suit, action, or other proceeding with respect to any such violation, right, or liability.

(E.O. 9280, 7 F.R. 10179; E.O. 9322, 8 F.R. 3807; E.O. 9334, 8 F.R. 5423; E.O. 9392, 8 F.R. 14783; FDO 79, 8 F.R. 12426, 13283)

Issued this 6th day of January 1944.

ROY F. HENDRICKSON,
Director of Food Distribution.

SUMMARY TO FOOD DISTRIBUTION ORDER NUMBER 79.102 AMENDMENT NUMBER 1

To permit milk dealers the maximum degree of flexibility in using their milk supplies consistent with the over-all purpose and effective administration of the milk conservation order (FDO 79), market agents in all milk sales areas established to date may establish sales quotas for milk, cream, and milk byproducts on a milk solids basis, instead of on the present basis of volume and butterfat. The delegation of authority, effective *January 1, 1944*, was granted by the Food Distribution Administration in Amendment 1 to Director Food Distribution Order 79.102.

The amendment does not affect total consumer supplies of milk used in fluid milk, cream and milk byproducts since dealers still must limit their deliveries to 100 percent of the fluid milk delivered in June and 75 percent of the milk used in cream and milk byproducts. However, with all quotas based on milk solids, and limitations on the use of solids in cream and milk byproducts both set at 75 percent of June use, cream and milk byproducts quotas are combined. With one quota for both groups authorized, the dealer can use his milk solids in either cream or byproducts as demand and supply dictate, provided that his cream deliveries do not exceed 100 percent of his June deliveries.

In addition, solids represented in milk byproducts and cream quotas may be transferred to fluid milk on a pound for pound basis, making it easier for dealers to make this shift to milk uses if it seems desirable.

Milk solids (such as protein, ash, lactose and butterfat) make up the total content of milk except for water.

rve
/
33F

FDO 79-103

DEC. 31, 1943

WAR FOOD ADMINISTRATION

[FDO 79.103]

PART 1401—DAIRY PRODUCTS

FLUID MILK AND CREAM IN THE MEMPHIS, TENN., METROPOLITAN AREA

Pursuant to the authority vested in me by Food Distribution Order No. 79, (8 F.R. 12426), issued on September 7, 1943, as amended, and to effectuate the purposes of such order, it is hereby ordered as follows:

§ 1401.136 *Quota restrictions*—(a) *Definitions.* When used in this order, unless otherwise distinctly expressed or manifestly incompatible with the intent hereof:

(1) Each term defined in Food Distribution Order No. 79, as amended, shall, when used herein, have the same meaning as is set forth for such term in Food Distribution Order No. 79, as amended.

(2) The term "FDO 79" means Food Distribution Order No. 79, issued on September 7, 1943, as amended.

(3) The term "sub-handler" means any handler, such as a peddler, vendor, sub-dealer, or secondary dealer, who purchases in a previously packaged and processed form milk, cream, or milk byproducts for delivery.

(4) The term "industrial user" means a person, as determined by the market agent, in the capacity of a manufacturer of products using as an ingredient therein milk, cream, or milk byproducts, which products are disposed of for resale to consumers off the premises where made.

(5) The term "base" means the total pounds of milk solids delivered by a handler within the sales area during the base period (i) in the form of milk, or (ii) in the form of cream and milk byproducts, minus the milk solids in quota-exempt deliveries of milk, and cream and milk byproducts, as described in (j) hereof. (For the purpose of this order, the milk solids content of milk, milk byproducts, and cream shall be computed as follows: Each hundredweight of milk, cream, or milk byproducts other than cottage, pot, or baker's cheese, shall be considered the equivalent of 9.375 pounds of milk solids plus the number of pounds of milk solids calculated by multiplying the pounds of butterfat in such milk, and cream and milk byproducts by 0.906; and each hundredweight of cottage, pot, or baker's cheese shall be considered the equivalent of 62.5 pounds of milk solids plus one pound of milk solids for each one percent of butterfat content of such cheese.)

(b) *Milk sales area.* The following area is hereby designated as a "milk sales area" to be known as the Memphis, Tennessee, metropolitan milk sales area, and is referred to hereinafter as the "sales area": The city of Memphis and all of Shelby County, Tennessee, and the city of West Memphis in Crittenden County, Arkansas.

(c) *Base period.* The calendar month of June 1943 is hereby designated as the base period for the sales area: *Provided,* That the month of May may be used as the base period for computing base and quota for deliveries to elementary, junior high, and high schools; and *Provided further,* That in the computations set forth in (e) hereof the total deliveries to elementary, junior high, and high schools in the base period shall be divided by the number of days such schools were in session in lieu of the total number of days in the base period as set forth in (e) (1) and the average daily deliveries so determined shall be multiplied by the number of days such schools are in session in each quota period in lieu of the number of days in the quota period as set forth in (e) (2).

(d) *Quota period.* Each calendar month, beginning with the effective date of this order, is hereby designated as a quota period for the sales area.

(e) *Handler quotas.* Quotas for each handler other than a subhandler or producer-handler shall be determined as follows:

(1) Divide his respective bases by the number of days in the base period;

(2) Multiply the foregoing result by the number of days in the quota period; and

(3) Multiply the aforesaid resulting amounts by 100 percent in the case of the base for milk, and 75 percent in the case of the base for cream and milk byproducts.

(f) *Quotas for handlers who are also producers.* Quotas for each handler who is also a producer and who purchases no milk shall be computed in accordance with (e) hereof, except:

(1) His base period shall be either June or December, whichever represents his larger total deliveries; and

(2) The applicable percentages shall be 100 percent in lieu of those specified in (e) (3).

(g) *Quota adjustments.* Each handler may increase his quota for milk within any quota period by one pound of milk solids ~~for each one pound of milk~~ solids he reduces his quota for cream and milk byproducts.

(h) *Cream deliveries.* The units of cream delivered subject to quota in any quota period shall not exceed 100 percent of the units of cream in his base, irrespective of the milk solids content of such deliveries.

(i) *Handler exemptions.* Quotas shall not apply to any handler who delivers in a quota period a daily average of less than 250 units of milk, cream, and milk byproducts. For the purpose of this order, a unit shall be the equivalent in volume of the following: (1) One quart of milk, buttermilk, or fluid milk byproducts; (2) one-half pint of cream; and (3) one-half pound of cottage, pot, or baker's cheese.

(j) *Quota exclusions and exemptions.* Deliveries of milk, milk byproducts, or cream (1) to other handlers, except for such deliveries to sub-handlers, (2) to plants engaged in the handling or processing of milk, milk byproducts, cream, or other dairy products from which no milk, milk byproducts, or cream, is delivered in the sales area, (3) to industrial users, and (4) to the agencies or groups specified in (d) of FDO 79, shall be excluded from the computation of deliveries in the base period and exempt from charges to quotas.

(k) *Transfers of bases.* The market agent is empowered to transfer base from one handler to another:

(1) Upon receipt of a request in writing from both handlers; and

(2) Upon application from a handler and written notice to the Director and to both handlers, (i) to permit deliveries to a purchaser not being served by a handler whose quota reflects deliveries to such purchaser in the base period, (ii) to permit a handler to serve an account which customarily rotates among several handlers inclusive of a contract let by a public agency or institution on a bid basis, and (iii) to permit a handler to serve an account which he is serving on the effective date of this order and which was served by another handler during the base period.

(l) *Consumer priorities.* In the distribution of milk subject to quotas established hereunder, a handler shall give preference in the order listed, taking into consideration the type of purchasers served by him in the base period, to:

(1) The need of children, expectant mothers, and invalids requiring milk;

(2) Homes and retail stores handling milk for consumption off the premises; and

(3) Establishments serving milk for consumption on the premises.

(m) *Petition for relief from hardship.* (1) Any person affected by FDO 79 or the provisions hereof who considers that compliance therewith would work an exceptional and unreasonable hardship on him, may file with the market agent a petition addressed to the Director. The petition shall contain the correct name, address and principal place of business of the petitioner, a full statement of the facts upon which the petition is based, and the hardship involved and the nature of the relief desired.

(2) Upon receiving such petition the market agent shall immediately investigate the representations and facts stated therein.

(3) After investigation, the petition shall be certified to the Director, but prior to certification the market agent may (i) deny the petition or (ii) grant temporary relief for a total period not to exceed 60 days.

(4) Denials or grants of relief by the market agent shall immediately inves-Director and may be affirmed, modified, or reversed by the Director.

(n) *Reports.* Each handler shall transmit to the market agent on forms prescribed by the market agent the following reports:

(1) Within 20 days following the effective date of this order, reports which show the information required by the market agent to establish such handler's quotas;

(2) Within 20 days following the close of each quota period, the information required by the market agent to establish volumes of deliveries of milk, cream, and milk byproducts during the preceding quota period; and

(3) Handlers exempt from quotas pursuant to (i) hereof shall, upon the request of the market agent, submit the information required by the market agent to establish volumes of deliveries of milk, cream, and milk byproducts.

(o) *Records.* Handlers shall keep and shall make available to the market agent such records of receipts, sales, deliveries, and production as the market agent shall require for the purpose of obtaining information which the Director may require for the establishment of quotas as prescribed in (b) of FDO 79.

(p) *Expense of administration.* Each handler shall pay to the market agent, within 20 days after the close of each calendar month, per hundredweigl byproducts, crear alent of cottage, delivered during t riod and subject t der the provision

(q) *Violations.* shall report all v tor together witl quired for the pr lations.

(r) *Bureau of* The record-keepi quirements of thi proved by the Bu accordance with t of 1942. Subsequ reporting requirer the approval of th pursuant to the I 1942.

(s) *Effective d.* take effect at 12:(ary 1, 1944.

(E.O. 9280, 7 F.R. 3807; E.O. 9334, 8 F.R. 14783; FDO 7

Issued this 31st

Acting Director o

TWELVE NEW MILK SALES AREAS NAMED

Milk sales in 12 metropolitan areas in Tennessee, North Carolina, Alabama, Georgia, and Michigan will be regulated under the Food Distribution Administration's fluid milk conservation and control program, beginning January 1, the War Food Administration said today.

The new milk sales areas are:

Memphis, Tenn. (FDO 79.103)	Birmingham, Ala. (FDO 79.109)
Chattanooga, Tenn. (FDO 79.104)	Montgomery, Ala. (FDO 79.110)
[illegible]	[illegible]

days in May will be used as the base period in determining quotas, rather than June. Milk dealers include all persons or firms engaged in the same or transfer of milk, but not such distributors as subhandlers ("peddlers"), retail stores, hotels or restaurants.

Producer distributors who purchase no milk will be permitted to sell as much milk as they sold in either June or December, whichever represents their larger total deliveries.

The order permits dealers to sell more fluid milk than their quotas allow, provided they use less milk in making cream

2. Homes and milk for consump

3. Establishmen consumption on t

Deliveries of mi products to other handlers; the Ar agencies or grou graph (d) of FI gaged in handlir milk byproducts, products from wl products, or crea sales area; and t users who use mi

WAR FOOD ADMINISTRATION
Food Distribution Administration
Washington 25, D. C.

ORRECTION NOTICE - FDO-79.103

n printing Food Distribution Order No. 79.103 the following error occurred:

n (m) (4) second line "immediately inves" appeared erroneously. This paraaph should read "Denials or grants of relief by the market agent shall be eviewed by the Director and may be affirmed, modified, or reversed by the irector."

WAR FOOD ADMINISTRATION

WAR FOOD ADMINISTRATION

[FDO 79-104]

PART 1401—DAIRY PRODUCTS

FLUID MILK AND CREAM IN THE CHATTANOOGA, TENN., METROPOLITAN AREA

Pursuant to the authority vested in me by Food Distribution Order No. 79 (8 F.R. 12426), issued on September 7, 1943, as amended, and to effectuate the purposes of such order, it is hereby ordered as follows:

§ 1401.144 *Quota restrictions*—(a) *Definitions*. When used in this order, unless otherwise distinctly expressed or manifestly incompatible with the intent hereof:

(1) Each term defined in Food Distribution Order No. 79, as amended, shall, when used herein, have the same meaning as is set forth for such term in Food Distribution Order No. 79, as amended.

(2) The term "FDO 79" means Food Distribution Order No. 79, issued on September 7, 1943, as amended.

(3) The term "sub-handler" means any handler, such as a peddler, vendor, sub-dealer, or secondary dealer, who purchases in a previously packaged and processed form milk, cream, or milk byproducts for delivery.

(4) The term "industrial user" means a person, as determined by the market agent, in the capacity of a manufacturer of products using as an ingredient therein milk, cream, or milk byproducts, which products are disposed of for resale to consumers off the premises where made.

(5) The term "base" means the total pounds of milk solids delivered by a handler within the sales area during the base period (i) in the form of milk, or (ii) in the form of cream and milk byproducts, minus the milk solids in quota-exempt deliveries of milk, and cream and milk byproducts, as described in (j) hereof. (For the purpose of this order, the milk solids content of milk, milk byproducts, and cream shall be computed as follows: Each hundredweight of milk, cream, or milk byproducts other than cottage, pot, or baker's cheese, shall be considered the equivalent of 9.375 pounds of milk solids plus the number of pounds of milk solids calculated by multiplying the pounds of butterfat in such milk, and cream and milk byproducts by .906; and each hundredweight of cottage, pot, or baker's cheese shall be considered the equivalent of 62.5 pounds of milk solids plus one pound of milk solids for each one percent of butterfat content of such cheese.)

(b) *Milk sales area*. The following area is hereby designated as a "milk sales area" to be known as the Chattanooga, Tennessee, metropolitan milk sales area, and is referred to hereinafter as the "sales area":

The city of Chattanooga and the civil districts 1, 2, 3, and 4 in Hamilton County, Tennessee; and the militia districts of Creek in Dade County, Ninth in Catoosa County, and Lookout Mountain, Lisbon, Rossville, and Chickamauga in Walker County, Georgia.

(c) *Base period*. The calendar month of June 1943 is hereby designated as the base period for the sales area: *Provided*, That the month of May may be used as the base period for computing base and quota for deliveries to elementary, junior high, and high schools; and *Provided further*, That in the computations set forth in (e) hereof the total deliveries to elementary, junior high, and high schools in the base period shall be divided by the number of days such schools were in session in lieu of the total number of days in the base period as set forth in (e) (1) and the average daily deliveries so determined shall be multiplied by the number of days such schools are in session in each quota period in lieu of the number of days in the quota period as set forth in (e) (2).

(d) *Quota period*. Each calendar month, beginning with the effective date of this order, is hereby designated as a quota period for the sales area.

(e) *Handler quotas*. Quotas for each handler other than a sub-handler or producer-handler shall be determined as follows:

(1) Divide his respective bases by the number of days in the base period;

(2) Multiply the foregoing result by the number of days in the quota period; and

(3) Multiply the aforesaid resulting amounts by 100 percent in the case of the base for milk, and 75 percent in the case of the base for cream and milk byproducts.

(f) *Quotas for handlers who are also producers*. Quotas for each handler who is also a producer and who purchases no milk shall be computed in accordance with (e) hereof, except:

(1) His base period shall be either June or December, whichever represents his larger total deliveries; and

(2) The applicable percentages shall be 100 percent in lieu of those specified in (e) (3).

(g) *Quota and adjustments*. Each handler may increase his quota for milk within any quota period by one pound of milk solids for each one pound of milk solids he reduces his quota for cream and milk byproducts.

(h) *Cream deliveries*. The units of cream delivered subject to quota in any quota period shall not exceed 100 percent of the units of cream in his base, irrespective of the milk solids content of such deliveries.

(i) *Handler exemptions*. Quotas shall not apply to any handler who delivers in a quota period a daily average of less than 200 units of milk, cream, and milk byproducts. For the purpose of this order, a unit shall be the equivalent in volume of the following: (1) One quart of milk, buttermilk, or fluid milk byproducts; (2) one-half pint of cream; and (3) one-half pound of cottage, pot, or baker's cheese.

(j) *Quota exclusions and exemptions*. Deliveries of milk, milk byproducts, or cream (1) to other handlers, except for such deliveries to sub-handlers, (2) to plants engaged in the handling or processing of milk, milk byproducts, cream or other dairy products from which no milk, milk byproducts, or cream, is delivered in the sales area, (3) to industrial users, and (4) to the agencies or groups specified in (d) of FDO 79, shall be excluded from the computation of deliveries in the base period and exempt from charges to quotas.

(k) *Transfers of bases*. The market agent is empowered to transfer base from one handler to another:

(1) Upon receipt of a request in writing from both handlers; and

(2) Upon application from a handler and written notice to the Director and to both handlers, (i) to permit deliveries to a purchaser not being served by a handler whose quota reflects deliveries to such purchaser in the base period, (ii) to permit a handler to serve an account which customarily rotates among several handlers inclusive of a contract let by a public agency or institution on a bid basis, and (iii) to permit a handler to serve an account which he is serving on the effective date of this order and which was served by another handler during the base period.

(l) *Consumer priorities*. In the distribution of milk subject to quotas estabıed hereunder, a handler shall give ference in the order listed, taking into sideration the type of purchasers ved by him in the base period, to:

1) The need of children, expectant thers, and invalids requiring milk;

2) Homes and retail stores handling k for consumption off the premises;

3) Establishments serving milk for sumption on the premises.

m) *Petition for relief from hardship.* Any person affected by FDO 79 or the visions hereof, who considers that npliance therewith would work an extional and unreasonable hardship on 1, may file with the market agent a ition addressed to the Director. The ition shall contain the correct name, lress and principal place of business he petitioner, a full statement of the ts upon which the petition is based, l the hardship involved and the nae of the relief desired.

2) Upon receiving such petition the rket agent shall immediately investie representations and facts stated rein.

3) After investigation, the petition ll be certified to the Director, but or to certification the market agent y (i) deny the petition or (ii) grant nporary relief for a total period not to eed 60 days.

(4) Denials or grants of relief by the market agent shall be reviewed by the Director and may be affirmed, modified, or reversed by the Director.

(n) *Reports.* Each handler shall transmit to the market agent on forms prescribed by the market agent the following reports:

(1) Within 20 days following the effective date of this order, reports which show the information required by the market agent to establish such handler's quotas;

(2) Within 20 days following the close of each quota period, the information required by the market agent to establish volumes of deliveries of milk, cream, and milk byproducts during the preceding quota period; and

(3) Handlers exempt from quotas pursuant to (i) hereof shall, upon the request of the market agent, submit the information required by the market agent to establish volumes of deliveries of milk, cream, and milk byproducts.

(o) *Records.* Handlers shall keep and shall make available to the market agent such records of receipts, sales, deliveries, and production as the market agent shall require for the purpose of obtaining information which the Director may require for the establishment of quotas as prescribed in (b) of FDO 79.

(p) *Expense of administration.* Each handler shall pay to the market agent, within 20 days after the close of e calendar month, an assessment of $ per hundredweight of each of milk, r byproducts, cream, and skim milk eq alent of cottage, pot, or baker's ch delivered during the preceding q period and subject to quota regulat under the provisions hereof.

(q) *Violations.* The market a shall report all violations to the Dire together with the information requ for the prosecution of such violations

(r) *Bureau of the Budget appr* The record-keeping and reporting quirements of this order have been proved by the Bureau of the Budge accordance with the Federal Reports of 1942. Subsequent record-keepin reporting requirements will be sut to the approval of the Bureau of Budget pursuant to the Federal Rep Act of 1942.

(s) *Effective date.* This order s take effect at 12:01 a. m., e. w. t., . uary 1, 1944.

(E.O. 9280, 7 F.R. 10179; E.O. 932 F.R. 3807; E.O. 9334, 8 F.R. 5423; 9392, 8 F.R. 14783; FDO 79, 8 F.R. 1 13283)

Issued this 31st day of December 1

C. W. KITCHEN,
Acting Director of Food Distributio

'ELVE NEW MILK SALES AREAS NAMED

Milk sales in 12 metropolitan areas in nnessee, North Carolina, Alabama, orgia, and Michigan will be regulated der the Food Distribution Administion's fluid milk conservation and ntrol program, beginning January 1, : War Food Administration said to-.

The new milk sales areas are:

mphis, Tenn. (FDO 79.103)	Birmingham, Ala. (FDO 79.109)
attanooga, Tenn. (FDO 79.104)	Montgomery, Ala. (FDO 79.110)
oxville, Tenn. (FDO 79.105)	Muskegon, Mich. (FDO 79.111)
shville, Tenn. (FDO 79.106)	Battle Creek, Mich. (FDO 79.112)
anta, Ga. (FDO 79.107)	Winston-Salem, N. C. (FDO 79.113)
umbus, Ga. (FDO 79.108)	Charlottee, N. C. (FDO 79.114)

Under the program, milk dealers will permitted to sell to all customers exot schools as much fluid milk as they d in June and three-fourths as much lk in cream and milk byproducts ıch as cottage cheese, chocolate milk d buttermilk) as they sold in June. liveries to elementary, junior high d high schools will be under the same strictions except the number of school days in May will be used as the base period in determining quotas, rather than June. Milk dealers include all persons or firms engaged in the same or transfer of milk, but not such distributors as subhandlers ("peddlers"), retail stores, hotels or restaurants.

Producer distributors who purchase no milk will be permitted to sell as much milk as they sold in either June or December, whichever represents their larger total deliveries.

The order permits dealers to sell more fluid milk than their quotas allow, provided they use less milk in making cream or byproducts. Since cream and milk byproducts are recognized as one quota group, dealers may sell more cream by cutting down on milk byproducts, or more byproducts by reducing the amount of milk used in cream, so long as they do not use more than 75 percent of the milk used for such purposes in June.

In distributing the milk, cream and byproducts allowed under their quotas, dealers are required to give preference to the following consumer groups, in the order listed, taking into consideration the type of purchasers they served in the base period:

1. Children, expectant mothers, and invalids requiring milk;

2. Homes and retail stores han milk for consumption off the prem

3. Establishments serving milk consumption on the premises.

Deliveries of milk, cream and mil products to other handlers, except handlers; the Armed Forces; i. e., agencies or groups specified in p graph (d) of FDO 79; to plants gaged in handling or processing milk byproducts, cream, or other products from which no milk, milk products, or cream is delivered in sales area; and to designated indu users who use milk, cream, or milk products in making products whic disposed of for resale to consumer the premises where made are exempt.

Consumers in the milk sales named today, as in others already d nated, generally will be able to pur as much milk under the milk cons tion program as they have been b in recent months. Fluid milk sale being stabilized, and sales of cream milk byproducts are being reduced, officials said, to help assure suffi milk for manufacturing the cheese, ter, evaporated milk and milk powde quired by the armed forces and civi for good nutrition and properly bala diets.

FDO 79-105

DEC. 31, 1943

WAR FOOD ADMINISTRATION

[FDO 79-105]

PART 1401—DAIRY PRODUCTS

FLUID MILK AND CREAM IN THE KNOXVILLE, TENN., METROPOLITAN AREA

Pursuant to the authority vested in me by Food Distribution Order No. 79 (8 F.R. 12426), issued on September 7, 1943, as amended, and to effectuate the purposes of such order, it is hereby ordered as follows:

§ 1401.138 *Quota restrictions*—(a) *Definitions.* When used in this order, unless otherwise distinctly expressed or manifestly incompatible with the intent hereof:

(1) Each term defined in Food Distribution Order No. 79, as amended, shall, when used herein, have the same meaning as is set forth for such term in Food Distribution Order No. 79, as amended.

(2) The term "FDO 79" means Food Distribution Order No. 79, issued on September 7, 1943, as amended.

(3) The term "sub-handler" means any handler, such as a peddler, vendor, sub-dealer, or secondary dealer, who purchases in a previously packaged and processed form milk, cream, or milk byproducts for delivery.

(4) The term "industrial user" means a person, as determined by the market agent, in the capacity of a manufacturer of products using as an ingredient therein milk, cream, or milk byproducts, which products are disposed of for resale to consumers off the premises where made.

(5) The term "base" means the total pounds of milk solids delivered by a handler within the sales area during the base period (i) in the form of milk, or (ii) in the form of cream and milk byproducts, minus the milk solids in quota-exempt deliveries of milk, and cream and milk byproducts, as described in (j) hereof. (For the purpose of this order, the milk solids content of milk, milk byproducts and cream shall be computed as follows: Each hundredweight of milk, cream, or milk byproducts other than cottage, pot, or baker's cheese, shall be considered the equivalent of 9.375 pounds of milk solids plus the number of pounds of milk solids calculated by multiplying the pounds of butterfat in such milk, and cream and milk byproducts by 0.906; and each hundredweight of cottage, pot, or baker's cheese shall be considered the equivalent of 62.5 pounds of milk solids plus one pound of milk solids for each one percent of butterfat content of such cheese.)

(b) *Milk sales area.* The following area is hereby designated as a "milk sales area" to be known as the Knoxville, Tennessee, metropolitan milk sales area, and is referred to hereinafter as the "sales area":

The city of Knoxville and Knox County, the towns of Maryville and Alcoa in Blount County, the town of Jefferson City in Jefferson County, and the towns of Lenoir City and Loudon in Loudon County, all in the State of Tennessee.

(c) *Base period.* The calendar month of June 1943 is hereby designated as the base period for the sales area: *Provided,* That the month of May may be used as the base period for computing base and quota for deliveries to elementary, junior high, and high schools; and *Provided further,* That in the computations set forth in (e) hereof the total deliveries to elementary, junior high, and high schools in the base period shall be divided by the number of days such schools were in session in lieu of the total number of days in the base period as set forth in (e) (1) and the average daily deliveries so determined shall be multiplied by the number of days such schools are in session in each quota period in lieu of the number of days in the quota period as set forth in (e) (2).

(d) *Quota period.* Each calendar month, beginning with the effective date of this order, is hereby designated as a quota period for the sales area.

(e) *Handler quotas.* Quotas for each handler other than a sub-handler or producer-handler shall be determined as follows:

(1) Divide his respective bases by the number of days in the base period;

(2) Multiply the foregoing result by the number of days in the quota period; and

(3) Multiply the aforesaid resulting amounts by 100 percent in the case of the base for milk, and 75 percent in the case of the base for cream and milk byproducts.

(f) *Quotas for handlers who are also producers.* Quotas for each handler who is also a producer and who purchases no milk shall be computed in accordance with (e) hereof, except:

(1) His base period shall be either June or December, whichever represents his larger total deliveries; and

(2) The applicable percentages shall be 100 percent in lieu of those specified in (e) (3).

(g) *Quota and adjustments.* Each handler may increase his quota for milk within any quota period by one pound of milk solids for each one pound of milk solids he reduces his quota for cream and milk byproducts.

(h) *Cream deliveries.* The units of cream delivered subject to quota in any quota period shall not exceed 100 percent of the units of cream in his base, irrespective of the milk solids content of such deliveries.

(i) *Handler exemptions.* Quotas shall not apply to any handler who delivers in a quota period a daily average of less than 200 units of milk, cream, and milk byproducts. For the purpose of this order, a unit shall be the equivalent in volume of the following: (1) One quart of milk, buttermilk, or fluid milk byproducts; (2) one-half pint of cream; and (3) one-half pound of cottage, pot, or baker's cheese.

(j) *Quota exclusions and exemptions.* Deliveries of milk, milk byproducts, or cream (1) to other handlers, except for such deliveries to sub-handlers, (2) to plants engaged in the handling or processing of milk, milk byproducts, cream or other dairy products from which no milk, milk byproducts, or cream, is delivered in the sales area, (3) to industrial users, and (4) to the agencies or groups specified in (d) of FDO 79, shall be excluded from the computation of deliveries in the base period and exempt from charges to quotas.

(k) *Transfers of bases.* The market agent is empowered to transfer base from one handler to another.

(1) Upon receipt of a request in writing from both handlers; and

(2) Upon application from a handler and written notice to the Director and to both handlers, (i) to permit deliveries to a purchaser not being served by a handler whose quota reflects deliveries to such purchaser in the base period, (ii) to permit a handler to serve an account which customarily rotates among several handlers inclusive of a contract let by a public agency or institution on a bid basis, and (iii) to permit a handler to serve an account which he is serving on the effective date of this order and which was served by another handler during the base period.

(l) *Consumer priorities.* In the distribution of milk subject to quotas established hereunder, a handler shall give preference in the order listed, taking into consideration the type of purchasers served by him in the base period, to:

(1) The need of children, expectant mothers, and invalids requiring milk;

(2) Homes and retail stores handling milk for consumption off the premises; and

(3) Establishments serving milk for consumption on the premises.

(m) *Petition for relief from hardship.* (1) Any person affected by FDO 79 or the provisions hereof, who considers that compliance therewith would work an exceptional and unreasonable hardship on him, may file with the market agent a petition addressed to the Director. The petition shall contain the correct name, address, and principal place of business of the petitioner, a full statement of the facts upon which the petition is based, and the hardship involved and the nature of the relief desired.

(2) Upon receiving such petition the market agent shall immediately investigate, representations and facts stated therein.

(3) After investigation, the petition shall be certified to the Director, but prior to certification the market agent may (i) deny the petition or (ii) grant temporary relief for a total period not to exceed 60 days.

(4) Denials or grants of relief by the market agent shall be reviewed by the Director and may be affirmed, modified, or reversed by the Director.

(n) *Reports.* Each handler shall transmit to the market agent on forms prescribed by the market agent the following reports:

(1) Within 20 days following the effective date of this order, reports which show the information required by the market agent to establish such handler's quotas;

(2) Within 20 days following the close of each quota period, the information required by the market agent to establish volumes of deliveries of milk, cream, and milk byproducts during the preceding quota period; and

(3) Handlers exempt from quotas pursuant to (i) hereof shall, upon the request of the market agent, submit the information required by the market agent to establish volumes of deliveries of milk, cream, and milk byproducts.

(o) *Records.* Handlers shall keep and shall make available to the market agent such records of receipts, sales, deliveries, and production as the market agent shall require for the purpose of obtaining information which the Director may require for the establishment of quotas as prescribed in (b) of FDO 79.

(p) *Expense of administration.* Each handler shall pay to the market agent,

with
cale
per
bypı
alen
deli
peri
und
(c
shal
toge
for
(ı
The
quir
prov
accc
of 1
repc
the
pur:
1942
(s
take
1, 1!
(E.C
380'
8 F.:
Is
Ac

TWELVE NEW MILK SALES AREAS NAMED

Milk sales in 12 metropolitan areas in Tennessee, North Carolina, Alabama, Georgia, and Michigan will be regulated under the Food Distribution Administration's fluid milk conservation and control program, beginning January 1, the War Food Administration said today.

The new milk sales areas are:

Memphis, Tenn. (FDO 79.103)	**Birmingham, Ala.** (FDO 79.109)
Chattanooga, Tenn. (FDO 79.104)	**Montgomery, Ala.** (FDO 79.110)
Knoxville, Tenn. (FDO 79.105)	**Muskegon, Mich.** (FDO 79.111)
Nashville, Tenn. (FDO 79.106)	**Battle Creek, Mich.** (FDO 79.112)
Atlanta, Ga. (FDO 79.107)	**Winston-Salem, N. C.** (FDO 79.113)
Columbus, Ga. (FDO 79.108)	**Charlottee, N. C.** (FDO 79.114)

Under the program, milk dealers will be permitted to sell to all customers except schools as much fluid milk as they sold in June and three-fourths as much milk in cream and milk byproducts (such as cottage cheese, chocolate milk and buttermilk) as they sold in June. Deliveries to elementary, junior high and high schools will be under the same restrictions except the number of school days in May will be used as the base period in determining quotas, rather than June. Milk dealers include all persons or firms engaged in the same or transfer of milk, but not such distributors as subhandlers ("peddlers"), retail stores, hotels or restaurants.

Producer distributors who purchase no milk will be permitted to sell as much milk as they sold in either June or December, whichever represents their larger total deliveries.

The order permits dealers to sell more fluid milk than their quotas allow, provided they use less milk in making cream or byproducts. Since cream and milk byproducts are recognized as one quota group, dealers may sell more cream by cutting down on milk byproducts, or more byproducts by reducing the amount of milk used in cream, so long as they do not use more than 75 percent of the milk used for such purposes in June.

In distributing the milk, cream and byproducts allowed under their quotas, dealers are required to give preference to the following consumer groups, in the order listed, taking into consideration the type of purchasers they served in the base period:

1. Children, expectant mothers, and invalids requiring milk;

2.
milk
3.
con
D
pro
ha
age
gra
gag
mil
pro
pro
sale
use
pro
dis
the
exe
(
na
na
as
tio
in
bei
mi
off
mi
ter,
qui
for
diet

FDO 79-106

DEC. 31, 1943

WAR FOOD ADMINISTRATION

[FDO 79-106]

PART 1401—DAIRY PRODUCTS

FLUID MILK AND CREAM IN THE NASHVILLE, TENN., METROPOLITAN SALES AREA

Pursuant to the authority vested in me by Food Distribution Order No. 79 (8 F.R. 12426), issued on September 7, 1943, as amended, and to effectuate the purposes of such order, it is hereby ordered as follows:

§ 1401.137 *Quota restrictions*—(a) *Definitions.* When used in this order, unless otherwise distinctly expressed or manifestly incompatible with the intent hereof:

(1) Each term defined in Food Distribution Order No. 79, as amended, shall, when used herein, have the same meaning as is set forth for such term in Food Distribution Order No. 79, as amended.

(2) The term "FDO 79" means Food Distribution Order No. 79, issued on September 7, 1943, as amended.

(3) The term "sub-handler" means any handler, such as a peddler, vendor, sub-dealer, or secondary dealer, who purchases in a previously packaged and processed form milk, cream, or milk byproducts for delivery.

(4) The term "industrial user" means a person, as determined by the market agent, in the capacity of a manufacturer of products using as an ingredient therein milk, cream, or milk byproducts, which products are disposed of for resale to consumers off the premises where made.

(5) The term "base" means the total pounds of milk solids delivered by a handler within the sales area during the base period (i) in the form of milk, or (ii) in the form of cream and milk byproducts, minus the milk solids in quota-exempt deliveries of milk, and cream and milk byproducts, as described in (j) hereof. (For the purpose of this order, the milk solids content of milk, milk byproducts, and cream shall be computed as follows: Each hundredweight of milk, cream, or milk byproducts other than cottage, pot, or baker's cheese, shall be considered the equivalent of 9.375 pounds of milk solids plus the number of pounds of milk solids calculated by multiplying the pounds of butterfat in such milk, and cream and milk byproducts by 0.906; and each hundredweight of cottage, pot, or baker's cheese shall be considered the equivalent of 62.5 pounds of milk solids plus one pound of milk solids for each one percent of butterfat content of such cheese.)

(b) *Milk sales area.* The following area is hereby designated as a "milk sales area" to be known as the Nashville, Tennessee, metropolitan milk sales area, and is referred to hereinafter as the "sales area":

The city of Nashville, and Civil Districts Nos. 1, 2, 3, 4, 5, 6, 7, 8, 10, 11, 12, and 13 all in Davidson County, Tennessee.

(c) *Base period.* The calendar month of June 1943 is hereby designated as the base period for the sales area: *Provided,* That the month of May may be used as the base period for computing base and quota for deliveries to elementary, junior high, and high schools; and *Provided further,* That in the computations set forth in (e) hereof the total deliveries to elementary, junior high, and high schools in the base period shall be divided by the number of days such schools were in session in lieu of the total number of days in the base period as set forth in (e) (1) and the average daily deliveries so determined shall be multiplied by the number of days such schools are in session in each quota period in lieu of the number of days in the quota period as set forth in (e) (2).

(d) *Quota period.* Each calendar month beginning with the effective date of this order, is hereby designated as a quota period for the sales area.

(e) *Handler quotas.* Quotas for each handler other than a sub-handler or producer-handler shall be determined as follows:

(1) Divide his respective bases by the number of days in the base period;

(2) Multiply the foregoing result by the number of days in the quota period; and

(3) Multiply the aforesaid resulting amounts by 100 percent in the case of the base for milk, and 75 percent in the case of the base for cream and milk byproducts.

(f) *Quotas for handlers who are also producers.* Quotas for each handler who is also a producer and who purchases no milk shall be computed in accordance with (e) hereof, except:

(1) His base period shall be either June or December, whichever represents his larger total deliveries; and

(2) The applicable percentages shall be 100 percent in lieu of those specified in (e) (3).

(g) *Quota and adjustments.* Each handler may increase his quota for milk within any quota period by one pound of milk solids for each one pound of milk solids he reduces his quota for cream and milk byproducts.

(h) *Cream deliveries.* The units of cream delivered subject to quota in any quota period shall not exceed 100 percent of the units of cream in his base, irrespective of the milk solids content of such deliveries.

(i) *Handler exemptions.* Quotas shall not apply to any handler who delivers in a quota period a daily average of less than 100 units of milk, cream, and milk byproducts. For the purpose of this order, a unit shall be the equivalent in volume of the following: (1) One quart of milk, buttermilk, or fluid milk byproducts; (2) one-half pint of cream; and (3) one-half pound of cottage, pot, or baker's cheese.

(j) *Quota exclusions and exemptions.* Deliveries of milk, milk byproducts, or cream (1) to other handlers, except for such deliveries to sub-handlers, (2) to plants engaged in the handling or processing of milk, milk byproducts, cream or other dairy products from which no milk, milk byproducts, or cream, is delivered in the sales area, (3) to industrial users, and (4) to the agencies or groups specified in (d) of FDO 79, shall be excluded from the computation of deliveries in the base period and exempt from charges to quotas.

(k) *Transfers of bases.* The market agent is empowered to transfer base from one handler to another:

(1) Upon receipt of a request in writing from both handlers; and

(2) Upon application from a handler and written notice to the Director and to both handlers, (i) to permit deliveries to a purchaser not being served by a handler whose quota reflects deliveries to such purchaser in the base period, (ii) to permit a handler to serve an account which customarily rotates among several handlers inclusive of a contract let by a public agency or institution on a bid basis, and (iii) to permit a handler to serve an account which he is serving on the effective date of this order and which was served by another handler during the base period.

(l) *Consumer priorities.* In the distribution of milk subject to quotas established hereunder, a handler shall give preference in the order listed, taking into consideration the type of purchasers served by him in the base period, to:

(1 The need of children, expectant mothers, and invalids requiring milk;

(2) Homes and retail stores handling milk for consumption off the premises; and

(3) Establishments serving milk for consumption on the premises.

(m) *Petition for relief from hardship.* (1) Any person affected by FDO 79 or the provisions hereof, who considers that compliance therewith would work an exceptional and unreasonable hardship on him, may file with the market agent a petition addressed to the Director. The petition shall contain the correct name, address and principal place of business of the petitioner, a full statement of the facts upon which the petition is based, and the hardship involved and the nature of the relief desired.

(2) Upon receiving such petition the market agent shall immediately investigate representations and facts stated therein.

(3) After investigation, the petition shall be certified to the Director, but prior to certification the market agent may (i) deny the petition or (ii) grant temporary relief for a total period not to exceed 60 days.

(4) Denials or grants of relief by the market agent shall be reviewed by the Director and may be affirmed, modified, or reversed by the Director.

(n) *Reports.* Each handler shall transmit to the market agent on forms prescribed by the market agent the following reports:

(1) Within 20 days following the effective date of this order, reports which show the information required by the market agent to establish such handler's quotas;

(2) Within 20 days following the close of each quota period, the information required by the market agent to establish volumes of deliveries of milk, cream, and milk byproducts during the preceding quota period; and

(3) Handlers exempt from quotas pursuant to (i) hereof shall, upon the request of the market agent, submit the information required by the market agent to establish volumes of deliveries of milk, cream, and milk byproducts.

(o) *Records.* Handlers shall keep and shall make available to the market agent such records of receipts, sales, deliveries, and production as the market agent shall require for the purpose of obtaining information which the Director may require for the establishment of quotas as prescribed in (b) of FDO 79.

(p) *Expense of administration.* Each handler shall pay to the market agent, within 20 days after the close of each calendar month, an assessment of $0.01 per hundredweight of each of milk, milk byproducts, cream, and skim mi[lk equiv]alent of cottage, pot, or baker'[s cheese] delivered during the precedin[g quota] period and subject to quota reg[ulation] under the provisions hereof.

(q) *Violations.* The marke[t agent] shall report all violations to th[e Direc]tor together with the informa[tion re]quired for the prosecution of suc[h viola]tions.

(r) *Bureau of the Budget a[pproval.]* The record-keeping and report[ing re]quirements of this order have b[een ap]proved by the Bureau of the Bu[dget in] accordance with the Federal Rep[orts Act] of 1942. Subsequent record-kee[ping or] reporting requirements will be su[bject to] the approval of the Bureau of the [Budget] pursuant to the Federal Reports [Act of] 1942.

(s) *Effective date.* This ord[er shall] take effect at 12:01 a. m., e. w. [t., Jan]uary 1, 1944.

(E.O. 9280, 7 F.R. 10179; E.O. 932[2, 8 F.R.] 3807; E.O. 9334, 8 F.R. 5423; E.O. [9392, 8] F.R. 14783; FDO 79, 8 F.R. 12426[)]

Issued this 31st day of Decemb[er 1943.]

C. W. Kitch[en,]
Acting Director of Food Distrib[ution.]

Twelve New Milk Sales Areas Named

Milk sales in 12 metropolitan areas in Tennessee, North Carolina, Alabama, Georgia, and Michigan will be regulated under the Food Distribution Administration's fluid milk conservation and control program, beginning January 1, the War Food Administration said today.

The new milk sales areas are:

Memphis, Tenn. (FDO 79.103)	Birmingham, Ala. (FDO 79.109)
Chattanooga, Tenn. (FDO 79.104)	Montgomery, Ala. (FDO 79.110)
Knoxville, Tenn. (FDO 79.105)	Muskegon, Mich. (FDO 79.111)
Nashville, Tenn. (FDO 79.106)	Battle Creek, Mich. (FDO 79.112)
Atlanta, Ga. (FDO 79.107)	Winston-Salem, N. C. (FDO 79.113)
Columbus, Ga. (FDO 79.108)	Charlottee, N. C. (FDO 79.114)

Under the program, milk dealers will be permitted to sell to all customers except schools as much fluid milk as they sold in June and three-fourths as much milk in cream and milk byproducts (such as cottage cheese, chocolate milk and buttermilk) as they sold in June. Deliveries to elementary, junior high and high schools will be under the same restrictions except the number of school days in May will be used as the base period in determining quotas, rather than June. Milk dealers include all persons or firms engaged in the same or transfer of milk, but not such distributors as subhandlers ("peddlers"), retail stores, hotels or restaurants.

Producer distributors who purchase no milk will be permitted to sell as much milk as they sold in either June or December, whichever represents their larger total deliveries.

The order permits dealers to sell more fluid milk than their quotas allow, provided they use less milk in making cream or byproducts. Since cream and milk byproducts are recognized as one quota group, dealers may sell more cream by cutting down on milk byproducts, or more byproducts by reducing the amount of milk used in cream, so long as they do not use more than 75 percent of the milk used for such purposes in June.

In distributing the milk, cream and byproducts allowed under their quotas, dealers are required to give preference to the following consumer groups, in the order listed, taking into consideration the type of purchasers they served in the base period:

1. Children, expectant mothers, and invalids requiring milk;

2. Homes and retail stores ha[ndling] milk for consumption off the pr[emises].

3. Establishments serving mi[lk for] consumption on the premises.

Deliveries of milk, cream and m[ilk by]products to other handlers, excep[t sub]handlers; the Armed Forces; i. [e., the] agencies or groups specified in [para]graph (d) of FDO 79; to plan[ts en]gaged in handling or processing [of] milk byproducts, cream, or othe[r milk] products from which no milk, m[ilk by]products, or cream is delivered [in the] sales area; and to designated ind[ustrial] users who use milk, cream, or m[ilk by]products in making products wh[ich are] disposed of for resale to consum[ption off] the premises where made are exempt.

Consumers in the milk sales [areas] named today, as in others already [desig]nated, generally will be able to pu[rchase] as much milk under the milk co[nserva]tion program as they have been [buying] in recent months. Fluid milk sa[les are] being stabilized, and sales of crea[m and] milk byproducts are being reduce[d,] officials said, to help assure su[fficient] milk for manufacturing the chees[e, but]ter, evaporated milk and milk pow[der re]quired by the armed forces and c[ivilians] for good nutrition and properly ba[lanced] diets.

F733F

Cr/D.

FDO 79-107

DEC. 31, 1943

WAR FOOD ADMINISTRATION

[FDO 79-107]

PART 1401—DAIRY PRODUCTS

FLUID MILK AND CREAM IN THE ATLANTA, GA., METROPOLITAN SALES AREA

Pursuant to the authority vested in me by Food Distribution Order No. 79 (8 F.R. 12426), issued on September 7, 1943, as amended, and to effectuate the purposes of such order, it is hereby ordered as follows:

§ 1401.141 *Quota restrictions*—(a) *Definitions.* When used in this order, unless otherwise distinctly expressed or manifestly incompatible with the intent hereof:

(1) Each term defined in Food Distribution Order No. 79, as amended, shall, when used herein, have the same meaning as is set forth for such term in Food Distribution Order No. 79, as amended.

(2) The term "FDO 79" means Food Distribution Order No. 79, issued on September 7, 1943, as amended.

(3) The term "sub-handler" means any handler, such as a peddler, vendor, sub-dealer, or secondary dealer, who purchases in a previously packaged and processed form milk, cream, or milk byproducts for delivery.

(4) The term "industrial user" means a person, as determined by the market agent, in the capacity of a manufacturer of products using as an ingredient therein milk, cream, or milk byproducts, which products are disposed of for resale to consumers off the premises where made.

(5) The term "base" means the total pounds of milk solids delivered by a handler within the sales area during the base period (i) in the form of milk, or (ii) in the form of cream and milk byproducts, minus the milk solids in quota-exempt deliveries of milk, and cream and milk byproducts, as described in (j) hereof. (For the purpose of this order, the milk solids content of milk, milk byproducts, and cream shall be computed as follows: Each hundredweight of milk, cream, or milk byproducts other than cottage, pot, or baker's cheese, shall be considered the equivalent of 9.375 pounds of milk solids plus the number of pounds of milk solids calculated by multiplying the pounds of butterfat in such milk, and cream and milk byproducts by 0.906; and each hundredweight of cottage, pot, or baker's cheese shall be considered the equivalent of 62.5 pounds of milk solids plus one pound of milk solids for each one percent of butterfat content of such cheese.)

(b) *Milk sales area.* The following area is hereby designated as a "milk sales area" to be known as the Atlanta, Georgia, metropolitan milk sales area, and is referred to hereinafter as the "sales area":

The city of Atlanta and the counties of Fulton, De Kalb and Cobb all in the State of Georgia.

(c) *Base period.* The calendar month of June 1943 is hereby designated as the base period for the sales area: *Provided*, That the month of May may be used as the base period for computing base and quota for deliveries to elementary, junior high, and high schools; and *Provided further*, That in the computations set forth in (e) hereof the total deliveries to elementary, junior high, and high schools in the base period shall be divided by the number of days such schools were in session in lieu of the total number of days in the base period as set forth in (e) (1) and the average daily deliveries so determined shall be multiplied by the number of days such schools are in session in each quota period in lieu of the number of days in the quota period as set forth in (e) (2).

(d) *Quota period.* Each calendar month, beginning with the effective date of this order, is hereby designated as a quota period for the sales area.

(e) *Handler quotas.* Quotas for each handler other than a sub-handler or producer-handler shall be determined as follows:

(1) Divide his respective bases by the number of days in the base period;

(2) Multiply the foregoing result by the number of days in the quota period; and

(3) Multiply the aforesaid resulting amounts by 100 percent in the case of the base for milk, and 75 percent in the case of the base for cream and milk byproducts.

(f) *Quotas for handlers who are also producers.* Quotas for each handler who is also a producer and who purchases no milk shall be computed in accordance with (e) hereof, except:

(1) His base period shall be either June or December, whichever represents his larger total deliveries; and

(2) The applicable percentages shall be 100 percent in lieu of those specified in (e) (3).

(g) *Quota and adjustments.* Each handler may increase his quota for milk within any quota period by one pound of milk solids for each one pound of milk solids he reduces his quota for cream and milk byproducts.

(h) *Cream deliveries.* The units of cream delivered subject to quota in any quota period shall not exceed 100 percent of the units of cream in his base, irrespective of the milk solids content of such deliveries.

(i) *Handler exemptions.* Quotas shall not apply to any handler who delivers in a quota period a daily average of less than 125 units of milk, cream, and milk byproducts. For the purpose of this order, a unit shall be the equivalent in volume of the following: (1) One quart of milk, buttermilk, or fluid milk byproducts; (2) one-half pint of cream; and (3) one-half pound of cottage, pot, or baker's cheese.

(j) *Quota exclusions and exemptions.* Deliveries of milk, milk byproducts, or cream (1) to other handlers, except for such deliveries to sub-handlers, (2) to plants engaged in the handling or processing of milk, milk byproducts, cream or other dairy products from which no milk, milk byproducts, or cream, is delivered in the sales area, (3) to industrial users, and (4) to the agencies or groups specified in (d) of FDO 79, shall be excluded from the computation of deliveries in the base period and exempt from charges to quotas.

(k) *Transfers of bases.* The market agent is empowered to transfer base from one handler to another:

(1) Upon receipt of a request in writing from both handlers; and

(2) Upon application from a handler and written notice to the Director and to both handlers, (i) to permit deliveries to a purchaser not being served by a handler whose quota reflects deliveries to such purchaser in the base period, (ii) to permit a handler to serve an account which customarily rotates among several handlers inclusive of a contract let by a public agency or institution on a bid basis, and (iii) to permit a handler to serve an account which he is serving on the effective date of this order and which was served by another handler during the base period.

(l) *Consumer priorities.* In the distribution of milk subject to quotas established hereunder, a handler shall give preference in the order listed, taking into consideration the type of purchasers served by him in the base period, to:

(1) The need of children, expectant mothers, and invalids requiring milk;

(2) Homes and retail stores handling milk for consumption off the premises; and

(3) Establishments serving milk for consumption on the premises.

(m) *Petition for relief from hardship.* (1) Any person affected by FDO 79 or the provisions hereof, who considers that compliance therewith would work an exceptional and unreasonable hardship on him, may file with the market agent a petition addressed to the Director. The petition shall contain the correct name, address and principal place of business of the petitioner, a full statement of the facts upon which the petition is based, and the hardship involved and the nature of the relief desired.

(2) Upon receiving such petition the market agent shall immediately investigate representations and facts stated therein.

(3) After investigation, the petition shall be certified to the Director, but prior to certification the market agent may (i) deny the petition or (ii) grant temporary relief for a total period not to exceed 60 days.

(4) Denials or grants of relief by the market agent shall be reviewed by the Director and may be affirmed, modified, or reversed by the Director.

(n) *Reports.* Each handler shall transmit to the market agent on forms prescribed by the market agent the following reports:

(1) Within 20 days following the effective date of this order, reports which show the information required by the market agent to establish such handler's quotas;

(2) Within 20 days following the close of each quota period, the information required by the market agent to establish volumes of deliveries of milk, cream, and milk byproducts during the preceding quota period; and

(3) Handlers exempt from quotas pursuant to (i) hereof shall, upon the request of the market agent, submit the information required by the market agent to establish volumes of deliveries of milk, cream, and milk byproducts.

(o) *Records.*—Handlers shall keep and shall make available to the market agent such records of receipts, sales, deliveries, and production as the market agent shall require for the purpose of obtaining information which the Director may require for the establishment of quotas as prescribed in (b) of FDO 79.

(p) *Expense of administration.* Each handler shall pay to the market agent, within 20 days after the close of each calendar month, an assessment of $0.015 per hundredweigl
milk byproducts, crean
equivalent of cottage,
cheese delivered durir
quota period and subjec
tions under the provisic

(q) *Violations.* Th
shall report all violatioi
together with the info
for the prosecution of :

(r) *Bureau of the .*
The record-keeping ai
quirements of this ord
proved by the Bureau
accordance with the
Act of 1942. Subsequer
or reporting requiremer
to the approval of th
Budget pursuant to the
Act of 1942.

(s) *Effective date:*
take effect at 12:01 a. m
1, 1944.

(E.O. 9280; 7 F.R. 10179
3807; E.O. 9334, 8 F.R.
8 F.R. 14783; FDO 79, 8

Issued this 31st day c

C.
Acting Director of Fo

TWELVE NEW MILK SALES AREAS NAMED

Milk sales in 12 metropolitan areas in Tennessee, North Carolina, Alabama, Georgia, and Michigan will be regulated under the Food Distribution Administration's fluid milk conservation and control program, beginning January 1, the War Food Administration said today.

The new milk sales areas are:

Memphis, Tenn. (FDO 79.103)	Birmingham, Ala. (FDO 79.109)
Chattanooga, Tenn. (FDO 79.104)	Montgomery, Ala. (FDO 79.110)
Knoxville, Tenn. (FDO 79.105)	Muskegon, Mich. (FDO 79.111)
Nashville, Tenn. (FDO 79.106)	Battle Creek, Mich. (FDO 79.112)
Atlanta, Ga. (FDO 79.107)	Winston-Salem, N. C. (FDO 79.113)
Columbus, Ga. (FDO 79.108)	Charlottee, N. C. (FDO 79.114)

Under the program, milk dealers will be permitted to sell to all customers except schools as much fluid milk as they sold in June and three-fourths as much milk in cream and milk byproducts (such as cottage cheese, chocolate milk and buttermilk) as they sold in June. Deliveries to elementary, junior high and high schools will be under the same restrictions except the number of school days in May will be used as the base period in determining quotas, rather than June. Milk dealers include all persons or firms engaged in the same or transfer of milk, but not such distributors as subhandlers ("peddlers"), retail stores, hotels or restaurants.

Producer distributors who purchase no milk will be permitted to sell as much milk as they sold in either June or December, whichever represents their larger total deliveries.

The order permits dealers to sell more fluid milk than their quotas allow, provided they use less milk in making cream or byproducts. Since cream and milk byproducts are recognized as one quota group, dealers may sell more cream by cutting down on milk byproducts, or more byproducts by reducing the amount of milk used in cream, so long as they do not use more than 75 percent of the milk used for such purposes in June.

In distributing the milk, cream and byproducts allowed under their quotas, dealers are required to give preference to the following consumer groups, in the order listed, taking into consideration the type of purchasers they served in the base period:

1. Children, expectant mothers, and invalids requiring milk;

2. Homes and retail
milk for consumption

3. Establishments s
consumption on the pr

Deliveries of milk, cr
products to other han
handlers; the Armed
agencies or groups s
graph (d) of FDO 7
gaged in handling or
milk byproducts, crea
products from which
products, or cream is
sales area; and to des
users who use milk, cr
products in making pr
disposed of for resale
the premises where
exempt.

Consumers in the
named today, as in oth
nated, generally will b
as much milk under t
tion program as they
in recent months. Fl
being stabilized, and s
milk byproducts are be
officials said, to help
milk for manufacturin
ter, evaporated milk an
quired by the armed f
for good nutrition and
diets.

vo

3F

WAR FOOD ADMINISTRATION
Office of Distribution
Washington 25, D. C.

CORRECTION NOTICE - FDO 79.107 Amend. 1

In printing Food Distribution Order No. 79.107 Amend. 1 the following errors occurred:

In paragraph four under Effective Date the word "Food" is misspelled. Also the effective time erroneously appeared. This should read "12:01 a. m. e. w. t. March 1, 1944.

Last paragraph "8 F. R. 5425" should read " 8 F. R. 5423." "8 F. R. 14785" should read "8 F. R. 14783."

FDO 79-107

AMDT. 1
FEB. 29, 1944

WAR FOOD ADMINISTRATION

[FDO 79-107, Amdt. 1]

PART 1401—DAIRY PRODUCTS

FLUID MILK AND CREAM IN THE ATLANTA, GA., METROPOLITAN SALES AREA

Pursuant to Food Distribution Order No. 79 (8 F.R. 12426), dated September 7, 1943, as amended, and to effectuate the purposes thereof, Food Distribution Order No. 79-107 (9 F.R. 140) relative to the conservation and distribution of fluid milk in the Atlanta, Georgia, milk sales area, issued by the Director of Food Distribution on December 31, 1943, is hereby amended by deleting therefrom in § 1401.141 (b), *Milk sales area*, the words "and Cobb" and inserting the word "and" after the word "Fulton" and before the word "De Kalb." The Atlanta, Georgia, milk sales area will then be described as follows:

"The city of Atlanta and the counties of Fulton and De Kalb, all in the State of Georgia."

The handler exemptions specified in § 1401.141 (i) are amended by deleting the numeral "125" and substituting therefor the numeral "250."

Effective date. This amendment of Food Distribution Order No. 79-107 shall become effective at 12:01 a. m., e. w. t., March 1, 1944. With respect to violations of said Food Distribution Order No. 79-107, rights accrued, or liabilities incurred prior to the effective time of this amendment, said Food Distribution Order No. 79-107, shall be deemed to be in full force and effect for the purpose of sustaining any proper suit, action, or other proceeding with respect to any such violation, right, or liability.

(E.O. 9280, 7 F.R. 10179; E.O. 9322, 8 F.R. 3807; E.O. 9334, 8 F.R. 5423; E.O. 9392, 8 F.R. 14783; FDO 79, 8 F.R. 12426, 13283)

Issued this 29th day of February 1944.

C. W. KITCHEN,
Acting Director of Food Distribution.

FDO 79-108

DEC. 31, 1943

WAR FOOD ADMINISTRATION

[FDO 79-108]

PART 1401—DAIRY PRODUCTS

FLUID MILK AND CREAM IN THE COLUMBUS, GA., SALES AREA

Pursuant to the authority vested in me by Food Distribution Order No. 79 (8 F.R. 12426), issued on September 7, 1943, as amended, and to effectuate the purposes of such order, it is hereby ordered as follows:

§ 1401.146 *Quota restrictions*—(a) *Definitions.* When used in this order, unless otherwise distinctly expressed or manifestly incompatible with the intent hereof:

(1) Each term defined in Food Distribution Order No. 79, as amended, shall, when used herein, have the same meaning as is set forth for such term in Food Distribution Order No. 79, as amended.

(2) The term "FDO 79" means Food Distribution Order No. 79, issued on September 7, 1943, as amended.

(3) The term "sub-handler" means any handler, such as a peddler, vendor, sub-dealer, or secondary dealer, who purchases in a previously packaged and processed form milk, cream, or milk byproducts for delivery.

(4) The term "industrial user" means a person, as determined by the market agent, in the capacity of a manufacturer of products using an an ingredient therein milk, cream, or milk byproducts, which products are disposed of for resale to consumers off the premises where made.

(5) The term "base" means the total pounds of milk solids delivered by a handler within the sales area during the base period (i) in the form of milk, or (ii) in the form of cream and milk byproducts, minus the milk solids in quota-exempt deliveries of milk, and cream and milk byproducts, as described in (j) hereof. (For the purpose of this order, the milk solids content of milk, milk byproducts, and cream shall be computed as follows: Each hundredweight of milk, cream, or milk byproducts other than cottage, pot, or baker's cheese, shall be considered the equivalent of 9.375 pounds of milk solids plus the number of pounds of milk solids calculated by multiplying the pounds of butterfat in such milk, and cream and milk byproducts by 0.906; and each hundredweight of cottage, pot, or baker's cheese shall be considered the equivalent of 62.5 pounds of milk solids plus one pound of milk solids for each one percent of butterfat content of such cheese.)

(b) *Milk sales area.* The following area is hereby designated as a "milk sales area" to be known as the Columbus, Georgia, milk sales area, and is referred to hereinafter as the "sales area":

The city of Columbus, Georgia, and the county of Muscogee in the State of Georgia, and the incorporated town of Phoenix-Girard located in Lee and Russell counties in the State of Alabama.

(c) *Base period.* The calendar month of June 1943 is hereby designated as the base period for the sales area: *Provided,* That the month of May may be used as the base period for computing base and quota for deliveries to elementary, junior high and high schools; and *Provided further,* That in the computations set forth in (e) hereof the total deliveries to elementary, junior high, and high schools in the base period shall be divided by the number of days such schools were in session in lieu of the total number of days in the base period as set forth in (e) (1) and the average daily deliveries so determined shall be multiplied by the number of days such schools are in session in each quota period in lieu of the number of days in the quota period as set forth in (e) (2).

(d) *Quota period.* Each calendar month, beginning with the effective date of this order, is hereby designated as a quota period for the sales area.

(e) *Handler quotas.* Quotas for each handler other than a sub-handler or producer-handler shall be determined as follows:

(1) Divide his respective bases by the number of days in the base period;

(2) Multiply the foregoing result by the number of days in the quota period; and

(3) Multiply the aforesaid resulting amounts by 100 percent in the case of the base for milk, and 75 percent in the case of the base for cream and milk byproducts.

(f) *Quotas for handlers who are also producers.* Quotas for each handler who is also a producer and who purchases no milk shall be computed in accordance with (e) hereof, except:

(1) His base period shall be either June or December, whichever represents his larger total deliveries; and

(2) The applicable percentages shall be 100 percent in lieu of those specified in (e) (3).

(g) *Quota and adjustments.* Each handler may increase his quota for milk within any quota period by one pound of milk solids for each one pound of milk solids he reduces his quota for cream and milk byproducts.

(h) *Cream deliveries.* The units of cream delivered subject to quota in any quota period shall not exceed 100 percent of the units of cream in his base, irrespective of the milk solids content of such deliveries.

(i) *Handler exemptions.* Quotas shall not apply to any handler who delivers in a quota period a daily average of less than 125 units of milk, cream, and milk byproducts. For the purpose of this order, a unit shall be the equivalent in volume of the following: (1) One quart of milk, buttermilk, or fluid milk byproducts; (2) one-half pint of cream; and (3) one-half pound of cottage, pot, or baker's cheese.

(j) *Quota exclusions and exemptions.* Deliveries of milk, milk byproducts, or cream (1) to other handlers, except for such deliveries to sub-handlers, (2) to plants engaged in the handling of processing of milk, milk byproducts, cream or other dairy products from which no milk, milk byproducts, or cream, is delivered in the sales area, (3) to industrial users, and (4) to the agencies or groups specified in (d) of FDO 79, shall be excluded from the computation of deliveries in the base period and exempt from charges to quotas.

(k) *Transfers of bases.* The market agent is empowered to transfer base from one handler to another:

(1) Upon receipt of a request in writing from both handlers; and

(2) Upon application from a handler and written notice to the Director and to both handlers, (i) to permit deliveries to a purchaser not being served by a handler whose quota reflects deliveries to such purchaser in the base period, (ii) to permit a handler to serve an account which customarily rotates among several handlers inclusive of a contract let by a public agency or institution on a bid basis, and (iii) to permit a handler to serve an account which he is serving on the effective date of this order and which was served by another handler during the base period.

(l) *Consumer priorities.* In the distribution of milk subject to quotas established hereunder, a handler shall give preference in the order listed, taking into consideration the type of purchasers served by him in the base period, to:

(1) The need of children, expectant mothers, and invalids requiring milk;

(2) Homes and retail stores handling milk for consumption off the premises; and

(3) Establishments serving milk for consumption on the premises.

(m) *Petition for relief from hardship.* (1) Any person affected by FDO 79 or the provisions hereof who considers that compliance therewith would work an exceptional and unreasonable hardship on him, may file with the market agent a petition addressed to the Director. The petition shall contain the correct name, address and principal place of business of the petitioner, a full statement of the facts upon which the petition is based, and the hardship involved and the nature of the relief desired.

(2) Upon receiving such petition the market agent shall immediately investigate representations and facts stated therein.

(3) After investigation, the petition shall be certified to the Director, but prior to certification the market agent may (i) deny the petition or (ii) grant temporary relief for a total period not to exceed 60 days.

(4) Denials or grants of relief by the market agent shall be reviewed by the Director and may be affirmed, modified, or reversed by the Director.

(n) *Reports.* Each handler shall transmit to the market agent on forms prescribed by the market agent the following reports:

(1) Within 20 days following the effective date of this order, reports which show the information required by the market agent to establish such handler's quotas;

(2) Within 20 days following the close of each quota period, the information required by the market agent to establish volumes of deliveries of milk, cream, and milk byproducts during the preceding quota period; and

(3) Handlers exempt from quotas pursuant to (i) hereof shall, upon the request of the market agent, submit the information required by the market agent to establish volumes of deliveries of milk, cream, and milk byproducts.

(o) *Records.* Handlers shall keep and shall make available to the market agent such records of receipts, sales, deliveries, and production as the market agent shall require for the purpose of obtaining information which the Director may require for the establishment of quotas as prescribed in (b) of FDO 79.

(p) *Expense of administration.* Each handler shall pay to the market agent, within 20 days after the close of each calendar month, an assessment of 0.015 per hundredweight of each of milk, milk byproducts, cream, and skim milk equivalent of cottage, pot, or baker's cheese delivered during the preceding quota period and subject to quota regulations under the provisions hereof.

(q) *Violations.* The market agent shall report all violations to the Director together with the information required for the prosecution of such violations.

(r) *Bureau of the Budget approval.* The record-keeping and reporting requirements of this order have been approved by the Bureau of the Budget in accordance with the Federal Reports Act of 1942. Subsequent record-keeping or reporting requirements will be subject to the approval of the Bureau of the Budget pursuant to the Federal Reports Act of 1942.

(s) *Effective date.* This order shall take effect at 12:01 a. m., e. w. t., January 1, 1944.

(E.O. 9280, 7 F.R. 10179; E.O. 9322, 8 F.R. 3807; E.O. 9334, 8 F.R. 5423; E.O. 9392, 8 F.R. 14783; FDO 79, 8 F.R. 12426, 13283)

Issued this 31st day of December 1943.

C. W. KITCHEN,
Acting Director of Food Distribution.

TWELVE NEW MILK SALES AREAS NAMED

Milk sales in 12 metropolitan areas in Tennessee, North Carolina, Alabama, Georgia, and Michigan will be regulated under the Food Distribution Administration's fluid milk conservation and control program, beginning January 1, the War Food Administration said today.

The new milk sales areas are:

Memphis, Tenn. (FDO 79.103)	Birmingham, Ala. (FDO 79.109)
Chattanooga, Tenn. (FDO 79.104)	Montgomery, Ala. (FDO 79.110)
Knoxville, Tenn. (FDO 79.105)	Muskegon, Mich. (FDO 79.111)
Nashville, Tenn. (FDO 79.106)	Battle Creek, Mich. (FDO 79.112)
Atlanta, Ga. (FDO 79.107)	Winston-Salem, N. C. (FDO 79.113)
Columbus, Ga. (FDO 79.108)	Charlottee, N. C. (FDO 79.114)

Under the program, milk dealers will be permitted to sell to all customers except schools as much fluid milk as they sold in June and three-fourths as much milk in cream and milk byproducts (such as cottage cheese, chocolate milk and buttermilk) as they sold in June. Deliveries to elementary, junior high and high schools will be under the same restrictions except the number of school days in May will be used as the base period in determining quotas, rather than June. Milk dealers include all persons or firms engaged in the same or transfer of milk, but not such distributors as subhandlers ("peddlers"), retail stores, hotels or restaurants.

Producer distributors who purchase no milk will be permitted to sell as much milk as they sold in either June or December, whichever represents their larger total deliveries.

The order permits dealers to sell more fluid milk than their quotas allow, provided they use less milk in making cream or byproducts. Since cream and milk byproducts are recognized as one quota group, dealers may sell more cream by cutting down on milk byproducts, or more byproducts by reducing the amount of milk used in cream, so long as they do not use more than 75 percent of the milk used for such purposes in June.

In distributing the milk, cream and byproducts allowed under their quotas, dealers are required to give preference to the following consumer groups, in the order listed, taking into consideration the type of purchasers they served in the base period:

1. Children, expectant mothers, and invalids requiring milk;
2. Homes and retail stores handling milk for consumption off the premises;
3. Establishments serving milk for consumption on the premises.

Deliveries of milk, cream and milk byproducts to other handlers, except subhandlers; the Armed Forces; i. e., the agencies or groups specified in paragraph (d) of FDO 79; to plants engaged in handling or processing milk, milk byproducts, cream, or other dairy products from which no milk, milk byproducts, or cream is delivered in the sales area; and to designated industrial users who use milk, cream, or milk byproducts in making products which are disposed of for resale to consumers off the premises where made are quota exempt.

Consumers in the milk sales areas named today, as in others already designated, generally will be able to purchase as much milk under the milk conservation program as they have been buying in recent months. Fluid milk sales are being stabilized, and sales of cream and milk byproducts are being reduced, FDA officials said, to help assure sufficient milk for manufacturing the cheese, butter, evaporated milk and milk powder required by the armed forces and civilians for good nutrition and properly balanced diets.

337

FDO 79-108
AMDT. 1
FEB. 2, 1944

WAR FOOD ADMINISTRATION

[FDO 79-108, Amdt. 1]

PART 1401—DAIRY PRODUCTS

FLUID MILK AND CREAM IN COLUMBUS, GA., SALES AREA

Pursuant to Food Distribution Order No. 79 (8 F.R. 12426), dated September 7, 1943, as amended, and to effectuate the purposes thereof, Food Distribution Order No. 79-108 (9 F.R. 142), relative to the conservation and distribution of fluid milk in the Columbus, Georgia, milk sales area, issued by the Director of Food Distribution on December 31, 1943, is hereby amended as follows:

Delete the description of the sales area in § 1401.146 (b) and insert, in lieu thereof, the following:

The city of Columbus, Georgia, and the county of Muscogee in the State of Georgia, and Phenix City located in Russell County in the State of Alabama.

The provisions of this amendment shall become effective at 12:01 a. m., e. w. t., February 1, 1944. With respect to violations of said Food Distribution Order No. 79-108, rights accrued, or liabilities incurred prior to the effective time of this amendment, said Food Distribution Order No. 79-108 shall be deemed to be in full force and effect for the purpose of sustaining any proper suit, action, or other proceeding with respect to any such violation, right, or liability.

(E.O. 9280, 7 F.R. 10179; E.O. 9322, 8 F.R. 3807; E.O. 9334, 8 F.R. 5423; E.O. 9392, 8 F.R. 14783; FDO 79, 8 F.R. 12426, 13283)

Issued this 2d day of February 1944.

C. W. KITCHEN,
Acting Director of Food Distribution.

Copy

FDO 79-109

DEC. 31, 1943

WAR FOOD ADMINISTRATION

[FDO 79-109]

PART 1401—DAIRY PRODUCTS

FLUID MILK AND CREAM IN THE BIRMINGHAM, ALA., METROPOLITAN SALES AREA

Pursuant to the authority vested in me by Food Distribution Order No. 79 (8 F.R. 12426), issued on September 7, 1943, as amended, and to effectuate the purposes of such order, it is hereby ordered as follows:

§ 1401.142 *Quota restrictions*—(a) *Definitions*. When used in this order, unless otherwise distinctly expressed or manifestly incompatible with the intent hereof:

(1) Each term defined in Food Distribution Order No. 79, as amended, shall, when used herein, have the same meaning as is set forth for such term in Food Distribution Order No. 79, as amended.

(2) The term "FDO 79" means Food Distribution Order No. 79, issued on September 7, 1943, as amended.

(3) The term "sub-handler" means any handler, such as a peddler, vendor, sub-dealer, or secondary dealer, who purchases in a previously packaged and processed form milk, cream, or milk byproducts for delivery.

(4) The term "industrial user" means a person, as determined by the market agent, in the capacity of a manufacturer of products using as an ingredient therein milk, cream, or milk byproducts, which products are disposed of for resale to consumers off the premises where made.

(5) The term "base" means the total pounds of milk solids delivered by a handler within the sales area during the base period (i) in the form of milk, or (ii) in the form of cream and milk byproducts, minus the milk solids in quota-exempt deliveries of milk, and cream and milk byproducts, as described in (j) hereof. (For the purpose of this order, the milk solids content of milk, milk byproducts, and cream shall be computed as follows: Each hundredweight of milk, cream, or milk byproducts other than cottage, pot, or baker's cheese, shall be considered the equivalent of 9.375 pounds of milk solids plus the number of pounds of milk solids calculated by multiplying the pounds of butterfat in such milk, and cream and milk byproducts by 0.906; and each hundredweight of cottage, pot, or baker's cheese shall be considered the equivalent of 62.5 pounds of milk solids plus one pound of milk solids for each one percent of butterfat content of such cheese.)

(b) *Milk sales area*. The following area is hereby designated as a "milk sales area" to be known as the Birmingham, Alabama, metropolitan milk sales area, and is referred to hereinafter as the "sales area":

The city of Birmingham and the territory within the following boundaries and located within Jefferson and Shelby counties, Alabama: Beginning at a point nine (9) miles due north of the northeast corner of the Jefferson County Courthouse, Birmingham division, thence running due west for fifteen (15) miles, thence running due south for eighteen (18) miles, thence running due east for twenty-eight (28) miles, thence running due north for eighteen (18) miles, thence running due west for thirteen (13) miles to the point of beginning.

(c) *Base period*. The calendar month of June 1943 is hereby designated as the base period for the sales area: *Provided*, That the month of May may be used as the base period for computing base and quota for deliveries to elementary, junior high, and high schools: *And provided further*, That in the computations set forth in (e) hereof the total deliveries to elementary, junior high, and high schools in the base period shall be divided by the number of days such schools were in session in lieu of the total number of days in the base period as set forth in (e) (1) and the average daily deliveries so determined shall be multiplied by the number of days such schools are in session in each quota period in lieu of the number of days in the quota period as set forth in (e) (2).

(d) *Quota period*. Each calendar month, beginning with the effective date of this order, is hereby designated as a quota period for the sales area.

(e) *Handler quotas*. Quotas for each handler other than a sub-handler or producer-handler shall be determined as follows:

(1) Divide his respective bases by the number of days in the base period;

(2) Multiply the foregoing result by the number of days in the quota period; and

(3) Multiply the aforesaid resulting amounts by 100 percent in the case of the base for milk, and 75 percent in the case of the base for cream and milk byproducts.

(f) *Quotas for handlers who are also producers*. Quotas for each handler who is also a producer and who purchases no milk shall be computed in accordance with (e) hereof, except:

(1) His base period shall be either June or December, whichever represents his larger total deliveries; and

(2) The applicable percentages shall be 100 percent in lieu of those specified in (e) (3).

(g) *Quota and adjustments*. Each handler may increase his quota for milk within any quota period by one pound of milk solids for each one pound of milk solids he reduces his quota for cream and milk byproducts.

(h) *Cream deliveries*. The units of cream delivered subject to quota in any quota period shall not exceed 100 percent of the units of cream in his base, irrespective of the milk solids content of such deliveries.

(i) *Handler exemptions*. Quotas shall not apply to any handler who delivers in a quota period a daily average of less than 125 units of milk, cream, and milk byproducts. For the purpose of this order, a unit shall be the equivalent in volume of the following: (1) One quart of milk, buttermilk, or fluid milk byproducts; (2) one-half pint of cream; and (3) one-half pound of cottage, pot, or baker's cheese.

(j) *Quota exclusions and exemptions*. Deliveries of milk, milk byproducts, or cream (1) to other handlers, except for such deliveries to sub-handlers, (2) to plants engaged in the handling or processing of milk, milk byproducts, cream or other dairy products from which no milk, milk byproducts, or cream, is delivered in the sales area, (3) to industrial users, and (4) to the agencies or groups specified in (d) of FDO 79, shall be excluded from the computation of deliveries in the base period and exempt from charges to quotas.

(k) *Transfers of bases*. The market agent is empowered to transfer base from one handler to another:

(1) Upon receipt of a request in writing from both handlers; and

(2) Upon application from a handler and written notice to the Director and to both handlers, (i) to permit deliveries to a purchaser not being served by a handler whose quota reflects deliveries to such purchaser in the base period, (ii) to permit a handler to serve an account which customarily rotates among several handlers inclusive of a contract let by a public agency or institution on a bid basis, and (iii) to permit a handler to

serve an account which he is serving on the effective date of this order and which was served by another handler during the base period.

(l) *Consumer priorities.* In the distribution of milk subject to quotas established hereunder, a handler shall give preference in the order listed, taking into consideration the type of purchasers served by him in the base period, to:

(1) The need of children, expectant mothers, and invalids requiring milk;

(2) Homes and retail stores handling milk for consumption off the premises; and

(3) Establishments serving milk for consumption on the premises.

(m) *Petition for relief from hardship.* (1) Any person affected by FDO 79 or the provisions hereof, who considers that compliance therewith would work an exceptional and unreasonable hardship on him, may file with the market agent a petition addressed to the Director. The petition shall contain the correct name, address and principal place of business of the petitioner, a full statement of the facts upon which the petition is based, and the hardship involved and the nature of the relief desired.

(2) Upon receiving such petition the market agent shall immediately investigate representations and facts stated therein.

(3) After investigation, the petition shall be certified to the Director, but prior to certification the market agent may (i) deny the petition or (ii) grant temporary relief for a total period not to exceed 60 days.

(4) Denials or grants of relief by the market agent shall be reviewed by the Director and may be affirmed, modified, or reversed by the Director.

(n) *Reports.* Each handler shall transmit to the market agent on forms prescribed by the market agent the following reports:

(1) Within 20 days following the effective date of this order, reports which show the information required by the market agent to establish such handler's quotas;

(2) Within 20 days following the close of each quota period, the information required by the market agent to establish volumes of deliveries of milk, cream, and milk byproducts during the preceding quota period; and

(3) Handlers exempt from quotas pursuant to (i) hereof shall, upon the request of the market agent, submit the information required by the market agent to establish volumes of deliveries of milk, cream, and milk byproducts.

(o) *Records.* Handlers shall keep and shall make available to the market agent such records of receipts, sales, deliveries, and production as the market agent shall require for the purpose of obtaining information which the Director may require for the establishment of quotas as prescribed in (b) of FDO 79.

(p) *Expense of administr*
handler shall pay to the m
within 20 days after the c
calendar month, an assessm
per hundredweight of each
byproducts, cream, and skin
alent of cottage, pot, or ba
delivered during the prec
period and subject to quot
under the provisions hereof

(q) *Violations.* The m
shall report all violations to
together with the informat
for the prosecution of such

(r) *Bureau of the Budg*
The record-keeping and r
quirements of this order h
proved by the Bureau of th
accordance with the Federa
of 1942. Subsequent recor
reporting requirements will
the approval of the Bureau
pursuant to the Federal R
1942.

(s) *Effective date.* This
take effect at 12:01 a. m.,
uary 1, 1944.

(E.O. 9280, 7 F.R. 10179;
F.R. 3807; E.O. 9334, 8 F.F
9392; 8 F.R. 14783; FDO 79,
13283)

Issued this 31st day of De

C. W.

Acting Director of Food D

TWELVE NEW MILK SALES AREAS NAMED

Milk sales in 12 metropolitan areas in Tennessee, North Carolina, Alabama, Georgia, and Michigan will be regulated under the Food Distribution Administration's fluid milk conservation and control program, beginning January 1, the War Food Administration said today.

The new milk sales areas are:

Memphis, Tenn. (FDO 79.103)	Birmingham, Ala. (FDO 79.109)
Chattahooga, Tenn. (FDO 79.104)	Montgomery, Ala. (FDO 79.110)
Knoxville, Tenn. (FDO 79.105)	Muskegon, Mich. (FDO 79.111)
Nashville, Tenn. (FDO 79.106)	Battle Creek, Mich. (FDO 79.112)
Atlanta, Ga. (FDO 79.107)	Winston-Salem, N. C. (FDO 79.113)
Columbus, Ga. (FDO 79.108)	Charlottee, N. C. (FDO 79.114)

Under the program, milk dealers will be permitted to sell to all customers except schools as much fluid milk as they sold in June and three-fourths as much milk in cream and milk byproducts (such as cottage cheese, chocolate milk and buttermilk) as they sold in June. Deliveries to elementary, junior high and high schools will be under the same restrictions except the number of school days in May will be used as the base period in determining quotas, rather than June. Milk dealers include all persons or firms engaged in the same or transfer of milk, but not such distributors as subhandlers ("peddlers"), retail stores, hotels or restaurants.

Producer distributors who purchase no milk will be permitted to sell as much milk as they sold in either June or December, whichever represents their larger total deliveries.

The order permits dealers to sell more fluid milk than their quotas allow, provided they use less milk in making cream or byproducts. Since cream and milk byproducts are recognized as one quota group, dealers may sell more cream by cutting down on milk byproducts, or more byproducts by reducing the amount of milk used in cream, so long as they do not use more than 75 percent of the milk used for such purposes in June.

In distributing the milk, cream and byproducts allowed under their quotas, dealers are required to give preference to the following consumer groups, in the order listed, taking into consideration the type of purchasers they served in the base period:

1. Children, expectant mothers, and invalids requiring milk;

2. Homes and retail sto
milk for consumption off t

3. Establishments servin
consumption on the premis

Deliveries of milk, cream
products to other handlers
handlers; the Armed Forc
agencies or groups specifi
graph (d) of FDO 79; t
gaged in handling or pro
milk byproducts, cream, o
products from which no m
products, or cream is deli
sales area; and to designat
users who use milk, cream
products in making produc
disposed of for resale to c
the premises where mad
exempt.

Consumers in the milk
named today, as in others a
nated, generally will be abl
as much milk under the m
tion program as they have
in recent months. Fluid n
being stabilized, and sales
milk byproducts are being
officials said, to help ass
milk for manufacturing the
ter, evaporated milk and mi
quired by the armed forces
for good nutrition and prop
diets.

)(

FDO 79-110

DEC. 31, 1943

WAR FOOD ADMINISTRATION

[FDO 79-110]

PART 1401—DAIRY PRODUCTS

FLUID MILK AND CREAM IN THE MONTGOMERY, ALA., METROPOLITAN SALES AREA

Pursuant to the authority vested in me by Food Distribution Order No. 79 (8 F.R. 12426), issued on September 7, 1943, as amended, and to effectuate the purposes of such order, it is hereby ordered as follows:

§ 1401.143 *Quota restrictions*—(a) *Definitions.* When used in this order, unless otherwise distinctly expressed or manifestly incompatible with the intent hereof:

(1) Each term defined in Food Distribution Order No. 79, as amended, shall, when used herein, have the same meaning as is set forth for such term in Food Distribution Order No. 79, as amended.

(2) The term "FDO 79" means Food Distribution Order No. 79, issued on September 7, 1943, as amended.

(3) The term "sub-handler" means any handler, such as a peddler, vendor, sub-dealer, or secondary dealer, who purchases in a previously packaged and processed form milk, cream, or milk byproducts for delivery.

(4) The term "industrial user" means a person, as determined by the market agent, in the capacity of a manufacturer of products using as an ingredient therein milk, cream, or milk byproducts, which products are disposed of for resale to consumers off the premises where made.

(5) The term 'base" means the total pounds of milk solids delivered by a handler within the sales area during the base period (i) in the form of milk, or (ii) in the form of cream and milk byproducts, minus the milk solids in quota exempt deliveries of milk, and cream and milk byproducts, as described in (j) hereof. (For the purpose of this order, the milk solids content of milk, milk byproducts, and cream shall be computed as follows: Each hundredweight of milk, cream, or milk byproducts other than cottage, pot, or baker's cheese, shall be considered the equivalent of 9.375 pounds of milk solids plus the number of pounds of milk solids calculated by multiplying the pounds of butterfat in such milk, and cream and milk byproducts by 0.906; and each hundredweight of cottage, pot, or baker's cheese shall be considered the equivalent of 62.5 pounds of milk solids plus one pound of milk solids for each one percent of butterfat content of such cheese.)

(b) *Milk sales area.* The following area is hereby designated as a "milk sales area" to be known as the Montgomery, Alabama, metropolitan milk sales area, and is referred to hereinafter as the "sales area":

The city of Montgomery and the county of Montgomery in the State of Alabama.

(c) *Base period.* The calendar month of June 1943 is hereby designated as the base period for the sales area: *Provided,* That the month of May may be used as the base period for computing base and quota for deliveries to elementary, junior high, and high schools; and *Provided further,* That in the computations set forth in (e) hereof the total deliveries to elementary, junior high, and high schools in the base period shall be divided by the number of days such schools were in session in lieu of the total number of days in the base period as set forth in (e) (1) and the average daily deliveries so determined shall be multiplied by the number of days such schools are in session in each quota period in lieu of the number of days in the quota period as set forth in (e) (2).

(d) *Quota period.* Each calendar month, beginning with the effective date of this order, is hereby designated as a quota period for the sales area.

(e) *Handler quotas.* Quotas for each handler other than a sub-handler or producer-handler shall be determined as follows:

(1) Divide his respective bases by the number of days in the base period;

(2) Multiply the foregoing result by the number of days in the quota period; and

(3) Multiply the aforesaid resulting amounts by 100 percent in the case of the base for milk, and 75 percent in the case of the base for cream and milk byproducts.

(f) *Quotas for handlers who are also producers.* Quotas for each handler who is also a producer and who purchases no milk shall be computed in accordance with (e) hereof, except:

(1) His base period shall be either June or December, whichever represents his larger total deliveries; and

(2) The applicable percentages shall be 100 percent in lieu of those specified in (e) (3).

(g) *Quota and adjustments.* Each handler may increase his quota for milk within any quota period by one pound of milk solids for each one pound of milk solids he reduces his quota for cream and milk byproducts.

(h) *Cream deliveries.* The units of cream delivered subject to quota in any quota period shall not exceed 100 percent of the units of cream in his base, irrespective of the milk solids content of such deliveries.

(i) *Handler exemptions.* Quotas shall not apply to any handler who delivers in a quota period a daily average of less than 150 units of milk, cream, and milk byproducts. For the purpose of this order, a unit shall be the equivalent in volume of the following: (1) One quart of milk, buttermilk, or fluid milk byproducts; (2) one-half pint of cream; and (3) one-half pound of cottage, pot, or baker's cheese.

(j) *Quota exclusions and exemptions.* Deliveries of milk, milk byproducts, or cream (1) to other handlers, except for such deliveries to sub-handlers, (2) to plants engaged in the handling or processing of milk, milk byproducts, cream or other dairy products from which no milk, milk byproducts, or cream, is delivered in the sales area, (3) to industrial users, and (4) to the agencies or groups specified in (d) of FDO 79, shall be excluded from the computation of deliveries in the base period and exempt from charges to quotas.

(k) *Transfers of bases.* The market agent is empowered to transfer base from one handler to another:

(1) Upon receipt of a request in writing from both handlers; and

(2) Upon application from a handler and written notice to the Director and to both handlers, (i) to permit deliveries to a purchaser not being served by a handler whose quota reflects deliveries to such purchaser in the base period, (ii) to permit a handler to serve an account which customarily rotates among several handlers inclusive of a contract let by a public agency or institution on a bid basis, and (iii) to permit a handler to serve an account which he is serving on the effective date of this order and which was served by another handler during the base period.

(l) *Consumer priorities.* In the distribution of milk subject to quotas established hereunder, a handler shall give preference in the order listed, taking into consideration the type of purchasers served by him in the base period, to:

(1) The need of children, expectant mothers, and invalids requiring milk;

(2) Homes and retail stores handling milk for consumption off the premises; and

(3) Establishments serving milk for consumption on the premises.

(m) *Petition for relief from hardship.* (1) Any person affected by FDO 79 or the provisions hereof, who considers that compliance therewith would work an exceptional and unreasonable hardship on him, may file with the market agent a petition addressed to the Director. The petition shall contain the correct name, address and principal place of business of the petitioner, a full statement of the facts upon which the petition is based, and the hardship involved and the nature of the relief desired.

(2) Upon receiving such petition the market agent shall immediately investigate representations and facts stated therein.

(3) After investigation, the petition shall be certified to the Director, but prior to certification the market agent may (i) deny the petition or (ii) grant temporary relief for a total period not to exceed 60 days.

(4) Denials or grants of relief by the market agent shall be reviewed by the Director and may be affirmed, modified, or reversed by the Director.

(n) *Reports.* Each handler shall transmit to the market agent on forms prescribed by the market agent the following reports:

(1) Within 20 days following the effective date of this order, reports which show the information required by the market agent to establish such handler's quotas;

(2) Within 20 days following the close of each quota period, the information required by the market agent to establish volumes of deliveries of milk, cream, and milk byproducts during the preceding quota period; and

(3) Handlers exempt from quotas pursuant to (i) hereof shall, upon the request of the market agent, submit the information required by the market agent to establish volumes of deliveries of milk, cream, and milk byproducts.

(o) *Records.* Handlers shall keep and shall make available to the market agent such records of receipts, sales, deliveries, and production as the market agent shall require for the purpose of obtaining information which the Director may require for the establishment of quotas as prescribed in (b) of FDO 79.

(p) *Expense of administration.* Each handler shall pay to the market agent, within 20 days after the close of each calendar month, an assessment of $0.015 per hundredweight of each of milk, milk byproducts, cream, and skim milk equivalent of cottage, pot, or baker's cheese delivered during the preceding quota period and subject to quota regulations under the provisions hereof.

(q) *Violations.* The market agent shall report all violations to the Director together with the information required for the prosecution of such violations.

(r) *Bureau of the Budget approval.* The record-keeping and reporting requirements of this order have been approved by the Bureau of the Budget in accordance with the Federal Reports Act of 1942. Subsequent record-keeping or reporting requirements will be subject to the approval of the Bureau of the Budget pursuant to the Federal Reports Act of 1942.

(s) *Effective date.* This order shall take effect at 12:01 a. m., e. w. t., January 1, 1944.

(E.O. 9280, 7 F.R. 10179; E.O. 9322, 8 F.R. 3807; E.O. 9334, 8 F.R. 5423; E.O. 9392, 8 F.R. 14783; FDO 79, 8 F.R. 12426, 13283)

Issued this 31st day of December 1943.

C. W. KITCHEN,
Acting Director of Food Distribution.

TWELVE NEW MILK SALES AREAS NAMED

Milk sales in 12 metropolitan areas in Tennessee, North Carolina, Alabama, Georgia, and Michigan will be regulated under the Food Distribution Administration's fluid milk conservation and control program, beginning January 1, the War Food Administration said today.

The new milk sales areas are:

Memphis, Tenn. (FDO 79.103)	Birmingham, Ala. (FDO 79.109)
Chattanooga, Tenn. (FDO 79.104)	Montgomery, Ala. (FDO 79.110)
Knoxville, Tenn. (FDO 79.105)	Muskegon, Mich. (FDO 79.111)
Nashville, Tenn. (FDO 79.106)	Battle Creek, Mich. (FDO 79.112)
Atlanta, Ga. (FDO 79.107)	Winston-Salem, N. C. (FDO 79.113)
Columbus, Ga. (FDO 79.108)	Charlottee, N. C. (FDO 79.114)

Under the program, milk dealers will be permitted to sell to all customers except schools as much fluid milk as they sold in June and three-fourths as much milk in cream and milk byproducts (such as cottage cheese, chocolate milk and buttermilk) as they sold in June. Deliveries to elementary, junior high and high schools will be under the same restrictions except the number of school days in May will be used as the base period in determining quotas, rather than June. Milk dealers include all persons or firms engaged in the same or transfer of milk, but not such distributors as subhandlers ("peddlers"), retail stores, hotels or restaurants.

Producer distributors who purchase no milk will be permitted to sell as much milk as they sold in either June or December, whichever represents their larger total deliveries.

The order permits dealers to sell more fluid milk than their quotas allow, provided they use less milk in making cream or byproducts. Since cream and milk byproducts are recognized as one quota group, dealers may sell more cream by cutting down on milk byproducts, or more byproducts by reducing the amount of milk used in cream, so long as they do not use more than 75 percent of the milk used for such purposes in June.

In distributing the milk, cream and byproducts allowed under their quotas, dealers are required to give preference to the following consumer groups, in the order listed, taking into consideration the type of purchasers they served in the base period:

1. Children, expectant mothers, and invalids requiring milk;

2. Homes and retail stores handling milk for consumption off the premises;

3. Establishments serving milk for consumption on the premises.

Deliveries of milk, cream and milk byproducts to other handlers, except subhandlers; the Armed Forces; i. e., the agencies or groups specified in paragraph (d) of FDO 79; to plants engaged in handling or processing milk, milk byproducts, cream, or other dairy products from which no milk, milk byproducts, or cream is delivered in the sales area; and to designated industrial users who use milk, cream, or milk byproducts in making products which are disposed of for resale to consumers off the premises where made are quota exempt.

Consumers in the milk sales areas named today, as in others already designated, generally will be able to purchase as much milk under the milk conservation program as they have been buying in recent months. Fluid milk sales are being stabilized, and sales of cream and milk byproducts are being reduced, FDA officials said, to help assure sufficient milk for manufacturing the cheese, butter, evaporated milk and milk powder required by the armed forces and civilians for good nutrition and properly balanced diets.

33 F

FDO 79-111

DEC. 31, 1943

WAR FOOD ADMINISTRATION

[FDO 79-111]

PART 1401—DAIRY PRODUCTS

FLUID MILK AND CREAM IN THE MUSKEGON, MICH., SALES AREA

Pursuant to the authority vested in me by Food Distribution Order No. 79 (8 F.R. 12426), issued on September 7, 1943, as amended, and to effectuate the purposes of such order, it is hereby ordered as follows:

§ 1401.140 *Quota restrictions*.—(a) *Definitions*. When used in this order, unless otherwise distinctly expressed or manifestly incompatible with the intent hereof:

(1) Each term defined in Food Distribution Order No. 79, as amended, shall, when used herein, have the same meaning as is set forth for such term in Food Distribution Order No. 79, as amended.

(2) The term "FDO 79" means Food Distribution Order No. 79, issued on September 7, 1943, as amended.

(3) The term "sub-handler" means any handler, such as a peddler, vendor, sub-dealer, or secondary dealer, who purchases in a previously packaged and processed form milk, cream, or milk byproducts for delivery.

(4) The term "industrial user" means a person, as determined by the market agent, in the capacity of a manufacturer of products using as an ingredient therein milk, cream, or milk byproducts, which products are disposed of for resale to consumers off the premises where made.

(5) The term "base" means the total pounds of milk solids delivered by a handler within the sales area during the base period (i) in the form of milk, or (ii) in the form of cream and milk byproducts, minus the milk solids in quota-exempt deliveries of milk, and cream and milk byproducts, as described in (j) hereof. (For the purpose of this order, the milk solids content of milk, milk byproducts, and cream shall be computed as follows: Each hundredweight of milk, cream, or milk byproducts other than cottage, pot, or baker's cheese, shall be considered the equivalent of 9.375 pounds of milk solids plus the number of pounds of milk solids calculated by multiplying the pounds of butterfat in such milk, and cream and milk byproducts by 0.906; and each hundredweight of cottage, pot, or baker's cheese shall be considered the equivalent of 62.5 pounds of milk solids plus one pound of milk solids for each one percent of butterfat content of such cheese.)

(b) *Milk sales area*. The following area is hereby designated as a "milk sales area" to be known as the Muskegon, Michigan, milk sales area, and is referred to hereinafter as the "sales area":

The cities of Muskegon, Muskegon Heights and North Muskegon and the townships of Laketon, Muskegon, Fruitport, and Norton, all in the county of Muskegon, Michigan.

(c) *Base period*. The calendar month of June 1943 is hereby designated as the base period for the sales area: *Provided*, That the month of May may be used as the base period for computing base and quota for deliveries to elementary, junior high, and high schools: *And provided further*, That in the computations set forth in (e) hereof the total deliveries to elementary, junior high, and high schools in the base period shall be divided by the number of days such schools were in session in lieu of the total number of days in the base period as set forth in (e) (1) and the average daily deliveries so determined shall be multiplied by the number of days such schools are in session in each quota period in lieu of the number of days in the quota period as set forth in (e) (2).

(d) *Quota period*. Each calendar month, beginning with the effective date of this order, is hereby designated as a quota period for the sales area.

(e) *Handler quotas*. Quotas for each handler other than a sub-handler or producer-handler shall be determined as follows:

(1) Divide his respective bases by the number of days in the base period;

(2) Multiply the foregoing result by the number of days in the quota period; and

(3) Multiply the aforesaid resulting amounts by 100 percent in the case of the base for milk, and 75 percent in the case of the base for cream and milk byproducts.

(f) *Quotas for handlers who are also producers*. Quotas for each handler who is also a producer and who purchases no milk shall be computed in accordance with (e) hereof, except:

(1) His base period shall be either June or December, whichever represents his larger total deliveries; and

(2) The applicable percentages shall be 100 percent in lieu of those specified in (e) (3).

(g) *Quota and adjustments*. Each handler may increase his quota for milk within any quota period by one pound of milk solids for each one pound of milk solids he reduces his quota for cream and milk byproducts.

(h) *Cream deliveries*. The units of cream delivered subject to quota in any quota period shall not exceed 100 percent of the units of cream in his base, irrespective of the milk solids content of such deliveries.

(i) *Handler exemptions*. Quotas shall not apply to any handler who delivers in a quota period a daily average of less than 300 units of milk, cream, and milk byproducts. For the purpose of this order, a unit shall be the equivalent in volume of the following: (1) One quart of milk, buttermilk, or fluid milk byproducts; (2) one-half pint of cream; and (3) one-half pound of cottage, pot, or baker's cheese.

(j) *Quota exclusions and exemptions*. Deliveries of milk, milk byproducts, or cream (1) to other handlers, except for such deliveries to sub-handlers, (2) to plants engaged in the handling or processing of milk, milk byproducts, cream or other dairy products from which no milk, milk byproducts, or cream, is delivered in the sales area, (3) to industrial users, and (4) to the agencies or groups specified in (d) of FDO 79, shall be excluded from the computation of deliveries in the base period and exempt from charges to quotas.

(k) *Transfers of bases*. The market agent is empowered to transfer base from one handler to another:

(1) Upon receipt of a request in writing from both handlers; and

(2) Upon application from a handler and written notice to the Director and to both handlers, (i) to permit deliveries to a purchaser not being served by a handler whose quota reflects deliveries to such purchaser in the base period, (ii) to permit a handler to serve an account which customarily rotates among several handlers inclusive of a contract let by a public agency or institution on a bid basis, and (iii) to permit a handler to serve an account which he is serving on the effective date of this order and which was served by another handler during the base period.

(l) *Consumer priorities*. In the distribution of milk subject to quotas established hereunder, a handler shall give preference in the order listed, taking into consideration the type of purchasers served by him in the base period, to:

(1) The need of children, expectant mothers, and invalids requiring milk;

MILK SALES AREAS NAMED

12 metropolitan areas in
rth Carolina, Alabama,
lichigan will be regulated
d Distribution Adminis-
milk conservation and
m, beginning January 1,
Administration said to-

k sales areas are:

	Birmingham, Ala. (FDO 79.109)
nn.	Montgomery, Ala. (FDO 79.110)
	Muskegon, Mich. (FDO 79.111)
	Battle Creek, Mich. (FDO 79.112)
	Winston-Salem, N. C. (FDO 79.113)
	Charlotte, N. C. (FDO 79.114)

rogram, milk dealers will
sell to all customers ex-
much fluid milk as they
ad three-fourths as much
n and milk byproducts
ge cheese, chocolate milk
) as they sold in June.
elementary, junior high
ls will be under the same
ept the number of school days in May will be used as the base period in determining quotas, rather than June. Milk dealers include all persons or firms engaged in the same or transfer of milk, but not such distributors as subhandlers ("peddlers"), retail stores, hotels or restaurants.

Producer distributors who purchase no milk will be permitted to sell as much milk as they sold in either June or December, whichever represents their larger total deliveries.

The order permits dealers to sell more fluid milk than their quotas allow, provided they use less milk in making cream or byproducts. Since cream and milk byproducts are recognized as one quota group, dealers may sell more cream by cutting down on milk byproducts, or more byproducts by reducing the amount of milk used in cream, so long as they do not use more than 75 percent of the milk used for such purposes in June.

In distributing the milk, cream and byproducts allowed under their quotas, dealers are required to give preference to the following consumer groups, in the order listed, taking into consideration the type of purchasers they served in the base period:

1. Children, expectant mothers, and invalids requiring milk;

2. Homes and retail stores handli
milk for consumption off the premis
3. Establishments serving milk
consumption on the premises.

Deliveries of milk, cream and milk b
products to other handlers, except su
handlers; the Armed Forces; i. e., t
agencies or groups specified in pa
graph (d) of FDO 79; to plants e
gaged in handling or processing mi
milk byproducts, cream, or other da
products from which no milk, milk b
products, or cream is delivered in t
sales area; and to designated industr
users who use milk, cream, or milk b
products in making products which a
disposed of for resale to consumers
the premises where made are quo
exempt.

Consumers in the milk sales are
named today, as in others already desi
nated, generally will be able to purcha
as much milk under the milk conserv
tion program as they have been buyi
in recent months. Fluid milk sales a
being stabilized, and sales of cream a
milk byproducts are being reduced, F
officials said, to help assure sufficie
milk for manufacturing the cheese, bu
ter, evaporated milk and milk powder r
quired by the armed forces and civilia
for good nutrition and properly balanc
diets.

WAR FOOD ADMINISTRATION
Food Distribution Administration
Washington 25, D. C.

FDO-79.112 Dairy Products

In printing Food Distribution Order No. 79.112 the following error occurred:

In Section 1401.139 (a) (2) "FD 79" should read "FDO-79"

FDO 79-112

DEC. 31, 1943

WAR FOOD ADMINISTRATION

[FDO 79-112]

PART 1401—DAIRY PRODUCTS

FLUID MILK AND CREAM IN THE BATTLE CREEK, MICH., SALES AREA

Pursuant to the authority vested in me by Food Distribution Order No. 79 (8 F.R. 12426), issued on September 7, 1943, as amended, and to effectuate the purposes of such order, it is hereby ordered as follows:

§ 1401.139 *Quota restrictions*—(a) *Definitions.* When used in this order, unless otherwise distinctly expressed or manifestly incompatible with the intent hereof:

(1) Each term defined in Food Distribution Order No. 79, as amended, shall, when used herein, have the same meaning as is set forth for such term in Food Distribution Order No. 79, as amended.

(2) The term "FD 79" means Food Distribution Order No. 79, issued on September 7, 1943, as amended.

(3) The term "sub-handler" means any handler, such as a peddler, vendor, sub-dealer, or secondary dealer, who purchases in a previously packaged and processed form milk, cream, or milk byproducts for delivery.

(4) The term "industrial user" means a person, as determined by the market agent, in the capacity of a manufacturer of products using as an ingredient therein milk, cream, or milk byproducts, which products are disposed of for resale to consumers off the premises where made.

(5) The term "base" means the total pounds of milk solids delivered by a handler within the sales area during the base period (i) in the form of milk, or (ii) in the form of cream and milk byproducts, minus the milk solids in quota-exempt deliveries of milk, and cream and milk byproducts, as described in (j) hereof. (For the purpose of this order, the milk solids content of milk, milk byproducts, and cream shall be computed as follows: Each hundredweight of milk, cream, or milk byproducts other than cottage, pot, or baker's cheese, shall be considered the equivalent of 9.375 pounds of milk solids plus the number of pounds of milk solids calculated by multiplying the pounds of butterfat in such milk, and cream and milk byproducts by 0.906; and each hundredweight of cottage, pot, or baker's cheese shall be considered the equivalent of 62.5 pounds of milk solids plus one pound of milk solids for each one percent of butterfat content of such cheese.)

(b) *Milk sales area.* The following area is hereby designated as a "milk sales area" to be known as the Battle Creek, Michigan, milk sales area, and is referred to hereinafter as the "sales area":

The city of Battle Creek and the townships of Emmett, Pennfield, Bedford, and Battle Creek, in Calhoun County, Michigan.

(c) *Base period.* The calendar month of June 1943 is hereby designated as the base period for the sales area: *Provided,* That the month of May may be used as the base period for computing base and quota for deliveries to elementary, junior high, and high schools; and *Provided further,* That in the computations set forth in (e) hereof the total deliveries to elementary, junior high, and high schools in the base period shall be divided by the number of days such schools were in session in lieu of the total number of days in the base period as set forth in (e) (1) and the average daily deliveries so determined shall be multiplied by the number of days such schools are in session in each quota period in lieu of the number of days in the quota period as set forth in (e) (2).

(d) *Quota period.* Each calendar month, beginning with the effective date of this order, is hereby designated as a quota period for the sales area.

(e) *Handler quotas.* Quotas for each handler other than a sub-handler or producer-handler shall be determined as follows:

(1) Divide his respective bases by the number of days in the base period;

(2) Multiply the foregoing result by the number of days in the quota period; and

(3) Multiply the aforesaid resulting amounts by 100 percent in the case of the base for milk, and 75 percent in the case of the base for cream and milk byproducts.

(f) *Quotas for handlers who are also producers.* Quotas for each handler who is also a producer and who purchases no milk shall be computed in accordance with (e) hereof, except:

(1) His base period shall be either June or December, whichever represents his larger total deliveries; and

(2) The applicable percentages shall be 100 percent in lieu of those specified in (e) (3).

(g) *Quota and adjustments.* Each handler may increase his quota for milk within any quota period by one pound of milk solids for each one pound of milk solids he reduces his quota for cream and milk byproducts.

(h) *Cream deliveries.* The units of cream delivered subject to quota in any quota period shall not exceed 100 percent of the units of cream in his base, irrespective of the milk solids content of such deliveries.

(i) *Handler exemptions.* Quotas shall not apply to any handler who delivers in a quota period a daily average of less than 100 units of milk, cream, and milk byproducts. For the purpose of this order, a unit shall be the equivalent in volume of the following: (1) One quart of milk, buttermilk, or fluid milk byproducts; (2) one-half pint of cream; and (3) one-half pound of cottage, pot, or baker's cheese.

(j) *Quota exclusions and exemptions.* Deliveries of milk, milk byproducts, or cream (1) to other handlers, except for such deliveries to sub-handlers, (2) to plants engaged in the handling or processing of milk, milk byproducts, cream or other dairy products from which no milk, milk byproducts, or cream, is delivered in the sales area, (3) to industrial users, and (4) to the agencies or groups specified in (d) of FDO 79, shall be excluded from the computation of deliveries in the base period and exempt from charges to quotas.

(k) *Transfers of bases.* The market agent is empowered to transfer base from one handler to another:

(1) Upon receipt of a request in writing from both handlers; and

(2) Upon application from a handler and written notice to the Director and to both handlers, (i) to permit deliveries to a purchaser not being served by a handler whose quota reflects deliveries to such purchaser in the base period, (ii) to permit a handler to serve an account which customarily rotates among several handlers inclusive of a contract let by a public agency or institution on a bid basis, and (iii) to permit a handler to serve an account which he is serving on the effective date of this order and which was served by another handler during the base period.

(l) *Consumer priorities.* In the distribution of milk subject to quotas established hereunder, a handler shall give preference in the order listed, taking into consideration the type of purchasers served by him in the base period, to:

(1) The need of children, expectant mothers, and invalids requiring milk;

(2) Homes and retail stores handling milk for consumption off the premises; and

(3) Establishments serving milk for consumption on the premises.

(m) *Petition for relief from hardship.* (1) Any person affected by FDO 79 or the provisions hereof, who considers that compliance therewith would work an exceptional and unreasonable hardship on him, may file with the market agent a petition addressed to the Director. The petition shall contain the correct name, address, and principal place of business of the petitioner, a full statement of the facts upon which the petition is based, and the hardship involved and the nature of the relief desired.

(2) Upon receiving such petition the market agent shall immediately investigate, representations and facts stated therein.

(3) After investigation, the petition shall be certified to the Director, but prior to certification the market agent may (i) deny the petition or (ii) grant temporary relief for a total period not to exceed 60 days.

(4) Denials or grants of relief by the market agent shall be reviewed by the Director and may be affirmed, modified, or reversed by the Director.

(n) *Reports.* Each handler shall transmit to the market agent on forms prescribed by the market agent the following reports:

(1) Within 20 days following the effective date of this order, reports which show the information required by the market agent to establish such handler's quotas;

(2) Within 20 days following the close of each quota period, the information required by the market agent to establish volumes of deliveries of milk, cream, and milk byproducts during the preceding quota period; and

(3) Handlers exempt from quotas pursuant to (i) hereof shall, upon the request of the market agent, submit the information required by the market agent to establish volumes of deliveries of milk, cream, and milk byproducts.

(o) *Records.* Handlers shall keep and shall make available to the market agent such records of receipts, sales, deliveries, and production as the market agent shall require for the purpose of obtaining information which the Director may require for the establishment of quotas as prescribed in (b) of FDO 79.

(p) *Expense of administration.* Each handler shall pay to the market agent, within 20 days after the close of each calendar month, an assessment of per hundredweight of each of milk byproducts, cream, and skim equivalent of cottage, pot, or b cheese delivered during the pre quota period and subject to quota lations under the provisions hereof

(q) *Violations.* The market shall report all violations to the Di together with the information re for the prosecution of such violatic

(r) *Bureau of the Budget app* The record-keeping and reportir quirements of this order have bee proved by the Bureau of the Bud accordance with the Federal Repor of 1942. Subsequent record-keep reporting requirements will be s to the approval of the Bureau Budget pursuant to the Federal R Act of 1942.

(s) *Effective date.* This order take effect at 12:01 a. m., e. w. t., ary 1, 1944.

(E.O. 9280, 7 F.R. 10179; E.O. 9 F.R. 3807; E.O. 9334. 8 F.R. 5423 9392, 8 F.R. 14783; FDO 79, 8 F.R. 13283)

Issued this 31st day of December

C. W. KITCHE

Acting Director of Food Distribut

TWELVE NEW MILK SALES AREAS NAMED

Milk sales in 12 metropolitan areas in Tennessee, North Carolina, Alabama, Georgia, and Michigan will be regulated under the Food Distribution Administration's fluid milk conservation and control program, beginning January 1, the War Food Administration said today.

The new milk sales areas are:

Memphis, Tenn. (FDO 79.103)	Birmingham, Ala. (FDO 79.109)
Chattanooga, Tenn. (FDO 79.104)	Montgomery, Ala. (FDO 79.110)
Knoxville, Tenn. (FDO 79.105)	Muskegon, Mich. (FDO 79.111)
Nashville, Tenn. (FDO 79.106)	Battle Creek, Mich. (FDO 79.112)
Atlanta, Ga. (FDO 79.107)	Winston-Salem, N. C. (FDO 79.113)
Columbus, Ga. (FDO 79.108)	Charlottee, N. C. (FDO 79.114)

Under the program, milk dealers will be permitted to sell to all customers except schools as much fluid milk as they sold in June and three-fourths as much milk in cream and milk byproducts (such as cottage cheese, chocolate milk and buttermilk) as they sold in June. Deliveries to elementary, junior high and high schools will be under the same restrictions except the number of school days in May will be used as the base period in determining quotas, rather than June. Milk dealers include all persons or firms engaged in the same or transfer of milk, but not such distributors as subhandlers ("peddlers"), retail stores, hotels or restaurants.

Producer distributors who purchase no milk will be permitted to sell as much milk as they sold in either June or December, whichever represents their larger total deliveries.

The order permits dealers to sell more fluid milk than their quotas allow, provided they use less milk in making cream or byproducts. Since cream and milk byproducts are recognized as one quota group, dealers may sell more cream by cutting down on milk byproducts, or more byproducts by reducing the amount of milk used in cream, so long as they do not use more than 75 percent of the milk used for such purposes in June.

In distributing the milk, cream and byproducts allowed under their quotas, dealers are required to give preference to the following consumer groups, in the order listed, taking into consideration the type of purchasers they served in the base period:

1. Children, expectant mothers, and invalids requiring milk;

2. Homes and retail stores har milk for consumption off the prer

3. Establishments serving milk consumption on the premises.

Deliveries of milk, cream and mil products to other handlers, except handlers; the Armed Forces; i. e agencies or groups specified in graph (d) of FDO 79; to plant gaged in handling or processing milk byproducts, cream, or other products from which no milk, mil products, or cream is delivered i sales area; and to designated indu users who use milk, cream, or mil products in making products whic disposed of for resale to consume the premises where made are exempt.

Consumers in the milk sales named today, as in others already nated, generally will be able to pur as much milk under the milk cons tion program as they have been b in recent months. Fluid milk sale being stabilized, and sales of crean milk byproducts are being reduced, officials said, to help assure suff milk for manufacturing the cheese ter, evaporated milk and milk powd quired by the armed forces and civ for good nutrition and properly bal diets.

FDO 79-113
DEC. 31, 1943

WAR FOOD ADMINISTRATION

[FDO 79-113]

PART 1401—DAIRY PRODUCTS

FLUID MILK AND CREAM IN THE WINSTON-SALEM, N. C., SALES AREA

Pursuant to the authority vested in me by Food Distribution Order No. 79 (8 F.R. 12426), issued on September 7, 1943, as amended, and to effectuate the purposes of such order, it is hereby ordered as follows:

§ 1401.147 *Quota restrictions*—(a) *Definitions.* When used in this order, unless otherwise distinctly expressed or manifestly incompatible with the intent hereof:

(1) Each term defined in Food Distribution Order No. 79, as amended, shall, when used herein, have the same meaning as is set forth for such term in Food Distribution Order No. 79, as amended.

(2) The term "FDO 79" means Food Distribution Order No. 79, issued on September 7, 1943, as amended.

(3) The term "sub-handler" means any handler, such as a peddler, vendor, sub-dealer, or secondary dealer, who purchases in a previously packaged and processed form milk, cream, or milk byproducts for delivery.

(4) The term "industrial user" means a person, as determined by the market agent, in the capacity of a manufacturer of products using as an ingredient therein milk, cream, or milk byproducts, which products are disposed of for resale to consumers off the premises where made.

(5) The term 'base" means the total pounds of milk solids delivered by a handler within the sales area during the base period (i) in the form of milk, or (ii) in the form of cream and milk byproducts, minus the milk solids in quota-exempt deliveries of milk, and cream and milk byproducts, as described in (j) hereof. (For the purpose of this order, the milk solids content of milk, milk byproducts, and cream shall be computed as follows: Each hundredweight of milk, cream, or milk byproducts other than cottage, pot, or baker's cheese, shall be considered the equivalent of 9.375 pounds of milk solids plus the number of pounds of milk solids calculated by multiplying the pounds of butterfat in such milk, and cream and milk byproducts by .906; and each hundredweight of cottage, pot, or baker's cheese shall be considered the equivalent of 62.5 pounds of milk solids plus one pound of milk solids for each one percent of butterfat content of such cheese.)

(b) *Milk sales area.* The following area is hereby designated as a "milk sales area" to be known as the Winston-Salem, North Carolina, milk sales area, and is referred to hereinafter as the "sales area":

The city of Winston-Salem in the county of Forsyth in the State of North Carolina.

(c) *Base period.* The calendar month of June 1943 is hereby designated as the base period for the sales area: *Provided,* That the month of May may be used as the base period for computing base and quota for deliveries to elementary, junior high and high schools: *And provided further,* That in the computations set forth in (e) hereof the total deliveries to elementary, junior high, and high schools in the base period shall be divided by the number of days such schools were in session in lieu of the total number of days in the base period as set forth in (e) (1) and the average daily deliveries so determined shall be multiplied by the number of days such schools are in session in each quota period in lieu of the number of days in the quota period as set forth in (e) (2).

(d) *Quota period.* Each calendar month, beginning with the effective date of this order, is hereby designated as a quota period for the sales area.

(e) *Handler quotas.* Quotas for each handler other than a sub-handler or producer-handler shall be determined as follows:

(1) Divide his respective bases by the number of days in the base period;

(2) Multiply the foregoing result by the number of days in the quota period; and

(3) Multiply the aforesaid resulting amounts by 100 percent in the case of the base for milk, and 75 percent in the case of the base for cream and milk byproducts.

(f) *Quotas for handlers who are also producers.* Quotas for each handler who is also a producer and who purchases no milk shall be computed in accordance with (e) hereof, except:

(1) His base period shall be either June or December, whichever represents his larger total deliveries; and

(2) The applicable percentages shall be 100 percent in lieu of those specified in (e) (3).

(g) *Quota and adjustments.* Each handler may increase his quota for milk within any quota period by one pound of milk solids for each one pound of milk solids he reduces his quota for cream and milk byproducts.

(h) *Cream deliveries.* The units of cream delivered subject to quota in any quota period shall not exceed 100 percent of the units of cream in his base, irrespective of the milk solids content of such deliveries.

(i) *Handler exemptions.* Quotas shall not apply to any handler who delivers in a quota period a daily average of less than 200 units of milk, cream, and milk byproducts. For the purpose of this order, a unit shall be the equivalent in volume of the following: (1) One quart of milk, buttermilk, or fluid milk byproducts; (2) one-half pint of cream; and (3) one-half pound of cottage, pot, or baker's cheese.

(j) *Quota exclusions and exemptions.* Deliveries of milk, milk byproducts, or cream (1) to other handlers, except for such deliveries to sub-handlers, (2) to plants engaged in the handling or processing of milk, milk byproducts, cream or other dairy products from which no milk, milk byproducts, or cream, is delivered in the sales area, (3) to industrial users, and (4) to the agencies or groups specified in (d) of FDO 79, shall be excluded from the computation of deliveries in the base period and exempt from charges to quotas.

(k) *Transfers of bases.* The market agent is empowered to transfer base from one handler to another:

(1) Upon receipt of a request in writing from both handlers; and

(2) Upon application from a handler and written notice to the Director and to both handlers, (i) to permit deliveries to a purchaser not being served by a handler whose quota reflects deliveries to such purchaser in the base period, (ii) to permit a handler to serve an account which customarily rotates among several handlers inclusive of a contract let by a public agency or institution on a bid basis, and (iii) to permit a handler to serve an account which he is serving on the effective date of this order and which was served by another handler during the base period.

(l) *Consumer priorities.* In the distribution of milk subject to quotas established hereunder, a handler shall give preference in the order listed, taking into consideration the type of purchasers served by him in the base period, to:

(1) The need of children, expectant mothers, and invalids requiring milk;

(2) Homes and retail stores handling milk for consumption off the premises; and

(3) Establishments serving milk for consumption on the premises.

(m) *Petition for relief from hardship.* (1) Any person affected by FDO 79 or the provisions hereof who considers that compliance therewith would work an exceptional and unreasonable hardship on him, may file with the market agent a petition addressed to the Director. The petition shall contain the correct name, address, and principal place of business of the petitioner, a full statement of the facts upon which the petition is based, and the hardship involved and the nature of the relief desired.

(2) Upon receiving such petition the market agent shall immediately investigate representations and facts stated therein.

(3) After investigation, the petition shall be certified to the Director, but prior to certification the market agent may (i) deny the petition or (ii) grant temporary relief for a total period not to exceed 60 days.

(4) Denials or grants of relief by the market agent shall be reviewed by the Director and may be affirmed, modified, or reversed by the Director.

(n) *Reports.* Each handler shall transmit to the market agent on forms prescribed by the market agent the following reports:

(1) Within 20 days following the effective date of this order, reports which show the information required by the market agent to establish such handler's quotas;

(2) Within 20 days following the close of each quota period, the information required by the market agent to establish volumes of deliveries of milk, cream, and milk byproducts during the preceding quota period; and

(3) Handlers exempt from quotas pursuant to (i) hereof shall, upon the request of the market agent, submit the information required by the market agent to establish volumes of deliveries of milk, cream, and milk byproducts.

(o) *Records.* Handlers shall keep and shall make available to the market agent such records of receipts, sales, deliveries, and production as the market agent shall require for the purpose of obtaining information which the Director may require for the establishment of quotas as prescribed in (b) of FDO 79.

(p) *Expense of administration.* Each handler shall pay to the market agent, within 20 days after the close of each calendar month, an assessment of $0.(per hundredweight of each of milk, m byproducts, cream, and skim milk equ alent of cottage, pot, or baker's che delivered during the preceding qu period and subject to quota regulatic under the provisions hereof.

(q) *Violations.* The market ag shall report all violations to the Direc together with the information requi for the prosecution of such violatio

(r) *Bureau of the Budget appro* The record-keeping and reporting quirements of this order have been proved by the Bureau of the Budget accordance with the Federal Reports of 1942. Subsequent record-keeping reporting requirements will be subject the approval of the Bureau of the Bud pursuant to the Federal Reports Act 1942.

(s) *Effective date.* This order sh take effect at 12:01 a. m., e. w. t., Ja ary 1, 1944.

(E.O. 9280, 7 F.R. 10179; E.O. 9322, 8 F 3807; E.O. 9334, 8 F.R. 5423; E.O. 93 8 F.R. 14783; FDO 79, 8 F.R. 12426, 132

Issued this 31st day of December 19

C. W. KITCHEN,
Acting Director of Food Distribution

TWELVE NEW MILK SALES AREAS NAMED

Milk sales in 12 metropolitan areas in Tennessee, North Carolina, Alabama, Georgia, and Michigan will be regulated under the Food Distribution Administration's fluid milk conservation and control program, beginning January 1, the War Food Administration said today.

The new milk sales areas are:

Memphis, Tenn. (FDO 79.103)	Birmingham, Ala. (FDO 79.109)
Chattanooga, Tenn. (FDO 79.104)	Montgomery, Ala. (FDO 79.110)
Knoxville, Tenn. (FDO 79.105)	Muskegon, Mich. (FDO 79.111)
Nashville, Tenn. (FDO 79.106)	Battle Creek, Mich. (FDO 79.112)
Atlanta, Ga. (FDO 79.107)	Winston-Salem, N. C. (FDO 79.113)
Columbus, Ga. (FDO 79.108)	Charlottee, N. C. (FDO 79.114)

Under the program, milk dealers will be permitted to sell to all customers except schools as much fluid milk as they sold in June and three-fourths as much milk in cream and milk byproducts (such as cottage cheese, chocolate milk and buttermilk) as they sold in June. Deliveries to elementary, junior high and high schools will be under the same restrictions except the number of school days in May will be used as the base period in determining quotas, rather than June. Milk dealers include all persons or firms engaged in the same or transfer of milk, but not such distributors as subhandlers ("peddlers"), retail stores, hotels or restaurants.

Producer distributors who purchase no milk will be permitted to sell as much milk as they sold in either June or December, whichever represents their larger total deliveries.

The order permits dealers to sell more fluid milk than their quotas allow, provided they use less milk in making cream or byproducts. Since cream and milk byproducts are recognized as one quota group, dealers may sell more cream by cutting down on milk byproducts, or more byproducts by reducing the amount of milk used in cream, so long as they do not use more than 75 percent of the milk used for such purposes in June.

In distributing the milk, cream and byproducts allowed under their quotas, dealers are required to give preference to the following consumer groups, in the order listed, taking into consideration the type of purchasers they served in the base period:

1. Children, expectant mothers, and invalids requiring milk;

2. Homes and retail stores handli milk for consumption off the premis

3. Establishments serving milk consumption on the premises.

Deliveries of milk, cream and milk b products to other handlers, except su handlers; the Armed Forces; i. e., t agencies or groups specified in pa graph (d) of FDO 79; to plants e gaged in handling or processing mi milk byproducts, cream, or other da products from which no milk, milk products, or cream is delivered in t sales area; and to designated industr users who use milk, cream, or milk b products in making products which disposed of for resale to consumers the premises where made are qu exempt.

Consumers in the milk sales ar named today, as in others already des nated, generally will be able to purch as much milk under the milk conser tion program as they have been buyi in recent months. Fluid milk sales being stabilized, and sales of cream a milk byproducts are being reduced, F officials said, to help assure suffici milk for manufacturing the cheese, b ter, evaporated milk and milk powder quired by the armed forces and civili for good nutrition and properly balan diets.

FDO 79-114

DEC. 31, 1943

WAR FOOD ADMINISTRATION

[FDO 79-114]

PART 1401—DAIRY PRODUCTS

FLUID MILK AND CREAM IN THE CHARLOTTE, N. C., SALES AREA

Pursuant to the authority vested in me by Food Distribution Order No. 79 (8 F.R. 12426), issued on September 7, 1943, as amended, and to effectuate the purposes of such order, it is hereby ordered as follows:

§ 1401.145 *Quota restrictions*—(a) *Definitions.* When used in this order, unless otherwise distinctly expressed or manifestly incompatible with the intent hereof:

(1) Each term defined in Food Distribution Order No. 79, as amended, shall, when used herein, have the same meaning as is set forth for such term in Food Distribution Order No. 79, as amended.

(2) The term "FDO 79" means Food Distribution Order No. 79, issued on September 7, 1943, as amended.

(3) The term "sub-handler" means any handler, such as a peddler, vendor, sub-dealer, or secondary dealer, who purchases in a previously packaged and processed form milk, cream, or milk byproducts for delivery.

(4) The term "industrial user" means a person, as determined by the market agent, in the capacity of a manufacturer of products using as an ingredient therein milk, cream, or milk byproducts, which products are disposed of for resale to consumers off the premises where made.

(5) The term "base" means the total pounds of milk solids delivered by a handler within the sales area during the base period (i) in the form of milk, or (ii) in the form of cream and milk byproducts, minus the milk solids in quota-exempt deliveries of milk, and cream and milk byproducts, as described in (j) hereof. (For the purpose of this order, the milk solids content of milk, milk byproducts, and cream shall be computed as follows: Each hundredweight of milk, cream, or milk byproducts other than cottage, pot, or baker's cheese, shall be considered the equivalent of 9.375 pounds of milk solids plus the number of pounds of milk solids calculated by multiplying the pounds of butterfat in such milk, and cream and milk byproducts by 0.906; and each hundredweight of cottage, pot, or baker's cheese shall be considered the equivalent of 62.5 pounds of milk solids plus one pound of milk solids for each one percent of butterfat content of such cheese.)

(b) *Milk sales area.* The following area is hereby designated as a "milk sales area" to be known as the Charlotte, North Carolina, milk sales area, and is referred to hereinafter as the "sales area":

The city of Charlotte and the township of Charlotte in the county of Mecklenburg in the State of North Carolina.

(c) *Base period.* The calendar month of June 1943 is hereby designated as the base period for the sales area: *Provided*, That the month of May may be used as the base period for computing base and quota for deliveries to elementary, junior high and high schools; and *Provided further*, That in the computations set forth in (e) hereof the total deliveries to elementary, junior high, and high schools in the base period shall be divided by the number of days such schools were in session in lieu of the total number of days in the base period as set forth in (e) (1) and the average daily deliveries so determined shall be multiplied by the number of days such schools are in session in each quota period in lieu of the number of days in the quota period as set forth in (e) (2).

(d) *Quota period.* Each calendar month, beginning with the effective date of this order, is hereby designated as a quota period for the sales area.

(e) *Handler quotas.* Quotas for each handler other than a sub-handler or producer-handler shall be determined as follows:

(1) Divide his respective bases by the number of days in the base period;

(2) Multiply the foregoing result by the number of days in the quota period; and

(3) Multiply the aforesaid resulting amounts by 100 percent in the case of the base for milk, and 75 percent in the case of the base for cream and milk byproducts.

(f) *Quotas for handlers who are also producers.* Quotas for each handler who is also a producer and who purchases no milk shall be computed in accordance with (e) hereof, except:

(1) His base period shall be either June or December, whichever represents his larger total deliveries; and

(2) The applicable percentages shall be 100 percent in lieu of those specified in (e) (3).

(g) *Quota and adjustments.* Each handler may increase his quota for milk within any quota period by one pound of milk solids for each one pound of milk solids he reduces his quota, for cream and milk byproducts.

(h) *Cream deliveries.* The units of cream delivered subject to quota in any quota period shall not exceed 100 percent of the units of cream in his base, irrespective of the milk solids content of such deliveries.

(i) *Handler exemptions.* Quotas shall not apply to any handler who delivers in a quota period a daily average of less than 200 units of milk, cream, and milk byproducts. For the purpose of this order, a unit shall be the equivalent in volume of the following: (1) One quart of milk, buttermilk, or fluid milk byproducts; (2) one-half pint of cream; and (3) one-half pound of cottage, pot, or baker's cheese.

(j) *Quota exclusions and exemptions.* Deliveries of milk, milk byproducts, or cream (1) to other handlers, except for such deliveries to sub-handlers, (2) to plants engaged in the handling or processing of milk, milk byproducts, cream or other dairy products from which no milk, milk byproducts, or cream, is delivered in the sales area, (3) to industrial users, and (4) to the agencies or groups specified in (d) of FDO 79, shall be excluded from the computation of deliveries in the base period and exempt from charges to quotas.

(k) *Transfers of bases.* The market agent is empowered to transfer base from one handler to another:

(1) Upon receipt of a request in writing from both handlers; and

(2) Upon application from a handler and written notice to the Director and to both handlers, (i) to permit deliveries to a purchaser not being served by a handler whose quota reflects deliveries to such purchaser in the base period, (ii) to permit a handler to serve an account which customarily rotates among several handlers inclusive of a contract let by a public agency or institution on a bid basis, and (iii) to permit a handler to serve an account which he is serving on the effective date of this order and which was served by another handler during the base period.

(l) *Consumer priorities.* In the distribution of milk subject to quotas established hereunder, a handler shall give preference in the order listed, taking into consideration the type of purchasers served by him in the base period, to:

(1) The need of children, expectant mothers, and invalids requiring milk;

(2) Homes and retail stores handling milk for consumption off the premises; and

(3) Establishments serving milk for consumption on the premises.

(m) *Petition for relief from hardship.* (1) Any person affected by FDO 79 or the provisions hereof who considers that compliance therewith would work an exceptional and unreasonable hardship on him, may file with the market agent a petition addressed to the Director. The petition shall contain the correct name, address and principal place of business of the petitioner, a full statement of the facts upon which the petition is based, and the hardship involved and the nature of the relief desired.

(2) Upon receiving such petition the market agent shall immediately investigate representations and facts stated therein.

(3) After investigation, the petition shall be certified to the Director, but prior to certification the market agent may (i) deny the petition or (ii) grant temporary relief for a total period not to exceed 60 days.

(4) Denials or grants of relief by the market agent shall be reviewed by the Director and may be affirmed, modified, or reversed by the Director.

(n) *Reports.* Each handler shall transmit to the market agent on forms prescribed by the market agent the following reports:

(1) Within 20 days following the effective date of this order, reports which show the information required by the market agent to establish such handler's quotas;

(2) Within 20 days following the close of each quota period, the information required by the market agent to establish volumes of deliveries of milk, cream, and milk byproducts during the preceding quota period; and

(3) Handlers exempt from quotas pursuant to (i) hereof shall, upon the request of the market agent, submit the information required by the market agent to establish volumes of deliveries of milk, cream, and milk byproducts.

(o) *Records.* Handlers shall keep and shall make available to the market agent such records of receipts, sales, deliveries, and production as the market agent shall require for the purpose of obtaining information which the Director may require for the establishment of quotas as prescribed in (b) of FDO 79.

(p) *Expense of administration.* Each handler shall pay to the market agent, within 20 days after the close of each calendar month, an assessment of $0.015 per hundredweight of each of milk, milk byproducts, cream, and skim milk equivalent of cottage, pot, or baker's cheese delivered during the preceding quota period and subject to quota regulations under the provisions hereof.

(q) *Violations.* The market agent shall report all violations to the Director together with the information required for the prosecution of such violations.

(r) *Bureau of the Budget approval.* The record-keeping and reporting requirements of this order have been approved by the Bureau of the Budget in accordance with the Federal Reports Act of 1942. Subsequent record-keeping or reporting requirements will be subject to the approval of the Bureau of the Budget pursuant to the Federal Reports Act of 1942.

(s) *Effective date.* This order shall take effect at 12:01 a. m., e. w. t., January 1, 1944.

(E.O. 9280, 7 F.R. 10179; E.O. 9322, 8 F.R. 3807; E.O. 9334, 8 F.R. 5423; E.O. 9392, 8 F.R. 14783; FDO 79, 8 F.R. 12426, 13283)

Issued this 31st day of December 1943.

C. W. KITCHEN,
Acting Director of Food Distribution.

TWELVE NEW MILK SALES AREAS NAMED

Milk sales in 12 metropolitan areas in Tennessee, North Carolina, Alabama, Georgia, and Michigan will be regulated under the Food Distribution Administration's fluid milk conservation and control program, beginning January 1, the War Food Administration said today.

The new milk sales areas are:

Memphis, Tenn. (FDO 79.103)	Birmingham, Ala. (FDO 79.109)
Chattanooga, Tenn. (FDO 79.104)	Montgomery, Ala. (FDO 79.110)
Knoxville, Tenn. (FDO 79.105)	Muskegon, Mich. (FDO 79.111)
Nashville, Tenn. (FDO 79.106)	Battle Creek, Mich. (FDO 79.112)
Atlanta, Ga. (FDO 79.107)	Winston-Salem, N. C. (FDO 79.113)
Columbus, Ga. (FDO 79.108)	Charlottee, N. C. (FDO 79.114)

Under the program, milk dealers will be permitted to sell to all customers except schools as much fluid milk as they sold in June and three-fourths as much milk in cream and milk byproducts (such as cottage cheese, chocolate milk and buttermilk) as they sold in June. Deliveries to elementary, junior high and high schools will be under the same restrictions except the number of school days in May will be used as the base period in determining quotas, rather than June. Milk dealers include all persons or firms engaged in the same or transfer of milk, but not such distributors as subhandlers ("peddlers"), retail stores, hotels or restaurants.

Producer distributors who purchase no milk will be permitted to sell as much milk as they sold in either June or December, whichever represents their larger total deliveries.

The order permits dealers to sell more fluid milk than their quotas allow, provided they use less milk in making cream or byproducts. Since cream and milk byproducts are recognized as one quota group, dealers may sell more cream by cutting down on milk byproducts, or more byproducts by reducing the amount of milk used in cream, so long as they do not use more than 75 percent of the milk used for such purposes in June.

In distributing the milk, cream and byproducts allowed under their quotas, dealers are required to give preference to the following consumer groups, in the order listed, taking into consideration the type of purchasers they served in the base period:

1. Children, expectant mothers, and invalids requiring milk;

2. Homes and retail stores handling milk for consumption off the premises;

3. Establishments serving milk for consumption on the premises.

Deliveries of milk, cream and milk byproducts to other handlers, except subhandlers; the Armed Forces; i. e., the agencies or groups specified in paragraph (d) of FDO 79; to plants engaged in handling or processing milk, milk byproducts, cream, or other dairy products from which no milk, milk byproducts, or cream is delivered in the sales area; and to designated industrial users who use milk, cream, or milk byproducts in making products which are disposed of for resale to consumers off the premises where made are quota exempt.

Consumers in the milk sales areas named today, as in others already designated, generally will be able to purchase as much milk under the milk conservation program as they have been buying in recent months. Fluid milk sales are being stabilized, and sales of cream and milk byproducts are being reduced, FDA officials said, to help assure sufficient milk for manufacturing the cheese, butter, evaporated milk and milk powder required by the armed forces and civilians for good nutrition and properly balanced diets.

7233+ Cop. 1

FDO 79-115

JAN. 13, 1944

WAR FOOD ADMINISTRATION

[FDO 79-115] A

PART 1401—DAIRY PRODUCTS

FLUID MILK AND CREAM IN THE MIAMI, FLA., METROPOLITAN SALES AREA

Pursuant to the authority vested in me by Food Distribution Order No. 79 (8 F.R. 12426), issued on September 7, 1943, as amended, and to effectuate the purposes of such order, it is hereby ordered as follows:

§ 1401.149 *Quota restrictions*—(a) *Definitions.* When used in this order, unless otherwise distinctly expressed or manifestly incompatible with the intent hereof:

(1) Each term defined in Food Distribution Order No. 79, as amended, shall, when used herein, have the same meaning as is set forth for such term in Food Distribution Order No. 79, as amended.

(2) The term "FDO 79" means Food Distribution Order No. 79, issued on September 7, 1943, as amended.

(3) The term "sub-handler" means any handler, such as a peddler, vendor, sub-dealer, or secondary dealer, who purchases in a previously packaged and processed form milk, cream, or milk byproducts for delivery.

(4) The term "industrial user" means a person, as determined by the market agent, in the capacity of a manufacturer of products using as an ingredient therein milk, cream, or milk byproducts, which products are disposed of for resale to consumers off the premises where made.

(5) The term "base" means the total pounds of milk solids delivered by a handler within the sales area during the base period (i) in the form of milk, or (ii) in the form of cream and milk byproducts, minus the milk solids in quota-exempt deliveries of milk, and cream and milk byproducts, as described in (j) hereof. (For the purpose of this order, the milk solids content of milk, milk byproducts, and cream shall be computed as follows: Each hundredweight of milk, cream, or milk byproducts other than cottage, pot, or baker's cheese, shall be considered the equivalent of 9.375 pounds of milk solids plus the number of pounds of milk solids calculated by multiplying the pounds of butterfat in such milk, and cream and milk byproducts by .906; and each hundredweight of cottage, pot, or baker's cheese shall be considered the equivalent of 62.5 pounds of milk solids plus one pound of milk solids for each one percent of butterfat content of such cheese.)

(b) *Milk sales area.* The following area is hereby designated as a "milk sales area" to be known as the Miami, Florida, metropolitan milk sales area, and is referred to hereinafter as the "sales area":

The city of Miami and the entire area included in the election precincts numbered 1 to 84, inclusive, that part of 85 comprising parts of Miami Springs town, 87 to 106, inclusive, and those parts of 107, 108, 109, 110, 111, 112, comprising parts of the cities of Coral Gables, Miami, and South Miami, all in Dade County, Florida.

(c) *Base period.* The calendar month of June 1943 is hereby designated as the base period for the sales area: *Provided,* That the month of May may be used as the base period for computing base and quota for deliveries to elementary, junior high and high schools: *And provided further,* That in the computation set forth in (e) hereof the total deliveries to elementary, junior high, and high schools in the base period shall be divided by the number of days such schools were in session in lieu of the total number of days in the base period as set forth in (e) (1) and the average daily deliveries so determined shall be multiplied by the number of days such schools are in session in each quota period in lieu of the number of days in the quota period as set forth in (e) (2).

(d) The remainder of the calendar month in which the provisions hereof become effective and each subsequent calendar month, respectively, is hereby designated as the quota period for the sales area.

(e) *Handler quotas.* Quotas for each handler other than a sub-handler or producer-handler shall be determined as follows:

(1) Divide his respective bases by the number of days in the base period;

(2) Multiply the foregoing result by the number of days in the quota period; and

(3) Multiply the aforesaid resulting amounts by 100 percent in the case of the base for milk, and 75 percent in the case of the base for cream and milk byproducts.

(f) *Quotas for handlers who are also producers.* Quotas for each handler who is also a producer and who purchases no milk shall be computed in accordance with (e) hereof, except:

(1) His base period shall be either June or December, whichever represents his larger total deliveries; and

(2) The applicable percentages shall be 100 percent in lieu of those specified in (e) (3).

(g) *Quota adjustments.* Each handler may increase his quota for milk within any quota period by one pound of milk solids for each one pound of milk solids he reduces his quota for cream and milk byproducts.

(h) *Cream deliveries.* The units of cream delivered subject to quota in any quota period shall not exceed 100 percent of the units of cream in his base, irrespective of the milk solids content of such deliveries.

(i) *Handler exemptions.* Quota shall not apply to any handler who delivers in a quota period a daily average of less than 100 units of milk, cream, and milk byproducts. For the purpose of this order, a unit shall be the equivalent in volume of the following: (1) One quart of milk, buttermilk, or fluid milk byproducts; (2) one-half pint of cream; and (3) one-half pound of cottage, pot, or baker's cheese.

(j) *Quota exclusions and exemptions.* Deliveries of milk, milk byproducts, or cream (1) to other handlers, except for such deliveries to sub-handlers, (2) to plants engaged in the handling or processing of milk, milk byproducts, cream or other dairy products from which no milk, milk byproducts, or cream, is delivered in the sales area, (3) to industrial users, and (4) to the agencies or groups specified in (d) of FDO 79, shall be excluded from the computation of deliveries in the base period and exempt from charges to quotas.

(k) *Transfers of bases.* The market agent is empowered to transfer base from one handler to another.

(1) Upon receipt of a request in writing from both handlers; and

(2) Upon application from a handler and written notice to the Director and to both handlers, (i) to permit deliveries to a purchaser not being served by a handler whose quota reflects deliveries to such purchaser in the base period, (ii) to permit a handler to serve an account which customarily rotates among several handlers inclusive of a contract let by a public agency or institution on a bid basis, and (iii) to permit a handler to serve an account which he is serving on the effective date of this order and which was served by another handler during the base period.

(l) *Consumer priorities.* In the distribution of milk subject to quotas established hereunder, a handler shall give preference in the order listed, taking

into consideration the type of purchasers served by him in the base period, to:

(1) The need of children, expectant mothers, and invalids requiring milk;

(2) Homes and retail stores handling milk for consumption off the premises; and

(3) Establishments serving milk for consumption on the premises.

(m) *Petition for relief from hardship.* (1) Any person affected by FDO 79 or the provisions hereof who considers that compliance therewith would work an exceptional and unreasonable hardship on him, may file with the market agent a petition addressed to the Director. The petition shall contain the correct name, address and principal place of business of the petitioner, a full statement of the facts upon which the petition is based, and the hardship involved and the nature of the relief desired.

(2) Upon receiving such petition the market agent shall immediately investigate representations and facts stated therein.

(3) After investigation, the petition shall be certified to the Director, but prior to certification the market agent may (i) deny the petition or (ii) grant temporary relief for a total period not to exceed 60 days.

(4) Denials or grants of relief by the market agent shall be reviewed by the Director and may be affirmed, modified, or reversed by the Director.

(n) *Reports.* Each handler shall transmit to the market agent on forms prescribed by the market agent the following reports:

(1) Within 20 days following the effective date of this order, reports which show the information required by the market agent to establish such handler's quotas;

(2) Within 20 days following the close of each quota period, the information required by the market agent to establish volumes of deliveries of milk, cream and milk byproducts during the preceding quota period; and

(3) Handlers exempt from quotas pursuant to (i) hereof shall, upon the request of the market agent, submit the information required by the market agent to establish volumes of deliveries of milk, cream, and milk byproducts.

(o) *Records.* Handlers shall keep and shall make available to the market agent such records of receipts, sales, deliveries, and production as the market agent shall require for the purpose of obtaining information which the Director may require for the establishment of quotas as prescribed in (b) of FDO 79.

(p) *Expense of administration.* Each handler shall pay to the market agent, within 20 days after the close of e calendar month, an assessment of $0 per hundredweight of each of milk, byproducts, cream, and skim equivalent of cottage, pot, or bal cheese delivered during the prece quota period and subject to quota reg tions under the provisions hereof.

(q) *Violations.* The market a shall report all violations to the Dire together with the information requ for the prosecution of such violations

(r) *Bureau of the Budget appro* The record-keeping and reporting quirements of this order have been proved by the Bureau of the Budge accordance with the Federal Reports of 1942. Subsequent record-keeping reporting requirements will be subjec the approval of the Bureau of the Bu pursuant to the Federal Reports Ac 1942.

(s) *Effective date.* This order s take effect at 12:01 a. m., e. w. t., Feb ary 1, 1944.

(E.O. 9280, 7 F.R. 10179; E.O. 932 F.R. 3807; E.O. 9334, 8 F.R. 5423; 9392, 8 F.R. 14783; FDO 79, 8 F.R. 12 13283)

Issued this 13th day of January 1

ROY F. HENDRICKSON,
Director of Food Distributio

War Food Administration:
Summary to FDO 79.115–79.121.

Seven New Milk Sales Areas Named

Milk sales in 7 metropolitan areas in Florida, North Carolina, South Carolina, Georgia, and Mississippi will be regulated under the Food Distribution Administration's fluid milk conservation and control program, beginning February 1.

The new milk sales areas are:

Miami, Fla., Metropolitan (FDO 79.115); Tampa-St. Petersburg, Fla. (FDO 79.116); Jacksonville, Fla. (FDO 79.117); Savannah, Ga. (FDO 79.118); Durham, N. C. (FDO 79.119); Charleston, S. C. (FDO 79.120); Jackson, Miss. (FDO 79.121).

Market agents who will administer the orders in each area will be named later.

Under the program, milk dealers will be permitted to deliver to all customers except schools as much fluid milk as they delivered in June and three-fourths as much milk in cream and milk byproducts (such as cottage cheese, chocolate milk and buttermilk) as they delivered in June. Deliveries to elementary, junior high and high schools will be under the same restrictions except the number of school days in May will be used as the base period in determining quotas, rather than June. Milk dealers include all persons or firms engaged in the delivery or transfer of milk, but not such distributors as subhandlers ("peddlers"), retail stores, hotels, or restaurants.

Producer distributors who purchase no milk will be permitted to deliver as much milk as they delivered in either June or December, whichever represents their larger total deliveries.

The order permits dealers to deliver more fluid milk than their quotas allow, provided they deliver less cream or milk byproducts. Since cream and milk byproducts are recognized as one quota group, dealers may deliver more cream by cutting down deliveries on milk byproducts, provided they do not deliver more cream than they delivered in the base period, or more byproducts by reducing the amount of milk solids used in cream.

In distributing the milk, cream and byproducts allowed under their quotas, dealers are required to give preference to the following consumer groups, in the order listed, taking into consideration the type of purchasers they served in the base period:

1. Children, expectant mothers, invalids requiring milk;

2. Homes and retail stores handl milk for consumption off the premi

3. Establishments serving milk consumption on the premises.

Deliveries of milk, cream and milk products to other dealers; to the arm forces; to plants engaged in handl or processing milk, byproducts and cre which are not distributed in the s area; and to designated industrial m ufacturers who use milk, cream, or n byproducts in making products wh are sold off the premises are qu exempt.

Consumers in the milk sales a named today, as in others already ignated, generally will be able to p chase as much milk under the milk c servation program as they have b buying in recent months. Fluid n sales are being stabilized, and sales cream and milk byproducts are be reduced, FDA officials said, to help sure sufficient milk for manufactu the cheese, butter, evaporated milk, milk powder required by the armed fo and civilians for good nutrition properly balanced diets.

FDO 79-115

AMDT. 1
MAR. 29, 1944
(Corrected Copy)

WAR FOOD ADMINISTRATION

(Corrected Copy)

[FDO 79-115, Amdt. 1]

PART 1401—DAIRY PRODUCTS

FLUID MILK AND CREAM IN MIAMI, FLA., METROPOLITAN SALES AREA

Pursuant to Food Distribution Order No. 79 (8 F.R. 12426), dated September 7, 1943, as amended, and to effectuate the purposes thereof, Food Distribution Order No. 79-115 (9 F.R. 632), relative to the conservation and distribution of fluid milk in the Miami, Florida, metropolitan milk sales area, issued by the Director of Food Distribution on January 13, 1944, is hereby amended by deleting therefrom the provisions in § 1401.149 (e) (3) and inserting, in lieu thereof, the following:

Multiply the aforesaid resulting amounts in the case of the base for milk as follows:

	Percent
January	115
February	120
March	130
April	110
May	110
June	90
July	80
August	80
September	85
October	90
November	90
December	100

and, in the case of the base for cream and milk byproducts as follows:

	Percent
January	86.25
February	90.00
March	97.50
April	82.50
May	82.50
June	67.50
July	60.00
August	60.00
September	63.75
October	67.50
November	67.50
December	75.00

The provisions of this amendment shall become effective at 12:01 a. m., e. w. t., April 1, 1944. With respect to violations of said Food Distribution Order No. 79-115, rights accrued, or liabilities incurred prior to the effective time of this amendment, said Food Distribution Order No. 79-115 shall be deemed to be in full force and effect for the purpose of sustaining any proper suit, action, or other proceeding with respect to any such violation, right, or liability.

(E.O. 9280, 7 F.R. 10179; E.O. 9322, 8 F.R. 3807; E.O. 9334, 8 F.R. 5423; E.O. 9392, 8 F.R. 14783; FDO 79, 8 F.R. 12426, 13283)

Issued this 29th day of March 1944.

LEE MARSHALL,
Director of Food Distribution.

WAR FOOD ADMINISTRATION
Food Distribution Administration
Washington 25, D. C.

E ·FDO 79-116 Dairy Products

Distribution Order No. 79-116 the following error occurred:

od (punctuation mark) was omitted after the word "period" at sentence beginning "Upon application from a handler."

pp. 1

FDO 79-116

JAN. 13, 1944

WAR FOOD ADMINISTRATION

[FDO 79-116] A

PART 1401—DAIRY PRODUCTS

FLUID MILK AND CREAM IN THE TAMPA-ST. PETERSBURG, FLA., SALES AREA

Pursuant to the authority vested in me by Food Distribution Order No. 79 (8 F.R. 12426), issued on September 7, 1943, as amended, and to effectuate the purposes of such order, it is hereby ordered as follows:

§ 1401.150 *Quota restrictions*—(a) *Definitions.* When used in this order, unless otherwise distinctly expressed or manifestly incompatible with the intent hereof:

(1) Each term defined in Food Distribution Order No. 79, as amended, shall, when used herein, have the same meaning as is set forth for such term in Food Distribution Order No. 79, as amended.

(2) The term "FDO 79" means Food Distribution Order No. 79, issued on September 7, 1943, as amended.

(3) The term "sub-handler" means any handler, such as a peddler, vendor, sub-dealer, or secondary dealer, who purchases in a previously packaged and processed form milk, cream, or milk byproducts for delivery.

(4) The term "industrial user" means a person, as determined by the market agent, in the capacity of a manufacturer of products using as an ingredient therein milk, cream, or milk byproducts, which products are disposed of for resale to consumers off the premises where made.

(5) The term "base" means the total pounds of milk solids delivered by a handler within the sales area during the base period (i) in the form of milk, or (ii) in the form of cream and milk byproducts, minus the milk solids in quota-exempt deliveries of milk, and cream and milk byproducts, as described in (j) hereof. (For the purpose of this order, the milk solids content of milk, milk byproducts, and cream shall be computed as follows: Each hundredweight of milk, cream, or milk byproducts other than cottage, pot, or baker's cheese, shall be considered the equivalent of 9.375 pounds of milk solids plus the number of pounds of milk solids calculated by multiplying the pounds of butterfat in such milk, and cream and milk byproducts by .906; and each hundredweight of cottage, pot, or baker's cheese shall be considered the equivalent of 62.5 pounds of milk solids plus one pound of milk solids for each one percent of butterfat content of such cheese.)

(b) *Milk sales area.* The following area is hereby designated as a "milk sales area" to be known as the Tampa-St. Petersburg, Florida, milk sales area, and is referred to hereinafter as the "sales area":

The cities of Tampa, in Hillsborough County, and St. Petersburg, in Pinellas County; the election precincts numbered 1 to 40, inclusive, 42, 43, 44, that part of 46 comprising part of Temple Terrace city, 58, 59, and 60, in Hillsborough County; the election precincts numbered 1 to 21, inclusive, 21A, and 22 to 47, inclusive, in Pinellas County, Florida.

(c) *Base period.* The calendar month of June 1943 is hereby designated as the base period for the sales area: *Provided*, That the month of May may be used as the base period for computing base and quota for deliveries to elementary, junior high and high schools: and *Provided further*, That in the computations set forth in (e) hereof the total deliveries to elementary, junior high, and high schools in the base period shall be divided by the number of days such schools were in session in lieu of the total number of days in the base period as set forth in (e) (1) and the average daily deliveries so determined shall be multiplied by the number of days such schools are in session in each quota period in lieu of the number of days in the quota period as set forth in (e) (2).

(d) The remainder of the calendar month in which the provisions hereof become effective and each subsequent calendar month, respectively, is hereby designated as the quota period for the sales area.

(e) *Handler quotas.* Quotas for each handler other than a sub-handler or producer-handler shall be determined as follows:

(1) Divide his respective bases by the number of days in the base period;

(2) Multiply the foregoing result by the number of days in the quota period; and

(3) Multiply the aforesaid resulting amounts by 100 percent in the case of the base for milk, and 75 percent in the case of the base for cream and milk byproducts.

(f) *Quotas for handlers who are also producers.* Quotas for each handler who is also a producer and who purchases no milk shall be computed in accordance with (e) hereof, except:

(1) His base period shall be either June or December, whichever represents his larger total deliveries; and

(2) The applicable percentages shall be 100 percent in lieu of those specified in (e) (3).

(g) *Quota adjustments.* Each handler may increase his quota for milk within any quota period by one pound of milk solids for each one pound of milk solids he reduces his quota for cream and milk byproducts.

(h) *Cream deliveries.* The units of cream delivered subject to quota in any quota period shall not exceed 100 percent of the units of cream in his base, irrespective of the milk solids content of such deliveries.

(i) *Handler exemptions.* Quota shall not apply to any handler who delivers in a quota period a daily average of less than 100 units of milk, cream, and milk byproducts. For the purpose of this order, a unit shall be the equivalent in volume of the following: (1) One quart of milk, buttermilk, or fluid milk byproducts; (2) one-half pint of cream; and (3) one-half pound of cottage, pot, or baker's cheese.

(j) *Quota exclusions and exemptions.* Deliveries of milk, milk byproducts, or cream (1) to other handlers, except for such deliveries to sub-handlers, (2) to plants engaged in the handling or processing of milk, milk byproducts, cream or other dairy products from which no milk, milk byproducts, or cream, is delivered in the sales area, (3) to industrial users, and (4) to the agencies or groups specified in (d) of FDO 79, shall be excluded from the computation of deliveries in the base period and exempt from charges to quotas.

(k) *Transfers of bases.* The market agent is empowered to transfer base from one handler to another.

(1) Upon receipt of a request in writing from both handlers; and

(2) Upon application from a handler and written notice to the Director and to both handlers, (i) to permit deliveries to a purchaser not being served by a handler whose quota reflects deliveries to such purchaser in the base period, (ii) to permit a handler to serve an account which customarily rotates among several handlers inclusive of a contract let by a public agency or institution on a bid basis, and (iii) to permit a handler to serve an account which he is serving on the effective date of this order and which was served by another handler during the base period

(l) *Consumer priorities* In the distribution of milk subject to quotas established hereunder, a handler shall give preference in the order listed, taking into consideration the type of purchasers served by him in the base period, to:

(1) The need of children, expectant mothers, and invalids requiring milk;

(2) Homes and retail stores handling milk for consumption off the premises; and

(3) Establishments serving milk for consumption on the premises.

(m) *Petition for relief from hardship.* (1) Any person affected by FDO 79 or the provisions hereof who considers that compliance therewith would work an exceptional and unreasonable hardship on him, may file with the market agent a petition addressed to the Director. The petition shall contain the correct name, address and principal place of business of the petitioner, a full statement of the facts upon which the petition is based, and the hardship involved and the nature of the relief desired.

(2) Upon receiving such petition the market agent shall immediately investigate representations and facts stated therein.

(3) After investigation, the petition shall be certified to the Director, but prior to certification the market agent may (i) deny the petition or (ii) grant temporary relief for a total period not to exceed 60 days.

(4) Denials or grants of relief by the market agent shall be reviewed by the Director and may be affirmed, modified, or reversed by the Director.

(n) *Reports.* Each handler shall transmit to the market agent on forms prescribed by the market agent the following reports:

(1) Within 20 days following the effective date of this order, reports which show the information required by the market agent to establish such handler's quotas;

(2) Within 20 days following the close of each quota period, the information required by the market agent to establish volumes of deliveries of milk, cream and milk byproducts during the preceding quota period; and

(3) Handlers exempt from quotas pursuant to (i) hereof shall, upon the request of the market agent, submit the information required by the market agent to establish volumes of deliveries of milk, cream, and milk byproducts.

(o) *Records.* Handlers shall keep and shall make available to the market agent such records of receipts, sales, deliveries, and production as the market agent shall require for the purpose of obtaining information which the Director may require for the establishment of quotas as prescribed in (b) of FDO 79.

(p) *Expense of administration.* Each handler shall pay to the market agent, within 20 days after the close of each calendar month, an assessment of $0.015 per hundredweight of each of milk, milk byproducts, cream, and skim milk equivalent of cottage, pot, or baker's cheese delivered during the preceding quota period and subject to quota regulations under the provisions hereof.

(q) *Violations.* The market agent shall report all violations to the Director together with the information required for the prosecution of such violations.

(r) *Bureau of the Budget approval.* The record-keeping and reporting requirements of this order have been approved by the Bureau of the Budget in accordance with the Federal Reports Act of 1942. Subsequent record-keeping or reporting requirements will be subject to the approval of the Bureau of the Budget pursuant to the Federal Reports Act of 1942.

(s) *Effective date.* This order shall take effect at 12:01 a. m., e. w. t., February 1, 1944.

(E.O. 9280, 7 F.R. 10179; E.O. 9322, 8 F.R. 3807; E.O. 9334, 8 F.R. 5423; E.O. 9392, 8 F.R. 14783; FDO 79, 8 F.R. 12426, 13283)

Issued this 13th day of January 1944.

ROY F. HENDRICKSON,
Director of Food Distribution.

War Food Administration:
Summary to FDO 79.115–79.121.

Seven New Milk Sales Areas Named

Milk sales in 7 metropolitan areas in Florida, North Carolina, South Carolina, Georgia, and Mississippi will be regulated under the Food Distribution Administration's fluid milk conservation and n program, beginning February ko trol

The new milk sales areas are:

Miami, Fla., Metropolitan (FDO 79.115); Tampa-St. Petersburg, Fla. (FDO 79.116); Jacksonville, Fla. (FDO 79.117); Savannah, Ga. (FDO 79.118); Durham, N. C. (FDO 79.119); Charleston, S. C. (FDO 79.120); Jackson, Miss. (FDO 79.121).

Market agents who will administer the orders in each area will be named later.

Under the program, milk dealers will be permitted to deliver to all customers except schools as much fluid milk as they delivered in June and three-fourths as much milk in cream and milk byproducts (such as cottage cheese, chocolate milk and buttermilk) as they delivered in June. Deliveries to elementary, junior high and high schools will be under the same restrictions except the number of school days in May will be used as the base period in determining quotas, rather than June. Milk dealers include all persons or firms engaged in the delivery or transfer of milk, but not such distributors as subhandlers ("peddlers"), retail stores, hotels, or restaurants.

Producer distributors who purchase no milk will be permitted to deliver as much milk as they delivered in either June or December, whichever represents their larger total deliveries.

The order permits dealers to deliver more fluid milk than their quotas allow, provided they deliver less cream or milk byproducts. Since cream and milk byproducts are recognized as one quota group, dealers may deliver more cream by cutting down deliveries on milk byproducts, provided they do not deliver more cream than they delivered in the base period, or more byproducts by reducing the amount of milk solids used in cream.

In distributing the milk, cream and byproducts allowed under their quotas, dealers are required to give preference to the following consumer groups, in the order listed, taking into consideration the type of purchasers they served in the base period:

1. Children, expectant mothers, and invalids requiring milk;

2. Homes and retail stores handling milk for consumption off the premises;

3. Establishments serving milk for consumption on the premises.

Deliveries of milk, cream and milk byproducts to other dealers; to the armed forces; to plants engaged in handling or processing milk, byproducts and cream which are not distributed in the sales area; and to designated industrial manufacturers who use milk, cream, or milk byproducts in making products which are sold off the premises are quota exempt.

Consumers in the milk sales areas named today, as in others already designated, generally will be able to purchase as much milk under the milk conservation program as they have been buying in recent months. Fluid milk sales are being stabilized, and sales of cream and milk byproducts are being reduced, FDA officials said, to help assure sufficient milk for manufacturing the cheese, butter, evaporated milk, and milk powder required by the armed forces and civilians for good nutrition and properly balanced diets.

33F
101
1

FDO 79-116
AMDT. 1
MAR. 29, 1944

WAR FOOD ADMINISTRATION

[FDO 79-116, Amdt. 1]

PART 1401—DAIRY PRODUCTS

FLUID MILK AND CREAM IN TAMPA-ST. PETERSBURG, FLA., SALES AREA

Pursuant to Food Distribution Order No. 79 (8 F.R. 12426), dated September 7, 1943, as amended, and to effectuate the purposes thereof, Food Distribution Order No. 79-116 (9 F.R. 633), relative to the conservation and distribution of fluid milk in the Tampa-St. Petersburg, Fla., milk sales area, issued by the Director of Food Distribution on January 13, 1944, is hereby amended as follows:

1. Delete from the heading of the order the word "-St. Petersburg", making the heading of the order read as follows: "Fluid Milk and Cream in Tampa, Fla., Sales Area."

2. Delete the description of the sales area in § 1401.150 (b) and insert in lieu thereof, the following:

(b) The city of Tampa, and the election precincts numbered 1 to 40, inclusive, 42, 43, 44, that part of 43 comprising part of Temple Terrace City, 58, 59, and 60, in Hillsborough County, Fla.

The provisions of this amendment shall become effective at 12:01 a. m., e. w. t., April 1, 1944. With respect to violations of said Food Distribution Order No. 79-116, rights accrued, or liabilities incurred prior to the effective time of this amendment, said Food Distribution Order No. 79-116, shall be deemed to be in full force and effect for the purpose of sustaining any proper suit, action, or other proceeding with respect to any such violation, right, or liability.

(E.O. 9280, 7 F.R. 10179; E.O. 9322, 8 F.R. 3607; E.O. 9334, 8 F.R. 5423; E.O. 9392, 8 F.R. 14783; FDO 79, 8 F.R. 12426, 13283)

Issued this 29th day of March 1944.

LEE MARSHALL,
Director of Food Distribution.

WAR FOOD ADMINISTRATION
Food Distribution Administration
Washington 25, D. C.

CORRECTION NOTICE - FDO 79.117 · Dairy Products

In printing Food Distribution Order No. 79.117 the following errors occurred:

(f) (1) In the sentence beginning "His base period" the word "Shall" is misspelled.

(i) In the sentence beginning "For the purpose" the comma has been omitted after the word "Order".

Cop. 1

FDO 79-117

JAN. 13, 1944

WAR FOOD ADMINISTRATION

[FDO 79-117] A

Part 1401—Dairy Products

FLUID MILK AND CREAM IN THE JACKSONVILLE, FLA., SALES AREA

Pursuant to the authority vested in me by Food Distribution Order No. 79 (8 F.R. 12426), issued on September 7, 1943, as amended, and to effectuate the purposes of such order, it is hereby ordered as follows:

§ 1401.148 *Quota restrictions*—(a) *Definitions.* When used in this order, unless otherwise distinctly expressed or manifestly incompatible with the intent hereof:

(1) Each term defined in Food Distribution Order No. 79, as amended, shall, when used herein, have the same meaning as is set forth for such term in Food Distribution Order No. 79, as amended.

(2) The term "FDO 79" means Food Distribution Order No. 79, issued on September 7, 1943, as amended.

(3) The term "sub-handler" means any handler, such as a peddler, vendor, sub-dealer, or secondary dealer, who purchases in a previously packaged and processed form milk, cream, or milk byproducts for delivery.

(4) The term "industrial user" means a person, as determined by the market agent, in the capacity of a manufacturer of products using as an ingredient therein milk, cream, or milk byproducts, which products are disposed of for resale to consumers off the premises where made.

(5) The term "base" means the total pounds of milk solids delivered by a handler within the sales area during the base period (i) in the form of milk, or (ii) in the form of cream and milk byproducts, minus the milk solids in quota-exempt deliveries of milk, and cream and milk byproducts, as described in (j) hereof. (For the purpose of this order, the milk solids content of milk, milk byproducts, and cream shall be computed as follows: Each hundredweight of milk, cream, or milk byproducts other than cottage, pot, or baker's cheese, shall be considered the equivalent of 9.375 pounds of milk solids plus the number of pounds of milk solids calculated by multiplying the pounds of butterfat in such milk, and cream and milk byproducts by .906; and each hundredweight of cottage, pot, or baker's cheese shall be considered the equivalent of 62.5 pounds of milk solids plus one pound of milk solids for each one percent of butterfat content of such cheese.)

(b) *Milk sales area.* The following area is hereby designated as a "milk sales area" to be known as the Jacksonville, Florida, milk sales area, and is referred to hereinafter as the "sales area":

The area included within the city of Jacksonville and Duval County in the State of Florida.

(c) *Base period.* The calendar month of June 1943 is hereby designated as the base period for the sales area: *Provided*, That the month of May may be used as the base period for computing base and quota for deliveries to elementary, junior high and high schools: *And provided further*, That in the computations set forth in (e) hereof the total deliveries to elementary, junior high, and high schools in the base period shall be divided by the number of days such schools were in session in lieu of the total number of days in the base period as set forth in (e) (1) and the average daily deliveries so determined shall be multiplied by the number of days such schools are in session in each quota period in lieu of the number of days in the quota period as set forth in (e) (2).

(d) The remainder of the calendar month in which the provisions hereof become effective and each subsequent calendar month, respectively, is hereby designated as the quota period for the sales area.

(e) *Handler quotas.* Quotas for each handler other than a sub-handler or producer-handler shall be determined as follows:

(1) Divide his respective bases by the number of days in the base period;

(2) Multiply the foregoing result by the number of days in the quota period; and

(3) Multiply the aforesaid resulting amounts by 100 percent in the case of the base for milk, and 75 percent in the case of the base for cream and milk byproducts.

(f) *Quotas for handlers who are also producers.* Quotas for each handler who is also a producer and who purchases no milk shall be computed in accordance with (e) hereof, except:

(1) His base period shal be either June or December, whichever represents his larger total deliveries; and

(2) The applicable percentages shall be 100 percent in lieu of those specified in (e) (3).

(g) *Quota adjustments.* Each handler may increase his quota for milk within any quota period by one pound of milk solids for each one pound of milk solids he reduces his quota for cream and milk byproducts.

(h) *Cream deliveries.* The units of cream delivered subject to quota in any quota period shall not exceed 100 percent of the units of cream in his base, irrespective of the milk solids content of such deliveries.

(i) *Handler exemptions.* Quota shall not apply to any handler who delivers in a quota period a daily average of less than 400 units of milk, cream, and milk byproducts. For the purpose of this order a unit shall be the equivalent in volume of the following: (1) One quart of milk, buttermilk, or fluid milk byproducts; (2) one-half pint of cream; and (3) one-half pound of cottage, pot, or baker's cheese.

(j) *Quota exclusions and exemptions.* Deliveries of milk, milk byproducts, or cream (1) to other handlers, except for such deliveries to sub-handlers, (2) to plants engaged in the handling or processing of milk, milk byproducts, cream or other dairy products from which no milk, milk byproducts, or cream, is delivered in the sales area, (3) to industrial users, and (4) to the agencies or groups specified in (d) of FDO 79, shall be excluded from the computation of deliveries in the base period and exempt from charges to quotas.

(k) *Transfers of bases.* The market agent is empowered to transfer base from one handler to another:

(1) Upon receipt of a request in writing from both handlers; and

(2) Upon application from a handler and written notice to the Director and to both handlers, (i) to permit deliveries to a purchaser not being served by a handler whose quota reflects deliveries to such purchaser in the base period, (ii) to permit a handler to serve an account which customarily rotates among several handlers inclusive of a contract let by a public agency or institution on a bid basis and (iii) to permit a handler to serve an account which he is serving on the effective date of this order and which was served by another handler during the base period.

(l) *Consumer priorities.* In the distribution of milk subject to quotas established hereunder, a handler shall give preference in the order listed, taking into consideration the type of purchasers served by him in the base period, to:

(1) The need of children, expectant mothers, and invalids requiring milk;

(2) Homes and retail stores handling milk for consumption off the premises; and

(3) Establishments serving milk for consumption on the premises.

(m) *Petition for relief from hardship.* (1) Any person affected by FDO 79 or the provisions hereof who considers that compliance therewith would work an exceptional and unreasonable hardship on him, may file with the market agent a petition addressed to the Director. The petition shall contain the correct name, address and principal place of business of the petitioner, a full statement of the facts upon which the petition is based, and the hardship involved and the nature of the relief desired.

(2) Upon receiving such petition the market agent shall immediately investigate representations and facts stated therein.

(3) After investigation, the petition shall be certified to the Director, but prior to certification the market agent may (i) deny the petition or (ii) grant temporary relief for a total period not to exceed 60 days.

(4) Denials or grants of relief by the market agent shall be reviewed by the Director and may be affirmed, modified, or reversed by the Director.

(n) *Reports.* Each handler shall transmit to the market agent on forms prescribed by the market agent the following reports:

(1) Within 20 days following the effective date of this order, reports which show the information required by the market agent to establish such handler's quotas;

(2) Within 20 days following the close of each quota period, the information required by the market agent to establish volumes of deliveries of milk, cream, and milk byproducts during the preceding quota period; and

(3) Handlers exempt from quotas pursuant to (i) hereof shall, upon the request of the market agent, submit the information required by the market agent to establish volumes of deliveries of milk, cream, and milk byproducts.

(o) *Records.* Handlers shall keep and shall make available to the market agent such records of receipts, sales, deliveries, and production as the market agent shall require for the purpose of obtaining information which the Director may require for the establishment of quotas as prescribed in (b) of FDO 79.

(p) *Expense of administration.* Each handler shall pay to the market agent, within 20 days after the close of each calendar month, an assessment of $0.015 per hundredweight of each of n byproducts, cream, and skim mi alent of cottage, pot, or baker delivered during the precedir period and subject to quota re under the provisions hereof.

(q) *Violations.* The marke shall report all violations to the together with the information for the prosecution of such viol

(r) *Bureau of the Budget* The record-keeping and repo quirements of this order have proved by the Bureau of the B accordance with the Federal Re of 1942. Subsequent record-k reporting requirements will be s the approval of the Bureau of th pursuant to the Federal Repor 1942.

(s) *Effective date.* This or take effect at 12:01 a. m., e. w. ary 1, 1944.

(E.O. 9280, 7 F.R. 10179; E.O. 93 3807; E.O. 9334, 8 F.R. 5423; E 8 F.R. 14783; FDO 79, 8 F.R. 1242

Issued this 13th day of Januar

ROY F. HENDRICK
Director of Food Distri

War Food Administration:
Summary to FDO 79.115–79.121.

Seven New Milk Sales Areas Named

Milk sales in 7 metropolitan areas in Florida, North Carolina, South Carolina, Georgia, and Mississippi will be regulated under the Food Distribution Administration's fluid milk conservation and control program, beginning February 1.

The new milk sales areas are:

Miami, Fla., Metropolitan (FDO 79.115); Tampa-St. Petersburg, Fla. (FDO 79.116); Jacksonville, Fla. (FDO 79.117); Savannah, Ga. (FDO 79.118); Durham, N. C. (FDO 79.119); Charleston, S. C. (FDO 79.120); Jackson, Miss. (FDO 79.121).

Market agents who will administer the orders in each area will be named later.

Under the program, milk dealers will be permitted to deliver to all customers except schools as much fluid milk as they delivered in June and three-fourths as much milk in cream and milk byproducts (such as cottage cheese, chocolate milk and buttermilk) as they delivered in June. Deliveries to elementary, junior high and high schools will be under the same restrictions except the number of school days in May will be used as the base period in determining quotas, rather than June. Milk dealers include all persons or firms engaged in the delivery or transfer of milk, but not such distributors as subhandlers ("peddlers"), retail stores, hotels, or restaurants.

Producer distributors who purchase no milk will be permitted to deliver as much milk as they delivered in either June or December, whichever represents their larger total deliveries.

The order permits dealers to deliver more fluid milk than their quotas allow, provided they deliver less cream or milk byproducts. Since cream and milk byproducts are recognized as one quota group, dealers may deliver more cream by cutting down deliveries on milk byproducts, provided they do not deliver more cream than they delivered in the base period, or more byproducts by reducing the amount of milk solids used in cream.

In distributing the milk, cream and byproducts allowed under their quotas, dealers are required to give preference to the following consumer groups, in the order listed, taking into consideration the type of purchasers they served in the base period:

1. Children, expectant moth invalids requiring milk;
2. Homes and retail stores milk for consumption off the p
3. Establishments serving consumption on the premises.

Deliveries of milk, cream and products to other dealers; to th forces; to plants engaged in or processing milk, byproducts a which are not distributed in area; and to designated industr ufacturers who use milk, cream byproducts in making produc are sold off the premises a exempt.

Consumers in the milk sal named today, as in others alre ignated, generally will be able chase as much milk under the r servation program as they h buying in recent months. Fl sales are being stabilized, and cream and milk byproducts a reduced, FDA officials said, to sure sufficient milk for manu the cheese, butter, evaporated r milk powder required by the arm and civilians for good nutri properly balanced diets.

23.3 Fo
Lt 1

FDO 79-118

JAN. 13, 1944

WAR FOOD ADMINISTRATION

[FDO 79-118]

PART 1401—DAIRY PRODUCTS

FLUID MILK AND CREAM IN THE SAVANNAH, GA., SALES AREA

Pursuant to the authority vested in me by Food Distribution Order No. 79 (8 F.R. 12426), issued on September 7, 1943, as amended, and to effectuate the purposes of such order, it is hereby ordered as follows:

§ 1401.151 *Quota restrictions*—(a) *Definitions.* When used in this order, unless otherwise distinctly expressed or manifestly incompatible with the intent hereof:

(1) Each term defined in Food Distribution Order No. 79, as amended, shall, when used herein, have the same meaning as is set forth for such term in Food Distribution Order No. 79, as amended.

(2) The term "FDO 79" means Food Distribution Order No. 79, issued on September 7, 1943, as amended.

(3) The term "sub-handler" means any handler, such as a peddler, vendor, sub-dealer, or secondary dealer, who purchases in a previously packaged and processed form milk, cream, or milk byproducts for delivery.

(4) The term "industrial user" means a person, as determined by the market agent, in the capacity of a manufacturer of products using as an ingredient therein milk, cream, or milk byproducts, which products are disposed of for resale to consumers off the premises where made.

(5) The term "base" means the total pounds of milk solids delivered by a handler within the sales area during the base period (i) in the form of milk, or (ii) in the form of cream and milk byproducts, minus the milk solids in quota-exempt deliveries of milk, and cream and milk byproducts, as described in (j) hereof. (For the purpose of this order, the milk solids content of milk, milk byproducts, and cream shall be computed as follows: Each hundredweight of milk, cream, or milk byproducts other than cottage, pot, or baker's cheese, shall be considered the equivalent of 9.375 pounds of milk solids plus the number of pounds of milk solids calculated by multiplying the pounds of butterfat in such milk, and cream and milk byproducts by .906; and each hundredweight of cottage, pot, or baker's cheese shall be considered the equivalent of 62.5 pounds of milk solids plus one pound of milk solids for each one percent of butterfat content of such cheese.)

(b) *Milk sales area.* The following area is hereby designated as a "milk sales area" to be known as the Savannah, Georgia, milk sales area, and is referred to hereinafter as the "sales area":

The city of Savannah and Chatham County, all in the State of Georgia.

(c) *Base period.* The calendar month of June 1943 is hereby designated as the base period for the sales area: *Provided,* That the month of May may be used as the base period for computing base and quota for deliveries to elementary, junior high and high schools: *And provided further,* That in the computations set forth in (e) hereof the total deliveries to elementary, junior high, and high schools in the base period shall be divided by the number of days such schools were in session in lieu of the total number of days in the base period as set forth in (e) (1) and the average daily deliveries so determined shall be multiplied by the number of days such schools are in session in each quota period in lieu of the number of days in the quota period as set forth in (e) (2).

(d) The remainder of the calendar month in which the provisions hereof become effective and each subsequent calendar month, respectively, is hereby designated as the quota period for the sales area.

(e) *Handler quotas.* Quotas for each handler other than a sub-handler or producer-handler shall be determined as follows:

(1) Divide his respective bases by the number of days in the base period;

(2) Multiply the foregoing result by the number of days in the quota period; and

(3) Multiply the aforesaid resulting amounts by 100 percent in the case of the base for milk, and 75 percent in the case of the base for cream and milk byproducts.

(f) *Quotas for handlers who are also producers.* Quotas for each handler who is also a producer and who purchases no milk shall be computed in accordance with (e) hereof, except:

(1) His base period shall be either June or December, whichever represents his larger total deliveries; and

(2) The applicable percentages shall be 100 percent in lieu of those specified in (e) (3).

(g) *Quota adjustments.* Each handler may increase his quota for milk within any quota period by one pound of milk solids for each one pound of milk solids he reduces his quota for cream and milk byproducts.

(h) *Cream deliveries.* The units of cream delivered subject to quota in any quota period shall not exceed 100 percent of the units of cream in his base, irrespective of the milk solids content of such deliveries.

(i) *Handler exemptions.* Quota shall not apply to any handler who delivers in a quota period a daily average of less than 100 units of milk, cream, and milk byproducts. For the purpose of this order, a unit shall be the equivalent in volume of the following: (1) One quart of milk, buttermilk, or fluid milk byproducts; (2) one-half pint of cream; and (3) one-half pound of cottage, pot, or baker's cheese.

(j) *Quota exclusions and exemptions.* Deliveries of milk, milk byproducts, or cream (1) to other handlers, except for such deliveries to sub-handlers, (2) to plants engaged in the handling or processing of milk, milk byproducts, cream or other dairy products from which no milk, milk byproducts, or cream, is delivered in the sales area, (3) to industrial users, and (4) to the agencies or groups specified in (d) of FDO 79, shall be excluded from the computation of deliveries in the base period and exempt from charges to quotas.

(k) *Transfers of bases.* The market agent is empowered to transfer base from one handler to another.

(1) Upon receipt of a request in writing from both handlers; and

(2) Upon application from a handler and written notice to the Director and to both handlers, (i) to permit deliveries to a purchaser not being served by a handler whose quota reflects deliveries to such purchaser in the base period, (ii) to permit a handler to serve an account which customarily rotates among several handlers inclusive of a contract let by a public agency or institution on a bid basis, and (iii) to permit a handler to serve an account which he is serving on the effective date of this order and which was served by another handler during the base period.

(l) *Consumer priorities.* In the distribution of milk subject to quotas established hereunder, a handler shall give preference in the order listed, taking into consideration the type of purchasers served by him in the base period, to:

(1) The need of children, expectant mothers, and invalids requiring milk;

(2) Homes and retail stores handling milk for consumption off the premises; and

(3) Establishments serving milk for consumption on the premises.

(m) *Petition for relief from hardship.* (1) Any person affected by FDO 79 or the provisions hereof who considers that compliance therewith would work an exceptional and unreasonable hardship on him, may file with the market agent a petition addressed to the Director. The petition shall contain the correct name, address and principal place of business of the petitioner, a full statement of the facts upon which the petition is based, and the hardship involved and the nature of the relief desired.

(2) Upon receiving such petition the market agent shall immediately investigate representations and facts stated therein.

(3) After investigation, the petition shall be certified to the Director, but prior to certification the market agent may (i) deny the petition or (ii) grant temporary relief for a total period not to exceed 60 days.

(4) Denials or grants of relief by the market agent shall be reviewed by the Director and may be affirmed, modified, or reversed by the Director.

(n) *Reports.* Each handler shall transmit to the market agent on forms prescribed by the market agent the following reports:

(1) Within 20 days following the effective date of this order, reports which show the information required by the market agent to establish such handler's quotas;

(2) Within 20 days following the close of each quota period, the information required by the market agent to establish volumes of deliveries of milk, cream and milk byproducts during the preceding quota period; and

(3) Handlers exempt from quotas pursuant to (i) hereof shall, upon the request of the market agent, submit the information required by the market agent to establish volumes of deliveries of milk, cream, and milk byproducts.

(o) *Records.* Handlers shall keep and shall make available to the market agent such records of receipts, sales, deliveries, and production as the market agent shall require for the purpose of obtaining information which the Director may require for the establishment of quotas as prescribed in (b) of FDO 79.

(p) *Expense of administration.* Each handler shall pay to the market agent, within 20 days after the close of each calendar month, an assessment of $0.015 per hundredweight of each of milk, milk byproducts, cream, and skim milk equivalent of cottage, pot, or baker's cheese delivered during the preceding quota period and subject to quota regulations under the provisions hereof.

(q) *Violations.* The market agent shall report all violations to the Director together with the information required for the prosecution of such violations.

(r) *Bureau of the Budget approval.* The record-keeping and reporting requirements of this order have been approved by the Bureau of the Budget in accordance with the Federal Reports Act of 1942. Subsequent record-keeping or reporting requirements will be subject to the approval of the Bureau of the Budget pursuant to the Federal Reports Act of 1942.

(s) *Effective date.* This order shall take effect at 12:01 a. m., e. w. t., February 1, 1944.

(E.O. 9280, 7 F.R. 10179; E.O. 9322, 8 F.R. 3807; E.O. 9334, 8 F.R. 5423; E.O. 9392, 8 F.R. 14783; FDO 79, 8 F.R. 12426, 13283)

Issued this 13th day of January 1944.

ROY F. HENDRICKSON,
Director of Food Distribution.

War Food Administration:
Summary to FDO 79.115–79.121.

Seven New Milk Sales Areas Named

Milk sales in 7 metropolitan areas in Florida, North Carolina, South Carolina, Georgia, and Mississippi will be regulated under the Food Distribution Administration's fluid milk conservation and control program, beginning February 1.

The new milk sales areas are:

Miami, Fla., Metropolitan (FDO 79.115); Tampa-St. Petersburg, Fla. (FDO 79.116); Jacksonville, Fla. (FDO 79.117); Savannah, Ga. (FDO 79.118); Durham, N. C. (FDO 79.119); Charleston, S. C. (FDO 79.120); Jackson, Miss. (FDO 79.121).

Market agents who will administer the orders in each area will be named later.

Under the program, milk dealers will be permitted to deliver to all customers except schools as much fluid milk as they delivered in June and three-fourths as much milk in cream and milk byproducts (such as cottage cheese, chocolate milk and buttermilk) as they delivered in June. Deliveries to elementary, junior high and high schools will be under the same restrictions except the number of school days in May will be used as the base period in determining quotas, rather than June. Milk dealers include all persons or firms engaged in the delivery or transfer of milk, but not such distributors as subhandlers ("peddlers"), retail stores, hotels, or restaurants.

Producer distributors who purchase no milk will be permitted to deliver as much milk as they delivered in either June or December, whichever represents their larger total deliveries.

The order permits dealers to deliver more fluid milk than their quotas allow, provided they deliver less cream or milk byproducts. Since cream and milk byproducts are recognized as one quota group, dealers may deliver more cream by cutting down deliveries on milk byproducts, provided they do not deliver more cream than they delivered in the base period, or more byproducts by reducing the amount of milk solids used in cream.

In distributing the milk, cream and byproducts allowed under their quotas, dealers are required to give preference to the following consumer groups, in the order listed, taking into consideration the type of purchasers they served in the base period:

1. Children, expectant mothers, and invalids requiring milk;

2. Homes and retail stores handling milk for consumption off the premises;

3. Establishments serving milk for consumption on the premises.

Deliveries of milk, cream and milk byproducts to other dealers; to the armed forces; to plants engaged in handling or processing milk, byproducts and cream which are not distributed in the sales area; and to designated industrial manufacturers who use milk, cream, or milk byproducts in making products which are sold off the premises are quota exempt.

Consumers in the milk sales areas named today, as in others already designated, generally will be able to purchase as much milk under the milk conservation program as they have been buying in recent months. Fluid milk sales are being stabilized, and sales of cream and milk byproducts are being reduced, FDA officials said, to help assure sufficient milk for manufacturing the cheese, butter, evaporated milk, and milk powder required by the armed forces and civilians for good nutrition and properly balanced diets.

WAR FOOD ADMINISTRATION
Food Distribution Administration
Washington 25, D. C.

CORRECTION NOTICE - FDO-79.119 Dairy Products

In printing Food Distribution Order No. 79.119 the following error occurred:

Section 1401.152 (4) In the phrase beginning "as determined by the market" after the word "market", the word "agent" was omitted. The phrase should read "as determined by the market agent."

oz.1

FDO 79-119

JAN. 13, 1944

WAR FOOD ADMINISTRATION

[FDO 79-119] A

PART 1401—DAIRY PRODUCTS

FLUID MILK AND CREAM IN THE DURHAM, N. C., SALES AREA

Pursuant to the authority vested in me by Food Distribution Order No. 79 (8 F.R. 12426), issued on September 7, 1943, as amended, and to effectuate the purposes of such order, it is hereby ordered as follows:

§ 1401.152 *Quota restrictions*—(a) *Definitions.* When used in this order, unless otherwise distinctly expressed or manifestly incompatible with the intent hereof:

(1) Each term defined in Food Distribution Order No. 79, as amended, shall, when used herein, have the same meaning as is set forth for such term in Food Distribution Order No. 79, as amended.

(2) The term "FDO 79" means Food Distribution Order No. 79, issued on September 7, 1943, as amended.

(3) The term "sub-handler" means any handler, such as a peddler, vendor, sub-dealer, or secondary dealer, who purchases in a previously packaged and processed form milk, cream, or milk byproducts for delivery.

(4) The term "industrial user" means a person, as determined by the market, in the capacity of a manufacturer of products using as an ingredient therein milk, cream, or milk byproducts, which products are disposed of for resale to consumers off the premises where made.

(5) The term "base" means the total pounds of milk solids delivered by a handler within the sales area during the base period (i) in the form of milk, or (ii) in the form of cream and milk byproducts, minus the milk solids in quota-exempt deliveries of milk, and cream and milk byproducts, as described in (j) hereof. (For the purposes of this order, the milk solids content of milk, milk byproducts, and cream shall be computed as follows: Each hundredweight of milk, cream, or milk byproducts other than cottage, pot, or baker's cheese, shall be considered the equivalent of 9.375 pounds of milk solids plus the number of pounds of milk solids calculated by multiplying the pounds of butterfat in such milk, and cream and milk byproducts by .906; and each hundredweight of cottage, pot, or baker's cheese shall be considered the equivalent of 62.5 pounds of milk solids plus one pound of milk solids for each one percent of butterfat content of such cheese.)

(b) *Milk sales area.* The following area is hereby designated as a "milk sales area" to be known as the Durham, North Carolina, milk sales area, and is referred to hereinafter as the "sales area":

The city of Durham and the townships of Durham and Patterson, all in Durham County, North Carolina.

(c) *Base period.* The calendar month of June 1943 is hereby designated as the base period for the sales area: *Provided,* That the month of May may be used as the base period for computing base and quota for deliveries to elementary, junior high and high schools: *And provided further,* That in the computations set forth in (e) hereof the total deliveries to elementary, junior high, and high schools in the base period shall be divided by the number of days such schools were in session in lieu of the total number of days in the base period as set forth in (e) (1) and the average daily deliveries so determined shall be multiplied by the number of days such schools are in session in each quota period in lieu of the number of days in the quota period as set forth in (e) (2).

(d) The remainder of the calendar month in which the provisions hereof become effective and each subsequent calendar month, respectively, is hereby designated as the quota period for the sales area.

(e) *Handler quotas.* Quotas for each handler other than a sub-handler or producer-handler shall be determined as follows:

(1) Divide his respective bases by the number of days in the base period;

(2) Multiply the foregoing result by the number of days in the quota period; and

(3) Multiply the aforesaid resulting amounts by 100 percent in the case of the base for milk, and 75 percent in the case of the base for cream and milk byproducts.

(f) *Quotas for handlers who are also producers.* Quotas for each handler who is also a producer and who purchases no milk shall be computed in accordance with (e) hereof, except:

(1) His base period shall be either June or December, whichever represents his larger total deliveries; and

(2) The applicable percentages shall be 100 percent in lieu of those specified in (e) (3).

(g) *Quota adjustments.* Each handler may increase his quota for milk within any quota period by one pound of milk solids for each one pound of milk solids he reduces his quota for cream and milk byproducts.

(h) *Cream deliveries.* The units of cream delivered subject to quota in any quota period shall not exceed 100 percent of the units of cream in his base, irrespective of the milk solids content of such deliveries.

(i) *Handler exemptions.* Quota shall not apply to any handler who delivers in a quota period a daily average of less than 100 units of milk, cream, and milk byproducts. For the purpose of this order, a unit shall be the equivalent in volume of the following: (1) One quart of milk, buttermilk, or fluid milk byproducts; (2) one-half pint of cream; and (3) one-half pound of cottage, pot, or baker's cheese.

(j) *Quota exclusions and exemptions.* Deliveries of milk, milk byproducts, or cream (1) to other handlers, except for such deliveries to sub-handlers, (2) to plants engaged in the handling or processing of milk, milk byproducts, cream or other dairy products from which no milk, milk byproducts, or cream, is delivered in the sales area, (3) to industrial users, and (4) to the agencies or groups specified in (d) of FDO 79, shall be excluded from the computation of deliveries in the base period and exempt from charges to quotas.

(k) *Transfers of bases.* The market agent is empowered to transfer base from one handler to another.

(1) Upon receipt of a request in writing from both handlers; and

(2) Upon application from a handler and written notice to the Director and to both handlers, (i) to permit deliveries to a purchaser not being served by a handler whose quota reflects deliveries to such purchaser in the base period, (ii) to permit a handler to serve an account which customarily rotates among several handlers inclusive of a contract let by a public agency or institution on a bid basis, and (iii) to permit a handler to serve an account which he is serving on the effective date of this order and which was served by another handler during the base period.

(l) *Consumer priorities.* In the distribution of milk subject to quotas established hereunder, a handler shall give preference in the order listed, taking into consideration the type of purchasers served by him in the base period, to:

(1) The need of children, expectant mothers, and invalids requiring milk;

(2) Homes and retail stores handling milk for consumption off the premises; and

(3) Establishments serving milk for consumption on the premises.

(m) *Petition for relief from hardship.* (1) Any person affected by FDO 79 or the provisions hereof who considers that compliance therewith would work an exceptional and unreasonable hardship on him, may file with the market agent a petition addressed to the Director. The petition shall contain the correct name, address and principal place of business of the petitioner, a full statement of the facts upon which the petition is based, and the hardship involved and the nature of the relief desired.

(2) Upon receiving such petition the market agent shall immediately investigate representations and facts stated therein.

(3) After investigation, the petition shall be certified to the Director, but prior to certification the market agent may (i) deny the petition or (ii) grant temporary relief for a total period not to exceed 60 days.

(4) Denials or grants of relief by the market agent shall be reviewed by the Director and may be affirmed, modified, or reversed by the Director.

(n) *Reports.* Each handler shall transmit to the market agent on forms prescribed by the market agent the following reports:

(1) Within 20 days following the effective date of this order, reports which show the information required by the market agent to establish such handler's quotas;

(2) Within 20 days following the close of each quota period, the information required by the market agent to establish volumes of deliveries of milk, cream and milk byproducts during the preceding quota period; and

(3) Handlers exempt from quotas pursuant to (i) hereof shall, upon the request of the market agent, submit the information required by the market agent to establish volumes of deliveries of milk, cream, and milk byproducts.

(o) *Records.* Handlers shall keep and shall make available to the market agent such records of receipts, sales, deliveries, and production as the market agent shall require for the purpose of obtaining information which the Director may require for the establishment of quotas as prescribed in (b) of FDO 79.

(p) *Expense of administration.* Each handler shall pay to the market agent, within 20 days after the close of each calendar month, an assessment of $0.015 per hundredweight of each of milk, milk byproducts, cream, and skim milk equivalent of cottage, pot, or baker's cheese delivered during the preceding quota period and subject to quota regulations under the provisions hereof.

(q) *Violations.* The market agent shall report all violations to the Director together with the information required for the prosecution of such violations.

(r) *Bureau of the Budget approval.* The record-keeping and reporting requirements of this order have been approved by the Bureau of the Budget in accordance with the Federal Reports Act of 1942. Subsequent record-keeping or reporting requirements will be subject to the approval of the Bureau of the Budget pursuant to the Federal Reports Act of 1942.

(s) *Effective date.* This order shall take effect at 12:01 a. m., e. w. t., February 1, 1944.

(E.O. 9280, 7 F.R. 10179; E.O. 9322, 8 F.R. 3807; E.O. 9334, 8 F.R. 5423; E.O. 9392, 8 F.R. 14783; FDO 79, 8 F.R. 12426, 13283)

Issued this 13th day of January 1944.

ROY F. HENDRICKSON,
Director of Food Distribution.

War Food Administration:
Summary to FDO 79.115–79.121.

Seven New Milk Sales Areas Named

Milk sales in 7 metropolitan areas in Florida, North Carolina, South Carolina, Georgia, and Mississippi will be regulated under the Food Distribution Administration's fluid milk conservation and control program, beginning February 1.

The new milk sales areas are:

Miami, Fla., Metropolitan (FDO 79.115); Tampa-St. Petersburg, Fla. (FDO 79.116); Jacksonville, Fla. (FDO 79.117); Savannah, Ga. (FDO 79.118); Durham, N. C. (FDO 79.119); Charleston, S. C. (FDO 79.120); Jackson, Miss. (FDO 79.121).

Market agents who will administer the orders in each area will be named later.

Under the program, milk dealers will be permitted to deliver to all customers except schools as much fluid milk as they delivered in June and three-fourths as much milk in cream and milk byproducts (such as cottage cheese, chocolate milk and buttermilk) as they delivered in June. Deliveries to elementary, junior high and high schools will be under the same restrictions except the number of school days in May will be used as the base period in determining quotas, rather than June. Milk dealers include all persons or firms engaged in the delivery or transfer of milk, but not such distributors as subhandlers ("peddlers"), retail stores, hotels, or restaurants.

Producer distributors who purchase no milk will be permitted to deliver as much milk as they delivered in either June or December, whichever represents their larger total deliveries.

The order permits dealers to deliver more fluid milk than their quotas allow, provided they deliver less cream or milk byproducts. Since cream and milk byproducts are recognized as one quota group, dealers may deliver more cream by cutting down deliveries on milk byproducts, provided they do not deliver more cream than they delivered in the base period, or more byproducts by reducing the amount of milk solids used in cream.

In distributing the milk, cream and byproducts allowed under their quotas, dealers are required to give preference to the following consumer groups, in the order listed, taking into consideration the type of purchasers they served in the base period:

1. Children, expectant mothers, and invalids requiring milk;

2. Homes and retail stores handling milk for consumption off the premises;

3. Establishments serving milk for consumption on the premises.

Deliveries of milk, cream and milk byproducts to other dealers; to the armed forces; to plants engaged in handling or processing milk, byproducts and cream which are not distributed in the sales area; and to designated industrial manufacturers who use milk, cream, or milk byproducts in making products which are sold off the premises are quota exempt.

Consumers in the milk sales areas named today, as in others already designated, generally will be able to purchase as much milk under the milk conservation program as they have been buying in recent months. Fluid milk sales are being stabilized, and sales of cream and milk byproducts are being reduced, FDA officials said, to help assure sufficient milk for manufacturing the cheese, butter, evaporated milk, and milk powder required by the armed forces and civilians for good nutrition and properly balanced diets.

WAR FOOD ADMINISTRATION
Food Distribution Administration
Washington 25, D. C.

In printing Food Distribution Order No. 79.120 the following errors occurred:

(m) After the heading "Petition for relief from hardship "the line "the provisions hereof who considers that" should be deleted.

(n) (1) In the sentence beginning "any person affected by FDO 79" several words have been omitted. Preceding the words "may file," the sentence should read, "Any person affected by FDO 79 or the provisions hereof who considers that compliance therwith would work an exceptional and unreasonable hardship on him,"

FDO 79-120

JAN. 13, 1944

WAR FOOD ADMINISTRATION

[FDO 79-120] A

PART 1401—DAIRY PRODUCTS

FLUID MILK AND CREAM IN THE CHARLESTON, S. C., SALES AREA

Pursuant to the authority vested in me by Food Distribution Order No. 79 (8 F.R. 12426), issued on September 7, 1943, as amended, and to effectuate the purposes of such order, it is hereby ordered as follows:

§ 1401.153 *Quota restrictions*—(a) *Definitions.* When used in this order, unless otherwise distinctly expressed or manifestly incompatible with the intent hereof:

(1) Each term defined in Food Distribution Order No. 79, as amended, shall, when used herein, have the same meaning as is set forth for such term in Food Distribution Order No. 79, as amended.

(2) The term "FDO 79" means Food Distribution Order No. 79, issued on September 7, 1943, as amended.

(3) The term "sub-handler" means any handler, such as a peddler, vendor, sub-dealer, or secondary dealer, who purchases in a previously packaged and processed form milk, cream, or milk byproducts for delivery.

(4) The term "industrial user" means a person, as determined by the market agent, in the capacity of a manufacturer of products using as an ingredient therein milk, cream, or milk byproducts, which products are disposed of for resale to consumers off the premises where made.

(5) The term "base" means the total pounds of milk solids delivered by a handler within the sales area during the base period (i) in the form of milk, or (ii) in the form of cream and milk byproducts, minus the milk solids in quota-exempt deliveries of milk, and cream and milk byproducts, as described in (j) hereof. (For the purpose of this order, the milk solids content of milk, milk byproducts, and cream shall be computed as follows: Each hundredweight of milk, cream, or milk byproducts other than cottage, pot, or baker's cheese, shall be considered the equivalent of 9.375 pounds of milk solids plus the number of pounds of milk solids calculated by multiplying the pounds of butterfat in such milk, and cream and milk byproducts by .906; and each hundredweight of cottage, pot, or baker's cheese shall be considered the equivalent of 62.5 pounds of milk solids plus one pound of milk solids for each one percent of butterfat content of such cheese.)

(b) *Milk sales area.* The following area is hereby designated as a "milk sales area" to be known as the Charleston, South Carolina, milk sales area, and is referred to hereinafter as the "sales area":

The city of Charleston and Charleston County, all in the State of South Carolina.

(c) *Base period.* The calendar month of June 1943 is hereby designated as the base period for the sales area: *Provided,* That the month of May may be used as the base period for computing base and quota for deliveries to elementary, junior high and high schools: *And Provided further,* That in the computations set forth in (e) hereof the total deliveries to elementary, junior high, and high schools in the base period shall be divided by the number of days such schools were in session in lieu of the total number of days in the base period as set forth in (e) (1) and the average daily deliveries so determined shall be multiplied by the number of days such schools are in session in each quota period in lieu of the number of days in the quota period as set forth in (e) (2).

(d) The remainder of the calendar month in which the provisions hereof become effective and each subsequent calendar month, respectively, is hereby designated as the quota period for the sales area.

(e) *Handler quotas.* Quotas for each handler other than a sub-handler or producer-handler shall be determined as follows:

(1) Divide his respective bases by the number of days in the base period;

(2) Multiply the foregoing result by the number of days in the quota period; and

(3) Multiply the aforesaid resulting amounts by 100 percent in the case of the base for milk, and 75 percent in the case of the base for cream and milk byproducts.

(f) *Quotas for handlers who are also producers.* Quotas for each handler who is also a producer and who purchases no milk shall be computed in accordance with (e) hereof, except:

(1) His base period shall be either June or December, whichever represents his larger total deliveries; and

(2) The applicable percentages shall be 100 percent in lieu of those specified in (e) (3).

(g) *Quota adjustments.* Each handler may increase his quota for milk within any quota period by one pound of milk solids for each one pound of milk solids he reduces his quota for cream and milk byproducts.

(h) *Cream deliveries.* The units of cream delivered subject to quota in any quota period shall not exceed 100 percent of the units of cream in his base, irrespective of the milk solids content of such deliveries.

(i) *Handler exemptions.* Quota shall not apply to any handler who delivers in a quota period a daily average of less than 250 units of milk, cream, and milk byproducts. For the purpose of this order, a unit shall be the equivalent in volume of the following: (1) One quart of milk, buttermilk, or fluid milk byproducts; (2) one-half pint of cream; and (3) one-half pound of cottage, pot, or baker's cheese.

(j) *Quota exclusions and exemptions.* Deliveries of milk, milk byproducts, or cream (1) to other handlers, except for such deliveries to sub-handlers, (2) to plants engaged in the handling or processing of milk, milk byproducts, cream or other dairy products from which no milk, milk byproducts, or cream, is delivered in the sales area, (3) to industrial users, and (4) to the agencies or groups specified in (d) of FDO 79, shall be excluded from the computation of deliveries in the base period and exempt from charges to quotas.

(k) *Transfers of bases.* The market agent is empowered to transfer base from one handler to another.

(1) Upon receipt of a request in writing from both handlers; and

(2) Upon application from a handler and written notice to the Director and to both handlers, (i) to permit deliveries to a purchaser not being served by a handler whose quota reflects deliveries to such purchaser in the base period, (ii) to permit a handler to serve an account which customarily rotates among several handlers inclusive of a contract let by a public agency or institution on a bid basis, and (iii) to permit a handler to serve an account which he is serving on the effective date of this order and which was served by another handler during the base period.

(l) *Consumer priorities.* In the distribution of milk subject to quotas established hereunder, a handler shall give preference in the order listed, taking into consideration the type of purchasers served by him in the base period, to:

(1) The need of children, expectant mothers, and invalids requiring milk;

(2) Homes and retail stores handling milk for consumption off the premises; and

(3) Establishments serving milk for consumption on the premises.

(m) *Petition for relief from hardship.* the provisions hereof who considers that

(1) Any person affected by FDO 79 or compliance therewith would work an exceptional and unreasonable hardship on him, may file with the market agent a petition addressed to the Director. The petition shall contain the correct name, address and principal place of business of the petitioner, a full statement of the facts upon which the petition is based, and the hardship involved and the nature of the relief desired.

(2) Upon receiving such petition the market agent shall immediately investigate representations and facts stated therein.

(3) After investigation, the petition shall be certified to the Director, but prior to certification the market agent may (i) deny the petition or (ii) grant temporary relief for a total period not to exceed 60 days.

(4) Denials or grants of relief by the market agent shall be reviewed by the Director and may be affirmed, modified, or reversed by the Director.

(n) *Reports.* Each handler shall transmit to the market agent on forms prescribed by the market agent the following reports:

(1) Within 20 days following the effective date of this order, reports which show the information required by the market agent to establish such handler's quotas;

(2) Within 20 days following the close of each quota period, the information required by the market agent to establish volumes of deliveries of milk, cream and milk byproducts during the preceding quota period; and

(3) Handlers exempt from quotas pursuant to (i) hereof shall, upon the request of the market agent, submit the information required by the market agent to establish volumes of deliveries of milk, cream, and milk byproducts.

(o) *Records.* Handlers shall keep and shall make available to the market agent such records of receipts, sales, deliveries, and production as the market agent shall require for the purpose of obtaining information which the Director may require for the establishment of quotas as prescribed in (b) of FDO 79.

(p) *Expense of administration.* Each handler shall pay to the market agent, within 20 days after the close of each calendar month, an assessment of $0.015 per hundredweight of each of milk, milk byproducts, cream, and skim milk equivalent of cottage, pot, or baker's cheese delivered during the preceding quota period and subject to quota regulations under the provisions hereof.

(q) *Violations.* The market agent shall report all violations to the Director together with the information required for the prosecution of such violations.

(r) *Bureau of the Budget approval.* The record-keeping and reporting requirements of this order have been approved by the Bureau of the Budget in accordance with the Federal Reports Act of 1942. Subsequent record-keeping or reporting requirements will be subject to the approval of the Bureau of the Budget pursuant to the Federal Reports Act of 1942.

(s) *Effective date.* This order shall take effect at 12:01 a. m., e. w. t., February 1, 1944.

(E.O. 9280, 7 F.R. 10179; E.O. 9322, 8 F.R. 3807; E.O. 9334, 8 F.R. 5423; E.O. 9392, 8 F.R. 14783; FDO 79, 8 F.R. 12426, 13283)

Issued this 13th day of January 1944.

ROY F. HENDRICKSON,
Director of Food Distribution.

War Food Administration:
Summary to FDO 79.115–79.121.

Seven New Milk Sales Areas Named

Milk sales in 7 metropolitan areas in Florida, North Carolina, South Carolina, Georgia, and Mississippi will be regulated under the Food Distribution Administration's fluid milk conservation and control program, beginning February 1.

The new milk sales areas are:

Miami, Fla., Metropolitan (FDO 79.115); Tampa-St. Petersburg, Fla. (FDO 79.116); Jacksonville, Fla. (FDO 79.117); Savannah, Ga. (FDO 79.118); Durham, N. C. (FDO 79.119); Charleston, S. C. (FDO 79.120); Jackson, Miss. (FDO 79.121).

Market agents who will administer the orders in each area will be named later.

Under the program, milk dealers will be permitted to deliver to all customers except schools as much fluid milk as they delivered in June and three-fourths as much milk in cream and milk byproducts (such as cottage cheese, chocolate milk and buttermilk) as they delivered in June. Deliveries to elementary, junior high and high schools will be under the same restrictions except the number of school days in May will be used as the base period in determining quotas, rather than June. Milk dealers include all persons or firms engaged in the delivery or transfer of milk, but not such distributors as subhandlers ("peddlers"), retail stores, hotels, or restaurants.

Producer distributors who purchase no milk will be permitted to deliver as much milk as they delivered in either June or December, whichever represents their larger total deliveries.

The order permits dealers to deliver more fluid milk than their quotas allow, provided they deliver less cream or milk byproducts. Since cream and milk byproducts are recognized as one quota group, dealers may deliver more cream by cutting down deliveries on milk byproducts, provided they do not deliver more cream than they delivered in the base period, or more byproducts by reducing the amount of milk solids used in cream.

In distributing the milk, cream and byproducts allowed under their quotas, dealers are required to give preference to the following consumer groups, in the order listed, taking into consideration the type of purchasers they served in the base period:

1. Children, expectant mothers, and invalids requiring milk;

2. Homes and retail stores handling milk for consumption off the premises;

3. Establishments serving milk for consumption on the premises.

Deliveries of milk, cream and milk byproducts to other dealers; to the armed forces; to plants engaged in handling or processing milk, byproducts and cream which are not distributed in the sales area; and to designated industrial manufacturers who use milk, cream, or milk byproducts in making products which are sold off the premises are quota exempt.

Consumers in the milk sales areas named today, as in others already designated, generally will be able to purchase as much milk under the milk conservation program as they have been buying in recent months. Fluid milk sales are being stabilized, and sales of cream and milk byproducts are being reduced, FDA officials said, to help assure sufficient milk for manufacturing the cheese, butter, evaporated milk, and milk powder required by the armed forces and civilians for good nutrition and properly balanced diets.

WAR FOOD ADMINISTRATION
Food Distribution Administration
Washington 25, D. C.

CORRECTION NOTICE - FDO 79.121 Dairy Products

In printing Food Distribution Order No. 79.121 the following error occurred:

Section 1401.154 (a) the heading "Definitions" is misspelled.

FDO 79-121

JAN. 13, 1944

WAR FOOD ADMINISTRATION

(b) *Milk sales area.* The following area is hereby designated as a "milk sales area" to be known as the Jackson, Mississippi, milk sales area, and is referred to hereinafter as the "sales area":

The city of Jackson and the area included in beats 1, 4, and 5, all in Hinds County, Mississippi.

(c) *Base period.* The calendar month of June 1943 is hereby designated as the base period for the sales area: *Provided*, That the month of May may be used as the base period for computing base and quota for deliveries to elementary, junior high and high schools: *And provided further*, That in the computation set forth in (e) hereof the total deliveries to elementary, junior high, and high schools in the base period shall be divided by the number of days such schools were in session in lieu of the total number of days in the base period as set forth in (e) (1) and the average daily deliveries so determined shall be multiplied by the number of days such schools are in session in each quota period in lieu of the number of days in the quota period as set forth in (e) (2).

(d) The remainder of the calendar month in which the provisions hereof become effective and each subsequent calendar month, respectively, is hereby designated as the quota period for the sales area.

(e) *Handler quotas.* Quotas for each handler other than a sub-handler or producer-handler shall be determined as follows:

(1) Divide his respective bases by the number of days in the base period;

(2) Multiply the foregoing result by the number of days in the quota period; and

(3) Multiply the aforesaid resulting amounts by 100 percent in the case of the base for milk, and 75 percent in the case of the base for cream and milk byproducts.

(f) *Quotas for handlers who are also producers.* Quotas for each handler who is also a producer and who purchases no milk shall be computed in accordance with (e) hereof, except:

(1) His base period shall be either June or December, whichever represents his larger total deliveries; and

(2) The applicable percentages shall be 100 percent in lieu of those specified in (e) (3).

(g) *Quota adjustments.* Each handler may increase his quota for milk within any quota period by one pound of milk solids for each one pound of milk solids he reduces his quota for cream and milk byproducts.

(h) *Cream deliveries.* The units of cream delivered subject to quota in any quota period shall not exceed 100 percent of the units of cream in his base, irrespective of the milk solids content of such deliveries.

(i) *Handler exemptions.* Quota shall not apply to any handler who delivers in a quota period a daily average of less than 200 units of milk, cream, and milk byproducts. For the purpose of this order, a unit shall be the equivalent in volume of the following: (1) One quart of milk, buttermilk, or fluid milk byproducts; (2) one-half pint of cream; and (3) one-half pound of cottage, pot, or baker's cheese.

(j) *Quota exclusions and exemptions.* Deliveries of milk, milk byproducts, or cream (1) to other handlers, except for such deliveries to sub-handlers, (2) to plants engaged in the handling or processing of milk, milk byproducts, cream or other dairy products from which no milk, milk byproducts, or cream, is delivered in the sales area, (3) to industrial users, and (4) to the agencies or groups specified in (d) of FDO 79, shall be excluded from the computation of deliveries in the base period and exempt from charges to quotas.

(k) *Transfers of bases.* The market agent is empowered to transfer base from one handler to another.

(1) Upon receipt of a request in writing from both handlers; and

(2) Upon application from a handler and written notice to the Director and to both handlers, (i) to permit deliveries to a purchaser not being served by a handler whose quota reflects deliveries to such purchaser in the base period, (ii) to permit a handler to serve an account which customarily rotates among several handlers inclusive of a contract let by a public agency or institution on a bid basis, and (iii) to permit a handler to serve an account which he is serving on the effective date of this order and which was served by another handler during the base period.

(l) *Consumer priorities.* In the distribution of milk subject to quotas established hereunder, a handler shall give preference in the order listed, taking into consideration the type of purchasers served by him in the base period, to:

(1) The need of children, expectant mothers, and invalids requiring milk;

(2) Homes and retail stores handling milk for consumption off the premises; and

(3) Establishments serving milk for consumption on the premises.

(m) *Petition for relief from hardship.* (1) Any person affected by FDO 79 or the provisions hereof who considers that compliance therewith would work an exceptional and unreasonable hardship on him, may file with the market agent a petition addressed to the Director. The petition shall contain the correct name, address and principal place of business of the petitioner, a full statement of the facts upon which the petition is based, and the hardship involved and the nature of the relief desired.

(2) Upon receiving such petition the market agent shall immediately investigate representations and facts stated therein.

(3) After investigation, the petition shall be certified to the Director, but prior to certification the market agent may (i) deny the petition or (ii) grant temporary relief for a total period not to exceed 60 days.

(4) Denials or grants of relief by the market agent shall be reviewed by the Director and may be affirmed, modified, or reversed by the Director.

(n) *Reports.* Each handler shall transmit to the market agent on forms prescribed by the market agent the following reports:

(1) Within 20 days following the effective date of this order, reports which show the information required by the market agent to establish such handler's quotas;

(2) Within 20 days following the close of each quota period, the information required by the market agent to establish volumes of deliveries of milk, cream and milk byproducts during the preceding quota period; and

(3) Handlers exempt from quotas pursuant to (i) hereof shall, upon the request of the market agent, submit the information required by the market agent to establish volumes of deliveries of milk, cream, and milk byproducts.

(o) *Records.* Handlers shall keep and shall make available to the market agent such records of receipts, sales, deliveries, and production as the market agent shall require for the purpose of obtaining information which the Director may require for the establishment of quotas as prescribed in (b) of FDO 79.

(p) *Expense of administration.* Each handler shall pay to the market agent, within 20 days after the close of each calendar month, an assessment of $0.015 per hundredweight of byproducts, cream, an alent of cottage, pot, delivered during the pr riod and subject to under the provisions h

(q) *Violations.* Tl shall report all violatic together with the inf for the prosecution of

(r) *Bureau of the* The record-keeping a quirements of this orc proved by the Bureau accordance with the F of 1942. Subsequent reporting requirements the approval of the Bu pursuant to the Feder 1942.

(s) *Effective date.* take effect at 12:01 a. ary 1, 1944.

(E.O. 9280, 7 F.R. 1017 3807; E.O. 9334, 8 F.R 8 F.R. 14783; FDO 79, 8

Issued this 13th day

ROY F.
Director of Fo

War Food Administration:
Summary to FDO 79.115–79.121.

Seven New Milk Sales Areas Named

Milk sales in 7 metropolitan areas in Florida, North Carolina, South Carolina, Georgia, and Mississippi will be regulated under the Food Distribution Administration's fluid milk conservation and control program, beginning February 1.

The new milk sales areas are:

Miami, Fla., Metropolitan (FDO 79.115); Tampa-St. Petersburg, Fla. (FDO 79.116); Jacksonville, Fla. (FDO 79.117); Savannah, Ga. (FDO 79.118); Durham, N. C. (FDO 79.119); Charleston, S. C. (FDO 79.120); Jackson, Miss. (FDO 79.121).

Market agents who will administer the orders in each area will be named later.

Under the program, milk dealers will be permitted to deliver to all customers except schools as much fluid milk as they delivered in June and three-fourths as much milk in cream and milk byproducts (such as cottage cheese, chocolate milk and buttermilk) as they delivered in June. Deliveries to elementary, junior high and high schools will be under the same restrictions except the number of school days in May will be used as the base period in determining quotas, rather than June. Milk dealers include all persons or firms engaged in the delivery or transfer of milk, but not such distributors as subhandlers ("peddlers"), retail stores, hotels, or restaurants.

Producer distributors who purchase no milk will be permitted to deliver as much milk as they delivered in either June or December, whichever represents their larger total deliveries.

The order permits dealers to deliver more fluid milk than their quotas allow, provided they deliver less cream or milk byproducts. Since cream and milk byproducts are recognized as one quota group, dealers may deliver more cream by cutting down deliveries on milk byproducts, provided they do not deliver more cream than they delivered in the base period, or more byproducts by reducing the amount of milk solids used in cream.

In distributing the milk, cream and byproducts allowed under their quotas, dealers are required to give preference to the following consumer groups, in the order listed, taking into consideration the type of purchasers they served in the base period:

1. Children, expecta invalids requiring milk

2. Homes and retai milk for consumption

3. Establishments s consumption on the pr

Deliveries of milk, cr products to other deal forces; to plants eng or processing milk, byp which are not distrib area; and to designate ufacturers who use mi byproducts in making are sold off the pre exempt.

Consumers in the named today, as in ot ignated, generally wil chase as much milk un servation program as buying in recent mo sales are being stabili cream and milk bypr reduced, FDA officials sure sufficient milk f the cheese, butter, eva milk powder required b and civilians for go properly balanced die

WAR FOOD ADMINISTRATION
Food Distribution Administration
Washington 25, D. C.

CORRECTION NOTICE- FDO 79,122 Dairy Products

In printing Food Distribution Order No. 79,122 the following error occurred:

Section 1401.155 (3) In the phrase "in a previously packaged and processed from" the work "from" should be "form," so the sentence will read" the term 'sub-handler' means any handler, such as a peddler, vendor, sub-dealer, or secondary dealer, who purchases in a previously packaged and processed form milk, cream, or milk byproducts for delivery."

1337
Cop. 1

FDO 79-122

JAN. 13, 1944

WAR FOOD ADMINISTRATION

[FDO 79-122] A

PART 1401—DAIRY PRODUCTS

FLUID MILK AND CREAM IN THE HOUSTON, TEX., SALES AREA

Pursuant to the authority vested in me by Food Distribution Order No. 79 (8 F.R. 12426), issued on September 7, 1943, as amended, and to effectuate the purposes of such order, it is hereby ordered as follows:

§ 1401.155 *Quota restrictions*—(a) *Definitions.* When used in this order, unless otherwise distinctly expressed or manifestly incompatible with the intent hereof:

(1) Each term defined in Food Distribution Order No. 79, as amended, shall, when used herein, have the same meaning as is set forth for such term in Food Distribution Order No. 79, as amended.

(2) The term "FDO 79" means Food Distribution Order No. 79, issued on September 7, 1943, as amended.

(3) The term "sub-handler" means any handler, such as a peddler, vendor, sub-dealer, or secondary dealer, who purchases in a previously packaged and processed from milk, cream, or milk byproducts for delivery.

(4) The term "industrial user" means a person, as determined by the market agent, in the capacity of a manufacturer of products using as an ingredient therein milk, cream, or milk byproducts, which products are disposed of for resale to consumers off the premises where made.

(5) The term "base" means the total pounds of milk solids delivered by a handler within the sales area during the base period (i) in the form of milk, or (ii) in the form of cream and milk byproducts, minus the milk solids in quota-exempt deliveries of milk, and cream and milk byproducts, as described in (j) hereof. (For the purpose of this order, the milk solids content of milk, milk byproducts, and cream shall be computed as follows: Each hundredweight of milk, cream, or milk byproducts other than cottage, pot, or baker's cheese, shall be considered the equivalent of 9.375 pounds of milk solids plus the number of pounds of milk solids calculated by multiplying the pounds of butterfat in such milk, and cream and milk byproducts by .906; and each hundredweight of cottage, pot, or baker's cheese shall be considered the equivalent of 62.5 pounds of milk solids plus one pound of milk solids for each one percent of butterfat content of such cheese.)

(b) *Milk sales area.* The following area is hereby designated as a "milk sales area" to be known as the Houston, Texas, milk sales area, and is referred to hereinafter as the "sales area":

The city of Houston, justices' precincts 1, 2, 8, and that part of justices' precinct 3 lying west of the San Jacinto River and that part of justices' precinct 3 east of the San Jacinto River which lies south of the Texas and New Orleans Railroad, all in Harris County, Texas.

(c) *Base period.* The calendar month of June 1943 is hereby designated as the base period for the sales area: *Provided*, That the month of May may be used as the base period for computing base and quota for deliveries to elementary, junior high and high schools: *And provided further*, That in the computations set forth in (e) hereof the total deliveries to elementary, junior high, and high schools in the base period shall be divided by the number of days such schools were in session in lieu of the total number of days in the base period as set forth in (e) (1) and the average daily deliveries so determined shall be multiplied by the number of days such schools are in session in each quota period in lieu of the number of days in the quota period as set forth in (e) (2).

(d) The remainder of the calendar month in which the provisions hereof become effective and each subsequent calendar month, respectively, is hereby designated as the quota period for the sales area.

(e) *Handler quotas.* Quotas for each handler other than a sub-handler or producer-handler shall be determined as follows:

(1) Divide his respective bases by the number of days in the base period;

(2) Multiply the foregoing result by the number of days in the quota period; and

(3) Multiply the aforesaid resulting amounts by 100 percent in the case of the base for milk, and 75 percent in the case of the base for cream and milk byproducts.

(f) *Quotas for handlers who are also producers.* Quotas for each handler who is also a producer and who purchases no milk shall be computed in accordance with (e) hereof, except:

(1) His base period shall be either June or December, whichever represents his larger total deliveries; and

(2) The applicable percentages shall be 100 percent in lieu of those specified in (e) (3).

(g) *Quota adjustments.* Each handler may increase his quota for milk within any quota period by one pound of milk solids for each one pound of milk solids he reduces his quota for cream and milk byproducts.

(h) *Cream deliveries.* The units of cream delivered subject to quota in any quota period shall not exceed 100 percent of the units of cream in his base, irrespective of the milk solids content of such deliveries.

(i) *Handler exemptions.* Quota shall not apply to any handler who delivers in a quota period a daily average of less than 200 units of milk, cream, and milk byproducts. For the purpose of this order, a unit shall be the equivalent in volume of the following: (1) One quart of milk, buttermilk, or fluid milk byproducts; (2) one-half pint of cream; and (3) one-half pound of cottage, pot, or baker's cheese.

(j) *Quota exclusions and exemptions.* Deliveries of milk, milk byproducts, or cream (1) to other handlers, except for such deliveries to sub-handlers, (2) to plants engaged in the handling or processing of milk, milk byproducts, cream or other dairy products from which no milk, milk byproducts, or cream, is delivered in the sales area, (3) to industrial users, and (4) to the agencies or groups specified in (d) of FDO 79, shall be excluded from the computation of deliveries in the base period and exempt from charges to quotas.

(k) *Transfers of bases.* The market agent is empowered to transfer base from one handler to another.

(1) Upon receipt of a request in writing from both handlers; and

(2) Upon application from a handler and written notice to the Director and to both handlers, (i) to permit deliveries to a purchaser not being served by a handler whose quota reflects deliveries to such purchaser in the base period, (ii) to permit a handler to serve an account which customarily rotates among several handlers inclusive of a contract let by a public agency or institution on a bid basis, and (iii) to permit a handler to serve an account which he is serving on the effective date of this order and which was served by another handler during the base period.

(l) *Consumer priorities.* In the distribution of milk subject to quotas established hereunder, a handler shall give preference in the order listed, taking into consideration the type of purchasers served by him in the base period, to:

(1) The need of children, expectant mothers, and invalids requiring milk;

(2) Homes and retail stores handling milk for consumption off the premises; and

(3) Establishments serving milk for consumption on the premises.

(m) *Petition for relief from hardship.* (1) Any person affected by FDO 79 or the provisions hereof who considers that compliance therewith would work an exceptional and unreasonable hardship on him, may file with the market agent a petition addressed to the Director. The petition shall contain the correct name, address and principal place of business of the petitioner, a full statement of the facts upon which the petition is based; and the hardship involved and the nature of the relief desired.

(2) Upon receiving such petition the market agent shall immediately investigate representations and facts stated therein.

(3) After investigation, the petition shall be certified to the Director, but prior to certification the market agent may (i) deny the petition or (ii) grant temporary relief for a total period not to exceed 60 days.

(4) Denials or grants of relief by the market agent shall be reviewed by the Director and may be affirmed, modified, or reversed by the Director.

(n) *Reports.* Each handler shall transmit to the market agent on forms prescribed by the market agent the following reports:

(1) Within 20 days following the effective date of this order, reports which show the information required by the market agent to establish such handler's quotas;

(2) Within 20 days following the close of each quota period, the information required by the market agent to establish volumes of deliveries of milk, cream and milk byproducts during the preceding quota period; and

(3) Handlers exempt from quotas pursuant to (i) hereof shall, upon the request of the market agent, submit the information required by the market agent to establish volumes of deliveries of milk, cream, and milk byproducts.

(o) *Records.* Handlers shall keep and shall make available to the market agent such records of receipts, sales, deliveries, and production as the market agent shall require for the purpose of obtaining information which the Director may require for the establishment of quotas as prescribed in (b) of FDO 79.

(p) *Expense of administration.* Each handler shall pay to the market agent, within 20 days after the close of each calendar month, an assessment of $0.015 per hundredweight of each of milk, milk byproducts, cream, and skim milk equivalent of cottage, pot, or baker's cheese delivered during the preceding quota period and subject to quota regulation under the provisions hereof.

(q) *Violations.* The market agent shall report all violations to the Director together with the information required for the prosecution of such violations.

(r) *Bureau of the Budget approval.* The record-keeping and reporting requirements of this order have been approved by the Bureau of the Budget in accordance with the Federal Reports Act of 1942. Subsequent record-keeping or reporting requirements will be subject to the approval of the Bureau of the Budget pursuant to the Federal Reports Act of 1942.

(s) *Effective date.* This order shall take effect at 12:01 a. m., e. w. t., February 1, 1944.

(E.O. 9280, 7 F.R. 10179; E.O. 9322, 8 F.R. 3807; E.O. 9334, 8 F.R. 5423; E.O. 9392, 8 F.R. 14783; FDO 79, 8 F.R. 12426, 13283)

Issued this 13th day of January 1944.

ROY F. HENDRICKSON,
Director of Food Distribution.

War Food Administration:
Summary to FDO–79.124–FDO 79.130.

Nine New Milk Sales Areas Named

Milk sales in 9 metropolitan areas in Texas, Louisiana, and Arkansas will be regulated under the Food Distribution Administration's Fluid milk conservation and control program, beginning February 1, 1944.

The new milk sales areas are:

Waco, Texas (FDO 79.123); Dallas, Texas (FDO 79.124); Ft. Worth, Texas (FDO 79.125); Austin, Texas (FDO 79.126); Galveston, Texas (FDO 79.127); San Antonio, Texas (FDO 79.128); Houston, Texas (FDO 79.122); Shreveport, Louisiana (FDO 79.129); Little Rock, Arkansas (FDO 79.130).

Market agents who will administer the orders in each area will be named later.

Under the program, milk dealers will be permitted to deliver to all customers except schools as much fluid milk as they delivered in June and three-fourths as much milk in cream and milk byproducts (such as cottage cheese, chocolate milk and buttermilk) as they sold in June. Deliveries to elementary, junior high and high schools will be under the same restrictions except the number of school days in May will be used as the base period in determining quotas, rather than June. Milk dealers include all persons or firms engaged in the delivery of transfer of milk, but not such distributors as subhandlers ("peddlers"), retail stores, hotels, or restaurants.

Producer distributors who purchase no milk will be permitted to deliver as much milk as they delivered in either June or December, whichever represents their larger total deliveries.

The order permits dealers to deliver more fluid milk than their quotas allow, provided they use less milk solids in deliveries of cream or milk byproducts. Since cream and milk byproducts are recognized as one quota group, dealers may deliver more cream, but not more than 100% of the deliveries of cream in the base period by cutting down on milk solids used in milk byproducts, or more byproducts by reducing the amount of milk solids used in cream.

In distributing the milk, cream and byproducts allowed under their quotas, dealers are required to give preference to the following consumer groups, in the order listed, taking into consideration the type of purchasers they served in the base period:

1. Children, expectant mothers, and invalids requiring milk;
2. Homes and retail stores handling milk for consumption off the premises.
3. Establishments serving milk for consumption on the premises.

Deliveries of milk, cream and milk byproducts to other dealers; to the Armed Forces; to plants engaged in handling or processing milk, byproducts and cream which are not distributed in the sales area; and to designated industrial manufacturers who use milk, cream, or milk byproducts in making products which are sold off the premises are quota exempt.

Consumers in the milk sales areas named today, as in others already designated, generally will be able to purchase as much milk under the milk conservation program as they have been buying in recent months. Fluid milk sales are being stabilized, and sales of cream and milk byproducts are being reduced, FDA officials said, to help assure sufficient milk for manufacturing the cheese, butter, evaporated milk, and milk powder required by the armed forces and civilians for good nutrition and properly balanced diets.

FDO 79-123

JAN. 13, 1944

WAR FOOD ADMINISTRATION

[FDO 79-123]

PART 1401—DAIRY PRODUCTS

FLUID MILK AND CREAM IN THE WACO, TEX. SALES AREA

Pursuant to the authority vested in me by Food Distribution Order No. 79 (8 F.R. 12426), issued on September 7, 1943, as amended, and to effectuate the purposes of such order, it is hereby ordered as follows:

§ 1401.156 *Quota restrictions*—(a) *Definitions.* When used in this order, unless otherwise distinctly expressed or manifestly incompatible with the intent hereof:

(1) Each term defined in Food Distribution Order No. 79, as amended, shall, when used herein, have the same meaning as is set forth for such term in Food Distribution Order No. 79, as amended.

(2) The term "FDO 79" means Food Distribution Order No. 79, issued on September 7, 1943, as amended.

(3) The term "sub-handler" means any handler, such as a peddler, vendor, sub-dealer, or secondary dealer, who purchases in a previously packaged and processed form milk, cream, or milk byproducts for delivery.

(4) The term "industrial user" means a person, as determined by the market agent, in the capacity of a manufacturer of products using as an ingredient therein milk, cream, or milk byproducts, which products are disposed of for resale to consumers off the premises where made.

(5) The term "base" means the total pounds of milk solids delivered by a handler within the sales area during the base period (i) in the form of milk, or (ii) in the form of cream and milk byproducts, minus the milk solids in quota-exempt deliveries of milk, and cream and milk byproducts, as described in (j) hereof. (For the purpose of this order, the milk solids content of milk, milk byproducts, and cream shall be computed as follows: Each hundredweight of milk, cream, or milk byproducts other than cottage, pot, or baker's cheese, shall be considered the equivalent of 9.375 pounds of milk solids plus the number of pounds of milk solids calculated by multiplying the pounds of butterfat in such milk, and cream and milk byproducts by .906; and each hundredweight of cottage, pot, or baker's cheese shall be considered the equivalent of 62.5 pounds of milk solids plus one pound of milk solids for each one percent of butterfat content of such cheese.)

(b) *Milk sales area.* The following area is hereby designated as a "milk sales area" to be known as the Waco, Texas, milk sales area, and is referred to hereinafter as the "sales area":

The city of Waco and justices' precincts 1 and that part of 4 comprising part of the city of Waco, all in McLennan County, Texas.

(c) *Base period.* The calendar month of June 1943 is hereby designated as the base period for computing base and quota for the sales area: *Provided,* That the month of May may be used as the base period for computing base and quota for deliveries to elementary, junior high and high schools: *And provided further,* That in the computations set forth in (e) hereof the total deliveries to elementary, junior high, and high schools in the base period shall be divided by the number of days such schools were in session in lieu of the total number of days in the base period as set forth in (e) (1) and the average daily deliveries so determined shall be multiplied by the number of days such schools are in session in each quota period in lieu of the number of days in the quota period as set forth in (e) (2).

(d) The remainder of the calendar month in which the provisions hereof become effective and each subsequent calendar month, respectively, is hereby designated as the quota period for the sales area.

(e) *Handler quotas.* Quotas for each handler other than a sub-handler or producer-handler shall be determined as follows:

(1) Divide his respective bases by the number of days in the base period;

(2) Multiply the foregoing result by the number of days in the quota period; and

(3) Multiply the aforesaid resulting amounts by 100 percent in the case of the base for milk, and 75 percent in the case of the base for cream and milk byproducts.

(f) *Quotas for handlers who are also producers.* Quotas for each handler who is also a producer and who purchases no milk shall be computed in accordance with (e) hereof, except:

(1) His base period shall be either June or December, whichever represents his larger total deliveries; and

(2) The applicable percentages shall be 100 percent in lieu of those specified in (e) (3).

(g) *Quota adjustments.* Each handler may increase his quota for milk within any quota period by one pound of milk solids for each one pound of milk solids he reduces his quota for cream and milk byproducts.

(h) *Cream deliveries.* The units of cream delivered subject to quota in any quota period shall not exceed 100 percent of the units of cream in his base, irrespective of the milk solids content of such deliveries.

(i) *Handler exemptions.* Quota shall not apply to any handler who delivers in a quota period a daily average of less than 200 units of milk, cream, and milk byproducts. For the purpose of this order, a unit shall be the equivalent in volume of the following: (1) One quart of milk, buttermilk, or fluid milk byproducts; (2) one-half pint of cream; and (3) one-half pound of cottage, pot, or baker's cheese.

(j) *Quota exclusions and exemptions.* Deliveries of milk, milk byproducts, or cream (1) to other handlers, except for such deliveries to sub-handlers, (2) to plants engaged in the handling or processing of milk, milk byproducts, cream or other dairy products from which no milk, milk byproducts, or cream, is delivered in the sales area, (3) to industrial users, and (4) to the agencies or groups specified in (d) of FDO 79, shall be excluded from the computation of deliveries in the base period and exempt from charges to quotas.

(k) *Transfers of bases.* The market agent is empowered to transfer base from one handler to another.

(1) Upon receipt of a request in writing from both handlers; and

(2) Upon application from a handler and written notice to the Director and to both handlers, (i) to permit deliveries to a purchaser not being served by a handler whose quota reflects deliveries to such purchaser in the base period, (ii) to permit a handler to serve an account which customarily rotates among several handlers inclusive of a contract let by a public agency or institution on a bid basis, and (iii) to permit a handler to serve an account which he is serving on the effective date of this order and which was served by another handler during the base period.

(l) *Consumer priorities.* In the distribution of milk subject to quotas established hereunder, a handler shall give preference in the order listed, taking into consideration the type of purchasers served by him in the base period, to:

(1) The need of children, expectant mothers, and invalids requiring milk;

(2) Homes and retail stores handling milk for consumption off the premises; and

(3) Establishments serving milk for consumption on the premises.

(m) *Petition for relief from hardship.* (1) Any person affected by FDO 79 or the provisions hereof who considers that compliance therewith would work an exceptional and unreasonable hardship on him, may file with the market agent a petition addressed to the Director. The petition shall contain the correct name, address and principal place of business of the petitioner, a full statement of the facts upon which the petition is based, and the hardship involved and the nature of the relief desired.

(2) Upon receiving such petition the market agent shall immediately investigate representations and facts stated therein.

(3) After investigation, the petition shall be certified to the Director, but prior to certification the market agent may (i) deny the petition or (ii) grant temporary relief for a total period not to exceed 60 days.

(4) Denials or grants of relief by the market agent shall be reviewed by the Director and may be affirmed, modified, or reversed by the Director.

(n) *Reports.* Each handler shall transmit to the market agent on forms prescribed by the market agent the following reports:

(1) Within 20 days following the effective date of this order, reports which show the information required by the market agent to establish such handler's quotas;

(2) Within 20 days following the close of each quota period, the information required by the market agent to establish volumes of deliveries of milk, cream and milk byproducts during the preceding quota period; and

(3) Handlers exempt from quota pursuant to (i) hereof shall, upon the request of the market agent, submit the information required by the market agent to establish volumes of deliveries of milk, cream, and milk byproducts.

(o) *Records.* Handlers shall keep and shall make available to the market agent such records of receipts, sales, deliveries, and production as the market agent shall require for the purpose of obtaining information which the Director may require for the establishment of quotas as prescribed in (b) of FDO 79.

(p) *Expense of administration.* Each handler shall pay to the market agent, within 20 days after the close of each calendar month, an assessment of $0.015 per hundredweight of each of milk, milk byproducts, cream, and skim milk equivalent of cottage, pot, or baker's cheese delivered during the preceding quota period and subject to quota regulations under the provisions hereof.

(q) *Violations.* The market agent shall report all violations to the Director together with the information required for the prosecution of such violations.

(r) *Bureau of the Budget approval.* The record-keeping and reporting requirements of this order have been approved by the Bureau of the Budget in accordance with the Federal Reports Act of 1942. Subsequent record-keeping or reporting requirements will be subject to the approval of the Bureau of the Budget pursuant to the Federal Reports Act of 1942.

(s) *Effective date.* This order shall take effect at 12:01 a. m., e. w. t., February 1, 1944.

(E.O. 9280, 7 F.R. 10179; E.O. 9322, 8 F.R. 3807; E.O. 9334, 8 F.R. 5423; E.O. 9392, 8 F.R. 14783; FDO 79, 8 F.R. 12426, 13283)

Issued this 13th day of January 1944.

ROY F. HENDRICKSON,
Director of Food Distribution.

War Food Administration:
Summary to FDO-79.124-FDO 79.130.

Nine New Milk Sales Areas Named

Milk sales in 9 metropolitan areas in Texas, Louisiana, and Arkansas will be regulated under the Food Distribution Administration's Fluid milk conservation and control program, beginning February 1, 1944.

The new milk sales areas are:

Waco, Texas (FDO 79.123); Dallas, Texas (FDO 79.124); Ft. Worth, Texas (FDO 79.125); Austin, Texas (FDO 79.126); Galveston, Texas (FDO 79.127); San Antonio, Texas (FDO 79.128); Houston, Texas (FDO 79.122); Shreveport, Louisiana (FDO 79.129); Little Rock, Arkansas (FDO 79.130).

Market agents who will administer the orders in each area will be named later.

Under the program, milk dealers will be permitted to deliver to all customers except schools as much fluid milk as they delivered in June and three-fourths as much milk in cream and milk byproducts (such as cottage cheese, chocolate milk and buttermilk) as they sold in June. Deliveries to elementary, junior high and high schools will be under the same restrictions except the number of school days in May will be used as the base period in determining quotas, rather than June. Milk dealers include all persons or firms engaged in the delivery of transfer of milk, but not such distributors as subhandlers ("peddlers"), retail stores, hotels, or restaurants.

Producer distributors who purchase no milk will be permitted to deliver as much milk as they delivered in either June or December, whichever represents their larger total deliveries.

The order permits dealers to deliver more fluid milk than their quotas allow, provided they use less milk solids in deliveries of cream or milk byproducts. Since cream and milk byproducts are recognized as one quota group, dealers may deliver more cream, but not more than 100% of the deliveries of cream in the base period by cutting down on milk solids used in milk byproducts, or more byproducts by reducing the amount of milk solids used in cream.

In distributing the milk, cream and byproducts allowed under their quotas, dealers are required to give preference to the following consumer groups, in the order listed, taking into consideration the type of purchasers they served in the base period:

1. Children, expectant mothers, and invalids requiring milk;
2. Homes and retail stores handling milk for consumption off the premises;
3. Establishments serving milk for consumption on the premises.

Deliveries of milk, cream and milk by products to other dealers; to the Armed Forces; to plants engaged in handling or processing milk, byproducts and cream which are not distributed in the sales area; and to designated industrial manufacturers who use milk, cream, or milk byproducts in making products which are sold off the premises are quota exempt.

Consumers in the milk sales areas named today, as in others already designated, generally will be able to purchase as much milk under the milk conservation program as they have been buying in recent months. Fluid milk sales are being stabilized, and sales of cream and milk byproducts are being reduced, FDA officials said, to help assure sufficient milk for manufacturing the cheese, butter, evaporated milk, and milk powder required by the armed forces and civilians for good nutrition and properly balanced diets.

FDO 79-124

JAN. 13, 1944

WAR FOOD ADMINISTRATION

[FDO 79-124] A

PART 1401—DAIRY PRODUCTS

FLUID MILK AND CREAM IN THE DALLAS, TEX., SALES AREA

Pursuant to the authority vested in me by Food Distribution Order No. 79 (8 F.R. 12426), issued on September 7, 1943, as amended, and to effectuate the purposes of such order, it is hereby ordered as follows:

§ 1401.157 *Quota restrictions*—(a) *Definitions.* When used in this order, unless otherwise distinctly expressed or manifestly incompatible with the intent hereof:

(1) Each term defined in Food Distribution Order No. 79, as amended, shall, when used herein, have the same meaning as is set forth for such term in Food Distribution Order No. 79, as amended.

(2) The term "FDO 79" means Food Distribution Order No. 79, issued on September 7, 1943, as amended.

(3) The term "sub-handler" means any handler, such as a peddler, vendor, sub-dealer, or secondary dealer, who purchases in a previously packaged and processed form milk, cream, or milk byproducts for delivery.

(4) The term "industrial user" means a person, as determined by the market agent, in the capacity of a manufacturer of products using as an ingredient therein milk, cream, or milk byproducts, which products are disposed of for resale to consumers off the premises where made.

(5) The term "base" means the total pounds of milk solids delivered by a handler within the sales area during the base period (i) in the form of milk, or (ii) in the form of cream and milk byproducts, minus the milk solids in quota-exempt deliveries of milk, and cream and milk byproducts, as described in (j) hereof. (For the purpose of this order, the milk solids content of milk, milk byproducts, and cream shall be computed as follows: Each hundredweight of milk, cream, or milk byproducts other than cottage, pot, or baker's cheese, shall be considered the equivalent of 9.375 pounds of milk solids plus the number of pounds of milk solids calculated by multiplying the pounds of butterfat in such milk, and cream and milk byproducts by .906; and each hundredweight of cottage, pot, or baker's cheese shall be considered the equivalent of 62.5 pounds of milk solids plus one pound of milk solids for each one percent of butterfat content of such cheese.)

(b) *Milk sales area.* The following area is hereby designated as a "milk sales area" to be known as the Dallas, Texas, milk sales area, and is referred to hereinafter as the "sales area":

The city of Dallas and justices' precincts 1, 2, 3, 7, and 8, all in Dallas County, Texas.

(c) *Base period.* The calendar month of June 1943 is hereby designated as the base period for the sales area: *Provided,* That the month of May may be used as the base period for computing base and quota for deliveries to elementary, junior high and high schools; *And provided further,* That in the computations set forth in (e) hereof the total deliveries to elementary, junior high, and high schools in the base period shall be divided by the number of days such schools were in session in lieu of the total number of days in the base period as set forth in (e) (1) and the average daily deliveries so determined shall be multiplied by the number of days such schools are in session in each quota period in lieu of the number of days in the quota period as set forth in (e) (2).

(d) The remainder of the calendar month in which the provisions hereof become effective and each subsequent calendar month, respectively, is hereby designated as the quota period for the sales area.

(e) *Handler quotas.* Quotas for each handler other than a sub-handler or producer-handler shall be determined as follows:

(1) Divide his respective bases by the number of days in the base period;

(2) Multiply the foregoing result by the number of days in the quota period; and

(3) Multiply the aforesaid resulting amounts by 100 percent in the case of the base for milk, and 75 percent in the case of the base for cream and milk byproducts.

(f) *Quotas for handlers who are also producers.* Quotas for each handler who is also a producer and who purchases no milk shall be computed in accordance with (e) hereof, except:

(1) His base period shall be either June or December, whichever represents his larger total deliveries; and

(2) The applicable percentages shall be 100 percent in lieu of those specified in (e) (3).

(g) *Quota adjustments.* Each handler may increase his quota for milk within any quota period by one pound of milk solids for each one pound of milk solids he reduces his quota for cream and milk byproducts.

(h) *Cream deliveries.* The units of cream delivered subject to quota in any quota period shall not exceed 100 percent of the units of cream in his base, irrespective of the milk solids content of such deliveries.

(i) *Handler exemptions.* Quota shall not apply to any handler who delivers in a quota period a daily average of less than 200 units of milk, cream, and milk byproducts. For the purpose of this order, a unit shall be the equivalent in volume of the following: (1) One quart of milk, buttermilk, or fluid milk byproducts; (2) one-half pint of cream; and (3) one-half pound of cottage, pot, or baker's cheese.

(j) *Quota exclusions and exemptions.* Deliveries of milk, milk byproducts, or cream (1) to other handlers, except for such deliveries to sub-handlers, (2) to plants engaged in the handling or processing of milk, milk byproducts, cream or other dairy products from which no milk, milk byproducts, or cream, is delivered in the sales area, (3) to industrial users, and (4) to the agencies or groups specified in (d) of FDO 79, shall be excluded from the computation of deliveries in the base period and exempt from charges to quotas.

(k) *Transfers of bases.* The market agent is empowered to transfer base from one handler to another.

(1) Upon receipt of a request in writing from both handlers; and

(2) Upon application from a handler and written notice to the Director and to both handlers, (i) to permit deliveries to a purchaser not being served by a handler whose quota reflects deliveries to such purchaser in the base period, (ii) to permit a handler to serve an account which customarily rotates among several handlers inclusive of a contract let by a public agency or institution on a bid basis, and (iii) to permit a handler to serve an account which he is serving on the effective date of this order and which was served by another handler during the base period.

(l) *Consumer priorities.* In the distribution of milk subject to quotas established hereunder, a handler shall give preference in the order listed, taking into consideration the type of purchasers served by him in the base period, to:

(1) The need of children, expectant mothers, and invalids requiring milk;

(2) Homes and retail stores handling milk for consumption off the premises; and

(3) Establishments serving milk for consumption on the premises.

(m) *Petition for relief from hardship.* (1) Any person affected by FDO 79 or the provisions hereof who considers that compliance therewith would work an exceptional and unreasonable hardship on him, may file with the market agent a petition addressed to the Director. The petition shall contain the correct name, address and principal place of business of the petitioner, a full statement of the facts upon which the petition is based, and the hardship involved and the nature of the relief desired.

(2) Upon receiving such petition the market agent shall immediately investigate representations and facts stated therein.

(3) After investigation, the petition shall be certified to the Director, but prior to certification the market agent may (i) deny the petition or (ii) grant temporary relief for a total period not to exceed 60 days.

(4) Denials or grants of relief by the market agent shall be reviewed by the Director and may be affirmed, modified, or reversed by the Director.

(n) *Reports.* Each handler shall transmit to the market agent on forms prescribed by the market agent the following reports:

(1) Within 20 days following the effective date of this order, reports which show the information required by the market agent to establish such handler's quotas;

(2) Within 20 days following the close of each quota period, the information required by the market agent to establish volumes of deliveries of milk, cream, and milk byproducts during the preceding quota period; and

(3) Handlers exempt from quotas pursuant to (i) hereof shall, upon the request of the market agent, submit the information required by the market agent to establish volumes of deliveries of milk, cream, and milk byproducts.

(o) *Records.* Handlers shall keep and shall make available to the market agent such records of receipts, sales, deliveries, and production as the market agent shall require for the purpose of obtaining information which the Director may require for the establishment of quotas as prescribed in (b) of FDO 79.

(p) *Expense of administration.* Each handler shall pay to the market agent, within 20 days after the close of each calendar month, an assessment of $0.015 per hundredweight of each of milk, milk byproducts, cream, and skim milk equivalent of cottage, pot, or baker's cheese delivered during the preceding quota period and subject to quota regulations under the provisions hereof.

(q) *Violations.* The market agent shall report all violations to the Director together with the information required for the prosecution of such violations.

(r) *Bureau of the Budget approval.* The record-keeping and reporting requirements of this order have been approved by the Bureau of the Budget in accordance with the Federal Reports Act of 1942. Subsequent record-keeping or reporting requirements will be subject to the approval of the Bureau of the Budget pursuant to the Federal Reports Act of 1942.

(s) *Effective date.* This order shall take effect at 12:01 a. m., e. w. t., February 1, 1944.

(E.O. 9280, 7 F.R. 10179; E.O. 9322, 8 F.R. 3807; E.O. 9334, 8 F.R. 5423; E.O. 9392, 8 F.R. 14783; FDO 79, 8 F.R. 12426, 13283)

Issued this 13th day of January 1944.

ROY F. HENDRICKSON,
Director of Food Distribution.

War Food Administration:
Summary to FDO-79.124-FDO 79.130.

Nine New Milk Sales Areas Named

Milk sales in 9 metropolitan areas in Texas, Louisiana, and Arkansas will be regulated under the Food Distribution Administration's Fluid milk conservation and control program, beginning February 1, 1944.

The new milk sales areas are:

Waco, Texas (FDO 79.123); Dallas, Texas (FDO 79.124); Ft. Worth, Texas (FDO 79.125); Austin, Texas (FDO 79.126); Galveston, Texas (FDO 79.127); San Antonio, Texas (FDO 79.128); Houston, Texas (FDO 79.122); Shreveport, Louisiana (FDO 79.129); Little Rock, Arkansas (FDO 79.130).

Market agents who will administer the orders in each area will be named later.

Under the program, milk dealers will be permitted to deliver to all customers except schools as much fluid milk as they delivered in June and three-fourths as much milk in cream and milk byproducts (such as cottage cheese, chocolate milk and buttermilk) as they sold in June. Deliveries to elementary, junior high and high schools will be under the same restrictions except the number of school days in May will be used as the base period in determining quotas, rather than June. Milk dealers include all persons or firms engaged in the delivery of transfer of milk, but not such distributors as subhandlers ("peddlers"), retail stores, hotels, or restaurants.

Producer distributors who purchase no milk will be permitted to deliver as much milk as they delivered in either June or December, whichever represents their larger total deliveries.

The order permits dealers to deliver more fluid milk than their quotas allow, provided they use less milk solids in deliveries of cream or milk byproducts. Since cream and milk byproducts are recognized as one quota group, dealers may deliver more cream, but not more than 100% of the deliveries of cream in the base period by cutting down on milk solids used in milk byproducts, or more byproducts by reducing the amount of milk solids used in cream.

In distributing the milk, cream and byproducts allowed under their quotas, dealers are required to give preference to the following consumer groups, in the order listed, taking into consideration the type of purchasers they served in the base period:

1. Children, expectant mothers, and invalids requiring milk;
2. Homes and retail stores handling milk for consumption off the premises;
3. Establishments serving milk for consumption on the premises.

Deliveries of milk, cream and milk byproducts to other dealers; to the Armed Forces; to plants engaged in handling or processing milk, byproducts and cream which are not distributed in the sales area; and to designated industrial manufacturers who use milk, cream, or milk byproducts in making products which are sold off the premises are quota exempt.

Consumers in the milk sales areas named today, as in others already designated, generally will be able to purchase as much milk under the milk conservation program as they have been buying in recent months. Fluid milk sales are being stabilized, and sales of cream and milk byproducts are being reduced, FDA officials said, to help assure sufficient milk for manufacturing the cheese, butter, evaporated milk, and milk powder required by the armed forces and civilians for good nutrition and properly balanced diets.

[FDO 79-125] A

PART 1401—DAIRY PRODUCTS

FLUID MILK AND CREAM IN THE FT. WORTH, TEX., SALES AREA

Pursuant to the authority vested in me by Food Distribution Order No. 79 (8 F.R. 12426), issued on September 7, 1943, as amended, and to effectuate the purposes of such order, it is hereby ordered as follows:

§ 1401.158 *Quota restrictions*—(a) *Definitions.* When used in this order, unless otherwise distinctly expressed or manifestly incompatible with the intent hereof:

(1) Each term defined in Food Distribution Order No. 79, as amended, shall, when used herein, have the same meaning as is set forth for such term in Food Distribution Order No. 79, as amended.

(2) The term "FDO 79" means Food Distribution Order No. 79, issued on September 7, 1943, as amended.

(3) The term "sub-handler" means any handler, such as a peddler, vendor, sub-dealer, or secondary dealer, who purchases in a previously packaged and processed form milk, cream, or milk byproducts for delivery.

(4) The term "industrial user" means a person, as determined by the market agent, in the capacity of a manufacturer of products using as an ingredient therein milk, cream, or milk byproducts, which products are disposed of for resale to consumers off the premises where made.

(5) The term "base" means the total pounds of milk solids delivered by a handler within the sales area during the base period (i) in the form of milk, or (ii) in the form of cream and milk byproducts, minus the milk solids in quota-exempt deliveries of milk, and cream and milk byproducts, as described in (j) hereof. (For the purpose of this order, the milk solids content of milk, milk byproducts, and cream shall be computed as follows: Each hundredweight of milk, cream, or milk byproducts other than cottage, pot, or baker's cheese, shall be considered the equivalent of 9.375 pounds of milk solids plus the number of pounds of milk solids calculated by multiplying the pounds of butterfat in such milk, and cream and milk byproducts by .906; and each hundredweight of cottage, pot, or baker's cheese shall be considered the equivalent of 62.5 pounds of milk solids plus one pound of milk solids for each one percent of butterfat content of such cheese.)

(b) *Milk sales area.* The following area is hereby designated as a "milk sales area" to be known as the Fort Worth, Texas, milk sales area, and is referred to hereinafter as the "sales area":

The city of Fort Worth and justices' precincts 1, 2, 5, and 6, all in Tarrant County, Texas.

(c) *Base period.* The calendar month of June 1943 is hereby designated as the base period for the sales area: *Provided,* That the month of May may be used as the base period for computing base and quota for deliveries to elementary, junior high and high schools: *And provided further,* That in the computations set forth in (e) hereof the total deliveries to elementary, junior high, and high schools in the base period shall be divided by the number of days such schools were in session in lieu of the total number of days in the base period as set forth in (e) (1) and the average daily deliveries so determined shall be multiplied by the number of days such schools are in session in each quota period in lieu of the number of days in the quota period as set forth in (e) (2).

(d) The remainder of the calendar month in which the provisions hereof become effective and each subsequent calendar month, respectively, is hereby designated as the quota period for the sales area.

(e) *Handler quotas.* Quotas for each handler other than a sub-handler or producer-handler shall be determined as follows:

(1) Divide his respective bases by the number of days in the base period;

(2) Multiply the foregoing result by the number of days in the quota period; and

(3) Multiply the aforesaid resulting amounts by 100 percent in the case of the base for milk, and 75 percent in the case of the base for cream and milk byproducts.

(f) *Quotas for handlers who are also producers.* Quotas for each handler who is also a producer and who purchases no milk shall be computed in accordance with (e) hereof, except:

(1) His base period shall be either June or December, whichever represents his larger total deliveries; and

(2) The applicable percentages shall be 100 percent in lieu of those specified in (e) (3).

(g) *Quota adjustments.* Each handler may increase his quota for milk within any quota period by one pound of milk solids for each one pound of milk solids he reduces his quota for cream and milk byproducts.

(h) *Cream deliveries.* The units of cream delivered subject to quota in any quota period shall not exceed 100 percent of the units of cream in his base, irrespective of the milk solids content of such deliveries.

(i) *Handler exemptions.* Quota shall not apply to any handler who delivers in a quota period a daily average of less than 200 units of milk, cream, and milk byproducts. For the purpose of this order, a unit shall be the equivalent in volume of the following: (1) One quart of milk, buttermilk, or fluid milk byproducts; (2) one-half pint of cream; and (3) one-half pound of cottage, pot, or baker's cheese.

(j) *Quota exclusions and exemptions.* Deliveries of milk, milk byproducts, or cream (1) to other handlers, except for such deliveries to sub-handlers, (2) to plants engaged in the handling or processing of milk, milk byproducts, cream or other dairy products from which no milk, milk byproducts, or cream, is delivered in the sales area, (3) to industrial users, and (4) to the agencies or groups specified in (d) of FDO 79, shall be excluded from the computation of deliveries in the base period and exempt from charges to quotas.

(k) *Transfers of bases.* The market agent is empowered to transfer base from one handler to another.

(1) Upon receipt of a request in writing from both handlers; and

(2) Upon application from a handler and written notice to the Director and to both handlers, (i) to permit deliveries to a purchaser not being served by a handler whose quota reflects deliveries to such purchaser in the base period, (ii) to permit a handler to serve an account which customarily rotates among several handlers inclusive of a contract let by a public agency or institution on a bid basis, and (iii) to permit a handler to serve an account which he is serving on the effective date of this order and which was served by another handler during the base period.

(l) *Consumer priorities.* In the distribution of milk subject to quotas established hereunder, a handler shall give preference in the order listed, taking into consideration the type of purchasers served by him in the base period, to:

(1) The need of children, expectant mothers, and invalids requiring milk;

(2) Homes and retail stores handling milk for consumption off the premises; and

(3) Establishments serving milk for consumption on the premises.

(m) *Petition for relief from hardship.* (1) Any person affected by FDO 79 or the provisions hereof who considers that compliance therewith would work an exceptional and unreasonable hardship on him, may file with the market agent a petition addressed to the Director. The petition shall contain the correct name, address and principal place of business of the petitioner, a full statement of the facts upon which the petition is based, and the hardship involved and the nature of the relief desired.

(2) Upon receiving such petition the market agent shall immediately investigate representations and facts stated therein.

(3) After investigation, the petition shall be certified to the Director, but prior to certification the market agent may (i) deny the petition or (ii) grant temporary relief for a total period not to exceed 60 days.

(4) Denials or grants of relief by the market agent shall be reviewed by the Director and may be affirmed, modified, or reversed by the Director.

(n) *Reports.* Each handler shall transmit to the market agent on forms prescribed by the market agent the following reports:

(1) Within 20 days following the effective date of this order, reports which show the information required by the market agent to establish such handler's quotas;

(2) Within 20 days following the close of each quota period, the information required by the market agent to establish volumes of deliveries of milk, cream and milk byproducts during the preceding quota period; and

(3) Handlers exempt from quotas pursuant to (i) hereof shall, upon the request of the market agent, submit the information required by the market agent to establish volumes of deliveries of milk, cream, and milk byproducts.

(o) *Records.* Handlers shall keep and shall make available to the market agent such records of receipts, sales, deliveries, and production as the market agent shall require for the purpose of obtaining information which the Director may require for the establishment of quotas as prescribed in (b) of FDO 79.

(p) *Expense of administration.* Each handler shall pay to the market agent, within 20 days after the close of each calendar month, an assessment of $0.015 per hundredweight of each of milk, milk byproducts, cream, and skim milk equivalent of cottage, pot, or baker's cheese delivered during the preceding quota period and subject to quota regulations under the provisions hereof.

(q) *Violations.* The market agent shall report all violations to the Director together with the information required for the prosecution of such violations.

(r) *Bureau of the Budget approval.* The record-keeping and reporting requirements of this order have been approved by the Bureau of the Budget in accordance with the Federal Reports Act of 1942. Subsequent record-keeping or reporting requirements will be subject to the approval of the Bureau of the Budget pursuant to the Federal Reports Act of 1942.

(s) *Effective date.* This order shall take effect at 12:01 a. m., e. w. t., February 1, 1944.

(E.O. 9280, 7 F.R. 10179; E.O. 9322, 8 F.R. 3807; E.O. 9334, 8 F.R. 5423; E.O. 9392, 8 F.R. 14783; FDO 79, 8 F.R. 12426, 13283)

Issued this 13th day of January 1944.

ROY F. HENDRICKSON,
Director of Food Distribution.

War Food Administration:
Summary to FDO-79.124-FDO 79.130.

Nine New Milk Sales Areas Named

Milk sales in 9 metropolitan areas in Texas, Louisiana, and Arkansas will be regulated under the Food Distribution Administration's Fluid milk conservation and control program, beginning February 1, 1944.

The new milk sales areas are:

Waco, Texas (FDO 79.123); Dallas, Texas (FDO 79.124); Ft. Worth, Texas (FDO 79.125); Austin, Texas (FDO 79.126); Galveston, Texas (FDO 79.127); San Antonio, Texas (FDO 79.128); Houston, Texas, (FDO 79.122); Shreveport, Louisiana (FDO 79.129); Little Rock, Arkansas (FDO 79.130).

Market agents who will administer the orders in each area will be named later.

Under the program, milk dealers will be permitted to deliver to all customers except schools as much fluid milk as they delivered in June and three-fourths as much milk in cream and milk byproducts (such as cottage cheese, chocolate milk and buttermilk) as they sold in June. Deliveries to elementary, junior high and high schools will be under the same restrictions except the number of school days in May will be used as the base period in determining quotas, rather than June. Milk dealers include all persons or firms engaged in the delivery of transfer of milk, but not such distributors as subhandlers ("peddlers"), retail stores, hotels, or restaurants.

Producer distributors who purchase no milk will be permitted to deliver as much milk as they delivered in either June or December, whichever represents their larger total deliveries.

The order permits dealers to deliver more fluid milk than their quotas allow, provided they use less milk solids in deliveries of cream or milk byproducts. Since cream and milk byproducts are recognized as one quota group, dealers may deliver more cream, but not more than 100% of the deliveries of cream in the base period by cutting down on milk solids used in milk byproducts, or more byproducts by reducing the amount of milk solids used in cream.

In distributing the milk, cream and byproducts allowed under their quotas, dealers are required to give preference to the following consumer groups, in the order listed, taking into consideration the type of purchasers they served in the base period:

1. Children, expectant mothers, and invalids requiring milk;
2. Homes and retail stores handling milk for consumption off the premises;
3. Establishments serving milk for consumption on the premises.

Deliveries of milk, cream and milk byproducts to other dealers; to the Armed Forces; to plants engaged in handling or processing milk, byproducts and cream which are not distributed in the sales area; and to designated industrial manufacturers who use milk, cream, or milk byproducts in making products which are sold off the premises are quota exempt.

Consumers in the milk sales areas named today, as in others already designated, generally will be able to purchase as much milk under the milk conservation program as they have been buying in recent months. Fluid milk sales are being stabilized, and sales of cream and milk byproducts are being reduced, FDA officials said, to help assure sufficient milk for manufacturing the cheese, butter, evaporated milk, and milk powder required by the armed forces and civilians for good nutrition and properly balanced diets.

FDO 79-126
JAN. 13, 1944

WAR FOOD ADMINISTRATION

[FDO 79-126]

PART 1401—DAIRY PRODUCTS

FLUID MILK AND CREAM IN THE AUSTIN, TEX., SALES AREA

Pursuant to the authority vested in me by Food Distribution Order No. 79 (8 F.R. 12426), issued on September 7, 1943, as amended, and to effectuate the purposes of such order, it is hereby ordered as follows:

§ 1401.159 *Quota restrictions*—(a) *Definitions.* When used in this order, unless otherwise distinctly expressed or manifestly incompatible with the intent hereof:

(1) Each term defined in Food Distribution Order No. 79, as amended, shall, when used herein, have the same meaning as is set forth for such term in Food Distribution Order No. 79, as amended.

(2) The term "FDO 79" means Food Distribution Order No. 79, issued on September 7, 1943, as amended.

(3) The term "sub-handler" means any handler, such as a peddler, vendor, sub-dealer, or secondary dealer, who purchases in a previously packaged and processed form milk, cream, or milk byproducts for delivery.

(4) The term "industrial user" means a person, as determined by the market agent, in the capacity of a manufacturer of products using as an ingredient therein milk, cream, or milk byproducts, which products are disposed of for resale to consumers off the premises where made.

(5) The term "base" means the total pounds of milk solids delivered by a handler within the sales area during the base period (i) in the form of milk, or (ii) in the form of cream and milk byproducts, minus the milk solids in quota-exempt deliveries of milk, and cream and milk byproducts, as decribed in (j) hereof. (For the purpose of this order, the milk solids content of milk, milk byproducts, and cream shall be computed as follows: Each hundredweight of milk, cream, or milk byproducts other than cottage, pot, or baker's cheese, shall be considered the equivalent of 9.375 pounds of milk solids plus the number of pounds of milk solids calculated by multiplying the pounds of butterfat in such milk, and cream and milk byproducts by .906; and each hundredweight of cottage, pot, or baker's cheese shall be considered the equivalent of 62.5 pounds of milk solids plus one pound of milk solids for each one percent of butterfat content of such cheese.)

(b) *Milk sales area.* The following area is hereby designated as a "milk sales area" to be known as the Austin, Texas, milk sales area, and is referred to hereinafter as the "sales area":

The city of Austin and justices' precincts 1, 2, 3, 5, and 6 in Travis County, all in the State of Texas.

(c) *Base period.* The calendar month of June 1943 is hereby designated as the base period for the sales area: *Provided,* That the month of May may be used as the base period for computing base and quota for deliveries to elementary, junior high and high schools: *And provided further,* That in the computations set forth in (e) hereof the total deliveries to elementary, junior high, and high schools in the base period shall be divided by the number of days such schools were in session in lieu of the total number of days in the base period as set forth in (e) (1) and the average daily deliveries so determined shall be multiplied by the number of days such schools are in session in each quota period in lieu of the number of days in the quota period as set forth in (e) (2)

(d) The remainder of the calendar month in which the provisions hereof become effective and each subsequent calendar month, respectively, is hereby designated as the quota period for the sales area.

(e) *Handler quotas.* Quotas for each handler other than a sub-handler or producer-handler shall be determined as follows:

(1) Divide his respective bases by the number of days in the base period;

(2) Multiply the foregoing result by the number of days in the quota period; and

(3) Multiply the aforesaid resulting amounts by 100 percent in the case of the base for milk, and 75 percent in the case of the base for cream and milk byproducts.

(f) *Quotas for handlers who are also producers.* Quotas for each handler who is also a producer and who purchases no milk shall be computed in accordance with (e) hereof, except:

(1) His base period shall be either June or December, whichever represents his larger total deliveries; and

(2) The applicable percentages shall be 100 percent in lieu of those specified in (e) (3).

(g) *Quota adjustments.* Each handler may increase his quota for milk within any quota period by one pound of milk solids for each one pound of milk solids he reduces his quota for cream and milk byproducts.

(h) *Cream deliveries.* The units of cream delivered subject to quota in any quota period shall not exceed 100 percent of the units of cream in his base, irrespective of the milk solids content of such deliveries.

(i) *Handler exemptions.* Quota shall not apply to any handler who delivers in a quota period a daily average of less than 200 units of milk, cream, and milk byproducts. For the purpose of this order, a unit shall be the equivalent in volume of the following: (1) One quart of milk, buttermilk, or fluid milk byproducts; (2) one-half pint of cream, and (3) one-half pound of cottage, pot, or baker's cheese.

(j) *Quota exclusions and exemptions.* Deliveries of milk, milk byproducts, or cream (1) to other handlers, except for such deliveries to sub-handlers, (2) to plants engaged in the handling or processing of milk, milk byproducts, cream or other dairy products from which no milk, milk byproducts, or cream, is delivered in the sales area, (3) to industrial users, and (4) to the agencies or groups specified in (d) of FDO 79, shall be excluded from the computation of deliveries in the base period and exempt from charges to quotas.

(k) *Transfers of bases.* The market agent is empowered to transfer base from one handler to another.

(1) Upon receipt of a request in writing from both handlers; and

(2) Upon application from a handler and written notice to the Director and to both handlers, (i) to permit deliveries to a purchaser not being served by a handler whose quota reflects deliveries to such purchaser in the base period, (ii) to permit a handler to serve an account which customarily rotates among several handlers inclusive of a contract let by a public agency or institution on a bid basis, and (iii) to permit a handler to serve an account which he is serving on the effective date of this order and which was served by another handler during the base period.

(l) *Consumer priorities.* In the distribution of milk subject to quotas established hereunder, a handler shall give preference in the order listed, taking

into consideration the type of purchasers served by him in the base period, to:

(1) The need of children, expectant mothers, and invalids requiring milk;

(2) Homes and retail stores handling milk for consumption off the premises; and

(3) Establishments serving milk for consumption on the premises.

(m) *Petition for relief from hardship.* (1) Any person affected by FDO 79 or the provisions hereof who considers that compliance therewith would work an exceptional and unreasonable hardship on him, may file with the market agent a petition addressed to the Director. The petition shall contain the correct name, address and principal place of business of the petitioner, a full statement of the facts upon which the petition is based, and the hardship involved and the nature of the relief desired.

(2) Upon receiving such petition the market agent shall immediately investigate representations and facts stated therein.

(3) After investigation, the petition shall be certified to the Director, but prior to certification the market agent may (i) deny the petition or (ii) grant temporary relief for a total period not to exceed 60 days.

(4) Denials or grants of relief by the market agent shall be reviewed by the Director and may be affirmed, modified, or reversed by the Director.

(n) *Reports.* Each handler shall transmit to the market agent on forms prescribed by the market agent the following reports:

(1) Within 20 days following the effective date of this order, reports which show the information required by the market agent to establish such handler's quotas;

(2) Within 20 days following the close of each quota period, the information required by the market agent to establish volumes of deliveries of milk, cream and milk byproducts during the preceding quota period; and

(3) Handlers exempt from quotas pursuant to (i) hereof shall, upon the request of the market agent, submit the information required by the market agent to establish volumes of deliveries of milk, cream, and milk byproducts.

(o) *Records.* Handlers shall keep and shall make available to the market agent such records of receipts, sales, deliveries, and production as the market agent shall require for the purpose of obtaining information which the Director may require for the establishment of quotas as prescribed in (b) of FDO 79.

(p) *Expense of administration.* Each handler shall pay to the market agent, within 20 days after the close of each calendar month, an assessment of per hundredweight of each of mill byproducts, cream, and skim milk alent of cottage, pot, or baker's delivered during the preceding period and subject to quota regu under the provisions hereof.

(q) *Violations.* The market shall report all violations to the tor together with the informati quired for the prosecution of suc lations.

(r) *Bureau of the Budget ap* The record-keeping and reporti quirements of this order have be proved by the Bureau of the Buc accordance with the Federal Repo of 1942. Subsequent record-keep reporting requirements will be s to the approval of the Bureau Budget pursuant to the Federal R Act of 1942.

(s) *Effective date.* This order take effect at 12:01 a. m., e. w. t., ary 1, 1944.

(E. O. 9280, 7 F.R. 10179; E.O. F. R. 3807; E.O. 9334, 8 F.R. 542 9392, 8 F.R.14783; FDO 79, 8 F.R. 13283)

Issued this 13th day of Januar

ROY F. HENDRICKSC
Director of Food Distribu

War Food Administration:
Summary to FDO-79.124-FDO-79.130.

Nine New Milk Sales Areas Named

Milk sales in 9 metropolitan areas in Texas, Louisiana, and Arkansas will be regulated under the Food Distribution Administration's fluid milk conservation and control program, beginning February 1, 1944.

The new milk sales areas are:

Waco, Texas (FDO 79.123); Dallas, Texas (FDO 79.124); Ft. Worth, Texas (FDO 79.125); Austin, Texas (FDO 79.126); Galveston, Texas (FDO 79.127); San Antonio, Texas (FDO 79.128); Houston, Texas (FDO 79.122); Shreveport, Louisiana (FDO 79.129); Little Rock, Arkansas (FDO 79.130).

Market agents who will administer the orders in each area will be named later.

Under the program, milk dealers will be permitted to deliver to all customers except schools as much fluid milk as they delivered in June and three-fourths as much milk in cream and milk byproducts (such as cottage cheese, chocolate milk and buttermilk) as they sold in June. Deliveries to elementary, junior high and high schools will be under the same restrictions except the number of school days in May will be used as the base period in determining quotas, rather than June. Milk dealers include all persons or firms engaged in the delivery of transfer of milk, but not such distributors as subhandlers ("peddlers"), retail stores, hotels, or restaurants.

Producer distributors who purchase no milk will be permitted to deliver as much milk as they delivered in either June or December, whichever represents their larger total deliveries.

The order permits dealers to deliver more fluid milk than their quotas allow, provided they use less milk solids in deliveries of cream or milk byproducts. Since cream and milk byproducts are recognized as one quota group, dealers may deliver more cream, but not more than 100% of the deliveries of cream in the base period by cutting down on milk solids used in milk byproducts, or more byproducts by reducing the amount of milk solids used in cream.

In distributing the milk, cream and byproducts allowed under their quotas, dealers are required to give preference to the following consumer groups, in the order listed, taking into consideration the type of purchasers they served in the base period:

1. Children, expectant mother invalids requiring milk;

2. Homes and retail stores ha milk for consumption off the pre

3. Establishments serving mil consumption on the premises.

Deliveries of milk, cream and mi products to other dealers; to the Forces; to plants engaged in handl processing milk, byproducts and which are not distributed in the area; and to designated industrial facturers who use milk, cream, o byproducts in making products are sold off the premises are exempt.

Consumers in the milk sales named today, as in others already nated, generally will be able to pu as much milk under the milk con tion program as they have been in recent months. Fluid milk sal being stabilized, and sales of crea milk byproducts are being reduced officials said, to help assure su milk for manufacturing the chees ter, evaporated milk, and milk p required by the Armed Forces and ians for good nutrition and pr balanced diets.

WAR FOOD ADMINISTRATION
Food Distribution Administration
Washington 25, D. C.

CORRECTION NOTICE- 79-127 Dairy Products

In printing Food Distribution Order No. 79-127 the following error occurred:

(j) (2) In the phrase "to plants engaged in the handling of processing" the word "of" should be "or" so the phrase will read "to plants engaged in the handling or processing of milk."

FDO 79-127
JAN. 13, 1944

WAR FOOD ADMINISTRATION

[FDO 79-127] A

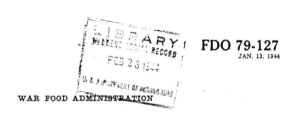

PART 1401—DAIRY PRODUCTS

FLUID MILK AND CREAM IN THE GALVESTON, TEX. SALES AREA

Pursuant to the authority vested in me by Food Distribution Order No. 79 (8 F.R. 12426), issued on September 7, 1943, as amended, and to effectuate the purposes of such order, it is hereby ordered as follows:

§ 1401.162 *Quota restrictions*—(a) *Definitions.* When used in this order, unless otherwise distinctly expressed or manifestly incompatible with the intent hereof:

(1) Each term defined in Food Distribution Order No. 79, as amended, shall, when used herein, have the same meaning as is set forth for such term in Food Distribution Order No. 79, as amended.

(2) The term "FDO 79" means Food Distribution Order No. 79, issued on September 7, 1943, as amended.

(3) The term "sub-handler" means any handler, such as a peddler, vendor, sub-dealer, or secondary dealer, who purchases in a previously packaged and processed form milk, cream, or milk byproducts for delivery.

(4) The term "industrial user" means a person, as determined by the market agent, in the capacity of a manufacturer of products using as an ingredient therein milk, cream, or milk byproducts, which products are disposed of for resale to consumers off the premises where made.

(5) The term "base" means the total pounds of milk solids delivered by a handler within the sales area during the base period (i) in the form of milk, or (ii) in the form of cream and milk byproducts, minus the milk solids in quota-exempt deliveries of milk, and cream and milk byproducts, as described in (j) hereof. (For the purpose of this order, the milk solids content of milk, milk byproducts, and cream shall be computed as follows: Each hundredweight of milk, cream, or milk byproducts other than cottage, pot, or baker's cheese, shall be considered the equivalent of 9.375 pounds of milk solids plus the number of pounds of milk solids calculated by multiplying the pounds of butterfat in such milk, and cream and milk byproducts by .906; and each hundredweight of cottage, pot, or baker's cheese shall be considered the equivalent of 62.5 pounds of milk solids plus one pound of milk solids for each one percent of butterfat content of such cheese.)

(b) *Milk sales area.* The following area is hereby designated as a "milk sales area" to be known as the Galveston, Texas, milk sales area, and is referred to hereinafter as the "sales area":

The city of Galveston and justices' precincts 1, 2, and 5, all in Galveston County, Texas.

(c) *Base period.* The calendar month of June 1943 is hereby designated as the base period for the sales area: *Provided,* That the month of May may be used as the base period for computing base and quota for deliveries to elementary, junior high and high schools: *And provided further,* That in the computations set forth in (e) hereof the total deliveries to elementary, junior high, and high schools in the base period shall be divided by the number of days such schools were in session in lieu of the total number of days in the base period as set forth in (e) (1) and the average daily deliveries so determined shall be multiplied by the number of days such schools are in session in each quota period in lieu of the number of days in the quota period as set forth in (e) (2).

(d) The remainder of the calendar month in which the provisions hereof become effective and each subsequent calendar month, respectively, is hereby designated as the quota period for the sales area.

(e) *Handler quotas.* Quotas for each handler other than a sub-handler or producer-handler shall be determined as follows:

(1) Divide his respective bases by the number of days in the base period;

(2) Multiply the foregoing result by the number of days in the quota period; and

(3) Multiply the aforesaid resulting amounts by 100 percent in the case of the base for milk, and 75 percent in the case of the base for cream and milk byproducts.

(f) *Quotas for handlers who are also producers.* Quotas for each handler who is also a producer and who purchases no milk shall be computed in accordance with (e) hereof, except:

(1) His base period shall be either June or December, whichever represents his larger total deliveries; and

(2) The applicable percentages shall be 100 percent in lieu of those specified in (e) (3).

(g) *Quota adjustments.* Each handler may increase his quota for milk within any quota period by one pound of milk solids for each one pound of milk solids he reduces his quota for cream and milk byproducts.

(h) *Cream deliveries.* The units of cream delivered subject to quota in any quota period shall not exceed 100 percent of the units of cream in his base, irrespective of the milk solids content of such deliveries.

(i) *Handler exemptions.* Quota shall not apply to any handler who delivers in a quota period a daily average of less than 200 units of milk, cream, and milk byproducts. For the purpose of this order, a unit shall be the equivalent in volume of the following: (1) One quart of milk, buttermilk, or fluid milk byproducts; (2) one-half pint of cream; and (3) one-half pound of cottage, pot, or baker's cheese.

(j) *Quota exclusions and exemptions.* Deliveries of milk, milk byproducts, or cream (1) to other handlers, except for such deliveries to sub-handlers, (2) to plants engaged in the handling of processing of milk, milk byproducts, cream or other dairy products from which no milk, milk byproducts, or cream, is delivered in the sales area, (3) to industrial users, and (4) to the agencies or groups specified in (d) of FDO 79, shall be excluded from the computation of deliveries in the base period and exempt from charges to quotas.

(k) *Transfers of bases.* The market agent is empowered to transfer base from one handler to another.

(1) Upon receipt of a request in writing from both handlers; and

(2) Upon application from a handler and written notice to the Director and to both handlers, (i) to permit deliveries to a purchaser not being served by a handler whose quota reflects deliveries to such purchaser in the base period, (ii) to permit a handler to serve an account which customarily rotates among several handlers inclusive of a contract let by a public agency or institution on a bid basis, and (iii) to permit a handler to serve an account which he is serving on the effective date of this order and which was served by another handler during the base period.

(l) *Consumer priorities.* In the distribution of milk subject to quotas established hereunder, a handler shall give preference in the order listed, taking into consideration the type of purchasers served by him in the base period, to:

(1) The need of children, expectant mothers, and invalids requiring milk;

(2) Homes and retail stores handling milk for consumption off the premises; and

(3) Establishments serving milk for consumption on the premises.

(m) *Petition for relief from hardship.* (1) Any person affected by FDO 79 or the provisions hereof who considers that compliance therewith would work an exceptional and unreasonable hardship on him, may file with the market agent a petition addressed to the Director. The petition shall contain the correct name, address and principal place of business of the petitioner, a full statement of the facts upon which the petition is based, and the hardship involved and the nature of the relief desired.

(2) Upon receiving such petition the market agent shall immediately investigate representations and facts stated therein.

(3) After investigation, the petition shall be certified to the Director, but prior to certification the market agent may (i) deny the petition or (ii) grant temporary relief for a total period not to exceed 60 days.

(4) Denials or grants of relief by the market agent shall be reviewed by the Director and may be affirmed, modified, or reversed by the Director.

(n) *Reports.* Each handler shall transmit to the market agent on forms prescribed by the market agent the following reports:

(1) Within 20 days following the effective date of this order, reports which show the information required by the market agent to establish such handler's quotas;

(2) Within 20 days following the close of each quota period, the information required by the market agent to establish volumes of deliveries of milk, cream, and milk byproducts during the preceding quota period; and

(3) Handlers exempt from quotas pursuant to (i) hereof shall, upon the request of the market agent, submit the information required by the market agent to establish volumes of deliveries of milk, cream, and milk byproducts.

(o) *Records.* Handlers shall keep and shall make available to the market agent such records of receipts, sales, deliveries, and production as the market agent shall require for the purpose of obtaining information which the Director may require for the establishment of quotas as prescribed in (b) of FDO 79.

(p) *Expense of administration.* Each handler shall pay to the market agent, within 20 days after the close of each calendar month, an assessment of $0.015 per hundredweight of each of milk, milk byproducts, cream, and skim milk e alent of cottage, pot, or baker's c delivered during the preceding period and subject to quota regul under the provisions hereof.

(q) *Violations.* The market shall report all violations to the Di together with the information rec for the prosecution of such violatio

(r) *Bureau of the Budget app* The record-keeping and reportin quirements of this order have bee proved by the Bureau of the Bud accordance with the Federal Repor of 1942. Subsequent record-keepi reporting requirements will be s to the approval of the Bureau o Budget pursuant to the Federal Re Act of 1942.

(s) *Effective date.* This order take effect at 12:01 a. m., e. w. t., F ary 1, 1944.

(E.O. 9280, 7 F.R. 10179; E.O. 9322, 3807; E.O. 9334, 8 F.R. 5423; E.O. 8 F.R. 14783; FDO 79, 8 F.R. 1 13283)

Issued this 13th day of January 19

ROY F. HENDRICKSON
Director of Food Distributi

War Food Administration:
Summary to FDO-79.124-FDO 79.130.

Nine New Milk Sales Areas Named

Milk sales in 9 metropolitan areas in Texas, Louisiana, and Arkansas will be regulated under the Food Distribution Administration's Fluid milk conservation and control program, beginning February 1, 1944.

The new milk sales areas are:

Waco, Texas (FDO 79.123); Dallas, Texas (FDO 79.124); Ft. Worth, Texas (FDO 79.125); Austin, Texas (FDO 79.126); Galveston, Texas (FDO 79.127); San Antonio, Texas (FDO 79.128); Houston, Texas (FDO 79.122); Shreveport, Louisiana (FDO 79.129); Little Rock, Arkansas (FDO 79.130).

Market agents who will administer the orders in each area will be named later.

Under the program, milk dealers will be permitted to deliver to all customers except schools as much fluid milk as they delivered in June and three-fourths as much milk in cream and milk byproducts (such as cottage cheese, chocolate milk and buttermilk) as they sold in June. Deliveries to elementary, junior high and high schools will be under the same restrictions except the number of school days in May will be used as the base period in determining quotas, rather than June. Milk dealers include all persons or firms engaged in the delivery of transfer of milk, but not such distributors as subhandlers ("peddlers"), retail stores, hotels, or restaurants.

Producer distributors who purchase no milk will be permitted to deliver as much milk as they delivered in either June or December, whichever represents their larger total deliveries.

The order permits dealers to deliver more fluid milk than their quotas allow, provided they use less milk solids in deliveries of cream or milk byproducts. Since cream and milk byproducts are recognized as one quota group, dealers may deliver more cream, but not more than 100% of the deliveries of cream in the base period by cutting down on milk solids used in milk byproducts, or more byproducts by reducing the amount of milk solids used in cream.

In distributing the milk, cream and byproducts allowed under their quotas, dealers are required to give preference to the following consumer groups, in the order listed, taking into consideration the type of purchasers they served i base period:

1. Children, expectant mothers, invalids requiring milk;
2. Homes and retail stores hand milk for consumption off the prem
3. Establishments serving milk consumption on the premises.

Deliveries of milk, cream and milk products to other dealers; to the A Forces; to plants engaged in handlir processing milk, byproducts and c which are not distributed in the area; and to designated industrial m facturers who use milk, cream, or byproducts in making products whic sold off the premises are quota exen

Consumers in the milk sales named today, as in others already d nated, generally will be able to purc as much milk under the milk conse tion program as they have been bu in recent months. Fluid milk sale being stabilized, and sales of cream milk byproducts are being reduced, officials said, to help assure suffi milk for manufacturing the cheese, ter, evaporated milk, and milk po required by the armed forces and ians for good nutrition and pro balanced diets.

WAR FOOD ADMINISTRATION
Food Distrubition Administration
Washington 25, D. C.

CORRECTION NOTICE- FDO 79-128 Dairy Products

In printing Food Distribution Order No, 79-128 the following error occurred:

(b) In the sentence beginning "The city of San Antonio" the word "Lean" is incorrect. The phrase should read "lying east of Leon Creek."

1337
Cop.1

FDO 79-128

JAN. 13, 1944

WAR FOOD ADMINISTRATION

[FDO 79-128]

PART 1401—DAIRY PRODUCTS

FLUID MILK AND CREAM IN THE SAN ANTONIO, TEX., SALES AREA

Pursuant to the authority vested in me by Food Distribution Order No. 79 (8 F.R. 12426), issued on September 7, 1943, as amended, and to effectuate the purposes of such order, it is hereby ordered as follows:

§ 1401.163 *Quota restrictions*—(a) *Definitions.* When used in this order, unless otherwise distinctly expressed or manifestly incompatible with the intent hereof:

(1) Each term defined in Food Distribution Order No. 79, as amended, shall, when used herein, have the same meaning as is set forth for such term in Food Distribution Order No. 79, as amended.

(2) The term "FDO 79" means Food Distribution Order No. 79, issued on September 7, 1943, as amended.

(3) The term "sub-handler" means any handler, such as a peddler, vendor, sub-dealer, or secondary dealer, who purchases in a previously packaged and processed form milk, cream, or milk byproducts for delivery.

(4) The term "industrial user" means a person, as determined by the market agent, in the capacity of a manufacturer of products using as an ingredient therein milk, cream, or milk byproducts, which products are disposed of for resale to consumers off the premises where made.

(5) The term "base" means the total pounds of milk solids delivered by a handler within the sales area during the base period (i) in the form of milk, or (ii) in the form of cream and milk byproducts, minus the milk solids in quota-exempt deliveries of milk, and cream and milk byproducts, as described in (j) hereof. (For the purpose of this order, the milk solids content of milk, milk byproducts, and cream shall be computed as follows: Each hundredweight of milk, cream, or milk byproducts other than cottage, pot, or baker's cheese, shall be considered the equivalent of 9.375 pounds of milk solids plus the number of pounds of milk solids calculated by multiplying the pounds of butterfat in such milk, and cream and milk byproducts by .906; and each hundredweight of cottage, pot, or baker's cheese shall be considered the equivalent of 62.5 pounds of milk solids plus one pound of milk solids for each one percent of butterfat content of such cheese.)

(b) *Milk sales area.* The following area is hereby designated as a "milk sales area" to be known as the San Antonio, Texas, milk sales area, and is referred to hereinafter as the "sales area":

The city of San Antonio and justices' precincts 1, 2, 6, 7, 8 and that part of justices' precinct 2 lying east of Lean Creek, all in Bexar County, Texas.

(c) *Base period.* The calendar month of June 1943 is hereby designated as the base period for the sales area: *Provided,* That the month of May may be used as the base period for computing base and quota for deliveries to elementary, junior high and high schools; *And provided further,* That in the computations set forth in (e) hereof the total deliveries to elementary, junior high, and high schools in the base period shall be divided by the number of days such schools were in session in lieu of the total number of days in the base period as set forth in (e) (1) and the average daily deliveries so determined shall be multiplied by the number of days such schools are in session in each quota period in lieu of the number of days in the quota period as set forth in (e) (2).

(d) The remainder of the calendar month in which the provisions hereof become effective and each subsequent calendar month, respectively, is hereby designated as the quota period for the sales area.

(e) *Handler quotas.* Quotas for each handler other than a sub-handler or producer-handler shall be determined as follows:

(1) Divide his respective bases by the number of days in the base period;

(2) Multiply the foregoing result by the number of days in the quota period; and

(3) Multiply the aforesaid resulting amounts by 100 percent in the case of the base for milk, and 75 percent in the case of the base for cream and milk byproducts.

(f) *Quotas for handlers who are also producers.* Quotas for each handler who is also a producer and who purchases no milk shall be computed in accordance with (e) hereof, except:

(1) His base period shall be either June or December, whichever represents his larger total deliveries; and,

(2) The applicable percentages shall be 100 percent in lieu of those specified in (e) (3).

(g) *Quota adjustments.* Each handler may increase his quota for milk within any quota period by one pound of milk solids for each one pound of milk solids he reduces his quota for cream and milk byproducts.

(h) *Cream deliveries.* The units of cream delivered subject to quota in any quota period shall not exceed 100 percent of the units of cream in his base, irrespective of the milk solids content of such deliveries.

(i) *Handler exemptions.* Quota shall not apply to any handler who deliveries in a quota period a daily average of less than 500 units of milk, cream, and milk byproducts. For the purpose of this order, a unit shall be the equivalent in volume of the following: (1) One quart of milk, buttermilk, or fluid milk byproducts; (2) one-half pint of cream; and (3) one-half pound of cottage, pot, or baker's cheese.

(j) *Quota exclusions and exemptions.* Deliveries of milk, milk byproducts, or cream (1) to other handlers, except for such deliveries to sub-handlers, (2) to plants engaged in the handling or processing of milk, milk byproducts, cream or other dairy products from which no milk, milk byproducts, or cream, is delivered in the sales area, (3) to industrial users, and (4) to the agencies or groups specified in (d) of FDO 79, shall be excluded from the computation of deliveries in the base period and exempt from charges to quotas.

(k) *Transfers of bases.* The market agent is empowered to transfer base from one handler to another.

(1) Upon receipt of a request in writing from both handlers; and

(2) Upon application from a handler and written notice to the Director and to both handlers, (i) to permit deliveries to a purchaser not being served by a handler whose quota reflects deliveries to such purchaser in the base period, (ii) to permit a handler to serve an account which customarily rotates among several handlers inclusive of a contract let by a public agency or institution on a bid basis, and (iii) to permit a handler to serve an account which he is serving on the effective date of this order and which was served by another handler during the base period.

(l) *Consumer priorities.* In the distribution of milk subject to quotas established hereunder, a handler shall give preference in the order listed, taking into consideration the type of purchasers served by him in the base period, to:

(1) The need of children, expectant mothers, and invalids requiring milk;

(2) Homes and retail stores handling milk for consumption off the premises; and

(3) Establishments serving milk for consumption on the premises.

(m) *Petition for relief from hardship.* (1) Any person affected by FDO 79 or the provisions hereof who considers that compliance therewith would work an exceptional and unreasonable hardship on him, may file with the market agent a petition addressed to the Director. The petition shall contain the correct name, address and principal place of business of the petitioner, a full statement of the facts upon which the petition is based, and the hardship involved and the nature of the relief desired.

(2) Upon receiving such petition the market agent shall immediately investigate representations and facts stated therein.

(3) After investigation, the petition shall be certified to the Director, but prior to certification the market agent may (i) deny the petition or (ii) grant temporary relief for a total period not to exceed 60 days.

(4) Denials or grants of relief by the market agent shall be reviewed by the Director and may be affirmed, modified, or reversed by the Director.

(n) *Reports.* Each handler shall transmit to the market agent on forms prescribed by the market agent the following reports:

(1) Within 20 days following the effective date of this order, reports which show the information required by the market agent to establish such handler's quotas;

(2) Within 20 days following the close of each quota period, the information required by the market agent to establish volumes of deliveries of milk, cream and milk byproducts during the preceding quota period; and

(3) Handlers exempt from quotas pursuant to (i) hereof shall, upon the request of the market agent, submit the information required by the market agent to establish volumes of deliveries of milk, and milk byproducts.

(o) *Records.* Handlers shall keep and shall make available to the market agent such records of receipts, sales, deliveries, and production, as the market agent shall require for the purpose of obtaining information which the Director may require for the establishment of quotas as prescribed in (b) of FDO 79.

(p) *Expense of administration.* Each handler shall pay to the market agent, within 20 days after the close of each calendar month, an assessment of $0.015 per hundredweight of each of milk, milk byproducts, cream, and skim milk equivalent of cottage, pot, or baker's cheese delivered during the preceding quota period and subject to quota regulations under the provisions hereof.

(q) *Violations.* The market agent shall report all violations to the Director together with the information required for the prosecution of such violations.

(r) *Bureau of the Budget approval.* The record-keeping and reporting requirements of this order have been approved by the Bureau of the Budget in accordance with the Federal Reports Act of 1942. Subsequent record-keeping or reporting requirements will be subject to the approval of the Bureau of the Budget pursuant to the Federal Reports Act of 1942.

(s) *Effective date.* This order shall take effect at 12:01 a. m., e. w. t., February 1, 1944.

(E.O. 9280, 7 F.R. 10179; E.O. 9322, 8 F.R. 3807; E.O. 9334, 8 F.R. 5423; E.O. 9392, 8 F.R. 14783; FDO 79, 8 F.R. 12426, 13283)

Issued this 13th day of January 1944.

ROY F. HENDRICKSON,
Director of Food Distribution.

War Food Administration:
Summary to FDO-79.124-FDO 79.130.

Nine New Milk Sales Areas Named

Milk sales in 9 metropolitan areas in Texas, Louisiana, and Arkansas will be regulated under the Food Distribution Administration's Fluid milk conservation and control program, beginning February 1, 1944.

The new milk sales areas are:

Waco, Texas (FDO 79.123); Dallas, Texas (FDO 79.124); Ft. Worth, Texas (FDO 79.125); Austin, Texas (FDO 79.126); Galveston, Texas (FDO 79.127); San Antonio, Texas (FDO 79.128); Houston, Texas (FDO 79.122); Shreveport, Louisiana (FDO 79.129); Little Rock, Arkansas (FDO 79.130).

Market agents who will administer the orders in each area will be named later.

Under the program, milk dealers will be permitted to deliver to all customers except schools as much fluid milk as they delivered in June and three-fourths as much milk in cream and milk byproducts (such as cottage cheese, chocolate milk and buttermilk) as they sold in June. Deliveries to elementary, junior high and high schools will be under the same restrictions except the number of school days in May will be used as the base period in determining quotas, rather than June. Milk dealers include all persons or firms engaged in the delivery of transfer of milk, but not such distributors as subhandlers ("peddlers"), retail stores, hotels, or restaurants.

Producer distributors who purchase no milk will be permitted to deliver as much milk as they delivered in either June or December, whichever represents their larger total deliveries.

The order permits dealers to deliver more fluid milk than their quotas allow, provided they use less milk solids in deliveries of cream or milk byproducts. Since cream and milk byproducts are recognized as one quota group, dealers may deliver more cream, but not more than 100% of the deliveries of cream in the base period by cutting down on milk solids used in milk byproducts, or more byproducts by reducing the amount of milk solids used in cream.

In distributing the milk, cream and byproducts allowed under their quotas, dealers are required to give preference to the following consumer groups, in the order listed, taking into consideration the type of purchasers they served in the base period:

1. Children, expectant mothers, and invalids requiring milk;
2. Homes and retail stores handling milk for consumption off the premises;
3. Establishments serving milk for consumption on the premises.

Deliveries of milk, cream and milk byproducts to other dealers; to the Armed Forces; to plants engaged in handling or processing milk, byproducts and cream which are not distributed in the sales area; and to designated industrial manufacturers who use milk, cream, or milk byproducts in making products which are sold off the premises are quota exempt.

Consumers in the milk sales areas named today, as in others already designated, generally will be able to purchase as much milk under the milk conservation program as they have been buying in recent months. Fluid milk sales are being stabilized, and sales of cream and milk byproducts are being reduced, FDA officials said, to help assure sufficient milk for manufacturing the cheese, butter, evaporated milk, and milk powder required by the armed forces and civilians for good nutrition and properly balanced diets.

7851
1401

FDO 79-128
AMDT. 1
JAN. 27, 1944

WAR FOOD ADMINISTRATION

[FDO 79-128, Amdt. 1]

PART 1401—DAIRY PRODUCTS

FLUID MILK AND CREAM IN SAN ANTONIO, TEX., SALES AREA

Pursuant to Food Distribution Order No. 79 (8 F.R. 12426), dated September 7, 1943, as amended, and to effectuate the purposes thereof, Food Distribution Order No. 79-128 (9 F.R. 648), relative to the conservation and distribution of fluid milk in the San Antonio, Texas, milk sales area, issued by the Director of Food Distribution on January 13, 1944, is amended by deleting the description of the sales area in § 1401.163 (b) and inserting, in lieu thereof, the following:

The city of San Antonio and justices' precincts 1, 3, 6, 7, 8 and that part of justices' precinct 2 lying east of Leon Creek, all in Bexar County, Texas.

The provisions of this amendment shall become effective at 12:01 a. m., e. w. t., February 1, 1944. With respect to violations of said Food Distribution Order No. 79-128, rights accrued, or liabilities incurred prior to the effective time of this amendment, said Director Food Distribution Order No. 79-128 shall be deemed to be in full force and effect for the purpose of sustaining any proper suit, action, or other proceeding with respect to any such violation, right, or liability.

(E.O. 9280, 7 F.R. 10179; E.O. 9322, 8 F.R. 3807; E.O. 9334, 8 F.R. 5423; E.O. 9392, 8 F.R. 14783; FDO 79, 8 F.R. 12426, 13283)

Issued this 27th day of January 1944.

LEE MARSHALL,
Director of Food Distribution.

FDO 79-128

AMDT. 2
FEB. 11, 1944

WAR FOOD ADMINISTRATION

[FDO 79-128. Amdt. 2]

PART 1401—DAIRY PRODUCTS

FLUID MILK AND CREAM IN SAN ANTONIO, TEX., SALES AREA

Pursuant to Food Distribution Order Uo. 79 (8 F.R. 12426), dated September 7, 1943, as amended, and to effectuate the purposes thereof, Food Distrbution Order No. 79-128 (9 F.R. 643), relative to the conservation and distribution of fluid milk in the San Antonio, Texas, milk sales area, issued by the Director of Food Distribution on January 13, 1944, as amended, is hereby further amended by deleting therefrom the provisions in § 1401.163 (b) and inserting, in lieu thereof, the following:

The city of San Antonio and all of the remaining territory within the boundary lines of Bexar County, in the State of Texas.

The provisions of this amendment shall become effective at 12:01 a. m., e. w. t., March 1, 1944. With respect to violations of said Food Distribution Order No. 79-128, as amended, rights accrued, or liabilities incurred prior to the effective time of this amendment, said Food Distribution Order No. 79-128, as amended, shall be deemed to be in full force and effect for the purpose of sustaining any proper suit, action, or other proceeding with respect to any such violation, right, or liability.

(E.O. 9280, 7 F.R. 10179; E.O. 9322, 8 F.R. 3807; E.O. 9334, 8 F.R. 5423; E.O. 9392, 8 F.R. 14783; FDO 79, 8 F.R. 12426, 13283)

Issued this 11th day of February 1944.

C. W. KITCHEN,
Acting Director of Food Distribution.

FDO 79-129

JAN. 13, 1944

WAR FOOD ADMINISTRATION

[FDO 79-129] A

PART 1401—DAIRY PRODUCTS

FLUID MILK AND CREAM IN THE SHREVEPORT, LA., SALES AREA

Pursuant to the authority vested in me by Food Distribution Order No. 79 (8 F.R. 12426), issued on September 7, 1943, as amended, and to effectuate the purposes of such order, it is hereby ordered as follows:

§ 1401.164 *Quota restrictions*—(a) *Definitions.* When used in this order, unless otherwise distinctly expressed or manifestly incompatible with the intent hereof:

(1) Each term defined in Food Distribution Order No. 79, as amended, shall, when used herein, have the same meaning as is set forth for such term in Food Distribution Order No. 79, as amended.

(2) The term "FDO 79" means Food Distribution Order No. 79, issued on September 7, 1943, as amended.

(3) The term "sub-handler" means any handler, such as a peddler, vendor, subdealer, or secondary dealer, who purchases in a previously packaged and processed form milk, cream, or milk byproducts for delivery.

(4) The term "industrial user" means a person, as determined by the market agent, in the capacity of a manufacturer of products using as an ingredient therein milk, cream, or milk byproducts, which products are disposed of for resale to consumers off the premises where made.

(5) The term "base" means the total pounds of milk solids delivered by a handler within the sales area during the base period (i) in the form of milk, or (ii) in the form of cream and milk byproducts, minus the milk solids in quota-exempt deliveries of milk, and cream and milk byproducts, as described in (j) hereof. (For the purpose of this order, the milk solids content of milk, milk byproducts, and cream shall be computed as follows: Each hundredweight of milk, cream, or milk byproducts other than cottage, pot, or baker's cheese, shall be considered the equivalent of 9.375 pounds of milk solids plus the number of pounds of milk solids calculated by multiplying the pounds of butterfat in such milk, and cream and milk byproducts by .906; and each hundredweight of cottage, pot, or baker's cheese shall be considered the equivalent of 62.5 pounds of milk solids plus one pound of milk solids for each one percent of butterfat content of such cheese.)

(b) *Milk sales area.* The following area is hereby designated as a "milk sales area" to be known as the Shreveport, Louisiana, milk sales area, and is referred to hereinafter as the "sales area":

The city of Shreveport, police jury ward 2 in Bossier Parish, and police jury ward 4 in Caddo Parish, all in the State of Louisiana.

(c) *Base period.* The calendar month of June 1943 is hereby designated as the base period for the sales area: *Provided*, That the month of May may be used as the base period for computing base and quota for deliveries to elementary, junior high and high schools; *And Provided further*, That in the computations set forth in (e) hereof the total deliveries to elementary, junior high, and high schools in the base period shall be divided by the number of days such schools were in session in lieu of the total number of days in the base period as set forth in (e) (1) and the average daily deliveries so determined shall be multiplied by the number of days such schools are in session in each quota period in lieu of the number of days in the quota period as set forth in (e) (2).

(d) The remainder of the calendar month in which the provisions hereof become effective and each subsequent calendar month, respectively, is hereby designated as the quota period for the sales area.

(e) *Handler quotas.* Quotas for each handler other than a sub-handler or producer-handler shall be determined as follows:

(1) Divide his respective bases by the number of days in the base period;

(2) Multiply the foregoing result by the number of days in the quota period; and

(3) Multiply the aforesaid resulting amounts by 100 percent in the case of the base for milk, and 75 percent in the case of the base for cream and milk byproducts.

(f) *Quotas for handlers who are also producers.* Quotas for each handler who is also a producer and who purchases no milk shall be computed in accordance with (e) hereof, except:

(1) His base period shall be either June or December, whichever represents his larger total deliveries; and,

(2) The applicable percentages shall be 100 percent in lieu of those specified in (e) (3).

(g) *Quota adjustments.* Each handler may increase his quota for milk within any quota period by one pound of milk solids for each one pound of milk solids he reduces his quota for cream and milk byproducts.

(h) *Cream deliveries.* The units of cream delivered subject to quota in any quota period shall not exceed 100 percent of the units of cream in his base, irrespective of the milk solids content of such deliveries.

(i) *Handler exemptions.* Quota shall not apply to any handler who delivers in a quota period a daily average of less than 200 units of milk, cream, and milk byproducts. For the purpose of this order, a unit shall be the equivalent in volume of the following: (1) One quart of milk, buttermilk, or fluid milk byproducts; (2) one-half pint of cream; and (3) one-half pound of cottage, pot, or baker's cheese.

(j) *Quota exclusions and exemptions.* Deliveries of milk, milk byproducts, or cream (1) to other handlers, except for such deliveries to sub-handlers, (2) to plants engaged in the handling or processing of milk, milk byproducts, cream or other dairy products from which no milk, milk byproducts, or cream, is delivered in the sales area, (3) to industrial users, and (4) to the agencies or groups specified in (d) of FDO 79, shall be excluded from the computation of deliveries in the base period and exempt from charges to quotas.

(k) *Transfers of bases.* The market agent is empowered to transfer base from one handler to another.

(1) Upon receipt of a request in writing from both handlers; and

(2) Upon application from a handler and written notice to the Director and to both handlers, (i) to permit deliveries to a purchaser not being served by a handler whose quota reflects deliveries to such purchaser in the base period, (ii) to permit a handler to serve an account which customarily rotates among several handlers inclusive of a contract let by a public agency or institution on a bid basis, and (iii) to permit a handler to serve an account which he is serving on the effective date of this order and which was served by another handler during the base period.

(l) *Consumer priorities.* In the distribution of milk subject to quotas established hereunder, a handler shall give preference in the order listed, taking into consideration the type of purchasers served by him in the base period, to:

(1) The need of children, expectant mothers, and invalids requiring milk;

(2) Homes and retail stores handling milk for consumption off the premises; and

(3) Establishments serving milk for consumption on the premises.

(m) *Petition for relief from hardship.* (1) Any person affected by FDO 79 or the provisions hereof who considers that compliance therewith would work an exceptional and unreasonable hardship on him, may file with the market agent a petition addressed to the Director. The petition shall contain the correct name, address and principal place of business of the petitioner, a full statement of the facts upon which the petition is based, and the hardship involved and the nature of the relief desired.

(2) Upon receiving such petition the market agent shall immediately investigate representations and facts stated therein.

(3) After investigation, the petition shall be certified to the Director, but prior to certification the market agent may (i) deny the petition or (ii) grant temporary relief for a total period not to exceed 60 days.

(4) Denials or grants of relief by the market agent shall be reviewed by the Director and may be affirmed, modified, or reversed by the Director.

(n) *Reports.* Each handler shall transmit to the market agent on forms prescribed by the market agent the following reports:

(1) Within 20 days following the effective date of this order, reports which show the information required by the market agent to establish such handler's quotas;

(2) Within 20 days following the close of each quota period, the information required by the market agent to establish volumes of deliveries of milk, cream and milk byproducts during the preceding quota period; and

(3) Handlers exempt from quotas pursuant to (i) hereof shall, upon the request of the market agent, submit the information required by the market agent to establish volumes of deliveries of milk, cream, and milk byproducts.

(o) *Records.* Handlers shall keep and shall make available to the market agent such records of receipts, sales, deliveries, and production as the market agent shall require for the purpose of obtaining information which the Director may require for the establishment of quotas as prescribed in (b) of FDO 79.

(p) *Expense of administration.* Each handler shall pay to the market agent, within 20 days after the close of each calendar month, an assessme per hundredweight of each o byproducts, cream, and skim alent of cottage, pot, or baker livered during the preceding and subject to quota regula the provisions hereof.

(q) *Violations.* The ma shall report all violations to together with the informati for the prosecution of such

(r) *Bureau of the Budge* The record-keeping and re quirements of this order ha proved by the Bureau of th accordance with the Federal of 1942. Subsequent record reporting requirements will b the approval of the Bureau o pursuant to the Federal Re 1942.

(s) *Effective date.* This take effect at 12:01 a. m., e. w ary 1, 1944.

(E.O. 9280, 7 F.R. 10179; E.O. 3807; E.O. 9334, 8 F.R. 5423; 8 F.R. 14783; FDO 79, 8 F.R. 1

Issued this 13th day of Ja

ROY F. HENDR
Director of Food Dis

War Food Administration.
Summary to FDO-79.124-FDO 79.130.

Nine New Milk Sales Areas Named

Milk sales in 9 metropolitan areas in Texas, Louisiana, and Arkansas will be regulated under the Food Distribution Administration's Fluid milk conservation and control program, beginning February 1, 1944.

The new milk sales areas are:

Waco, Texas (FDO 79.123); Dallas, Texas (FDO 79.124); Ft. Worth, Texas (FDO 79.125); Austin, Texas (FDO 79.126); Galveston, Texas (FDO 79.127); San Antonio, Texas (FDO 79.128); Houston, Texas (FDO 79.122); Shreveport, Louisiana (FDO 79.129); Little Rock, Arkansas (FDO 79.130).

Market agents who will administer the orders in each area will be named later.

Under the program, milk dealers will be permitted to deliver to all customers except schools as much fluid milk as they delivered in June and three-fourths as much milk in cream and milk byproducts (such as cottage cheese, chocolate milk and buttermilk) as they sold in June. Deliveries to elementary, junior high and high schools will be under the same restrictions except the number of school days in May will be used as the base period in determining quotas, rather than June. Milk dealers include all persons or firms engaged in the delivery of transfer of milk, but not such distributors as subhandlers ("peddlers"), retail stores, hotels, or restaurants.

Producer distributors who purchase no milk will be permitted to deliver as much milk as they delivered in either June or December, whichever represents their larger total deliveries.

The order permits dealers to deliver more fluid milk than their quotas allow, provided they use less milk solids in deliveries of cream or milk byproducts. Since cream and milk byproducts are recognized as one quota group, dealers may deliver more cream, but not more than 100% of the deliveries of cream in the base period by cutting down on milk solids used in milk byproducts, or more byproducts by reducing the amount of milk solids used in cream.

In distributing the milk, cream and byproducts allowed under their quotas, dealers are required to give preference to the following consumer groups, in the order listed, taking into consideration the type of purchasers they se base period:

1. Children, expectant mo invalids requiring milk;
2. Homes and retail store milk for consumption off th
3. Establishments serving consumption on the premises

Deliveries of milk, cream ar products to other dealers; to Forces; to plants engaged in l processing milk, byproducts which are not distributed i area; and to designated indus facturers who use milk, crea byproducts in making product sold off the premises are quot

Consumers in the milk named today, as in others alr nated, generally will be able as much milk under the mil tion program as they have b in recent months. Fluid mi being stabilized, and sales of milk byproducts are being re officials said, to help assur milk for manufacturing the c ter; evaporated milk, and m required by the armed force ians for good nutrition an balanced diets.

F.1

FDO 79-130

JAN. 13, 1944

WAR FOOD ADMINISTRATION

[FDO 79-130]

PART 1401—DAIRY PRODUCTS

FLUID MILK AND CREAM IN THE LITTLE ROCK, ARK., SALES AREA

Pursuant to the authority vested in me by Food Distribution Order No. 79 (8 F.R. 12426), issued on September 7, 1943, as amended, and to effectuate the purposes of such order, it is hereby ordered as follows:

§ 1401.166 *Quota restrictions*—(a) *Definitions.* When used in this order, unless otherwise distinctly expressed or manifestly incompatible with the intent hereof:

(1) Each term defined in Food Distribution Order No. 79, as amended, shall, when used herein, have the same meaning as is set forth for such term in Food Distribution Order No. 79, as amended.

(2) The term "FDO 79" means Food Distribution Order No. 79, issued on September 7, 1943, as amended.

(3) The term "sub-handler" means any handler, such as a peddler, vendor, sub-dealer, or secondary dealer, who purchases in a previously packaged and processed form milk, cream, or milk byproducts for delivery.

(4) The term "industrial user" means a person, as determined by the market agent, in the capacity of a manufacturer of products using as an ingredient therein milk, cream, or milk byproducts, which products are disposed of for resale to consumers off the premises where made.

(5) The term "base" means the total pounds of milk solids delivered by a handler within the sales area during the base period (i) in the form of milk, or (ii) in the form of cream and milk byproducts, minus the milk solids in quota-exempt deliveries of milk, and cream and milk byproducts, as described in (j) hereof. (For the purpose of this order, the milk solids content of milk, milk byproducts, and cream shall be computed as follows: Each hundredweight of milk, cream, or milk byproducts other than cottage, pot, or baker's cheese, shall be considered the equivalent of 9.375 pounds of milk solids plus the number of pounds of milk solids calculated by multiplying the pounds of butterfat in such milk, and cream and milk byproducts by .906; and each hundredweight of cottage, pot, or baker's cheese shall be considered the equivalent of 62.5 pounds of milk solids plus one pound of milk solids for each one percent of butterfat content of such cheese.)

(b) *Milk sales area.* The following area is hereby designated as a "milk sales area" to be known as the Little Rock, Arkansas, milk sales area, and is referred to hereinafter as the "sales area":

The city of Little Rock and the townships of Badgett, Big Rock, and Hill, all in Pulaski County, Arkansas.

(c) *Base period.* The calendar month of June 1943 is hereby designated as the base period for the sales area: Provided, That the month of May may be used as the base period for computing base and quota for deliveries to elementary, junior high and high schools; and *Provided further,* That in the computations set forth in (e) hereof the total deliveries to elementary, junior high, and high schools in the base period shall be divided by the number of days such schools were in session in lieu of the total number of days in the base period as set forth in (e) (1) and the average daily deliveries so determined shall be multiplied by the number of days such schools are in session in each quota period in lieu of the number of days in the quota period as set forth in (e) (2).

(d) The remainder of the calendar month in which the provisions hereof become effective and each subsequent calendar month, respectively, is hereby designated as the quota period for the sales area.

(e) *Handler quotas.* Quotas for each handler other than a sub-handler or producer-handler shall be determined as follows:

(1) Divide his respective bases by the number of days in the base period;

(2) Multiply the foregoing result by the number of days in the quota period; and

(3) Multiply the aforesaid resulting amounts by 100 percent in the case of the base for milk, and 75 percent in the case of the base for cream and milk byproducts.

(f) *Quotas for handlers who are also producers.* Quotas for each handler who is also a producer and who purchases no milk shall be computed in accordance with (e) hereof, except:

(1) His base period shall be either June or December, whichever represents his larger total deliveries; and,

(2) The applicable percentages shall be 100 percent in lieu of those specified in (e) (3).

(g) *Quota adjustments.* Each handler may increase his quota for milk within any quota period by one pound of milk solids for each one pound of milk solids he reduces his quota for cream and milk byproducts.

(h) *Cream deliveries.* The units of cream delivered subject to quota in any quota period shall not exceed 100 percent of the units of cream in his base, irrespective of the milk solids content of such deliveries.

(i) *Handler exemptions.* Quota shall not apply to any handler who delivers in a quota period a daily average of less than 200 units of milk, cream, and milk byproducts. For the purpose of this order, a unit shall be the equivalent in volume of the following: (1) One quart of milk, buttermilk, or fluid milk byproducts; (2) one-half pint of cream; and (3) one-half pound of cottage, pot, or baker's cheese.

(j) *Quota exclusions and exemptions.* Deliveries of milk, milk byproducts, or cream (1) to other handlers, except for such deliveries to sub-handlers, (2) to plants engaged in the handling or processing of milk, milk byproducts, cream or other dairy products from which no milk, milk byproducts, or cream, is delivered in the sales area, (3) to industrial users, and (4) to the agencies or groups specified in (d) of FDO 79, shall be excluded from the computation of deliveries in the base period and exempt from charges to quotas.

(k) *Transfers of bases.* The market agent is empowered to transfer base from one handler to another.

(1) Upon receipt of a request in writing from both handlers; and

(2) Upon application from a handler and written notice to the Director and to both handlers, (i) to permit deliveries to a purchaser not being served by a handler whose quota reflects deliveries to such purchaser in the base period, (ii) to permit a handler to serve an account which customarily rotates among several handlers inclusive of a contract let by a public agency or institution on a bid basis, and (iii) to permit a handler to serve an account which he is serving on the effective date of this order and which was served by another handler during the base period.

(l) *Consumer priorities.* In the distribution of milk subject to quotas established hereunder, a handler shall give preference in the order listed, taking into consideration the type of purchasers served by him in the base period, to:

(1) The need of children, expectant mothers, and invalids requiring milk;

(2) Homes and retail stores handling milk for consumption off the premises; and

(3) Establishments serving milk for consumption on the premises.

(m) *Petition for relief from hardship.* (1) Any person affected by FDO 79 or the provisions hereof who considers that compliance therewith would work an exceptional and unreasonable hardship on him, may file with the market agent a petition addressed to the Director. The petition shall contain the correct name, address and principal place of business of the petitioner, a full statement of the facts upon which the petition is based, and the hardship involved and the nature of the relief desired.

(2) Upon receiving such petition the market agent shall immediately investigate representations and facts stated therein.

(3) After investigation, the petition shall be certified to the Director, but prior to certification the market agent may (i) deny the petition or (ii) grant temporary relief for a total period not to exceed 60 days.

(4) Denials or grants of relief by the market agent shall be reviewed by the Director and may be affirmed, modified, or reversed by the Director.

(n) *Reports.* Each handler shall transmit to the market agent on forms prescribed by the market agent the following reports:

(1) Within 20 days following the effective date of this order, reports which show the information required by the market agent to establish such handler's quotas;

(2) Within 20 days following the close of each quota period, the information required by the market agent to establish volumes of deliveries of milk, cream, and milk byproducts during the preceding quota period; and

(3) Handlers exempt from quotas pursuant to (i) hereof shall, upon the request of the market agent, submit the information required by the market agent to establish volumes of deliveries of milk, cream, and milk byproducts.

(o) *Records.* Handlers shall keep and shall make available to the market agent such records of receipts, sales, deliveries, and production as the market agent shall require for the purpose of obtaining information which the Director may require for the establishment of quotas as prescribed in (b) of FDO 79.

(p) *Expense of administration.* Each handler shall pay to the market agent, within 20 days after the close of each

calendar month, an asses
per hundredweight of ea
byproducts, cream, and s
alent of cottage, pot, or
delivered during the p
period and subject to qu
under the provisions her

(q) *Violations.* The
shall report all violations
together with the infor
to the prosecution of suc

(r) *Bureau of the B*
The record-keeping and
quirements of this order
proved by the Bureau o
accordance with the Fed
of 1942. Subsequent re
reporting requirements
to the approval of the
Budget pursuant to the
Act of 1942.

(s) *Effective date.* T
take effect at 12:01 a. m.
ary 1, 1944.

(E.O. 9280, 7 F.R. 10179;
3807; E.O. 9334, 8 F.R.
8 F.R. 14783; FDO 79, 8 F.

Issued this 13th day o

ROY F. H
Director of Food

War Food Administration:
Summary to FDO–79,124–FDO 79.130.

Nine New Milk Sales Areas Named

Milk sales in 9 metropolitan areas in Texas, Louisiana, and Arkansas will be regulated under the Food Distribution Administration's Fluid milk conservation and control program, beginning February 1, 1944.

The new milk sales areas are:

Waco, Texas (FDO 79.123); Dallas, Texas (FDO 79.124); Ft. Worth, Texas (FDO 79.125); Austin, Texas (FDO 79.126); Galveston, Texas (FDO 79.127); San Antonio, Texas (FDO 79.128); Houston, Texas (FDO 79.122); Shreveport, Louisiana (FDO 79.129); Little Rock, Arkansas (FDO 79.130).

Market agents who will administer the orders in each area will be named later.

Under the program, milk dealers will be permitted to deliver to all customers except schools as much fluid milk as they delivered in June and three-fourths as much milk in cream and milk byproducts (such as cottage cheese, chocolate milk and buttermilk) as they sold in June. Deliveries to elementary, junior high and high schools will be under the same restrictions except the number of school days in May will be used as the base period in determining quotas, rather than June. Milk dealers include all persons or firms engaged in the delivery of transfer of milk, but not such distributors as subhandlers ("peddlers"), retail stores, hotels, or restaurants.

Producer-distributors who purchase no milk will be permitted to deliver as much milk as they delivered in either June or December, whichever represents their larger total deliveries.

The order permits dealers to deliver more fluid milk than their quotas allow, provided they use less milk solids in deliveries of cream or milk byproducts. Since cream and milk byproducts are recognized as one quota group, dealers may deliver more cream, but not more than 100% of the deliveries of cream in the base period by cutting down on milk solids used in milk byproducts, or more byproducts by reducing the amount of milk solids used in cream.

In distributing the milk, cream and byproducts allowed under their quotas, dealers are required to give preference to the following consumer groups, in the order listed, taking into consideration the type of purchasers th
base period:

1. Children, expectan
invalids requiring milk;

2. Homes and retail
milk for consumption o

3. Establishments ser
consumption on the pre

Deliveries of milk, cre
products to other dealer
Forces; to plants engage
processing milk, byprod
which are not distribut
area; and to designated
facturers who use milk,
byproducts in making pr
sold off the premises are

Consumers in the m
named today, as in othe
nated, generally will be
as much milk under the
tion program as they h
in recent months. Flu
being stabilized, and sal
milk byproducts are bei
officials said, to help
milk for manufacturing
ter, evaporated milk, a
required by the armed
ians for good nutritio
balanced diets.

7337

FDO 79-131

JAN. 21, 1944

WAR FOOD ADMINISTRATION

[FDO 79-131] A

PART 1401—DAIRY PRODUCTS

FLUID MILK AND CREAM IN GREENSBORO, N. C., SALES AREA

Pursuant to the authority vested in me by Food Distribution Order No. 79 (8 F.R. 12426), issued on September 7, 1943, as amended, and to effectuate the purposes of such order, it is hereby ordered as follows:

§ 1401.168 *Quota restrictions*—(a) *Definitions*. When used in this order, unless otherwise distinctly expressed or manifestly incompatible with the intent hereof:

(1) Each term defined in Food Distribution Order No. 79, as amended, shall, when used herein, have the same meaning as is set forth for such term in Food Distribution Order No. 79, as amended.

(2) The term "FDO 79" means Food Distribution Order No. 79, issued on September 7, 1943, as amended.

(3) The term "sub-handler" means any handler, such as a peddler, vendor, sub-dealer, or secondary dealer, who purchases in a previously packaged and processed form milk, cream, or milk byproducts for delivery.

(4) The term "industrial user" means a person, as determined by the market agent, in the capacity of a manufacturer of products using as an ingredient therein milk, cream, or milk byproducts, which products are disposed of for resale to consumers off the premises where made.

(5) The term "base" means the total pounds of milk solids delivered by a handler within the sales area during the base period (i) in the form of milk, or (ii) in the form of cream and milk byproducts, minus the milk solids in quota-exempt deliveries of milk, and cream and milk byproducts, as described in (j) hereof. (For the purpose of this order, the milk solids content of milk, milk byproducts, and cream shall be computed as follows: Each hundredweight of milk, cream, or milk byproducts other than cottage, pot, or baker's cheese, shall be considered the equivalent of 9.375 pounds of milk solids plus the number of pounds of milk solids calculated by multiplying the pounds of butterfat in such milk, and cream and milk byproducts by .906; and each hundredweight of cottage, pot, or baker's cheese shall be considered the equivalent of 62.5 pounds of milk solids plus one pound of milk solids for each one percent of butterfat content of such cheese.)

(b) *Milk sales area*. The following area is hereby designated as a "milk sales area" to be known as the Greensboro, North Carolina, sales area, and is referred to hereinafter as the "sales area":

The cities of Greensboro and High Point, and the townships of Gilmer, High Point and Morehead all in Guilford County, North Carolina.

(c) *Base period*. The calendar month of June 1943 is hereby designated as the base period for the sales area: *Provided*, That the month of May may be used as the base period for computing base and quota for deliveries to elementary, junior high, and high schools: *And provided further*, That in the computations set forth in (e) hereof the total deliveries to elementary, junior high, and high schools in the base period shall be divided by the number of days such schools were in session in lieu of the total number of days in the base period as set forth in (e) (1) and the average daily deliveries so determined shall be multiplied by the number of days such schools are in session in each quota period in lieu of the number of days in the quota period as set forth in (e) (2).

(d) The remainder of the calendar month in which the provisions hereof become effective and each subsequent calendar month, respectively, is hereby designated as the quota period for the sales area.

(e) *Handler quotas*. Quotas for each handler other than a sub-handler or producer-handler shall be determined as follows:

(1) Divide his respective bases by the number of days in the base period;

(2) Multiply the foregoing result by the number of days in the quota period; and

(3) Multiply the aforesaid resulting amounts by 100 percent in the case of the base for milk, and 75 percent in the case of the base for cream and milk byproducts.

(f) *Quotas for handlers who are also producers*. Quotas for each handler who is also a producer and who purchases no milk shall be computed in accordance with (e) hereof, except:

(1) His base period shall be either June or December, whichever represents his larger total deliveries; and

(2) The applicable percentages shall be 100 percent in lieu of those specified in (e) (3).

(g) *Quota adjustments*. Each handler may increase his quota for milk within any quota period by one pound of milk solids for each one pound of milk solids he reduces his quota for cream and milk byproducts.

(h) *Cream deliveries*. The units of cream delivered subject to quota in any quota period shall not exceed 100 percent of the units of cream in his base, irrespective of the milk solids content of such deliveries.

(i) *Handler exemptions*. Quota shall not apply to any handler who delivers in a quota period a daily average of less than 200 units of milk, cream and milk byproducts. For the purpose of this order, a unit shall be the equivalent in volume of the following: (1) One quart of milk, buttermilk, or fluid milk byproducts; (2) one-half pint of cream; and (3) one-half pound of cottage, pot, or baker's cheese.

(j) *Quota exclusions and exemptions*. Deliveries of milk, milk byproducts, or cream (1) to other handlers, except for such deliveries to sub-handlers, (2) to plants engaged in the handling or processing of milk, milk byproducts, cream or other dairy products from which no milk, milk byproducts, or cream, is delivered in the sales area, (3) to industrial users, and (4) to the agencies or groups specified in (d) of FDO 79, shall be excluded from the computation of deliveries in the base period and exempt from charges to quotas.

(k) *Transfers of bases*. The market agent is empowered to transfer base from one handler to another:

(1) Upon receipt of a request in writing from both handlers; and

(2) Upon application from a handler and written notice to the Director and to both handlers, (i) to permit deliveries to a purchaser not being served by a handler whose quota reflects deliveries to such purchaser in the base period, (ii) to permit a handler to serve an account which customarily rotates among several handlers inclusive of a contract let by a public agency or institution on a bid basis and (iii) to permit a handler to serve an account which he is serving on the effective date of this order and which was served by another handler during the base period.

(l) *Consumer priorities*. In the distribution of milk subject to quotas established hereunder, a handler shall give preference in the order listed, taking into consideration the type of purchasers served by him in the base period, to:

(l) The need of children, expectant mothers, and invalids requiring milk;

(2) Homes and retail stores handling milk for consumption off the premises; and

(3) Establishments serving milk for consumption on the premises.

(m) *Petition for relief from hardship.* (1) Any person affected by FDO 79 or the provisions hereof who considers that compliance therewith would work an exceptional and unreasonable hardship on him, may file with the market agent a petition addressed to the Director. The petition shall contain the correct name, address and principal place of business of the petitioner, a full statement of the facts upon which the petition is based, and the hardship involved and the nature of the relief desired.

(2) Upon receiving such petition the market agent shall immediately investigate representations and facts stated therein.

(3) After investigation, the petition shall be certified to the Director, but prior to certification the market agent may (i) deny the petition or (ii) grant temporary relief for a total period not to exceed 60 days.

(4) Denials or grants of relief by the market agent shall be reviewed by the Director and may be affirmed, modified or reversed by the Director.

(n) *Reports.* Each handler shall transmit to the market agent on forms prescribed by the market agent the following reports:

(1) Within 20 days following the effective date of this order, reports which show the information required by the market agent to establish such handler's quotas;

(2) Within 20 days following the close of each quota period, the information required by the market agent to establish volumes of deliveries of milk, cream, and milk byproducts during the preceding quota period; and

(3) Handlers exempt from quotas pursuant to (i) hereof shall, upon the request of the market agent, submit the information required by the market agent to establish volumes of deliveries of milk, cream, and milk byproducts.

(o) *Records.* Handlers shall keep and shall make available to the market agent such records of receipts, sales, deliveries, and production as the market agent shall require for the purpose of obtaining information which the Director may require for the establishment of quotas as prescribed in (b) of FDO 79.

(p) *Expense of administration.* Each handler shall pay to the market agent, within 20 days after the cl
calendar month, an assessme
per hundredweight of eac
milk byproducts, cream, an
equivalent of cottage, pot,
cheese delivered during th
quota period and subject to
lations under the provisions

(q) *Violations.* The ma
shall report all violations to
together with the informati
for the prosecution of such

(r) *Bureau of the Budge*
The record-keeping and re
quirements of this order ha
proved by the Bureau of th
accordance with the Federal
of 1942. Subsequent record
reporting requirements will b
the approval of the Bureau o
pursuant to the Federal Re
1942.

(s) *Effective date.* This
take effect at 12:01 a. m., e
ruary 1, 1944.

(E.O. 9280, 7 F.R. 10179; E.O.
3807; E.O. 9334, 8 F.R. 5423
8 F.R. 14783; FDO 79, 8
13283)

Issued this 21st day of Jan

LEE M
Director of Food Dis

War Food Administration.
Summary to FDO 79.131 & 79.132.

TWO NEW MILK SALES AREAS NAMED

Milk sales in 2 metropolitan areas in North Carolina will be regulated under the Food Distribution Administration's fluid milk conservation and control program, beginning February 1, 1944.

The new milk sales areas are:

Asheville, N. C. (FDO 79.132)
Greensboro, N. C. (FDO 79.131)

A. J. Drost, with offices in Charlotte, N. C., will administer the orders in these areas. He also will be market agent of the milk conservation orders in previously-established milk sales areas in Charlotte, Winston-Salem, N. C., and Roanoke, Va. (The order in the Roanoke area has been administered by the Washington, D. C. Office.)

Under the program, milk dealers will be permitted to deliver to all customers except schools as much fluid milk as they delivered in June and three-fourths as much milk in cream and milk byproducts (such as cottage cheese, chocolate milk and buttermilk) as they delivered in June. Deliveries to elementary, junior high and high schools will be under the same restrictions except the number of school days in May will be used as the base period in determining quotas, rather than June. Milk dealers include all persons or firms engaged in the sale or transfer of milk, but not such distributors as subhandlers ("peddlers"), retail stores, hotels or restaurants.

Producer-distributors who purchase no milk will be permitted to deliver as much milk as they delivered in either June or December, whichever represents their larger total deliveries.

The order permits dealers to deliver more fluid milk than their quotas allow, provided they use less milk solids in making cream or milk byproducts. Since cream and milk byproducts are recognized as one quota group, dealers may deliver more milk solids in cream by cutting down on milk byproducts, or more milk solids in milk byproducts by reducing the amount of milk solids used in cream, so long as they do not deliver more than 100 percent of the milk solids delivered as cream in June.

In distributing the milk, cream and byproducts allowed under their quotas, dealers are required to give preference to the following consumer groups, in the order listed, taking into consideration the type of purchasers they served in the base period:

1. Children, expectant m
invalids requiring milk;

2. Homes and retail stor
milk for consumption off the

3. Establishments serving
consumption on the premise

Deliveries of milk, cream a
products to other dealers, to
Forces; to plants engaged in
processing milk, byproducts
which are not distributed i
area; and to designated indu
ufacturers who use milk, cre
byproducts in making proc
are sold off the premises ar
empt.

Consumers in the milk
named today, as in others al
nated, generally will be able
as much milk under the mil
tion program as they have l
in recent months. Fluid mi
being stabilized, and sales of
milk byproducts are being re
officials said, to help assu
milk for manufacturing the
ter, evaporated milk, and n
required by the armed force
ians for good nutrition a
balanced diets.

137
p. 1

FDO 79-132
JAN. 21, 1944

WAR FOOD ADMINISTRATION

[FDO 79-132]

PART 1401—DAIRY PRODUCTS

FLUID MILK AND CREAM IN ASHEVILLE, N. C., SALES AREA

Pursuant to the authority vested in me by Food Distribution Order No. 79 (8 F.R. 12426), issued on September 7, 1943, as amended, and to effectuate the purposes of such order, it is hereby ordered as follows:

§ 1401.167 *Quota restrictions* — (a) *Definitions.* When used in this order, unless otherwise distinctly expressed or manifestly incompatible with the intent hereof:

(1) Each term defined in Food Distribution Order No. 79, as amended, shall, when used herein, have the same meaning as is set forth for such term in Food Distribution Order No. 79, as amended.

(2) The term "FDO 79" means Food Distribution Order No. 79, issued on September 7, 1943, as amended.

(3) The term "sub-handler" means any handler, such as a peddler, vendor, sub-dealer, or secondary dealer, who purchases in a previously packaged and processed form milk, cream, or milk byproducts for delivery.

(4) The term "industrial user" means a person, as determined by the market agent, in the capacity of a manufacturer of products using as an ingredient therein milk, cream, or milk byproducts, which products are disposed of for resale to consumers off the premises where made.

(5) The term "base" means the total pounds of milk solids delivered by a handler within the sales area during the base period (i) in the form of milk or (ii) in the form of cream and milk byproducts, minus the milk solids in quota-exempt deliveries of milk, and cream and milk byproducts, as described in (j) hereof. (For the purpose of this order, the milk solids content of milk, milk byproducts, and cream shall be computed as follows: Each hundredweight of milk, cream, or milk products, other than cottage, pot, or baker's cheese, shall be considered the equivalent of 9.375 pounds of milk solids plus the number of pounds of milk solids calculated by multiplying the pounds of butterfat in such milk, and cream and milk byproducts by .906; and each hundredweight of cottage, pot, or baker's cheese shall be considered the equivalent of 62.5 pounds of milk solids plus one pound of milk solids for each one percent of butterfat content of such cheese.)

(b) *Milk sales area.* The following area is hereby designated as a "milk sales area" to be known as the Asheville, North Carolina, Milk sales area, and is referred to hereinafter as the "sales area":

The city of Asheville and the townships of Asheville, Lower Hominy, Swannanoa, and that part of the township of Limestone comprising part of the town of Biltmore Forest, all in Buncombe County, North Carolina.

(c) *Base period.* The calendar month of June 1943 is hereby designated as the base period for the sales area: *Provided*, That the month of May may be used as the base period for computing base and quota for deliveries to elementary, junior high, and high schools: *And provided further*, That in the computations set forth in (e) hereof the total deliveries to elementary, junior high, and high schools in the base period shall be divided by the number of days such schools were in session in lieu of the total number of days in the base period as set forth in (e) (1) and the average daily deliveries so determined shall be multiplied by the number of days such schools are in session in each quota period in lieu of the number of days in the quota period as set forth in (e) (2).

(d) The remainder of the calendar month in which the provisions hereof become effective and each subsequent calendar month, respectively, is hereby designated as the quota period for the sales area.

(e) *Handler quotas.* Quotas for each handler other than a sub-handler or producer-handler shall be determined as follows:

(1) Divide his respective bases by the number of days in the base period;

(2) Multiply the foregoing results by the number of days in the quota period; and

(3) Multiply the aforesaid resulting amounts by 100 percent in the case of the base for milk, and 75 percent in the case of the base for cream and milk byproducts.

(f) *Quotas for handlers who are also producers.* Quotas for each handler who is also a producer and who purchases no milk shall be computed in accordance with (e) hereof, except:

(1) His base period shall be either June or December, whichever represents his larger total deliveries; and,

(2) The applicable percentages shall be 100 percent in lieu of those specified in (e) (3).

(g) *Quota adjustments.* Each handler may increase his quota for milk within any quota period by one pound of milk solids for each one pound of milk solids he reduces his quota for cream and milk byproducts.

(h) *Cream deliveries.* The units of cream delivered subject to quota in any quota period shall not exceed 100 percent of the units of cream in his base, irrespective of the milk solids content of such deliveries.

(i) *Handler exemptions.* Quota shall not apply to any handler who delivers in a quota period a daily average of less than 200 units of milk, cream and milk byproducts. For the purpose of this order, a unit shall be the equivalent in volume of the following: (1) One quart of milk, buttermilk, or fluid milk byproducts; (2) one-half pint of cream; and (3) one-half pound of cottage, pot, or baker's cheese.

(j) *Quota exclusions and exemptions.* Deliveries of milk, milk byproducts, or cream (1) to other handlers, except for such deliveries to sub-handlers, (2) to plants engaged in the handling or processing of milk, milk byproducts, cream or other dairy products from which no milk, milk byproducts, or cream, is delivered in the sales area, (3) to industrial users, and (4) to the agencies or groups specified in (d) of FDO 79 shall be excluded from the computation of deliveries in the base period and exempt from charges to quotas.

(k) *Transfers of bases.* The market agent is empowered to transfer base from one handler to another.

(1) Upon receipt of a request in writing from both handlers; and

(2) Upon application from a handler and written notice to the Director and to both handlers, (i) to permit deliveries to a purchaser not being served by a handler whose quota reflects deliveries to such purchaser in the base period, (ii) to permit a handler to serve an account which customarily rotates among several handlers inclusive of a contract let by a public agency or institution on a bid basis, and (iii) to permit a handler to serve an account which he is serving on the effective date of this order and which was served by another handler during the base period.

(l) *Consumer priorities.* In the distribution of milk subject to quotas established hereunder, a handler shall give preference in the order listed, taking into consideration the type of purchasers served by him in the base period, to:

(1) The need of children, expectant mothers, and invalids requiring milk;

(2) Homes and retail stores handling milk for consumption off the premises; and

(3) Establishments serving milk for consumption on the premises.

(m) *Petition for relief from hardship.* (1) Any person affected by FDO 79 or the provisions hereof who considers that compliance therewith would work an exceptional and unreasonable hardship on him, may file with the market agent a petition addressed to the Director. The petition shall contain the correct name, address and principal place of business of the petitioner, a full statement of the facts upon which the petition is based, and the hardship involved and the nature of the relief desired.

(2) Upon receiving such petition the market agent shall immediately investigate representations and facts stated therein.

(3) After investigation, the petition shall be certified to the Director, but prior to certification the market agent may (i) deny the petition or (ii) grant temporary relief for a total period not to exceed 60 days.

(4) Denials or grants of relief by the market agent shall be reviewed by the Director and may be affirmed, modified, or reversed by the Director.

(n) *Reports.* Each handler shall transmit to the market agent on forms prescribed by the market agent the following reports:

(1) Within 20 days following the effective date of this order, reports which show the information required by the market agent to establish such handler's quotas;

(2) Within 20 days following the close of each quota period, the information required by the market agent to establish volumes of deliveries of milk, cream and milk byproducts during the preceding quota period; and

(3) Handlers exempt from quotas pursuant to (i) hereof shall, upon the request of the market agent, submit the information required by the market agent to establish volumes of deliveries of milk, cream, and milk byproducts.

(o) *Records.* Handlers shall keep and shall make available to the market agent such records of receipts, sales, deliveries, and production as the market agent shall require for the purpose of obtaining information which the Director may require for the establishment of quotas as prescribed in (b) of FDO 79.

(p) *Expense of administration.* Ea[ch] handler shall pay to the market age[nt] within 20 days after the close of ea[ch] calendar month, an assessment of $0.0[...] per hundredweight of each of milk, mi[lk] byproducts, cream, and skim milk equi[v]alent of cottage, pot, or baker's chee[se] delivered during the preceding quota p[e]riod and subject to quota regulatio[n] under the provisions hereof.

(q) *Violations.* The market age[nt] shall report all violations to the Direct[or] together with the information requir[ed] for the prosecution of such violations.

(r) *Bureau of the Budget approv[al].* The record-keeping and reporting r[e]quirements of this order have been a[p]proved by the Bureau of the Budget [in] accordance with the Federal Reports A[ct] of 1942. Subsequent record-keeping [or] reporting requirements will be subje[ct] to the approval of the Bureau of t[he] Budget pursuant to the Federal Repor[ts] Act of 1942.

(s) *Effective date.* This order sh[all] take effect at 12:01 a. m., e. w. t., Fe[b]ruary 1st, 1944.

(E.O. 9280, 7 F.R. 10179; E.O. 9322, 8 F.[R.] 3807; E.O. 9334, 8 F.R. 5423; E.O. 93[9...] 8 F.R. 14783; FDO 79, 8 F.R. 12426, 1328[...])

Issued this 21st day of January 1944.

LEE MARSHALL,
Director of Food Distribution.

War Food Administration,
Summary to FDO 79.131 & 79.132.

TWO NEW MILK SALES AREAS NAMED.

Milk sales in 2 metropolitan areas in North Carolina will be regulated under the Food Distribution Administration's fluid milk conservation and control program, beginning February 1, 1944.

The new milk sales areas are:

Asheville, N. C. (FDO 79.132)
Greensboro, N. C. (FDO 79.131)

A. J. Drost, with offices in Charlotte, N. C., will administer the orders in these areas. He also will be market agent of the milk conservation orders in previously-established milk sales areas in Charlotte, Winston-Salem, N. C., and Roanoke, Va. (The order in the Roanoke area has been administered by the Washington, D. C. Office.)

Under the program, milk dealers will be permitted to deliver to all customers except schools as much fluid milk as they delivered in June and three-fourths as much milk in cream and milk byproducts (such as cottage cheese, chocolate milk and buttermilk), as they delivered in June. Deliveries to elementary, junior high and high schools will be under the same restrictions except the number of school days in May will be used as the base period in determining quotas, rather than June. Milk dealers include all persons or firms engaged in the sale or transfer of milk, but not such distributors as subhandlers ("peddlers"), retail stores, hotels or restaurants.

Producer-distributors who purchase no milk will be permitted to deliver as much milk as they delivered in either June or December, whichever represents their larger total deliveries.

The order permits dealers to deliver more fluid milk than their quotas allow, provided they use less milk solids in making cream or milk byproducts. Since cream and milk byproducts are recognized as one quota group, dealers may deliver more milk solids in cream by cutting down on milk byproducts, or more milk solids in milk byproducts by reducing the amount of milk solids used in cream, so long as they do not deliver more than 100 percent of the milk solids delivered as cream in June.

In distributing the milk, cream and byproducts allowed under their quotas, dealers are required to give preference to the following consumer groups, in the order listed, taking into consideration the type of purchasers they served in the base period:

1. Children, expectant mothers, an[d] invalids requiring milk;

2. Homes and retail stores handlin[g] milk for consumption off the premises;

3. Establishments serving milk f[or] consumption on the premises;

Deliveries of milk, cream and milk b[y]products to other dealers, to the Arme[d] Forces; to plants engaged in handling [or] processing milk, byproducts and crea[m] which are not distributed in the sal[es] area; and to designated industrial ma[n]ufacturers who use milk, cream, or mi[lk] byproducts in making products whic[h] are sold off the premises are quota e[x]empt.

Consumers in the milk sales are[as] named today, as in others already desi[g]nated, generally will be able to purcha[se] as much milk under the milk conserv[a]tion program as they have been buyi[ng] in recent months. Fluid milk sales a[re] being stabilized, and sales of cream a[nd] milk byproducts are being reduced, FD[A] officials said, to help assure sufficie[nt] milk for manufacturing the cheese, bu[t]ter, evaporated milk, and milk powd[er] required by the armed forces and civi[l]ians for good nutrition and proper balanced diets.

FDO 79-133
JAN. 27, 1944

WAR FOOD ADMINISTRATION

[FDO 79-133]

PART 1401—DAIRY PRODUCTS

FLUID MILK AND CREAM IN EL PASO, TEX., SALES AREA

Pursuant to the authority vested in me by Food Distribution Order No. 79 (8 F.R. 12426), issued on September 7, 1943, as amended, and to effectuate the purposes of such order, it is hereby ordered as follows:

§ 1401.161 *Quota restrictions*—(a) *Definitions*. When used in this order, unless otherwise distinctly expressed or manifestly incompatible with the intent hereof:

(1) Each term defined in Food Distribution Order No. 79, as amended, shall, when used herein, have the same meaning as is set forth for such term in Food Distribution Order No. 79, as amended.

(2) The term "FDO 79" means Food Distribution Order No. 79, issued on September 7, 1943, as amended.

(3) The term "sub-handler" means any handler, such as a peddler, vendor, sub-dealer, or secondary dealer, who purchases in a previously packaged and processed form milk, cream, or milk byproducts for delivery.

(4) The term "industrial user" means a person, as determined by the market agent, in the capacity of a manufacturer of products using as an ingredient therein milk, cream, or milk byproducts, which products are disposed of for resale to consumers off the premises where made.

(5) The term "base" means the total pounds of milk solids delivered by a handler within the sales area during the base period (i) in the form of milk, or (ii) in the form of cream and milk byproducts, minus the milk solids in quota-exempt deliveries of milk, and cream and milk byproducts, as described in (j) hereof. (For the purpose of this order, the milk solids content of milk, milk byproducts, and cream shall be computed as follows: Each hundredweight of milk, cream, or milk byproducts other than cottage, pot, or baker's cheese, shall be considered the equivalent of 9.375 pounds of milk solids plus the number of pounds of milk solids calculated by multiplying the pounds of butterfat in such milk, and cream and milk byproducts by .906; and each hundredweight of cottage, pot, or baker's cheese shall be considered the equivalent of 62.5 pounds of milk solids plus one pound of milk solids for each one percent of butterfat content of such cheese.)

(b) *Milk sales area*. The following area is hereby designated as a "milk sales area" to be known as the El Paso, Texas, milk sales area, and is referred to hereinafter as the "sales area":

The city of El Paso; that part of justices' precinct 1 south of North Line Drive extended and North Line Drive, northwest of U. S. Highway 54, south of Hercules Drive, east of Diana Drive, south of Gas Line Road, and southwest of the Southern Pacific Railroad; that part of justices' precinct 2 south of the north boundary of Fort Bliss Military Reservation to the intersection of U. S. Highway 62, and south of U. S. Highway 62; and the entire area of justices' precinct 8; all in El Paso County, Texas.

(c) *Base period*. The calendar month of June 1943 is hereby designated as the base period for the sales area: *Provided*, That the month of May may be used as the base period for computing base and quota for deliveries to elementary, junior high and high schools: *And provided further*, That in the computations set forth in (e) hereof the total deliveries to elementary, junior high, and high schools in the base period shall be divided by the number of days such schools were in session in lieu of the total number of days in the base period as set forth in (e) (1) and the average daily deliveries so determined shall be multiplied by the number of days such schools are in session in each quota period in lieu of the number of days in the quota period as set forth in (e) (2).

(d) The remainder of the calendar month in which the provisions hereof become effective and each subsequent calendar month, respectively, is hereby designated as the quota period for the sales area.

(e) *Handler quotas*. Quotas for each handler other than a sub-handler or producer-handler shall be determined as follows:

(1) Divide his respective bases by the number of days in the base period;

(2) Multiply the foregoing result by the number of days in the quota period; and

(3) Multiply the aforesaid resulting amounts by 100 percent in the case of the base for milk, and 75 percent in the case of the base for cream and milk byproducts.

(f) *Quotas for handlers who are also producers*. Quotas for each handler who is also a producer and who purchases no milk shall be computed in accordance with (e) hereof, except:

(1) His base period shall be either June or December, whichever represents his larger total deliveries; and,

(2) The applicable percentages shall be 100 percent in lieu of those specified in (e) (3).

(g) *Quota adjustments*. Each handler may increase his quota for milk within any quota period by one pound of milk solids for each one pound of milk solids he reduces his quota for cream and milk byproducts.

(h) *Cream deliveries*. The units of cream delivered subject to quota in any quota period shall not exceed 100 percent of the units of cream in his base, irrespective of the milk solids content of such deliveries.

(i) *Handler exemptions*. Quota shall not apply to any handler who delivers in a quota period a daily average of less than 200 units of milk, cream, and milk byproducts. For the purpose of this order, a unit shall be the equivalent in volume of the following: (1) One quart of milk, buttermilk, or fluid milk byproducts; (2) one-half pint of cream; and (3) one-half pound of cottage, pot, or baker's cheese.

(j) *Quota exclusions and exemptions*. Deliveries of milk, milk byproducts, or cream (1) to other handlers, except for such deliveries to sub-handlers, (2) to plants engaged in the handling or processing of milk, milk byproducts, cream or other dairy products from which no milk, milk byproducts, or cream, is delivered in the sales area, (3) to industrial users, and (4) to the agencies or groups specified in (d) of FDO 79, shall be excluded from the computation of deliveries in the base period and exempt from charges to quotas.

(k) *Transfers of bases*. The market agent is empowered to transfer base from one handler to another:

(1) Upon receipt of a request in writing from both handlers; and

(2) Upon application from a handler and written notice to the Director and to both handlers, (i) to permit deliveries to a purchaser not being served by a handler whose quota reflects deliveries to such purchaser in the base period, (ii) to permit a handler to serve an account which customarily rotates among several handlers inclusive of a contract let by a public agency or institution on a bid basis, and (iii) to permit a handler to serve an account which he is serving

on the effective date of this order and which was served by another handler during the base period.

(l) *Consumer priorities.* In the distribution of milk subject to quotas established hereunder, a handler shall give preference in the order listed, taking into consideration the type of purchasers served by him in the base period, to:

(1) The need of children, expectant mothers, and invalids requiring milk;

(2) Homes and retail stores handling milk for consumption off the premises; and

(3) Establishments serving milk for consumption on the premises.

(m) *Petition for relief from hardship.* (1) Any person affected by FDO 79 or the provisions hereof who considers that compliance therewith would work an exceptional and unreasonable hardship on him, may file with the market agent a petition addressed to the Director. The petition shall contain the correct name, address and principal place of business of the petitioner, a full statement of the facts upon which the petition is based, and the hardship involved and the nature of the relief desired.

(2) Upon receiving such petition the market agent shall immediately investigate representations and facts stated thereon.

(3) After investigation, the petition shall be certified to the Director, but prior to certification the market agent may (i) deny the petition or (ii) grant temporary relief for a total period not to exceed 60 days.

(4) Denials or grants of relief by the market agent shall be reviewed by the Director and may be affirmed, modified, or reversed by the Director.

(n) *Reports.* Each handler shall transmit to the market agent on forms prescribed by the market agent the following reports:

(1) Within 20 days following the effective date of this order, reports which show the information required by the market agent to establish such handler's quotas;

(2) Within 20 days following the close of each quota period, the information required by the market agent to establish volumes of deliveries of milk, cream and milk byproducts during the preceding quota period; and

(3) Handlers exempt from quotas pursuant to (i) hereof shall, upon the request of the market agent, submit the information required by the market agent to establish volumes of deliveries of milk, cream, and milk byproducts.

(o) *Records.* Handlers shall keep and shall make available to the market agent such records of receipts, sales, deliveries, and production as the market agent shall require for the purpose of obtaining information which the Director may require for the establishment of quotas as prescribed in (b) of FDO 79.

(p) *Expense of administration.*
handler shall pay to the market
within 20 days after the close of eac
endar month, an assessment of $0.0
hundredweight of each of milk, mi
products, cream, and skim milk eq
lent of cottage, pot, or baker's chee
livered during the preceding quot
riod and subject to quota regulatior
der the provisions hereof.

(q) *Violations.* The market
shall report all violations to the Di
together with the information req
for the prosecution of such violatio

(r) *Bureau of the Budget app*
The record-keeping and reportin
quirements of this order have bee
proved by the Bureau of the Bud
accordance with the Federal Repor
of 1942. Subsequent record-keepi
reporting requirements will be subj
the approval of the Bureau of the B
pursuant to the Federal Reports A
1942.

(s) *Effective date.* This order
take effect at 12:01 a. m., e. w. t.,
ruary 1, 1944.

(E.O. 9280, 7 F.R. 10179; E.O. 9322,
3807; E.O. 9334, 8 F.R. 5423; E.O.
8 F.R. 14783; FDO 79, 8 F.R. 12426, 1

Issued this 27th day of January

LEE MARSHALL
Director of Food Distributi

War Food Administration,
Summary to FDO 79.134, 79.133, 79.135.

Milk sales in 3 metropolitan areas in Texas will be regulated under the War Food Administration's fluid Milk conservation and control program, beginning February 1, 1944. The New milk sales areas are:

Corpus Christi, (FDO 79.134).

El Paso (FDO 79.133), Ben H. King, 810 14th St., Denver, Colo.

Amarillo, (FDO 79.135), M. M. Morehouse, 406 W. 34th St., Kansas City 2, Missouri.

The Market Agent who will administer the order for Corpus Christi will be named later.

Under the program, milk dealers will be permitted to deliver to all customers except schools as much fluid milk as they delivered in June and three-fourths as much milk in cream and milk byproducts (such as cottage cheese, chocolate milk and buttermilk) as they sold in June. Deliveries to elementary, junior high and high schools will be under the same restrictions except the number of school days in May will be used as the base period in determining quotas, rather than June. Milk dealers include all persons or firms engaged in the delivery or transfer of milk, but not such distributors as subhandlers ("peddlers"), retail stores, hotels, or restaurants.

Producer-distributors who purchase no milk will be permitted to deliver as much milk as they delivered in either June or December, whichever represents their larger total deliveries.

The order permits dealers to deliver more fluid milk than their quotas allow, provided they use less milk solids in deliveries of cream or milk byproducts. Since cream and milk byproducts are recognized as one quota group, dealers may deliver more cream, but not more than 100% of the deliveries of cream in the base period by cutting down on milk solids used in milk byproducts, or more byproducts by reducing the amount of milk solids used in cream.

In distributing the milk, cream and byproducts allowed under their quotas, dealers are required to give preference to the following consumer groups, in the order listed, taking into consideration the type of purchasers they served in the base period:

1. Children, expectant mothers,
invalids requiring milk;

2. Homes and retail stores han
milk for consumption off the premis

3. Establishments serving milk
consumption on the premises.

Deliveries of milk, cream and mil
products to other dealers; to the A
Forces; to plants engaged in handli
processing milk, byproducts and c
which are not distributed in the
area; and to designated industrial
ufacturers who use milk cream, or
byproducts in making products
are sold off the premises are
exempt.

Consumers in the milk sales
named today, as in others already
nated, generally will be able to pur
as much milk under the milk cons
tion program as they have been b
in recent months. Fluid milk sale
being stabilized, and sales of crean
milk byproducts are being reduced,
officials said, to help assure suff
milk for manufacturing the cl
butter, evaporated milk, and milk
der required by the armed force
civilians for good nutrition and pr
balanced diets.

FDO 79-134

JAN. 27, 1944

WAR FOOD ADMINISTRATION

[FDO 79-134] A

PART 1401—DAIRY PRODUCTS

FLUID MILK AND CREAM IN CORPUS CHRISTI, TEX., SALES AREA

Pursuant to the authority vested in me by Food Distribution Order No. 79 (8 F. R. 12426), issued on September 7, 1943, as amended, and to effectuate the purposes of such order, it is hereby ordered as follows:

§ 1401.160 *Quota restrictions* — (a) *Definitions.* When used in this order, unless otherwise distinctly expressed or manifestly incompatible with the intent hereof:

(1) Each term defined in Food Distribution Order No. 79, as amended, shall, when used herein, have the same meaning as is set forth for such term in Food Distribution Order No. 79, as amended.

(2) The term "FDO 79" means Food Distribution Order No. 79, issued on September 7, 1943, as amended.

(3) The term "sub-handler" means any handler, such as a peddler, vendor, sub-dealer, or secondary dealer, who purchases in a previously packaged and processed form milk, cream, or milk byproducts for delivery.

(4) The term "industrial user" means a person, as determined by the market agent, in the capacity of a manufacturer of products using as an ingredient therein milk, cream, or milk byproducts, which products are disposed of for resale to consumers off the premises where made.

(5) The term 'base" means the total pounds of milk solids delivered by a handler within the sales area during the base period (i) in the form of milk, or (ii) in the form of cream and milk byproducts, minus the milk solids in quota-exempt deliveries of milk, and cream and milk byproducts, as described in (j) hereof. (For the purpose of this order, the milk solids content of milk, milk byproducts, and cream shall be computed as follows: Each hundredweight of milk, cream, or milk byproducts other than cottage, pot, or baker's cheese, shall be considered the equivalent of 9.375 pounds of milk solids plus the number of pounds of milk solids calculated by multiplying the pounds of butterfat in such milk, and cream and milk byproducts by .906; and each hundredweight of cottage, pot, or baker's cheese shall be considered the equivalent of 62.5 pounds of milk solids plus one pound of milk solids for each one percent of butterfat content of such cheese.)

(b) *Milk sales area.* The following area is hereby designated as a "milk sales area" to be known as the Corpus Christi, Texas, milk sales area, and is referred to hereinafter as the "sales area":

The city of Corpus Christi and the remainder of the area included in justices' precinct 1, all in Nueces County, Texas.

(c) *Base period.* The calendar month of June 1943 is hereby designated as the base period for the sales area: *Provided,* That the month of May may be used as the base period for computing base and quota for deliveries to elementary, junior high and high schools: *And provided further,* That in the computations set forth in (e) hereof the total deliveries to elementary, junior high and high schools in the base period shall be divided by the number of days such schools were in session in lieu of the total number of days in the base period as set forth in (e) (1) and the average daily deliveries so determined shall be multiplied by the number of days such schools are in session in each quota period in lieu of the number of days in the quota period as set forth in (e) (2).

(d) The remainder of the calendar month in which the provisions hereof become effective and each subsequent calendar month, respectively, is hereby designated as the quota period for the sales area.

(e) *Handler quotas.* Quotas for each handler other than a sub-handler or produoer-handler shall be determined as follows:

(1) Divide his respective bases by the number of days in the base period;

(2) Multiply the foregoing result by the number of days in the quota period; and

(3) Multiply the aforesaid resulting amounts by 100 percent in the case of the base for milk, and 75 percent in the case of the base for cream and milk byproducts.

(f) *Quotas for handlers who are also producers.* Quotas for each handler who is also a producer and who purchases no milk shall be computed in accordance with (e) hereof, except:

(1) His base period shall be either June or December, whichever represents his larger total deliveries; and

(2) The applicable percentages shall be 100 percent in lieu of those specified in (e) (3).

(g) *Quota adjustments.* Each handler may increase his quota for milk within any quota period by one pound of milk solids for each one pound of milk solids he reduces his quota for cream and milk byproducts.

(h) *Cream deliveries.* The units of cream delivered subject to quota in any quota period shall not exceed 100 percent of the units of cream in his base, irrespective of the milk solids content of such deliveries.

(i) *Handler exemptions.* Quota shall not apply to any handler who delivers in a quota period a daily average of less than 200 units of milk, cream, and milk byproducts. For the purpose of this order, a unit shall be the equivalent in volume of the following: (1) One quart of milk, buttermilk, or fluid milk byproducts; (2) one-half pint of cream; and (3) one-half pound of cottage, pot, or baker's cheese.

(j) *Quota exclusions and exemptions.* Deliveries of milk, milk byproducts, or cream (1) to other handlers, except for such deliveries to sub-handlers, (2) to plants engaged in the handling or processing of milk, milk byproducts, cream or other dairy products from which no milk, milk byproducts, or cream, is delivered in the sales area, (3) to industrial users, and (4) to the agencies or groups specified in (d) of FDO 79, shall be excluded from the computation of deliveries in the base period and exempt from charges to quotas.

(k) *Transfers of bases.* The market agent is empowered to transfer base from one handler to another.

(1) Upon receipt of a request in writing from both handlers; and

(2) Upon application from a handler and written notice to the Director and to both handlers, (i) to permit deliveries to a purchaser not being served by a handler whose quota reflects deliveries to such purchaser in the base period, (ii) to permit a handler to serve an account which customarily rotates among several handlers inclusive of a contract let by a public agency or institution on a bid basis, and (iii) to permit a handler to serve an account which he is serving on the effective date of this order and which was served by another handler during the base period.

(l) *Consumer priorities.* In the distribution of milk subject to quotas established hereunder, a handler shall give preference in the order listed, taking

into consideration the type of purchasers served by him in the base period, to:

(1) The need of children; expectant mothers, and invalids requiring milk;

(2) Homes and retail stores handling milk for consumption off the premises; and

(3) Establishments serving milk for consumption on the premises.

(m) *Petition for relief from hardship.* (1) Any person affected by FDO 79 or the provisions hereof who considers that compliance therewith would work an exceptional and unreasonable hardship on him, may file with the market agent a petition addressed to the Director. The petition shall contain the correct name, address and principal place of business of the petitioner, a full statement of the facts upon which the petition is based, and the hardship involved and the nature of the relief desired.

(2) Upon receiving such petition the market agent shall immediately investigate representations and facts stated therein.

(3) After investigation, the petition shall be certified to the Director, but prior to certification the market agent may (i) deny the petition or (ii) grant temporary relief for a total period not to exceed 60 days.

(4) Denials or grants of relief by the market agent shall be reviewed by the Director and may be affirmed, modified, or reversed by the Director.

(n) *Reports.* Each handler shall transmit to the market agent on forms prescribed by the market agent the following reports:

(1) Within 20 days following the effective date of this order, reports which show the information required by the market agent to establish such handler's quotas:

(2) Within 20 days following the close of each quota period, the information required by the market agent to establish volumes of deliveries of milk, cream and milk byproducts during the preceding quota; and

(3) Handlers exempt from quotas pursuant to (i) hereof shall, upon the request of the market agent, submit the information required by the market agent to establish volumes of deliveries of milk, cream, and milk byproducts.

(o) *Records.* Handlers shall keep and shall make available to the market agent such records of receipts, sales, deliveries, and production as the market agent shall require for the purpose of obtaining information which the Director may require for the establishment of quotas as prescribed in (b) of FDO 79.

(p) *Expense of administration.* Each handler shall pay to the market agent, within 20 days after the close of each calendar month, an assessment of $0.01 per hundredweight of each of milk, milk byproducts, cream, and skim milk equivalent of cottage, pot, or baker's cheese delivered during the preceding quota period and subject to quota regulation under the provisions hereof.

(q) *Violations.* The market agent shall report all violations to the Director together with the information required for the prosecution of such violations.

(r) *Bureau of the Budget approval.* The record-keeping and reporting requirements of this order have been approved by the Bureau of the Budget in accordance with the Federal Reports Act of 1942. Subsequent record-keeping or reporting requirements will be subject to the approval of the Bureau of the Budget pursuant to the Federal Reports Act of 1942.

(s) *Effective date.* This order shall take effect at 12:01 a. m., e. w. t., February 1, 1944.

(E.O. 9280, 7 F.R. 10179; E.O. 9322, 8 F.R. 3807; E.O. 9334, 8 F.R. 5423; E.O. 9392, 8 F.R. 14783; FDO 79, 8 F.R. 12426, 13283)

Issued this 27th day of January 1944.

LEE MARSHALL,
Director of Food Distribution.

War Food Administration,
Summary to FDO 79.134, 79.133, 79.135.

Milk sales in 3 metropolitan areas in Texas will be regulated under the War Food Administration's fluid Milk conservation and control program, beginning February 1, 1944. The New milk sales areas are:

Corpus Christi, (FDO 79.134).

El Paso (FDO 79.133), Ben H. King, 810 14th St., Denver, Colo.

Amarillo, (FDO 79.135), M. M. Morehouse, 406 W. 34th St., Kansas City 2, Missouri.

The Market Agent who will administer the order for Corpus Christi will be named later.

Under the program, milk dealers will be permitted to deliver to all customers except schools as much fluid milk as they delivered in June and three-fourths as much milk in cream and milk byproducts (such as cottage cheese, chocolate milk and buttermilk) as they sold in June. Deliveries to elementary, junior high and high schools will be under the same restrictions except the number of school days in May will be used as the base period in determining quotas, rather than June. Milk dealers include all persons or firms engaged in the delivery or transfer of milk, but not such distributors as subhandlers ("peddlers"), retail stores, hotels, or restaurants.

Producer-distributors who purchase no milk will be permitted to deliver as much milk as they delivered in either June or December, whichever represents their larger total deliveries.

The order permits dealers to deliver more fluid milk than their quotas allow, provided they use less milk solids in deliveries of cream or milk byproducts. Since cream and milk byproducts are recognized as one quota group, dealers may deliver more cream, but not more than 100% of the deliveries of cream in the base period by cutting down on milk solids used in milk byproducts, or more byproducts by reducing the amount of milk solids used in cream.

In distributing the milk, cream and byproducts allowed under their quotas, dealers are required to give preference to the following consumer groups, in the order listed, taking into consideration the type of purchasers they served in the base period:

1. Children, expectant mothers, and invalids requiring milk;

2. Homes and retail stores handling milk for consumption off the premises;

3. Establishments serving milk for consumption on the premises.

Deliveries of milk, cream and milk byproducts to other dealers; to the Armed Forces; to plants engaged in handling or processing milk, byproducts and cream which are not distributed in the sales area; and to designated industrial manufacturers who use milk cream, or milk byproducts in making products which are sold off the premises are quota exempt.

Consumers in the milk sales areas named today, as in others already designated, generally will be able to purchase as much milk under the milk conservation program as they have been buying in recent months. Fluid milk sales are being stabilized, and sales of cream and milk byproducts are being reduced, FDA officials said, to help assure sufficient milk for manufacturing the cheese, butter, evaporated milk, and milk powder required by the armed forces and civilians for good nutrition and properly balanced diets.

WAR FOOD ADMINISTRATION
Office of Distribution
Washington 25, D. C.

CORRECTION NOTICE - FDO 79.135 Dairy Products.

In printing Food Distribution Order No. 79.135 the following error occurred:

In paragraph (j) (2) fourth line the word "no" was deleted. This sentence should read "to plants engaged in the handling or processing of milk, milk byproducts, cream or other dairy products from which no milk..."

FDO 79-135
JAN. 27, 1944

WAR FOOD ADMINISTRATION

[FDO 79-135]

PART 1401—DAIRY PRODUCTS

FLUID MILK AND CREAM IN AMARILLO, TEX., SALES AREA

Pursuant to the authority vested in me by Food Distribution Order No. 79 (8 F.R. 12426), issued on September 7, 1943, as amended, and to effectuate the purposes of such order, it is hereby ordered as follows:

§ 1401.165 *Quota restrictions*—(a) *Definitions.* When used in this order, unless otherwise distinctly expressed or manifestly incompatible with the intent hereof:

(1) Each term defined in Food Distribution Order No. 79, as amended, shall, when used herein, have the same meaning as is set forth for such term in Food Distribution Order No. 79, as amended.

(2) The term "FDO 79" means Food Distribution Order No. 79, issued on September 7, 1943, as amended.

(3) The term "sub-handler" means any handler, such as a peddler, vendor, sub-dealer, or secondary dealer, who purchases in a previously packaged and processed form milk, cream, or milk byproducts for delivery.

(4) The term "industrial user" means a person, as determined by the market agent, in the capacity of a manufacturer of products using as an ingredient therein milk, cream, or milk byproducts, which products are disposed of for resale to consumers off the premises where made.

(5) The term "base" means the total pounds of milk solids delivered by a handler within the sales area during the base period (i) in the form of milk, or (ii) in the form of cream and milk byproducts, minus the milk solids in quota-exempt deliveries of milk, and cream and milk byproducts, as described in (j) hereof. (For the purpose of this order, the milk solids content of milk, milk byproducts, and cream shall be computed as follows: Each hundredweight of milk, cream, or milk byproducts other than cottage, pot, or baker's cheese, shall be considered the equivalent of 9.375 pounds of milk solids plus the number of pounds of milk solids calculated by multiplying the pounds of butterfat in such milk, and cream and milk byproducts by .906; and each hundredweight of cottage, pot, or baker's cheese shall be considered the equivalent of 62.5 pounds of milk solids plus one pound of milk solids for each one percent of butterfat content of such cheese.)

(b) *Milk sales area.* The following area is hereby designated as a "milk sales area" to be known as the Amarillo, Texas, milk sales area, and is referred to hereinafter as the "sales area":

The city of Amarillo, and the remainder of the area included in justices' precinct 1 in Potter County, all in the State of Texas.

(c) *Base period.* The calendar month of June 1943 is hereby designated as the base period for the sales area: *Provided,* That the month of May may be used as the base period for computing base and quota for deliveries to elementary, junior high and high schools; and *Provided further,* That in the computations set forth in (e) hereof the total deliveries to elementary, junior high, and high schools in the base period shall be divided by the number of days such schools were in session in lieu of the total number of days in the base period as set forth in (e) (1) and the average daily deliveries so determined shall be multiplied by the number of days such schools are in session in each quota period in lieu of the number of days in the quota period as set forth in (e) (2).

(d) The remainder of the calendar month in which the provisions hereof become effective and each subsequent calendar month, respectively, is hereby designated as the quota period for the sales area.

(e) *Handler quotas.* Quotas for each handler other than a sub-handler or producer-handler shall be determined as follows:

(1) Divide his respective bases by the number of days in the base period;

(2) Multiply the foregoing result by the number of days in the quota period; and

(3) Multiply the aforesaid resulting amounts by 100 percent in the case of the base for milk, and 75 percent in the case of the base for cream and milk byproducts.

(f) *Quotas for handlers who are also producers.* Quotas for each handler who is also a producer and who purchases no milk shall be computed in accordance with (e) hereof, except:

(1) His base period shall be either June or December, whichever represents his larger total deliveries; and

(2) The applicable percentages shall be 100 percent in lieu of those specified in (e) (3).

(g) *Quota adjustments.* Each handler may increase his quota for milk within any quota period by one pound of milk solids for each one pound of milk solids he reduces his quota for cream and milk byproducts.

(h) *Cream deliveries.* The units of cream delivered subject to quota in any quota period shall not exceed 100 percent of the units of cream in his base, irrespective of the milk solids content of such deliveries.

(i) *Handler exemptions.* Quota shall not apply to any handler who delivers in a quota period a daily average of less than 200 units of milk, cream, and milk byproducts. For the purpose of this order, a unit shall be the equivalent in volume of the following: (1) One quart of milk, buttermilk, or fluid milk byproducts; (2) one-half pint of cream; and (3) one-half pound of cottage, pot, or baker's cheese.

(j) *Quota exclusions and exemptions.* Deliveries of milk, milk byproducts, or cream (1) to other handlers, except for such deliveries to sub-handlers, (2) to plants engaged in the handling or processing of milk, milk byproducts, cream or other dairy products from which milk, milk byproducts, or cream, is delivered in the sales area, (3) to industrial users, and (4) to the agencies or groups specified in (d) of FDO 79, shall be excluded from the computation of deliveries in the base period and exempt from charges to quotas.

(k) *Transfers of bases.* The market agent is empowered to transfer base from one handler to another.

(1) Upon receipt of a request in writing from both handlers; and

(2) Upon application from a handler and written notice to the Director and to both handlers, (i) to permit deliveries to a purchaser not being served by a handler whose quota reflects deliveries to such purchaser in the base period, (ii) to permit a handler to serve an account which customarily rotates among several handlers inclusive of a contract let by a public agency or institution on a bid basis, and (iii) to permit a handler to serve an account which he is serving on the effective date of this order and which was served by another handler during the base period.

(l) *Consumer priorities.* In the distribution of milk subject to quotas established hereunder, a handler shall give preference in the order listed, taking into consideration the type of purchasers served by him in the base period, to:

(1) The need of children, expectant mothers, and invalids requiring milk;

(2) Homes and retail stores handling milk for consumption off the premises; and

(3) Establishments serving milk for consumption on the premises.

(m) *Petition for relief from hardship.* (1) Any person affected by FDO 79 or the provisions hereof who considers that compliance therewith would work an exceptional and unreasonable hardship on him may file with the market agent a petition addressed to the Director. The petition shall contain the correct name, address and principal place of business of the petitioner, a full statement of the facts upon which the petition is based, and the hardship involved and the nature of the relief desired.

(2) Upon receiving such petition the market agent shall immediately investigate representations and facts stated therein.

(3) After investigation, the petition shall be certified to the Director, but prior to certification the market agent may (i) deny the petition or (ii) grant temporary relief for a total period not to exceed 60 days.

(4) Denials or grants of relief by the market agent shall be reviewed by the Director and may be affirmed, modified, or reversed by the Director.

(n) *Reports.* Each handler shall transmit to the market agent on forms prescribed by the market agent the following reports:

(1) Within 20 days following the effective date of this order, reports which show the information required by the market agent to establish such handler's quotas;

(2) Within 20 days following the close of each quota period, the information required by the market agent to establish volumes of deliveries of milk, cream and milk byproducts during the preceding quota period; and

(3) Handlers exempt from quotas pursuant to (i) hereof shall, upon the request of the market agent, submit the information required by the market agent to establish volumes of deliveries of milk, cream, and milk byproducts.

(o) *Records.* Handlers shall keep and shall make available to the market agent such records of receipts, sales, deliveries, and production as the market agent shall require for the purpose of obtaining information which the Director may require for the establishment of quotas as prescribed in (b) of FDO 79.

(p) *Expense of administration.* Each handler shall pay to the market agent, within 20 days after the close of each calendar month, an assessment of $0.015 per hundredweight of each of milk, milk byproducts, cream, and skim milk equivalent of cottage, pot, or baker's cheese delivered during the preceding quota period and subject to quota regulations under the provisions hereof.

(q) *Violations.* The market agent shall report all violations to the Director together with the information required for the prosecution of such violations.

(r) *Bureau of the Budget approval.* The record-keeping and reporting requirements of this order have been approved by the Bureau of the Budget in accordance with the Federal Reports Act of 1942. Subsequent record-keeping or reporting requirements will be subject to the approval of the Bureau of the Budget pursuant to the Federal Reports Act of 1942.

(s) *Effective date.* This order shall take effect at 12:01 a. m., e. w. t., February 1, 1944.

(E.O. 9280, 7 F.R. 10179; E.O. 9322, 8 F.R. 3807; E.O. 9334, 8 F.R. 5423; E.O. 9392, 8 F.R. 14783; FDO 79, 8 F.R. 12426, 13283)

Issued this 27th day of January 1944.

LEE MARSHALL,
Director of Food Distribution.

War Food Administration,
Summary to FDO 79.134, 79.133, 79.135.

Milk sales in 3 metropolitan areas in Texas will be regulated under the War Food Administration's fluid Milk conservation and control program, beginning February 1, 1944. The New milk sales areas are:

Corpus Christi, (FDO 79.134).

El Paso (FDO 79.133), Ben H. King, 810 14th St, Denver, Colo.

Amarillo, (FDO 79.135), M. M. Morehouse, 406 W. 34th St, Kansas City 2, Missouri.

The Market Agent who will administer the order for Corpus Christi will be named later.

Under the program, milk dealers will be permitted to deliver to all customers except schools as much fluid milk as they delivered in June and three-fourths as much milk in cream and milk byproducts (such as cottage cheese, chocolate milk and buttermilk) as they sold in June. Deliveries to elementary, junior high and high schools will be under the same restrictions except the number of school days in May will be used as the base period in determining quotas, rather than June. Milk dealers include all persons or firms engaged in the delivery or transfer of milk, but not such distributors as subhandlers ("peddlers"), retail stores, hotels, or restaurants.

Producer-distributors who purchase no milk will be permitted to deliver as much milk as they delivered in either June or December, whichever represents their larger total deliveries.

The order permits dealers to deliver more fluid milk than their quotas allow, provided they use less milk solids in deliveries of cream or milk byproducts. Since cream and milk byproducts are recognized as one quota group, dealers may deliver more cream, but not more than 100% of the deliveries of cream in the base period by cutting down on milk solids used in milk byproducts, or more byproducts by reducing the amount of milk solids used in cream.

In distributing the milk, cream and byproducts allowed under their quotas, dealers are required to give preference to the following consumer groups, in the order listed, taking into consideration the type of purchasers they served in the base period:

1. Children, expectant mothers, and invalids requiring milk;
2. Homes and retail stores handling milk for consumption off the premises;
3. Establishments serving milk for consumption on the premises.

Deliveries of milk, cream and milk byproducts to other dealers; to the Armed Forces; to plants engaged in handling or processing milk, byproducts and cream which are not distributed in the sales area; and to designated industrial manufacturers who use milk cream, or milk byproducts in making products which are sold off the premises are quota exempt.

Consumers in the milk sales areas named today, as in others already designated, generally will be able to purchase as much milk under the milk conservation program as they have been buying in recent months. Fluid milk sales are being stabilized, and sales of cream and milk byproducts are being reduced, FDA officials said, to help assure sufficient milk for manufacturing the cheese, butter, evaporated milk, and milk powder required by the armed forces and civilians for good nutrition and properly balanced diets.

FDO 79-136

FEB. 1, 1944

WAR FOOD ADMINISTRATION

[FDO 79-136] A

PART 1401—DAIRY PRODUCTS

FLUID MILK AND CREAM IN AUGUSTA, GA., SALES AREA

Pursuant to the authority vested in me by Food Distribution Order No. 79 (8 F.R. 12426), issued on September 7, 1943, as amended, and to effectuate the purposes of such order, it is hereby ordered as follows:

§ 1401.171 *Quota restrictions*—(a) *Definitions.* When used in this order, unless otherwise distinctly expressed or manifestly incompatible with the intent hereof:

(1) Each term defined in Food Distribution Order No. 79, as amended, shall, when used herein, have the same meaning as is set forth for such term in Food Distribution Order No. 79, as amended.

(2) The term "FDO 79" means Food Distribution Order No. 79, issued on September 7, 1943, as amended.

(3) The term "sub-handler" means any handler, such as a peddler, vendor, sub-dealer, or secondary dealer, who purchases in a previously packaged and processed form milk, cream, or milk byproducts for delivery.

(4) The term "industrial user" means a person, as determined by the market agent, in the capacity of a manufacturer of products using as an ingredient therein milk, cream, or milk byproducts, which products are disposed of for resale to consumers off the premises where made.

(5) The term "base" means the total pounds of milk solids delivered by a handler within the sales area during the base period (i) in the form of milk, or (ii) in the form of cream and milk byproducts, minus the milk solids in quota-exempt deliveries of milk, and cream and milk byproducts, as described in (j) hereof. (For the purpose of this order, the milk solids content of milk, milk byproducts, and cream shall be computed as follows: Each hundredweight of milk, cream, or milk byproducts other than cottage, pot, or baker's cheese, shall be considered the equivalent of 9.375 pounds of milk solids plus the number of pounds of milk solids calculated by multiplying the pounds of butterfat in such milk, and cream and milk byproducts by .906; and each hundredweight of cottage, pot, or baker's cheese shall be considered the equivalent of 62.5 pounds of milk solids plus one pound of milk solids for each one percent of butterfat content of such cheese.)

(b) *Milk sales area.* The following area is hereby designated as a "milk sales area" to be known as the Augusta, Georgia, sales area, and is referred to hereinafter as the "sales area":

The city of Augusta and the militia districts numbered 119, 120, 123, 600 and 1,269, in Richmond County, Georgia, and the townships of Langley and Schultz in Aiken County, South Carolina.

(c) *Base period.* The calendar month of June 1943 is hereby designated as the base period for the sales area: *Provided,* That the month of May may be used as the base period for computing base and quota for deliveries to elementary, junior high and high schools; and *Provided further,* That in the computations set forth in (e) hereof the total deliveries to elementary, junior high, and high schools in the base period shall be divided by the number of days such schools were in session in lieu of the total number of days in the base period as set forth in (e) (1) and the average daily deliveries so determined shall be multiplied by the number of days such schools are in session in each quota period in lieu of the number of days in the quota period as set forth in (e) (2).

(d) The remainder of the calendar month in which the provisions hereof become effective and each subsequent calendar month, respectively, is hereby designated as the quota period for the sales area.

(e) *Handler quotas.* Quotas for each handler other than a sub-handler or producer-handler shall be determined as follows:

(1) Divide his respective bases by the number of days in the base period;

(2) Multiply the foregoing result by the number of days in the quota period; and

(3) Multiply the aforesaid resulting amounts by 100 percent in the case of the base for milk, and 75 percent in the case of the base for cream and milk byproducts.

(f) *Quotas for handlers who are also producers.* Quotas for each handler who is also a producer and who purchases no milk shall be computed in accordance with (e) hereof, except:

(1) His base period shall be either June or December, whichever represents his larger total deliveries; and,

(2) The applicable percentages shall be 100 percent in lieu of those specified in (e) (3).

(g) *Quota adjustments.* Each handler may increase his quota for milk within any quota period by one pound of milk solids for each one pound of milk solids he reduces his quota for cream and milk byproducts.

(h) *Cream deliveries.* The units of cream delivered subject to quota in any quota period shall not exceed 100 percent of the units of cream in his base, irrespective of the milk solids content of such deliveries.

(i) *Handler exemptions.* Quota shall not apply to any handler who delivers in a quota period a daily average of less than 200 units of milk, cream and milk byproducts. For the purpose of this order, a unit shall be the equivalent in volume of the following: (1) One quart of milk, buttermilk, or fluid milk byproducts; (2) one-half pint of cream; and (3) one-half pound of cottage, pot, or baker's cheese.

(j) *Quota exclusions and exemptions.* Deliveries of milk, milk byproducts, or cream (1) to other handlers, except for such deliveries to sub-handlers, (2) to plants engaged in the handling or processing of milk, milk byproducts, cream or other dairy products from which no milk, milk byproducts, or cream, is delivered in the sales area, (3) to industrial users, and (4) to the agencies or groups specified in (d) of FDO 79, shall be excluded from the computation of deliveries in the base period and exempt from charges to quotas.

(k) *Transfers of bases.* The market agent is empowered to transfer base from one handler to another.

(1) Upon receipt of a request in writing from both handlers; and

(2) Upon application from a handler and written notice to the Director and to both handlers, (i) to permit deliveries to a purchaser not being served by a handler whose quota reflects deliveries to such purchaser in the base period, (ii) to permit a handler to serve an account which customarily rotates among several handlers inclusive of a contract let by a public agency or institution on a bid basis, and (iii) to permit a handler to serve an account which he is serving on the effective date of this order and which was served by another handler during the base period.

(l) *Consumer priorities.* In the distribution of milk subject to quotas established hereunder, a handler shall give preference in the order listed, taking into consideration the type of purchasers served by him in the base period, to:

(1) The need of children, expectant mothers, and invalids requiring milk;

(2) Homes and retail stores handling milk for consumption off the premises; and

(3) Establishments serving milk for consumption on the premises.

(m) *Petition for relief from hardship.* (1) Any person affected by FDO 79 or the provisions hereof who considers that compliance therewith would work an exceptional and unreasonable hardship on him, may file with the market agent a petition addressed to the Director. The petition shall contain the correct name, address and principal place of business of the petitioner, a full statement of the facts upon which the petition is based, and the hardship involved and the nature of the relief desired.

(2) Upon receiving such petition the market agent shall immediately investigate representations and facts stated therein.

(3) After investigation, the petition shall be certified to the Director, but prior to certification the market agent may (i) deny the petition or (ii) grant temporary relief for a total period not to exceed 60 days.

(4) Denials or grants of relief by the market agent shall be reviewed by the Director and may be affirmed, modified, or reversed by the Director.

(n) *Reports.* Each handler shall transmit to the market agent on forms prescribed by the market agent the following reports:

(1) Within 20 days following the effective date of this order, reports which show the information required by the market agent to establish such handler's quotas;

(2) Within 20 days following the close of each quota period, the information required by the market agent to establish volumes of deliveries of milk, cream and milk byproducts during the preceding quota period; and

(3) Handlers exempt from quotas pursuant to (i) hereof shall, upon the request of the market agent, submit the information required by the market agent to establish volumes of deliveries of milk, cream, and milk byproducts.

(o) *Records.* Handlers shall keep and shall make available to the market agent such records of receipts, sales, deliveries, and production as the market agent shall require for the purpose of obtaining information which the Director may require for the establishment of quotas as prescribed in (b) of FDO 79.

(p) *Expense of administration.* Each handler shall pay to the market agent, within 20 days after the close of each calendar month, an assessment of $0.015 per hundredweight of each of milk, m byproducts, cream, and skim milk equ alent of cottage, pot, or baker's che delivered during the preceding qu period and subject to quota regulati under the provisions hereof.

(q) *Violations.* The market ag shall report all violations to the Direc together with the information requi for the prosecution of such violations.

(r) *Bureau of the Budget approv* The record-keeping and reporting quirements of this order have been proved by the Bureau of the Budget accordance with the Federal Reports of 1942. Subsequent record-keeping reporting requirements will be subj to the approval of the Bureau of Budget pursuant to the Federal Repo Act of 1942.

(s) *Effective date.* This order sh take effect at 12:01 a. m., e. w. t., Feb ary 15, 1944.

(E.O. 9280, 7 F.R. 10179; E.O. 9322, 8 F 3807; E.O. 9334, 8 F.R. 5423; E.O. 939 F.R. 14783; FDO 79, 8 F.R. 12426, 13283)

Issued this 1st day of February 1944.

C. W. KITCHEN,
Acting Director of Food Distribution

War Food Administration

Summary to FDO–79.136, 79.137, 79.138, 79.139

Milk sales in 4 metropolitan areas in Georgia, Alabama, and South Carolina will be regulated under the War Food Administration's fluid milk conservation and control program, beginning February 15, 1944.

The new milk sales areas and the market agents who will administer the programs in each, are:

Augusta, Ga. (FDO 79.136) and Macon, Ga. (FDO 79.138), Paul H. Fight, Western Union Building (Temp.), Atlanta, Ga.

Mobile, Ala. (FDO 79.139), Frank M. Stewart % Milk Control Board, Montgomery, Ala.

Columbia, S. C. (FDO 79.137), A. J. Drost, County Agent's Office (Temp.), Meckenburg County Court House Charlotte, N. C.

Under the program, milk dealers will be permitted to deliver to all customers except schools as much fluid milk as they delivered in June and three-fourths as much milk in cream and milk byproducts (such as cottage cheese, chocolate milk and buttermilk) as they sold in June. Deliveries to elementary, junior high and high schools will be under the same restrictions except the number of school days in May will be used as the base period in determining quotas, rather than June. Milk dealers include all persons or firms engaged in the sale or transfer of milk, but not such distributors as subhandlers ("peddlers"), retail stores, hotels, or restaurants.

Producer-distributors who purchase no milk will be permitted to deliver as much milk as they delivered in either June or December whichever represents their larger total deliveries.

The order permits dealers to deliver more fluid milk than their quotas allow, provided they use less milk solids in deliveries of cream or milk by-products. Since cream and milk by-products are recognized as one quota group, dealers may deliver more milk solids in cream by cutting down on milk products, or more milk solids in milk by-products by reducing the amount of milk solids used in cream, so long as they do not deliver more than 100% of the milk solids delivered in June.

In distributing the milk, cream and by-products allowed under their quotas, dealers are required to give preference to the following consumer groups, in the order listed, taking into consideration the type of purchasers they served in base period:

1. Children, expectant mothers, a invalids requiring milk;
2. Homes and retail stores handli milk for consumption off the premis
3. Establishments serving milk for co sumption on the premises.

Deliveries of milk, cream and milk products to other dealers; to the Arm Forces; to plants engaged in handling processing milk, by-products and cre which are not distributed in the sa area; and to designated industrial ma facturers who use milk, cream, or m by-products in making products wh are sold off the premises are qu exempt.

Consumers in the milk sales ar named today, as in others already des nated, generally will be able to purch as much milk under the milk conser tion program as they have been buy in recent months. Fluid milk sales being stabilized, and sales of cream milk by-products are being reduced, F. Officials said, to help assure suffici milk for manufacturing the cheese, b ter, evaporated milk, and milk powder quired by the armed forces and civili for good nutrition and properly balan diets.

7337
Cop. 1

FDO 79-137

FEB. 1, 1944.

WAR FOOD ADMINISTRATION

[FDO 79-137] A

PART 1401—DAIRY PRODUCTS

FLUID MILK AND CREAM IN COLUMBIA, S. C., SALES AREA

Pursuant to the authority vested in me by Food Distribution Order No. 79 (8 F.R. 12426), issued on September 7, 1943, as amended, and to effectuate the purposes of such order, it is hereby ordered as follows:

§ 1401.172 *Quota restrictions*—(a) *Definitions.* When used in this order, unless otherwise distinctly expressed or manifestly incompatible with the intent hereof:

(1) Each term defined in Food Distribution Order No. 79, as amended, shall, when used herein, have the same meaning as is set forth for such term in Food Distribution Order No. 79, as amended.

(2) The term "FDO 79" means Food Distribution Order No. 79, issued on September 7, 1943, as amended.

(3) The term "sub-handler" means any handler, such as a peddler, vendor, sub-dealer, or secondary dealer, who purchases in a previously packaged and processed form milk, cream, or milk byproducts for delivery.

(4) The term "industrial user" means a person, as determined by the market agent, in the capacity of a manufacturer of products using as an ingredient therein milk, cream, or milk byproducts, which products are disposed of for resale to consumers off the premises where made.

(5) The term "base" means the total pounds of milk solids delivered by a handler within the sales area during the base period (i) in the form of milk, or (ii) in the form of cream and milk byproducts, minus the milk solids in quota-exempt deliveries of milk, and cream and milk byproducts, as described in (j) hereof. (For the purpose of this order, the milk solids content of milk, milk byproducts, and cream shall be computed as follows: Each hundredweight of milk, cream, or milk byproducts other than cottage, pot, or baker's cheese, shall be considered the equivalent of 9.375 pounds of milk solids plus the number of pounds of milk solids calculated by multiplying the pounds of butterfat in such milk, and cream and milk byproducts by .906; and each hundredweight of cottage, pot, or baker's cheese shall be considered the equivalent of 62.5 pounds of milk solids plus one pound of milk solids for each one percent of butterfat content of such cheese.)

(b) *Milk sales area.* The following area is hereby designated as a "milk sales area" to be known as the Columbia, South Carolina, sales area, and is referred to hereinafter as the "sales area":

The city of Columbia and the school districts of Columbia, Hyatt Park, Edgewood, Olympia, and St. Andrews in Richland County, and the township of Congaree in Lexington County, all in the State of South Carolina.

(c) *Base period.* The calendar month of June 1943 is hereby designated as the base period for the sales area: *Provided,* That the month of May may be used as the base period for computing base and quota for deliveries to elementary, junior high and high schools; *And provided further,* That in the computations set forth in (e) hereof the total deliveries to elementary, junior high and high schools in the base period shall be divided by the number of days such schools were in session in lieu of the total number of days in the base period as set forth in (e) (1) and the average daily deliveries so determined shall be multiplied by the number of days such schools are in session in each quota period in lieu of the number of days in the quota period as set forth in (e) (2).

(d) The remainder of the calendar month in which the provisions hereof become effective and each subsequent calendar month, respectively, is hereby designated as the quota period for the sales area.

(e) *Handler quotas.* Quotas for each handler other than a sub-handler or producer-handler shall be determined as follows:

(1) Divide his respective bases by the number of days in the base period;

(2) Multiply the foregoing result by the number of days in the quota period; and

(3) Multiply the aforesaid resulting amounts by 100 percent in the case of the base for milk, and 75 percent in the case of the base for cream and milk byproducts.

(f) *Quotas for handlers who are also producers.* Quotas for each handler who is also a producer and who purchases no milk shall be computed in accordance with (e) hereof, except:

(1) His base period shall be either June or December, whichever represents his larger total deliveries; and,

(2) The applicable percentages shall be 100 percent in lieu of those specified in (e) (3).

(g) *Quota adjustments.* Each handler may increase his quota for milk within any quota period by one pound of milk solids for each one pound of milk solids he reduces his quota for cream and milk byproducts.

(h) *Cream deliveries.* The units of cream delivered subject to quota in any quota period shall not exceed 100 percent of the units of cream in his base, irrespective of the milk solids content of such deliveries.

(i) *Handler exemptions.* Quota shall not apply to any handler who delivers in a quota period a daily average of less than 200 units of milk, cream and milk byproducts. For the purpose of this order, a unit shall be the equivalent in volume of the following: (1) One quart of milk, buttermilk, or fluid milk byproducts; (2) one-half pint of cream; and (3) one-half pound of cottage, pot, or baker's cheese.

(j) *Quota exclusions and exemptions.* Deliveries of milk, milk byproducts, or cream (1) to other handlers, except for such deliveries to sub-handlers, (2) to plants engaged in the handling or processing of milk, milk byproducts, cream or other dairy products from which no milk, milk byproducts, or cream, is delivered in the sales area, (3) to industrial users, and (4) to the agencies or groups specified in (d) of FDO 79, shall be excluded from the computation of deliveries in the base period and exempt from charges to quotas.

(k) *Transfers of bases.* The market agent is empowered to transfer base from one handler to another.

(1) Upon receipt of a request in writing from both handlers; and

(2) Upon application from a handler and written notice to the Director and to both handlers, (i) to permit deliveries to a purchaser not being served by a handler whose quota reflects deliveries to such purchaser in the base period, (ii) to permit a handler to serve an account which customarily rotates among several handlers inclusive of a contract let by a public agency or institution on a bid basis, and (iii) to permit a handler to serve an account which he is serving on the effective date of this order and which was served by another handler during the base period.

(l) *Consumer priorities.* In the distribution of milk subject to quotas established hereunder, a handler shall give preference in the order listed, taking into consideration the type of purchasers served by him in the base period, to:

(1) The need of children, expectant mothers, and invalids requiring milk;

(2) Homes and retail stores handling milk for consumption off the premises; and

(3) Establishments serving milk for consumption on the premises.

(m) *Petition for relief from hardship.* (1) Any person affected by FDO 79 or the provisions hereof who considers that compliance therewith would work an exceptional and unreasonable hardship on him, may file with the market agent a petition addressed to the Director. The petition shall contain the correct name, address and principal place of business of the petitioner, a full statement of the facts upon which the petition is based, and the hardship involved and the nature of the relief desired.

(2) Upon receiving such petition the market agent shall immediately investigate representations and facts stated therein.

(3) After investigation, the petition shall be certified to the Director, but prior to certification the market agent may (i) deny the petition or (ii) grant temporary relief for a total period not to exceed 60 days.

(4) Denials or grants of relief by the market agent shall be reviewed by the Director and may be affirmed, modified, or reversed by the Director.

(n) *Reports.* Each handler shall transmit to the market agent on forms prescribed by the market agent the following reports:

(1) Within 20 days following the effective date of this order, reports which show the information required by the market agent to establish such handler's quotas;

(2) Within 20 days following the close of each quota period, the information required by the market agent to establish volumes of deliveries of milk, cream and milk byproducts during the preceding quota period; and

(3) Handlers exempt from quotas pursuant to (i) hereof shall, upon the request of the market agent, submit the information required by the market agent to establish volumes of deliveries of milk, cream, and milk byproducts.

(o) *Records.* Handlers shall keep and shall make available to the market agent such records of receipts, sales, deliveries, and production as the market agent shall require for the purpose of obtaining information which the Director may require for the establishment of quotas as prescribed in (b) of FDO 79.

(p) *Expense of administration.* Each handler shall pay to the market agent, within 20 days after the close of each calendar month, an assessment of $0.015 per hundredweight of each of milk, milk byproducts, cream, and skim milk equivalent of cottage, pot, or baker's cheese delivered during the preceding quota period and subject to quota regulations under the provisions hereof.

(q) *Violations.* The market agent shall report all violations to the Director together with the information required for the prosecution of such violations.

(r) *Bureau of the Budget approval.* The record-keeping and reporting requirements of this order have been approved by the Bureau of the Budget in accordance with the Federal Reports Act of 1942. Subsequent record-keeping or reporting requirements will be subject to the approval of the Bureau of the Budget pursuant to the Federal Reports Act of 1942.

(s) *Effective date.* This order shall take effect at 12:01 a. m., e. w. t., February 15, 1944.

(E.O. 9280, 7 F.R. 10179; E.O. 9322, 8 F.R. 3807; E.O. 9334, 8 F.R. 5423; E.O. 9392, 8 F.R. 14783; FDO 79, 8 F.R. 12426, 13283)

Issued this 1st day of February 1944.

C. W. KITCHEN,
Acting Director of Food Distribution.

War Food Administration

Summary to FDO-79.136, 79.137, 79.138, 79.139

Milk sales in 4 metropolitan areas in Georgia, Alabama, and South Carolina will be regulated under the War Food Administration's fluid milk conservation and control program, beginning February 15, 1944.

The new milk sales areas and the market agents who will administer the programs in each, are:

Augusta, Ga. (FDO 79.136) and Macon, Ga. (FDO 79.138), Paul H. Ficht, Western Union Building (Temp.), Atlanta, Ga.

Mobile, Ala. (FDO 79.139), Frank M. Stewart % Milk Control Board, Montgomery, Ala.

Columbia, S. C. (FDO 79.137), A. J. Drost, County Agent's Office (Temp.), Meckenburg County Court House Charlotte, N. C.

Under the program, milk dealers will be permitted to deliver to all customers except schools as much fluid milk as they delivered in June and three-fourths as much milk in cream and milk byproducts (such as cottage cheese, chocolate milk and buttermilk) as they sold in June. Deliveries to elementary, junior high and high schools will be under the same restrictions except the number of school days in May will be used as the base period in determining quotas, rather than June. Milk dealers include all persons or firms engaged in the sale or transfer of milk, but not such distributors as subhandlers ("peddlers"), retail stores, hotels, or restaurants.

Producer-distributors who purchase no milk will be permitted to deliver as much milk as they delivered in either June or December whichever represents their larger total deliveries.

The order permits dealers to deliver more fluid milk than their quotas allow, provided they use less milk solids in deliveries of cream or milk by-products. Since cream and milk by-products are recognized as one quota group, dealers may deliver more milk solids in cream by cutting down on milk products, or more milk solids in milk by-products by reducing the amount of milk solids used in cream, so long as they do not deliver more than 100% of the milk solids delivered in June.

In distributing the milk, cream and byproducts allowed under their quotas, dealers are required to give preference to the following consumer groups, in the order listed, taking into consideration the type of purchasers they served in the base period:

1. Children, expectant mothers, and invalids requiring milk;
2. Homes and retail stores handling milk for consumption off the premises;
3. Establishments serving milk for consumption on the premises.

Deliveries of milk, cream and milk byproducts to other dealers; to the Armed Forces; to plants engaged in handling of processing milk, by-products and cream which are not distributed in the sales area; and to designated industrial manufacturers who use milk, cream, or milk by-products in making products which are sold off the premises are quota exempt.

Consumers in the milk sales areas named today, as in others already designated, generally will be able to purchase as much milk under the milk conservation program as they have been buying in recent months. Fluid milk sales are being stabilized, and sales of cream and milk by-products are being reduced, FDA Officials said, to help assure sufficient milk for manufacturing the cheese, butter, evaporated milk, and milk powder required by the armed forces and civilians for good nutrition and properly balanced diets.

FDO 79-138

WAR FOOD ADMINISTRATION

[FDO 79-138]

PART 1401—DAIRY PRODUCTS

FLUID MILK AND CREAM IN MACON, GA., SALES AREA

Pursuant to the authority vested in me by Food Distribution Order No. 79 (8 F.R. 12426), issued on September 7, 1943, as amended, and to effectuate the purposes of such order, it is hereby ordered as follows:

§ 1401.173 *Quota restrictions*—(a) *Definitions.* When used in this order, unless otherwise distinctly expressed or manifestly incompatible with the intent hereof:

(1) Each term defined in Food Distribution Order No. 79, as amended, shall, when used herein, have the same meaning as is set forth for such term in Food Distribution Order No. 79, as amended.

(2) The term "FDO 79" means Food Distribution Order No. 79, issued on September 7, 1943, as amended.

(3) The term "sub-handler" means any handler, such as a peddler, vendor, sub-dealer, or secondary dealer, who purchases in a previously packaged and processed form milk, cream, or milk byproducts for delivery.

(4) The term "industrial user" means a person, as determined by the market agent, in the capacity of a manufacturer of products using as an ingredient therein milk, cream, or milk byproducts, which products are disposed of for resale to consumers off the premises where made.

(5) The term "base" means the total pounds of milk solids delivered by a handler within the sales area during the base period (i) in the form of milk, or (ii) in the form of cream and milk byproducts, minus the milk solids in quota-exempt deliveries of milk, and cream and milk byproducts, as described in (j) hereof. (For the purpose of this order, the milk solids content of milk, milk byproducts, and cream shall be computed as follows: Each hundredweight of milk, cream, or milk byproducts other than cottage, pot, or baker's cheese, shall be considered the equivalent of 9.375 pounds of milk solids plus the number of pounds of milk solids calculated by multiplying the pounds of butterfat in such milk, and cream and milk byproducts by .906; and each hundredweight of cottage, pot, or baker's cheese shall be considered the equivalent of 62.5 pounds of milk solids plus one pound of milk solids for each one percent of butterfat content of such cheese.)

(b) *Milk sales area.* The following area is hereby designated as a "milk sales area" to be known as the Macon, Georgia, sales area, and is referred to hereinafter as the "sales area":

The city of Macon and the militia districts of Godfrey, East Macon, and Vineville, all in Bibb County, Georgia.

(c) *Base period.* The calendar month of June 1943 is hereby designated as the base period for the sales area: *Provided,* That the month of May may be used as the base period for computing base and quota for deliveries to elementary, junior high and high schools; and *Provided further,* That in the computations set forth in (e) hereof the total deliveries to elementary, junior high, and high schools in the base period shall be divided by the number of days such schools were in session in lieu of the total number of days in the base period as set forth in (e) (1) and the average daily deliveries so determined shall be multiplied by the number of days such schools are in session in each quota period in lieu of the number of days in the quota period as set forth in (e) (2).

(d) The remainder of the calendar month in which the provisions hereof become effective and each subsequent calendar month, respectively, is hereby designated as the quota period for the sales area.

(e) *Handler quotas.* Quotas for each handler other than a sub-handler or producer-handler shall be determined as follows:

(1) Divide his respective bases by the number of days in the base period;

(2) Multiply the foregoing result by the number of days in the quota period; and

(3) Multiply the aforesaid resulting amounts by 100 percent in the case of the base for milk, and 75 percent in the case of the base for cream and milk byproducts.

(f) *Quotas for handlers who are also producers.* Quotas for each handler who is also a producer and who purchases no milk shall be computed in accordance with (e) hereof, except:

(1) His base period shall be either June or December, whichever represents his larger total deliveries; and,

(2) The applicable percentages shall be 100 percent in lieu of those specified in (e) (3).

(g) *Quota adjustments.* Each handler may increase his quota for milk within any quota period by one pound of milk solids for each one pound of milk solids he reduces his quota for cream and milk byproducts.

(h) *Cream deliveries.* The units of cream delivered subject to quota in any quota period shall not exceed 100 percent of the units of cream in his base, irrespective of the milk solids content of such deliveries.

(i) *Handler exemptions.* Quota shall not apply to any handler who delivers in a quota period a daily average of less than 200 units of milk, cream and milk byproducts. For the purpose of this order, a unit shall be the equivalent in volume of the following: (1) One quart of milk, buttermilk, or fluid milk byproducts; (2) one-half pint of cream; and (3) one-half pound of cottage, pot, or baker's cheese.

(j) *Quota exclusions and exemptions.* Deliveries of milk, milk byproducts, or cream (1) to other handlers, except for such deliveries to sub-handlers, (2) to plants engaged in the handling or processing of milk, milk byproducts, cream or other dairy products from which no milk, milk byproducts, or cream, is delivered in the sales area, (3) to industrial users, and (4) to the agencies or groups specified in (d) of FDO 79, shall be excluded from the computation of deliveries in the base period and exempt from charges to quotas.

(k) *Transfers of bases.* The market agent is empowered to transfer base from one handler to another.

(1) Upon receipt of a request in writing from both handlers; and

(2) Upon application from a handler and written notice to the Director and to both handlers, (i) to permit deliveries to a purchaser not being served by a handler whose quota reflects deliveries to such purchaser in the base period, (ii) to permit a handler to serve an account which customarily rotates among several handlers inclusive of a contract let by a public agency or institution on a bid basis, and (iii) to permit a handler to serve an account which he is serving on the effective date of this order and which was served by another handler during the base period.

(l) *Consumer priorities.* In the distribution of milk subject to quotas established hereunder, a handler shall give preference in the order listed, taking

into consideration the type of purchasers served by him in the base period, to:

(1) The need of children, expectant mothers, and invalids requiring milk;

(2) Homes and retail stores handling milk for consumption off the premises; and

(3) Establishments serving milk for consumption on the premises.

(m) *Petition for relief from hardship*: (1) Any person affected by FDO 79 or the provisions hereof who considers that compliance therewith would work an exceptional and unreasonable hardship on him, may file with the market agent a petition addressed to the Director. The petition shall contain the correct name, address and principal place of business of the petitioner, a full statement of the facts upon which the petition is based, and the hardship involved and the nature of the relief desired.

(2) Upon receiving such petition the market agent shall immediately investigate representations and facts stated therein.

(3) After investigation, the petition shall be certified to the Director, but prior to certification the market agent may (i) deny the petition or (ii) grant temporary relief for a total period not to exceed 60 days.

(4) Denials or grants of relief by the market agent shall be reviewed by the Director and may be affirmed, modified, or reversed by the Director.

(n) *Reports*. Each handler shall transmit to the market agent on forms prescribed by the market agent the following reports:

(1) Within 20 days following the effective date of this order, reports, which show the information required by the market agent to establish such handler's quotas;

(2) Within 20 days following the close of each quota period, the information required by the market agent to establish volumes of deliveries of milk, cream and milk byproducts during the preceding quota period; and

(3) Handlers exempt from quotas pursuant to (i) hereof shall, upon the request of the market agent, submit the information required by the market agent to establish volumes of deliveries of milk, cream, and milk byproducts.

(o) *Records*. Handlers shall keep and shall make available to the market agent such records of receipts, sales, deliveries, and production as the market agent shall require for the purpose of obtaining information which the Director may require for the establishment of quotas as prescribed in (b) of FDO 79.

(p) *Expense of administration*. Each handler shall pay to the market agent, within 20 days after the close of each calendar month, an assessment of $0.015 per hundredweight of each of milk, milk byproducts, cream, and skim milk equivalent of cottage, pot, or baker's cheese delivered during the preceding quota period and subject to quota regulations under the provisions hereof.

(q) *Violations*. The market agent shall report all violations to the Director together with the information required for the prosecution of such violations.

(r) *Bureau of the Budget approval*. The record-keeping and reporting requirements of this order have been approved by the Bureau of the Budget in accordance with the Federal Reports Act of 1942. Subsequent record-keeping or reporting requirements will be subject to the approval of the Bureau of the Budget pursuant to the Federal Reports Act of 1942.

(s) *Effective date*. This order shall take effect at 12:01 a. m., e. w. t., February 15, 1944.

(E.O. 9280, 7 F.R. 10179; E.O. 9322, 8 F.R. 3807; E.O. 9334, 8 F.R. 5423; E.O. 9392, 8 F.R. 14783; FDO 79, 8 F.R. 12426, 13283)

Issued this 1st day of February 1944.

C. W. KITCHEN,
Acting Director of Food Distribution.

War Food Administration

Summary to FDO–79.136, 79.137, 79.138, 79.139

Milk sales in 4 metropolitan areas in Georgia, Alabama, and South Carolina will be regulated under the War Food Administration's fluid milk conservation and control program, beginning February 15, 1944.

The new milk sales areas and the market agents who will administer the programs in each, are:

Augusta, Ga. (FDO 79.136) and Macon, Ga. (FDO 79.138), Paul H. Ficht, Western Union Building (Temp.), Atlanta, Ga.

Mobile, Ala. (FDO 79.139), Frank M. Stewart % Milk Control Board, Montgomery, Ala.

Columbia, S. C. (FDO 79.137), A. J. Drost, County Agent's Office (Temp.), Meckenburg County Court House Charlotte, N. C.

Under the program, milk dealers will be permitted to deliver to all customers except schools as much fluid milk as they delivered in June and three-fourths as much milk in cream and milk by-products (such as cottage cheese, chocolate milk and buttermilk) as they sold in June. Deliveries to elementary, junior high and high schools will be under the same restrictions except the number of school days in May will be used as the base period in determining quotas, rather than June. Milk dealers include all persons or firms engaged in the sale or transfer of milk, but not such distributors as subhandlers ("peddlers"), retail stores, hotels, or restaurants.

Producer-distributors who purchase no milk will be permitted to deliver as much milk as they delivered in either June or December whichever represents their larger total deliveries.

The order permits dealers to deliver more fluid milk than their quotas allow, provided they use less milk solids in deliveries of cream or milk by-products. Since cream and milk by-products are recognized as one quota group, dealers may deliver more milk solids in cream by cutting down on milk products, or more milk solids in milk by-products by reducing the amount of milk solids used in cream, so long as they do not deliver more than 100% of the milk solids delivered in June.

In distributing the milk, cream and by-products allowed under their quotas, dealers are required to give preference to the following consumer groups, in the order listed, taking into consideration the type of purchasers they served in the base period:

1. Children, expectant mothers, and invalids requiring milk;

2. Homes and retail stores handling milk for consumption off the premises;

3. Establishments serving milk for consumption on the premises.

Deliveries of milk, cream and milk by-products to other dealers; to the Armed Forces; to plants engaged in handling of processing milk, by-products and cream which are not distributed in the sales area; and to designated industrial manufacturers who use milk, cream, or milk by-products in making products which are sold off the premises are quota exempt.

Consumers in the milk sales areas named today, as in others already designated, generally will be able to purchase as much milk under the milk conservation program as they have been buying in recent months. Fluid milk sales are being stabilized, and sales of cream and milk by-products are being reduced, FDA Officials said, to help assure sufficient milk for manufacturing the cheese, butter, evaporated milk, and milk powder required by the armed forces and civilians for good nutrition and properly balanced diets.

FDO 79-139
FEB. 1, 1944

WAR FOOD ADMINISTRATION

[FDO 79-139]

PART 1401—DAIRY PRODUCTS

FLUID MILK AND CREAM IN MOBILE, ALA., SALES AREA

Pursuant to the authority vested in me by Food Distribution Order No. 79 (8 F.R. 12426), issued on September 7, 1943, as amended, and to effectuate the purposes of such order, it is hereby ordered as follows:

§ 1401.174 *Quota restrictions*—(a) *Definitions.* When used in this order, unless otherwise distinctly expressed or manifestly incompatible with the intent hereof:

(1) Each term defined in Food Distribution Order No. 79, as amended, shall, when used herein, have the same meaning as is set forth for such term in Food Distribution Order No. 79, as amended.

(2) The term "FDO 79" means Food Distribution Order No. 79, issued on September 7, 1943, as amended.

(3) The term "sub-handler" means any handler, such as a peddler, vendor, sub-dealer, or secondary dealer, who purchases in a previously packaged and processed form milk, cream, or milk byproducts for delivery.

(4) The term "industrial user" means a person, as determined by the market agent, in the capacity of a manufacturer of products using as an ingredient therein milk, cream, or milk byproducts, which products are disposed of for resale to consumers off the premises where made.

(5) The term "base" means the total pounds of milk solids delivered by a handler within the sales area during the base period (i) in the form of milk, or (ii) in the form of cream and milk byproducts, minus the milk solids in quota-exempt deliveries of milk, and cream and milk byproducts, as described in (j) hereof. (For the purpose of this order, the milk solids content of milk, milk byproducts, and cream shall be computed as follows: Each hundredweight of milk, cream, or milk byproducts other than cottage, pot, or baker's cheese, shall be considered the equivalent of 9.375 pounds of milk solids plus the number of pounds of milk solids calculated by multiplying the pounds of butterfat in such milk, and cream and milk byproducts by .906; and each hundredweight of cottage, pot, or baker's cheese shall be considered the equivalent of 62.5 pounds of milk solids plus one pound of milk solids for each one percent of butterfat content of such cheese.)

(b) *Milk sales area.* The following area is hereby designated as a "milk sales area" to be known as the Mobile, Alabama, sales area; and is referred to hereinafter as the "sales area":

The city of Mobile, Alabama and an area included within a radius of ten (10) miles of the northeast corner of the Mobile County Court House.

(c) *Base period.* The calendar month of June 1943 is hereby designated as the base period for the sales area: *Provided,* That the month of May may be used as the base period for computing base and quota for deliveries to elementary, junior high and high schools; and *Provided further,* That in the computations set forth in (e) hereof the total deliveries to elementary, junior high, and high schools in the base period shall be divided by the number of days such schools were in session in lieu of the total number of days in the base period as set forth in (e) (1) and the average daily deliveries so determined shall be multiplied by the number of days such schools are in session in each quota period in lieu of the number of days in the quota period set forth in (e) (2).

(d) The remainder of the calendar month in which the provisions hereof become effective and each subsequent calendar month, respectively, is hereby designated as the quota period for the sales area.

(e) *Handler quotas.* Quotas for each handler other than a sub-handler or producer-handler shall be determined as follows:

(1) Divide his respective bases by the number of days in the base period;

(2) Multiply the foregoing result by the number of days in the quota period; and

(3) Multiply the aforesaid resulting amounts by 100 percent in the case of the base for milk, and 75 percent in the case of the base for cream and milk byproducts.

(f) *Quotas for handlers who are also producers.* Quotas for each handler who is also a producer and who purchases no milk shall be computed in accordance with (e) hereof, except:

(1) His base period shall be either June or December, whichever represents his larger total deliveries; and,

(2) The applicable percentages shall be 100 percent in lieu of those specified in (e) (3).

(g) *Quota adjustments.* Each handler may increase his quota for milk within any quota period by one pound of milk solids for each one pound of milk solids he reduces his quota for cream and milk byproducts.

(h) *Cream deliveries.* The units of cream delivered subject to quota in any quota period shall not exceed 100 percent of the units of cream in his base, irrespective of the milk solids content of such deliveries.

(i) *Handler exemptions.* Quota shall not apply to any handler who delivers in a quota period a daily average of less than 150 units of milk, cream and milk byproducts. For the purpose of this order, a unit shall be the equivalent in volume of the following: (1) One quart of milk, buttermilk, or fluid milk byproducts; (2) one-half pint of cream; and (3) one-half pound of cottage, pot, or baker's cheese.

(j) *Quota exclusions and exemptions.* Deliveries of milk, milk byproducts, or cream (1) to other handlers, except for such deliveries to sub-handlers, (2) to plants engaged in the handling or processing of milk, milk byproducts, cream or other dairy products from which no milk, milk byproducts, or cream, is delivered in the sales area, (3) to industrial users, and (4) to the agencies or groups specified in (d) of FDO 79, shall be excluded from the computation of deliveries in the base period and exempt from charges to quotas.

(k) *Transfers of bases.* The market agent is empowered to transfer base from one handler to another.

(1) Upon receipt of a request-in-writing from both handlers; and

(2) Upon application from a handler and written notice to the Director and to both handlers, (i) to permit deliveries to a purchaser not being served by a handler whose quota reflects deliveries to such purchaser in the base period, (ii) to permit a handler to serve an account which customarily rotates among several handlers inclusive of a contract let by a public agency or institution on a bid basis, and (iii) to permit a handler to serve an account which he is serving on the effective date of this order and which was served by another handler during the base period.

(l) *Consumer priorities.* In the distribution of milk subject to quotas established hereunder, a handler shall give preference in the order listed, taking into consideration the type of purchasers served by him in the base period, to:

(1) The need of children, expectant mothers, and invalids requiring milk;

(2) Homes and retail stores handling milk for consumption off the premises; and

(3) Establishments serving milk for consumption on the premises.

(m) *Petition for relief from hardship.* (1) Any person affected by FDO 79 or the provisions hereof who considers that compliance therewith would work an exceptional and unreasonable hardship on him, may file with the market agent a petition addressed to the Director. The petition shall contain the correct name, address and principal place of business of the petitioner, a full statement of the facts upon which the petition is based, and the hardship involved and the nature of the relief desired.

(2) Upon receiving such petition the market agent shall immediately investigate representations and facts stated therein.

(3) After investigation, the petition shall be certified to the Director, but prior to certification the market agent may (i) deny the petition or (ii) grant temporary relief for a total period not to exceed 60 days.

(4) Denials or grants of relief by the market agent shall be reviewed by the Director and may be affirmed, modified, or reversed by the Director.

(n) *Reports.* Each handler shall transmit to the market agent on forms prescribed by the market agent the following reports:

(1) Within 20 days following the effective date of this order, reports which show the information required by the market agent to establish such handler's quotas;

(2) Within 20 days following the close of each quota period, the information required by the market agent to establish volumes of deliveries of milk, cream and milk byproducts during the preceding quota period; and

(3) Handlers exempt from quotas pursuant to (i) hereof shall, upon the request of the market agent, submit the information required by the market agent to establish volumes of deliveries of milk, cream, and milk byproducts.

(o) *Records.* Handlers shall keep and shall make available to the market agent such records of receipts, sales, deliveries, and production as the market agent shall require for the purpose of obtaining information which the Director may require for the establishment of quotas as prescribed in (b) of FDO 79.

(p) *Expense of administration.* Each handler shall pay to the market agent, within 20 days after the close of each calendar month, an assessm per hundredweight of each byproducts, cream, and skin alent of cottage, pot, or b delivered during the prec period and subject to quot under the provisions hereof

(q) *Violations.* The m shall report all violations t tor together with the inf quired for the prosecuti violations.

(r) *Bureau of the Bud* The record-keeping and r quirements of this order h proved by the Bureau of t accordance with the Federa of 1942. Subsequent recor reporting requirements wi to the approval of the B Budget pursuant to the Fe Act of 1942.

(s) *Effective date.* This take effect at 12:01 a. m., e. ary 15, 1944.

(E.O. 9280, 7 F.R. 10179; E.C 3807; E.O. 9334, 8 F.R. 5423 F.R. 14783; FDO 79, 8 F.R. 12

Issued this 1st day of Feb

C. W.

Acting Director of Food D

War Food Administration

Summary to FDO-79.136, 79.137, 79.138, 79.139

Milk sales in 4 metropolitan areas in Georgia, Alabama, and South Carolina will be regulated under the War Food Administration's fluid milk conservation and control program, beginning February 15, 1944.

The new milk sales areas and the market agents who will administer the programs in each, are:

Augusta, Ga. (FDO 79.136) and Macon, Ga. (FDO 79.138), Paul H. Ficht, Western Union Building (Temp.), Atlanta, Ga.

Mobile, Ala. (FDO 79.139), Frank M. Stewart % Milk Control Board, Montgomery, Ala.

Columbia, S. C. (FDO 79.137), A. J. Drost, County Agent's Office (Temp.), Meckenburg County Court House Charlotte, N. C.

Under the program, milk dealers will be permitted to deliver to all customers except schools as much fluid milk as they delivered in June and three-fourths as much milk in cream and milk byproducts (such as cottage cheese, chocolate milk and buttermilk) as they sold in June. Deliveries to elementary, junior high and high schools will be under the same restrictions except the number of school days in May will be used as the base period in determining quotas, rather than June. Milk dealers include all persons or firms engaged in the sale or transfer of milk, but not such distributors as subhandlers ("peddlers"), retail stores, hotels, or restaurants.

Producer-distributors who purchase no milk will be permitted to deliver as much milk as they delivered in either June or December whichever represents their larger total deliveries.

The order permits dealers to deliver more fluid milk than their quotas allow, provided they use less milk solids in deliveries of cream or milk by-products. Since cream and milk by-products are recognized as one quota group, dealers may deliver more milk solids in cream by cutting down on milk products, or more milk solids in milk by-products by reducing the amount of milk solids used in cream, so long as they do not deliver more than 100% of the milk solids delivered in June.

In distributing the milk, cream and by-products allowed under their quotas, dealers are required to give preference to the following consumer groups, in the order listed, taking into consideration the type of purchasers they s base period:

1. Children, expectant r invalids requiring milk;

2. Homes and retail sto milk for consumption off t

3. Establishments serving sumption on the premises.

Deliveries of milk, cream products to other dealers; Forces; to plants engaged i processing milk, by-produc which are not distributed area; and to designated ind facturers who use milk, cr by-products in making pr are sold off the premise exempt.

Consumers in the milk named today, as in others a nated, generally will be abl as much milk under the m tion program as they have in recent months. Fluid n being stabilized, and sales milk by-products are being Officials said, to help ass milk for manufacturing the ter, evaporated milk, and mi quired by the armed forces for good nutrition and prop diets.

3 F
D 2

FDO 79-140

FEB. 29, 1944

WAR FOOD ADMINISTRATION

[FDO 79-140]

PART 1401—DAIRY PRODUCTS

DELEGATION OF AUTHORITY TO CHIEF, DAIRY AND POULTRY BRANCH, OFFICE OF DISTRIBUTION, WITH RESPECT TO FLUID MILK AND CREAM

Pursuant to the authority vested in the Director by Food Distribution Order No. 79 (8 F.R. 12426), issued by the War Food Administrator on September 7, 1943, as amended, and in order to effectuate the purposes thereof, it is hereby ordered, as follows:

§ 1401.169 *Delegation of authority*—(a) *Definitions*. When used herein, unless otherwise distinctly expressed or manifestly incompatible with the intent hereof:

(1) The term "FDO 79" means Food Distribution Order No. 79, issued by the War Food Administrator on September 7, 1943, as amended.

(2) Each term defined in FDO 79 shall, when used herein, have the same meaning as set forth in said FDO 79.

(b) *Authority delegated*. The authority vested in the Director is hereby delegated to the Chief of the Dairy and Poultry Branch, Office of Distribution, to review, and after such review, to affirm, modify, or reverse:

(1) Rulings made by a market agent pursuant to Food Distribution Order No. 79-102 (8 F.R. 16313) issued by the Director on November 30, 1943, as amended; and

(2) Transfers and apportionment of quotas, or denials of such by the market agent, as provided in any order heretofore or hereafter issued by the Director allocating milk, cream, or milk byproducts pursuant to FDO 79.

(c) *Retention of authority by Director*. Nothing contained herein shall be construed to abrogate any power or authority vested in the Director by FDO 79.

(d) *Effective date*. The provisions hereof shall become effective at 12:01 a. m., e. w. t., February 29, 1944.

(E.O. 9280, 7 F.R. 10179; E.O. 9322, 8 F.R. 3807; E.O. 9334, 8 F.R. 5423; E.O. 9392, 8 F.R. 14783; FDO 79, 8 F.R. 12426, 13283)

Issued this 29th day of February 1944.

C. W. KITCHEN,
Acting Director of Food Distribution.

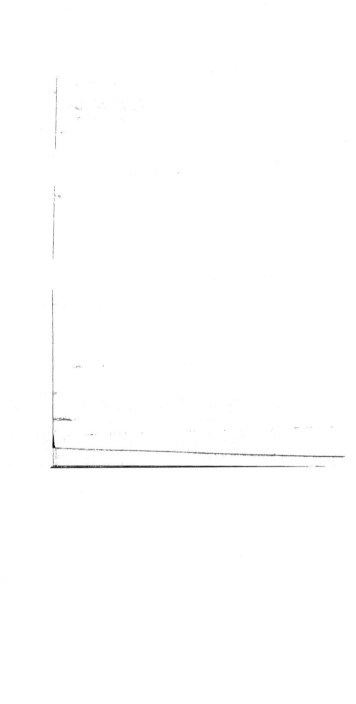

F. 733 F
cop 1

FDO 79-141

MAR. 1, 1944

WAR FOOD ADMINISTRATION

[FDO 79-141]

PART 1401—DAIRY PRODUCTS

FLUID MILK AND CREAM IN GREATER PROVIDENCE, R. I., SALES AREA

Pursuant to the authority vested in me by Food Distribution Order No. 79 (8 F.R. 12426), issued on September 7, 1943, as amended, and to effectuate the purposes of such order, *it is hereby ordered* as follows:

§ 1401.176 *Quota restrictions*—(a) *Definitions.* When used in this order, unless otherwise distinctly expressed or manifestly incompatible with the intent hereof:

(1) Each term defined in Food Distribution Order No. 79, as amended, shall, when used herein, have the same meaning as is set forth for such term in Food Distribution Order No. 79, as amended.

(2) The term "FDO 79" means Food Distribution Order No. 79, issued on September 7, 1943, as amended.

(3) The term "sub-handler" means any handler who (i) receives in a previously packaged and processed form milk, milk byproducts, or cream for delivery, and (ii) does not operate facilities for the processing and bottling of fluid milk.

(b) *Milk sales area.* The following area is hereby designated as a "milk sales area" to be known as the Greater Providence, Rhode Island, sales area, and is referred to hereinafter as the "sales area":

The territory included within the boundaries of the following cities and towns in Rhode Island:

Barrington, Bristol, Central Falls, Coventry, Cranston, Cumberland, East Greenwich, East Providence, Jamestown, Johnston, Lincoln, Middletown, Newport, North Providence, North Smithfield, Pawtucket, Portsmouth, Providence, Smithfield, Warren, Warwick, West Warwick, and Woonsocket;

The following cities and towns in Massachusetts:

Attleboro, Bellingham, Blackstone, Franklin, Millville, North Attleboro, Plainville, Seekonk, and Wrentham.

(c) *Base period.* The calendar month of June 1943 is hereby designated as the base period for the sales area.

(d) *Quota periods.* The remainder of the calendar month in which the provisions hereof become effective and each subsequent calendar month, respectively, are hereby designated as quota periods for the sales area.

(e) *Handler quotas.* Quotas for each handler in the sales area in each quota period shall be calculated in terms of pounds of each of the items for which percentages are specified in (3) below and shall be determined as follows:

(1) Divide the total deliveries of each such item made in the sales area by such handler during the base period, after excluding the quota-exempt deliveries described in (i) hereof, by the number of days in the base period;

(2) Multiply the result of the foregoing calculation by the number of days in the quota period;

(3) Multiply the aforesaid resulting amount by the following applicable percentage: (i) Milk, 100 percent; (ii) Butterfat in milk. -- percent; (iii) Cream, 75 percent; (iv) Butterfat in cream, 75 percent; (v) Milk byproducts other than cottage, pot, or bakers' cheese, 75 percent; and (vi) Cottage, pot, or bakers' cheese, 75 percent of skim milk equivalent. (For the purpose of this order, one pound of cottage, pot, or bakers' cheese shall be considered as the equivalent of 7 pounds of skim milk.)

(f) *Quota limitations.* No handler shall, during any quota period, make deliveries in the sales area in excess of his respective quotas, except as set out in (i) hereof: *Provided,* That a handler may, after application to and approval by the market agent, secure an increase in milk quotas through an equivalent reduction as determined by the market agent, in cream and milk byproducts quotas, and an increase in milk byproducts quota through an equivalent reduction as determined by the market agent, in cream quotas.

(g) *Quotas for handlers who are also producers.* Quotas for handlers who are also producers and who purchase no milk shall be computed in accordance with (e) hereof, except that the applicable percentages shall be 100 percent in lieu of the percentages specified in (e) (3).

(h) *Handler exemptions.* Quotas shall not apply to any handler who delivers in a quota period a daily average of less than 300 units of milk, cream, and milk byproducts. For the purpose of this order, a unit shall be the equivalent in volume of the following: (1) milk, one quart of milk; (2) cream, one-half pint of cream; and (3) milk byproduct, one quart of skim milk, buttermilk, flavored milk drink, or other beverage containing more than 85 percent of skim milk, or one-half pound of cottage, pot, or bakers' cheese.

(i) *Quota exclusions and exemptions.* Deliveries of milk, milk byproducts, or cream (1) to other handlers, except for such deliveries to sub-handlers, (2) to plants engaged in the handling or processing of milk, milk byproducts, or cream from which no milk byproducts, or cream is delivered in the sales area, and (3) to the agencies or groups specified in (d) of FDO 79, shall be excluded from the computation of deliveries in the base period and exempt from charges to quotas.

(j) *Transfers and apportionment of quotas.* The market agent is empowered to deduct an amount of base period deliveries to purchasers from the total of deliveries made by a handler or other person in the base period upon the application and a showing of unreasonable hardship by the handler making deliveries to such purchasers on the effective date of this order, and to add the amount of such deliveries to the total base period deliveries of the applicant handler. Denials of transfers or transfers granted by the market agent shall be reviewed by the Director upon application.

(k) *Petition for relief from hardships.* (1) Any person affected by FDO 79 or the provisions hereof who considers that compliance therewith would work an exceptional and unreasonable hardship on him, may file with the market agent a petition addressed to the Director. The petition shall contain the correct name, address and principal place of business of the petitioner, a full statement of the facts upon which the petition is based, and the hardship involved and the nature of the relief desired.

(2) Upon receiving such petition, the market agent shall immediately investigate the representations and facts stated therein.

(3) After investigation, the petition shall be certified to the Director, but prior to certification the market agent may (i) deny the petition, or (ii) grant temporary relief for a total period not to exceed 60 days.

(4) Denials or grants of relief by the market agent shall be reviewed by the Director and may be affirmed, modified, or reversed by the Director.

(l) *Reports.* Each handler shall transmit to the market agent on forms prescribed by the market agent the following reports:

(1) Within 20 days following the effective date of this order, reports which show the information required by the market agent to establish such handlers' quotas;

(2) Within 20 days following the close of each quota period, the information required by the market agent to establish volumes of deliveries of milk, cream, and milk byproducts during the preceding quota period; and

(3) Handlers exempt from quotas pursuant to (h) hereof shall, upon the request of the market agent, submit the information required by the market agent to establish volumes of deliveries of milk, cream, and milk byproducts.

(m) *Records.* Handlers shall keep and shall make available to the market agent such records of receipts, sales, deliveries, and production as the market agent shall require for the purpose of obtaining information which the Director may require for the establishment of quotas as prescribed in (b) of FDO 79.

(n) *Distribution schedules.* The distribution schedules, if any, to be followed by the handlers in making deliveries shall be made effective in the terms of approval by the Director of such schedules.

(o) *Expense of administration.* Each handler shall pay to the market agent, within 20 days after the close of each calendar month an assessment of $0.015 per hundredweight of each of milk, cream, skim milk, buttermilk, flavored milk drinks, beverages containing more than 85 percent of skim milk, and skim milk equivalent of cottage, pot, or bakers' cheese delivered during the preceding quota period and subject to quota regulations under the provisions hereof.

(p) *Violations.* The market agent shall report all violations to the Director together with the information required for the prosecution of such violations, except in a case where a handler has made deliveries in a quota period in excess of a quota in an amount not to ex-

FDO 79-142

MAR. 1, 1944

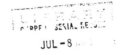

WAR FOOD ADMINISTRATION

[FDO 79-142]

PART 1401—DAIRY PRODUCTS

CONSERVATION AND DISTRIBUTION OF FLUID MILK AND CREAM IN CONN. SALES AREA

Pursuant to the authority vested in me by Food Distribution Order No. 79 (8 F.R. 12426), issued on September 7, 1943, as amended, and to effectuate the purposes of such order, it is hereby ordered as follows:

§ 1401.175 *Quota restrictions*—(a) *Definitions.* When used in this order, unless otherwise distinctly expressed or manifestly incompatible with the intent hereof:

(1) Each term defined in Food Distribution Order No. 79, as amended, shall, when used herein, have the same meaning as is set forth for such term in Food Distribution Order No. 79, as amended.

(2) The term "FDO 79" means Food Distribution Order No. 79, issued on September 7, 1943, as amended.

(3) The term "subhandler" means any handler, such as a peddler, vendor, subdealer, or secondary dealer, who purchases in a previously packaged and processed form milk, milk byproducts, or cream for delivery.

(b) *Milk sales area.* The entire area of the State of Connecticut is hereby designated as the "milk sales area" to be known as the Connecticut sales area, and is referred to hereinafter as the "sales area."

(c) *Base period.* The calendar month of June 1943 is hereby designated as the base period for the sales area.

(d) *Quota periods.* The remainder of the calendar month in which the provisions hereof become effective and each subsequent calendar month, respectively, are hereby designated as quota periods for the sales area.

(e) *Handler quotas.* Quotas for each handler in the sales area in each quota period shall be calculated in terms of pounds of each of the items for which percentages are specified in (3) below and shall be determined as follows:

(1) Divide the total deliveries of each such item made in the sales area by such handler during the base period, after excluding the quota-exempt deliveries described in (i) hereof, by the number of days in the base period;

(2) Multiply the result of the foregoing calculation by the number of days in the quota period;

(3) Multiply the aforesaid resulting amount by the following applicable percentage: (i) Milk: 100 percent; (ii) Butterfat in milk: — percent; (iii) Cream: 75 percent; (iv) Butterfat in cream: 75 percent; (v) Milk byproducts other than cottage, pot, or baker's cheese: 75 percent; and (vi) Cottage, pot, or baker's cheese: 75 percent of skim milk equivalent. (For the purpose of this order, one pound of cottage, pot, or baker's cheese shall be considered as the equivalent of 7 pounds of skim milk.)

(f) *Quota limitations.* No handler shall, during any quota period, make deliveries in the sales area in excess of his respective quotas, except as set out in (i) hereof: *Provided*, That a handler may, after application to and approval by the market agent, secure an increase in milk quotas through an equivalent reduction as determined by the market agent, in cream and milk byproducts quotas, and an increase in milk byproducts quota through an equivalent reduction as determined by the market agent in cream quotas.

(g) *Quotas for handlers who are also producers.* Quotas for handlers who are also producers and who purchase no milk shall be 100 percent of the total production of such handlers in the base period.

(h) *Handler exemptions.* Quotas shall not apply to any handler who delivers in a quota period a daily average of less than 300 units of milk, cream, or milk byproducts. For the purpose of this order, a unit shall be the equivalent in volume of the following: (1) milk, one quart of milk; (2) cream, one-half pint of cream; and (3) milk byproduct, one quart of skim milk, buttermilk, flavored milk drink, or other beverage, containing more than 85 percent of skim milk, or one-half pound of cottage, pot, or baker's cheese.

(i) *Quota exclusions and exemptions.* Deliveries of milk, milk byproducts, or cream (1) to other handlers, except for such deliveries to sub-handlers; (2) to plants engaged in the handling or processing of milk, milk byproducts, or cream, from which no milk, milk byproducts, or cream is delivered in the sales area; (3) to nursery, elementary, junior high, and high schools; and (4) to the agencies or groups specified in (d) of FDO 79, shall be excluded from the computation of deliveries in the base period and exempt from charges to quotas.

(j) *Transfers and apportionment of quotas.* The market agent is empowered to deduct an amount of base period deliveries to purchasers from the total of deliveries made by a handler or other person in the base period upon the application and a showing of unreasonable hardship by the handler making deliveries to such purchasers on the effective date of this order, and to add the amount of such deliveries to the total base period deliveries of the applicant handler. Denials of transfers or transfers granted by the market agent shall be reviewed by the Director upon application.

(k) *Petition for relief from hardship.* (1) Any person affected by FDO 79 or the provisions hereof, who considers that compliance therewith would work exceptional and unreasonable hardship on him, may file with the market agent a petition addressed to the Director. The petition shall contain the correct name, address and principal place of business of the petitioner, a full statement of the facts upon which the petition is based, and the hardship involved and the nature of the relief desired.

(2) Upon receiving such petition, the market agent shall immediately investigate the representations and facts stated therein.

(3) After investigation, the petition shall be certified to the Director, but prior to certification the market agent may (i) deny the petition, or (ii) grant temporary relief for a total period not to exceed 60 days.

(4) Denials or grants of relief by the market agent shall be reviewed by the Director and may be affirmed, modified, or reversed by the Director.

(l) *Reports.* Each handler shall transmit to the market agent on forms prescribed by the market agent the following reports:

(1) Within 20 days following the effective date of this order, reports which show the information required by the market agent to establish such handlers' quotas;

(2) Within 20 days following the close of each quota period, the information required by the market agent to establish volumes of deliveries of milk, cream, and milk byproducts during the preceding quota period; and

(3) Handlers exempt from quotas pursuant to (h) hereof shall, upon the request of the market agent, submit the information required by the market agent to establish volumes of deliveries of milk, cream, and milk byproducts.

(m) *Records.* Handlers shall keep and shall make available to the market agent such records of receipts, sales, deliveries, and production as the market agent shall require for the purpose of obtaining information which the Director may require for the establishment of quotas as prescribed in (b) of FDO 79.

(n) *Distribution schedules.* The distribution schedules, if any, to be fol-

SUMMARY TO FOOD DISTRIBUTION ORDER NO. 79-142, AMENDMENT 1

The War Food Administration has amended Food Distribution Order No. 79-142, effective April 1, 1944, by deleting Section 1401.175 (g) entitled "Quotas for handlers who are also producers". Because of this deletion, quotas allotted to producer-handlers are based on sales of milk, cream and by-products during June 1943 rather than production during that month.

-3F

FDO 79-142
AMDT. 1
MAR. 29, 1944

WAR FOOD ADMINISTRATION

[FDO 79-142, Amdt. 1]

PART 1401—DAIRY PRODUCTS

FLUID MILK AND CREAM IN CONNECTICUT SALES AREA

Pursuant to Food Distribution Order No. 79 (8 F.R. 12426), dated September 7, 1943, as amended, and to effectuate the purposes thereof, Food Distribution Order No. 79-142 (9 F.R. 2534), relative to the conservation and distribution of fluid milk in the Connecticut milk sales area, issued by the Director of Food Distribution on March 1, 1944, is hereby amended as follows:

Delete the provisions in § 1401.175 (g).

The provisions of this amendment shall become effective at 12:01 a. m., e. w. t., April 1, 1944. With respect to violations of said Food Distribution Order No. 79-142, rights accrued, or liabilities incurred prior to the effective time of this amendment, said Food Distribution Order No. 79-142, shall be deemed to be in full force and effect for the purpose of sustaining any proper suit, action, or other proceeding with respect to any such violation, right, or liability.

(E.O. 9280, 7 F.R. 10179; E.O. 9322, 8 F.R. 3807; E.O. 9334, 8 F.R. 5423; E.O. 9392, 8 F.R. 14783; FDO 79, 8 F.R. 12426, 13283)

Issued this 29th day of March 1944.

LEE MARSHALL,
Director of Food Distribution.

GPO—WFA 518—p. 2

733F cop 1

FDO 79-143

APR. 5, 1944

WAR FOOD ADMINISTRATION

[FDO 79-143]

PART 1401—DAIRY PRODUCTS

FLUID MILK AND CREAM IN ST. PETERSBURG, FLA., SALES AREA

Pursuant to the authority vested in me by Food Distribution Order No. 79 (8 F.R. 12426), issued on September 7, 1943, as amended, and to effectuate the purposes of such order, it is hereby ordered as follows:

§ 1401.177 *Quota restrictions*—(a) *Definitions.* When used in this order, unless otherwise distinctly expressed or manifestly incompatible with the intent hereof:

(1) Each term defined in Food Distribution Order No. 79, as amended, shall, when used herein, have the same meaning as is set forth for such term in Food Distribution Order No. 79, as amended.

(2) The term "FDO 79" means Food Distribution Order No. 79, issued on September 7, 1943, as amended.

(3) The term "sub-handler" means any handler, such as a peddler, vendor, sub-dealer, or secondary dealer, who purchases in a previously packaged and processed form milk, cream, or milk byproducts for delivery.

(4) The term "industrial user" means a person, as determined by the market agent, in the capacity of a manufacturer of products using as an ingredient therein milk, cream, or milk byproducts, which products are disposed of for resale to consumers off the premises where made.

(5) The term "base" means the total pounds of milk solids delivered by a handler within the sales area during the base period (i) in the form of milk, or (ii) in the form of cream and milk byproducts, minus the milk solids in quota-exempt deliveries of milk, and cream and milk byproducts, as described in (j) hereof. (For the purpose of this order, the milk solids content of milk, milk byproducts, and cream shall be computed as follows: Each hundredweight of milk, cream, or milk byproducts other than cottage, pot, or baker's cheese, shall be considered the equivalent of 9.375 pounds of milk solids plus the number of pounds of milk solids calculated by multiplying the pounds of butterfat in such milk, and cream and milk byproducts by .906; and each hundredweight of cottage, pot, or baker's cheese shall be considered the equivalent of 62.5 pounds of milk solids plus one pound of milk solids for each one percent of butterfat content of such cheese.)

(b) *Milk sales area.* The following area is hereby designated as a "milk sales area" to be known as the St. Petersburg, Florida, milk sales area, and is referred to hereinafter as the "sales area":

The city of St. Petersburg, and the election precincts numbered 1 to 21, inclusive, 21-A, and 22 to 47, inclusive, in Pinellas County, Florida.

(c) *Base period.* The calendar month of June 1943 is hereby designated as the base period for the sales area: *Provided,* That the month of May may be used as the base period for computing base and quota for deliveries to elementary, junior high, and high schools: and *Provided further,* That in the computations set forth in (e) hereof the total deliveries to elementary, junior high, and high schools in the base period shall be divided by the number of days such schools were in session in lieu of the total number of days in the base period as set forth in (e) (1) and the average daily deliveries so determined shall be multiplied by the number of days such schools are in session in each quota period in lieu of the number of days in the quota period as set forth in (e) (2).

(d) *Quota period.* The remainder of the calendar month in which the provisions hereof become effective and each subsequent calendar month, respectively, is hereby designated as the quota period for the sales area.

(e) *Handler quotas.* Quotas for each handler other than a sub-handler or producer-handler shall be determined as follows:

(1) Divide his respective bases by the number of days in the base period;

(2) Multiply the foregoing result by the number of days in the quota period; and

(3) Multiply the aforesaid resulting amounts in the case of the base for milk as follows:

	Percent		Percent
January	110	July	80
February	120	August	80
March	130	September	85
April	110	October	90
May	100	November	100
June	90	December	105

And, in the case of the base for cream and milk byproducts as follows:

	Percent		Percent
January	82.50	July	60.00
February	90.00	August	60.00
March	97.50	September	63.75
April	82.50	October	67.50
May	75.00	November	75.00
June	67.50	December	78.75

(f) *Quotas for handlers who are also producers.* Quotas for each handler not a cooperative association and who delivers no milk, cream, or milk byproducts, other than that produced by him from his own cows located on the premises held by him on the effective date of this order shall be computed in accordance with (e) hereof, except:

(1) His base period shall be either June or December, whichever represents his larger total deliveries; and

(2) The applicable percentages shall be 100 percent in lieu of those specified in (e) (3).

(g) *Quota adjustments.* Each handler may increase his quota for milk within any quota period by one pound of milk solids for each one pound of milk solids he reduces his quota for cream and milk byproducts.

(h) *Cream deliveries.* The units of cream delivered subject to quota in any quota period shall not exceed 100 percent of the units of cream in his base, irrespective of the milk solids content of such deliveries.

(i) *Handler exemptions.* Quota shall not apply to any handler who is also a producer and who delivers in a quota period a daily average of less than 100 units of milk, cream, and milk byproducts.

For the purpose of this order, a unit shall be the equivalent in volume of the following: (1) One quart of milk, buttermilk, or fluid milk byproducts; (2) one-half pint of cream; and (3) one-half pound of cottage, pot, or baker's cheese.

(j) *Quota exclusions and exemptions.* Deliveries of milk, milk byproducts, or cream (1) to other handlers, except for such deliveries to sub-handlers, (2) to plants engaged in the handling or processing of milk, milk byproducts, cream or other dairy products from which no milk, milk byproducts, or cream is delivered in the sales area, (3) to industrial users, and (4) to the agencies or groups specified in (d) of FDO 79, shall be excluded from the computation of deliveries in the base period and exempt from charges to quotas.

(k) *Transfers of bases.* The market agent is empowered to transfer base from one handler to another:

(1) Upon receipt of a request in writing from both handlers; and

(2) Upon application from a handler and written notice to the Director and to both handlers, (i) to permit deliveries to a purchaser not being served by a handler whose quota reflects deliveries to such purchaser in the base period, (ii) to permit a handler to serve an account which customarily rotates among several handlers inclusive of a contract let by a public agency or institution on a bid basis, and (iii) to permit a handler to serve an account which he is serving on the effective date of this order and which was served by another handler during the base period.

(l) *Consumer priorities.* In the distribution of milk subject to quotas established hereunder, a handler shall give preference in the order listed, taking into consideration the type of purchasers served by him in the base period, to:

(1) The need of children, expectant mothers, and invalids requiring milk;

(2) Homes and retail stores handling milk for consumption off the premises; and

(3) Establishments serving milk for consumption on the premises.

(m) *Petition for relief from hardship.* (1) Any person affected by FDO 79 or the provisions hereof who considers that compliance therewith would work an exceptional and unreasonable hardship on him may file with the market agent a petition addressed to the Director. The petition shall contain the correct name, address and principal place of business of the petitioner, a full statement of the facts upon which the petition is based, and the hardship involved and the nature of the relief desired.

(2) Upon receiving such petition the market agent shall immediately investigate representations and facts stated therein.

(3) After investigation, the petition shall be certified to the Director, but prior to certification the market agent may (i) deny the petition or (ii) grant temporary relief for a total period not to exceed 60 days.

(4) Denials or grants of relief by the market agent shall be reviewed by the Director and may be affirmed, modified, or reversed by the Director.

(n) *Reports.* Each handler shall transmit to the market agent on forms prescribed by the market agent the following reports:

(1) Within 20 days following the effective date of this order, reports which show the information required by the market agent to establish such handler's quotas;

(2) Within 20 days following the close of each quota period, the information required by the market agent to establish volumes of deliveries of milk, cream and milk byproducts during the preceding quota period; and

(3) Handlers exempt from quotas pursuant to (i) hereof shall, upon the request of the market agent, submit the information required by the market agent to establish volumes of deliveries of milk, cream, and milk byproducts.

WAR FOOD ADMINISTRATION

[FDO 79-144]

PART 1401—DAIRY PRODUCTS

FLUID MILK AND CREAM IN WORCESTER, MASS., SALES AREA

Pursuant to the authority vested in me by Food Distribution Order No. 79 (8 F.R. 12426), issued on September 7, 1943, as amended, and to effectuate the purposes of such order, it is hereby ordered as follows:

§ 1401.178 *Quota restrictions*—(a) *Definitions.* When used in this order, unless otherwise distinctly expressed or manifestly incompatible with the intent hereof:

(1) Each term defined in Food Distribution Order No. 79, as amended, shall, when used herein, have the same meaning as is set forth for such term in Food Distribution Order No. 79, as amended.

(2) The term "FDO 79" means Food Distribution Order No. 79, issued on September 7, 1943, as amended.

(3) The term "sub-handler" means any handler, who (i) receives in a previously packaged and processed form milk, milk byproducts, or cream for delivery, and (ii) does not operate facilities for the processing and bottling of fluid milk.

(b) *Milk sales area.* The following area is hereby designated as a "milk sales area" to be known as the Worcester, Massachusetts, sales area, and is referred to hereinafter as the "sales area:"

The city of Marlboro and the towns of Hudson and Hopkinton in Middlesex County, Massachusetts.

In Worcester County, Massachusetts, the city of Worcester and the following towns: Auburn, Berlin, Boylston, Clinton, Grafton, Holden, Hopedale, Leicester, Mendon, Milford, Millbury, Northbridge, Northboro, Paxton, Shrewsbury, Southboro, Spencer, Upton, Uxbridge, Westboro, and West Boylston.

(c) *Base period.* The calendar month of June 1943, is hereby designated as the base period for the sales area.

(d) *Quota period.* The remainder of the calendar month in which the provisions hereof become effective and each subsequent calendar month, respectively, is hereby designated as a quota period for the sales area.

(e) *Handler quotas.* Quotas for each handler in the sales area in each quota period shall be calculated in terms of pounds of each of the items for which percentages are specified in (3) below and shall be determined as follows:

(1) Divide the total deliveries of each such item made in the sales area by such handler during the base period, after excluding the quota exempt deliveries described in (i) hereof, by the number of days in the base period;

(2) Multiply the result of the foregoing calculation by the number of days in the quota period;

(3) Multiply the aforesaid resulting amount by the following applicable percentage: (i) Milk, 100 percent; (ii) butterfat in milk, xxx percent; (iii) cream, 75 percent; (iv) butterfat in cream, 75 percent; (v) milk, byproducts other than cottage, pot, or baker's cheese, 75 percent; and (vi) cottage, pot, or baker's cheese, 75 percent of skim milk equivalent. (For the purpose of this order, one pound of cottage, pot, or baker's cheese shall be considered as the equivalent of 7 pounds of skim milk.)

(f) *Quota limitations.* No handler shall, during any quota period, make deliveries in the sales area in excess of his respective quotas, except as set out in (i) hereof: *Provided,* That a handler may, after application to and approval by the market agent, secure an increase in milk quotas through an equivalent reduction as determined by the market agent, in cream and milk byproducts quotas, and an increase in milk byproducts quota through an equivalent reduction, as determined by the market agent, in cream quotas.

(g) *Quotas for handlers who are also producers.* Quotas for handlers who are also producers and who purchase no milk shall be computed in accordance with (e) hereof, except that the applicable percentages shall be 100 percent in lieu of the percentages specified in (e) (3).

(h) *Handler exemptions.* Quotas shall not apply to any handler who delivers in a quota period a daily average of less than 300 units of milk, cream, and milk byproducts. For the purpose of this order, a unit shall be the equivalent in volume of the following:

(1) Milk, one quart of milk;

(2) Cream, one-half pint of cream; and

(3) Milk byproduct, one quart of skim milk, buttermilk, flavored milk drink, or other beverage containing more than 85 percent of skim milk, or one-half pound of cottage, pot, or baker's cheese.

(i) *Quota exclusions and exemptions.* Deliveries of milk, milk byproducts, or cream (1) to other handlers, except for such deliveries to sub-handlers, (2) to plants engaged in the handling or processing of milk, milk byproducts, or cream from which no milk, milk byproducts, or cream is delivered in the sales area, (3) to nursery, elementary, junior high, and high schools, and (4) to the agencies or groups specified in (d) of FDO 79, shall be excluded from the computation of deliveries in the base period and exempt from charges to quotas.

(j) *Transfers and apportionment of quotas.* The market agent is empowered to deduct an amount of base period deliveries to purchasers from the total of deliveries made by a handler or other person in the base period upon the application and a showing of unreasonable hardship by the handler making deliveries to such purchasers on the effective date of this order, and to add the amount of such deliveries to the total base period deliveries of the applicant handler. Denials of transfers or transfers granted by the market agent shall be reviewed by the Director upon application.

(k) *Petition for relief from hardship.* (1) Any person affected by FDO 79 or the provisions hereof who considers that compliance therewith would work an exceptional and unreasonable hardship on him, may file with the market agent a petition addressed to the Director. The petition shall contain the correct name, address and principal place of business of the petitioner, a full statement of the facts upon which the petition is based, and the hardship involved and the nature of the relief desired.

(2) Upon receiving such petition, the market agent shall immediately investigate the representations and facts stated therein.

(3) After investigation, the petition shall be certified to the Director, but prior to certification the market agent may (i) deny the petition, or (ii) grant temporary relief for a total period not to exceed 60 days.

(4) Denials or grants of relief by the market agent shall be reviewed by the Director and may be affirmed, modified, or reversed by the Director.

(l) *Reports.* Each handler shall transmit to the market agent on forms prescribed by the market agent the following reports:

(1) Within 20 days following the effective date of this order, reports which show the information required by the market agent to establish such handler's quotas;

(2) Within 20 days following the close of each quota period, the information required by the market agent to establish volumes of deliveries of milk, cream, and milk byproducts during the preceding quota period; and

(3) Handlers exempt from quotas pursuant to (h) hereof shall, upon the request of the market agent, submit the information required by the market agent to establish volumes of deliveries of milk, cream, and milk byproducts.

(m) *Records.* Handlers shall keep and shall make available to the market agent such records of receipts, sales, deliveries, and production as the market agent shall require for the purpose of obtaining information which the Director may require for the establishment of quotas as prescribed in (b) of FDO 79.

(n) *Distribution schedules.* The distribution schedules, if any, to be followed by the handlers in making deliveries shall be made effective in the terms of approval by the Director of such schedules.

(o) *Expense of administration.* Each handler shall pay to the market agent, within 20 days after the close of each calendar month, an assessment of $0.015 per hundredweight of each of milk, cream, skim milk, buttermilk, flavored milk drinks, beverages containing more than 85 percent of skim milk, and skim milk equivalent of cottage, pot, or baker's cheese delivered during the preceding quota period and subject to quota regulations under the provisions hereof.

(p) *Violations.* The market agent shall report all violations to the Director together with the information required for the prosecution of such violations, except in a case where a handler has made deliveries in a quota period in excess of a quota in an amount not to exceed 5 percent of such quota, and in the succeeding quota period makes deliveries below that quota by at least the same percent.

(q) *Bureau of the Budget approval.* The record keeping and reporting requirements of this order have been approved by the Bureau of the Budget in accordance with the Federal Reports Act of 1942. Subsequent record keeping or reporting requirements will be subject to the approval of the Bureau of the Budget pursuant to the Federal Reports Act of 1942.

(r) *Effective date.* This order shall take effect at 12:01 a.m., e. w. t., May 1, 1944.

(E. O. 9280, 7 F.R. 10179; E.O. 9322, 8 F.R. 3807; E.O. 9334, 8 F.R. 5423; E.O. 9392, 8 F.R. 14783)

Issued this 5th day of April 1944.

LEE MARSHALL,
Director of Distribution.

Lightning Source UK Ltd.
Milton Keynes UK
UKHW012303301218
334781UK00009B/584/P

9 780260 413468